Tel. 443-414-5597

3ds max

and its applications

Release 4

D0921968

Eric K. Augspurger
Technical Illustrator/Technical Writer
Lansing, Illinois

Blake J. Fisher
Graphic Designer/Technical Writer
Springfield, Illinois

Publisher
The Goodheart-Willcox Company, Inc.
Tinley Park, Illinois

autodesk®
authorized publisher

Library of Congress Catalog Card Number 01-033400
International Standard Book Number 1-56637-856-7
1 2 3 4 5 6 7 8 9 10 02 05 04 03 02 01

Library of Congress Cataloging-in-Publication Data

Augspurger, Eric K.
  3ds max and its applications: release 4/Eric K.
  Augspurger, Blake J. Fisher.
      p. cm.
  ISBN 1-56637-856-7
  1. Computer animation. 2. Computer graphics 3. 3ds Max 4
(Computer file)
      I. Fisher, Blake J. II. Title.
TR897.7 .A92 2001
006.6'96--dc21   2001033400
                                                      CIP

Introduction

This is a very "hands-on" book designed to help you learn 3ds max, the industry standard in computer rendering and animation. It is not a tutorial, it is a learn-by-example text. This text presents the basic information needed to get started, then allows you to "jump in" and start modeling. The best way to learn is by doing, and with this book, you do just that.

This book is specifically designed for education. It is designed both for an instructor in a classroom setting and a student learning 3ds max in a classroom setting. However, the hands-on approach also makes this book exceptionally suited for an individual learner as well.

Using This Text

This book is divided into five sections—*Getting Started, Moving to Realism, Making It Real, Objects in Motion,* and *Introduction to NURBS.* The book progresses in "looping circles," like a spring. Each section builds on skills learned in the previous section(s).

The first section, *Getting Started,* presents an overview of 3ds max and its setup. Then, creating 3D objects and 2D shapes is covered. Finally, basic model editing is presented along with an introduction to materials and rendering. This section allows you to create simple, yet interesting models in a short period of time.

The second section, *Moving to Realism,* presents more detailed modeling and editing techniques. Lighting theory and cameras are also covered. An introduction to creating your own materials is presented. Finally, adding motion to a scene is introduced. New functions and applications, such as lights and cameras, are introduced in this section. However, the fundamental skills learned in the first section are applied and built on.

The third section, *Making It Real,* presents material allowing you to create very realistic rendered models. Motion control is also discussed. Creating advanced materials, material mapping, and lighting effects are also covered. While this section introduces advanced functions and applications of 3ds max, the skills learned in the first two sections are further built upon.

The fourth section, *Objects in Motion,* presents advanced motion control topics. These topics include inverse kinematics, systems, and space warps. This section also covers particle generators called particle systems.

The final section, *Introduction to NURBS,* presents an introduction to NURBS as a tool for modeling organic objects. The basic knowledge and skills needed to model using NURBS are covered. In addition, incorporating NURBS into an animated scene is covered.

Features of This Book

Throughout the book, keyboard alternatives to commands are identified in the margin next to the discussion of the command, like the one shown here. This particular key combination is for saving the current model.

Toolbar buttons corresponding to commands are also shown in the margin. For example, the button for drawing a box is shown in the margin here.

Box

In traditional animation, a "cel" is a single frame of the animation. Throughout this book, you will find Help Cels. These present useful information and are intended to help you be more efficient, point out important features, or suggest a course of action. They appear as shown below.

Help Cel

A Help Cel contains information you should find useful. Be sure to read each one.

Each chapter contains several Exercises throughout the chapter. Exercises are presented after a command, application, or feature is discussed. They are designed to be completed immediately to reinforce the just-presented material. Exercises are, by design, fairly basic so they can be completed in a few minutes. This allows you to quickly move on to the next topic.

At the end of the chapter, there is a Chapter Snapshot section. This section lists the topics discussed in the chapter. Each topic appears with the page number(s) where the item is discussed to allow quick reference.

The chapter ends with a Chapter Test. The test allows you to measure your progress. Each chapter test covers material presented in that chapter only.

In addition, a Modeling Problems section appears at the end of the chapter. The modeling problems are designed to utilize primarily the commands and functions presented in the chapter. However, as you progress through the book, the modeling problems will require you to apply previously learned functions and applications as well. Where exercises are by design fairly basic, the chapter modeling problems are more involved. Each may take an hour or more to complete, depending on your ability, and are designed as out-of-class laboratory assignments.

The modeling problems in each chapter are divided into three general categories—Beginner, Intermediate, and Advanced. This allows you to select problems based on your skill level. Beginner problems are identified with a wireframe-model icon. Intermediate problems are identified with a color-shaded icon. The Advanced problems are identified with a rendered object icon. These icons are shown in the margin here. The top icon is the Beginner icon. The bottom icon is the Advanced icon.

At the end of each of the five sections is a tutorial. Each Section Tutorial allows you to apply the material presented in the section. General procedures are given, such as "draw a five-unit cube in the Top viewport." However, specific commands and methods on how to use commands are *not* discussed. You must determine this on your own. At the end of the tutorial is a section with discussion questions about the tutorial. These questions are designed to be discussed in groups with other students in the class. Each tutorial is progressively more advanced.

Fonts Used in This Book

This book makes extensive use of font changes to identify commands, features, or important terms. Keys, information typed on the keyboard, status line displays, prompt line displays, and file names appear in sans serif, roman typeface. The parts of 3ds max, such as dialog box names, toolbar buttons, and items in the **Command Panel** always appear in **sans serif, bold** typeface. Important terms always appear in *serif, **bold italic*** typeface. *Serif, italic* typeface is used for emphasis for terms such as *not* or *never*.

About the Authors

Eric K. Augspurger is a technical illustrator, technical writer, and editor specializing in 3D modeling and animation. He received a Bachelor of Science degree in Industrial Technology from Illinois State University. He also has a Master of Science degree in Industrial Technology with an emphasis on Industrial Training, also from Illinois State University.

Mr. Augspurger is experienced using AutoCAD, 3D Studio, Adobe Photoshop, Corel DRAW!, and various word processing and desktop publishing software. Mr. Augspurger has approximately 20 years of drafting experience in both traditional (manual) and CAD drafting. In addition, he has nearly 10 years experience in editing and writing technical material and several years of technical illustration experience for industry.

Blake J. Fisher is a graphic designer and technical writer specializing in 3D modeling and display graphics. He received a Bachelor of Arts degree in English from Northern Illinois University. Mr. Fisher is experienced using AutoCAD, 3D Studio, Adobe Photoshop, Adobe Illustrator, Corel DRAW!, and various word processing and desktop publishing software. Mr. Fisher has approximately 5 years of experience in the design and production of large-scale display graphics.

Feedback

Your comments and input are very valuable. Please direct any comments you have to:

Managing Editor—Technology
Goodheart-Willcox Publisher
18604 West Creek Drive
Tinley Park, IL 60477

Trademarks

AutoCAD, 3D Studio, 3ds max, and 3D Studio VIZ are registered trademarks of Autodesk, Inc. Other trademarks are registered by their respective owners.

Contents

Section One: Getting Started

Chapter 4: Creating Basic 2D Geometry (Shapes) 106

Chapter 5: Model Editing 132

Section Two: Moving to Realism

Section Three: Making It Real

Section Four: Objects in Motion

Section Five: Introduction to NURBS

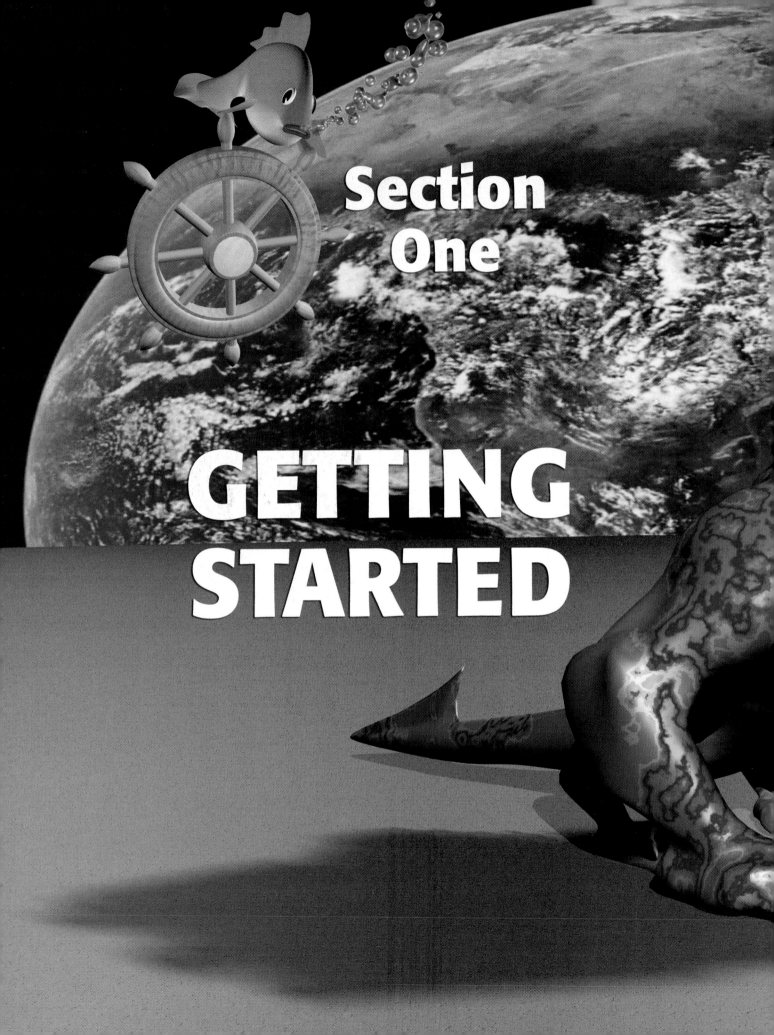

Section One

GETTING STARTED

Three-dimensional models can be seen throughout the world in entertainment and design. The
fundamentals of three-dimensional space, basic
3ds max objects, and rendering presented in
Section One will provide the foundation on
which to build your 3D skills.

(Original model supplied by Autodesk)

Chapter

1

Getting Started Modeling

Objectives

After completing this chapter, you will be able to:

- Identify different elements of the 3ds max interface.
- Describe the functions of the elements of the 3ds max interface.
- Explain the drawing planes used by 3ds max.
- Set up a modeling session.

Introduction to Advanced Computer Graphics

Computer graphics is the field of creating visual images using a computer. This is a very broad field that covers everything from computer-aided drafting (CAD) to two-dimensional (2D) painting and drawing to three-dimensional (3D) modeling and animation. There are many different software programs designed for a variety of different computer graphics applications. These programs are typically available for the most popular computer platforms, or operating systems. Many of the 2D painting and drawing programs have traditionally been available on the Apple Macintosh platform. Most of the CAD and 3D modeling programs have traditionally been available on the PC platform or the UNIX platform. Now, quality CAD, 2D paint/draw, and 3D modeling programs are available for all platforms. The software 3ds max and its sister software 3D Studio VIZ are industry standards for 3D modeling, rendering, and animation.

The 3ds max software was formerly called 3D Studio MAX. Starting with Release 4, the official name of the software is 3ds max. However, when talking about the software, it is still common to refer to it as "3D studio" or "max."

Computer Graphics Terminology

There are many technical terms used in the field of computer graphics. It is important to know these terms in order to understand the software, technologies, and processes of computer graphics. It is also important to know these terms to be an effective and knowledgeable communicator in the field of computer graphics. Some of the major terms used in the field of computer graphics are covered below. Study these carefully and be sure you understand them.

- *Rendering.* This is the process of applying color and textures to the objects in a scene to create a realistic appearance. Rendering can be done using a computer, with 3ds max for example, or by hand, with charcoal, airbrushes, and other tools.
- *Bitmap.* This is a type of electronic graphic file where the image is made up of a series of "dots." The computer does not see a line as a line, but rather as a series of dots. When these dots are viewed on the screen, they appear as a line. The disadvantage of bitmaps is they cannot be scaled very well. When they are scaled, especially to a larger size, they tend to have "jaggies." This is when the object, such as a line, appears to be made of large blocks, instead of one smooth entity. Photorealistic images are bitmaps. There are several common types of bitmap files, including BMP, PCX, TIFF, JPEG, and AVI.
- *Vector.* This is a type of electronic graphic file where the image is made up of lines, circles, arcs, and other line-based objects. The computer sees each object as its mathematical definition. The big advantage of this file type is that objects can be easily edited, scaled, or otherwise altered without losing any of their appearance. Adobe Illustrator, AutoCAD, and 3ds max are vector-based programs. However, a rendering from 3ds max is a bitmap.
- *Paint programs.* These are computer programs that typically create bitmapped images. Most photo editing software can generically be called paint programs.
- *Draw programs.* These are computer programs that typically create vector-based images. Most CAD software can generically be called draw programs.
- *Animation.* An animation is a series of images displayed quickly to trick the brain into seeing motion. There is no actual motion in an animation. Rather, several similar images are played back-to-back very quickly. The brain sees one image, and the differences between each actual image as motion.
- *Two-dimensional.* This describes "flat" space. A two-dimensional object is located using coordinates on two axes. Two-dimensional objects usually have X and Y coordinates, but X/Z and Y/Z coordinates also create 2D objects.
- *Three-dimensional.* This describes space with "volume." Everything you see around you is a 3D object; even a flat sheet of paper has three dimensions. Three-dimensional objects have X, Y, and Z coordinates. Coordinate systems are discussed later in this chapter.

Introduction to 3ds max

3ds max is an advanced software program for creating and rendering models. Models can be rendered as still images, or motion can be added to create a rendered animation. The final, rendered product can range from very realistic to fantastic, Figure 1-1. The following sections cover the basics of how 3ds max is organized.

Figure 1-1. A—This model of a '57 Chevy looks like an actual car. **B**—Fantasy or SciFi images and animations can also be created in 3ds max. (Discreet, a division of Autodesk)

A

B

3ds max Interface

When 3ds max is first started, or launched, the screen appears as shown in Figure 1-2. There are certain basic features to the interface. These must be understood to effectively use 3ds max.

Figure 1-2. The default 3ds max layout.

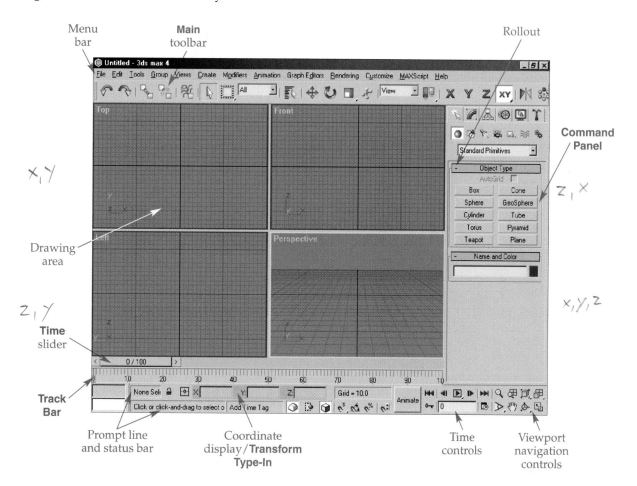

Menu bar — Main toolbar — Rollout — Command Panel — Drawing area — Time slider — Track Bar — Prompt line and status bar — Coordinate display/**Transform Type-In** — Time controls — Viewport navigation controls

Along the top of the screen is the *menu bar*. This bar contains several
pull-down menus. *Pull-down menus* are used to access various
commands. The standard Windows pull-down menus **File**, **Edit**, and **Help**
are found in the menu bar. In addition, the 3ds max pull-down menus
Tools, **Group**, **Views**, **Create**, **Modifiers**, **Animation**, **Graph Editors**,
Rendering, **Customize**, and **MAXScript** are located in the menu bar.

Below the menu bar is the **Main** toolbar. This is displayed in a docked
position by default. A *floating toolbar* is displayed on top of 3ds max
screen elements. A *docked toolbar* is displayed so that it is not floating
on top of any screen elements. To make a docked toolbar floating, move
the cursor to the double vertical lines on the far left of the toolbar. The
cursor changes to an arrow with two overlapping rectangles. Pick and
hold down the left mouse button, and then drag the toolbar away from
its docked position. An outline of the toolbar is displayed as you drag
the toolbar. Release the mouse button to float the toolbar. To dock a
floating toolbar, pick and hold on its title bar, and then drag the toolbar
to the top, bottom, or either side of the screen. You can also dock a
toolbar by right-clicking on the title bar, selecting **Dock** from the shortcut
menu which appears, and selecting the docked location in the cascading
menu. See Figure 1-3. A docked toolbar can be made floating using the
shortcut menu as well.

Figure 1-3. A toolbar can be docked using the shortcut menu.

In 3D Studio MAX R3, the *tab panel* is located below the menu bar by default. This feature still exists in 3ds max; however, it is not displayed by default. The tab panel allows you to "tab" between the display of several different toolbars. To display the tab panel, right-click on the **Main** toolbar and select **Tab Panel** from the shortcut menu. Refer to Figure 1-3.

Taking up most of the 3ds max display is the *drawing area.* By default, this is a four-viewport configuration with the Top, Front, Left, and Perspective viewports displayed. You can display from one to four viewports in a variety of configurations. Changing the viewport configuration is discussed later in this chapter.

On the right side of the display is the **Command Panel**. There are six different panels. The **Create** panel is displayed on top by default. Picking a tab at the top of the **Command Panel** displays a different panel. Most of the 3ds max modeling and animating tools are located in one of the six panels. The **Command Panel** can be made to float. To do so, pick and hold on the top of the **Command Panel**. Then, drag it away from its docked position. You can also right-click on the top of the **Command Panel** and float it using the shortcut menu.

Each panel in the **Command Panel** may have several *rollouts.* These are expanded and collapsed to show or hide various commands. An expanded rollout has a minus sign (–) next to the name, indicating it can be collapsed. A collapsed rollout has a plus sign (+) next to the name, indicating it can be expanded.

The rollouts on a given panel can be rearranged. To do so, pick and hold on the rollout name. Then, drag the rollout to a new location in the panel. A blue line indicates where the rollout will be placed as you drag. Release the mouse button when the rollout is where you want it. In addition, the **Command Panel** can be made "two column." Move your cursor to the left side of the **Command Panel** until it changes to the standard Windows resize cursor. Then, pick and drag to the left, creating a two-column **Command Panel**. Reverse the process to return the **Command Panel** to a one-column setup.

Below the viewports is the **Time** slider. This indicates the current frame of the animation and the total number of frames. In addition, this slider can be dragged to get a quick preview of the animation.

Below the **Time** slider is the **Track Bar**. This shows the frame numbers or animation time, any animation keys for the selected object, and the current frame in the animation. The **Track Bar** can be used as a quick alternative to **Track View**. **Track View** is introduced later in this chapter.

The *prompt line* and *status bar* are located below the **Track Bar**. These areas display information and provide prompts related to the active command and the scene. The snap command buttons are also located in the status bar.

The *coordinate display* is located next to the prompt line. It consists of the three coordinate boxes labeled **X:**, **Y:**, and **Z:**. The values listed indicate the X, Y, and Z coordinates corresponding to the position of the cursor in the current viewport. The boxes can also be used to enter transform values when applying move, rotate, or scale transforms. Transforms are discussed in Chapter 5, *Model Editing*.

⑥ The *time controls* are located in the bottom portion of the screen near the right corner. These tools are used to move through or play an animation, and to make certain animation configuration settings. The **Toggle Animation Mode** button, labeled **Animate**, is used to turn the animation mode on or off. To create an animation, you must first be in animation mode. The text box in the time controls area is used to jump to a specific frame by typing a frame number and pressing [Enter].

⑦ At the very bottom-right corner of the display are the *viewport navigation controls.* These tools are used to zoom, pan, and rotate the view in a viewport.

Right-Click Menus

A *right-click menu* is a menu that appears next to the cursor when the right mouse button is picked. An example, discussed earlier in this chapter, is the menu used to dock or float the **Main** toolbar. For simplicity in this text, right-click menus are called *shortcut menus*. However, in the 3ds max documentation, these menus are called right-click menus. 3ds max has many shortcut menus. These are discussed as you progress through this text.

New to 3ds max r4 is the *quad menu.* This is a shortcut menu accessed by right-clicking anywhere in any viewport, except on the viewport label. The quad menu provides quick access to various commands without having to find the command in a pull-down menu or the **Command Panel**. The contents of the quad menu vary, depending on what is selected or what command is active. The quad menu may display up to four "panels" or "quadrants," as shown in Figure 1-4.

The right-side quadrants of the quad menu display generic commands. These commands, such as **Move**, **Properties**..., and **Hide Selection**, are common to all objects. The left-side quadrants display options specific to the active command or selected object. Some of the commands and options in the quad menu may have cascading submenus, as shown in Figure 1-4. The quad menu can be customized to contain frequently used commands and options.

The last command or option selected in the quad menu is highlighted the next time the menu is displayed. Each quadrant can display a "last-used" command. To close the quad menu, right-click anywhere or left-click outside of the menu.

Material Editor

Adding materials to the objects created in 3ds max is essential to creating realistic scenes. The **Material Editor** is used to select, create, and assign materials, Figure 1-5. When opened, it appears floating on top of the 3ds max display. By default, six "blank" material samples are displayed. The features and functions of the **Material Editor** are discussed later in this text.

"M" p 210

Figure 1-4. The quad menu is accessed by right-clicking anywhere in a viewport, except on the viewport label.

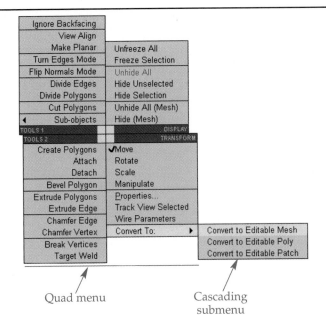

Quad menu   Cascading submenu

Figure 1-5. The **Material Editor** is used to define and apply materials.

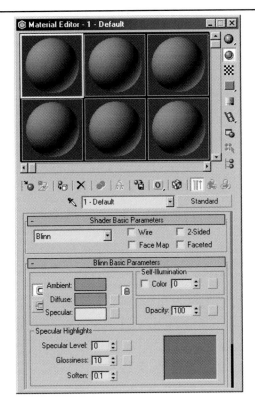

Track View

Track View is an important tool used in creating animations. It allows you to control the visibility and timing of objects and cameras for an animation. You can also add sound and replace objects using **Track View**. When open, **Track View** appears floating on top of the 3ds max display, Figure 1-6. **Track View** can also be displayed in a viewport. **Track View** is discussed in detail later in Chapter 16, *Using Track View.*

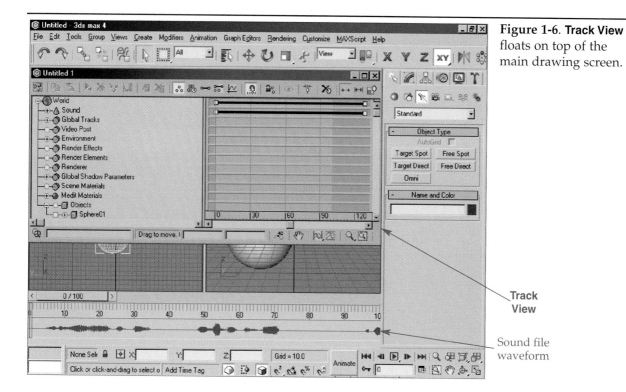

Figure 1-6. **Track View** floats on top of the main drawing screen.

Track View

Sound file waveform

Video Post

The **Video Post** is a feature of 3ds max that allows you to composite various types of events. These events include a rendering of the current scene, bitmap images, and image processing functions. The **Video Post** appears similar to **Track View**. The dialog box shows when each event occurs in the finished video. Each event is associated with a track that has a range bar. **Video Post** is not discussed in this text.

Expert Mode

The 3ds max screen contains many elements. Often, especially in a complex model, you may want to display only the drawing area. Expert mode allows you to hide all elements of 3ds max except the menu bar, viewports, **Time** slider, and **Track Bar**. See Figure 1-7. To enter expert mode, select **Expert Mode** from the **Views** pull-down menu or press [Ctrl][X] on the keyboard. To exit expert mode, press [Ctrl][X] again or pick the **Cancel Expert Mode** button at the bottom of the screen.

As you progress through this book, you will learn various keyboard shortcuts. When in expert mode, you need to use keyboard shortcuts to activate commands.

Figure 1-7. Expert mode hides most of the 3ds max elements, allowing the viewports to be displayed larger.

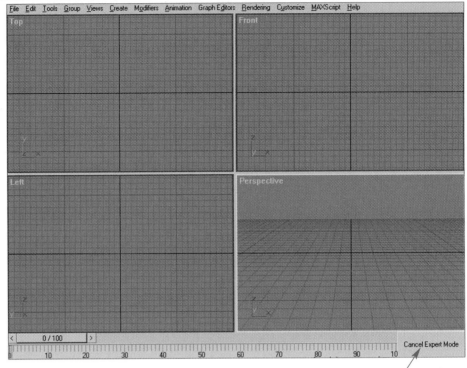

Pick to cancel expert mode

Understanding the 3ds max Drawing Planes

3ds max uses the same method of defining objects in 3D space as most CAD software. In addition, as with most CAD software, there are different planes that can be drawn on to create objects.

Coordinate Systems

The *Cartesian coordinate system* is used by 3ds max to define objects in three dimensions. This coordinate system uses three axes—X, Y, and Z. These axes intersect at right angles (90°) at a point called the *origin*. Every point or feature on an object can be defined in three-dimensional space using coordinates defined on these three axes in relation to the origin. See Figure 1-8.

Home Grid

A *grid* is like graph paper. It is a series of vertical and horizontal lines that intersect each other at right angles (90°). 3ds max has two basic types of grids. These are the home grid and grid objects.

The planes defined by the X, Y, and Z axes of the Cartesian coordinate system are called the world coordinate system by many CAD software programs. 3ds max refers to the world coordinate system as the *home grid.* Two axes of the world coordinate system define each of the three planes of the home grid. Objects are always drawn on a plane unless keyboard entry is used.

The home grid can be turned on or off, but it cannot be rotated or changed. In order to create objects that are not aligned with the home grid, 3ds max has "helpers" called **grid objects.** These can be placed at any angle and location. Then, when a grid object is made the current grid, objects are placed on that grid and not the home grid. Grid objects are similar to user coordinate systems in AutoCAD.

Orthographic Views

There are six standard orthographic views that can be displayed in a viewport. An **orthographic view** looks perpendicular to one of the coordinate system planes. For each orthographic view, there is an opposite view. The six views are front, back, left, right, top, and bottom. See Figure 1-9.

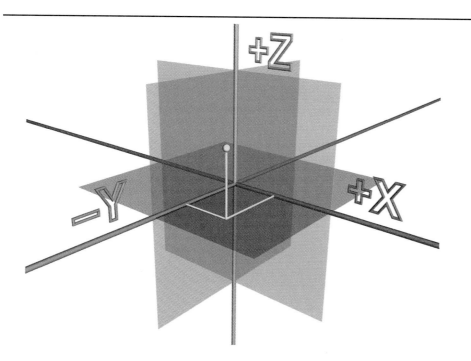

Figure 1-8. The Cartesian coordinate system is used by 3ds max to define points in three-dimensional space. The yellow dot shown here can be located with an X, Y, and Z coordinate. The three intersecting planes are called the home grid.

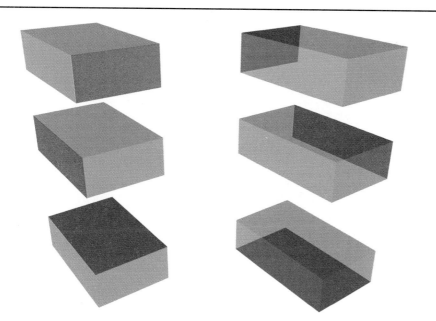

Figure 1-9. The six orthographic views are, starting with the top-left object shown here, front, back, left, right, top, and bottom.

Basic Setup

There are basic features of 3ds max that should be set up when first starting a model. These include the viewport configuration, unit setup, snap settings, and grid settings. While these can be, and often are, changed during the modeling process, making basic settings before beginning the model helps create a "starting point."

Viewport Configuration

The *viewport configuration* is how the drawing viewports are arranged on screen. By default, 3ds max has a configuration of four equally sized viewports. This is a commonly used configuration. However, you may find that a different configuration works best for you.

The active viewport is indicated by a thick yellow line surrounding the viewport. To make a different viewport active, simply pick in the viewport. However, it is a good habit to right-click in a viewport to make it active. In this way, you do not accidentally initiate a command.

To change the viewport configuration, select **Viewport Configuration**... from the **Customize** pull-down menu. This displays the **Viewport Configuration** dialog box. You can also open this dialog box by right-clicking on the viewport label (name) and picking **Configure**... from the shortcut menu. There are several features of this dialog box that are discussed throughout this text. However, to change the basic configuration, select the **Layout** tab. See Figure 1-10.

To select a new configuration, pick an image tile at the top of the dialog box. There are 14 different configurations to choose from. Once you have selected the configuration, the preview at the bottom of the dialog box changes to reflect the new configuration. To change the view displayed in a viewport, pick in the viewport on the preview image. A shortcut menu appears, as shown in Figure 1-10. Select the view you want displayed from the menu. The current view has a check mark next to it in the menu.

Figure 1-10. The **Layout** tab of the **Viewport Configuration** dialog box is used to set the viewport configuration. Picking in the layout image tiles displays a shortcut menu from which you can select the view to display.

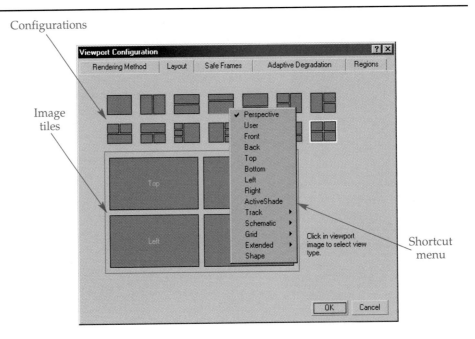

Configurations

Image tiles

Shortcut menu

Once you have the configuration setup as you want it, pick the **OK** button to close the dialog box. The drawing area is updated to display the new configuration.

You can quickly change the view in the current viewport using keyboard shortcut keys. The most common are: [F] for Front, [K] for Back, [L] for Left, [R] for Right, [T] for Top, [B] for Bottom, [C] for Camera, [U] for User, and [P] for Perspective.

Help Cel

Once a viewport configuration is set, you can adjust the size of the viewports. Move your cursor to the vertical or horizontal line separating viewports. Then, pick and drag to a new viewport size. Viewports must be adjusted in pairs.

Display Mode

In each viewport, you have a choice of several different levels of detail for the display of objects. The **Smooth + Highlights** option displays objects in a low-resolution rendering. This provides the best view of the objects, short of an actual rendering. On the other end of the spectrum is the **Bounding Box** option. This option simply displays each object as a box that surrounds the object. However, as with all computer display settings, the better the display, the slower the performance.

To change the display mode of a viewport, right-click on the viewport label (name) to display the shortcut menu. Then, select the option you want from the menu. You can also set the display mode in the **Rendering Method** tab of the **Viewport Configuration** dialog box discussed earlier. The different options are explained in the sections that follow.

You can also use ActiveShade in a viewport. ActiveShade is a feature new to 3ds max 4. It allows you to quickly preview changes made to lights and materials. ActiveShade is discussed in more detail later in this book.

Smooth + Highlights

The **Smooth + Highlights** option displays objects shaded with smoothing groups and lights applied. This is a low-resolution display, but it is the most realistic display short of an actual rendering. Maps can also be displayed on objects when this option is active. Shaded viewports can display self-illuminated materials and specular highlights.

Even though the effect of lights is displayed with this option, it is only an approximation of the final rendering. The display tends to be lighter than the actual rendering.

Wireframe

The **Wireframe** option displays objects as wireframes. This is a good option to use in all orthographic viewports, with the **Smooth + Highlights** option used in a Perspective or Camera viewport. Wireframe mode allows you to see the shape and movement of objects, but no materials or highlights are applied.

Edged Faces

The **Edged Faces** option in the viewport label shortcut menu is only available if the current viewport is already in a shaded mode. When **Edged Faces** is selected in a shaded viewport, both the wireframe edges of the objects and the shaded surfaces are displayed. This can be useful when editing meshes in a shaded display.

Smooth

The **Smooth** option is located in the **Other** cascading menu in the viewport label shortcut menu. This option applies smoothing groups to objects in the viewport. However, highlights are not shown in the viewport. This option provides slightly better computer performance than the **Smooth + Highlights** option.

Facets + Highlights

The **Facets + Highlights** option is located in the **Other** cascading menu in the viewport label shortcut menu. It displays highlights on the objects. However, smoothing groups are not applied to the objects. Therefore, a sphere does not appear as a globe, but more like a soccer ball. Since smoothing groups are not applied to objects, this option provides very good computer performance.

Facets

The **Facets** option is located in the **Other** cascading menu in the viewport label shortcut menu. It produces shaded objects, but smoothing groups and highlights are not applied. This is the same as the **Facets + Highlights** option without the highlights.

Lit Wireframes

The **Lit Wireframes** option is located in the **Other** cascading menu in the viewport label shortcut menu. It displays objects as wireframes. However, unlike the **Wireframe** option, highlights are applied to the objects.

Bounding Box

The **Bounding Box** option is located in the **Other** cascading menu in the viewport label shortcut menu. It displays objects as the bounding box that surrounds each object. This is the option that provides the best computer performance, but it also gives the least-detailed view of objects.

Viewport Transparency

You can set how objects with transparent materials are displayed in shaded viewports. These options are set in the **Transparency** area of the **Rendering Method** tab in the **Viewport Configuration** dialog box. The three available options are **None**, **Stipple**, and **Blend**. When the **None** radio button is on, objects with transparent materials are displayed opaque, or solid. Picking the **Stipple** radio button displays objects with transparent materials as a pattern of "see-through" dots. This is the method used by previous releases of 3D Studio MAX. When the **Blend** radio button is on, objects with transparent materials are displayed closer to how they will appear when rendered. See Figure 1-11.

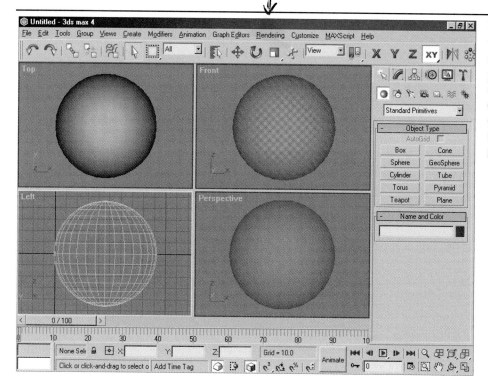

Figure 1-11. There are three options for displaying transparent materials in a shaded viewport. Clockwise from the top left, these are: **None**, **Stipple**, and **Blend**.

Unit Setup

Setting up your model with the proper units of measurement is essential if you are sharing data (drawings) with other programs, such as AutoCAD. Without using the same units, objects shared with other programs can become nonsense. A toothpick might be ten feet tall or a planet might be the size of a golf ball. If your **3ds max** model will *never* be shared with other programs, the generic drawing units can be used. Otherwise, set up the correct units of measurement before beginning your model.

When units are changed from generic units, coordinates are displayed in those values. Also, values typed in text boxes are considered by **3ds max** to be in the units you set up. **3ds max** also automatically performs a unit conversion. For example, if you set up units as centimeters and enter a value of 1'1", **3ds max** automatically converts this value to 33.02 cm.

To set up the units for your model, pick **Units Setup**... from the **Customize** pull-down menu. The **Units Setup** dialog box is displayed, Figure 1-12. The **Generic Units** radio button is selected by default. Pick

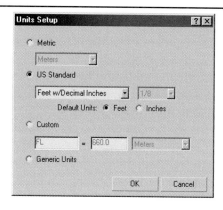

Figure 1-12. The **Units Setup** dialog box is used to define units for the model.

the **Metric**, **US Standard**, or **Custom** radio button to use units other than the generic units.

When you pick one of these radio buttons other than **Generic**, you will need to define the specific units. For example, if you pick the **Metric** radio button, you need to specify millimeters, centimeters, meters, or kilometers in the drop-down list.

If you pick the **US Standard** radio button, you must make a selection from the left drop-down list. If you select a fractional unit option, you must also specify the precision in the right drop-down list. Finally, if you select US Standard "feet with inches" units, you must pick the radio button to indicate whether feet or inches are the default units when entered in a text box.

Picking the **Custom** radio button allows you to define your own units. The left text box is where you enter an abbreviation for your units. This is simply a label and can be anything you want it to be. However, it should be something that makes sense. The middle text box is where you define how many of the units specified in the drop-down list equal one unit of your custom units. There are only a few practical applications for custom units.

Once you have made the proper selections in the **Units Setup** dialog box, pick the **OK** button. The model is now set up with the units you specified.

Precision Drawing Tools

Creating precise models is particularly important to those who are creating realistic, "real-world" scenes. There are various tools in 3ds max that help you create precise models. These include snaps, grids, and the ability to align objects. Aligning objects is discussed later in this text. Snaps and grids should be familiar to anyone who has used CAD software.

Snap Setup

Snaps allow the cursor to "lock onto" specific parts of an object or grid. There are different types of snaps. There are the 2D, 2.5D, and 3D object snaps; angle snap; and percent snap. There is also the spinner snap. The settings for object snaps, angle snap, and percent snap are changed in the **Grid and Snap Settings** dialog box. This is accessed by right-clicking on the **Snap Toggle** flyout, **Angle Snap Toggle** button, or **Percent Snap** button located at the bottom of the screen. The snap settings are stored in the 3dsmax.ini file, not the individual drawing files.

In the **Snaps** tab of the **Grid and Snap Settings** dialog box, you can pick which object snaps are active, Figure 1-13A. As soon as a check box in this dialog box is checked (or unchecked), the snap is activated (or deactivated). The dialog box does not need to be closed first, and, in fact, can remain open as you draw. Depending on which object snaps are active during a command, a cyan (blue) helper cursor appears, indicating what is being snapped to. The helper cursor appears the same as the related icon in the **Grid and Snap Settings** dialog box.

The angle snap is set in the **Options** tab of the **Grid and Snap Settings** dialog box. See Figure 1-13B. *Angle snap* defines the angular increments that will be used for actions such as rotating an object. For example, if angle snap is on and set to 5°, when rotating an object, you will only be

Figure 1-13. A—The **Snaps** tab of the **Grid and Snap Settings** dialog box is used to turn specific snaps on and off. The helper cursor for a snap appears in the viewports like the icon in the dialog box. B—The angle snap setting is changed in the **Options** tab of the **Grid and Snap Settings** dialog box.

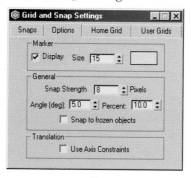

A   B

able to rotate it to 5°, 10°, 15°, and so on. To change the angle snap, enter a value in the **Angle (deg):** spinner. By default, this is set to 5°.

Next to the **Angle (deg):** spinner is the **Percent:** spinner. The value in this spinner determines the increments for any command that uses a percentage value, such as scale. By default, this is set to 10%. To change this value, simply enter a new value in the spinner.

Also in the **Options** tab, you can turn the display of the snap helper cursor on and off. When the **Display** check box in the **Marker** area is checked, the helper cursor is displayed when snap is on. When unchecked, the helper cursor is not displayed. This setting does *not* turn snap on and off.

Help Cel

You can also temporarily access a snap during a command by holding the [Shift] key and right-clicking. Then, select **Standard** and the snap from the shortcut menu.

2D, 2.5D, 3D Snap

3ds max has three different ways to snap to objects and grids in three-dimensional space. There are 2D, 2.5D, and 3D snaps for each of the object snaps. These are available in the **Snap Toggle** flyout at the bottom of the screen. A *flyout* is indicated by the small black triangle in the corner of the button. A flyout contains other commands that can be accessed if the button is held down. The last command used in a flyout is the button displayed on a toolbar. Only one command in a flyout can be active at a time. To turn on the current snap, which is indicated by the button in the flyout, either pick the button or press the [S] key on the keyboard. Picking the button or pressing the [S] key again turns the snap off.

When **2D Snap** is on, any object snap is applied to the current grid only. Any Z axis dimension is ignored. When **2.5D Snap** is on, object snaps are applied to the current grid and objects projected onto the current grid. When **3D Snap** is on, object snaps are applied to three-dimensional space. See Figure 1-14.

2D Snap

2.5D Snap

3D Snap

Figure 1-14. The three different modes of snap allow snapping to the object in 3D space, a projection of the object on the current grid, or only to points on the current grid.

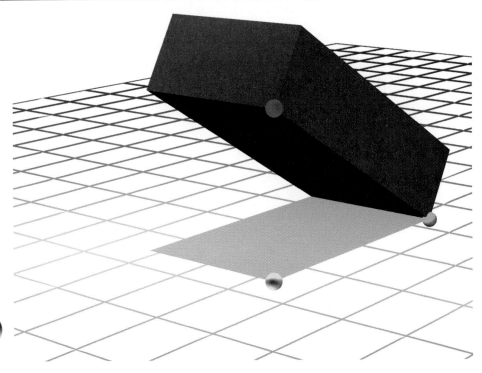

2D   3D   2.5D

Grid Setup

As discussed earlier, 3ds max has two basic types of grids. These are the home grid and grid objects. The spacing between grid lines and other features of grids can be changed using the **Grid and Snap Settings** dialog box.

The **Home Grid** tab has settings for the home grid. See Figure 1-15A. In the **Grid Spacing** area, enter a value for the size of the smallest square. This value is in the current drawing units. You should pick values that "make sense" in your current model. For example, if you are drawing an architectural model, you might make the grid spacing equal to 1 inch.

In the **Major Lines every Nth** area, enter a value for how often a major grid line should be displayed. A major grid line is displayed thicker and helps break up the grid into smaller visual sections. For example, if an architectural model is using a grid spacing of 1 inch, the major grid line may be set for every 12 lines. This makes the major grid line spacing equal to 1 foot.

At the bottom of the **Home Grid** tab, you can choose whether the changes are applied to the current viewport only or to all viewports. Also, the **Inhibit Grid Subdivision Below Grid Spacing** check box, when checked, prevents a "new" grid from appearing when you zoom in past the smallest grid box. If unchecked, when you zoom in past the smallest grid box, the box is subdivided using the current grid spacing. This may get quite confusing, but may be necessary in some instances.

The **User Grids** tab of the **Grid and Snap Settings** dialog box is used to specify certain settings for grid objects. See Figure 1-15B. When checked, the **Activate grids when created** check box automatically makes a newly created grid object current. This is unchecked by default, meaning grid objects must be manually turned on after they are created.

Figure 1-15. A—Changes to the home grid settings are made in the **Home Grid** tab of the **Grid and Snap Settings** dialog box. B—Certain settings for grid objects are made in the **User Grids** tab of the **Grid and Snap Settings** dialog box.

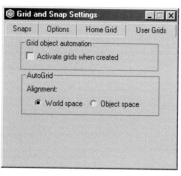

A   B

The **AutoGrid** area is used to specify whether an AutoGrid is created in world or object space. An AutoGrid is a temporary grid object placed on an existing object while in an object creation command. An AutoGrid can only be activated after an object creation command has been invoked. This is accomplished by checking the **AutoGrid** check box at the top of the **Object Type** rollout when creating an object.

Exercise 1-1

1) Set up a four-viewport configuration with three small viewports on the left and one large viewport on the right. Select **Viewport Configuration**... from the **Customize** pull-down menu. The small viewports should be the Top, Front, and Left views and the large viewport should be the Perspective view.
2) Open the **Units Setup** dialog box and set the unit type as **US Standard**. Select **Feet w/Fractional Inches** as the units and **1/4** as the precision.
3) Open the **Grid and Snap Settings** dialog box. In the **Home Grid** tab, set the **Grid Spacing** to 1′0″ and the **Major Lines every Nth** setting to 10.
4) In the **Snaps** tab, turn on the **Grid Points** snap by making sure there is a check in that check box.
5) Close the **Grid and Snap Settings** dialog box and turn on the **3D Snap** button.

Exercise

Viewport Navigation Controls

Earlier in this chapter, you learned how to adjust the viewport configuration. In addition to this, you must also be able to move the view *in* each viewport. Without being able to do this, it would be impossible to effectively model. 3ds max has several commands that allow you to adjust the view in a viewport. These can generally be grouped into three categories—zooming, panning, and rotating a view.

Zoom

Zoom All

Z

Esc

Zoom Extents

Zoom Extents All

Ctrl Alt Z

Ctrl Shift Z

Zoom Extents Selected

Zoom Extents All Selected

Region Zoom

Field-of-View

Ctrl W

Zooming

Zooming is a function common to most computer graphics programs. *Zooming* is changing the magnification of a view. This can be either increasing (zooming in) or decreasing (zooming out) the magnification.

The **Zoom** and **Zoom All** commands function similarly. The only difference between the two is that **Zoom** affects the current viewport only, while **Zoom All** affects all viewports the same. To use either of these commands, pick the **Zoom** or **Zoom All** button in the viewport navigation controls. These are located at the bottom-right corner of the screen. The [Z] key can also be used to activate the **Zoom** command. After picking one of these buttons, it is depressed and the background of the button turns orange. This indicates that you are in a navigation mode. A navigation mode is active until canceled by right-clicking or pressing the [Esc] key. To use the **Zoom** or **Zoom All** command, pick in a viewport and hold. Then, drag the mouse up to zoom in or down to zoom out.

The **Zoom Extents** and **Zoom Extents All** commands also function similarly. **Zoom Extents** affects only the current viewport. **Zoom Extents All** affects all viewports. Picking these buttons zooms the viewport(s) to the extents of the model. This may be in or out, depending on the current zoom level. The *scene extents* is an imaginary box that encloses all objects. The two **Zoom Extents** commands are not navigation modes. This means that the command is invoked and exited immediately when the button is picked. The keyboard shortcut [Ctrl][Alt][Z] activates the **Zoom Extents** command. The keyboard shortcut [Ctrl][Shift][Z] activates the **Zoom Extents All** command.

The **Zoom Extents** and **Zoom Extents All** buttons are flyouts. The **Zoom Extents** flyout contains the **Zoom Extents Selected** button. The **Zoom Extents All** flyout contains the **Zoom Extents All Selected** button. These commands zoom to the extents of the selected objects, not all objects.

The final zoom command is **Region Zoom**. Picking this button or pressing [Ctrl][W] allows you to drag a window around the area you want to magnify. This is a navigation mode command and can only be used in one viewport at a time. **Region Zoom** is similar to "window zooms" found in many CAD and illustration programs. If a camera or perspective viewport is active, the **Region Zoom** button is replaced by the **Field-of-View** button. Field of view is explained in Chapter 11, *Cameras*.

Help Cel

To undo a zoom, select **Undo** from the **Views** pull-down menu or press [Shift][Z].

Panning

Panning is moving the view around in the current viewport without changing the magnification. If you think of the model as a sheet of paper and the viewport as a window, panning is like moving the paper so that different portions can be seen through the window. See Figure 1-16.

To pan the view in the current viewport, pick the **Pan** button or press [Ctrl][P] on the keyboard. The cursor changes to the pan cursor. Pick and hold in the viewport. Then, drag the view as needed. Release the button when done. To end the command, right-click or press the [Esc] key.

If you hold down the [Shift] key before picking in the viewport, the viewport can only be panned along the axis first moved. For example, if you hold the [Shift] key, pick in the viewport, and first move along the X axis, you can pan the view along the X axis only. Holding down the [Ctrl] key accelerates the pan.

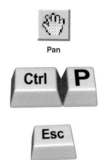

Help Cel

To undo a pan, select **Undo** from the **Views** pull-down menu or press [Shift][Z].

Rotating a View

The Perspective viewport provides a three-dimensional view of your model. However, the current perspective view may not always show what you want to see. Therefore, it may be necessary to rotate the view in 3D space. Any viewport can be rotated, including camera viewports. If one of the standard orthographic viewports—Top, Bottom, Left, Right, Front, or Back—is rotated, it becomes a User viewport. A User viewport is simply one that contains a view defined by the user.

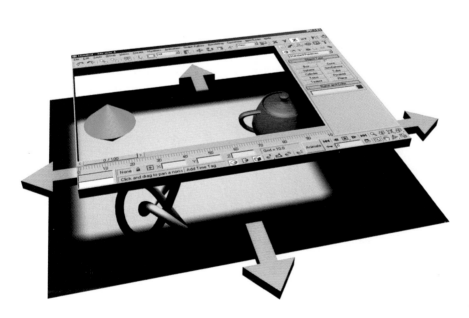

Figure 1-16. You can think of panning as moving a sheet of paper below the viewport. Only the objects "below" the viewport are visible in the viewport.

Arc Rotate

Orbit Camera

To rotate the view in a viewport, first activate the viewport. Then, pick the **Arc Rotate** button located in the viewport navigation controls. If the current viewport is a camera viewport, the button is replaced by the **Orbit Camera** button. Both of these commands are navigational modes. They remain active until you right-click or press [Esc] to end the command.

In a noncamera viewport, the view rotation trackball is displayed after picking the button. The *view rotation trackball* is a yellow circle with square "handles" at the four quadrants. See Figure 1-17. Picking and dragging inside the circle rotates the view about the viewing plane. Picking and dragging outside the circle rotates the view about the axis perpendicular to the viewing plane.

Arc Rotate Selected

Arc Rotate SubObject

The **Arc Rotate** and **Orbit Camera** buttons are flyouts. The keyboard shortcut [Ctrl][R] activates whichever command was last used in the flyout. Contained in the **Arc Rotate** flyout are the **Arc Rotate Selected** and **Arc Rotate SubObject** buttons. **Arc Rotate** uses the center of the view as the center for rotation. **Arc Rotate Selected** uses the center of the selection as the center for rotation. **Arc Rotate SubObject** uses the center of the current sub-object selection as the center for rotation. Sub-object selection is discussed later in this text.

Pan Camera

Contained in the **Orbit Camera** flyout is the **Pan Camera** button. The **Orbit Camera** command rotates the camera about the target. The **Pan Camera** command rotates the target about the camera. In a camera viewport, the view rotation trackball is not displayed.

Help Cel

Generally, right-clicking can be used to cancel any command.

Figure 1-17. The view rotation trackball allows you to adjust a 3D view in the viewport.

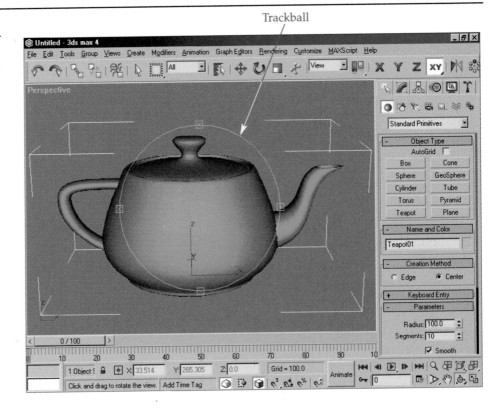

Maximizing a Viewport

With more than one viewport displayed, parts of your model may become quite small and hard to see. While you can reconfigure the display for a single viewport, there is a much easier way. The **Min/Max Toggle** button, located in the viewport navigation controls, switches the current viewport to a single viewport configuration. Picking the button again returns to the previous viewport configuration. The [W] key can also be used to toggle between a single viewport and the previous configuration.

Min/Max Toggle

Exercise 1-2

1) Open the file Angus Face.max located in the 3ds max \Scenes folder. This file is installed when 3ds max is installed. When prompted, do not save the file from Exercise 1-1. Note: The rectangles displayed in the viewport are called the "safe frame." This is discussed later in the book. Ignore them for this exercise.
2) Open the **Viewport Configuration** dialog box. Switch to a configuration with three small viewports on the left and one large viewport on the right. Perform a zoom extents in all viewports.
3) Change the large viewport to the Right view. Perform a zoom extents.
4) Change the top small viewport to the Left view. Perform a zoom extents.
5) Change the middle small viewport to the Top view. Perform a zoom extents.
6) Change the bottom small viewport to the Front view. Perform a zoom extents.
7) Change the large viewport to the Perspective view. Perform a zoom extents. Then, rotate the view to obtain a display close to the original display when the file was opened.
8) Change the display mode of the Perspective viewport to **Wireframe**. Then, change the display back to **Smooth + Highlights**.

Exercise

Saving Your Work and Resetting 3ds max

It is very important to save your work often. By doing so, you can minimize the amount of work that needs to be replicated in case of a computer crash or power failure. Also, there are a couple of different ways to "clear" 3ds max and start fresh.

Saving Your Work

Save and save often. Also, always save your work before performing an action where you are not quite sure of the results, or if you think the computer may crash during the command.

To save your work, pick **Save** from the **File** pull-down menu or press [Ctrl][S]. If you have already saved the file at least once before, the file is saved with the same name. If the file has not been saved, or if you pick **Save As**... from the **File** pull-down menu, the **Save File As** dialog box appears. See Figure 1-18. This is a standard Windows "save" dialog box. Switch to the drive and folder where you want to save the file and enter a name in the **File name:** text box. Then, pick the **Save** button or press [Enter] to save the file.

Resetting 3ds max

To "clear" 3ds max and start fresh, pick **Reset** from the **File** pull-down menu. If changes have been made since the last time the file was saved, a dialog box appears indicating this and asks if you want to save the changes, Figure 1-19A. Then, a dialog box appears asking if you want to reset 3ds max, Figure 1-19B. Pick the **Yes** button and 3ds max is reset to its default settings. Picking **New**... from the **File** pull-down menu or pressing [Ctrl][N] also clears 3ds max. However, current settings such as the viewport configuration and grid setup are retained.

Figure 1-18. The **Save File As** dialog box is used to save your model to the folder of your choice using a name you specify.

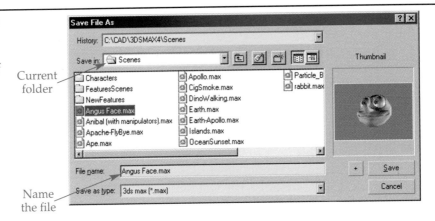

Figure 1-19. A—This dialog box appears if you try to close or reset without first saving the current scene. B—This dialog box appears when you reset 3ds max.

A

B

Exercise 1-3

Exercise

1) Reset 3ds max without saving.
2) Set up 3ds max as described in Exercise 1-1.
3) Save the setup as section01.max in the folder of your choice.
4) Reset 3ds max.

Chapter Snapshot

Chapter Test

Answer the following questions on a separate sheet of paper.

1) Define the following terms.
    a) computer graphics
    b) rendering
    c) bitmap
    d) vector
    e) paint program
    f) draw program
    g) animation
    h) two-dimensional
    i) three-dimensional

2) Identify the following parts of the 3ds max interface.

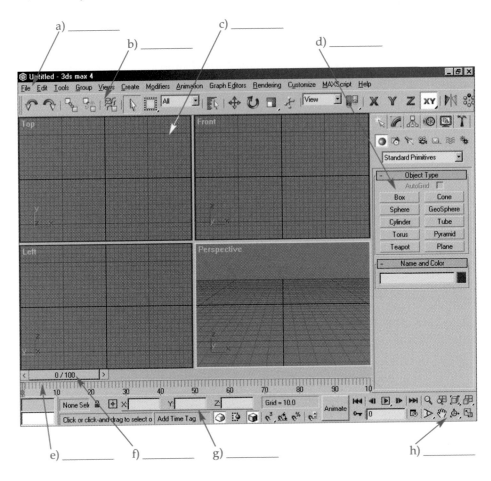

3) A toolbar and the **Command Panel** can be _____ or docked.
4) The _____ is accessed by right-clicking anywhere in any viewport, except on the viewport label.
5) Define expert mode.
6) What is the **Material Editor** used for?
7) List the six standard orthographic views.
8) What is **Track View** used for?
9) List what the following keyboard shortcuts do.
    a) F
    b) K
    c) L
    d) R
    e) T
    f) B
    g) C
    h) U
    i) P
10) ActiveShade allows you to _____.
11) List the eight display modes.
12) List the three options for viewport transparency.
13) What are the four types of units that can be set up on 3ds max?
14) What is the purpose of **Snap**?

15) What is the home grid?
16) How do **Zoom Extents** and **Zoom Extents All** differ?
17) When panning in a viewport, how do you limit the movement to one axis only?
18) What keyboard key is used to switch the current viewport to a single-viewport configuration?
19) How does resetting 3ds max differ from selecting **New**... in the **File** pull-down menu?
20) What does the [Ctrl][S] key combination do?

Creating Basic 3D Geometry (Standard Primitives)

Objectives

After completing this chapter, you will be able to:
- Explain what a standard primitive is.
- Define parametric modeling.
- Draw 3ds max standard primitives.

3ds max has several basic building blocks called ***standard primitives.*** These are basic geometric shapes, such as boxes and spheres. As you will see in this section of the text, complex scenes can be created from these simple shapes.

3ds max is a ***parametric modeling program.*** This means that the parameters, or dimensions, of an object can be changed after the object is created. All standard primitives can be drawn using the cursor to specify parameters or by entering parameters using the keyboard.

Help Cel

When using the **Command Panel**, you can "pan" the panel up and down. Move the cursor to an open area of the panel. The cursor changes to the "pan hand." Then, pick, hold, and pan the panel.

Create

Geometry

Box

Box

Box

A *box* is a simple, six-sided object. A box only has three parameters—length, width, and height. To create a box, first select **Create** in the **Command Panel**. Then, pick the **Geometry** button. Select **Standard Primitives** in the drop-down list and then pick the **Box** button in the **Object Type** rollout.

You can also pick **Standard Primitives** in the **Create** pull-down menu. Then, pick **Box** in the cascading menu. This opens the **Create** tab in the **Command Panel** and selects the **Box** button.

In the **Creation Method** rollout, you can specify how the box is created. Picking the **Box** radio button allows a box to be created with different dimensions for the length, width, and height. This is the

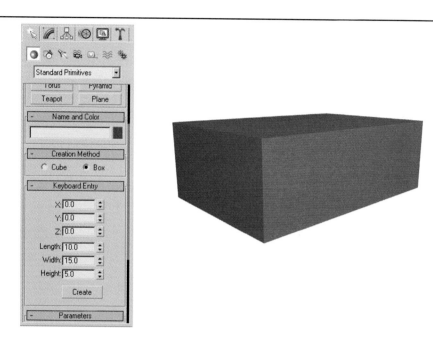

Figure 2-1. A box has length, width, and height parameters.

default. Picking the **Cube** radio button creates a box with equal values for the length, width, and height.

To draw a box using the cursor, simply pick a point for the first corner of the box. Then drag the cursor to the other corner of the first face. This defines the length and width. Next, drag and pick to define the height.

To draw a box using the keyboard, expand the **Keyboard Entry** rollout by picking on it. See Figure 2-1. Then, enter values in the **Length:**, **Width:**, and **Height:** spinners. The X, Y, and Z coordinates of the center of the first face can also be entered in this rollout. Finally, pick the **Create** button to draw the box.

Once the box is created, a name can be entered in the **Name and Color** rollout. The color of the box can also be changed by picking the color swatch and then selecting a new color in the **Object Color** dialog box. See Figure 2-2.

The values in the **Length Segs:**, **Width Segs:**, and **Height Segs:** spinners in the **Parameters** rollout determine how many divisions there are along each axis of the box. These divisions are called *segments.* The number of

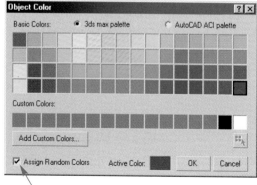

Random colors are assigned when checked

Figure 2-2. The **Object Color** dialog box is used to change an object's display color. By default, 3ds max randomly assigns display colors to new objects.

segments is important if the box will be modified. For example, if the box is bent, you may want to use a greater number of segments so the bend is curved rather than square. The **Generate Mapping Coordinates** check box at the bottom of the **Parameters** rollout is used to automatically calculate mapping coordinates for the box being created. By default, this option is off. Mapping is discussed later in this text.

Help Cel

By default, 3ds max automatically assigns a new color to each newly created object.

Exercise 2-1

1) Select **Create** in the **Command Panel**. Then, pick the **Geometry** button and select **Standard Primitives** from the drop-down list.
2) Pick **Box** in the **Object Type** rollout.
3) Draw a box using the **Keyboard Entry** rollout. Use your own dimensions.
4) Draw another box using the cursor.
5) Reset 3ds max. Do not save the file.

Create

Geometry

Sphere

Sphere

Sphere

A *sphere* is a simple ball. A sphere has only one parameter—a radius. 3ds max has two types of spheres. These are sphere and geosphere. The geosphere primitive is discussed in the next section. To draw a sphere, first select **Create** in the **Command Panel**. Then, pick the **Geometry** button. Select **Standard Primitives** in the drop-down list and then pick the **Sphere** button in the **Object Type** rollout.

You can also pick **<u>S</u>tandard Primitives** in the **<u>C</u>reate** pull-down menu. Then, pick **Sphere** in the cascading menu. This opens the **Create** tab in the **Command Panel** and selects the **Sphere** button.

In the **Creation Method** rollout, you can specify how the sphere is created. Picking the **Center** radio button specifies the first point picked as the center of the sphere. Picking the **Edge** radio button specifies the first point picked as the first corner of the sphere's bounding box. These options do not apply when drawing the sphere using the **Keyboard Entry** rollout.

To draw a sphere using the keyboard, first expand the **Keyboard Entry** rollout by picking on it. Then, enter the radius for the sphere in the **Radius:** spinner. Finally, pick the **Create** button to draw the sphere. The X, Y, and Z coordinates of the center of the sphere can also be specified in this rollout. See Figure 2-3.

To draw a sphere using the cursor, pick a location in the viewport for the center of the sphere. If the **Edge** radio button is picked in the **Creation Method** rollout, the first point is one corner of the sphere's

Figure 2-3. A sphere has a radius parameter.

bounding box. Then, drag the cursor to set the radius of the sphere. When you have the radius you want, release the mouse button.

Once the sphere is created, a name can be entered in the **Name and Color** rollout. The object color can also be changed by picking the color swatch and selecting a new color in the **Object Color** dialog box.

The **Segments:** spinner in the **Parameters** rollout allows you to set the number of segments for the sphere. The **Smooth** check box is located below the **Segments:** spinner. When checked, the **Smooth** check box applies smoothing to the sphere. When unchecked, the sphere has abrupt transitions between faces. This gives the sphere a faceted appearance.

A *hemisphere* is a portion of a complete sphere. Perhaps the most common type of hemisphere is a sphere sliced down the middle. When you think of the northern or southern hemisphere of Earth, this is one half of a complete sphere. To create a hemisphere, enter a value other than 0 in the **Hemisphere:** spinner in the **Parameters** rollout. A value of 0.25 creates 3/4 of a sphere. A value of 0.5 creates half a sphere.

Below the **Hemisphere:** spinner are the **Chop** and **Squash** radio buttons. When **Chop** is selected and a hemisphere is created, the faces are not altered. The sphere is simply "cut" at the level specified in the **Hemisphere:** spinner. When **Squash** is selected, the hemisphere has the same number of faces as the complete sphere. The faces are scaled to fit in the dimensions of the hemisphere.

Checking the **Slice On** check box in the **Parameters** rollout enables the **Slice From:** and **Slice To:** spinners. These spinners allow you to specify where the sphere "starts" and "stops" around its local Z axis by entering a starting degree value and an ending degree value. In this way, you can create portions of a sphere. For example, suppose you are modeling Earth and need to show its core. You could use the slice option to create a model of Earth you can see into. See Figure 2-4.

The **Base To Pivot** check box, when checked, shifts the sphere on its local Z axis so the pivot point is tangent to the surface of the sphere.

Figure 2-4. By slicing a sphere, you can create a model of Earth showing its core.

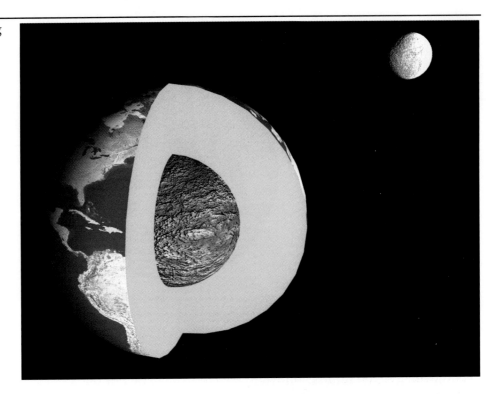

When unchecked, the pivot is the center of the sphere. This is the default. The **Generate Mapping Coordinates** check box at the bottom of the **Parameters** rollout is used to automatically calculate mapping coordinates for the sphere being created. By default, this option is off. Mapping is discussed later in this text.

Exercise

Exercise 2-2

1) Select **Create** in the **Command Panel**. Then, pick the **Geometry** button and select **Standard Primitives** from the drop-down list.
2) Pick **Sphere** in the **Object Type** rollout.
3) Draw a sphere using the **Keyboard Entry** rollout. Use your own dimensions.
4) Draw another sphere using the cursor.
5) Uncheck the **Smooth** check box. Notice the difference between the objects in the Perspective viewport.
6) Enter a value of 0.3 in the **Hemisphere:** spinner.
7) Pick the **Base To Pivot** check box so it is checked.
8) Reset 3ds max. Do not save the file.

GeoSphere

A *geosphere* is a geodesic sphere. You can choose between three types of polygonal "solids" that make up the geosphere. Remember, however, that 3ds max creates surfaced objects and not solid objects. A geosphere is smoother and has a more regular surface than a sphere. To draw a geosphere, first select **Create** in the **Command Panel**. Then, pick the **Geometry** button. Select **Standard Primitives** in the drop-down list and then pick the **GeoSphere** button in the **Object Type** rollout.

You can also pick **S̲tandard Primitives** in the **C̲reate** pull-down menu. Then, pick **G̲eoSphere** in the cascading menu. This opens the **Create** tab in the **Command Panel** and selects the **GeoSphere** button.

In the **Geodesic Base Type** area of the **Parameters** rollout, you can select between three types of polygonal solids that make up the geosphere. Selecting the **Tetra** radio button creates a surface made up of tetrahedrons and triangular faces. This is the least refined of the three options. Selecting the **Octa** radio button creates a surface made up of octagons and triangular faces. Selecting the **Icosa** radio button creates a surface made up of 20-sided polygons and equilateral triangles. This is the most refined of the three options. If you draw a geosphere and set the **Segments:** value to 1, you can pick the three radio buttons to see the different base polygonal shapes.

In the **Creation Method** rollout, you can specify how the geosphere is created. Picking the **Center** radio button specifies the first point picked as the center of the geosphere. Picking the **Diameter** radio button specifies the first point picked as one point on the diameter of the geosphere. Where you release the mouse button is the opposite side of the diameter. These options do not apply when drawing the geosphere using the **Keyboard Entry** rollout.

To draw a geosphere using the keyboard, first expand the **Keyboard Entry** rollout by picking on it. Then, enter a radius in the **Radius:** spinner and pick the **Create** button. See Figure 2-5. You can also specify the X, Y, and Z coordinates of the geosphere center in this rollout.

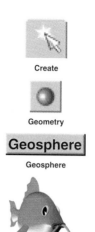

Create

Geometry

Geosphere

Geosphere

Figure 2-5. A geosphere, like a sphere, has a radius parameter.

To draw a geosphere using the cursor, pick in the viewport to specify the center of the geosphere. Then, drag the cursor to specify the radius of the geosphere. Once you have the radius as you want it, release the mouse button.

Once the geosphere is created, a name can be entered in the **Name and Color** rollout. The object color can also be changed by picking the color swatch and selecting a new color in the **Object Color** dialog box.

At the bottom of the **Parameters** rollout are four check boxes. The **Smooth** check box applies smoothing to the geosphere when checked. Checking the **Hemisphere** check box creates one half of a geosphere. This is similar to entering 0.5 in the **Hemisphere:** spinner and picking the **Squash** radio button for a sphere. Checking the **Base to Pivot** check box shifts the geosphere on its local Z axis so the pivot point is tangent to the geosphere. Checking this when **Hemisphere** is checked has no effect.

The **Generate Mapping Coordinates** check box at the bottom of the **Parameters** rollout is used to automatically calculate mapping coordinates for the geosphere being created. By default, this option is off. Mapping is discussed later in this text.

Exercise

Exercise 2-3

1) Select **Create** in the **Command Panel**. Then, pick the **Geometry** button and select **Standard Primitives** from the drop-down list.
2) Pick **GeoSphere** in the **Object Type** rollout.
3) Draw a geosphere using the **Keyboard Entry** rollout. Select the **Tetra** radio button in the **Parameters** rollout. Also, uncheck the **Smooth** check box. Use your own dimensions.
4) Draw another geosphere using the cursor. Pick the **Icosa** radio button in the **Parameters** rollout. Also, uncheck the **Smooth** check box, if checked. Looking at the Perspective viewport, compare this geosphere with the first one. Now, check the **Smooth** check box.
5) Draw a third geosphere using either the cursor or the keyboard. Check the **Hemisphere** check box in the **Parameters** rollout.
6) Reset 3ds max. Do not save the file.

Create

Geometry

Cylinder

Cylinder

Cylinder

A *cylinder* is like a round pencil. It has two parameters—a radius and a height. You can also set the number of segments for the height and ends of the cylinder. To draw a cylinder, first select **Create** in the **Command Panel**. Then, pick the **Geometry** button. Select **Standard Primitives** in the drop-down list and then pick the **Cylinder** button in the **Object Type** rollout.

You can also pick **Standard Primitives** in the **Create** pull-down menu. Then, pick **Cylinder** in the cascading menu. This opens the **Create** tab in the **Command Panel** and selects the **Cylinder** button.

In the **Creation Method** rollout, you can specify how the cylinder is created. Picking the **Center** radio button specifies the first point picked as the center of the first (bottom) face of the cylinder. Picking the **Edge**

Figure 2-6. A cylinder has radius and height parameters.

radio button specifies the first point picked as the first corner of a box enclosing the first face of the cylinder. These options do not apply when drawing the cylinder using the **Keyboard Entry** rollout.

To draw a cylinder using the keyboard, first expand the **Keyboard Entry** rollout by picking on it. Then, enter a radius in the **Radius:** spinner and a height in the **Height:** spinner. Finally, pick the **Create** button. See Figure 2-6. You can also specify the X, Y, and Z coordinates of the center of the first face in this rollout.

To draw a cylinder using the cursor, pick a point in the viewport as the center of the first face. Then, drag the cursor to set the radius. Once the radius is set, release the mouse button and move the cursor up or down to set the height of the cylinder.

Once the cylinder is created, a name can be entered in the **Name and Color** rollout. The object color can also be changed by picking the color swatch and selecting a new color in the **Object Color** dialog box.

The number of segments for the height and the ends can be set in the **Parameters** rollout. The value in the **Height Segments:** spinner determines how many divisions there are on the height of the cylinder. As with a box, if the cylinder is to be modified, too few height segments may result in an unwanted shape. The value in the **Cap Segments:** spinner determines the number of segments on each end of the cylinder. Usually, this value can be very low and in many cases set to 1. The value in the **Sides:** spinner determines how many sides the cylinder has. A low value can be used to produce polygonal objects. For example, if you uncheck the **Smooth** check box and draw a cylinder with six sides, you can use this object as the body of a pencil or ballpoint pen.

Just as with a sphere, a cylinder can be sliced. Checking the **Slice On** check box in the **Parameters** rollout applies the values in the **Slice From:** and **Slice To:** spinners. These spinners allow you to specify where the circle portion of the cylinder "starts" and "stops" around its local Z axis. In this way, you can create portions of a cylinder.

The **Generate Mapping Coordinates** check box at the bottom of the **Parameters** rollout is used to automatically calculate mapping coordinates for the cylinder being created. By default, this option is off. Mapping is discussed later in this text.

Exercise

Exercise 2-4

1) Select **Create** in the **Command Panel**. Then, pick the **Geometry** button and select **Standard Primitives** from the drop-down list.
2) Pick **Cylinder** in the **Object Type** rollout.
3) Draw a cylinder using the **Keyboard Entry** rollout with the Front viewport active. Use your own dimensions.
4) Check the **Slice On** check box in the **Parameters** rollout. Enter values in the **Slice From:** and **Slice To:** spinners. Observe how different values affect the object.
5) Draw another cylinder using the keyboard with the Top viewport active.
6) Draw a third cylinder using the cursor. Make the Left viewport active before entering parameters. How does this cylinder differ from the others?
7) Reset 3ds max. Do not save the file.

Create

Geometry

Tube

Tube

Tube

A *tube* is a cylinder with a hole down the middle, similar to a drinking straw. There are three parameters to a tube—an inner radius, an outer radius, and a height. To draw a tube, first select **Create** in the **Command Panel**. Then, pick the **Geometry** button. Select **Standard Primitives** in the drop-down list and then pick the **Tube** button in the **Object Type** rollout.

You can also pick **Standard Primitives** in the **Create** pull-down menu. Then, pick **Tube** in the cascading menu. This opens the **Create** tab in the **Command Panel** and selects the **Tube** button.

In the **Creation Method** rollout, you can specify how the tube is created. Picking the **Center** radio button specifies the first point picked as the center of the first (bottom) face of the tube. Picking the **Edge** radio button specifies the first point picked as the first corner of a box enclosing the first face of the tube. These options do not apply when drawing the tube using the **Keyboard Entry** rollout.

To draw a tube using the keyboard, first expand the **Keyboard Entry** rollout by picking on it. Then, enter a radius in both the **Inner Radius:** and **Outer Radius:** spinners and a height in the **Height:** spinner. Pick the **Create** button to create the tube. See Figure 2-7. You can also specify the X, Y, and Z coordinates of the center of the first face in this rollout.

To draw a tube using the cursor, pick in the viewport to set the center of the first face (or point on diameter) and drag to set the first radius. Once the first radius is set, release the mouse button. Then, move the cursor and pick to set the second radius. If you move the cursor

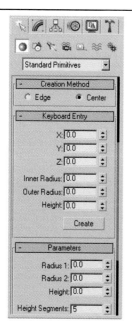

Figure 2-7. A tube has a height parameter and two radius parameters.

inside the first radius, the first radius is the outer radius and the second radius is the inner radius. If you move the cursor *outside* the first radius, the first radius is the inner radius and the second radius is the outer radius. Once both radii are set, move the cursor up or down and pick to set the height.

Once the tube is created, a name can be entered in the **Name and Color** rollout. The object color can also be changed by picking the color swatch and selecting a new color in the **Object Color** dialog box.

Just as with a cylinder, the number of segments can be set in the **Parameters** rollout. The value in the **Height Segments:** spinner determines how many divisions there are on the height of the tube. The value in the **Cap Segments:** spinner determines the number of segments on each end of the tube. The value in the **Sides:** spinner determines how many sides the tube has. Checking the **Smooth** check box applies smoothing to the tube.

Also, just as with a cylinder, the **Slice On** check box in the **Parameters** rollout applies the values in the **Slice From:** and **Slice To:** spinners. These spinners allow you to specify where the circle portion of the tube "starts" and "stops" around its Z axis. In this way, you can create portions of a tube. The slice values apply to both radii.

The **Generate Mapping Coordinates** check box at the bottom of the **Parameters** rollout is used to automatically calculate mapping coordinates for the tube being created. By default, this option is off. Mapping is discussed later in this text.

Exercise

Exercise 2-5

1) Select **Create** in the **Command Panel**. Then, pick the **Geometry** button and select **Standard Primitives** from the drop-down list.
2) Pick **Tube** in the **Object Type** rollout.
3) Draw a tube using the **Keyboard Entry** rollout. Use your own dimensions.
4) Check the **Slice On** check box in the **Parameters** rollout. Enter values in the **Slice From:** and **Slice To:** spinners. Observe how different values affect the object.
5) Draw another tube using the keyboard with the Front viewport active. Uncheck the **Smooth** check box and enter a value of 8 in the **Sides:** spinner.
6) Draw a third tube using the cursor. Make the Top viewport active before entering parameters. Check the **Smooth** check box and enter a value of 32 in the **Sides:** spinner. How does this tube differ from the others?
7) Reset 3ds max. Do not save the file.

Create

Geometry

Cone

Cone

Cone

A *cone* is like a cylinder with end faces of different diameters. Often, one diameter is zero, creating a pointed cone. To draw a cone, first select **Create** in the **Command Panel**. Then, pick the **Geometry** button. Select **Standard Primitives** in the drop-down list and then pick the **Cone** button in the **Object Type** rollout.

You can also pick **Standard Primitives** in the **Create** pull-down menu. Then, pick **Cone** in the cascading menu. This opens the **Create** tab in the **Command Panel** and selects the **Cone** button.

In the **Creation Method** rollout, you can specify how the cone is created. Picking the **Center** radio button specifies the first point picked as the center of the cone's base. Picking the **Edge** radio button specifies the first point picked as the first corner of a box enclosing the first face of the cone. These options do not apply when drawing the cone using the **Keyboard Entry** rollout.

To draw a cone using the keyboard, first expand the **Keyboard Entry** rollout by picking on it. Then, enter values in the **Radius 1:** and **Radius 2:** spinners. Also enter a value in the **Height:** spinner. Finally, pick the **Create** button to create the cone. See Figure 2-8. The **Radius 1:** value applies to the first end face. This is the bottom if a positive height is entered or the top if a negative height is entered. You can also specify the X, Y, and Z coordinates of the center of the first face in this rollout.

To draw a cone using the cursor, pick in the viewport to set the center of the first face. Drag the cursor and release the mouse button to set the first radius. Then, move the cursor up or down and pick to set the height. Finally, move the cursor up or down and pick to set the second radius.

Once the cone is created, a name can be entered in the **Name and Color** rollout. The object color can also be changed by picking the color swatch and selecting a new color in the **Object Color** dialog box.

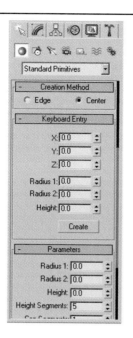

Figure 2-8. A cone has a height parameter and two radius parameters.

Just as with a cylinder, the number of segments can be set in the **Parameters** rollout. The value in the **Height Segments:** spinner determines how many divisions there are on the height of the cone. The value in the **Cap Segments:** spinner determines the number of segments on each end of the cone. The value in the **Sides:** spinner determines how many sides the cone has. Checking the **Smooth** check box applies smoothing to the cone.

Also, just as with a cylinder, the **Slice On** check box in the **Parameters** rollout applies the values in the **Slice From:** and **Slice To:** spinners. These spinners allow you to specify where the circle portion of the cone "starts" and "stops" around its Z axis. Both radii use the same slice values.

The **Generate Mapping Coordinates** check box at the bottom of the **Parameters** rollout is used to automatically calculate mapping coordinates for the cone being created. By default, this option is off. Mapping is discussed later in this text.

Help Cel

When drawing a cone, the **Radius 2:** value can be larger than the **Radius 1:** value. However, the **Radius 1:** value cannot be 0.

Exercise

Exercise 2-6

1) Select **Create** in the **Command Panel**. Then, pick the **Geometry** button and select **Standard Primitives** from the drop-down list.
2) Pick **Cone** in the **Object Type** rollout.
3) Draw a cone using the **Keyboard Entry** rollout. Use your own dimensions. Make the **Radius 2:** value larger than the **Radius 1:** value.
4) Check the **Slice On** check box in the **Parameters** rollout. Enter values in the **Slice From:** and **Slice To:** spinners. Observe how different values affect the object.
5) Draw another cone using the keyboard with the Left viewport active. Uncheck the **Smooth** check box and enter a value of 4 in the **Sides:** spinner.
6) Draw a third cone using the cursor. Make the Top viewport active before entering parameters. Check the **Smooth** check box and enter a value of 32 in the **Sides:** spinner. How does this cone differ from the others?
7) Reset 3ds max. Do not save the file.

Create

Geometry

Pyramid

Pyramid

A *pyramid* has a rectangular face on one end and comes to a point at the other end. There are three parameters for a pyramid—width, depth, and height. To draw a pyramid, first select **Create** in the **Command Panel**. Then, pick the **Geometry** button. Select **Standard Primitives** in the drop-down list and then pick the **Pyramid** button in the **Object Type** rollout.

You can also pick **Standard Primitives** in the **Create** pull-down menu. Then, pick **Pyramid** in the cascading menu. This opens the **Create** tab in the **Command Panel** and selects the **Pyramid** button.

In the **Creation Method** rollout, you can specify how the pyramid is created. Picking the **Center** radio button specifies the first point picked as the center of the first face of the pyramid. Picking the **Base/Apex** radio button specifies the first point picked as the first corner of a box enclosing the first face of the pyramid. With both options, the *apex,* or top, of the pyramid must be set with another mouse drag/pick. These options do not apply when drawing the pyramid using the **Keyboard Entry** rollout.

To draw a pyramid using the keyboard, first expand the **Keyboard Entry** rollout by picking on it. Then, enter values in the **Width:** and **Depth:** spinners to define the size of the base. Also, enter a height in the **Height:** spinner. Then, pick the **Create** button. See Figure 2-9. You can also specify the X, Y, and Z coordinates of the center of the base in this rollout.

To draw a pyramid using the cursor, pick in the viewport and drag to define the width and depth of the base. Release the mouse button and then move the cursor up or down and pick to set the height.

Once the pyramid is created, a name can be entered in the **Name and Color** rollout. The object color can also be changed by picking the color swatch and selecting a new color in the **Object Color** dialog box.

Figure 2-9. A pyramid has width, depth, and height parameters.

The number of segments the pyramid has can be set independently for the width, depth, and height in the **Parameters** rollout. The value in the **Width Segs:** spinner determines the number of segments on the pyramid's X axis. The value in the **Depth Segs:** spinner determines the number of segments on the pyramid's Y axis. The value in the **Height Segs:** spinner determines the number of segments on the pyramid's Z axis.

The **Generate Mapping Coordinates** check box at the bottom of the **Parameters** rollout is used to automatically calculate mapping coordinates for the pyramid being created. By default, this option is off. Mapping is discussed later in this text.

Exercise 2-7

1) Select **Create** in the **Command Panel**. Then, pick the **Geometry** button and select **Standard Primitives** from the drop-down list.
2) Pick **Pyramid** in the **Object Type** rollout.
3) Draw a pyramid in the Top viewport using the cursor. Draw a second pyramid in the Front viewport. Use your own dimensions.
4) Draw a pyramid using the keyboard with the Left viewport active.
5) Draw a pyramid with a base that has six sides. Draw a fourth pyramid with a base that has four sides, but one quarter sliced away. Hint: Neither of these can be drawn using the **Pyramid** object.
6) Reset 3ds max. Do not save the file.

Exercise

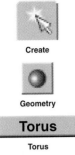

Create

Geometry

Torus

Torus

Torus

A *torus* is like a doughnut. It has a major radius and a minor radius. The *major radius* is the overall radius. The *minor radius* is the radius of the cross section. To draw a torus, first select **Create** in the **Command Panel**. Then, pick the **Geometry** button. Select **Standard Primitives** in the drop-down list and then pick the **Torus** button in the **Object Type** rollout.

You can also pick **S̲tandard Primitives** in the **C̲reate** pull-down menu. Then, pick **To̲rus** in the cascading menu. This opens the **Create** tab in the **Command Panel** and selects the **Torus** button.

In the **Creation Method** rollout, you can specify how the torus is created. Picking the **Center** radio button specifies the first point picked as the center of the torus. Picking the **Edge** button specifies the first point picked as a point on the major diameter. These options do not apply when drawing the torus using the **Keyboard Entry** rollout.

To draw a torus using the keyboard, first expand the **Keyboard Entry** rollout by picking on it. Then, enter values in the **Major Radius:** and **Minor Radius:** spinners. Pick the **Create** button to create the torus. See Figure 2-10. You can also specify the X, Y, and Z coordinates of the center of the torus in this rollout.

To draw a torus using the cursor, pick in the viewport to specify the center (or point on diameter) of the torus. Drag the cursor and pick to set the major radius. Then, drag the cursor and pick to set the minor radius.

Once the torus is created, a name can be entered in the **Name and Color** rollout. The object color can also be changed by picking the color swatch and selecting a new color in the **Object Color** dialog box.

Additional settings can be made in the **Parameters** rollout. The value in the **Segments:** spinner determines the number of segments around the circumference of the torus. The value in the **Sides:** spinner determines the number of segments in the circle cross section of the torus. In the **Smooth:** area, you can set how smoothing groups are applied to the torus. Picking the **All** radio button applies smoothing groups to both

Figure 2-10. A torus has major radius and minor radius parameters. The major radius sets the overall size of the torus. The minor radius sets the size of the circular cross section.

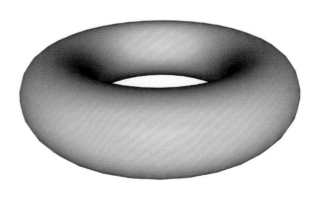

segments and sides. Picking the **None** radio button applies no smoothing groups at all. Picking the **Sides** radio button applies smoothing groups to the sides only. This produces a banded effect. Picking the **Segments** radio button applies smoothing groups to the segments around the circumference of the cross-sectional circle only. This produces a ribbed effect.

Checking the **Slice On** check box in the **Parameters** rollout applies the values in the **Slice From:** and **Slice To:** spinners. These spinners allow you to specify where the circumference of the torus "starts" and "stops" around its Z axis.

A torus has two other parameters. These are *rotation* and *twist.* The value in the **Rotation:** spinner determines how much the circular cross section of the torus is rotated. This can be animated to represent various cutters or tools, for example. The value in the **Twist:** spinner determines how much the circular cross section of the torus is twisted from the first segment to the last. Its cross section is progressively rotated until the degree of twist is reached at the final segment.

The **Generate Mapping Coordinates** check box at the bottom of the **Parameters** rollout is used to automatically calculate mapping coordinates for the torus being created. By default, this option is off. Mapping is discussed later in this text.

Exercise 2-8

1) Select **Create** in the **Command Panel**. Then, pick the **Geometry** button and select **Standard Primitives** from the drop-down list.
2) Pick **Torus** in the **Object Type** rollout.
3) Draw a torus in the Left viewport using the cursor. Draw a second torus in the Top viewport. Use your own dimensions.
4) Draw a torus using the keyboard with the Front viewport active. Check the **Slice On** check box. Enter 90 in the **Slice From:** spinner and 180 in the **Slice To:** spinner.
5) Enter 6 in the **Sides:** spinner. Then, enter 360 in the **Twist:** spinner.
6) Reset 3ds max. Do not save the file.

Exercise

Plane

A *plane* is a special type of flat, rectangular polygon. It is designed to be scaled up when performing a render. However, the actual plane that is drawn can be very small. In addition, any type of transform or modifier can be applied to the plane. This allows you to create a large surface, such as ground, from a small object. In this manner, regeneration time while modeling is reduced. It also helps to keep the model from getting too cluttered.

To draw a plane, first select **Create** in the **Command Panel**. Then, pick the **Geometry** button. Select **Standard Primitives** in the drop-down list and then pick the **Plane** button in the **Object Type** rollout.

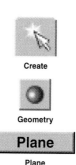

Create

Geometry

Plane

Plane

You can also pick **Standard Primitives** in the **Create** pull-down menu. Then, pick **Plane** in the cascading menu. This opens the **Create** tab in the **Command Panel** and selects the **Plane** button.

In the **Creation Method** rollout, you can specify how the plane is created. Picking the **Rectangle** radio button specifies the first point picked as the corner of a rectangular plane. Picking the **Square** radio button specifies the first point picked as the center of a square plane. These options do not apply when drawing the plane using the **Keyboard Entry** rollout.

The value in the **Length Segs:** spinner in the **Parameters** rollout determines the number of segments on the plane's Y axis. The value in the **Width Segs:** spinner determines the number of segments on the plane's X axis. These values are only important if the plane will be modified to create something other than a flat object.

To draw a plane using the keyboard, first open the **Keyboard Entry** rollout by picking on it. Then, enter values for the length and width in the **Length:** and **Width:** spinners. Finally, pick the **Create** button to create the plane. See Figure 2-11.

To draw a plane using the cursor, pick in the viewport to set the first corner or center of the plane. Then, drag the cursor to the opposite corner of the plane. When the opposite corner is where you want it, release the mouse button to create the plane.

Once the plane is created, you must set the multipliers used for rendering. These are found in the **Render Multipliers** area of the **Parameters** rollout. The value in the **Scale:** spinner is the factor by which the plane is scaled at rendering time. For example, if 10 is entered, the plane is rendered at 10 times the current size. Remember, a plane does not have a thickness. The value in the **Density:** spinner is the factor by which the density of the mesh is scaled. If the plane will remain flat, this value can stay set at 1. On the other hand, if a modifier is applied to simulate a surface such as hilly terrain, then the mesh density is important. A message at the bottom of the **Render Multipliers** area indicates the

Figure 2-11. A plane has length and width parameters. When rendered, the plane is scaled by the value set in the **Parameters** rollout. The rendered plane shown here is viewed at an angle.

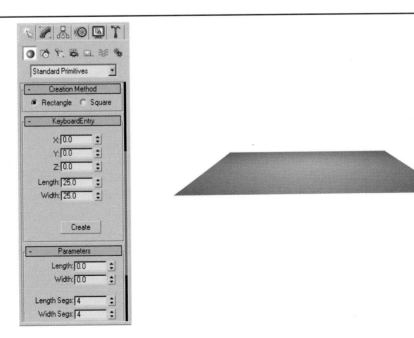

total number of faces on the plane. This number should be kept as low as possible, within reason, to help system performance.

Also, after the plane is created, a name can be entered in the **Name and Color** rollout. The object color can be changed by picking the color swatch and selecting a new color in the **Object Color** dialog box.

The **Generate Mapping Coordinates** check box at the bottom of the **Parameters** rollout is used to automatically calculate mapping coordinates for the plane being created. By default, this option is off. Mapping is discussed later in this text.

Exercise 2-9

1) Select **Create** in the **Command Panel**. Then, pick the **Geometry** button and select **Standard Primitives** from the drop-down list.
2) Pick **Plane** in the **Object Type** rollout.
3) Draw a plane in the Left viewport using the cursor. Use your own dimensions.
4) Draw a second plane using the keyboard with the Top viewport active. Use your own dimensions.
5) Reset 3ds max. Do not save the file.

Exercise

Teapot

A *teapot* is a primitive often used to test materials and lighting. It is a traditional object used in computer graphics because it has a variety of surfaces and curves. A teapot can also be incorporated into scenes. Like all 3ds max primitives, it is a parametric object. As such, the entire teapot, or just parts of the teapot, can be created.

Create

Geometry

Teapot

To draw a teapot, first select **Create** in the **Command Panel**. Then, pick the **Geometry** button. Select **Standard Primitives** in the drop-down list and then pick the **Teapot** button in the **Object Type** rollout.

You can also pick **S̲tandard Primitives** in the **C̲reate** pull-down menu. Then, pick **Teapot** in the cascading menu. This opens the **Create** tab in the **Command Panel** and selects the **Teapot** button.

In the **Creation Method** rollout, you can specify how the teapot is created. Picking the **Center** radio button specifies the first point picked as the center of the bottom of the teapot. Picking the **Edge** button specifies the first point picked as the first corner of a box enclosing the bottom face of the teapot. These options do not apply when drawing the teapot using the **Keyboard Entry** rollout.

To draw a teapot using the keyboard, first open the **Keyboard Entry** rollout by picking on it. Then, enter a radius in the **Radius:** spinner. This value is the radius of the body. The other parts are sized automatically when you pick the **Create** button. See Figure 2-12.

To draw a teapot using the cursor, pick in the viewport to set the center (or corner) of the bottom face of the body. Then, drag the cursor to set the radius of the body.

Figure 2-12. A teapot is created by specifying the radius of the body.

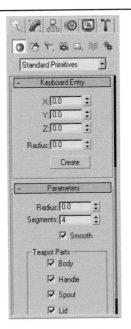

Figure 2-13. Four parts create a teapot. These parts can be created individually or in combinations.

The number of segments for the teapot is set in the **Segments:** spinner. This spinner is located in the **Parameters** rollout. The segments value is the number of divisions in each quadrant of the body, as viewed from the top. The minimum value of 1 produces a four-sided body. This value also produces the spout and handle as flat objects.

A teapot has four parts—a body, lid, handle, and spout. After the teapot is created, you can specify which parts you want to keep. See Figure 2-13. This is done in the **Teapot Parts** area of the **Parameters** rollout. By default, all four check boxes are checked. This means an entire teapot is drawn. Uncheck any check box for a part you do *not* want to display. You can always edit the object later and turn on parts as needed. You can also use parts of a teapot as other objects. For example, drawing the body and handle quickly creates a coffee mug. Checking the **Smooth** check box applies smoothing groups to all elements of the teapot.

Once the teapot is created, a name can be entered in the **Name and Color** rollout. The object color can also be changed by picking the color swatch and selecting a new color in the **Object Color** dialog box.

The **Generate Mapping Coordinates** check box at the bottom of the **Parameters** rollout is used to automatically calculate mapping coordinates for the teapot being created. By default, this option is off. Mapping is discussed later in this text.

Exercise 2-10

1) Select **Create** in the **Command Panel**. Then, pick the **Geometry** button and select **Standard Primitives** from the drop-down list.
2) Pick the **Teapot** button. Draw a teapot in the viewport of your choice.
3) Experiment with the teapot by checking and unchecking the check boxes in the **Teapot Parts** area of the **Parameters** rollout.
4) Reset 3ds max. Do not save the file.

Moving, Rotating, and Scaling

When you move, rotate, or scale an object, you are transforming the object. The operation is called a *transform* or transformation. This is covered in detail in Chapter 5. A brief introduction to the basic transform operations is provided here.

To *move* an object, pick the **Select and Move** button on the **Main** toolbar. Then, pick and move the object as needed.

To *rotate* an object, pick the **Select and Rotate** button on the **Main** toolbar. Then, pick and rotate the object as needed.

To *scale* an object, pick the **Select and Scale** flyout button on the **Main** toolbar. Then, pick and scale the object as needed.

Select and Move

Select and Rotate

Select and Scale

Chapter Snapshot

Chapter Test

Answer the following questions on a separate sheet of paper.
1) Define parametric modeling.
2) What is a standard primitive?
3) What is the purpose of the **Generate Mapping Coordinates** check box?
4) How is a hemisphere created?
5) When the **Smooth** check box is checked, what is the effect on the object?
6) Which rollout is used to name an object?
7) How is the display color of an object changed?
8) Name the three radio buttons that let you set the type of polygons used for a geosphere.
9) What is the purpose of the **Height Segments:** spinner used when creating a cylinder?
10) How is a tube different from a cylinder?
11) How do you create a pointed cone?
12) What are the **Slice From:** and **Slice To:** spinners used for?
13) A pyramid has _____ sides on its bottom face.
14) What are the two parameters required to draw a torus?
15) What is the function of a plane object?
16) What is the default thickness of a plane?
17) When drawing a plane, what effect does the value in the **Scale:** spinner have on the plane?
18) What parameter is required to draw a teapot?
19) List the parts of a teapot.
20) How can a coffee mug be quickly drawn using only one object?

Modeling Problems

Draw the following models. Use the basic primitives presented in this chapter. Choose object colors similar to those shown. When finished, save each model as p02-xx.max in the folder of your choice.

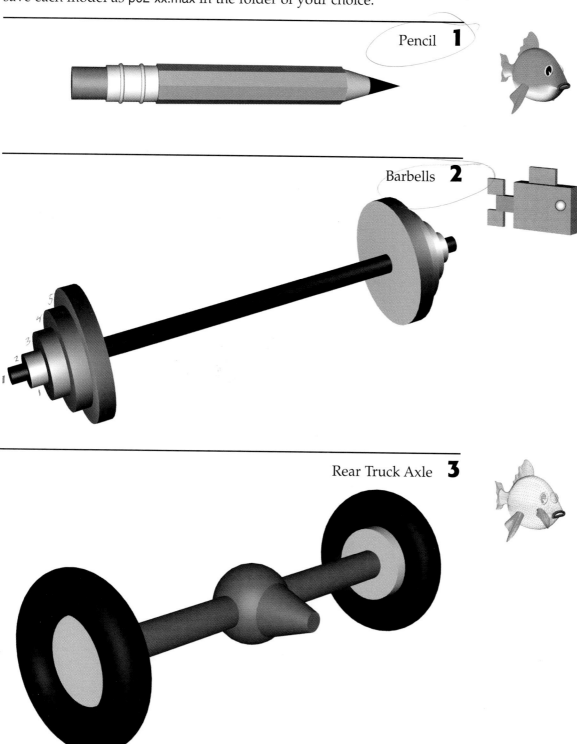

Pencil **1**

Barbells **2**

Rear Truck Axle **3**

4 Stove

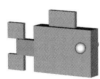

5 Window Frame and Panes

Lamppost **6**

Antique Movie Projector **7**

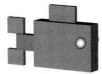

8 Double Scoop Ice Cream Cone

9 Chair

Desk **10**

Chapter 3

Creating Extended Primitives and Patch Grids

Objectives

After completing this chapter, you will be able to:

- Define extended primitives.
- Create various extended primitives.
- Define patch grids.
- Create a quad patch grid.
- Create a tri patch grid.

Extended Primitives

In Chapter 2, the standard primitives available in 3ds max are explained. In addition to standard primitives, 3ds max has several extended primitives. Like standard primitives, *extended primitives* are predefined geometric shapes. However, extended primitives are slightly more refined than standard primitives. For example, a box is a standard primitive. A *chamfered* box, or a box with chamfered edges, is an extended primitive. The following sections explain the extended primitives available in 3ds max.

Hedra

Create

Geometry

Hedra
Hedra

A *hedra* is one of a family of polyhedrons. There are several different polyhedrons you can create. These include tetrahedron, cubic polyhedron, octahedron, dodecahedron, icosahedron, and two different star-shaped polyhedrons.

A hedra has several parameters that need to be specified. These include the family type, family parameters, axis scaling, vertex type, and radius. These settings are all located in the **Parameters** rollout, Figure 3-1. To create a hedra, first select **Create** in the **Command Panel**. Then, pick the **Geometry** button. Select **Extended Primitives** in the drop-down list and then pick the **Hedra** button in the **Object Type** rollout.

You can also pick **Extended Primitives** in the **Create** pull-down menu. Then, pick **Hedra** in the cascading menu. This opens the **Create** tab in the **Command Panel** and selects the **Hedra** button.

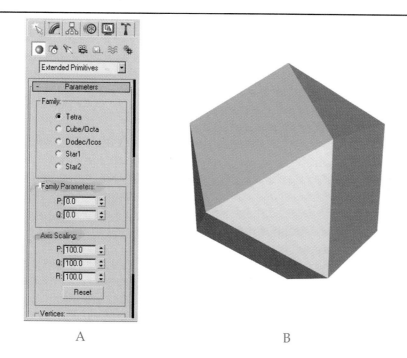

Figure 3-1. A—The **Parameters** rollout for a hedra. B—A sample hedra.

A   B

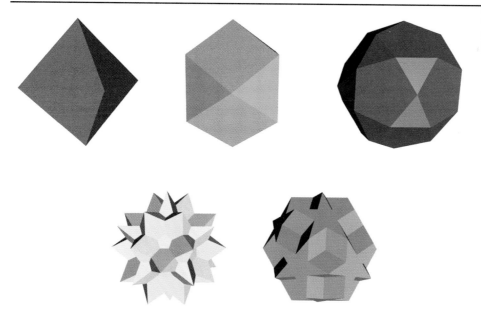

Figure 3-2. A hedra can have one of five basic shapes.

The radius defines the actual size of the object. The radius must be initially set using the cursor. Pick a point for the center of the hedra and drag the cursor to set the radius. This radius can be any value. Next, in the **Parameters** rollout, enter the exact radius in the **Radius:** spinner and press the [Enter] key. Now, other parameters of the object can be set.

The family setting defines the shape of the polyhedron, Figure 3-2. The type is specified using the radio buttons in the **Family:** area of the **Parameters** rollout. Picking the **Tetra** radio button creates a tetrahedron. Picking the **Cube/Octa** radio button creates a cubic or octahedral polyhedron, depending on the settings in the **Family Parameters:** area. Picking the **Dodec/Icos** radio button creates a dodecahedron or icosahedron, depending on the settings in the **Family Parameters:** area. The **Star1** and **Star2** radio buttons allow you to create two different star-shaped polyhedrons.

The **Family Parameters:** area of the **Parameters** rollout has two spinners. The **P:** and **Q:** spinners are related to each other and modify the vertices and faces of the polyhedron. These spinner values cannot exceed 1.0 when added together. For example, the **P:** spinner may have a value of 0.7 and the **Q:** spinner a value of 0.0. However, the **Q:** spinner cannot be set any higher than 0.3 in this example.

A polyhedron can have up to three shapes of facets, including triangles, squares, and pentagons. The **Axis Scaling:** area of the **Parameters** rollout has three spinners, one for each possible shape. By default, the **P:**, **Q:**, and **R:** spinners have a value of 100.0, for 100%. Changing the scaling on these axes in effect pushes the facets into or pulls them out of the object. Picking the **Reset** button sets all three spinners back to 100%.

The type of vertex is specified in the **Vertices:** area of the **Parameters** rollout. There are three options. Picking the **Basic** radio button limits the number of vertices to the minimum required. Picking the **Center** radio button places an additional vertex in the center of a facet. This is the default setting if an axis is scaled. Picking the **Center & Sides** radio button places additional vertices at the center of the facet and each edge. This option produces the greatest number of faces.

Once the hedra is created, a name can be entered in the **Name and Color** rollout. The color of the hedra can also be changed by picking the color swatch and then selecting a new color in the **Object Color** dialog box.

The **Generate Mapping Coords** check box at the bottom of the **Parameters** rollout is used to automatically calculate mapping coordinates for the hedra being created. By default, this option is off. Mapping is discussed in detail later in this text.

Help Cel

Changing between hedra family types can be animated. The change is instantaneous with no transition.

Exercise

Exercise 3-1

1) Select **Create** in the **Command Panel**. Then, pick the **Geometry** button and select **Extended Primitives** from the drop-down list.
2) Pick **Hedra** in the **Object Type** rollout.
3) Draw a hedra in any viewport. Use your own dimensions.
4) In the **Family:** area of the **Parameters** rollout, pick the different radio buttons. Observe how each type differs.
5) Pick the **Tetra** radio button. Then, enter 0.25 in the **P:** spinner in the **Family Parameters:** area of the **Parameters** rollout. Observe how the object changes.
6) In the **Axis Scaling:** area, enter 75.0 in the **Q:** spinner. Observe how the object changes. Enter 250.0 in the **R:** spinner. Again, observe how the object changes.
7) Reset 3ds max. Do not save the file.

Chamfer Box

A *chamfer box* is the same as the box standard primitive, but with rounded or chamfered edges, Figure 3-3. A chamfer box has the same length, width, and height parameters as a box, and an additional fillet radius parameter. To create a chamfer box, first select **Create** in the **Command Panel**. Then, pick the **Geometry** button. Select **Extended Primitives** in the drop-down list and then pick the **Chamfer Box** button in the **Object Type** rollout.

You can also pick **Extended Primitives** in the **Create** pull-down menu. Then, pick **Chamfer Box** in the cascading menu. This opens the **Create** tab in the **Command Panel** and selects the **Chamfer Box** button.

In the **Creation Method** rollout, you can specify how the chamfer box is created. Picking the **Box** radio button allows a chamfer box to be created with different dimensions for the length, width, and height. This is the default. Picking the **Cube** radio button creates a chamfer box with equal values for the length, width, and height.

In the **Parameters** rollout, you can specify the number of segments for the length, width, height, and fillet. Setting the number of fillet segments to 1.0 creates a square chamfer. A higher number of segments creates a rounded edge, called a fillet. The number of segments for the length, width, and height is important if a modifier will be applied to the chamfer box. To set the number of segments, simply enter a value in the appropriate spinner.

To draw a chamfer box using the cursor, simply pick a point for the first corner of the box. Then drag the cursor to the other corner of the first face and release. This defines the length and width. Next, drag and pick to define the height. Finally, move the cursor up and down and pick to set the fillet radius. If drawing a cube, you only need to pick the center and drag to set the overall dimensions.

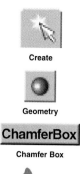
Create

Geometry

ChamferBox
Chamfer Box

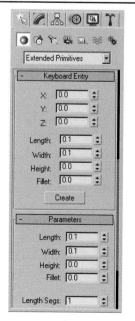

Figure 3-3. A—The **Parameters** rollout for a chamfer box. B—A sample chamfer box.

A

B

To draw a chamfer box using the keyboard, expand the **Keyboard Entry** rollout. Then, enter values in the **Length:**, **Width:**, and **Height:** spinners. Also, specify the fillet radius in the **Fillet:** spinner. The X, Y, and Z coordinates of the center of the first face can also be entered in this rollout. Finally, pick the **Create** button to draw the chamfer box.

Once the chamfer box is created, a name can be entered in the **Name and Color** rollout. The color of the chamfer box can also be changed by picking the color swatch and then selecting a new color in the **Object Color** dialog box.

The **Generate Mapping Coords** check box at the bottom of the **Parameters** rollout is used to automatically calculate mapping coordinates for the chamfer box being created. By default, this option is off. Mapping is discussed later in this text.

Also at the bottom of the **Parameters** rollout is the **Smooth** check box. This option is on by default and applies smoothing groups to the faces of the object. When off, the fillet is faceted.

Exercise

Exercise 3-2

1) Select **Create** in the **Command Panel**. Then, pick the **Geometry** button and select **Extended Primitives** from the drop-down list.
2) Pick **Chamfer Box** in the **Object Type** rollout.
3) Draw a chamfer box using the cursor. Use your own dimensions.
4) In the **Parameters** rollout, enter 1.0 in the **Fillet Segs:** spinner. Uncheck the **Smooth** check box.
5) Draw another chamfer box using the keyboard. Use your own dimensions.
6) In the **Parameters** rollout, enter 3.0 in the **Fillet Segs:** spinner. Check the **Smooth** check box.
7) Reset 3ds max. Do not save the file.

Chamfer Cylinder

Create

Geometry

Chamfer Cyl

Just as a chamfer box is a box primitive with curved edges, a *chamfer cylinder* is a cylinder with curved edges. See Figure 3-4. As with a cylinder, a chamfer cylinder has radius and height parameters. It also has a fillet parameter, just as with a chamfer box. As with a cylinder, the number of segments on the height and ends of the chamfer cylinder can be set. In addition, the number of fillet segments can be set, as with a chamfer box. To draw a chamfer cylinder, first select **Create** in the **Command Panel**. Then, pick the **Geometry** button. Select **Extended Primitives** in the drop-down list and then pick the **Chamfer Cyl** button in the **Object Type** rollout.

You can also pick **Extended Primitives** in the **Create** pull-down menu. Then, pick **Chamfer Cylinder** in the cascading menu. This opens the **Create** tab in the **Command Panel** and selects the **Chamfer Cyl** button.

In the **Creation Method** rollout, you can specify how the chamfer cylinder is created. Picking the **Center** radio button specifies the first point picked as the center of the first face of the chamfer cylinder.

A   B

Picking the **Edge** radio button specifies the first point picked as one point on the first face of the chamfer cylinder. The second point picked is directly opposite the first. These options do not apply when drawing the chamfer cylinder using the **Keyboard Entry** rollout.

To draw a chamfer cylinder using the keyboard, first expand the **Keyboard Entry** rollout by picking on it. Then, enter a radius in the **Radius:** spinner and a height in the **Height:** spinner. Also, enter a fillet radius in the **Fillet:** spinner. Then, pick the **Create** button. You can also specify the X, Y, and Z coordinates of the center of the first face in this rollout.

To draw a chamfer cylinder using the cursor, pick a point in a viewport and drag the cursor to set the radius of the first face. Once the radius is set, release the mouse button, move the cursor up or down, and pick to set the height of the cylinder. Finally, move the cursor up and down and then pick to set the fillet radius.

Once the chamfer cylinder is created, a name can be entered in the **Name and Color** rollout. The object color can also be changed by picking the color swatch and selecting a new color in the **Object Color** dialog box.

The number of segments for the height, ends, and fillets can be set in the **Parameters** rollout. The value in the **Height Segs:** spinner determines how many divisions there are on the height of the chamfer cylinder. The value in the **Cap Segs:** spinner determines the number of segments on each end of the chamfer cylinder. The value in the **Fillet Segs:** spinner determines how many segments each fillet has. The **Sides:** spinner sets the number of sides around the circumference of the chamfer cylinder.

Just as with a cylinder, a chamfer cylinder can be sliced. The **Slice On** check box in the **Parameters** rollout applies the values in the **Slice From:** and **Slice To:** spinners. These spinners allow you to specify where the circle portion of the chamfer cylinder "starts" and "stops" around its Z axis. In this way, you can create portions of a chamfer cylinder. See Figure 3-5.

Figure 3-5. A chamfer cylinder without slice and with slice.

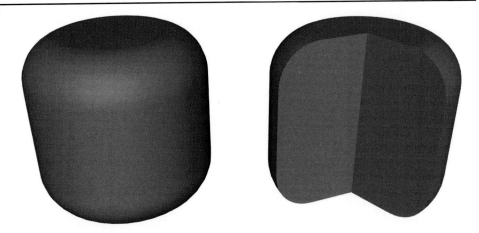

The **Generate Mapping Coords** check box at the bottom of the **Parameters** rollout is used to automatically calculate mapping coordinates for the chamfer cylinder being created. By default, this option is off. Mapping is discussed in detail later in this text.

Also in the **Parameters** rollout is the **Smooth** check box. This option is on by default and applies smoothing groups to the faces of the object.

Exercise

Exercise 3-3

1) Select **Create** in the **Command Panel**. Then, pick the **Geometry** button and select **Extended Primitives** from the drop-down list.
2) Pick **Chamfer Cyl** in the **Object Type** rollout.
3) Draw a chamfer cylinder using the cursor. Use your own dimensions.
4) In the **Parameters** rollout, enter 1.0 in the **Fillet Segs:** spinner. Uncheck the **Smooth** check box.
5) Draw another chamfer cylinder using the keyboard. Use your own dimensions.
6) In the **Parameters** rollout, enter 10.0 in the **Fillet Segs:** spinner. Check the **Smooth** check box.
7) Reset 3ds max. Do not save the file.

Create

Geometry

Capsule

Capsule

Capsule

A *capsule* is similar in appearance to a chamfer cylinder. However, there are fewer parameters and, as a result, slightly less control. A capsule is simply a cylinder with two end caps that are hemispheres of the same diameter as the cylinder. See Figure 3-6. You specify a radius and a height. To create a capsule, first select **Create** in the **Command Panel**. Then, pick the **Geometry** button. Select **Extended Primitives** in the drop-down list and then pick the **Capsule** button in the **Object Type** rollout.

A   B

Figure 3-6. A—The **Parameters** rollout for a capsule. B—A sample capsule.

You can also pick **Extended Primitives** in the **Create** pull-down menu. Then, pick **Capsule** in the cascading menu. This opens the **Create** tab in the **Command Panel** and selects the **Capsule** button.

In the **Creation Method** rollout, you can specify how the capsule is created. Picking the **Center** radio button specifies that the first point picked is tangent to the hemisphere and on the object's Z axis. Picking the **Edge** radio button specifies the first point picked as one point on the cylinder part of the object, if projected onto the current drawing plane. The second point picked is directly opposite the first. Simply think of these two options in terms of those used for drawing a cylinder, since they are really the same. These options do not apply when drawing the capsule using the **Keyboard Entry** rollout.

To draw a capsule using the cursor, pick in a viewport and drag the cursor to set the radius of the capsule. Then, drag the cursor up or down and pick to set the height of the capsule. The end caps are automatically created.

To draw a capsule using the keyboard, expand the **Keyboard Entry** rollout by picking on it. Then, enter values in the **Radius:** and **Height:** spinners. The X, Y, and Z coordinates of the point tangent to the first hemisphere on the Z axis can also be entered in this rollout. Finally, pick the **Create** button to draw the capsule.

Once the capsule is created, a name can be entered in the **Name and Color** rollout. The color of the capsule can also be changed by picking the color swatch and then selecting a new color in the **Object Color** dialog box.

The number of height segments and sides the capsule has can be set in the **Parameters** rollout. The value in the **Height Segs:** spinner determines how many divisions there are on the cylinder portion of the capsule. The value in the **Sides:** spinner determines the number of sides around the circumference of the capsule. This value also determines the number of segments the hemisphere portions have.

Figure 3-7. There are two ways to specify the height of a capsule.

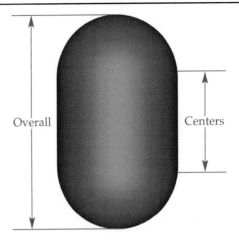

Overall

Centers

Below the **Radius:** and **Height:** spinners in the **Parameters** rollout are two radio buttons. Picking the **Overall** radio button specifies that the value in the **Height:** spinner is the distance between the peak of each hemisphere. In other words, it specifies the total height of the capsule. Picking the **Centers** radio button specifies that the height value is for the cylinder portion of the capsule only. The height of the two hemispheres must be added to get the total height of the object. See Figure 3-7. These radio buttons are also found in the **Keyboard Entry** rollout for use when creating a capsule using the keyboard.

Just as with a cylinder, a capsule can be sliced. The **Slice On** check box in the **Parameters** rollout applies the values in the **Slice From:** and **Slice To:** spinners. These spinners allow you to specify where the capsule "starts" and "stops" around its Z axis. In this way, you can create portions of a capsule.

The **Generate Mapping Coords** check box at the bottom of the **Parameters** rollout is used to automatically calculate mapping coordinates for the capsule being created. By default, this option is off. Mapping is discussed in detail later in this text.

Also in the **Parameters** rollout is the **Smooth** check box. This option is on by default and applies smoothing groups to the faces of the object.

Exercise

Exercise 3-4

1) Select **Create** in the **Command Panel**. Then, pick the **Geometry** button and select **Extended Primitives** from the drop-down list.
2) Pick **Capsule** in the **Object Type** rollout.
3) Draw a capsule using the cursor. Use your own dimensions.
4) In the **Parameters** rollout, pick the **Overall** radio button. Then, pick the **Centers** radio button. Observe the difference in the object.
5) Check the **Slice On** check box.
6) Enter 90.0 in the **Slice From:** spinner and 270.0 in the **Slice To:** spinner.
7) Reset 3ds max. Do not save the file.

Oil Tank

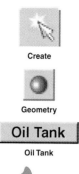

Create

Geometry

Oil Tank

Oil Tank

An *oil tank* is like a capsule, except you have control over the parameters of the hemisphere end caps. See Figure 3-8. As with a capsule, you must specify a radius and height. In addition, you must also specify the height of the end caps. To create an oil tank, first select **Create** in the **Command Panel**. Then, pick the **Geometry** button. Select **Extended Primitives** in the drop-down list and then pick the **Oil Tank** button in the **Object Type** rollout.

You can also pick **Extended Primitives** in the **C̲reate** pull-down menu. Then, pick **Oil Tank** in the cascading menu. This opens the **Create** tab in the **Command Panel** and selects the **Oil Tank** button.

In the **Creation Method** rollout, you can specify how the oil tank is created. Picking the **Center** radio button specifies that the first point picked is tangent to the hemisphere and on the object's Z axis. Picking the **Edge** radio button specifies that the first point picked is one point on the cylinder part of the object, if projected onto the current drawing plane. The second point picked is directly opposite the first. Simply think of these two options in terms of drawing a cylinder. These options do not apply when drawing the oil tank using the **Keyboard Entry** rollout.

As with a capsule, the height specified for an oil tank can be the overall height or the height of the cylinder portion. Picking the **Overall** radio button means that the height specified is the overall height of the object. Picking the **Centers** radio button means that the height specified is the height of the cylinder portion of the object. These radio buttons are found in the **Parameters** rollout and in the **Keyboard Entry** rollout.

An oil tank has a *blend parameter.* This value is set in the **Blend:** spinner found in the **Parameters** rollout and the **Keyboard Entry** rollout. When the blend value is 0, there is a hard edge between the end caps and the cylinder. This is especially noticeable if the **Cap Height:** value is

A

B

Figure 3-8. A—The **Parameters** rollout for an oil tank. B—A sample oil tank.

Figure 3-9. An oil tank can have a blend between the top and sides, as shown on the right.

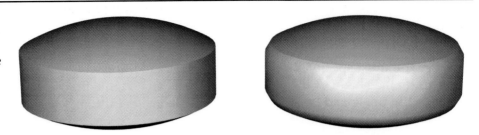

small. When the blend value is greater than 0, a bevel is created between the cylinder and the end caps, making a smooth transition. The size of the bevel is determined by the value entered. See Figure 3-9.

To draw an oil tank using the keyboard, first expand the **Keyboard Entry** rollout by picking on it. Then, enter a radius in the **Radius:** spinner and a height in the **Height:** spinner. Also, enter a height for the end caps in the **Cap Height:** spinner. Pick the appropriate radio button to specify if the height is measured between centers or overall. Then, pick the **Create** button. You can also specify the X, Y, and Z coordinates of the center of the first face in this rollout.

To draw an oil tank using the cursor, pick a point in a viewport and drag the cursor to set the radius of the oil tank. Once the radius is set, release the mouse button and move the cursor up or down and pick to set the height of the oil tank. Finally, move the cursor up and down and then pick to set the height of the end caps.

Once the oil tank is created, a name can be entered in the **Name and Color** rollout. The object color can also be changed by picking the color swatch and selecting a new color in the **Object Color** dialog box.

The number of segments the height has and the number of sides the oil tank has can be set in the **Parameters** rollout. The value in the **Height Segs:** spinner determines how many divisions there are on the height of the cylinder portion of the oil tank. The value in the **Sides:** spinner determines the number of sides the cylinder portion has. This value also determines the number of segments used for the end caps.

Just as with a cylinder, an oil tank can be sliced. The **Slice On** check box in the **Parameters** rollout applies the values in the **Slice From:** and **Slice To:** spinners. These spinners allow you to specify where the oil tank "starts" and "stops" around its Z axis. See Figure 3-10.

Figure 3-10. An oil tank can be sliced.

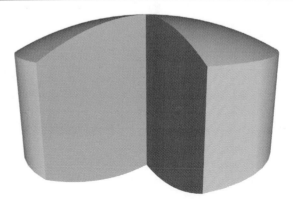

The **Generate Mapping Coords** check box at the bottom of the **Parameters** rollout is used to automatically calculate mapping coordinates for the oil tank being created. By default, this option is off. Mapping is discussed in detail later in this text.

Also in the **Parameters** rollout is the **Smooth** check box. This option is on by default and applies smoothing groups to the faces of the object.

Exercise 3-5

1) Select **Create** in the **Command Panel**. Then, pick the **Geometry** button and select **Extended Primitives** from the drop-down list.
2) Pick **Oil Tank** in the **Object Type** rollout.
3) Draw an oil tank using the cursor. Use your own dimensions.
4) In the **Parameters** rollout, pick the **Overall** radio button. Then, pick the **Centers** radio button. Observe the difference in the object.
5) Change the value in the **Blend:** spinner and observe the effect on the object. Reset the value to 0.
6) Change the value in the **Cap Height:** spinner. Observe the effect on the object.
7) Reset 3ds max. Do not save the file.

Spindle

A *spindle* is like an oil tank. However, the end caps are cones instead of hemispheres. See Figure 3-11. To create a spindle, first select **Create** in the **Command Panel**. Then, pick the **Geometry** button. Select **Extended Primitives** in the drop-down list and then pick the **Spindle** button in the **Object Type** rollout.

Create

Geometry

Spindle

You can also pick **Extended Primitives** in the <u>C</u>reate pull-down menu. Then, pick **S**pindle in the cascading menu. This opens the **Create** tab in the **Command Panel** and selects the **Spindle** button.

In the **Creation Method** rollout, you can specify how the spindle is created. Picking the **Center** radio button specifies the first point picked as the apex of the first end cap cone. Picking the **Edge** radio button specifies the first point picked as one point on the cylinder part of the object, if projected onto the current drawing plane. The second point picked is directly opposite the first. These options do not apply when drawing the spindle using the **Keyboard Entry** rollout.

As with a capsule and oil tank, the height specified for a spindle can be the overall height or the height of the cylinder portion. Picking the **Overall** radio button means the height specified is the overall height of the object. Picking the **Centers** radio button means the height specified is the height of the cylinder portion of the object. These radio buttons are found in the **Parameters** rollout and in the **Keyboard Entry** rollout.

Like an oil tank, a spindle has a blend parameter. When the blend value is greater than 0, a bevel is created between the cylinder and the end caps, making a smooth transition. The size of the bevel is determined by

Figure 3-11. A—The **Parameters** rollout for a spindle. B—A sample spindle.

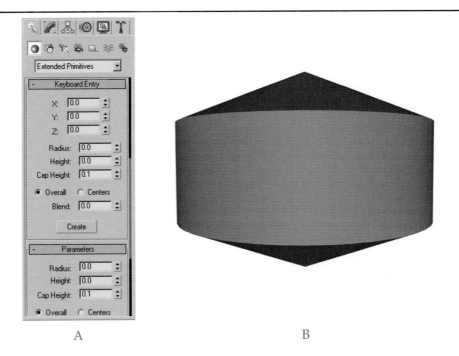

A   B

the value entered in the **Blend:** spinner in the **Parameters** rollout or the **Keyboard Entry** rollout.

To draw a spindle using the keyboard, first expand the **Keyboard Entry** rollout by picking on it. Then, enter a radius in the **Radius:** spinner and a height in the **Height:** spinner. Also, enter a height for the end caps in the **Cap Height:** spinner. Pick the appropriate radio button to specify if the height is measured between centers or overall. Then, pick the **Create** button. You can also specify the X, Y, and Z coordinates of the apex of the first end cap in this rollout.

To draw a spindle using the cursor, pick a point in a viewport and drag the cursor to set the radius. Once the radius is set, release the mouse button and move the cursor up or down and pick to set the height of the spindle. Finally, move the cursor up and down and then pick to set the height of the end caps.

Once the spindle is created, a name can be entered in the **Name and Color** rollout. The object color can also be changed by picking the color swatch and selecting a new color in the **Object Color** dialog box.

The number of segments the height and the caps have and the number of sides the spindle has can be set in the **Parameters** rollout. The value in the **Height Segs:** spinner determines how many divisions there are on the height of the cylinder portion of the spindle. The value in the **Cap Segs:** spinner determines the number of vertical segments on the end caps. The value in the **Sides:** spinner determines the number of sides the cylinder portion has. This value also determines the number of radial segments used for the end caps.

A spindle can be sliced. The **Slice On** check box in the **Parameters** rollout applies the values in the **Slice From:** and **Slice To:** spinners. These spinners allow you to specify where the spindle "starts" and "stops" around its Z axis.

The **Generate Mapping Coords** check box at the bottom of the **Parameters** rollout is used to automatically calculate mapping coordinates for the spindle being created. By default, this option is off. Mapping is discussed in detail later in this text.

Also in the **Parameters** rollout is the **Smooth** check box. This option is on by default and applies smoothing groups to the faces of the object.

Exercise 3-6

1) Select **Create** in the **Command Panel**. Then, pick the **Geometry** button and select **Extended Primitives** from the drop-down list.
2) Pick **Spindle** in the **Object Type** rollout.
3) Draw a spindle using the cursor. Use your own dimensions.
4) In the **Parameters** rollout, pick the **Overall** radio button. Then, pick the **Centers** radio button. Observe the difference in the object.
5) Change the value in the **Blend:** spinner and observe the effect on the object. Reset the value to 0.
6) Change the value in the **Cap Height:** spinner. Observe the effect on the object.
7) Change the value in the **Sides:** spinner to 3. Observe the effect on the end caps and cylinder portion. Change the value in the **Cap Segs:** spinner to 10. Observe the effect on the end caps and cylinder portion.
8) Reset 3ds max. Do not save the file.

Prism

A *prism* is a three-sided object with two triangular ends and a height, similar to a three-sided cylinder. See Figure 3-12. The advantage of a prism is that the number of segments can be independently set for each side. To create a prism, first select **Create** in the **Command Panel**. Then, pick the **Geometry** button. Select **Extended Primitives** in the drop-down list and then pick the **Prism** button in the **Object Type** rollout.

Create

Geometry

Prism

You can also pick **Extended Primitives** in the <u>C</u>reate pull-down menu. Then, pick <u>P</u>rism in the cascading menu. This opens the **Create** tab in the **Command Panel** and selects the **Prism** button.

In the **Creation Method** rollout, you can specify the form of the prism base. Picking the **Isosceles** radio button specifies that the base of the prism is an isosceles triangle. This type of triangle has two equal sides. Picking the **Base/Apex** radio button specifies that the base of the prism is a scalene triangle. This type of triangle can have unequal sides. These options do not apply when drawing the prism using the **Keyboard Entry** rollout.

To draw a prism using the cursor, pick a point for the first corner of the base triangle. If the **Isosceles** radio button is on, the left-right movement of the cursor defines the length of the unequal side. The up-down movement defines the length of the equal sides. Release the mouse button to set the size of the triangle. Next, move the cursor up or down to define the height. If the **Base/Apex** radio button is on, pick the first point and drag the cursor right-left to set the length of the first side.

Figure 3-12. A—The **Parameters** rollout for a prism. B—A sample prism.

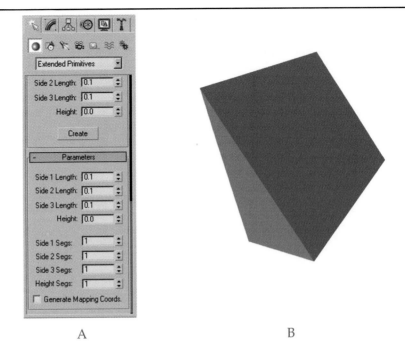

A   B

Release the mouse button and drag the cursor to set the length of the remaining sides and the location of the third vertex. Finally, move the cursor up or down and pick to set the height of the prism.

To draw a prism using the keyboard, expand the **Keyboard Entry** rollout by picking on it. Then, enter values in the **Side 1 Length:**, **Side 2 Length:**, and **Side 3 Length:** spinners. Also, enter a height value in the **Height:** spinner. The X, Y, and Z coordinates of the center of the first face can also be entered in this rollout. Finally, pick the **Create** button to draw the prism.

Once the prism is created, a name can be entered in the **Name and Color** rollout. The color of the prism can also be changed by picking the color swatch and then selecting a new color in the **Object Color** dialog box.

In the **Parameters** rollout, you can specify the number of segments for each side of the prism. You can also set the number of height segments on the prism. To set the number of segments for each side, enter values in the **Side 1 Segs:**, **Side 2 Segs:**, and **Side 3 Segs:** spinners. These values also determine the number of segments on each end face. To set the number of height segments, enter a value in the **Height Segs:** spinner.

The **Generate Mapping Coords** check box at the bottom of the **Parameters** rollout is used to automatically calculate mapping coordinates for the prism. By default, this option is off. Mapping is discussed in detail later in this text.

Exercise 3-7

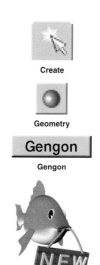

1) Select **Create** in the **Command Panel**. Then, pick the **Geometry** button and select **Extended Primitives** from the drop-down list.
2) Pick **Prism** in the **Object Type** rollout.
3) Pick the **Isosceles** radio button in the **Creation Method** rollout. Draw a prism using the cursor. Use your own dimensions.
4) Pick the **Base/Apex** radio button in the **Creation Method** rollout. Draw another prism using the cursor. Use your own dimensions.
5) In the **Parameters** rollout, change the **Side 1 Segs:** spinner to 3, the **Side 2 Segs:** spinner to 6, and the **Side 3 Segs:** spinner to 12.
6) Reset 3ds max. Do not save the file.

Gengon

A *gengon* is like a prism, except the base is a regular polygon. The number of sides on the polygon can be set. In addition, the polygon can be filleted between its sides. See Figure 3-13. To create a gengon, first select **Create** in the **Command Panel**. Then, pick the **Geometry** button. Select **Extended Primitives** in the drop-down list and then pick the **Gengon** button in the **Object Type** rollout.

Create

Geometry

Gengon

Gengon

You can also pick **Extended Primitives** in the **Create** pull-down menu. Then, pick **Gengon** in the cascading menu. This opens the **Create** tab in the **Command Panel** and selects the **Gengon** button.

In the **Creation Method** rollout, you can specify how the polygon base is created. Picking the **Center** radio button specifies the first point picked as the center of the polygon. Picking the **Edge** radio button specifies the first point picked as one point on the diameter of a circle circumscribed about the polygon. The second point picked is directly opposite the first.

A   B

Figure 3-13. A—The **Parameters** rollout for a gengon. B—A sample five-sided gengon.

These options do not apply when drawing the gengon using the **Keyboard Entry** rollout.

To draw a gengon using the cursor, pick a point and drag the cursor to set the radius. Next, move the cursor up or down and pick to define the height. Finally, move the cursor up and down and pick to set the fillet radius. By default, the gengon has five sides. This can be changed in the **Parameters** rollout.

To draw a gengon using the keyboard, expand the **Keyboard Entry** rollout by picking on it. Then, enter values in the **Sides:**, **Radius:**, and **Height:** spinners. Also, enter a fillet radius in the **Fillet:** spinner. If you do not want fillets between the polygon edges, enter 0 in this spinner. The X, Y, and Z coordinates of the center of the first face can also be entered in this rollout. Finally, pick the **Create** button to draw the gengon.

Once the gengon is created, a name can be entered in the **Name and Color** rollout. The object color can also be changed by picking the color swatch and then selecting a new color in the **Object Color** dialog box.

The number of segments on the sides, height, and fillets can be set in the **Parameters** rollout. Enter values in the **Side Segs:**, **Height Segs:**, and **Fillet Segs:** spinners. If you do not want fillets between the edges of the polygon, you can either enter 0 in the **Fillet:** spinner or set the number of fillet segments to 0. To set the number of sides the polygon has, enter a value in the **Sides:** spinner.

The **Generate Mapping Coords** check box at the bottom of the **Parameters** rollout is used to automatically calculate mapping coordinates for the gengon being created. By default, this option is off. Mapping is discussed in detail later in this text.

Also in the **Parameters** rollout is the **Smooth** check box. This option is on by default and applies smoothing groups to the faces of the object.

Exercise

Exercise 3-8

1) Select **Create** in the **Command Panel**. Then, pick the **Geometry** button and select **Extended Primitives** from the drop-down list.
2) Pick **Gengon** in the **Object Type** rollout.
3) Draw a gengon using the cursor. Use your own dimensions.
4) In the **Parameters** rollout, change the number of sides to eight.
5) Change the value in the **Fillet:** spinner to 0. Observe the shape of the object. Increase the **Fillet:** value. Notice how the object has changed.
6) Change the **Fillet Segs:** value to 0. Notice how the object has changed. Enter 5 in the **Fillet Segs:** spinner. How has the object changed?
7) Reset 3ds max. Do not save the file.

L-Ext

An *L-Ext,* or L-Extrusion, is an L-shaped object. It can be used to quickly create walls, fences, and other objects. See Figure 3-14. To create an L-Ext, first select **Create** in the **Command Panel**. Then, pick the **Geometry** button. Select **Extended Primitives** in the drop-down list and then pick the **L-Ext** button in the **Object Type** rollout.

You can also pick **Extended Primitives** in the <u>C</u>**reate** pull-down menu. Then, pick **L-Extrusion** in the cascading menu. This opens the **Create** tab in the **Command Panel** and selects the **L-Ext** button.

In the **Creation Method** rollout, you can specify how the L-shaped base is created. Picking the **Corners** radio button specifies the first point picked as the first corner of a box surrounding the first face. The second point is the opposite corner. Picking the **Center** button specifies the first point picked as the center of a box surrounding the first face. The second point is a corner of the box. These options do not apply when drawing the L-Ext using the **Keyboard Entry** rollout.

To draw an L-Ext using the cursor, pick a point and drag the cursor to set the overall length and width of the object. Then, move the cursor up or down and pick to set the height of the object. Finally, move the cursor up and down and pick to set the thickness of the legs.

To draw an L-Ext using the keyboard, expand the **Keyboard Entry** rollout by picking on it. Then, specify the overall width and length of the L-Ext by entering values in the **Side Length:** and **Front Length:** spinners. Also, enter the thickness, or width, of each leg in the **Side Width:** and **Front Width:** spinners. Enter the overall height of the L-Ext in the **Height:** spinner. The X, Y, and Z coordinates of the center of the box enclosing the first face can also be entered in this rollout. Finally, pick the **Create** button to draw the L-Ext object.

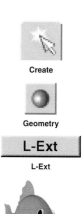

Create

Geometry

L-Ext

L-Ext

Figure 3-14. A—The **Parameters** rollout for an L-Ext. B—A sample L-Ext.

A

B

Once the L-Ext is created, a name can be entered in the **Name and Color** rollout. The color can also be changed by picking the color swatch and then selecting a new color in the **Object Color** dialog box.

The number of segments on the sides of each leg and the height can be set in the **Parameters** rollout. The values in the **Side Segs:** and **Front Segs:** spinners determine the number of vertical segments on the sides of the L-Ext. The value in the **Width Segs:** spinner sets the number of vertical segments on the thickness, or width, of each leg. To set the number of segments on the object's height, or horizontal segments, enter a value in the **Height Segs:** spinner. All of these values are set to 1 by default. It is only necessary to increase the number of segments if a modifier will be applied to the object.

The **Generate Mapping Coords** check box at the bottom of the **Parameters** rollout is used to automatically calculate mapping coordinates for the object being created. By default, this option is off. Mapping is discussed in detail later in this text.

Help Cel

When using the cursor to draw an L-Ext, each leg of the L is drawn with the same thickness, or width. To have legs of different thickness, you must either draw the L-Ext using the keyboard or edit the parameters after the object is drawn.

Exercise

Exercise 3-9

1) Select **Create** in the **Command Panel**. Then, pick the **Geometry** button and select **Extended Primitives** from the drop-down list.
2) Pick **L-Ext** in the **Object Type** rollout.
3) Pick the **Corners** radio button in the **Creation Method** rollout. Draw an L-Ext using the cursor. Use your own dimensions.
4) Draw another L-Ext using the keyboard. Enter different values in the **Side Width:** and **Front Width:** spinners.
5) In the **Parameters** rollout, enter 2 in the **Sides Segs:** spinner. Observe how the object changes.
6) Enter 3 in the **Front Segs:** spinner. Observe how the object changes.
7) Enter 4 in the **Width Segs:** spinner. Observe how the object changes.
8) Enter 5 in the **Height Segs:** spinner. Observe how the object changes.
9) Reset 3ds max. Do not save the file.

C-Ext

A *C-Ext,* or C-Extrusion, is like an L-Ext, except it is a C-shaped object. See Figure 3-15. To create a C-Ext, first select **Create** in the **Command Panel**. Then, pick the **Geometry** button. Select **Extended Primitives** in the drop-down list and then pick the **C-Ext** button in the **Object Type** rollout.

You can also pick **Extended Primitives** in the <u>C</u>reate pull-down menu. Then, pick **C-Extrusion** in the cascading menu. This opens the **Create** tab in the **Command Panel** and selects the **C-Ext** button.

In the **Creation Method** rollout, you can specify how the C-shaped base is created. Picking the **Corners** radio button specifies the first point picked as the first corner of a box surrounding the first face. The second point is the opposite corner. Picking the **Center** radio button specifies the first point picked as the center of a box surrounding the first face. The second point is a corner of the box. These options do not apply when drawing the C-Ext using the **Keyboard Entry** rollout.

To draw a C-Ext using the cursor, pick a point and drag the cursor to set the overall length and width of the object. Then, move the cursor up or down and pick to set the height of the object. Finally, move the cursor up and down and pick to set the thickness of the legs.

To draw a C-Ext using the keyboard, expand the **Keyboard Entry** rollout by picking on it. Enter values in the **Front Length:** and **Back Length:** spinners. These values can be different. Also, enter the length of the side in the **Side Length:** spinner. The thickness, or width, of each leg is set in the **Back Width:**, **Side Width:**, and **Front Width:** spinners. Enter the overall height of the C-Ext in the **Height:** spinner. The X, Y, and Z coordinates of the center of the box that encloses the first face can also be entered in this rollout. Finally, pick the **Create** button to draw the C-Ext object.

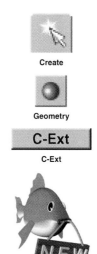

Create

Geometry

C-Ext

C-Ext

A

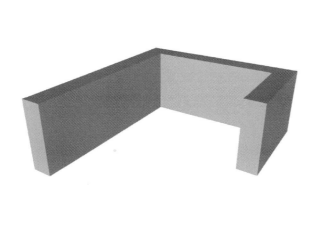

B

Figure 3-15. A—The **Parameters** rollout for a C-Ext. B—A sample C-Ext.

Once the C-Ext is created, a name can be entered in the **Name and Color** rollout. The color can also be changed by picking the color swatch and then selecting a new color in the **Object Color** dialog box.

The number of segments on the sides of each leg and the height can be set in the **Parameters** rollout. The values in the **Back Segs:**, **Side Segs:**, and **Front Segs:** spinners determine the number of vertical segments on the sides of the C-Ext. The value in the **Width Segs:** spinner sets the number of vertical segments on the thickness, or width, of each leg. To set the number of segments on the object's height, or horizontal segments, enter a value in the **Height Segs:** spinner.

The **Generate Mapping Coords** check box at the bottom of the **Parameters** rollout is used to automatically calculate mapping coordinates for the object being created. By default, this option is off. Mapping is discussed in detail later in this text.

Help Cel

When using the cursor to draw a C-Ext, each leg is drawn with the same thickness, or width. Also, the lengths of the back and front legs are the same. To have legs of different thickness or different front and back lengths, you must either draw the C-Ext using the keyboard or edit the parameters after the object is drawn.

Exercise

Exercise 3-10

1) Select **Create** in the **Command Panel**. Then, pick the **Geometry** button and select **Extended Primitives** from the drop-down list.
2) Pick **C-Ext** in the **Object Type** rollout.
3) Draw a C-Ext using the keyboard. Use different values in the **Back Length:**, **Side Length:**, and **Front Length:** spinners. Also enter different values in the **Back Width:**, **Side Width:**, and **Front Width:** spinners.
4) In the **Parameters** rollout, enter 2 in the **Back Segs:** spinner. Observe how the object changes.
5) Enter 3 in the **Side Segs:** spinner. Observe how the object changes.
6) Enter 4 in the **Front Segs:** spinner. Observe how the object changes.
7) Enter 5 in the **Width Segs:** spinner. Observe how the object changes.
8) Enter 6 in the **Height Segs:** spinner. Observe how the object changes.
9) Reset 3ds max. Do not save the file.

Torus Knot

A *torus knot* is similar to a torus. However, it is in a complex, knotted form. This object might be used to model a knot of rope or string. Where a standard torus uses a 2D curve as the path, a torus knot uses a 3D curve. This curve is called the *base curve* and can be a circle or a knot. See Figure 3-16. There are many settings for a torus knot.

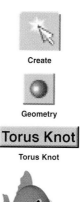

Create

Geometry

Torus Knot

Torus Knot

To create a torus knot, first select **Create** in the **Command Panel**. Then, pick the **Geometry** button. Select **Extended Primitives** in the drop-down list and then pick the **Torus Knot** button in the **Object Type** rollout.

You can also pick **Extended Primitives** in the <u>C</u>reate pull-down menu. Then, pick **Torus Knot** in the cascading menu. This opens the **Create** tab in the **Command Panel** and selects the **Torus Knot** button.

In the **Creation Method** rollout, you can specify how the overall size of the torus knot is determined. Picking the **Diameter** radio button specifies the first point picked as a point on the overall diameter of the torus knot. The second point is opposite the first. Picking the **Radius** radio button specifies the first point picked as the center of the overall diameter of the torus knot. The second point sets the radius. These options do not apply when drawing the torus knot using the **Keyboard Entry** rollout.

To draw a torus knot using the cursor, simply pick a point and drag to set the overall size of the knot. Then, move the cursor and pick to set the diameter of the cross section.

To draw a torus knot using the keyboard, expand the **Keyboard Entry** rollout by picking on it. Then, enter a value in the **Major Radius:** spinner to set the overall size of the torus knot. Enter a value in the **Minor Radius:** spinner to set the size of the circular cross section. The X, Y, and Z coordinates of the center of the circular projection can also be entered in this rollout. Finally, pick the **Create** button to draw the torus knot.

Once the torus knot is created, a name can be entered in the **Name and Color** rollout. The color can also be changed by picking the color swatch and then selecting a new color in the **Object Color** dialog box.

After the torus knot is created, there are several parameters that can be changed in the **Parameters** rollout. These are discussed in the next section.

Figure 3-16. The base curve for a torus knot can be a knot or a circle.

Torus Knot Parameters

In the **Base Curve** area of the **Parameters** rollout, you can specify whether the base curve is a circle or knot. By default, the **Knot** radio button is checked and the object is created as a knot. Picking the **Circle** radio button changes the base curve to a circle. The radius of the base curve, the major radius, can be changed in this area. Also, the number of segments along the base curve can be set in this area.

There are four spinners at the bottom of the **Base Curve** area. When the **Knot** radio button is on, the **P:** and **Q:** spinners are active and the **Warp Count:** and **Warp Height:** spinners are inactive. When the **Circle** radio button is on, the **P:** and **Q:** spinners are inactive and the **Warp Count:** and **Warp Height:** spinners are active. The value in the **P:** spinner determines how many turns there are around the object's Z axis. The value in the **Q:** spinner determines how many up-down bends there are from the object's XY plane. The minimum value for either spinner is 1.0. See Figure 3-17A. Setting both of these spinners to the same value creates a circular torus. The value in the **Warp Count:** spinner determines how many "bumps" there are around the circumference of the circle. The value in the **Warp Height:** spinner determines how "big" the bumps are. See Figure 3-17B.

In the **Cross Section** area, the parameters for the cross section of the torus knot are set. The radius of the cross section, the minor radius, and the number of sides the cross section has are set in the **Radius:** and **Sides:** spinners. The value in the **Eccentricity:** spinner determines the shape of the cross section. A value of 1 creates a circular cross section. Other values create an elliptical cross section. The value in the **Twist:** spinner sets the number of turns the cross section rotates through along the length of the path. See Figure 3-18. The value in the **Lumps:** spinner sets the number of bulges placed along the length of the path. The value in the **Lump Height:** spinner determines how big each "lump" is. The **Lump Offset:** spinner allows you to shift the lumps along the length of the path.

Figure 3-17. A—This torus knot has a **P:** value of 2 and a **Q:** value of 3. B—This torus knot has a circle base curve with a **Warp Count:** value of 3 and a **Warp Height:** value of 2. The blue line represents the warp height.

A   B

Figure 3-18. This torus knot, shown cut open, has a **Twist:** value of 4 and a **Lump Height:** value of 0.5.

The radio buttons in the **Smooth:** area determine how smoothing groups are applied to the object. Picking the **All** radio button applies smoothing to all faces of the torus knot. Picking the **Sides** radio button applies smoothing only to the side segments. Picking the **None** radio button leaves the torus knot faceted (no smoothing is applied).

At the bottom of the **Parameters** rollout is the **Mapping Coordinates** area. Checking the **Generate Mapping Coords** check box automatically calculates mapping coordinates for the torus knot. In addition, there are four spinners in this area that allow you to specify mapping offsets and tiling. Mapping is discussed in detail later in this text.

Exercise 3-11

1) Select **Create** in the **Command Panel**. Then, pick the **Geometry** button and select **Extended Primitives** from the drop-down list.
2) Pick **Torus Knot** in the **Object Type** rollout.
3) Draw a torus knot using the cursor.
4) In the **Base Curve** area of the **Parameters** rollout, pick the **Circle** radio button.
5) Enter 4 in the **Warp Count:** spinner. Change the value in the **Warp Height:** spinner to something other than 0. Observe how the object changes.
6) In the **Cross Section** area, enter 0.75 in the **Eccentricity:** spinner and 2.0 in the **Twist:** spinner. Observe the change in the object.
7) In the **Cross Section** area, enter 4.0 in the **Lumps:** spinner and 0.25 in the **Lump Height:** spinner. Observe how the object changes.
8) In the **Base Curve** area, pick the **Knot** radio button. Observe how the object changes. Which settings are retained?
9) Reset 3ds max. Do not save the file.

Exercise

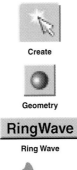

Create

Geometry

RingWave

Ring Wave

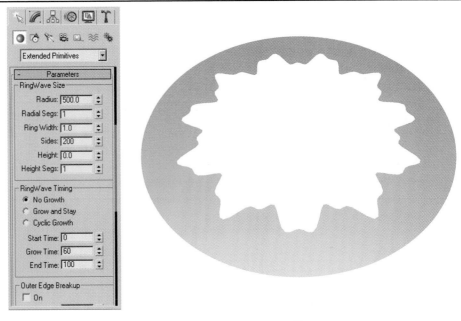

Ring Wave

A *ring wave* is a circular object that can have irregular inner and outer surfaces. See Figure 3-19. Ring waves can be used for many different special effects since the irregularity can be animated. Outer space explosions found in SciFi movies are a common example of animated ring waves. To create a ring wave, first select **Create** in the **Command Panel**. Then, pick the **Geometry** button. Select **Extended Primitives** in the drop-down list and then pick the **Ring Wave** button in the **Object Type** rollout.

You can also pick **Extended Primitives** in the **Create** pull-down menu. Then, pick **Ring Wave** in the cascading menu. This opens the **Create** tab in the **Command Panel** and selects the **Ring Wave** button.

A ring wave must be drawn using the cursor. Pick a point for the center of the ring wave. Then, drag the cursor to set the outer radius. Next, drag the cursor to set the inner radius. Once the ring wave is created, a name can be entered in the **Name and Color** rollout. The color can also be changed by picking the color swatch and then selecting a new color in the **Object Color** dialog box. Then, use the **Parameters** rollout to finish creating the ring wave.

The **Ring Wave Size** area is where the basic size of the ring wave is set. The value in the **Radius:** spinner is the radius to the outside of the ring wave. The value in the **Radial Segs:** spinner sets the number of segments on the face between the outer and inner radii. These are concentric circles. The value in the **Ring Width:** spinner sets how wide the ring face is and determines the inner radius. The value in the **Sides:** spinner sets the number of sides around the circumference of the ring wave. This number should be high if the ring wave will be animated. The ring wave can be given a height in the **Height:** spinner, and the number of height segments can be set in the **Height Segs:** spinner. However, a ring wave is not usually given a height in a typical application.

Figure 3-19. A—The **Parameters** rollout for a ring wave. B—A sample ring wave.

A

B

The settings in the **Ring Wave Timing** area are used to animate a ring wave from a zero radius to the value in the **Radius:** spinner. This is how an outer space explosion is created. The three radio buttons in this area determine how the ring wave grows. The three spinners set the time for the growth.

Picking the **No Growth** radio button specifies that the ring wave does not increase in size over time. It appears on the frame indicated in the **Start Time:** spinner. It disappears on the frame indicated in the **End Time:** spinner.

Picking the **Grow and Stay** radio button specifies that the ring wave begins to appear in the frame specified in the **Start Time:** spinner. The number of frames indicated in the **Grow Time:** spinner is how many frames it takes the ring wave to grow to its maximum size. The ring disappears on the frame indicated in the **End Time:** spinner.

Picking the **Cyclic Growth** radio button specifies that the ring wave begins to appear on the frame specified in the **Start Time:** spinner. It will grow to its full size over the number of frames indicated in the **Grow Time:** spinner. The ring will then repeat this growth until the frame indicated in the **End Time:** spinner is reached. This gives the appearance of repeated explosions from the center point.

The **Outer Edge Breakup** and **Inner Edge Breakup** areas have the same parameter settings. These settings determine the "breakup" of the edges. The settings in the **Outer Edge Breakup** area are applied to the outer edge. The settings in the **Inner Edge Breakup** area are applied to the inner edge. In order for the settings to be applied, the **On** check box must be checked. The value in the **Major Cycles:** spinner sets the number of waves around the circumference of the ring wave. The value in the **Minor Cycles:** spinner sets the number of smaller, random waves inside of each major wave.

Major waves and minor waves both have **Width Flux:** and **Crawl Time:** settings. The value in the **Width Flux:** spinner is a percentage that sets the size of the wave. The value in the **Crawl Time:** spinner is the number of frames it takes a single wave to travel the entire circumference of the ring wave.

Hose

A *hose* is an extended primitive that appears similar to a shock absorber boot or a bellows. See Figure 3-20. A hose can have one of three basic shapes. In addition, a hose can be "free" or linked to one or two objects.

To create a hose, first select **Create** in the **Command Panel**. Then, pick the **Geometry** button. Select **Extended Primitives** in the drop-down list and then pick the **Hose** button in the **Object Type** rollout. You can also pick **Extended Primitives** in the <u>C</u>reate pull-down menu. Then, pick **Hose** in the cascading menu. This opens the **Create** tab in the **Command Panel** and selects the **Hose** button.

Pick in a viewport and drag to set the overall diameter of the hose. Then, move the cursor up and down and pick to set the height of the hose. There are many parameters which need to be set for a hose. These are discussed in the following sections.

Create

Geometry

Hose

Hose

Figure 3-20. A—The **Parameters** rollout for a hose. B—A sample hose.

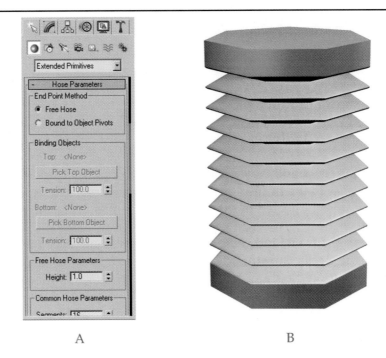

A   B

Hose Type

A hose can be created as one of two types—free or bound. A free hose is created by picking the **Free Hose** radio button in the **End Point Method** area of the **Parameters** rollout. When this radio button is on, the height of the hose can be set in the **Height:** spinner located in the **Free Hose Parameters** area of the **Parameters** rollout. A free hose may be used to create turned wooden legs on a table, for example.

A bound hose is created by picking the **Bound to Object Pivots** radio button in the **End Point Method** area of the **Parameters** rollout. When this radio button is on, the options in the **Binding Objects** area are enabled. Using the buttons in this area, you can select objects to which the hose is bound at the pivot point. This means as you move one of the "binding" objects, the hose changes shape based on the movement. Linking, binding, and animation are discussed later in this book.

Use the two buttons in the **Binding Objects** area to select a top and bottom object. The terms "top" and "bottom" are just labels, and just as easily could have been called "one" and "two." Once an object is selected, the object name is displayed above the button. The two **Tension:** spinners are used to set how close to the object a bend in the hose occurs as the object is moved. The higher the value, the farther away the bend occurs from the object.

Hose Shape

A hose can have one of three basic shapes. These shapes are round, rectangular, and D-shaped. You can set the basic shape by picking the **Round Hose**, **Rectangular Hose**, or **D-Section Hose** radio button in the **Hose Shape** area of the **Parameters** rollout. Once a radio button is selected, the options related to that shape are enabled below the button.

The **Diameter:** spinner under the **Round Hose** radio button sets the maximum diameter of the hose. The **Sides:** spinner sets the number of sides the hose has.

The **Width:** and **Depth:** spinners under the **Rectangular Hose** radio button set the cross-sectional size of the hose. The **Fillet:** spinner sets a radius by which the corners of the cross section are rounded. The **Fillet Segs:** spinner value must be 1 or greater to see the fillet. The **Rotation:** spinner allows you to rotate the rectangular cross section about the hose's Z axis.

The **Width:** and **Depth:** spinners under the **D-Section Hose** radio button set a rectangular cross-sectional size for the hose. The value in the **Round Sides:** spinner is the number of segments used to create the round "D." The minimum value is 2. The **Fillet:** spinner sets a radius by which the square corners of the cross section are rounded. The **Fillet Segs:** spinner value must be 1 or greater to see the fillet. The **Rotation:** spinner allows you to rotate the D-shaped cross section about the hose's Z axis.

Common Parameters

The options in the **Common Hose Parameters** area need to be set, regardless of the type or shape of hose. The value in the **Segments:** spinner is the number of segments along the length of the hose. At the bottom of the **Common Hose Parameters** area is the **Generate Mapping Coords** check box. When checked, mapping coordinates are automatically assigned to the object. Also, the **Renderable** check box must be checked for the hose to appear in a rendering. The **Smoothing** radio buttons determine how smoothing groups are applied to the hose. These options are similar to those used for a torus.

Near the top of the **Common Hose Parameters** area is the **Flex Section Enable** check box. When this is unchecked, the hose appears similar to a cylinder, such as a common garden hose. When checked, the hose appears similar to a bellows, and the four spinners below the check box are enabled.

The **Starts:** spinner determines where the flexible section begins along the hose. The value in the spinner is a percentage of the total length. The flexible section begins the specified percentage from the hose's start. The start is defined as the end where the default pivot point is located. The **Ends:** spinner specifies a percentage of the length from the hose's start where the flexible section ends.

The **Cycles:** spinner determines how many bends are in the flexible section. The number of segments must be high enough to allow for all bends to be displayed. The **Diameter:** spinner sets the secondary diameter of the flexible section. The value is a percentage of the main hose diameter. A negative percentage makes the diameter smaller than the overall diameter. A positive percentage makes the diameter larger than the overall diameter.

Exercise

Exercise 3-12

1) Select **Create** in the **Command Panel**. Then, pick the **Geometry** button and select **Extended Primitives** from the drop-down list.
2) Pick **Hose** in the **Object Type** rollout.
3) Draw a hose in the Top viewport. Make the hose approximately 100 units in diameter and 300 units tall.
4) Set the hose as a free hose.
5) Set the hose so the flexible section starts at 25% and ends at 75%. Set the cycles to 10 and the number of segments to 40.
6) Change the hose shape to **D-Section Hose**. Observe the results.
7) Change the hose shape to **Rectangular Hose**. Observe the results.
8) Increase the **Fillet:** and **Fillet Segs:** spinner values to 10 each. Observe the results.
9) Reset 3ds max. Do not save the file.

Patch Grids

Patch grids are flat 2D objects that can be modified or transformed into 3D surfaces. Patch grids are a good starting point for creating organic, or "life form," objects. There are two kinds of patch grid objects. These are quad patch and tri patch.

Create

Geometry

Quad Patch

Quad Patch

A *quad patch* is a flat, rectangular object made up of 36 visible rectangular faces. See Figure 3-21. Each visible face is actually two triangular faces, making the total number of faces 72. To create a patch grid, first select **Create** in the **Command Panel**. Then, pick the **Geometry** button. Select **Patch Grids** in the drop-down list and then pick the **Quad Patch** button in the **Object Type** rollout.

To draw a quad patch using the cursor, simply pick a point for the first corner of the patch grid. Then, drag the cursor to the other corner of the patch grid. This defines the length and width.

To draw a quad patch using the keyboard, expand the **Keyboard Entry** rollout by picking on it. Then, enter values in the **Length:** and **Width:** spinners. The X, Y, and Z coordinates of the center of the patch grid can also be entered in this rollout. Finally, pick the **Create** button to draw the patch grid.

Once the patch grid is created, a name can be entered in the **Name and Color** rollout. The color can also be changed by picking the color swatch and then selecting a new color in the **Object Color** dialog box.

In the **Parameters** rollout, you can change the number of segments for both the length and width. This increases the number of faces. The minimum number of faces is 36 and results from a value of 1 in the **Length Segs:** and **Width Segs:** spinners. Each visible rectangular face is subdivided by the number that appears in these spinners.

The **Generate Mapping Coords** check box at the bottom of the **Parameters** rollout is used to automatically calculate mapping coordinates for the object being created. By default, this option is off. Mapping is discussed in detail later in this text.

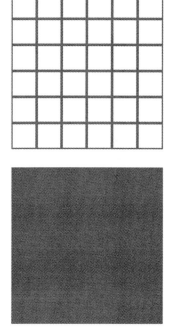

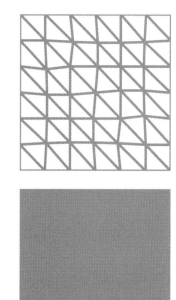

Figure 3-21. A quad patch is shown on the left. On the right is a tri patch. Notice the distortion in the middle of the tri patch.

Tri Patch

A *tri patch* is very similar to a quad patch. It consists of 72 triangular faces, all visible. See Figure 3-21. Unlike a quad patch, the number of segments cannot be increased. To create a tri patch, first select **Create** in the **Command Panel**. Then, pick the **Geometry** button. Select **Patch Grids** in the drop-down list and then pick the **Tri Patch** button in the **Object Type** rollout.

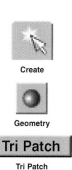

Create

Geometry

Tri Patch

Tri Patch

To draw a tri patch using the cursor, simply pick a point for the first corner of the patch grid. Then, drag the cursor to the other corner of the patch grid. This defines the length and width.

To draw a tri patch using the keyboard, expand the **Keyboard Entry** rollout by picking on it. Then, enter values in the **Length:** and **Width:** spinners. The X, Y, and Z coordinates of the center of the patch grid can also be entered in this rollout. Finally, pick the **Create** button to draw the patch grid.

Once the patch grid is created, a name can be entered in the **Name and Color** rollout. The color can also be changed by picking the color swatch and then selecting a new color in the **Object Color** dialog box.

The **Generate Mapping Coordinates** check box at the bottom of the **Parameters** rollout is used to automatically calculate mapping coordinates for the object being created. By default, this option is off. Mapping is discussed in detail later in this text.

Exercise

Exercise 3-13

1) Select **Create** in the **Command Panel**. Then, pick the **Geometry** button and select **Patch Grids** from the drop-down list.
2) Pick **Quad Patch** in the **Object Type** rollout.
3) Draw a quad patch of any size.
4) In the **Parameters** rollout, change the value in the **Length Segs:** spinner to 3. Observe the change in the object.
5) Pick **Tri Patch** in the **Object Type** rollout.
6) Draw a tri patch of any size. Notice how it differs from the quad patch.
7) Reset 3ds max. Do not save the file.

Chapter Snapshot

Chapter Test

Answer the following questions on a separate sheet of paper.

1) Define extended primitives.
2) Define patch grids.
3) List the two types of patch grids.
4) How do the two types of patch grids differ from each other?
5) When drawing a hedra, what is the purpose of the **P:** and **Q:** spinners in the **Family Parameters:** area of the **Parameters** rollout?
6) How many different shapes of facets can a hedra have?
7) What additional parameter does a chamfer box have over a box?
8) When drawing a chamfer cylinder, what does the value in the **Height Segs:** spinner determine?
9) What is a capsule?
10) How does an oil tank differ from a capsule?
11) How does a spindle differ from an oil tank?
12) What is a prism?
13) How does a gengon differ from a prism?
14) What is a typical use for L-Ext and C-Ext objects?
15) How does a torus knot differ from a standard torus?
16) When drawing a torus knot, what does the **Warp Count:** value determine?
17) What does the **Warp Height:** value determine when drawing a torus knot?

18) What is a common use for a ring wave?
19) What is the **Ring Wave Timing** area of the **Parameters** rollout used for?
20) List the three basic shapes for a hose.

Modeling Problems

Draw the following models. Use the 3ds max objects presented in this and earlier chapters. Choose object colors similar to those shown. When finished, save each model as p03-xx.max in the folder of your choice.

Chair **1**

Construction Barricade and Cones **2**

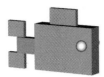

3 Toy Top

4 Accordion

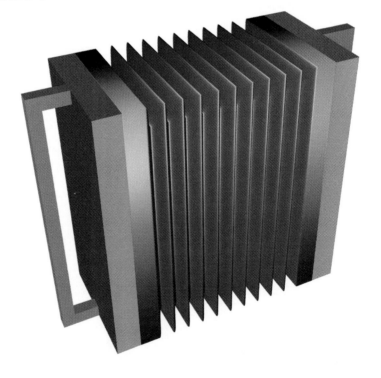

Croquet Mallet, Wicket, and Ball **5**

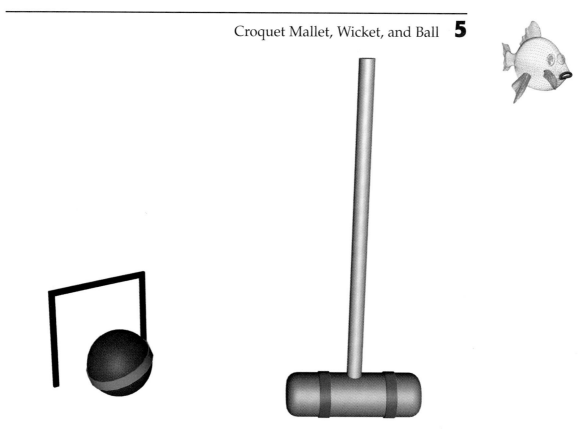

Toy Rocket **6**

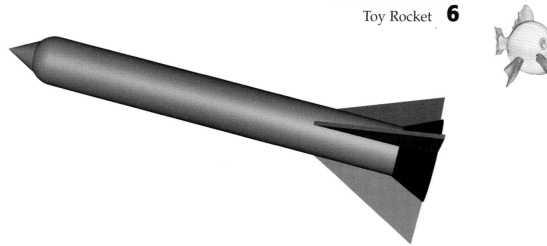

7 Brayer/Roller

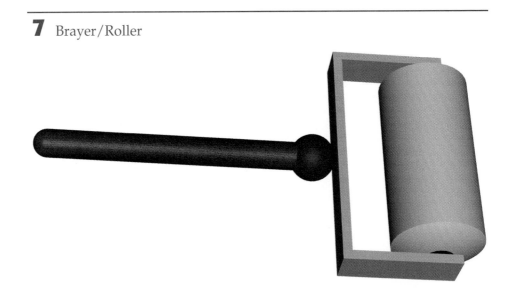

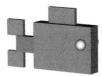

8 Residential Home

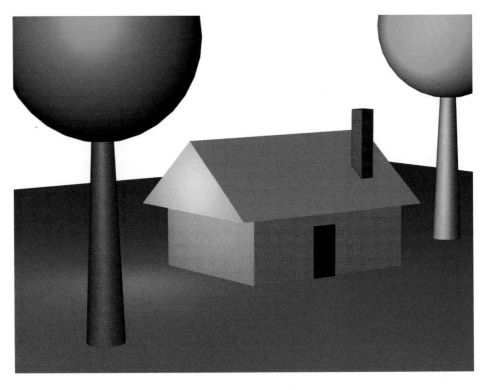

Toy Helicopter **9**

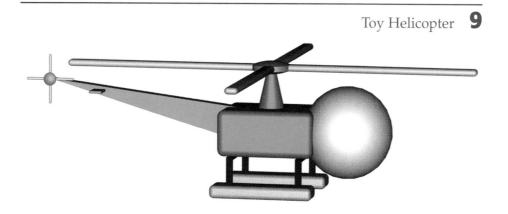

Books and Bookends **10**

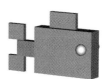

Creating Basic 2D Geometry (Shapes)

Objectives

After completing this chapter, you will be able to:

- Define a 3ds max shape.
- Identify the types of 3ds max spline shapes.
- Create various 3ds max shapes.
- Create text.
- Create a section.

3ds max has several different types of basic building blocks created as splines, or 2D geometry. 3ds max calls these splines *shapes.* Shapes are used to create 3D objects. They can also be used as paths for lofting and for movement.

A *spline* is simply a line segment between two endpoints. The segment can be straight or curved. Spline shapes in 3ds max include lines, rectangles, circles, ellipses, arcs, donuts, NGons, stars, text, helixes, and sections. The commands to draw these shapes are accessed by picking **Create** in the **Command Panel** followed by picking the **Shapes** button, and then selecting **Splines** from the drop-down list. Splines can also be drawn by selecting **Shapes** in the **Create** pull-down menu, and then picking the spline in the cascading menu. This chapter introduces the various spline shapes and discusses how they are used to create basic 2D geometry.

The Rendering and Interpolation Rollouts for Splines

When creating a spline, all types have the same options in the **Rendering** rollout. The settings in this rollout determine the properties of the spline when rendered. At the top of the rollout are two radio buttons. The settings made with the **Renderer** radio button on are used when the scene is rendered. The settings made with the **Viewport** radio button on are used for the display in shaded viewports. To enable the **Viewport** radio button, the **Display Render Mesh** and **Use Viewport Settings** check boxes at the bottom of the rollout must be checked.

By default, splines are not rendered. This is because splines are generally used to create final objects. However, a spline can be set to render by checking the **Renderable** check box in the **Rendering** rollout. A circle is used as the cross section for the rendered spline. The value in the **Thickness:** spinner determines the diameter of the rendered spline. The value in the **Sides:** spinner determines the number of segments in the circular cross section. The **Angle:** spinner is used to rotate the cross section around the spline's Z axis. Checking the **Generate Mapping Coordinates** check box automatically calculates mapping coordinates for the spline.

When the **Display Render Mesh** check box is checked, the settings in the **Thickness:**, **Sides:**, and **Angle:** spinners are reflected in shaded viewports. The settings displayed are for the **Viewport** radio button. Once settings are made, the mesh display can be turned on and off by checking and unchecking the **Display Render Mesh** check box.

In addition to the **Rendering** rollout, all splines except helixes and sections have the **Interpolation** rollout. The settings in this rollout determine how the spline is created. When the **Adaptive** check box is checked, 3ds max automatically adjusts the number of steps in a spline to produce a smoothed curve. When the **Adaptive** check box is unchecked, the **Optimize** check box can be checked and the **Steps:** spinner is enabled. The value in the **Steps:** spinner determines the number of steps between each spline vertex. If the **Optimize** check box is checked, 3ds max removes steps on straight-line segments, as they are not needed.

Help Cel

When the **Adaptive** and **Optimize** check boxes are unchecked, you can control the exact number of vertices in an object. This is important for certain operations, such as morphing.

AutoGrid

The **AutoGrid** feature allows you to automatically create and activate a temporary drawing grid. A *grid* is a construction plane. A grid is a special type of 3ds max object called a helper.

The AutoGrid feature can be activated when drawing a spline shape. To do so, check the **AutoGrid** check box in the **Object Type** rollout. If you pick the first point of a spline on the face of an existing object, a temporary grid is created and activated on that face. The spline is created on the plane defined by the face you picked on. This allows you to quickly draw on a plane other than the home grid.

Line

A *line* is a basic spline. It can be made up of one or more straight or curved segments. In addition, a line can be open or closed. See Figure 4-1. To draw a line, pick **Create** in the **Command Panel**. Then, pick the **Shapes** button. Select **Splines** in the drop-down list and then pick the **Line** button in the **Object Type** rollout.

Create

Shapes

Line

Line

Figure 4-1. A—The **Creation Method** rollout for a line. B—Three sample splines.

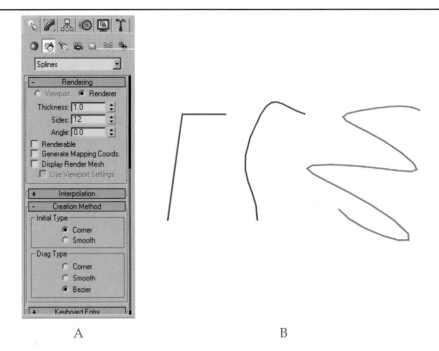

A   B

You can also pick **Shapes** in the <u>C</u>reate pull-down menu. Then, pick **Line** in the cascading menu. This opens the **Create** tab in the **Command Panel** and selects the **Line** button.

Notice that the **Start New Shape** check box in the **Object Type** rollout is checked by default. When this check box is unchecked, you can draw different shapes and they are added to the current shape, even if the shapes do not touch. When checked, drawing different shapes creates separate shapes. You learn more about this in Chapter 5.

In the **Creation Method** rollout, you can control how the line is drawn. In the **Initial Type** area, you can specify how the vertices are created when points are picked using single mouse picks. Picking the **Corner** radio button makes each vertex a corner. This means that the line leads straight out of the first vertex and straight into the next. In other words, straight line segments are created. Picking the **Smooth** radio button specifies that a smooth curve is drawn between vertices. The shape of the curve is determined by the number and position of vertices.

In the **Drag Type** area of the **Creation Method** rollout, you can specify the type of vertex drawn when points are dragged. *Dragging* is picking a point and, while holding the mouse button down, dragging to set the vertex control point. There are three options. The **Corner** and **Smooth** radio buttons function the same as those in the **Initial Type** area. Picking the **Bezier** radio button creates a Bézier curve through the vertices. Unlike a smooth curve, a Bézier curve can be adjusted by altering the control points.

Help Cel

The vertex control points for corner and smooth vertices are nonadjustable. Only control points for Bézier vertices can be adjusted.

To draw a line using the keyboard, expand the **Keyboard Entry** rollout. In the **X:**, **Y:**, and **Z:** spinners, enter the coordinates of the first vertex. Then, pick the **Add Point** button. Enter the coordinates of the second vertex in the spinners and pick the **Add Point** button again. Continue until all vertices are entered. If you wish to close the line, pick the **Close** button. A segment is drawn from the last vertex entered to the first vertex. If the line is to remain open, pick the **Finish** button to end the command. The type of vertices drawn using the keyboard is controlled in the **Initial Type** area of the **Creation Method** rollout.

To draw a line using the cursor, first set the vertex type in the **Initial Type** and **Drag Type** areas of the **Creation Method** rollout. Then, simply pick points in the current viewport to define the segments of the line. Pick or pick and drag as needed, depending on the settings in the **Creation Method** rollout. When done, right-click to end the command. If you pick the last point on top of the first point, a dialog box appears asking if you want to close the spline. Answer yes or no in the dialog box.

When using the mouse to create a line, you can press and hold the [Shift] key to constrain new line segments to 90° increments based on world space coordinates. This is called **Rectilinear Snap**. Pressing and holding the [Ctrl] key constrains the new line segments to angle increments determined by the current angle snap setting without turning **Angle Snap** on. One segment (two vertices) must be created before the angle constraint will work.

Once the line is created, a name can be entered in the **Name and Color** rollout. The color of the line can also be changed by picking the color swatch and then selecting a new color in the **Object Color** dialog box.

Exercise

Exercise 4-1

1) Select **Create** in the **Command Panel**. Then, pick the **Shapes** button and select **Splines** from the drop-down list.
2) Pick **Line** in the **Object Type** rollout.
3) In the **Creation Method** rollout, pick the **Smooth** radio button in the **Initial Type** area. Pick the **Corner** radio button in the **Drag Type** area.
4) Pick a point in the viewport as the first vertex. Pick another point as the second vertex. Pick a third point. Notice how the line is curved as you draw it.
5) Pick and drag a fourth, fifth, and sixth point. Notice how the new line segments are straight lines.
6) Right-click to end the command.
7) With the **Line** button still active in the **Object Type** rollout, uncheck the **Start New Shape** check box.
8) Draw another line picking points of your choice. Notice how these new segments are part of the previous line. You can see this because the transform coordinate center icon moves as you draw the line.
9) Reset 3ds max. Do not save the file.

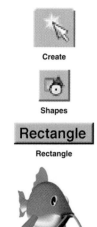

Create

Shapes

Rectangle

Rectangle

Rectangle

A *rectangle* is a spline with four straight-line segments at right angles to each other. The corners of a rectangle can be square, or they can have a radius. See Figure 4-2. To draw a rectangle, pick **Create** in the **Command Panel**. Then, pick the **Shapes** button. Select **Splines** in the drop-down list and then pick the **Rectangle** button in the **Object Type** rollout.

You can also pick **Shapes** in the **Create** pull-down menu. Then, pick **Rectangle** in the cascading menu. This opens the **Create** tab in the **Command Panel** and selects the **Rectangle** button.

Check the **Start New Shape** check box in the **Object Type** rollout to create a new shape. Uncheck it to make the rectangle part of the previous shape.

In the **Creation Method** rollout, you can specify how the rectangle is created. Picking the **Edge** radio button allows you to pick opposite corners of the rectangle. Picking the **Center** radio button specifies the first point picked as the center of the rectangle. The second point picked is a corner of the rectangle. These settings do not apply when drawing a rectangle using the keyboard.

To draw a rectangle using the keyboard, open the **Keyboard Entry** rollout. Enter the length and width of the rectangle in the **Length:** and **Width:** spinners. Enter a radius for the corners in the **Corner Radius:** spinner. If the corners are square, this value should be 0. You can also specify the X, Y, and Z coordinates of the center of the rectangle in this rollout. Finally, pick the **Create** button to draw the rectangle.

To draw a rectangle using the cursor, simply pick in the current viewport to set the first point. Depending on the settings in the **Creation Method** rollout, this may be the first corner or the center of the rectangle. Next, drag the cursor to the other corner to set the size of the rectangle. If you hold down the [Ctrl] key while dragging, a square is drawn.

Figure 4-2. A—The **Parameters** rollout for a rectangle. B—A sample rectangle.

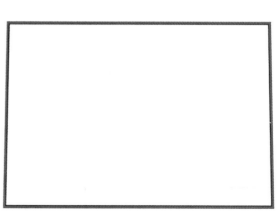

A

B

Once the rectangle is created, a name can be entered in the **Name and Color** rollout. The color of the rectangle can also be changed by picking the color swatch and then selecting a new color in the **Object Color** dialog box.

Help Cel

The vertices of a rectangle are Bézier corner vertices.

Exercise 4-2

1) Select **Create** in the **Command Panel**. Then, pick the **Shapes** button and select **Splines** from the drop-down list.
2) Pick **Rectangle** in the **Object Type** rollout.
3) In the **Creation Method** rollout, pick the **Center** radio button.
4) Draw a rectangle using the cursor. Use your own dimensions.
5) Draw another rectangle using the keyboard. Use your own dimensions. Enter a value in the **Corner Radius:** spinner. Do not make the value too large.
6) Reset 3ds max. Do not save the file.

Circle

A *circle* is a closed spline with a regular curve through each of its four Bézier vertices. See Figure 4-3. To draw a circle, pick **Create** in the **Command Panel**. Then, pick the **Shapes** button. Select **Splines** in the drop-down list and then pick the **Circle** button in the **Object Type** rollout.

Create

Shapes

Circle

You can also pick **Shapes** in the **Create** pull-down menu. Then, pick **Circle** in the cascading menu. This opens the **Create** tab in the **Command Panel** and selects the **Circle** button.

Check the **Start New Shape** check box in the **Object Type** rollout to create a new shape. Uncheck it to make the circle part of the previous shape.

In the **Creation Method** rollout, you can specify how the circle is created. Picking the **Edge** radio button allows you to pick opposite sides of the circle. Picking the **Center** radio button specifies the first point picked as the center of the circle. The second point picked is on the circumference of the circle. These settings do not apply when drawing a circle using the keyboard.

To draw a circle using the keyboard, open the **Keyboard Entry** rollout. Enter the radius of the circle in the **Radius:** spinner. You can also specify the X, Y, and Z coordinates of the center of the circle in this rollout. Finally, pick the **Create** button to draw the circle.

To draw a circle using the cursor, simply pick in the current viewport to set the first point. Depending on the settings in the **Creation Method** rollout, this may be a point on the circumference of the circle or the center point. Next, drag the cursor to set the size of the circle.

Figure 4-3. A—The **Parameters** rollout for a circle. B—A sample circle.

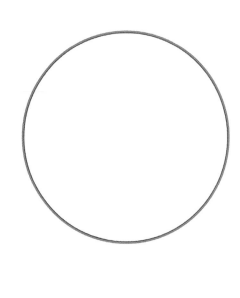

A   B

Once the circle is created, a name can be entered in the **Name and Color** rollout. The color of the circle can also be changed by picking the color swatch and then selecting a new color in the **Object Color** dialog box.

Exercise 4-3

1) Select **Create** in the **Command Panel**. Then, pick the **Shapes** button and select **Splines** from the drop-down list.
2) Pick **Circle** in the **Object Type** rollout.
3) In the **Creation Method** rollout, pick the **Edge** radio button.
4) Draw a circle using the cursor. Use your own dimensions.
5) Draw another circle in a different viewport using the keyboard. Use your own dimensions.
6) Reset 3ds max. Do not save the file.

Create

Shapes

Arc

Arc

Arc

An *arc* is a curved line with four Bézier vertices. The arc can be open or closed. See Figure 4-4. To draw an arc, pick **Create** in the **Command Panel**. Then, pick the **Shapes** button. Select **Splines** in the drop-down list and then pick the **Arc** button in the **Object Type** rollout.

You can also pick **Shapes** in the **Create** pull-down menu. Then, pick **Arc** in the cascading menu. This opens the **Create** tab in the **Command Panel** and selects the **Arc** button.

Check the **Start New Shape** check box in the **Object Type** rollout to create a new shape. Uncheck it to make the arc part of the previous shape.

In the **Creation Method** rollout, you can specify how the arc is created. There are two options. These options do not apply when creating an arc using the keyboard. When the **End-End-Middle** radio

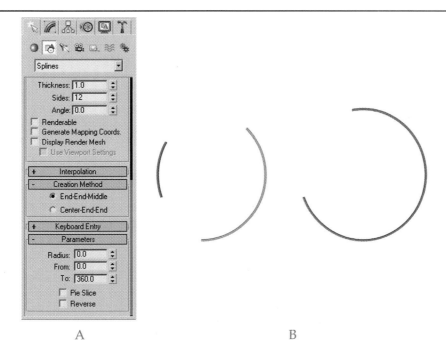

Figure 4-4. A—The **Parameters** rollout for an arc. B—Three sample arcs.

A   B

button is selected, two end points of the arc are picked, and then the midpoint of the arc is set. When the **Center-End-End** radio button is selected, the first point picked sets the center. The next two points define the endpoints of the arc.

To draw an arc using the keyboard, expand the **Keyboard Entry** rollout by picking on it. Then, enter a radius value in the **Radius:** spinner. The values in the **From:** and **To:** spinners are in degrees. These values determine where the arc starts and stops, as measured about the arc's center point. The X, Y, and Z coordinates of the center of the arc can also be entered in this rollout. Finally, pick the **Create** button to draw the arc.

To draw an arc using the cursor, pick the appropriate radio button in the **Creation Method** rollout. Then, pick in the viewport to set the first point. Holding the mouse button down, drag the cursor to the next point and release. Finally, move the cursor and pick to set the shape of the arc.

In the **Parameters** rollout, you can make the arc a *pie slice.* Checking the **Pie Slice** check box draws a line from each endpoint of the arc to its center. See Figure 4-5. You can also reverse the direction of the arc by checking the **Reverse** check box. This makes the first vertex the last and vice versa.

Once the arc is created, a name can be entered in the **Name and Color** rollout. The color of the arc can also be changed by picking the color swatch and then selecting a new color in the **Object Color** dialog box.

Help Cel

If the **Pie Slice** option is on, the first and last vertices are on top of each other.

Figure 4-5. The three arcs from Figure 4-4 with the **Pie Slice** option turned on.

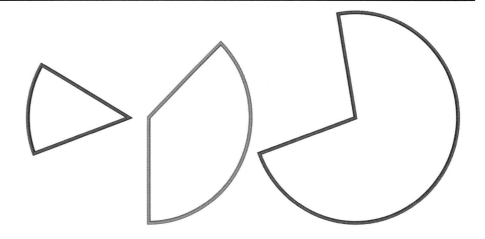

Exercise

Exercise 4-4

1) Select **Create** in the **Command Panel**. Then, pick the **Shapes** button and select **Splines** from the drop-down list.
2) Pick **Arc** in the **Object Type** rollout.
3) In the **Creation Method** rollout, pick the **End-End-Middle** radio button.
4) Draw an arc using the cursor. Use your own dimensions.
5) Draw another arc using the cursor with the **Center-End-End** radio button selected in the **Creation Method** rollout. Use your own dimensions.
6) How are the two creation methods different?
7) Draw another arc using either the keyboard or the cursor. Check the **Pie Slice** check box in the **Parameters** rollout.
8) Reset 3ds max. Do not save the file.

Create

Shapes

Ellipse

Ellipse

Ellipse

An *ellipse* is a regular, closed circular spline with a major axis and minor axis. See Figure 4-6. An ellipse has four Bézier vertices. To draw an ellipse, pick **Create** in the **Command Panel**. Then, pick the **Shapes** button. Select **Splines** in the drop-down list and then pick the **Ellipse** button in the **Object Type** rollout.

You can also pick **Shapes** in the **Create** pull-down menu. Then, pick **Ellipse** in the cascading menu. This opens the **Create** tab in the **Command Panel** and selects the **Ellipse** button.

Check the **Start New Shape** check box in the **Object Type** rollout to create a new shape. Uncheck it to make the ellipse part of the previous shape.

In the **Creation Method** rollout, you can specify how the ellipse is created. There are two options. These options do not apply when creating an ellipse using the keyboard. If the **Edge** radio button is on, the two points you pick are corners of an imaginary box surrounding the ellipse. If the **Center** radio button is on, the first point you pick is the center of the ellipse. The second point is one corner of the bounding box.

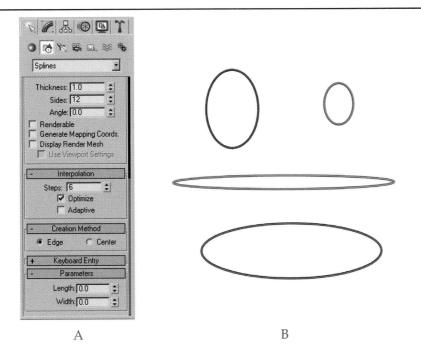

Figure 4-6. A—The **Parameters** rollout for an ellipse. B—Four sample ellipses.

A   B

To draw an ellipse using the keyboard, open the **Keyboard Entry** rollout by picking on it. Then, enter values in the **Length:** and **Width:** spinners. These values define the major and minor axes. You can also enter the X, Y, and Z coordinates of the ellipse center in this rollout. Finally, pick the **Create** button to draw the ellipse.

Once the ellipse is created, a name can be entered in the **Name and Color** rollout. The color of the ellipse can also be changed by picking the color swatch and then selecting a new color in the **Object Color** dialog box.

Exercise 4-5

1) Select **Create** in the **Command Panel**. Then, pick the **Shapes** button and select **Splines** from the drop-down list.
2) Pick **Ellipse** in the **Object Type** rollout.
3) In the **Creation Method** rollout, pick the **Edge** radio button.
4) Draw an ellipse using the cursor. Use your own dimensions.
5) Draw another ellipse using the keyboard. Use your own dimensions.
6) Reset 3ds max. Do not save the file.

NGon

An *NGon* is a regular, closed spline with three or more sides. The sides can be straight line segments or circular. See Figure 4-7. The vertices of an NGon are Bézier corner vertices. To draw an NGon, pick **Create** in the **Command Panel**. Then, pick the **Shapes** button. Select **Splines** in the drop-down list and then pick the **NGon** button in the **Object Type** rollout.

Create

Shapes

NGon

Figure 4-7. A—The **Parameters** rollout for an NGon. B—Three sample NGons.

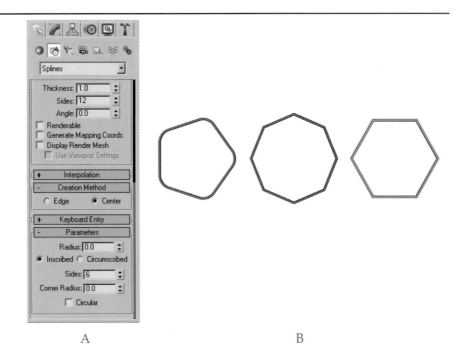

A   B

You can also pick **Shapes** in the **Create** pull-down menu. Then, pick **NGon** in the cascading menu. This opens the **Create** tab in the **Command Panel** and selects the **NGon** button.

Check the **Start New Shape** check box in the **Object Type** rollout to create a new shape. Uncheck it to make the NGon part of the previous shape.

In the **Creation Method** rollout, you can specify how the NGon is created. There are two options. These options do not apply when creating an NGon using the keyboard. If the **Edge** radio button is on, the two points you pick are corners of an imaginary box surrounding the NGon. If the **Center** radio button is on, the first point you pick is the center of the NGon. The second point is one corner of the bounding box.

In the **Parameters** rollout, you can specify if the NGon is inscribed or circumscribed. If the **Inscribed** radio button is on, the NGon fits inside of an imaginary circle defined by the **Radius:** spinner value. If the **Circumscribed** radio button is on, the imaginary circle fits inside the NGon. You can also set how many sides the NGon has by entering a value in the **Sides:** spinner. The **Corner Radius:** spinner is used to round the corners. Checking the **Circular** check box makes the NGon a circle with the number of segments set in the **Sides:** spinner.

To draw an NGon using the keyboard, expand the **Keyboard Entry** rollout by picking on it. Enter a radius value for the imaginary circle in the **Radius:** spinner. The settings in the **Parameters** rollout determine the number of sides and if the NGon is inscribed or circumscribed. Enter a corner radius value in the **Corner Radius:** spinner. A value of 0 creates square corners. You can also enter the X, Y, and Z coordinates of the center of the NGon in this rollout. Finally, pick the **Create** button to draw the NGon.

To draw an NGon using the cursor, set the number of sides in the **Parameters** rollout. Also, specify whether the NGon is to be inscribed or circumscribed. Then, pick in the viewport to set the first point. Holding the mouse button down, drag the cursor and release to set the second point.

Once the NGon is created, a name can be entered in the **Name and Color** rollout. The color of the NGon can also be changed by picking the color swatch and then selecting a new color in the **Object Color** dialog box.

Exercise 4-6

1) Select **Create** in the **Command Panel**. Then, pick the **Shapes** button and select **Splines** from the drop-down list.
2) Pick **NGon** in the **Object Type** rollout.
3) In the **Creation Method** rollout, pick the **Edge** radio button.
4) Draw an NGon using the cursor. Use your own dimensions.
5) In the **Parameters** rollout, set the number of sides to 5. Also, enter a corner radius. Use a value that is about 1/4 of the NGon radius.
6) Reset 3ds max. Do not save the file.

Donut

A *donut* is a closed spline consisting of two concentric circles. Each circle contains four Bézier vertices. When lofted or extruded, a donut creates a tube. See Figure 4-8. To draw a donut, pick **Create** in the **Command Panel**. Then, pick the **Shapes** button. Select **Splines** in the drop-down list and then pick the **Donut** button in the **Object Type** rollout.

You can also pick **Shapes** in the <u>C</u>reate pull-down menu. Then, pick <u>D</u>onut in the cascading menu. This opens the **Create** tab in the **Command Panel** and selects the **Donut** button.

Check the **Start New Shape** check box in the **Object Type** rollout to create a new shape. Uncheck it to make the donut part of the previous shape.

Create

Shapes

Donut

Donut

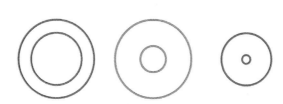

Figure 4-8. A—The **Parameters** rollout for a donut. B—Three sample donuts.

A

B

In the **Creation Method** rollout, you can specify how the donut is created. There are two options. These options do not apply when creating a donut using the keyboard. If the **Edge** radio button is on, the two points you pick are corners of an imaginary box surrounding the donut. If the **Center** radio button is on, the first point you pick is the center of the donut. The second point is one corner of the bounding box.

To draw a donut using the keyboard, expand the **Keyboard Entry** rollout by picking on it. Then, enter radius values in the **Radius 1:** and **Radius 2:** spinners. If Radius 1 is larger than Radius 2, then Radius 1 is the radius of the outer circle. You can also specify the X, Y, and Z coordinates of the center of the donut in this rollout. Finally, pick the **Create** button to draw the donut.

To draw a donut using the cursor, pick in the viewport and drag to set the first radius. Release the mouse button, move the mouse to set the second radius, and pick to create the donut.

Once the donut is created, a name can be entered in the **Name and Color** rollout. The color of the donut can also be changed by picking the color swatch and then selecting a new color in the **Object Color** dialog box.

Exercise

Exercise 4-7

1) Select **Create** in the **Command Panel**. Then, pick the **Shapes** button and select **Splines** from the drop-down list.
2) Pick **Donut** in the **Object Type** rollout.
3) In the **Creation Method** rollout, pick the **Edge** radio button.
4) Draw a donut using the cursor. Use your own dimensions.
5) Draw another donut using the keyboard. Use your own dimensions.
6) Reset 3ds max. Do not save the file.

Star

Create

Shapes

Star

Star

A *star* is a closed spline that can be created with as few as 3 points or as many as 100 points. See Figure 4-9. The vertices of a star are Bézier vertices. A star has two radii which define the overall size of the shape. In addition, the outer and inner points can have fillets applied independently. To draw a star, pick **Create** in the **Command Panel**. Then, pick the **Shapes** button. Select **Splines** in the drop-down list and then pick the **Star** button in the **Object Type** rollout.

You can also pick **Shapes** in the **C**reate pull-down menu. Then, pick **St**ar in the cascading menu. This opens the **Create** tab in the **Command Panel** and selects the **Star** button.

Check the **Start New Shape** check box in the **Object Type** rollout to create a new shape. Uncheck it to make the star part of the previous shape.

To draw a star using the keyboard, first set the number of points in the **Points:** spinner in the **Parameters** rollout. Then, expand the **Keyboard Entry** rollout by picking on it. Enter values in the **Radius 1:** and **Radius 2:** spinners. The larger of these two values is the overall size of the star. The

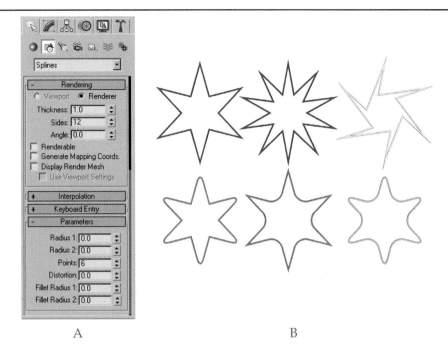

A   B

Figure 4-9. A—The **Parameters** rollout for a star. B—Six sample stars, all with the same **Radius 1:** and **Radius 2:** spinner values.

smaller of these two values is the radius of the inner points. If you want a fillet applied to either the inner or outer points, enter a value in the **Fillet Radius 1:** or **Fillet Radius 2:** spinner. You can also specify the X, Y, and Z coordinates of the center of the star in this rollout. Finally, pick the **Create** button to draw the star.

To draw a star using the cursor, first set the number of points in the **Parameters** rollout. Then, pick a point in the viewport as the center of the star. Drag and release to set the first radius. Next, move the cursor and pick to set the second radius. Finally, in the **Parameters** rollout, enter fillet values for the inner and outer points.

In the **Parameters** rollout, the value in the **Distortion:** spinner determines how much the outer points are rotated about the center of the star. By default, this is zero. Entering a value other than zero produces a saw-like effect. See Figure 4-10.

Once the star is created, a name can be entered in the **Name and Color** rollout. The color of the star can also be changed by picking the color swatch and then selecting a new color in the **Object Color** dialog box.

Figure 4-10. A star with increasing distortion. The one on the left has no distortion. The one on the right has the most distortion.

Exercise

Exercise 4-8

1) Select **Create** in the **Command Panel**. Then, pick the **Shapes** button and select **Splines** from the drop-down list.
2) Pick **Star** in the **Object Type** rollout.
3) Draw a star using the cursor. Use your own dimensions.
4) Change the **Distortion:** spinner value in the **Parameters** rollout and observe the change in the star.
5) Draw another star using the keyboard. Use your own dimensions. Enter values in the **Fillet Radius 1:** and **Fillet Radius 2:** spinners.
6) Reset 3ds max. Do not save the file.

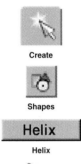

Create

Shapes

Helix

Helix

Helix

A *helix* is a spiral-shaped spline. A helix is typically drawn in three dimensions, but it can also lie flat on a plane. A helix has two radii, one at the start of the spiral and one at the end. The helix is a smooth curve between these radii. See Figure 4-11. The vertices of a helix are corner vertices. As such, it takes many vertices to create a smooth curve.

To draw a helix, pick **Create** in the **Command Panel**. Then, pick the **Shapes** button. Select **Splines** in the drop-down list and then pick the **Helix** button in the **Object Type** rollout.

You can also pick **Shapes** in the **Create** pull-down menu. Then, pick **Helix** in the cascading menu. This opens the **Create** tab in the **Command Panel** and selects the **Helix** button.

Check the **Start New Shape** check box in the **Object Type** rollout to create a new shape. Uncheck it to make the helix part of the previous shape.

In the **Creation Method** rollout, you can specify how the helix is created. There are two options. These options do not apply when creating a helix using the keyboard. If the **Edge** radio button is on, the

Figure 4-11. A—The **Parameters** rollout for a helix. B—Three samples of how a helix can be drawn.

A   B

two points you pick are points on the diameter of the helix. If the **Center** radio button is on, the first point you pick is the center of the helix. The second point is a point on the diameter of the helix.

To draw a helix using the keyboard, expand the **Keyboard Entry** rollout by picking on it. Then, enter values in the **Radius 1:** and **Radius 2:** spinners. Radius 1 is the radius at the start of the helix. Radius 2 is the radius at the end of the helix. Enter a value for the height in the **Height:** spinner. If the helix is to lie on a plane, this value is zero. You can also enter the X, Y, and Z coordinates of the center of the helix in this rollout. Finally, pick the **Create** button to draw the helix.

To draw a helix using the cursor, pick in the viewport to set the first point of Radius 1. Drag the cursor and release to set the second point of Radius 1. Next, move the cursor and pick to set the height of the helix. Finally, move the cursor and pick to set Radius 2.

In the **Parameters** rollout, you can set the number of turns the helix has by entering a value in the **Turns:** spinner. A helix also has a bias setting. The value in the **Bias:** spinner can be from –1.0 to 1.0. A setting of –1.0 forces the coils of the helix toward the start of the helix. A value of 0.0 evenly distributes the coils. A value of 1.0 forces the coils toward the end of the helix. See Figure 4-12. The **CW** (clockwise) and **CCW** (counterclockwise) radio buttons at the bottom of the **Parameters** rollout set which direction the helix turns.

Once the helix is created, a name can be entered in the **Name and Color** rollout. The color of the helix can also be changed by picking the color swatch and then selecting a new color in the **Object Color** dialog box.

Figure 4-12. The effect of bias on a helix. On the left, there is no bias. In the middle, there is positive bias applied. On the right, there is negative bias applied.

Exercise 4-9

1) Select **Create** in the **Command Panel**. Then, pick the **Shapes** button and select **Splines** from the drop-down list.
2) Pick **Helix** in the **Object Type** rollout.
3) In the **Creation Method** rollout, pick the **Edge** radio button.
4) Draw a helix using the cursor. Use your own dimensions.
5) In the **Parameters** rollout, increase the number of turns. Then, change the **Bias:** spinner value and observe the results.
6) Reset 3ds max. Do not save the file.

Text

Create

Shapes

Text

Text

Text in the form of spline shapes can be created using Type 1 PostScript or TrueType fonts. The type of vertices in the text spline will vary based on the font used and the text drawn. To draw text, pick **Create** in the **Command Panel**. Then, pick the **Shapes** button. Select **Splines** in the drop-down list and then pick the **Text** button in the **Object Type** rollout.

You can also pick **Shapes** in the **Create** pull-down menu. Then, pick **Text** in the cascading menu. This opens the **Create** tab in the **Command Panel** and selects the **Text** button.

Check the **Start New Shape** check box in the **Object Type** rollout to create a new shape. Uncheck it to make the text part of the previous shape.

At the top of the **Parameters** rollout is the font drop-down list. See Figure 4-13. All available fonts are shown in this list. Choose the font you want to use.

Below the font drop-down list are the style buttons. You can choose to have the text appear normal, italicized, underlined, or italicized and underlined. You can also pick to have the text aligned to the left, aligned to the center, aligned to the right, or fully justified. Full justification specifies that the text aligns to both the left and right.

Help Cel

The text alignment options only apply to multiple lines of text.

Below the style buttons in the **Parameters** rollout are the **Size:**, **Kerning:**, and **Leading:** spinners. The value in the **Size:** spinner determines the vertical size of the text in the current drawing units. The **Kerning:** spinner allows you to adjust the distance between letters. The value in the **Leading:** spinner determines the spacing between lines of text.

Figure 4-13. A—The **Parameters** rollout for text. B—Select an installed font by picking from the drop-down list.

A

B

The **Text:** edit box is where text is entered. By default, the text MAX Text appears in this box. To enter your own text, simply pick in this box and backspace over the default text. Then, enter your text. Think of this edit box as a small word processor. The text is not displayed in the font selected in the drop-down list. It will be, however, when the text is placed in the viewport.

At the bottom of the **Parameters** rollout is the **Update** area. When the **Manual Update** check box is unchecked, the text in the viewport is dynamically updated as the text is edited. If this check box is checked, the text in the viewport is not updated until the **Update** button is picked. This button is greyed out until the **Manual Update** check box is checked.

To place the text, simply pick a point in the viewport and hold. Then, drag the text into the correct location and release. Once the text is created, a name can be entered in the **Name and Color** rollout. The color of the text can also be changed by picking the color swatch and then selecting a new color in the **Object Color** dialog box.

Exercise 4-10

1) Select **Create** in the **Command Panel**. Then, pick the **Shapes** button and select **Splines** from the drop-down list.
2) Pick **Text** in the **Object Type** rollout.
3) In the **Parameters** rollout, type My Own Words in the **Text:** edit box.
4) Pick in a viewport to place the text.
5) In the **Parameters** rollout, select a different font. Check the **Manual Update** check box.
6) Change the text to read My New Words. Notice that the text in the viewport has not changed. Pick the **Update** button to change the text in the viewport.
7) Reset 3ds max. Do not save the file.

Exercise

Section

Drawing a *section* generates splines based on the cross-sectional dimensions of other existing objects. See Figure 4-14. The vertices of the resulting spline are corner vertices. To draw a section, pick **Create** in the **Command Panel**. Then, pick the **Shapes** button. Select **Splines** in the drop-down list and then pick the **Section** button in the **Object Type** rollout.

You can also pick **Shapes** in the **Create** pull-down menu. Then, pick **Section** in the cascading menu. This opens the **Create** tab in the **Command Panel** and selects the **Section** button.

Check the **Start New Shape** check box in the **Object Type** rollout to create a new shape. Uncheck it to make the spline created by the section part of the previous shape.

Start by drawing a section of any size in the viewport. A section appears as a rectangular object. The first point picked is the center point of the section object. Drag and pick to set the length and width of the

Create

Shapes

Section

Figure 4-14. The splines resulting from creating a section at three different vertical positions on a teapot.

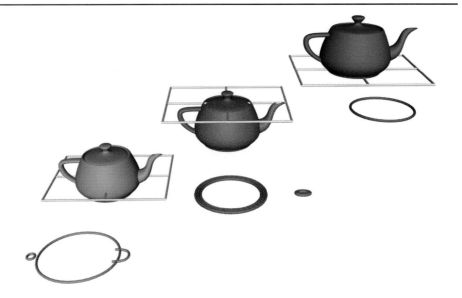

section object. At this point, you can enter a name for the object in the **Name and Color** rollout. The color of the section object can also be changed by picking the color swatch and then selecting a new color in the **Object Color** dialog box.

After the section is drawn, there are several parameters that need to be set. First, in the **Section Size** rollout, you can enter an exact size for the section. The size is only important if the section extents are set to **Section Boundary**. This is discussed later in this section.

At the top of the **Section Parameters** rollout is the **Create Shape** button. This button is used to generate a new spline based on the cross section where the section cuts the object. In this rollout, there are also the **Update:** and **Section Extents** areas.

The radio buttons in the **Update:** area allow you to set how the cross section is updated. Picking the **When Section Moves** radio button automatically updates the display of the cross section as the section object is moved. Picking the **When Section Selected** radio button updates the display of the cross section whenever the section object is selected. However, the display is not updated as the section object is moved. Picking the **Manually** radio button updates the display of the cross section only when the **Update Section** button in this area is selected. This button must also be picked if the **When Section Selected** radio button is on and the section object is moved.

The **Section Extents** area allows you to set the extents of the section. When the **Infinite** radio button is selected, the section object has no boundaries. This means that the section object can be next to another object without touching it and still create a cross section. When the **Section Boundary** radio button is selected, cross sections are only created for objects the section object touches.

At the bottom of the **Section Parameters** rollout is a color swatch. This is the display color of the cross section created by the section object. This, however, is not the display color of the resulting spline. To change the color, simply pick the color swatch and select a different color in the **Color Selector:** dialog box.

To create a cross section using a section object, first create the object you want to "slice." Next, draw a section. Move and rotate the section as necessary. The cross section that will be generated is displayed in yellow (or the color you set). See Figure 4-15. Finally, pick the **Create Shape** button in the **Section Parameters** rollout to generate the spline. The **Name Section Shape** dialog box appears. See Figure 4-16. Enter a name in the **Name:** text box and pick the **OK** button to create the spline.

Once the spline is created, it can be selected and given a new name in the **Name and Color** rollout. The display color can also be set in this rollout.

Help Cel

If a section object is transformed (moved, rotated, or scaled) after it is initially drawn, the **Create Shape** button must be accessed in the **Modify** tab. Using this tab is discussed in detail in Chapter 5.

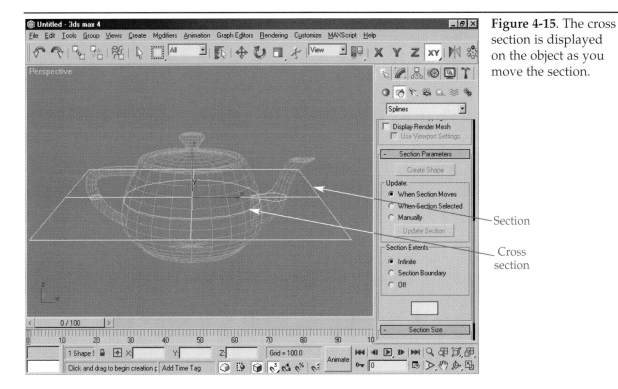

Figure 4-15. The cross section is displayed on the object as you move the section.

Section

Cross section

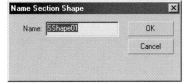

Figure 4-16. The **Name Section Shape** dialog box is used to name the spline resulting from the section operation.

Exercise

Exercise 4-11

1) Select **Create** in the **Command Panel**. Then, pick the **Geometry** button and select **Standard Primitives** from the drop-down list.
2) Pick **Teapot** in the **Object Type** rollout.
3) Draw a teapot in the Top viewport centered on the world origin using your own dimensions.
4) Select **Create** in the **Command Panel**. Then, pick the **Shapes** button and select **Splines** from the drop-down list.
5) Pick **Section** in the **Object Type** rollout.
6) Draw a section in the Front viewport. Move it as necessary to intersect the teapot. Make sure the **Infinite** radio button is selected in the **Section Parameters** rollout.
7) Notice the cross section shape indicated by the yellow lines. Pick the **Create Shape** button. If you moved the section since it was created, you must access this button in the **Modify** tab of the **Command Panel**. The cross section is now a spline.
8) Reset 3ds max. Do not save the file.

Chapter Snapshot

Chapter Test

Answer the following questions on a separate sheet of paper.

1) What is a 3ds max shape?
2) What are the settings in the **Interpolation** rollout used for?
3) How is a spline object made so it can be rendered?
4) A line is made up of one or more _____ or _____ segments.
5) What is the purpose of the **Start New Shape** check box?
6) When drawing a line, what do the settings in the **Initial Type** and **Drag Type** areas of the **Creation Method** rollout determine?
7) A rectangle can have _____ or _____ corners.
8) When creating a circle, the settings in the **Creation Method** rollout apply only when using the _____.
9) The two radio buttons in the **Creation Method** rollout for an arc are _____ and _____.
10) An ellipse is a closed circular spline with _____ and _____ axes.
11) If the **Pie Slice** check box is checked, a line is drawn from each endpoint of an arc to _____.
12) An NGon must have at least _____ sides.
13) A circumscribed NGon fits _____ the imaginary circle defined by the **Radius:** spinner value.

14) When lofted or extruded, a donut creates a _____.
15) A star can have as few as _____ and as many as _____ points.
16) The _____ points of a star can be filleted.
17) A helix is a _____ spline.
18) A value of –1.0 in the **Bias:** spinner forces the coils of a helix _____.
19) Splines can be created from text using _____ or _____ fonts.
20) A section generates splines based on _____.

Modeling Problems

Draw the following models. Use the 3ds max objects presented in this and earlier chapters. Choose object colors similar to those shown. When finished, save each model as p04-xx.max in the folder of your choice.

Pie Chart **1**

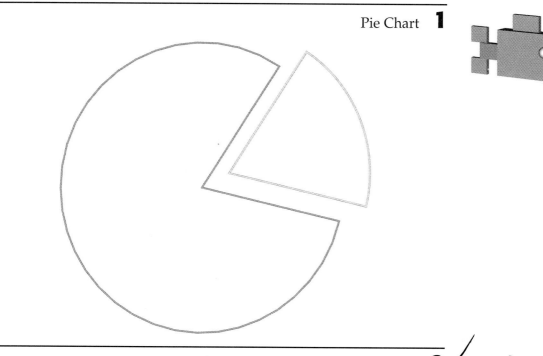

Wireframe Bar Stock **2**

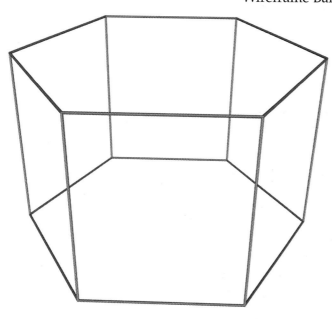

3 Wireframe Allen Head Bolt

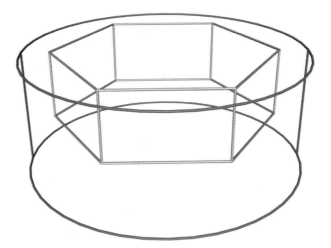

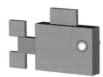

4 Nameplate

Outdoor Sign **5**

Pinball Mechanism **6**

7 Holiday Tree

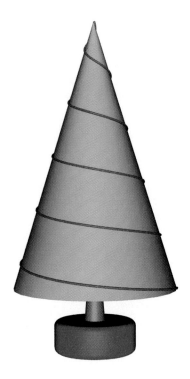

8 Shock Absorber

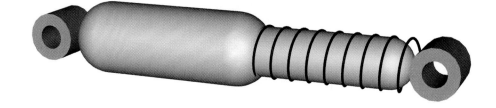

Three-Dimensional Arrowhead **9**

Teapot and Steam **10**

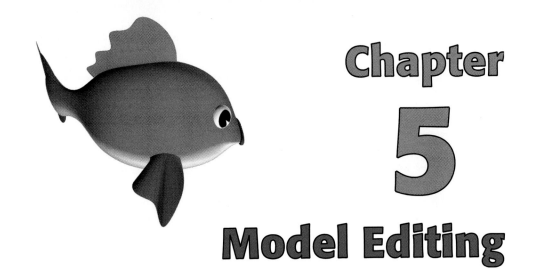

Chapter
5
Model Editing

Objectives

After completing this chapter, you will be able to:

- Describe the different ways to reverse actions in 3ds max.
- Explain different ways to select objects.
- Define transforms.
- Define modifiers.
- Transform objects.
- Apply modifiers.
- Explain sub-object mode.
- Edit splines.
- Hide and display objects.
- Group, align, array, and mirror objects using 3ds max tools.

As you may have already discovered, there are many situations where you need to edit objects created during the modeling process. There are many types of editing tools available in 3ds max. In addition to the transform tools (move, rotate, and scale) introduced earlier in this text, 3ds max provides many types of object modifiers that can be applied to create unique shapes. This chapter introduces the basic editing tools and modifiers available in 3ds max.

Undo/Redo and Hold/Fetch

When creating a model, there will almost always be at least one instance where you want to reverse the last thing you did. There are two different ways you can do this in 3ds max. The **Undo** function allows you to step back through the previous commands. The **Hold** and **Fetch** functions allow you to create and restore a "mini-save" of the file.

Undo/Redo

The **Undo** function is a standard Windows function used to reverse the last action. You can sequentially "retrace" your actions. By default, you can step back 20 times. However, you can set up 3ds max to allow you to step back up to 500 times. This is set by selecting **Preferences**... from the **Customize** pull-down menu. When the **Preference Settings** dialog box appears, select the **General** tab. In the **Scene Undo** area, enter a value in the **Levels:** spinner. This is the number of steps you can go back with the **Undo** function. Pick the **OK** button to close the dialog box.

To undo an action, pick the **Undo** button on the **Main** toolbar, pick **Undo** from the **Edit** pull-down menu, or press [Ctrl][Z] on the keyboard. When using the pull-down menu, the entry **Undo** is followed by the action that will be undone. You can continue to undo the number of actions as set in the **Preference Settings** dialog box.

Any action that is undone can be redone in reverse order. To do this, pick the **Redo** button on the **Main** toolbar, pick **Redo** from the **Edit** pull-down menu, or press [Ctrl][A]. When using the pull-down menu, the entry **Redo** is followed by the action that will be redone. If no action has been undone, the redo function is unavailable.

Hold/Fetch

The **Undo** function can only go back so far. The **Hold** and **Fetch** functions allow you to go back as far as you want. This is because a "mini-saved" version of the model is created. The hold and fetch functions are especially useful when a series of commands is about to be used. Then, if the result is not what you want, you can simply "fetch" the model instead of stepping back through several undos. Also, if your machine happens to crash in the middle of the sequence, the undo function cannot be used. However, the fetch function can still be used.

To "hold" a model, select **Hold** from the **Edit** pull-down menu or press [Alt][Ctrl][H] on the keyboard. The model is saved in a file named maxhold.mx and is a .max file with a different extension. This file is saved in a folder specified in the AutoBackup path. To "fetch" the model, select **Fetch** from the **Edit** pull-down menu or press [Alt][Ctrl][F] on the keyboard. A dialog box appears asking if you want to fetch. See Figure 5-1. Pick **OK** to restore the "held" file.

To change the AutoBackup path, select **Configure Paths**... from the **Customize** pull-down menu. Then, pick the **General** tab in the **Configure Paths** dialog box. This tab displays several entries and their corresponding paths. Select the AutoBackup entry and pick the **Modify**... button. See Figure 5-2. The **Choose Directory for AutoBackup** dialog box appears. This is a standard Windows "explorer-type" dialog box. Simply select a new drive and folder for the AutoBackup path and pick the **Use Path** button. Then, pick the **OK** button in the **Configure Paths** dialog box.

Figure 5-1. Before you fetch, you are asked to confirm the action.

Figure 5-2. The **General** tab of the **Configure Paths** dialog box is used to change the AutoBackup path.

Path

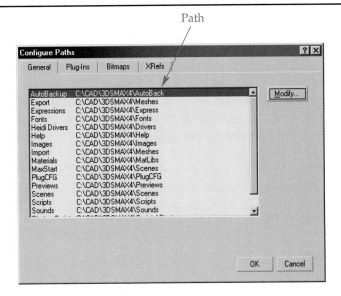

Exercise

Exercise 5-1

1) Reset 3ds max.
2) Draw a box in any viewport.
3) Select **Hold** from the **Edit** pull-down menu.
4) Draw a sphere in any viewport.
5) Draw a cylinder in any viewport.
6) Draw a teapot in any viewport.
7) Pick the **Undo** button. What happened?
8) Pick the **Redo** button. What happened?
9) Press [Alt][Ctrl][F] on the keyboard. What happened?
10) Reset 3ds max without saving the file.

Selecting Objects

There are almost no instances where all changes to an object are made right after it is created. This being the case, you will need to select the various objects in your scene during the modeling process. There are several ways of doing this.

Selecting Objects Using the Cursor

Select object

The most basic way of selecting objects is to pick them with the cursor. To do this, pick the **Select object** button on the **Main** toolbar. Then, place the cursor over the object you want to select and press the left mouse button. If you want to select more than one object, after the first object is selected, hold down the [Ctrl] key and pick the other objects. All of the selected objects together are called a *selection set.* To remove objects from the selection set, hold down the [Alt] key and pick the objects to remove them.

Rectangular Selection Region

You can select multiple objects at the same time using the **Select object** button by dragging a *region,* or window. The shape of the region is determined by the currently selected button in the **Selection Region** flyout on the **Main** toolbar. The default button is the **Rectangular Selection Region** button.

This button allows you to drag a rectangular window around objects to select them. Any object inside the window is selected. Picking the flyout and holding it down allows you to select other buttons. The **Circular Selection Region** button allows you to draw a circular window to select objects. The **Fence Selection Region** button allows you to draw a series of straight lines to create an irregularly shaped window. Double-click when the last point is selected and the fence is closed. See Figure 5-3.

Circular Selection Region

Fence Selection Region

You can set whether the selection region is a "window" or a "crossing." When set to window, objects must be completely inside of the region. When set to crossing, objects can be inside or touching the region. To set this, pick **Region** from the **Edit** pull-down menu. Then, in the cascading menu, select either **Window** or **Crossing**. The current setting has a check mark next to it.

You can select all objects in the scene by picking **Select All** from the **Edit** pull-down menu. To deselect all objects, pick **Select None** from the **Edit** pull-down menu. Picking **Select Invert** from the **Edit** pull-down menu selects all currently unselected objects and deselects all currently selected objects.

Selecting Objects by Name

All objects in a scene have a name. You can select objects by their name using a dialog box. To do this, pick the **Select by Name** button on the **Main** toolbar, pick **Name** from the **Select By** cascading menu in the **Edit** pull-down menu, or press the [H] key on the keyboard. The **Select Objects** dialog box appears. See Figure 5-4.

Select by Name

On the left side of this dialog box is a list of names for all currently visible objects. In the **List Types** area on the right side of the dialog box, check the object types you want displayed in the list. By default, all types are listed. In the **Sort** area, specify how you want the names arranged. By default, names appear in the list in alphabetical order. In

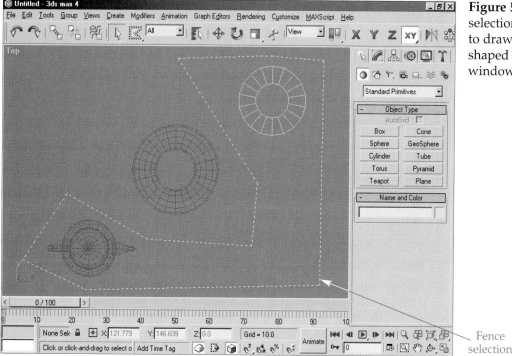

Figure 5-3. A fence selection allows you to draw an irregularly shaped selection window.

Fence selection

Figure 5-4. The **Select Objects** dialog box allows you to select objects by name.

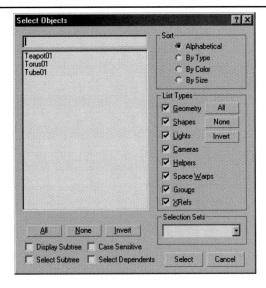

the **Selection Sets** area is a drop-down list. If any selection sets have been named, they appear in this list. Picking a selection set name in this drop-down list highlights the names of the objects in the selection set in the list at the left of the dialog box.

To select an object, pick its name in the list at the left of the dialog box. By holding down the [Ctrl] key, you can pick multiple objects. Holding down the [Shift] key allows you to pick two object names. Any objects between the two are also selected. When you have all objects picked in the list, pick the **Select** button to close the dialog box and select the objects.

Help Cel

It is possible to have two different objects in the scene with identical names. When naming objects, be sure you are not duplicating an existing name.

Exercise

Exercise 5-2

1) Draw six objects of your choice. Use standard primitives, extended primitives, or shapes.
2) Pick the **Select object** button and select a single object with the cursor.
3) Add three more objects to the selection set by holding down the [Ctrl] key and picking them with the cursor.
4) Remove one object by holding down the [Alt] key and picking it with the cursor.
5) Pick **Select Invert** from the **Edit** pull-down menu. What happened?
6) Pick **Select None** from the **Edit** pull-down menu.
7) Pick the **Selection Region** flyout and select the **Fence Selection Region** button. Pick points to create a fence around two of the objects. Double-click to complete the fence.
8) Press the [H] key on the keyboard. Select three objects in the **Select Objects** dialog box.
9) Reset 3ds max without saving.

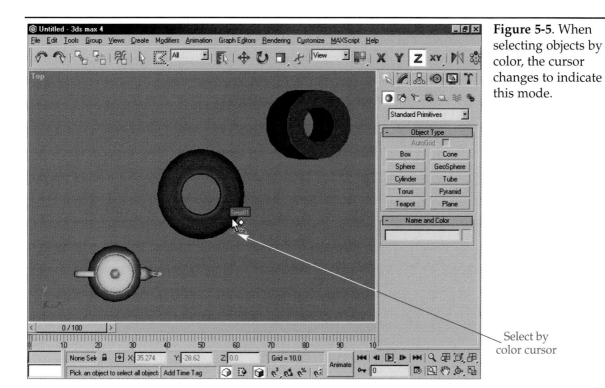

Figure 5-5. When selecting objects by color, the cursor changes to indicate this mode.

Select by color cursor

Selecting Objects by Color

You can select all objects in the scene that have the same display color. To do so, pick **Color** in the **Select By** cascading menu of the **Edit** pull-down menu. The cursor changes to indicate you are in the "select by color" mode. See Figure 5-5. Pick an object of the color you want to select. All objects with that same display color are selected.

By default, 3ds max assigns random display colors to new objects. For the "select by color" feature to be useful, the random color feature should be turned off and colors manually assigned. To turn the random colors feature off, open the **Object Color** dialog box. The easiest way to do this is to pick the color swatch in the **Name and Color** rollout. You do not have to select an object to do this. In the **Object Color** dialog box, uncheck the **Assign Random Colors** check box at the bottom left. See Figure 5-6. Also, pick a color you want to be the current color. The

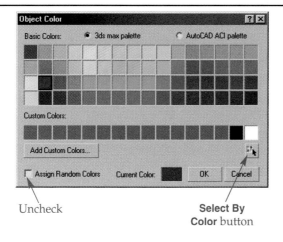

Figure 5-6. To make selecting by color useful, objects should not be created with randomly assigned colors.

Uncheck

Select By Color button

Select by Color

current color is indicated in the **Current Color:** color swatch. Then, pick the **OK** button. All new objects will have the color you selected. The **Select By Color** button can also be found in the **Object Color** dialog box.

By default, 3ds max uses its own color palette. However, you can also use the standard AutoCAD ACI or add custom colors to the 3ds max palette. To use the AutoCAD ACI, pick the **AutoCAD ACI palette** radio button at the top of the **Object Color** dialog box. To add custom colors, pick the **3ds max palette** radio button at the top of the **Object Color** dialog box. Then, pick an unused swatch in the **Custom Colors:** area and pick the **Add Custom Colors...** button. The **Color Selector: Add Color** dialog box appears. See Figure 5-7. Make color settings as you want them, and then pick the **Add Color** button. Close the **Color Selector: Add Color** dialog box. The new color now appears in the **Object Color** dialog box.

Help Cel

If you are running a medium- or low-resolution display, such as 800 x 600, the **Color Selector: Add Color** dialog box may "disappear" off the screen. If this happens, pick anywhere on the **Object Color** dialog box to make it "on top." Then, press the [Esc] key or pick the **Cancel** button to close both dialog boxes. Next, open the **Object Color** dialog box again. Move the cursor to the title bar, pick and hold, and drag the dialog box down to make room for the **Color Selector: Add Color** dialog box on screen.

Figure 5-7. You can define custom object display colors in the **Color Selector: Add Color** dialog box.

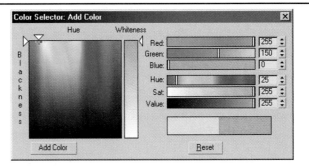

Exercise 5-3

1) In the **Name and Color** rollout in the **Command Panel**, pick the color swatch to open the **Object Color** dialog box.
2) Pick the **AutoCAD ACI palette** radio button. The available colors match the ACI.
3) Pick the **3ds max palette** radio button.
4) Select an unused color swatch in the **Custom Colors:** area. Pick the **Add Custom Colors...** button.
5) In the **Color Selector: Add Color** dialog box, pick a color of your choice. Then, pick the **Add Color** button.
6) Close the **Color Selector: Add Color** dialog box. The new color appears in the **Object Color** dialog box.
7) Close the **Object Color** dialog box and reset 3ds max without saving.

Select and Transform Tools

There are three tools that allow you to select an object and immediately transform it. Transforms are introduced in Chapter 2, and are discussed in the next section. By combining the commonly used transforms of move, rotate, and scale with a selection tool, a step is removed. The **Select and Move**, **Select and Rotate**, and **Select and Scale** transform tools are discussed later in this chapter.

Locking a Selection Set

It is often useful to lock a selection set. By locking the selection, you cannot accidentally deselect the objects or select other objects. In complex models, you will probably find yourself locking and unlocking selections quite frequently.

There are two ways to lock a selection. First, select all objects you want in the locked selection set. Then, you can either press the spacebar or pick the **Selection Lock Toggle** button next to the prompt line. With either method, the button is depressed. To unlock the selection, either press the spacebar or pick the button again. The button is no longer depressed, and you can select other objects.

Selection Lock Toggle

Transforms vs Modifiers

When an object is created, its position, rotation, and scale in relation to the world coordinate system are stored in a transformation matrix. This is a table internal to 3ds max. Any change made to the position (moving), rotation (rotating), or scale (scaling) is called a *transformation,* or *transform.* Transforms can be applied in any order.

Modifiers are used to change an object's form or shape in some way. For example, if you have a cylinder and apply a bend modifier to one end, you can end up with a candy cane. See Figure 5-8. Unlike transforms, modifiers can have different effects when applied in different orders. Modifiers are some of the most powerful tools of 3ds max. Some basic modifiers are introduced later in this chapter. Modifiers are covered in detail in Chapter 8.

At any given time (one frame), an object can have many modifiers. However, an object can only have one set of transforms. Transforms can change from frame to frame, but on a single frame, an object can have only one position, one rotation, and one scale.

Figure 5-8. This candy cane is created by applying a twist modifier and then a bend modifier to a simple cylinder.

Transforms

As discussed in the previous section, a transform alters an object's position, rotation, or scale in relation to the world. When performing a transform, it is often helpful to restrict the cursor movement to one or two axes. In addition, when transforming objects, it is important to understand the transform coordinate center. The following sections cover these topics.

Restricting Cursor Movement

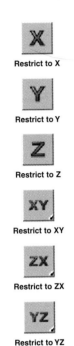

Restrict to X

Restrict to Y

Restrict to Z

Restrict to XY

Restrict to ZX

Restrict to YZ

The Cartesian coordinate system is used by 3ds max. This location system consists of the X, Y, and Z axes. Any point can be defined in 3D space using the three axes. When transforming objects, you will often need to restrict the cursor movement to one or two of these axes only. There are several ways to do this.

On the **Main** toolbar are the "restrict" buttons. See Figure 5-9. There is a button for each axis and a flyout. The flyout contains buttons that restrict the cursor movement to a plane (or two axes). Only one button can be active at a time.

You can also restrict cursor movement by using the transform gizmo. Whenever an object and a transform tool are selected, the transform gizmo is displayed. See Figure 5-10. This is a tripod that appears in the object's bounding box. By picking on one of the axes, the transform is restricted to that axis, regardless of the button selected. If you pick the transform gizmo "corner," the transform is restricted to that plane. The axes to which the transform will be restricted turn yellow to indicate the restriction.

When you pick an axis on the transform gizmo, the corresponding restrict button on the **Main** toolbar becomes active. In addition, after the transform, it remains active. Make sure you pay attention to this feature if you use the transform gizmo.

The transform gizmo is not enabled by default. To enable the transform gizmo, select **Preferences**... from the **Customize** pull-down menu. Then, pick the **Viewports** tab. At the bottom of the tab is the **Transform Gizmo** area. Check the **On** check box to enable the transform gizmo.

Transform Coordinate Center

Use Pivot Point Center

Use Selection Center

The buttons in the **Transform Center** flyout on the **Main** toolbar are used to determine the center point for rotation and scale transforms. When the **Use Pivot Point Center** button is selected, each object in the selection set is transformed about its own pivot point. See Figure 5-11. When the **Use Selection Center** button is selected, each object in the selection set is transformed about the center point of the selection. When

---

Figure 5-9. Transforms can be restricted to an axis or plane by picking the appropriate button on the **Main** toolbar.

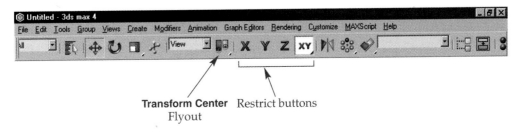

Transform Center   Restrict buttons
Flyout

the **Use Transform Coordinate Center** button is selected, the current coordinate system origin is used as the transform center. It is important to pay attention to which button is selected before performing a transform. If you do not, you may be "undoing" your work often.

Use Transform Coordinate Center

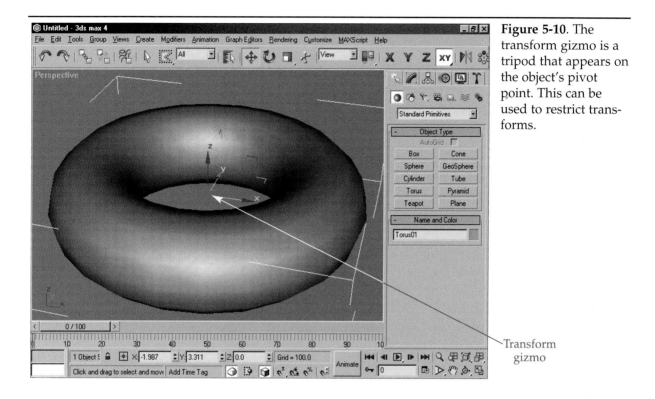

Figure 5-10. The transform gizmo is a tripod that appears on the object's pivot point. This can be used to restrict transforms.

Transform gizmo

Figure 5-11. Rotation and scale transforms can be centered at one of three locations. If the three orange objects are all selected, the red, green, and blue dots represent the three possible transform centers.

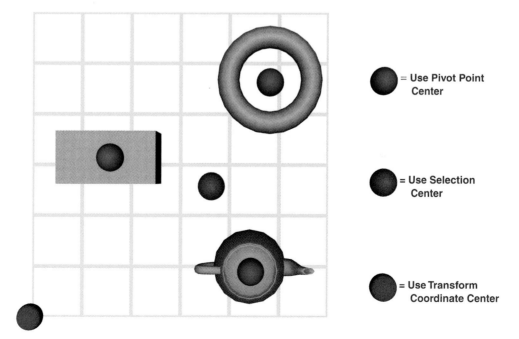

Moving Objects

Select and Move

The **Select and Move** button on the **Main** toolbar is used to move objects. With the object selected or unselected, pick this button in the toolbar. Then, pick on the object and move it to the new location. If the selection is locked by pressing the spacebar, you can pick anywhere in the active viewport. Use the appropriate viewport(s) to complete the operation. Restrict the cursor movement as necessary. See Figure 5-12. You can also use the **Transform Type-In**, which is discussed later in this chapter.

Rotating Objects

Select and Rotate

The **Select and Rotate** button on the **Main** toolbar is used to rotate objects. With the object selected or unselected, pick this button in the toolbar. Then, pick on the object and rotate it as needed. If the selection is locked by pressing the spacebar, you can pick anywhere in the viewport. Restrict the cursor movement as necessary. See Figure 5-13. The center point of rotation is determined by the transform coordinate center.

Figure 5-12. Moving an object. The rotation and scale of the object are unchanged.

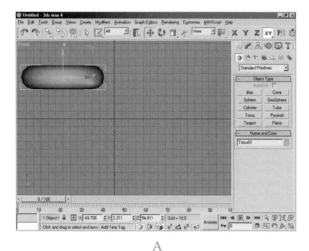
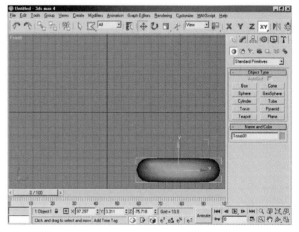

A

B

Figure 5-13. Rotating an object. The scale and position of the object are unchanged. The position of the object is defined by its pivot point.

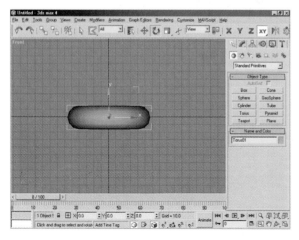
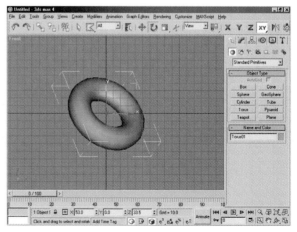

A

B

When necessary, angle snap can be used for precise rotation. You can also use the **Transform Type-In**, discussed later in this chapter.

Scaling Objects

There are three buttons located in the **Select and Scale** flyout on the **Main** toolbar. The **Select and Uniform Scale** button is used to scale an object by the same amount on all axes. The **Select and Non-Uniform Scale** button is used to scale the object on the current "restricted" axis only. The **Select and Squash** button is used to scale the object down on one axis while scaling up the other two axes proportionally. See Figure 5-14. You can also scale the object using the **Transform Type-In**, discussed in the next section.

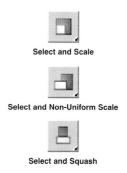

Select and Scale

Select and Non-Uniform Scale

Select and Squash

A little planning is required when using nonuniform scaling and squashing. Both these operations are applied *after* all modifiers applied to an object, even if the modifier is applied after the operation. If you pick the **Select and Non-Uniform Scale** or **Select and Squash** button, you receive a warning stating this. If modifiers will not be applied, you can use the command normally. If modifiers will be applied, you will need to collapse the modifier stack to an editable mesh after using the command and *before* applying modifiers. However, this removes the parameters of the original object. The modifier stack is discussed in detail later in this chapter.

Help Cel

An easy, and perhaps better, alternative to collapsing the stack before using squash or nonuniform scale is to apply an xform modifier. This modifier is discussed in Chapter 8.

Figure 5-14. The sphere on the left is squashed to create the object on the right.

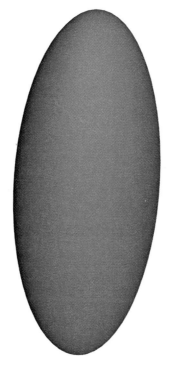

Transform Type-In

The **Transform Type-In** allows you to enter precise values for transforms using the keyboard. You can enter absolute coordinates or offsets. The **Transform Type-In** dialog boxes can be used for any operation displaying the axis tripod or a transform gizmo.

To open the **Transform Type-In**, first select an object and activate the button on the **Main** toolbar for the transform to perform. Then, right-click on any of the transform buttons in the **Main** toolbar, select **Transform Type-In**... from the **Tools** pull-down menu, or press the [F12] key. See Figure 5-15. The "type-in" dialog box displayed corresponds to the transform that is active. There is a "type-in" for each of the move, rotate, and scale transforms.

The offsets entered in the **Transform Type-In** dialog boxes are measured from the transform center, or pivot point, of the object. Offset values revert to 0 after an operation. Absolute values are always measured from the world coordinate system origin, except for scale transforms. Absolute values for a scale transformation are measured from the object's transform center.

Offset Mode Transform Type-In

The transform type-in feature is also available on the status bar at the bottom of the screen. You can select between absolute mode and offset mode by selecting the button next to the type-in boxes (spinners). With the correct mode selected, enter values in the **X:**, **Y:**, and **Z:** spinners. Remember, the transform is based on which "select and transform" button is selected on the **Main** toolbar.

Absolute Mode Transform Type-In

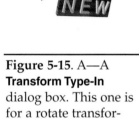

Figure 5-15. A—A **Transform Type-In** dialog box. This one is for a rotate transformation. B—The transform type-in feature is also available on the status bar.

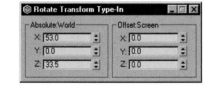

A

Pick to switch modes   Enter values

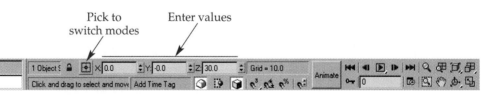

B

Exercise 5-4

1) Draw the objects shown below. Use your own dimensions.
2) Make the Top viewport active. Pick the **Select and Rotate** button and then the **Y** restrict button. Rotate the teapot 45 degrees.
3) Select the cone. Restrict the movement to the X axis. Rotate it 90 degrees.
4) Make the Front viewport active. Select the torus. Pick the **Select and Uniform Scale** button and restrict the transform to the Y axis. Also, pick the **Use Transform Coordinate Center** button. Scale the torus to 57%.
5) Pick the **Select and Rotate** button. In the Front viewport, select all three objects. Restrict the transform to the Z axis. Then, pick the **Use Pivot Point Center** button.
6) Rotate the objects 45 degrees. Notice how the objects rotate.
7) Reset 3ds max without saving.

Cloning (Copying) Objects

A *clone* is an identical replica of an object. The clone can be created as a copy, an instance, or a reference object. A *copy* and the original object are completely independent of each other. The original can be altered and modified without affecting the copy. On the other hand, the copy can be altered and modified without affecting the original.

An *instance* is also a clone of the original object. The original and the instance have separate transforms, but all modifiers and edits are shared. If the original is edited, the instance is automatically changed to reflect the edit. If a modifier is placed on the instance, it is also placed on the original.

A *reference object* is like an instance. The difference is that the relationship between an instance and the original object is a two-way street; however, the relationship between a reference object and the original object is a *one-way* street. Modifiers applied to and edits to the original object are transferred to the reference object. However, modifiers applied to the reference object are *not* transferred back to the original object. The parameters of the reference object cannot be changed.

You can quickly clone an object. With any of the three transform buttons on the **Main** toolbar active, press the [Shift] key before selecting an object. Then, transform the object as necessary. The transforms are applied to the clone rather than the original object. The original object remains in its original location. You can also clone an object by selecting **Clone** in the **Edit** pull-down menu. With this method, the clone is not transformed.

With either method, the **Clone Options** dialog box is displayed. See Figure 5-16. The dialog box is opened when the mouse button is released to complete the transform with the "shift" method. With the menu method, the dialog box is displayed when the pull-down menu item is selected. In this dialog box, you can name the clone and select whether it is a copy, instance, or reference object. Picking the **OK** button creates the clone.

Help Cel

When more than one object is selected and cloned, the **Clone Options** dialog box appears only once. You can enter a name for the first clone. All other clones are given the same name with a sequential number.

Introduction to Modifiers and "The Stack"

An object can have an unlimited number of modifiers applied to it. However, it is important to keep in mind that the order in which modifiers are applied to an object can have different effects. For example, if a five-sided gengon is tapered, then twisted, and finally bent, the object in Figure 5-17A is produced. However, if the same modifiers are applied in reverse order, the object shown in Figure 5-17B is produced. All modifiers applied to an object are stored in the modifier stack. The modifier stack is displayed in the **Modify** tab of the **Command Panel**.

There are two basic types of modifiers. *Object space modifiers (OSMs)* are applied to an object based on its local coordinate center. The object can be moved and rotated without affecting the modifier. *World space modifiers (WSMs)* are applied to an object in relation to the world space origin. The effect of the modifier is increased the closer an object is to the world space origin. The effect is decreased the farther an object is from the world space origin.

Figure 5-16. The **Clone Options** dialog box appears when cloning an object.

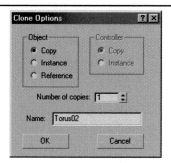

Figure 5-17. A—A five-sided gengon tapered, then twisted, and finally bent. B—The same five-sided gengon bent, then twisted, and finally tapered. Notice the huge difference in the shape of the objects.

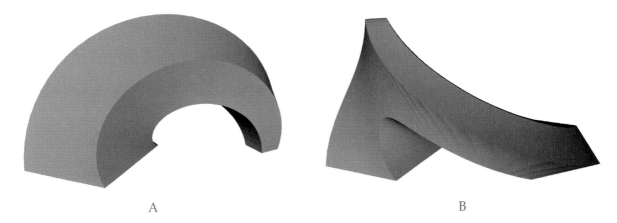

A   B

Help Cel

When modifiers will be applied to an object, it is important that the original object is created with enough segments in order to produce a desired effect. If you try to bend a cylinder with only one height segment, you will see why this is important.

The Modifier Stack

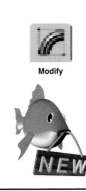

Modify

The *modifier stack* stores all modifiers applied to an object in the order they are applied. Modifiers can be removed from the stack. The order in which modifiers are applied can also be changed. Remember, applying modifiers in different orders produces different effects.

To edit the modifier stack for an object, first select the object. Then, pick **Modify** in the **Command Panel**. The modifier stack, or "stack," is displayed at the top of the tab, as shown in Figure 5-18. With 3ds max r4,

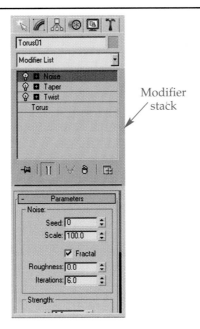

Modifier stack

Figure 5-18. The modifier stack is displayed at the top of the **Modify** tab in the **Command Panel**.

the modifier stack and the way in which modifiers are applied have changed significantly over previous releases of 3D Studio MAX.

The stack, or list, displays all modifiers applied to the object. Selecting a modifier name in the stack displays the rollouts for that modifier. The modifier's parameters can be changed in the rollouts. Selecting a different modifier in the stack displays its rollouts and allows you to change the parameters of that modifier.

Pin Stack

The **Pin Stack** button is used to lock the modifier stack to the selected object. In other words, you can "pin" an object and select other objects, and the **Modify** tab always displays the "pinned" object. The **Pin Stack** button is depressed and turns yellow when on. If other objects are selected with the "pinned" object and another modifier is applied to the selection set, the modifier is only applied to the "pinned" object. The stack remains locked until the **Pin Stack** button is selected again to turn it off. Selecting another **Command Panel** tab also "unpins" the object.

To the left of each modifier in the stack is the **Active/inactive** icon, which looks like a lightbulb. This icon turns the modifier on and off. This allows you to see the effect of deleting the modifier without actually deleting it. The icon is "inactive" when the lightbulb is dark and "active" when the lightbulb is light.

The **Show end result on/off toggle** is used to control the display of the modifiers in the stack. When this button is on (depressed), the object is displayed in the viewports as it appears with all modifiers in the stack applied. If this button is off, the effects of the modifiers up to and including the modifier selected in the stack are shown on the object.

Make Unique

The **Make unique** button is used to make an instanced (referenced) modifier unique to the object. Picking the **Remove modifier from the stack** button permanently deletes the modifier selected in the stack from the object. The **Configure Modifier Sets** button is used to display modifier set buttons in the **Modify** tab, and is discussed later in this chapter.

Help Cel

Right-clicking on an object or modifier name in the stack displays a shortcut menu. If the current object can be converted to a different type of object and no modifiers are applied, the shortcut menu lists the types of objects to convert to. You can also convert an object using the quad menu.

Managing the Modifier Stack

A sample modifier stack is shown in Figure 5-19. At the bottom of the stack is the original geometry. This always appears at the bottom. While modifiers can be moved around in the list, they cannot be placed below the original object. If any world space modifiers are applied to the object, they appear at the very top of the list above all object space modifiers. They can be reordered, but must remain above all OSMs. Modifiers are applied to the object in order, from the bottom of the stack to the top.

To rearrange the order of a modifier in the stack, first highlight the name of the modifier. Then, pick and hold on the name, and drag it to the new location in the stack. As you drag, a blue line appears between modifier names. If you release the mouse button, the modifier is moved to the location of the blue line. Also, the name of the modifier appears next to the cursor as you drag, similar to moving a file in Windows Explorer.

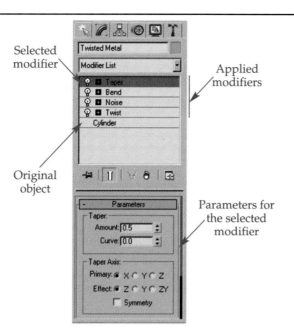

Selected modifier

Applied modifiers

Original object

Parameters for the selected modifier

Figure 5-19. A sample modifier stack. The base object is at the bottom of the list. All modifiers appear in the order in which they were applied, from bottom to top.

You can rename a modifier in the stack to be more meaningful to your application. For example, the name Neck, Bend, Forward is more descriptive than Bend. To rename a modifier in the stack, highlight the modifier. Then, right-click to display a shortcut menu. See Figure 5-20A. Select **Rename** from the top of the shortcut menu. A text box appears in place of the modifier name in the stack with the current name highlighted. See Figure 5-20B. Type a new name and press [Enter]. Keep in mind, you are renaming the modifier in the stack, not the modifier itself. If you apply the modifier again or to another object, it is applied using the original name. Also, you are not changing the effect of the modifier in any way.

To remove a modifier from the stack, first highlight the modifier name. The modifier can be removed in one of two ways. First, you can pick the **Remove modifier from the stack** button. Second, you can right-click on the modifier name and select **Delete** from the shortcut menu. Refer to Figure 5-20A. Once you remove a modifier from the stack, it is permanently deleted. To put the modifier back, you must reapply it and redefine its parameters.

Remove modifier from the stack

Copying and Pasting Modifiers

You can cut, copy, and paste modifiers, just as you might do with text in a word processor. To place a copy of a modifier at a different location in the stack, highlight the name of the modifier to copy. Then, right-click to display the shortcut menu. Pick **Copy** in the shortcut menu. Then, highlight the modifier in the stack where you want the modifier placed *above*. Finally, right-click and select **Paste** in the shortcut menu. If you want to place the copy as an instance, pick **Paste Instanced** in the shortcut menu. The instance and the original modifier names are italicized to indicate an instance.

If you want to move the modifier, pick **Cut** from the shortcut menu. Then, paste the modifier where you want it in the stack. Simply picking **Cut** in the shortcut menu without pasting the modifier back into the stack is another way to delete a modifier from the stack.

Figure 5-20.
A—Right-clicking on a modifier name in the stack displays this shortcut menu, which offers several options. B—You can rename modifiers in the stack to be more meaningful to your application.

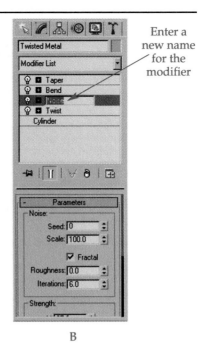

Enter a new name for the modifier

A   B

A modifier can be cut or copied from the stack on one object and pasted into the stack on another object. In this case, you might paste the modifier as an instance.

If a modifier in the stack is an instance, picking the **Make unique** button turns it into a copy. You can also right-click on the modifier name in the stack and select **Make Unique** from the shortcut menu. The modifier is no longer affected by changes in the original modifier from which it was instanced.

Make unique

Collapsing the Stack

When you collapse the stack, all the parameters and modifiers are applied to create a mesh object. The parameters and modifiers can no longer be changed. This can be thought of as taking a snapshot of the current state of the object and turning that into a mesh. Collapsing the stack simplifies the model and can save system resources. However, generally speaking, there is no turning back. Collapsing should be done when you are absolutely sure you no longer need to change parameters or modifier settings.

To collapse the entire stack, right-click anywhere on the stack to display the shortcut menu. Then, pick **Collapse All** from the menu. The entire stack is collapsed into a mesh. To collapse the stack from a certain modifier down to the bottom, select the modifier name in the stack and right-click to display the shortcut menu. Then, select **Collapse To** from the menu. The stack is collapsed from the bottom up to, and including, the highlighted modifier. When collapsing the stack, the warning dialog box shown in Figure 5-21 appears.

Help Cel

Collapsing the stack also removes animation keys for animated parameters and modifiers.

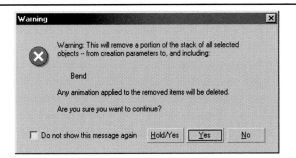

Figure 5-21. Before the stack is collapsed, you are warned and given a last chance to cancel the operation.

Sub-Object Mode

Most objects in 3ds max consist of other, "sub" objects. Even a straight line is made up of two vertices and one segment. Learning to work with objects at the sub-object level is important in mastering 3ds max.

Entering sub-object mode has changed significantly in 3ds max r4. To work at the sub-object level, first select an object or shape to be edited. Then, pick **Modify** in the **Command Panel**. In the modifier stack, select the item you want to edit at the sub-object level. This may be a modifier or the original object. Finally, pick the plus sign (+) next to the item name to display the sub-object tree. See Figure 5-22. When you pick a sub-object in the tree, its name is highlighted in yellow. The rollouts and parameters for that sub-object are displayed at the bottom of the **Modify** tab.

Sub-object mode for editable splines, meshes, and patch objects can be entered directly by picking the appropriate "level" button at the top of the **Selection** rollout in the **Modify** tab. Sub-object mode can also be entered directly by right-clicking on the object in a viewport to display the quad menu. Then, select **Sub-objects** in the upper-left quadrant. Finally, select the sub-object in the cascading menu.

If the selected object has modifiers applied, you can enter sub-object mode using the quad menu. The modifier that is currently selected in the stack is the one for which you can enter sub-object

Modify

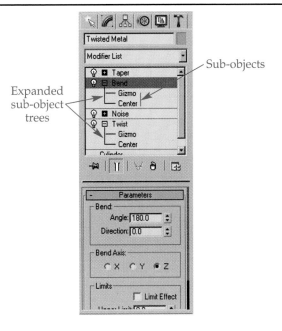

Expanded sub-object trees

Sub-objects

Figure 5-22. Pick the plus sign (+) next to an item in the stack to display the sub-object tree. Then, select a sub-object for editing.

mode. To enter sub-object mode for a different modifier, you must first select that modifier in the stack. Then, you can enter sub-object mode using the quad menu or by expanding the stack.

To exit sub-object mode, select a top-level item in the modifier stack. The name of the top-level item is highlighted in dark grey. If the sub-object tree is collapsed and the top-level name remains highlighted in yellow, you are still in sub-object mode. If you reselect a top-level item for which sub-object mode was previously active, the name is highlighted in yellow and the previous sub-object mode is made active, even if the sub-object tree remains collapsed.

Help Cel

You must exit sub-object mode before you can select other shapes and objects.

Gizmo

A *gizmo* is a wireframe object surrounding an object when a modifier is applied to that object. See Figure 5-23. As the parameters of the modifier are changed, the gizmo is modified and transfers the changes to the object. Each modifier that uses a gizmo has its own gizmo. A gizmo can be transformed (moved, rotated, and scaled) in the same way as other objects in 3ds max. Doing so alters the effects of the modifier on the object. Transforming a gizmo is done at the sub-object level.

By default, a gizmo is displayed orange. This can be changed in the **Colors** tab of the **Customize User Interface** dialog box. Open this dialog box by picking **Customize User Interface** from the **Customize** pull-down menu. Then, select **Gizmos** in the **Elements:** drop-down list. Finally, select **Gizmos** in list below the **Elements:** drop-down list, and change the color using the color swatch to the right.

Some modifiers also have a center point. The modifier is applied in relation to this center. The center can be moved at the sub-object level. Moving the center point alters the effects of the modifier on the object.

Figure 5-23. The gizmo appears as an orange wireframe box surrounding the object.

Help Cel

Not all modifiers use a gizmo.

Applying Modifiers

Modifiers are grouped in 3ds max by the type of function they perform. There are 12 different groups. These groups are:

- Selection modifiers
- Patch/spline editing
- Mesh editing
- Animation modifiers
- UV coordinates
- Cache tools
- Subdivision surfaces
- Free form deformers
- Parametric deformers
- Surface
- NURBS editing
- Conversion modifiers (available only in the **Modify** tab)

Each group may contain WSMs and OSMs. WSMs are indicated by an asterisk before the modifier name.

There are two basic ways to apply a modifier. First, you can use the **Modifiers** pull-down menu. Second, you can pick the **Modifier List** drop-down list in the **Modify** tab of the **Command Panel**. See Figure 5-24. Both the pull-down menu and the drop-down list are organized by "group." Locate the group containing the modifier you wish to apply. Next, locate the modifier and select it. The modifier then appears in the modifier stack. Finally, select the modifier in the stack and adjust its parameters as needed.

The following sections cover selected modifiers. These modifiers are frequently used and will allow you to create more advanced models. Other modifiers are discussed in Chapter 8, *Modeling with Modifiers.*

A

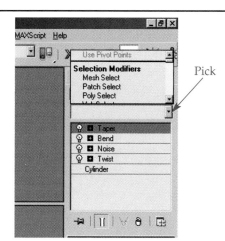

B

Figure 5-24. A—Using the **Modifiers** pull-down menu to apply a modifier. B—Using the **Modifier List** drop-down list to apply a modifier.

Help Cel

The **Modifier List** drop-down list in the **Modify** tab is "selection sensitive." Only the modifiers that can be applied to the current selection are displayed in the drop-down list. In the **Modifiers** pull-down menu, any modifiers invalid for the current selection are greyed out.

Displaying Buttons

As just explained, you can apply a modifier using the **Modifiers** pull-down menu or the **Modifier List** drop-down list. While many users will find these two methods useful, others may find them cumbersome. This may be especially true for those who have used previous releases of 3D Studio MAX. If you like, you can display buttons that can be used to apply modifiers. Accessing modifiers in this manner is similar to how certain modifiers are applied in previous releases of 3D Studio MAX.

Configure Modifier Sets

To display modifier buttons, select **Modify** in the **Command Panel**. At the bottom of the modifier stack, pick the **Configure Modifier Sets** button. A shortcut menu is displayed. See Figure 5-25A. Select **Show Buttons** from the menu. The modifier set (group) indicated by a chevron (>) in the menu is displayed with buttons above the modifier stack. See Figure 5-25B. Pick the **Configure Modifier Sets** button again and select a different set from the shortcut menu to display the buttons in that set.

If you pick **Configure Modifier Sets** in the shortcut menu, the **Configure Modifier Sets** dialog box is opened. This dialog box allows you to alter existing modifier sets or create new ones of your own. This feature is not covered in this text. However, it is very similar to standard "customizing" functions in other software, such as Microsoft Word or AutoCAD.

Figure 5-25.
A—Picking the **Configure Modifier Sets** button displays this shortcut menu.
B—Buttons are displayed for the **Selection Modifiers** modifier set.

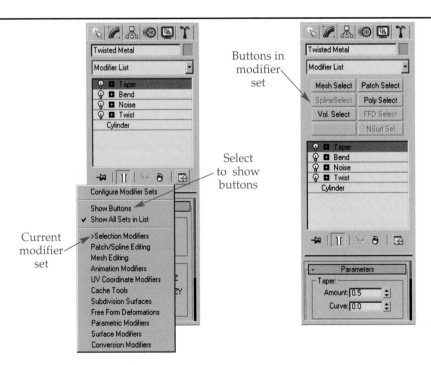

A

B

Help Cel

If you are displaying modifier set buttons, you will probably need to have a high resolution monitor setting, such as 1280 × 1024. You may also want to make the **Command Panel** two columns wide. Otherwise, the **Modify** tab will be mostly taken up by the modifier stack and modifier buttons.

Introduction to Parametric Deformer Modifiers

Parametric deformer modifiers are used to change the shape of an object based on parameters you enter. For example, you can bend an object a specified number of degrees. The bend, taper, twist, and noise parametric deformer modifiers are covered in the following sections. Also, refer to Chapter 8, *Modeling with Modifiers*, for further discussions on modifiers.

Bend Modifier

The *bend modifier* allows you to put a bend into an object. See Figure 5-26. The bend is applied to the X, Y, or Z axis. By applying the modifier twice, you can produce a bend on two axes. You can apply the bend over the entire object, or you can specify a portion of the object to bend.

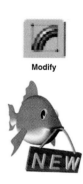
Modify

To apply a bend modifier, select the object to bend. Then, open the **Modifier List** drop-down list in the **Modify** tab of the **Command Panel**. Finally, select **Bend** in the **Parametric Modifiers** area of the list. You can also select **Parametric Deformers** in the **Modifiers** pull-down menu, and then **Bend** in the cascading menu. The bend modifier appears in the modifier stack and the **Parameters** rollout is displayed at the bottom of the **Modify** tab. Also, the gizmo is displayed on the object.

In the **Bend:** area of the **Parameters** rollout, specify the amount of the bend in the **Angle:** spinner. This value is measured in degrees from the horizontal plane defined by the local axes and based on the bend axis. In the **Direction:** spinner, enter a value to "rotate" the bend in the horizontal plane.

In the **Bend Axis:** area of the **Parameters** rollout, pick the **X**, **Y**, or **Z** radio button. This specifies which of the object's local axes the bend is applied around. It is important to remember that these are the local axes, not the world axes.

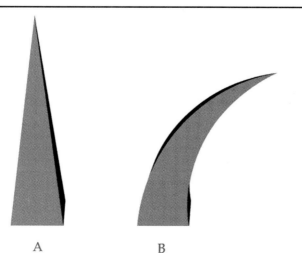

A　　　　B

Figure 5-26. On the left is a pyramid. On the right, a bend modifier is applied to the pyramid.

Finally, you can limit the bend to a portion of the object. In the **Limits** area of the **Parameters** rollout, check the **Limit Effect** check box. Then, enter values in the **Upper Limit:** and **Lower Limit:** spinners. These values set the distance from the modifier center point beyond which the modifier no longer affects the object.

The bend modifier has two sub-objects. These are gizmo and center. Enter sub-object mode and adjust the sub-objects as needed.

Exercise

Exercise 5-5

1) Draw a cylinder in any viewport. Use your own dimensions, but make it tall and thin.
2) In the **Parameters** rollout, enter 15.0 in the **Height Segments:** spinner. Use more segments if your cylinder is very tall.
3) With the cylinder selected, apply a bend modifier.
4) In the **Parameters** rollout for the bend modifier, enter 45.0 in the **Angle:** spinner.
5) Enter 45.0 in the **Direction:** spinner.
6) Reset 3ds max without saving.

Taper Modifier

Modify

The *taper modifier* scales the ends of an object on either side of the gizmo center. One end is scaled up and the opposite end is equally scaled down. For some objects, the gizmo center is by default on one end of the object. Therefore, it can appear as though only one end is being scaled. See Figure 5-27.

To apply a taper modifier, select the object to taper. Then, open the **Modifier List** drop-down list in the **Modify** tab of the **Command Panel**. Finally, select **Taper** in the **Parametric Modifiers** area of the list. You can also select **Parametric Deformers** in the **Modifiers** pull-down menu, and then **Taper** in the cascading menu. The taper modifier appears in the

Figure 5-27. On the left is a cylinder. In the middle, the cylinder is tapered with the gizmo center located on the top end. On the right, the cylinder is tapered with the center located on the bottom end.

modifier stack and the **Parameters** rollout is displayed at the bottom of the **Modify** tab. Also, the gizmo is displayed on the object.

In the **Taper:** area of the **Parameters** rollout, specify the amount and shape of the taper. The value in the **Amount:** spinner is the amount of taper. The value in the **Curve:** spinner applies a curve to the gizmo sides to produce a different shape of taper. Both values can range from –10.0 to 10.0, where 0.0 is no taper or no curve.

The **Taper Axis:** area is used to determine how the taper is applied on one of the object's local axes. The **Primary:** radio buttons set the central axis. The **Effect:** radio buttons determine the direction of the taper from the primary axis. These radio buttons change, depending on which primary axis is selected. When the **Symmetry** check box is checked, the resulting taper is symmetrical about the primary axis.

In the **Limits** area of the **Parameters** rollout, you can limit the taper to a portion of the object. Check the **Limit Effect** check box. Then, enter values in the **Upper Limit:** and **Lower Limit:** spinners. These values set the distance from the modifier center point beyond which the modifier no longer affects the object.

The taper modifier has two sub-objects. These are gizmo and center. Enter sub-object mode and adjust the sub-objects as needed.

Exercise 5-6

1) Draw a tube in the Front or Left viewport. Use your own dimensions, but make the height about three times the diameter.
2) With the tube selected, apply a taper modifier.
3) In the **Taper:** area of the **Parameters** rollout for the taper modifier, enter 1.0 in the **Amount:** spinner. Pick the **Zoom Extents All** button if necessary to see the entire object.
4) Enter –2.0 in the **Curve:** spinner.
5) In the **Taper Axis:** area of the **Parameters** rollout, pick the **X** radio button as the primary axis. Observe the result.
6) Pick the **Y** radio button as the primary axis. Observe the result.
7) Pick the **Z** radio button as the primary axis. Observe the result.
8) With the **Z** radio button as the primary axis, pick the **X Effect:** radio button. Observe the result.
9) Pick the **Y Effect:** radio button. Observe the result.
10) Pick the **XY Effect:** radio button. Observe the result.
11) Reset 3ds max without saving.

Figure 5-28. The torus on the left has a twist modifier applied to create the object shown on the right.

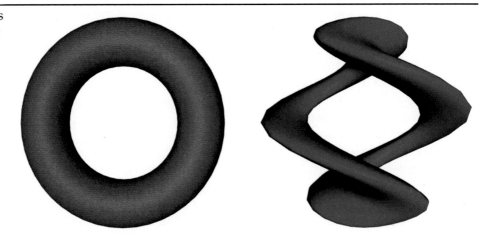

Modify

Twist Modifier

A *twist modifier* does just that, it twists an object's geometry around one of the local axes. See Figure 5-28. The gizmo center aligns with the object's pivot point. The gizmo center can be moved using sub-object mode.

To apply a twist modifier, select the object to twist. Then, open the **Modifier List** drop-down list in the **Modify** tab of the **Command Panel**. Finally, select **Twist** in the **Parametric Modifiers** area of the list. You can also select **Parametric Deformers** in the **Modifiers** pull-down menu, and then **Twist** in the cascading menu. The twist modifier appears in the modifier stack and the **Parameters** rollout is displayed at the bottom of the **Modify** tab. Also, the gizmo is displayed on the object.

In the **Twist:** area of the **Parameters** rollout, enter the amount of twist in the **Angle:** spinner. This value is the number of degrees the object is twisted around the selected local axis. In the **Bias:** spinner, you can enter a value to shift the twist to one end of the object. The effect of this setting is similar to that of the **Bias:** setting for a helix shape. The value can be from −100 to 100. A value of 0 evenly spreads the twist along the length of the object.

In the **Twist Axis:** area of the **Parameters** rollout, select a local axis around which to twist the object. The three radio buttons allow you to select the X, Y, or Z local axis.

In the **Limits** area of the **Parameters** rollout, you can limit the twist to a portion of the object. Check the **Limit Effect** check box. Then, enter values in the **Upper Limit:** and **Lower Limit:** spinners. These values set the distance from the modifier center point beyond which the modifier no longer affects the object.

The twist modifier has two sub-objects. These are gizmo and center. Enter sub-object mode and adjust the sub-objects as needed.

Exercise 5-7

1) Draw a five-sided gengon in the Top viewport. Use your own dimensions, but make the height about four times the diameter.
2) With the gengon selected, apply a twist modifier using the pull-down menu.
3) In the **Twist:** area of the **Parameters** rollout, enter 30.0 in the **Angle:** spinner.
4) In the **Twist Axis:** area of the **Parameters** rollout, pick the **X** radio button. Observe the result.
5) Pick the **Y** radio button in the **Twist Axis:** area. Observe the result.
6) Pick the **Z** radio button in the **Twist Axis:** area. Observe the result.
7) Reset 3ds max without saving.

Noise Modifier

The *noise modifier* produces irregularities in the surface of an object. All objects in the real world have slight variations in their surfaces. The noise modifier can be used to simulate this. Noise can also be used to simulate water or ground terrain. See Figure 5-29. Noise is often animated. For example, when used to simulate water, animated noise represents ripples or waves on the surface of the water.

To apply a noise modifier, select the object to which you want noise added. Then, open the **Modifier List** drop-down list in the **Modify** tab of the **Command Panel**. Finally, select **Noise** in the **Parametric Modifiers** area of the list. You can also select **Parametric Deformers** in the **Modifiers** pull-down menu, and then **Noise** in the cascading menu. The noise modifier appears in the modifier stack and the **Parameters** rollout is displayed at the bottom of the **Modify** tab. Also, the gizmo is displayed on the object.

Modify

The **Noise:** area of the **Parameters** rollout is used to specify the "shape" of the noise. The value in the **Seed:** spinner is a starting point from which noise is randomly generated. This value can be anything from 0 to 100,000,000. The value in the **Scale:** spinner defines how smooth or jagged the noise effect is. Higher values produce a very smooth noise effect. Lower values produce a jagged noise effect. The default value is 100. Setting this value to 1 or 0 produces a very "spiky" effect on the object.

Also in the **Noise:** area of the **Parameters** rollout is the **Fractal** check box. When checked, this produces a fractal-based noise effect. A *fractal* is a random, nonrepeating mathematical equation. The **Roughness:** and **Iterations:** spinners are also enabled when the **Fractal** check box is checked. These spinners are used to control the fractal. A low value in the **Roughness:** spinner produces a smooth fractal. Higher values produce a fractal that is more rough. The value in the **Iterations:** spinner can be thought of as how many "times" the fractal is "applied." A low value produces a smoother surface than a high value. The value can be from 1 to 10. Entering a value of 1 is the same as unchecking the **Fractal** check box.

The settings in the **Strength:** area of the **Parameters** rollout are used to set the strength of the noise. When the modifier is first applied, the values in the **X:**, **Y:**, and **Z:** spinners are 0. This means the noise has no strength or,

Figure 5-29. A—This flat quad patch can be quickly turned into sand dunes. B—After a noise modifier is applied, the quad patch becomes sand dunes.

A

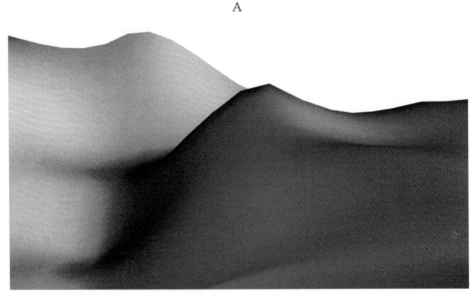

B

in effect, is not applied. To add strength, enter a value in the appropriate spinner. If you are creating water, for example, using a patch grid, you will only want to apply strength on one axis (the Z axis). In this way, the overall size of the object is not changed, rather only the "elevation."

The **Animation:** area of the **Parameters** rollout is used to define a sinusoidal wave form the noise modifier will use over the length of an animation. In effect, this sets up a boundary to help limit extreme variants of noise. To animate noise, first check the **Animate Noise** check box. The value in the **Frequency:** spinner determines how quickly the noise "vibrates." A low value produces a gentle flow. A high value produces a very "jiggly" noise effect. The value in the **Phase:** spinner shifts the sinusoidal wave form along the time segment. Animation is covered in more detail later in this text.

The noise modifier has two sub-objects. These are gizmo and center. Enter sub-object mode and adjust the sub-objects as needed.

Help Cel

The **Noise:** and **Strength:** settings can be animated without the **Animate Noise** check box checked.

Exercise 5-8

1) In the Top viewport, draw a quad patch. Using generic units, make it 200 units square and set the length and width segments to 10.
2) Make the Perspective viewport active and maximize it by pressing the [W] key on the keyboard.
3) With the patch grid selected, apply a noise modifier using the **Modify** tab.
4) In the **Strength:** area of the **Parameters** rollout, enter 10.0 in the **Z:** spinner.
5) In the **Noise:** area of the **Parameters** rollout, enter 10.0 in the **Scale:** spinner. Notice the result.
6) Enter 100.0 in the **Scale:** spinner.
7) Check the **Fractal** check box. Notice the change in the object.
8) In the **Strength:** area, change the **Z:** spinner value to 50.0 and observe the change in the object.
9) Reset 3ds max without saving.

Introduction to Mesh Editing Modifiers

Mesh editing modifiers are used to alter the mesh of a mesh object. The shape of the object may or may not be changed. For example, you can increase the subdivisions on a mesh by using a tessellate modifier. On the other hand, you can create a mesh object from a spline by applying an extrude modifier. The extrude and face extrude mesh editing modifiers are covered in the next sections. Also, refer to Chapter 8, *Modeling with Modifiers,* for further discussions on modifiers.

Extrude Modifier

The *extrude modifier* is used to make a 2D spline a three-dimensional object. It gives a height or thickness to the spline. See Figure 5-30. The spline you extrude can be closed or open.

Figure 5-30. The text spline object on the top is extruded to create the object shown on the bottom.

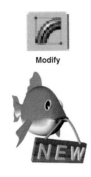

Modify

To apply an extrude modifier, select the spline you want to extrude. Then, open the **Modifier List** drop-down list in the **Modify** tab of the **Command Panel**. Finally, select **Extrude** in the **Mesh Editing** area of the list. You can also select **Mesh Editing** in the **Modifiers** pull-down menu, and then **Extrude** in the cascading menu. The extrude modifier appears in the modifier stack and the **Parameters** rollout is displayed at the bottom of the **Modify** tab. This modifier does not have a gizmo. Also, there are no sub-objects for this modifier.

At the top of the **Parameters** rollout is the **Amount:** spinner. The value in this spinner is the number of units of height given to the spline. The value in the **Segments:** spinner is the number of height segments assigned to the 3D mesh object.

In the **Capping** area of the **Parameters** rollout, you can set the properties for the ends of the extruded object. The **Cap Start** and **Cap End** check boxes determine if caps are placed on the ends. When checked, a cap is placed on the end indicated by the check box. The **Morph** and **Grid** radio buttons are used to determine how the segments on the end caps are calculated. Picking the **Morph** radio button calculates evenly distributed faces. This is important for morphing operations. Picking the **Grid** radio button arranges the faces in a square grid and simply trims the faces at the edge. This option should be used in most cases.

In the **Output** area of the **Parameters** rollout, you can select what type of object is generated by the extrude modifier. You can select a patch, mesh, or NURBS object. In most cases, you will be generating a mesh object.

Checking the **Generate Mapping Coordinates** check box at the bottom of the **Parameters** rollout automatically calculates mapping coordinates for the extruded object. Checking the **Generate Material IDs** check box assigns material ID 3 to the sides and ID 1 and ID 2 to the ends. Material IDs are covered later in this text. The **Use Shape IDs** check box is only available when the **Generate Material IDs** check box is checked. When it is checked, the material IDs assigned to the spline are carried over to the extruded object.

The **Smooth** check box is at the very bottom of the **Parameters** rollout. When this check box is checked, smoothing groups are applied to the extruded object. When unchecked, the extruded object appears faceted.

Face Extrude Modifier

The *face extrude modifier* is used to extrude a selected face along its normals. A *normal* is a vector, or invisible line, coming straight out of a face in one direction only. When using a face extrude modifier, a mesh select modifier can be used to select the face(s) at the sub-object level. The mesh select modifier is discussed in Chapter 8, *Modeling with Modifiers*. As the face is extruded, new faces are created along the sides of the extrusion from the extruded face to the original object. The extrusion can be negative or positive. In addition, the extrusion can be tapered inward or outward. By applying the face extrude modifier again, you can create another "step" of extrusion. See Figure 5-31. The parameters of a face extrude modifier can be animated.

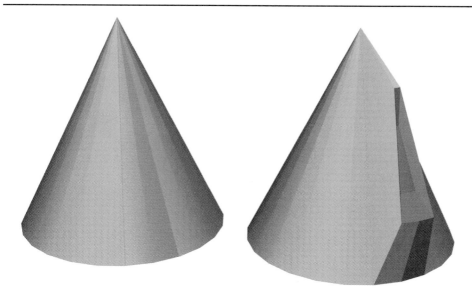

Figure 5-31. The face extrude modifier is used to extrude selected faces. The purple faces on the left-hand sphere are extruded out with a taper, then extruded in with a taper.

To apply a face extrude modifier, make a selection at the face sub-object level. The mesh select modifier, discussed in Chapter 8, can be used for this on objects which are not editable meshes. Then, open the **Modifier List** drop-down list in the **Modify** tab of the **Command Panel**. Finally, select **Face Extrude** in the **Mesh Editing** area of the list. You can also select **Mesh Editing** in the **Modifiers** pull-down menu, and then **Face Extrude** in the cascading menu. The face extrude modifier appears in the modifier stack and the **Parameters** rollout is displayed at the bottom of the **Modify** tab. This modifier does not have a gizmo. It does, however, have an extrude center sub-object.

In the **Parameters** rollout are the **Amount:** and **Scale:** spinners. The value in the **Amount:** spinner is the distance in current drawing units that the face is extruded. The value in the **Scale:** spinner is the percentage of the original face size used for the extruded face. A scale of 100% means the extruded face is the same size as the original face. A scale of 50% means the extruded face is half the original size.

When the **Extrude From Center** check box is checked, each vertex is extruded in a radial manner from the modifier center. As the center is moved at the sub-object level, the effect of the modifier is changed. When this check box is unchecked, the faces are extruded from the center of the object.

Help Cel

Extruding a face on an editable mesh at the sub-object level is very similar to using the face extrude modifier.

Exercise

Exercise 5-9

1) Pick **Create** in the **Command Panel**. Pick the **Shapes** button and then **Splines** in the drop-down list. Then, pick the **Line** button in the **Object Type** rollout. Draw an irregular, closed spline. Use both straight and curved segments.
2) With the spline selected, apply an extrude modifier.
3) In the **Parameters** rollout, enter a value in the **Amount:** spinner.
4) Uncheck the **Cap Start** and **Cap End** check boxes. What happened?
5) Check the **Cap Start** check box. Observe the result.
6) Check the **Cap End** check box. Observe the result.
7) Reset 3ds max without saving.

Introduction to Patch/Spline Editing Modifiers

Patch/spline editing modifiers are used to alter the mesh of a patch object or spline. The shape of the object may or may not be changed. For example, you can normalize the steps on a spline by using a normalize spline modifier. On the other hand, you can create a mesh from a spline by applying a lathe modifier to rotate the spline about an axis. The lathe and edit spline patch/spline editing modifiers are covered in the next sections. Also, refer to Chapter 8, *Modeling with Modifiers,* for further discussions on modifiers.

Lathe Modifier

The *lathe modifier* is used to revolve a spline around an axis to create a 3D object. If the spline is open, a one-sided surface is created. If the spline is closed, a two-sided ("solid") object is created. See Figure 5-32.

Figure 5-32. The red profile has a lathe modifier applied to create the red bottle. Notice it is a one-sided surface, as indicated by the white showing through. When the profile is closed by adding the yellow spline, the yellow bottle is created when the lathe modifier is applied. This is a "solid" object.

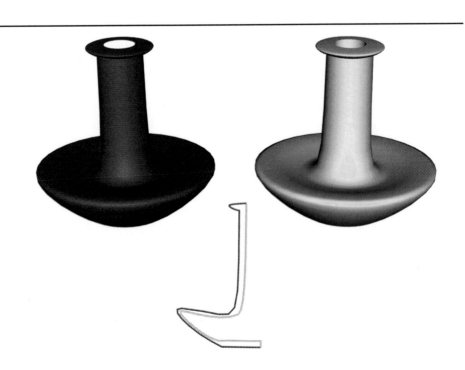

To apply a lathe modifier, select the spline you want to rotate about an axis. Then, open the **Modifier List** drop-down list in the **Modify** tab of the **Command Panel**. Finally, select **Lathe** in the **Patch/Spline Editing** area of the list. You can also select **Patch/Spline Editing** in the **Modifiers** pull-down menu, and then **Lathe** in the cascading menu. The lathe modifier appears in the modifier stack and the **Parameters** rollout is displayed at the bottom of the **Modify** tab. This modifier does not have a gizmo. It does, however, have an axis sub-object.

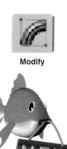

Modify

At the top of the **Parameters** rollout, enter the amount of rotation in the **Degrees:** spinner. A value of 360° rotates the object completely around the axis set in the **Direction** area. The value in the **Segments:** spinner determines how many segments are placed around the axis of revolution when the object is created.

The buttons in the **Direction** area of the **Parameters** rollout determine which local axis of the object is used as the axis of rotation. The spline can only be revolved around one axis.

Checking the **Weld Core** check box simplifies the object by welding overlapping vertices that lie on the axis of revolution. This option should not be used if the object will be morphed.

Checking the **Flip Normals** check box reverses the normals on an object. This determines which side of a face is the "top." Depending on how the spline was drawn and the direction of rotation the lathe modifier uses, the resulting object may appear to be "inside out." Checking the **Flip Normals** check box corrects this problem.

The options in the **Capping** area of the **Parameters** rollout are the same as those for the extrude modifier discussed previously. Checking the **Cap Start** and **Cap End** check boxes places caps on the ends. These are only used when the spline is rotated less than 360 degrees.

The buttons in the **Align** area of the **Parameters** rollout determine how the spline is aligned with the axis of revolution. Picking the **Min** button aligns the axis of revolution with the minimum extents of the spline, as viewed in the viewport. Picking the **Center** button aligns the axis with the center of the extents. Picking the **Max** button aligns the axis with the maximum extents of the object. See Figure 5-33. The minimum and maximum extents are opposite each other. If the object does not appear correctly after picking one of these buttons, pick one of the other buttons.

In the **Output** area of the **Parameters** rollout, you can select what type of object is generated by the lathe modifier. You can select a patch, mesh, or NURBS object. In most cases, you will be generating a mesh object.

Checking the **Generate Mapping Coords.** check box at the bottom of the **Parameters** rollout automatically calculates mapping coordinates for the revolved object. If the spline is revolved less than 360° and "capped," coordinates are generated for the caps as well.

Checking the **Generate Material IDs** check box assigns material ID 3 to the sides and ID 1 and ID 2 to the ends. Material IDs are covered later in this text. The **Use Shape IDs** check box is only available when the **Generate Material IDs** check box is checked. When it is checked, the material IDs assigned to the spline are carried over to the revolved object.

The **Smooth** check box is at the very bottom of the **Parameters** rollout. When this check box is checked, smoothing groups are applied to the revolved object. When unchecked, the revolved object appears faceted.

Figure 5-33. The profile has a lathe modifier applied. On the left, the **Min** align button is selected. In the middle, the **Center** align button is selected. On the right, the **Max** align button is selected.

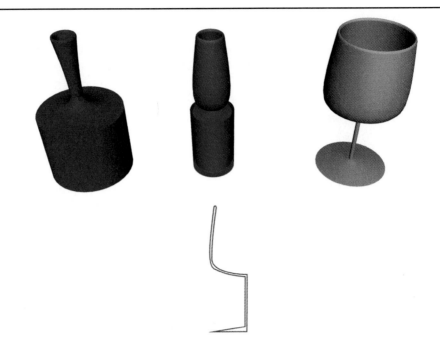

Exercise

Exercise 5-10

1) In the Front or Left viewport, draw an L-shaped line with two segments.
2) With the line selected, apply a lathe modifier using the pull-down menu.
3) In the **Parameters** rollout, enter 270.0 in the **Degrees:** spinner. If the object appears inside out, check the **Flip Normals** check box.
4) In the **Direction** area of the **Parameters** rollout, pick the **Y** button.
5) In the **Align** area, pick the **Min** button. Observe the result.
6) Pick the **Center** button. Observe the result.
7) Pick the **Max** button. Observe the result.
8) Reset 3ds max without saving.

Editing Splines and Applying the Edit Spline Modifier

Splines are often edited to create more complex shapes. See Figure 5-34. A spline is edited in sub-object mode. In order to do this, you must either convert the spline to an editable spline or apply an edit spline modifier. The *edit spline modifier* allows you to edit a spline, such as a rectangle, without converting it to an editable spline. By not converting the spline, you retain access to the spline's original parameters. The line spline object is automatically converted to an editable spline when it is created.

To convert a spline into an editable spline, select the object. Then, pick **Modify** in the **Command Panel**. Right-click on the modifier stack to display the shortcut menu. Then, pick **Editable Spline** in the **Convert To:** area of the menu. You can also right-click on the object in a viewport and select **Convert To:** in the lower-right quadrant of the quad menu. Then, in the cascading menu, select **Convert to Editable Spline**. The spline is

Modify

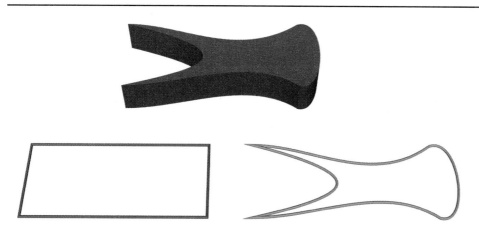

Figure 5-34. The rectangle on the left is edited to create the shape on the right. The shape is then extruded to create the object shown on the top.

converted to an editable spline and is no longer a parametric shape. There are three sub-objects. These are vertex, segment, and spline.

To apply an edit spline modifier, select the spline. Then, open the **Modifier List** drop-down list in the **Modify** tab of the **Command Panel**. Finally, select **Edit Spline** in the **Patch/Spline Editing** area of the list. You can also select **Patch/Spline Editing** in the **Modifiers** pull-down menu, and then **Edit Spline** in the cascading menu. The edit spline modifier appears in the modifier stack and the **Parameters** rollout is displayed at the bottom of the **Modify** tab. This modifier does not have a gizmo. The modifier has the same three sub-objects as an editable spline. These sub-objects are discussed in the following sections.

Help Cel

Applying an edit spline modifier allows you to edit a noneditable spline, such as a rectangle, while maintaining the ability to change its parameters. In many cases, this can be a great timesaving technique.

Vertex

A *vertex* is a point on a spline. See Figure 5-35. To edit a vertex, expand the sub-object tree in the modifier stack. Then, select **Vertex** in the tree. You can also enter vertex sub-object mode directly by picking the **Vertex** button at the top of the **Selection** rollout. Finally, you can enter sub-object mode using the quad menu. Right-clicking on the object in a viewport displays the quad menu. In the upper-left quadrant, you can select **Sub-objects**. Then, select **Vertex** in the cascading menu.

Vertex

You can move a vertex using the **Select and Move** tool. You can also change the type of vertex. Right-click on the vertex to display the quad menu. In the upper-left quadrant of the quad menu, change the type of the vertex. A vertex can be a smooth, Bézier, corner, or Bézier corner vertex.

Select and Move

A *smooth vertex* curves the segments leading into and out of the vertex. See Figure 5-35. The amount of curvature is determined by the distance between vertices. In this way, 3ds max attempts to produce the smoothest curve possible. This type of curve is not adjustable.

A *Bézier vertex* has adjustable handles called Bézier handles. See Figure 5-35. The shape of the curve is determined by the position and

Figure 5-35. There are various sub-objects in an editable spline.

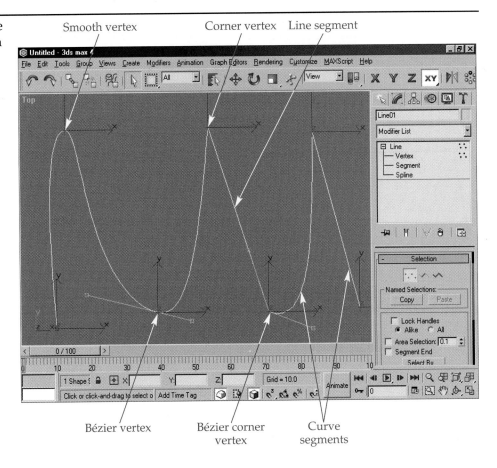

Smooth vertex   Corner vertex   Line segment

Bézier vertex   Bézier corner vertex   Curve segments

length of the handles. The handles are locked together, so the curve is smooth leading into and out of the vertex.

A *corner vertex* is not adjustable. Sharp corners are produced with this type of vertex. See Figure 5-35.

Like a Bézier vertex, a ***Bézier corner vertex*** has Bézier handles. Each handle can be adjusted independently to change the shape of the curve. See Figure 5-35.

Segment

A *segment* is the line between two vertices. A segment can be either a line or a curve. Even when it is a curve, a segment can be straight. However, if set to a line, it cannot be curved. See Figure 5-35. To edit a spline segment, expand the sub-object tree in the modifier stack. Then, select **Segment** in the tree. You can also enter segment sub-object mode directly by picking the **Segment** button at the top of the **Selection** rollout. Finally, you can enter sub-object mode using the quad menu. Right-clicking on the object in a viewport displays the quad menu. In the upper-left quadrant, you can select **Sub-objects**. Then, select **Segment** in the cascading menu.

You can move, rotate, or scale a segment using transform tools. You can also right-click on the segment to display the quad menu. In the upper-left quadrant of the quad menu, you can change the type of the segment to a line or curve.

Segment

Spline

A *spline sub-object* consists of all vertices and segments of the base shape. The spline can be transformed. However, transformations are done at the sub-object level with respect to the transform gizmo. If the base shape is transformed, the transformation gizmo is transformed as well. This is a subtle difference, but one that may be used effectively.

To edit a spline at the spline sub-object level, expand the sub-object tree in the modifier stack. Then, select **Spline** in the tree. You can also enter spline sub-object mode directly by picking the **Spline** button at the top of the **Selection** rollout. Finally, you can enter sub-object mode using the quad menu. Right-clicking on the object in a viewport displays the quad menu. In the upper-left quadrant, you can select **Sub-objects**. Then, select **Spline** in the cascading menu.

Spline

Rollouts

When editing splines, different rollouts appear in the **Modify** tab, depending on whether you convert the spline to an editable spline or apply an edit spline modifier. The **Rendering** and **Interpolation** rollouts found with editable splines are not available with the edit spline modifier. This is because the base object remains parametric. The options found in these rollouts can be accessed by picking the base object in the modifier stack and modifying the parameters.

The **Selection** rollout contains the options for selecting sub-objects. You can enter sub-object mode directly by picking the buttons at the top of the rollout. The spline can then be edited in sub-object mode, as discussed in the previous sections.

The **Geometry** rollout for the edit spline modifier and an editable spline provides additional ways to edit the spline. This rollout is discussed in the next section.

Geometry Rollout

When first opened, most of the options in the **Geometry** rollout are greyed out. As you select different sub-object levels, the options applying to the level are enabled. There are many options available in this rollout. Some of the more commonly used options are discussed here.

At the top of the rollout is the **Create Line** button. Picking this button allows you to add spline segments to the selected spline. The new segments do not have to be connected to the existing spline. If the existing spline is open, the line you create can be attached to the open vertices. When the cursor is over a vertex the line can connect to, the pointer changes to indicate this. The **PolyConnect** check box next to the **Create Line** button must be checked to connect vertices. If unchecked, you can place vertices directly on top of each other without connecting them. Right-click or pick the **Create Line** button again to exit this mode.

Create Line

The **Attach** button allows you to make another spline in the scene part of the selected spline. Select the button and then pick the spline you want to add. The cursor changes when over a valid spline object. Right-click or pick the **Attach** button again to exit this mode.

Attach

The **Attach Mult.** (attach multiple) button allows you to attach several splines to the selected spline all at once. Picking this button displays the **Attach Multiple** dialog box. See Figure 5-36. This dialog box is a variation of the **Select Objects** dialog box. Only the names of valid spline shapes

Attach Mult.

Figure 5-36. You can attach multiple splines at the same time using the **Attach Multiple** dialog box.

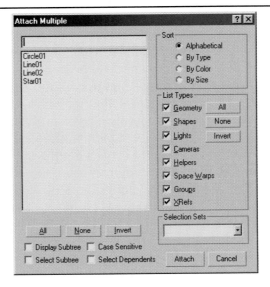

are listed in the **Attach Multiple** dialog box, regardless of the settings in the **List Types** area. When checked, the **Reorient** check box in the **Geometry** rollout aligns the local coordinate system of any attached splines to the local coordinate system of the selected spline. This also works with the **Attach** button.

The **Break** button is enabled when in vertex or segment sub-object mode. It is used to break a spline at a selected point. In effect, this inserts two unconnected vertices at the same point. To break a spline at the segment sub-object level, pick the **Break** button. Then, pick a point on the spline where you want the break. The cursor changes to indicate you are breaking the spline. To break a vertex, select the vertex at the vertex sub-object level and pick the **Break** button. After a spline is broken, the new vertices can then be further modified.

You can insert additional vertices on a spline to create new segments. To do so, pick the **Insert** button. Then, pick a point on the segment where you want to insert the vertex. The cursor changes to indicate a valid segment. See Figure 5-37. Next, move the cursor and pick to place the new vertex. As you move the cursor, two rubberband lines are attached to the new vertex. Continue adding vertices to the segment as needed. Right-click or pick the **Insert** button again to exit this mode.

When in vertex sub-object selection mode, you can set a new first vertex for the spline. This can be useful when lofting multiple shapes. The first vertex is indicated by a small box around it. All other vertices appear as small plus signs (+). To set a new first vertex, select the vertex you want to make first. Then, pick the **Make First** button in the **Geometry** rollout. The box moves to the selected vertex, indicating it is now the first vertex.

The **Fuse** option moves all selected vertices to the center of the selection. However, despite the name of this option, the vertices are not connected, but rather placed on top of one another. To use this option, select more than one vertex. Then, pick the **Fuse** button in the **Geometry** rollout. The vertices are moved to the center of the selection. This option can only be used in vertex sub-object selection mode.

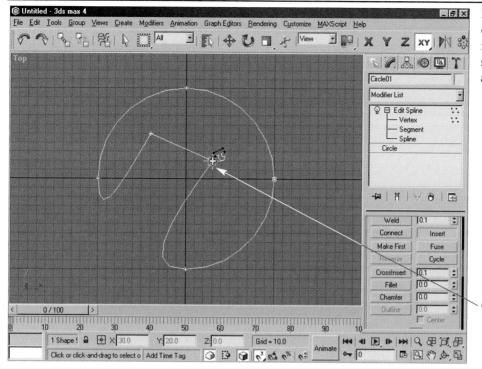

Cursor with snap on

Help Cel

The **Insert** option requires that the shape of the curve be changed. To insert a vertex without changing the shape of the curve, refine the curve as explained in the following section, *Refining a Segment.*

Refining a Segment

You can add vertices between the endpoints of a spline segment. This is called *refining.* Refining differs from inserting a vertex in that the curve of the spline is not altered. The options in the **Refine** area are available when in vertex or segment sub-object selection mode. To refine a segment, pick the **Refine** button. Then, pick on the segment where you want the new vertex. The cursor changes to indicate a valid segment. Right-click or pick the **Refine** button again to exit this mode.

Refine

How the vertex is placed when refining is controlled by the options in the **Refine** area. If the **Connect** check box is checked and more than one vertex is added, the new vertices are connected by a segment. The segment is independent of the base spline and appears when **Refine** mode is exited. Vertices are also added to the base spline at the points picked. In addition, checking the **Connect** check box enables the remaining options.

When the **Linear** check box is checked, the vertices of the new, "connected" segment are corner vertices. When this check box is unchecked, the new vertices are smooth vertices. However, in both cases the vertices added to the base spline are Bézier vertices.

The **Bind first** and **Bind last** check boxes perform similar functions. When checked, they force either the first or last vertex placed when refining to be bound to the center of the selected segment. A *bound vertex* is displayed in black, when in vertex sub-object mode. It cannot be moved, but its type can be changed and adjusted. The bound vertex is placed in the center of the segment, regardless of where on the segment you pick.

When the **Closed** check box is checked, the first and last vertices of a refinement are connected. This creates a closed spline. When unchecked, the first and last vertices are not closed. The vertices added to the base spline are not connected regardless of this check box setting.

Trimming, Extending, and Exploding Splines

The **Trim** option is used to remove overlapping spline segments. To use this option, two or more attached splines must overlap. Also, this can only be used at the spline sub-object level. Pick the **Trim** button in the **Geometry** rollout and then pick the portion of the overlap to trim. The vertices are not automatically joined. However, since they are on top of each other, they can be easily welded.

Welding vertices connects them into a single vertex. Select two overlapping vertices while in vertex sub-object mode. Then, pick the **Weld** button in the **Geometry** rollout. The two original vertices are replaced with a single vertex. The spinner next to the **Weld** button defines the maximum distance allowed between vertices that can be welded. Vertices that are farther apart than this distance cannot be welded.

The **Extend** option is used to extend a segment to another segment. The segment to which you are extending must be attached to the spline. This option can only be used at the spline sub-object level. Pick the **Extend** button in the **Geometry** rollout and then pick on the end of the segment you want to extend. A straight line segment is added from the end vertex to the closest segment, tangent to the curve leading into the end vertex. You can then use the **Trim** option to make the two segments meet at an exact location.

The **Explode** option breaks up a single spline into multiple splines based on the segments. In other words, each segment of the original spline becomes its own spline. This option can only be used at the spline sub-object level. If the **Splines** radio button is on, the new segments are all attached to each other. If the **Objects** radio button is on, the new segments become new shapes. The **Explode** dialog box also appears asking you to name the new objects. See Figure 5-38.

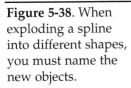

Help Cel

Two unattached splines can be selected and an edit spline modifier applied to both. This allows you to extend and trim the two splines without attaching them together.

Figure 5-38. When exploding a spline into different shapes, you must name the new objects.

Using Boolean Operations on Splines

Boolean operations are used to create unique objects from two objects. In most cases, Boolean operations are performed on two objects that overlap or intersect. Boolean operations are discussed in more detail in Chapter 6. Using Boolean operations on splines can be a quick way to create complex splines that might otherwise take a long time to create. The splines must be closed, attached, and on the same plane. Also, the Boolean operation must be done at the spline sub-object level. You can perform union, subtraction, and intersection operations. After the operation, the first spline selected is modified and the second spline is deleted. See Figure 5-39.

To perform a Boolean, first select the spline sub-object you want to keep. Then, pick the **Boolean** button in the **Geometry** rollout. It remains depressed until the operation is completed. Pick the **Union**, **Subtraction**, or **Intersection** button to set the type of operation. Next, pick the second spline sub-object for the operation. Right-click to exit this mode.

You can continue to pick "second" objects while in Boolean mode. You can also switch between Boolean types by picking a different button.

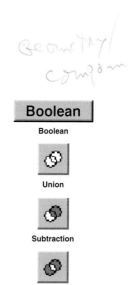

Boolean

Boolean

Union

Subtraction

Intersection

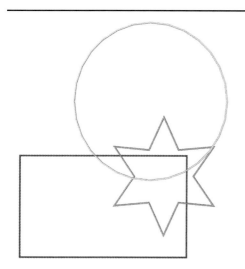

Figure 5-39. Boolean operations can be performed on splines. In this example, an intersection is created from the rectangle and star, and the resulting object is unioned to the circle.

Exercise

Exercise 5-11

1) Draw a rectangle and a circle as shown below. Use your own dimensions.
2) Apply an edit spline modifier to the circle.
3) Attach the rectangle to the circle.
4) At the vertex sub-object level, move the right-most vertex of the circle so it is inside the rectangle.
5) Change the two left vertices of the rectangle to smooth types.
6) At the spline sub-object level, trim the circle outside of the rectangle on the top and bottom. Then, trim the rectangle to the right of the circle.
7) At the segment sub-object level, delete the two right-hand segments in the circle.
8) At the spline sub-object level, extend the remaining two circle segments to meet the rectangle. Then, trim the rectangle to form a closed shape.
9) At the vertex sub-object level, weld the ends of the rectangle to the circle.
10) Save the model as ex05-11.max in the folder of your choice.

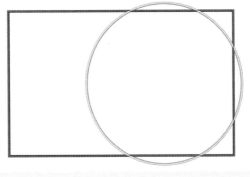

Hiding and Displaying Objects

As you create complex models, you will find your drawing screen can quickly become a tangled mess of lines. It is often helpful to temporarily turn off the display of objects. This has two effects. First, it makes the drawing screen less cluttered. Second, screen regeneration time is reduced. To turn the display of objects on or off, select the **Display** tab in the **Command Panel**. See Figure 5-40. You have several options.

Display

Hiding by Category

In the **Hide by Category** rollout, there are several check boxes that allow you to hide all items of a particular type. For example, if you check the **Lights** and **Cameras** check boxes, all lights and cameras are hidden in all viewports. If you have a viewport displaying the camera or spotlight view, that view is still displayed. In addition, the effect of lights are still applied to the model. If you pick the **All** button, all categories are selected and hidden. If you pick the **None** button, all categories are displayed. Picking the **Invert** button flip-flops the checked and unchecked check boxes.

All

All

None

None

Invert

Invert

Figure 5-40. The **Display** tab is used to hide and unhide objects.

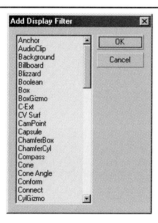

Figure 5-41. The **Add Display Filter** dialog box allows you to add custom categories that can then be hidden in the **Display** tab of the **Command Panel**.

At the bottom of the **Hide by Category** rollout is the display filters list. This list allows you to assign custom categories to hide. By default, **Bones, IK Chain Object**, and **Point** are displayed as the custom categories. To add a custom category, pick the **Add** button next to the filters list. The **Add Display Filter** dialog box appears. See Figure 5-41. Select a category from the list and pick **OK**. That category now appears in the display filters list. To hide any of the categories in the display filters list, pick on the name so it is highlighted. To unhide the category, hold the [Ctrl] key and pick the name again. You can pick multiple categories in the display filters list by holding the [Ctrl] key and picking the names.

Hiding Individual Items

The **Hide** rollout is used to turn the display of individual items on and off. Picking the **Hide Selected** button hides all currently selected items, such as objects, lights, and cameras. Picking the **Hide Unselected** button hides all items *not* currently selected.

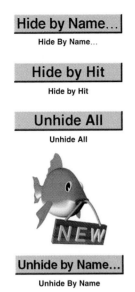

Picking the **Hide by Name...** button opens the **Hide Objects** dialog box. This is a variation of the **Select Objects** dialog box. It allows you to pick multiple objects to hide by their name.

Picking the **Hide by Hit** button allows you to pick multiple objects in the viewport using the cursor. Pick the button a second time or right-click to exit this mode.

Picking the **Unhide All** button displays all items. Picking the **Unhide by Name...** button opens the **Unhide Objects** dialog box. This, like the **Hide Objects** dialog box, is a variation of the **Select Objects** dialog box.

You can hide the selected object or all unselected objects using the quad menu. In addition, the quad menu contains options to unhide all objects.

Grouping Objects

Often, several objects "stay together" after being created. For example, a window might contain molding, a sill, glass, and hardware. In this case, all of these objects are always together. The glass is never moved outside of the window, for example. Therefore, the window "group" is moved as a whole.

In 3ds max, you can assign objects to a group. The group can be transformed or modified as a whole. In addition, a group has a pivot point of its own. To create a group, select the objects. Then, select **Group** from the **Group** pull-down menu. In the **Group** dialog box which appears, name the group. The **Group** pull-down menu contains other commands for working with groups.

Aligning Objects

You can quickly align an object with another in 3ds max. To align objects, select the first object. Then, pick **Align...** from the **Tools** pull-down menu, press the [Alt][A] key combination, or pick the **Align** button on the **Main** toolbar. The cursor changes to indicate "align" mode. Select a second object to align the first object with. The **Align Selection** dialog box is displayed. See Figure 5-42. The name of the object to which you are aligning appears in the title bar of the dialog box.

To align the position of the object, select the point of reference on the first object and the second object in the **Current Object:** and **Target**

Figure 5-42. The **Align Selection** dialog box is used to align a selected object with another object.

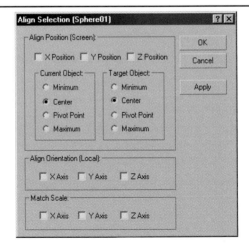

Object: areas of the dialog box. The first object is the "current object." You can pick the minimum position, center, pivot point, or maximum position. Think of minimum and maximum as "left" and "right" or "top" and "bottom." These positions are based on the current viewport, when the current reference coordinate system is **View**. The maximum Y position is different in the Top viewport and the Left viewport, for example.

Once the references are set, pick which axis to align. You can pick one, two, or all three axes by checking the check boxes at the top of the dialog box. You can apply the alignment by picking the **OK** button to close the dialog box. You can also pick the **Apply** button. This keeps the dialog box open so you can enter a new alignment for a different axis.

The alignment position is based on the current selection in the **Reference Coordinate System** drop-down list on the **Main** toolbar. This is by default set to **View**, and the **Align** command uses screen coordinates for this setting. The current reference coordinate system is indicated in the **Align Position** label in the **Align Selection** dialog box.

Help Cel

If you select multiple objects and align them with another object, the selected objects are *not* treated as a group. All selected objects are individually aligned to the target.

Mirroring Objects

You can mirror objects about a centerline in 3ds max. The mirrored objects can be clones of the original objects, or you can move the original objects to the mirrored location. To create a mirror, select the object to mirror. Then, pick **Mirror...** in the **Tools** pull-down menu or pick the **Mirror Selected Objects** button on the **Main** toolbar. The **Mirror** dialog box appears, Figure 5-43.

Mirror Selected Objects

The mirror operation is based on the current selection in the **Reference Coordinate System** drop-down list on the **Main** toolbar. The current reference coordinate system is indicated in the title bar of the **Mirror** dialog box. This is by default set to **View**, and the **Mirror** command uses screen coordinates for this setting.

Figure 5-43. The **Mirror** dialog box is used to mirror objects.

In the **Mirror Axis:** area of the **Mirror** dialog box, you must define the axis about which the object is mirrored. You can choose the X, Y, or Z axis as the mirror axis. In addition, you can choose a mirror axis that is a combination of the XY, YZ, or ZX axes. Remember, the mirror axis specified is based on the current reference coordinate system. The value in the **Offset:** spinner is the distance between the mirrored object's pivot point and the pivot point of the original object.

In the **Clone Selection:** area of the **Mirror** dialog box, pick a radio button to determine if the original is cloned, and, if so, what type of clone is created. Below the **Clone Selection:** area, you can specify to mirror IK limits and bones. Bones and IK are discussed in Chapter 21.

The **Mirror** command is actually, like a nonuniform scale or squash, applied after all modifiers. However, you do not get any warning messages to this effect. In some instances, especially advanced animations, this may not be acceptable. If you need the mirror applied before certain modifiers, use the mirror parametric deformer modifier. This places the mirror command in the stack where it can be managed. The mirror modifier has the same **Mirror Axis:** and **Offset:** options found in the **Mirror** dialog box. However, you can only choose to have a copy or no copy. Instances and references are unavailable.

Help Cel

There are many times when the **Mirror** command can be used without problems. If you plan your projects, you should be able to identify up front when you can use the **Mirror** command and when you should use the mirror modifier.

Arrays

Array

An *array* is an arrangement of clones of an original object. The array can be a rectangular array in two or three dimensions. The array can also be polar, or angular, in two or three dimensions. To create an array of an existing object, select the object. Then, pick the **Array** button on the **Main** toolbar or pick **Array...** from the **Tools** pull-down menu. The **Array** dialog box appears. See Figure 5-44.

The two most important areas of the **Array** dialog box are the **Array Transformation** and **Array Dimensions** areas. The settings in these two areas actually define the array.

The radio buttons in the **Type of Object** area allow you to make the clones in the array copies, instances, or references. At the right side of the **Array** dialog box is the **Total in Array:** display box. The value in this box is the total number of objects that will be generated by the settings in the dialog box. As you change settings, this number is updated. If you pick the **Reset All Parameters** button, all settings in the dialog box are returned to default settings. When all settings are made for the array, pick the **OK** button to close the dialog box and create the array.

Help Cel

Develop the habit of defining the array transformation first, then the array dimensions. The array dimensions build on the array transformations. This good practice will usually save you time.

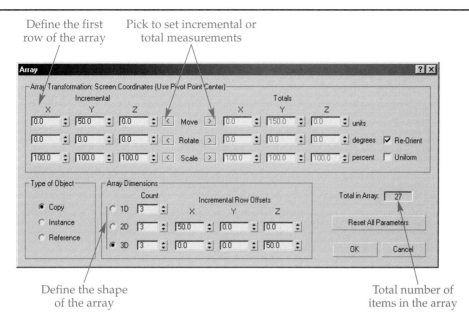

Define the first row of the array

Pick to set incremental or total measurements

Define the shape of the array

Total number of items in the array

Figure 5-44. The **Array** dialog box is used to create rectangular and polar arrays.

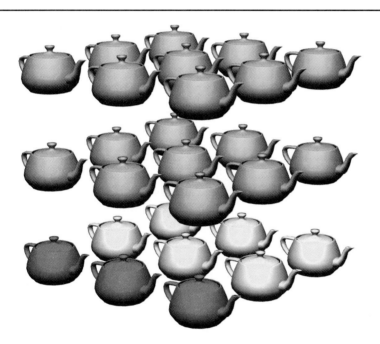

Figure 5-45. The red teapots are the first defined row of the array. The 2D "plane" includes the red and yellow teapots. The 3D "volume" is all the teapots.

Array Transformation

The **Array Transformation** area of the **Array** dialog box is used to define the first row in an array. In Figure 5-45, the first row is represented by the red teapots. This first row is then copied in 2D or 3D space, based on other settings in the dialog box. You can set the movement, rotation, and scale of the objects in the array. For each transformation, you choose incremental or total measurements. In addition, the transform can be applied on the X, Y, and Z axes.

By default, the array is set for incremental transformation. This means the values set for transformation are applied over and over until the total number of objects is reached. For example, if you specify a move transformation of 25 incremental units and a total of 10 objects, the *total* distance from the first object to the last in the first row is 250 units

(25 units applied 10 times). Incremental transformations are specified on the left side of the **Array Transformation** area.

To specify total measurements for the transformations, first pick the arrow button next to the transform name so it points to the "total" (right) side of the **Array Transformation** area. Then, enter values for the transformations in the spinners on the right side. These values represent the total measurement from the first object to the last object in the first row. For example, if you specify a move transformation of 25 total units and a total of 10 objects, the distance *between each object* is 2.5 units (25 units divided equally over 10 objects). Compare this example to the previous example.

Help Cel

By entering values on more than one axis, you can create a "diagonal" first row, and, thus, a "diagonal" array.

Array Dimensions

Once the first row of the array is defined, you need to define the shape of the array. The array can be one-dimensional, two-dimensional, or three-dimensional. A *one-dimensional array* is simply the first row. A *two-dimensional array* is a plane. A *three-dimensional array* has volume. To set the shape of the array, pick the **1D**, **2D**, or **3D** radio button in the **Array Dimensions** area of the **Array** dialog box.

When creating a one-dimensional array, you need to set the total number of objects in the first row. In the **Array Dimensions** area, pick the **1D** radio button and then enter the total number of objects in the row in the **Count** spinner. Then, simply pick the **OK** button in the dialog box to create the array. The first row defined in the **Array Transformation** area is the entire array. This is represented by the red teapots in Figure 5-45.

To create a two-dimensional array, you must first define the first row, or 1D array. This includes the total number of objects in the first row. Then, you must define values for the first "plane" of the array. In other words, you must set how many times the first row defined in the **Array Transformation** area is copied on an XY, YZ, or XZ plane. This is represented by the red and yellow teapots in Figure 5-45. Pick the **2D** radio button to enable the **X**, **Y**, and **Z** offset spinners. Then, enter *incremental offsets* for repeating the first row. Finally, you must enter the number of times the first row is repeated in the **2D Count** spinner. Pick the **OK** button in the dialog box to create the array.

To create a three-dimensional array, you must first define the first row, followed by the "plane" of the array, and finally the "volume" of the array. In other words, you must specify how many times the first row defined in the **Array Transformation** area is copied to create a plane, and how many times that plane is copied to create an array in three dimensions. This is represented by all the teapots in Figure 5-45. Pick the **3D** radio button to enable all **X**, **Y**, and **Z** offset spinners. Set the number of objects in the first row using the **1D Count** spinner. Then, enter incremental offsets to define the plane in the **2D X**, **Y**, and **Z** spinners. Also, enter the number of times the first row is repeated in the **2D Count** spinner. Next, enter incremental offsets to define the volume in the **3D X**, **Y**, and **Z** spinners. Finally, enter the number of times the plane is repeated in the **3D Count** spinner. The total number of objects in the array is the value in the **1D Count** spinner times the value in the **2D Count** spinner times the value in the **3D Count** spinner. Pick the **OK** button to create the array.

Help Cel

The settings in the **Array** dialog box are based on the current reference coordinate system and which button is selected in the **Transform Center** flyout.

Exercise

Exercise 5-12

1) Reset 3ds max. Then, draw a sphere approximately 30 units in diameter.
2) Move the sphere to the bottom-left corner of the Top viewport.
3) Pick the **Array** button on the **Main** toolbar.
4) In the **Array Transformation** area of the **Array** dialog box, enter 40.0 in the **X** incremental move spinner. Also, enter 50.0 in the **X**, **Y**, and **Z** incremental scale spinners.
5) In the **Array Dimensions** area of the **Array** dialog box, pick the **3D** radio button. Then, enter 3.0 in the **1D**, **2D**, and **3D Count** spinners. The total number of objects in the array should be indicated as 27.
6) Enter –100.0 in the **2D** incremental offset **Y** spinner. Enter 30.0 in the **3D** incremental offset **Z** spinner.
7) Pick the **OK** button to create the rectangular array. Your model should look like the one shown on the next page.
8) In the Left viewport, draw a cylinder approximately 10 units in diameter and 150 units in height.
9) In the Top viewport, move the cylinder to the right of the rectangular array.
10) In the **Transform Center** flyout on the **Main** toolbar, select the **Use Selection Center** button. Also, make sure the current coordinate system in the **Reference Coordinate System** drop-down list on the **Main** toolbar is **View**.
11) With the Top viewport active, open the **Array** dialog box. Pick the **Reset All Parameters** button.
12) In the **Array Transformation** area of the dialog box, pick the right-hand arrow button next to **Rotate** to specify a total measurement. Enter 360.0 in the **Z** spinner for **Rotate**.
13) In the **Array Dimensions** area of the dialog box, pick the **2D** radio button. Enter 10.0 in the **1D Count** spinner. Enter 10.0 in the **2D Count** spinner.
14) Enter 10.0 in the **2D** incremental offset **Z** spinner. Pick the **OK** button to create the array. Your array should look like the one shown on the next page.
15) Pick the **Undo** button on the **Main** toolbar.
16) Activate the Left viewport and open the **Array** dialog box. Notice the last settings are still shown. Pick the **OK** button to draw an array with the same settings as the last.
17) Why is the new array different? Undo the array.
18) Activate the Front viewport and draw an array using the same settings. How does this array differ from the previous two?

(continued on page 182)

Exercise

Exercise 5-12 *(Continued from page 181)*

19) Undo the array and activate the Top viewport. Draw the array again so your model looks like the rendering shown below.
20) Save the scene as ex05-12.max in the folder of your choice.

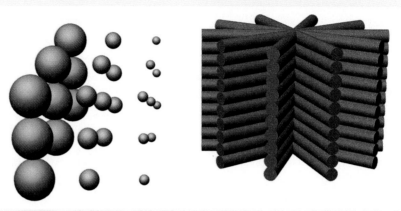

Spacing Tool

The spacing tool functions much like the **Array** tool, but it allows you to pick a path along which to distribute the cloned objects. These cloned objects can be copies, instances, or reference objects of the original. The path can be a spline or a NURBS curve. You also have the option of picking two points in space, which define the endpoint and starting point of a straight path. The spacing tool can be used to add legs to the body of an insect, or to distribute oars along the edge of a ship's hull.

Spacing Tool

To create a series of cloned objects using the spacing tool, pick the **Spacing Tool** button from the **Array** flyout on the **Main** toolbar, select **Spacing Tool**... from the **Tools** pull-down menu, or press [Shift][I] on the keyboard. This opens the **Spacing Tool** dialog box, which is modeless. See Figure 5-46.

Select the object you wish to clone and distribute, if the object is not already selected. Next, select either the **Pick Path** or **Pick Points** button in the **Spacing Tool** dialog box to determine a path. If you choose the **Pick Path** button, select a spline or curve to serve as the path. If you choose the **Pick Points** button, pick two points in space that define an imaginary straight line to use as a path.

The **Parameters** area contains controls that determine how the cloned objects are arranged. Checking the check box next to each option activates it. Selecting a spacing method from the drop-down list automatically activates all associated parameters. Activating different combinations of parameters will automatically set the appropriate spacing method.

The **Count:** spinner setting determines how many clones are created. The **Spacing:** spinner setting determines the distance between the clones. The **Start Offset:** spinner setting determines the distance between the starting point of the path and the first cloned object. The **End Offset:** spinner setting determines the distance between the endpoint of the path and the last cloned object.

The **Context** area in the dialog box contains two radio buttons that allow you to select the way in which the distance between the cloned

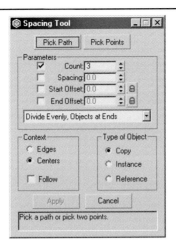

Figure 5-46. The **Spacing Tool** dialog box is used to space copies of an object along a path.

objects is measured. When the **Edges** radio button is selected, the distance between successive objects is measured between the facing edges of the objects. When the **Centers** radio button is selected, the distance is measured between the centers of the objects. Checking the **Follow** check box aligns the pivots of the cloned objects to the normals of the path.

The **Type of Object** area in the dialog box contains three radio buttons that determine the type of cloned objects created. The cloned objects can be copies, instances, or references. The help window at the bottom of the dialog box displays instructions and information while creating the distribution.

Chapter Snapshot

Chapter Test

Answer the following questions on a separate sheet of paper.

1) What is the difference between **Undo** and **Hold**?
2) What is the difference between **Redo** and **Fetch**?
3) List three ways to select objects.
4) Which selection method uses the currently selected button in the **Selection Region** flyout?
5) Which button in the **Selection Region** flyout allows you to draw an irregular window?
6) What is the keyboard shortcut to the **Select Objects** dialog box?
7) Why would you turn off the **Assign Random Colors** feature?
8) A transform is any change made to the _____, _____, or _____ of an object.
9) A modifier changes the _____ or _____ of an object.
10) How many modifiers can an object have in any given frame?
11) A maximum of _____ move transforms can be applied to an object in any given frame.
12) Name the two basic types of modifiers.
13) The _____ is used to manage the modifiers placed on an object.
14) What does collapsing the stack do?
15) Define gizmo.
16) List two ways to restrict cursor movement.
17) What are the buttons in the **Transform Center** flyout used for?
18) What is sub-object mode used for?
19) How do you enter sub-object mode?
20) Name the sub-objects found in a spline.
21) Which tool allows you to place copies of an object equally spaced along a spline?
22) What is the purpose of the **Mirror** command?
23) What do the settings in the **Array Transformation** area of the **Array** dialog box define?
24) What do the settings in the **Array Dimensions** area of the **Array** dialog box define?
25) Give the keyboard shortcut used to open the **Align Selection** dialog box.

Modeling Problems

Draw the following models. Use the 3ds max objects presented in this and earlier chapters. Unless otherwise indicated, use your own dimensions. Choose object colors similar to those shown. When finished, save each model as p05-xx.max in the folder of your choice.

Vanity **1**

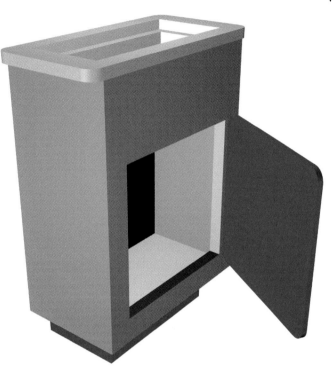

Fireplace and Chimney **2**

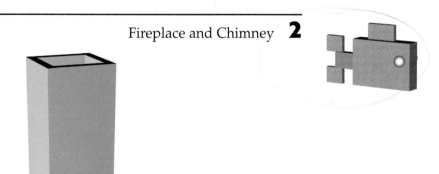

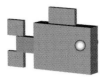

3 Cane

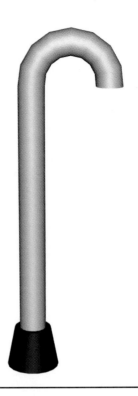

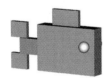

4 Ottoman

Roof Truss System **5**

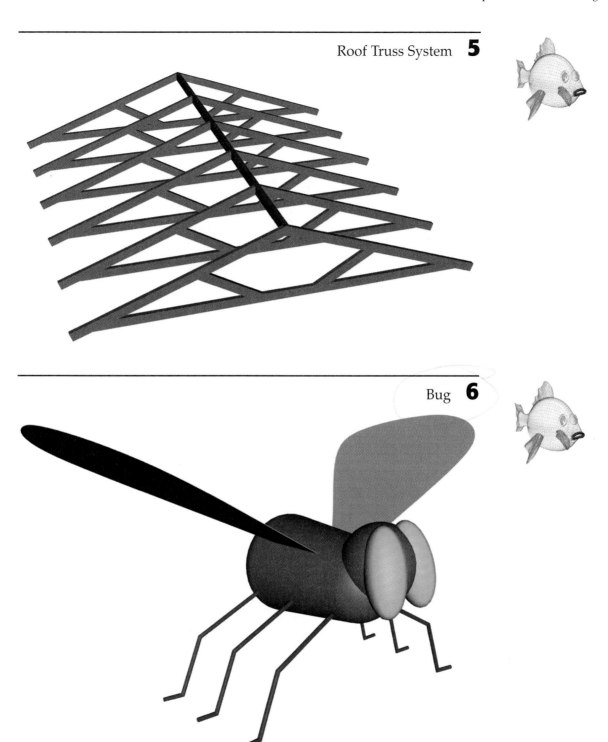

Bug **6**

7 Chair

8 Lantern

Flower and Vase **9**

Table **10**

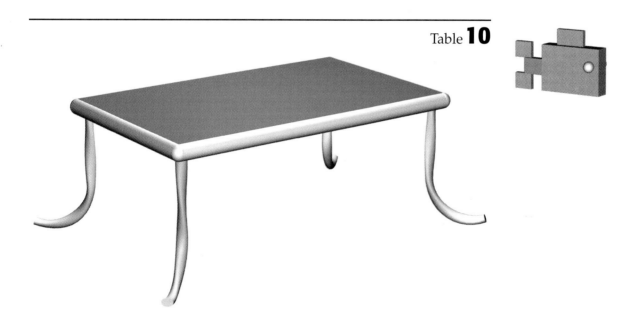

Chapter 6

Creating Compound Objects

Objectives

After completing this chapter, you will be able to:
- Define loft objects.
- Create basic loft objects.
- Define Boolean objects.
- Create basic Boolean objects.
- Define terrain objects.
- Create terrain objects.

Compound objects use two or more objects or shapes to create new, complex objects. There are nine types of compound objects that can be created in 3ds max. These objects are loft, Boolean, terrain, scatter, connect, ShapeMerge, conform, morph, and mesher objects. The loft, Boolean, and terrain compound object types are discussed in this chapter. The morph, connect, ShapeMerge, and mesher object types are discussed in Chapter 9, *Creating Advanced Compound Objects.*

To create a compound object, pick **Create** in the **Command Panel**. Then, pick the **Geometry** button and select **Compound Objects** from the drop-down list. Finally, in the **Object Type** rollout, select the button corresponding to the type of compound object you want to create.

Create

Geometry

Loft Objects

A *loft object* is a spline that is extruded, or lofted, along a path. See Figure 6-1. This is similar to applying an extrude modifier, except you can use a spline you create as the axis of extrusion. You also have more control over the resulting object. Once a loft is created, it can be converted to a NURBS surface, if so desired.

There are very few shapes that cannot be lofted. However, if you attempt to "get" an invalid shape, the prompt line displays the reason that the shape is invalid. You can usually correct the problem with the shape and then loft it.

To create a loft object, first draw a spline you want to loft. This is called the *shape.* Also draw a spline to use as the path. Then, with one of the splines selected, pick **Create** in the **Command Panel**. Pick the

Create

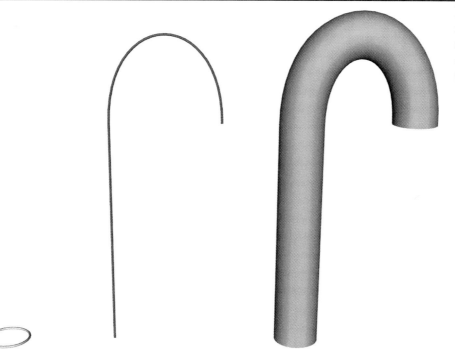

Figure 6-1. The circle is lofted along the cane-shaped path to create the object on the right.

Geometry button and select **Compound Objects** from the drop-down list. Finally, pick the **Loft** button in the **Object Type** rollout.

It is important to put some thought into which object is selected first. If the path is selected first, then you must "get" a shape to place on the path. The resulting loft object is generated along the Z axis of the path in the same location as the path. If the shape is selected first, then you must "get" a path. The resulting loft object is generated along the Z axis of the shape in the same location as the shape. Also, the shape is always perpendicular to the path in the resulting loft object.

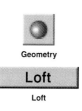

Geometry

Loft

Loft

Help Cel

In many cases, creating a loft object is a better choice over applying an extrude modifier, even if the path is straight. You have more control over the resulting object. In addition, an extruded object often does not react well when used in a Boolean operation. Boolean operations are discussed later in this chapter.

Creation Method Rollout

The **Creation Method** rollout is where you "get" either the path or shape for lofting. If the shape is selected, pick the **Get Path** button. Then, select the path in any viewport. When you move the cursor over the path, the cursor changes shape. See Figure 6-2. If the path is selected first, pick the **Get Shape** button and pick the shape in any viewport.

At the bottom of the **Creation Method** rollout are three radio buttons. Picking the **Move** radio button moves the shape (or path) to the path (or shape). Picking the **Copy** radio button places a copy of the shape (or path) on the path (or shape). Picking the **Instance** radio button places an instance of the shape (or path) on the path (or shape).

Figure 6-2. The cursor changes to indicate a valid path for lofting.

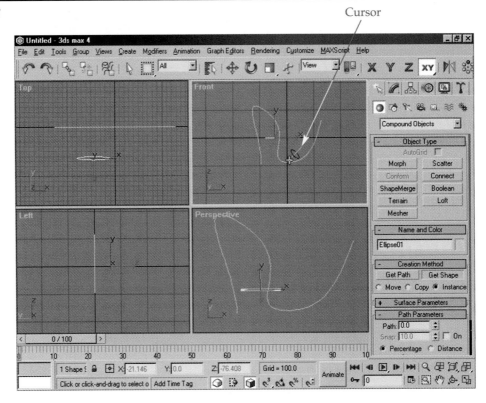

Help Cel

If you think the shape or path may need to be changed at some point, use an instance. Modifying the original spline may be easier than using sub-object mode on the loft object.

Surface Parameters Rollout

The **Surface Parameters** rollout is used to control the appearance of the loft object's surface. You can specify whether to apply smoothing and generate mapping coordinates. You can also specify what type of object is generated by the loft.

In the **Smoothing** area of the **Surface Parameters** rollout are the **Smooth Length** and **Smooth Width** check boxes. Checking the **Smooth Length** check box places smoothing groups along the path. Checking the **Smooth Width** check box places smoothing groups around the circumference of the path; in other words, around the shape.

In the **Mapping** area, you can set 3ds max to automatically generate mapping coordinates for the loft object. Checking the **Apply Mapping** check box applies mapping coordinates to the loft object and enables the other options in this area. The value in the **Length Repeat:** spinner is the number of times the map is tiled along the path. The bottom of the map is placed at the first vertex of the path. The value in the **Width Repeat:** spinner is the number of times the map is tiled around the shape. The left side of the map is placed at the first vertex of the shape. Checking the **Normalize** check box evenly spaces the map tiling along both the length and width of the loft object. When unchecked, map tiling is based on the location of vertices. This may produce bunched-up tiling. Mapping is discussed in detail later in this text.

The **Materials** area is used to automatically generate material IDs. When the **Generate Material IDs** check box is checked, material IDs are calculated for the loft object. When the **Use Shape IDs** check box is checked, the material IDs for the shape are carried over to the loft object. Material IDs are used for multi/sub-object materials, which are discussed in detail later in this text.

In the **Output** area, you can set what type of object is created. Pick the **Patch** radio button to create the loft object as a patch. Pick the **Mesh** radio button to create the loft object as a mesh. In most cases, a mesh is generated.

Help Cel

Materials and material mapping are discussed in detail in Chapter 17 and Chapter 18.

Path Parameters Rollout

The **Path Parameters** rollout is used to control the placement of multiple shapes on a path. See Figure 6-3. This is discussed in detail in Chapter 9. The settings in this rollout are not needed to create a basic loft object.

Skin Parameters Rollout

The settings in the **Skin Parameters** rollout are used to control the mesh or patch that is the surface of the loft object. In the **Capping** area, you can specify whether or not the ends are capped. Also, you can set how the faces on the end caps are calculated. The options in this area are the same as those for the extrude modifier discussed in Chapter 5.

The options in the **Display** area determine how the loft object is shown in the viewports. When the **Skin** check box is checked, the skin of the loft object is displayed in all viewports. When unchecked, the loft object is displayed as the path and the shapes only. When the **Skin in Shaded** check box is checked, the loft object is displayed with skin in shaded viewports only. This check box has no effect if the **Skin** check box

Figure 6-3. The **Path Parameters** rollout for a loft object.

Figure 6-4. The skin is displayed for the object on the right. Skin is not displayed for the object on the left. Note: The two objects are shown on the same screen for illustration purposes only.

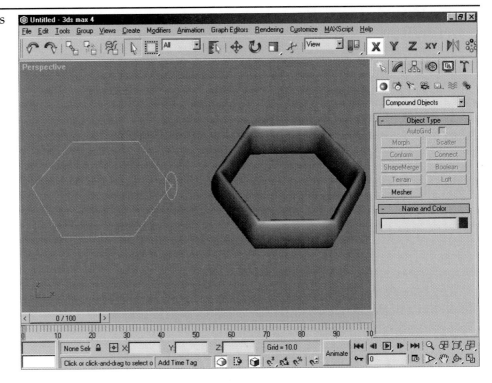

is checked. See Figure 6-4. The current settings in the **Display** area are used for the next loft object created. To use different settings, make the changes either before or after lofting a new object.

At the top of the **Options** area are the **Path Steps:** and **Shape Steps:** spinners. The value in the **Path Steps:** spinner determines how many levels, or steps, are placed between each main division along the path. A shape is placed at each step. The value in the **Shape Steps:** spinner determines how many steps are placed between each vertex around the shape.

When the **Optimize Shapes** check box is checked, 3ds max removes shape steps on straight segments of the shape or multiple shapes. This reduces the complexity of the loft object. Checking the **Optimize Path** check box removes steps on straight line segments of the path. This check box is only enabled when the **Path Steps** radio button is selected in the **Path Parameters** rollout.

When the **Adaptive Path Steps** check box is checked, 3ds max analyzes the loft object and attempts to create the "best" skin. This is done by adjusting where the main divisions are along the path. When this check box is unchecked, main divisions are placed at the path vertices only. This check box is disabled when the **Path Steps** radio button is selected in the **Path Parameters** rollout.

When the **Contour** check box is checked, the shape "rotates" to follow the curvature of the path. When unchecked, the shape maintains the same orientation that it has at the first level. When the **Banking** check box is checked, the shape rotates about the path as the path curves. You can think of this as an oval race track. The asphalt (a box) rotates and banks through the curves of the oval (the path).

Checking the **Constant Cross-Section** check box scales shapes at angles in the path to maintain a constant width of the loft object. When this is unchecked, the shape maintains its original dimensions along the entire length of the path. In some cases, this can cause the loft object to be pinched at angles in the path.

When the **Linear Interpolation** check box is checked, the skin is generated with straight edges between shapes. When unchecked, the skin is generated with curved edges. This option is off by default.

The **Flip Normals** check box is used to turn a loft object inside out. Depending on how the shapes and path are drawn, the loft object may initially be inside out. Checking this check box flips the normals so the loft object is rendered correctly. Normals are discussed in Chapter 5.

When the **Quad Sides** check box is checked, the faces between sections of the loft that have the same number of sides are four-sided. All other faces are three-sided. When unchecked, all faces are three-sided. This feature can help to optimize large models.

The **Transform Degrade** check box is used to turn the display of the loft object's skin on or off when transforming in sub-object mode. When the check box is checked, the skin is turned off during sub-object transforms. This can make things easier to see and transform.

Exercise 6-1

Exercise

1) Draw the three sets of splines shown below. Use your own dimensions.
2) Select the first path. Then, "get" the shape and loft it. Notice where the resulting loft object is placed.
3) Select the second shape using the **Select object** button. Then, "get" the path and loft it. Notice where the resulting loft object is placed.
4) Loft the third shape along the path. Notice the shape of the lofted object.
5) In the **Options** area of the **Skin Parameters** rollout, change the **Path Steps:** spinner value to 1. Notice how the object changes.
6) Change the **Path Steps:** spinner value to 10. Notice how the object changes.
7) Reset 3ds max without saving.

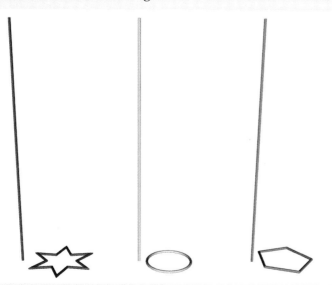

Boolean Objects

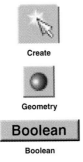

Create

Geometry

Boolean

Boolean

A *Boolean object* is created from two objects. The two original objects are called *operands.* Operands typically overlap, but do not need to for certain Boolean operations. There are four types of Boolean operations in 3ds max. See Figure 6-5. These are union, subtraction, intersection, and cut.

To create a Boolean object, first create the two objects on which to perform the operation. These can be primitives, extrusions, lathe objects, or lofts. With one of the objects selected, pick **Create** in the **Command Panel**. Pick the **Geometry** button and select **Compound Objects** from the drop-down list. Finally, pick the **Boolean** button in the **Object Type** rollout. If the selected object is not valid for a Boolean operation, the **Boolean** button is greyed out.

Union

A *union* operation combines the two operands to create one object. The overlapping portions of the two operands are removed. If the operands do not overlap, a single object is created with two detached components. To combine objects, select the **Union** radio button in the **Operation** area of the **Parameters** rollout. Then, proceed as described in the section, *Completing the Boolean.*

Subtraction

A *subtraction* operation removes one operand from the other. This is commonly used to create hollow objects or to create holes. To subtract one object from another, pick the **Subtraction (A-B)** or **Subtraction (B-A)** radio button in the **Operation** area of the **Parameters** rollout. The first selected operand is identified as A and the second operand is identified as B. Then, proceed as described in the section, *Completing the Boolean.*

Intersection

An *intersection* operation creates a new object from the overlapping portion of the two operands. The portions not overlapping are removed. This is the opposite of a union operation. To create an intersection, pick the **Intersection** radio button in the **Operation** area of the **Parameters** rollout. Then, proceed as described in the section, *Completing the Boolean.*

Figure 6-5. The two purple objects on the left are used for Boolean operations. The light blue object is unioned. The green object is an intersection. The yellow object is a subtraction. The red object is cut.

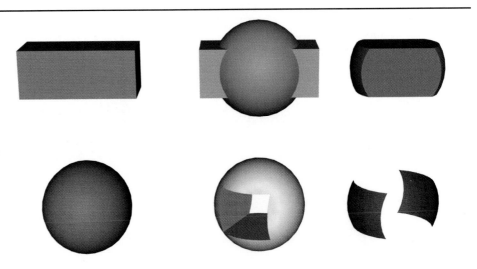

Cut

The *cut* Boolean operation uses operand B to slice operand A. To create a cut object, pick the **Cut** radio button in the **Operation** area of the **Parameters** rollout. Then, pick the type of cut.

Picking the **Refine** radio button adds vertices, edges, and faces where operand B intersects operand A. This helps "clean up" operand A at the intersection. Picking the **Split** radio button also refines the intersection, but creates two elements belonging to the same mesh.

Picking the **Remove Inside** radio button deletes all faces of operand A lying inside operand B. This is similar to the subtraction operation, but it does not add any faces or vertices to operand A.

Picking the **Remove Outside** radio button keeps all faces of operand A lying inside operand B and deletes those outside. This is similar to the intersection operation, but it does not add any faces or vertices to operand A.

After picking the **Cut** radio button and the type of cut, proceed as described in the next section, *Completing the Boolean.*

Completing the Boolean

To complete the Boolean, you must specify the second object, or operand B. To do this, select the **Pick Operand B** button in the **Pick Boolean** rollout. Then, select the second object. In the **Pick Boolean** rollout, you must also specify if operand B is moved to the Boolean object, copied, placed as an instance, or placed as a reference object.

If you are performing multiple Booleans on one object, it is important to pick the **Boolean** button in the **Object Type** rollout to complete the first operation and start the second. For example, if you are adding two spheres to a box, union the first sphere to the box. Then, pick the **Boolean** button and union the second sphere to the box/sphere object. If you do not pick the **Boolean** button again, the second time you select the **Pick Operand B** button, you are merely selecting a different operand B for the first operation.

Display/Update Rollout

In the **Display:** area of the **Display/Update** rollout, you can set how the Boolean is displayed. Picking the **Result** radio button displays only the end result of the operation. Picking the **Result + Hidden Ops** radio button displays the end result of the operation as well as wireframes of the operands. Picking the **Operands** radio button displays the two operands, but not the end result.

In the **Update:** area of the **Display/Update** rollout, you can set when a Boolean is updated after its operands are modified. By default, the update is automatic, as indicated by the **Always** radio button being selected. Picking the **When Rendering** radio button updates the Boolean only when a rendering is performed, or when the **Update** button at the bottom of the rollout is picked. When the **Manually** radio button is selected, the Boolean is only updated when the **Update** button is picked.

Operands with Materials

Performing a Boolean operation on objects that have materials assigned requires a little planning. Materials are introduced in Chapter 7, *Introduction to Materials and Rendering.* If operand A has a material assigned but operand B does not, operand B inherits the material from operand A. If operand B has a material assigned but operand A does not, operand A inherits the material from operand B.

Now, here is where it gets a bit tricky. If both operand A and operand B have materials assigned to them, the resulting Boolean object has a sub-object material created from the two operand materials. See Figure 6-6. This can produce unwanted results that can be hard to fix. The easiest way to remedy this problem is to assign the same material to both objects. Then perform the Boolean operation.

Extracting Operands

The operands of a Boolean object can be extracted as an instance or a copy. This allows the original objects to be used for other operations, animations, or features. In addition, if extracted as an instance, the instance can be altered and the Boolean object is automatically updated to reflect the change.

To extract an operand, first select its name in the **Operands** area in the **Parameters** rollout. This must be done in the **Modify** tab of the **Command Panel**, not in the **Create** tab. Then, pick the **Instance** or **Copy** radio button. Finally, pick the **Extract Operand** button. The object is placed into the scene using the original object's name plus a sequential number.

Figure 6-6. A—A multi/sub-object material shown in the **Material Editor**. B—When the sphere with the red material is subtracted from the box with the blue material, a red and blue multi/sub-object material is created, as shown at the bottom.

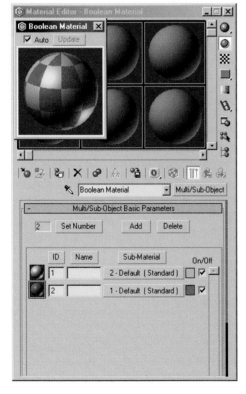
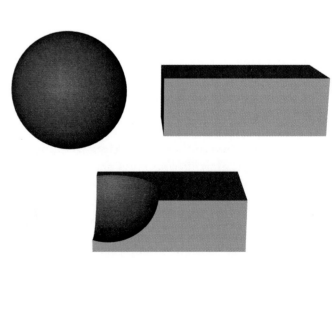

A   B

Exercise 6-2

1) Draw a cylinder, a box, two tori, and two spheres, as shown below. Use your own dimensions. Move and rotate the objects as necessary to position them as shown below.
2) Union the box to the middle of the cylinder.
3) Subtract one torus from the cylinder.
4) Create an intersection object using the other torus and one sphere.
5) Union the remaining sphere to the end of the cylinder.
6) Save the scene as ex06-02.max in the folder of your choice.

Exercise

Terrain

A *terrain* compound object is a three-dimensional object generated from splines used as contour lines. *Contour lines* are the curved lines that you see on a terrain map. They are used to indicate the elevation and shape of the ground. See Figure 6-7.

To create a terrain object, first create the contour lines. Often, these lines are imported from other software, such as AutoCAD. In order to correctly create the terrain, the contour lines must be at the proper elevation when viewed from the side. Next, select all of the contour lines. Then, pick **Create** in the **Command Panel**. Pick the **Geometry** button and select **Compound Objects** from the drop-down list. Then, pick the **Terrain** button in the **Object Type** rollout. 3ds max automatically calculates the faces needed to generate the three-dimensional object.

Create

Geometry

Terrain

Pick Operand Rollout

The **Pick Operand** button in the **Pick Operand** rollout allows you to add additional spline contours to the terrain object. Select the button and then pick the splines to add. You can add multiple splines sequentially. 3ds max automatically calculates the new terrain.

The four radio buttons in the rollout are similar to those for a Boolean operation. They determine how the new contours are added to the terrain. If the **Move** radio button is selected, the original contour data is moved into the terrain object. In effect, the original is deleted from the scene. Selecting the **Copy**, **Reference**, or **Instance** radio button places a

Figure 6-7. A terrain object is created from contour lines (splines).

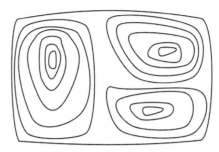

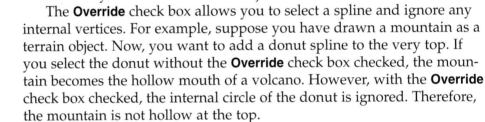

clone of the original in the terrain. If the **Reference** or **Instance** radio button is selected, the original can be edited later. The changes are then automatically added to the terrain object.

The **Override** check box allows you to select a spline and ignore any internal vertices. For example, suppose you have drawn a mountain as a terrain object. Now, you want to add a donut spline to the very top. If you select the donut without the **Override** check box checked, the mountain becomes the hollow mouth of a volcano. However, with the **Override** check box checked, the internal circle of the donut is ignored. Therefore, the mountain is not hollow at the top.

Parameters Rollout

In the **Operands** area of the **Parameters** rollout is a box with a list of all operands in the terrain object. All operand names are preceded by Op and a number. You can remove an operand from the terrain by highlighting it in the list and picking the **Delete Operand** button.

In the **Form** area of the **Parameters** rollout, you can set what form the final object takes. See Figure 6-8. Picking the **Graded Surface** radio button creates a surface that is "empty" on the bottom. Picking the **Graded Solid** radio button essentially caps the bottom and edges, creating a "solid" object. Picking the **Layered Solid** button creates terrain that resembles traditional architectural foam or cardboard terrain models. This is similar to extruding the contour lines to the proper height and combining them with a union Boolean operation.

The **Stitch Border** check box is used when the spline operands are open, not closed. When on, this check box prevents additional triangular faces from being created at the edge. Checking the **Retriangulate** check box forces 3ds max to use a more precise mathematical formula to

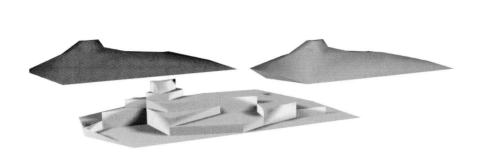

Figure 6-8. The three ways to display a terrain object. The results of the graded surface option (red) and graded solid option (blue) appear very similar. A terrain object displayed with the layered solid option (yellow) resembles an architectural foam model.

calculate the terrain. This is usually only necessary when the default calculation creates sharp bends or folds in the terrain object. The effect of this check box can be easily seen if you display the terrain as a layered solid. Then, check and uncheck the **Retriangulate** check box.

The setting in the **Display** area of the **Parameters** rollout determines how the terrain is shown in the viewports. Picking the **Terrain** radio button displays only the "skin" of the terrain. Picking the **Contours** radio button displays only the operands. Picking the **Both** radio button displays the skin with the operands over the top.

The setting in the **Update** area of the **Parameters** rollout determines when 3ds max calculates a change made to the terrain object. Picking the **Always** radio button makes 3ds max calculate the change immediately. Picking the **When Rendering** radio button makes 3ds max wait to calculate the change until a rendering is performed, or until the **Update** button at the bottom of this area is selected. Picking the **Manually** radio button specifies that 3ds max will not calculate the change until the **Update** button is selected.

Simplification Rollout

The settings in the **Simplification** rollout are used to adjust the complexity of the terrain object. See Figure 6-9. In the **Horizontal** area, you can set how many vertices of the operands are used to create the terrain. Picking the **No Simplification** radio button uses all of the vertices on the operands. This results in the most detailed object, but also the most complex. Picking the **Use 1/2 of Points** radio button uses half of the vertices on each operand to create the terrain. Picking the **Use 1/4 of Points** radio button uses one fourth of the vertices on each operand to create the terrain.

The interpolation radio buttons in the **Horizontal** area are used to increase the number of vertices on the splines used to create the terrain object. Picking the **Interpolate Points *2** radio button doubles the number of vertices. Picking the **Interpolate Points *4** button quadruples the number of vertices. Each of these options refines the terrain object, but also increases the complexity of the object.

In the **Vertical** area, you can set how many of the operands are used to create the terrain. Picking the **No Simplification** radio button uses all selected operands to create the terrain. Picking the **Use 1/2 of Lines** radio

Figure 6-9. The green terrain object is the red object simplified. Notice the green object is much "blockier."

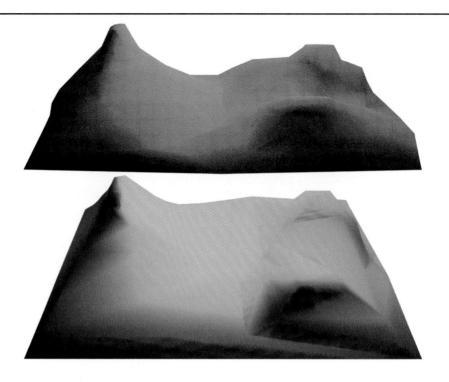

button uses half of the selected operands to create the terrain. Picking the **Use 1/4 of Lines** radio button uses one fourth of the selected operands to create the terrain.

Color by Elevation Rollout

The **Color by Elevation** rollout is used to calculate and apply color to the terrain object. This generates an object similar to the terrain on a colored relief map. See Figure 6-10. At the top of this rollout are two display boxes. The **Maximum Elev.** box shows the Z coordinate of the "top" of the object. The **Minimum Elev.** box shows the Z coordinate of the "bottom" of the object. Both of these boxes are for display only. The values cannot be changed.

The value in the **Reference Elev.** spinner is the Z coordinate of an elevation used by 3ds max as "sea level." After entering a value, pick the **Create Defaults** button in the **Zones by Base Elevation** area to create zones. The Z coordinate of the bottom of each generated zone is

Figure 6-10. A terrain object can have colors represent different elevations.

displayed in the list. This Z coordinate is relative to the "sea level" elevation value entered in the **Reference Elev.** spinner.

The **Color Zone** area is used to change the default colors assigned to
the zones by 3ds max. The value in the **Base Elev.:** spinner indicates the
current elevation. Remember, the elevations are listed in the box in the
Zones by Base Elevation area of the rollout. The **Base Color:** color swatch
indicates the current color of the elevation.

To change the color, pick the color swatch and choose a new color in
the **Color Selector:** dialog box. Then, pick the **Modify Zone** button. To
delete a zone, highlight the elevation in the list or enter the elevation in
the **Base Elev.:** spinner. Then, pick the **Delete Zone** button. To add a zone,
enter the elevation in the **Base Elev.:** spinner. Then, pick the **Add Zone**
button. A new color for the zone can also be set.

The **Blend to Color Above** radio button is used to create a gradient, or
blend, of color from the current zone to the zone above it. Picking the **Solid
to Top of Zone** radio button prevents 3ds max from blending the colors.

Help Cel

If a material is applied to the terrain object, the elevation colors are no
longer visible and are not rendered.

Exercise 6-3

1) Draw the splines shown below. Approximate the shapes.
2) Move the splines to provide "elevation."
3) Select the "bottom" three splines. Create a terrain object.
4) Add the "top" three splines to the object.
5) Add colors by elevation to the object.
6) Save the scene as ex06-03.max in the folder of your choice.

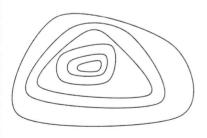

Chapter Snapshot

Chapter Test

Answer the following questions on a separate sheet of paper.
1) What is a compound object?
2) What is a loft object?
3) How can you tell if a shape is invalid when creating a loft object?
4) When creating a loft object, which spline is selected first?
5) What are the three ways to place the shape or path you "get" for a loft object in the resulting object?
6) If the **Smooth Length** check box in the **Surface Parameters** rollout is checked, what is the effect on the loft object?
7) If mapping coordinates are generated for the loft object, why would you check the **Normalize** check box?
8) How do you display the skin of a loft object in shaded viewports only?
9) When would you check the **Flip Normals** check box for a loft object?
10) List the types of Boolean operations in 3ds max.
11) The original object in a Boolean operation is called _____.
12) Which Boolean operation combines overlapping objects and removes the overlapped portion?
13) A subtraction Boolean operation is often used to _____.
14) When applying an intersection Boolean operation, the resulting object is created from the portions that are _____.
15) The cut Boolean operation is used to _____.
16) If both objects in the Boolean operation have different materials applied, the resulting object has the _____ type material.
17) A terrain object generates a 3D object from _____.
18) The **Override** check box is used to _____ when creating a terrain object.
19) The settings in the **Simplification** rollout for a terrain object are used to _____.
20) The _____ rollout is used to calculate and apply color to a terrain object.

Modeling Problems

Draw the following models. Use the 3ds max objects presented in this and earlier chapters. Choose object colors similar to those shown. When finished, save each model as p06-xx.max in the folder of your choice.

Bracket Handle **1**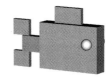

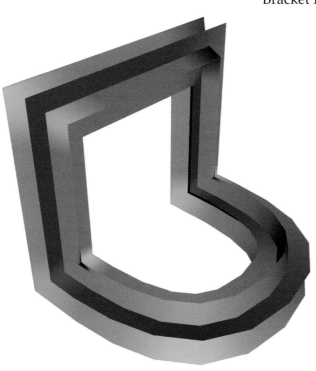

Thor's Hammer **2**

3 Chair

4 Door with Frosted Glass

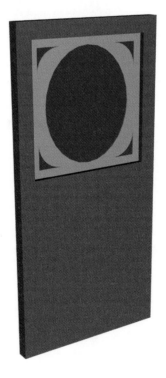

Mountain Peak **5**

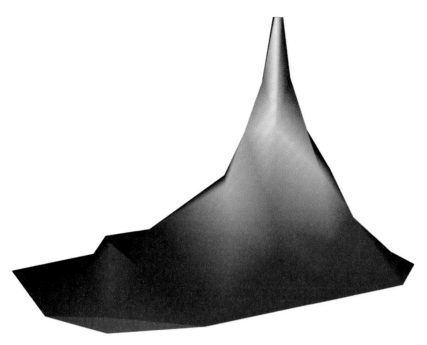

Faucet Casting **6**

7 Odin's Sword

8 Bathroom Vanity and Sink

Picture Frame and Molding **9**

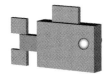

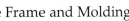

Ice Cream Parlor **10**

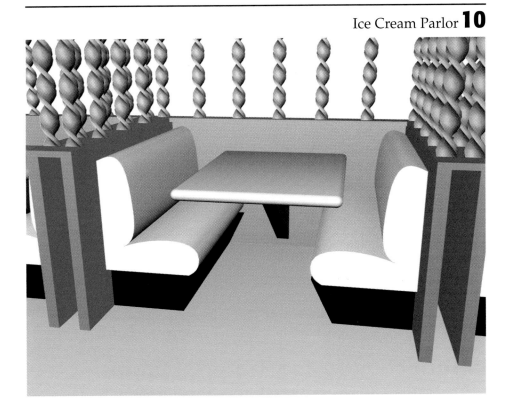

Introduction to Materials and Rendering

Objectives

After completing this chapter, you will be able to:

- Define rendering.
- Explain materials.
- Get a material from a library.
- Apply a material to an object.
- Create a rendering.
- Save a rendering to a file.
- Explain ActiveShade.
- Display an ActiveShade viewport.

What Is Rendering?

Rendering is applying color and shading to an object. Traditional artists use paint, charcoal, pencil, chalk, or other media to create the final image. In 3ds max, you model objects and apply materials to the objects. The computer can then render, or color, the objects based on the materials.

What Is a Material?

A *material* is a set of data defining how the object should appear when rendered by 3ds max. The color of the object, how light reflects off the object, and any surface textures are some of the things that a material can define. See Figure 7-1. For example, if you assign the material Metal_Chrome to an object, you are really telling 3ds max to render the object with a silver color that is very shiny. 3ds max then calculates how the object should appear based on the scene you have created.

Introduction to the Material Editor

The **Material Editor** is the "control room" for materials. You can import materials, create new materials, modify the existing materials, and assign materials to objects. The **Material Editor** is a "modeless" dialog box. This means you can continue to work in the background without having to close it. It can also be minimized to make room on

Figure 7-1. By assigning different materials to a dog model, the result can be a wood carving, metal robot, or stone sculpture.

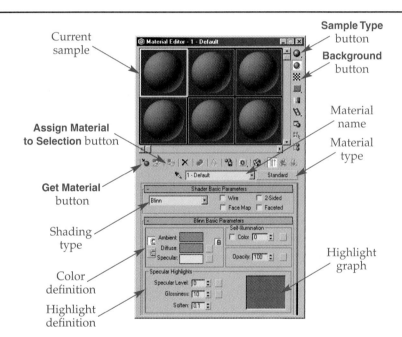

Figure 7-2. The default appearance of the **Material Editor**.

screen. To open the **Material Editor**, pick the **Material Editor** button on the **Main** toolbar, select **Material Editor…** from the **Rendering** pull-down menu, or press [M] on the keyboard. There are several parts to the **Material Editor**. See Figure 7-2.

Material Editor

In the top portion of the **Material Editor** are the material samples. By default, six "blank" samples are displayed in three columns and two rows. The current sample is indicated by the white box around the sample. You can also display 15 or 24 samples. To do so, right-click in the current sample to display the shortcut menu. Then, pick the sample configuration from the bottom of the menu. There are always 24 samples, regardless of how many are displayed. To see any samples that are not visible, as in a 3 x 2 or 5 x 3 configuration, use the scroll bars next to the sample slots or the pan cursor.

The name of the current material is shown in the drop-down list below the material samples. It is also displayed in the **Material Editor** title bar. To rename a material, pick in the drop-down list text box (not the arrow). Then, type a new name and press the [Enter] key. The material is renamed.

At the bottom of the **Material Editor** are rollouts. These rollouts are used to set various properties for the current material. These are discussed in detail in Chapters 13, 17, and 18.

To quickly create a very basic material, pick the **Diffuse:** color swatch. Then, in the **Color Selector:** dialog box, pick a color. Close the **Color Selector:** dialog box. The material can now be applied, as discussed later in this chapter. This process creates the most basic material. More detailed material definitions are explained in Chapters 13, 17, and 18.

Help Cel

By default, the material sample slots are "blank" because the file medit.mat found in the 3ds max \matlibs folder contains no definitions. If this file has been deleted or was not installed, the default sample slots contain basic materials of various colors.

Material Libraries

A *material library* is a file where material definitions are stored. By saving materials to a library, you do not have to recreate the same material over and over for different models. A material library can have as many materials as needed. Material libraries can be copied, merged, and deleted.

You may want to have several different material libraries for different projects. In this way, you can modify existing materials to meet the needs of the project without losing the original material.

Getting a Material from a Material Library

Get Material

Materials stored in a material library are not automatically available in the **Material Editor**. In order to use a saved material in your model, you must first "get" the material from the library. To do this, open the **Material Editor** and select a material sample. Be sure that you do not need that sample. Getting a material completely replaces the material definition for the current sample. With a sample selected, pick the **Get Material** button in the **Material Editor**. You can also pick **Material/Map Browser...** from the **Rendering** pull-down menu. The **Material/Map Browser** is opened. Like the **Material Editor**, this is also a modeless dialog box. When a material is selected in the **Material/Map Browser**, it is placed in the **Material Editor**.

Material/Map Browser

The **Material/Map Browser** works in conjunction with the **Material Editor**. Think of the **Material/Map Browser** as the "file manager" for materials. See Figure 7-3. Most of the **Material/Map Browser** is taken up by the material/map list, which is located on the right side. There are scroll bars to navigate through the list. What is displayed in the material/map list is determined by which radio button is selected in the **Browse From:** area on the left side of the dialog box.

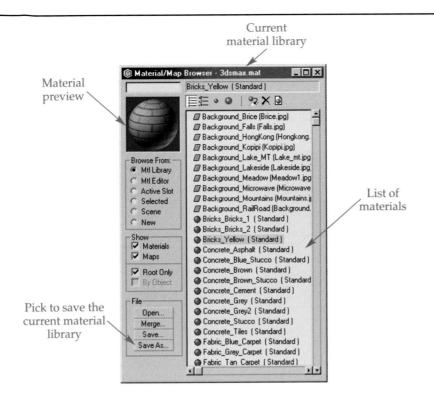

Current material library

Material preview

Pick to save the current material library

List of materials

Figure 7-3. The **Material/Map Browser.**

Picking the **Mtl Library** radio button in the **Browse From:** area displays the materials in the current material library. The name of the library is displayed in the title bar of the **Material/Map Browser**. Using the buttons in the **File** area, you can open a different material library, merge materials from a different library into the current one, and save the material library.

Picking the **Mtl Editor** radio button in the **Browse From:** area displays the materials defined in the sample slots of the **Material Editor**. Using the **Save As...** button in the **File** area, you can quickly save the materials defined in the **Material Editor** as a new material library.

Picking the **Active Slot** radio button in the **Browse From:** area displays the material defined in the current sample slot in the **Material Editor**. Picking the **Selected** radio button displays only the materials assigned to the currently selected objects. Picking the **Scene** radio button displays all materials assigned in the current scene. Picking the **New** radio button displays the types of 3ds max materials that can be created.

At the top of the **Material/Map Browser** is a text box. Typing the first few characters of a material name here "jumps" the list to matching names. For example, typing woo jumps the list to the first material name that starts with woo, such as Wood_Ash. Below the text box is a sample display. A rendered sample of the selected material appears in this area.

Along the top of the **Material/Map Browser** are several buttons. These buttons control how the material/map list is displayed. See Figure 7-4. Picking the **View List** button displays only the names of materials. Picking the **View List + Icons** button displays both material names and a small icon representation of the material. Picking the **View Small Icons** button displays only icons, in a small size. Picking the **View Large Icons** button displays the name and large icons. These buttons are radio buttons; only one can be selected at a time.

View List

View List + Icons

View Small Icons

View Large Icons

Figure 7-4. Materials can be displayed in one of four ways in the **Material/Map Browser**.

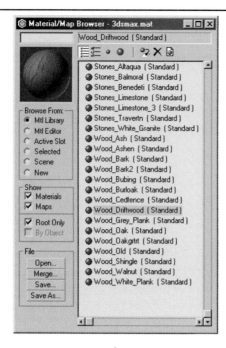

A

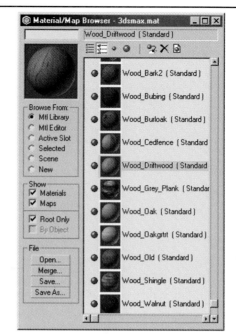

B

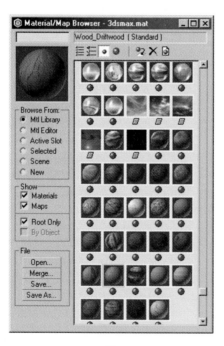

C

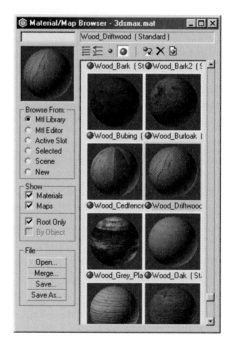

D

To place a material from the browser into the **Material Editor**, locate the name in the material/map list. Then, double-click on the material name. The material is placed into the current material sample in the **Material Editor**. The browser remains open.

Exercise 7-1

1) Draw two boxes and an oil tank, as shown below.
2) Open the **Material Editor**. Pick the **Get Material** button to open the **Material/Map Browser**.
3) Pick the **Mtl Library** button in the **Browse From:** area.
4) Scroll down in the material/map list to the material Metal_Galvanized. Highlight the name to get a preview. Then, double-click to place it in the **Material Editor**.
5) Select a different material sample slot in the **Material Editor**.
6) Get the material Stones_Limestone from the **Material/Map Browser**.
7) Select a different material sample slot in the **Material Editor**.
8) Get the material Wood_White_Plank.
9) Close the **Material/Map Browser** and the **Material Editor**.
10) Save the scene as ex07-01.max and leave 3ds max open. This scene is used in later exercises.

Exercise

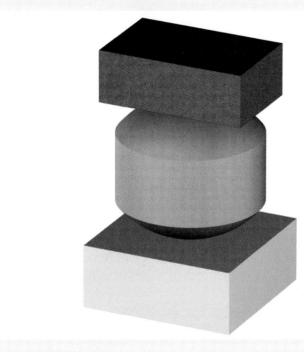

Applying Materials

There are two basic ways of applying a material to an object. One way is to pick, hold, and drag the material sample into a viewport and drop it onto an object. In a simple model, this may be the easiest method. However, in a more complex model, this method may become difficult.

You can also apply a material to a selected object. To do this, select the object and open the **Material Editor**. You can select multiple objects to apply the same material to all objects in the selection. Then, make the sample of the material you want to assign current. Finally, pick the **Assign Material to Selection** button in the **Material Editor**. The material is assigned to all selected objects. Since the **Material Editor** is modeless, you can leave it open and select other objects. Different materials can then be applied to the new selection.

Assign Material to Selection

Help Cel

There are other, more advanced ways to assign materials. These methods are discussed later in this text.

Exercise 7-2

1) If you have not already completed Exercise 7-1, do so now.
2) Select the oil tank using the **Select object** button.
3) Open the **Material Editor**. Make the Metal_Galvanized material sample current.
4) Pick the **Assign Material to Selection** button.
5) Press the [H] key on the keyboard and select the lower box.
6) Make the Stones_Limestone material sample current.
7) Pick the **Assign Material to Selection** button.
8) Drag the Wood_White_Plank material into the viewport and drop it onto the top box.
9) Save the scene as ex07-02.max and leave 3ds max open.

Introduction to the Render Scene Dialog Box

Render Scene

Shift **R**

F10

Just as the **Material Editor** can be thought of as the control room for materials, the **Render Scene** dialog box is the control room for rendering the scene. See Figure 7-5. To open the **Render Scene** dialog box, pick the **Render Scene** button on the **Main** toolbar, select <u>R</u>ender... from the **Rendering** pull-down menu, or press [Shift][R] or [F10] on the keyboard. Many features in this dialog box are covered in detail in later chapters. For now, the basics of this dialog box are covered.

The **Render Scene** dialog box is made up of four rollouts. The **Common Parameters** rollout contains settings that apply to all 3ds max renderings. This rollout is discussed here and in later chapters. The other rollouts are beyond the scope of this text.

In the **Time Output** area of the **Common Parameters** rollout, you specify which frames of the animation are rendered. If you are creating a still image without any motion, you render a single frame. Picking the **Single** radio button specifies that only the current frame is rendered. Picking the **Active Time Segment:** radio button specifies that the active time segment is rendered. Time segments are discussed later in this text. Picking the **Range:** radio button allows you to specify a range of frames to render. Picking the **Frames** radio button allows you to specify a series of nonsequential frames to render, such as 1, 8, and 15.

In the **Output Size** area of the **Common Parameters** rollout, you specify the pixel dimensions of the rendering. You can select from several preset sizes, or you can enter your own dimensions in the **Width:** and **Height:** spinners. This area is discussed in more detail later in this text.

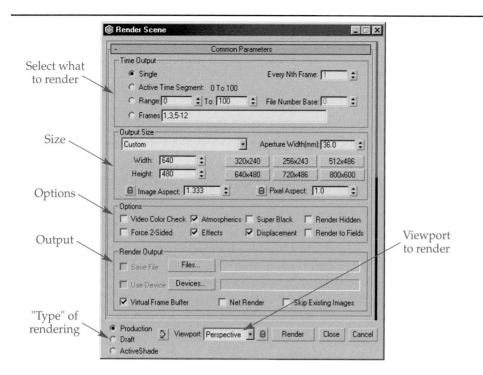

Select what to render

Size

Options

Output

"Type" of rendering

Viewport to render

Figure 7-5. The **Render Scene** dialog box.

In the **Options** area of the **Common Parameters** rollout, you can pick several options. These options are discussed later in this text.

In the **Render Output** area of the **Common Parameters** rollout, you can specify to save the rendering to a file or to an output device. An output device is a film or video recorder. This option is not covered in this text. Saving the rendering to a file is covered later in this chapter.

At the bottom of the **Render Scene** dialog box are the **Production**, **Draft**, and **ActiveShade** radio buttons. You can make settings in the **Common Parameters** rollout for each of these buttons independently. The **Quick Render** flyout on the **Main** toolbar has the **Quick Render (Production)**, **Quick Render (Draft)**, and **Quick Render (ActiveShade)** buttons. See Figure 7-6. Picking the **Quick Render (Production)** button renders the scene with the settings made while the **Production** radio button is on. Picking the **Quick Render (Draft)** button renders the scene with the settings made while the **Draft** radio button is on.

Quick Render (Production)

Quick Render (Draft)

Quick Render (ActiveShade)

Figure 7-6. The **Quick Render** flyout on the **Main** toolbar contains the **Quick Render (Production)**, **Quick Render (Draft)**, and **Quick Render (ActiveShade)** buttons.

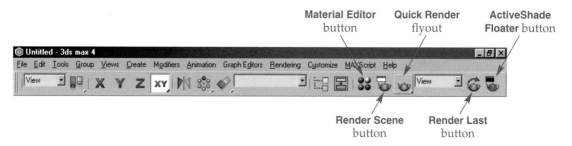

Material Editor button

Quick Render flyout

ActiveShade Floater button

Render Scene button

Render Last button

The **ActiveShade** radio button is new to 3ds max r4. When selected, the parameters for ActiveShade are displayed. ActiveShade allows you to create a dynamically updated, accurate preview rendering. This feature is discussed later in this chapter.

Assigning low-resolution settings to the **Quick Render (Draft)** button, you can quickly render a scene in a small size by picking the button on the **Main** toolbar. This allows you to see how things are fitting together. Then, you can produce a finished rendering using the settings assigned to the **Quick Render (Production)** button. Since these buttons are on the **Main** toolbar, you can accomplish both "types" of renderings without having to open the **Render Scene** dialog box.

The **Viewport:** drop-down list at the bottom of the dialog box allows you to specify which viewport is rendered. By default, the current viewport is displayed in the list. Only the viewports in the current viewport configuration are available in this list.

The lock button next to the **Viewport:** drop-down list allows you to lock the selected viewport as the "rendering" viewport. In this way, you can close the dialog box, adjust the scene in various viewports, and then render the scene using the **Quick Render** buttons without having to worry about which viewport is current.

Once all settings have been made, pick the **Render** button at the bottom of the **Render Scene** dialog box to render the scene. If you have made settings but do not want to render the scene at this time, pick the **Close** button. Pick the **Cancel** button to exit the dialog box without saving any changes you made. When the **ActiveShade** radio button is on, the **Render** button is replaced with the **ActiveShade** button. Picking this button launches the ActiveShade floating window. ActiveShade is discussed later in this chapter.

Rendering a Still Image

A *still image* is a single frame of the animation. To render a still image, open the **Render Scene** dialog box. In the **Time Output** area of the **Common Parameters** rollout, pick the **Single** radio button. In the **Output Size** area, pick a button representing the resolution, or "size," you want. You can also enter a custom size in the **Width:** and **Height:** spinners. For computer displays, still images are typically rendered to 640 x 480 or 800 x 600. Keep in mind, the larger the size, the longer the rendering time. Also, make sure the correct viewport is displayed in the **Viewport:** drop-down list at the bottom of the dialog box. Finally, pick the **Render** button to render the image.

Once you pick the **Render** button, the **Rendering** dialog box and the render window are displayed. See Figure 7-7. The **Rendering** dialog box shows the status of the rendering and provides an overview. There are no actual changes that can be made. However, you can pause or cancel the rendering. The render window is where the final rendered image is displayed. When the rendering is complete, the **Rendering** dialog box automatically closes. To return to the model, close the render window and the **Render Scene** dialog box.

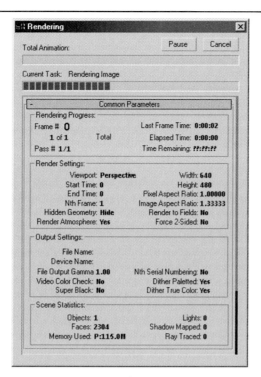

A

B

Figure 7-7. A—The **Rendering** dialog box displays the progress of the rendering. B—The completed rendering is shown in the render window.

Help Cel

If you have the "production" or "draft" **Quick Render** button set up for a single frame, you can simply pick the appropriate button in the flyout to render the current viewport.

Exercise

Exercise 7-3

1) If you have not completed Exercise 7-1 and Exercise 7-2, do so now.
2) Pick the **Render Scene** button on the **Main** toolbar.
3) Make sure the **Production** radio button at the bottom of the dialog box is on. Then, in the **Time Output** area, pick the **Single** radio button. In the **Output Size** area, pick the **640x480** button. Also, pick Perspective from the **Viewport:** drop-down list and pick the lock button so it is on (depressed).
4) Pick the **Draft** radio button. Make sure the **Single** radio button is on in the **Time Output** area. Pick the **320x240** button in the **Output Size** area.
5) Pick the **Close** button to close the **Render Scene** dialog box.
6) Make the Perspective viewport active. Then, pick the **Quick Render (Draft)** button on the **Main** toolbar.
7) When the rendering is complete, close the render window. Also, make the Top viewport active.
8) Pick the **Quick Render (Production)** button on the **Main** toolbar. When the rendering is complete, close the render window.
9) How did the two renderings differ? Why?
10) Save the file as ex07-03.max and leave 3ds max open.

Saving a Rendered Image to a File

When you render an image, you are not automatically saving it to a file. In order to do so, you must set the **Render Scene** dialog box to save to a file. First open the **Render Scene** dialog box. Make the other settings as necessary. Then, pick the **Files...** button in the **Render Output** area. The **Render Output File** dialog box is displayed. See Figure 7-8.

Switch to the drive and folder where you want to save the file. Then, enter a name in the **File name:** text box. Next, select a file type from the **Save as type:** drop-down list. Most still images are saved in BMP, TIFF, or JPEG format. Then, pick the **Save** button. Once you select a file type

Figure 7-8. The **Render Output File** dialog box is used to specify a file to render to.

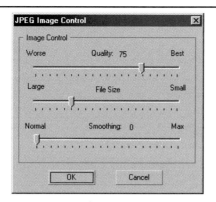

Figure 7-9. When rendering to a file, there are options to be set. These depend on the type of file specified. This dialog box is used to set options for a JPEG file.

and pick **Save**, a dialog box appears for you to make settings specific to that file type. For example, when you pick the JPEG file type, the dialog box shown in Figure 7-9 appears. In this dialog box, you need to set the image quality, file size, and smoothing level for the JPEG file. Once you make the settings, you are returned to the **Render Scene** dialog box.

Notice that the **Save File** check box in the **Render Output** area is now enabled and checked. If you uncheck this check box, the file is not saved. The path and file name are also displayed next to the **Files...** button. Finally, pick the **Render** button to render the scene. The render window and the **Rendering** dialog box appear. After the scene is rendered, the **Rendering** dialog box is closed and the image is saved to the file.

To view a file, pick **View Image File...** from the **File** pull-down menu. In the **View File** dialog box, change to the drive and folder where the file is located. Pick the file from the file list and pick the **Open** button. The file is displayed.

Help Cel

The **Quick Render** button corresponding to the radio button active (**Production** or **Draft**) when you set the rendering to save to a file is also set to save to a file.

Exercise 7-4

1) If you have not yet completed Exercise 7-1 and Exercise 7-2, do so now.
2) Make the Perspective viewport active.
3) Open the **Render Scene** dialog box and make sure the **Production** radio button is on.
4) Pick the **Files...** button in the **Render Output** area.
5) In the **Render Output File** dialog box, name the file ex07-04 and select the JPEG file type. Pick the **Save** button.
6) In the **JPEG Image Control** dialog box, accept the default settings by picking the **OK** button.
7) In the **Render Scene** dialog box, pick the **Render** button. When the rendering is complete, close the render window and the **Render Scene** dialog box.
8) Use 3ds max to view the file.
9) Save the scene as ex07-04.max in the folder of your choice.

ActiveShade

ActiveShade is an interactive preview rendering window. The rendering automatically updates when a change is made to lighting or materials. ActiveShade can be displayed in a viewport or as a floating window. See Figure 7-10.

ActiveShade produces a higher-resolution rendering than a preview rendering. Preview renderings are typically used for animations, and are discussed in Chapter 15. While ActiveShade provides a higher-resolution rendering than what is displayed in a shaded viewport, it does not provide quite the same quality as a final rendering. The advantage of ActiveShade is the preview generates automatically.

ActiveShade creates a preview in two stages. First, ActiveShade is *initialized*. This involves evaluating the scene and preparing it for the second stage. Initialization is done to make the second stage as fast as possible. The second stage is called *updating*. It is important to understand this two stage process to better understand how the ActiveShade commands work.

Displaying ActiveShade

ActiveShade Floater

To display ActiveShade as a floating window, first activate the viewport you want rendered. Then, pick the **ActiveShade Floater** button on the **Main** toolbar. The **Quick Render (ActiveShade)** button can also be found in the **Quick Render** flyout. You can also display ActiveShade as a floating window by picking **ActiveShade Floater** in the **Rendering** pull-down menu.

To display ActiveShade in a viewport, first display the view you want rendered in the viewport. Then, pick **ActiveShade Viewport** in the **Rendering** pull-down menu. You can also right-click on the viewport label. Then, pick **Views** in the shortcut menu. Finally, pick **ActiveShade** in the cascading menu.

Figure 7-10.
ActiveShade can be displayed as a floating window or in a viewport. The lower-left viewport shown here is an ActiveShade viewport. Compare that viewport to the Perspective viewport on the lower right.

ActiveShade viewport

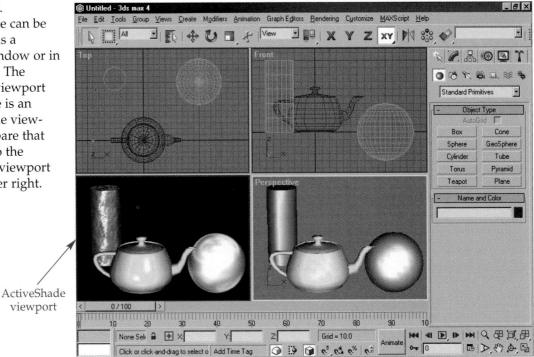

Help Cel

When a viewport is displayed as an ActiveShade viewport, it cannot be displayed full screen. In addition, a full-screen viewport cannot be displayed as an ActiveShade viewport.

ActiveShade Commands

When you display the quad menu in ActiveShade, there are several commands available. See Figure 7-11. The **Close** command in the upper-left quadrant closes ActiveShade. If ActiveShade is displayed in a viewport, this command returns the viewport to its previous view.

There are three options in the lower-left quadrant. The **Act Only on Mouse Up** option is on by default, as indicated by a check mark. This means the ActiveShade display is updated only when the mouse button is released when changing light or material parameters. Otherwise, the display is updated immediately. When the **Auto Initialization** option is on, a map change to a material initializes the ActiveShade display. Mapped materials are discussed later in this text. When the **Auto Update** option is on, a change made to lighting or nonmapped materials updates the display. Otherwise, you must manually update the display.

The **Tools** quadrant, which is the lower-right quadrant, contains several options. The **Initialize** option is used to reinitialize the ActiveShade display after changing a mapped material or object geometry. The **Update** option is used to update the shading in the display. The **Select Object** option allows you to pick an object in the ActiveShade viewport. This option is not available in the floating window. The **Toggle Toolbar** option allows you to turn the **ActiveShade** toolbar on and off in the viewport. The spacebar can also be used to turn the toolbar on and off. This option is not available in the floating window.

The **Draw Region** option allows you to limit ActiveShade to a portion of the scene. This option is available in the ActiveShade viewport *and* in the floating window. To use the **Draw Region** option, first turn it on. A check mark appears next to the option when it is on. Then, draw a rectangular area in the ActiveShade viewport or floating window. Now, only the portion of the scene inside the rectangle is updated when parameters in the scene are changed. Turning the option off in the quad menu does not actually turn the option off. To turn the option off, pick outside of the rectangular region in the ActiveShade viewport or floating window. The **Draw Region** option must be checked in the quad menu in order to turn the region off.

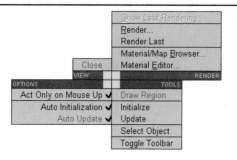

Figure 7-11. The quad menu for ActiveShade.

Help Cel

ActiveShade previews still images only. It cannot be used to preview an animation.

Chapter Snapshot

Chapter Test

Answer the following questions on a separate sheet of paper.

1) Define rendering.
2) List three media that have been traditionally used to produce renderings.
3) What is a material in 3ds max?
4) The _____ is the "control room" for materials.
5) What is a modeless dialog box?
6) What is the maximum number of materials that can be displayed at one time in the **Material Editor**?
7) What are the two locations where a material name is displayed in the **Material Editor**?
8) Define material library.
9) Why should material libraries be used?
10) To use a saved material in your model, you must _____ the material.
11) The **Material/Map Browser** is the _____ for materials.
12) In the **Material/Map Browser**, how do you display the materials in the current material library?
13) How do you place a material listed in the **Material/Map Browser** into the **Material Editor**?
14) List two basic ways of applying a material to an object.
15) The **Render Scene** dialog box is the _____ for rendering a scene.
16) List three ways to open the **Render Scene** dialog box.
17) What is the purpose of the **Production** and **Draft** buttons in the **Render Scene** dialog box and on the **Main** toolbar?
18) How do you save a rendered image to a file?
19) After a rendered image is saved, how do you view the file?
20) _____ provides an interactive rendered preview of the scene.

Modeling Problems

Draw the following models. Use the 3ds max objects presented in this and earlier chapters. Do *not* use Boolean operations to create the objects. Use only basic primitives, extended primitives, and loft objects. When creating objects, make sure the "generate mapping coordinates" option is turned on. Choose and assign materials as shown. When needed, define very basic materials by changing color in the **Diffuse:** color swatch. When finished, save each scene as p06-xx.max in the folder of your choice.

Security Wall **1**

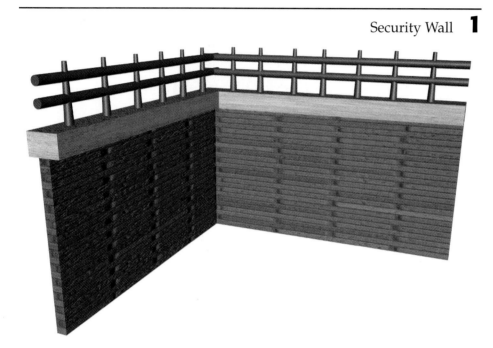

Dock of the Bay **2**

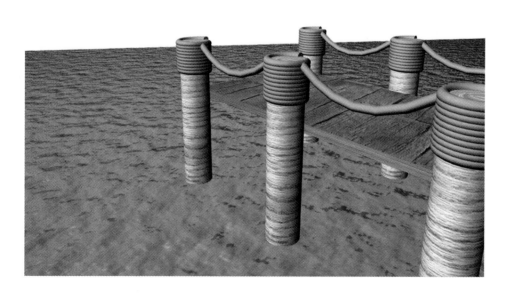

3 Cartoon Bee

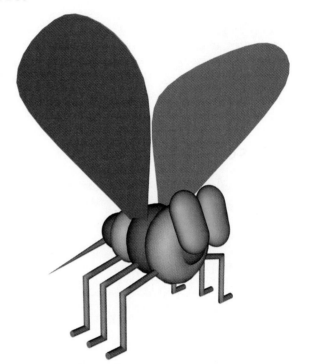

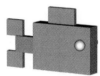

4 Jet Plane

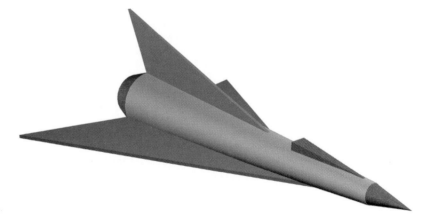

Snork 2000 Security System **5**

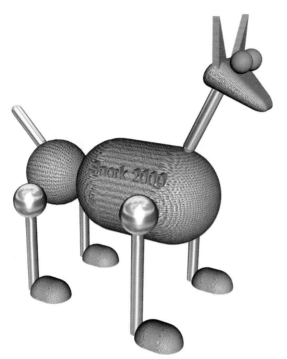

Cabinets and Countertop **6**

7 Rear Axle and Tires for a Hot Rod
(the rim profile is shown in yellow)

8 Charcoal Grill

Cape Cod Style House **9**

Love Seat Sofa **10**

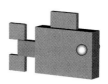

Section One Tutorial

Overview

For the Section One Tutorial, you will create a simplified model of William Shakespeare's Globe Theater. This model demonstrates that even with only the basic 3ds max skills learned so far, a fairly detailed model can be created. In order to complete the model, you will need to draw on the skills presented in the first section. It is important to have a grasp of the basic skills. The following sections in the text build on this foundation. p35

Start by opening the section01.max file saved in Exercise 1-3. If you did not save the file, complete the exercise before continuing. Figure T1-1 shows a final rendering of the model. Looking at the model, it can be broken down into several basic components. There are the ground and background, the trees and bushes, and the building itself. Tackle the model in stages, starting with the building.

Help Cel

Save often. Also, change viewport configurations and maximize viewports as needed.

Building

The building makes up most of the model. After all, the theater is what you are presenting. The rest of the model just adds detail. The building consists of walls, a roof, exposed timbers, and an entrance. Each of these is modeled separately.

Figure T1-1. The completed Section One Tutorial.

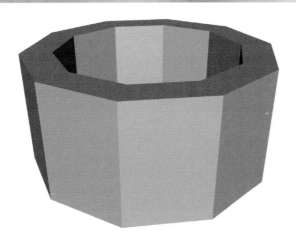

Figure T1-2. The "drill" object is subtracted to create the walls.

Walls

This model of the theater has 10 sides. Historians think the real-life theater probably had 20 or 24 sides. But, as this is a simplified model, 10 sides will do. In the Top viewport, draw a 10-sided gengon with a radius of 100′, a fillet of 0′, and a height of 90′. Center the gengon on the world origin. Check the **Generate Mapping Coordinates** check box. Name this object Walls.

Draw a second gengon centered on the first with a radius of 75′, a fillet of 0′, and a height greater than 90′. Check the **Generate Mapping Coordinates** check box for this object as well. Name this object Wall Drill. Center the "drill" object vertically on the Walls object. Then, subtract the drill from the walls. See Figure T1-2. The walls are now complete.

Help Cel

It is important to have the **Generate Mapping Coordinates** check box checked. Otherwise, mapping coordinates must be applied in order for the material you will apply to render correctly. Mapping coordinates are discussed in detail later in the text.

Roof

The roof is a triangle lofted along an ngon path. In the Top viewport, draw a 10-sided ngon centered on the walls. The ngon should have an inscribed radius of 87′6″ so it is centered inside the walls. This will serve as the path for lofting the roof.

Next, in the Front viewport, move the ngon to the top of the walls. Then, draw a triangle using the **Line** button. Make the triangle 60′ across the base and 30′ tall. See Figure T1-3. Then, loft the triangle along the ngon path. Name the object Roof. Move the roof if necessary so it sits on top of the walls.

The roof and walls are now complete. See Figure T1-4. Does your roof look like the one in the figure or does it look more like a round donut? If it is round, adjust the loft object as necessary to produce the 10-sided roof.

Timbers

When creating the exposed timbers, you may find it easier to hide the roof. Then, in the Top viewport, draw a box 1′ by 2′ by 90′ tall. Name it Timber01 and place it at one corner of one side. It will be easiest if you work on a side that is "flat" to the viewport, such as the "bottom" side. See Figure T1-5. Make a copy named Timber02. Place it at the other corner of the same side.

Figure T1-3. The dimensions of the triangle to loft for the roof.

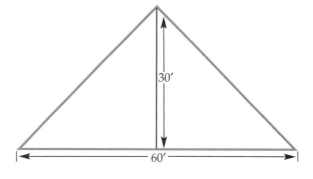

Figure T1-4. The completed walls with the completed roof on top.

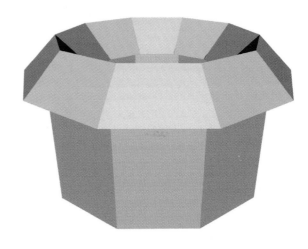

Figure T1-5. The location of the first timber. This is a partial top view.

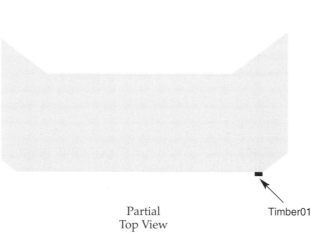

Partial
Top View

Timber01

Now, draw three horizontal timbers on the same side. See Figure T1-6. The timbers should be 2' by 1' by 60'. The ends of the horizontal timbers should be "inside" of the vertical timbers (the ends of the horizontal pieces will overlap the vertical pieces). Place one of the three timbers on the bottom, one on the top, and one in the middle. Name these timbers Timber03, Timber04, and Timber05.

Draw four more timbers to form an X in the top square and the bottom square. See Figure T1-7. Each timber should be 2' by 1' by 74'. Rotate the timbers so the ends are "inside" of the vertical and horizontal timbers. Name these timbers Timber06, Timber07, Timber08, and Timber09.

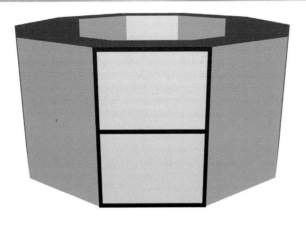

Figure T1-6. The vertical and horizontal timbers placed for the first side.

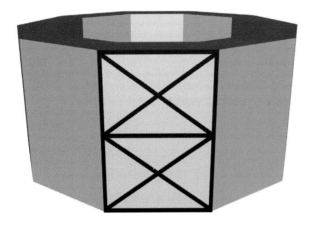

Figure T1-7. The crossing timbers placed for the first side.

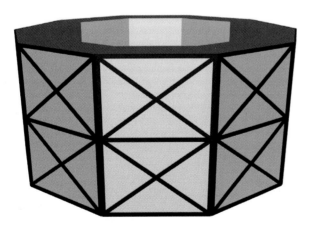

Figure T1-8. Timbers are placed on all 10 sides.

Spacing tool p.182

s+i

follow ingon

    The exposed timbers are completed for one of the 10 sides. Select the timbers and create a group called Timber Side 01. Then, copy and rotate the group to create the timbers for the other nine sides. Each copy needs to be rotated 36° (360° divided by 10 sides). Name the groups Timber Side 02, Timber Side 03, and so on. After rotating the copy, move it into the correct position. See Figure T1-8.

Help Cel

An array is the easiest way to create the remaining timbers. Create the array in the Top viewport with the reference coordinate system set to **World** and the **Use Transform Coordinate Center** button active. However, in order for this to work correctly, the walls must be centered on the world origin.

Entrance

With the walls, roof, and timbers in place, creating the entrance will finish the building portion of the model. First draw a box in the Top viewport 40′ wide and 30′ tall sticking out 20′ from one side of the walls. It is easiest if you work with a side "flat" to the view. Name the object Entrance House.

Next, in the Front or Left viewport, draw a triangle with a base 46′ wide and a height of 15′ at its apex. See Figure T1-9. Loft this triangle along a straight 25′ path. Name the object Entrance Roof. Place it on top of the Entrance House object and flush to the walls.

On each of the two front corners of the Entrance House object, draw a 3′ radius cylinder 60′ tall. Name the cylinders Tower01 and Tower02. Each of these will go through the roof of the entrance. Top each cylinder with a cone having a Radius 1 of 5′, Radius 2 of 0′, and height of 10′. Name the cones Tower Roof01 and Tower Roof02.

Finally, draw an arched door shape and extrude it 1′. Center this on the front of the entrance. Name the object Door. The entrance is now complete. See Figure T1-10.

Figure T1-9. The dimensions of the triangle to loft for the entrance roof.

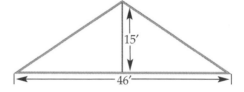

Figure T1-10. The entrance is finished.

Help Cel

If you want to add some flags to the tops of the towers, try using thin cylinders as flagpoles and extruding small triangles as the flags.

Trees and Bushes

Add a couple of trees behind the theater and a few bushes in front. The trees and bushes are very simplified. Draw a cone with a Radius 1 of 15', a Radius 2 of 5', and a height of 150'. Name it Tree Trunk01. Place it somewhere behind the theater. Draw another cone with the same radii, but a height of 200'. Name it Tree Trunk02. Place it behind the theater as well. Draw a sphere on top of each cone. Use your own dimensions. These spheres represent the "volume" of the leaves. Name the spheres Leaves01 and Leaves02.

Now, draw two long thin capsules to represent bushes along the entrance. The capsules should have a radius of about 4', and they should be about 75' long. Name these objects Bush01 and Bush02. Place them at ground level leading up to the doorway. See Figure T1-11.

Help Cel

A noise modifier can help make the tree leaves and bushes look less like simple objects.

Ground and Background

The ground and background are simply flat quad patches. In the Top viewport, draw a quad patch about 2000' square. Name this object Ground. Center the object on the theater. Also, make sure it is placed vertically at ground level.

In the Front viewport, draw another quad patch about 2000' square. Name this object Sky. Place it at the back edge of the Ground object.

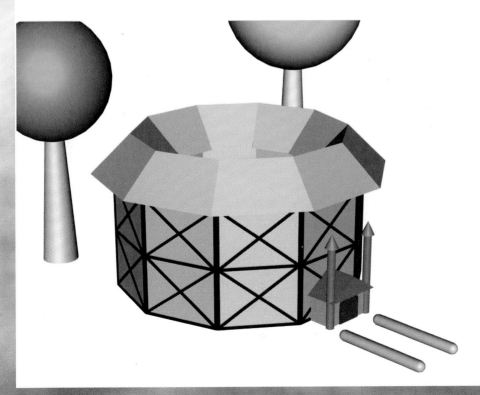

Figure T1-11. Trees and bushes are added to the scene.

Assigning Materials

There are only a few basic materials needed to finish the model. Most of these are located in the default 3ds max material library. You must also define two simple materials. Select the first material sample slot in the **Material Editor**. Define a light blue material by changing the diffuse color. Assign this material to the background. Next, define a dark green material in the second material sample slot. Assign it to the Leaves01 and Leaves02 objects.

Next, get the material Ground_Grass and assign it to the ground. Also get the material Wood_Bark and assign it to the tree trunks. Get the material Ground_Foliage and assign it to the bushes.

Get the material Concrete_Stucco. Assign it to the Walls object. Also assign it to the Entrance House, Tower01, and Tower02 objects.

Get the material Wood_Cedfence. Assign it to the Roof object. Also assign it to the Entrance Roof object and the two tower roof objects.

Finally, get the material Wood_Old. Select the timber groups and ungroup them. Then, assign the material to each timber. Also, assign the material to the door object.

Create a rendering of the scene. See Figure T1-12. Adjust the Perspective viewport as necessary to get a good view of the model. Save the rendering to a file.

Figure T1-12. The final rendering of the tutorial.

Discussion Questions

1) When the triangle was lofted to form the roof, did the resulting object sit on top of the walls or did you have to move it up? Why?
2) After the roof was lofted, what did you do to make it 10-sided instead of rounded?
3) When rotating the copies of the timber groups, where was each group rotated about?
4) Why were the timber groups ungrouped before applying the material? If you do not know the answer, try applying the material before ungrouping. Then, render the scene.
5) In the final scene, there are a few obviously unrealistic features. What are they? Can you come up with some ideas on how the problems might be fixed?

Section Two

MOVING TO REALISM

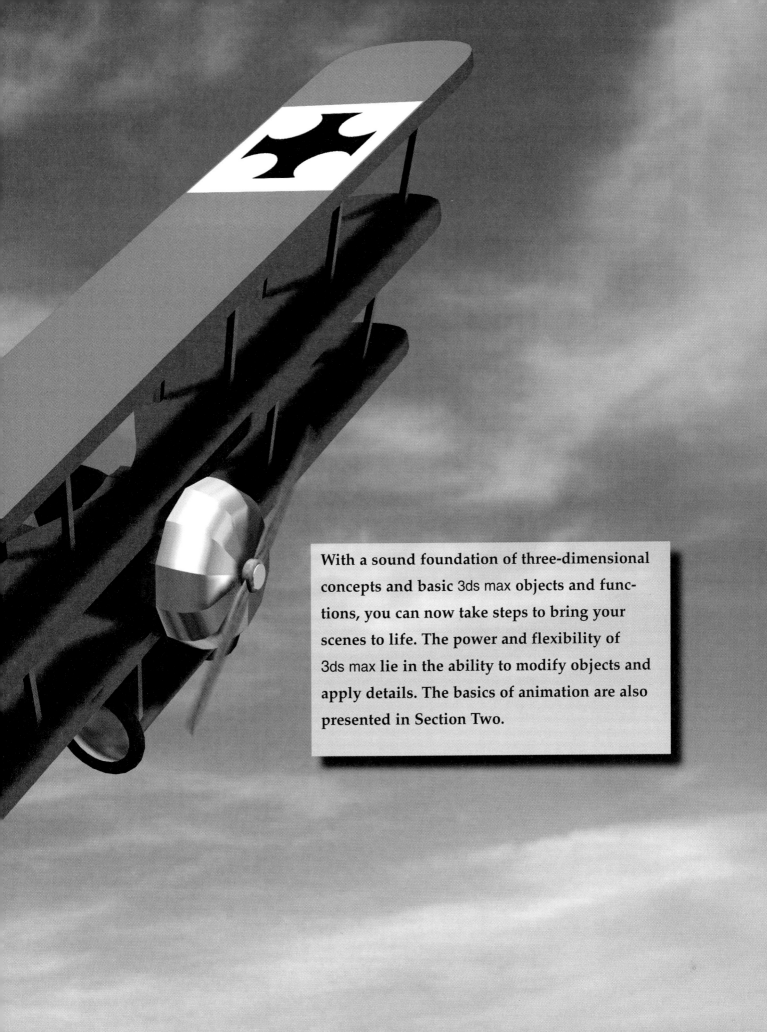

With a sound foundation of three-dimensional concepts and basic 3ds max objects and functions, you can now take steps to bring your scenes to life. The power and flexibility of 3ds max lie in the ability to modify objects and apply details. The basics of animation are also presented in Section Two.

Modeling with Modifiers

Objectives

After completing this chapter, you will be able to:

- Describe the functions of the mesh select and patch select modifiers.
- Explain how an object with an edit patch modifier applied differs from an editable patch object.
- Define FFD.
- Identify the types of materials used with a material modifier.
- Explain the uses for xform and linked xform modifiers.
- Identify applications for a normalize spline modifier.
- List the major differences between world space modifiers and object space modifiers.

Modifiers are used to change an object's form or shape. In other words, they modify an object. Using modifiers can be considered an editing function because you "edit" the base object. However, modifiers should be considered modeling tools. The power of 3ds max lies in the ability to apply and animate modifiers. As discussed in Chapter 5, modifiers are grouped by the type of function they perform. There are 12 different groups. These groups are:

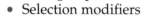

- Selection modifiers
- Surface
- Patch/spline editing
- Mesh editing
- Parametric deformers
- Free form deformers
- Animation modifiers
- UV coordinates
- Cache tools
- Subdivision surfaces
- NURBS editing
- Conversion modifiers

Each group may contain world space modifiers (WSMs) and object space modifiers (OSMs). WSMs are indicated by an asterisk before the modifier name.

This chapter covers selected modifiers from these modifier categories. However, 3ds max has many more than those covered here. One of the keys to effectively using modifiers is to know what a modifier does. One of the best ways of learning this is to experiment with each modifier. The basic principles of the modifiers presented in this chapter will get you "thinking" like a modifier. Once you are able to think like a modifier, it is easy to experiment with other modifiers.

Help Cel

The **Modifier List** drop-down list in the **Modify** tab is "selection sensitive." Only the modifiers that can be applied to the current selection are displayed in the drop-down list. In the **Modifiers** pull-down menu, the modifiers invalid for the current selection are greyed out.

Selection Modifiers

Selection modifiers are used to create sub-object selections. In general, a selection modifier creates a "branch" or "Y" in the modifier tree. In other words, once you apply a selection modifier, all other modifiers applied to the object after the selection are actually applied to the sub-object selection. This holds true until another selection modifier is applied.

There are seven selection modifiers available in the **Modifiers** pull-down menu. These are the mesh select, patch select, spline select, volume select, FFD (free form deformation) select, NURBS curve select, and NURBS surface select modifiers. The mesh select and patch select modifiers are discussed in the next sections.

Mesh Select

The *mesh select modifier* allows you to create a sub-object selection. This selection can then be modified independently without modifying the entire object. A common application for this is to select a portion of an object and then apply a sub-object material to the selection. See Figure 8-1.

Figure 8-1. This fireplace is a single object. A mesh select modifier was applied in conjunction with a sub-object material.

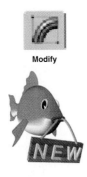

Modify

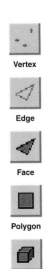

Vertex

Edge

Face

Polygon

Element

To apply a mesh select modifier, first select the object. Then, open the **Modifier List** drop-down list in the **Modify** tab of the **Command Panel**. Finally, pick **Mesh Select** in the **Selection Modifiers** area of the list. You can also pick **Selection Modifiers** in the **Modifiers** pull-down menu, and then pick **Mesh Select** in the cascading menu. The mesh select modifier appears in the modifier stack. The **Mesh Select Parameters** and **Soft Selection** rollouts are displayed at the bottom of the **Modify** tab.

Below the modifier stack, the **Show end result on/off toggle** is automatically turned off. However, if another modifier is applied and then you return to the **Mesh Select** level in the stack, this button can be turned on. The original mesh object is displayed as an orange wireframe. The end result is displayed as a white wireframe.

The **Mesh Select Parameters** rollout allows you to work with sub-objects and selection sets, and control display properties. See Figure 8-2. At the top of the rollout are five buttons allowing you to directly enter sub-object mode. Picking one of these buttons is the same as picking that sub-object in the modifier stack. You can select a single item, such as a vertex, with the cursor. You can also select multiple items using the [Ctrl] key or a region selection. When in sub-object mode for a mesh select modifier, the transform buttons are disabled. To apply a transform to a mesh sub-object selection, use the xform or linked xform modifier. These modifiers are discussed later in this chapter.

A selection set is named by picking in the **Named Selection Sets** drop-down list text box on the **Main** toolbar. This is located next to the **Align** button. Type a name for the selection set and press [Enter]. All named selection sets appear in this drop-down list. The sub-object level at which the selection set is created must be active to see the selection set.

Once a selection set is created, other modifiers can be applied to the items in the set. The modifiers affect only the items in the set. The object as a whole is not affected. For example, if you select the bottom portion of a cylinder, you can add a taper modifier to create a machine tool cutter bit. See Figure 8-3.

Figure 8-2. The **Mesh Select Parameters** rollout for a mesh select modifier.

Figure 8-3. A taper modifier was applied after a mesh select modifier to create the tapered end of this machine tool cutter.

Exercise 8-1

1) Draw a teapot using your own dimensions.
2) Apply a mesh select modifier. At the vertex sub-object level, select the vertices on the handle.
3) Name the selection set Handle. Then, apply a taper modifier to the selection set.
4) Apply another mesh select modifier. At the face sub-object level, select the faces on the lid's handle.
5) Name the selection set Lid Knob. Then, apply a bend modifier to the selection set.
6) Apply a third mesh select modifier. At the face sub-object level, select the faces on the spout.
7) Name the selection set Spout. Then, apply a noise modifier to the selection set.
8) Save the scene as ex08-01.max in the folder of your choice.

Patch Select

The *patch select* modifier works in the same way as the mesh select modifier. However, you can select sub-objects as if the object is a patch object. A *patch object* is a collection of Bézier patches. Patch objects are good to use when creating gentle curved surfaces, such as the fenders on a car. Patch objects are also discussed in the section *Edit Patch Modifier* later in this chapter.

Modify

To apply a patch modifier, first select the object. Then, open the **Modifier List** drop-down list in the **Modify** tab of the **Command Panel**. Finally, pick **Patch Select** in the **Selection Modifiers** area of the list. You can also pick **Selection Modifiers** in the **Modifiers** pull-down menu, and then pick **Patch Select** in the cascading menu. The patch select modifier appears in the modifier stack. The **Parameters** and **Soft Selection** rollouts are displayed at the bottom of the **Modify** tab.

The patch select modifier has four sub-objects. These are vertex, edge, patch, and element. To enter sub-object mode, expand the tree in the modifier stack. Then, select the sub-object level. You can also enter sub-object mode directly by picking the appropriate button at the top of the **Parameters** rollout. Make a sub-object selection and apply other modifiers as needed.

When the patch select modifier is highlighted in the modifier stack, the transform tools are disabled. To apply a transform to a patch sub-object selection, use the xform or linked xform modifier.

Help Cel

Objects can be permanently converted to patch objects, but the object's original parameters are lost.

Surface Modifiers

Surface modifiers, generally speaking, are used to work with the surface of an object. For example, you can use the material modifier to apply the components of a multi/sub-object material to different parts of an object. There are three modifiers in the surface modifiers category available in the **Modifiers** pull-down menu. These are the material, material by element, and disp approx modifiers. The material and disp approx modifiers are introduced in the next sections.

Material

Modify

The *material modifier* is used to change the material ID of the object or sub-object selection to which it is applied. This modifier is essential to applying multi/sub-object materials. You can use the material modifier with selection modifiers to create one object with several different materials. See Figure 8-4A. You can also use this modifier to animate material changes, such as the sequence of a stoplight. See Figure 8-4B. This modifier is covered in detail in Chapter 17.

To apply a material modifier, first select the object. Then, open the **Modifier List** drop-down list in the **Modify** tab of the **Command Panel**. Finally, pick **Material** in the **Surface Modifiers** area of the list. You can also pick **Surface** in the **Modifiers** pull-down menu, and then pick **Material** in the cascading menu. The material modifier appears in the modifier stack. The **Parameters** rollout is displayed at the bottom of the **Modify** tab.

A

B

Figure 8-4. A—The material applied to this sphere is a multi/sub-object material. B—Animating the material IDs can create the effect of a stoplight changing from green to yellow to red.

Displacement Approximation

The *disp approx,* or displacement approximation, modifier is used in conjunction with displacement mapping. Mapping is discussed in detail in Chapter 18. Displacement mapping is used to deform an object's surface geometry. A displacement mapped material can be applied to an editable mesh object without using a modifier. However, to apply the same material to a "non-mesh" object, the disp approx modifier must be applied. This modifier simulates a conversion of the object to an editable mesh. However, using the modifier stack, you still have access to the object's original parameters.

The disp approx modifier does not allow access to the sub-objects of an editable mesh. You must use a mesh select or edit mesh modifier to gain access to editable mesh sub-objects. If these modifiers are applied, displacement mapping can be used on the object. However, the effect may be different, and unwanted, than when the disp approx modifier is applied.

Modify

To apply a disp approx modifier, first select the object. Then, open the **Modifier List** drop-down list in the **Modify** tab of the **Command Panel**. Finally, pick **Disp Approx** in the **Surface Modifiers** area of the list. You can also pick **Surface** in the **Modifiers** pull-down menu, and then pick **Disp Approx** in the cascading menu. The disp approx modifier appears in the modifier stack. The **Displacement Approx** (approximation) rollout is displayed at the bottom of the **Modify** tab.

Help Cel

Applying a disp approx modifier may result in different displacement mapping in comparison to converting the object into an editable mesh.

Patch/Spline Editing Modifiers

Patch/spline editing modifiers are used to alter the mesh of a patch object or spline. The shape of the object may or may not be changed. For example, you can normalize the steps on a spline by using a normalize spline modifier. On the other hand, you can turn a network of splines into a mesh by applying a surface modifier. There are 10 patch/spline editing modifiers available in the **Modifiers** pull-down menu. The edit patch, normalize spline, and surface modifiers are covered in the next sections.

Edit Patch

The *edit patch modifier* allows you to edit an object as if it is an editable patch object. With the edit patch modifier, the base object is not actually converted to an editable patch. The advantage of this, as with the edit spline and edit mesh modifiers, is the base object remains parametric. You can go back in the stack at any time and change the base object's parameters.

Modify

To apply an edit patch modifier, first select the object. Then, open the **Modifier List** drop-down list in the **Modify** tab of the **Command Panel**. Finally, pick **Edit Patch** in the **Patch/Spline Editing** area of the list. You can also pick **Patch/Spline Editing** in the **Modifiers** pull-down menu, and then pick **Edit Patch** in the cascading menu. The edit patch modifier appears in the modifier stack. The **Selection**, **Soft Selection**, **Geometry**, and **Surface Properties** rollouts are displayed at the bottom of the **Modify** tab. See Figure 8-5.

Figure 8-5. The **Selection** rollout for an edit patch modifier.

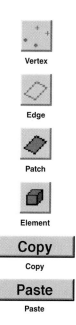

There are four sub-object modes at which you can edit a patch. These are vertex, edge, patch, and element. You can select the mode by expanding the sub-object tree in the modifier stack and selecting the mode. You can also enter the sub-object mode directly by picking the **Vertex**, **Edge**, **Patch**, or **Element** button at the top of the **Selection** rollout.

The **Selection** rollout also provides options for working with named selection sets and filters. Picking the **Copy** button in the **Named Selections:** area opens the **Copy Named Selection** dialog box. See Figure 8-6. Picking a selection in this dialog box copies it to a buffer. Then, you can use the **Paste** button in the **Named Selections:** area to paste the selection onto another object.

The check boxes in the **Filter** area allow you to limit what can be selected. If the **Vertices** check box is unchecked, you cannot select any vertex on the object. If the **Vectors** check box is unchecked, you cannot select any of the vector control points. See Figure 8-7. Unchecking one of the check boxes greys out the other and keeps it checked. By default, both of these check boxes are checked, meaning you can select both vertices and vector control points.

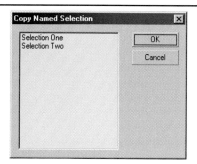

Figure 8-6. You can copy named selections to a buffer and then paste them onto an object.

Figure 8-7. The vertices are filtered, so you can only select vectors.

Vector

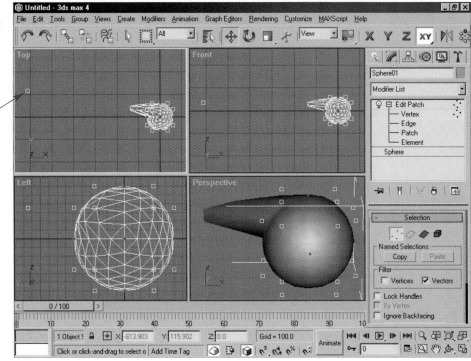

Below the **Filter** area is the **Lock Handles** check box. When checked, this locks the handles of a vertex so they move together. When one handle is moved, the other handles mirror the movement about the vertex. Unless you are in **Vertex** sub-object mode, this check box has no effect. Also, this check box only applies to corner vertices. The handles of a coplanar vertex are automatically locked.

At the very bottom of the **Selection** rollout is a status line. This indicates what is currently selected.

The **Geometry** rollout contains options for editing the patch object. In addition, depending on which sub-object level is selected, other rollouts may be displayed to allow further refinement of the patch.

Help Cel

Once an edit patch modifier is applied, editing the object is identical to editing an editable patch object.

Exercise 8-2

1) Draw a capsule similar to the one shown below. Use your own dimensions.
2) Apply an edit patch modifier. At the patch sub-object level, select the middle of the capsule. Name the selection Middle.
3) Scale the selection to about 50%.
4) Select the top of the capsule while still at the patch sub-object level. Name the selection Top.
5) Apply a bend modifier to the selection with an angle of about 150°. Set the bend axis as the X axis.
6) Apply another edit patch modifier. At the vertex sub-object level, select the vertices on the bottom of the capsule. Name the selection Bottom.
7) Move the vertices straight down until the capsule is about twice its original height.
8) Save the model as ex08-02.max in the folder of your choice.

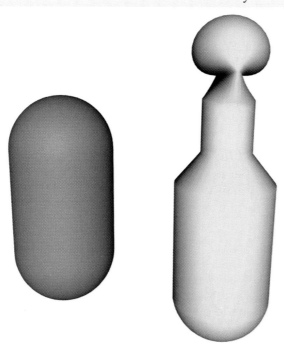

Normalize Spline

The *normalize spline modifier* is used to equally space vertices along the length of a spline. This is often done when the line is used as a motion path to generate a constant velocity.

To apply a normalize spline modifier, select the spline. Then, open the **Modifier List** drop-down list in the **Modify** tab of the **Command Panel**. Finally, pick **Normalize Spl.** in the **Patch/Spline Editing** area of the list. You can also pick **Patch/Spline Editing** in the **M**odifiers pull-down menu, and then pick **Normalize Spline** in the cascading menu. The normalize spline modifier appears as **Normalize Spl.** in the modifier stack. The **Parameters** rollout is displayed at the bottom of the **Modify** tab. See Figure 8-8.

Modify

NEW

Figure 8-8. The **Parameters** rollout for a normalize spline modifier.

The value in the **Seg Length:** spinner is a relative length of each segment. For example, if 20 is entered, 3ds max attempts to equally divide the entire spline into segments 20 units long. The original vertices are ignored when this modifier is applied.

Surface

The *surface modifier* generates a patch grid from a combination of splines. This modifier is most commonly used to generate organic objects, such as animals or SciFi characters. See Figure 8-9. Where the spline segments form three- or four-sided polygons, the modifier creates a patch. An edit patch modifier can be placed in the stack above the surface modifier to further refine the patch surface.

There are a few basic rules for the splines used with the surface modifier. First, whenever splines cross, each spline should have a vertex. Also, the intersecting splines must form three- or four-sided polygons. The spline can be made up of individual splines, but they must all be attached to each other. Finally, make sure you have enough splines so 3ds max can accurately calculate the patch surface.

Modify

To apply a surface modifier, select the attached splines. Then, open the **Modifier List** drop-down list in the **Modify** tab of the **Command Panel**. Finally, pick **Surface** in the **Patch/Spline Editing** area of the list. You can also pick **Patch/Spline Editing** in the **Modifiers** pull-down menu, and then pick **Surface** in the cascading menu. The surface modifier appears in the modifier stack. The **Parameters** rollout is displayed at the bottom of the **Modify** tab. See Figure 8-10.

The **Spline Options** area sets how the splines are treated. The value in the **Threshold:** spinner is the distance in current drawing units used to weld vertices. For example, if the units are generic and the **Threshold:** value is 1.5, any vertex 1.5 units from a given vertex is welded to that vertex. Checking the **Flip Normals** check box reverses the direction of normals on the resulting patch. Checking the **Remove interior patches** check box deletes patches inside of the object. For example, if several

Figure 8-9. A—The network of splines is created for use with the surface modifier. B—The surface modifier is applied to the spline network. (Discreet, a division of Autodesk)

Figure 8-10. The **Parameters** rollout for a surface modifier.

closed cross sections are used to create the surface, patches might also be created inside the cross section. These are not needed. Checking this check box removes these patches. Checking the **Use only selected segs.** check box applies the surface modifier only to segments selected with the edit spline modifier, if below the surface modifier in the stack.

The **Patch Topology** area is used to set the number of steps between each spline vertex. The higher the value in the **Steps:** spinner, the smoother the curve produced by the modifier. This value is the number of steps between *each* vertex. Therefore, keep the value low to reduce polygon count.

Exercise

Exercise 8-3

1) Draw three ngon shapes. Set one to have three sides, one to have four sides, and one to have five sides.
2) Apply a surface modifier to each ngon. What happened? Why?
3) Reset 3ds max without saving.
4) Draw a spline with three segments similar to the profile shown below on the top right.
5) Copy the spline four times. Adjust each copy to get variations between the cross sections.
6) Connect the endpoints of each cross section. Use the endpoint snap.
7) Connect all splines together to create a single network.
8) Apply a surface modifier to the spline network.
9) Rotate the object or **Perspective** view to see the surface.
10) Save the model as ex08-03.max in the folder of your choice.

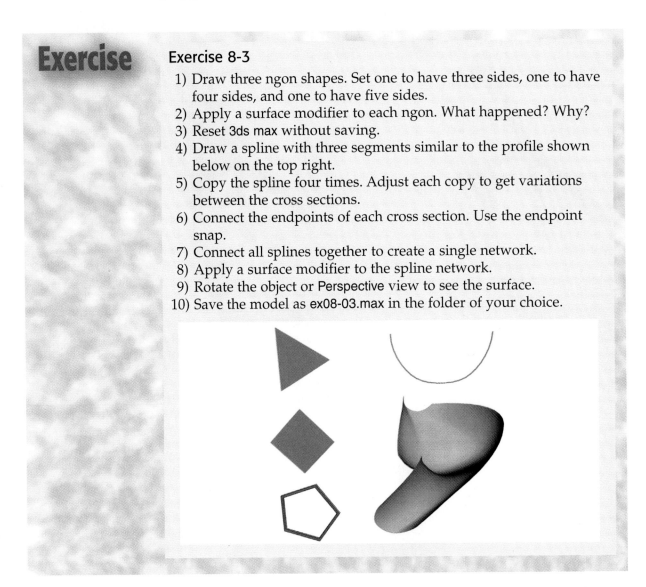

Mesh Editing Modifiers

Mesh editing modifiers are used to alter the mesh of a mesh object. The shape of the object may or may not be changed. For example, you can use the delete mesh modifier to delete a sub-object selection. On the other hand, you can increase the surface subdivisions of a mesh object using the tessellate modifier. There are 11 mesh editing modifiers available in the **Modifiers** pull-down menu. These are the delete mesh, edit mesh, face extrude, extrude, normal, smooth, tessellate, STL check, cap holes, vertex paint, and optimize modifiers. The edit mesh, delete mesh, and tessellate modifiers are discussed in the next sections.

Edit Mesh

The *edit mesh modifier* allows you to edit an object as if it is an editable mesh object. With the edit mesh modifier, the base object is not actually converted to an editable mesh. The advantage of this, as with the edit spline and edit patch modifiers, is that the base object remains parametric. You can go back in the stack at any time and change the base object's parameters. The edit mesh modifier is used in a very similar manner to how the edit spline and edit patch modifiers are used.

To apply an edit mesh modifier, first select the object. Then, open the **Modifier List** drop-down list in the **Modify** tab of the **Command Panel**. Finally, pick **Edit Mesh** in the **Mesh Editing** area of the list. You can also pick **M̲esh Editing** in the **M̲odifiers** pull-down menu, and then pick **Edit Mesh** in the cascading menu. The edit mesh modifier appears in the modifier stack. The **Selection**, **Soft Selection**, and **Edit Geometry** rollouts are displayed at the bottom of the **Modify** tab.

There are five sub-object modes at which you can edit a mesh. These are vertex, edge, face, polygon, and element. You can select the mode by expanding the sub-object tree in the modifier stack and selecting the mode. You can also enter the sub-object mode directly by picking the **Vertex**, **Edge**, **Face**, **Polygon**, or **Element** button at the top of the **Selection** rollout.

Modify

Face　Vertex

Polygon　Edge

Element

Help Cel

Once an edit mesh modifier is applied, editing the object is identical to editing an editable mesh object.

Delete Mesh

The *delete mesh modifier* allows you to remove portions of an object. While this can be done with standard sub-object editing methods, using a modifier keeps the base object parametric. See Figure 8-11.

For example, if you select several vertices in sub-object mode and press the [Delete] key, the vertices are permanently removed from the object. However, the object must be an editable mesh. On the other hand, you can apply a mesh select modifier to select vertices. Then, apply the

Delete

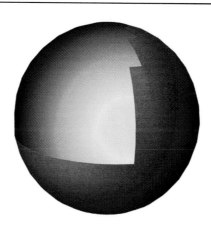

Figure 8-11. A portion of the sphere on the left was selected using a mesh select modifier. The selection then had a delete mesh modifier applied, as shown on the right.

Modify

delete mesh modifier to the selection. The base object remains parametric. Also, the deleted vertices can be restored later by simply removing the delete mesh modifier from the stack.

To apply a delete mesh modifier, first make a sub-object selection on the object. This selection can consist of vertices, faces, edges, patches, etc. Then, open the **Modifier List** drop-down list in the **Modify** tab of the **Command Panel**. Finally, pick **Delete Mesh** in the **Mesh Editing** area of the list. You can also pick **Mesh Editing** in the **Modifiers** pull-down menu, and then pick **Delete Mesh** in the cascading menu. The selected sub-objects are removed from the object and the delete mesh modifier appears in the modifier stack. There are no rollouts associated with the delete mesh modifier, nor are there any sub-objects.

Help Cel

If you apply the delete mesh modifier to an object without a sub-object selection, the entire object is deleted. This is probably not what you want.

Exercise

Exercise 8-4

1) Draw a sphere using your own dimensions.
2) Apply a mesh select modifier to the sphere. At the vertex sub-object level, select the middle of the sphere.
3) Apply a delete mesh modifier to the selection. See the figure below. Note: A 2-sided material has been applied for illustration purposes.
4) Save the model as ex08-04.max in the folder of your choice.

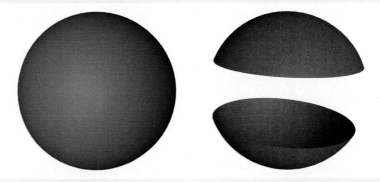

Tessellate

The *tessellate modifier* is used to subdivide faces on an object. This is done to add smoothness for rendering. Subdividing faces also ensures animated joints, such as those in bones systems, have enough faces to provide smooth motion. See Figure 8-12.

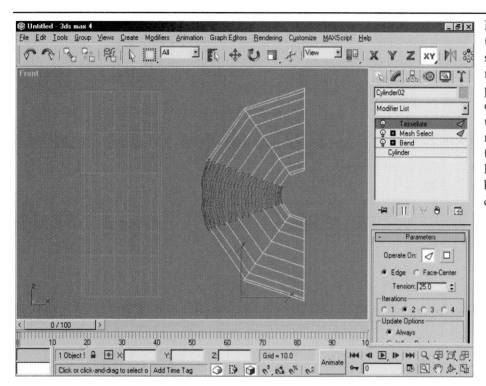

Figure 8-12. The tessellate modifier subdivides faces. The middle (yellow) portion of this cylinder was selected using a mesh select modifier. The selection then had a tessellate modifier applied before the entire cylinder was bent.

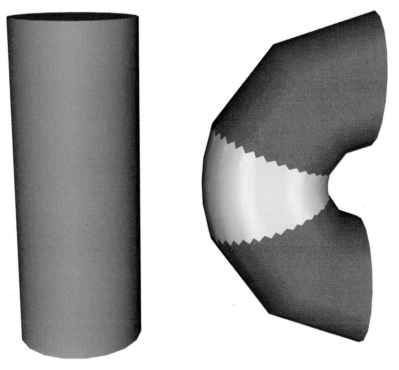

Modify

Faces

Polygons

To apply a tessellate modifier, first select the object or make a sub-object selection. Then, open the **Modifier List** drop-down list in the **Modify** tab of the **Command Panel**. Finally, pick **Tessellate** in the **Mesh Editing** area of the list. You can also pick **Mesh Editing** in the **Modifiers** pull-down menu, and then pick **Tessellate** in the cascading menu.

At the top of the **Parameters** rollout are the **Operate On:** buttons. These buttons determine the elements to which the modifier is applied. When the **Faces** button is on, 3ds max treats selected elements as triangular faces. When the **Polygons** button is on, 3ds max treats selected elements as polygon facets.

When the **Face-Center** radio button is on, the selection is subdivided from the center of each item to its vertices. When the **Edge** radio button is on, the selection is subdivided from the middle of each edge. Also, a tension can be specified when the **Edge** radio button is on. A value of 0 in the **Tension:** spinner means that the new faces are flat. A positive value makes the new faces convex. A negative value makes the new faces concave.

The **Iterations** area is used to determine how many times the selection is subdivided. You can pick the **1**, **2**, **3**, or **4** radio button to have the selection subdivided that many times. If you need more than four subdivisions, apply the modifier a second time.

The **Update Options** area allows you to set when the object is updated. By default, the **Always** radio button is on, resulting in updates when a change is made. However, on a complex model, you may want to change this setting to **Manually** or **When Rendering** to save regeneration time.

Help Cel

Never use the tessellate modifier on an object to be morphed. Also, tessellation can quickly create an object with far too many faces. Use this modifier with care.

Exercise 8-5

1) Draw a box using your own dimensions. Set the number of length, width, and height segments to 4.
2) Apply a mesh select modifier. At the face sub-object level, select the middle faces on the top of the box.
3) Apply a tessellate modifier to the selection. Set the iterations to 2. Notice how the selection no longer has straight-edged boundaries.
4) Save the model as **ex08-05.max** in the folder of your choice.

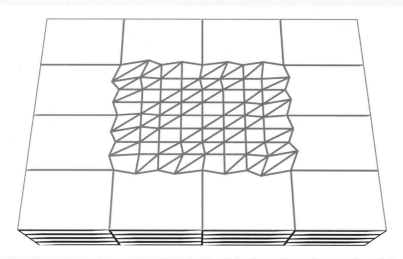

Parametric Deformer Modifiers

Parametric deformer modifiers are used to change the shape of an object based on parameters you enter. For example, you can bend an object a specified number of degrees. There are 19 parametric deformer modifiers available in the **Modifiers** pull-down menu. The displace, lattice, push, and xform modifiers are covered in the next sections.

Displace

The *displace modifier* is used to distort the surface of an object. This modifier is often used to emboss an object with a bitmap image or a procedural map. Using an animation as the bitmap, you can create a moving force field effect, for example. See Figure 8-13. The displacement can also be applied directly to the gizmo instead of through a bitmap. In this case, you would most likely apply the modifier to a sub-object selection set.

To apply a displace modifier, first select the object or make a sub-object selection. Then, open the **Modifier List** drop-down list in the **Modify** tab of the **Command Panel**. Finally, pick **Displace** in the **Parametric Modifiers** area of the list. You can also pick **Parametric Deformers** in the **Modifiers** pull-down menu, and then pick **Displace** in the cascading menu. The displace modifier appears in the modifier stack. The **Parameters** rollout appears at the bottom of the **Modify** tab. This modifier has one sub-object—its gizmo.

Modify

Figure 8-13. A force field effect can be created with a displace modifier. A—The unmodified object. B—The force field beginning to affect the left side of the object.

A

B

C

D

Figure 8-13. C—The force field passing through the middle of the object. D—The force field exiting the right side of the object.

In the **Displacement:** area of the **Parameters** rollout, specify the amount of displacement. The value in the **Strength:** spinner determines how much the selection is displaced. Values greater than 0 move the selection away from the gizmo. Values less than zero move the selection toward the gizmo. Entering a value in the **Decay:** spinner decreases the strength of the displacement the farther it is from the gizmo center.

Using a Bitmap for Displace

The **Image:** area of the **Parameters** rollout is used to specify a map or bitmap as the source for displacement. 3ds max uses shades of grey to determine the displacement pattern. Any areas of pure white displace the farthest away from the gizmo. Areas of pure black project the most toward the gizmo.

The center of projection is determined by the value in the **Center:** spinner in the **Displacement:** area. Check the **Luminance Center** check box. Then, enter a value in the spinner. The default value of 0.5 corresponds to a grey value of 128. This is one half of 256 shades of grey. A value of 0.0 corresponds to a grey value of 0, or pure black. A value of 1.0 corresponds to a grey value of 256, or pure white.

To assign a bitmap as the basis for displacement, pick the top button under **Bitmap:** in the **Image:** area. By default, this button is labeled **None**. The **Select Displacement Image** dialog box is opened. See Figure 8-14. Select a bitmap image and then pick the **Open** button. The selection is displaced based on the greyscale equivalent of the image. To remove the bitmap, pick the **Remove Bitmap** button.

To assign a procedural map as the basis for displacement, pick the top button below **Map:**. By default, this button is labeled **None**. The **Material/Map Browser** is opened. See Figure 8-15. Select a procedural map and then pick **OK**. The selection is displaced based on the greyscale equivalent of the procedural map. To remove the procedural map, pick the **Remove Map** button. Mapping is discussed in detail in Chapter 18.

You can apply both a bitmap and a procedural map. In addition, you can apply two bitmaps by selecting the **Bitmap** procedural map.

The **Blur:** spinner at the bottom of the **Image:** area is used to soften the edges of a bitmap or procedural map. The default value of 0.0 produces hard edges. Increasing the value softens the edges. The maximum value is 10.0.

Help Cel

If you are using a procedural map for displacement, define the map in the **Material Editor** first. Then, "get" the map from the **Material Editor** using the **Material/Map Browser**.

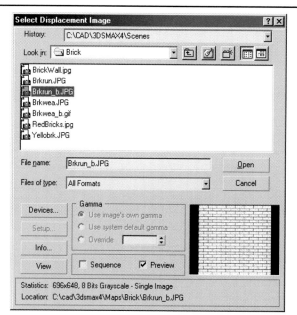

Figure 8-14.
A—Selecting a bitmap to use with the displace modifier. B—The effect on the object before and after the modifier is applied.

A

B

Setting Mapping Coordinates

The **Map:**, **Channel:**, and **Alignment:** areas of the **Parameters** rollout are used to specify how the map is placed on the object. These options are the same as the corresponding options used with the UVW map modifier. The UVW modifier is used to properly align maps on an object. It is discussed in detail in Chapter 17.

Figure 8-15.
A—Selecting a
checker procedural
map to use with the
displace modifier.
B—The effect on the
object before and after
the modifier is
applied.

A

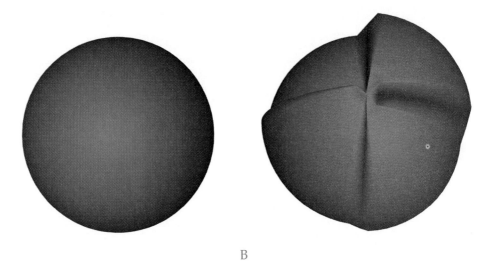

B

Exercise 8-6

1) Draw an oil tank as shown below. Use your own dimensions.
2) Apply a displace modifier to the oil tank.
3) Set the mapping to planar and the alignment to "fit."
4) Assign the Brice.jpg file as a bitmap for displacement. This file is located in the 3ds max \Maps\Backgrounds folder.
5) Set the displacement strength to about 25. Depending on the size of your oil tank, this value may need to be higher or lower.
6) Rotate the object or Perspective view to see the displacement.
7) Save the model as ex08-06.max in the folder of your choice.

Lattice

The *lattice modifier* creates a wireframe object based on the segments and edges of an object. See Figure 8-16. You can also have one of three polygon shapes placed at the intersection of the "wires," or struts.

To apply a lattice modifier, select the object. Then, open the **Modifier List** drop-down list in the **Modify** tab of the **Command Panel**. Finally, select **Lattice** in the **Parametric Modifiers** area of the list. You can also select **Parametric Deformers** in the **Modifiers** pull-down menu, and then pick **Lattice** in the cascading menu. The lattice modifier appears in the modifier stack and the **Parameters** rollout is displayed at the bottom of the **Modify** tab. There are no sub-objects for this modifier.

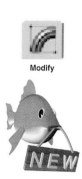

Modify

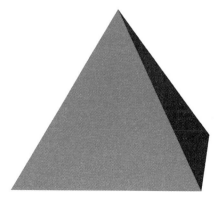
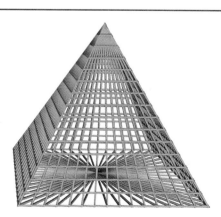

Figure 8-16. The object on the right is created by applying a lattice modifier to the object on the left.

In the **Geometry** area of the **Parameters** rollout, specify if you want the wireframe to be on the struts, at the joints, or both. In the **Struts** rollout, specify the size of the strut. Also, set the number of sides and segments for each strut. In the **Joints** area, specify the shape of each joint and its size. You can also assign material IDs to the struts and joints individually. Finally, in the **Mapping Coordinates** area, set how mapping coordinates are applied to the object.

Exercise

Exercise 8-7

1) Draw a torus knot using your own dimensions. You may want to reduce the number of sides and segments so as not to "bog down" your computer.
2) Apply a lattice modifier to the torus knot.
3) Adjust the radius settings of the struts and the joints to obtain a proportional lattice.
4) Set the struts to smooth.
5) Change the joint type to icosa.
6) Display only the joints. Increase the joint radius if necessary.
7) Save the model as ex08-07.max in the folder of your choice.

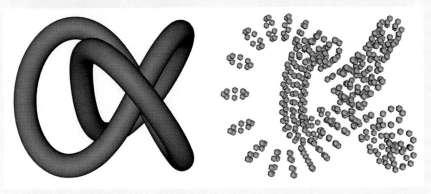

Push

The *push modifier* allows you to scale an object up (out) or down (in) along the normals of its faces. The normals are calculated as the average of all vertex normals. The modifier can also be applied to sub-object selections.

Modify

To apply a push modifier, select the object or make a sub-object selection. Then, open the **Modifier List** drop-down list in the **Modify** tab of the **Command Panel**. Finally, select **Push** in the **Parametric Modifiers** area of the list. You can also select **Parametric Deformers** in the **Modifiers** pulldown menu, and then pick **Push** in the cascading menu. The push modifier appears in the modifier stack and the **Parameters** rollout is displayed at the bottom of the **Modify** tab. See Figure 8-17. There are no sub-objects for this modifier. In the **Push Value:** spinner, enter the number of units to push the selection. Positive values push outward. Negative values push inward.

Figure 8-17. The **Parameters** rollout for a push modifier.

Exercise 8-8

1) Draw a sphere. Use your own dimensions.
2) Apply a mesh select modifier. At the face sub-object level, select the middle portion of the sphere.
3) Apply a push modifier to the selection. Enter a positive push value, such as 40.
4) Apply another mesh select modifier. At the face sub-object level, select the top portion of the sphere.
5) Apply a push modifier to the selection. Enter a negative push value, such as –15.
6) Rotate the object or Perspective view to see the effects of the push.
7) Save the model as ex08-08.max in the folder of your choice.

Exercise

Xform

Xform is an abbreviation for transform. Applying an *xform modifier* is the only way to animate sub-object transformations when the "select" modifiers are used. The xform modifier can also be used to place a transform into the modifier stack. The *linked xform modifier* is a variation of the xform modifier, where the transform is controlled by the transform of another object. The linked xform modifier is discussed later in this chapter.

Modify

To apply an xform modifier, first select the object or make a sub-object selection. Then, open the **Modifier List** drop-down list in the **Modify** tab of the **Command Panel**. Finally, select **XForm** in the **Parametric Modifiers** area of the list. You can also select **Parametric Deformers** in the **Modifiers** pull-down menu, and then pick **XForm** in the cascading menu. The xform modifier appears in the modifier stack. There are no rollouts associated with this modifier.

The modifier has center and gizmo sub-objects. The transformation is applied at the gizmo sub-object level. Expand the sub-object tree and highlight **Gizmo**. Apply any transforms needed. If you are animating the selection, make sure you have first turned on the **Toggle Animation Mode** button. You can also transform the gizmo's center at the sub-object level.

Free Form Deformer Modifiers

A *free form deformation (FFD) modifier* surrounds the object with a box. The box is made up of a lattice and control points. The lattice and control points can be adjusted to deform the object. See Figure 8-18. There are five free form deformer modifiers available in the **Modifiers** pull-down menu. These are the FFD 2x2x2, FFD 3x3x3, FFD 4x4x4, FFD box, and FFD cylinder modifiers. All five are very similar.

FFD Types

There are several different types of FFD modifiers. The FFD box modifier is designed to be used with boxes. The FFD cylinder modifier is designed to be used with cylinders and tubes. With these two types, you can set the number of control points in the lattice.

The other three types of FFDs are named based on the number of control points. These are FFD 2x2x2, FFD 3x3x3, and FFD 4x4x4. The numbers relate to the number of control points on each edge of the lattice box. For example, the FFD 4x4x4 modifier has 4 control points on each axis of the lattice box. This makes a total of 16 on each face of the lattice box for a total of 96 control points in the lattice. The number of control points cannot be changed with these three types of FFDs.

Applying and Using FFDs

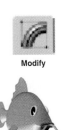

Modify

To apply an FFD modifier, first select the object or make a sub-object selection. Then, open the **Modifier List** drop-down list in the **Modify** tab of the **Command Panel**. Finally, select the type of FFD you want to use in the **Free Form Deformations** area of the list. You can also select **Free Form Deformers** in the **Modifiers** pull-down menu, and then pick the type of FFD in the cascading menu. The selected modifier appears in the modifier stack. The **FFD Parameters** rollout appears at the bottom of the **Modify** tab. This rollout is discussed later in this chapter.

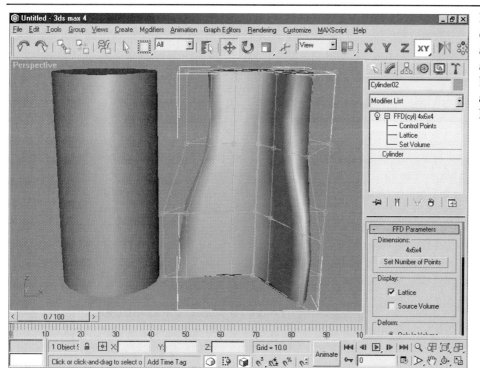

A

Figure 8-18. A—The object on the right has an FFD modifier applied and adjusted. B—The object before and after applying the FFD modifier.

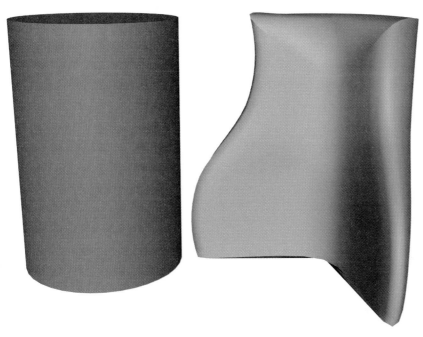

B

Sub-Object Levels

There are three sub-object levels to an FFD. These are **Control Points**, **Lattice**, and **Set Volume**. To enter sub-object mode, expand the sub-object tree in the modifier stack. Then, pick the appropriate sub-object level.

The *control points* are the "vertices" of the lattice. By transforming the control points, you change the shape of the lattice. This, in turn, deforms the object. You can select single or multiple control points using standard 3ds max selection methods.

The *lattice* is the box surrounding the object. You can transform the lattice in relation to the object. By moving the lattice so it "splits" the object, you can apply the FFD to only a portion of the object. You can also animate the lattice transformation. For example, if you make the lattice into the shape of a wave, you can animate the wave passing through the object.

The *set volume* sub-object level is designed to allow fitting the lattice closely to the object. For example, if the object is irregularly shaped, a standard "box" lattice does not closely match the shape of the object. By transforming the control points and lattice at the set volume sub-object level, you can make the lattice conform to the object's surface. See Figure 8-19. Transforms applied at the set volume sub-object level do not affect the object, only the shape of the lattice.

Help Cel

When transforming control points in sub-object mode, it is often helpful to lock the selection with the space bar. This ensures the transform is not accidentally applied to a different control point.

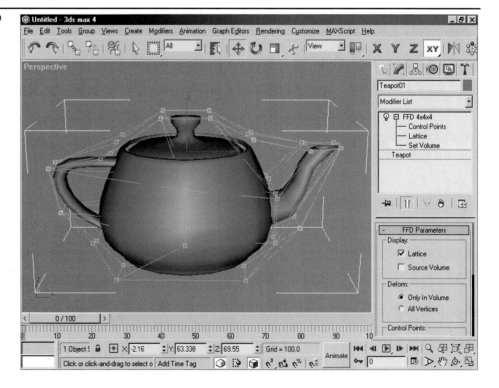

Figure 8-19. The FFD 4x4x4 lattice is adjusted to better fit the shape of the teapot.

FFD Parameters Rollout

The information in the **FFD Parameters** rollout depends on which type of FFD is applied. The FFD box and FFD cylinder parameters rollouts have all the information found in the FFD 2x2x2, FFD 3x3x3, and FFD 4x4x4 parameters rollouts, plus additional information. See Figure 8-20.

The **Display:** area is used to control how the lattice is displayed in the viewport. When the **Lattice** check box is checked, lines are drawn between the control points of the lattice. When unchecked, only the control points are displayed in the viewport. When the **Source Volume** check box is unchecked, the lattice displays its shape with transforms applied. When checked, the original shape of the lattice is displayed.

The **Deform:** area determines how the deformation is applied to the object. When the **Only In Volume** radio button is on, only the portion of the object lying inside of the lattice is deformed. When the **All Vertices** radio button is on, the deformation is applied to the entire object, even if a portion of it lies outside of the lattice. The deformation is applied as a continuation of the lattice, not a relocation.

The **Control Points:** area provides some tools for working with control points. Picking the **Reset** button returns all control points to their position prior to transforms. This allows you to easily start over. Picking the **Animate All** button places controllers in **Track View** for each control point. A controller is automatically placed in **Track View** for an individual control point if it is animated, regardless of this setting. **Track View** is discussed later in this text.

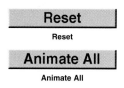

Reset

Animate All

When the **Conform to Shape** button is picked, 3ds max attempts to place the lattice on the object as a skin. This is determined by a straight line from the object's center to the control point. The control point is then moved to where the line intersects the object. See Figure 8-21. When the **Inside Points** check box is checked, any control points inside the object are moved. When the **Outside Points** check box is checked, any control

Conform to Shape

A

B

Figure 8-20.
A—The **FFD Parameters** rollout for 2x2x2, 3x3x3, and 4x4x4 FFD modifiers.
B—The **FFD Parameters** rollout for box and cylindrical FFD modifiers.

Figure 8-21. The object on the left has a 4x4x4 FFD modifier applied. On the right, the same object has the **Conform to Shape** option turned on. Note: Both object gizmos are shown for illustration purposes only.

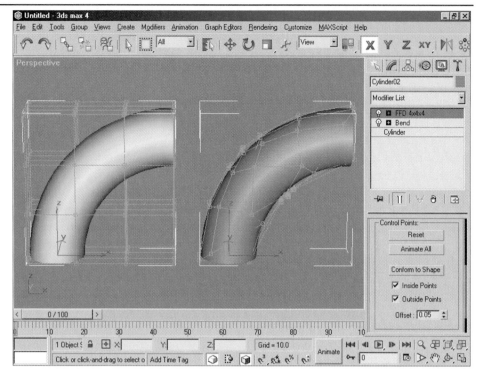

points outside the object are moved. When both are checked, all control points are moved. The value in the **Offset:** spinner is the number of drawing units the control points are placed from the object's surface.

In addition to the features described above, the **FFD Parameters** rollout for the FFD box and FFD cylinder modifiers have other options. At the top of the rollout is the **Dimensions:** area. This displays the number of vertices on each lattice axis. Picking the **Set Number of Points** button displays the **Set FFD Dimensions** dialog box. See Figure 8-22. In this dialog box, you can set the number of control points on each axis of the lattice. Make sure you change the number of control points *before* applying any transformations.

The **Deform:** area has additional options as well. When the **All Vertices** radio button is on, the **Falloff:** spinner is enabled. The value in

Set Number of Points

Figure 8-22. A—Setting the number of control points for an FFD box modifier. B—Setting the number of control points for an FFD cylinder modifier.

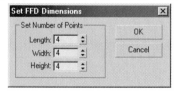

A

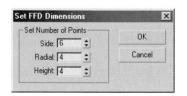

B

this spinner determines the distance from the lattice beyond which the deformation is not applied. The units for this spinner are determined by the size of the lattice. The lattice is 1.0 units wide, long, and tall. Therefore, unless the lattice is square, the value in the **Falloff:** spinner has different effects on different sides of the object.

Also in the **Deform:** area are the **Tension:** and **Continuity:** spinners. These values control how much effect the deformation has on the object. Tension and continuity are discussed in detail in Chapter 16.

The **Selection:** area is an additional option area available with the FFD box and FFD cylinder modifiers. This area contains three buttons that act as filters and can be turned on in any combination. They allow you to select all control points on the specified axis when only one point is selected. For example, if the **All X** button is on and you pick a corner control point, all of the control points in line with that point on the X axis are selected. If the **All X** and **All Y** buttons are on, all the control points in line with the selected point on the X and Y axes are selected. See Figure 8-23.

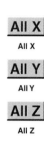

All X

All Y

All Z

Animating FFDs

Animating an FFD modifier is easy. After the modifier is applied, move to the first keyframe. Then, turn on the **Toggle Animation Mode** button. Enter the sub-object mode at which you want to animate. Then, apply the transformations. Continue to the next keyframe, and so on. After exiting animation mode, you can fine-tune the animation using **Track View**. This is discussed in Chapter 16. Animation is introduced in Chapter 14.

Toggle Animation Mode

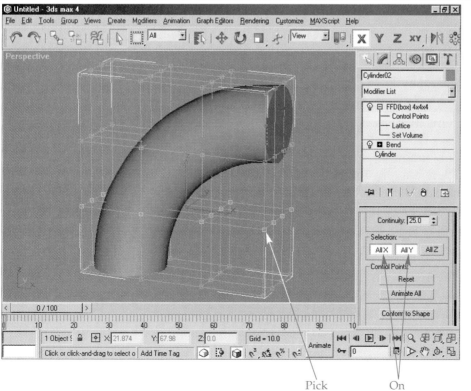

Figure 8-23. You can select all vertices on one or more axes by turning on the buttons in the **Selection:** area and picking a single control point.

Pick　　On

Exercise

Exercise 8-9

1) Draw a sphere using your own dimensions.
2) Apply an FFD 4x4x4 modifier to the sphere.
3) At the control points sub-object level, select the middle four points on one side. Move the points out to form a spike.
4) Repeat the procedure with the middle four points on the other five sides of the lattice.
5) At the lattice sub-object level, move the gizmo left and right. Observe how the deformation changes as the gizmo (lattice) is moved.
6) Undo the lattice transformation.
7) Save the model as ex08-09.max in the folder of your choice.

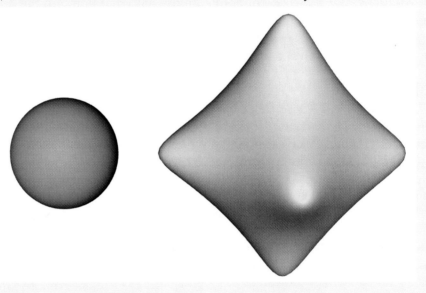

Animation Modifiers

Animation modifiers are designed to automate certain animatable items. For example, by applying a melt modifier, you can animate any object "melting." While a similar effect can be achieved by animating an FFD modifier, the melt modifier automates and simplifies the process. There are nine animation modifiers available in the **Modifiers** pull-down menu. These include the skin, morpher, flex, melt, linked xform, path deform, and patch deform modifiers. There are also two surf deform modifiers. One surf deform modifier is an object space modifier and the other is a world space modifier, as indicated by the asterisk in front of its name. The flex, linked xform, melt, and skin modifiers are discussed in the next sections.

Flex

The *flex modifier* is a spring-based system. It is used to make a portion of the object "lag" as the object is moved. For example, the top of a "whip" antenna on a truck can be made to lag behind the bottom as the truck moves forward. See Figure 8-24. The effects of the flex modifier

Figure 8-24. The antenna on this toy truck lags behind as the truck is moved because of the flex modifier applied to the antenna.

are only visible in an animation. The object to which the modifier is applied must be animated in some way to produce an effect. Using the whip antenna example, if the modifier is applied to the antenna but the truck does not move, the modifier has no effect.

To apply a flex modifier, first select the object or make a sub-object selection. Then, open the **Modifier List** drop-down list in the **Modify** tab of the **Command Panel**. Finally, select **Flex** in the **Animation Modifiers** area of the list. You can also select **Animation Modifiers** in the **Modifiers** pull-down menu, and then pick **Flex** in the cascading menu. The flex modifier appears in the modifier stack. The **Parameters, Simple Soft Bodies, Weights and Painting, Forces and Deflectors, Advanced Parameters**, and **Advanced Springs** rollouts are also displayed at the bottom of the **Modify** tab. See Figure 8-25.

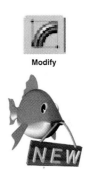

Modify

The flex modifier has three sub-object levels. These are **Center, Edge Vertices**, and **Weights & Springs**. To enter sub-object mode, expand the sub-object tree in the modifier stack. Then, pick the appropriate sub-object level.

Parameters Rollout

The value in the **Flex:** spinner in the **Parameters** rollout is the amount of flex used for the effect. The higher this value, the more pronounced the effect of the modifier. The value in the **Strength:** spinner determines the stiffness of the spring. Higher values make the spring stiffer. The value in the **Sway:** spinner is the number of frames it takes the object to stop flexing.

The **Use Chase Springs** check box is used to make the object or selection attempt to follow, or chase, its "original" position. As used here, the "original" position means the movement of the object as if no flex modifier is applied. When the **Use Chase Springs** check box is unchecked, the flex of the object or selection is based on weights only. This option is on for most applications, especially for organic models.

Figure 8-25. The **Parameters** rollout for a flex modifier.

When the **Use Weights** check box is checked, any custom weight "painted" onto the object is used for the flex effect. When unchecked, the entire object or selection is treated with the default weights.

At the bottom of the **Parameters** rollout is a drop-down list. This list allows you to select the type of equation used to calculate the flex effect. This equation is called a "solver." The most basic of the solvers is the **Euler** solver. The most complex solver is the **Runge-Kutta4** solver. The **Midpoint** solver is in between the two others in terms of complexity. The more complex the solver, the more accurate the calculation of the effect. Of course, the more complex the solver, the more computer resources are required.

The **Samples:** spinner at the bottom of the **Parameters** rollout sets how many times the flex effect is calculated on each frame. The default value is 5. Prior to 3ds max Release 4, this value was 1 and could not be changed.

Weights and Painting Rollout

The **Weights and Painting** rollout is used to apply custom weights to the object. By applying weights, you can refine the movement of the flex modifier. Weights must be applied at the sub-object level, but it can be any sub-object level. Once in sub-object mode, pick the **Paint** button in the **Weights and Painting** rollout. Next, move the cursor over a vertex. The cursor changes to the "paint" cursor. See Figure 8-26. As you paint on the vertex, more and more weight is added. The vertices change color to reflect added weight, as shown in Figure 8-26. Pick the button again or right-click to exit "paint mode."

As you edit the object at a sub-object level, the color-coded effect of weights is displayed on the object in all viewports. Blue portions of the object are affected least. Red portions of the object are affected most.

The **Strength:** spinner in the **Paint Weights** area determines the amount of weight added when you "paint." A negative value removes weight. The **Radius:** spinner sets the size of the brush in current drawing units. The **Feather:** spinner is used to set the softness of the "brush." A value of 1.0 creates a soft brush.

| Paint |

Paint

Less
weight

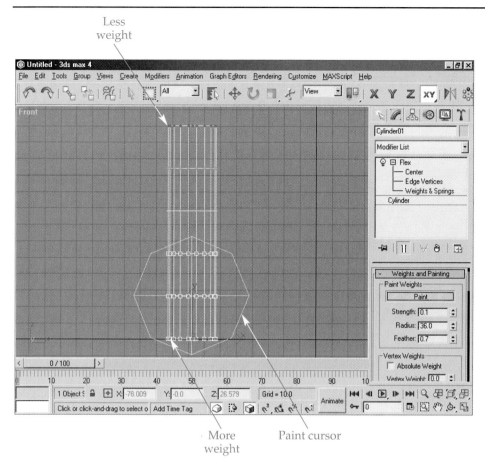

Figure 8-26. When applying a flex modifier, you can "paint" weight onto the object. Vertex color indicates the amount of weight.

More
weight

Paint cursor

The **Vertex Weights** area allows you to manually set the weight assigned to selected vertices. When the **Absolute Weight** check box is checked, the weight assigned to the selected vertices is absolute, not relative. The settings in this area must be applied at the weights and springs sub-object level.

Forces and Deflectors Rollout

The **Forces and Deflectors** rollout is used to add space warps to control the flex. To add a force space warp, pick the **Add** button in the **Forces** area. Then, select the force space warp in a viewport. The name of the space warp appears in the list in the **Forces** area. To add a deflector space warp, pick the **Add** button in the **Deflectors** area. Then, select the deflector space warp in a viewport. The name of the deflector appears in the list in the **Deflectors** area. You can add more than one space warp to the modifier.

Simple Soft Bodies Rollout

The settings in the **Simple Soft Bodies** rollout are used to automate the creation of springs for a soft-body object. A *soft-body object* is an organic object, such as a dog's tail. A spring is "attached" between adjacent vertices and holds them together. If you are not happy with the settings automatically calculated by 3ds max, you can use the **Advanced Springs** rollout to manually set springs.

First, enter values in the **Stretch:** and **Stiffness:** spinners. The **Stretch:** value is the amount of stretch allowed on the edges of an object or selection. The **Stiffness:** value represents the rigidity of the object or selection. In other words, it is the resistance to flex of an object or selection. The **Stretch:** and **Stiffness:** values are affected by each other. When making adjustments, change one setting and preview the motion. Then, adjust the other setting if necessary.

Create Simple Soft Body

Once the **Stretch:** and **Stiffness:** values are set, you can tell 3ds max to calculate the springs. Pick the **Create Simple Soft Body** button. After the springs are calculated, you can adjust the **Stretch:** and **Stiffness:** values as needed. The changes are immediately applied, so you do not have to pick the button again.

Advanced Parameters and Advanced Springs Rollouts

The **Advanced Parameters** rollout is used to specify a starting and ending frame for the flex effect. If the **Affect All Points** check box is checked, the modifier ignores sub-object selections. The **Set Reference** button is used to update the viewports after the center sub-object is edited.

The **Advanced Springs** rollout is used to add precise springs. These settings should be used when the simple soft body settings do not provide the needed control. When making settings in this rollout, you should be at the weights and springs sub-object level.

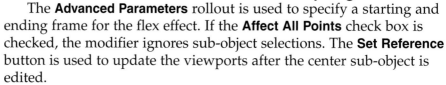

Exercise

Exercise 8-10

1) Draw a tall, thin cylinder. Draw a sphere on one end. Union the two objects.
2) Move the object so it is on one side of the Perspective viewport.
3) Apply a flex modifier to the object.
4) Drag the **Time** slider to frame 50. Turn on the **Toggle Animation Mode** button. Note: Animation is discussed in detail in Chapter 14.
5) Move the object to the other side of the Perspective viewport. The object may appear abnormally stretched at this point.
6) Drag the **Time** slider to frame 100.
7) Move the object back to its original position.
8) Turn off the **Toggle Animation Mode** button.
9) Pick the **Play Animation** button.
10) Observe the motion.
11) Save the model as ex08-10.max in the folder of your choice.

Linked Xform

The *linked xform modifier* is a variation of the xform modifier discussed earlier in this chapter. Unlike the xform modifier, the transform of a linked xform modifier is controlled by the transform of another object. Applying a linked xform or xform modifier is the only way to animate sub-object transformations when the "select" modifiers are used. The linked xform modifier, like the xform modifier, can be used to place a transform into the modifier stack.

To apply a linked xform modifier, first select the object or make a sub-object selection. Then, open the **Modifier List** drop-down list in the **Modify** tab of the **Command Panel**. Finally, select **Linked XForm** in the **Animation Modifiers** area of the list. You can also select **Animation Modifiers** in the **Modifiers** pull-down menu, and then pick **Linked XForm** in the cascading menu. The linked xform modifier appears in the modifier stack. The **Parameters** rollout appears at the bottom of the **Modify** tab. See Figure 8-27.

At the top of the **Parameters** rollout is the **Control Object:** area. A status line appears in this area indicating the name of the control object. The *control object* is the object from which transforms are inherited. When the modifier is first applied, there is no control object. To assign a control object, select the **Pick Control Object** button. Then, select an object in the viewport. That object's name is then displayed in the **Control Object:** area. Now, you can transform and animate the control object. All transforms are passed to the object with the linked xform modifier.

Melt

The *melt modifier* is used to make an object appear as if it is melting. See Figure 8-28. It can be applied to an entire object or to a sub-object selection. There are four preset "material melts" to choose from, or you can define your own.

To apply a melt modifier, first select the object or make a sub-object selection. Then, open the **Modifier List** drop-down list in the **Modify** tab of the **Command Panel**. Finally, select **Melt** in the **Animation Modifiers** area of

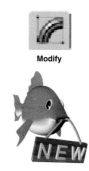

Modify

Pick Control Object

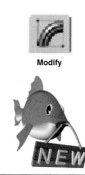

Modify

Figure 8-27. The **Parameters** rollout for a linked xform modifier. The object Torus01 is set as the control object.

Figure 8-28. The object on the bottom is created by applying a melt modifier to the object on the top. Which "melt" was used? Why is it not centered?

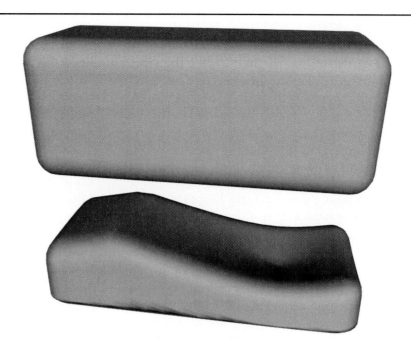

Figure 8-29. The **Parameters** rollout for the melt modifier.

the list. You can also select **Animation Modifiers** in the **Modifiers** pull-down menu, and then pick **Melt** in the cascading menu. The melt modifier appears in the modifier stack. The **Parameters** rollout appears at the bottom of the **Modify** tab. See Figure 8-29. The melt modifier has center and gizmo sub-objects.

The value in the **Amount:** spinner in the **Melt** area determines the decay. In other words, this value sets how much the object is melted. The value can range from 0.0 to 1000.0. A value of 0.0 produces no melting.

The **Spread** area is used to determine how big a puddle the melted object makes. The value in the **% of Melt:** spinner is a percentage of the melted height. For example, if this spinner is set to 50% and the object has melted 10 "units" down, the puddle or bulge is roughly 5 "units" wide.

The **Solidity** area is used to set how the center of the object melts. Materials such as metal and glass tend to melt more on the outside of the object than the inside. Materials such as plastic tend to melt more on the inside than the outside. There are four preset "materials" to choose from. To the right of each radio button, the solidity value is displayed. In addition, you can pick the **Custom:** radio button and enter your own value in the spinner. This value can range from 0.2 to 30.0. The higher the solidity value, the more the object melts on the "outside."

In the **Axis to Melt** area, you can pick the object's local axis to which the modifier is applied. The melt is normally in the positive-to-negative direction. However, if you check the **Flip Axis** check box, the direction is from negative to positive.

You can transform the gizmo at the sub-object level. In this way, you can apply the melt unevenly to the object. You can also transform the center at the sub-object level to change the center of modification.

Help Cel

If you are animating the melt modifier, make sure the **Toggle Animation Mode** button is on. Make sure you are on the proper keyframe before making changes to the parameters. Also, do not confuse picking a "melt material" with applying a material to the object.

Exercise 8-11

1) Draw a sphere using your own dimensions.
2) Apply a melt modifier. Set the melt amount to about 50. Set the melt axis to Z.
3) Pick the **Ice (Default)** radio button in the **Solidity** area. Note the shape of the sphere.
4) Pick the **Glass** radio button. How did the sphere change?
5) Pick the **Jelly** radio button. How did the sphere change?
6) Pick the **Plastic** radio button.
7) Rank the solidity types from "most melt" to "least melt."
8) Save the model as **ex08-11.max** in the folder of your choice.

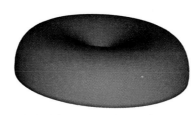

Skin

The *skin modifier* allows you to deform an object with another object. This modifier is most often used with a bones system. See Figure 8-30. However, it can be used with other objects to produce various effects.

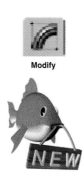

Modify

To apply the skin modifier, you must first have other objects in the scene to use as "bones." Select the object to which you want the modifier applied. Then, open the **Modifier List** drop-down list in the **Modify** tab of the **Command Panel**. Finally, select **Skin** in the **Animation Modifiers** area of the list. You can also select **Animation Modifiers** in the M**o**difiers pull-down menu, and then pick **Skin** in the cascading menu. The skin modifier appears in the modifier stack. The **Parameters, Display, Advance Params** (advanced parameters), and **Gizmos** rollouts appear at the bottom of the **Modify** tab. The skin modifier has an envelope sub-object.

Most of the features of this modifier are beyond the scope of this text. However, a brief tutorial is presented here. This is designed to allow you to use the skin modifier at its most basic level. The following tutorial simulates a "hole" in outer space.

First, draw a box in the Top viewport 250 units in length, 350 units in width, and –5 units in height. Change the length, width, and height segments to 50 each. Next, draw a sphere with a radius of 50 units in about the center of the box. Rotate the Perspective view so you are looking nearly straight down on the box. In the Left or Front viewport, move the sphere straight down so it is below the box.

Select the box and apply the skin modifier. Then, in the **Parameters** rollout, pick the **Add Bone** button. The **Select Bones** dialog box appears. This is a variation of the **Select Objects** dialog box. All objects in the

Figure 8-30. The skin modifier is designed to be used with a bones system.

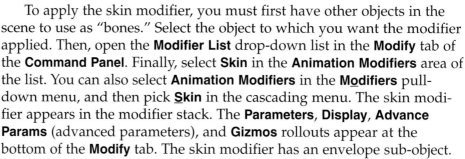

Bone hierarchy

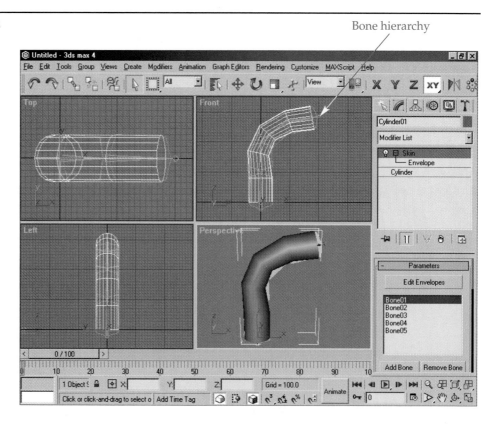

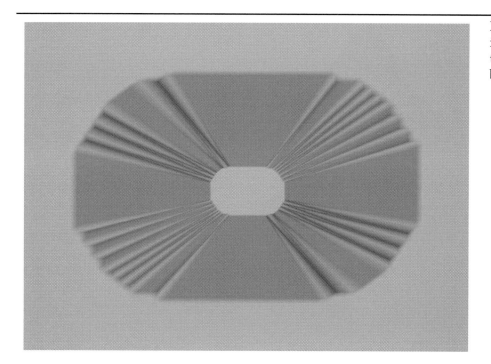

Figure 8-31. A "hole" in space created using the skin modifier on a box.

scene that can be used as a bone for the selected object appear in the list. As there is only one valid object, the sphere is the only object in the list. Select it and pick the **Select** button. The sphere's name appears in the list at the top of the **Parameters** rollout.

Now, select the sphere in either the Left or Front viewport. Move it straight down and watch the Perspective viewport. As you move the sphere down, a "hole" in space appears in the box. See Figure 8-31. If you animate the transformation of the sphere, the hole is animated as well.

World Space Modifiers

World space modifiers (WSMs) are applied to an object in the same way as object space modifiers. However, the effects of the modifier are based on world space, not object space. Therefore, as an object is moved around in the scene, the effect of the modifier changes, even if the parameters remain unchanged. See Figure 8-32.

The WSMs available in 3ds max are the camera map, displace mesh, displace NURBS, map scaler, patch deform, path deform, point cache, surface mapper, and surf deform modifiers. These are all located in the **Modifier List** drop-down list in the **Modify** tab of the **Command Panel**. In addition, some can be found in the **Modifiers** pull-down menu. The WSMs are indicated in both the drop-down list and pull-down menu by an asterisk before the name. Once applied, a WSM can be fine-tuned or adjusted in the **Command Panel**.

The *camera map WSM* applies UVW mapping based on world coordinates and the position of a specified camera. As the camera or object is moved, the mapping is adjusted in relation to world space coordinates. The OSM version of this modifier uses an object's local coordinates, as opposed to world coordinates.

The *displace mesh WSM* is used in conjunction with displacement mapping or the disp approx object space modifier. The displace mesh

Figure 8-32. A—The red object is assigned as the patch for a patch deform WSM applied to the orange box. B—As the box is moved in space, the effect of the modifier changes based on world coordinates.

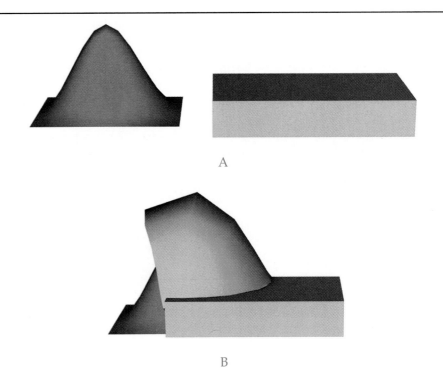

A

B

WSM shows the end result of these two operations. This is done to temporarily show an object's displacement to allow other objects to be positioned correctly. This is also done to create a snapshot object at a certain point in an animated displacement.

The *displace NURBS WSM* is used to convert a NURBS model into a mesh object. This modifier can be used to see displacement mapping on a NURBS model. In addition, you can generate a mesh object based on the displacement-mapped NURBS model using the **Snapshot** command.

The *map scaler WSM* is used to retain the scale of an applied map. This allows you to scale or resize the object while maintaining the scale of a previously applied map.

The *patch deform WSM* is used to deform an object based on a patch in relation to world space coordinates. As the object or patch is moved, the deformation changes based on world space. The *path deform WSM* works in the same way, except a spline is used for the deformation. The *surf deform WSM* also works in the same way, except a NURBS surface is used as the source for deformation.

The *point cache WSM* is used to record animated information as changes in vertex location. This vertex information is then saved to a file. The information can be retrieved from the file for animation playback in instances where computing the animation playback bogs down the system. You can also use the data to apply the same animated parameters to different objects in the scene. There is also an object space modifier version of this modifier that operates in object space.

The *surface mapper WSM* is used to take the mapping coordinates applied to a NURBS surface and assign them to an object. This can be used to apply one set of mapping coordinates to several objects. As the objects or source NURBS surfaces are moved in the scene, the mapping is adjusted based on world coordinates.

Modeling with Modifiers

The following short tutorial demonstrates how modifiers can be used as modeling tools. Not all of the modifiers presented in this chapter are used. The tutorial model is a simple rowboat on water. See Figure 8-33. As you progress through the tutorial, procedures and dimensions are given. However, information about where to find specific commands in 3ds max is not given. You will need to use what you have learned to find what you need to complete the tutorial. When complete, you will have a basic understanding of how modifiers can be used as modeling tools. As you progress through this book, you will learn more advanced modeling, lighting, and material techniques, which will allow you to construct a more detailed model.

The water is the easiest part of the model to create. Draw a quad patch in the Top viewport. Make it 500 units square. Also, make both the length and width segment values 5. Name the object Water. Next, apply a noise modifier. Make the noise fractal. Set the X strength to 100, the Y strength to 150, and the Z strength to 5. Finally, open the **Material Editor** and get the material Ground_Water from the material library. Assign this to the Water object.

At this point, you may want to change the rendering background color to represent the sky. Use a light blue, almost white color. To do this, select **Environment...** from the **Rendering** pull-down menu. In the **Background:** area of the **Common Parameters** rollout in the **Environment** dialog box, pick the color swatch. In the color selector, set the new color. Then, close all dialog boxes. Now, zoom in on the water in the Perspective viewport. See Figure 8-34.

Since the water is very large compared to the rest of the model, it is a good idea to hide it at this point. Refer to Chapter 5 for a review of

Figure 8-33. A rendering of the completed tutorial.

Figure 8-34. The completed water object.

hiding/displaying objects if necessary. Now, create the rowboat. This object is created using a network of splines and the surface modifier. Start by creating the splines as shown in Figure 8-35. First draw the splines for the cross sections as straight lines. Then, modify the vertices in sub-object mode to get the shape you want. Finally, connect the cross sections with more splines. You can use your own dimensions and shapes. However, when connecting the cross sections, be sure to use the **Endpoint** snap to precisely locate the splines. The Perspective viewport may be the best one to use when connecting the cross sections.

With the spline network completed, attach all splines together as one spline. Name the spline Rowboat. Then, apply the surface modifier. Define a material in the **Material Editor** by setting a light yellow diffuse color, and apply it to the rowboat. You will need to check the **2-Sided** check box in the **Shader Basic Parameters** rollout. Adjust the Perspective viewport and render it. Display the Water object and render the viewport again.

You may notice that the scene is a bit dark. You can use lights to fix the problem. Lights are covered in Chapter 10 and Chapter 19.

Help Cel

The **2-Sided** check box must be checked because the surface is one-sided. If you do not enable this option, you will not be able to see the "other side" of the rowboat when it is rendered.

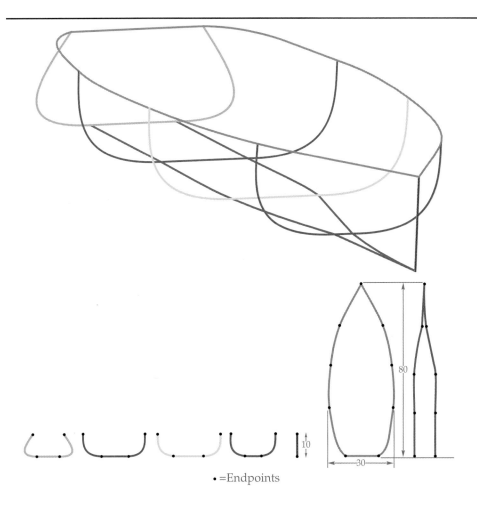

Figure 8-35. The spline network used to create the rowboat.

• =Endpoints

Next, the oars need to be created. This is done in three steps. The handle is created, the blade is created, and then the two are joined in a Boolean operation. To make the handle, draw the spline profile shown in Figure 8-36A. Then, apply the lathe modifier. Next, draw a box 10 x 3 x .25 with 10 segments on each axis. Apply a push modifier with a value of 0.25. Next, apply a taper modifier with a taper of –1.0 and a curve of 0.25. Make the primary taper axis X with the effect on ZY. Finally, union the two pieces with a Boolean operation. Make a copy of the completed oar. Move and rotate the oars as needed. Turn the water back on if hidden and render the scene. See Figure 8-36B.

Finally, a lobster trap needs to be made and placed over the side of the boat. This is done using a standard cylinder primitive and a lattice modifier, Figure 8-37. First draw a cylinder with a radius of 5 units and a height of 15 units. Slice the cylinder 180°. Next, apply a lattice modifier. Set the radius for the struts and joints to a small value, such as 0.1 or 0.2 units. Get the material Wood_Old from the material library and apply it to the trap. Finally, position the trap over the side of the boat. The final scene is shown in Figure 8-33.

Figure 8-36. A—The profile used to create the handle portion of the oar. B—The completed oars placed in the scene.

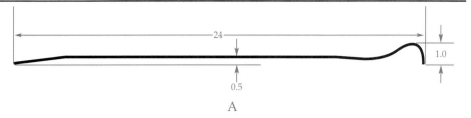

A

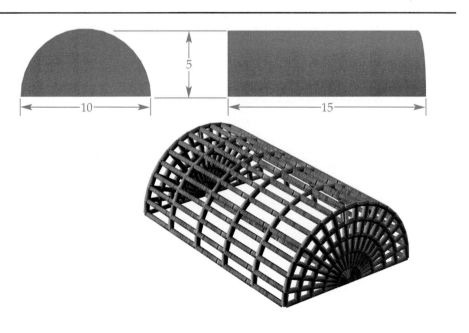

B

Figure 8-37. The dimensions of the cylinder used to create the lobster trap.

Chapter Snapshot

Chapter Test

Answer the following questions on a separate sheet of paper.

1) What is the purpose of the mesh select modifier?
2) Which type of material is used with the material modifier?
3) What is a displacement approximation modifier used for?
4) How does applying an edit patch modifier to a parametric object differ from converting the object into an editable patch object?
5) When is the normalize spline modifier used?
6) The surface modifier generates a patch grid from what type of object?
7) Why would you use the delete mesh modifier instead of deleting items at the sub-object level?
8) What function does the tessellate modifier perform?
9) What effect can be created with the displace modifier?
10) The lattice modifier produces what type of object?
11) What does the push modifier do?
12) What do the xform and linked xform modifiers allow you to do?
13) How does the xform modifier differ from the linked xform modifier?
14) What does FFD stand for?
15) Which FFD modifiers allow you to set the number of control points?
16) If a melt modifier has a high solidity value, what effect is produced on the object?
17) What does the flex modifier do?
18) The skin modifier is designed to be used with _____.
19) What is the main difference between world space modifiers and object space modifiers?
20) What is the purpose of the point cache modifier?

Modeling Problems

For each of the following problems, start by drawing the object on the left. Use your own dimensions. Then, use modifiers to approximately create the object shown on the right. In most cases, more than one modifier must be used. When complete, save each model as p08-xx.max in the folder of your choice.

1 Cylinder Deformation

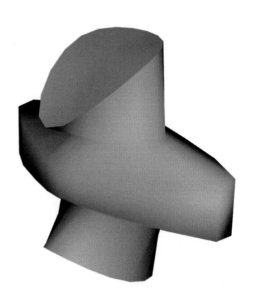

2 Pyramid Deformation

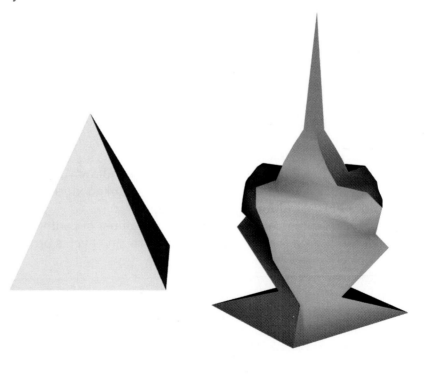

Teapot Deformation **3**

Capsule Deformation **4**

Torus Deformation **5**

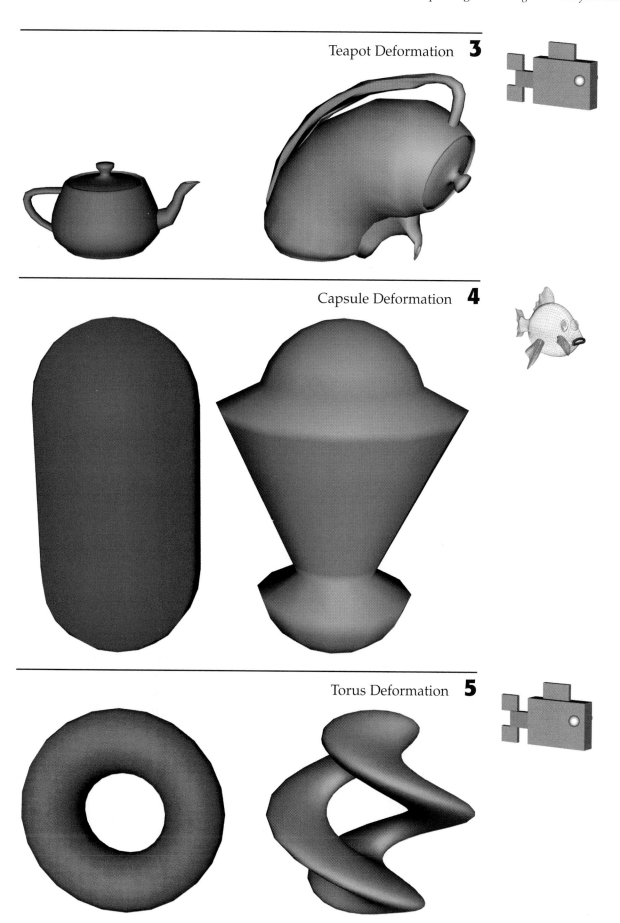

6 Chamfer Box Deformation

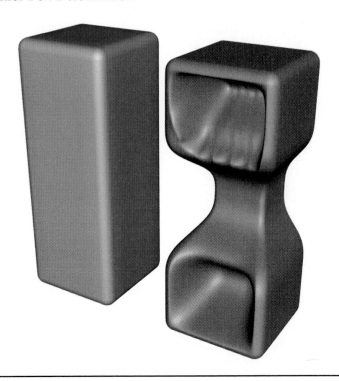

7 Sphere Deformation

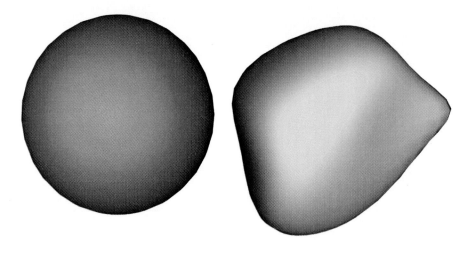

Box Deformation **8**

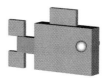

Palm Tree **9**

Computer Monitor **10**

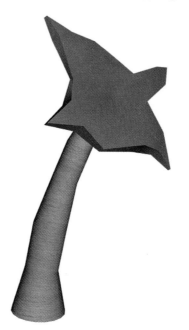

Chapter 9

Creating Advanced Compound Objects

Objectives

After completing this chapter, you will be able to:

- Explain how to loft multiple shapes.
- Create complex loft objects.
- Explain the purpose of the **Snap:** spinner for a loft object.
- Identify components of the **Deformation** dialog box.
- Define deformations.
- Apply deformations.
- Remove a twist from a loft object.
- Explain morph, connect, ShapeMerge, and mesher objects.

Complex Loft Objects

In Chapter 6, you learned how to create a simple loft object using a single shape and a path. While this procedure allows you to create objects beyond the 3ds max primitives, it may have seemed a bit primitive itself. However, lofting is a very powerful modeling tool. Using advanced lofting procedures, you can quickly create very complex loft objects. This can be done by adjusting the path and skin parameters, applying deformations, and lofting multiple shapes.

Skin Parameters

The **Skin Parameters** rollout is used to control the mesh or patch that is the surface of the loft object. This rollout contains the **Capping**, **Options**, and **Display** areas. See Figure 9-1. This rollout is covered in detail in Chapter 6. Refer to that chapter if you need to review.

Path Parameters

The **Path Parameters** rollout is used to control the placement of multiple shapes on a path. See Figure 9-2. The ability to have more than one shape on a single loft object is one of the keys to creating complex loft objects. See Figure 9-3. This section discusses the options in the **Path Parameters** rollout. The next section describes how to loft multiple shapes.

Figure 9-1. The **Skin Parameters** rollout is used to control the surface of the loft object.

Figure 9-2. The **Path Parameters** rollout is used to control the placement of shapes along the path.

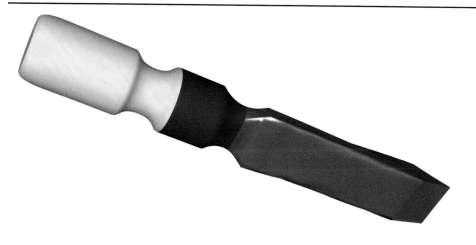

Figure 9-3. Multiple shapes were lofted to create this chisel.

The value in the **Path:** spinner indicates the current level on the path. The current level is where any shape "put" on the path is placed. It is indicated in the viewports by a small yellow X. The value in the spinner can be expressed as a percentage of the path length, an absolute distance from the first vertex, or as path steps. What is displayed in the spinner is determined by the three radio buttons. Notice when moving between levels using the spinner that the loft object is displayed as the path and the shapes only, without the end result.

The **Snap:** spinner is used to set snap increments for adjusting the **Path:** spinner. To activate the spinner, check the **On** check box. Then, enter a value in the **Snap:** spinner. What the value represents is determined by the three radio buttons. For example, if you pick the **Percentage** radio button, check the **On** check box, and enter 20 in the **Snap:** spinner, when the **Path:** spinner is adjusted, the value jumps in 20% increments.

The three radio buttons at the bottom of the **Path Parameters** rollout determine what the values in the **Path:** and **Snap:** spinners represent. If the **Percentage** radio button is picked, the values are a percentage of the total path length. The first vertex on the path is represented by 0% and the last vertex is represented by 100%. If the **Distance** radio button is picked, the values in the spinners are absolute distances from the first vertex. The maximum value for a spinner is the absolute length of the path. If the **Path Steps** radio button is picked, the values in the spinners are steps. Also, the total number of steps is shown in parentheses next to the **Path:** spinner. For example, if the **Path Steps** radio button is picked and the value in the **Path:** spinner is 4, this means the current level is the fourth step from the first vertex.

When you pick the **Path Steps** radio button, a warning dialog box appears asking you to verify your action, Figure 9-4. The reason this dialog box appears is each step can only have one shape. If the loft object has more shapes than path steps, using this option will force 3ds max to delete one or more extra shapes. However, with the **Percentage** and **Distance** options, you can have a virtually unlimited number of shapes on the path.

Pick Shape

Previous Shape

Next Shape

At the very bottom of the **Path Parameters** rollout are the **Pick Shape**, **Previous Shape**, and **Next Shape** buttons. The **Pick Shape** button allows you to set the current level to that of the shape you pick. After you pick the button, move the cursor in the viewport to the shape you want to pick. The cursor changes to indicate when you are over a shape. See Figure 9-5. The value in the **Path:** spinner reflects the level of the shape. The **Snap:** spinner **On** check box is unchecked. The **Previous Shape** and **Next Shape** buttons allow you to set the current level to that of the shape on either side of the current level.

Help Cel

The **Pick Shape** button is disabled when creating a loft object. It is only available in the **Modify** tab of the **Command Panel**.

Figure 9-4. This warning appears when the **Path Steps** radio button is picked.

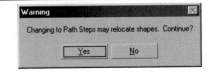

Cursor

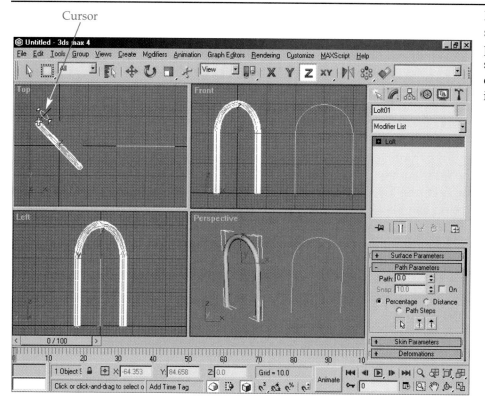

Figure 9-5. When setting the current path level to that of a selected shape, the cursor changes to indicate a valid shape.

Exercise 9-1

1) Draw the simple loft object shown below. Use your own dimensions.
2) With the Perspective viewport active, switch to a single viewport configuration. Adjust the display as necessary.
3) Change the display mode to wireframe.
4) In the **Modify** tab of the **Command Panel**, expand the **Path Parameters** rollout. Make sure the **Percentage** radio button is selected.
5) Activate the **Snap:** spinner. Using the **Path:** spinner, change to different levels on the path. Observe the yellow X in the viewport.
6) Pick the **Path Steps** radio button. Answer **Yes** in the dialog box that appears.
7) Using the **Path:** spinner, change to different levels on the path. Notice the difference in how the X moves.
8) Reset 3ds max without saving.

Exercise

Lofting Multiple Shapes

There are two basic ways to loft multiple shapes. First, when creating the loft object, multiple shapes can be added to the path. Second, the loft object can be created as one shape lofted along the path. Then, using the **Modify** tab of the **Command Panel**, other shapes can be added. The procedure is basically the same for both methods.

First, create a simple loft with the path and one of the shapes. See Figure 9-6. Keep the loft object selected. If you unselect the loft object, you will have to use the **Modify** tab of the **Command Panel**. Next, expand the **Path Parameters** rollout if not already open. Using the **Path:** spinner, move to the level where you want to add the next shape. The **Snap** option can be very useful.

With the correct level set, pick the **Get Shape** button in the **Creation Method** rollout. Move the cursor in the viewport and pick the shape you want to add. See Figure 9-7. Continue adding shapes at different levels as needed. Remember, a level can only have one shape. If you switch to a level that already has a shape and get a new one, the old shape is replaced.

Get Shape

Figure 9-6. A complex loft object often starts as a simple loft object, such as a circle lofted along a straight line.

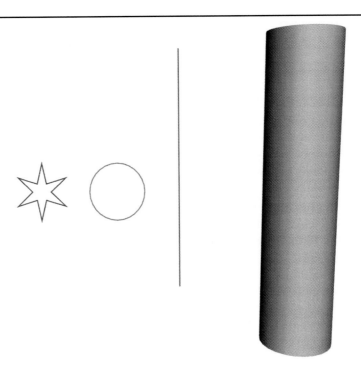

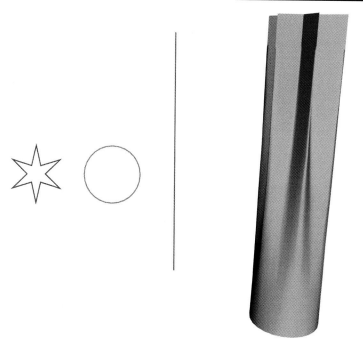

Figure 9-7. When the star shape is added to the original loft object, a more complex object is created.

Exercise 9-2

Exercise

1) Draw the six shapes shown below. Use your own dimensions.
2) Select the helix. This is the path for the loft object.
3) Loft the ellipse along the helix.
4) Add the star at the 25% level.
5) Add the square at the 40% and 60% levels.
6) Add the circle at the 75% level.
7) Add the six-sided NGon at the 100% level.
8) Make the Perspective viewport current and its shading mode **Smooth + Highlights**, if not already selected. Using the **Arc Rotate** button, rotate the view. Notice the loft's transitions between shapes.
9) Reset 3ds max without saving.

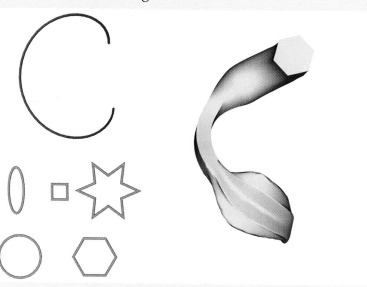

Figure 9-8. Various deformation tools are applied to the simple loft object on the bottom to create the complex loft object shown on the top.

Deformations

The *deformation tools* allow you to fine-tune a loft object. See Figure 9-8. They include **Scale**, **Twist**, **Teeter**, **Bevel**, and **Fit**. These tools are not available when creating the loft object. They must be accessed through the **Modify** tab of the **Command Panel**. The interface for these tools is a graph, as explained in the next sections.

With a loft object selected, expand the **Deformations** rollout in the **Modify** tab of the **Command Panel**. See Figure 9-9. Then, pick the button corresponding to the deformation you want to apply. Once a deformation is applied, the **Enable/Disable** button to the right of the deformation button is depressed. This is a toggle allowing you to turn the settings for a deformation on or off.

Modify

Enable/Disable

Figure 9-9. Deformations are applied to a loft object in the **Deformations** rollout of the **Modify** tab.

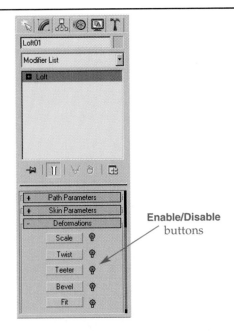

Enable/Disable buttons

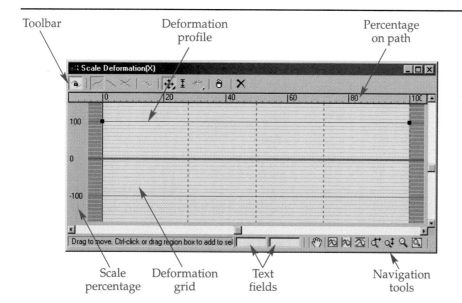

Toolbar   Deformation profile   Percentage on path

Scale percentage   Deformation grid   Text fields   Navigation tools

Figure 9-10. Each deformation tool has its own **Deformation** dialog box. These dialog boxes all share a common layout, except for the one used with the **Fit** deformation.

Deformation Dialog Box

Other than the **Fit** deformation, the deformation tools use dialog boxes sharing a common layout. However, each deformation tool has its own **Deformation** dialog box. See Figure 9-10.

At the left of the dialog box is the 0% point on the path. At the right of the dialog box is the 100% point on the path. A ruler along the top of the graph indicates the percentage. Also, the vertical axis in the dialog box represents the percentage of the deformation being applied. A ruler along the left side of the graph indicates the percentage.

In the middle of the dialog box is the deformation grid. This is where the graph of the deformation is displayed. The light-colored area in the middle of the graph is the active area. This defines the "boundaries" of the object.

The X axis is displayed by default. It appears as a red line. The Y axis can also be displayed. It appears as a green line. Both axes can be displayed at the same time. Each appears in its own color. The axis currently displayed appears in the dialog box title bar.

Tools

Along the top of the deformation dialog box is a toolbar. The first button from the left is the **Make Symmetrical** button. When this button is on (depressed), the changes made in the dialog box are applied equally to both the X and Y axes. When off, changes can be made independently on each axis.

The next three buttons from the left control which axis is displayed. Picking the **Display X Axis** button displays the X axis on the graph as a red line. Picking the **Display Y Axis** button displays the Y axis on the graph as a green line. This also turns off the display of the X axis. Picking the **Display XY Axes** button shows both the X and the Y axes on the graph.

The **Swap Deform Curves** button is used to flip-flop the settings for the X and Y axes. This button only has an effect when the **Make Symmetrical** button is off.

The **Move Control Point** button functions in much the same way as the **Select and Move** transform. It is used to move an existing control point. Pick the button and then a control point on the graph. You can then drag the

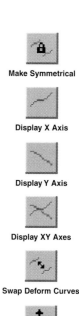

Make Symmetrical

Display X Axis

Display Y Axis

Display XY Axes

Swap Deform Curves

Move Control Point

control point up and down to change the percentage of deformation. You can also drag the control point left and right to a different percentage level on the path. The button is a flyout. Contained in the flyout are buttons that constrain movement to either the vertical or horizontal directions.

The **Scale Control Point** button is used to scale control points while maintaining the ratio to one another. This button does not allow you to move the selected points to a different percentage level on the path. It is used most often when multiple points are selected.

The **Insert Control Point** button is used to add new control points to the graph. Pick the button and then pick a point on the graph where you want to add a control point. The point added is by default a corner-type vertex. However, contained in the flyout is the **Insert Bezier Point** button. This button allows you to insert a Bézier corner control point. You cannot move a control point using these buttons.

The **Delete Control Point** button allows you to delete a point by selecting it. Picking the **Reset Curve** button removes all added control points and changes the curve to the default setting.

Making Adjustments

The deformation curve starts as a straight line with a control point at the beginning and end of the line. By inserting and adjusting additional control points between these two, you can quickly create complex loft objects.

Control points are added by picking the **Insert Control Point** or **Insert Bezier Point** button on the toolbar and then picking on the line where you want to insert the point. Once a point is inserted, pick the **Move Control Point** or **Scale Control Point** button to move or scale the point.

When using these tools, it can be difficult to place a new point at an exact location. It is also difficult to move a control point to an exact location. However, there is an easy way to insert, move, or scale control points. At the bottom of the **Deformation** dialog box are two text fields. See Figure 9-10. The left-hand text box indicates the percent position on the path of the current control point. The right-hand text box indicates the amount of deformation at the current control point. Once a point is inserted or selected, you can enter values in these text boxes to precisely locate or move the control point.

You can select multiple control points and move or scale them at the same time. To select multiple control points, hold down the [Ctrl] key and pick the points with the cursor. You can also drag a window around the points. Holding the [Alt] key allows you to remove points from the selection set.

In addition to adjusting the position and scale of a control point, you can adjust its curve. To switch between control point types, right-click on a control point. Then, pick **Corner, Bezier-Smooth,** or **Bezier-Corner** from the shortcut menu. Bézier-type control points can be refined using their handles. Pick a Bézier control point and the handles are displayed. See Figure 9-11. Then, adjust the handles using the **Move Control Point** button to obtain the curve you want.

Scale Control Point

Insert Control Point

Insert Bezier Point

Delete Control Point

Reset Curve

Help Cel

You can place more than one point at the same path percentage point. However, a point cannot be moved to the left of its left-hand neighbor or to the right of its right-hand neighbor.

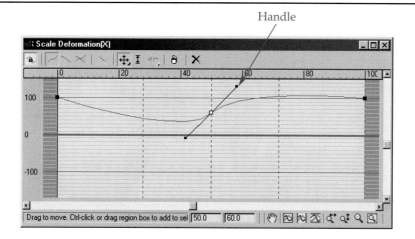

Handle

Figure 9-11. By adjusting Bézier handles, you can change the shape of the deformation curve.

Navigation Controls

At the bottom-right corner of the **Deformation** dialog box is the navigation controls toolbar. The toolbar buttons allow you to pan and zoom to get a better view of the deformation curve. The buttons available are **Pan, Zoom Extents, Zoom Horizontal Extents, Zoom Vertical Extents, Zoom Horizontally, Zoom Vertically, Zoom**, and **Zoom Region**. Some of these work in the same way as the standard 3ds max navigation controls. The ones that do not are explained below.

Picking the **Zoom Horizontal Extents** button zooms the horizontal extents, but retains the current vertical zoom. Picking the **Zoom Horizontally** button allows you to zoom horizontally while maintaining the current vertical zoom.

Picking the **Zoom Vertical Extents** button zooms to the vertical extents, but maintains the current horizontal zoom. Picking the **Zoom Vertically** button allows you to zoom along the vertical axis while maintaining the current horizontal zoom.

Pan

Zoom Vertically

Zoom Extents

Zoom Region

Zoom Vertical Extents

Zoom

Zoom Horizontal Extents

Help Cel

You can use the [Ctrl][Z] key combination to undo a change in the **Deformation** dialog box.

Scale

The *scale deformation* allows you to scale the profile of the loft object. The scaling can be done on the object's X or Y axis, or on both axes. The Z axis is the loft path. This deformation can be used to create complex objects from a single, simple lofted shape. See Figure 9-12.

To apply a scale deformation, pick the **Scale** button in the **Deformations** rollout. The **Scale Deformation** dialog box is opened. This dialog box represents the profile of the loft object as a graph. See Figure 9-13. Add, move, and scale control points as necessary to obtain the shape you want. Make any adjustments to Bézier control point handles as well. Any points above the 100% line mean the cross section is larger than the original shape. Points below the 0% line are mirrored on the opposite side of the profile.

Scale

Scale

Figure 9-12. A scale deformation can be applied to the object on the left to produce the object on the right.

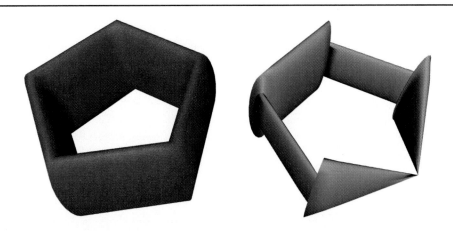

Figure 9-13. The **Scale Deformation** dialog box showing the deformation for the object in Figure 9-12.

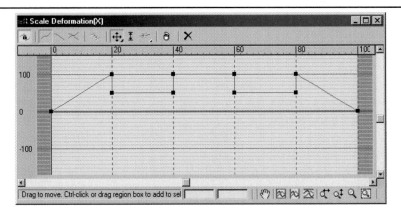

Exercise

Exercise 9-3

1) Reset 3ds max. Set the units to generic.
2) Loft a 10-unit radius circle along a 200-unit long straight path.
3) Using the scale deformation, add three control points and adjust the profile of the loft object to create the baseball bat shown below.
4) Apply a wood material to the baseball bat.
5) Render the scene to a file named ex09-03.jpg in the folder of your choice.
6) Save the scene as ex09-03.max in the folder of your choice.

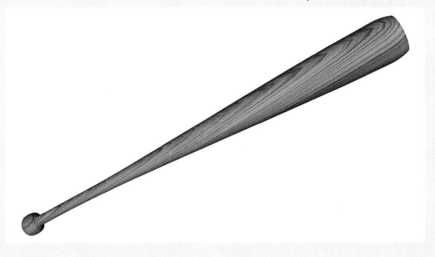

Twist

The *twist deformation* allows you to twist a loft object along its path. See Figure 9-14. The deformation specifies the amount of rotation about the path.

To apply the twist deformation, select the **Twist** button in the **Deformations** rollout. The **Twist Deformation** dialog box is opened, Figure 9-15. Notice the "axis buttons" at the top are greyed out. This is because the twist must be around the Z axis (the path).

A single red line shows the amount of twist for the loft object. By default, this is 0. Add, move, and scale control points as necessary to obtain the shape you want. Make any adjustments to Bézier control point handles as well. Positive values produce a counterclockwise twist, as viewed looking down the positive Z axis toward the first path vertex. Negative values produce a clockwise twist.

Twist

Twist

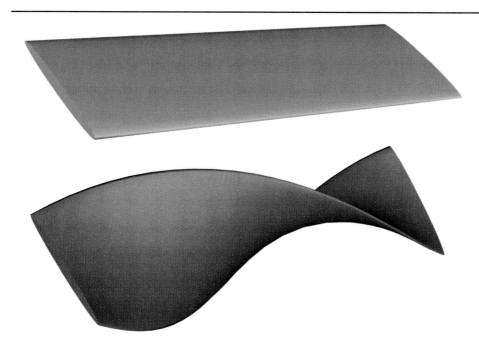

Figure 9-14. A twist deformation is applied to the top object to create the bottom object.

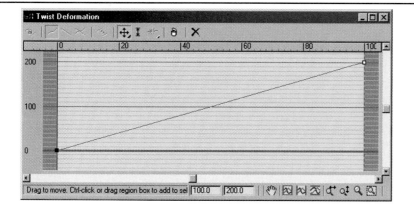

Figure 9-15. The **Twist Deformation** dialog box showing the deformation for the object in Figure 9-14.

Exercise

Exercise 9-4

1) Draw the simple loft object shown below on the left. Create it as an ellipse lofted along a larger ellipse.
2) Using the twist deformation, insert a control point at the 50% path point.
3) Enter a twist amount of 180 at the 0% and 100% path points.
4) The object now looks like a Möbius strip. Apply the material Fabric_Tan_Carpet to the loft object.
5) Render the scene to a file named ex09-04.jpg.
6) Save the scene as ex09-04.max in the folder of your choice.

Teeter

The *teeter deformation* rotates a cross-sectional shape about the loft object's X or Y axis, Figure 9-16. This is what 3ds max does for curved loft paths when you check the **Contour** check box in the **Skin Parameters** rollout. However, the teeter deformation allows you to manually control this function, even on loft objects with straight paths.

To apply a teeter deformation, pick the **Teeter** button in the **Deformations** rollout. The **Teeter Deformation** dialog box appears, Figure 9-17. The shape can be rotated about its X or Y axis, or about both axes. By default, there are 0 degrees of rotation on the X and Y axes. Add, move, and scale control points as necessary to obtain the shape you want. Make any adjustments to Bézier control point handles as well. Positive values rotate the shape counterclockwise around the shape's positive axis. Negative values rotate the shape clockwise.

Figure 9-16. The object on the left has a teeter deformation applied to its middle section to produce the object on the right.

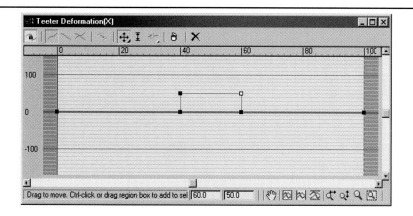

Figure 9-17. The **Teeter Deformation** dialog box showing the deformation for the object in Figure 9-16.

Exercise

Exercise 9-5

1) Draw a circle and a straight line. Loft the circle along the line.
2) Using the teeter deformation, place control points at the 20%, 50%, and 80% path locations.
3) Set the amount of teeter at the 50% control point to 100. See the object shown below.
4) Render the scene to a file named ex09-05.jpg.
5) Save the scene as ex09-05.max in the folder of your choice.

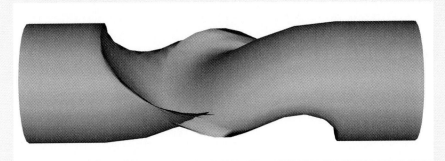

Bevel

The *bevel deformation* provides a way of adding a bevel to a loft object, Figure 9-18. While the same effect can be achieved using the scale deformation, the bevel deformation is independent and measured in current drawing units. This allows flexibility.

To apply a bevel deformation, pick the **Bevel** button in the **Deformations** rollout. The **Bevel Deformation** dialog box is opened, Figure 9-19. The bevel is placed on both the X and Y axes. Add, move, and scale control points as necessary to obtain the shape you want. Make any adjustments to Bézier control point handles as well. Positive values move the shape closer to the path. Negative values move the shape farther away from the path.

The **Bevel Deformation** dialog box has three additional buttons contained in a flyout. These are **Normal Bevel**, **Adaptive (Linear)**, and **Adaptive (Cubic)**. The selected button determines the type of bevel produced. With normal beveling, the beveled shape always remains parallel to the original. Adaptive linear beveling changes the length of the bevel linearly based on the angle produced. Adaptive cubic beveling changes the length of the bevel to a greater degree on steep angles than on shallow angles. This produces an effect that may only be seen in certain instances.

Bevel

Bevel

Normal Bevel

LIN

Adaptive Linear

CUB

Adaptive Cubic

Help Cel

Use the bevel deformation in small increments. Bevels are small and, as such, a large value can quickly create an unrecognizable object.

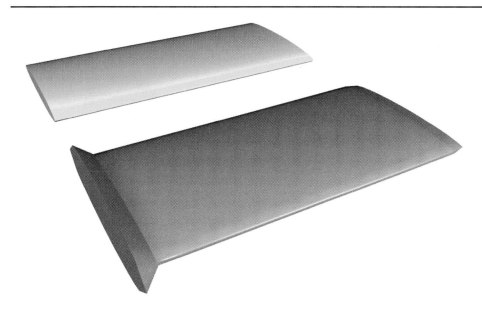

Figure 9-18. A bevel deformation is applied to the ends of the top object to create the bottom object.

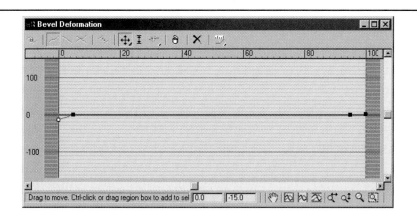

Figure 9-19. The **Bevel Deformation** dialog box showing the deformation for the object in Figure 9-18. Notice the small values for the bevel.

Exercise

Exercise 9-6

1) Draw the loft object shown below on the left.
2) Using the bevel deformation, insert control points at the 25%, 50%, and 75% path locations.
3) Set the bevel at the 25% and 75% control points to 35.
4) Set the bevel at the 50% control point to 25.
5) Assign the material Concrete_Brown_Stucco to the object.
6) Render the scene to a file named ex09-06.jpg in the folder of your choice.
7) Save the scene as ex09-06.max in the folder of your choice.

Fit

The *fit deformation* forces the loft object to fit inside profile shapes you define, Figure 9-20. The deformation can be applied to the object's X or Y axis, or to both axes. The final shape of the loft object is more dependent on the "fit shapes" than on the lofted shape or the shape of the path. The scale of the lofted shape is adjusted along the path so it matches the fit shape. This is almost as if you are "importing" the fit shapes as curves into the **Scale Deformation** dialog box.

To apply a fit deformation, pick the **Fit** button in the **Deformations** rollout. The **Fit Deformation** dialog box is opened. In addition to the standard **Deformation** dialog box buttons, this dialog box has several other buttons. See Figure 9-21.

Picking the **Mirror Horizontally** button mirrors the fit shape about the horizontal axis. Picking the **Mirror Vertically** button mirrors the fit shape about the vertical axis. If the X and Y axes have different fit shapes, only the displayed shapes are mirrored. If only one shape is displayed, the other shape is not mirrored.

Fit

Mirror Horizontally

Mirror Vertically

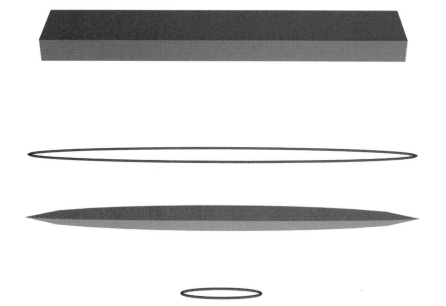

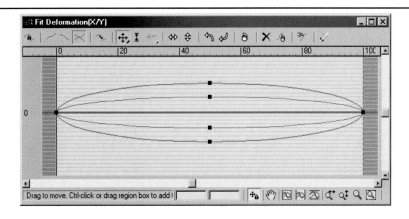

Figure 9-20. The two splines are used as fit shapes for the top object (shown in blue) to create the bottom object (shown in orange).

Figure 9-21. The **Fit Deformation** dialog box showing the shapes for the object in Figure 9-20. Notice the additional features of this dialog box as compared to the other **Deformation** dialog boxes.

Picking the **Rotate 90 CCW** button rotates the fit shape 90° counterclockwise. Picking the **Rotate 90 CW** button rotates the fit shape 90° clockwise. As with the mirror buttons, only displayed shapes are affected. If the X and Y axes have different fit shapes and only one is displayed, the other is not rotated.

Picking the **Delete Curve** button removes the fit shape. If both fit shapes are displayed, then both are removed. If the **Make Symmetrical** button is on, the fit shape is removed from both axes, even if only one is displayed.

The **Get Shape** button is used to select a fit shape and load it into the **Fit Deformation** dialog box. Select the button and then move the cursor in a viewport. Pick the shape to use as a fit shape. You can also use the [H] key or the **Select by Name** button to select an object by its name. When you pick the shape, it is placed on the currently displayed axis in the **Fit Deformation** dialog box. If both axes are displayed or the **Make Symmetrical** button is on, the shape is placed on both axes. The fit shapes can then be independently modified in the dialog box.

When the **Generate Path** button is picked, the current path is replaced by a new path, which is a straight line. This can produce some unexpected results, so use it with caution.

Rotate 90 CCW

Rotate 90 CW

Delete Curve

Get Shape

Select by Name

Generate Path

Reset Curve

Lock Aspect

The **Reset Curve** button works slightly differently with the fit deformation as compared to other deformation types. When the button is picked in the **Fit Deformation** dialog box, the displayed fit shape is replaced with a 100-unit square. If the **Make Symmetrical** button is on, the square is placed on both axes even if only one is displayed.

Included in the navigation controls area of the **Fit Deformation** dialog box is the **Lock Aspect** button. When this button is on, zooming is automatically done on both the horizontal and vertical axes. When off, the axes can be zoomed independently.

Help Cel

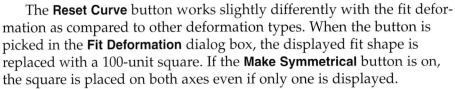

While deformations are powerful modeling tools, they are also powerful animation tools. Many of the objects that can be created with deformations can just as easily be created using standard methods. However, by creating the objects using deformations, you can animate them in ways that would be nearly impossible if the objects were originally created using standard methods.

Exercise

Exercise 9-7

1) Draw the two splines shown below on the left.
2) Draw a simple loft object of a circle lofted along a straight line.
3) Using the fit deformation, assign the "T" as a fit shape on the object's X axis.
4) Assign the ellipse as a fit shape on the object's Y axis.
5) Apply the material Metal_Dark_Gold to the object.
6) Render the scene to a file named ex09-07.jpg in the folder of your choice.
7) Save the scene as ex09-07.max in the folder of your choice.

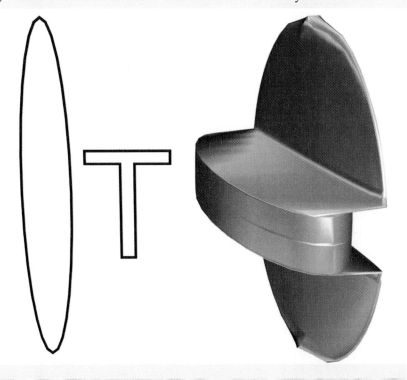

Sub-Object Editing

A loft object has two components that can be edited at the sub-object level. These are the path and the shape. If multiple shapes are lofted, each one can be edited independently. Selecting either **Shape** or **Path** in the modifier stack replaces all rollouts in the **Command Panel** with new ones.

Path Commands

When the loft path is selected for sub-object editing, the **Path Commands** rollout appears in the **Command Panel**. This rollout contains the **Put...** button. Picking this button displays the **Put To Scene** dialog box shown in Figure 9-22. This dialog box allows you to place either a copy or an instance of the loft object's path into the scene as a separate object. Enter a name for the new object in the **Name:** field, pick the **Copy** or **Instance** radio button, and then pick the **OK** button. If you place the path in the scene as an instance, changes made to the clone are transferred to the loft object.

Once you select the path in the modifier stack, the original path spline appears in the stack. If you select the original path spline in the modifier stack, you can edit it at the sub-object level. For example, if the original path spline is a line with three vertices, you can enter sub-object mode and move the middle vertex. To exit sub-object mode, pick **Path** in the stack to return to that sub-object level. Then, pick **Loft** in the stack to completely exit sub-object mode.

Shape Commands

When the loft shape is selected for sub-object editing, the **Shape Commands** rollout appears in the **Command Panel**. See Figure 9-23. At

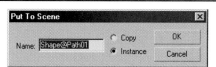

Figure 9-22. This dialog box appears when you put a path to the scene.

Figure 9-23. The **Shape Commands** rollout appears when editing a loft shape at the sub-object level.

the bottom of the rollout is the **Put** area with the **Put...** button. As with the **Put...** button in the **Path Commands** rollout, picking this button opens the **Put To Scene** dialog box. In order to put a shape into the scene, the shape must be selected on the loft object.

At the top of the rollout is the **Path Level:** spinner. This spinner indicates the current level along the path of the selected shape. The spinner, along with most of the buttons in the rollout, is unavailable until a shape is selected. To select a shape, pick the **Select Object** button or one of the transform buttons on the **Main** toolbar. Then, select the shape *on the loft object.* Adjusting the value in the **Path Level:** spinner moves the shape along the path. The shape is moved along the path, even if the **Select and Rotate** button or one of the **Select and Scale** buttons is used to pick the shape.

Below the **Path Level:** spinner is the **Compare** button. Picking this button opens the **Compare** dialog box. This dialog box is discussed in the next section.

Reset Shape

Select and Rotate

Select and Scale

Select and Move

You can use transform tools to transform a shape in the loft object. The **Select and Rotate** button allows you to rotate the shape about the path. The **Select and Scale** flyout allows you to scale the current shape. The **Select and Move** button allows you to move the shape in relation to the path. If the transform is restricted to the local Z axis, you can move the shape *along* the path, just as you would with the **Path Level:** spinner. The **Reset** button located below the **Compare** button allows you to undo all rotations or scaling. It has no effect on any movement of the shape.

Picking the **Delete** button deletes the current shape from the loft object. The shape can be added again later using the method for lofting multiple shapes.

The **Align** area contains several buttons allowing you to control how the shape is placed in relation to the path. These buttons are **Left**, **Right**, **Top**, **Bottom**, **Center**, and **Default**. The alignment is determined by looking down the loft object's positive Z axis toward the first path vertex. Picking the **Default** button aligns the shape so the path passes through its pivot point. While this is often the center of the object, sometimes it is not. Therefore, picking the **Default** button and the **Center** button may produce different results. The alignment buttons do not "reset" when picked. In other words, if you pick the **Right** button and then the **Top** button, the shape is aligned to the top right "corner."

Compare Dialog Box

The **Compare** dialog box is used to align the vertices of multiple shapes in a loft object. For example, if you loft a circle and a square along a straight path, the resulting loft object may appear twisted, Figure 9-24. This is because the first vertices of the shapes do not align. The **Compare** dialog box is used to correct this problem. It is opened by picking the **Compare** button in the **Shape Commands** rollout.

Compare

When the dialog box is first opened, it is empty. You must "get" shapes by selecting the **Pick Shape** button. Then, select the shapes on the loft object you want to compare. A plan, or top, view of the shapes is displayed in the **Compare** dialog box, Figure 9-25. The first vertex of each shape is shown as a small square. The object is to get all of the first vertices to align. To do this, use the **Select and Rotate** button and rotate the shape *on the loft object.* You can watch the coordinate display to get an exact rotation. However, this process is often an approximation, so you must sometimes "eyeball" the rotation.

Picking the **Reset** button removes all shapes from the dialog box. This button has no effect on the model itself. There are also four navigation controls at the bottom right of the dialog box. These are **Zoom Extents, Pan, Zoom,** and **Zoom Region**. These buttons work in the **Compare** dialog box in the same way that the standard 3ds max viewport navigation controls work in viewports.

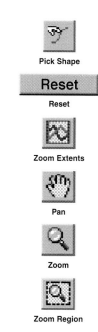

Pick Shape

Reset

Zoom Extents

Pan

Zoom

Zoom Region

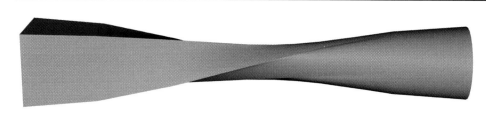

Figure 9-24. When lofting different shapes, the resulting object may appear twisted due to misalignment of the first vertices.

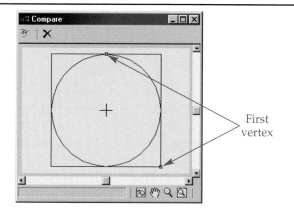

First vertex

Figure 9-25. The **Compare** dialog box is used to align the first vertex of each shape in a loft object.

Exercise

Exercise 9-8

1) Draw a circle and a rectangle. Loft the circle along a straight line path. Place the rectangle at the 40% and 60% path locations. Place the circle at the 100% path location. See the object shown on the top in the illustration below.
2) Remove the "twist" from the object. Use the **Compare** dialog box at the shape sub-object level.
3) Assign the material Wood_Ash to the object.
4) Render the scene to a file named ex09-08.jpg in the folder of your choice.
5) Save the scene as ex09-08.max in the folder of your choice.

Advanced Compound Objects

Compound objects are introduced in Chapter 6. You learned how to create basic loft objects, Boolean objects, and terrain objects. Advanced loft objects are covered in the first part of this chapter. This section covers more advanced types of compound objects. These include morph, connect, ShapeMerge, and mesher objects.

Morph

Morphing is perhaps one of the most recognizable 3D animation techniques. It can be seen in TV commercials, movies, and video games. *Morphing* involves one object changing into another object, Figure 9-26. In terms of 3ds max, morphing refers to matching the vertices of the starting object to the final object over a series of frames. The starting object is called the *seed* or *base object*. The final object is called the *target.*

There are some rules to follow for objects to be morphed. First, both objects must be mesh objects or patch objects. You cannot mix and match object types. Second, all objects must have the same number of vertices. This is one of the reasons you need to plan your models carefully. It is easy to do things early in the modeling process, such as optimizing a shape, that can make it impossible to morph the object.

Morph Object vs Morpher Modifier

3ds max has a compound object called a *morph object*. It also has a morpher modifier. Applying the morpher modifier generally allows more flexibility than modeling with the morph object. The modifier can

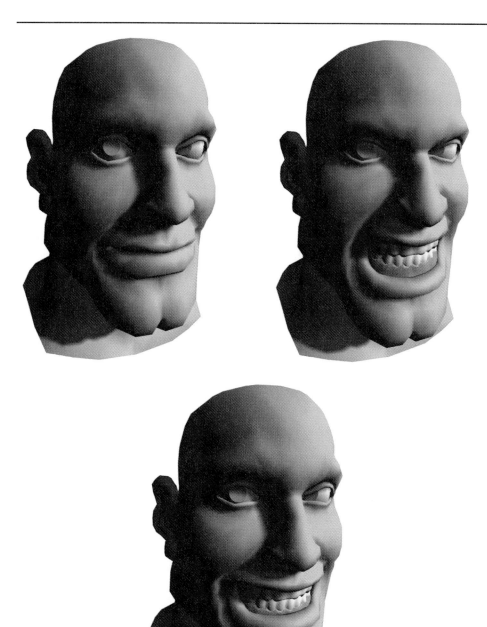

Figure 9-26. The face object is morphed to create a sneer. Morphing is commonly used to animate facial expressions and talking. (Discreet, a division of Autodesk)

be applied and managed in the modifier stack. This allows the seed and target to be modified prior to the morpher modifier being applied. The modifier can, in certain situations, be easier to use in **Track View** as well. **Track View** is covered in Chapter 16. However, the morph object is still an important modeling tool.

Making a Morph

The most important thing to keep in mind when creating seeds and targets is they *must* have the same number of vertices. This requires planning. An easy way to do this is to make a copy of the seed. Then,

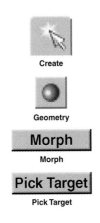

Create

Geometry

Morph

Morph

Pick Target

Pick Target

Create Morph Key

Create Morph Key

modify the copy to obtain what you want as the target. It can be much easier to do this once and then animate a morph rather than trying to animate all of the adjustments required.

Once you have a valid seed and a target created, select the seed. Then, pick the **Create** tab in the **Command Panel**. Pick the **Geometry** button and select **Compound Objects** from the drop-down list. In the **Object Type** rollout, pick the **Morph** button.

In the **Pick Targets** rollout, select the appropriate radio button to create a copy, instance, or reference, or to move the target. Then, select the **Pick Target** button and select the target object in the viewport. Both the seed and the target are displayed in the **Morph Targets:** list in the **Current Targets** rollout. See Figure 9-27.

Now, if you pick the **Play Animation** button, the object is fully morphed in all frames. This is because the seed is set to be 100% morphed on frame 0. In order to correctly morph the object, animation keys must be set. Keys are explained in detail in Chapter 16. To set a morph animation key, move to the frame where the object should be fully morphed. Then, select the target in the **Morph Targets:** list and pick the **Create Morph Key** button at the bottom of the **Current Targets** rollout. A key is added and displayed on the **Track Bar**. See Figure 9-28. Also notice a key is added at frame 0. The **Toggle Animation Mode** button does *not* need to be on to do this.

To finish, the keys need to be modified. Right-click on the key at frame 0 to display a shortcut menu. Then, select *objectname:***Morph** from the menu to open the **Key Info** dialog box. See Figure 9-29. This dialog box shows information about the key. In the **Targets:** list, the seed and the target are each displayed with a percentage. At frame 0, the seed is currently 0% and the target is 100%. That is why the object appears fully morphed. Highlight the seed in the list and change the value in the **Percentage:** spinner to 100. This makes the object 100% the seed at frame 0. Pick the right arrow at the top of the **Key Info** dialog box to move to the next key. This key should be set so that the object is 100% the target. If you add a third key, you can make the object morph from the seed to the target and back to the seed.

Figure 9-27. The morph seed and target are displayed in the **Current Targets** rollout.

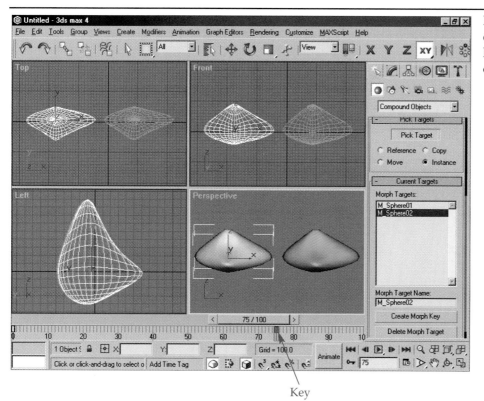

Figure 9-28. When objects are morphed, keys are added for the objects.

Key

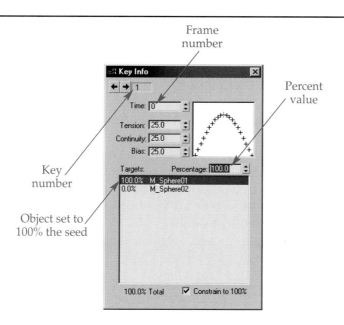

Figure 9-29. The **Key Info** dialog box is used to adjust keys for an object.

Frame number

Percent value

Key number

Object set to 100% the seed

Exercise

Exercise 9-9

1) Draw a 10-unit cube. Increase the number of segments on each side to 10. Name the cube Object Start.
2) Make a copy of the cube. Name it Object End.
3) Apply an FFD modifier to Object End. Create a shape of your own design, such as the one shown below.
4) Create a morph object using Object Start.
5) Move to frame 100. Assign Object End as the target.
6) Adjust the keys as needed so the object is 100% Object Start on frame 0, and 100% Object End on frame 100.
7) Pick the **Play Animation** button.
8) Observe the animated morph. Then, reset 3ds max without saving.

Connect

The *connect compound object* is used to connect the open ends of two objects. In order to create this object, the two base objects must have faces deleted to create openings in the objects. See Figure 9-30.

To create a connect object, select one of the two objects with holes. Then, pick the **Create** tab in the **Command Panel** and pick the **Geometry** button. Select **Compound Objects** from the drop-down list and pick the **Connect** button in the **Object Type** rollout.

In the **Pick Operand** rollout, select the **Pick Operand** button and pick the second object. The angle between the "holes" on the two objects must be less than 90°. The two objects are then connected between their holes with a *bridge.*

You can adjust the connection in the **Interpolation** area of the **Parameters** rollout. The value in the **Segments:** spinner determines the number of segments used to make the bridge. The **Tension:** spinner is used to adjust the curvature of the bridge. A value of 0 produces no curve. Do not set this value too high.

The smoothing of the bridge is controlled in the **Smoothing** area of the **Parameters** rollout. Checking the **Bridge** check box applies smoothing to the bridge. When you check the **Ends** check box, 3ds max attempts to smooth the edges between the operands and the bridge.

You can extract a copy or instance of an operand. This can be done by using the **Extract Operand** button in the **Operands** area in the **Parameters**

Create

Geometry

Connect

Pick Operand

Pick Operand

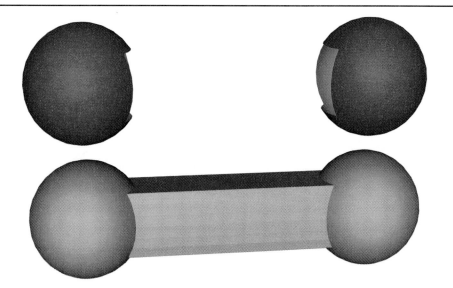

Figure 9-30. The connect compound object connects the two top objects (shown in red) between the holes in each. The resulting object is shown on the bottom (in orange).

rollout. However, this button is only available in the **Modify** tab after creating the object. To extract an operand, open the **Modify** tab and highlight the operand name in the **Operands** area in the **Parameters** rollout. Also, pick either the **Instance** or **Copy** radio button. Then, pick the **Extract Operand** button. The copy or instance is placed on top of the operand.

Exercise

Exercise 9-10

1) Draw two spheres.
2) Using the mesh select and delete mesh modifiers, remove a portion of each sphere. The portions removed should approximately face each other.
3) Render the scene to a file named ex09-10a.jpg in the folder of your choice.
4) Create a connect compound object from the two spheres. Adjust the tension as needed.
5) Render the scene to a file named ex09-10b.jpg in the folder of your choice.
6) Save the scene as ex09-10.max in the folder of your choice.

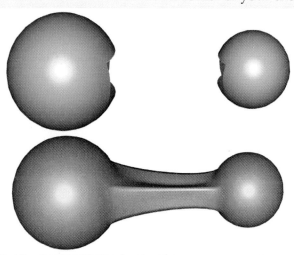

Figure 9-31. The red brick and green text shown on the top are the original objects. On the lower left, the text is merged and "cut" from the brick. On the lower right, the text is merged with the brick and the brick is removed.

ShapeMerge

The *ShapeMerge compound object* is created from a mesh object and a shape. The shape can be imbedded in the mesh object or subtracted from it. See Figure 9-31. To create a ShapeMerge object, select a mesh object. Then, pick **Create** in the **Command Panel**. Pick the **Geometry** button and select **Compound Objects** from the drop-down list. Then, pick the **ShapeMerge** button in the **Object Type** rollout.

Create

Geometry

ShapeMerge

ShapeMerge

Pick Shape

Pick Shape

In the **Pick Operand** rollout, select the **Pick Shape** button. Select the shape in the viewport. The shape is projected plan to the mesh object in the viewport where it is selected. Therefore, the shape must be properly located before picking it. However, it can be moved later using sub-object editing.

In the **Operation** area of the **Parameters** rollout, select the **Merge** radio button to merge the shape with the mesh object. This can be useful if you are going to extrude the faces later. Pick the **Cookie Cutter** radio button if you want to use the shape as a cutting edge. This can be used to remove the shape from the mesh object. Checking the **Invert** check box flip-flops the effects of both the **Merge** and **Cookie Cutter** options.

Help Cel

Creating a ShapeMerge compound object requires tremendous computer resources. Keep the object and the shape as simple as possible. Otherwise, you may crash your computer.

Exercise 9-11

1) Draw a box. Increase the number of segments to 5 on each side.
2) Draw text of your first name. Use the Arial font. Size the text so it will fit "inside" the box.
3) Create a ShapeMerge compound object. Select the box first. Then, pick the text as the shape. This may take a few seconds to complete. If you have a long name, you might want to use your initials.
4) Create a cookie cutter with the text removed from the box.
5) Assign the material Stones_Balmoral to the box.
6) Render the scene to a file named ex09-11.jpg in the folder of your choice.
7) Save the scene as ex09-11.max in the folder of your choice.

Mesher

The *mesher compound object* creates instances of other animated objects. It is designed primarily to be used with particle systems. However, a mesher compound object can be used with any type of object. One huge advantage of this object is you can, in effect, apply modifiers to a particle system. Particle systems are covered in Chapter 22.

To create a mesher object, pick **Create** in the **Command Panel**. Then, pick the **Geometry** button and select **Compound Objects** from the drop-down list. Pick the **Mesher** button in the **Object Type** rollout. The **Parameters** rollout is displayed, Figure 9-32. Finally, draw the mesher object in the viewport. The size of the mesher object is not important. The object looks like a pyramid until a particle system or other object is assigned to it.

Once the mesher object is created, a particle system or other object must be assigned to it. This must be done in the **Modify** tab. In the **Parameters** rollout, select the button below the **Pick object** label. By

Create

Geometry

Mesher

Mesher

Figure 9-32. The
Parameters rollout for
a mesher object.

default, the button is labeled **None**, which is replaced by the selected object's name. Once you select the button, pick the object.

The value in the **Time Offset:** spinner determines how the instanced, animated geometry matches to the animation of the original geometry. For example, if you are using the mesher object with a particle system and enter –1.0 in the spinner, the particles "generated" from the mesher object begin one frame *earlier* than the particle system. A value of 1.0 means they start one frame *later*.

When the **Build Only At Render Time** check box is on, the mesher object does not display instanced geometry until rendered. The **Update** button just below this check box is used to manually update the mesher object. This button should be picked when the offset timing is changed or the original instanced geometry is altered.

You can use the mesher object's default bounding box to control the effects of the object or you can choose to match the bounding box of another object. By using a custom bounding box, the size of the bounding box remains static. If the default mesher bounding box is used, especially with a particle system, the bounding box can change in size over the animation. To pick a new bounding box, check the **Custom Bounding Box** check box. Then, select the **Pick Bounding Box** button. Finally, select an object to match its bounding box. Modifiers are now applied to the mesher object in reference to the custom bounding box. Below the **Pick Bounding Box** button is a display showing the coordinates of the bounding box.

Help Cel

Transforms applied to the original geometry are not applied to the mesher object, even if an xform modifier is applied to the original.

Chapter Snapshot

Chapter Test

Answer the following questions on a separate sheet of paper.
1) Which rollout is used to loft multiple shapes?
2) Define current level.
3) What are the three ways the value in the **Path:** spinner can be displayed?
4) How is the current path level indicated in viewports?
5) What is the purpose of the value in the **Snap:** spinner for loft objects?
6) Which radio button(s) allow a virtually unlimited number of shapes on the path of a loft object?
7) What is the purpose of the **Pick Shape** button at the bottom of the **Path Parameters** rollout?
8) How can you add loft shapes to an existing loft object?
9) What do deformation tools allow you to do?
10) How can you apply a deformation when creating a loft object?
11) Which deformation tools use a dialog box with a common layout?
12) Briefly describe the **Deformation** dialog box layout.
13) What is the purpose of the **Make Symmetrical** button in the **Deformation** dialog box?
14) In what color are the X and Y axes displayed in the **Deformation** dialog box?
15) What does the **Reset Curve** button do in all of the **Deformation** dialog boxes except the **Fit Deformation** dialog box?
16) What are the three types of control points that can be used on a deformation curve?
17) What does the fit deformation do?
18) How do you remove a twist from a loft object created from a square and a circle shape?
19) What are the two conditions that must be met for morphing two objects?
20) With what type of object is the mesher compound object designed to be used?

Modeling Problems

Draw the following models. Use the 3ds max objects presented in this and earlier chapters. Start by drawing the objects shown on the left. Then, apply modifiers, deformations, and transforms as needed to complete the model. You may also need to make copies of some objects. Choose object colors as shown. When finished, save each model as p09-xx.max in the folder of your choice.

1 Cartoon Snake

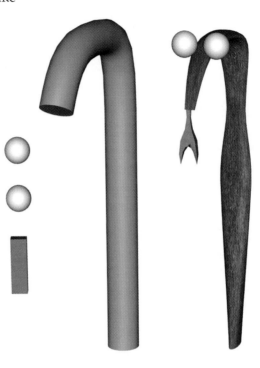

2 Cartoon Hog

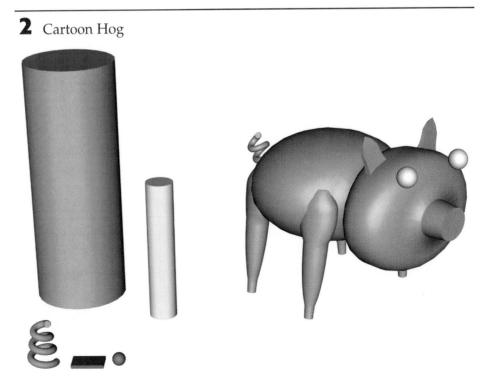

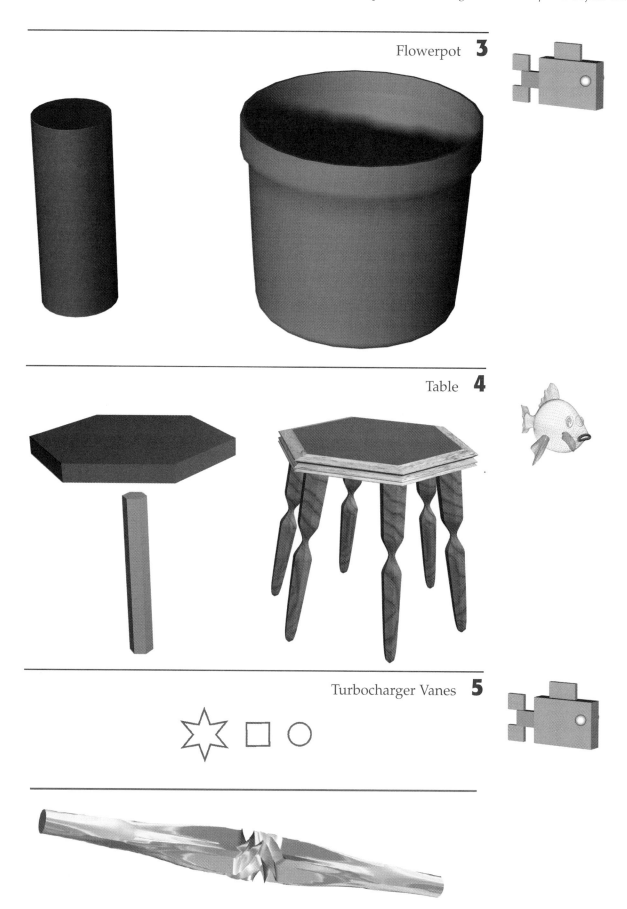

Flowerpot **3**

Table **4**

Turbocharger Vanes **5**

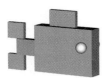

6 Candlestick

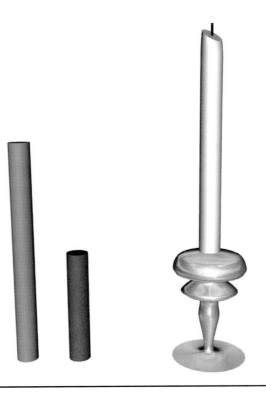

7 Candy Cane

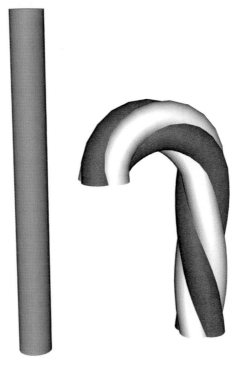

Jack **8**

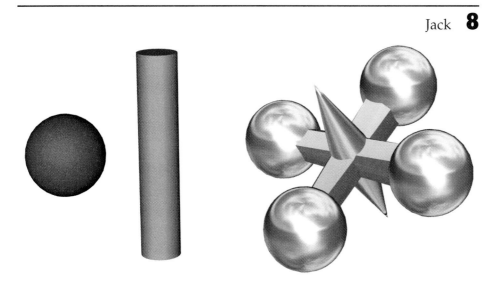

Cartoon Refrigerator **9**

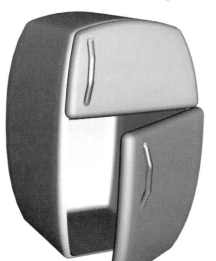

Alien Head **10**

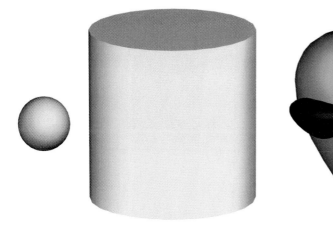

Objectives

After completing this chapter, you will be able to:

- Explain what a light is in relation to 3D modeling and animation.
- Identify the four types of lighting in 3ds max.
- Create different types of lights.
- Summarize lighting theory.

What Are Lights?

Lights in 3ds max perform the same function as the lights you have in your home—they provide illumination. See Figure 10-1. Where the lights in your home illuminate a room, the lights in 3ds max illuminate a scene. There are four types of lights in 3ds max. These are omni lights,

Figure 10-1. Lights are used to provide illumination in a scene. Where lights are placed and how they are set up can greatly affect the mood of a scene. Here, the lights in this scene help communicate a night or evening setting.

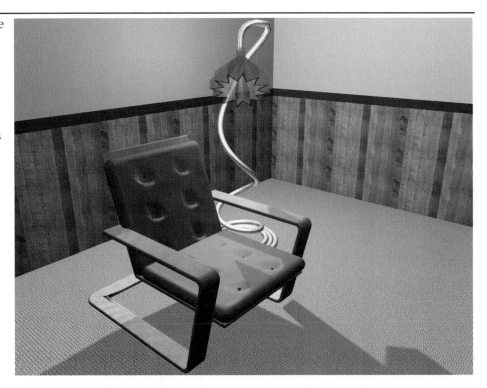

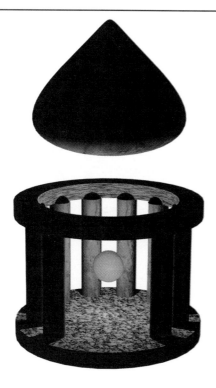

Figure 10-2. In this scene, an orange-tinted omni light is placed in the center of the temple inside the orb. As you can see, all interior surfaces are illuminated by the omni light.

spotlights, directional lights, and ambient light. Once created, omni lights, spotlights, and directional lights can be converted between the three types. This is done in the **Modify** tab of the **Command Panel**.

Omni Lights

An *omni light* is a single point with rays projecting in all directions. See Figure 10-2. Omni lights can cast shadows and can also be used as projectors. Omni lights can be set with or without falloff. *Falloff*, or *attenuation*, is when the intensity of the light decreases over distance. This distance can be set as a range.

To create an omni light, select **Create** in the **Command Panel**. Then, pick the **Lights** button and select **Omni** in the **Object Type** rollout.

You can also pick **Lights** in the **Create** pull-down menu. Then, pick **Omni Light** in the cascading menu. This opens the **Create** tab in the **Command Panel** and selects the **Omni** button.

Finally, pick a location in the viewport to place the omni light. Once the light is created, it can be named in the **Name and Color** rollout. You can also pick the color swatch to open the **Object Color** dialog box. However, changing this color has no effect on the light or its displayed color.

There are several rollouts associated with an omni light. See Figure 10-3. Settings in the **General Parameters** and **Attenuation Parameters** rollouts are discussed later in this chapter. The other rollouts are discussed in Chapter 19, *Lighting Effects.*

Create

Lights

Omni

Omni

Figure 10-3. The roll-outs for an omni light.

Exercise

Exercise 10-1

1) Draw the objects shown below.
2) Place an omni light in the middle of the objects. Notice the effect in the Perspective viewport.
3) Delete the first omni light.
4) Place two more omni lights "outside" the objects. Notice the effect.
5) Reset 3ds max without saving.

Turning Default Lighting into Omni Lights

3ds max has default lighting based on either one or two omni lights. Once an omni light, spotlight, or direction light is placed in the scene, the default lighting is "deleted." To set the number of lights used for default lighting, open the **Viewport Configuration** dialog box. This is done by selecting **Viewport Configuration**... from the **Customize** pull-down menu or by right-clicking on a viewport name and selecting **Configure**... from the shortcut menu. In the **Rendering Options** area of the **Rendering Method** tab, select either the **1 Light** or **2 Lights** radio button. By default, the **1 Light** radio button is on.

The default lighting can be converted into two omni lights. This allows you to make changes to the lights. This feature only works when the **2 Lights** radio button is on. With the **2 Lights** radio button on, select **Add Default Lights to Scene** from the **Views** pull-down menu. The **Add Default Lights to Scene** dialog box appears. See Figure 10-4.

Even though the **2 Lights** radio button must be on for this feature to work, you do not have to convert both lights. Checking the **Add Default Key Light** check box adds an omni light in front and to the left of the scene. Checking the **Add Default Fill Light** check box adds an omni light behind and to the right of the scene. See Figure 10-5. The value in the **Distance Scaling:** spinner determines how far the omni lights are placed from the world origin (0,0,0). The default value is 1.0 and is a relative value. In other words, it is not in current drawing units. Finally, pick the **OK** button to close the dialog box and place the omni lights.

A

Figure 10-4. A—You can add one or both of the default lights to the scene. B—This scene has no lights placed yet.

B

Figure 10-5. Default lighting added to the scene in Figure 10-4.

Exercise

Exercise 10-2

1) Draw the objects shown below.
2) Convert the default lighting into omni lights.
3) Notice the location of the new omni lights in the scene.
4) Reset 3ds max without saving.

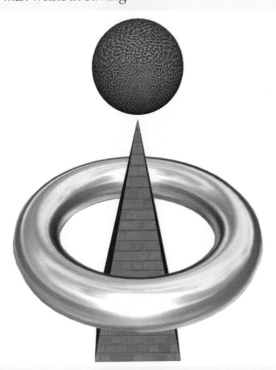

Spotlights

A *spotlight* has rays projecting in a cone in one direction from a source. See Figure 10-6. Spotlights in 3ds max are just like those you might see at a sports event or concert. There are two types of spotlights—target and free. To create a spotlight, pick **Create** in the **Command Panel**. Then pick the **Lights** button. Finally, pick either the **Target Spot** or **Free Spot** button in the **Object Type** rollout.

You can also pick **Lights** in the **Create** pull-down menu. Then, pick **Target Spotlight** or **Free Spotlight** in the cascading menu. This opens the **Create** tab in the **Command Panel** and selects the **Target Spot** or **Free Spot** button.

A *target spotlight* has a target that must be placed in addition to the light itself. The target and the spotlight can be transformed together or independently. Pick a point in the viewport and hold down the mouse button. This point is the location of the spotlight. Next, drag the mouse to the location of the target and release.

A *free spotlight* has no target and can be aimed anywhere. Pick a point (single click) in the viewport for the location of the light. The spotlight is initially aimed directly "down" in the viewport, but can be transformed later.

Once a spotlight is created, it can be named in the **Name and Color** rollout. The **Object Color** dialog box can be opened by picking on the color swatch, but this setting has no effect on the light.

There are several other rollouts associated with spotlights. The **General Parameters** and **Attenuation Parameters** rollouts are discussed later in this chapter. The remaining rollouts are discussed in Chapter 19, *Lighting Effects*.

Create

Lights

Target Spot

Free Spot

Figure 10-6. The rays from a spotlight project in a cone.

Exercise

Exercise 10-3

1) Draw the objects shown below.
2) Create a target spotlight located as shown below. Notice the effect in the Perspective viewport.
3) Delete the spotlight.
4) Place a free spotlight as shown below. Notice the effect in the Perspective viewport.
5) Reset 3ds max without saving.

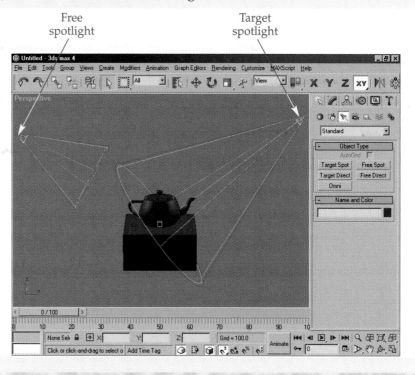

Free spotlight · Target spotlight

Create

Lights

Target Direct

Free Direct

Directional Lights

Directional lights have rays projecting in one direction from a source, like spotlights. However, unlike spotlights, the rays are projected parallel, rather than in a cone. See Figure 10-7. Directional lights are called *direct lights* or direction lights in 3ds max. Direct lights are typically used to simulate sunlight or other "far away" light sources.

There are two types of direct lights—target and free. To create a direct light, pick **Create** in the **Command Panel**. Then, pick the **Lights** button. Finally, pick either the **Target Direct** or **Free Direct** button in the **Object Type** rollout.

You can also pick **Lights** in the **Create** pull-down menu. Then, pick **Target Directional Light** or **Directional Light** in the cascading menu. This opens the **Create** tab in the **Command Panel** and selects the **Target Direct** or **Free Direct** button.

A *target direct light* has a target that must be placed in addition to the light itself. The target and the direct light can be transformed together or independently. Pick a point in the viewport and hold down

Figure 10-7. The rays from a direct light project parallel to each other and perpendicular to the light.

the mouse button. This point is the location of the direct light. Next, drag the mouse to the location of the target and release.

A *free direct light* has no target and can be aimed anywhere. Pick a point in the viewport for the location of the light. The direct light is initially aimed directly "down" in the viewport, but can be transformed later.

Once a direct light is created, it can be named in the **Name and Color** rollout. The **Object Color** dialog box can be opened by picking on the color swatch, but this setting has no effect on the light.

There are several other rollouts associated with direct lights. The **General Parameters** and **Attenuation Parameters** rollouts are discussed later in this chapter. The remaining rollouts are discussed in Chapter 19, *Lighting Effects*.

Help Cel

There is another way to simulate sunlight in 3ds max. This is with the sunlight system, discussed in Chapter 20 of this text. The sunlight system automatically creates and controls a free direct light based on geography.

Exercise

Exercise 10-4

1) Draw the objects shown below.
2) Place a free direct light as shown below. Notice the effect in the Perspective viewport.
3) Delete the direct light. Place a free spotlight in the same location. Notice the difference in the Perspective viewport.
4) Reset 3ds max without saving.

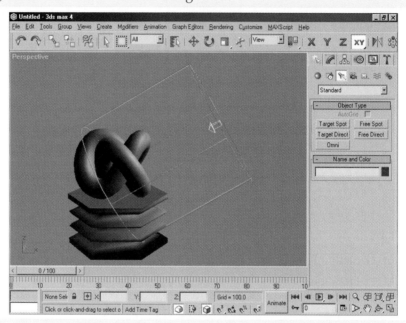

General Parameters Rollout

The settings in the **General Parameters** rollout are common to all types of lights except ambient light. See Figure 10-8. In this rollout, you can set the color of the light and its intensity, and also determine which objects the light affects. The **General Parameters** rollout is available when creating the light, or it can be accessed in the **Modify** tab of the **Command Panel**.

You can switch between light types. At the top of the rollout is the **Type:** drop-down list. This list identifies the current type of light. You can select a different type from the list to change the light. The drop-down list is disabled when creating a light and must be accessed in the **Modify** tab.

You can think of the **On** check box as the light switch. When the check box is checked, the light is on. When unchecked, the light is off. When the **Cast Shadows** check box is checked, the light produces shadows where appropriate in the scene.

The brightness, or *intensity,* of the light is set in the **Multiplier:** spinner. The default value of 1.0 provides a starting point. The required intensity of the light will vary from scene to scene. The distance from the light to the objects also affects how intense the light must be.

Light Color

Next to the **On:** check box is a color swatch. This is the color of light produced by the light. Pick on the swatch to open the color selector and choose a new color. The corresponding values of the selected color appear

Figure 10-8. The settings in the **General Parameters** rollout are common to all lights, except ambient light.

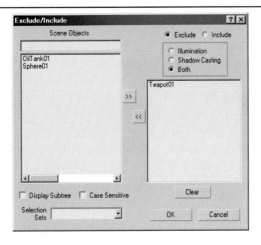

Figure 10-9. You can limit which objects a light affects using the **Exclude/Include** dialog box.

in the **R:**, **G:**, **B:**, **H:**, **S:**, and **V:** spinners. The color of the light can also be changed by adjusting these spinners. The color swatch updates as you change the spinner values. Changing the color of a light can be animated.

Excluding Objects

Picking the **Exclude**... button opens the **Exclude/Include** dialog box. See Figure 10-9. This dialog box allows you to limit the number of objects the light affects when the scene is rendered.

The **Exclude** and **Include** radio buttons at the top right of the dialog box determine if the objects selected are affected (included) or not (excluded). By default, a light affects all objects in the scene.

You can exclude illumination of an object's surface or eliminate the shadow an object casts. Picking the **Illumination** radio button turns off the illuminating effect of the light on an object's surface. Picking the **Shadow Casting** radio button turns off the shadows of the object the light will create. Picking the **Both** radio button turns off illumination and shadow casting. If the **Include** radio button is on, picking these buttons turns *on* illumination and/or shadow casting.

On the left of the dialog box is a list of **Scene Objects**. These are all objects in the scene. To exclude (or include) an object, highlight the name in the list on the left. Then, pick the **>>** button to place it in the list on the right. The list on the right displays the objects excluded from (or included in) the light's effect. To remove an object from the list at the right, highlight the name in the right-hand list and pick the **<<** button. Picking the **Clear** button removes all objects from the right-hand list.

Any saved selection sets appear in the **Selection Sets** drop-down list. To highlight all objects in a selection set in the left-hand list, pick the name of the set in the drop-down list.

Finally, to exclude (or include) the objects in the list at the right, pick the **OK** button to close the dialog box. Picking the **Cancel** button closes the dialog box without accepting the settings.

Help Cel

The effects of excluding an object from a light cannot be seen in a shaded viewport. The scene must be rendered to see the effect. The effect also appears in an ActiveShade display.

Setting How a Light Affects Surfaces

The **Affect Surfaces:** area of the **General Parameters** rollout has settings that allow fine-tuning of how a light affects the surface of objects. These controls can help you add the subtle lighting details to a scene that make it an exceptional scene.

The **Contrast:** spinner is used to adjust the contrast between the areas of the object illuminated by diffuse and ambient light. The default value of 0.0 produces a normal contrast. This is used in most scenes. However, a high contrast value is often used in SciFi space scenes where there is typically an abrupt change between ambient and diffuse light illumination.

The value in the **Soften Diff. Edge:** spinner sets the transition between diffuse and ambient illumination. The default value of 50.0 provides an average transition that can be used in most scenes. The value can be increased to a maximum of 100.0 to help eliminate unwanted "hard" transitions. The value can be reduced to a minimum of 0.0 to produce a hard transition.

The **Diffuse**, **Specular**, and **Ambient Only** check boxes allow you to set which portions of the object the light affects. When the **Diffuse** check box is checked, the light affects the diffuse color portion of the object. When the **Specular** check box is checked, the light affects the specular portion of the object. When the **Ambient Only** check box is checked, only the ambient portion of the object is affected by the light. The other two check boxes and the other controls in the **Affect Surfaces:** area are greyed out, as is the **Cast Shadows** check box.

Exercise

Exercise 10-5

1) Draw the objects shown below.
2) Add three spotlights to the scene.
3) Adjust the properties of the three spotlights to produce the shadows and illumination shown below.
4) Reset 3ds max without saving.

Attenuation Parameters Rollout

Attenuation describes the property of a light's intensity decreasing over distance. This effect is similar to the headlights on your car only illuminating for a certain distance. In 3ds max, without attenuation, a light has the same intensity no matter the distance from the light. The attenuation for an omni light, spotlight, or direct light is set in the **Attenuation Parameters** rollout. See Figure 10-10.

The values in the **Near Attenuation:** area set the distance from the light where the illumination starts, or "fades in." The value in the **Start:** spinner specifies the distance from the light, in current drawing units, where the light begins to fade in. The value in the **End:** spinner is the distance from the light where the illumination is first generated at 100%. For near attenuation to be on, the **Use** check box must be checked. Otherwise, the light is generated at 100% illumination at the source. Checking the **Show** check box displays a gizmo-like wireframe in the viewports representing the near attenuation.

The values in the **Far Attenuation:** area set the distance from the light where the illumination reaches zero. The value in the **Start:** spinner specifies the distance from the light, in current drawing units, where the light begins to fade out. The value in the **End:** spinner is the distance from the light where the illumination is 0%. For far attenuation to be on, the **Use** check box must be checked. Otherwise, the light continues at 100% illumination to infinity... and beyond. Checking the **Show** check box displays a gizmo-like wireframe in the viewports representing the far attenuation.

The settings in the **Decay** area offer another way to add attenuation to a light. These settings may provide the solution when standard attenuation settings do not produce the desired results. You can choose between three different types of illumination decay. The type of decay is selected in the **Type:** drop-down list. The **None** type applies no decay to the illumination. The near and far attenuation settings are the only settings applied. The **Inverse Square** type uses the mathematical equation that physicists use in "the real world" to calculate light properties. However, in the "digital world," this may not provide enough illumination. The **Inverse** type provides a "near-real-world" effect on the scene that may be more applicable to the digital world. The value in the **Start:** spinner sets the distance from the light, in current drawing units, where the illumination decay of the light begins. Checking the **Show** check box displays a gizmo-like wireframe in the viewports, which represents the attenuation.

Figure 10-11 shows the effect of different attenuation settings. Notice how different the rendered scenes appear.

Figure 10-10. The **Attenuation Parameters** rollout is used to set how a light's intensity decreases over distance.

Figure 10-11. The effect of attenuation settings on a scene. A—Near falls off at 250, far at 600. B—Near falls off at 225, far at 600.

A

B

Figure 10-11. C—Near falls off at 225, far at 300. D—Near falls off at 0, far at 150.

C

D

Help Cel

When using a decay setting, it is dependent on near attenuation settings. With no attenuation, decay starts at the light. When near attenuation is set, decay begins at that point. Far attenuation has no effect on decay.

Ambient Light

Ambient light is the overall light in a scene. It is like outdoor lighting just before sunrise. Ambient light has the same intensity everywhere in the scene. It does not have directional rays and therefore does not cast shadows. If a scene is rendered with only ambient light, all objects appear as silhouettes. See Figure 10-12. To set ambient light, select **Environment...** in the **Rendering** pull-down menu. This opens the **Environment** dialog box. See Figure 10-13.

In the **Global Lighting:** area of the **Common Parameters** rollout in the **Environment** dialog box, you can set the color of ambient light. You can also change the intensity of ambient light and add a color tint to all lights in the scene. To change the color of ambient light, pick the **Ambient:** color swatch. Then, in the **Color Selector: Ambient Light** dialog box, pick a color. Close the color selector to return to the **Environment** dialog box.

To change the intensity of ambient light, enter a value other than 1.0 in the **Level:** spinner. This, in effect, changes the intensity of all lights in the scene.

To add a color tint to *all* lights, pick the **Tint:** color swatch. Then, pick a color in the **Color Selector: Global Light Tint** dialog box. Close the color selector to return to the **Environment** dialog box.

Changes made to ambient light should be made carefully and in small increments. It is too easy to fall into the trap of "fixing" lighting problems by adjusting ambient light. Doing so usually makes the scene look fake and computer-generated. The level of ambient light should almost never be changed. Tints, however, can be used effectively in many instances, such as simulating a harvest moon.

Exposure Control

Exposure control is used to adjust the rendered output of a scene, much like a photographer adjusts exposure before taking a picture. Exposure control can adjust for bright and dim spots in the scene. To set exposure control, open the **Environment** dialog box and expand the **Exposure Control** rollout if not already expanded.

Figure 10-12. A—This scene includes two spotlights for illumination. B—When the spotlights are turned off, only ambient light illuminates the scene. Notice how the background is not affected by lighting.

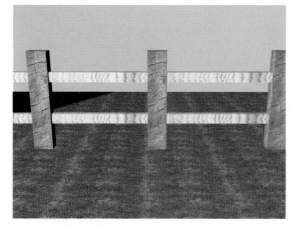

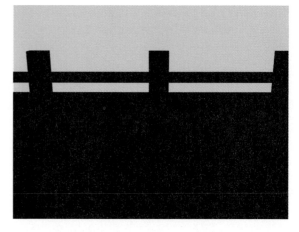

A

B

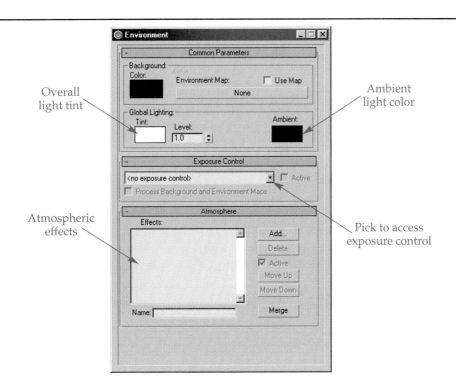

Figure 10-13.
The **Environment** dialog box.

In the drop-down list, select the exposure control to use for the scene. By default, 3ds max is supplied with one type called **Automatic Exposure Control**. Aftermarket software developers may offer other plug-ins. The **Active** check box turns the control on and off. When the **Process Background and Environment Maps** check box is checked, exposure control is applied to these items.

When **Automatic Exposure Control** is selected in the drop-down list, the **Automatic Exposure Control Parameters** rollout appears in the **Environment** dialog box. This rollout is used to fine-tune the control. When the **Chromatic Adaptation:** check box is checked, color correction is applied to the scene using the color in the color swatch. When the **Color Differentiation** check box is on, colors with low levels of illumination are rendered as grey.

The **Physical Scale:** spinner is used to lighten or dim all lights in the scene. The default value of 1500.0 is a starting value. Increasing the value lightens the scene. Decreasing the value dims the scene. The **Exposure Value:** spinner is used to lighten or dim the entire scene. This effect is similar to opening the rendering in photo editing software and adjusting the brightness. Both of these spinners can be animated.

Help Cel

Generally, exposure control is a very subtle effect. The impact on a scene may not be obvious. Also, the effects of exposure control are not displayed in an ActiveShade view.

Lighting Theory

One of the most important parts of any 3D scene is the lighting. Often, however, the lighting is also one of the most neglected parts of a 3D scene. It is all too easy to get caught up in the intricacies of creating realistic objects with realistic materials, and then just throw some lights into the scene and render it. However, realistic lighting of a 3D scene can make the

difference between a poor or average 3D rendering or animation that is obviously computer-generated and an exceptional one that is very realistic.

Lighting a Scene

There are two general approaches to lighting a scene. The first approach is often found in video production or "sitcom" television. This approach is to flood the scene with light so virtually everything is illuminated. This is very easy to do and requires very few adjustments as the actors move around the scene. However, the next time you watch a sitcom, look at the room (or scene) on the TV and then look at the room you are sitting in. Odds are the room you are sitting in has many shadows and is *not* flooded with light. This approach to lighting does not produce very realistic scenes.

The second approach is used in traditional photography and cinematography. This is called *triangle lighting,* and is used for the basis of all lighting. It is called triangle lighting because three lights are used to illuminate the scene. Figure 10-14 shows a scene illuminated with traditional triangle lighting. The three lights used in triangle lighting are the key light, fill light, and backlight.

Key Light

The first light is called the *key light.* It provides the primary illumination to the scene. The exact location will depend on the particular model that you are lighting and the "mood" you want to create. See Figure 10-14. Lighting moods are covered later in this chapter.

Fill Light

The second light is called the *fill light,* or *flood light.* This light is used to eliminate or reduce unwanted shadows in the scene. The location of the fill light is determined by the shadows cast by the key light. This will vary from model to model, and even object to object. In some cases, more than one fill light may be needed. Refer to Figure 10-14.

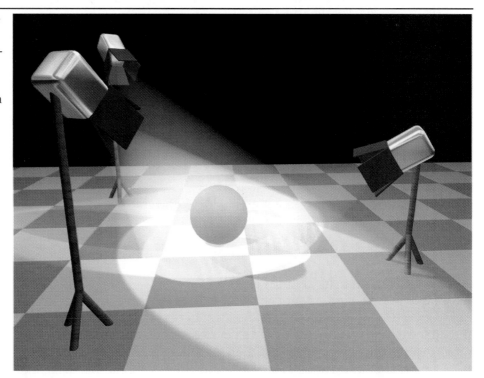

Figure 10-14. Triangle lighting is used in traditional cinematography. The light on the left in front is the key light. The light on the right is the fill light. The light on the left in the back is the backlight.

Backlight

The third light is called the *backlight.* This light is used to add a sense of depth to the scene by bringing the objects out of the background. The location and intensity of the backlight are determined by the effect the fill light has on the scene. Backlighting is generally placed after the key light and fill light. Refer to Figure 10-14.

Lighting Moods

By simply changing the lighting in a scene, the mood can be drastically changed. Changing the lighting can also make a scene that originally appeared as if it was shot in daylight look as if it is now midnight.

There are five basic types of mood lighting. These are high key, low key, frontal, side, and cross key. Cross key lighting is not commonly used in traditional cinematography and is not discussed here. The other four types are discussed next.

High Key Lighting

High key lighting is used for interior scenes illuminated with daylight. See Figure 10-15. The key light is placed in front of and above the objects. How far it is placed in front and above will depend on the specific model. Traditionally, the key light is placed at about a 45° angle above the objects.

The fill light is placed in front of the objects and perhaps to one side. This will depend greatly on where the shadows are cast from the key light. However, the intensity of the fill light should be about 1/2 that of the key light, or slightly above.

The backlight is placed behind the objects. Traditionally, the backlight is placed either above the objects or at "ground" level. The intensity of the backlight should be about 1 1/2 times that of the key light.

Low Key Lighting

Low key lighting is used for nighttime scenes. See Figure 10-16. The key light is placed in front of the objects and usually higher than in a high key setup. Also, the key light is often placed to one side of the center of the objects.

The fill light is placed in front of the objects and perhaps to one side. The intensity of the fill light is traditionally about 15% of the key light. The backlight is set just as it is with a high key setup.

Frontal Lighting

Frontal lighting produces overhead lighting for scenes that should appear to have ceiling lighting fixtures in the scene. See Figure 10-17. This lighting is set up like high key lighting, except that the key light is placed high above the objects and directly in front, not off to one side. The key light should illuminate both "halves" of the scene equally.

Side Lighting

Side lighting produces lighting as if the objects are illuminated by sunlight or a street lamp outside a window. See Figure 10-18. The key light should be placed at about "eye level" and in front of the model. Looking at the scene from the side, the light and target should be at nearly the same level. The fill light and backlights are set up as they are for high key lighting.

Figure 10-15. High key lighting is used for interior scenes illuminated with daylight.

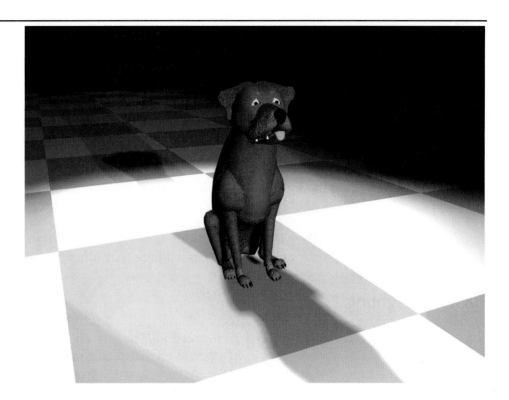

Figure 10-16. Low key lighting is used for nighttime scenes. Compare this figure with Figure 10-15.

Figure 10-17. Frontal lighting is used to simulate overhead lighting. Compare this figure with Figure 10-15 and Figure 10-16.

Figure 10-18. Side lighting is used to provide illumination from a light through a window. A cross-shaped gobo is used on the light here to simulate shadows from mullions in the window. Side lighting does not have to be from the "side" of the model. It is placed at the "front" in this figure.

Help Cel

When using side lighting, the effect can be enhanced by using a window-shaped gobo on a projector spotlight for the key light.

Chapter Snapshot

Chapter Test

Answer the following questions on a separate sheet of paper.
1) What is a light in 3ds max?
2) List the four types of lights in 3ds max.
3) A(n) _____ has rays that project in all directions.
4) Define falloff (attenuation).
5) Default lighting can be turned into which type of light?
6) In order to turn default lighting into light objects, the _____ radio button must be on.
7) A(n) _____ has rays that project in one direction but are not parallel.
8) What is the difference between a "target" light and a "free" light?
9) A(n) _____ has rays that project in one direction and are parallel.
10) Which lights can be either "free" or "target" lights?
11) A(n) _____ is commonly used to simulate sunlight or extremely distant light sources.
12) The _____ rollout is used to set the color of the light and its intensity.
13) Exposure control is used to _____.
14) _____ is like outdoor light just before sunrise.
15) Name the three lights used in triangle lighting.
16) In triangle lighting, the _____ light produces the primary illumination for the scene.
17) In triangle lighting, the _____ light is used to eliminate unwanted shadows in the scene.
18) In triangle lighting, the _____ adds a sense of depth to the scene.
19) What is mood lighting used for?
20) List the four basic types of mood lighting used in traditional cinematography.

Modeling Problems

Draw the following models. Use the 3ds max objects presented in this and earlier chapters. Use your own dimensions. Choose object colors similar to those shown. Define and assign basic materials where appropriate. Add lights to each model as necessary. Pay attention to the shadows shown in each figure. Also pay attention to light color. When finished, save each model as p10-xx.max in the folder of your choice.

Table and Lamp **1**

Candle and Holder **2**

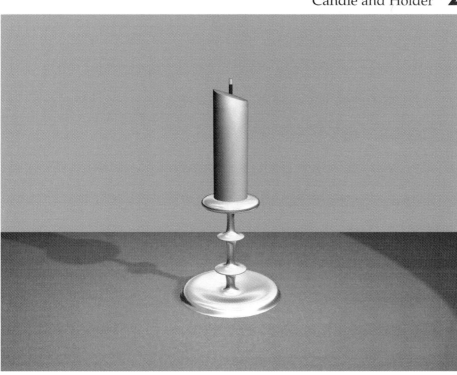

3 Desktop Lamp

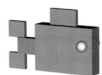

4 Colored Lights

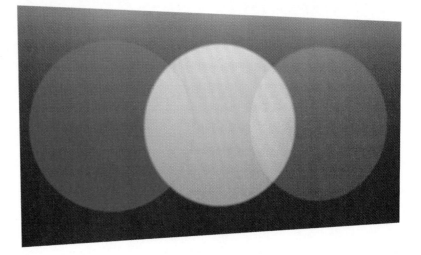

Teapot Shadow Study **5**

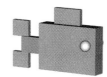

Tori Shadow Study **6**

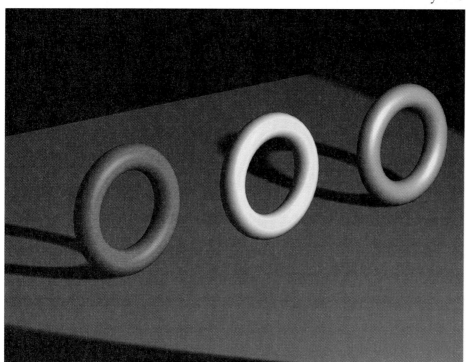

7 Motel Sign with Neon Lights

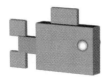

8 Pyramid Shadow Study

Sofa and Sunlight **9**

Wall Sconce Lights **10**

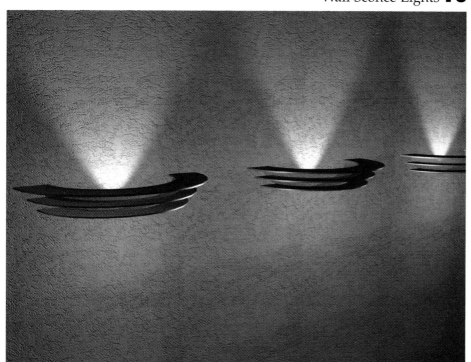

Chapter 11

Cameras

Objectives

After completing this chapter, you will be able to:

● Define what a camera is in 3ds max.
● Create cameras.
● Define safe frame.
● Explain camera matching.
● Animate a camera.
● Link a camera to an object for animation.

What Are Cameras?

Cameras in 3ds max are like still and video cameras used in the real world. While the Perspective viewport can provide a 3D viewpoint for the scene, there are limitations to what can be displayed. For example, if the viewport is changed to a different view, it can be nearly impossible to obtain the exact same Perspective view again later. A camera, on the other hand, provides virtually unlimited possibilities for displaying a scene.

In the real world, different types of cameras are used for still photography and video or cinematic photography. In 3ds max, however, there is no distinction. What determines if the camera is a still or video camera is whether you are rendering a single frame (still) or multiple frames (an animation).

Many special effects can be created with cameras. For example, a camera can be animated. Suppose you are animating the view from an airplane cockpit as it may be seen by the pilot. If the plane performs a roll, you can make the camera roll as well. You can also make a camera follow, or "look at," an object in the scene during an animation.

A common use of 3ds max in the architecture and civil engineering fields is to show what a planned building may look like in relation to existing structures. See Figure 11-1. A feature of 3ds max called camera matching can be used to help do this.

A

B

Figure 11-1. A—This photo is of a recently purchased lot for a vacation cabin. B—The architect uses 3ds max to show how a proposed cabin will look on the site.

Creating Cameras

There are two basic types of cameras in 3ds max. See Figure 11-2. The *target camera* type consists of a camera and a target. The camera and target can be moved independently or together. The *free camera* type does not have a visible target. This type of camera can be easier to animate and is often used for walkthrough animations.

To create a camera, select **Create** in the **Command Panel**. Then, pick the **Cameras** button. The only selection that can be made in the drop-down list is **Standard**. However, if you have third-party plug-ins installed, other options may be available. Finally, in the **Object Type** rollout, pick the button corresponding to the type of camera you want to create.

After the camera is created, it can be named in the **Name and Color** rollout. You cannot change the display color of a camera in this rollout. If multiple cameras will be created, it can be useful to name each one. For example, Left Camera and Right Camera are more meaningful than Camera01 and Camera02.

Both camera types have the same parameters. These parameters are discussed in the *Camera Parameters* section in this chapter.

Creating a Target Camera

A target camera must be drawn using the cursor. The first point you pick is the location of the camera. Hold down the mouse button and drag the cursor to the location where you want the target. Then, release to place the target. The camera and target can be moved to precise locations using the transform tools. The camera and target appear in the viewports as shown in Figure 11-3. After the camera is created, the parameters need to be set. Refer to the *Camera Parameters* section in this chapter.

Create

Cameras

Target

Target Camera

Free

Free Camera

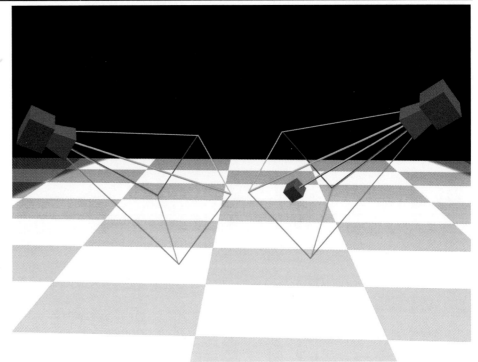

Figure 11-2. The camera on the left is a free camera. The camera on the right is a target camera. Notice the target (small cube).

Camera

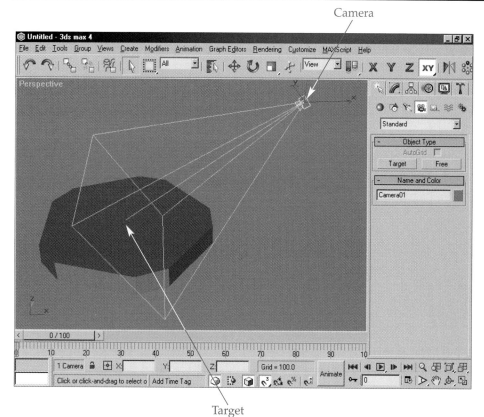

Target

Figure 11-3. A target camera as it appears in a viewport.

Creating a Free Camera

Like a target camera, a free camera must be drawn using the cursor. Since a free camera does not have a target, only one point needs to be picked. The picked point is the location of the camera. The camera is created perpendicular to the current construction grid. The camera points down along the negative Z axis of the current construction grid. However, the camera can be transformed after it is created. A free camera appears in the viewports as shown in Figure 11-4.

In addition to the camera parameters shared with a target camera, a free camera also has the **Target Distance:** spinner. This spinner is located in the **Parameters** rollout in the **Command Panel**. The value in the **Target Distance:** spinner sets the distance to an invisible target. The invisible target is used when the free camera is orbited using the **Orbit Camera** button. This button replaces the **Arc Rotate** button if the current viewport is a camera viewport.

Orbit Camera

Help Cel

The **Target Distance:** spinner is also available for a target camera. This spinner is located in the **Parameters** rollout and can be used to change the distance between the camera and target by transforming the target. However, it may be easier to use the **Select and Move** button to transform the target in a viewport.

Figure 11-4. A free camera as it appears in a viewport.

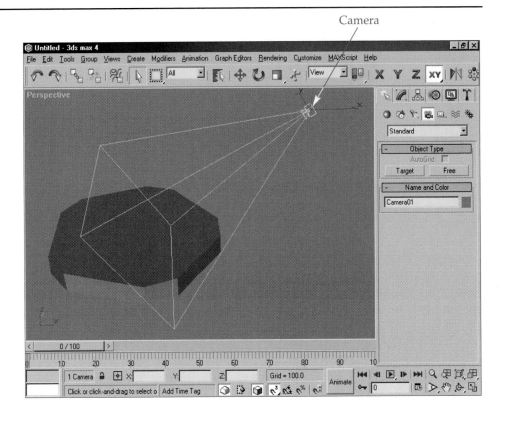

Camera

Figure 11-5. The **Parameters** rollout for a camera.

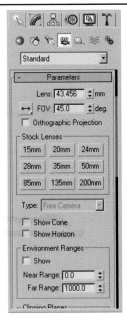

Camera Parameters

Target cameras and free cameras have the same parameters. These parameters can be set in the **Parameters** rollout in the **Modify** tab of the **Command Panel**. See Figure 11-5. These parameters can also be set when the camera is created while the camera is still selected.

At the top of this rollout is the **Lens:** spinner. The value in this spinner is the focal length of the camera measured in millimeters. You can select from common, real-world lenses by picking the appropriate button in the **Stock Lenses** area. The value in the **Lens:** spinner changes to match the lens selected.

The value in the **FOV:** spinner sets the field of view for the camera. The *field of view (FOV)* refers to how much the camera can "see" from side-to-side. You can think of FOV as the width of the camera. The FOV value is measured in degrees.

Horizontal FOV

Vertical FOV

Field of view is by default calculated horizontally. However, by picking the appropriate button in the **FOV** flyout, you can change the direction to vertical or diagonal. Which button is selected in the **FOV** flyout determines how the value in the **FOV:** spinner affects the camera.

Checking the **Orthographic Projection** check box applies orthographic projection to the camera viewport. Unchecking the check box applies perspective projection. A *perspective projection* has foreshortening and appears more realistic.

The **Type:** drop-down list allows you to switch between camera types. The current type is displayed in the drop-down list. If you switch to a free camera from a target camera, any animation applied to the target camera's target is lost.

Checking the **Show Cone** check box displays the FOV cone in all viewports except camera viewports, whether or not the camera is selected. When a camera is selected, the cone always shows. When unselected, the cone does not show unless the **Show Cone** check box is checked. The **Show Horizon** check box is used to turn on the display of the camera's horizon line in a camera viewport. When unchecked, the horizon line is not displayed.

The **Environment Ranges** area is used to set the near and far limits for environmental effects. Environmental effects are discussed in Chapter 15. Checking the **Show** check box displays rectangles in the non-camera viewports to represent the limits.

The **Clipping Planes** area is used to set the "starting" and "ending" points for what the camera "sees." These distances are measured along the camera's local Z axis. Anything closer than the near clipping plane or farther than the far clipping plane is ignored when the scene is rendered. This can be useful when test rendering a large scene. To set the clipping planes, check the **Clip Manually** check box and enter values in the **Near Clip:** and **Far Clip:** spinners. The planes are displayed in the viewports as red rectangles.

The **Multi-Pass Effect** area of the **Parameters** rollout is used to apply depth of field or motion blur to a camera. *Depth of field* describes the effect of a camera blurring objects near it or far from it. The objects "in focus" are the subjects of the camera. *Motion blur* is used to simulate the effect of objects moving. This effect is exaggerated on fan blades or a hummingbird's wings.

To apply a multi-pass effect to the camera, select either **Motion Blur** or **Depth of Field** from the drop-down list. For the effect to be rendered, the **Enable** check box must be checked. Checking this check box enables the **Preview** button. To preview the multi-pass effect in the camera viewport, move to the frame you want to preview and pick the **Preview** button.

When the **Render Effects Per Pass** check box is checked, any rendering effects are applied on each pass of the multi-pass effect. Otherwise, the rendering effect is placed on the last pass. Turning this option off can speed up rendering. Rendering effects are covered in Chapter 15.

When you make a selection in the drop-down list, a rollout corresponding to your selection appears in the **Command Panel**. Refer to the next sections for discussion on these rollouts.

Help Cel

In addition to the multi-pass camera motion blur, there are other ways to add motion blur, including object motion blur and the motion blur rendering effect. These are discussed in Chapter 14 and Chapter 15.

Exercise

Exercise 11-1

1) Draw the vase shown below. Use your own dimensions.
2) Create a target camera. Place the target and camera as shown below.
3) Name the camera Camera-Target.
4) Create a free camera, placed as shown below.
5) Set the free camera focal distance to the stock 35 mm lens.
6) Name the camera Camera-Free.
7) Save the scene as ex11-01.max in the folder of your choice.

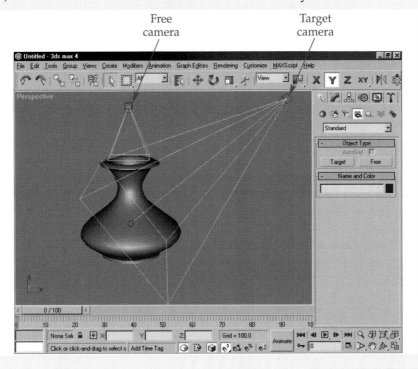

Depth of Field

A "real life" camera produces an image with the foreground and background elements out of focus, or blurred. Only the main subject is in focus. By using different lenses and settings, this effect can be adjusted. As previously discussed, in **3ds max**, you can apply a depth of field effect to a camera. The effect is adjustable. It works by applying an offset to multiple rendering passes, thus creating a blur. Once you have selected **Depth of Field** in the **Multi-Pass Effects** area of the **Parameters** rollout for a camera, the **Depth of Field Parameters** rollout appears. See Figure 11-6. The settings in this rollout are discussed in the following sections.

Help Cel

Depth of field can also be applied as a rendering effect. Rendering effects are discussed in Chapter 15.

Focal Depth

When the **Use Target Distance** check box in the **Focal Depth** area is checked, the distance from the camera to its target is used to calculate rendering offsets. In other words, the target is the point about which offsets are applied. When the check box is unchecked, the value in the **Focal Depth:** spinner defines the offset point. The value in this spinner is relative and can range from 0 to 100. A value of 100 is essentially infinity, resulting in no depth of field. Using a **Focal Depth:** setting tends to apply an overall blur to the scene.

Sampling

The **Sampling** area of the **Depth of Field Parameters** rollout is used to set how the rendered offsets are calculated and displayed. When the **Display Passes** check box is checked, each rendering pass is displayed in the viewport preview as it is generated. When unchecked, only the final

Figure 11-6. The **Depth of Field Parameters** rollout.

result is displayed. When the **Use Original Location** check box is on, the first pass is displayed at the camera's location. When unchecked, all passes (including the first) are offset.

The **Total Passes:** spinner sets the number of rendering passes used to calculate the effect. The higher this number, the more detailed the final effect. However, increasing the value also increases rendering time.

The **Sample Radius:** spinner determines the "size" of the offset. In other words, this spinner controls how blurry of an effect is generated. The higher the value in the spinner, the more the effect is blurred. The value can be set to nearly one million, but there is a practical limit.

The **Sample Bias:** spinner controls the "regularity" of the effect. Increasing the value can produce a more even effect. Reducing the value allows the effect to "stray" from the sample radius, producing a random effect. The value can range from 0 to 1, with 0.5 the default.

Pass Blending

The **Pass Blending** area of the **Depth of Field Parameters** rollout is used to set how multiple rendered passes are composited, or blended, to create the final rendered effect. The rendering passes are composited with random weight applied to each pass. This is done to prevent moiré or streaks. When the **Normalize Weights** check box is checked, a smooth effect results. When unchecked, the effect is sharp, but it tends to be grainy.

Each rendered pass is blended using dithering. The value in the **Dither Strength:** spinner determines how much dithering is applied. The higher the value, the more dithering. However, more dithering usually results in a grainy image.

The **Tile Size:** spinner sets the size of a single dithering "tile." This value can range from 0 to 100, with 32 the default. The higher the value, the larger a tile. Small tiles produce a cleaner image, but increase rendering times.

Scanline Renderer Parameters

Antialiasing is used to soften the edge between two colors. Without antialiasing, a sharp transition is produced. On diagonal or curved edges, a blocky "stairstep" effect results without antialiasing. The **Scanline Renderer Parameters** area of the **Depth of Field Parameters** rollout is used to disable antialiasing and the filtering pass. When the **Disable Filtering** check box is checked, the filtering pass is eliminated. When the **Disable Antialiasing** check box is checked, antialiasing is not calculated. These check boxes affect the depth of field effect only.

Camera Motion Blur

As objects move in the "real world," the motion is often too fast for a camera to capture or the naked eye to see. For example, the propeller on an airplane moves so fast that the eye sees a circular blur of the propeller color. The wings of a hummingbird are another example of where motion is too fast for the eye or a camera to capture. Motion blur added to a 3ds max camera simulates this real-world effect by rendering multiple passes. The passes are offset and blended to produce the final

Figure 11-7. The **Motion Blur Parameters** rollout.

rendered image. Once you have selected **Motion Blur** in the **Multi-Pass Effects** area of the **Parameters** rollout for a camera, the **Motion Blur Parameters** rollout appears. See Figure 11-7. The settings in this rollout are discussed in the following sections.

Sampling

The **Sampling** area of the **Motion Blur Parameters** rollout is used to set how the rendered offsets are calculated and displayed. When the **Display Passes** check box is checked, each rendering pass is displayed in the viewport preview as it is generated. When unchecked, only the final result is displayed.

The **Total Passes:** spinner sets the number of rendering passes used to calculate the motion blur. The higher this number, the more detailed the final effect. However, increasing the value also increases rendering time.

The **Duration (frames):** spinner sets the number of frames in which the motion blur is calculated. By default, motion blur is calculated on the current frame only. Increasing the value in this spinner increases the number of frames for the effect. The number of frames is "split" so that the effect is applied to the same number of frames before and after the current frame.

The **Bias:** spinner controls the "shift" of the motion blur to or away from the current frame. Increasing the value shifts the blur toward the frames following the current frame. This, in effect, shifts the blur away from the current frame. Reducing the value shifts the blur toward the frames before the current frame. This, in effect, shifts the blur to the current frame. The bias value can range from 0 to 1, with 0.5 the default.

Pass Blending

The options in the **Pass Blending** area of the **Motion Blur Parameters** rollout are the same as those for depth of field. They are used to set how multiple rendered passes are composited, or blended, to create the final rendered effect. The rendering passes are composited with random weight applied to each pass. This is done to prevent moiré or streaks. When the **Normalize Weights** check box is checked, a smooth effect results. When unchecked, the effect is sharp, but it tends to be grainy.

Each rendered pass is blended using dithering. The value in the **Dither Strength:** spinner determines how much dithering is applied. The higher the value, the more dithering. However, more dithering usually results in a grainy image.

The **Tile Size:** spinner sets the size of a single dithering "tile." This value can range from 0 to 100, with 32 the default. The higher the value, the larger a tile. Small tiles produce a cleaner image, but increase rendering times.

Scanline Renderer Parameters

The options in the **Scanline Renderer Params** (parameters) area of the **Motion Blur Parameters** rollout are used to disable antialiasing and the filtering pass. When the **Disable Filtering** check box is checked, the filtering pass is eliminated. When the **Disable Antialiasing** check box is checked, antialiasing is not calculated. These check boxes affect the camera motion blur effect only.

Safe Frame

The *safe frame* shows the area in a camera viewport that will be rendered. The frame is represented by three rectangles showing the overall, action, and title zones. A yellow rectangle indicates the overall size of the rendered image. An orange rectangle indicates the action safe zone. All movement in an animation should occur inside this rectangle to ensure nothing is "chopped off." A cyan rectangle indicates the title safe zone. Any text or labels should be placed inside this rectangle.

To display the safe frame, right-click on a camera or perspective viewport label. Then, pick **Show Safe Frame** from the shortcut menu. See Figure 11-8. To turn off the safe frame, select **Show Safe Frame** from the shortcut menu again. You can also toggle the safe frame on and off by pressing [Shift][F] on the keyboard.

Safe frame can also be turned on and off in the **Viewport Configuration** dialog box. Select the **Safe Frames** tab in the dialog box. Then, to turn on safe frame for the active viewport, check the **Show Safe Frames in Active View** check box. To turn off safe frame in the viewport, uncheck the check box.

Figure 11-8. Showing the safe frame in a camera viewport.

Exercise 11-2

1) Open ex11-01.max if not already open.
2) Change the Perspective viewport to the Camera-Free viewport.
3) Display the safe frame in the Camera-Free viewport.
4) Save the scene as ex11-02.max and reset 3ds max.

Introduction to Camera Matching

The purpose of *camera matching* is to match the perspective of the camera to that of a bitmap image. This is a very useful tool for architects and civil engineers. For example, suppose an architect plans to make a presentation to a city council on a proposed building. By taking a photo of the site, scanning the photo, and using the 3ds max camera matching feature, the architect can create a 3D model of the new building based on the existing site. The city council can then "see" the new building in place. This feature can also be very useful in film production where computer-generated characters are placed into a scene with live-action characters.

The next sections introduce two ways to match a camera to a bitmap image. Both methods involve displaying the bitmap as a background in a viewport.

Viewport Background

To display a bitmap image as the background of a viewport, first select the viewport. Then, select **Viewport Background**... from the **Views** pull-down menu or press [Alt][B] on the keyboard. The **Viewport Background** dialog box is displayed, Figure 11-9. In the **Background Source** area, pick the **Files**... button. In the **Select Background Image** dialog box that appears, pick the bitmap you want to use as the viewport background. Pick the **Open** button to close the **Select Background Image** dialog box. Then, close the **Viewport Background** dialog box.

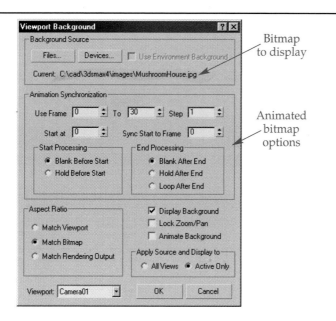

Figure 11-9. Setting a viewport background image.

Bitmap to display

Animated bitmap options

The image is displayed as the background once the **Viewport Background** dialog box is closed. You can turn the display of the image on and off by right-clicking on the viewport label to display the shortcut menu. Then, select **Show Background** from the menu. The display is toggled on or off.

Help Cel

The current environment background can be used as the viewport background by checking the **Use Environment Background** check box in the **Viewport Background** dialog box.

Matching Perspective Using the Horizon

A simple way to match a camera to a bitmap image is to use the camera's horizon. First, create a camera. Then, change to the camera viewport and turn the horizon line on. This procedure is discussed earlier in this chapter. It may be helpful to turn off the grid display. Next, orbit and move the camera until the horizon line matches the natural horizon of the bitmap image. See Figure 11-10.

Figure 11-10. The background image and the camera horizon line displayed in the camera viewport.

Exercise 11-3

1) Draw a simple "stick figure," such as the one shown below.
2) Create a target camera. Adjust the camera so it is to the right of the stick figure and slightly above.
3) Change the Perspective viewport to the Camera viewport.
4) Display the bitmap meadow1.jpg as the background in the Camera viewport. This file is located in the 3ds max \Maps\Backgrounds folder.
5) Turn on the horizon in the Camera viewport. Turn off the grid.
6) Adjust the camera until its horizon line matches the horizon of the bitmap. Refer to the figure shown below.
7) Save the scene as ex11-03.max in the folder of your choice and reset 3ds max.

Horizon line

Matching a Camera to a Viewport

The **Camera Match** function is a special utility that comes with 3ds max. It allows you to create a camera exactly matching the perspective of a bitmap image. This is much more involved than the method of camera matching previously discussed. However, it is also a much more exact method. In order to use this method, you must know exact "real world" distances of at least five points in the scanned image.

To use the **Camera Match** utility, first set the viewport background to the image you will be using. Then, identify at least five points on the image to use as reference points. These points are called *CamPoints.* To draw CamPoints, select **Create** in the **Command Panel**. Then, pick the **Helpers** button. Select **Camera Match** from the drop-down list. Finally, select the **CamPoint** button in the **Object Type** rollout and pick the points on the bitmap to use as references. See Figure 11-11.

Next, move the CamPoints to the correct distances in relation to each other. This step is crucial to matching the camera to the bitmap. Then, pick **Utilities** in the **Command Panel**. Pick the **Camera Match** button in the **Utilities** rollout.

Create

Helpers

CamPoint

CamPoint

Utilities

Camera Match

Camera Match

Figure 11-11.
CamPoints placed to use as references for camera matching.

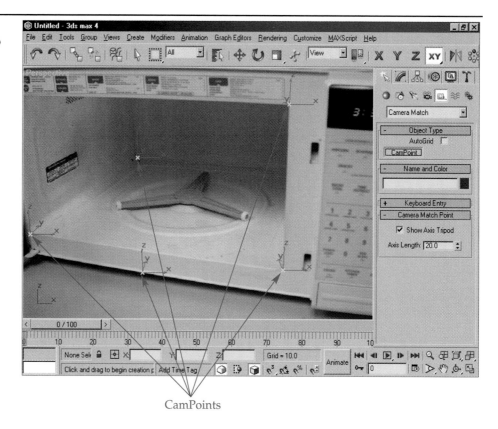

CamPoints

Figure 11-12.
Selecting CamPoints to use with the **Camera Match** utility.

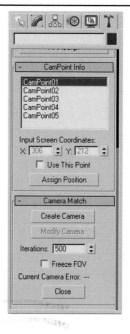

At the top of the **CamPoint Info** rollout is a list of all CamPoints in the scene. See Figure 11-12. You must use at least five CamPoints. Individually highlight the CamPoints you want to use in the list and check the **Use This Point** check box at the bottom of the rollout. Finally, pick the **Create Camera** button in the **Camera Match** rollout to create the camera. The camera is a free camera and can now be selected and named just like any other camera.

This is merely an introduction to the **Camera Match** utility. There are many other options and features with this utility. As you develop your

Create Camera

3ds max skills, experiment with this utility. Note: When placing CamPoints in relation to each other with the **Camera Match** utility, you *must* know the *exact* distances for the points in order to create a usable camera.

Animating Cameras

You can animate a camera just as you would an object. A camera can be moved or rolled. In addition, the target of a target camera can be animated independent of the camera. Also, it can be useful to make a camera follow a path or always "look at" an object as it moves.

Linking to Objects

Linking is used to create a relationship between objects where the transformation of one object is passed to another. Linking is covered in detail in Chapter 12. The movement of a camera or camera target can be linked to an object for animation.

For example, suppose you are modeling race cars crossing the finish line. You might want to show the finish from the perspective of somebody standing at the finish line. The person's view will naturally follow the cars as they race past. By linking a camera's target to the car models, the camera will automatically follow the cars as they race past the viewer (camera). See Figure 11-13.

Figure 11-13. As the race car speeds past, the camera follows the car because the target of the camera is linked to the car.

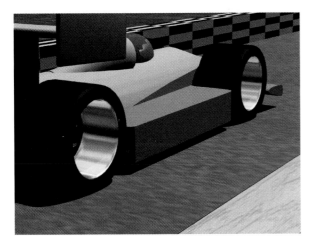

Select and Link

To link a camera target to an object, first create the object and the camera. Then, pick the **Select and Link** button in the **Main** toolbar. Pick the target to select it and hold down the mouse button. Drag the cursor to the object. A line appears from the target to the cursor. When the cursor is over an object, the link cursor appears. Release the mouse button to link the object. The object momentarily flashes white as 3ds max records the link. Now, when the object moves, the camera target moves with it.

This same procedure can be used to link a camera to an object. A camera is often linked to a dummy object to make animating the camera easier. Dummy objects are discussed in Chapter 14.

Following a Path

A common type of architectural application is called a ***walkthrough.*** This is where the view moves through a building as though the viewer is walking. To create this effect in 3ds max, a free camera is made to follow a path. The path is the line of motion that the viewer will take when "walking through" the building.

Another example of using a path is showing what a person riding a motorcycle sees while racing around a track. In this case, the camera *and* parts of the motorcycle, such as the handlebars, must follow the path. See Figure 11-14.

Figure 11-14. As the supersport motorcycle moves around the track, the camera follows the path showing what the rider sees. Notice how the front portion of the motorcycle does not move from frame to frame.

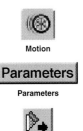

Motion

Parameters

Parameters

Assign Controller

To make a free camera follow a path, a ***controller*** is assigned to the camera. First, create the camera and a spline representing the path. The path is usually drawn as a line. Next, select the camera and pick **Motion** in the **Command Panel**. Pick the **Parameters** button at the top of the panel. In the **Assign Controller** rollout, pick the **Position** controller in the hierarchical tree. Then, pick the **Assign Controller** button. See Figure 11-15.

In the **Assign Position Controller** dialog box that appears, select **Path Constraint** from the list and pick the **OK** button. See Figure 11-16. The **Path Parameters** rollout now appears on the panel. Next, pick the **Add Path** button. In the viewport, select the spline drawn as the path.

Now, when the **Play Animation** button is picked, the camera follows the path. However, the camera may not "turn" with the path. The **Path Options:** area of the **Path Parameters** rollout allows you to adjust how the camera moves along the path. Checking the **Follow** check box makes the camera align to the path. Which path axis the camera aligns to is set in the **Axis:** area of the rollout. Checking the **Bank** check box in the **Path Options:** area allows the camera to lean into turns. This option is used in Figure 11-14. The amount of lean is determined by the value in the **Bank Amount:** spinner. The value in the **Smoothness:** spinner determines how quickly the camera "reacts" to the curves of the path.

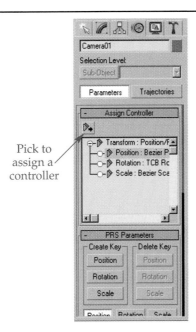

Pick to assign a controller

Figure 11-15. Setting a free camera to follow a path starts in the **Motion** tab of the **Command Panel**.

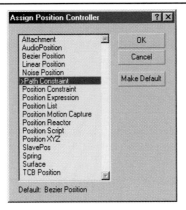

Figure 11-16. Selecting **Path Constraint** as the position controller for a camera.

To make a target camera follow a path, create the path, the camera, and a dummy object. Link both the camera and target to the dummy. Then, assign the path controller to the dummy object using the same procedure previously described for a free camera. This simplifies the process, rather than having independent path controllers for both the camera and target.

You can add multiple paths to a single path controller. By weighting the effect of each path, the motion produced is a blend of all paths assigned to the controller.

Help Cel

Using the procedure described here, you can assign any of the available controllers to any object as appropriate. Controllers can be powerful tools in 3ds max.

Exercise

Exercise 11-4

1) Draw the pylons and spline path shown below. Use your own dimensions.
2) Create a free camera and locate it as shown below. Change the Perspective viewport to the Camera viewport.
3) Assign a path constraint position controller to the camera. Use the curved spline as the path.
4) Pick the **Play Animation** button to preview the motion. Do this with the Top viewport active and then with the Camera viewport active.
5) Set the camera to follow the path and bank.
6) Preview the motion again in both the Top and Camera viewports.
7) Save the scene as ex11-04.max and reset 3ds max.

Chapter Snapshot

Chapter Test

Answer the following questions on a separate sheet of paper.
1) Define a camera in relation to 3ds max.
2) List the different types of cameras in 3ds max.
3) How do the types of cameras in 3ds max differ?
4) What effect does changing the display color of a camera in the **Name and Color** rollout have on the scene?
5) A camera must be drawn using _____.
6) A _____ camera has an invisible target used when the camera is orbited.
7) When a camera is created, unselected, and selected again, its parameters are set in the _____ rollout of the _____ tab of the **Command Panel**.
8) The value in the **Lens:** spinner is the _____ of the camera.
9) What are the functions of the buttons in the **Stock Lenses** area?
10) Define field of view.
11) What do the buttons in the **FOV** flyout allow you to do?
12) The **Type:** drop-down list in the **Parameters** rollout for a camera allows you to _____.
13) What are clipping planes?
14) What is camera motion blur used for?
15) Define safe frame.
16) What is the purpose of camera matching?
17) List two ways to perform camera matching.
18) Give one example of when you may use linking with a camera.
19) Define walkthrough.
20) What type of camera is typically used for a walkthrough?

Modeling Problems

Draw the following models. Use the 3ds max objects presented in this and earlier chapters. Use your own dimensions unless otherwise indicated. Choose object colors similar to those shown. Create and assign basic materials as appropriate. Add lights as needed. Be sure to match any shadows or light color shown. When finished, save each model as p11-xx.max in the folder of your choice.

1 Camera Path Around Pylons
Draw the pylons shown here. Also, draw the spline to use as a path for a camera. Finally, draw a camera and set it up to follow the path.

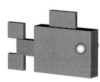

2 Corkscrew Path
Draw the bar stock and corkscrew spline shown below. Use your own dimensions. Create a free camera and set it up to follow the corkscrew.

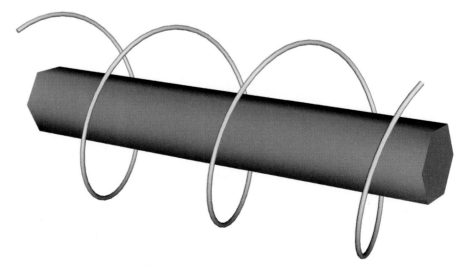

Floor Plan **3**

Draw the walls shown below. Use your own dimensions. Add doorways and windows as needed. Assign materials as appropriate. Add two spotlights to the scene. Position the lights to obtain shadows similar to those shown. Draw the spline shown. Use it as a path for a free camera.

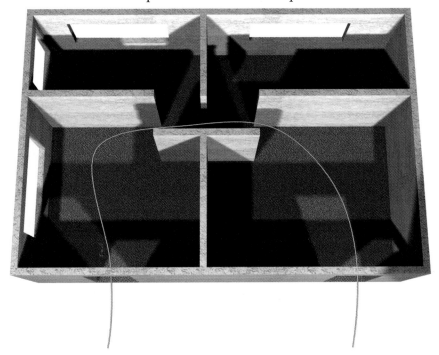

Ferris Wheel **4**

Draw the simple Ferris wheel shown here. Then, create a circle centered on the wheel. Finally, create a camera and set it up to follow the circle path.

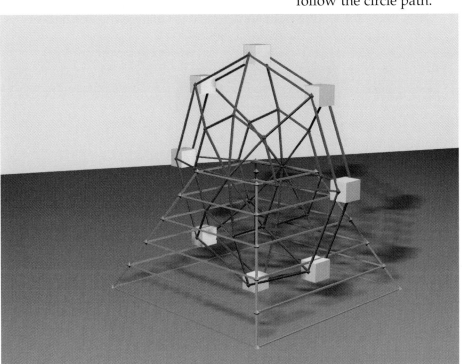

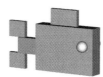

5 Car and Road

Draw the objects shown. Use your own dimensions. Add lights and apply materials as needed. Create a free camera showing a view similar to the rendering. Create a path as needed so the camera follows the road.

6 Bug Walk

Draw the objects shown below using your own dimensions. Assign materials similar to those shown. Transparent glass materials can be found in the RayTraced_01 material library. Create a free camera and set it up to follow the path shown below. Change the Perspective viewport to display the camera view.

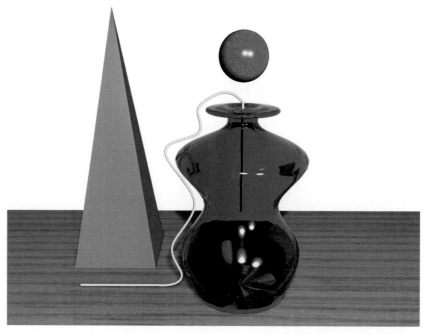

Teapot Study **7**

Draw the teapot and quad patch shown below. Add two spotlights to produce the shadows shown. Change the light color as needed. Create a free camera and an appropriate path to produce the renderings shown.

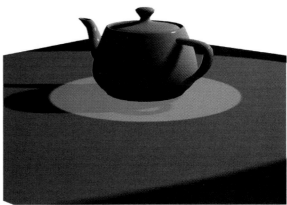

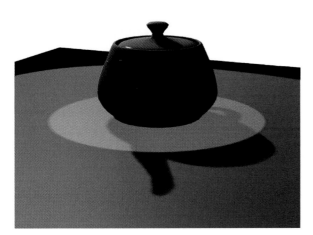

Football Helmet **8**

Draw the football helmet shown below. Use your own dimensions. Add lights and assign materials as needed. Create a free camera. Change the **Perspective** viewport to show the camera view. Then, position the camera to look out of the helmet. Add a viewport background or place other objects in front of the helmet.

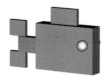

9 Colored Tube

Draw a tube using your own dimensions. Define a basic white material and assign it to the tube. Create a camera and position it inside the tube. Add lights as needed to create the colored shadows shown.

10 Steel Production

Draw the steel-making ladle and lance shown below. Use your own dimensions. Add lights and assign materials as appropriate. Create a free camera and set it up to follow the path shown below.

Race Car **11**

Draw the portion of the race car that can be seen from the cockpit, as shown here. Create a free camera and place it so the view is from the driver's seat. The camera should follow the track path. Select and link all objects to the camera.

Chapter 12

Hierarchy and Linking

Objectives

After completing this chapter, you will be able to:

- Explain a hierarchy and list several advantages to its use.
- Define terms used to describe hierarchies.
- List the two types of hierarchical relationships 3ds max can create.
- Explain the two general rules that apply to hierarchies.
- Link child objects to parent objects.
- Adjust pivot points.
- Specify inheritance.
- Lock object transformations.
- Assign a link constraint.

Introduction to Creating a Hierarchy

The ability to create a hierarchy is one of the most important tools an animator can have. A hierarchy can be used to create complex motion, simulate joint functions, or to simplify the animation process. For example, cameras and targets are often linked to a dummy object when creating a walkthrough animation. This way, only the dummy object needs to be animated instead of both the camera and its target.

A *hierarchy* in 3ds max is a relationship that occurs when an object's movement, rotation, or scale is controlled by that of another object. The object being controlled is called the *child.* The object doing the controlling is called the *parent.* A parent object is often controlled by a parent of its own. This "grandparent" is called an *ancestor* of the first child object. A child object that has no children itself is called a *leaf.* See Figure 12-1. This whole relationship may be easiest to understand if you think of it as a family tree.

For example, suppose you have modeled a plane. All of the objects in the plane must follow the position and rotation of the fuselage, or body, of the plane. Therefore, the wings, tail, landing gear, and propeller are made child objects of the parent object fuselage. See Figure 12-2. By doing this, to move or bank the plane, only the fuselage needs to be animated. The other objects automatically inherit the movement and rotation of the fuselage. In addition, in the case of the propeller, the child objects can be rotated or moved independent of the parent.

3ds max has two types of hierarchical relationships that can be created. The first type is created using linking and is called forward kinematics. This is a basic type of hierarchy construction and is discussed in this chapter. A more advanced type of hierarchical relationship, called inverse kinematics (IK), also uses links. This is discussed in Chapter 21.

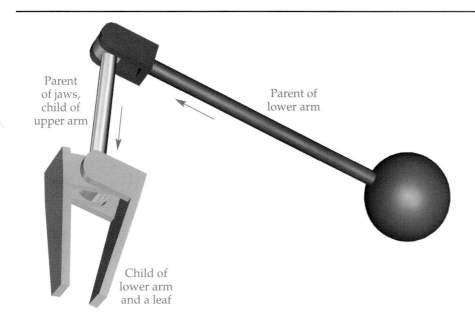

Figure 12-1. Terminology associated with hierarchies.

Parent of jaws, child of upper arm

Parent of lower arm

Child of lower arm and a leaf

Figure 12-2. A—If not properly linked, moving the fuselage can result in parts of the triplane being left behind. B—When properly linked, the fuselage can be moved and banked. All parts of the triplane correctly follow the motion of the fuselage.

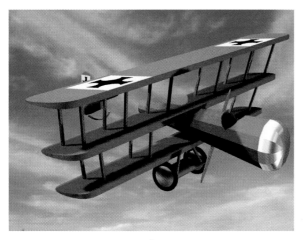

A

B

Linking (Forward Kinematics)

Often, the terms "linking" and "forward kinematics" are used interchangeably. However, they are really separate processes. *Linking* is establishing the relationship between a parent and a child. *Forward kinematics (FK)* is the process of animating a child object based on the transformation of a parent object.

Forward kinematics is a one-way relationship. If the child is transformed, the parent is not affected. Linking only relates to transforms. Modifiers applied to a parent are not linked to the child.

Of the two types of hierarchical relationships (FK and IK), a linked forward kinematic hierarchy is the easiest to create. However, linking still requires careful planning. If you do not put a little thought into the process before linking objects, you can quickly create a useless mess. This is even more critical when linking objects for an inverse kinematic hierarchy. In addition, by creating a logical hierarchy, the movement in your scene will appear more realistic.

In general, the parent object should move much less than the child object. If you select a parent object that moves a lot, you may find yourself making many adjustments to the child objects. An exception to this rule occurs when dummy objects are used to simplify motion. In this case, the dummy object is the parent object. All child objects are linked to the dummy. The dummy is then transformed, thus eliminating the need to transform each individual child. Dummy objects are discussed in Chapter 14.

Planning a logical relationship between objects is perhaps the most important consideration when creating a hierarchy. For example, if you are animating a dog's mouth, there are several ways you can link objects. You can link the lower jaw to the tongue. If you animate the jaw opening and closing by rotating the tongue, everything should work. See Figure 12-3A. However, if you later decide to make the tongue wag, the jaw will also wag. See Figure 12-3B. A more logical hierarchy for this example is linking the teeth to the lower jaw and the tongue to the lower jaw. You could also

Figure 12-3. A—The tongue is rotated down and the jaw follows. B—However, if the tongue wags from side-to-side, the jaw incorrectly follows the motion.

A   B

link the tongue to the teeth, since the teeth do not move independent of the jaw.

All links should be established before animating the scene. The linking and unlinking of objects cannot normally be animated. In addition, any links established are active throughout the entire animation, regardless of which frame they are created in.

While linking and unlinking cannot normally be animated, a link constraint can be applied to an object. This allows you to set up different parent objects on different frames of an animation. Using a link constraint is discussed later in the chapter.

Help Cel

Modifiers are not linked between a parent and its children. However, you can achieve this effect by placing an instance of a parent's modifier in the child's modifier stack.

Exercise 12-1

1) Make a simple sketch of the stick figure shown below.
2) Develop a hierarchy for the objects.
3) Sketch a chart showing the hierarchy.
4) Using standard or extended primitives, draw the stick figure in 3ds max.
5) Save the scene as ex12-01.max in the folder of your choice.

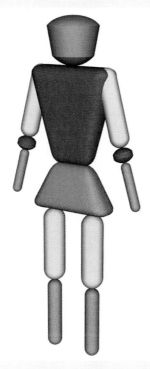

Creating Links

Creating links is easy. The process involves first selecting an object that is the child. Then, you link the child to the object that is its parent.

Select and Link

Pick the **Select and Link** button on the **Main** toolbar. Next, select the child object by picking on it. Hold the mouse button and drag the cursor to the parent object. A dashed rubber band is attached to the cursor as you drag it. When the cursor is over a valid parent object, the link cursor appears. See Figure 12-4. Release the mouse button to link the objects. The parent object flashes once to indicate the link is established. You can also use the [H] key to select a parent object by its name. Simply select the child with the **Select and Link** button active using a single pick. Then, press the [H] key.

Unlink Selection

Removing a link is just as easy. Simply select the child object. Then, pick the **Unlink Selection** button on the **Main** toolbar. The link from the child to the parent is removed. However, any children the selected object may have remain linked to the selected object. To remove all links in a tree, pick the **Select Object** button and double-click on the top parent object. This selects the entire tree from the parent object down. Then, pick the **Unlink Selection** button. All links in the tree are removed.

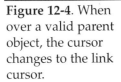

Help Cel

After you link an object, pick the **Select object** button. This "sets" the link. Otherwise, it is very easy to accidentally link a different object.

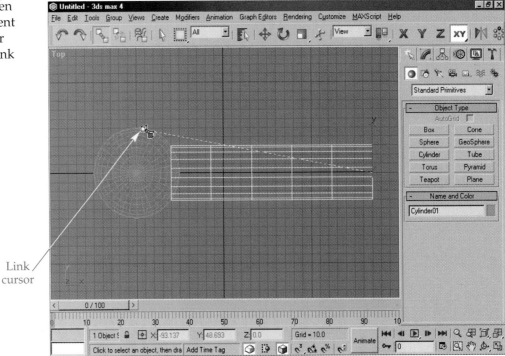

Figure 12-4. When over a valid parent object, the cursor changes to the link cursor.

Link cursor

Exercise 12-2

1) Open ex12-01.max if not already open.
2) Using the sketch you made in Exercise 12-1, link the objects to create a hierarchy.
3) Save the scene as ex12-02.max in the folder of your choice.

Pivot Points

Pivot point location is extremely important to creating hierarchies. The *pivot point,* or *transform center,* of an object is the point about which transforms are applied. Any transform inherited from a parent object is also applied to the child object about the parent's pivot point.

All objects have a default pivot point. For example, the default pivot point for a sphere is its center. However, this may not be the best location for your model. As an example, rotating a sphere about its center really has no effect. However, rotating the sphere about a point on its surface produces a noticeable effect. See Figure 12-5. To do this, the pivot point must be moved from its default location.

To adjust the pivot point on an object, first select the object. Then, pick the **Hierarchy** tab in the **Command Panel**. See Figure 12-6. Below the object's name, pick the **Pivot** button.

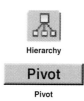

Hierarchy

Pivot

Pivot

Help Cel

For a transform to be applied about an object's pivot point, the **Use Pivot Point Center** button must be selected in the **Transform Center** flyout on the **Main** toolbar.

Adjust Pivot Rollout

In the **Move/Rotate/Scale:** area of the **Adjust Pivot** rollout, you can control if the pivot, object, or hierarchy is affected. You can think of these options as sub-object editing modes. The functions of these selection buttons are discussed next. Refer to Figure 12-7 as you go through each example.

Figure 12-5. On the left, the sphere is rotated about its default pivot point location. You cannot see any change. On the right, the pivot point is relocated to the center of the box. Now, when the sphere is rotated, it rotates about the center of the box.

Figure 12-6. The
Hierarchy tab in the
Command Panel is
used to adjust an
object's pivot point.

Figure 12-7. These are
examples of how the
buttons in the
Move/Rotate/Scale:
area affect the object
and pivot point. In
the examples shown,
the pyramid is linked
to the sphere. Note:
These objects are
shown in one view-
port for illustration
purposes.

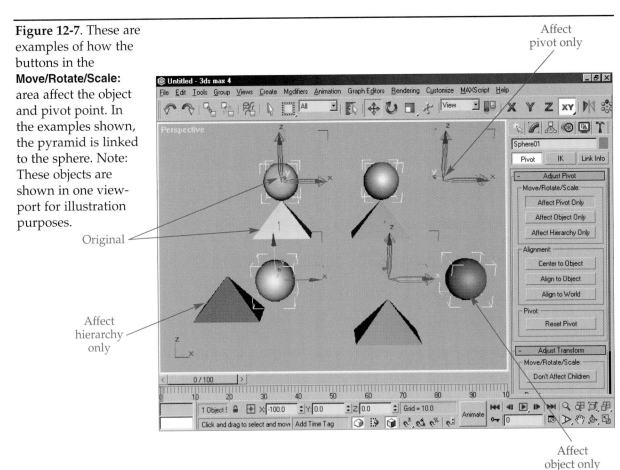

If the **Affect Pivot Only** button is picked, transforms are applied to the object's pivot point and not to the object. To change the location of an object's pivot point, make sure this button is on (depressed). Then, using the select and transform tools on the **Main** toolbar, move or rotate the pivot point to the new location. A pivot point cannot be scaled. Then, pick the **Affect Pivot Only** button to exit this editing mode. See Figure 12-7. Now, when the object is transformed, the transform is applied about the new pivot point location.

The **Affect Object Only** button is somewhat like the **Affect Pivot Only** button. However, the object is transformed while the pivot remains in the same location. See Figure 12-7. In effect, this relocates the pivot point. Keep in mind, however, the object is actually moved in the scene. This may not be acceptable for your model.

The **Affect Hierarchy Only** button is primarily designed to be used with bones systems. When this button is on, the position of the hierarchy below the selected object is rotated or scaled. See Figure 12-7. However, it cannot be moved. An individual object's pivot point is not transformed. This allows you to match an existing hierarchy, such as a bones network, to mating geometry, such as a character.

The options in the **Alignment:** area work with the **Affect Pivot Only** and **Affect Object Only** buttons. When the **Affect Hierarchy Only** button is selected, this area is greyed out. When the **Affect Pivot Only** button is selected, the pivot is transformed. When the **Affect Object Only** button is selected, the object is transformed. The buttons in the **Alignment:** area change depending on which button is selected in the **Move/Rotate/Scale:** area. Picking the **Center to Object** button or **Center to Pivot** button centers the pivot on the object, or the object on the pivot. Picking the **Align to Object** button or **Align to Pivot** button aligns the pivot or object to the transform matrix. Picking the **Align to World** button aligns the pivot or object to the world coordinate axes.

Picking the **Reset Pivot** button in the **Pivot:** area realigns the pivot point to the default location. This is the location of the pivot point when the object is created. Picking the **Reset Pivot** button relocates the pivot point regardless of which button in the **Move/Rotate/Scale:** area is selected.

Adjust Transform Rollout

The **Adjust Transform** rollout is used to transform an object without affecting any children it may have. To do this, first select the object. Then, pick the **Don't Affect Children** button in the **Move/Rotate/Scale:** area of the **Adjust Transform** rollout. Make any transforms necessary to the object. Until the **Don't Affect Children** button is turned off, the transforms are not passed on to the child objects.

Picking the **Transform** button in the **Reset:** area aligns the object's local axes to the world coordinate system. Picking the **Scale** button updates the transformation matrix to the current scale level of the object. These functions do not affect any children the object may have. There also may be no visible change in the object.

Exercise

1) Open the file ex12-02.max if not already open.
2) On the sketch you made in Exercise 12-1, determine the best location for each object's pivot point. Mark it with an X.
3) Move object pivot points as necessary. Refer to your sketch.
4) Align all pivot points to the world. You may need to first rotate some objects.
5) Save the scene as ex12-03.max in the folder of your choice.

Parent-Child Inheritance

Transforms, not modifiers, are passed from a parent to a child. The child inherits the movement, rotation, and scale of the parent object. However, you may not want all transforms to be inherited. Or, you may want a child object to inherit a transform from a particular axis of the parent object, not all axes. Fortunately, you can specify which transforms are inherited and for which axes.

Hierarchy

Link Info

Link Info

To specify inheritance, select the child object. Then, open the **Hierarchy** tab in the **Command Panel**. Below the object's name, pick the **Link Info** button. This displays the **Locks** and **Inherit** rollouts. See Figure 12-8.

The **Locks** rollout is used to prevent a transform on any of the object's local axes. By default, all transforms are applied on all axes. However, there will be many times when you need to change this. The **Locks** rollout contains the **Move:**, **Rotate:**, and **Scale:** areas. Each area has a check box for each of the X, Y, and Z local axes. To limit the transform, simply check the appropriate check box for the appropriate transform. Any checked check box indicates the transform *cannot* be applied along that axis. For example, to prevent an object being moved along its X and Z axes, check the **X** and **Z** check boxes in the **Move:** area. See Figure 12-9.

The **Inherit** rollout is used to set what the child inherits from the parent. By default, a child object inherits all transforms on all axes.

Figure 12-8. The parent-child inheritance is set in the **Locks** and **Inherit** rollouts of the **Hierarchy** tab of the **Command Panel**.

However, this can be changed. The **Inherit** rollout contains the **Move:**, **Rotate:**, and **Scale:** areas. Each of these areas has check boxes for the X, Y, and Z axes. To specify a transform inheritance, simply check the appropriate check box for the appropriate transform. Any checked check box indicates that the transform *is* inherited along that axis. This may seem logically the reverse of the **Locks** rollout. Also, even if a transform is limited in the **Locks** rollout, the corresponding axis will still inherit transforms if specified in the **Inherit** rollout. See Figure 12-10.

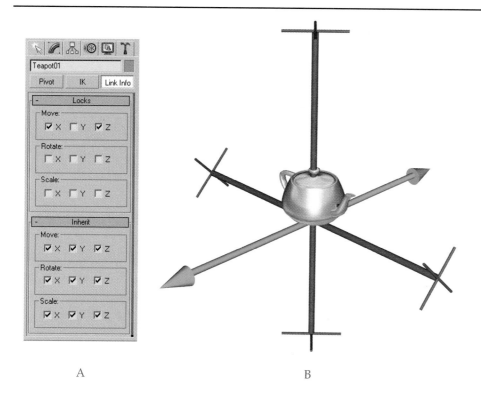

A

B

Figure 12-9.
A—Locking transformations for an object. B—The object can move on its Y axis, but not on its X and Z axes.

A

B

Figure 12-10.
A—Setting inheritance for a linked object.
B—The cylinder is linked to the box (top). The cylinder is set to inherit Z axis rotation and, therefore, does not inherit the box's Y axis rotation (middle). When the cylinder is set to inherit Y axis rotation, it rotates with the box (bottom).

Help Cel

Before establishing links in a hierarchy, first align all pivot points to the world coordinate axes whenever possible. This can help you identify the correct axes when locking transforms and making inheritance settings. There will be situations, however, where an object's pivot point should not be aligned to the world.

Exercise

Exercise 12-4

1) Open ex12-03.max if not already open.
2) Using the sketch you made in Exercise 12-1, determine what transforms each object should inherit from its parent. Make notes on your sketch.
3) Set inherit properties for each object based on your notes.
4) Save the scene as ex12-04.max in the folder of your choice.

Linking Application

To demonstrate how linking works, the door and window combination shown in Figure 12-11 will be linked in the following example. First, start by modeling the door, door frame, window, and window frame. You can use the dimensions given in Figure 12-12 or your own dimensions. Then, assemble the pieces together to form the complete door.

The first step in creating a hierarchy is planning. So, look at the door model. Obviously, the door frame should not move. Also, anytime the door is opened, the window and window frame must move with the door. However, the window and window frame can also be opened, but the frame cannot move independent of the window. Therefore, the

Figure 12-11. This door and window combination will be properly linked. The sphere is shown to give depth to the scene.

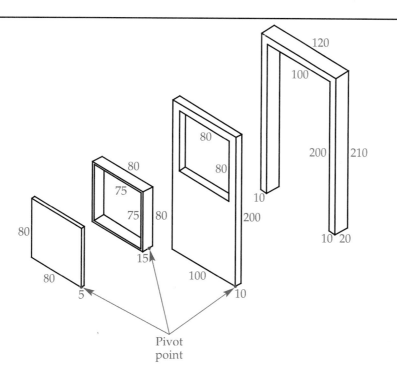

Figure 12-12.
Suggested dimensions for creating the door and window combination. Move the pivot points to the locations shown here.

window frame must follow the movement of the window. After planning out the hierarchy, the linking for the model is:

• Window frame to window (or, window to window frame).
• Window to door (or window frame to door).
• Door to door frame.

The last link is created so the entire unit can be moved without disturbing the hierarchy. If the door unit needs to be moved to a different location, you can simply move the door frame and all other parts of the unit follow.

With the hierarchy planned, the next step is to adjust pivot points as necessary. The pivot point for each object is shown in Figure 12-12. The default location of an object's pivot point can vary greatly, depending on how you create the object. However, the procedure for moving pivot points is the same. First, select the object. Next, open the **Hierarchy** tab in the **Command Panel**. Pick the **Pivot** button and then the **Affect Pivot Only** button. Now, any transforms are applied to the pivot point and not the object.

Use the transformation buttons on the **Main** toolbar to locate the pivot point as needed. When the pivot point is correctly located, pick the next object and locate its pivot point. When finished with the last object, pick the **Affect Pivot Only** button again. Transforms are now applied to the object and not the pivot.

It is always a good idea to align pivot points to the world before establishing any links. After all of the objects are in the proper position and all pivot points are correctly located, it is time to link objects. You do not have to link objects in order. However, doing so can help you keep track of which objects are linked and which ones have not yet been linked.

Select the window frame. This object never moves unless the window glass moves. Therefore, link it to the glass (or vice versa). Pick

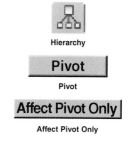

Hierarchy

Pivot

Pivot

Affect Pivot Only

Affect Pivot Only

the **Select and Link** button on the **Main** toolbar. Then, drag from the window frame to the glass. The link cursor appears when over the glass. Release the mouse button to create the link. The parent object (glass) flashes as the link is established.

In addition to linking the window frame to the glass, you also want to make sure the frame cannot be moved by itself. To do this, select the frame, open the **Hierarchy** tab in the **Command Panel**, and pick the **Link Info** button. In the **Locks** rollout, check all of the check boxes. See Figure 12-13. This prevents the window frame being moved, rotated, or scaled on any of its axes. Also, the frame and glass will only rotate about the Z axis. It is good practice to set an object to inherit only the transforms it should. Therefore, set the rotation inheritance to the Z axis.

Next, the window glass needs to be linked to the door. Select the glass using the **Select and Link** button. Now, press the [H] key to open the **Select Parent** dialog box. See Figure 12-14. This dialog box is very similar

Link Info

Link Info

Figure 12-13. Locking transformations for the window frame.

Figure 12-14. Linking the glass to the door using the [H] key to select by name.

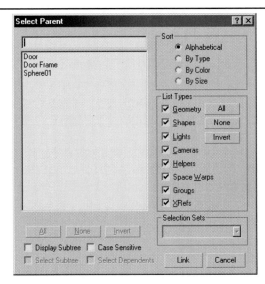

to the **Select Objects** dialog box. However, notice the "OK" button is the **Link** button. Also, notice only valid parent objects are listed. Select the door from the list and pick the **Link** button.

Now, you want to prevent the window glass from being transformed. In the **Locks** rollout, check all check boxes in the **Move:** and **Scale:** areas. However, you *do* want to be able to rotate it about its vertical axis. In the figures in the book, this is the Z axis, but it may be different for your model. Therefore, in the **Rotate:** area of the **Locks** rollout, check the **X** and **Y** check boxes. Leaving the **Z** check box unchecked allows the glass to be rotated about its Y (vertical) axis.

Finally, use either the cursor or the [H] key to select and link the door to the frame. Also, limit all transforms except rotation about the door's vertical axis. With the door frame as the ancestor (top-level parent) object, the entire unit can be moved, scaled, or rotated by transforming the door frame.

With the proper hierarchy created, the door can open and close. The window and window frame follow. See Figure 12-15A. Also, the window can be opened and closed independent of the door. The window frame follows. See Figure 12-15B. In addition, the window can be opened, and then the door opened. The window remains open as the door is opened. See Figure 12-15C. The window frame always follows the glass.

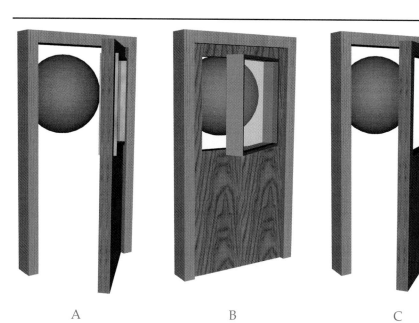

A   B   C

Figure 12-15. A—The window follows the door when the door is rotated open. B—The window can rotate open by itself. C—If the window is first rotated open and then the door is opened, the window stays in the same relative position.

Exercise

Exercise 12-5

1) Open ex12-04.max if not already open.
2) Rotate the right upper arm away from the body.
3) Rotate the right elbow in toward the body.
4) Rotate the left upper arm away from the body.
5) Rotate the upper torso around the waist.
6) Bend the upper torso down. The model should look similar to the one shown below.
7) Save the scene as ex12-05.max in the folder of your choice.

Introduction to Using Link Constraints

A *link constraint* allows you to animate a child object "switching" parent objects during an animation. Animation is discussed in Chapter 14. To apply a link constraint, select the child object. Then, pick **Motion** in the **Command Panel**. In the **Assign Controller** rollout, select **Transform** in the hierarchical tree. If you select **Position**, **Rotation**, or **Scale**, you will not be able to assign a link constraint. Next, pick the **Assign Controller** button. Finally, in the **Assign Transform Controller** dialog box that appears, select **Link Constraint**. The **Link Params** (parameters) rollout appears in the **Command Panel**. See Figure 12-16.

To link the child to parent objects, pick the **Add Link** button. Then, move to the frame in the animation where you want the link to become active. Moving around in an animation is discussed in Chapter 14. Once on the correct frame, pick the parent object in a viewport. Repeat this procedure for all parents of the child. When finished, pick the **Add Link** button again or right-click to end the command.

Motion

Assign Controller

Add Link

Add Link

Figure 12-16.
Applying a link constraint allows you to animate switching of parent objects.

You can also apply a link constraint to a selected object using a pull-down menu. You should first be on the frame where you want the link to become active. Then, pick **Constraints** in the **Animation** pull-down menu. Finally, pick **Link Constraint** in the cascading menu. The "link rubber band" appears from the selected object's pivot point. Select the parent object. Then, continue using the above procedure until all parents are specified.

This is intended as an introduction only. Once you learn about animation in Chapter 14, design your own scenes and animations. Then, apply link constraints to your scenes. As you apply link constraints to your own scenes, you will gain experience in how this feature works.

Help Cel

To remove the link constraint, assign the **Position/Rotation/Scale** controller to the transform.

Chapter Snapshot

Chapter Test

Answer the following questions on a separate sheet of paper.

1) Define hierarchy.
2) List three things a hierarchy can be used for.
3) Define:
   - a) ancestor
   - b) parent
   - c) child
   - d) leaf
4) What are the two types of hierarchical relationships that can be created in 3ds max?
5) List two basic rules that apply to hierarchies.
6) How can you animate linking an object to different parents?
7) Once a link is created in frame 50 of 100 using the **Select and Link** button, for how many frames is the link active?
8) What is the basic process for creating a link?
9) How do you unlink an object?
10) How can you unlink *all* objects in a tree all at once?
11) What is a pivot point?
12) Which tab in the **Command Panel** is used to adjust a pivot point?
13) What effect does scaling a pivot point have on the final transformation?
14) What is the purpose of the **Adjust Transform** rollout?
15) How do you specify parent-child inheritance for transforms?
16) How do you specify parent-child inheritance for modifiers?
17) What three areas appear in the **Inherit** rollout?
18) How do you set a child to inherit movement along the X axis only?
19) In the **Locks** rollout, what does a check in one of the check boxes mean?
20) Does an inherited transform override a locked transform or vice versa?

Modeling Problems

Draw the following models. Use the 3ds max objects presented in this and earlier chapters. Create a linked hierarchy for each scene. Apply materials as needed, similar to those shown. Add lights and cameras as needed to create the shadows and views shown. When finished, save each model as p12-xx.max in the folder of your choice.

Yard Swing **1**

The swing should pivot about the top of the ropes. The boards making up the swing should follow the rotation of the ropes.

Ceiling Fan **2**

The blades of the fan should rotate about the center of the hub.

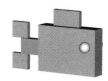

3 Robot Arm

There should be four points of movement for the arm assembly. The wrist should rotate about the lower arm. The lower arm should rotate about the first elbow. The upper arm (closest to the base) should rotate about the second elbow. The second elbow should rotate about the black base. Finally, the black base should rotate on top of the blue base.

4 Desk and Drawers

The hardware and drawer face of each drawer should match the movement of the drawer.

Antique Chest **5**

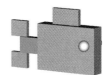

Refer to the hinge detail to create the hinge. The hinge should pivot about the center of the cylinder portion of the hinge. The chest lid should follow the rotation of the hinge.

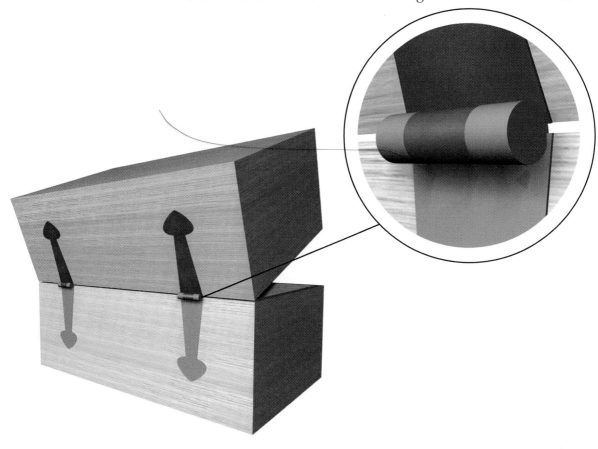

Toy Gyroscope **6**

The yellow cross members should rotate about the center cylinder. The red wheel should match the rotation of the cross members. The outer "cage" should rotate as the center cylinder rotates.

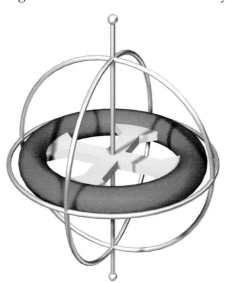

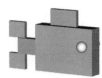

7 Wooden Fences and Gate
Each half of the gate should rotate about the center of the vertical columns.

8 Concert Lighting
Draw the scaffolding shown. Draw three colored spheres to represent spotlights. Draw three colored spotlights centered on the outside of the spheres. The spotlights should point to the center of the sphere, even as the sphere moves.

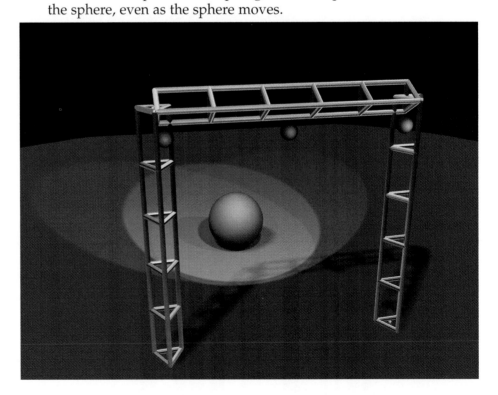

Robot Quadruped **9**

Move and adjust pivot points as needed to create lifelike quadruped movement.

Robot Biped **10**

Move and adjust pivot points as needed to create lifelike biped movement.

Chapter 13

Creating Basic Materials

Objectives

After completing this chapter, you will be able to:

- List the types of materials you can create with 3ds max.
- Explain the characteristics of different shading types.
- Identify the components of a material's color.
- Explain opacity.
- Create basic materials.

Material Types

There are several different material types in 3ds max. Each type provides a starting point for creating different materials, and each has its own unique properties. Consider an analogy using bread. There is rye, wheat, and white bread. In addition, there are dinner rolls, French loaves, and family style loaves. You can put butter and blackberry jam on a slice of each type of bread, and they all have the same general color. However, each type of bread still has its own qualities, such as texture or overall color of the bread. Material types in 3ds max are the same way. Assigning a standard material to a sphere produces a different result from assigning a raytrace material, even if the colors are the same. See Figure 13-1.

There are 10 material types in 3ds max. These include standard, raytrace, and matte/shadow. The other seven types are called *compound material types.* This is because they create a material by combining other materials. Compound material types include blend, composite, double sided, morpher, multi/sub-object, shellac, and top/bottom. Only the standard material type is discussed in this chapter. The other material types are discussed in Chapters 17 and 18.

Standard Material

The *standard material type* has very basic settings. It is the default type of material in 3ds max. This material type allows you to quickly create materials of different, uniform colors. Even though a material is a uniform, single color, you see variations in the color in a rendering 3ds max uses four types of color to produce realistic object shading. The

Figure 13-1. The material on the left is a standard material. The material on the right has the same color definitions, but it is a raytrace material. Notice the sharper reflection.

four types of color are ambient, diffuse, specular, and filter. In Chapter 7, you learned the very basics of changing an object's diffuse color. In addition to those three colors, some real-world objects produce their own light. This light can add to the coloring of the object. A glowing match ember is an example. This is called *self-illumination* and can be defined in 3ds max. In addition to color types, there are several different shading types available in 3ds max.

To create a material, first open the **Material Editor**. Do this by picking the **Material Editor** button on the **Main** toolbar, selecting **Material Editor**... from the **Rendering** pull-down menu, or pressing [M] on the keyboard. Then, make the necessary settings to the material.

Material Editor

Help Cel

By default, the material sample slots in the **Material Editor** are "blank" because the file medit.mat found in the 3ds max \matlibs folder contains no definitions. If this file has been deleted or was not installed, the default sample slots contain basic materials of various colors.

Shading Types

The **Shader Basic Parameters** rollout in the **Material Editor** is where the type of shading is set for the material. See Figure 13-2. There are seven different shading types available. Each type produces a slightly different effect when the material is rendered. To select a shading type, pick the name from the drop-down list. The different shading types are discussed in the next sections. In addition to selecting a shading type, the **Shader Basic Parameters** rollout allows you to set the material as wireframe, 2-sided, face mapped, or faceted.

Figure 13-2. Selecting a shading type in the **Shader Basic Parameters** rollout.

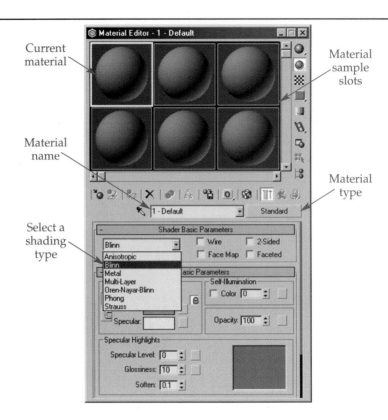

Current material

Material sample slots

Material name

Material type

Select a shading type

Checking the **Wire** check box forces the material to render as a wireframe. The diameter of the "wire" is set in the **Size:** spinner in the **Wire** area of the **Extended Parameters** rollout.

The **2-Sided** check box is used to force 3ds max to apply the material to both sides of an object. Setting this option increases rendering time, but it may solve some problems where portions of an object disappear in the final rendering. Making the material 2-sided may be the easiest solution. This check box should also be checked for transparent materials such as glass. In this way, both the inside and outside surfaces of a bottle can be seen.

The **Face Map** check box is only checked if the material is a mapped material. Material mapping is covered in Chapter 18. When this check box is checked, any map defined for the material is applied to each face of the object. This also eliminates the need to apply mapping coordinates, if face mapping is appropriate.

The **Faceted** check box is used to create a faceted object. In effect, checking this check box removes any smoothing groups that may be applied to the object.

Help Cel

Once a shading type is selected, the material's **Basic Parameters** rollout changes to reflect the selection.

Blinn and Phong

The Phong and Blinn shading types have the same parameters, but they create slightly different results. See Figure 13-3. *Phong shading* applies smoothing groups to adjacent facets of an object. Phong shading also

Figure 13-3. The object on the left is rendered with Blinn shading. Notice the soft highlight when compared to the object on the right. The object on the right is rendered with Phong shading. Both objects have the same color definitions.

renders strong, circular highlights. This is useful when creating very shiny materials. *Blinn shading* is a variation of Phong shading. The main difference is that the highlights produced with Blinn shading are slightly softer than those produced with Phong shading. The default shading type is Blinn.

The **Basic Parameters** rollout is where the basic properties of the material are defined. The rollout is named **Blinn Basic Parameters** for the Blinn shading type and **Phong Basic Parameters** for the Phong shading type. See Figure 13-4. Both shading types have ambient, diffuse, and specular color components. In addition, the specular highlights can be fine-tuned. Also, both types have self-illumination and opacity settings. These are all discussed later in this chapter.

Metal

As you might guess, the *Metal shading* type is designed to be used for metallic surfaces. This shading type calculates a specular color based on the ambient and diffuse colors. Because of this, the Metal shading type produces a distinctive transition between material colors. See Figure 13-5. This accurately reproduces the effect found on most metals.

The **Metal Basic Parameters** rollout is where the basic properties of the material are defined. See Figure 13-6. The Metal shading type has ambient and diffuse color components. There are also self-illumination and opacity settings. Even though there is not a specular color component, the specular highlight can be fine-tuned. However, the spinners in the **Specular Highlights** area function a bit differently from those of the other shading types. All these settings are discussed later in this chapter.

Figure 13-4. A—The **Blinn Basic Parameters** rollout. B—The **Phong Basic Parameters** rollout.

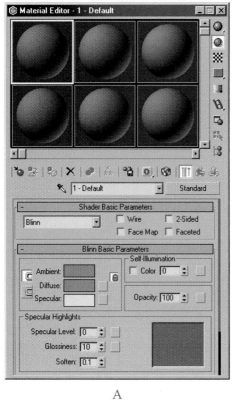

A

B

Figure 13-5. This object is rendered with the Metal shading type. It has the same color definitions as the objects shown in Figure 13-3.

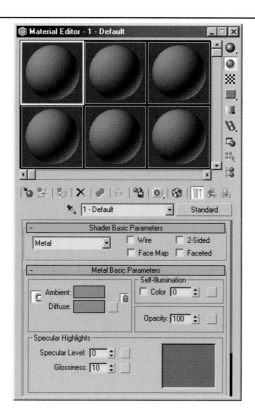

Figure 13-6. The **Metal Basic Parameters** rollout.

Anisotropic

The *Anisotropic shading* type can create elliptical highlights. See Figure 13-7. These highlights are called anisotropic highlights. An anisotropic highlight is calculated by "looking" at the material from two different vantage points. The Anisotropic shading type is good for organic materials, such as hair, fur, or grass.

The **Anisotropic Basic Parameters** rollout is where the basic properties of the material are defined. See Figure 13-8. The Anisotropic shading type has ambient, diffuse, and specular color components. There are also self-illumination and opacity settings. In addition, there is a diffuse level setting. The specular highlight can be fine-tuned. However, the settings differ slightly from those for other shading types. All these settings are discussed later in this chapter.

Multi-Layer

The *Multi-Layer shading* type is based on the Anisotropic type. However, instead of one anisotropic highlight, there are two. See Figure 13-9. Each highlight can be independently controlled. This produces a more intricate shading result than that produced by the Anisotropic shading type.

The **Multi-Layer Basic Parameters** rollout is where the basic properties of the material are defined. See Figure 13-10. The Multi-Layer shading type has ambient, diffuse, and two specular color components. There are self-illumination, opacity, and diffuse level settings, just as with the Anisotropic shading type. However, there is also a roughness setting. There are also two independent areas where the two specular highlights can be fine-tuned. All these settings are discussed later in this chapter.

Figure 13-7. This object is rendered with the Anisotropic shading type. Compare this to the objects shown in Figure 13-3 and Figure 13-5.

Figure 13-8. The **Anisotropic Basic Parameters** rollout.

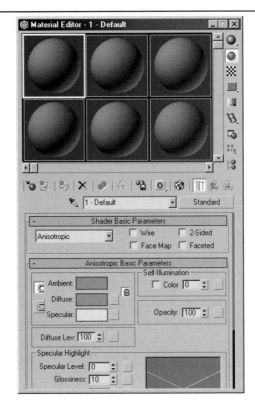

Figure 13-9. This object is rendered with the Multi-Layer shading type. The second anisotropic highlight on this object is light red. Compare this object to the one shown in Figure 13-7.

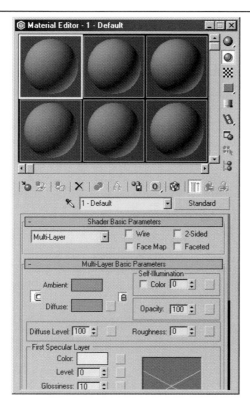

Figure 13-10. The **Multi-Layer Basic Parameters** rollout.

Figure 13-11. This object is rendered with the Oren-Nayar-Blinn shading type. Compare it to the Blinn-shaded object in Figure 13-3.

Oren-Nayar-Blinn

The *Oren-Nayar-Blinn shading* type is a variation of the Blinn shading type. However, there is more control over the diffuse color. This shading type is good for dull or matte materials, such as rubber or clay. See Figure 13-11.

The **Oren-Nayar-Blinn Basic Parameters** rollout is where the basic properties of the material are defined. See Figure 13-12. Like the Blinn shading type, the Oren-Nayar-Blinn shading type has ambient, diffuse, and specular color components. There are self-illumination and opacity settings, and the specular highlight can be fine-tuned. In addition, there are diffuse level and roughness settings, as with the Multi-Layer shading type.

Strauss

The *Strauss shading* type is used for metallic materials. However, it does not have as many settings as the Metal shading type. See Figure 13-13. The **Strauss Basic Parameters** rollout is where the basic properties of the material are defined. The Strauss shading type has only a diffuse color component. There are no ambient, specular, or self-illumination settings. There is an opacity setting.

There are also glossiness and metalness settings. These are used to define the strength and size of the highlight. The color of the specular highlight and the ambient portion of the material are calculated based on these settings and the diffuse color.

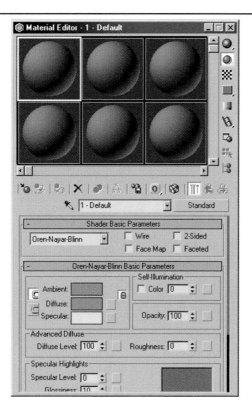

Figure 13-12. The **Oren-Nayar-Blinn Basic Parameters** rollout.

Figure 13-13. This object is rendered with the Strauss shading type. Compare this object to the Metal-shaded object in Figure 13-5.

Exercise

Exercise 13-1

1) Open the **Material Editor**.
2) Get the material Metal_Grey_Plain from the 3dsmax.mat material library.
3) Starting with Anisotropic, select each shading type in order from the drop-down list. It is important to select Strauss last.
4) Notice the differences between each shading type.
5) Why was it important to select Strauss last?
6) Reset 3ds max without saving.

SuperSampling Rollout

Supersampling is a function used to add antialiasing to the rendered scene. *Antialiasing* smoothes the "jaggies" of a rendered image by blending colored pixels. While this softens the jaggies, it can also produce a blurry image if not used properly. However, antialiasing generally improves the image quality. Supersampling is used in addition to the antialiasing used for textures, shadows, highlights, and raytracing. In general, only use supersampling when normal antialiasing is not adequate.

To turn on supersampling, check the **Enable Sampler** check box in the **SuperSampling** rollout in the **Material Editor**. See Figure 13-14. Then, pick the sampling method from the drop-down list. The default sampling method is Max 2.5 Star. This is the supersampling method used in 3D Studio MAX R2.5. A brief description of the selected method appears below the drop-down list.

Figure 13-14. The **SuperSampling** rollout.

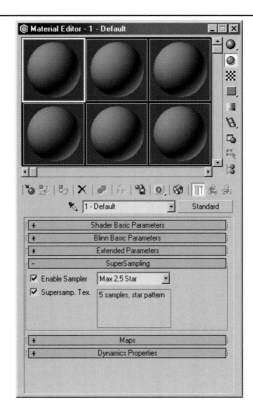

You will need to experiment with the different types of sampling to see which one works best for your application. Make changes to the settings for the sampling type as needed.

Material Color

Any material color is made up of different color components. Even a material which is a solid color consists of multiple colors, each a slight variation of the "solid color." 3ds max uses a combination of four base colors to define a material color. These are ambient, diffuse, specular, and filter color. See Figure 13-15. Depending on which shading type is selected, these colors may be automatically calculated by 3ds max or manually set.

Ambient, Diffuse, and Specular Color

The *ambient color* of a material is the color illuminated by ambient light. This is the color of the object in shadows and is generally the darkest color component of a material. The diffuse color of a material is the main color. When you look at a material and see a color, generally you see the *diffuse color*. For example, when you say an apple is red, you are really saying the apple has a red diffuse color. The *specular color* is the color of the highlight. This is the shiny part of the material.

To set the ambient, diffuse, or specular color of the material, pick the **Ambient:**, **Diffuse:**, or **Specular:** color swatch in the **Basic Parameters** rollout in the **Material Editor**. If the shading type is Metal, there is no **Specular:** color swatch. If the shading type is Strauss, there is only the **Color:** color swatch, which is the diffuse color. Pick the color swatch to change the color. Then, in the color selector, pick the color you want to use. Finally, close the color selector. The color swatch indicates the color selected.

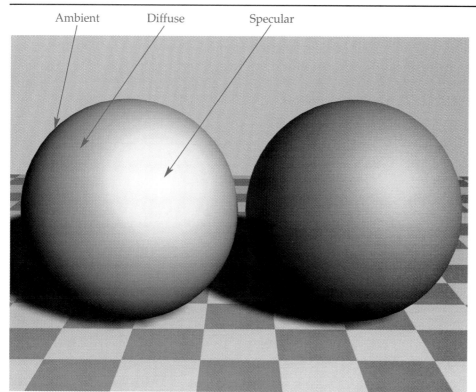

Ambient   Diffuse   Specular

Figure 13-15. The basic colors used to define a material color are specular, diffuse, ambient, and filter color. The object on the right is the same as the object on the left, except it is slightly transparent. The object has a red filter color.

Figure 13-16. You can lock the ambient color to the diffuse color. You can also lock the specular color to the diffuse color.

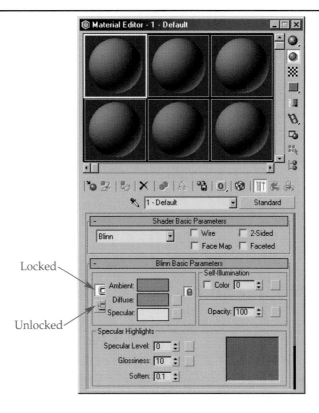

You can lock the ambient and diffuse colors, or the diffuse and specular colors. To do this, pick one of the lock buttons next to the color swatches. See Figure 13-16. When locked, the button is depressed. Now, any changes made to one color are transferred to the other, locked color. You can lock all three colors by picking both lock buttons. By default, the ambient and diffuse colors are locked.

You can copy a color from one swatch to another. To do this, pick and hold the color swatch. Then, drag and drop it onto the other color swatch. The **Copy or Swap Colors** dialog box shown in Figure 13-17 appears. Pick the **Copy** button if you want to copy the color. Pick the **Swap** button if you want to flip-flop the color swatches. Pick the **Cancel** button to cancel the operation.

Figure 13-17. This dialog box appears when you drag and drop a color swatch onto another color swatch in the **Material Editor**.

Exercise 13-2

Exercise

1) Open the **Material Editor**.
2) Select the first material sample. Select the Blinn shading type.
3) Pick the lock button to unlock the diffuse and ambient colors. Change the diffuse color to a bright orange. What happened?
4) Change the specular color to pure white (255). How did the material sample change? It probably did not change at all. This is because the default material sample, which you are modifying, has a specular level setting of 0. In order to see the specular color, this setting needs to be increased, as discussed later in this chapter.
5) Pick the lock button to lock the diffuse and ambient colors. What happened?
6) Select the second material sample. Select the Phong shading type.
7) Change the ambient color to bright blue. What happened to the material sample?
8) Unlock the diffuse and ambient colors. Change the diffuse color to a dark red (R150). What happened to the material sample?
9) Swap the ambient and diffuse colors by dragging one color swatch onto the other. How did the material sample change?
10) Reset 3ds max without saving.

Filter Color

The *filter color* of an object is the color of white light passing through the object. For example, sunlight shining through a green glass bottle projects a green shadow. See Figure 13-18. This is the filter color. The filter color is set in the **Advanced Transparency** area of the **Extended Parameters** rollout in the **Material Editor**. The material's opacity must be less than 100 for the filter color to be used. Opacity is discussed later in this chapter.

Pick the **Filter:** radio button to turn on filter color. Then, pick the color swatch and choose a color in the color selector. A map can also be assigned by picking the map button next to the color swatch. Mapping is discussed in Chapter 18.

Help Cel

Only raytraced shadows are tinted with the filter color.

Self-Illumination

Self-illumination replaces any shadows on the surface of the material with color. This gives the illusion that the material is generating light. However, no illumination is created. For example, if you create a neon sign, you would create a material with self-illumination. You would also need to create an omni light with the same color placed in the center of the sign. This light provides the actual illumination in the scene. See Figure 13-19. It is important to remember that materials in 3ds max do not provide illumination to a scene.

Figure 13-18. This green glass vase has a green filter color. As light passes through the glass, it transmits green into the shadow.

Figure 13-19. Four omni lights are used to provide illumination from the neon sign, as shown in the camera viewport on the bottom. The sign has self-illuminated materials. The omni lights provide the colored light to the scene, as shown in the ActiveShade viewport on the top.

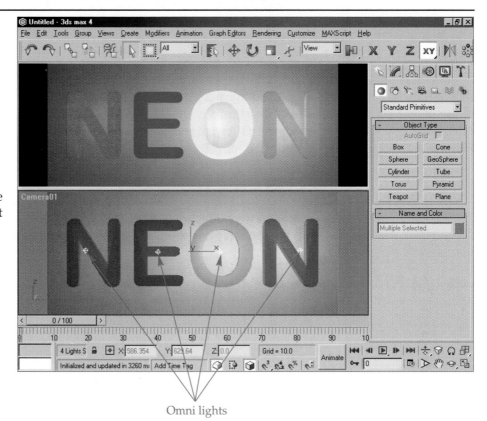

Omni lights

By default, the self-illumination color is the diffuse color. Entering a value in the spinner in the **Self-Illumination** area of the **Basic Parameters** rollout in the **Material Editor** specifies what percent of shadow is replaced with the diffuse color. Increasing the self-illumination has the same effect on the object as increasing the overall intensity of ambient light in the scene.

If you check the **Color** check box, the spinner is replaced with a color swatch. You can then pick the swatch and choose a color in the color selector. This allows you to use a color different from the diffuse color for self-illumination. For example, you might assign a bright orange self-illumination color to glowing charcoal briquettes.

A map can also be assigned as a self-illumination color. This is generally done when a diffuse color map is used. Both maps are generally related to each other. To assign a map, pick the map button at the right of the **Self-Illumination** area. Mapping is discussed in Chapter 18.

Opacity

Opacity is a measure of how transparent a material is. A material with an opacity value of 100 is completely opaque, or not at all transparent. A material with an opacity value of 0 is completely transparent. See Figure 13-20.

Opacity is set in the **Opacity:** spinner in the **Basic Parameters** rollout in the **Material Editor**. The value in the spinner is the percentage of opacity. An opacity map can also be assigned to the material by picking the map button next to the spinner. Mapping is discussed in Chapter 18.

Help Cel

When creating transparent materials, it is often helpful to pick the **Background** button on the right side of the **Material Editor**. This displays a colored checkerboard behind the material sample.

Figure 13-20. Varying degrees of opacity. The object on the far left is 100% opaque.

Exercise

Exercise 13-3

1) Open the **Material Editor**.
2) Select the first material sample.
3) Make the diffuse color a bright red and the ambient color a dark red. Notice the appearance of the material sample.
4) Check the **Color** check box in the **Self-Illumination** area. Change the self-illumination color to a dark yellow (R80, G80, B0). How did the material sample change?
5) Change the opacity to 50%. How did the sample change? Pick the **Background** button. Can you notice a difference?
6) Reset 3ds max without saving.

Specular Highlights

The *specular highlight* is the shiny part of a material. Setting the color of the highlight is discussed earlier in this chapter. In addition to the color, the shape and appearance of the specular highlight can be fine-tuned. These settings are found in the **Specular Highlights** area of the **Basic Parameters** rollout in the **Material Editor**. See Figure 13-21.

The **Specular Level:** spinner is used to set the intensity, or brightness, of the specular highlight. This value can range from 0 to 999. The default value is 0.

The **Glossiness:** spinner is used to set the size of the highlight. The higher the value, the smaller the highlight. A very glossy material, such

Figure 13-21. The **Specular Highlights** area of the **Basic Parameters** rollout is used to define the specular highlight.

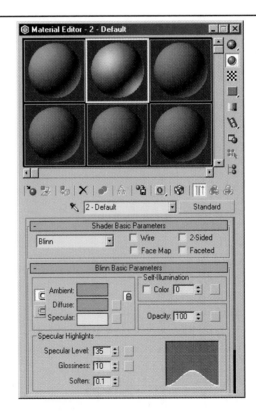

as plastic, has a very small specular highlight. This value can range from 0 to 100, with 10 the default.

The **Soften:** spinner is used to soften the edges of the specular highlight. This value can range from 0.0 to 1.0, with 0.1 the default. The default setting may need to be changed when the **Specular Level:** value is high and the **Glossiness:** value is low.

At the right of the **Specular Highlights** area is the highlight graph. This is a graphic representation of the **Specular Level:** and **Glossiness:** settings. As the specular level is increased, the bell curve in the graph becomes taller. As the glossiness is increased, the bell curve becomes thinner.

Help Cel

Earlier versions of 3D Studio referred to the "specular" component as "shininess."

Metal Specular Highlights

The specular highlight settings function a bit differently for the Metal shading type. The values in the **Specular Level:** and **Glossiness:** spinners do not form a bell curve. As you make changes to the specular level and glossiness, the difference becomes apparent in the highlight graph. See Figure 13-22. In addition, the **Soften:** spinner is not available.

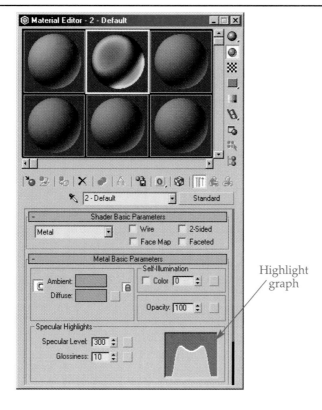

Figure 13-22. The specular highlight for a Metal-shaded object is slightly different from that of other types. Notice the graph.

Highlight graph

Exercise

Exercise 13-4
1) Open the **Material Editor**.
2) Select a material sample. Select the Phong shading type.
3) Set the diffuse color to a medium green. Set the ambient color to an appropriate dark green. Make the specular color pure white (255).
4) Change the value in the **Specular Level:** spinner to 50. What happened to the material sample? What happened to the highlight graph?
5) Change the value in the **Glossiness:** spinner to 50. What happened to the material sample? What happened to the highlight graph?
6) Change the value in the **Glossiness:** spinner to 0. How did the material sample and highlight graph change?
7) Change the value in the **Soften:** spinner to 0.0. How did the material sample change? Enter 1.0 in the **Soften:** spinner. How is this different?
8) Reset 3ds max without saving.

Other Settings

In addition to the basic parameters discussed above, some shading types have other settings specific to the type. These settings include diffuse level, roughness, anisotropy, and orientation.

Diffuse Level

The **Diffuse Level:** spinner controls the intensity, or brightness, of the material's diffuse color. See Figure 13-23. This setting is available with the Anisotropic, Multi-Layer, and Oren-Nayar-Blinn shading types. The diffuse level can range from 0 to 400, with 100 as the default. A map can also be assigned to the diffuse level by picking the map button next to the spinner. Mapping is discussed in Chapter 18.

Roughness

The **Roughness:** spinner controls the transition from diffuse color to ambient color. This transition determines if the material is matte or shiny. As the value in the spinner is increased, the material becomes more matte. See Figure 13-24. The **Roughness:** spinner is available with the Multi-Layer and Oren-Nayar-Blinn shading types. The value can range from 0 to 100. The default is 50 for Oren-Nayar-Blinn shading and 0 for Multi-Layer shading. At 0, the transition between diffuse and ambient color is the same as that produced with the Blinn shading type.

Anisotropy and Orientation

The **Anisotropy:** and **Orientation:** spinners are available with the Anisotropic and Multi-Layer shading types. The Multi-Layer shading type has two sets of specular highlights.

Figure 13-23. These two objects have the same material, except the object on the right has its **Diffuse Level:** value increased.

Figure 13-24. These two objects have the same material, except the object on the right has a higher **Roughness:** value. Notice how it appears less shiny and more matte.

Figure 13-25. The highlight graph for the Anisotropic shading type is three-dimensional.

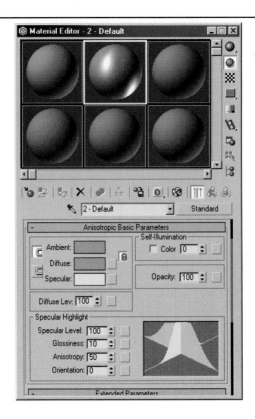

The **Anisotropy:** spinner controls the shape of the highlight. The highlight graph for the Anisotropic shading type is three-dimensional. See Figure 13-25. One axis remains constant, based on the specular level. The other axis changes based on the value in the **Anisotropy:** spinner. The higher the value, the thinner the highlight. At 0, the highlight is circular.

The **Orientation:** spinner controls how the highlight is placed on the material. Changing this value changes the orientation of the highlight. The highlight graph does not change. However, the material sample does reflect the setting in this spinner.

Exercise

Exercise 13-5

1) Open the **Material Editor**.
2) Select a material sample. Pick the Multi-Layer shading type.
3) Set the diffuse color to a deep red. Set the ambient color to a near-black red.
4) In the **First Specular Layer** area, set the first specular color to pure white (255).
5) Set the first **Level:** spinner to 50. Also set the first **Anisotropy:** spinner to 50. How did the material sample change? How did the highlight graph change?
6) In the **Second Specular Layer** area, set the second specular color to yellow (R255, G255).
7) Set the second **Level:** spinner to 100. Set the second **Anisotropy:** spinner to 75. Set the second **Orientation:** spinner to 100. How did the material sample change?
8) Reset 3ds max without saving.

Chapter Snapshot

Chapter Test

Answer the following questions on a separate sheet of paper.

1) What is the purpose of having different material types?
2) How many material types are there in 3ds max?
3) Define compound material type.
4) Where is a material created?
5) How do you activate the function in Question 4? List three different methods.
6) What effect does checking the **Wire** check box in the **Shader Basic Parameters** rollout have on the material?
7) What effect does checking the **2-Sided** check box in the **Shader Basic Parameters** rollout have on the material?
8) When would you check the **2-Sided** check box?
9) What effect does checking the **Faceted** check box in the **Shader Basic Parameters** rollout have?
10) How many shading types are there in 3ds max?
11) What is the main difference between Blinn and Phong shading?
12) Which color component cannot be set for the Metal shading type?
13) Which shading type is the Multi-Layer type based on?
14) What is the function of supersampling?
15) List the four color components used by 3ds max to define a material color.
16) How can you swap the colors defined in two color swatches?
17) If the ambient color is locked to the specular color, what must also be true?
18) Which color component is set in the **Extended Parameters** rollout?
19) What type of light is simulated by a material with self-illumination?
20) Define opacity.

Modeling Problems

Draw the following models using your own dimensions. Apply materials as needed, similar to those shown. Add lights and cameras as needed to create the shadows and views shown. When finished, save each model as p13-xx.max in the folder of your choice.

1 Transparent Sphere
Adjust the color, opacity, and filter color as needed to reproduce the scene shown here. Add lights and a camera as necessary.

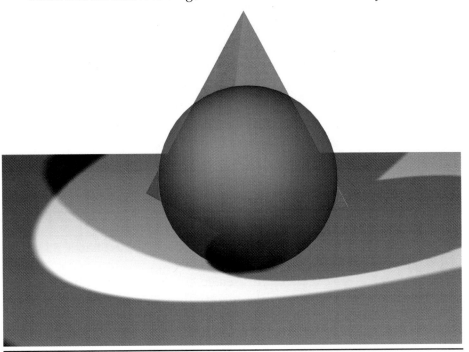

2 Shiny Sphere
Adjust the color and other material parameters as needed to reproduce the scene shown here. Add lights and a camera as necessary.

Dinner Scene **3**

Draw the objects and define the materials needed to reproduce the scene shown. Add lights and a camera as necessary. Pay attention to how the shadows are cast.

Snowman **4**

Draw the objects and define the materials needed to reproduce the scene shown. Some materials can be found in the default 3ds max material library. Add lights and a camera as necessary. Pay attention to how the shadows are cast.

5 Bumper and License Plate
Create the partial view of the license plate, holder, bumper, and hood shown here. Define the materials needed to complete the scene. Add lights and a camera as necessary.

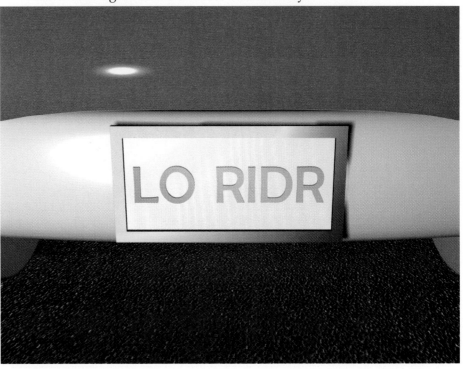

6 White Ware Display
Draw the plate, holder, and cabinet shown here. Create a green glass material for the front of the cabinet, as shown. Add lights and a camera as needed to reproduce the scene.

Transparent Drinking Glasses **7**

Draw the objects shown. Define the materials needed to reproduce the scene. Pay attention to opacity and filter color. Add lights and a camera to the scene as needed.

Concentric Spheres **8**

Draw the five spheres shown here. The largest sphere contains all other spheres. Define the materials needed to reproduce the scene. Add lights as needed to create the shadows shown.

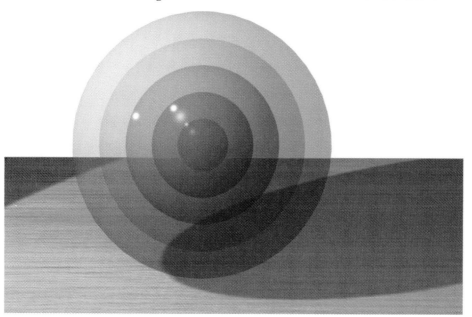

9 CD Jewel Case
Draw the CD and jewel case shown here. Define the materials needed to complete the scene. Add lights and a camera as necessary.

10 Clock
Create the clock. Define the materials needed to reproduce the scene.

Residential Windows with Mullions **11**

Draw the window shown here. There are two pieces of glass and the mullions are sandwiched between the two panes.

Glass Bottle **12**

Draw the glass bottle shown here. Add lights as needed to define the scene.

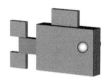

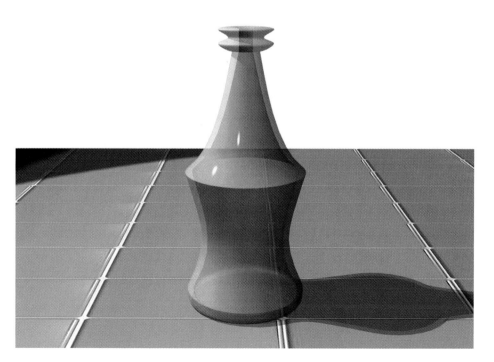

Chapter 14

Animating a Scene

Objectives

After completing this chapter, you will be able to:

- Define animation.
- Compare cel animation to **3ds max** animation.
- Explain keys.
- Set the animation length.
- Define object motion blur and image motion blur.
- Apply motion blur.
- Use the **Snapshot** tool.
- Define a dummy object.
- Use a dummy object.

Introduction to Animation

When you view an animation, whether created in **3ds max** or a Saturday morning cartoon, you see motion. However, there is no actual motion. An *animation* creates the illusion of motion. What you see as movement is actually a series of still images with small differences. When the images are displayed fast enough, the brain cannot distinguish them as individual still images. The slight differences between the images are interpreted by the brain as motion. Think of the simple cartoons you may have created on the edge of your notebook as a kid. See Figure 14-1. This is the same basic process used to create an animation in **3ds max**.

There are several different types of animation. Cartoons are an example of a type of animation that has been around a long time. Stop motion photography is another type that has been around for many years. This type of photography is used for "claymation" type animations. Animatronics is a special type of animation where an object is automated, animated, and filmed, similar to filming a puppet.

Cel (Traditional) Animation

Traditional animations, such as cartoons, are called *cel animations.* An artist draws a series of still images with minor differences between each image. Each individual still image is called a *frame* or *cel.* See Figure 14-2.

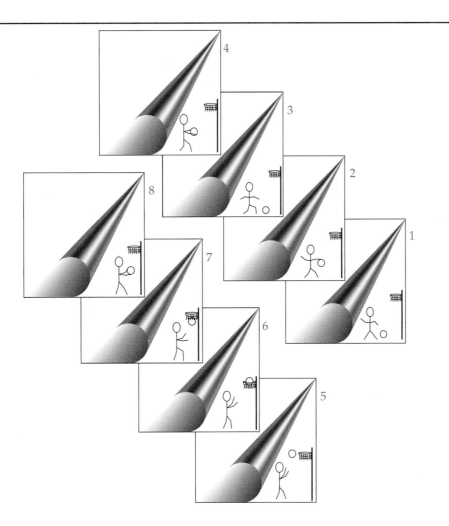

Figure 14-1. A very basic form of animation is the "notebook cartoons" you may have created as a kid.

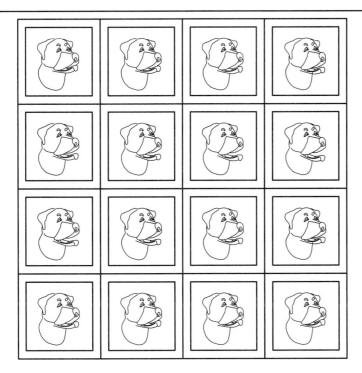

Figure 14-2. Traditional cel animation involves creating a series of drawings with very small differences between each.

The lead artist draws the image in special frames called keyframes. *Keyframes* are certain frames in the animation where a particular action must take place, such as a closed door being completely opened. After the lead artist has drawn the keyframes, the assistant artists draw the frames between the keyframes. The frames in between keyframes are called *tweens.*

Computer Animation

When creating an animation in 3ds max, the same basic process used with cel animation is employed. Objects have keyframes specified for their movement. 3ds max then calculates the tweens for the animation. Think of yourself as the lead artist and 3ds max as the assistant artist. When a keyframe is specified, 3ds max saves information about the related action as an *animation key.* This key can be edited, adjusted, or removed.

In many respects, 3ds max animation is most like animatronics. You do not draw objects again and again in each cel. Rather, the objects are automated and the 3ds max camera "films" the movement. See Figure 14-3.

Figure 14-3. Animation in 3ds max is similar to animatronics in that objects are automated and "filmed." (Discreet, a division of Autodesk)

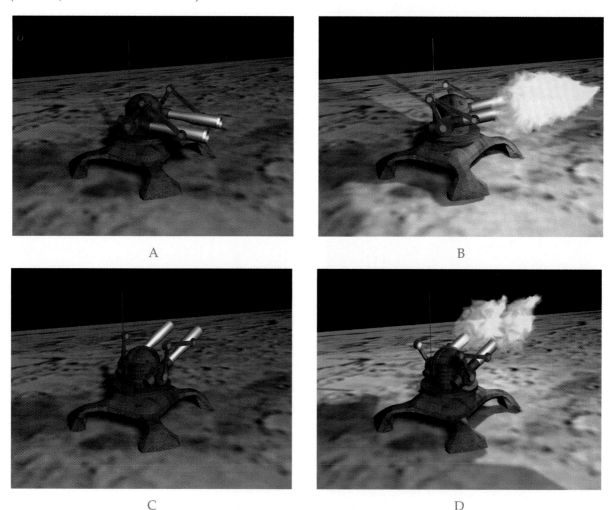

A

B

C

D

Storyboards

Storyboards are used to show the motion in an animation before creating the animation. Originally developed in the early part of the 20th century, a storyboard can be thought of as an "animation script." The important frames, or keyframes, are indicated on the storyboard. This allows animators to see how the frames fit together. Animators can also determine how many frames are required in between keyframes. All but the most simple animations should start as a sketch on a storyboard.

Professional animators often use storyboards as presentation material for clients. The storyboard then becomes part of the contract. The animator is required to stick to the storyboard animation. Also, changes or alterations by the client can be documented as "charge for" alterations.

Storyboards can be as simple as sketches. Preprinted storyboard templates can also be purchased. These are often useful for client presentations. In addition, there are several software packages that can be used for creating storyboards. A sample storyboard is shown in Figure 14-4.

Animating a Scene in 3ds max

Animating a scene in 3ds max is easy. After objects are created, the basic process is:

- Determining keyframes.
- Entering animation mode.
- Creating keys.

The following sections discuss how each of these procedures is incorporated into the animation process.

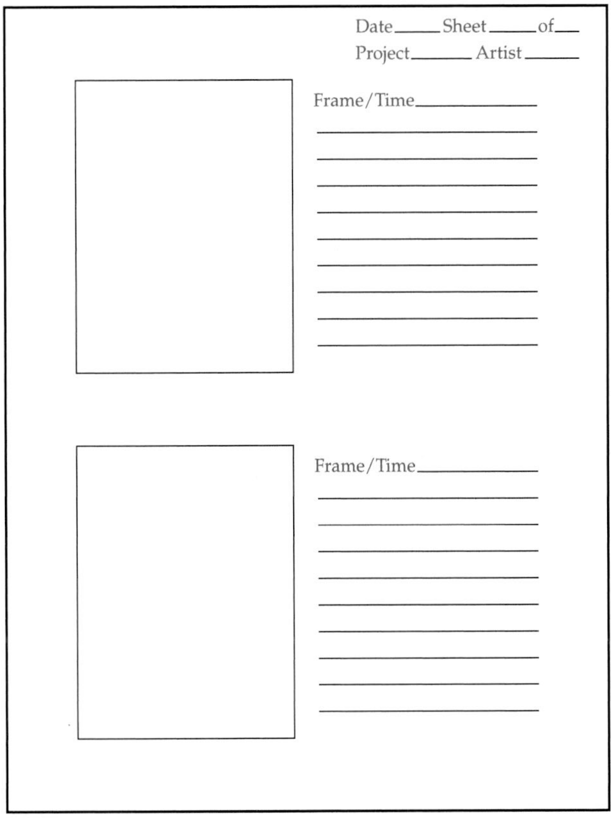

Figure 14-4. Storyboards are a must for creating all but the most basic animations.

Animation Length

Before setting the animation length, you need to determine how long the animation needs to be. Different output devices display frames at different rates. For example, a computer typically displays frames at a rate of 30 per second. A cartoon, however, is typically displayed at 24 frames per second. Therefore, a one-minute animation intended for computer display needs to be 1800 frames long. That same animation transferred to film as a cartoon only needs to be 1440 frames long.

Time Configuration

Once you have determined the number of frames needed, you can set 3ds max to that number of frames. It is important to do this before creating keyframes. While you can adjust the length later, you will have to adjust existing animation keys as well. To set the animation length, pick the **Time Configuration** button in the time controls. You can also right-click on any of the time controls buttons. The **Time Configuration** dialog box is displayed. See Figure 14-5.

The radio buttons in the **Frame Rate** area allow you to set a specific frames per second speed. This setting is only important if you are sending the animation to a recording device. If you are sending the animation to the hard drive, leave this setting to the default **NTSC**.

The settings in the **Time Display** area determine how time is displayed by 3ds max. These settings are most important when sending the animation to a recording device.

If the **Real Time** check box is checked in the **Playback** area, 3ds max will skip frames during viewport playback in an attempt to match the actual speed set in the **Frame Rate** area. Unchecking this check box forces 3ds max to display all frames during viewport playback.

The **Animation** area is where the length of the animation is set. The values in this area are displayed as the number of frames if the **Frames** radio button is selected in the **Time Display** area. The value in the **Length:** spinner is the total length of the animation. The **Start Time:** and **End Time:** spinners set the current time segment. This allows you to render a portion of the total animation. These values can be lower than 0, if necessary. The value in the **Current Time:** spinner is the frame shown in the

Figure 14-5. The **Time Configuration** dialog box is used to set the length of the animation. It is also used to set the frame rate for the animation. The frame rate must match that of the playback device.

Animation length settings

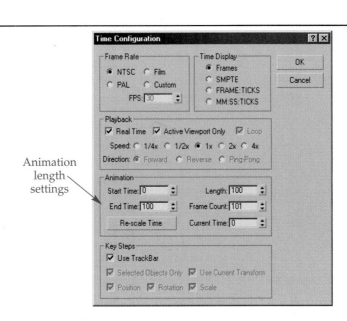

viewports and represented by the **Time** slider. Changing this value changes the current frame displayed in the viewports. Picking the **Rescale Time** button forces any existing animation to fit inside the time segment specified by the **Start Time:** and **End Time:** spinners.

As you make changes in the **Time Configuration** dialog box, 3ds max updates settings. For example, if you change the **Current Time:** value, you may notice that the **Time** slider at the bottom of the drawing area moves. However, this is not a modeless dialog box. You must close the dialog box to continue working.

Exercise

Exercise 14-1

1) Draw the inline skate and pylon shown below. Use your own dimensions.
2) Design a logical linked hierarchy and assign it to the skate. Make the top part of the skate the top of the hierarchy.
3) Create and assign appropriate materials. Use the chrome material in the default material library for the bracket.
4) Open the **Time Configuration** dialog box.
5) Pick the **NTSC** radio button in the **Frame Rate** area.
6) Pick the **Frames** radio button in the **Time Display** area, if not already on.
7) In the **Animation** area, set the **Length:** spinner to 300. This will create an animation 10 seconds long.
8) Save the scene as ex14-01.max in the folder of your choice.

Moving Between Frames

In order to create an animation in 3ds max, you must know how to move between frames. In the previous section, you learned how to do this using the **Time Configuration** dialog box. However, this is a time-consuming and inefficient method. Fortunately, there are much easier ways to move between frames.

If you pick and hold the **Time** slider, you can move it left and right. The current frame is displayed both on the slider and in the current

Previous Frame

Next Frame

Go to Start   Go to End

frame field in the time controls. When the frame you are moving to is displayed, release the mouse button. Also, picking the left or right arrow on the **Time** slider advances one frame in the arrow direction.

If you pick in the current frame field in the time controls, you can type a new frame number. Pressing the [Enter] key then moves to that frame. Also, the **Previous Frame**, **Next Frame**, **Go to Start**, and **Go to End** buttons are in the time controls. These buttons allow you to move one frame at a time or jump to the first or last frame of the current time segment. The buttons work much like the "play" buttons on a home CD or DVD player.

Help Cel

Only the frames in the current time segment can be accessed. To access frames outside the current time segment, you need to redefine the current time segment in the **Time Configuration** dialog box.

Creating Keys

Keys contain information about an action performed on a keyframe. A keyframe contains at least one key, and a key is always on a keyframe. Before creating any animation keys, you must determine which frames are keyframes. For example, on frame 30, assume you want a door to be fully open. This means that frame 30 is a keyframe for the door. Each object, camera, light, etc., can have multiple keyframes and keys. Once you have determined the keyframes for each object, it is time to add the keys.

First, select the object to which you are going to assign keys. Next, move to the first keyframe. It is often easiest to assign all keys for one object, then move on to the next object. Finally, pick the **Toggle Animation Mode** button to turn animation mode on. The button turns red to indicate you are in animation mode. The current viewport also has a red line around it. In addition, the background behind the **Time** slider turns red. Now, animate the object as needed. The animation can be a transformation, a change in the object's parameters, a change in a modifier's parameters, or just about anything. There are very few limitations placed on what can be animated. Whenever the value in a spinner is animated, red corners appear around the spinner to indicate it has animation keys. See Figure 14-6. Continue adding keys on the required keyframes until all objects are animated.

Once keys have been created for the object in the keyframe, a key is displayed in the track bar below the **Time** slider as a red box. See Figure 14-7. You can move the key to a different frame by dragging it along the **Time** slider with the cursor. You can also delete the key by highlighting it and pressing the [Delete] key. A highlighted key is white. Only the keys for the currently selected object are displayed in the track bar. If no object is selected, no keys appear in the track bar.

Continue adding keys for the object by moving to the next keyframe and performing the next animation. It is very important to remember to have the **Toggle Animation Mode** button turned on *before* adding the next key. If you are not in animation mode, any "animation" you add is really a change made to the scene and is transferred to frame 0. Frame 0 is the base frame where all modeling should be completed.

After all keys have been added to all objects, exit animation mode by picking the **Toggle Animation Mode** button. The button is no longer

Animate

Toggle Animation Mode

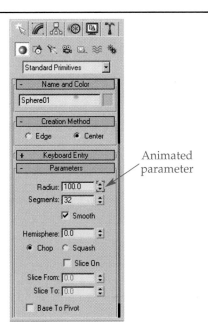

Figure 14-6. An animated spinner (parameter) has a red box around the spinner buttons.

Animated parameter

depressed and red. Now, you can pick the **Play Animation** button in the time controls to see the animated objects in the current viewport.

Play Animation

You may notice that the objects do not move quite as you expected. This is because 3ds max tries to make all movement "organic" or lifelike. To do this, the software "floats" the movement into and out of a key. This floating can be adjusted, along with many other features, using a feature of 3ds max called **Track View**. Chapter 16 explains editing keys using **Track View**.

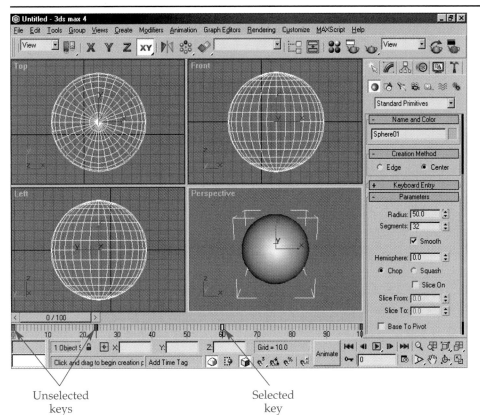

Figure 14-7. Keys for a selected object appear below the **Time** slider.

Unselected keys

Selected key

Exercise

Exercise 14-2

1) Open ex14-01.max if it is not already open.
2) Create one copy of the skate to form a pair. Do not link the skates to one another. Also, copy the pylon several times to form a slalom. See below.
3) Animate the objects by transforming them as shown below. Tilt the skates as they move through the slalom. Be sure you are in animation mode before adding the keys. Exit animation mode when finished adding keys.
4) Make the Perspective viewport current. Pick the **Play Animation** button.
5) Pick the **Stop** button when done viewing the animation.
6) Select the left skate (top object in the hierarchy). Pick the first key below the **Time** slider. Move it to frame 25. Pick the second key and move it to frame 75. Continue moving all keys for the left skate "up" by 25 frames. Leave the last key at frame 300 unchanged.
7) Play the animation again in the Perspective viewport. How is the animation different?
8) Save the file as ex14-02.max.

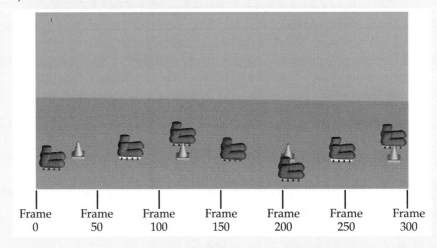

| Frame 0 | Frame 50 | Frame 100 | Frame 150 | Frame 200 | Frame 250 | Frame 300 |

Motion Blur

In Chapter 11, you learned how to apply motion blur to a scene using a camera. You can also add motion blur to an individual object. This "streaks" the object from frame to frame. See Figure 14-8. There are two types of motion blur that can be added to an object—object and image. There is one main difference between object motion blur and image motion blur. Object motion blur is designed to simulate a fast-moving object. Image motion blur, on the other hand, is designed to simulate a slow shutter speed on a real-word camera. This is a subtle distinction, and the difference in a rendering can be subtle as well.

To add motion blur, select the object to which you want motion blur applied. Then, right-click on the object and pick **Properties**... from the quad menu or pick **Object Properties**... in the **Edit** pull-down menu. The **Object Properties** dialog box appears, Figure 14-9.

Figure 14-8. A—The propeller is animated, but no motion blur is applied. B—The same scene with object motion blur applied to the propeller.

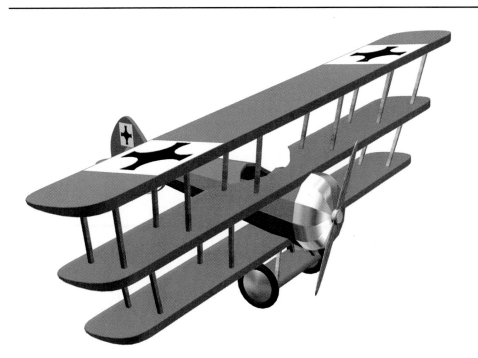

A

B

Figure 14-9. The **Object Properties** dialog box is used to add object or image motion blur to an object.

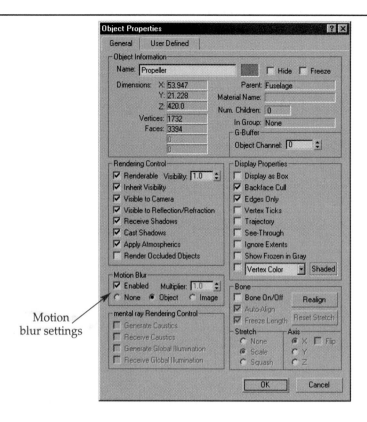

Motion blur settings

In the **General** tab of the **Object Properties** dialog box, check the **Enabled** check box in the **Motion Blur** area. If the **None** radio button is on, no motion blur is applied. If the **Object** radio button is on, object motion blur is applied. If the **Image** radio button is on, image motion blur is applied. In addition, with image motion blur, you must specify a value in the **Multiplier:** spinner. This value determines the "length" of a streak for image motion blur.

Once you have specified motion blur for the object, close the **Object Properties** dialog box. The next time the scene is rendered, motion blur is calculated and applied to the object.

Help Cel

For either object or image motion blur to be rendered, the appropriate **Apply** check box must be checked in the **MAX Default Scanline A-Buffer** rollout of the **Render Scene** dialog box. These are both checked by default.

Snapshot

Snapshot

The **Snapshot** tool allows you to clone animated objects. As with other cloning methods, you can create a copy, instance, or reference. You can also create the clone as a mesh object. By creating the clone as a mesh, you can create a new object based on the animated deformations of an object on any frame.

To create a snapshot, select the animated object. Then, move to the frame from which to generate the clone. Finally, pick the **Snapshot** button from the **Array** flyout on the **Main** toolbar or select **Snapshot**…

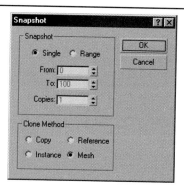

Figure 14-10. The **Snapshot** dialog box allows you to clone an animated object over time.

from the **Tools** pull-down menu. The **Snapshot** dialog box appears. See Figure 14-10.

In the **Snapshot** area, specify if the clone is to be a single clone or multiple clones over a range of frames. If the **Range** radio button is on, you must set the first and last frame in the range using the **To:** and **From:** spinners. You must also specify how many clones are created over that range. If the **Single** radio button is on, only one clone is created based on the state of the selected object on the current frame.

In the **Clone Method** area, you must specify what type of clone is created. Picking the **Copy**, **Reference**, and **Instance** radio buttons create standard clone objects. Picking the **Mesh** radio button creates a mesh object based on the state of the selected object.

Finally, pick the **OK** button to create the clone(s). The animated transforms applied to the original object are *not* copied to the clone. However, materials are copied, and, if animated, the animation is copied, too. Also, animated parameters of the original object are transferred to the clone.

You can use the **Snapshot** tool on particle systems. The output can be a mesh object. In this way, you can have a static clone of the particle system. As an example, you might use this method to create a frozen water spray. Particle systems are covered in Chapter 22.

Dummy Objects

A *dummy object* is a special helper object in 3ds max. It is always a cube with a pivot point in its center. See Figure 14-11. A dummy is not rendered and has no parameters to change. The primary purpose of a dummy is to help animate objects or groups of objects. A dummy provides a single point to which other objects can be linked. The dummy is then animated and all its children follow.

As mentioned in Chapter 11, a dummy can also be used to help animate a target camera. Both the camera and its target are linked to the dummy. Then, the dummy is animated. The camera and its target follow the dummy.

Creating Dummy Objects

To create a dummy, pick **Create** in the **Command Panel**. Then, pick the **Helpers** button. Select **Standard** in the drop-down list and pick the **Dummy** button in the **Object Type** rollout. Finally, pick and drag in a viewport to draw the dummy.

Create

Helpers

Dummy

Figure 14-11. A dummy object is a cube used to assist in animating other objects. Dummy objects are not rendered.

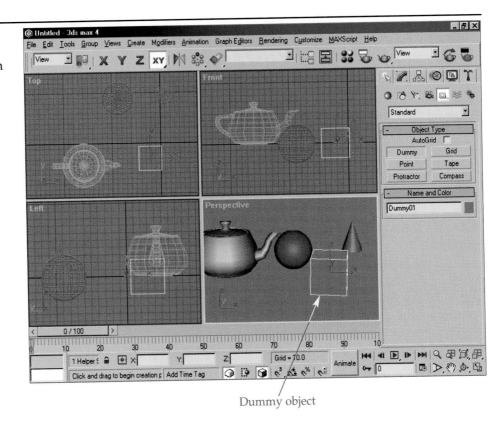

Dummy object

It does not matter if you create a big dummy or a small dummy. The dummy should be large enough to easily see and select. However, do not make the dummy too big or it may make it hard to select other objects.

Once the dummy is created, it can be named in the **Name and Color** rollout. The display color of the dummy cannot be changed, even though there is a color swatch in this rollout. A dummy has no parameters. If you want to make the dummy bigger or smaller after it is created, use the **Select and Scale** tool.

Using Dummy Objects

Select and Link

Hierarchy

Link Info

Using a dummy object is easy. First create the dummy. Then, use the **Select and Link** button to link objects to the dummy. Finally, pick **Hierarchy** in the **Command Panel** and the **Link Info** button. Make the appropriate settings in the **Inherit** and **Locks** rollouts.

Now, identify keyframes for the objects linked to the dummy. Then, assign animation keys to the dummy object for those keyframes. When the animation is played, the linked objects will follow the dummy's motion. The dummy object will appear if the animation is previewed in the viewport. However, it will not appear in the final rendering. Dummy objects are not rendered. See Figure 14-12.

Figure 14-12. When the scene in Figure 14-11 is rendered, you can see the dummy object is not rendered.

Exercise 14-3

1) Open ex14-02.max if it is not already open.
2) Delete all of the animation keys for both skates. Reposition the objects at the beginning of the slalom on frame 0.
3) Create two dummy objects, one named Left Big Dummy and the other named Right Big Dummy.
4) Link the left skate to the Left Big Dummy. Link the right skate to the Right Big Dummy. Then, link Left Big Dummy to Right Big Dummy.
5) Adjust pivot points and inherits as necessary.
6) Animate the Right Big Dummy through the slalom. Move keys as needed after they are created.
7) Preview the animation in the Perspective viewport. Notice how the skates move in relation to the dummy objects.
8) Save the scene as ex14-03.max.

Exercise

Chapter Snapshot

Chapter Test

Answer the following questions on a separate sheet of paper.
1) How is motion produced in an animation?
2) Give an example of cel animation.
3) Define keyframe.
4) Define tweens.
5) What is an animation key?
6) The basic process of creating an animation in 3ds max is _____, _____, and _____.
7) To determine the animation length, you need to know the _____ and the _____.
8) List two ways to open the **Time Configuration** dialog box.
9) What is the function of the **Real Time** check box in the **Playback** area of the **Time Configuration** dialog box?
10) What do the **Start Time:** and **End Time:** spinners do?
11) What is the function of the **Re-scale Time** button?
12) List three ways to move between animation frames.
13) How do you turn animation mode on?
14) How is animation mode indicated on screen?
15) Once a key is created, how can it be deleted?
16) Why does movement float into and out of keys?
17) _____ motion blur is designed to simulate a fast-moving object, while _____ motion blur is designed to simulate a slow shutter speed on a camera.
18) What is the function of the **Snapshot** tool?
19) What parameters does a dummy object have?
20) How do you create a dummy object?

Modeling Problems

Draw the following models using your own dimensions. Use the 3ds max objects presented in this and earlier chapters. Create and apply basic materials as needed, similar to those shown. Add lights and cameras as needed to create the shadows and views shown. When finished, save each model as p14-xx.max in the folder of your choice.

Antique Fan **1**

Draw the antique fan shown. Adjust pivot points and link objects as needed. Create and assign basic materials similar to those shown. Animate the rotation of the fan blades several complete turns. Add motion blur to the blades. Also, animate the rotation of the "head" of the fan 30° and then back to its original position.

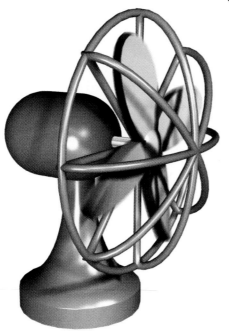

Refrigerator **2**

Draw the refrigerator and components shown. Create and assign basic materials similar to those shown. Pay attention to color, opacity, and glossiness. Add lights as needed. Be sure to place lighting inside the refrigerator. Animate the door open on frame 30. Slide the drawers out and then in by frame 60. Animate the door closed on frame 100. *(Note: There will be some motion problems with this animation. You will learn how to fix the motion in Chapter 16.)*

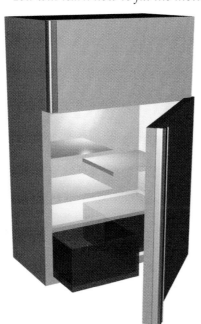

3 Truckasaurus

Draw a monster truck similar to the one shown. Create and assign basic materials as needed. Adjust pivots and create a hierarchy. Animate the wheels rotating several complete turns. Also, move the truck out of the view for its initial position. Then, from frame 0 to frame 100, the truck should move across the view.

4 Airplane

Draw the airplane shown. Adjust pivots and create a hierarchy as needed. Define and apply basic materials similar to those shown. Animate the propeller rotating several complete turns. Also, add two or three "banks" of the plane.

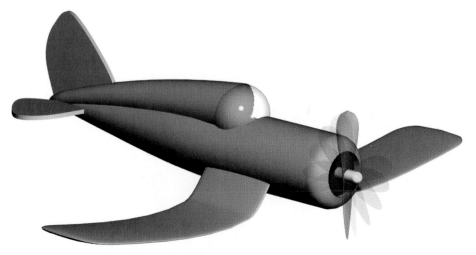

Meditation Swing **5**

Create the frame, balls, and strings shown below. Adjust the pivots and create a hierarchy as needed. Define basic materials or use materials from the default 3ds max material library as needed. Animate the left ball up on frame 25 and down on frame 50. The right ball should move up from frame 50 to frame 100. *(Note: There will be some motion problems with this animation. You will learn how to fix the motion in Chapter 16.)*

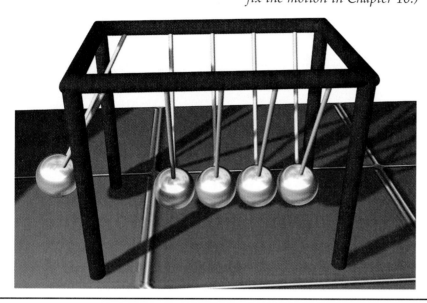

Ferris Wheel **6**

Draw the simple Ferris wheel shown below. Adjust pivots and create a hierarchy as needed. The gondolas should always "hang" from the bottom of the cross members. Create and apply basic materials similar to those shown. Use materials from the default 3ds max material library as needed. Animate the rotation of the Ferris wheel several turns.

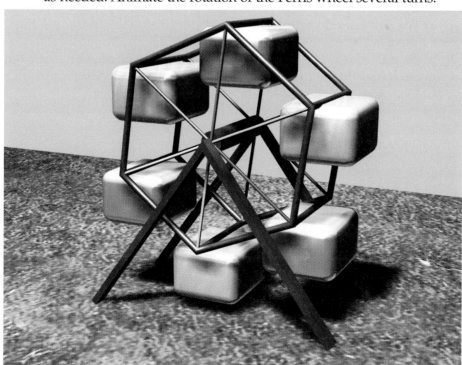

7 Sphere and Torus

Draw a sphere. Then, draw a torus centered on the sphere. Animate the parameters of the torus to "squeeze" the sphere. You will need to use a mesh select modifier and an xform modifier on the sphere. The torus should squeeze the sphere to frame 50. Then, both objects should return to their original sizes on frame 100.

8 Toy Cannon

Draw the cannon, cannonball, and smoke shown below. Create and apply basic materials similar to those shown. Animate the scene as follows.

a) The smoke and cannonball should start inside the cannon. Adjust the parameters for the smoke as needed.

b) On frame 50, the cannonball and smoke should be out of the cannon.

c) On frame 75, the cannonball should be out of the view.

d) On frame 100, the smoke should be out of the view.

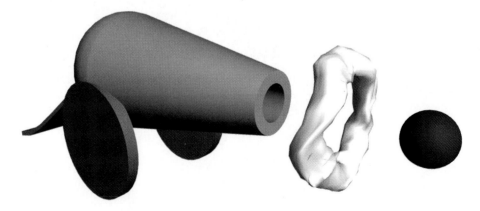

Candle **9**

Draw the candle and wick shown below. Create and apply basic materials. The candle wax is slightly transparent. Animate a melt modifier for the candle. Animate the height of the wick to match the melting of the candle.

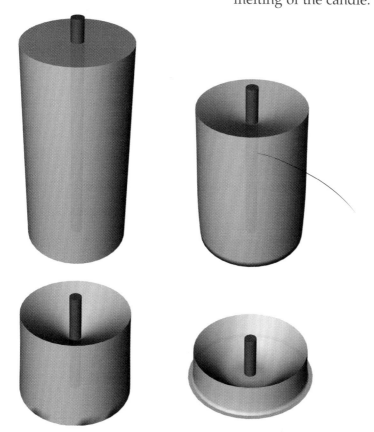

Umbrella **10**

Draw the umbrella shown. The top of the umbrella is a "squashed" hemisphere. Using an xform modifier, animate the umbrella open and closed.

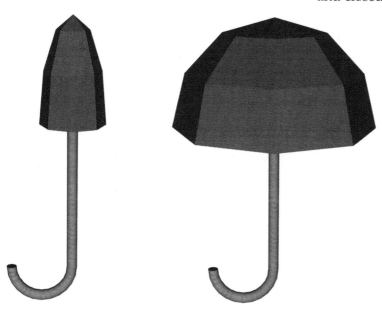

Chapter 15

Rendering an Animation

Objectives

After completing this chapter, you will be able to:

- Explain the purpose of a preview animation.
- Create a preview animation.
- Change the background.
- Set the animation output size.
- Define alpha channel and explain its purpose.
- Explain and apply rendering effects.
- Render a final animation.

Previewing an Animation

Rendering a final animation can take many hours to complete. The more complex a scene is, the longer it will take to render the final animation. Therefore, you should only render a final animation when you are sure the scene is complete. ActiveShade provides a rendered preview of a viewport on any frame. However, this is limited to a single frame. To check an animation for correct movement before creating the final rendering, you can create a preview.

A *preview animation* is a low-color, low-resolution rendering of the animation. A preview animation does not provide the rendering quality of ActiveShade or a final rendering. However, a preview can show the effects of multi-pass camera settings.

To create a preview, select **Make Preview**... from the **Rendering** pull-down menu. The **Make Preview** dialog box is displayed. See Figure 15-1. This dialog box is discussed in the next section.

The Make Preview Dialog Box

At the top of the **Make Preview** dialog box is the **Preview Range** area. In this area, you set the range of frames to be previewed. Picking the **Active Time Segment** radio button includes all frames of the active time segment in the preview. Picking the **Custom Range:** radio button allows you to specify a starting and ending frame in the spinners located below the radio button.

In the **Frame Rate** area, the value in the **Playback FPS:** spinner sets the number of frames played per second in the preview. The **Every Nth**

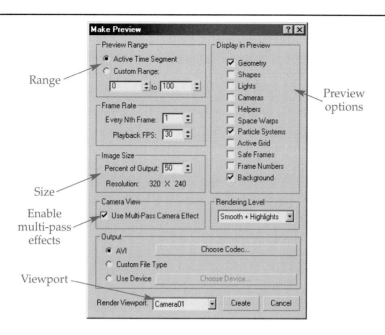

Figure 15-1. The **Make Preview** dialog box is used to set up and make a preview animation.

Frame: spinner allows you to skip frames in the preview. Entering a value of 1 in this spinner includes every frame in the preview. A value of 3 means every third frame is included in the preview.

The setting in the **Image Size** area determines the dimensions of the preview. This is tied to the output size set in the **Render Scene** dialog box. Setting the output size is discussed later in this chapter. The current output size is listed under the **Percent of Output:** spinner. The value in the spinner is what percent of the output size the preview will be. For example, if 50 is entered in the spinner, the preview will be half of the output size.

In the **Display in Preview** area, there are several check boxes allowing you to specify what to include in the preview. For example, you can check the **Frame Numbers** check box to have 3ds max render the number of the current frame in the upper-left corner of the preview. See Figure 15-2. There are also check boxes for geometry, shapes, lights, cameras, helpers, and background. A check in any of these boxes includes that item in the preview.

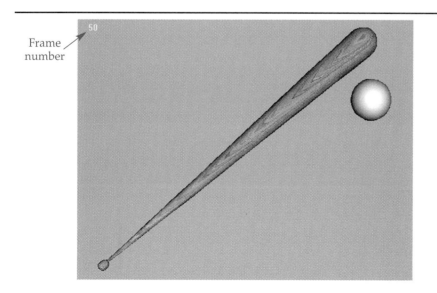

Figure 15-2. If the **Frame Numbers** option is used, each frame is numbered in the upper-left corner.

The **Rendering Level** area allows you to choose the level of detail in the preview. The options in the drop-down list are the same as those for the display mode in a viewport. The highest level of detail is produced by the **Smooth + Highlights** option. The lowest level of detail is produced by the **Bounding Box** option.

The **Render Viewport:** drop-down list at the bottom of the dialog box allows you to specify which viewport will be rendered. Only the names of viewports displayed in the current viewport configuration appear in the list.

After all settings have been made in the dialog box, pick the **Create** button to create the preview. The viewports are replaced with the preview rendering. See Figure 15-3. Each frame is rendered. The progress is shown at the bottom of the screen. To cancel the preview, pick the **Cancel** button.

Help Cel

The first time in a modeling session that you render to a file, you may be prompted to specify options for the file type. The file type for a preview is specified in the **Output** area. The settings for the default AVI file type can be set ahead of time by picking the **Choose Codec**... button.

Viewing the Preview

Once a preview is created, it is automatically played in Windows Media Player. See Figure 15-4. When done viewing the preview, close Media Player to return to 3ds max.

A preview can be viewed again later by selecting **View Preview**... from the **Rendering** pull-down menu. This opens Media Player and plays the preview animation. Close Media Player when done viewing the preview.

Figure 15-3. A preview being rendered.

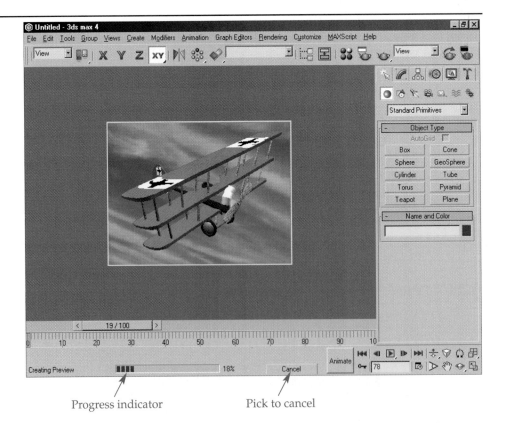

Progress indicator   Pick to cancel

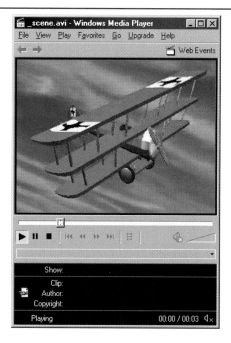

Figure 15-4. Previews are played in Windows Media Player.

Exercise 15-1

1) Draw the objects shown below. Use your own dimensions.
2) Add basic materials of your choice. Do not try to match the checkerboard pattern.
3) Animate the scene. You can use the suggested movement given below or your own ideas.
4) Create a camera. Change the Perspective viewport to the Camera viewport. Adjust the view to show the objects at the farthest extents of motion.
5) Make a preview of the Camera viewport.
6) View the preview animation.
7) Save the file as ex15-01.max in the folder of your choice.

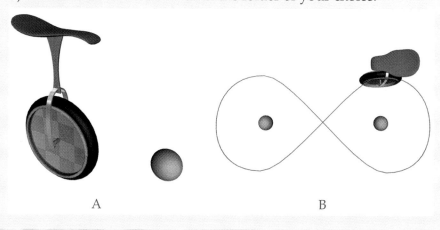

A   B

Render Scene

Rendering the Animation

A final animation is rendered using the **Render Scene** dialog box. See Figure 15-5. This is the same dialog box used to render a still image. The difference is you must specify which frames to render and save the rendering to file. To open the **Render Scene** dialog box, select **Render**... from the **Rendering** pull-down menu, pick the **Render Scene** button on the **Main** toolbar, or press [Shift][R].

If you are rendering an animation and you do not save the rendering to a file, the animation is lost. Fortunately, 3ds max warns you of this situation. When a rendering is initiated for a series of frames, but no file is specified, the warning dialog box shown in Figure 15-6 appears. Previous releases of 3D Studio did not provide this warning.

Setting What to Render

In the **Time Output** area of the **Render Scene** dialog box, you must set which frames to render. Since this is an animation, you do *not* want to select the **Single** radio button. Instead, select the **Active Time Segment:**, **Range:**, or **Frames** radio button.

Picking the **Active Time Segment:** radio button renders the entire time segment. Picking the **Range:** radio button allows you to specify a starting and ending frame. Picking the **Frames** radio button allows you to specify only certain frames. This option is not often used when rendering an animation.

Setting the Output Size

The **Output Size** area of the **Render Scene** dialog box is where you set the overall size of the rendering. You can pick one of the six preset buttons. You can also enter a custom size in the **Width:** and **Height:** spinners. These values are in pixels. The drop-down list has several options

---

Figure 15-5. The **Render Scene** dialog box is used to set up and render the final animation.

Frames to render

Output size settings

Rendering options

Check to save to file

Specify production or draft

File name and path

Viewport

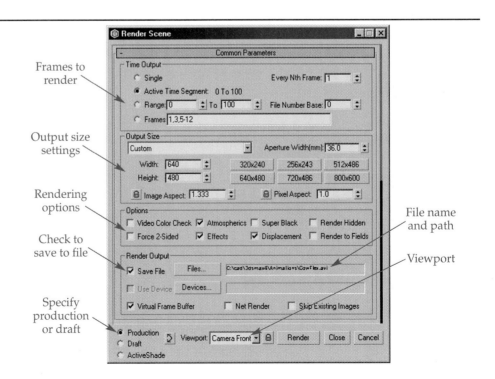

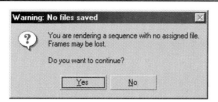

Figure 15-6. A warning dialog box appears when you attempt to render a series of frames without specifying a file.

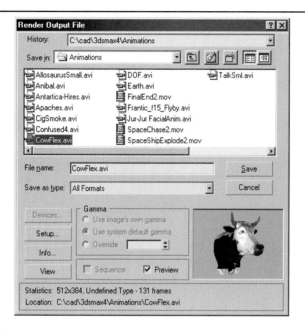

Figure 15-7. Specifying a file name and type in the **Render Output File** dialog box. This is the same dialog box used to save a still image.

for industry-standard sizes. Included in this list are HDTV (video), 4″ x 5″, and several 35 mm options. If you are producing an animation for a specific industry, you can select the format from this drop-down list. If the format is not listed, select **Custom** and enter the dimensions in the **Width:** and **Height:** spinners.

Rendering the Animation

To render the animation, you *must* specify a file to save it to. If you do not save the animation to a file, you will never be able to see it. 3ds max will only render each frame on screen. In the **Render Output** area, pick the **Files**... button. The **Render Output File** dialog box is displayed. See Figure 15-7. Specify a name and location for the file. Also, select an animation file type from the **Save as type:** drop-down list or type the extension of the file type after the file name. The three most common animation file types are AVI (*.avi), Autodesk Flic Image (*.flc, *.fli, *.cel), and Quicktime Movie (*.mov).

Pick the **Save** button after you have named the file and selected the file type. If this is the first time in this drawing session that you have used this file type, a dialog box appears for you to make file-type-specific settings. Which dialog box appears depends on which file type is selected.

When the **Render Scene** dialog box reappears, the **Save File** check box is now checked. This must be checked for the file to be saved. The name and path of the file also appear next to the **Files**... button.

To render the animation, make sure the viewport you want to render appears in the drop-down list at the bottom of the **Render Scene** dialog box. Then, pick the **Render** button. The **Rendering** dialog box appears showing the progress and current settings. The render window also appears. See Figure 15-8. Each frame is rendered and appears in the render window. When the animation is complete, the **Rendering** dialog

Figure 15-8. A—The render window shows each frame as it is rendered. B—The **Rendering** dialog box is displayed while the final animation is rendering. It shows the status of the rendering.

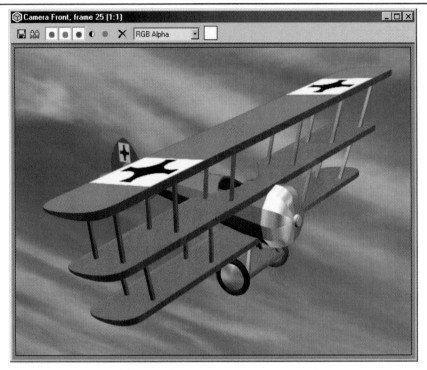

A

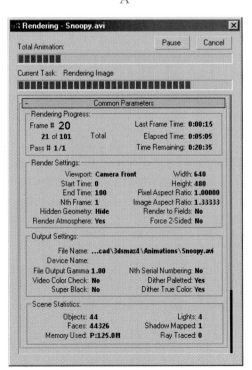

B

box closes. The final rendered frame appears in the render window. Close the render window and the **Render Scene** dialog box to return to the drawing display.

You can set up the **Production** and **Draft** rendering buttons to your advantage. For example, you may want to set up the **Production** button to save a final rendered animation to file. On the other hand, you can use the **Draft** button to perform still image renderings.

Help Cel

If you select a file type that is not an animation type, such as TIFF, the animation is rendered to a series of still image files.

Viewing an Animation

To view a saved animation, select **View Image File**... from the **File** pull-down menu. Change to the drive and folder where the animation file is saved. Then, select it from the list and pick the **Open** button. The appropriate playback device, such as Media Player, is opened and the animation is played.

You can also view a rendered animation directly in Media Player, if saved in a format it can view. You can launch Media Player from the Windows Start menu. Then, locate the animation file and open it. If Media Player is not enabled for the codec you used to render the file, you will need to update your system's codecs. Most animation codecs are available on the Internet through various sources.

Exercise 15-2

1) Open ex15-01.max if it is not already open.
2) Open the **Render Scene** dialog box.
3) Pick the **Draft** radio button at the bottom of the dialog box.
4) In the **Time Output** area, set the rendering to frames 1, 25, 50, 75, and 100.
5) Set the **Output Size** value to 640 x 480.
6) In the **Render Output** area, make sure the **Save File** check box is unchecked.
7) Pick the **Production** radio button.
8) In the **Time Output** area, set the rendering to **Active Time Segment**.
9) Set the **Output Size** value to 320 x 240.
10) In the **Render Output** area, set to save the animation to a file named ex15-02.avi in the folder of your choice.
11) Close the **Render Scene** dialog box and make the Camera viewport active.
12) Pick the **Quick Render (Draft)** button on the **Main** toolbar. Notice what happens. Close the render window when done.
13) Pick the **Quick Render (Production)** button on the **Main** toolbar. Notice what happens. Close the render window when done.
14) Play the rendered animation using 3ds max.
15) Save the scene as ex15-02.max in the folder of your choice. Reset 3ds max.

Environments and Background

To understand the environment in 3ds max, think of a movie set. 3ds max is the entire set. The objects you create are the actors and props. Just as on a movie set, lights and cameras are also placed. Often, a movie set includes a painted background image. Fog or smoke is sometimes created and sprayed onto the set for added effect. These two elements are controlled in 3ds max with *environment* settings. Adding a background is covered in this section. Fog is covered in Chapter 19.

The **Environment** dialog box is used to make environment settings. See Figure 15-9. To open this dialog box, pick **Environment...** from the **Rendering** pull-down menu. This dialog box was used in Chapter 10 to set the ambient light.

The *background* appears behind all objects in the final rendering. Think of it as the painted background on a movie set in front of which the actors perform. The background is set in the **Common Parameters** rollout of the **Environment** dialog box.

By default, the background is simply rendered as black. To change the color, pick the **Color:** swatch in the **Background:** area. Then, select a new color in the color selector. Finally, close the color selector. The next time the scene is rendered, the color you just picked is used as the background.

Using a single color as the background presents many limitations. You can expand the possibilities by using a map. To set the map, pick the **Environment Map:** button in the **Background:** area. This button is initially labeled **None**. The **Material/Map Browser** is displayed. See Figure 15-10. Select the type of map you want to use and close the browser. The name of the map now appears on the **Environment Map:** button. The **Use Map** check box is also checked. If you uncheck this check box, the color displayed in the color swatch is used as the background.

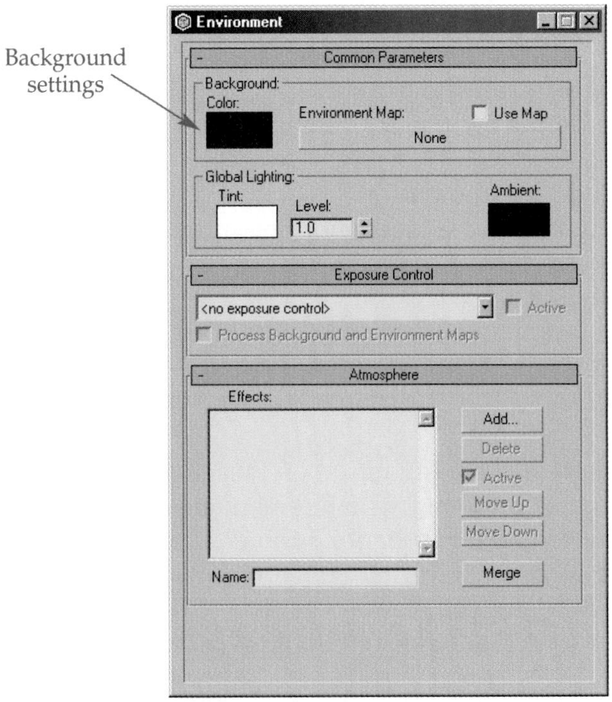

Figure 15-9. The **Environment** dialog box is used to set up a background and atmospheric effects.

Background settings

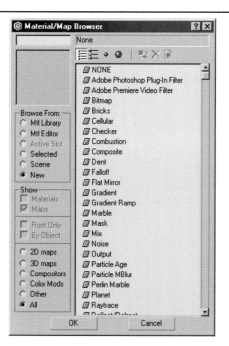

Figure 15-10. The **Material/Map Browser** is used to select a map for the background.

For example, to use a bitmap as the background, pick the **Environment Map:** button. Then, in the **Material/Map Browser**, pick the **Bitmap** type. The **Select Bitmap Image File** dialog box appears. This is a standard "file browser" dialog box. Locate the bitmap you want to use and pick the **Open** button. The name of the file appears on the **Environment Map:** button in parentheses. The first part of the button label, such as **Map #**x, refers to the location in the **3ds max** database. Mapping is discussed in detail in Chapter 18. To use a map type other than the **Bitmap** type as a background, you should read that chapter first.

Help Cel

To have access to various settings for a map, you must apply it to some component of a material. Then, when assigning it as the environment background, "get" it from the **Material Editor**.

Exercise

Exercise 15-3

1) Draw the air boat shown below. Use your own dimensions.
2) Using the **Environment** dialog box, set the background to a solid color of your choice, such as light blue.
3) Render the Perspective viewport.
4) Using the **Environment** dialog box, set the background to a map. Use the **Bitmap** type and select the Fresnel_Water2.jpg bitmap in the 3ds max \images folder.
5) Render the Perspective viewport again.
6) Save the scene as ex15-03.max in the folder of your choice and reset 3ds max.

Rendering Effects

Rendering effects are "special effects" applied to the final rendered image after the rendering is complete. For example, you may add a rendering "star" effect to a model of the sun breaking on the horizon, as seen from space. See Figure 15-11. There are several rendering effects that are supplied with 3ds max. In addition, many other rendering effects are available as aftermarket plug-ins from various software developers. The rendering effects covered in this chapter include film grain, motion blur, depth of field, and several lens effects.

Figure 15-11. A—This model of the sun cresting on the horizon does not have any rendering effects. B—The lens effects star and glow are added to the model.

A

B

To add a rendering effect to the scene, pick **Effects**... from the **Rendering** pull-down menu. The **Rendering Effects** dialog box appears. See Figure 15-12A. Any effects currently in the scene are listed in the **Effects:** list box at the left. To add a new effect to the scene, pick the **Add**... button. The **Add Effect** dialog box appears. See Figure 15-12B. Select an effect from the list and pick the **OK** button. The new effect now appears in the **Effects:** list box. At the bottom of the **Rendering Effects** dialog box are rollouts specific to the highlighted effect. These are discussed in the next sections.

To remove an effect from the scene, highlight the name in the list. Then, pick the **Delete** button. To turn the effect off without deleting it, uncheck the **Active** check box. To rearrange the order in which effects are applied, use the **Move Up** and **Move Down** buttons to move the highlighted effect in the list. The **Merge** button allows you to merge effects from other saved 3ds max files.

The settings in the **Preview** area are used to control how the effect is updated and previewed. The **Effects:** radio buttons determine which effects are previewed. When the **All** radio button is on, all effects in the scene appear in the preview. When the **Current** radio button is on, only the highlighted effect appears in the preview.

Figure 15-12. A—The **Rendering Effects** dialog box is used to add and manage rendering effects. B—Adding a rendering effect to the scene.

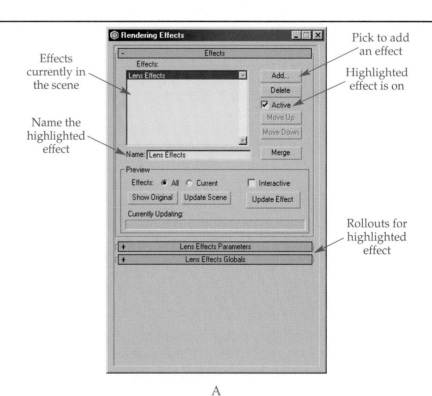

When the **Interactive** check box is checked, a preview is automatically generated in the render window whenever a change that impacts the effect is made. When unchecked, the preview is manually generated by picking the **Update Effect** button. Any changes made to the scene are not reflected in the update. Picking the **Update Scene** button generates the preview with an update of the scene and the rendering effect.

Picking the **Show Original** button previews the scene without any effects applied. This button changes to the **Show Effects** button after previewing the scene without effects. Picking this button previews the scene with effects applied. At the bottom of the **Preview** area is a status bar that displays the status of a preview generation. Except in very large scenes, you may not actually see the progress.

Help Cel

Rendering effects are not displayed in an ActiveShade view.

Alpha Channel

The alpha channel is an important part of creating a 3D scene. Many functions of 3ds max create, use, or affect the alpha channel. Some rendering effects have settings to determine how the effect is applied to the alpha channel. In addition, some materials and environmental effects either use or affect the alpha channel. Also, the alpha channel is *very* important when compositing images or animations.

The *alpha channel* basically provides a way of defining transparency in an image. The renderings created in 3ds max are defined in RGB. In other words, the colors in the rendering are defined by a combination of red, green, and blue. By adding the alpha channel, the transparency of the rendered objects can also be specified.

For example, when you render a solid (opaque) object on a background, none of the background shows through the object. Therefore, it is very easy to simply "lift" the object off the background and composite it onto another image. However, if the object is transparent, "lifting" the rendered object off the background also lifts the portion of the background that can be seen through the object, even if the background is white. See Figure 15-13A. By creating an alpha channel, on the other hand, the rendered transparent object can be composited without "lifting" the background that can be seen through the object. The transparency of the object is maintained in the composited image. The background in the composited image shows through the transparent object. See Figure 15-13B.

Help Cel

The alpha channel has many uses when working with 3ds max. When creating materials, the alpha channel is often used as a mask in conjunction with a bitmap applied as a map. Material mapping is discussed in Chapter 18.

Lens Effects

Lens effects are rendering effects that simulate various real-life effects produced by a camera. Sometimes these effects are unintentional. However, skilled photographers often use these "errors" to produce interesting visual effects. There are seven different lens effects supplied

Figure 15-13. The sphere and box will be composited onto the background. A—Using "cut and paste," the transparency is not retained. B—Using the alpha channel and properly compositing the images, transparency is retained.

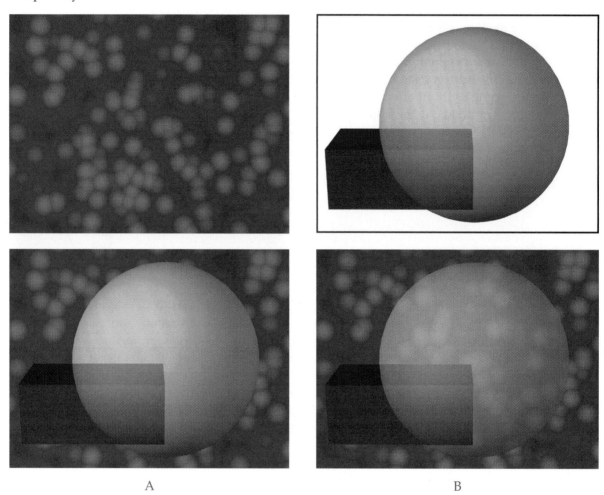

A   B

with 3ds max. Many of these effects are typically applied to lights. However, they can also be applied to objects. Refer to the section *Adding Lens Effects to Objects* in this chapter.

Lens effects can be applied by first selecting **Lens Effects** from the **Add Effect** dialog box. Once the lens effect category is added to the scene, you must select the specific effect in the **Lens Effect Parameters** rollout. The list on the left is the available lens effects. To add an effect to the scene, highlight it in the left list. Then, pick the **>** button to place it in the list at the right. This list contains the lens effects defined for the scene. To remove a specific lens effect from the scene, highlight its name in the right-hand list and pick the **<** button.

Once a specific lens effect is added to the scene, highlight its name in the right-hand list. Then, finalize the parameters in the "element" rollout. The "element" rollouts differ slightly for each of the effects. The specific parameters of each lens effect are outside the scope of this text. However, the next sections briefly introduce the glow, ring, ray, star, and streak effects. The intention is to introduce you to these effects and allow you to experiment on your own.

Glow

The *glow* lens effect produces, as you might expect, a glowing halo around a light or object. See Figure 15-14. Glow can be used to simulate a bright star or an outdoor "bug light." It might also be used with a fire effect for a candle or other flame. Keep in mind, however, that glow does

A

B

Figure 15-14. A glow lens effect added to an omni light.
A—Before.
B—After.

not add illumination to a scene. By adding glow to the particles in a particle system, you can create fireflies or pulses of superheated plasma from a SciFi plasma rifle.

Particle systems are discussed in Chapter 22. The fire atmospheric effect, called combustion in previous releases of 3D Studio MAX, is discussed in Chapter 19.

Ring

The *ring* lens effect produces a detached colored ring around a light or object. See Figure 15-15. Unlike glow, the effect is typically separated from the light or object. The ring effect can be used to help simulate a streetlight at night or in fog. By animating the size, you can use a ring with a ring array to help simulate a SciFi explosion. Creating a ring array is discussed in Chapter 20.

Ray

The *ray* lens effect produces straight lines streaking from the center of a light or object. See Figure 15-16. This effect can be used to simulate a sparkling star or scratches in a glass window. If tied to the particles in a particle system, the ray effect can also be used to simulate a photon cannon for a SciFi scene.

Star

The *star* lens effect produces an effect similar to that of the ray lens effect. However, it is limited to a maximum of 30 rays. See Figure 15-17. The rays in a star effect are also much larger than those produced with the ray lens effect. The star effect can be used in situations similar to those where the ray lens effect might be used.

Streak

The *streak* lens effect produces a wide, straight band through the scene. The band is centered on the light or object. See Figure 15-18. This effect can be used for many applications, from simulating the limitation of real-world cameras to SciFi space effects.

Figure 15-15. A ring lens effect added to an object. A—Before. B—After.

A   B

Figure 15-16. A ray lens effect added to an object. A—Before. B—After.

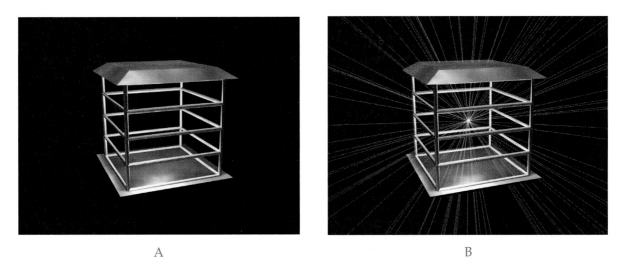

A

B

Figure 15-17. A star lens effect added to an object. A—Before. B—After.

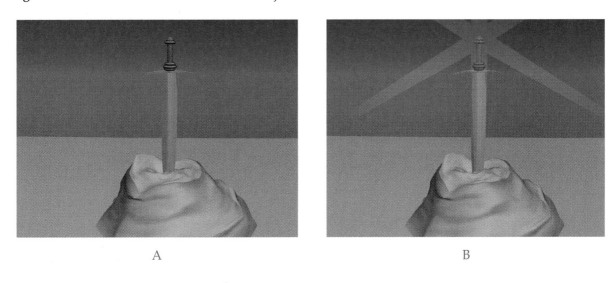

A

B

Figure 15-18. A streak lens effect added to omni lights. A—Before. B—After.

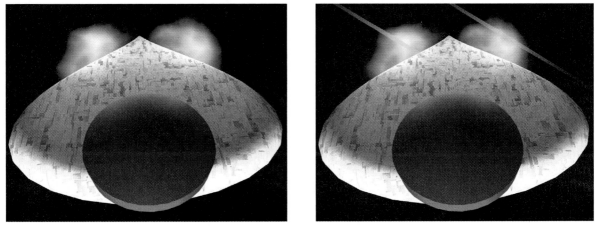

A

B

Adding Lens Effects to Objects

In order to add lens effects to objects instead of lights, you must use object IDs. An *object ID* is simply a number used to identify an object or a group of objects in the scene. This is somewhat similar to using material IDs, which is discussed in Chapter 18. By first assigning an object ID to an object, you can then tell 3ds max to apply a rendering effect to all objects in the scene with that ID.

First, select the object to which you want the lens effect applied. Then, open the **Object Properties** dialog box by right-clicking on the object and picking **Properties**... from the quad menu. You can also select **Object Properties**... from the **Edit** pull-down menu. In the **Object Properties** dialog box, locate the **G-Buffer** area. See Figure 15-19A. Enter an ID number in the **Object Channel:** spinner. It is important that this number be either unique, or the same as all other objects to which the effect will be applied. There can be over 65,000 different object IDs in a scene. Finally, close the **Object Properties** dialog box by picking the **OK** button. Do *not* pick the Windows "close" X button, as this is the same as picking the **Cancel** button.

Now, open the **Rendering Effects** dialog box and open the "element" rollout for the lens effect. Next, pick the **Options** tab. See Figure 15-19B. Many of the options found in this tab are beyond the scope of this text. In the **Apply Element To:** area, check the **Image Centers** check box if not already checked. Then, in the **Image Sources** area, enter the object ID number in the **Object ID** spinner. Also, check the check box if not already checked. The effect is now applied to *all* objects in the scene with that ID number. *Note:* Checking the **Image** check box applies the effect to the image and checking the **Lights** check box applies the effect to the light selected in the drop-down list in the **Lens Effects Globals** rollout.

The **Image Filters** area of the **Options** tab is used to set the portion of the object to which the effect is applied. The settings in this area really determine which pixels of all objects with the selected object ID are used to render the effect. When the **All** check box is checked, all possible pixels are used. When the **Edge** check box is checked, only the pixels at the boundary edge of the object are used. When the **Perim** check box is checked, only the pixels on the perimeter of the object are selected. This produces an eclipse effect. Checking the **Perim Alpha** check box produces a similar, but more precise, effect based on an object's alpha channel. The **Bright** and **Hue** check boxes and spinners allow you to filter the effect by the brightness and color of objects.

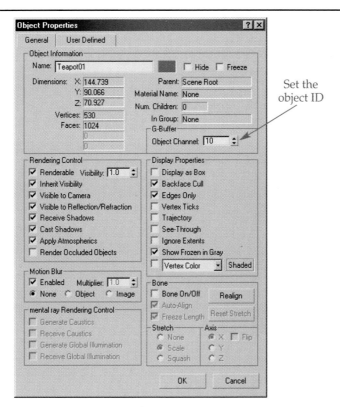

Figure 15-19.
A—Changing an object's ID in the **Object Properties** dialog box. B—Setting an effect to be applied to all objects with a specified ID.

Exercise

Exercise 15-4

1) Draw an omni light and two spheres. Place the objects as shown below.
2) Using the **Object Properties** dialog box, change the object ID of the small sphere to 10.
3) Using the **Rendering Effects** dialog box, add a ring and a ray lens effects to the scene.
4) For the ray effect, pick the omni light as the light.
5) For the ring effect, set it up so the effect is applied to all objects with the object ID of 10.
6) Render a single frame.
7) Experiment by adjusting the parameters of each lens effect. Change one parameter at a time and rerender the scene.
8) When finished experimenting, save the scene as ex15-04.max in the folder of your choice.

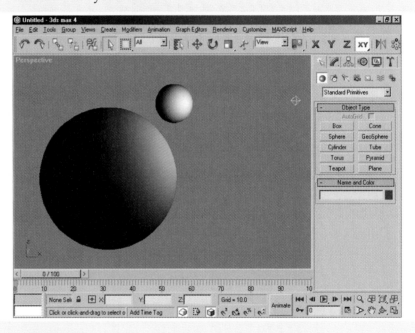

Film Grain

For various reasons, real-world motion cameras tend to produce a grainy effect. In the digital world, this may be called pixelation. Sometimes this is due to limitations in the camera or film itself. Sometimes, motion picture film degrades slightly over time. Think about watching an older movie on TV or the big screen. Just looking at it, you can tell it is older. The *film grain* rendering effect allows you to simulate "real-world" film grain. See Figure 15-20. You may use this strictly as an effect, or you may use this to match the quality of a film into which your animation will be composited.

Once you have "added" the film grain effect to your scene, the **Film Grain Parameters** rollout appears in the **Rendering Effects** dialog box. In the **Grain:** spinner, set the amount of film grain. This value can range

A

B

Figure 15-20. The film grain rendering effect can be used to match the graininess of an existing film or to simply produce a grainy effect. A—Before. B—After. (*Note:* The effect is very subtle. You may want to compare the two renderings under a magnifying glass.)

from 0.0 to 1.0, with 0.2 as the default. When the **Ignore Background** check box is checked, the effect is not applied to the background. If your animation is to be composited into a film and you are trying to match its grain, this option may be useful.

Motion Blur and Depth of Field

In Chapter 11, you learned how to apply motion blur and depth of field to a camera. These can both be added to a scene using rendering effects. These effects are designed to reproduce "real-world" camera effects. As explained in Chapter 14, image motion blur is designed to simulate a slow shutter speed, not a fast-moving object. Image motion blur and depth of field can be applied to a camera, as you learned in Chapter 11, or they can be applied as rendering effects.

Once the *motion blur rendering effect* is "added" to the scene, the **Motion Blur Parameters** rollout appears in the **Rendering Effects** dialog box. See Figure 15-21A. The value in the **Duration:** spinner, in effect, determines how long the camera shutter is open between frames. A value of 1.0 means the shutter is open for the entire time between frames. A value of 0.5 means the shutter is open half the time, thus reducing the effect of the motion blur. Values higher than 1.0, up to the maximum of 100, increase the effect of the motion blur. When the **Work with transparency** check box is checked, motion blur is applied to any object that can be seen through a transparent object.

Once the *depth of field rendering effect* is "added" to the scene, the **Depth of Field Parameters** rollout appears in the **Rendering Effects** dialog box. See Figure 15-21B. When the **Affect Alpha** check box at the top of the rollout is checked, the rendering effect is reflected in the alpha channel.

The **Cameras** area of the **Depth of Field Parameters** rollout is used to assign the effect to cameras in the scene. To assign the effect to a camera, select the **Pick Cam.** button. Then, pick the camera in a viewport. The drop-down list in the **Cameras** area shows all cameras to which the effect

Figure 15-21. A—Adding motion blur as a rendering effect. B—Adding depth of field as a rendering effect.

A

B

is applied. To remove the effect from a camera, select the camera in the drop-down list and pick the **Remove** button.

The **Focal Point** area of the **Depth of Field Parameters** rollout is used to determine the focal point for the effect. This is the point about which the effect is applied. If you pick the **Use Camera** radio button, the camera's target is used as the focal point for the effect. To manually set a focal point, pick the **Focal Node** radio button to turn it on. Then, select the **Pick Node** button and pick an object in the viewport. A selectable object, such as a primitive or light, must be used as the focal point.

The settings in the **Focal Parameters** area of the **Depth of Field Parameters** rollout determine the actual effect. When the **Use Camera** radio button is on, the final effect is determined by the parameters of the camera. To manually set the parameters, pick the **Custom** radio button. Then, enter values in the four spinners. The values in the **Horiz Focal Loss** and **Vert Focal Loss** spinners determine the amount of blur in the horizontal and vertical directions. The **Focal Range** spinner specifies the distance from the focal point where the image remains in focus. The distance is measured in current drawing units on either side of the focal point along the camera's local Z axis. The **Focal Limit** spinner determines the distance from the focal point where the "maximum blur" is reached. Beyond this point, the image is not additionally blurred.

Help Cel

Keep in mind, all rendering effects are applied "on top of" the final rendered image and do not provide illumination to the scene.

Chapter Snapshot

Chapter Test

Answer the following questions on a separate sheet of paper.
1) What is a preview animation?
2) Why should a preview animation be used?
3) How is the **Make Preview** dialog box opened?
4) What is the highest level of shading detail that can be rendered in a preview?
5) What is the output size of a preview based on?
6) What device is used to play a preview?

7) When rendering an animation, which radio button should *not* be picked in the **Time Output** area of the **Render Scene** dialog box?
8) List the three most common animation file types.
9) In order to view a rendered animation, what must be done in the **Render Output** area of the **Render Scene** dialog box?
10) What is an environment in 3ds max?
11) What is a background?
12) What is the default background setting?
13) How do you assign a map as a background?
14) What is a rendering effect?
15) When are rendering effects placed into the rendering?
16) Lens effects can be applied to _____ or objects.
17) Briefly explain how to assign a lens effect to an object.
18) When a lens effect is applied to an object, what is the purpose of the **Image Filters** area?
19) The film grain rendering effect is used to _____.
20) Which two camera effects can also be assigned as rendering effects?

Modeling Problems

Draw the following models using your own dimensions. Create and apply materials as needed, similar to those shown. Add lights and cameras as needed to create the shadows and views shown. When finished, save each model as p15-xx.max in the folder of your choice.

1 Holiday Tree

Draw the holiday tree shown. Add colored spheres to represent colored lights. Add a colored omni light in front of each sphere. Adjust the parameters of each omni light. Then, animate the omni lights on and off to create flashing lights. Render the animation to a file named p15-01.avi in the folder of your choice.

Jack-O'-Lantern **2**
Draw the jack-o'-lantern shown. Place an omni light inside the pumpkin. Animate the parameters of the omni light to simulate a flickering candle. Render the animation to a file named p15-02.avi in the folder of your choice.

CD Jewel Case **3**
Open p13-09.max from Chapter 13. Save the scene as p15-03.max in the folder of your choice. Adjust the pivot point of the jewel case lid as needed. Animate the scene as follows.
a) On frame 25, the case should open.
b) On frame 50, the CD should move out of the case.
c) On frame 75, the CD should "flip" three times.
d) On frame 100, the CD should return to its original position.
Render the animation to a file named p15-03.avi in the folder of your choice.

Desktop Lamp **4**
Open p10-03.max from Chapter 10. Save the scene as p15-04.max in the folder of your choice. Sketch a hierarchy for the lamp. Adjust pivot points as needed. Link objects to create the hierarchy. Be sure to link the spotlight (and target, if present) to match the motion as needed. Move the lamp so its initial position is "back" and slightly "closed." Animate the lamp as follows.
a) On frame 30, the lamp should extend and open.
b) On frame 50, the light should turn on.
c) On frame 75, the light should turn off.
d) On frame 100, the lamp should return to its initial position.
Render the animation to a file named p15-04.avi in the folder of your choice.

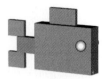

5 Antique Fan
Open p14-01.max from Chapter 14. Render the animation you defined to complete that problem. Save the animation as p15-05.avi and save the scene as p15-05.max in the folder of your choice.

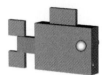

6 Airplane
Open p14-04.max from Chapter 14. Render the animation you defined to complete that problem. Save the animation as p15-06.avi and save the scene as p15-06.max in the folder of your choice.

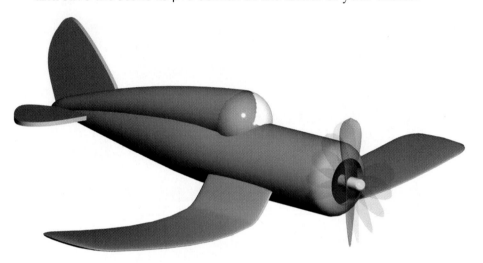

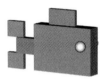

7 Meditation Swing
Open p14-05.max from Chapter 14. Render the animation you defined to complete that problem. Save the animation as p15-07.avi and save the scene as p15-07.max in the folder of your choice.

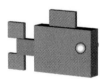

8 Truckasaurus
Open p14-03.max from Chapter 14. Render the animation you defined to complete that problem. Save the animation as p15-08.avi and save the scene as p15-08.max in the folder of your choice.

Ferris Wheel **9**

Open p14-06.max from Chapter 14. Render the animation you defined to complete that problem. Save the animation as p15-09.avi and save the scene as p15-09.max in the folder of your choice.

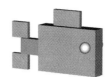

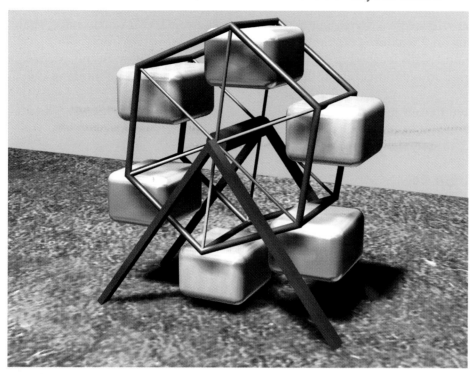

Toy Gyroscope **10**

Open p12-06.max from Chapter 12. Save the scene as p15-10.max in the folder of your choice. Animate rotation of the center shaft several turns. The cross members and wheel should follow the shaft. Also, animate several "tilts" of the gyroscope frame. Render the animation to a file named p15-10.avi in the folder of your choice.

Section Two Tutorial

Overview

In this tutorial, you will create a diving submersible. See Figure T2-1. You may have seen machines similar to this on TV nature programs. This model requires you to apply skills learned in this section and skills learned in the first section. Upon completion of this model, you should have a sound foundation of basic 3ds max skills to build on in the following advanced sections.

The model is created in four general steps. The first step is to create the geometry. The second step is to assemble the geometry. The third step is to define and apply materials. The fourth and final step is to animate the model and render the scene.

Help Cel

Save and save often. It is up to you to determine how often to save. However, a general rule of thumb is every 10 to 15 minutes.

Creating Geometry

Looking at Figure T2-1, the submersible can be broken down into five generic components. These are the body, sphere, propulsion units (2), diving planes (4), and arms (2). These components are modeled separately and then combined to form the completed submersible.

Start by resetting 3ds max. Use the default four-viewport configuration. Also use generic units. Use snap and other drawing tools as needed throughout the tutorial. Which tools are used and in which situations will depend on your personal preferences for modeling.

Figure T2-1. The completed tutorial model.

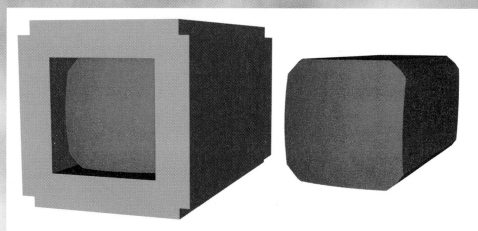

Figure T2-2. On the left, four boxes are placed around the oil tank object. On the right, the boxes are subtracted from the oil tank.

Body

The body begins as a simple oil tank object. Draw an oil tank in the Left viewport with a radius of 100 units and an overall height of 400 units. The cap height should be 25 units. Set the number of sides to 25.

Now, create four boxes to use as construction objects. The boxes will be subtracted from the oil tank. When you draw the boxes, make them large enough to overlap the oil tank. From a point of tangency, each box should be moved 20 units "into" the oil tank. See Figure T2-2. Then, subtract the boxes from the oil tank. Name the object Body.

The basic shape of the body is created. However, it is solid. To hollow out the inside, clone a copy of the body. Scale the clone to 90% on the object's X and Y axes. Scale the clone to 105% on the object's Z axis. Move the clone on its Z axis so one end is about 5 units "inside" the body. The other end should stick out of the body. Subtract the clone from the body.

The final part of the body that needs to be created is the hatch. In the Top viewport, draw a 40-unit radius cylinder toward the back of the body. The cylinder should be tall enough to go through the skin of the body. Subtract the cylinder from the body.

Draw a 40-unit radius circle centered on the hole just created. Loft the circle along a 20-unit straight line. Then, scale down the top end of the loft object to form a button shape. Name the object Hatch Lid. Add a handle created from a torus and two cylinders. A third cylinder can be used for the "stem." Union the parts of the handle and name the new object Hatch Handle. Position the hatch and handle on top of the body. See Figure T2-3.

Sphere

The sphere portion of the submersible, as you probably can guess, starts as a sphere object. Draw a 150-unit radius sphere. The sphere does not have to be in the correct location. It will be relocated later. Increase the number of segments to 48. Name the object Sphere Front. Then, clone a copy of the sphere. Scale the copy to 90% and, with the copy centered on the original, subtract it from Sphere Front.

Now, the portholes need to be created. In the Top viewport, draw a 60-unit radius cylinder centered on the sphere. Increase the number of sides to 36. The height should be tall enough to overlap the "skin." Move the cylinder to overlap the top of the sphere. See Figure T2-4. Name the object Drill01. Clone a copy named Drill Top and hide Drill01. Subtract Drill Top from the sphere.

Draw a donut shape on top of the hole. Make the outer radius 65 units and the inner radius 55 units. Vertically position the donut just below the surface of the sphere. Extrude the donut 20 units and name it Porthole01. Draw two cylinder cross members centered inside

Figure T2-3. The body is hollowed out and a hatch is created. Refer to the detail at the lower right when creating the handle.

Figure T2-4. The cylinder will be subtracted to create the porthole opening.

the porthole. Give them a radius of 2 units and a height of 120 units. Union the cross members to the porthole ring. Also, draw a cylinder with a radius of 60 units and a height of 1 unit. Name it Glass01. Vertically and horizontally center the glass in the porthole. See Figure T2-5.

To create the other portholes, first unhide Drill01. Then, group Porthole01 with Glass01 and Drill01. Name the group Port Construct01. Using the **Hierarchy** tab in the **Command Panel**, move the group's pivot point to the "visual" center of the sphere. Remember, the sphere is not exactly a complete sphere anymore. Then, copy and rotate Port Construct01 90° and then again –90° in the Left viewport. Be sure to rotate the group about the pivot point. This creates the left and right portholes. In the Front viewport, copy and rotate Port Construct01 90° and then once more 150°. This creates the front and bottom portholes.

Ungroup all of the groups. Then, subtract the "drill" objects from Sphere Front. Drill01 will not need to be subtracted since its "hole" is already created. The sphere is now complete. See Figure T2-6.

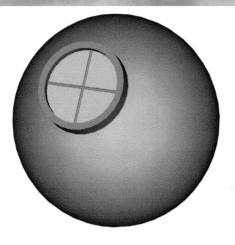

Figure T2-5. The first porthole and glass created. The sphere has been rotated for illustration purposes.

Figure T2-6. All portholes in their correct locations.

Propulsion Units

Each propulsion unit consists of a tube and propeller. The tube is simply a capsule object. Later, you will apply a transparent material to show the propeller inside. In the Left viewport, draw a capsule with a radius of 30 units and a height of 250 units. Increase the number of sides to 24 or 36. Name the capsule Prop Tube01.

Next, draw a four-pointed star centered on the capsule. Make the outer radius 27 units and the inner radius 5 units. Apply an edit spline modifier and create the basic propeller shape shown in Figure T2-7. You may find it easiest to convert each vertex to smooth, then to Bézier to refine the shape. Extrude the shape 2 units and name it Propeller01.

Apply a mesh select modifier to the object. At the vertex sub-object level, select the vertices of one "blade." Apply a twist modifier to the selection. Rotate the twist gizmo 45° and then set the twist angle to 30° on the object's X axis. Repeat this for the other three blades.

Finally, move the propeller inside the front of the tube. The propeller should be just inside the cylinder portion of the capsule. Select the propeller and tube and move them into position on the body. Then, copy both to the other side of the body.

Diving Planes

To create the four diving planes, first draw the shape shown in Figure T2-8. This shape is a rectangle 20 units by 60 units with an edit spline modifier applied. Next, loft the shape

Figure T2-7. The yellow shape is a four-pointed star with an edit spline modifier. The completed propeller is shown inside a propulsion tube. The tube has a transparent material to show the propeller.

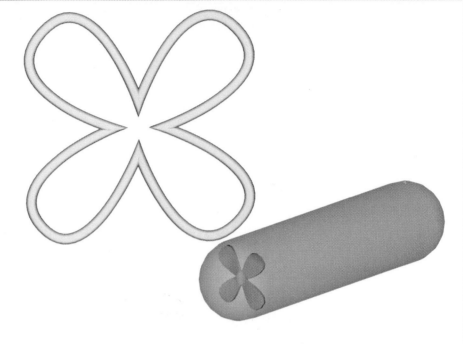

Figure T2-8. The red shape is lofted to form the plane. Make three copies of the completed dive plane.

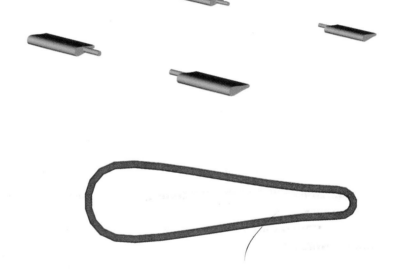

along a 160-unit straight line path. Name the object Dive Plane01. Copy the object three times, as shown in Figure T2-8.

Draw a cylinder centered in each of the shapes with a radius of 6 units and a height of 50 units. Finally, union each dive plane with its cylinder.

Arms

The arms are perhaps the most complicated part of the model. However, each arm is made up of four basic parts. There is the upper arm, lower arm, and two jaw parts. These are constructed separately to simplify modeling. Later in the tutorial, you will assemble the pieces into the completed arms. You may want to create the arms in a separate file and merge them into the scene.

Figure T2-9. A rectangle is modified to get the shape for a bracket. The shape is lofted.

Upper Arm

The upper arm consists of a basic sphere, a basic cylinder, and a compound object. Start by drawing a sphere with a radius of 30 units. Next, draw a cylinder with a radius of 5 units and a height of 200 units. Move the cylinder so one end is in the center of the sphere. Union the two objects. Name the new object Upper Arm01.

Now, draw the shape shown in Figure T2-9. Start with a 20-unit by 30-unit rectangle. Modify one end to get the curve. Loft the shape along a 20-unit straight line path. Finally, draw a 50 x 50 x 10 unit box. Vertically center the box inside the lofted shape. Horizontally position the box to create a bracket with a uniform thickness of 5 units. Subtract the box from the lofted shape.

Finally, center the bracket on the end of the cylinder opposite the sphere. Union the bracket to the upper arm. See Figure T2-10. The upper arm is complete.

Lower Arm

The lower arm is a cylinder with a pivot on each end. Draw a cylinder with a radius of 5 units and a height of 100 units. Name this cylinder Lower Arm01. The two pivots are simply cylinders unioned to the ends. Draw a cylinder with a radius of 10 units and a height of 10 units. The height fits in the bracket on the upper arm. Align the cylinder with one end of Lower Arm01. The center of the cylinder should be on the end face of Lower Arm01. See Figure T2-11. Finally, copy the cylinder to the other end of Lower Arm01 and union all three objects. The lower arm is complete.

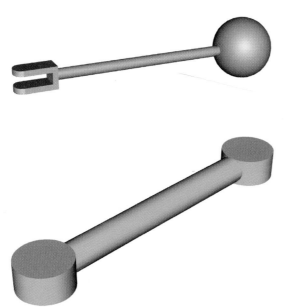

Figure T2-10. A completed upper arm.

Figure T2-11. A completed lower arm.

Jaw Parts

The jaws are constructed from two separate parts. Start by drawing the shape shown on the left in Figure T2-12. Make sure you have the seven vertices indicated. Next, extrude the shape 30 units. Name the object Jaw Right01.

Apply a mesh select modifier. Select the vertices on the long portion, as indicated in Figure T2-12. Apply a taper modifier to the selection. Enter 0.5 as the taper amount. Move the gizmo center so the taper starts at the edge of the selection. Apply the taper to one axis only. Repeat the entire process with the shape shown on the right in Figure T2-12. Name the object Jaw Left01.

On the right jaw, draw a 50 x 50 x 20 unit box. Subtract it from the jaw to create the bracket. On the left jaw, subtract a 50 x 50 x 10 unit box from the middle of the bracket. Subtract two additional boxes from the top and bottom so the bracket tabs are 5 units thick. See Figure T2-13.

Figure T2-12. Start creating the jaw by drawing this shape. Be sure to have the seven vertices indicated here. The red vertices are selected for the taper modifier.

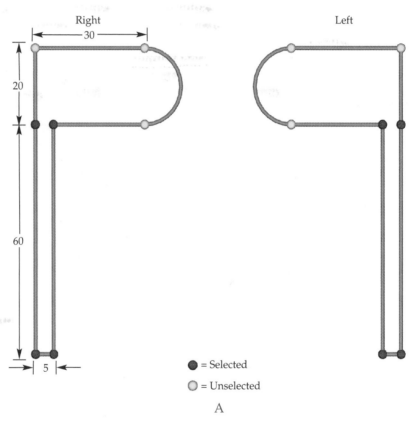

A

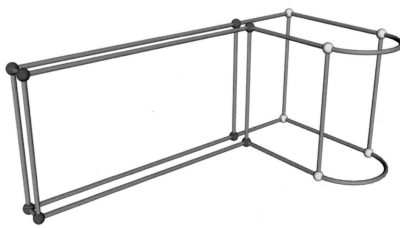

B

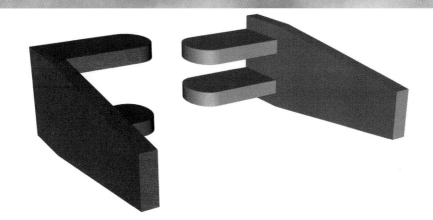

Figure T2-13. A completed set of jaws with left and right sides. Notice the brackets are different.

Ocean

Since this is a submersible, the animation will be of an underwater scene. Therefore, an underwater background needs to be created. Also, the sandy ocean floor needs to be created. The ocean floor is drawn as a large patch grid, about 5000 units square. Name the object Ocean Bottom. The underwater background is set up later as an environment background.

Assembling Geometry

Now that all geometry is created, it is time to assemble the submersible. If you created the different parts as separate files, merge all parts into a single file.

Linking Objects

Before moving any objects, you should link components. First, link the hatch handle to the hatch lid. Next, link the hatch lid to the body of the submersible. Link all portholes and glass to the front sphere. Finally, link each propeller to its propulsion tube. The jaws and arms also need to be linked. This is covered in the next section.

Linking the Arm

Move the jaws so they align with one pivot on the lower arm. Move the upper arm so it aligns with the opposite lower arm pivot. See Figure T2-14. It is very important to keep the jaws, lower arm, and upper arm in the same plane. Do not rotate the pieces yet. You first need to adjust the pivot points and limit transformations.

Move the pivot point of one jaw so it is centered in the lower arm pivot (cylinder). Rotate the pivot point so the Z axis comes out of the cylinder. Then, lock the rotation transformations on the X and Y axes. Repeat this process with the other jaw. See Figure T2-15.

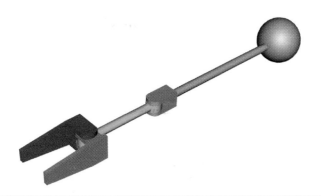

Figure T2-14. A completed, assembled arm.

Figure T2-15. The pivot point for the left jaw is relocated.

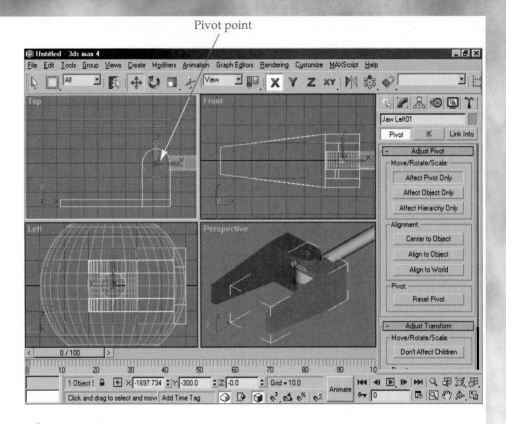

Move the pivot point of the lower arm to the center of the upper pivot (cylinder). Rotate the pivot point so the Z axis comes out of the cylinder. Then, lock the rotation transformations on the X and Y axes.

The pivot point for the upper arm should be in the middle of the sphere portion. Move the pivot if necessary. Make sure the Z axis of the pivot matches those of the other arm components (comes out). Rotation transformations should not be locked on any axis. Now, link the jaws to the lower arm and the lower arm to the upper arm.

Adjusting Pivots

The pivot point for each propeller should be in the center of its hub. The pivot point is probably already in the center. If not, move it as necessary. Also make sure the Z axis comes out of the propeller. Then, lock the rotation transformations on the X and Y axes.

Move the pivot point for the hatch to one edge. See Figure T2-16. The Z axis should point straight up from the body. Then, lock the rotation transformations on the Z and Y (or X) axes.

Moving Objects

Move the sphere so the open end of the body is just inside the sphere. Since the porthole assemblies are linked to the sphere, they move with it. Then, union the body and the sphere, selecting the body as operand A. The linking to the sphere is lost in this operation. Therefore, link the portholes and glass to the new body object. Also, move the pivot point of the new body object to where the sphere and box portions of the body meet. Rotate the pivot so the Z axis points up.

Move the dive planes into position. Center the dive plane pivots on the cylindrical portion of each plane. Link the dive planes and the propulsion tubes to the body. See Figure T2-17.

Move the arm assembly so the sphere of the upper arm is located on the lower right of the body sphere. Place the arm sphere below the "middle" portholes. The pivot point should

Pivot point

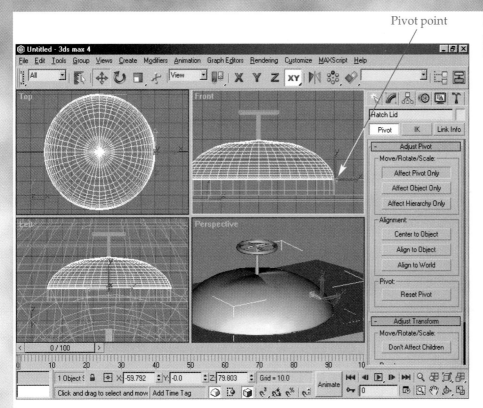

Figure T2-16. The pivot point for the hatch is relocated.

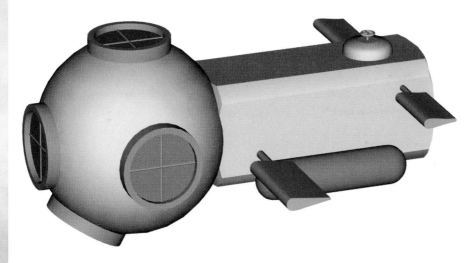

Figure T2-17. The four dive planes and the two propulsion tubes in their correct locations.

be on the surface of the body sphere. Copy the arm to the other side of the body sphere so there are two. See Figure T2-18. Link the upper arms of both arm assemblies to the body. Finally, "fold" the arms closed as shown in Figure T2-18.

Defining and Applying Materials

Assign the bitmap water1.tga as the background. This file is located in the 3ds max \Maps\Water folder.

For the ocean bottom, define a new material named Sand Bottom. Set the diffuse color to a light tan. The ambient color should be a darker version of the diffuse color. Assign the material to the Ocean Bottom object.

Figure T2-18. The two arms in their correct locations. Notice the position and rotation of the arms.

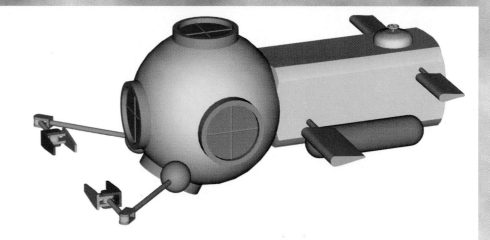

The main body and the hatch are yellow. Define a new material named Body Yellow. Set the diffuse color to a bright yellow. Set the ambient color to a darker version of the diffuse color. Assign the material to the Body and Hatch Lid objects.

The propulsion tubes have an orange, transparent material. Define a new material named Prop Tubes. Set the ambient and diffuse colors to a bright orange. Set the opacity to 50. Assign the material to the two Prop Tube objects.

The Prop Tubes material is the basis for the diving planes material. Copy the definition to a new sample slot. Change the name to Diving Planes. Then, set the opacity to 100. Finally, assign the material to all four Dive Planes.

The hatch handle, upper and lower arms, and jaws all have the same material applied. Get the material Metal_Grey_Plain from the default 3ds max material library. Assign the material to all arms, all jaw components, and the hatch handle.

Get the material Metal_Dark_Gold from the default 3ds max material library. Assign the material to all five porthole rings.

For the porthole glass, create a new material named Port Glass. Set the diffuse color to medium grey. Set the ambient color to black. Set the opacity to 25. Finally, assign the material to all five pieces of glass.

Get the material Metal_Black_Plain from the default 3ds max material library. Assign the material to both propellers.

All materials are assigned. However, three lights need to be added. Create an omni light in the middle of the sphere portion of the body. Name the light Dashboard. Set the multiplier to 1.0 and exclude all objects except the body. Link the light to the body. This light will simulate the light from instruments and lighting inside the submersible. You may want to set the light to cast shadows.

Next, create a free spotlight named Searchlight. Position it on the outside surface of the bottom porthole. Set the target distance so the light's cone touches the ocean floor. Set the multiplier to 1.0. Link the light to the body. This light is used to simulate a searchlight beneath the submersible.

Finally, create a free direct light named Sun. Position the light far above the ocean floor and centered on it. Set the multiplier between 0.3 and 0.5, lower if necessary. Also, set the falloff to about 3000 and the hotspot to about 2700. The light should cover the entire ocean floor. This light will simulate the small amount of illumination the sun provides to the bottom of the ocean.

Camera and
target

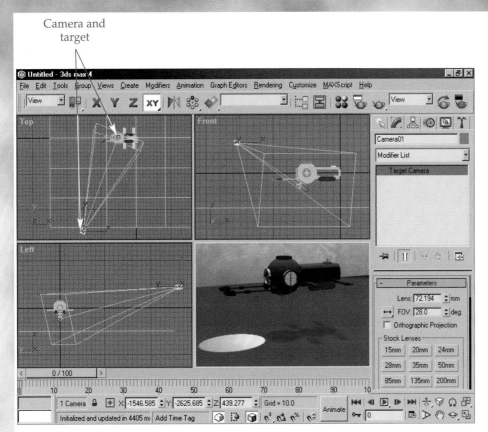

Figure T2-19. Locate the camera target in the middle of the Ocean Bottom object. Tilt the camera down slightly.

Animating and Rendering

Now you are ready to animate and render the scene. First, create a target camera pointing to the middle of the ocean floor. Tilt the camera slightly down. See Figure T2-19. Next, change the Perspective viewport to the Camera viewport. Fine-tune the camera view as needed.

You can choose the length of your animation. The default of 100 frames works, but 250 frames may allow more time to produce slow, underwater motion. Determine what motion you want in the animation. Make the submersible move as you like. However, make the sub:

1) Move into the camera view and pause. See Figure T2-20.
2) While the sub pauses, make one arm extend, reach down to the ocean bottom to "pick up" an object, and bring the jaws in front of the front porthole. You can model a rock or shell and add it to the scene if you like.
3) Move the sub off the screen with its arm still in front of the porthole. See Figure T2-21. As the submersible moves, the propellers should rotate inside the propulsion tubes. Also, the dive planes should rotate as the sub moves through the water. You may want to animate the Dashboard and Searchlight multipliers slightly. This can help simulate murky water.

You can fine-tune the movement using **Track View**. This is discussed in Chapter 16. For example, you may not want the arms to rotate until the submersible pauses. Also, the default key transitions produce motion that "floats" through keys. You can adjust this, as you will learn in the next section of the text. However, this model is an example of where the default Bézier transitions may produce the best motion. The Bézier motion curve makes the sub float in the water, simulating underwater ocean currents. The arms should, perhaps, have a more mechanical movement. After learning how to adjust key transitions in the next section, you may want to revisit this model and fine-tune the movement even more.

Figure T2-20. The submersible should pause while one arm extends to the ocean bottom.

Figure T2-21. The jaws should remain in front of the port-hole as the submersible moves off screen.

Make a preview animation. Then, make any adjustments necessary. Finally, render four or five still images of different frames. If you have time and hard drive space, render the animation to an AVI file. Be aware this may take an hour or more. The final file may be 10MB or larger.

Help Cel

If you are having problems properly rotating the arms, make sure you are using the **Use Pivot Point Center** button when rotating the objects. Also, make sure the appropriate coordinate system is selected in the drop-down list on the **Main** toolbar.

Discussion Questions

1) When scaling the "drill" objects, how did you make sure they stayed centered with the original objects?
2) When drawing the donut shape for the porthole, how did you center it on the sphere?
3) How did you position the cross members of the porthole on the "ring?"
4) After the edit spline modifier was applied to the star, how did you get the propeller shape?
5) Why were the portholes and glass linked to the sphere before it was unioned to the body?
6) Why is it important to lock the transformations for the arms and jaws?
7) When creating the sphere portion of the submersible, what must be done to correctly rotate the portholes about the sphere?
8) The ocean floor is created as a quad patch. What other type of object can be used for the ocean floor? Why is this perhaps a better choice over a single quad patch?

Section Three

MAKING IT REAL

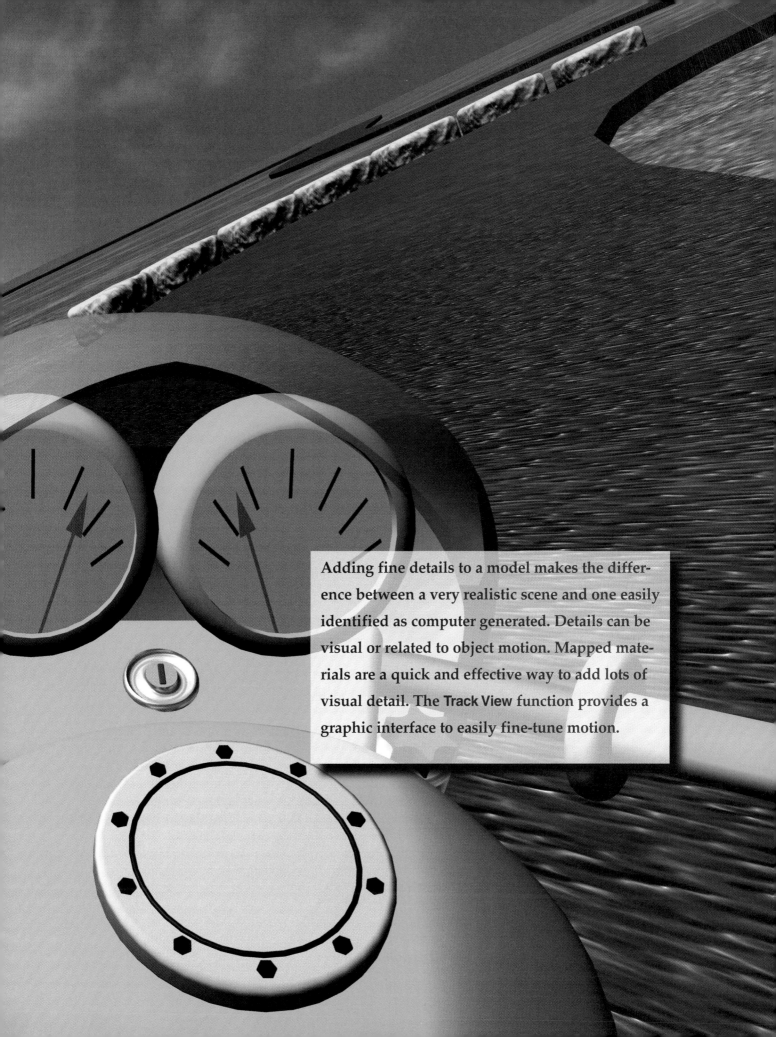

Adding fine details to a model makes the difference between a very realistic scene and one easily identified as computer generated. Details can be visual or related to object motion. Mapped materials are a quick and effective way to add lots of visual detail. The Track View function provides a graphic interface to easily fine-tune motion.

Chapter 16

Using Track View

Objectives

After completing this chapter, you will be able to:

● Define **Track View**.
● Identify parts of the **Track View** interface.
● Add and adjust keys.
● Explain the purpose of block controllers.
● Use block controllers.
● Control object visibility using **Track View**.
● Add notes using **Track View**.
● Add sound using **Track View**.
● Explain **Schematic View**.
● Link objects in **Schematic View**.

What Is Track View?

Track View provides a schematic interface for managing animation keys and controllers. You can move, delete, add, and clone keys. You can also adjust continuity into and out of keys. **Track View** allows you to add sound to the scene, insert and manage notes about the scene, and edit blocks of time.

Track View is opened by selecting **Track View** in the **Graph Editors** pull-down menu to display the cascading menu. If **Track View** has not yet been opened for the current model, select either **Open Track View** or **New Track View** from the cascading menu. You can also pick the **Open Track View** button on the **Main** toolbar. **Track View** is displayed on top of the viewports. **Track View** is a modeless dialog box. This means it can be left open or minimized while you continue to work in 3ds max.

Open Track View

You can save up to 13 different **Track View** layouts. Once a layout is saved, it appears at the bottom of the **Track View** cascading menu. If **Track View** is opened but not saved, the layout appears as **Untitled** at the bottom of the menu.

Track View can be displayed in a viewport. To do this, open the **Viewport Configuration** dialog box by selecting **Viewport Configuration**... from the **Customize** pull-down menu. In the **Layout** tab, click in the layout configuration image tile. In the shortcut menu, select **Track**. In the cascading menu, select the name of the layout to open or **New**. Finally, close the **Viewport Configuration** dialog box. **Track View** is then displayed in that viewport. See Figure 16-1.

Track View Layout

Track View has three basic components. At the top and bottom are two toolbars. On the left side of the **Track View** dialog box is the hierarchy tree. Finally, on the right side of the **Track View** dialog box is the edit window. See Figure 16-2.

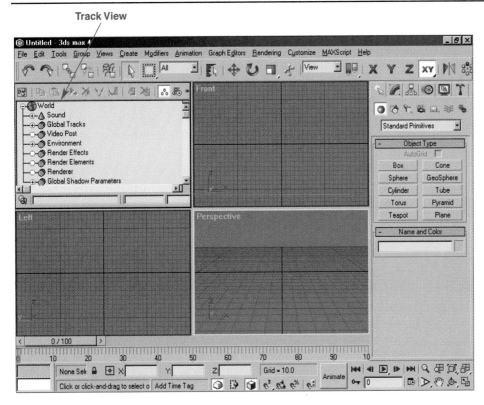

Figure 16-1. **Track View** can be displayed in a viewport.

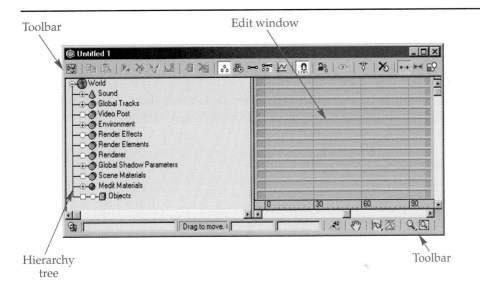

Figure 16-2. The basic layout of **Track View**.

Hierarchy Tree

World

The *hierarchy tree* displays all items in the scene in a tree view. Picking the plus sign (+) next to any branch expands the branch. Picking the minus sign (–) next to any expanded branch collapses the branch.

At the top of the tree is the **World** level. This is the root of the entire tree. All items in the hierarchy tree can be traced directly back to the world. The next level in the tree contains branches for sound, global tracks, video post, environment, render effects, render elements, renderer, global shadow parameters, scene materials, medit materials, and objects.

The **Sound** branch of the hierarchy tree is used to add sound to the animation. This level is also used to synchronize the animation to the sound file. When sound is added to the animation, a wave form is displayed in the edit window.

The **Global Tracks** branch of the hierarchy tree allows you to define global controllers. You can point to a global controller from other tracks. Then, as the global controller is changed, all tracks pointing to it are also changed.

The **Video Post** branch of the hierarchy tree is used to manage animated parameters for the **Video Post**. **Video Post** is not covered in this text.

The **Environment** branch of the hierarchy tree is used to manage environmental effects. These include background, ambient light, fog, and volumetric lighting.

The **Render Effects** branch of the hierarchy tree is used to manage rendering effects. These effects are added in the **Rendering Effects** dialog box.

The **Render Elements** branch shows the elements selected for rendering. These are specified in the **Render Elements** rollout of the **Render Scene** dialog box. This rollout is not covered in this text.

The **Renderer** branch of the hierarchy tree allows you to manage parameters of the renderer. For example, you can use this branch to animate renderer parameters.

The **Global Shadow Parameters** branch of the hierarchy tree is used to manage global shadow parameters. Any light with the **Use Global Settings** check box checked has its shadow parameters managed in this branch.

The **Scene Materials** branch of the hierarchy tree contains instance settings for all materials in the scene. Making changes in this branch also applies the changes to the material in the scene.

The **Medit Materials** branch of the hierarchy tree contains instance settings for all materials currently in the **Material Editor**. This includes materials that may not be assigned in the scene as well as those already assigned. Making a change in this branch also applies the change in the **Material Editor**. If the material is applied in the scene, the change is applied in the scene as well.

The **Objects** branch contains the hierarchy for all objects in the scene. In this branch, you control object transformation and visibility.

Hierarchy Category Icons

Any item in the hierarchy tree falls into one of seven categories. Which category the item falls into can be quickly identified by the icon to the left of the item name.

Objects have a yellow cube next to their name. The name of the branch is the name of the object. When the object branch is expanded, any transforms, modifiers, or materials applied to the object are displayed as branches (or leaves).

Object

Controllers are indicated by a green triangle next to their name. Controllers are the only items in the **Track View** hierarchy that can have animation keys. For example, transforms are controllers. Therefore, transforms have animation keys that can be adjusted in **Track View**.

Controllers

Material definitions are indicated by a blue sphere next to their name. The name of the branch is the material name appearing in the **Material Editor**.

Material

A green parallelogram indicates the item is a *map*. Any given map may have several branches and leaves below it. You can expand a map branch to display its hierarchy, or sub-levels. Animated components of a map are controllers and have green triangles next to their names.

Maps

A *modifier* is indicated by an orange diamond next to its name. The branches below the modifier contain all items the modifier affects. This icon also identifies *space warps*.

Modifier

A *container* is a branch item with multiple branches below it that completely define something in the scene. For example, assume you have drawn a cone and applied a taper modifier to the cone. The cone branch is a container because all branches below it define the cone. In addition, the modified object branch is a container because all branches below it, including the cone container, define a modified object. Containers are indicated by a light blue cylinder next to their name.

Container

Sound parameters are identified by a green cone next to their name. All sound parameters in **Track View** are contained in the **Sound** branch of the hierarchy tree.

Sound

Toolbars

Track View has two toolbars. The main toolbar at the top of the **Track View** dialog box contains tools for editing tracks and function curves. Depending on the size of the **Track View** window, you may need to pan this toolbar left or right to see all of it. The other toolbar is at the bottom of the **Track View** windows. It contains tools such as **Zoom** and **Pan** for navigating in **Track View**. The **Track View** buttons are explained as you progress through this chapter.

There are three general categories for the buttons on the main toolbar. The buttons in the "edit mode" group are used to change what is displayed for editing in the edit window. These buttons are located in the middle of the toolbar. The "edit" buttons are used to make changes in the edit window. Which buttons are displayed depend on the current edit mode. The edit buttons are located on the right-hand side of the toolbar. The "world" buttons apply to all items. Changing edit modes has no effect on the world buttons. These buttons are located on the left-hand side of the toolbar.

Edit Window

The edit window of **Track View** is where changes are made to tracks, keys, and function curves. The active time segment is displayed in the edit window with a light grey background. Frames outside of the active time segment are displayed with a dark grey background. The current frame is indicated by a vertical purple line. As you drag the **Time** slider below the main 3ds max drawing area, the purple line in the **Track View** edit window moves to reflect the change. See Figure 16-3.

Tracks

A *track* is a "channel" containing information about a single item. All editable parameters appear in the track. For example, suppose you animate the scale of a teapot once to 150% on frame 10. The object's scale track then contains the information indicating the object is scaled to 150% on frame 10. There are two types of tracks.

The first type is called a *range track.* This type of track indicates the entire range of frames in which an item is animated. See Figure 16-4. Using the previous example, there is a range track for the teapot and the teapot's transformation. Both of these range tracks are from frame 0 to frame 10. If you animate a twist modifier for the teapot on frame 75, the

---

Figure 16-3. The current frame is indicated in the **Track View** edit window by a vertical line.

Current frame indicator

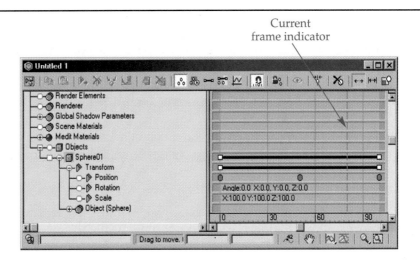

Figure 16-4. Range tracks indicate the total range of frames for the animated item.

Range tracks

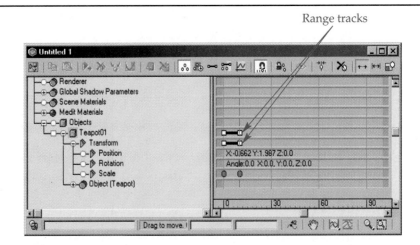

range track for the teapot is from frame 0 to frame 75. The range track for the teapot's transformation remains from frame 0 to frame 10. The range track for the teapot's twist modifier is from frame 0 to frame 75.

The second type of track is called an ***animation track.*** Animation tracks contain the values for animated parameters. The values are usually stored in keys. Using the previous example, the teapot's scale track has a key at frame 0 for 100% and a key at frame 10 for 150%. If the twist modifier has an angle animated from 0° to 180°, the teapot modifier's angle track has a key at frame 0 for 0° and a key at frame 75 for 180°. See Figure 16-5.

Keys

A *key* stores animated information. Each key is associated with a keyframe. The *keyframe* is the frame where the parameters are changed. The key contains the parameters. The parameters can be changed by editing the key. The keyframe can be changed by moving the key to a different frame. Keys are displayed in a track as filled circles. See Figure 16-6. Selected keys are filled white. Unselected keys are filled dark grey.

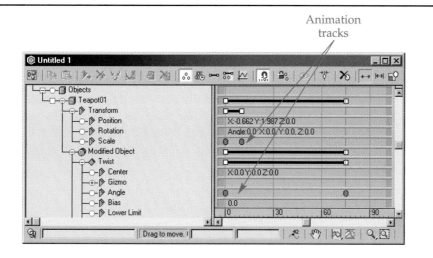

Figure 16-5. Animation tracks contain keys for the animated values.

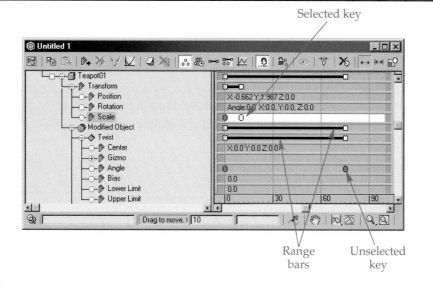

Figure 16-6. Keys mark the keyframes and hold parameters. Also, a range bar is displayed in a range track. It graphically represents the range of frames for the animated item.

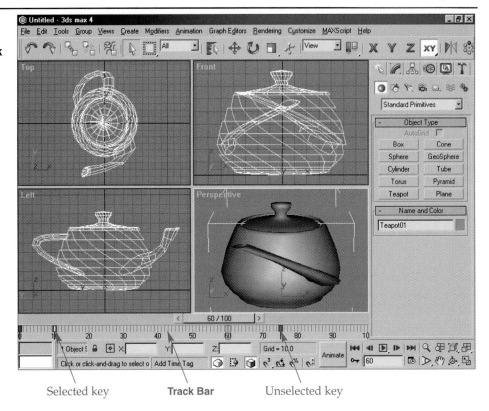

Figure 16-7. Keys for a selected object are displayed in the **Track Bar** below the **Time** slider.

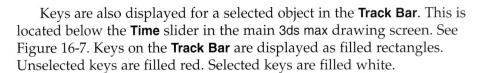

Selected key   Track Bar   Unselected key

Keys are also displayed for a selected object in the **Track Bar**. This is located below the **Time** slider in the main 3ds max drawing screen. See Figure 16-7. Keys on the **Track Bar** are displayed as filled rectangles. Unselected keys are filled red. Selected keys are filled white.

Help Cel

Keys are usually displayed in **Track View** as filled circles. However, they can also be displayed as points on a function curve.

Range Bars

A *range bar* is a black line graphically indicating the range of frames for the animated parameter. Refer to Figure 16-6. Range bars appear in range tracks. In some cases, range bars can also appear in animation tracks. You can increase or decrease the number of frames in the range by moving either end of the range bar. The keys within the range are scaled accordingly. You can also reposition the entire range without changing the number of frames. This is done by picking in the middle of the range bar and dragging the entire bar to a new location in the track.

Function Curves

Animation tracks can be displayed as function curves. A *function curve* allows you to see how parameters change over time. See Figure 16-8. The curve itself is an editable spline. You can modify the shape of the curve to control how the parameter changes.

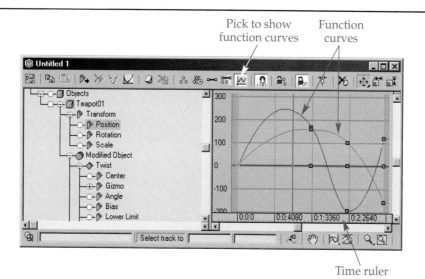

Pick to show function curves

Function curves

Figure 16-8.
Animation tracks can be displayed as function curves. Also, the time ruler in **Track View** indicates frames or time, depending on the settings in the **Time Configuration** dialog box.

Time ruler

You can edit the Bézier handles of a function curve. To do so, right-click on the key in the function curve to open the key info dialog box. Then, select the custom tangent tile from the image tile flyouts. The Bézier handles are now displayed on the function curve in **Track View** and can be edited. The key info dialog box is discussed in detail later in this chapter.

Time Ruler

The *time ruler* is located at the bottom of the **Track View** edit window. See Figure 16-8. This ruler indicates time in frames or time units. The units displayed are controlled by the settings in the **Time Configuration** dialog box.

Sample Model

The best way to learn how to use **Track View** is to experiment. To do this, you will first need to create and animate a simple model. The next two sections cover the steps for creating and animating the space garage scene shown in Figure 16-9.

Creating the Model

First, create the garage portion of the model. Draw a box 500 x 500 x 200 units in the Top viewport. Next, draw a sphere centered on the box with a radius of 350 units. Make the sphere a hemisphere using a 0.5 value. The bottom of the hemisphere should be on the same plane as the bottom of the box. The corners of the box form the pillars for the garage. Create a copy of the sphere by selecting **Clone** from the **Edit** pull-down menu. Then, subtract the copy from the box. Rename the box object Pillars. See Figure 16-10.

Create a box object to trim off the front of the sphere. This is where the door will be located. One edge of the "trim object" should be flush with the pillars. Also, make sure the object is large enough to trim the sphere. Then, subtract the box from the sphere.

Figure 16-9. The final frame of the space garage animation.

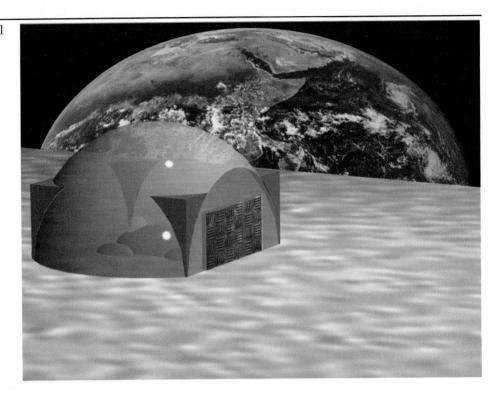

Figure 16-10. The sphere subtracted from the box creates the pillars of the space garage shown here.

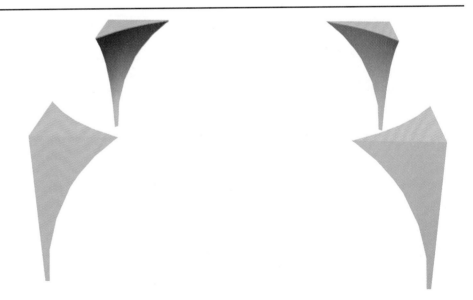

Now you need to hollow out the garage. Clone a copy of the sphere. Then, scale the copy to 90% using the **Scale Transform Type-In** dialog box. Finally, subtract the copy from the sphere. Name the sphere Dome.

Draw the door in the Front or Left viewport, depending on which "side" of the sphere you subtracted. Create the door as a box 150 x 300 x 10 units. Center it on the flat side of the dome with its bottom edge touching the bottom edge of the dome. It should be slightly inside the sphere. Name the object Door. Create a clone of the door to use as a "drill object." Increase the height of the copy from 10 to 80 units. Reposition the copy as needed so it overlaps the dome. Then, subtract the door copy from the dome to create the doorway. See Figure 16-11. The garage portion is complete.

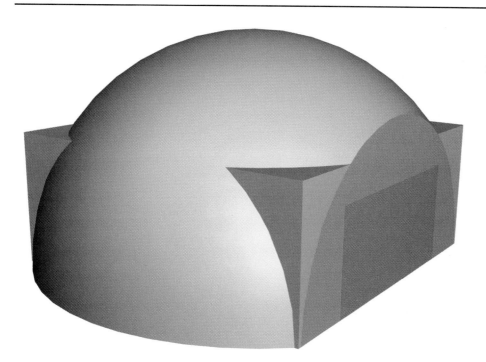

Figure 16-11. The completed space garage before materials are applied.

Now the space car needs to be drawn. The body and four fenders are all based on a sphere. In the Top viewport, draw a sphere with a radius of 40 units. Make it a hemisphere using a value of 0.5. Then, use the **Select and Squash** button to obtain a shape similar to the fenders shown in Figure 16-12. Next, make four copies of the first fender. Uniformly scale one copy up to about 250% for the body. Arrange the fenders on the body as you like. Then, union all five objects together. Name the new object Space Car.

To create the canopy, draw a sphere with a radius of 30. Name it Canopy. Move the sphere into a position you like. Then, clone a copy. Subtract the copy from the Space Car body. Finally, link the canopy to the body. The space car is ready to be parked in the garage. See Figure 16-12.

To create the ground, draw a very large quad patch underneath all objects. If you like, you can add a background. The background in the figures is the bitmap Earth2.jpg located in the 3ds max \Maps\Space folder.

Add materials of your choice. The Dome and Canopy objects should have transparent materials, as shown in Figure 16-12. Add lights and a camera. Position the camera to show a view similar to Figure 16-12.

Animating the Model

To animate the model, the first thing you need to do is reposition the pivot point for the door. Repositioning pivots is discussed in Chapter 12. Move the pivot point to the upper, "outside" corner. See Figure 16-13. This allows the door to swing open properly.

Now, you are ready to add animation. The animation is simple. The car starts off screen, moves into the view, turns, waits for the door to open, and moves into the garage as the door closes. Start by moving the car off screen on frame 0. Also, rotate the car so that it must make a 90° turn before entering the garage.

Figure 16-12. The space car is created and added to the scene. Materials are applied to the objects. Lights, a camera, and a background are also added to the scene.

Figure 16-13. The pivot point of the garage door is repositioned to allow for correct rotation.

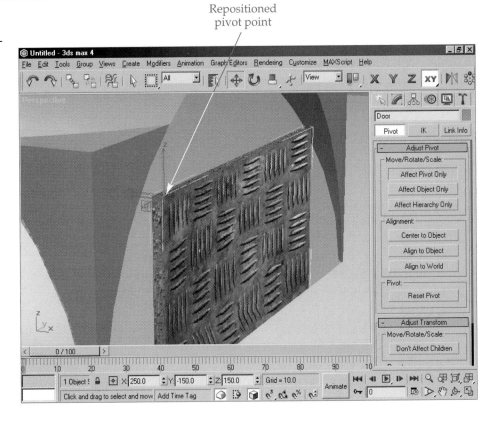

Repositioned pivot point

The first keyframe for the car is frame 40. In this frame, the car must be rotated 90° and in line with the garage door. See Figure 16-14. Then, in frame 50 the car should move straight forward to just in front of the door. Finally, in frame 75 the car should move straight forward into the garage and stop.

The first keyframe for the door is frame 70. In this frame, the door should be fully rotated open. The other keyframe for the door is frame 100, the last frame of the animation. In this frame, the door should be fully closed behind the car.

After adding all keyframes, make a preview animation. Then, play the animation. You will see a couple of problems. First, the car "slides" through the curve. Secondly, the car does not wait for the door to open. Finally, the door begins opening and begins closing before it should.

Editing Keys

All of the problems with the animation are due to the default settings 3ds max assigns to keys. By default, 3ds max attempts to produce smooth motion in an animation. While this sometimes results in acceptable motion, often it produces undesirable results. Using **Track View**, you can easily correct these problems.

Changing Time Position

The first problem we will address is the door. Currently the door starts opening at the beginning of the animation. However, it should not start to open until the space car is in front of it on frame 50. This is very easy to correct.

In **Track View**, expand the **Objects** branch until the door's rotation track is visible. See Figure 16-15. Next, make sure the **Edit Keys** mode button and the **Move Keys** edit button are both on in the main **Track View** toolbar. Then,

Edit Keys

Move Keys

Figure 16-14. The car in its correct location on frame 40 of the animation.

Figure 16-15.
Adjusting the first key for the door so the door will not begin to open until frame 50.

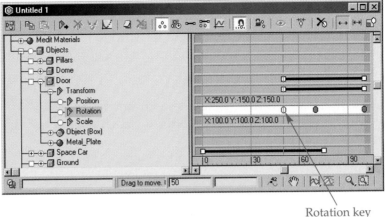

Rotation key
moved to frame 50

move the cursor to the first key in the rotation track. You can pick the key and drag it to frame 50. You can also pick the key to select it and then type 50 in the left-hand text box at the bottom of **Track View** and press [Enter].

Now, make another preview. Notice how the door does not start to open until frame 50. However, another problem has presented itself. The space car now drives through the door. This will be taken care of later.

Copying Keys

Now that the door opens correctly, it needs to be set up to stay open until the car is inside the garage. This is in frame 75. The rotation key for the door at frame 70 contains parameters for the door rotated fully open. This key can be copied to frame 75 in **Track View**. The result is the door stays open from frame 70 to 75. To copy the key, hold down the [Shift] keyboard key and pick the animation key. Then, drag the copy to frame 75.

Help Cel

It may at first appear as though the door is still closing too soon. This is because the door is "floating" through the controllers. This problem is corrected later.

Adding Keys

The car now needs some attention. If you make another preview, you can see the car does not wait for the door to open. It just drives right through the door. You can copy the car's position key at frame 50 to frame 70 to solve the problem. However, you can also add a key at frame 70 and adjust its properties.

Add Keys

To add a key, pick the **Add Keys** button in the main **Track View** toolbar. Then, pick in the car's position track at frame 70. Now, make a preview. You probably do not see any difference. This is because the key took the parameters at that point on the function curve between the other two keys. In other words, even though a key was added, the parameters have not changed. Right-click on the new key. The key info dialog box is displayed. See Figure 16-16. This dialog box is used to adjust the parameters of the key. The same information is found in the **Key Info (Basic)** rollout in the **Motion** tab of the **Command Panel**.

Motion

Key number

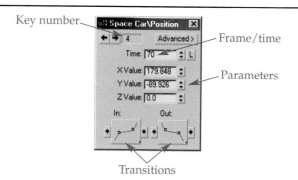

Frame/time

Parameters

Transitions

Figure 16-16. The key info dialog box for the fourth key in the car's position track.

At the top of the key info dialog box is the number of the key. If there are 5 keys for the track and you are on the middle key, the number is 3. The small arrows next to the number allow you to move forward and backward through the keys for the track. In the middle of the dialog box are the values for the key. Since this is a position key, X, Y, and Z values are displayed.

Pick the "back" arrow to move to the key at frame 50. Make note of the X, Y, and Z values. Then, move forward to the new key. The X, Y, and Z values must match. Otherwise, the car will move from frame 50 to frame 70. After you enter matching values, you can close the dialog box.

Now make and view a preview. Notice how the car waits for the door to open before moving forward. The car also has a "bounce" to it. This is due to the default transition assigned by 3ds max.

Editing Transitions

By default, 3ds max assigns a Bézier curve as the transition into and out of a key. This smooth transition produces an organic feel to the motion. However, for mechanical motion, such as for the door or the car, a smooth transition results in a bounce or wobble.

At the bottom of the key info dialog box are two image tiles. The curve on each tile shows how an object moves into and out of the key. What is being changed is actually the tangency of the Bézier handles for the key. You can change the image tile by picking on it and selecting a different curve from the flyout. You can also pick the left and right arrows next to the image tile to cycle through the curves.

The car should move into frame 70 with a mechanical motion. This also means that it must move out of frame 50 with the same mechanical motion. Move to the key at frame 70. Then, change the **In:** image tile to the square curve. See Figure 16-17. Next, move back to the key at frame 50. Notice the **Out:** image tile automatically changed to match the **In:** tile for frame 70.

Mechanical transition

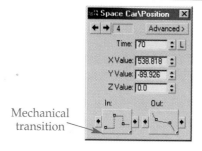

Figure 16-17. The transition into the key is changed to a mechanical transition.

Tension, Continuity, and Bias (TCB)

Make another preview. Notice the car now patiently waits for the door to open before driving inside. However, the door still has a slight bounce to its rotation. A rotation key has a slightly different type of default transition controller. This is called a tension, continuity, and bias (TCB) controller.

A TCB controller is similar to a Bézier controller. However, instead of tangent Bézier handles to control the shape of the motion curve, a TCB controller uses spinners to set values. A TCB controller typically allows more control of motion into and out of a key.

Bézier controllers can be converted to TCB controllers. For example, expand the hierarchy tree in **Track View** so the position controller of the space car is displayed. Highlight the track and pick the **Assign Controller** button on the main toolbar. The **Assign Position Controller** dialog box is displayed. See Figure 16-18. The name of the dialog box reflects the type of track, such as position in this example. Select **TCB Position** from the list to assign a TCB controller to the position track. For this example, pick the **Cancel** button to keep the controller a Bézier controller.

The key info dialog box for a TCB controller key is shown in Figure 16-19. This key is in the rotation track for the door. The key info dialog box has the key number and forward/back arrows found in the Bézier key info dialog box. There are also spinners for the parameters of the key.

The graph at the right of the key info dialog box displays the shape of the motion curve. By default, this is a smooth curve into and out of the key. The key is displayed as a red plus sign (+).

The **Tension:** spinner setting determines the shape of the motion curve. A high value produces a sharp curve. A low value produces a rounded curve.

Assign Controller

Figure 16-18. The **Assign Position Controller** dialog box is used to change the type of controller.

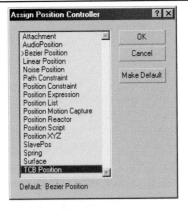

Figure 16-19. A key info dialog box for a TCB controller key.

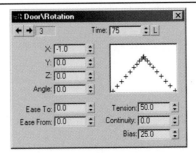

The **Continuity:** spinner setting controls the tangency of the curve to the key. The default setting of 25 produces a smooth tangency into and out of the key. A value of 0 produces a straight line into and out of the key. A value higher than 25 produces a curve that goes up, then down into and out of the key.

The **Bias:** spinner setting shifts the curve before or after the key. The default value of 25 places the top of the curve at the key. Values lower than 25 place the top of the curve before the key. Values greater than 25 place the top of the curve after the key.

The **Ease To:** and **Ease From:** spinners set the speed of motion into and out of the key. The default value of 0 has no effect. Increasing the value in the spinner decreases the speed of motion into or out of the key.

For all garage door keys, the curve needs to be sharp, have a straight tangency into and out of the key, and have its top at the key. Enter 50 in the **Tension:** spinner and 0 in the **Continuity:** spinner. Leave the value in the **Bias:** spinner at the default of 25. Also leave the **Ease To:** and **Ease From:** spinners set at the default of 0.

Finishing the Space Garage

Make another preview of the scene. The car waits for the door to open before pulling into the garage. The "bounce" in the door is also fixed. However, the car still slides through the turn. If your space driver is a hot rodder, this may be the effect you are looking for. However, if your space driver is a bit more conservative, the car should not slide through the curve.

Solving this problem is easy. Open **Track View**. Expand the hierarchy tree so the rotation track for the space car is displayed. Using the **Move Keys** button, move the key currently at frame 0 to about frame 20 or 25.

Move Keys

Make a final preview. Notice the car does not start turning until frame 20. See Figure 16-20. If you like, render a final animation to file.

Figure 16-20. In the final animation, the space car begins to turn on frame 20 and not before.

Using Track View to Control Visibility

There are times when you need to turn the display of an object on and off during an animation. You can use the **Display** tab in the **Command Panel** to turn the display of an object on and off. However, this cannot be animated. To control the display of an object during an animation, a *visibility track* must be added in **Track View**.

Add Visibility Track

To add a visibility track to an object, first determine the keyframes for visibility. Then, open **Track View**. Navigate through the hierarchy tree until the object is displayed. Highlight the object's name in the hierarchy and pick the **Add Visibility Track** button on the main **Track View** toolbar. A visibility controller now appears in the hierarchy below the object's name. However, notice in the edit window there are no keys.

Add Keys

To add keys, pick the **Add Keys** button on the main **Track View** toolbar. Then, pick in the visibility track where the first keyframe should be. After the key is added, you can move it to an exact frame by picking in the text box at the bottom of **Track View**. See Figure 16-21. Then, type the frame number and press [Enter].

Finally, you need to adjust the key info. Open the key info dialog box for the first key by right-clicking on the key. See Figure 16-22. The **Value:** spinner sets the visibility. A value of 0 means the object is completely invisible. A value of 1 means the object is completely visible. You can enter values greater than 1 and less than 0. Doing this, in effect, shifts the transition toward one key or the other. In other words, the transition is not applied smoothly between the keys.

With the default transition settings, the object will fade in and fade out. See Figure 16-23. However, in many cases you will need an abrupt, instantaneous change in visibility. For example, if you are using a particle system or combustion effect to explode the object on frame 10,

Figure 16-21. A visibility track is used to control an object's visibility in an animation.

Keys added to visibility track

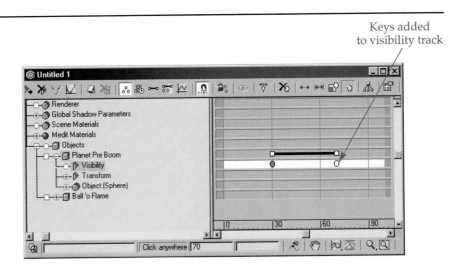

Figure 16-22. A value of 0 for a visibility key means the object is invisible. A value of 1 means the object is completely visible.

Figure 16-23. To create an instantaneous change in visibility, a mechanical transition must be used. Otherwise, the object fades in and out, as shown here.

the original object needs to be fully visible through frame 9, but not at all after that. Just as with motion, you can change the transition using the key info dialog box. To produce an instantaneous change in visibility, select the square, mechanical transition.

Help Cel

You can also add a visibility track by right-clicking on an object and selecting **P**roperties... from the quad menu. Then, in the **General** tab of the **Object Properties** dialog box, set the visibility in the **Rendering Control** area.

Exercise 16-1

1) Draw two spheres, one inside the other. Make the larger sphere red and about twice the size of the smaller one. Make the smaller sphere blue.
2) Add a camera and two spotlights to the scene. Switch the Perspective viewport to the Camera viewport. Adjust the viewport to get a good view of the sphere.
3) Make a final rendering of all frames. Save the animation to a file named ex16-01a.avi in the folder of your choice.
4) Add a visibility track for the large sphere. Add and adjust the keys necessary to make the sphere fully visible from frame 0 to frame 50. Change the default transition to mechanical.
5) Render another final rendering animation of all frames. Save the file as ex16-01b.avi in the folder of your choice.
6) Save the scene as ex16-01.max in the folder of your choice.

Exercise

Block Controller

A *block controller* allows you to group tracks from different objects. The group is called a *block*. The block can then be used to recreate the animation anywhere in time. A block controller is a global controller.

For example, suppose you are modeling a ninja and a samurai fighting for a 3D game application. Each figure has certain "ninja moves" that will be repeated over and over through the match. After animating a move the first time, you can group the tracks defining the move. Then, the group, or block, can be added each time the figure performs the move.

Assign Controller

To create a block controller, first animate the motion. Then, open **Track View**. Expand **Global Tracks** in the hierarchy tree. Then, expand **Block Control** and select the **Available** track. Pick the **Assign Controller** button on the main toolbar. The **Assign Constant Controller** dialog box is displayed. See Figure 16-24. Pick **MasterBlock** from the list and pick the **OK** button. A master block track is added to **Track View**.

The **Master Block Parameters** dialog box is displayed. See Figure 16-25. This dialog box is used to add tracks to the block controller. You can also right-click on the master block track in the **Track View** edit window and select **Properties** from the shortcut menu. Pick the **Add** button to add tracks to the block. The **Track View Pick** dialog box is displayed.

In the **Track View Pick** dialog box, expand the hierarchy tree to show the tracks for the items you want to add. See Figure 16-26. Notice only the items having keys are displayed, not all items. Also notice all tracks

Figure 16-24.
Assigning a master block controller.

Figure 16-25. The **Master Block Parameters** dialog box is used to add tracks to the block controller.

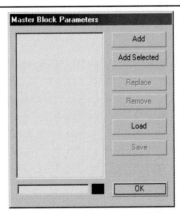

are greyed out except tracks containing keys. Pick the animated track you want to add. You can pick multiple tracks by pressing the [Ctrl] key and picking the tracks. Then, pick the **OK** button. The **Block Parameters** dialog box is displayed.

In the **Block Parameters** dialog box, enter a name for the block. See Figure 16-27. You can pick the color swatch and choose a color for the block. This is the color displayed in **Track View**. The **Start:** and **End:** spinners set the time range for the block. For example, if the animated move starts on frame 15 and ends on frame 75, enter 15 in the **Start:** spinner and 75 in the **End:** spinner. Pick the **OK** button to close the **Block Parameters** dialog box.

The name of the block is now displayed in the **Master Block Parameters** dialog box. You can define more blocks by picking the **Add** button again. If you are done defining blocks, pick the **OK** button to close the dialog box.

Now you need to add the block to the scene using **Track View**. Right-click on the master block track in the **Track View** edit window. In the shortcut menu, select the name of the block you defined. The block is displayed in the color you selected earlier. Drag the block to align its starting point on the correct frame.

You can add the block again at a point later in the animation. You can also go back and delete the original keys. Then, you can place a block "on top of" the original animation section.

Help Cel

The keys in a block are copies of the original keys, not instances. Therefore, if you make a change to the original key, the change is not transferred to the block.

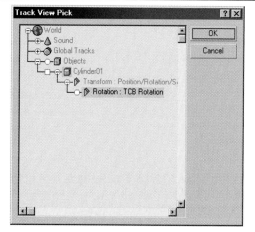

Figure 16-26. Adding tracks to a block controller.

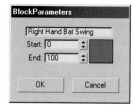

Figure 16-27. Naming a block for use with a block controller.

Exercise

Exercise 16-2

1) Draw the objects shown below. Use your own dimensions.
2) Examine the joints. Then, create a logical hierarchy and link the objects. Set inheritance and pivots as needed.
3) There will be two moves by the paddle, one swinging at a high ball and one swinging at a low ball. Animate both of these moves so the paddle starts and ends in approximately the same "middle" position.
4) Create a block controller for each move. Name one High Ball and the other Low Ball.
5) Using the block controllers, animate several Ping-Pong® balls coming at the paddle one at a time. Vary between high and low balls. For simplicity, you can make the paddle miss the ball each time.
6) Make a preview animation.
7) Make any adjustments needed. Then, render a low-resolution (320x240) animation. Save the animation as ex16-02.avi in the folder of your choice.
8) Save the scene as ex16-02.max in the folder of your choice.

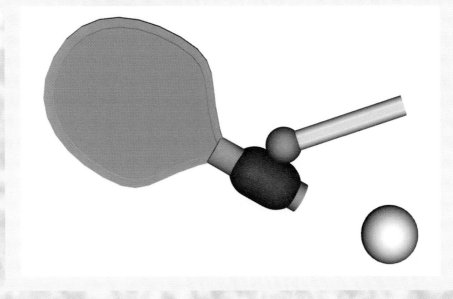

Adding and Managing Notes

Notes can be added to tracks in **Track View**. This can be useful in keeping track of keys, indicating why you set parameters the way you did or other important things. A note is actually a note track added below a selected track. To add a note track, select a track in **Track View**. Then, pick the **Add Note Track** button on the main toolbar. A note track is added below the selected track. See Figure 16-28. You may need to expand a branch to see the note track.

Add Note Track

Once the note track is added, you need to add keys. Pick the **Add Keys** button and pick in the note track at the frame where you want the note. A note key looks like a little notepad. The note can be edited by right-clicking on the key to open the **Notes** dialog box. See Figure 16-29.

Add Keys

Type the note in the text box. Then, close the **Notes** dialog box. The first line of the note appears next to the key. Therefore, you should use a very short description in the first line of the note. From the second line down, type a more lengthy note if necessary.

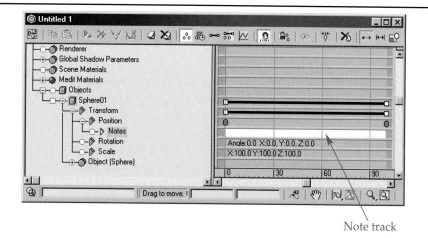

Figure 16-28. A note can be added as a key in a note track.

Note track

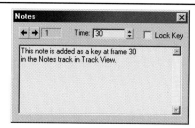

Figure 16-29. Instead of a key info dialog box, the **Notes** dialog box is displayed for adding and editing a note.

Exercise 16-3

1) Draw a sphere, teapot, and prism. Use your own dimensions.
2) Open **Track View**. Add a note track for each of the objects.
3) For the sphere, add a key in the note track at frame 30. Modify the note so it reads "This is the sphere at frame 30."
4) For the teapot, add a key in the note track at frame 65. Modify the note so it reads "The teapot should not move before this frame."
5) For the prism, add a key in the note track at frame 12. Modify the note so it reads "Light should begin to shine through the prism on this frame."
6) Save the scene as ex16-03.max in the folder of your choice.

Exercise

Adding Sound

Sound can be added to an animation. This is most often done to synchronize the animation to the sound. A temporary or "low res" sound file is used to save computer resources. The actual sound file is then composited with the animation later using separate software. You can also use the built-in metronome to "pace" the animation. In some cases, such as creating an animation to be played back on a computer, the "low res" sound file is acceptable for the final product and can be rendered directly to the animation.

Choose Sound

To add a sound track, open **Track View** and highlight the **Sound** track. Right-click in the track to open the **Sound Options** dialog box. See Figure 16-30. In the **Audio** area of the dialog box, pick the **Choose Sound** button. Select a sound file in the **Open Sound** dialog box and pick the **Open** button. Then, pick the **OK** button in the **Sound Options** dialog box to close it.

The waveform for the sound is displayed in **Track View**. See Figure 16-31. If the **Real Time** check box in the **Time Configuration** dialog box is checked, the sound plays when you play the animation. If the check box is unchecked, the sound file does not play.

You can shift the waveform ahead or back in the animation. However, you cannot rescale the wave form. To do this, you must edit the sound file in external software.

Help Cel

To match the total length of a sound file to the length of the animation, multiply the sound file length (in seconds) by the animation playback rate (in frames per second). The result is the minimum total number of animation frames needed to contain the sound file. For example, a 3-second sound file played at 30 fps needs a minimum of 90 frames to play the entire sound file.

Figure 16-30. The **Sound Options** dialog box is used to add a sound file to the scene.

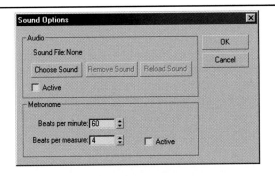

Figure 16-31. A sound file is displayed in **Track View** as a waveform.

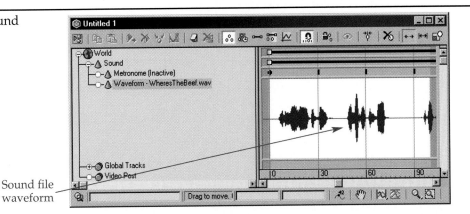

Sound file waveform

Exercise 16-4

1) Set the total number of frames to 130.
2) Draw two thin chamfer boxes similar to the ones shown below. Move the pivot point of each box to one edge.
3) Animate the boxes open and shut twice, like lips. The first time, animate them open slightly. The second time, animate them open a bit more.
4) Create two block controllers, one for the small opening and one for the larger opening. Name the "small" one Little Mouth. Name the "large" one Big Mouth.
5) Open **Track View**. Add the sound file WheresTheBeef.wav located in the 3ds max \sounds folder.
6) Using the block controllers, animate the box "lips" to synchronize with the wave file.
7) Adjust the Perspective viewport as necessary. Then, make a preview animation.
8) Make any adjustments necessary to the animation.
9) Render a final animation with the sound file. Save the animation as ex16-04.avi in the folder of your choice.
10) Save the scene as ex16-04.max in the folder of your choice.

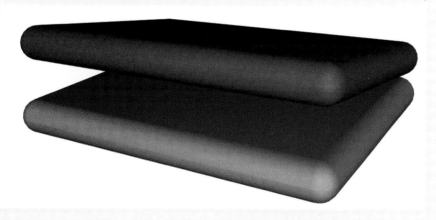

Exercise

Introduction to Schematic View

Schematic View is an interface that displays all objects in a scene as a flowchart. See Figure 16-32. It allows you to select, name, and copy modifiers between objects. In addition, you can create a linked hierarchy using **Schematic View**. To open **Schematic View**, select **Schematic View** from the **Graph Editors** pull-down menu. Then, pick **Open Schematic View** in the cascading menu. You can also pick the **Open Schematic View** button on the **Main** toolbar.

Open Schematic View

Overview

Objects are displayed in **Schematic View** as boxes. References between objects appear as connecting lines with arrows. A red triangle below the box indicates a reference below the object. Below the object is called *downstream.* Above the object is called *upstream.*

You can rearrange the boxes however you like. The reference lines and arrows remain attached as you move the boxes. For example, you may want to rearrange the flowchart in **Schematic View** to resemble the biped character you have modeled. With the chart resembling the actual shape of the character, selecting components is easy.

Figure 16-32.
Schematic View is used to display the objects in a scene as a flowchart.

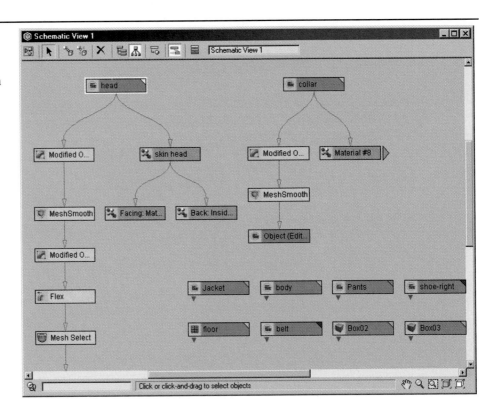

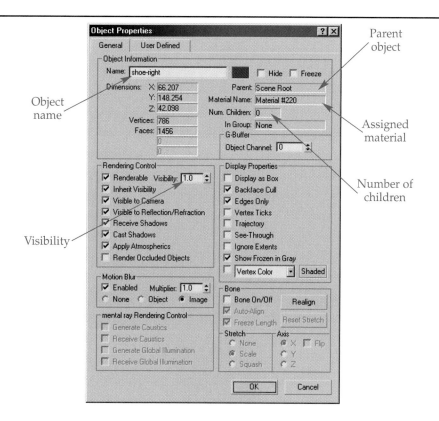

Figure 16-33. An object can be renamed in **Schematic View** using the **Object Properties** dialog box. Various other properties of the object can also be changed in this dialog box.

To select an object using **Schematic View**, simply double-click on the object's box. The object is selected in the viewports. To rename an object in **Schematic View**, right-click on the object's box and select **Properties**... from the shortcut menu. The **Object Properties** dialog box is displayed. See Figure 16-33. Enter a new name in the **Name:** text box in the **General** tab and then close the dialog box. The **Object Properties** dialog box can be used to change other settings for the object as well.

Creating Links Using Schematic View

Schematic View can be used to quickly create links. Once the objects are drawn, open **Schematic View**. Then, select a child to be linked and pick the **Link** button on the **Schematic View** toolbar. See Figure 16-34A. Pick on the child object box and drag the cursor to the parent object box to which you want it linked. This is just like linking in a viewport. Once the objects are linked, the flowchart reflects the reference. See Figure 16-34B. Continue linking objects as necessary.

Link

Figure 16-34.
A—Unlinked objects in **Schematic View**.
B—The objects after they have been linked in **Schematic View**.

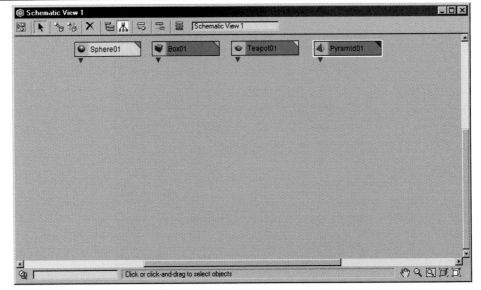

A

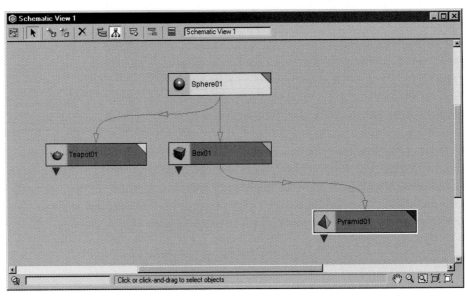

B

Exercise 16-5

1) Draw and locate the objects shown below. Use your own dimensions. Name the cylinders Top String, Middle String01, Middle String02, Bottom String01, Bottom String02, Bottom String03, and Bottom String04. Name the cross pieces Top Beam, Bottom Left Beam, and Bottom Right Beam.

2) Open **Schematic View**. Maximize the window. Zoom as needed to display all objects.

3) Rename the four pyramids to Object One, Object Two, Object Three, and Object Four.

4) Using the **Link** button on the **Schematic View** toolbar, link the objects. Start by linking Object One to its corresponding "bottom string." Then link the bottom string to its corresponding "bottom beam." Continue linking on up the hierarchy in this manner. Similarly, link the remaining geometry.

5) Close **Schematic View**. Verify proper linking by rotating the parts of the mobile from the top.

6) Add rotation animation of your own design. Render the animation to a file named **ex16-05.avi** in the folder of your choice.

7) Save the scene as **ex16-05.max** in the folder of your choice.

Exercise

Chapter Snapshot

Chapter Test

Answer the following questions on a separate sheet of paper.

1) Define **Track View**.
2) How do you display **Track View** in a viewport?
3) What are the three basic parts of **Track View**?
4) What part of the **Track View** hierarchy tree is the root of the entire tree?
5) The **Global Tracks** branch of the **Track View** hierarchy tree is used to _____.
6) The **Objects** branch of the **Track View** hierarchy tree contains _____.
7) In the **Track View** hierarchy tree, _____ have a yellow cube next to their name.
8) Controllers have a _____ icon next to their name in the **Track View** hierarchy tree.
9) A _____ icon in the **Track View** hierarchy tree indicates a map.
10) Define container.
11) **Track View** has two toolbars. Which one contains tools for editing tracks and function curves?
12) The edit window of **Track View** is used to _____.
13) List the two types of tracks.
14) Define key.
15) Which type of track can be displayed as a function curve?
16) What does a range bar indicate?
17) How can you copy a key within a track?
18) The default transition assigned by 3ds max attempts to create _____.
19) How does a TCB controller differ from a Bézier controller?
20) What is a block controller used for?

Modeling Problems

Draw the following models using your own dimensions. Create and apply materials as needed, similar to those shown. Add lights and cameras as needed to create the shadows and views shown. When finished, save each model as p16-xx.max in the folder of your choice.

Double Hung Window **1**

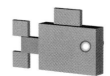

Draw the window and frame shown. Link each piece of glass to its corresponding frame. Create and assign basic materials as needed. Animate the window open and closed. Adjust the key transitions as needed so the window does not float past the window sill when closing. Render the animation to a file named p16-01.avi in the folder of your choice.

2 Refrigerator

Open p14-02.max from Chapter 14. Save the scene as p16-02.max in the folder of your choice. Adjust the animation so the door is open on frame 30 and stays open until frame 90. The drawers should not slide until the door is fully open. Adjust the drawer animations so one slides out and in from frame 30 to frame 60. Then, animate the other drawer out and in from frame 60 to frame 90. The door should be closed on frame 100. Also, the light inside the refrigerator should be on only when the door is open. Render the animation to a file named p16-02.avi in the folder of your choice.

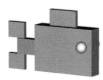

3 Light Switch

Draw the light switch and switch plate shown. Create and apply basic materials as needed. Several wood materials can be found in the default 3ds max material library, if you would like to use them. Animate the switch "on" and "off" several times. Adjust key transitions as necessary so the switch does not float into the switch plate. Render the animation to a file named p16-03.avi in the folder of your choice.

4 Truckasaurus

Open p14-03.max from Chapter 14. Save the scene as p16-04.max in the folder of your choice. Animate the truck so it begins on one side of the screen, moves to the other side, pauses for several frames, and reverses to its original location. Be sure to match the rotation of the wheels to the movement of the truck. Render the animation to a file named p16-04.avi in the folder of your choice.

Airplane **5**

Open p14-04.max from Chapter 14. Save the scene as p16-05.max in the folder of your choice. Animate the plane so it begins flying right-side-up, rolls and flies upside-down for 50 frames, and rolls to fly right-side-up at the end of the animation. Render the animation to a file named p16-05.avi in the folder of your choice.

Drop Forge **6**

Draw the drop forge, part blank (sphere), and part shown. Create and assign basic materials as needed. Animate the top platen closed on frame 50, remaining closed until frame 60, and open on frame 60. Adjust the transitions as needed. Remember, this is a machine. The sphere should turn into the finished part on frame 50. Render the animation to a file named p16-06.avi in the folder of your choice.

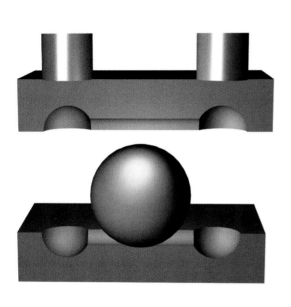

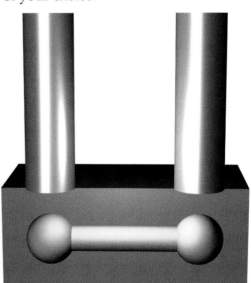

7 Pinball Mechanism

Draw the pinball mechanism shown. The spring is a "renderable" helix. Create and apply basic materials as needed. Adjust pivots and link objects as needed. Animate the mechanism as shown. The handle should be drawn back on frame 25 and return to its original position on frame 35. Be sure to make the spring follow the motion of the handle. Render the animation to a file named p16-07.avi in the folder of your choice.

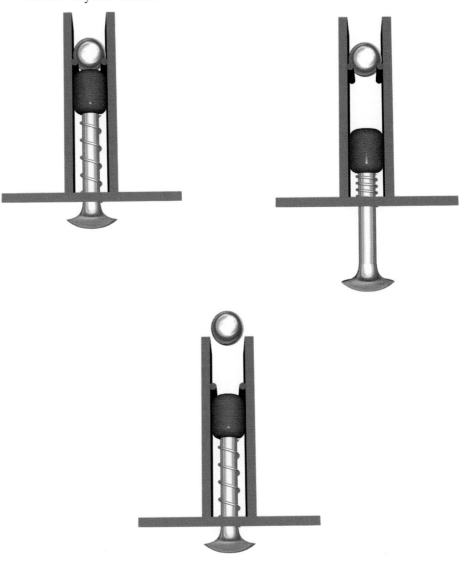

Linchpin **8**
Draw the linchpin joint shown. Adjust pivots and create a hierarchy as needed. Apply basic materials as needed. Animate the joint rotating back and forth. Adjust key transitions so the arm does not float into the coupling. Render the animation to a file named p16-08.avi in the folder of your choice.

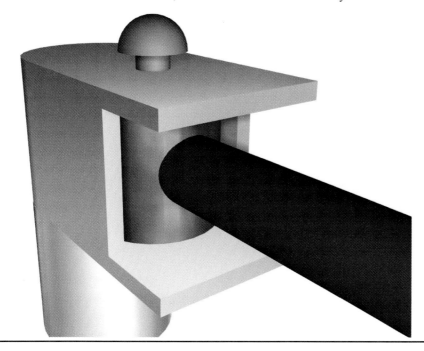

Meditation Swing **9**
Open p15-07.max from Chapter 15. Save the scene as p16-09.max in the folder of your choice. Adjust key transitions as needed to correct the motion problems. Render the animation to a file named p16-09.avi in the folder of your choice.

10 Space Blaster

Draw the space blaster shown. The "at rest" position should have the barrel down. Animate rotation of the base and barrel. Add a fireball of your own design. Add and animate lights as necessary. The barrel should recoil on firing and the blaster should fire twice during the animation. Keep in mind, the fireball will only be visible while the blaster fires. Also, the fireball momentarily adds bright illumination to the scene. Render the animation to a file named p16-10.avi in the folder of your choice.

Portable CD Player **11**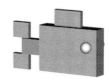

Draw the portable CD player shown here. Animate the lid opening, staying open as the CD comes out, and closing. Adjust key transitions as needed. Render the animation to a file named p16-11.avi in the folder of your choice.

Chapter 17

Creating Advanced Materials

Objectives

After completing this chapter, you will be able to:

● List the material types in 3ds max.
● Explain the material tree.
● Use the **Material/Map Navigator**.
● Explain each material type.
● Create materials of the various types.
● Explain the material modifier.
● List the map types in 3ds max.
● Explain the UVW map modifier.
● Apply and adjust a UVW map modifier.
● Animate a material.

In Chapter 13, you learned how to create basic materials using the standard material type. You learned the various shading types and how to make color settings for basic materials. Also, adding antialiasing to a rendered image using supersampling was introduced. Antialiasing is a method of improving rendered image quality.

Basic, standard-type materials often serve well in many applications. In general, however, the standard material type lacks the fine control necessary to create very realistic and believable scenes. In addition to the standard type, 3ds max has nine advanced material types. See Figure 17-1.

Help Cel

An unused material sample slot is one containing a material not assigned in the scene. It can, however, contain a material definition.

Material Types

As discussed in Chapter 13, the standard material type has very basic settings. It is the default type of material in 3ds max and allows you to quickly create materials of different, uniform colors. The advanced material types 3ds max has are raytrace, matte/shadow, and a group of types called compound materials. The *compound materials* include the blend, composite, double sided, morpher, multi/sub-object, shellac, and top/bottom types.

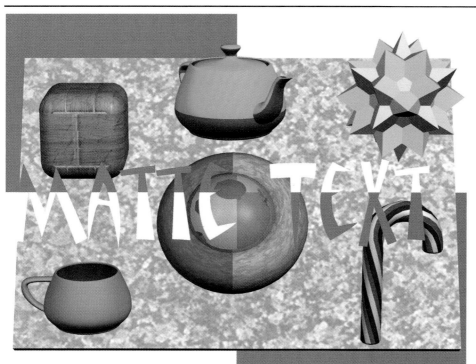

Figure 17-1. There are 10 types of materials in 3ds max. Each has its own characteristics.

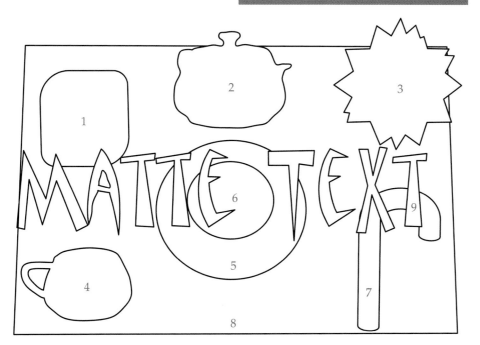

1 - Composite
2 - Top/Bottom
3 - Standard
4 - Double Sided
5 - Blend
6 - Raytrace
7 - Multi/Sub-Object
8 - Shellac
9 - Matte/Shadow
Not Shown - Morpher

To create a new material, open the **Material Editor**. Then, select an unused material sample slot. Finally, pick the material type button located to the right of the material name drop-down list. This is by default labeled **Standard**, indicating the material is the standard type. See Figure 17-2A. The **Material/Map Browser** is displayed.

To start defining a new material from scratch, pick the **New** radio button in the **Browse From:** area to display the 10 material types. See Figure 17-2B. Then, select a material type from the list and pick the **OK** button. Finally, complete the material definition in the **Material Editor**. You can also use an existing material from the material library, **Material Editor**, selected object, or current scene as a starting point by picking the appropriate button in the **Browse From:** area.

If the material type you choose is a compound material and the sample slot selected contains a material, you are prompted to discard or keep the old material. See Figure 17-3. Picking the **Discard old material?** radio button completely removes the existing material definition. Picking the **Keep old material as sub-material?** radio button uses the existing material definition as a component of the new compound material. If the new material type is standard, raytrace, or matte/shadow, the existing material definition is simply removed.

Climbing the Material Tree

Go to Parent

Go Forward to Sibling

Material/Map Navigator

All material types, especially compound materials, can have many levels in their corresponding material hierarchy or tree. The *material tree* can be confusing and it is easy to get lost. You can move directly up or down the tree by using the **Go to Parent** and **Go Forward to Sibling** buttons located just below the material sample area in the **Material Editor**. If the button is greyed out, you are already at the top or bottom. The "default" materials only have one level in the material tree.

3ds max also has a graphic interface for moving through the material tree. This is called the **Material/Map Navigator**. See Figure 17-4. It is displayed by picking the **Material/Map Navigator** button located to the right of the material samples. The **Material/Map Navigator** displays the material tree for the material in the selected sample slot. It is modeless, so you can keep it open and select different materials. Climbing up or down the tree is easy using the navigator. Simply pick on a level to highlight it. The settings corresponding to that level are displayed in the **Material Editor**.

You can use the buttons at the top of the **Material/Map Navigator** to display the tree as a list, list and icons, small icons, or large icons. The list or list and icons format may be the most useful setting.

Materials and maps can be dragged from the **Material/Map Navigator** and dropped onto sample slots or material/map buttons. This makes it easy to copy materials or maps from one material definition to another. This technique can also be used to copy maps up or down a material's own tree.

Help Cel

When working with material levels, you may quickly find yourself lost in the material tree. To avoid this, give your materials, sub-materials, and maps logical names. Default names, such as 6-Default or Map #21, provide no logical meaning.

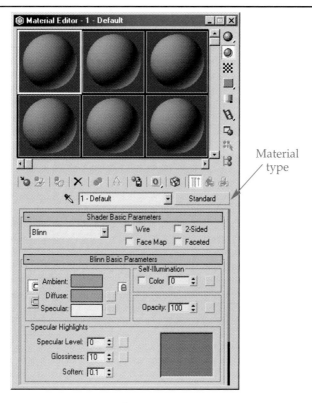

A

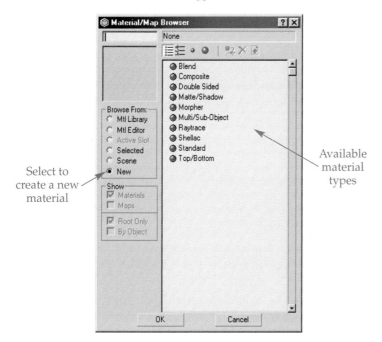

B

Figure 17-2. A—The type of material is set by picking the material type button in the **Material Editor**. B—Picking this button opens the **Material/Map Browser**.

Figure 17-3. When the new material type is a compound material, you are given the option of keeping the existing material as a sub-material.

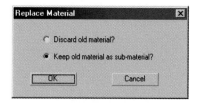

Figure 17-4. Using the **Material/Map Navigator** is a quick way to climb the material tree.

Exercise

Exercise 17-1

1) Start 3ds max and open the **Material Editor**.
2) Select a material sample slot and get the material Concrete_Asphalt.
3) Open the **Material/Map Navigator**. Make a list of the sub-components of the material.
4) Select a different sample slot. Get the material Ground_Water.
5) Using the **Material/Map Navigator**, make a list of the sub-components. How many levels does this material have?
6) Reset 3ds max without saving.

Blend

The *blend material* type allows you to mix, or blend, two different materials and apply the blend as a single material. The amount of blend can be animated over time or controlled by a mask. See Figure 17-5.

Once the material type is set to blend, the **Blend Basic Parameters** rollout is displayed in the **Material Editor**. See Figure 17-6. At the top of the rollout are the **Material 1:** and **Material 2:** buttons. The labels on these buttons are the material names. Picking a button moves you down a level in the material. You can then define the material as needed. Finally, return to the parent level of the material.

You may find it easier to first define the two materials in different sample slots. Then, drag each sample and drop it on one of the material buttons. When you do this, you are asked if you want to place a copy or an instance of the material in the tree. Choose which method you want to use.

The check boxes to the right of the material buttons are used to turn the materials on and off. When checked, the material is on and rendered.

Figure 17-5. The material on the left-hand sphere is blended with the material on the middle sphere to produce the material on the right-hand sphere.

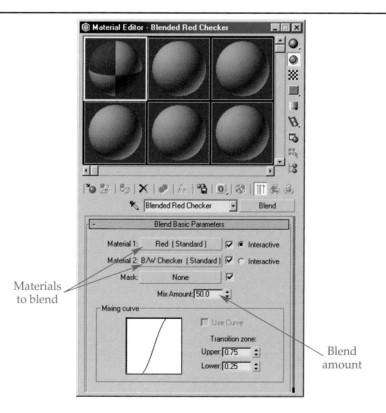

Figure 17-6. The **Blend Basic Parameters** rollout is used to define a blend material.

When unchecked, the material is off and not rendered. The **Interactive** radio buttons determine which material is displayed in shaded viewports. Only one can be displayed.

Below the material buttons is the **Mask:** button. The label on this button is the name of the mask specified. You can use a bitmap file or a procedural map. Procedural maps are discussed later in this chapter. The greyscale values of the map control the amount of the mix. For example, if a black and white checker pattern is used, the materials are mixed in a checker pattern. Use the check box next to the **Mask:** button to turn the mask on and off. When the mask is on, the **Mix Amount:** spinner is disabled.

The **Mix Amount:** spinner determines how much of each material is displayed. This is only active when a mask is not turned on. The value in the spinner is the percentage of **Material 2:** displayed. Therefore, a value of 100 means no percentage of **Material 1:** is displayed. This spinner can be animated to simulate a color morphing.

The **Mixing curve** area is used to set the transition between colors when a mask is specified. To apply the curve settings, the **Use Curve** check box must be checked. This check box is enabled when a mask is specified. The **Upper:** and **Lower:** spinners under the **Transition zone:** label set the transition between the materials. If the values are the same, the materials meet at a hard edge. The farther apart the two values, the softer the edge. The values can range from 0 to 1. The graph at the left of the **Mixing curve** area represents the settings.

Exercise

Exercise 17-2

1) Open the **Material Editor** and activate the first material sample slot.
2) Get the material Wood_Ashen from the default 3ds max material library.
3) Rename the material Wood Base.
4) Change the material type to blend. When prompted, keep the existing material as a sub-material.
5) Pick the **Material 2:** button. This moves you down to the Material 2 level in the hierarchy.
6) Change the material color to a light blue. Also rename the material Blue Wash.
7) Navigate back up the hierarchy to the blend level.
8) Change the mix amount to about 50. Also, rename the top-level material (at this level) Wood With Blue Wash.
9) Draw a thin box in any viewport using your own dimensions.
10) Apply the material Wood With Blue Wash to the box. Render the scene to a file named ex17-02.jpg in the folder of your choice.
11) Save the scene as ex17-02.max in the folder of your choice.

Composite

The *composite material* type is similar to the blend type. It allows you to layer, or composite, up to 10 different materials. See Figure 17-7. The mix amounts can be animated to simulate morphing materials.

Once the material type is set to composite, the **Composite Basic Parameters** rollout is displayed in the **Material Editor**. See Figure 17-8. This rollout is essentially a list of 10 materials you select to composite. At the top of the rollout is the **Base Material:** button. The label on this

Figure 17-7. The three materials on the spheres in the background are composited to create the material on the sphere in the foreground.

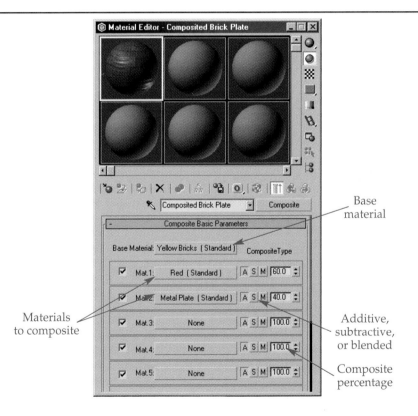

Figure 17-8. The **Composite Basic Parameters** rollout is used to define a composite material.

button is the name of the base material. Pick the button to define a new base material. The base material is displayed if all other materials are set to 0%.

Below the **Base Material:** button are the **Mat. 1:** through **Mat. 9:** buttons. The labels on these buttons are the names of selected materials. If the button is labeled **None**, pick it to select a material in the **Material/Map Browser**. If the button has a material name, picking the button navigates to that material's definition in the material tree. The nine materials are composited over the top of the base material. To the left of the nine buttons are check boxes used to turn the materials on and off. When one is checked, the material to the right of the check box is turned on.

In the **Composite Type** column next to each of the nine materials are three buttons and a spinner. The spinner sets the percentage of the material composited on top of the base material. This value can be animated.

The three buttons determine if additive color, subtractive color, or blending is used to composite the material. When the **A** button is on, additive color is used. This means the color of the base material is added to the color of the composited material. When the **S** button is on, subtractive color is used. This means the color of the composited material is subtracted from the color of the base material. When the **M** button is on, the materials are blended just as with the blend material type.

Help Cel

The composite percentage assigned to a material should not be too high.

Exercise

Exercise 17-3

1) Open the **Material Editor** and activate the first material sample slot.
2) Get the material Concrete_Tiles from the default 3ds max material library.
3) Rename the material Tile Base.
4) Change the material type to composite. When prompted, keep the existing material as a sub-material.
5) Activate an unused material sample slot. Get the material Concrete_Stucco from the material library.
6) Activate an unused material sample slot. Change the material color to a light purple. Name the material Purple.
7) Activate the Tile Base material sample slot. Navigate to the composite level in the hierarchy, if not already there.
8) Drag and drop the Concrete_Stucco material sample onto the **Mat. 1:** button. Select to make a copy.
9) Drag and drop the Purple material sample onto the **Mat. 2:** button. Select to make a copy.
10) Change the percentage of the Purple material to about 40. Change the percentage of the Concrete_Stucco material to about 35.
11) Draw a cube of your own dimensions. Apply the composite material to the cube.
12) Render the scene to a file named ex17-03.jpg in the folder of your choice.
13) Save the scene as ex17-03.max in the folder of your choice.

Figure 17-9. The materials on the two coffee cups in the background are used to create the double sided material on the coffee cup in the foreground.

Double Sided

The *double sided material* type allows you to assign different materials to the front and back faces of an object. See Figure 17-9. This is a variation of a two-sided material. You can also set how much of one material can be seen through the other.

Once the material type is set to double sided, the **Double Sided Basic Parameters** rollout is displayed. See Figure 17-10. In this rollout are the **Facing Material:** button and the **Back Material:** button. The labels on these buttons are the names of the materials selected. Pick a button to define a new material. The check boxes next to the buttons are used to turn the materials on and off. When checked, the material is on.

At the top of the rollout is the **Translucency:** spinner. The value in this spinner is a percentage of how much the back material shows through to the facing material. At 0, none of the back material shows through. At 100, the back material completely covers the facing material.

Figure 17-10. The **Double Sided Basic Parameters** rollout is used to define a double sided material.

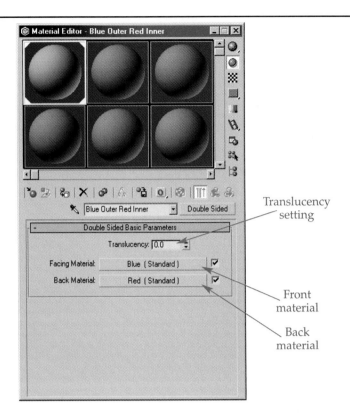

Translucency setting

Front material

Back material

Exercise

Exercise 17-4

1) Reset 3ds max.
2) Draw a teapot of your own dimensions. Using the **Modify** tab in the **Command Panel**, remove the lid and spout.
3) Open the **Material Editor**.
4) Select the first material sample slot. Change the material color to what you want for the outside of the cup. Name the material Outside.
5) Activate the second material sample slot. Change the material color to what you want for the inside of the cup. Use a color that is very different from the "outside" color. Name the material Inside.
6) Activate the first material sample slot and change the material type to double sided. When prompted, keep the existing material as a sub-material.
7) Drag and drop the Inside material sample onto the **Back Material:** button.
8) Rename the double sided material Cup. Change the translucency as needed.
9) Assign the material Cup to the teapot object.
10) Render the scene to a file named ex17-04.jpg in the folder of your choice.
11) Save the scene as ex17-04.max in the folder of your choice.

Matte/Shadow

The *matte/shadow material* type creates a matte object. A *matte object* is invisible in the scene because it is rendered with the environment background. However, the object will block the view of any objects behind it. In addition, a matte object can receive shadows. This is an easy way to cast shadows "onto" the background. See Figure 17-11. Matte objects can also receive reflections.

Once the material is set to matte/shadow, the **Matte/Shadow Basic Parameters** rollout is displayed. See Figure 17-12. Also notice the material sample slot no longer displays a sample object.

When the **Opaque Alpha** check box in the **Matte** area is *not* checked, the matte object does not make an alpha channel. The rendered image is then suitable for compositing. See Figure 17-13. When the **Opaque Alpha** check box is checked, the matte object creates an alpha channel.

The **Atmosphere** area determines if the matte object receives fog atmospheric effects. Fog is discussed in Chapter 19. When the **Apply Atmosphere** check box is checked, fog is applied to the matte object. When the **At Background Depth** radio button is on, 3ds max first renders the fog in the scene and then renders any shadows. When the **At Object Depth** radio button is on, 3ds max first renders any shadows and then renders the fog. This can produce a falloff effect on the shadows.

The **Shadow** area determines if and how the matte object receives shadows. For the object to receive shadows, the **Receive Shadows** check box must be checked. When the **Affect Alpha** check box is checked, the shadows are rendered to the alpha channel. This check box is greyed out unless the **Opaque Alpha** check box in the **Matte** area is unchecked.

Figure 17-11. The wood material on the deck shown in A is replaced in B with a matte/shadow material. Notice how the shadows appear to be cast onto the background.

A   B

The **Shadow Brightness:** spinner in the **Shadow** area determines the relative intensity of shadows received by the matte object. At a value of 0.0, the shadow is completely the color shown in the **Color:** swatch. At a value of 1.0, the shadows are in effect not shown.

The **Reflection** area determines if and how the matte object receives reflections. To have the object receive reflections, pick the **Map:** button to display the **Material/Map Browser**. Then, select a map to use as a reflection and close the browser. Mapping is discussed in detail in Chapter 18. The check box next to the **Map:** button is used to turn the reflection on and off. Once a map is specified, the **Amount:** spinner is enabled. This is used to control the percentage of the reflection map to use. The value can be animated.

Figure 17-12. The **Matte/Shadow Basic Parameters** rollout is used to define a matte material.

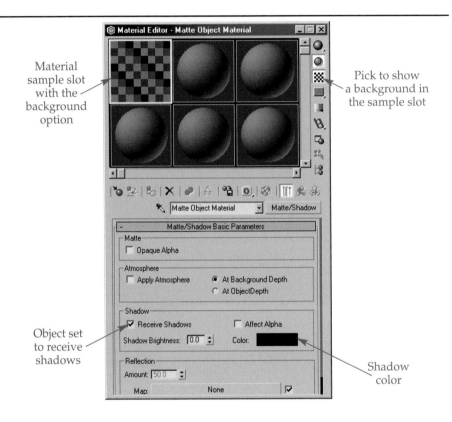

Material sample slot with the background option

Pick to show a background in the sample slot

Object set to receive shadows

Shadow color

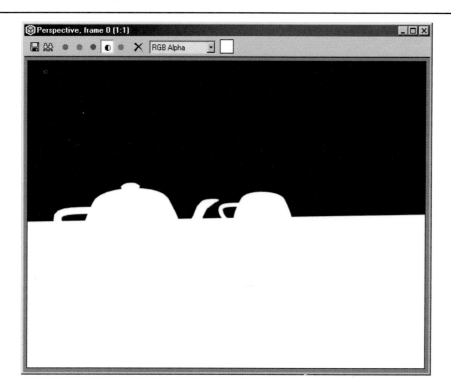

A

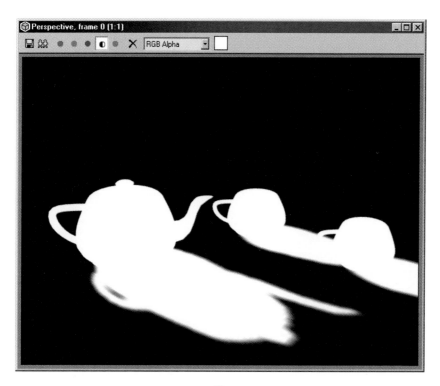

B

Figure 17-13. A—The matte object from Figure 17-11 creates an alpha channel (the white box at the bottom). B—The matte object from Figure 17-11 is set up so it does not create an alpha channel. Notice how the shadows do create an alpha channel.

Exercise

Exercise 17-5

1) Reset 3ds max and draw the objects shown below. Use your own dimensions.
2) Illuminate the scene as necessary. Set up one spotlight to cast shadows, as shown below. Make sure the shadows are strong.
3) Set the environment background to the bitmap kopipi.jpg found in the 3ds max \Maps\Backgrounds folder.
4) Add a camera. Change the Perspective viewport to the Camera viewport. Adjust the view as necessary.
5) Render the Camera viewport to a file named ex17-05a.jpg in the folder of your choice.
6) Open the **Material Editor** and select an unused material sample slot.
7) Change the material type to matte/shadow. Set up the material to receive shadows. Apply the matte material to the "ground" object beneath the boat.
8) Render the Camera viewport to a file named ex17-05b.jpg in the folder of your choice. Notice how the shadows appear on the background.
9) Save the scene as ex17-05.max in the folder of your choice.

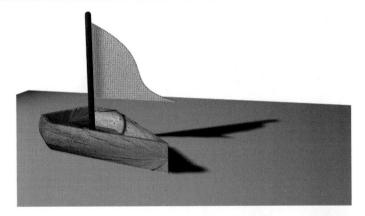

Morpher

The *morpher material* type is used with the morpher modifier. It allows you to morph materials as an object is being morphed. There are 100 channels in the morpher material type. These are mapped directly to the 100 channels in the morpher modifier. Once a morpher material is applied to an object with a morpher modifier, the modifier is used to control the morphing of the material. This material type can be used to animate skin tones or seasonal leaf changes. The morpher material type is not covered in this book.

Multi/Sub-Object

The *multi/sub-object material* type is used in conjunction with the mesh select and material modifiers. The mesh select modifier is discussed in Chapter 8. The material modifier is discussed later in this chapter. A multi/sub-object material allows you to assign up to 1000 distinctly different materials to a single object. However, in practice you will probably never use more than five or ten sub-materials. See Figure 17-14.

Once the material is set to the multi/sub-object type, the **Multi/Sub-Object Basic Parameters** rollout is displayed. See Figure 17-15. By default, the material is set to have 10 sub-materials. This is indicated by the value to the left of the **Set Number** button and by the 10 "material buttons." To change this number, pick the **Set Number** button. The **Set Number of Materials** dialog box is opened. See Figure 17-16. Enter the number of sub-materials you want to use in the **Number of Materials:** spinner and pick the **OK** button. You can always change this number later if needed.

Set Number

Figure 17-14. The sphere in the foreground has a multi/sub-object material applied, which is created from the materials shown on the spheres in the background.

Figure 17-15. The
**Multi/Sub-Object Basic
Parameters** rollout is
used to define a
multi/sub-object
material.

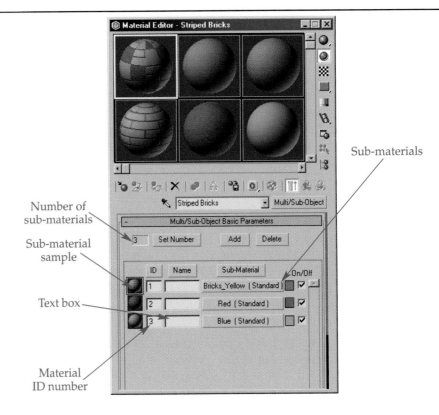

Sub-materials

Number of
sub-materials

Sub-material
sample

Text box

Material
ID number

Figure 17-16. You can
have up to 1000 sub-
materials, but there is
a practical limit.

The **Sub-Material** "material buttons" are assigned default materials.
The labels on the buttons indicate which materials are assigned. Picking
a button allows you to define a different material. You can also assign a
new diffuse color by picking the color swatch to the right of the button.
This opens the **Color Selector** dialog box. Finally, you can drag and drop
a material sample onto the material button.

The check boxes to the right of the color swatches are used to turn
the sub-materials on and off. When checked, the sub-material is on. This
cannot be animated.

To the left of the "material buttons" are the **Name** text boxes. You can
enter custom names in these text boxes. This does not rename the sub-
material. To rename a sub-material, you must navigate the material tree
to that material level and rename it there.

At the left of the **Name** text boxes are the **ID** text boxes. These are the
material ID numbers used by the material modifier. To change a sub-
material's ID, type a new number in the text box and press [Enter]. It is
important to use the material ID number to your advantage to be effective using the material modifier.

On the far left are small rendered samples of the sub-materials. These
are used to provide a quick view of the sub-material. There are no
settings associated with the samples.

You can add more sub-materials to the definition. First, you can simply increase the number of sub-materials using the **Set Number** button. Second, you can pick the **Add** button. Doing so adds a single additional sub-material at the bottom of the list.

To delete a sub-material from the definition, first highlight the sub-material sample. A white box appears around the sample. Then, pick the **Delete** button. The sub-material is removed from the definition.

You can sort the sub-material list by ID, custom name, or material name. To sort by material ID, pick the **ID** button. To sort by the custom names you entered, pick the **Name** button. To sort by the name assigned to the sub-material, pick the **Sub-Material** button.

Once all the sub-materials are defined, apply the material to objects before using the material modifier. If you try to use the material modifier and then define a multi/sub-object material for the object, you will get unwanted results.

If the object is an editable mesh, a multi/sub-object material can be created by first making sub-object selections. You can also select faces using the edit mesh modifier. Then, drag materials from the **Material Editor** onto the selections. The multi/sub-object material is compiled as you drop more materials onto the object. To make changes to the material at a later time, get the material from the scene. This method creates multi/sub-object materials as instances of the original materials.

Exercise 17-6

1) Reset 3ds max and open the **Material Editor**.
2) Select the first material sample slot.
3) Name the material Tri Sub. Change the material type to multi/sub-object. When prompted, discard the old material.
4) Set the number of "sub" materials to 3.
5) Pick the first sub-material button. Define a bright yellow color. Name the material at this level Yellow.
6) Return to the multi/sub-object material level.
7) Pick the second sub-material button. Define a bright orange color. Name the material at this level Orange.
8) Return to the multi/sub-object material level.
9) Pick the third sub-material button. Define a deep red color. Name the material at this level Red.
10) Close the **Material Editor**. Save the scene as ex17-06.max in the folder of your choice. This material is used later in Exercise 17-10.

Raytrace

The *raytrace material* type is a very complex material. It is used to produce very realistic, raytraced images. Raytracing follows the path of light rays as they move through a scene, reflecting off objects as they go. A shiny, raytraced material reflects other objects in the scene. See Figure 17-17.

There are many controls for a raytraced material. Once a material is set to the raytrace type, the **Raytrace Basic Parameters, Extended Parameters, Raytracer Controls, Maps,** and **Dynamics Properties** rollouts are displayed. The **Raytrace Basic Parameters** and **Raytracer Controls** rollouts are discussed here. The **Extended Parameters** and **Dynamics Properties** rollouts are discussed later in this chapter. The options in the **Maps** rollout are covered in Chapter 18. Most of the time, the options in the **Raytrace Basic Parameters** rollout are the only settings you will need to change. The other rollouts provide more advanced features and settings.

Raytrace Basic Parameters Rollout

The **Raytrace Basic Parameters** rollout appears similar to the **Basic Parameters** rollout for a standard material type. See Figure 17-18. It is used to control the object color and shading, reflectivity, and refractivity, and to apply environment or bump maps.

Help Cel

Raytracing uses a lot of computer resources. When options are used, especially supersampling, even the fastest of computers can slow to a crawl. Use raytracing when needed, but do not use it when unneeded.

Figure 17-17. The sphere on the left has a standard material applied to it. The sphere on the right has a material applied to it with the same color definitions, but it is a raytrace material.

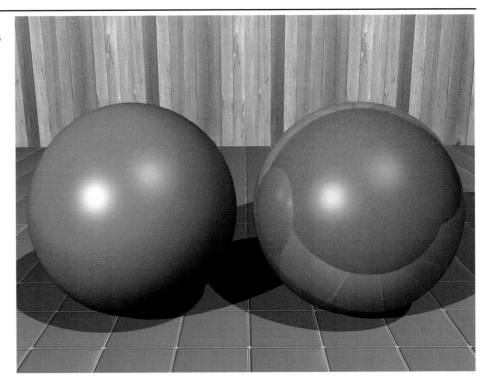

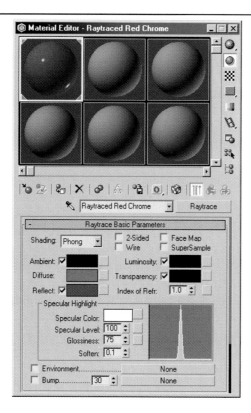

Figure 17-18. The **Raytrace Basic Parameters** rollout is used to define the basic color components of a raytrace material.

Shading

At the top of the rollout, you can set the shading type. Not all of the standard shading types are available with raytraced materials. You can select from Phong, Blinn, Metal, and Constant. *Constant shading* produces an effect similar to that of a standard material with Phong shading and the **Faceted** option on.

Next to the **Shading:** drop-down list are check boxes for **2-Sided**, **Wire**, **Face Map**, and **SuperSample**. The first three options work in the same manner as those for the standard material type, as discussed in Chapter 13. Checking the **SuperSample** check box applies supersampling to the rendered object. The standard material type has a separate rollout, the **SuperSampling** rollout, to control this option. Refer to Chapter 13 for a discussion on supersampling.

Color Components

There are five color swatches in the rollout to control the material's color components. Colors are set in a manner similar to setting color for the standard material type. You can also assign maps by picking the small button next to a color swatch to open the **Material/Map Browser**. However, even though the color components have names similar to those for the standard material type, they perform different functions, as described below.

The **Ambient:** color setting controls how much ambient light is absorbed by the material. This is very different from the ambient component of a standard material. The darker the color, the more ambient light is absorbed. On the other side of the coin, the lighter the color, the more ambient light is reflected. When the check box next to **Ambient:** is on, the color swatch controls absorption. When unchecked, the color swatch is replaced with a spinner. The value in the spinner is a greyscale percentage, where 100 is pure white.

The **Diffuse:** color setting controls the color of the object, minus its specular highlight. Set the color by picking the color swatch and selecting a new color in the color selector. A map can be assigned using the **Material/Map Browser** by picking the small button next to the color swatch. This function is the same as that for the standard material type. However, when reflection is 100%, the diffuse color cannot be seen on the object.

The **Reflect:** color setting acts as a filter. If a color other than black, white, or grey is set in the color swatch, reflections are tinted with that color. See Figure 17-19. Shades of grey also determine how reflective the object is. If the color swatch is black, the object does not reflect. If the color swatch is white, the object reflects everything and becomes nearly invisible. If the check box is unchecked, the color swatch is replaced with a spinner. The value in the spinner is a greyscale percentage, where 100 is pure white. You can also assign a reflection map using the **Material/Map Browser** by picking the small button next to the color swatch. This is the same reflection map that can be assigned in the **Maps** rollout.

The **Luminosity:** color component is similar to self-illumination with the standard material type. However, it is not tied to the diffuse color. To change the color, pick the color swatch to open the color selector. If the check box is unchecked, the color swatch is replaced with a spinner. The label changes from **Luminosity:** to **Self-Illum:**. The value in the spinner is a greyscale percentage, where 100 is pure white. A luminosity map can also be assigned using the **Material/Map Browser** by picking the small button next to the color swatch. This is the same luminosity map that can be assigned in the **Maps** rollout.

Figure 17-19. The raytrace materials on these two cups are the same with one exception. The material applied to the cup on the right has a green tint added to its reflections.

Figure 17-20. A green **Transparency:** color is applied to the material shown on the cup on the left to create the material shown on the cup on the right.

The **Transparency:** color component sets how opaque the object is. It also acts as a filter to tint light as it passes through the object. See Figure 17-20. Black creates a completely opaque material. White creates a completely transparent material. To change the color, pick the color swatch to open the color selector. If the check box is unchecked, the color swatch is replaced with a spinner. The value in the spinner is a greyscale percentage, where 100 is pure white. A transparency map can also be assigned using the **Material/Map Browser** by picking the small button next to the color swatch. This is the same transparency map that can be assigned in the **Maps** rollout.

Refraction

The **Index of Refr:** spinner is used to set the index of refraction for the material. An index of refraction is an indication of how much light rays are bent as they pass through a material. See Figure 17-21. A perfect vacuum has an index of refraction of 1.0. Air is very close to this with an index of refraction of 1.0003. Pure water has an index of refraction of about 1.3. Glass is typically between 1.5 and 1.7, depending on the type. The maximum value is 10, but values higher than 2.5 or 3.0 can really only be used for fantasy or SciFi applications. A refraction map, or IOR map, can be specified by picking the small button next to the spinner or by using the **Maps** rollout.

Specular Highlight

The **Specular Highlight** area controls the color and shape of the specular highlight. As changes are made in this area, the graph at the right reflects the settings.

The **Specular Color:** swatch is the color of specular highlights. You can change this color in the color selector by picking the color swatch. You can assign a specular map by picking the small button next to the color swatch or by using the **Maps** rollout.

Figure 17-21. Index of refraction is a measure of how much light bends as it travels through an object. The sphere on the left has a low IOR. Therefore, the cylinder behind it is not very distorted as seen through the sphere. However, the object on the right has a high IOR. Therefore, the cylinder appears very distorted.

The **Specular Level:** spinner sets the intensity of the specular highlight. This value can be set well over 1,000,000. However, there is a practical upper limit. You can specify a specular level map by picking the small button next to the spinner or by using the **Maps** rollout.

The **Glossiness:** spinner controls the size of the specular highlight. The higher the value, the smaller and more compact the highlight. The maximum value is 200. A glossiness map can be specified by picking the small button next to the spinner or by using the **Maps** rollout.

The **Soften:** spinner is used to soften the edges of the specular highlight. A very low value produces a very sharp edge. A high value produces a soft edge. The maximum value is 10. However, a value this high often eliminates all highlights.

Environment and Bump

The **Environment** setting is used to override the environment map. The check box turns this effect on and off. The label on the button is the name of the specified map. To change or set the overriding environment map, pick the button. Then, select a map in the **Material/Map Browser**. This can also be done in the **Maps** rollout. If an overriding map is not specified or is turned off, reflection and refraction use the overall environment map specified in the **Environment** dialog box.

A bump map can be applied using the **Bump** settings in the **Raytrace Basic Parameters** rollout. The check box is used to turn bump mapping on and off. The spinner is used to set the amount, or depth, of the bumps. To select a bump map, pick the button next to the **Bump** label. Then, select a map in the **Material/Map Browser**. The bump map option in the **Maps** rollout can also be used to assign the map. This bump mapping works just the same as that for the standard material type. Bump mapping is discussed in Chapter 18.

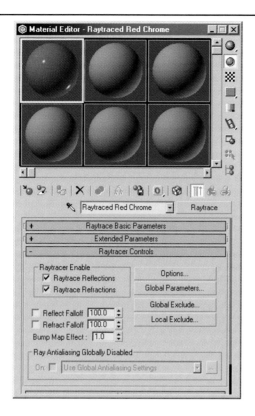

Figure 17-22. The **Raytracer Controls** rollout is used to fine-tune the raytrace engine.

Raytracer Controls Rollout

The options in the **Raytracer Controls** rollout specify how the raytrace engine works. See Figure 17-22. The **Raytracer Enable** area is used to turn raytraced reflections and refractions on or off. By default, both the **Raytrace Reflections** and **Raytrace Refractions** check boxes are on (checked).

The **Reflect Falloff** and **Refract Falloff** spinners are used to set falloff for reflections and refraction. When the check box is checked, the value in the spinner is used to calculate falloff. The checked/unchecked status of the check boxes cannot be animated. However, the spinners can be animated.

The **Bump Map Effect:** spinner is used to scale the bump map value in the **Raytrace Basic Parameters** rollout. The value is multiplied by the **Bump Map Effect:** spinner value.

Picking the **Options...** button displays the **Raytracer Options** dialog box. See Figure 17-23. This dialog box allows you to turn a number of options, including antialiasing, on or off. This can be done globally for all raytrace materials or locally for just the current raytrace material. All options, except antialiasing, are on by default.

Picking the **Global Parameters...** button displays the **Global Raytracer Settings** dialog box. See Figure 17-24. This dialog box is used to control ray depth and global antialiasing, and to manually set rendering acceleration.

Picking the **Global Exclude...** button displays the global **Exclude/Include** dialog box. This is similar to the dialog box used to exclude objects from lighting. See Figure 17-25. This dialog box allows you to pick objects in the scene to exclude from raytracing. For example, if you have two spheres and a box in the scene, but you only want one sphere to reflect on the box, you need to exclude the other sphere. Any object excluded globally is excluded from *all* raytrace materials in the scene, not just the current material.

Figure 17-23. The
Raytracer Options
dialog box is used to
make settings for a
raytraced material.

Figure 17-24. Certain
raytrace parameters
can be set globally,
or for all raytrace
operations.

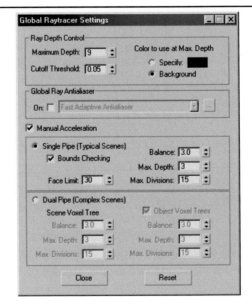

Figure 17-25. You can
select objects to
exclude from raytrace
operations.

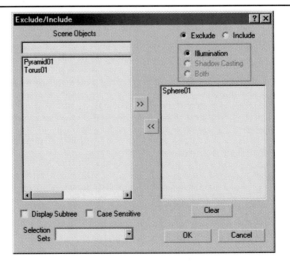

Picking the **Local Exclude...** button displays the local **Exclude/Include** dialog box. This dialog box looks and functions exactly the same as the global **Exclude/Include** dialog box. Even the title bar is the same. However, any object excluded using this dialog box is only excluded from the *current* raytrace material.

> **Local Exclude...**
>
> Local Exclude...

The **Raytraced Reflection and Refraction Antialiaser** area is disabled unless global antialiasing is turned on. When it is enabled, the drop-down list in this area allows you to use the global settings, or override the settings by selecting one of two other antialiasing options.

Exercise 17-7

Exercise

1) Reset 3ds max. Then, draw two spheres and two patch grids as shown below. Use your own dimensions.
2) Open the **Material Editor**. Select an unused material sample slot and get the material Concrete_Tiles from the default 3ds max material library.
3) Select an unused material sample slot and get the material Wood_Cedfence from the material library.
4) Apply the material Concrete_Tiles to the "floor" patch grid. Apply the material Wood_Cedfence to the "wall" patch grid.
5) Select an unused material sample slot. Change the material type to raytrace. Name the material My Ray.
6) Define diffuse and ambient colors of your choice.
7) Set the spinner value for the **Reflect:** color component to 75. This results in a dark grey color.
8) Apply the material My Ray to the two spheres.
9) Add lights as necessary to illuminate the scene.
10) Render the scene to a file named ex17-07.jpg in the folder of your choice.
11) Save the scene as ex17-07.max in the folder of your choice.

Shellac

The *shellac material* type superimposes a second material on top of a first material. The first material is called the *base material.* The second material is called the *shellac material.* The effect produced is the same as that produced by a two-material composite using additive colors. See Figure 17-26.

Once the material is set to the shellac type, the **Shellac Basic Parameters** rollout is displayed. See Figure 17-27. The **Base Material:** and

Figure 17-26. The materials on the two cups in the background are used to create the shellac material shown on the cup in the foreground.

Figure 17-27. The **Shellac Basic Parameters** rollout is used to define a shellac material.

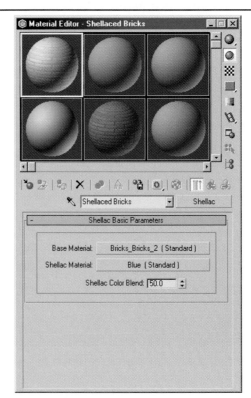

Shellac Material: buttons are labeled with the names of the materials assigned. 3ds max assigns a standard type material to each of these by default. The default base material is a bright red. The default shellac material is a bright blue. To change the material, pick the button. You are placed at that level in the material tree. Then, redefine the material. You can also drag a material sample and drop it onto the button.

The **Shellac Color Blend:** spinner is used to set the blend. At a value of 0.0, only the base material is rendered. Increasing this value increases the amount of the shellac material superimposed on the base material. The upper limit to this value is in the neighborhood of a trillion. By "shellacking" at over 100%, you can saturate the base material with the shellac material. The **Shellac Color Blend:** spinner can be animated.

Exercise 17-8

1) Reset 3ds max. Then draw three spheres of the same size.
2) Open the **Material Editor**.
3) Select an unused material sample slot. Then, get the material Wood_Shingle from the default 3ds max material library.
4) Select an unused material sample slot. Define a standard material of light color, such as light red. Name the material Light Shellac.
5) Select an unused material sample slot. Change the material type to shellac. When prompted, discard the old material. Name the material My Shellac.
6) Drag and drop the Wood_Shingle material sample onto the **Base Material:** button. Place it as an instance.
7) Drag and drop the Light Shellac material sample onto the **Shellac Material:** button. Place it as an instance.
8) Change the **Shellac Color Blend:** setting to about 50.
9) Assign the Wood_Shingle material to the left-hand sphere.
10) Assign the Light Shellac material to the middle sphere.
11) Assign the My Shellac material to the right-hand sphere.
12) Add lights as necessary to illuminate the scene.
13) Render the scene to a file named ex17-08.jpg in the folder of your choice.
14) Save the scene as ex17-08.max in the folder of your choice.

Top/Bottom

The *top/bottom material* type allows you to assign one material to the top of an object and a different material to the bottom. See Figure 17-28. The top of the object is defined by the faces with normals pointing up. For most objects, this is not just simply the top half of the object. The part of the object that is up and the part that is down is set in the material definition.

Once the material is set to the top/bottom type, the **Top/Bottom Basic Parameters** rollout is displayed. See Figure 17-29. The **Top Material:** and **Bottom Material:** buttons are labeled with the names of the materials assigned. 3ds max assigns a standard type material to each of these by default. To change the material, pick the button. You are placed at that level in the material tree. Then, redefine the material. You can also drag a material sample and drop it onto the button. Picking the **Swap** button reverses the top and bottom materials. The check box next to each material button turns the material on and off.

Swap

The **Coordinates:** area is used to define what is up and what is down. When the **World** radio button is on, the top is defined as normals pointing up the positive world Z axis. This stays the same as the object is transformed. In effect, transforming the object can change how the material is applied to the object. See Figure 17-30. When the **Local** radio button is on, the top is defined as normals pointing up the positive *local* Z axis. As the object is transformed, the material remains applied in the same way.

The value in the **Blend:** spinner is a percentage of overlap between the two sub-materials. For example, a value of 5 means that there is a 5% overlap. The value in the **Position:** spinner is a "height" percentage of the object where the material changes from one sub-material to the other. For example, a value of 25 means that the change takes place at 25% of the height, as measured from the bottom of the object. Both of these spinners can be animated.

Figure 17-28. The materials shown on the two mugs in the background are used to create the top/bottom material shown on the mug in the foreground.

Chapter Seventeen *Creating Advanced Materials* **559**

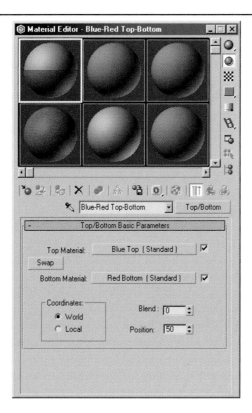

Figure 17-29. The **Top/Bottom Basic Parameters** rollout is used to define a top/bottom material.

Figure 17-30. When the coordinates of a top/bottom material are set to world, the material does not rotate as the object rotates.

Exercise

Exercise 17-9

1) Reset 3ds max and then draw a teapot of your own dimensions. Add any lights necessary to illuminate the scene.
2) Open the **Material Editor**.
3) Select the first material sample slot. Get the material Metal_Chrome from the default 3ds max material library. Make it two-sided by checking the **2-Sided** check box.
4) Select the second material sample slot. Modify the dark grey standard material as you like.
5) Select the third material sample slot. Change the material type to top/bottom. When prompted, discard the old material. Name the material Chrome Stuff.
6) Drag and drop the Metal_Chrome material sample onto the **Top Material:** button. Place it as an instance.
7) Drag and drop the dark grey material sample onto the **Bottom Material:** button. Place it as an instance.
8) Assign the Chrome Stuff material to the teapot.
9) Render the scene to a file named ex17-09.jpg in the folder of your choice.
10) Save the scene as ex17-09.max in the folder of your choice.

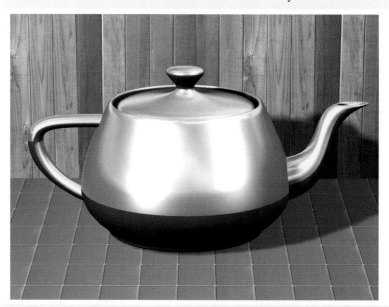

Extended Parameters

The standard and raytrace material types both have an **Extended Parameters** rollout in the **Material Editor**. This rollout provides advanced options beyond those found in the **Basic Parameters** rollout. The rollout is different for each material. The options are discussed in the following sections.

Standard Material

The **Extended Parameters** rollout for a standard material contains the **Advanced Transparency**, **Reflection Dimming**, and **Wire** areas. See Figure 17-31. The **Advanced Transparency** area is used to control the falloff of transparency. This is only a factor for transparent materials. The **Falloff:** radio buttons determine if the material is more transparent on the inside (**In**) or outside (**Out**). The **Amt:** spinner determines the transparency at the most outside or most inside point. This is the opposite of opacity—100% transparent is 0% opaque.

The **Type:** radio buttons in the **Advanced Transparency** area determine how the transparency is calculated. Activating the **Filter:** radio button adds the color in the color swatch to the color of objects behind the transparent object. See Figure 17-32. You can also assign a map in the **Material/Map Browser** by picking the small button next to the color swatch. Activating the **Subtractive** radio button subtracts the transparent material's color from objects behind it. Activating the **Additive** radio button adds the transparent material's color to objects behind it.

The **Index of Refraction:** spinner sets the index of refraction for the material. The higher the index of refraction, the more an object appears distorted when viewed through the material.

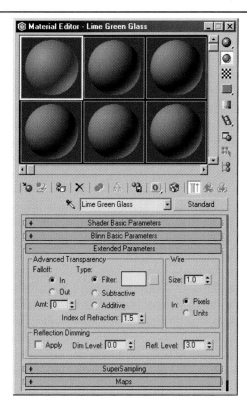

Figure 17-31. Additional settings for a standard material type can be found in the **Extended Parameters** rollout.

Figure 17-32. The mug in the foreground has the same green transparent material applied to the left-hand mug in the background, except the yellow color of the right-hand mug in the background is added as a filter color. Notice how the mug in the foreground has a more lime green color than the one in the background.

The **Wire** area is used to control the "wire size" when the material is set to **Wire** in the **Shader Basic Parameters** rollout. The value in the **Size:** spinner sets the diameter. The units for the **Size:** spinner value are set with the **In:** radio buttons. Picking the **Pixels** radio button measures the diameter in pixels. The wireframe object is always rendered with this diameter, no matter how near or far the object is from the camera. Picking the **Units** radio button measures the diameter in the current drawing units. The closer the wireframe object moves to the camera, the larger the wire appears.

The controls in the **Reflection Dimming** area are used to adjust reflections in shadows. See Figure 17-33. In real life, a reflection in a shadow is not typically as strong as one not in a shadow. The **Apply** check box is used to turn dimming on and off. The **Dim Level:** spinner sets the amount of dimming. A value of 1.0 specifies 100% dimming in the shadows. The **Refl. Level:** spinner sets the intensity of all reflections not in shadows. This value is a multiplier for the current illumination level. Increasing the reflection level compensates for dimming being applied. The default value of 3.0 works for most situations.

Raytrace Material

As is the case with a standard material, the **Extended Parameters** rollout for a raytrace material is used to control advanced transparency and wire size. See Figure 17-34. In addition, it is used to control special effects.

The options in the **Special Effects** area are used to apply additional lighting, translucency, and fluorescence to the raytraced material. The **Extra Lighting:** color swatch is additional light added to the material. The **Translucency:** color swatch is the color used to simulate a translucent effect. A translucent material emits a light and "breaks up" the image of objects behind it. The **Fluorescence:** color swatch is the color used to simulate fluorescence. A fluorescent material emits light when struck by radiation.

Figure 17-33. The object on the right has reflection dimming applied. Otherwise, the two materials are identical. Notice the difference in the reflections at the bottom of the objects.

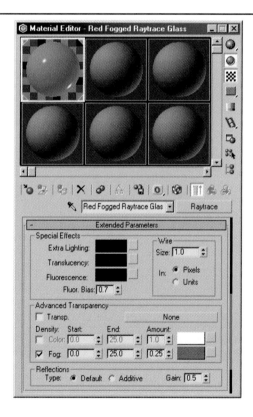

Figure 17-34. Additional settings for a raytrace material type can be found in the **Extended Parameters** rollout.

Fluorescent lights use this principle. The **Fluor. Bias:** spinner is used to adjust the effect of fluorescence. The higher the value, the greater the effect. Setting each of these color swatches to black means no effect is applied. You can select a map for any of these three effects using the **Material/Map Browser** by picking the small button next to the appropriate color swatch.

The settings in the **Wire** area work the same as those for a standard material. The value in the **Size:** spinner sets the diameter of the wire. The units for the **Size:** spinner value are set with the **In:** radio buttons. Picking the **Pixels** radio button measures the diameter in pixels. Picking the **Units** radio button measures the diameter in the current drawing units.

The **Advanced Transparency** area provides controls to fine-tune the material's transparency. The **Transp.** setting overrides the scene's environment map. This is applied to transparency only. The check box turns the effect on and off. Pick the button to select a map using the **Material/Map Browser**.

The **Density:** controls have no effect if the material is completely opaque. The **Color:** and **Fog:** check boxes must also be checked to enable the corresponding settings. The **Color:** setting tints any object inside the transparent material, such as water inside a red glass bottle. The **Fog:** setting fills the interior of the transparent material with a self-illuminate, opaque fog. This can be used to simulate frost between window panes on a cold winter day. See Figure 17-35. Both of these settings are based on thickness. The **Start:** and **End:** spinners specify the beginning and end of the effect in drawing units. The **Amount:** spinner sets the amount, or density, of the effect. The color swatches are the colors of the applied effects. You can assign maps for these effects in the **Material/Map Browser** by picking the small buttons next to the color swatches.

The **Reflections** area allows you to control how reflections are rendered. When the **Default** radio button is on, the reflection appears on top of the diffuse color. Diffuse color cannot be seen through the reflection. When the **Additive** radio button is on, the reflection is added to the diffuse color. This is similar to additive transparency for the standard material type. The value in the **Gain:** spinner determines how bright the reflection is. A value of 0 produces the brightest reflection. A value of 1.0 produces no reflection.

Figure 17-35. The raytrace material applied to the object on the left has a red fog applied to create the raytrace material for the object shown on the right.

Dynamics Properties

The standard and raytrace material types both have a **Dynamics Properties** rollout. The options in this rollout determine how objects react when they collide during an animation. These properties are used by the **Dynamics** utility. The **Dynamics Properties** rollout is the same for both material types. The default values simulate a hardened steel surface coated with Teflon®.

The value in the **Bounce Coefficient:** spinner determines how much "energy" is lost in the collision. The default value of 1.0 results in no loss of energy. A value of 0.0 results in a complete loss of energy. This means there will be no bounce.

The value in the **Static Friction:** spinner determines how easy it is to start an object sliding along a surface. The default value of 0.0 means no energy is required. A static friction value of 1.0 produces the effect of being glued.

The value in the **Sliding Friction:** spinner determines how easy an object slides over a surface. Once the static friction value has been overcome, the sliding friction value is used. The higher the value, the less likely the object will remain in motion. The default value is 0.0.

Material Modifier

The *material modifier* is used to apply different materials to different parts of a single object. It is used in conjunction with the multi/sub-object material type discussed earlier in this chapter. The multi/sub-object material must be defined and applied before applying the modifier. The material modifier is also used in conjunction with the mesh select modifier to select faces. The material modifier then assigns a material ID to the selection. This material ID corresponds to the ID in the defined multi/sub-object material.

To use the material modifier, first define a multi/sub-object material and apply it to the object. Then, use the mesh select modifier to select a series of faces. See Figure 17-36. If the object is already an editable mesh object, you do not need to apply the mesh select modifier. You can make the sub-object selection directly on the object.

With the sub-object selection still selected, open the **Modifier List** drop-down list in the **Modify** tab of the **Command Panel**. Then, select **Material** from the list in the **Surface Modifiers** area. You can also pick **Surface** from the **Modifiers** pull-down menu, and then **Material** in the cascading menu. The **Parameters** rollout is displayed. The **Material ID:** spinner is used to set a material ID. This number should correspond to the ID number of the defined sub-material you want applied. See Figure 17-37.

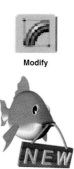

Modify

Next, apply another mesh select modifier and select a different series of faces. Apply another material modifier to that selection. Assign a different material ID. Continue in this manner until all of the sub-materials have been assigned as needed.

If you assign a material ID higher than the highest ID in the material, the modifier starts "counting over." For example, if the material has three sub-materials and you assign a material ID of 5 to the selection, the sub-material used is actually material ID 2.

Figure 17-36. The mesh select modifier is used to make sub-object selections for use with the material modifier.

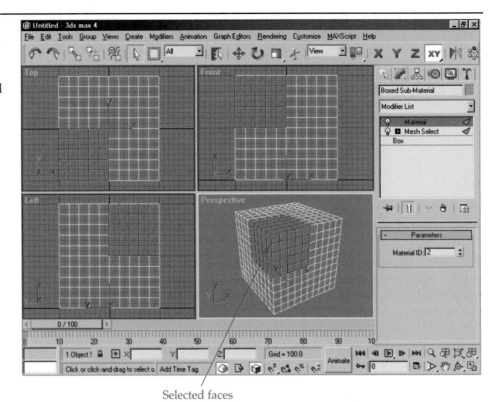

Selected faces

Figure 17-37. A multi/sub-object material is applied to the object in Figure 17-36.

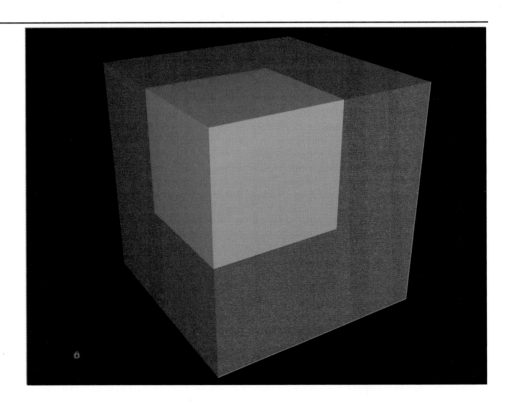

Help Cel

Some objects, by default, apply a different material ID to each "side" of the object. When using a multi/sub-object material on these objects, you may need to apply a material modifier to the entire object first to "normalize" the IDs. This applies the same material ID to all parts of the object. Then, apply additional material modifiers to sub-object selections as needed.

Exercise 17-10

Exercise

1) Open the scene ex17-06.max saved in Exercise 17-6. Save the scene as ex17-10.max in the folder of your choice.
2) Draw a chamfer cylinder. Bend it as shown below.
3) Assign the material Tri Sub to the object.
4) Apply a mesh select modifier to the object. At the face sub-object level, select the middle of the object.
5) With the sub-object selection still selected, apply a material modifier to the selection. Change the material ID parameter to 2.
6) Apply another mesh select modifier to the object. At the face sub-object level, select the top of the object.
7) Apply a material modifier to this sub-object selection. Change the material ID parameter to 3.
8) Add any lights necessary to illuminate the scene.
9) Render the scene to a file named ex17-10.jpg in the folder of your choice.
10) Save the scene.

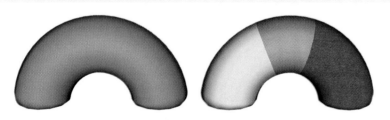

Introduction to Maps

Maps are simply images applied to a material. Maps can be applied to just about every component of a material definition, from diffuse color to opacity. A material with at least one map assigned to it is called a *mapped material.* Maps provide a quick and effective way to provide realism to any scene. In addition, maps can drastically reduce modeling and rendering times. It can take much less time to render a brick-mapped material as opposed to multiple mesh objects used to create a brick wall.

There are five general categories used by 3ds max for maps. These are 2D maps, 3D maps, compositors, color modifiers, and "other." The categories are based on how 3ds max handles the map and are listed in the **Material/Map Browser.** They are introduced here and discussed further in Chapter 18.

2D Maps

The *2D maps* are used to apply pictures and patterns to a material. The maps in this category include the bitmap, brick, checker, gradient, gradient ramp, and swirl maps. Also included with 3ds max are two filters from Adobe Systems. A combustion map designed for use with Discreet's Combustion effect is also included.

3D (Procedural) Maps

The *3D maps* are often called *procedural maps.* These maps calculate a pattern through the entire material, not just on the surface, as with 2D maps. The maps in this category include the cellular, dent, falloff, marble, noise, particle age, particle motion blur, perlin marble, planet, smoke, speckle, splat, stucco, water, and wood maps.

Compositor Maps

The maps in this category layer, or composite, other maps. This category includes the composite, mask, mix, and RGB multiply maps.

Color Modifier Maps

The color modifier maps are generally used with another type of map. They adjust the color components of the second map. This category includes the output, RGB tint, and vertex color maps.

Other Maps

The "other" category contains maps that do not fall into the other four categories. These include the flat mirror, raytrace, reflect/refract, and thin wall refraction maps. As you can see, these all deal with reflection and refraction.

UVW Map Modifier

The *UVW map modifier* is used to place and adjust mapping coordinates on an object. Mapped materials require mapping coordinates. *Mapping coordinates* tell 3ds max how to place the map on the rendered object. See Figure 17-38.

Some objects can be created with mapping coordinates automatically generated. Often, these default coordinates do not meet your needs. Other objects require that mapping coordinates be assigned to them. In addition, after some operations, such as Booleans, the default mapping coordinates may no longer be acceptable or even available. A warning appears when rendering a scene containing an object that needs UVW mapping. See Figure 17-39. UVW is used by 3ds max as another way of labeling the local XYZ axes on a given object.

To apply a UVW map modifier, select the object. Then, open the **Modifier List** drop-down list in the **Modify** tab of the **Command Panel**. Finally, select **UVW Map** in the **UV Coordinate Modifiers** area of the list. You can also select **UV Coordinates** in the **Modifiers** pull-down menu, and then **UVW Map** in the cascading menu. The **Parameters** rollout is displayed. See Figure 17-40.

Modify

Figure 17-38. The default mapping coordinates for the mug produce the pattern on the left. The UVW map modifier is used to change the mapping coordinates and create the pattern shown on the right.

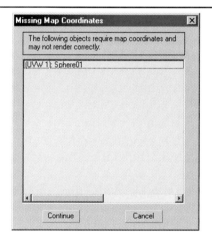

Figure 17-39. If any materials applied in the scene require mapping coordinates for the objects to which they are assigned, this dialog box appears when you attempt to render the scene.

Mapping Area

The **Mapping:** area of the UVW map modifier **Parameters** rollout is used to set the type of mapping coordinates and the tiling. There are seven different types of mapping coordinates. These are planar, cylindrical, spherical, shrink wrap, box, face, and XYZ to UVW. Each type has a radio button in the **Mapping:** area. To select the type of mapping coordinates, pick the appropriate radio button.

Figure 17-40. The **Parameters** rollout of the UVW map modifier is used to set the shape, size, and tiling for mapping coordinates.

A

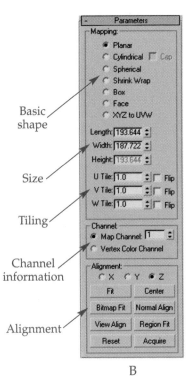

B

The *planar map* type projects the map onto the object from a flat plane. See Figure 17-41A. This type is used for objects where only one face can be seen or for very thin objects, such as paper.

The *cylindrical map* type projects the map onto the object from a cylinder. See Figure 17-41B. In effect, the map is wrapped around the object. The seam where the two edges of the map meet can often be seen. You can also choose to apply the map to the ends of the cylinder by checking the **Cap** check box.

The *spherical map* type projects the map onto the object from a sphere. See Figure 17-41C. The seams where the two edges of the map meet and at the two poles are often visible.

The *shrink wrap map* type is based on spherical coordinates. However, the corners of the map are removed, or truncated. These edges are then joined at a single pole. See Figure 17-41D. With some maps, this can hide the seams that may otherwise be visible.

The *box map* type projects six planar maps onto the object in a box shape. See Figure 17-41E. The plane most closely matching the normal of a face is projected onto that face.

The *face map* type projects a copy of the map onto every face of the object. See Figure 17-41F. This is generally used for objects with a small number of faces.

Figure 17-41. The different shapes of mapping. A—Planar. B—Cylindrical. C—Spherical. D—Shrink wrap (compare to C). E—Box. F—Face. G—The sphere is squashed without XYZ to UVW mapping. Notice the spots do not stretch. H—The sphere is squashed with XYZ to UVW mapping. Notice the spots stretch with the sphere.

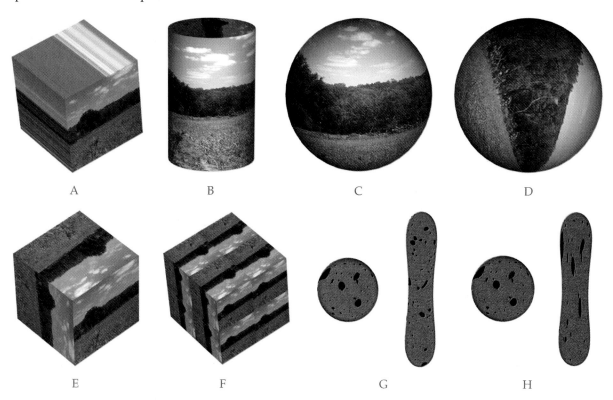

A   B   C   D

E   F   G   H

The *XYZ to UVW map* type is used with procedural-mapped materials. The XYZ coordinates of the procedural map are translated into the UVW mapping coordinates. The effect is tying the mapping coordinates to the current shape of the object. If the object is stretched, squashed, or otherwise modified, the coordinates are adjusted to match the new shape. See Figure 17-41G and Figure 17-41H.

The **Length:**, **Width:**, and **Height:** spinners in the **Mapping:** area are used to set the size of the modifier gizmo. These values are in current drawing units.

The **U Tile:**, **V Tile:**, and **W Tile:** spinners in the **Mapping:** area set the tiling for the map. *Tiling* is the number of times the map is repeated within the dimensions of the gizmo. For example, if the **U Tile:** spinner is set to 3, the map is repeated three times on the gizmo's X axis. Remember, UVW stands for XYZ. The **Flip** check box is used to reverse the direction of the map about the given axis.

Exercise

Exercise 17-11

1) Reset 3ds max and draw a cube. Subtract a smaller cube from the first to create an object similar to that shown below.
2) Open the **Material Editor**. Get the material Concrete_Stucco from the default 3ds max material library. Assign the material to the object.
3) Render the scene. Notice the **Missing Map Coordinates** dialog box appears. Pick the **Continue** button.
4) Assign a UVW map modifier to the object. Use box mapping. Render the scene again. This time, the "missing" dialog box should not appear.
5) Change the U, V, and W tiling each to 5.
6) Render the scene to a file named ex17-11.jpg in the folder of your choice.
7) Save the scene as ex17-11.max in the folder of your choice.

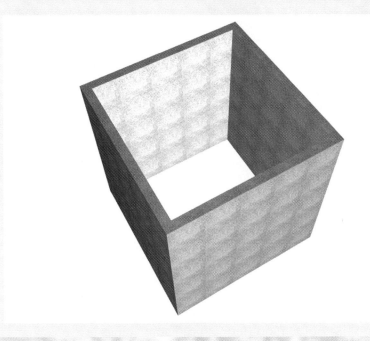

Channel Area

The **Channel:** area of the UVW map modifier **Parameters** rollout allows you to assign more than one set of mapping coordinates to an object. See Figure 17-42. Every object can have up to 99 UVW map channels. The default mapping coordinates generated by 3ds max always use map channel 1. The UVW map modifier applied to map channel 1 overrides the default coordinates.

Picking the **Map Channel:** radio button assigns the UVW map to the channel specified in the spinner. Picking the **Vertex Color Channel** radio button assigns the UVW map to the object based on vertex color. This option is used with the **Assign Vertex Colors** utility. This utility is not covered in this text.

The material assigned to the object must be mapped. In addition, the map must be assigned to the appropriate channel. This is done in the **Coordinates** rollout at the map level in the material tree. See Figure 17-43. In the **Mapping:** drop-down list, pick **Explicit Map Channel**. Then, enter the channel number in the **Map Channel:** spinner.

Figure 17-42. Using channels, you can have different mapping coordinate settings on the same object. Notice how the swirl stays the same but the checker pattern has different tiling.

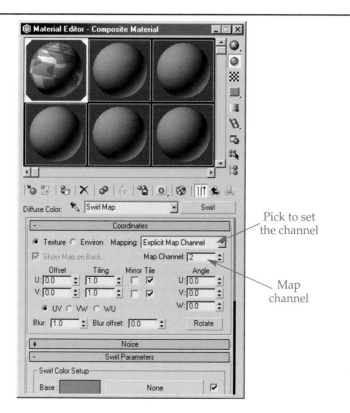

Figure 17-43. Setting a channel for a map.

Pick to set the channel

Map channel

Help Cel

You may experience problems when attempting to use a procedural map with different channels. Assign the procedural map to channel 1. Then, use a 2D map for the other channels.

Exercise

Exercise 17-12

1) Reset 3ds max and then draw the body and handle of a teapot. Use your own dimensions.
2) Open the **Material Editor**. Create a composite material of Metal_Plate and Wood_Shingle. Use Metal_Plate as the base material. Make one of the sub-materials 2-sided.
3) Assign the composite material to the teapot object.
4) Apply a UVW map modifier to the teapot object using the spherical shape. Render the scene.
5) At the diffuse map level of the Metal_Plate material, assign the **Map Channel** as 2.
6) Apply another UVW map modifier to the teapot. In the **Channel:** area of the **Parameters** rollout, assign the **Map Channel:** value as 2.
7) Change the U, V, and W tiling each to 5.
8) Render the scene again. This time save the image to a file named ex17-12.jpg in the folder of your choice.
9) Notice the Metal_Plate tiling has changed, but the Wood_Shingle tiling has remained the same. Save the scene as ex17-12.max in the folder of your choice.

Alignment Area

The **Alignment:** area of the UVW map modifier **Parameters** rollout defines how the gizmo is aligned to the object. The **X**, **Y**, and **Z** radio buttons determine which gizmo axis aligns with the object's local Z axis.

Picking the **Fit** button centers the gizmo on the object. It also makes the gizmo fit around the object's extents. The shape of the gizmo is not affected.

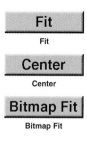

Picking the **Center** button centers the gizmo on the object. It does not change the size or shape of the gizmo.

Picking the **Bitmap Fit** button displays the **Select Image** dialog box. The image you pick in this dialog box is used to determine the size of the gizmo. When planar mapping is applied, the aspect ratio (height-to-width ratio) of the gizmo is forced to match that of the bitmap. When cylindrical mapping is applied, the height of the gizmo is forced to match the height of the bitmap.

The **Normal Align** button is used to change the origin and direction of the gizmo's normals. Pick the button to enter this mode. Then, pick a point on the object for the origin. Drag the mouse to set the direction of the gizmo normals. Pick the **Normal Align** button again to exit this mode.

Picking the **View Align** button orients the gizmo so its normals are pointing straight out of the current viewport. The size of the gizmo and location of its center remain unchanged.

Picking the **Region Fit** button allows you to pick and drag in a viewport to define the size and location of the gizmo. Pick the button again or right-click to exit this mode. Unless the view is plan to the **Alignment:** axis, you cannot drag in that viewport. In other words, if you are looking "down" the alignment axis, you can drag in the viewport. You can also drag in the Perspective, User, and camera viewport.

Picking the **Reset** button clears the current gizmo size and position. The **Fit** button is used to reset the gizmo to its "default" size and location.

Picking the **Acquire** button allows you to copy UVW mapping coordinates from another object in the scene. Pick the **Acquire** button and then select the object in the viewport. The **Acquire UVW Mapping** dialog box is displayed. See Figure 17-44. Picking the **Acquire Relative** radio button places a copy of the gizmo on top of the current object. Picking the **Acquire Absolute** radio button places a copy of the gizmo on top of the selected (second) object.

Gizmo

You can transform the UVW map modifier's gizmo at the sub-object level. This allows you to reposition the map on an object. It also allows you to adjust the scale of the mapping. If you set a mapped material to show the map in viewports, you can roughly see how the transforms affect the map. However, this should not take the place of a render to

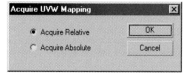

Figure 17-44. You can copy mapping coordinates from other objects in the scene.

Figure 17-45. The gizmo on the left-hand object is displayed in orange. This indicates you are *not* in sub-object mode. The yellow gizmo on the right-hand object indicates you are in sub-object mode. Note: These two gizmos are shown in the same viewport for illustration purposes.

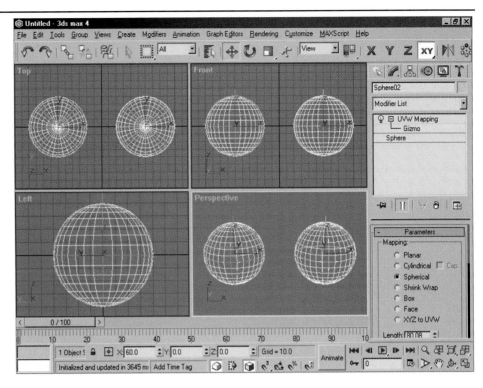

Toggle Animation Mode

check the changes. Changes made to the gizmo are reflected in ActiveShade after an initialization.

When not in sub-object mode, the gizmo is displayed in orange. See Figure 17-45. A short line indicates the top of the map. When in sub-object mode, the gizmo is displayed in yellow. Also, the right side of the map is displayed as a green line.

Animated Materials

There are several different ways to animate a material. Many material components, such as color, map percentages, and noise, can be animated. The **Specular Level:** spinner can be animated, as can the **Glossiness:** and **Soften:** spinners. In fact, most spinners in a material definition can be animated. To animate any of these features, move to the animation frame where you want to place the keyframe. Then, turn on the **Toggle Animation Mode** button and change the spinner, color, or feature in the **Material Editor**.

Another way to animate a material is to use a bitmap. An animated bitmap (AVI) can be used for any component that accepts maps, such as diffuse color. Simply apply the animated bitmap in the same way a single-frame bitmap is applied.

You can animate a transition between materials. Use the blend material type and animate the **Mix Amount:** spinner. You can also animate material ID changes. However, this produces a sharp change between materials. UVW map channel changes cannot be animated.

The number of ways to animate a material is nearly unlimited. For any given effect, there is undoubtedly more than one way to achieve the end result. This introduction should provide you with a basic understanding of how materials can be animated. The only real way to get a good grasp on the topic is to experiment with 3ds max and create animated materials.

To preview an animated material, simply pick the **Play Animation** button with the **Material Editor** open. You can also pick the **Make Preview** flyout button in the **Material Editor**. The three buttons in this flyout are **Make Preview**, **Play Preview**, and **Save Preview**. They allow you to make, play, and save a preview of an animated material. When you pick the **Make Preview** button, the **Create Material Preview** dialog box is opened. Make settings as necessary and pick the **OK** button. The **Material Editor** is temporarily hidden as the preview is generated. Unlike a scene preview, you cannot see each individual frame as it is rendered. When complete, the preview is played in Windows Media Player.

Play Animation

Make Preview

Play Preview

Save Preview

Exercise 17-13

1) Reset 3ds max and then draw a sphere. Use your own dimensions.
2) Open the **Material Editor**. Activate the first material sample slot. Name the material Groovy.
3) Define a bright blue material.
4) Move the **Time** slider to frame 25. Pick the **Toggle Animation Mode** button so it is on (red).
5) In the **Material Editor**, redefine the material color as bright red.
6) Move the **Time** slider to frame 50.
7) In the **Material Editor**, redefine the material color as bright green.
8) Move the **Time** slider to frame 75.
9) In the **Material Editor**, redefine the material color as bright yellow.
10) Move the **Time** slider to frame 100.
11) In the **Material Editor**, redefine the material color as the same bright blue originally used.
12) Pick the **Toggle Animation Mode** button to turn it off.
13) Pick the **Play Animation** button with the **Material Editor** open. Notice the preview of the material.
14) Assign the material to the sphere. Render the animation to a file named ex17-13.avi in the folder of your choice.
15) Save the file as ex17-13.max in the folder of your choice.

Exercise

Chapter Snapshot

Chapter Test

Answer the following questions on a separate sheet of paper.

1) List the compound material types.
2) When are you prompted to keep or discard the old material?
3) What is the material tree?
4) How can you move through the material tree graphically?
5) What is the purpose of the blend material type?
6) What is the purpose of the **Interactive** setting for a blend material?
7) How does the composite material type differ from the blend material type?
8) The _____ material type is a variation of a 2-sided material.
9) What is a matte object?
10) The _____ material type is used in conjunction with the material modifier.
11) If you drag and drop a material onto an editable mesh sub-object selection, which type of material is created?
12) How does raytracing work?
13) Which shading types are available with a raytraced material?
14) The _____ material type superimposes a second material on top of a first material.
15) How is the top defined for a top/bottom material?
16) Transparency falloff applies to _____ materials only.
17) What is the purpose of reflection dimming?
18) What do dynamics properties control?
19) Define maps.
20) What is the purpose of the UVW map modifier?
21) What does UVW stand for?
22) List the seven types of mapping coordinates.
23) What is the purpose of the **Channel:** area of the UVW map modifier's **Parameters** rollout?
24) How can you animate a material by only applying a bitmap?
25) Transforming a UVW map gizmo at the sub-object level allows you to _____.

Modeling Problems

Follow the directions in each problem to create and apply the materials needed. When necessary, draw the objects shown using your own dimensions. Add lights and cameras as needed. When finished, save each scene as p17-xx.max in the folder of your choice.

Bug **1**

Open p05-06.max from Chapter 5. Save the scene as p17-01.max in the folder of your choice. Define a shiny brown material for the body. Define a transparent yellow material for the wings. Define a shiny, transparent green material for the eyes. Adjust pivot points and create a hierarchy. Animate the wings flapping and the bug moving around the screen. Render the animation to a file named p17-01.avi in the folder of your choice.

Ice Cream Parlor **2**

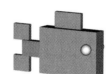

Open p06-10.max from Chapter 6. Save the scene as p17-02.max in the folder of your choice. Create a composite material based on Wood_Cedfence and a bright red material. Apply this material to the table. Apply a fabric material to the seats. Create a shiny material of your choice of color for the twisted columns. Apply Concrete_Tiles to the floor. Render the scene to a file named p17-02.jpg in the folder of your choice.

Snork 2000 Security System **3**

Open p07-05.max from Chapter 7. Save the scene as p17-03.max in the folder of your choice. Define a composite material based on Fabric_Tan_Carpet and a bright-colored material of your own definition. Apply this to the head, body, and feet. Create a transparent black material for the eyes. Adjust pivot points and create a hierarchy. Animate the head turning one way and then the other. Also animate the Snork raising up on its hind legs and returning to a normal position. Render the animation to a file named p17-03.avi in the folder of your choice.

Desktop Lamp **4**

Open p10-03.max from Chapter 10. Save the scene as p17-04.max in the folder of your choice. Define a composite material based on Metal_Chrome and a bright material of your own definition. Apply this material to the base and lamp head. Define a blend material based on Fabric_Tan_Carpet and a bright material of your own definition. Apply this material to the arms of the lamp. Render the scene to a file named p17-04.jpg in the folder of your choice.

5 Ferris Wheel

Open p14-06.max from Chapter 14. Save the scene as p17-05.max in the folder of your choice. Define a top/bottom material based on two bright materials of your own definition. Apply this material to the gondolas. Apply and adjust a UVW map modifier as needed. Define a bright, shiny transparent material using a color of your own choice. Apply this material to the spokes of the Ferris wheel. Add colored lights along each spoke. Link the lights to the spokes. Animate the wheel through several rotations (this should be done in Problem 14-6). Render the animation to a file named p17-05.avi in the folder of your choice.

6 Robot Biped

Open p12-10.max from Chapter 12. Save the scene as p17-06.max in the folder of your choice. Define a top/bottom material based on a bright red and a black material. Assign this material to the head, shoulders, elbows, and knees. Define a composite material based on Fabric_Tan_Carpet and a bright material of your own definition. Apply this material to the torso, arms, and legs. Define a blend material based on Metal_Chrome and Fabric_Tan_Carpet. Apply this material to the hands and feet. Apply and adjust UVW map modifiers as needed. Render the scene to a file named p17-06.jpg in the folder of your choice.

7 Holiday Tree

Open p15-01.max from Chapter 15. Save the scene as p17-07.max in the folder of your choice. Define a composite material based on the green material used for the tree and Ground_Grass. Apply this material to the tree. Define three shellac materials using a base material of Metal_Chrome. Each shellac material should have a bright, shiny material of your choice used as the shellac. Apply these to the ornaments. Render the scene to a file named p17-07.jpg in the folder of your choice.

8 Double Hung Window

Open p16-01.max from Chapter 16. Save the scene as p17-08.max in the folder of your choice. Define a composite material based on Wood_Cedfence and a white material of your own definition. Apply this material to the outer frame. Apply the material Wood_Oak to the inner frame. Define a composite material based on the glass material defined in Problem 16-1 and Metal_Chrome. The value for the chrome should be very low. Apply this material to the glass. Render the scene to a file named p17-08.jpg in the folder of your choice.

Tree Shadows **9**

Draw a tree similar to the one shown below. Define a composite material based on Wood_Bark and a dark brown material of your own definition. Apply this material to the trunk. Define a composite material based on Ground_Grass and a green and white top/bottom material of your own definition. Apply this to the branches. Set up the environment background as Magma-Snowscape2.jpg in the 3ds max \images folder. Draw a quad patch behind the three. Apply a matte/shadow material to it. Add shadow-casting lights to the scene. Render the scene to a file named p17-09.jpg in the folder of your choice.

Toy Helicopter **10**

Open p03-09.max from Chapter 3. Save the scene as p17-10.max in the folder of your choice. Define a shiny, transparent material for the canopy. Define a matte black material for the rotor blades and legs. Define a matte yellow material for the body. Define a bright orange material for the pontoons. Adjust pivots as needed and create a hierarchy. Animate the rotation of the main and tail rotors. Also, animate movement of the entire helicopter. Render the animation to a file named p17-10.avi in the folder of your choice.

Chapter 18

Material Mapping

Objectives

After completing this chapter, you will be able to:

- Define maps.
- List the five categories of maps.
- List material components that can be mapped.
- Apply various maps to material components.

Map Types

Maps are simply images applied to a material. Maps provide a quick and effective way to provide realism to any scene. In addition, maps can drastically reduce modeling and rendering times.

As explained in Chapter 17, there are five general categories used by 3ds max for maps. These are 2D maps, 3D maps, compositors, color modifiers, and "other" maps. The categories are based on how 3ds max handles the map.

There are a total of 33 different map types within the five categories. See Figure 18-1. The types covered in this chapter are bitmap, bricks, cellular, checker, dent, flat mirror, marble, particle age, raytrace, and wood. Once you know how to create and set these types of maps, you should be able to explore the other types of maps.

The *combustion map* type is for use with Discreet's Combustion software. In order to use this map type, you must have that software properly installed. The combustion software does not come with 3ds max. The combustion map type supersedes the paint map type found in 3D Studio MAX R3.1.

Maps can be assigned to most components of a material definition. Components that can be mapped are covered later in this chapter. To assign a map to any of these components, pick the appropriate "material/map" button in the **Material Editor** to open the **Material/Map Browser**.

Shared Rollouts

There are several rollouts in the **Material Editor** common to different map types. These include the **Coordinates**, **Output**, and **Noise** rollouts. The settings in these shared rollouts are the same for different map types.

Figure 18-1. 3ds max has 33 different types of maps.

Map Type	Category	Effect
Bitmap	2D	Applies a bitmap image.
Bricks	2D	Creates a brick/mortar pattern.
Cellular	3D	Used to create patterns such as mosaics, bubbles, and pebbles.
Checker	2D	Applies a two-color checkerboard pattern.
Combustion	2D	Used with Discreet's Combustion software.
Composite	Compositor	Is made up of other materials, in the same way a composite material is made up of other materials.
Dent	3D	Applies a random, fractal pattern. Used most often as a bump map.
Falloff	3D	Assigns one of two defined colors to faces based on their normals.
Flat Mirror	Other	Applies a reflection of surrounding materials. Must be used on a flat surface.
Gradient	2D	Applies a gradient of two to three colors.
Gradient Ramp	2D	Similar to the gradient map type, but allows more than three colors to be used.
Marble	3D	Applies a marbled effect from colored veins on a background of a different color.
Mask	Compositor	Applies two maps, the first visible through the second.
Mix	Compositor	Applies a mix of two colors or maps, similar to the blend material type.
Noise	3D	Applies random noise.
Output	Color Modifier	Applies output settings to maps that do not normally have them.
Paint		No longer available in 3ds max r4, superseded by the combustion map type.
Particle Age	3D	Used with a particle system to change the particle color over its life.
Particle MBlur	3D	Used with a particle system to change the opacity of a particle's edge based on its velocity. Used to create motion blur on the particle.
Perlin Marble	3D	Applies a marbled effect using a different mathematical algorithm from the marble map type.
Planet	3D	Simulates the colors on the surface of a planet using fractals.
Raytrace	Other	Applies raytraced reflections and refractions.
Reflect/Refract	Other	Applies reflections and refractions based on the objects in the scene.
RGB Multiply	Compositor	Combines two maps by multiplying their RGB values. Typically used for bump maps.
RGB Tint	Color Modifier	Used to adjust the RGB color of an object.
Smoke	3D	Applies a fractal-based pattern of turbulence.
Speckle	3D	Applies a granite-like speckled pattern based on two colors.
Splat	3D	Applies a fractal-based pattern similar to splattered paint.
Stucco	3D	Used to create bump maps that simulate a stucco surface. Can also be used for diffuse color mapping.
Swirl	2D	Applies a swirling, vortex pattern based on two colors or maps.
Thin Wall Refraction	Other	Applies an effect similar to the refraction created by a pane of glass.
Vertex Color	Color Modifier	Renders any assigned vertex colors.
Water	3D	Applies randomly generated, circular wave centers.
Wood	3D	Applies a wood grain pattern based on two colors or maps.

NEW (Combustion)

NEW (Paint)

Coordinates

The **Coordinates** rollout is used to set mapping coordinates for the map. These are different from mapping coordinates set for the object. However, the two work hand-in-hand. There is a common **Coordinates** rollout for 2D maps and a slightly different one common to some 3D maps.

2D Maps

The options in the **Coordinates** rollout are the same for the different map types in the 2D maps category. See Figure 18-2. Picking the **Texture** radio button applies the map as a texture on the surface of an object. The **Mapping:** drop-down list specifies if the coordinates are tied to an explicit map channel, a vertex color channel, planar mapping based on world coordinates, or planar mapping based on local coordinates. When tied to an explicit map channel, the **Map Channel:** spinner is used to specify which channel. This is used with the UVW map modifier.

Picking the **Environ** radio button applies the map as an environmental map. The coordinates can be tied to a spherical, cylindrical, or shrink-wrap environment, or the screen. You can then "get" the map from the **Material Editor** when assigning an environmental background.

When planar mapping is used for a rendering, checking the **Show Map on Back** check box projects the map onto faces with normals projecting opposite the map. In shaded viewports, maps always project through regardless of this setting.

The spinners in the **Offset** column are used to move the map on a plane. The spinners in the **Tiling** column are used to set the number of times the map repeats on a plane. The plane for both of these columns is determined by the **UV**, **VW**, and **WU** radio buttons. The labels for the spinners adjust accordingly. The **Mirror** check boxes are used to mirror

Figure 18-2. Making coordinate settings for a 2D map.

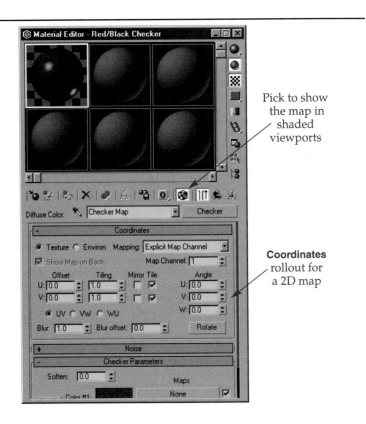

Pick to show the map in shaded viewports

Coordinates rollout for a 2D map

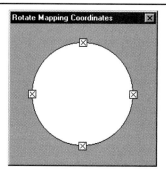

the map on the specified axis. The **Tile** check boxes are used to turn tiling on and off for the specified axis.

The **U:**, **V:**, and **W:** spinners in the **Angle** column are used to rotate the map about the specified axis. Picking the **Rotate** button displays the **Rotate Mapping Coordinates** dialog box. See Figure 18-3. This dialog box allows you to dynamically rotate the mapping coordinates in a manner similar to using **Arc Rotate** to adjust a viewport. Using the cursor, pick on the circle and rotate it. The angle settings and material sample change to reflect the rotation. It can be helpful to position the dialog box so you can see these change as you rotate the coordinates.

The **Blur:** spinner is used to blur the map. The amount of blur is based on the distance from the viewer. When applied to objects in the distance, the map is blurred more than when it is applied to objects in the foreground. The **Blur:** value can range from 0.01 to 100. The **Blur offset:** spinner is used to blur the map regardless of distance. This value can range from 0.0 to 1.0.

3D Maps

Several 3D map types, including cellular, dent, marble, and wood, have the same options in the **Coordinates** rollout. The **Source:** drop-down list is used to specify if the coordinates are tied to world coordinates, local coordinates, an explicit map channel, or a vertex color channel. See Figure 18-4. When set to an explicit map channel, the **Map Channel:** spinner is used to specify which channel. This is used with the UVW map modifier.

The **X:**, **Y:**, and **Z:** spinners are used to adjust coordinates on those axes. The spinners in the **Offset** column are used to shift the map along the specified axis. The spinners in the **Tiling** column are used to increase or decrease the number of times the map is repeated on the specified axis. The spinners in the **Angle:** column are used to rotate the map about the specified axis.

The **Blur:** spinner is used to blur the map. The amount of blur is based on the distance from the viewer. When applied to objects in the distance, the map is blurred more than when it is applied to objects in the foreground. The **Blur:** value can range from 0.01 to 100. The **Blur offset:** spinner is used to blur the map regardless of distance. This value can range from –0.1 to 1.0.

Output

The **Output** rollout is used to fine-tune the color of a 2D map. It is common to the bitmap, gradient, and gradient ramp map types. See

Figure 18-5. You can also adjust the bump effect of the map when it is used as a bump map. Bump mapping is discussed later in this chapter.

The **Invert** check box is used to create a negative image of the map. The effect is the same as looking at a negative of a photograph. The **Clamp** check box is used to limit the top end of colors to 1 when an RGB

Figure 18-4. Making coordinate settings for a 3D map.

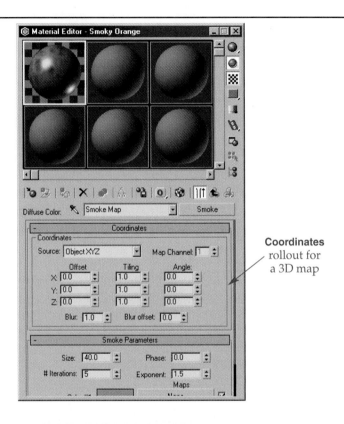

Coordinates rollout for a 3D map

Figure 18-5. The **Output** rollout is used to fine-tune the color of a 2D map.

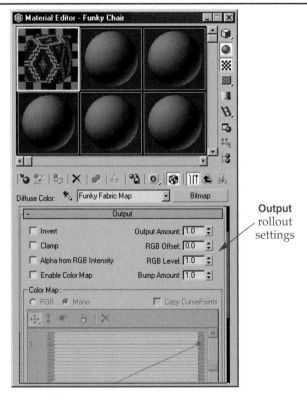

Output rollout settings

offset is used. When the **Alpha from RGB Intensity** check box is checked, an alpha channel is generated based on the RGB intensity of the map.

The **Output Amount:** spinner controls how much of the map is mixed when used as a map for a composite material. The **RGB Offset:** spinner is used to increase the RGB levels by the value in the spinner. The **RGB Level:** spinner is used to change the saturation of the map's colors. The **Bump Amount:** spinner is used to increase or decrease the bump effect of the map without affecting other components.

Checking the **Enable Color Map** check box enables the options in the **Color Map:** area. This area allows you to adjust the color tone of the map. The graph interface is similar to the interface used for loft deformation tools. Watch the material sample slot as you make changes to see the effect.

Noise

The **Noise** rollout allows you to apply noise to a 2D map and is common to each type. See Figure 18-6. Checking the **On** check box turns on the noise effect. Checking the **Animate:** check box allows you to automatically animate the noise.

The value in the **Amount:** spinner is a percentage. It represents the strength of the noise. The value in the **Levels:** spinner is the number of times the noise pattern is applied. The value in the **Size:** spinner sets the relative scale for the pattern. Low values tend to produce "white noise."

The **Phase:** spinner is used to animate the noise. This value is the relative speed of the noise during the animation. Higher values create "faster" noise.

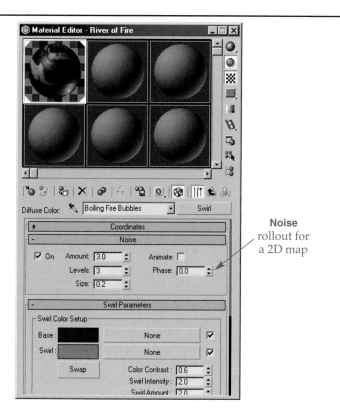

Figure 18-6. Noise can be added to a 2D map.

Noise rollout for a 2D map

Bitmap

The *bitmap map* type allows you to assign a bitmap image to the material. You can use a still image, such as a TIFF, PCX, or TGA file. You can also use an animated bitmap, such as an AVI file.

Once you select the bitmap type in the **Material/Map Browser**, the **Select Bitmap Image File** dialog box is displayed. Specify the bitmap and pick the **Open** button. You are then placed at the map level in the material tree. Several rollouts are displayed in the **Material Editor**. See Figure 18-7.

Bitmap Parameters

Reload

The **Bitmap:** button in the **Bitmap Parameters** rollout displays the complete path for the bitmap assigned. If you pick the **Reload** button, the image is reinitialized. Do this if you have made a change to the bitmap file since first applying the image.

The settings in the **Filtering** area determine how 3ds max processes the image when rendering. The **Pyramidal** option is acceptable for most instances. The **Summed Area** option produces a higher-quality reproduction, but uses more RAM.

The **Mono Channel Output:** area determines how the bitmap image is rendered to the mono channel. If the image has no alpha channel created for it, the RGB levels of the image must be used. Opacity and specular material components use a mono, or single-color, channel.

The **RGB Channel Output:** area determines how the bitmap is rendered to the RGB channel. If the image has no alpha channel created for it, the RGB levels of the image must be used. Ambient, diffuse, specular, and other components use RGB values.

Figure 18-7. The bitmap level of a material tree. Other rollouts can be seen by panning the panel.

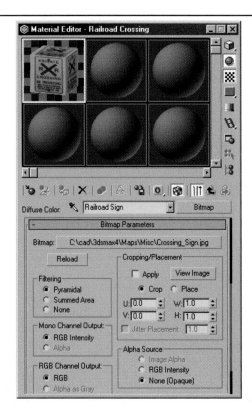

The **Alpha Source** area determines how an alpha channel is calculated for the bitmap image. The alpha channel can be used as a mask so only a portion of the bitmap image appears in the rendering. If the image does not contain an alpha channel, the RGB levels of the image are used. You can also turn on the image for alpha channel calculations.

The **Cropping/Placement** area allows you to fine-tune how the bitmap is placed as a map. The **Apply** check box must be checked for the settings in this area to be used. Picking the **View Image** button displays the image in a dialog box. See Figure 18-8.

View Image

View Image

If the **Crop** radio button is on, the settings in the **Cropping/Placement** area determine how the image is cropped. *Cropping* is like cutting off edges of the image. The scale remains unchanged, but the overall size of the object is decreased. Cropping removes a portion of the image.

If the **Place** radio button is on, the settings in the **Cropping/Placement** area determine how the image is placed. By changing the placement size, the scale of the image is changed. However, unlike cropping, the entire image remains intact.

The **U:** and **V:** spinners are used to adjust the bitmap's location. The **W:** and **H:** spinners are used to adjust the cropping or placement (scale) of the bitmap.

When the **Place** radio button is on, the **Jitter Placement:** check box and spinner are enabled. This setting allows you to specify the amount of random offset. The check box must be checked to turn on this option.

Time

The **Time** rollout is used to control the timing of animated bitmaps. The **Start Frame:** spinner sets the frame in which the animation begins to play. The value in the **Playback Rate:** spinner is a multiplier used to speed up or slow down the playback of the animation.

The **End Condition** area is used to set what happens when the entire animation has been played. If the **Loop** radio button is on, the animation plays over and over from the first frame. If the **Ping Pong** radio button is on, the animation plays forward, then in reverse, then forward. If the **Hold** radio button is on, the last frame of the animation is displayed until the entire scene animation has been rendered.

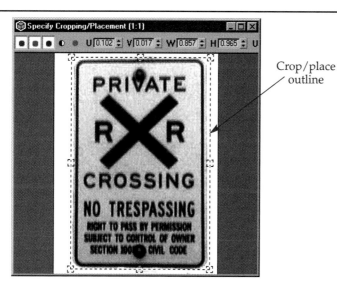

Crop/place outline

Figure 18-8. You can adjust the cropping and placement of a bitmap.

Help Cel

If you want to start the animation playback on a certain frame, you have to use the **Hold** option. The **Loop** and **Ping Pong** options will simply "wrap" the animation back to frame 0. The end of the animation is, therefore, played at the beginning of the scene animation.

Exercise

Exercise 18-1

1) Open the **Material Editor** and select an unused sample slot.
2) Set the material type to standard.
3) Set the shading type to Metal. Unlock the ambient and diffuse colors.
4) Pick the button next to the diffuse color swatch in the **Metal Basic Parameters** rollout. This opens the **Material/Map Browser** to assign a map as the diffuse color.
5) Select the bitmap map type.
6) In the **Select Bitmap Image File** dialog box, locate the file Oldmetal.jpg in the 3ds max \Maps\Metal folder.
7) Draw a sphere and a cube in any viewport. Use your own dimensions.
8) Assign the material you just defined to both objects.
9) Render the scene to a file named ex18-01.jpg in the folder of your choice.
10) Save the file as ex18-01.max in the folder of your choice.

Bricks

The *bricks map* type is used to apply a pattern of bricks and mortar. You can choose from seven preset architectural configurations or define your own. Once you select the bricks type in the **Material/Map Browser**, you are placed at the map level in the material tree. Several rollouts are displayed in the **Material Editor**. See Figure 18-9.

Standard Controls

The **Standard Controls** rollout is where you select a custom or preset configuration. The preset configurations are running bond, common Flemish bond, English bond, ½ running bond, stack bond, fine running bond, and fine stack bond. See Figure 18-10. Select the configuration you want to use from the drop-down list. If you want to define your own configuration, select **Custom Bricks** from the list.

Advanced Controls

The **Advanced Controls** rollout allows you to fine-tune the appearance of all configurations. You can change the brick and mortar color. You can also change color variance and assign texture maps. At the top of the rollout is the **Show Texture Swatches** check box. When checked, texture assigned as a map for the bricks or mortar is displayed in the color swatches.

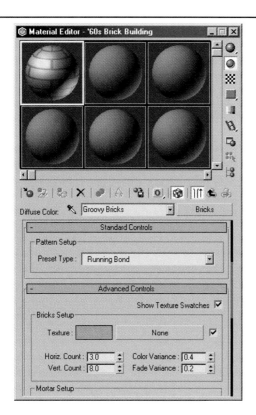

Figure 18-9. The bricks map level of a material tree. Other rollouts can be seen by panning the panel.

Figure 18-10. Examples of brick patterns. The first seven from the top left are presets. In order, they are running bond, common Flemish bond, English bond, ½ running bond, stack bond, fine running bond, and fine stack bond. The last two are custom brick definitions.

The **Bricks Setup** area is used to define the bricks portion of the map. You can change the color by picking the color swatch to open the color selector. You can also assign a map by picking the button to open the **Material/Map Browser**. If a map is specified, either the **Texture:** or **Show Texture Swatches** check box must be unchecked for you to pick on the color swatch.

The **Horiz. Count:** and **Vert. Count:** spinners in the **Bricks Setup** area determine how many bricks there are in the horizontal and vertical directions. The **Color Variance:** spinner determines how much variance in color there is between bricks. The **Fade Variance:** spinner determines how much variance there is in brick fading or weathering.

The **Mortar Setup** area is used to define the mortar portion of the map. The mortar is the "lines" between the bricks. Pick the color swatch to change the color in the color selector. Pick the button to assign a map in the **Material/Map Browser**. If a map is specified, either the **Texture:** or **Show Texture Swatches** check box must be unchecked for you to pick on the color swatch.

The **Horizontal Gap:** and **Vertical Gap:** spinners set the horizontal and vertical widths of the mortar. The values are relative to the size of the mapping coordinates. By default, these values are locked together. To enter different horizontal and vertical values, pick the **Lock** button to turn it off.

Lock

Unlock

The **% Holes:** spinner is used to add missing bricks to the pattern. This value defines the percentage of bricks that are missing. Mortar is displayed in the hole. The **Rough:** spinner sets how rough the edges are between the mortar and brick when rendered.

The **Random Seed:** spinner in the **Miscellaneous** area contains a value related to the randomly generated color pattern. If you have more than one object with the same brick pattern, use the same seed to create similar bricks. To create bricks that look completely different, as from a different manufactured batch, use a different seed. If you pick the **Swap Texture Entries** button, the texture settings for bricks and mortar are flip-flopped.

Swap Texture Entries

Custom Bricks

To create a custom brick pattern, first pick **Custom Bricks** from the **Preset Type:** drop-down list in the **Standard Controls** rollout. If you want to use one of the preset patterns as a starting point, first select that name in the list and *then* pick **Custom Bricks**. In the **Advanced Controls** rollout, define the color, texture mapping, and other settings.

The **Stacking Layout** area of the **Advanced Controls** rollout is used to define horizontal shifting of color in a row. Rows are shifted the number of units specified in the **Line Shift:** spinner. Rows are randomly shifted the number of units specified in the **Random Shift:** spinner. The "row shift" is the shift in color, not a shift in the mortar/brick pattern.

The **Row and Column Editing** area of the **Advanced Controls** rollout is used to fine-tune the mortar/brick pattern. The **Row Modify** settings determine the rows that are changed. For example, if the **Per Row:** spinner is set to 3, every third row is scaled by the amount in the **Change:** spinner. The **Column Modify** settings determine the columns that are changed. This works with the **Row Modify** settings. See Figure 18-11. The check boxes turn the "change" effects on and off.

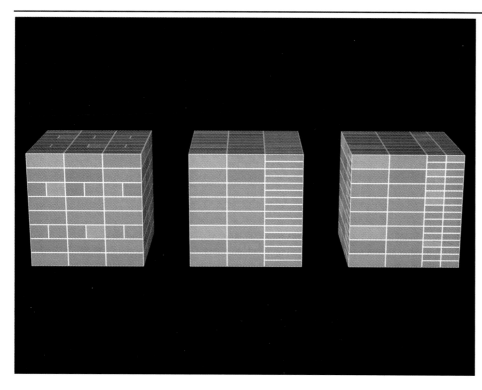

Figure 18-11. You can create custom brick patterns. The three patterns shown here have basically the same definitions. However, the row and column editing differs. On the left, 3 per row with a change of 0.5. In the middle, 3 per column with a change of 0.5. On the right, 1 per row with a change of 0.5 and 3 per column with a change of 0.5.

Exercise 18-2

1) Open the **Material Editor** and select an unused material sample slot.
2) Set the material type to standard and the shading type to Blinn.
3) Pick the button next to the diffuse color swatch in the **Blinn Basic Parameters** rollout. This opens the **Material/Map Browser** to assign a map to the diffuse color.
4) Assign a brick map.
5) At the map level, specify the bricks as fine running bond.
6) Select another unused material sample.
7) Assign a brick map as a diffuse color map.
8) At the map level, define a custom brick pattern of your choice.
9) Draw two boxes in any viewport using your own dimensions.
10) Assign the two materials you just defined to the boxes.
11) Render the scene to a file named ex18-02.jpg in the folder of your choice.
12) Save the file as ex18-02.max in the folder of your choice.

Exercise

Cellular

The *cellular map* type is a 3D procedural map used to simulate pebbles, bubbles, sand, mosaics, and many other surfaces made up of randomly sized patterns. See Figure 18-12. A cellular map is made up of cells and two-colored divisions between cells.

Once you select the cellular type in the **Material/Map Browser**, you are placed at the map level in the material tree. The **Coordinates, Cellular Parameters**, and **Output** rollouts are displayed in the **Material Editor**. See Figure 18-13. The **Coordinates** and **Output** rollouts are discussed earlier in this chapter.

The **Cell Color:** area of the **Cellular Parameters** rollout is used to set the color for the cell portion of the map. You can set a color by picking the color swatch. You can also assign a texture map using the **Material/Map Browser** by picking the button. The check box next to the button must be checked to apply the texture map. The **Variation:** spinner sets the percentage of cells that have randomly varied colors. By default, this is set to 0%.

The **Division Colors:** area is used to set the color for the divisions between cells. The division color is a mix between two colors and/or maps. The top color in the rollout appears directly next to the cells. The bottom color appears "in the middle" between cells. Set the two colors by picking the color swatches. One or both components can also have a texture map. Select the map in the **Material/Map Browser** by picking the appropriate button. The check box next to the button must be checked for the texture map to be applied.

The **Cell Characteristics:** area is used to set the size and shape of individual cells. You can choose between a base shape that is circular or chip-like. Picking the **Circular** radio button creates round cells, producing a bubble-like map. Picking the **Chips** radio button creates a pattern of

Figure 18-12. A cellular map is used for the alien skin on this model.

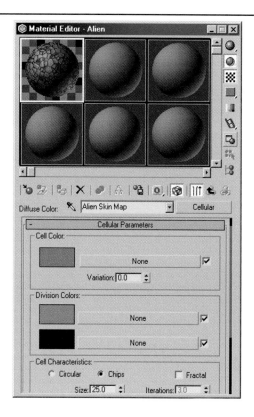

Figure 18-13. The cellular map level of a material tree. Other rollouts can be seen by panning the panel.

straight-edged cells, like a mosaic or sand pattern. Chips may also be used when creating skin.

The value in the **Size:** spinner is the relative size of all cells, or the entire map. The value in the **Spread:** spinner is the relative size of each individual cell. The **Bump Smoothing:** spinner is used to correct for aliasing that may appear when the map is used as a bump map. This value does not need to be changed unless aliasing is a problem.

You can make the cell pattern based on fractal equations by checking the **Fractal** check box. Checking this check box also enables the **Iterations:** and **Roughness:** spinners. The value in the **Iterations:** spinner is the number of times the fractal pattern is applied within the map area. The **Roughness:** spinner is used to increase or decrease the bump effect when the map is used as a bump map. When the **Adaptive** check box is checked, the number of iterations is increased if the object is close to the viewer, and decreased when farther from the view. This can help reduce rendering time.

The **Thresholds:** area is used to set the size of cells and divisions relative to the equation used to calculate the map. The value in the **Low:** spinner adjusts the size of cells. The value in the **Mid:** spinner adjusts the size of the color next to the cells, relative to the second (middle) color. The value in the **High:** spinner adjusts the size of the entire division. The default values are 0.0, 0.5, and 1.0, respectively.

Help Cel

The cellular map type can be used as a bump map, even when the **Fractal** check box is unchecked. However, you will not be able to change the **Roughness:** setting, as this spinner is disabled.

Exercise

Exercise 18-3

1) Open the **Material Editor** and select an unused material sample slot.
2) Pick the button next to the diffuse color swatch. This opens the **Material/Map Browser** to assign a map to the diffuse color.
3) Assign a cellular map.
4) At the map level, define the cell color as a dark green. Set the **Variation:** spinner to about 10 or 15.
5) Copy the cell color swatch to the first division color swatch. Darken the green just slightly.
6) Copy the cell color swatch to the second division color swatch.
7) Draw a sphere and a box in any viewport using your own dimensions.
8) Assign the material to both objects.
9) Render the scene to a file named ex18-03a.jpg in the folder of your choice.
10) In the **Material Editor**, navigate to the map level of the material if not already there. Change the cell color to a very light red.
11) Render the scene to a file named ex18-03b.jpg in the folder of your choice. How does the second rendering differ from the first?
12) Save the scene as ex18-03.max in the folder of your choice.

Checker

The *checker map* type is a 2D map. It is a checkerboard pattern based on two colors. A checker map can be used for a variety of applications, from tablecloths to chessboards. See Figure 18-14.

Once you select the checker type in the **Material/Map Browser**, you are placed at the map level in the material tree. The **Coordinates**, **Noise**, and **Checker Parameters** rollouts are displayed in the **Material Editor**. See Figure 18-15. The **Coordinates** and **Noise** rollouts are discussed earlier in this chapter.

Set the two colors for the checker pattern by picking the color swatches in the **Checker Parameters** rollout. Texture maps can also be applied using the **Material/Map Browser** by picking the **Maps** buttons. The corresponding check box must be checked to apply the map. Picking the **Swap** button flip-flops the colors or maps. The **Soften:** spinner is used to blur, or soften, the edges between the checker tiles.

Swap

Help Cel

Use a very low value in the **Soften:** spinner. Even a value as low as 1.0 can create so much blur that the checker pattern is lost.

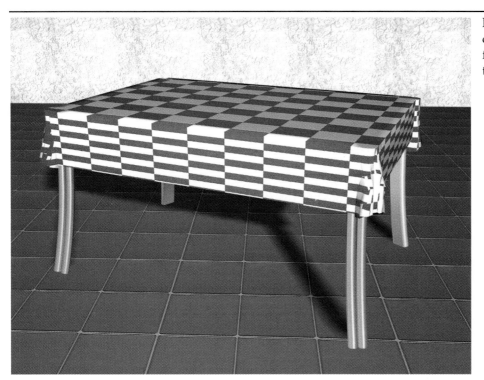

Figure 18-14. A checker map is used for the tablecloth on this table.

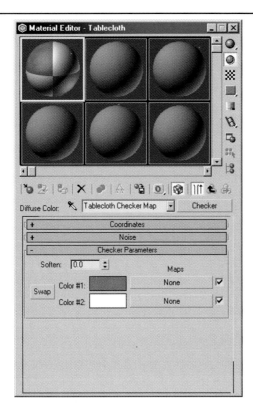

Figure 18-15. The checker map level of a material tree.

Exercise

Exercise 18-4

1) Draw the frame and playing surface of the chessboard shown below. Use four boxes to create the frame and another box to create the playing surface.
2) Using the **Material Editor**, get the material Wood_Oak from the default 3ds max material library.
3) Apply the wood material to the four boxes forming the frame. Render the scene.
4) In the **Material Editor**, select an unused material sample slot.
5) Pick the button next to the diffuse color swatch. This opens the **Material/Map Browser** to assign a map to the diffuse color.
6) Assign a checker map.
7) Apply the checkered material to the playing surface and render the scene. How does the material appear?
8) In the **Material Editor**, navigate to the map level of the checkered material, if not already there.
9) In the **Coordinates** rollout, assign tiling of 4.0 to both the **U:** and **V: Tiling** spinners. Make sure the **Tile** check boxes are also checked. As an alternative, a UVW map modifier can be used to adjust mapping coordinates.
10) Render the scene to a file named ex18-04.jpg in the folder of your choice.
11) Save the scene as ex18-04.max in the folder of your choice.

Dent

The *dent map* type is a 3D procedural map designed specifically for use as a bump map. It can be used for other map assignments, however. A dent map produces a random, fractal-based pattern. This map type is useful for "dirtying up" a scene, such as making a starship look battered by space debris or battles. See Figure 18-16.

Once you select the dent type in the **Material/Map Browser**, you are placed at the map level in the material tree. The **Coordinates** and **Dent Parameters** rollouts are displayed in the **Material Editor**. See Figure 18-17. The **Coordinates** rollout is discussed earlier in this chapter.

The value in the **Size:** spinner in the **Dent Parameters** rollout sets the relative size of each dent. The larger the dent, the fewer dents in the pattern. Increasing the value in the **Strength:** spinner increases the depth of the dents. The value in the **Iterations:** spinner determines how many times the fractal equation is applied to create the dent pattern.

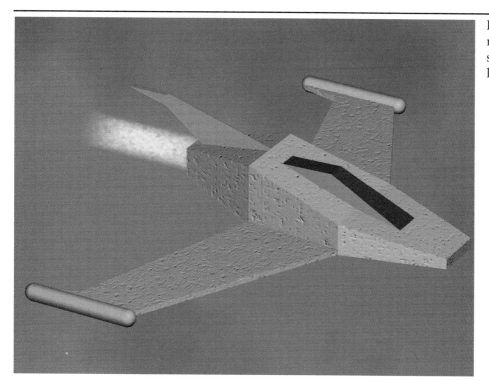

Figure 18-16. A dent map is used on this starfighter to make it look "beat up."

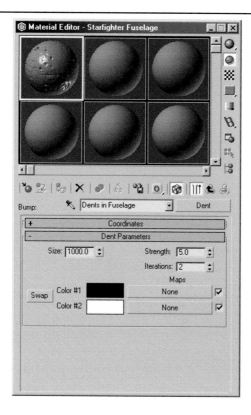

Figure 18-17. The dent map level of a material tree.

The colors in the color swatches are used to calculate the dent pattern. By default, the colors are black and white. However, any color can be used. The greyscale component of colors is used for the calculation. Therefore, if you change the colors to a dark blue and a very light red, the effect is not much different from that produced with black and white. Maps can also be specified using the **Material/Map Browser** by picking the **Maps** buttons. Picking the **Swap** button flip-flops the color/map settings.

Swap

Exercise 18-5

1) Draw two spheres in any viewport using your own dimensions.
2) In the **Material Editor**, select an unused material sample slot.
3) In the **Maps** rollout, pick the button next to the **Bump** spinner. This feature is discussed later in this chapter. Assign a dent map.
4) At the map level of the material tree, make sure the colors are the default black and white. Change the size value to 500 and the strength to 50.
5) Assign the material to one of the spheres.
6) In the **Material Editor**, select an unused material sample slot.
7) In the **Maps** rollout, assign a dent map as the bump map, as you did before.
8) At the map level of the material tree, define the colors as dark blue in place of black and light red in place of white. Change the size value to 500 and the strength to 50.
9) Assign the second material to the second sphere.
10) Render the scene to a file named ex18-05.jpg in the folder of your choice.
11) How do the two materials differ? Why?
12) Save the scene as ex18-05.max in the folder of your choice.

Flat Mirror

The *flat mirror map* type is designed specifically to be used as a reflection map on flat objects. It produces a reflection of surrounding objects in the scene on the surface of the object to which it is applied. The entire surface of the object must be flat to have an effect. See Figure 18-18. The flat mirror map type belongs to the "other" category of map types.

Once you select the reflection map as the flat mirror type in the **Material/Map Browser**, you are placed at the map level in the material tree. The **Flat Mirror Parameters** rollout is displayed in the **Material Editor**. See Figure 18-19.

The **Blur** area of the **Flat Mirror Parameters** rollout is used to blur the reflected image. This is primarily done to avoid aliasing in the rendered image. However, you can also do this to "fog up" a reflection, such as one on a steamed-up bathroom mirror. Check the **Apply Blur:** check box to blur the reflection. The value in the **Blur:** spinner determines how much the image is blurred.

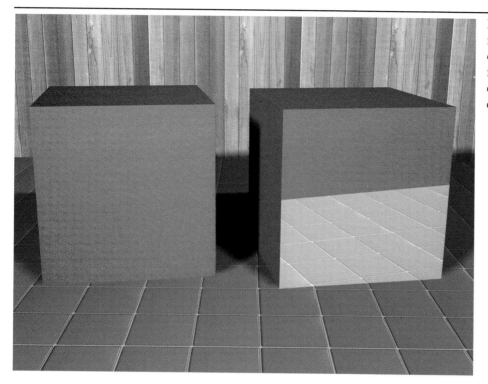

Figure 18-18. A flat mirror map is used to create reflections on a flat surface, as shown on the right-hand cube.

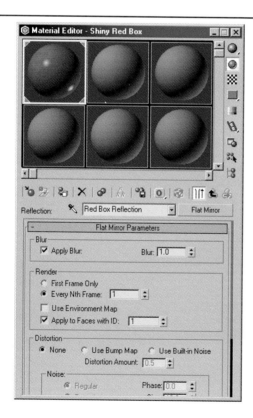

Figure 18-19. The flat mirror map level of a material tree.

The **Render** area is used to specify how the reflection is rendered. When the **First Frame Only** radio button is on, the reflection is calculated and rendered on the first frame of the animation only. If you are rendering a still image, this is acceptable. However, if you are rendering an animation, more than likely the reflection should be recalculated throughout the animation. Pick the **Every Nth Frame:** radio button. Then, enter a value in the spinner. The reflection is calculated on those frames. For example, if you enter 2 in the spinner, the reflection is recalculated every other frame.

The **Use Environment Map** check box sets whether or not the environment is reflected. When checked, the environment shows in the reflection. The **Apply to Faces with ID:** spinner and check box are used to assign the map to faces with a specific material ID. Check the check box and enter the ID number in the spinner. This can be used in conjunction with the material modifier to set material IDs. If the check box is *not* checked, the map must be applied as a multi/sub-object material.

The **Distortion** area is used to make the flat-object reflection look as though it is on an irregular object. For example, by adding distortion to a flat mirror on a flat quad patch, you can simulate reflections on water. See Figure 18-20. Picking the **None** radio button turns off distortion. Picking the **Use Bump Map** radio button enables the **Distortion Amount:** spinner. The spinner sets how much of the material's bump map is used to distort the reflection. Picking the **Use Built-in Noise** radio button allows you to set the phase, size, and levels of noise generated by 3ds max. You can also specify the type of noise generated by picking the **Regular**, **Fractal**, or **Turbulence** radio button in the **Noise:** area.

Figure 18-20.
Distortion is used on the flat mirror map assigned to the water to simulate ripples. Notice how the reflection of the boat is distorted. The water is simply a flat quad patch.

Exercise 18-6

1) Draw objects to create the medicine chest shown below. Draw the mirrored doors as quad patches. Draw a sphere in front of the chest to use for the reflection. Add lights and a camera.

2) In the **Material Editor**, select an unused material sample slot. Define a light blue standard material with Metal shading. Assign it to the frame.

3) Select another unused material sample slot. Define a bright orange standard material. Assign it to the sphere.

4) Select a third unused material sample slot. Define a light grey standard material with Blinn shading. Name the material Mirror Left.

5) Copy the Mirror Left material sample to an unused material sample slot. Name the copy Mirror Right.

6) Activate the Mirror Left material sample. In the **Maps** rollout, pick the button next to the **Reflection** spinner. This feature is discussed later in this chapter. Assign a flat mirror map.

7) Navigate to the map level of the Mirror Left material, if not already there. Make sure the **Apply Blur:** check box is checked. Then, change the **Blur:** spinner value to 35. Check the **Apply to Faces with ID:** check box and enter 1 in the spinner.

8) Activate the Mirror Right material sample. In the **Maps** rollout, pick the button next to the **Reflection** spinner. Assign a flat mirror map.

9) Navigate to the map level of the Mirror Right material, if not already there. Uncheck the **Apply Blur:** check box. Check the **Apply to Faces with ID:** check box and enter 1 in the spinner.

10) Assign the Mirror Left material to the left-hand door. Assign the Mirror Right material to the right-hand door.

11) Render the scene to a file named ex18-06.jpg in the folder of your choice. Notice how the two mirrors differ.

12) Save the file as ex18-06.max in the folder of your choice.

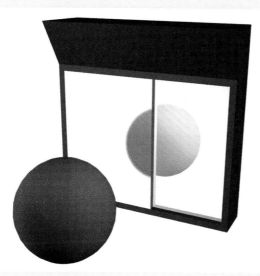

Marble

The *marble map* type is a 3D procedural map. It creates veins of three different colors based on two specified colors. The third color is automatically calculated. This map produces the effect of marble stone. See Figure 18-21. The *Perlin marble map* type is similar to this map type, but it produces a different pattern.

Once you select the marble type in the **Material/Map Browser**, you are placed at the map level in the material tree. The **Coordinates** and **Marble Parameters** rollouts are displayed in the **Material Editor**. See Figure 18-22. The **Coordinates** rollout is discussed earlier in this chapter.

Swap

The **Size:** spinner sets the relative distance between veins. The **Vein width:** spinner sets the relative width of individual veins. You can set the colors by picking the color swatches. You can also specify texture maps by picking the **Maps** buttons. The check boxes must be checked to apply the maps. Picking the **Swap** button flip-flops the color or map settings.

Figure 18-21. A marble map is used to create the marble material on this candlestick holder.

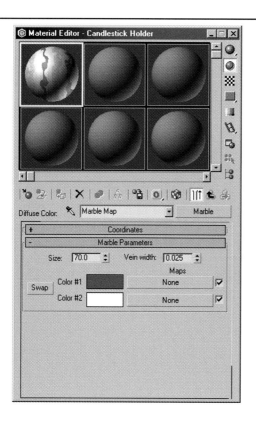

Figure 18-22. The marble map level of a material tree.

Exercise 18-7

Exercise

1) Create the simple bowl and table shown below.
2) In the **Material Editor**, select an unused material sample slot.
3) Pick the button next to the diffuse color swatch. Assign a marble map.
4) At the map level, define a marble pattern appearing similar to the one shown on the bowl.
5) Assign the marble material to the bowl.
6) Get a wood material from the default **3ds max** material library. Assign it to the table.
7) Add lights and a camera as necessary.
8) Render the scene to a file named **ex18-07.jpg** in the folder of your choice.
9) Make any necessary adjustments to the material at the map level.
10) Save the scene as **ex18-07.max** in the folder of your choice.

Particle Age

The *particle age map* type is used with particle systems. This is a 3D procedural map type that allows you to change a particle's color or map based on its age. See Figure 18-23. Particle systems are introduced in Chapter 22.

Once you select the particle age type in the **Material/Map Browser**, you are placed at the map level in the material tree. The **Particle Age Parameters** and **Output** rollouts are displayed in the **Material Editor**. See Figure 18-24. The **Output** rollout is discussed earlier in this chapter.

In the **Particle Age Parameters** rollout, you can specify three colors and/or maps for the particle, and at what age the particle transforms to the color. Set a color or choose a map for **Color #1**, **Color #2**, and **Color #3**. The check boxes must be checked to apply the maps. In the **Age #1**, **Age #2**, and **Age #3** spinners, enter age values for when the particle will be the corresponding color. These values are percentages of the particle's life.

Raytrace

The *raytrace map* type produces raytraced reflections and refractions. It belongs to the "other" category of map types and is similar to a raytraced material. See Figure 18-25. However, the raytrace map has more detailed attenuation controls. In addition, a raytrace-mapped material often renders much faster than an equivalent raytraced material.

Once you select the raytrace type in the **Material/Map Browser**, you are placed at the map level in the material tree. Several rollouts are displayed in the **Material Editor**. See Figure 18-26. These are discussed in the next sections.

Figure 18-23. A particle age map is used to change the color of particles based on their age. In this scene, the particles generated from the candlestick holder start out red, change to yellow, and end their life blue.

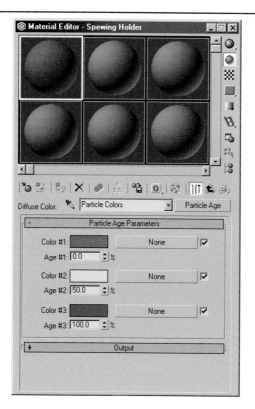

Figure 18-24. The particle age map level of a material tree.

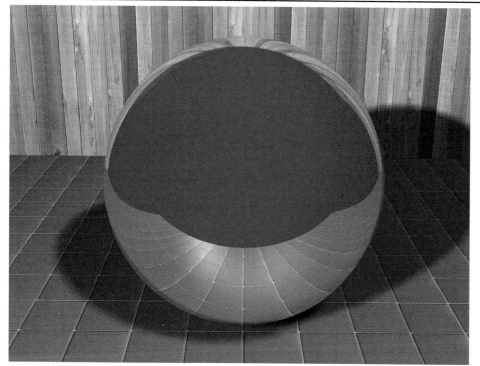

Figure 18-25. The sharp, strong reflection on this sphere is created with a raytrace map assigned as a reflection map.

Figure 18-26. The raytrace map level of a material tree. There are several rollouts.

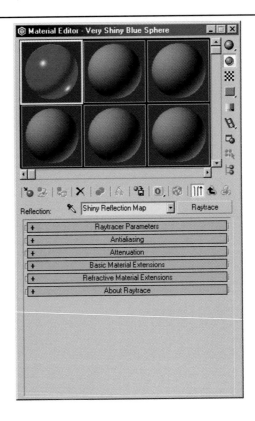

Raytracer Parameters

The **Trace Mode** area of the **Raytracer Parameters** rollout allows you to specify if reflection or refraction is calculated. See Figure 18-27. When the **Auto Detect** radio button is on, 3ds max creates a reflection when the map is assigned as a reflection map. When assigned as a refraction map, 3ds max automatically creates a refraction. If the map is assigned to any other component, such as a bump map, you must manually set which is created. Do this by picking either the **Reflection** or **Refraction** radio button.

The **Background** area allows you to specify how the background is calculated into the reflection or refraction. By default, the **Use Environment Settings** radio button is on. This calculates the current global environment into the reflection or refraction. If you pick the radio button next to the color swatch, the solid color in the swatch is used in place of the current environmental settings. If you pick the radio button next to the "map" button, the map specified using the button is calculated in place of the environmental settings.

Picking the **Options...** button opens the **Raytracer Options** dialog box. Picking the **Global Parameters...** button opens the **Global Raytracer Settings** dialog box. Picking the **Global Exclude...** button opens the global **Exclude/Include** dialog box. Picking the **Local Exclude...** button opens the local **Exclude/Include** dialog box. These are the same dialog boxes discussed in Chapter 17.

Antialiasing

The raytrace map type, by default, uses the global environmental settings for antialiasing. However, you can manually override these settings for an individual map using the **Antialiasing** rollout. See Figure 18-28.

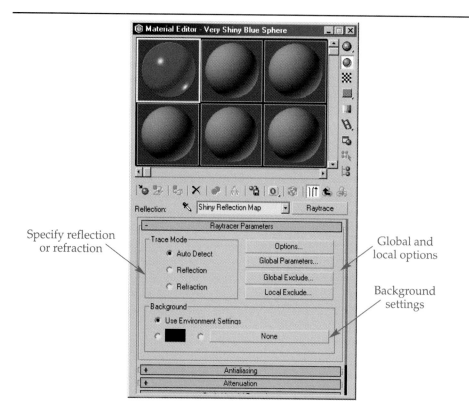

Figure 18-27. The **Raytracer Parameters** rollout at the raytrace map level of a material tree.

Specify reflection or refraction

Global and local options

Background settings

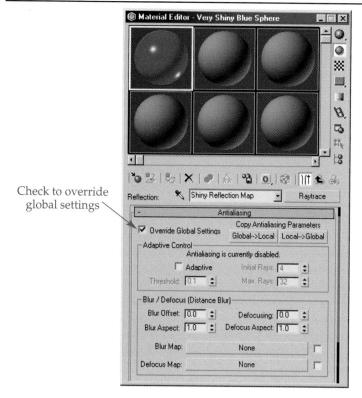

Figure 18-28. The **Antialiasing** rollout at the raytrace map level of a material tree.

Check to override global settings

Global-->Local

Local-->Global

To override the global settings, you must first check the **Override Global Settings** check box. This enables all of the options in the **Antialiasing** rollout. The **Copy Antialiasing Parameters** buttons allow you to copy defined parameters between global and local settings. Picking the **Global—>Local** button copies the global settings into the **Antialiasing** rollout. These settings can be used as a starting point for the new definition. You can also make changes in this rollout and replace the global settings by picking the **Local—>Global** button.

The **Adaptive Control** area is used to fine-tune the antialiasing properties. A message is displayed at the top of this area indicating the state of antialiasing in the **Raytracer Options** dialog box. Checking the **Adaptive** check box enables the options in this area and applies the settings to the map. The value in the **Initial Rays:** spinner is the number of rays cast by each pixel. However, the actual number of rays, including reflected rays, cannot exceed the value in the **Max. Rays:** spinner. A value of 0 in the **Threshold:** spinner casts the maximum number of rays. A value of 1 casts the minimum number of rays.

The **Blur/Defocus (Distance Blur)** area is used to blur the image. Blur settings affect the sharpness of reflected and refracted images regardless of viewing distance. On the other hand, defocus settings affect sharpness based on distance. The value in the **Blur Offset:** spinner is a measure of the number of pixels a reflected or refracted image is blurred. The value in the **Defocusing:** spinner is also a measure of the number of pixels blurred. However, the image is blurred more in the distance than in the foreground. The **Blur Aspect:** spinner sets the height-width aspect ratio of the blur. The **Defocus Aspect:** spinner sets the ratio for distance blurring. Normally, the default value of 1.0 is acceptable for both of these settings. The **Blur Map:** and **Defocus Map:** buttons allow you to specify texture maps to control the blurring. The check boxes must be checked to apply the maps.

Attenuation

The **Attenuation** rollout is used to control the length of projected rays. See Figure 18-29. This can lead to faster renderings, since without attenuation, or falloff, a ray travels forever.

You can pick which type of attenuation is used in the **Falloff Type:** drop-down list. You can choose linear, inverse square, exponential, or custom falloff. The falloff is calculated for the range specified in the **Start:** and **End:** spinners. These values are measured in current drawing units. If exponential falloff is specified, the **Exponent:** spinner is enabled. The value in this spinner is the exponent used for calculating the falloff.

The **Color:** radio buttons determine what a ray fades to as it falls off. By default, the ray fades to the background. This is indicated by the **Background** radio button being on. You can also pick the **Specify:** radio button and set a color in the color swatch.

When **Custom Falloff** is selected in the **Falloff Type:** drop-down list, the options in the **Custom Falloff** area are enabled. The curve graphically displays the settings at the right of this area. The value in the **Near:** spinner is the strength of the ray at the beginning of the range. The value in the **Far:** spinner is the strength at the end of the range. The **Control 1:** spinner is used to control the shape of the curve at the beginning. The **Control 2:** spinner is used to control the shape of the curve at the end.

Basic Material Extensions

The **Basic Material Extensions** rollout allows you to fine-tune the colors of the raytrace map. See Figure 18-30. The **Reflectivity/Opacity Map** area allows you to specify a texture map to control the intensity of the reflection or refraction. You must pick the button and specify a map to enable the other

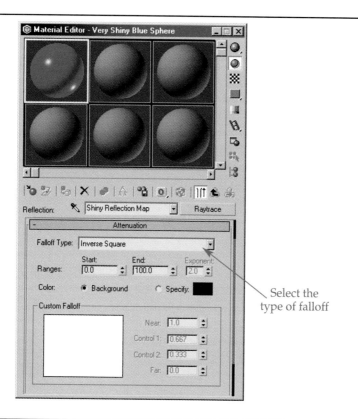

Figure 18-29. The **Attenuation** rollout at the raytrace map level of a material tree.

Select the type of falloff

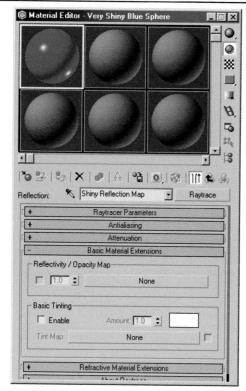

Figure 18-30. The **Basic Material Extensions** rollout at the raytrace map level of a material tree.

options in this area. The check box turns the effect of the map on and off. The spinner sets the amount of the raytraced image applied to the material.

The **Basic Tinting** area allows you to add a color tint to the reflected image. The material's diffuse color component is not affected by this setting. The **Enable** check box turns the tinting effect on and off. The **Amount:** spinner determines how much of the color in the color swatch is added to the reflection. Pick the color swatch to set a new color. The **Tint Map:** button allows you to assign a texture map. The check box next to the button turns the texture map on and off.

Refractive Material Extensions

The **Refractive Material Extensions** rollout allows you to fine-tune the refraction effect produced by the map. See Figure 18-31. The **Color Density (Filter)** area allows you to set the color transmitted by the material. For example, light passing through green glass transmits a green color. Check the **Enable** check box to activate the settings in this area. The transmission color is set by picking the color swatch. The **Amount:** spinner determines how much of the transmission color is used. The **Start Dist:** and **End Dist:** spinners are used to set the "thickness" of the material. These values are in current drawing units. A texture map can be assigned by picking the **Color Map:** button. The check box must be checked to apply the map.

The **Fog** area is used to add a self-illuminated, opaque fog inside the material. This is similar to the fog component of a raytrace type material discussed in Chapter 17. The **Enable** check box turns the effect on and off. The color of the fog is set by picking the color swatch. The **Amount:** spinner determines how much of the fog color is used. The **Start Dist:** and **End Dist:** spinners are used to set the "thickness" of the material. These values are in current drawing units. A texture map can be assigned by picking the **Color Map:** button. The check box must be checked to apply the map.

Figure 18-31. The **Refractive Material Extensions** rollout at the raytrace map level of a material tree.

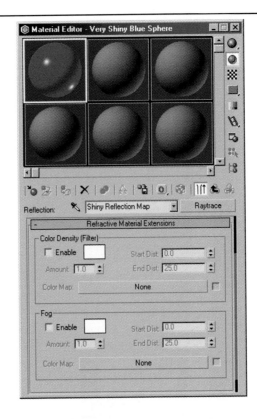

Exercise 18-8

1) Draw objects similar to the ones shown below. Use your own dimensions. Add lights and a camera as necessary.
2) In the **Material Editor**, get a wood material from the default 3ds max material library. Then, assign it to the "table."
3) In the **Material Editor**, select an unused material sample slot. Define a bright orange standard material. Use Metal shading. Apply this material to the cylinder.
4) Select an unused material sample slot in the **Material Editor**. Define a bright blue standard material. Use Phong shading. Change the specular level and glossiness to create a very shiny, plastic material. Assign this material to the pyramid.
5) Select another unused material sample slot in the **Material Editor**. Define a deep red standard material. Use Strauss shading. Use a **Glossiness:** value of about 80 and a **Metalness:** value of about 30. Assign this material to the box.
6) Select another unused material sample slot in the **Material Editor**. Define a bright yellow standard material. Use Oren-Nayar-Blinn shading. Make it very shiny and assign it to the sphere.
7) Render the scene to a file named ex18-08a.jpg in the folder of your choice.
8) Open the **Material Editor** and make the yellow material current. Then, open the **Maps** rollout and pick the button next to the **Reflection** spinner.
9) Assign a raytrace map. At the map level, pick the **Reflection** radio button. In the **Background** area, pick the radio button next to the color swatch. Then, define a dark grey color for the swatch (**Value:** of about 100).
10) Render the scene to a file named ex18-08b.jpg in the folder of your choice.
11) Compare the two renderings. How are they different? Why did you change the background color for the map from the environment setting? Why was a dark grey used instead of black?
12) Save the scene as ex18-08.max in the folder of your choice.

Wood

The *wood map* type is a 3D procedural map that creates a wood-grain pattern based on two specified colors or maps. See Figure 18-32. It is most often used as a diffuse color map, but it can also be used as a bump map.

Once you select the wood type in the **Material/Map Browser**, you are placed at the map level in the material tree. The **Coordinates** and **Wood Parameters** rollouts are displayed in the **Material Editor**. See Figure 18-33. The **Coordinates** rollout is discussed earlier in this chapter.

The **Grain Thickness:** spinner in the **Wood Parameters** rollout determines the relative width of the grain. This value will most likely vary greatly from a large object to a small object.

The "noise" spinners determine the pattern of the wood grain. The **Radial Noise:** spinner sets the waviness of the "rings" of the wood. The rings are found by cutting a tree across its trunk. The **Axial Noise:** spinner sets the waviness of the length of the wood. See Figure 18-34.

Swap

Use the color swatches to set the two colors for the wood. Pick the **Maps** buttons to specify texture maps instead of solid colors. The check boxes must be checked to apply the maps. Picking the **Swap** button flip-flops the color/map settings.

Figure 18-32. A wood map is used as a diffuse color map and a bump map to create this block of wood.

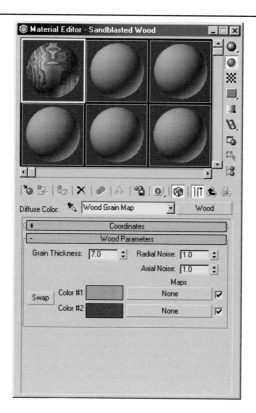

Figure 18-33. The wood map level in a material tree.

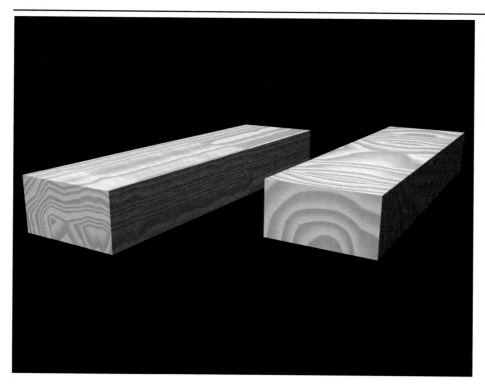

Figure 18-34. These two materials are the same except for noise. On the left, radial noise is applied. On the right, axial noise is applied.

Exercise

Exercise 18-9

1) Draw the coffee table shown below. Use your own dimensions. Add lights and a camera as necessary.
2) In the **Material Editor**, select an unused material sample slot. Pick the button next to the diffuse color swatch.
3) Assign a wood map.
4) At the map level, define a light tan wood. Adjust the parameters as necessary to get a grain pattern you like.
5) Assign the wood material to the coffee table.
6) Render the scene to a file named ex18-09.jpg in the folder of your choice. The tiling of the material on the table is probably not what you expected or want. Adjust the tiling in the **Coordinates** rollout for the wood map. Render the scene again if necessary, overwriting the existing file.
7) Save the scene as ex18-09.max in the folder of your choice.

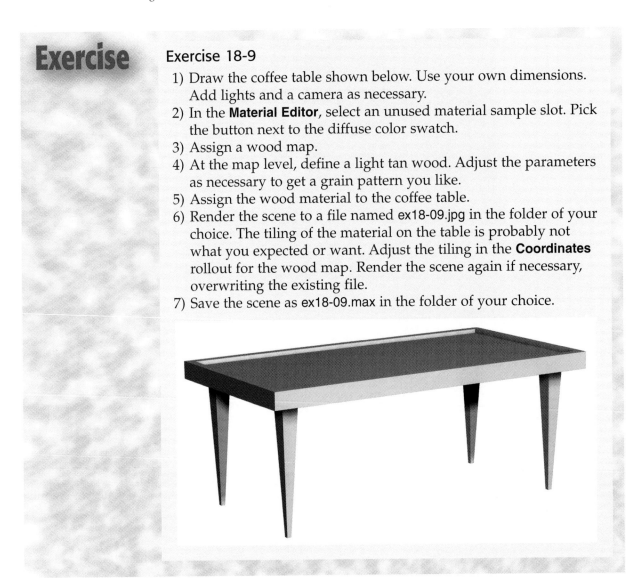

Mapping Material Components

Maps can be applied to just about every component of a material definition, from diffuse color to opacity. A material with at least one map assigned to it is called a *mapped material.* Material maps are applied in the **Maps** rollout of the **Material Editor**. See Figure 18-35.

At first, the terminology used to describe various mapping functions might get confusing. There are map types, such as checker, brick, and bitmap. There are also material components that are mapped, such as diffuse color. These components are called by their "mapping name," such as diffuse color mapping. Do not confuse this with a map type. A *map type*, such as checker, is used *for* diffuse color mapping. Once you gain experience working with maps, you will be able to recognize which names are map types and which ones are mapped material components.

Help Cel

Mapped components can be animated by applying an animated bitmap (AVI) or by animating settings, such as percentages or color settings.

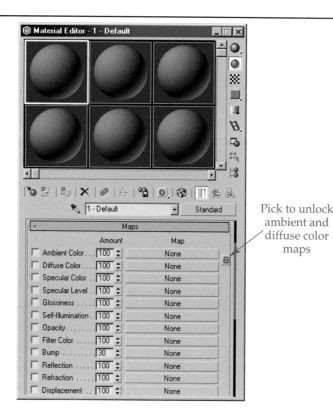

Figure 18-35. Using the **Maps** rollout, maps can be assigned to nearly every component of a material definition.

Pick to unlock ambient and diffuse color maps

Ambient Color Mapping

Ambient color mapping allows you to specify a texture map for the ambient color portion of the material definition. To specify an ambient map, pick the button next to **Ambient Color** in the **Maps** rollout of the **Material Editor**. This button is enabled after picking the **Lock** button to the right of the "map" buttons to unlock the ambient and diffuse color mapping components. You can also assign an ambient map by picking the small square button next to the ambient color swatch in the **Basic Parameters** rollout. This button appears when you pick the **Lock** button to the right of the "map" buttons. After defining and assigning the map, enter a percentage in the spinner in the **Maps** rollout. This determines how much of the ambient map is displayed. At a setting of 100, the ambient color defined for the material does not show through the ambient map. See Figure 18-36. The check box in the **Maps** rollout is used to turn the effects of the map on and off.

Lock

Diffuse Color Mapping

Diffuse color mapping allows you to specify a texture map for the diffuse color portion of the material definition. If the diffuse and ambient colors are locked, the texture map specified for the diffuse component is used for the ambient component. To specify a diffuse map, pick the button next to **Diffuse Color** in the **Maps** rollout of the **Material Editor**. You can also pick the small square button next to the diffuse color swatch in the **Basic Parameters** rollout. After assigning and defining the map, enter a percentage in the spinner in the **Maps** rollout. This determines how much of the diffuse map is displayed. At a setting of 100, the diffuse color defined for the material does not show through the diffuse map. See Figure 18-37. The check box is used to turn the effects of the map on and off.

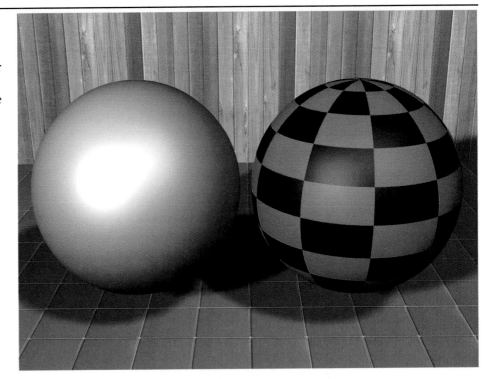

Diffuse Roughness Mapping

Diffuse roughness mapping allows you to use a map to control the roughness of the material. This material component is only available with the Oren-Nayar-Blinn and Multi-Layer shading types. White areas in the map increase the roughness of the material. Black areas in the map have no roughness (a roughness of 0). To specify a roughness map, pick the button next to **Diff. Roughness** in the **Maps** rollout of the **Material Editor**. After assigning and defining the map, enter a percentage in the spinner. This sets the amount of roughness based on the map. At a setting of 0, the roughness map is not applied. See Figure 18-38. The check box is used to turn the effects of the map on and off.

Diffuse Level Mapping

Diffuse level mapping allows you to assign a texture map to control the intensity of the diffuse color. A map allows you to have different intensities at different locations on an object. This mapping is only available with the Anisotropic, Oren-Nayar-Blinn, and Multi-Layer shading types. To specify the map, pick the button next to **Diffuse Level** in the **Maps** rollout of the **Material Editor**. After assigning and defining the map, enter a percentage in the spinner. This determines how much of the map is used to affect the diffuse color. At a setting of 100, the diffuse color is completely determined by the map. The check box is used to turn the effects of the map on and off.

Specular Color Mapping

Specular color mapping allows you to specify a texture map for the specular color portion of the material definition. To specify the map, pick the button next to **Specular Color** in the **Maps** rollout of the **Material Editor**. You can also pick the small square button next to the specular color swatch in the **Basic Parameters** rollout. After assigning and defining the map, enter a percentage in the spinner in the **Maps** rollout. This determines how much of the specular map is displayed. At a setting of 100, the specular color defined for the material does not show through the map. See Figure 18-39. The check box is used to turn the effects of the map on and off.

Figure 18-38. The material on the left-hand sphere has a checker map applied to the roughness component to create the material on the right-hand sphere. Notice how some parts of the sphere appear more dull than others.

Figure 18-39. The material on the left-hand sphere has a checker map applied to the specular color to create the material on the right-hand sphere. Notice how the map is only applied in the specular portion of the material.

Specular Level Mapping

Specular level mapping allows you to assign a texture map to control the intensity of specular highlights. The color (hue) of specular highlights is not affected. A map allows you to have different intensities at different locations on an object. To specify the map, pick the button next to **Specular Level** in the **Maps** rollout of the **Material Editor**. You can also pick the small square button next to the **Specular Level:** spinner in the **Basic Parameters** rollout. After assigning and defining the map, enter a percentage in the spinner in the **Maps** rollout. This determines how much of the map is used to affect the specular intensity. At a setting of 100, the intensity of the specular highlight is completely determined by the map. See Figure 18-40. The check box is used to turn the effects of the map on and off.

Glossiness Mapping

Glossiness mapping allows you to assign a texture map to control the glossiness, or shininess, of the material. Color from the texture map is *not* added to the color of the material. Using a map to control glossiness allows different parts of an object to be more or less glossy than others. See Figure 18-41. Glossiness mapping can also be used to simulate an irregular surface using a flat object.

To specify the map, pick the button next to **Glossiness** in the **Maps** rollout of the **Material Editor**. You can also pick the small square button next to the **Glossiness:** spinner in the **Basic Parameters** rollout. After assigning and defining the map, enter a percentage in the spinner in the **Maps** rollout. This determines how much of the map is used to affect the glossiness. At a setting of 100, the shiny portions of the material are determined solely by the map. The check box is used to turn the effects of the map on and off.

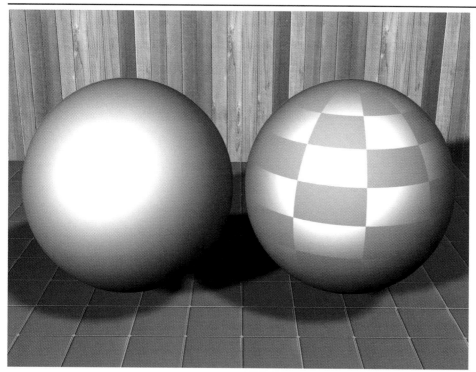

Figure 18-40. The material on the left-hand sphere has a checker map applied to the specular level component to create the material on the right-hand sphere. Notice how the map affects the intensity of the specular highlight, but does not affect any other portion of the material.

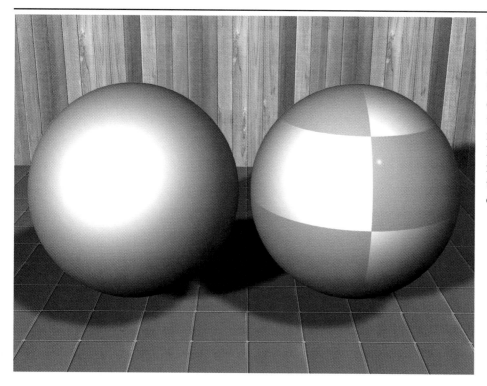

Figure 18-41. The material on the left-hand sphere has a checker map applied to the glossiness component to create the material on the right-hand sphere. Notice the difference in glossiness in the two "middle" checkers.

Self-Illumination Mapping

Self-illumination is used to simulate the effect of a material giving off light. This is done by replacing shadows with the diffuse color or a color you specify. Remember, 3ds max materials cannot actually provide illumination. Therefore, self-illumination only simulates this effect. A self-illumination map is used to control the self-illumination of the material.

See Figure 18-42. Self-illuminated areas of a material do not receive light or shadows.

To specify the map, pick the button next to **Self-Illumination** in the **Maps** rollout of the **Material Editor**. You can also pick the small square button in the **Self-Illumination** area of the **Basic Parameters** rollout. After assigning and defining the map, enter a percentage in the spinner in the **Maps** rollout. This determines how much of the map is used for self-illumination. At a setting of 100, self-illumination is controlled entirely by the map. The check box is used to turn the effects of the map on and off.

Opacity Mapping

Opacity mapping allows you to use a texture map to determine transparency, or opacity, for the material. Black portions of the map produce completely transparent areas on the material. White portions produce completely opaque areas. See Figure 18-43.

To specify the map, pick the button next to **Opacity** in the **Maps** rollout of the **Material Editor**. You can also pick the small square button next to the **Opacity:** spinner in the **Basic Parameters** rollout. After assigning and defining the map, enter a percentage in the spinner in the **Maps** rollout. This determines how the map controls opacity. At a setting of 100, black portions of the map create completely transparent areas. At a setting of 50, black portions create areas of 50% transparency. The check box is used to turn the effects of the map on and off.

Filter Color Mapping

Filter color is the color transmitted as light passes through a transparent object. The filter color of a transparent object is added to the color

Figure 18-42. The material on the left-hand sphere has a checker map applied to the self-illumination color to create the material on the right-hand sphere. The effect is most noticeable in the shadows at the edge of the object.

of items behind the object. Filter color mapping allows you to use a texture map to control the filter color. See Figure 18-44.

To specify the map, pick the button next to **Filter Color** in the **Maps** rollout of the **Material Editor**. You can also pick the small square button next to the **Filter:** color swatch in the **Extended Parameters** rollout. After assigning and defining the map, enter a percentage in the spinner in the

Figure 18-43. The material on the left-hand sphere has a checker map applied to the opacity component to create the material on the right-hand sphere.

Figure 18-44. The material on the left-hand sphere has a checker map applied to the filter color to create the material on the right-hand sphere. Notice how some parts of the sphere filter blue while other portions filter the same as those on the original object.

Maps rollout. This determines how much of the map is used for filter color. At a setting of 100, the filter color is determined solely by the map. At a setting of 50, the filter color is calculated as 50% from the map and 50% from the color defined in the **Extended Parameters** rollout. The check box is used to turn the effects of the map on and off.

Anisotropy Mapping

Anisotropy mapping allows you to use a map to control the shape of the anisotropic highlight for the material. See Figure 18-45. This material component is only available with the Anisotropic and Multi-Layer shading types. Greyscale patterns often produce a better highlight than black and white patterns.

To specify the map, pick the button next to **Anisotropy** in the **Maps** rollout of the **Material Editor**. You can also pick the small square button next to the **Anisotropy:** spinner in the **Basic Parameters** rollout. After assigning and defining the map, enter a percentage in the spinner in the **Maps** rollout. This determines how much the map controls the shape of the anisotropic highlight. At a setting of 100, the shape is determined primarily by the map. At a setting of 0, the anisotropy settings in the **Basic Parameters** rollout determine the shape. The check box is used to turn the effects of the map on and off.

Orientation Mapping

Orientation mapping is used to control the orientation of an anisotropic highlight. See Figure 18-46. This material component is only available with the Anisotropic and Multi-Layer shading types. Greyscale patterns often produce a better highlight than black and white patterns.

Figure 18-45.
Anisotropic mapping can be used to control the shape of an anisotropic highlight.

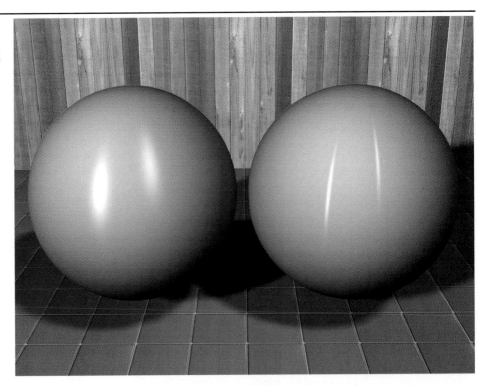

Figure 18-46.
Orientation mapping can be used to control the orientation of an anisotropic highlight. A checker map is used on the right-hand object.

Also, the map defined for this material component is often used as a bump map as well.

To specify the map, pick the button next to **Orientation** in the **Maps** rollout of the **Material Editor**. You can also pick the small square button next to the **Orientation:** spinner in the **Basic Parameters** rollout. After assigning and defining the map, enter a percentage in the spinner in the **Maps** rollout. This determines how much the map controls the position or orientation of the anisotropic highlight. At a setting of 100, the position is determined primarily by the map. At a setting of 0, the orientation setting in the **Basic Parameters** rollout determines the position. The check box is used to turn the effects of the map on and off.

Metalness Mapping

Metalness is a measure of how metallic a material appears. This material component is only available with the Strauss shading type. Metalness mapping allows you to use a texture map to apply different metalness values to different portions of a material. See Figure 18-47. Black portions of the map produce low metalness values. White portions of the map produce high metalness values.

To specify the map, pick the button next to **Metalness** in the **Maps** rollout of the **Material Editor**. You can also pick the small square button next to the **Metalness:** spinner in the **Strauss Basic Parameters** rollout. After assigning and defining the map, enter a percentage in the spinner in the **Maps** rollout. This determines how much of the metalness is based on the map. At a setting of 100, all metalness values are determined by the map. At a setting of 0, the metalness setting in the **Basic Parameters** rollout determines metalness. The check box is used to turn the effects of the map on and off.

Bump Mapping

Bump mapping is used to simulate a raised or bumpy surface. Black portions of the map appear "below" the surface. White areas appear "above" the surface. This allows you to use flat geometry instead of modeling the irregular surface. See Figure 18-48.

Figure 18-47. The material on the left-hand sphere has a checker map applied to the metalness component to create the material on the right-hand sphere. Look at the portion of the sphere in shadows to see the effect.

Figure 18-48. A cellular map is applied to the bump map component to create the material on the right-hand sphere.

To specify the map, pick the button next to **Bump** in the **Maps** rollout of the **Material Editor**. After assigning and defining the map, enter a percentage in the spinner in the **Maps** rollout. This determines how large the bumps are. At a setting of 0, the bumps have no "height" and are not applied. The check box is used to turn the effects of the map on and off.

Reflection Mapping

A reflection map is applied to simulate a reflection. See Figure 18-49. Often, a bitmap image is used as a reflection map on a very shiny material, such as chrome. To specify the map, pick the button next to **Reflection** in the **Maps** rollout of the **Material Editor**. After assigning and defining the map, enter a percentage in the spinner in the **Maps** rollout. This determines how much of the map is displayed and how much of the material's color shows through. At a setting of 100, the reflection map is fully displayed with the tinting from the base material colors. The check box is used to turn the effects of the map on and off.

Most of the time, a reflection map uses a low setting, such as 25 or 50. A very low value can add a subtle touch of realism to simulate a highly polished surface. A very high value tends to make the map act more like a decal than a realistic reflection.

Refraction Mapping

Refraction mapping is used to control the refraction of objects being seen through the transparent material. To specify the map, pick the button next to **Refraction** in the **Maps** rollout of the **Material Editor**. After assigning and defining the map, enter a percentage in the spinner. This determines how much of the map is displayed. At a setting of 100, the refraction map is fully displayed. At a lower setting, the refraction

Figure 18-49. A raytrace map is used as a reflection map on the right-hand sphere.

setting of the base material controls most of the refraction effect. The check box is used to turn the effects of the map on and off.

Displacement Mapping

Displacement mapping produces an effect similar to that of bump mapping. However, unlike bump mapping, displacement mapping deforms geometry on the object. See Figure 18-50. White portions of the map "push out of," or displace, the object more than the darker portions. Displacement mapping can be applied to editable meshes, patches, and NURBS surfaces. Other objects must have a disp approx modifier applied first. If you do not apply the disp approx modifier first, you will end up with very bizarre results.

To specify the map, pick the button next to **Displacement** in the **Maps** rollout of the **Material Editor**. After assigning and defining the map, enter a percentage in the spinner in the **Maps** rollout. This determines how much the geometry is displaced. The check box is used to turn the effects of the map on and off.

Figure 18-50. The material on the left-hand sphere has a checker map applied to the displacement component to create the material on the right-hand sphere. The right-hand sphere was first converted to an editable mesh.

Exercise 18-10

1) Draw a sphere on a quad patch "table." Use your own dimensions. Add lights and a camera as necessary.
2) In the **Material Editor**, get the material Concrete_Tiles from the default 3ds max material library. Assign the material to the quad patch. Apply a UVW map modifier and adjust mapping coordinates as necessary.
3) In the **Material Editor**, select an unused material sample slot. Define a bright red, shiny material with Blinn shading.
4) In the **Maps** rollout, assign a checker map to the diffuse color. Define the "checkers" as red and white. In the **Maps** rollout, set the diffuse color map percentage to about 25.
5) In the **Maps** rollout, assign a cellular map as the bump map. Use the default settings for the cellular map. In the **Maps** rollout, change the bump map percentage to 10.
6) In the **Maps** rollout, assign a raytrace map as the reflection map. In the **Background** area of the **Raytracer Parameters** rollout, pick the radio button next to the color swatch. Then, define a dark grey color for the color swatch (**Value:** of about 100).
7) Apply this new material to the sphere.
8) Render the scene to a file named ex18-10.jpg in the folder of your choice.
9) Make any adjustments to the material as necessary.
10) Save the file as ex18-10.max in the folder of your choice.

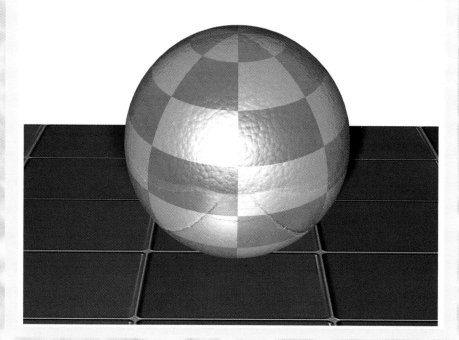

Raytrace Material Component Mapping

A raytrace material type has some of the same material components as the standard material type. For example, a raytrace material can have ambient color mapping or diffuse color mapping. However, there are some additional material components unique to a raytrace material. These are discussed in the next sections.

Reflect

A reflect, or reflection, map for a raytraced material controls which portions of the material reflect. Black portions of the map do not reflect. White portions of the map produce reflections. See Figure 18-51.

To specify the map, pick the button next to **Reflect** in the **Maps** rollout of the **Material Editor**. You can also pick the small square button next to the **Reflect:** spinner in the **Raytrace Basic Parameters** rollout. After assigning and defining the map, enter a percentage in the spinner in the **Maps** rollout. This determines how much the map controls reflections. At a setting of 100, the reflection is completely controlled by the map. The check box is used to turn the effects of the map on and off.

Transparency

Transparency mapping allows you to use a texture map to control transparency of a raytrace material. Black portions of the map are completely opaque. White portions are completely transparent. This effect is similar to that of opacity mapping for a standard material. However, filter color is also added to transparent portions.

To specify the map, pick the button next to **Transparency** in the **Maps** rollout of the **Material Editor**. You can also pick the small square button next to the **Transparency:** spinner in the **Raytrace Basic Parameters** rollout.

Figure 18-51. The raytrace material on the left-hand sphere has a checker map applied as a reflection map to create the raytrace material on the right-hand sphere.

After assigning and defining the map, enter a percentage in the spinner in the **Maps** rollout. This determines how much the map controls transparency. At a setting of 100, transparency is completely controlled by the map. The check box is used to turn the effects of the map on and off.

Luminosity

Luminosity mapping allows you to use a texture map to control the luminosity of a raytrace material. Luminosity is self-illumination, but it is not tied to the diffuse color. If the **Luminosity:** check box in the **Raytrace Basic Parameters** rollout is unchecked, this material component becomes self-illumination mapping.

To specify the map, pick the button next to **Luminosity** in the **Maps** rollout of the **Material Editor**. You can also pick the small square button next to the **Luminosity:** spinner in the **Raytrace Basic Parameters** rollout. After assigning and defining the map, enter a percentage in the spinner in the **Maps** rollout. This determines how much of the luminosity, or self-illumination, is provided by the map. At a setting of 100, the luminosity is provided entirely by the map. The check box is used to turn the effects of the map on and off.

Index of Refraction (IOR)

The index of refraction (IOR) determines how much light is bent as it passes through a transparent raytraced object. IOR for a raytrace material is covered in Chapter 17. You can use a map to control the IOR. The light and dark areas of the map increase or decrease the refraction of the material. Using the same map as a bump map, you can create glass objects with irregular surfaces without actually modeling the surface.

To specify the map, pick the button next to **IOR** in the **Maps** rollout of the **Material Editor**. You can also pick the small square button next to the **Index of Refr:** spinner in the **Raytrace Basic Parameters** rollout. After assigning and defining the map, enter a percentage in the spinner in the **Maps** rollout. This determines how much the map influences refraction. At a setting of 100, all light refraction is based on the map. The check box is used to turn the effects of the map on and off.

Extra Lighting

Extra lighting is light added to a raytrace material. This is similar to adding more ambient light to only the material, not the scene. Extra lighting mapping allows you to use a map to add ambient light to the raytrace material. See Figure 18-52. Black portions of the map do not add extra light. All other colors are added to the ambient light portion of the material.

To specify the map, pick the button next to **Extra Lighting** in the **Maps** rollout of the **Material Editor**. You can also pick the small square button next to the **Extra Lighting:** color swatch in the **Extended Parameters** rollout. After assigning and defining the map, enter a percentage in the spinner in the **Maps** rollout. This determines how much extra light is added from the map. At a setting of 100, all of the extra light that can be provided by the map is added to the material. The check box is used to turn the effects of the map on and off.

Figure 18-52. The raytrace material on the left-hand sphere has a green/black checker map applied to the extra lighting component to create the raytrace material on the right-hand sphere.

Translucency

A translucent material diffuses, or breaks up, light as it passes through the material. This makes objects behind the translucent object appear blurry or fuzzy. The material may also add color to the light as it is diffused. This translucent color is not tied to the viewing angle, unlike diffuse color. A translucency map uses a texture map to control the translucent properties of the raytrace material.

To specify the map, pick the button next to **Translucency** in the **Maps** rollout of the **Material Editor**. You can also pick the small square button next to the **Translucency:** color swatch in the **Extended Parameters** rollout. After assigning and defining the map, enter a percentage in the spinner in the **Maps** rollout. This determines how much of the material's translucency is provided by the map. At a setting of 100, the map completely controls the material's translucency. The check box is used to turn the effects of the map on and off.

Fluorescence

A fluorescent material gives off light when struck by radiation. Materials in 3ds max cannot provide illumination to a scene. However, a raytrace material can make an object look as though it is providing illumination. When combined with lights to provide the actual illumination, this can simulate a fluorescent material. A map can be used to control the fluorescent effect of the material. Black areas of the map do not add fluorescence to the material. All other colors add fluorescent illumination to the material.

To specify the map, pick the button next to **Fluorescence** in the **Maps** rollout of the **Material Editor**. You can also pick the small square button next to the **Fluorescence:** color swatch in the **Extended Parameters** rollout. After assigning and defining the map, enter a percentage in the spinner in the **Maps** rollout. This determines how much extra light is added from the map. At a setting of 100, the full effect of the map is applied. This can be used to simulate a neon light pattern. When a low value is used in conjunction with a bump map, skin is "given life." The check box is used to turn the effects of the map on and off.

Color Density

The color density component controls the color within the transparent raytrace material. This color is transmitted by light passing through the material. Color density is based on the thickness of the object. A texture map can be used to control the color density of a raytraced material. Black areas of the map do not increase the color density. All other colors are added to the "inside" color of the material. Color density mapping does not affect the color of the shadow.

To specify the map, pick the button next to **Color** in the **Maps** rollout of the **Material Editor**. You can also pick the small square button next to the **Color:** color swatch under the **Density:** label in the **Extended Parameters** rollout. The check box must be checked to pick the square button. After assigning and defining the map, enter a percentage in the spinner in the **Maps** rollout. This determines how much of the map is added to the "inside" color of the material. At a setting of 100, all of the color that can be provided by the map is added to the "inside" material color. The check box is used to turn the effects of the map on and off.

Help Cel

For color density mapping to have any effect, the color density settings in the **Advanced Transparency** area of the **Extended Parameters** rollout must be activated.

Fog Color

Fog color mapping is used to control the density fog of a raytraced material. Density fog is a self-illuminated, opaque fog rendered inside of a raytraced material. The effect is slightly different from that of color density. Density fog, like color density, is based on the thickness of the object.

A map can be used to control the density fog. Black areas of the map have no effect on the density fog. All other colors control both the density and color of the fog. See Figure 18-53.

To specify the map, pick the button next to **Fog** in the **Maps** rollout of the **Material Editor**. You can also pick the small square button next to the **Fog:** color swatch under the **Density:** label in the **Extended Parameters** rollout. The check box must be checked to pick the square button. After assigning and defining the map, enter a percentage in the spinner in the **Maps** rollout. This determines how much of the map is added to the density fog. At a setting of 100, all of the color that can be provided by the map is added to the density fog. The check box is used to turn the effects of the map on and off.

Figure 18-53. The transparent raytrace material on the left-hand sphere has a green/black checker map applied to the fog component to create the transparent raytrace material on the right-hand sphere.

Help Cel

For fog color mapping to have any effect, the fog color settings in the **Advanced Transparency** area of the **Extended Parameters** rollout must be activated.

Environment and Transparent Environment Mapping

The **Environment** and **Trans.** (transparent environment) mapping entries in the **Maps** rollout for a raytrace material are the same as those found in the **Basic Parameters** and **Extended Parameters** rollouts. These are discussed in Chapter 17. If you assign a map to the **Environment** component in the **Maps** rollout, that map also appears in the **Basic Parameters** rollout next to **Environment**. If you assign a transparent environment map in the **Maps** rollout, that map also appears in the **Extended Parameters** rollout next to the **Transp.** setting.

Notice in the **Maps** rollout that the spinners for these two items are greyed out. You cannot adjust the percentages for environment or transparent environment mapping. The check boxes in the **Maps** rollout turn the mapping on and off. The state of these check boxes is reflected in the corresponding check boxes in the "parameter" rollouts.

Exercise 18-11

1) Open ex18-10.max created in Exercise 18-10. Save the scene as ex18-11.max in the folder of your choice.
2) In the **Material Editor**, select the red material and change it from a standard type to a raytrace type. Doing this not only changes the type, but removes all map definitions.
3) In the **Maps** rollout, assign a checker map to the diffuse color. Define the "checkers" as bright red and white. Change the tiling to 2 for both the **U:** and **V:** values. In the **Maps** rollout, set the diffuse map percentage to 100.
4) In the **Maps** rollout, assign a checker map to the transparency. Use the default definition for the checkers. In the **Maps** rollout, set the transparency map percentage to 50.
5) In the **Maps** rollout, assign a raytrace map to the reflection. At the map level, change the background setting to the color swatch and make it dark grey. In the **Maps** rollout, set the reflect percentage to 50.
6) In the **Maps** rollout, assign a cellular map to the extra lighting. Use the default definition for the map. In the **Maps** rollout, change the extra lighting percentage to 15.
7) Render the scene to a file named ex18-11.jpg in the folder of your choice.
8) Make any adjustments to the material definition and render the scene again as necessary.
9) Save the scene.

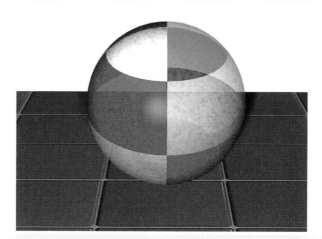

Chapter Snapshot

Chapter Test

Answer the following questions on a separate sheet of paper.
1) Define map.
2) List the five general categories of maps.
3) What is the function of the **Coordinates** rollout for a map?
4) What is a map's **Output** rollout used for?
5) Which category of maps has the **Noise** rollout?
6) What is the function of the bitmap map type?
7) The **Time** rollout for a bitmap map type is used to _____.
8) The bricks map type applies a pattern of _____ and _____.
9) List two types of surfaces the cellular map type can be used for.
10) The checker map type uses _____ colors to create the pattern.
11) The dent map type is designed to be mapped to which material component?
12) What type of object is the flat mirror map type designed to be used on?
13) When using the marble map type, how many colors create the pattern?
14) The particle age map type is used with _____.
15) How does the raytrace map type differ from the raytrace material type?

16) The wood map type creates a wood grain pattern based on _____.
17) Briefly describe how to assign a map to a material component.
18) What does the spinner next to a material component in the **Maps** rollout do?
19) For which material components are the spinners in the **Maps** rollout disabled?
20) How can you remove the effect of a map without actually removing the map?

Modeling Problems

Draw the objects shown below using your own dimensions. Save the scene as p18-00.max in the folder of your choice. This scene is used for all problems in this chapter. Follow the specific directions given in each problem. Define the materials as needed to reproduce each scene shown. The material type and shading mode are listed in each problem. The mapped component and type of map are also listed. You will need to match the material type/shading and mapped component/type to the correct objects based on the renderings. Add lights and a camera as necessary. Be sure to pay attention to shadow location and light color.

1 **Material type/shading:** Standard/Blinn (2), Raytrace/Phong (2), Raytrace Metal
Map types: Bump/Cellular, Diffuse/Checker
Open p18-00.max and save it as p18-01.max in the folder of your choice. Define the materials needed to complete the scene. Add lights as needed. Render the scene to a file named p18-01.jpg in the folder of your choice.

2 **Material type/shading:** Standard/Anisotropic, Standard/Blinn (2) Standard/Strauss, Standard/Metal
Map types: Diffuse Color/Checker, Opacity/Checker, Diffuse Color/Stucco, Bump/Stucco
Open p18-00.max and save it as p18-02.max in the folder of your choice. Define the materials needed to complete the scene. Add lights as needed. Use at least one target spotlight with its target in the center of the scene. Animate the spotlight around the scene. Render the animation to a file named p18-02.avi in the folder of your choice.

Material type/shading: Standard/Blinn, Standard/Phong, and materials from the default material library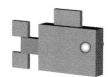

Map types: None (except those on the materials from the material library)

Open p18-00.max and save it as p18-03.max in the folder of your choice. Define the materials needed to complete the scene. Add lights as needed. Render the scene to a file named p18-03.jpg in the folder of your choice.

Material type/shading: Raytrace/Phong (4), Standard/Blinn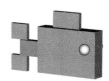

Map types: Diffuse Color/Checker

Open p18-00.max and save it as p18-04.max in the folder of your choice. Define the materials needed to complete the scene. Add lights as needed. Render the scene to a file named p18-04.jpg in the folder of your choice.

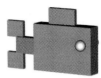

5 **Material type/shading:** Standard/Blinn (2), Standard/Strauss, Multi/Sub-Object, Shellac
Map types: Diffuse Color/Wood, Bump/Wood
Open p18-00.max and save it as p18-05.max in the folder of your choice. Define the materials needed to complete the scene. Add lights as needed. Render the scene to a file named p18-05.jpg in the folder of your choice.

6 **Material type/shading:** Standard/Blinn (5)
Map types: Diffuse Color/Wood, Diffuse Color/Bricks
(Bricks definition uses cellular and stucco maps)
Open p18-00.max and save it as p18-06.max in the folder of your choice. Define the materials needed to complete the scene. Add lights as needed. Render the scene to a file named p18-06.jpg in the folder of your choice.

Material type/shading: Standard/Blinn (2), Standard/Multi-Layer, Composite (2)

Map types: Diffuse Color/Bricks, Diffuse Color/Checker, Reflection/Raytrace

7

Open p18-00.max and save it as p18-07.max in the folder of your choice. Define the materials needed to complete the scene. Add lights as needed. Render the scene to a file named p18-07.jpg in the folder of your choice.

Material type/shading: Standard/Oren-Nayar-Blinn, Standard/Anisotropic (2), Standard/Blinn (2)

Map types: Diffuse Color/Checker

8

Open p18-00.max and save it as p18-08.max in the folder of your choice. Define the materials needed to complete the scene. Add lights as needed. Animate the target of the colored spotlight back and forth across the scene. Render the animation to a file named p18-08.avi in the folder of your choice.

9 **Material type/shading:** Raytrace/Phong
Map types: Reflect/Raytrace
Open p18-00.max and save it as p18-09.max in the folder of your choice. Define the materials needed to complete the scene. Add lights as needed. Render the scene to a file named p18-09.jpg in the folder of your choice. Due to the number of raytrace calculations in this scene, the rendering may take an hour or more.

10 **Material type/shading:** Standard/Blinn (3), Raytrace/Phong
Map types: Reflection/Raytrace (2), Diffuse Color/Marble, Diffuse Color/Cellular
Open p18-00.max and save it as p18-10.max in the folder of your choice. Define the materials needed to complete the scene. Add lights as needed. Render the scene to a file named p18-10.jpg in the folder of your choice.

Material type/shading: Standard/Blinn (4), Standard/Phong (1) **11**
Map types: Diffuse Color/Cellular (2), Diffuse Color/Checker (1),
Displacement/Checker (1), Opacity/Cellular (1),
Reflection/Raytrace (3)

Open p18-00.max and save it as p18-11.max in the folder of your
choice. Define the materials needed to complete the scene. Add
lights as needed. Render the scene to a file named
p18-11.jpg in the directory of your choice.

Chapter 19
Lighting Effects

Objectives

After completing this chapter, you will be able to:

- Create a colored light.
- Adjust the hotspot, falloff, and shape of a light.
- Create a projector from a light.
- Adjust shadow parameters.
- Animate lights.
- Add and set up atmospheric effects.

Colored Lights

One of the easiest lighting effects to create is colored lights. These can be used in a variety of applications. A colored light might be used to provide a special effect to an outdoor sign. Several color spotlights might be used in a concert or sporting event scene. In addition, since a material cannot produce illumination, a colored omni light might be placed behind a neon sign to simulate the colored illumination from the sign.

Modify

To change the color of a light, select the light and then pick **Modify** in the **Command Panel**. In the **General Parameters** rollout, pick the color swatch to open the color selector. Pick a color and close the dialog box. When the scene is rendered, the color in the swatch is added to all objects the light strikes.

Generally, do not use colored lights to illuminate most of the scene. There are a couple of exceptions. For example, if you model a black-smith's forge, you may want to add an omni light to the scene with a bright red tint. This can help give the scene an overall hot look. See Figure 19-1. Another example is an outdoor scene. You may want to add an omni or directional light with a light blue tint. This can help simulate light from a bright blue sky.

Help Cel

The color of a light can also be set when creating the light.

Figure 19-1. A red omni light is used to convey the heat generated by this blacksmith's forge.

Exercise 19-1

1) Draw a quad patch in the Top viewport. Draw a sphere on top of the quad patch, as shown below.
2) Get the material Concrete_Tiles from the default 3ds max material library. Assign the material to the quad patch.
3) In the **Material Editor**, define a white, shiny material. Assign the material to the sphere.
4) Add two spotlights to the scene. Place one on each side of the sphere.
5) Render the scene to a file named ex19-01a.jpg in the folder of your choice.
6) Change the left-hand light so it casts a light blue color.
7) Change the right-hand light so it casts a bright orange color.
8) Render the scene to a file named ex19-01b.jpg in the folder of your choice.
9) Compare the two renderings. How do they differ?
10) Save the scene as ex19-01.max in the folder of your choice.

Hotspot, Falloff, and Light Shape

Directional lights (direct lights) and spotlights have settings for the hotspot and the falloff. In addition, you can choose between a circular light pattern and a rectangular light pattern.

The *falloff* is where the light illumination fades to darkness. The *hotspot* is the part of the light cone that provides the most intense illumination. It is located in the center of the falloff. See Figure 19-2. The falloff must always be greater than the hotspot.

To change the size of the falloff or hotspot, select the light and pick **Modify** in the **Command Panel**. In the **Spotlight Parameters** rollout for a spotlight or the **Directional Parameters** rollout for a directional light, adjust the **Hotspot:** and **Falloff:** spinners as needed.

To set the shape of the light, pick either the **Circle** or **Rectangle** radio button in the **Spotlight Parameters** or **Directional Parameters** rollout. If you pick the **Rectangle** radio button, you must also specify the aspect ratio. The *aspect ratio* is the height-to-width ratio. You can match the light's aspect ratio to that of a bitmap by picking the **Bitmap Fit...** button. This opens the **Select Image File to Fit** dialog box. See Figure 19-3. Choose a bitmap file to match the aspect ratio. This affects the aspect ratio only. No pattern or image is applied.

At the top of the rollout is the **Overshoot** check box. When this check box is on, the spotlight or directional light casts light in all directions. However, shadows are only cast within the light's falloff. This check box is found in both the **Spotlight Parameters** rollout and the **Directional Parameters** rollout.

Figure 19-2. The hotspot is the inner cone of a spotlight, shown here in yellow. The falloff is the outermost point where a light provides illumination, shown here in white.

Figure 19-3. You can set a light's aspect ratio to match that of a bitmap.

Exercise 19-2

1) Draw the home movie screen shown below. Use your own dimensions.
2) Create and apply materials as needed.
3) Create a target spotlight. Place the target in the middle of the screen. The light should be perpendicular to the screen.
4) Adjust the hotspot and falloff. The hotspot should fill most of the movie screen. The falloff should be just larger than the hotspot.
5) Render the scene to a file named **ex19-02a.jpg** in the folder of your choice.
6) Change the spotlight shape to rectangular. Then, use the file **Frantic_f15_Flyby.avi** or any other AVI file as a "bitmap fit." The **Frantic_f15_Flyby.avi** file is located in the **3ds max \Animations** folder.
7) Render the scene to a file named **ex19-02b.jpg** in the folder of your choice.
8) Compare the two renderings. How has the screen changed?
9) Adjust the hotspot and falloff of the spotlight if necessary so it fills the movie screen.
10) Save the scene as **ex19-02.max** in the folder of your choice.

Exercise

Projectors

You can turn an omni light, directional light, or spotlight into a projector. A common use for this is to simulate light passing through leaves or the muntins of a window. See Figure 19-4. This special effect simulates the effect of gobos in theatrical lighting. An animated bitmap can be used to further enhance the effect of light passing through organic objects, such as leaves or grass.

Spotlight and Directional Light Projectors

Modify

To make a spotlight a projector, select the light. Then, pick **Modify** in the **Command Panel**. In the **Projector Map:** area of the **Spotlight Parameters** rollout, pick the **Map:** button to open the **Material/Map Browser**. Select the type of map to use. If you want to use a bitmap, select **Bitmap** from the list. This opens the **Select Bitmap Image File** dialog box. Select the bitmap you want to use. To use a different type of map, define it in the **Material Editor** and "get" it from there. Once the map is specified, the name of the map appears on the **Map:** button in the rollout. The check box is used to turn the projector effect on and off.

A directional light is made a projector in the same way a spotlight is made a projector. In the **Projector Map:** area of the **Directional Parameters** rollout, use the **Map:** button to specify a map. The check box turns the projector effect on and off for the light.

Omni Light Projector

The interface for making an omni light a projector is the same as that for spotlights and directional lights. However, omni lights have a separate **Projector Parameters** rollout. See Figure 19-5. Use the **Map:** button to specify a map. The check box turns the projector effect on and off.

Figure 19-4. A projector spotlight is used to create the effect of light passing through the leaves on a tree. The tree is modeled as just the trunk—no leaves were modeled.

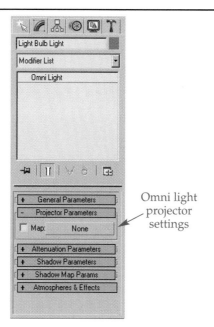

Figure 19-5. The **Projector Parameters** rollout is used to turn an omni light into a projector.

Omni light projector settings

Exercise 19-3

1) Open ex19-02.max if not already open. If you have not completed Exercise 19-2, do so now.
2) Change the total number of frames from 100 to 95.
3) Set up the spotlight as a projector. Use the file Frantic_f15_Flyby.avi (or the file you specified in Exercise 19-2, if different) as the projector map.
4) Render a single frame of the animation. Do not save it to a file.
5) Make any adjustments to the scene you feel necessary.
6) Render the entire animation to a file named ex19-03.avi in the folder of your choice.
7) When the rendering is complete, view the animation.
8) Save the scene as ex19-03.max in the folder of your choice.

Shadow and Shadow Map Parameters

There are two basic types of shadows that 3ds max lights can create. These are *shadow-mapped* and *raytraced shadows*. See Figure 19-6. Each type has its own unique properties. The default shadow type is shadow mapped. This type is generally acceptable in most applications. It also requires less computer resources to render.

Shadow-Mapped Shadows

The shadow cast by a shadow-mapped light is really a bitmap image. The image is calculated by 3ds max during the rendering process, just before the final rendering is created. This type of shadow does not receive color from transparent objects. However, color can be received

Figure 19-6. The shadow behind the sphere on the left is produced by a shadow-mapped light. The shadow behind the sphere on the right is produced by a raytraced light. Notice how sharp the right-hand shadow is compared to the left-hand shadow.

from colored lights. You can also change the color of the shadow. By default, shadows are black.

The edge of the shadow is very soft. The parameters of a shadow-mapped shadow can be adjusted to produce a sharper shadow. However, this increases the computer resources required to render the scene. Quick rendering time is one advantage of shadow-mapped shadows.

Raytraced Shadows

A raytraced shadow is calculated by tracing the path of rays from the light. This type of shadow produces a very clean, sharp edge. Raytraced shadows are much more accurate than shadow-mapped shadows. However, the big downside to raytraced shadows is the increased rendering time over shadow-mapped shadows.

Shadow Parameters

The **Shadow Parameters** rollout is used to set a light to cast shadows. It is also used to control how the shadow is created. The **Shadow Parameters** rollout is displayed for spotlights, directional lights, and omni lights. See Figure 19-7.

The **On** check box in the **Object Shadows:** area sets the light to cast shadows. When unchecked, the light does not cast shadows. This check box performs the same function as the **Cast Shadows** check box in the **General Parameters** rollout for the light. By default, lights do not cast shadows.

The drop-down list is used to set what type of shadow is cast. You can select between shadow-mapped and raytraced shadows. By default, a light casts shadow-mapped shadows.

When the **Use Global Settings** check box is checked, the global settings are used. Global settings affect all lights of the same type in the

Figure 19-7. The **Shadow Parameters** rollout is used to cast and define shadows.

same manner. When this check box is checked, the **Shadow Map Params** and **Ray Traced Shadow Params** rollouts display the global settings. When unchecked, these rollouts display the parameters for the selected light only. The only way to tell if global or local parameters are displayed is by viewing the state of this check box.

The **Color:** swatch sets the color of the shadow. The default color is black, which is used in most applications. By changing the color of the shadow, you can simulate the color of a transparent object showing on a shadow-mapped shadow.

The value in the **Dens.**, or density, spinner sets how dark or light a shadow appears. Increasing the value makes the shadow darker. Decreasing the value makes the shadow lighter. A negative value renders the opposite color.

The **Map:** button is used to set a shadow map. Do not confuse this with the shadow-mapped shadow 3ds max creates. This shadow map is blended with both shadow-mapped and raytraced shadows. See Figure 19-8. Picking the button opens the **Material/Map Browser**. Once a map is specified, its name appears on the button. The check box is used to turn the shadow map on and off.

When the **Light Affects Shadow Color** check box is on, the color of the light is blended with the shadow. This can be used to simulate the color of a transparent object showing on a shadow-mapped shadow. By default, this check box is off.

The **Atmosphere Shadows:** area allows you to set atmospheric effects to cast shadows. Atmospheric effects are discussed later in this chapter. Normally, atmospheric effects do not cast shadows. Check the check box in this area to turn on shadow casting for atmospheric effects. This is independent of shadow casting for objects. A light can be set to cast shadows through an atmospheric effect but not behind objects. The **Opacity:** spinner sets the percentage of opacity for the shadows. The **Color Amount:** spinner sets the percentage of color passed on to the shadow from the effect. Both of these spinners are set to 100% by default.

Figure 19-8. A cellular map is used as a shadow map for this sphere.

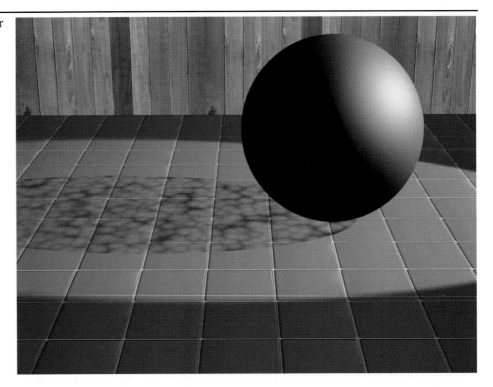

Shadow Map Parameters

There are two **Shadow Map Parameters** rollouts. The **Shadow Map Params** rollout is used for shadow-mapped shadows. The **Ray Traced Shadow Params** rollout is used for raytraced shadows. The settings in these rollouts are local to the selected light. However, if the **Use Global Settings** check box in the **Shadow Parameters** rollout is checked, the settings are for all lights of the same type as that of the selected light.

The **Bias:** spinner in the **Shadow Map Params** rollout is used to adjust the position of the shadow. Increasing the value moves the shadow away from the object that casts it. Decreasing the value moves the shadow toward the object. When the **Absolute Map Bias** check box at the bottom of the rollout is checked, bias is computed relative to the object. When the check box is off, bias is computed relative to the world.

The value in the **Size:** spinner in the **Shadow Map Params** rollout sets the size of the shadow map. This value is measured as horizontal pixels multiplied by vertical pixels, or pixels squared.

The value in the **Sample Range:** spinner in the **Shadow Map Params** rollout sets the size of the sampling area within the shadow. The higher the value, the softer the edge of the shadow. Generally, use a value between 2 and 5.

The **Bias:** spinner in the **Ray Traced Shadow Params** rollout is used to adjust the position of the shadow. See Figure 19-9. Increasing the value moves the shadow away from the object that casts it. Decreasing the value moves the shadow toward the object. The value in the **Max Quadtree Depth:** spinner adjusts the raytrace tree. Increasing the value allows for a larger tree, creating a higher-quality shadow. However, this also increases the rendering time.

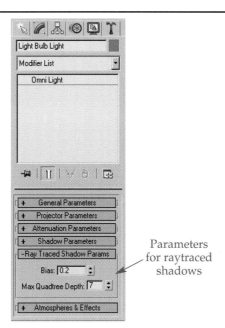

Parameters
for raytraced
shadows

Figure 19-9. The **Ray Traced Shadow Params** rollout is used to adjust the position of a raytraced shadow.

Exercise 19-4

Exercise

1) Draw a quad patch. Then, draw a sphere resting on the quad patch.
2) Create a target spotlight. Set the light to cast shadow-mapped shadows. Place the target in the center of the sphere.
3) Adjust the spotlight parameters so the hotspot is about the size of the sphere. Make the falloff about 10 units larger.
4) Get the material Concrete_Tiles from the default 3ds max material library. Apply it to the quad patch.
5) In the **Material Editor**, define a bright blue material. Assign the material to the sphere.
6) Render the scene to a file named ex19-04a.jpg in the folder of your choice.
7) Change the spotlight shadow to a raytraced shadow.
8) Render the scene to a file named ex19-04b.jpg in the folder of your choice.
9) Compare the two renderings. How do the shadows differ? How are they similar?
10) Save the scene as ex19-04.max in the folder of your choice.

Animating Lights

You can animate lights by animating transforms. You can also link lights to other animated objects. For example, you may link spotlights to a car for the headlights. You can also animate the light parameters. Most of the parameter definitions for a light can be animated. For example, you may want to animate a wide hotspot down to a very narrow beam of light. An animated bitmap can be applied as a shadow map or projector. In addition, the color of a light can be animated over time.

Exercise

Exercise 19-5

1) In the **Material Editor**, assign a cellular map as the diffuse color for any material sample. Adjust the cell parameters as you like.
2) Draw a quad patch and a sphere. Assign materials to the objects as you like.
3) Draw a spotlight. Place it so the sphere casts a shadow on the quad patch. Set up the light to cast shadows.
4) Assign a shadow map to the spotlight. When the **Material/Map Browser** appears, get the cellular map defined in the **Material Editor**.
5) In the **Material Editor**, animate the parameters for the cellular map you defined earlier. Make sure the **Toggle Animation Mode** button is on.
6) Render the animation to a file named ex19-05.avi in the folder of your choice. Render all frames.
7) When the rendering is complete, view the animation. Notice the animated shadow.
8) Save the scene as ex19-05.max in the folder of your choice.

Atmospheric Effects

An *atmospheric effect* is a plug-in used to produce environmental effects such as fog, fire, or special lighting. Many third-party developers offer plug-ins for 3ds max. However, 3ds max comes with several atmosphere plug-ins. Some of these atmospheric effects are applied to a special helper object in 3ds max called an *atmospheric apparatus.* Some atmospheric effects do not use an apparatus, but rather are applied to the entire scene or to a light. The atmospheric effects that come with 3ds max are fire, fog, volumetric fog, and volumetric light. The fire effect is called combustion in previous releases of 3D Studio MAX.

Help Cel

There are special rendering effects in 3ds max, such as lens effects. These effects have a dialog box similar to the **Environment** dialog box used for atmospheric effects. A review of this material, covered in Chapter 15, may be beneficial before learning about atmospheric effects.

Atmospheric Apparatus

An *atmospheric apparatus* is a special gizmo that accepts atmospheric plug-in effects. There are three types of atmospheric apparatus. These are based on the shape of the gizmo, which can be a box, sphere, or cylinder. See Figure 19-10. Just as a modifier is tied to an object's gizmo, the atmospheric effect is tied to the atmospheric apparatus. The fire and volumetric fog atmospheric effects both use an atmospheric apparatus.

Create

To draw an atmospheric apparatus, pick **Create** in the **Command Panel.** Then, pick the **Helpers** button. In the drop-down list, pick **Atmospheric Apparatus.** In the **Object Type** rollout, select the button corresponding to

Helpers

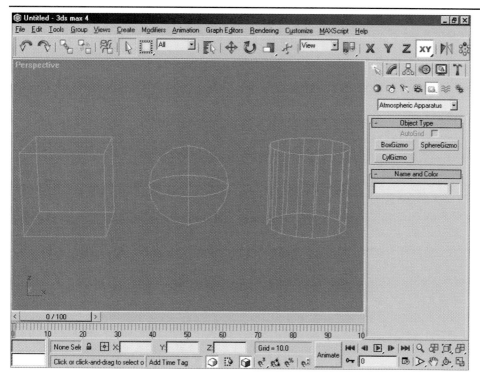

Figure 19-10. An atmospheric apparatus is a gizmo used to add atmospheric effects, such as fire, to a scene. An apparatus can be (from left) a box, sphere, or cylinder.

the shape you want to use. Finally, draw the apparatus in the viewport. The gizmo can be named in the **Name and Color** rollout, or in the text box at the top of the **Modify** tab. The display color cannot be changed, however. This color is controlled by 3ds max system preferences.

You can change the shape of the atmospheric apparatus by scaling and rotating it. This changes the shape of the effect. For a sphere apparatus, you can choose to create a hemisphere by checking the **Hemisphere** check box. In addition, in the **Gizmo Parameters** rollout for all types, you can change the seed. The seed is a starting point for the effect. Each apparatus in the scene should have a different seed. Otherwise, very similar effects are produced. Picking the **New Seed** button assigns a new, randomly generated seed to the apparatus.

After the apparatus is created, an atmospheric effect must be applied to it. With the apparatus selected, pick **Modify** in the **Command Panel**. In the **Atmospheres** rollout, pick the **Add** button. See Figure 19-11. The **Add Atmosphere** dialog box appears. See Figure 19-12. The list on the left of the **Add Atmosphere** dialog box shows all of the atmospheric effects available for the apparatus. Picking the **Existing** radio button displays only effects already defined in the current scene. Picking the **New** radio button displays all atmospheric effects loaded into 3ds max that can be applied to the apparatus. Select an effect from the list at the left and then pick the **OK** button to close the dialog box. Finally, in the **Atmospheres** rollout, highlight the effect and pick the **Setup** button. The **Environment** dialog box appears, allowing you to set the parameters for the effect. The settings for each effect are discussed in the next sections.

A single gizmo can have multiple effects assigned to it. Pick the **Add** button in the **Atmospheres** rollout and repeat the above process. To remove an atmospheric effect from an apparatus, highlight the effect's name in the **Atmospheres** rollout. Then, pick the **Delete** button. The effect is removed from the apparatus.

BoxGizmo

SphereGizmo

CylGizmo

New Seed

Modify

Add

Figure 19-11. An atmospheric effect is added to an atmospheric apparatus in the **Atmospheres** rollout.

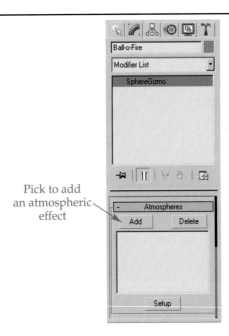

Pick to add an atmospheric effect

Figure 19-12. The **Add Atmosphere** dialog box is used to choose which atmospheric effect to assign to the atmospheric apparatus.

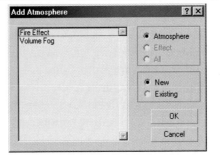

If you need to change the properties of the effect at a later time, high-light its name in the **Atmospheres** rollout. Then, pick the **Setup** button to open the **Environment** dialog box. You can also enter the **Environment** dialog box directly by picking **Environment...** from the **Rendering** pull-down menu. Finally, adjust the properties in the **Environment** dialog box.

Help Cel

In the **Atmosphere** rollout of the **Environment** dialog box, you can rename the atmospheric effect. If you are going to use more than one application of the same effect, you should rename each one. This will help keep things organized.

Fire

The fire effect, or simply "fire," is a cloud-like effect. It is used to produce flames, fire balls, and explosions. Fire can also be used for smoke, steam, fog effects, animated mud, or turbulent water. By using nonstandard color combinations, such as blue and magenta, you can also create SciFi effects such as a nebula. See Figure 19-13. In previous releases of 3D Studio MAX, the fire effect is called combustion.

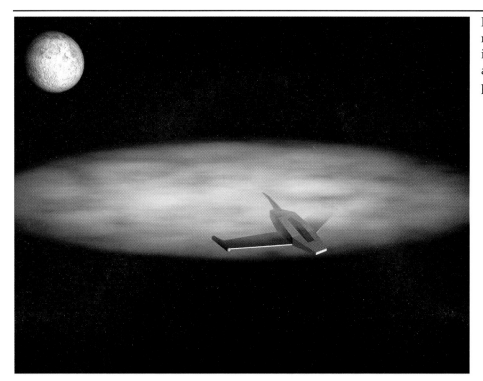

Figure 19-13. The nebula the starfighter is emerging from is actually a fire atmospheric effect.

To set up the fire effect, open the **Environment** dialog box. This can be done using the **Setup** button in the **Atmospheres** rollout for the atmospheric apparatus. You can also open the dialog box by selecting **Environment...** from the <u>R</u>endering pull-down menu. Then, highlight the fire name in the **Effects:** list in the **Atmosphere** rollout of the dialog box. The **Fire Effect Parameters** rollout appears. See Figure 19-14.

The **Gizmos:** area of the **Fire Effect Parameters** rollout allows you to assign the effect to, or remove the effect from, an atmospheric apparatus. The names of any gizmos the effect is currently assigned to appear in the drop-down list. The effect can be assigned to more than one gizmo. Picking the **Remove Gizmo** button removes the effect from the gizmo currently displayed in the drop-down list. Selecting the **Pick Gizmo** button allows you to choose an apparatus in the viewports. Pressing the [H] key to open the **Pick Object** dialog box is an effective way to select an apparatus.

Remove Gizmo

Pick Gizmo

The **Colors:** area allows you to define the colors used for the effect. By using unusual colors, such as purple and pink, you can create a SciFi nebula. The **Inner Color:** color is the most dense portion of the effect. For a flame, this is usually the hottest portion. Therefore, the default color is yellow. The **Outer Color:** color is the least dense portion of the effect. For a flame, this portion is cooler than the inside. Therefore, the default color is dark red. The **Smoke Color:** color is used only for the **Explosion** option. To change any color, pick the color swatch and select a new color in the color selector.

The **Shape:** area is used to define the overall shape of the effect. The **Flame Type:** radio buttons define the basic type of fire. Picking the **Tendril** radio button creates a flame effect similar to a campfire with "fingers" of flame. Picking the **Fire Ball** radio button creates a flame effect more similar to an explosion. See Figure 19-15. The value in the **Stretch:** spinner stretches the effect along the gizmo's Z axis. A value of 1 specifies no stretch, a value

Figure 19-14. The **Fire Effect Parameters** rollout in the **Environment** dialog box is used to define a fire effect.

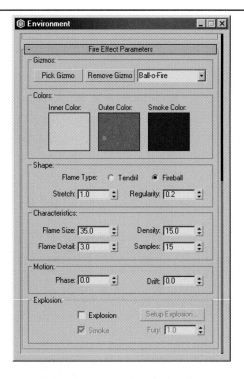

Figure 19-15. The fire effect on the left is set to fire ball. The fire effect on the right uses the exact same settings, except it is set to tendril.

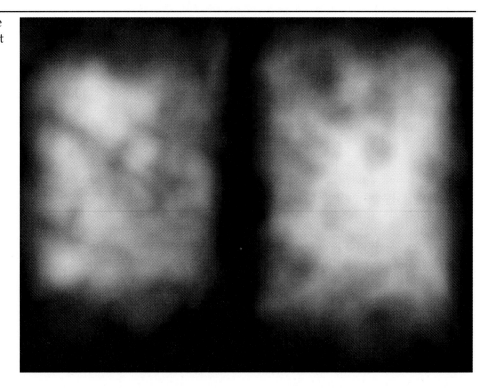

less than 1 compresses the effect, and a value greater than 1 stretches the effect. The value in the **Regularity:** spinner determines how the effect fills the gizmo. A value of 1 forces the effect to completely fill the gizmo. A very low value "shrinks" the effect inside the gizmo.

The **Characteristics:** area is used to define how the fire burns. See Figure 19-16. The **Flame Size:** setting determines the size of individual flames within the gizmo. The **Flame Detail:** setting determines color

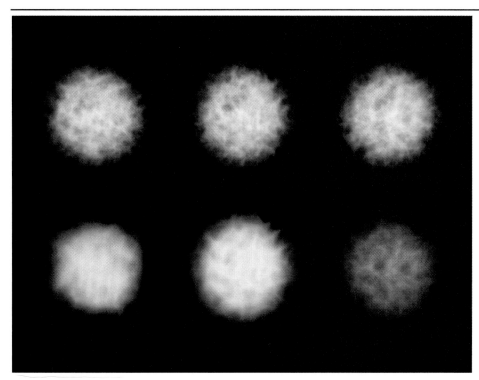

Figure 19-16. The three fire effects shown on the top have the same settings. At the bottom left, the flame size is increased. At the bottom middle, the flame detail is decreased. At the bottom right, the flame density is decreased.

change and the sharpness of the flame edges. You can also use this setting to make the flame "hotter." The **Density:** setting determines how bright and opaque the flame is. This also can be used to make the flame "hotter." The **Samples:** setting determines the sampling rate used by 3ds max to render the effect.

The **Motion:** area is used to define the movement or flicker of the flames. The **Phase:** spinner controls the rate of "burn" for the flame. The **Drift:** spinner sets how fast or slow a flame rises on the gizmo's Z axis. This value is low for cool, slow-burning fires.

The **Explosion:** area is used to automate the animation of an explosion. Check the **Explosion** check box to turn on this option. Pick the **Setup Explosion...** button to open the **Setup Explosion Phase Curve** dialog box. See Figure 19-17. In this dialog box, you can specify a starting and ending frame for the explosion. The **Phase:** spinner in the **Motion:** area is automatically animated over the range of frames specified.

The **Fury:** spinner is used to vary the **Phase:** spinner value. Fury determines the rolling, or "violent," effect of the explosion. If the **Smoke** check box is on, the explosion fades to the color set in the **Smoke Color:** swatch in the **Colors:** area.

Setup Explosion...

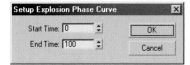

Figure 19-17. The **Setup Explosion Phase Curve** dialog box is used to set the starting and ending frames for a fire effect set as an explosion.

Help Cel

When the **Explosion** option is used, the value in the **Phase:** spinner indicates the state of the explosion. From 0 to 100, the explosion starts and builds to peak density. From 100 to 200, the explosion burns and generates smoke (if the **Smoke** option is on). From 200 to 300, the explosion fades away. A value over 300 has no effect on an explosion.

Exercise

Exercise 19-6

1) Draw the campfire logs and stone ring shown below. Use your own dimensions.
2) Define your own materials or get materials from the material library as appropriate. Apply materials to the objects.
3) Draw a cylindrical atmospheric apparatus in the middle of the logs. Use a nonuniform scale and squash to deform the apparatus as necessary.
4) Apply a fire atmospheric effect to the apparatus.
5) Define the fire effect to create gentle, climbing fingers of flame.
6) Render a couple frames of the animation as still images. You do not need to save the images. Make adjustments to the flame as necessary.
7) Add lights and a camera as necessary.
8) Render the final animation to a file named ex19-06.avi in the folder of your choice.
9) Save the file as ex19-06.max in the folder of your choice.

Fog

The fog and volumetric fog atmospheric effects are used to simulate fog, smoke, and steam. See Figure 19-18. They can also be used to simulate plasma or nebulas for SciFi applications. There are two types of fog—volumetric (volume) fog and plain fog. Volume fog is applied to an atmospheric apparatus. Fog is applied to the scene.

Help Cel

Use fog carefully. Too much fog can easily wipe out a scene, and perhaps your computer in the process. Rendering fog involves a *lot* of computations.

Volume Fog

To set up the volume fog effect, open the **Environment** dialog box. This can be done using the **Setup** button in the **Atmospheres** rollout for the atmospheric apparatus. You can also open the dialog box by selecting **Environment...** from the **Rendering** pull-down menu. Then, highlight the volume fog name in the **Effects:** list in the **Atmosphere** rollout of the dialog box. The **Volume Fog Parameters** rollout appears. See Figure 19-19.

The **Gizmos:** area of the **Volume Fog Parameters** rollout allows you to add or change gizmos to which the effect is applied. The names of any gizmos the effect is currently assigned to appear in the drop-down list. The effect can be assigned to more than one gizmo. Picking the **Remove Gizmo** button removes the effect from the gizmo currently displayed in the drop-down list. Selecting the **Pick Gizmo** button allows you to choose an apparatus in the viewports. The **Soften Gizmo Edges:** spinner is used

Figure 19-18. Volumetric fog is used to create steam rising from the manhole cover.

Figure 19-19. The **Volume Fog Parameters** rollout in the **Environment** dialog box is used to define a volumetric fog effect.

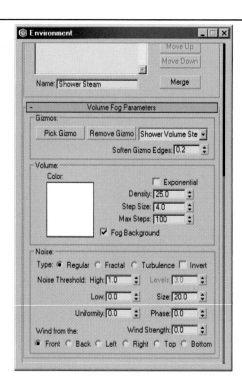

to soften or feather the edges of the fog. A value of 1.0 produces the softest edges possible.

The **Volume:** area is used to set the color and density of the fog. Pick the color swatch and choose a new color in the color selector. This can be animated by setting new colors on different animated frames. If the **Exponential** check box is checked, the density of the fog increases exponentially with distance. Otherwise, the density is linear. The **Density:** spinner sets the density of the fog. The **Step Size:** spinner sets the sampling size 3ds max uses to render the fog. The **Max Steps:** spinner sets an upper limit to sampling. This is used to prevent high rendering times. When the **Fog Background** check box is checked, the fog effect is applied to the background.

The **Noise:** area is used to generate noise in the fog. You can choose between the **Regular**, **Fractal**, and **Turbulence** types. Checking the **Invert** check box reverses the thin-dense effect of the fog. The **High:**, **Low:**, and **Uniformity: Noise Threshold:** spinners are used to limit the noise effect. The **Size:** and **Levels:** spinners control the size of the fog "bubbles." The **Levels:** spinner is active when the type of noise is set to **Fractal** or **Turbulence**. The **Phase:** spinner controls the wind effect on the fog. This value can be thought of as the speed of the wind. If the phase is not animated, the fog will not move. The **Wind Strength:** spinner sets the strength or force of the wind. The higher the value, the faster the fog moves in the direction of the wind. Finally, you can set the direction of the wind by picking one of the **Wind from the:** radio buttons.

Fog

The *fog*, or "plain" fog, atmospheric effect is used to produce fog or smoke. Many other effects can be achieved as well, such as a dust storm. There are two basic types of fog—standard and layered. Plain fog, unlike volumetric fog, is applied to the entire scene, not to an apparatus.

To set up the effect for plain fog, open the **Environment** dialog box. Then, pick the **Add...** button in the **Atmosphere** rollout. Select **Fog** in the **Add Atmospheric Effect** dialog box and pick the **OK** button. Then, highlight the fog name in the **Effects:** list in the **Atmosphere** rollout of the **Environment** dialog box. The **Fog Parameters** rollout appears. See Figure 19-20.

In the **Fog:** area, you can change the color of the fog by picking the color swatch. You can also assign environmental color and opacity maps by picking the buttons. By default, the **Fog Background** check box is on to apply the fog effect to the background. Finally, you can choose between standard and layered fog.

When the **Standard** radio button is selected in the **Fog:** area, the **Standard:** area of the rollout is enabled. Checking the **Exponential** check box increases fog density exponentially with distance. This should be unchecked for most applications. The **Near %:** spinner sets the density of the fog nearest the camera or viewer. The **Far %:** spinner sets the density of the fog at the camera's far range.

When the **Layered** radio button is selected in the **Fog:** area, the **Layered:** area of the rollout is enabled. The **Top:** and **Bottom:** spinner values set the range, or layer, where the fog is applied, in world units. The **Density:** spinner sets the density of the fog. The **Falloff:** radio buttons allow you to have the fog fade to 0 density at the top or bottom. By default, the **None** radio button is on.

You can also add horizontal noise to the fog by checking the **Horizon Noise** check box. The **Size:**, **Angle:**, and **Phase:** spinners are enabled. These are used to add noise to the horizon of the fog layer. Often, this can provide the added element of realism needed for the scene.

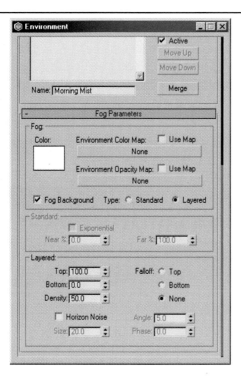

Figure 19-20. The **Fog Parameters** rollout in the **Environment** dialog box is used to define plain fog.

Help Cel

You can create multiple layers of fog by applying the fog effect several times. Each one remains independent of the others. However, this increases the calculations involved when rendering.

Exercise

Exercise 19-7

1) Draw a large quad patch. Increase the number of segments and apply noise to create terrain similar to that shown below.
2) Define your own ground material or use the material Ground_Grass in the default 3ds max material library.
3) Using the **Environment** dialog box, set up plain fog. Make the fog layered.
4) Define the fog to create the effect of early morning mist in the valleys, similar to the scene below.
5) In the **Material Editor**, define a gradient map for the diffuse color on any unused material sample. Define the gradient from blue to white, as shown on the background below.
6) In the **Environment** dialog box, set the background as the gradient map you defined in the **Material Editor**.
7) Render the scene to a file named ex19-07.jpg in the folder of your choice.
8) Make any adjustments as necessary. Render the scene again if necessary.
9) Save the scene as ex19-07.max in the folder of your choice.

Volumetric Lighting

Volumetric light uses the interaction of lights with the atmosphere to create lighting effects. Volumetric lighting, or "volume light," is used to produce a fog-like effect within the light's sphere of influence. Therefore, the effect is tied to a light instead of an atmospheric apparatus. For example, if volume light is applied to a spotlight, the "fog" is only visible within the spotlight's cone. Objects outside the cone are not affected. See Figure 19-21. Volumetric light is applied to a spotlight, omni light, or directional light.

To assign volumetric light to a light, select the light and pick **Modify** in the **Command Panel**. Open the **Atmospheres & Effects** rollout and pick the **Add** button. The **Add Atmosphere or Effect** dialog box is opened. Pick the **Atmosphere** radio button on the right side of the dialog box to display only the atmospheric effects. Then, pick **Volume Light** from the list at the left and the **OK** button.

You can also make a new volumetric light effect available in the scene without initially assigning it to a light. Open the **Environment** dialog box. Then, pick the **Add...** button in the **Atmosphere** rollout. Finally, select **Volume Light** in the **Add Atmospheric Effect** dialog box. Use the **Pick Light** and **Remove Light** buttons and the drop-down list in the **Lights:** area of the **Volume Light Parameters** rollout to manage the effect.

To set up volume light, open the **Environment** dialog box. This can be done using the **Setup** button in the **Atmospheres & Effects** rollout for the light. You can also open the dialog box by selecting **Environment...** from the **Rendering** pull-down menu. Highlight the volume light name in the **Effects:** list. The **Volume Light Parameters** rollout appears. See Figure 19-22. In the **Lights:** area, you can add and remove lights to which the effect is applied. Lights to which the effect is currently applied appear in the drop-down list.

Figure 19-21. Volumetric lighting affects objects inside a light's sphere of influence. In this example, most of the teapot is unaffected by the volumetric lighting effect.

Figure 19-22. The **Volume Light Parameters** rollout in the **Environment** dialog box is used to define a volumetric lighting effect.

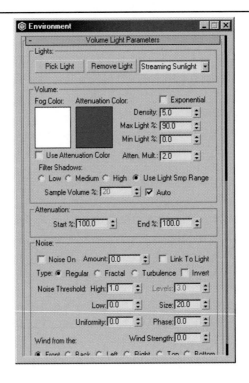

The **Volume:** area is used to determine the colors, density, and other settings for the effect. This area has two color swatches. The color in the **Fog Color:** swatch is the base color of the fog through which the light shines. The color in the **Attenuation Color:** swatch is the color to which the fog falls off. This color should generally be a neutral color, and is often a darker color. The default color is a bright blue. Check the **Use Attenuation Color** check box to apply the attenuation color to the fog. The value in the **Atten. Mult.:** spinner is a multiplier used for the attenuation color.

The **Filter Shadows:** radio buttons at the bottom of the **Volume:** area allow you to adjust the quality of the effect. These buttons set the sampling rate. Picking the **Use Light Smp Range** radio button bases the sampling rate on the light's shadow parameters. By default, the **Auto** check box is on. This enters a preset value in the **Sample Volume %:** spinner based on which radio button is selected. However, you can manually enter a value by unchecking the **Auto** check box.

The value in the **Density:** spinner of the **Volume:** area sets the density of the fog. If the **Exponential** check box is checked, the density of the effect increases exponentially with distance. Otherwise, the density is linear. The values in the **Max Light %:** and **Min Light %:** spinners determine the maximum and minimum glow the light produces in the fog. The **Max Light %:** spinner sets a maximum glow for the effect. The **Min Light %:** spinner sets a minimum glow. If this spinner value is higher than 0, it produces an effect similar to that of increasing ambient light. Objects outside the light's sphere of influence are affected.

The **Attenuation:** area is used to set a range for the effect's attenuation. These settings are based on the light's settings. The **Start %:** spinner determines the percentage of the light's start range where the effect begins to fall off. The **End %:** spinner determines the percentage of the light's end range where the effect falls off to 0.

The **Noise:** area is used to add noise to the volume light. The settings in this area are similar to those for volume fog. Check the **Noise On** check box to apply noise. The value in the **Amount:** spinner determines the percentage of noise applied. This value can range from 0 to 1. Checking the **Link To Light** check box "moves" the effect when the light is moved. When unchecked, the effect is based on world coordinates. There are three types of noise to choose from—regular, fractal, and turbulence. Checking the **Invert** check box reverses the noise effect of the fog.

If noise is used, set the **Noise Threshold:** and **Uniformity:** spinners. The noise threshold sets a maximum noise limit. Decreasing the uniformity thins the "fog" in the light. The value in the **Size:** spinner determines the size of the "fog" tendrils. The **Phase:** spinner is used to animate the wind effect on the "fog." The phase must be animated to see a movement in the light effect. The **Wind Strength:** spinner value is the force of the wind. The higher the value, the faster the "fog" moves through the light in the direction of the wind. The direction of the wind is set at the bottom of the **Noise:** area by picking the appropriate radio button.

Exercise

Exercise 19-8

1) Open ex19-03.max from Exercise 19-3. Save the scene as ex19-08.max in the folder of your choice.
2) Using the **Modify** tab of the **Command Panel**, add a volumetric lighting effect to the projector spotlight.
3) Render a single frame of the animation toward the middle, such as frame 50. You do not need to save the file.
4) Make any adjustments to the volumetric lighting as needed. The effect should be just noticeable. It should not appear as a solid cone of light.
5) Add a wall behind the screen and light.
6) When satisfied with the scene, render it to a file named ex19-08.avi in the folder of your choice.
7) Save the scene.

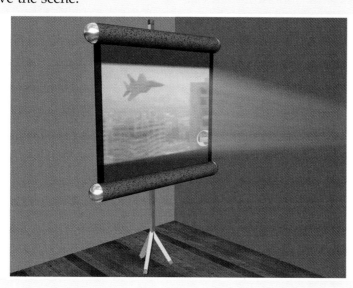

Chapter Snapshot

Chapter Test

Answer the following questions on a separate sheet of paper.
1) When the color of a light is changed, what is the effect on objects the light strikes?
2) Define falloff.
3) Define hotspot.
4) Which lights have a hotspot and falloff?
5) When can the hotspot be greater than the falloff?
6) Which lights can have their shape changed and to what shapes?
7) How can you turn a light into a projector?
8) Which lights can be used as projectors?
9) List two examples of where you might use a projector light.
10) What are the two basic types of shadows 3ds max lights can create?
11) What is the main difference between the two shadow types?
12) Which atmospheric effect can be used to model an exploding nebula for a SciFi application?
13) What type of shadow is the default cast by lights?
14) How do you set a light to cast shadows?
15) List two ways to animate a light.
16) Define atmospheric apparatus.
17) Which **Command Panel** tab is used to create an atmospheric apparatus?
18) Which atmospheric effects use an atmospheric apparatus?
19) Define volume light.
20) How do you create a volume light effect?

Modeling Problems

Draw the following objects using your own dimensions. Define and apply materials as needed. Add lights and a camera as needed. Pay attention to shadow location and color. Render each scene to a file named p19-xx.jpg in the folder of your choice. When finished, save each scene as p19-xx.max in the folder of your choice.

Red Glass Bottle **1**

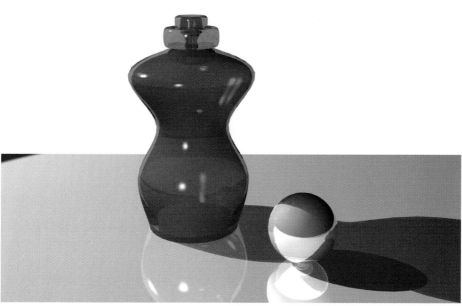

Salt and Pepper Shakers with Glass Bowl **2**

3 Fireplace

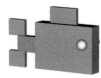

4 Candle

Oil Lamp **5**

Television **6**

Use an AVI file located in the 3ds max \Animations folder or an AVI file of your choice as the projector. Render a final animation of your scene to a file named p19-06.avi in the folder of your choice.

7 Starfighter

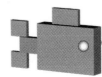

8 Fog

Space Nebula **9**

Open problem p19-07.max and save it as p19-09.max in the folder of your choice. Then, create the nebula and place the starfighter in it, as shown below.

Escaping Starfighter **10**

Open problem p19-09.max and save it as p19-10.max in the folder of your choice. Then, add several tiny explosions on the surface of the starfighter. Also, create one large explosion from which the starfighter is escaping.

Section Three Tutorial

Overview

For the Section Three tutorial, you will create an animation of a farmer's windmill. You will also add details such as a barn, ground, and a sky background. To complete the tutorial, you will need to create basic objects, apply modifiers, create hierarchies, and use a dummy object. You will also need to create and apply advanced materials and an atmospheric effect.

Figure T3-1 shows a final rendering of the model. Start by looking at the model and determining basic components into which the scene can be divided. For example, you can draw the windmill first, then the barn, and finally the ground and sky.

Help Cel

Save and save often. It is up to you to determine how often to save. However, a general rule of thumb is every 10 to 15 minutes. Also, you will probably want to perform test renderings during the modeling process. Use the **Quick Render (Draft)** and **Quick Render (Production)** settings and **ActiveShade** to your advantage.

Drawing the Windmill

To make the windmill easier to draw, break it into two general parts. The "lower" part of the windmill consists of the concrete pad, the tower, the two support braces, the pump, and the pump shaft. See Figure T3-2. The rest of the parts, including the gearbox, fin, and vanes, compose the "upper" part of the windmill. See Figure T3-3.

Figure T3-1. The Section Three tutorial model with extra details added.

Figure T3-2. The objects for the lower part of the windmill.

Figure T3-3. The objects for the upper part of the windmill.

Lower Part

Start drawing the lower portion of the windmill by creating the concrete pad. Draw the pad as a chamfer box in the Top viewport. You will use generic units for this model. The chamfer box is 400 units square and 20 units high. The fillet is 10 units. Increase the fillet segments to 5 or a little lower. Name the chamfer box Pad. Finally, position the object so it is centered on the world XY origin, if not already.

To create the tower, draw a four-sided cone in the Top viewport centered on the Pad object. Make the first radius 200 units and the second radius 50 units. The cone is 800 units high. Increase the height segments to 6. Rotate the cone so its flat sides match the flat sides of the concrete pad. Turn off smoothing for the cone and name it Tower. To finish the tower, apply a lattice modifier. Set it to display struts only. Make the struts five-sided with a radius of 3 and smoothed. Align the bottom of the tower with the bottom of the pad.

If you look at Figure T3-2, there are two support plates. The first support plate is in the middle of the tower. Draw a box 175 units square and 5 units in height. Name the box Plate, Middle. Then, center the plate in the middle of the tower. The second support plate is on top of the tower. Draw a box 70 units square and 5 units in height. Name the box Plate, Top. In the Top viewport, center the plate on the tower. Then, in the Left or Front viewport, vertically center the plate on the very top strut of the tower.

Notice in Figure T3-2 that each support plate has a guide hole through it. To finish the support plates, you must drill these holes. Use a 10-unit radius cylinder to drill the holes. The hole is in the center of each support plate.

The tall vertical shaft running to the "upper" portion of the windmill is drawn as a 5-unit radius cylinder. The cylinder is 950 units in height. Name the cylinder Pump Shaft. In the Top viewport, center the shaft on the tower and pad. The shaft should extend about 75 units below the bottom of the pad. This vertical location is not critical at this point. The vertical position of the shaft can be adjusted later.

The pump consists of three objects. See Figure T3-4. Draw a cylinder with a radius of 15 units and a height of 200 units. Position the cylinder on top of the pad. Then, position the cylinder so it is centered with one edge of the pad and offset on the other edge, as shown in Figure T3-4. It should be just inside the frame. Next, draw a sphere with a radius of 30 units. Center the sphere on top of the cylinder. The center of the sphere should be on the end of the cylinder. Finally, union the cylinder with the sphere. Name the object Pump Base.

To finish the pump, the pump spigot needs to be created. Draw the spline shown in Figure T3-5. Then, extrude the spline 175 units and name the object Pump Spigot. Finally, apply a taper of –0.5 on the Z axis with the effect on the X axis only. These axes may be

Figure T3-4. The pump is made from three simple objects. Also, notice the correct positioning of the pump inside the frame and the angle on the pump spigot.

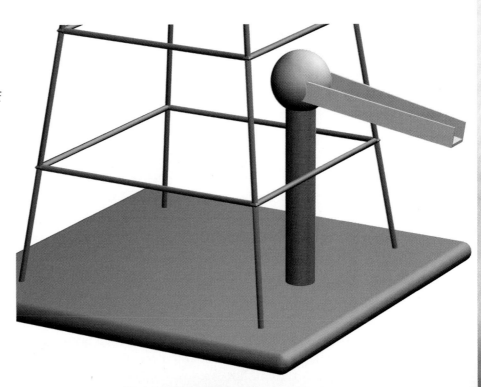

different for you, depending on how you created the spline. Finally, position the spigot on the Pump Base as shown in Figure T3-4.

To complete the lower portion of the windmill, a linkage needs to be created between the Pump Shaft and the Pump Base. See Figure T3-6. Draw the linkage as two 10-unit radius cylinders 10 units in height with a box in between them. The box is 20 units wide and 10 units high. The length of the box is determined by the distance from the pump base to the pump shaft. For example, if the center of the cylinder portion of the pump base and the center of the pump shaft are 80 units apart, make the length of the box 90 units (the center-to-center distance of 80 plus 10 for the radius of the cylinder portions of the linkage). In this way, one end of the box is enclosed inside the cylinder portion of the pump base.

Center the two "linkage" cylinders on the pump shaft. Then, position the box in between the cylinders, as shown in Figure T3-6. Union the three objects and name the resulting object Pump Linkage. Vertically position the linkage on the pump shaft toward the bottom, similar to the position shown in Figure T3-2. You may need to adjust the vertical position later.

Figure T3-5. The spline used to form the pump spigot.

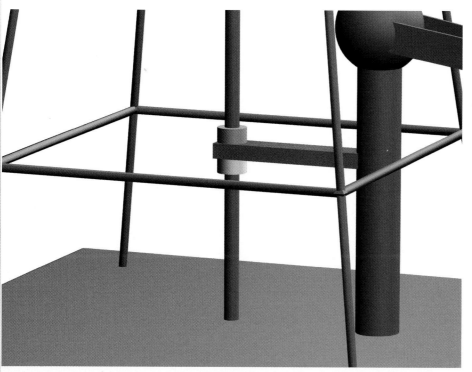

Figure T3-6. The pump linkage is made from two cylinders and a box. Also, notice the correct positioning of the linkage.

Upper Part

The upper portion of the windmill may appear more complex. It really is not any more complex, there are just more parts. To make it easier to draw, the upper portion is divided into the vanes, the gearbox, and the tailfin.

Help Cel

You may find it easier to model as objects are added to the scene by hiding any objects you do not need displayed.

Vanes

There are six vanes on the windmill centered on a hub. Each vane is made up of a wooden vane and a metal piece connecting the vane to the hub. Refer to Figure T3-3.

Start by drawing the hub. In the Left viewport, draw an oil tank with a radius of 30 units. Place the center of the oil tank at a world Z coordinate of 900 units. Make the overall height of the oil tank 10 units and the cap height 4.95 units. Increase the number of sides to 36 and name the object Hub, Vanes. In the Top viewport, move the hub so its left-hand edge is 140 units from the center of the tower (world origin) to locate it as shown in Figure T3-3.

Next, begin creating one of the vanes. The first vane will be cloned and rotated to create the other five vanes. Draw the "vane spline" shown in Figure T3-7. Center it left-to-right on the hub in the Left viewport. Also, place the shape above the hub. The bottom edge of the spline should be tangent to the top of the hub. Name the spline Vane Shape. Now, draw a straight line 5 units in length. The line can be drawn anywhere in any viewport. Name the line Vane Path. Select the Vane Shape spline. Create a loft object by "getting" the Vane Path spline as the path. Name the resulting loft object Vane01. If necessary, move Vane01 in the Front viewport so it is centered front-to-back on the hub.

Figure T3-7. The splines used to form one vane and one vane holder.

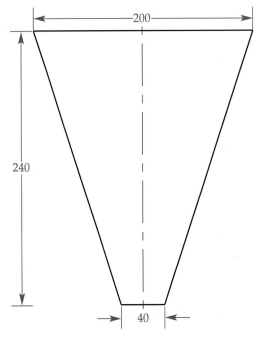

Vane

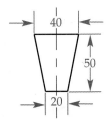

Vane Holder

Figure T3-8. One vane and one vane holder are correctly positioned on the hub.

Now, create the metal piece connecting the vane to the hub. Draw the "vane holder" spline shown in Figure T3-7. Center it left-to-right on the hub in the Left viewport. Then, move the spline vertically to overlap the hub and the vane, as shown in Figure T3-8. Name the spline Vane Plate Shape. Next, draw a straight line 10 units in length named Vane Plate Path. Select the Vane Plate Shape spline. Create a loft object by "getting" the Vane Plate Path spline as the path. Name the resulting loft object Vane Plate01. If necessary, move Vane Plate01 in the Front viewport so it is centered front-to-back on the hub and Vane01. See Figure T3-8.

Now, the vane and vane plate need to have curvature added. Apply a bend modifier to Vane01. Set the bend angle to 25° on the Y axis. The Y axis should be the "long" axis of the vane. Also, the angle should "cup" the vane toward the front of the windmill. If it cups in the other direction, use a value of –25°. Apply a bend modifier to Vane Plate01 using the same settings. Finally, in the Top viewport, rotate Vane01 30° counterclockwise.

One end of the vane plate needs to be rotated to match the vane. However, the other end must match the hub. Therefore, a twist modifier must be applied to Vane Plate01. Set the twist angle to 30° around the object's "long" axis. The object should twist to match the rotation of the vane. Hint: Move the center of the modifier's gizmo to obtain the correct twist.

Finally, the vane and vane plate need to be copied five times. To do this, first move the pivot point of each object to the center of the hub. Next, rotate five copies of the vane about the pivot point. A copy should be placed every 60° around the hub. Finally, rotate five copies of the vane plate about the pivot point in 60° intervals. See Figure T3-9.

Help Cel

When the twist modifier is applied to the vane plate, the surfaces of the vane plate will not exactly match the surfaces of the vane.

Gearbox and Axle

The gearbox is drawn as three simple objects. See Figure T3-10. First, draw a cylinder in the Top viewport with a radius of 35 units and a height of 5 units. Center the cylinder on the tower and name it Gearbox Plate. Also, increase the number of sides to 36. In the Front or Left viewport, move the cylinder up so it sits on top of the Plate, Top object.

Now, draw a box in the Top viewport 70 units by 70 units by 110 units tall. Set the length, width, and height segments to 5. Center the box on the tower and name it Gearbox. In the Left or Front viewport, move the box up so it sits on top of the Gearbox Plate object. Next,

Figure T3-9. All vanes and vane holders are correctly positioned.

Figure T3-10. The gearbox is made from three simple objects. The orange object is a box with a taper modifier applied.

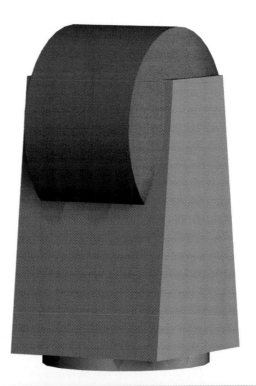

apply a taper modifier of –0.4 to the Z axis with the effect on the Y axis (or X axis) only. Refer to Figure T3-10.

The last part of the gearbox is a simple oil tank. In the Left viewport, draw an oil tank with a radius of 40 units centered on the Hub object. Make the overall height 70 units and the cap height 10 units. Increase the number of sides to 36. Center the oil tank front-to-back on the Gearbox object. Finally, union the oil tank with the Gearbox. Name the resulting object Gearbox Unit.

Now, the axle for the vane assembly needs to be created. First, draw a circle with a radius of 4 units in any viewport. Name the circle Axle Shape. Next, draw the spline shown in Figure T3-11 in the Front viewport. Center the spline in the gearbox as shown in Figure T3-3. Name the spline Axle Path. Finally, select Axle Path and create a loft object by "getting" the Axle Shape spline. Name the resulting loft object Axle. Move the pivot point of the loft object to the center of the main axle shaft and align it to the world, as shown in Figure T3-11. The axle and hub should rotate about the same point, when viewed in the Left viewport.

Tailfin and Frame

To draw the frame for the tailfin, first create a cylinder in the Top viewport with a radius of 5 units and a height of 30 units. The center of the cylinder should be in line with the axle centerline and 200 units "behind" the center of the tower. In the Left or Front viewport, vertically center the cylinder on the centerline of the axle. Name the cylinder Tail Frame Pivot.

Next, draw a box 170 units by 40 units by 5 units high in the Top viewport. Name the box Tail Frame Top. In the Top viewport, the "40-unit dimension" should be centered with the centerline of the axle. Also, one edge should align with the gearbox and the opposite edge should be tangent to the cylinder. See Figure T3-12. In the Left or Front viewport, move the bracket vertically so it sits on top of the cylinder. Its top edge should also be roughly flush with the top edge of the box portion of the gearbox. However, it may be slightly above or below the top edge. Apply a taper of 0.75 on one axis only to the Tail Frame Top box to get the final shape of the bracket, as shown in Figure T3-12. You will need to move the center of the modifier's gizmo. If the taper is in the wrong direction, change the value to negative.

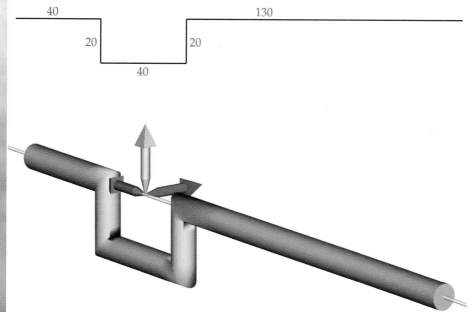

Figure T3-11. The path for the axle. The lofted axle is shown here rendered with its pivot point correctly located.

Now, clone a copy of the bracket. In the Left or Front viewport, move the copy down vertically so its top edge is flush with the bottom of the cylinder. Finally, union Tail Frame Pivot and the two brackets. Name the resulting object Tail Frame Bracket.

To create the tailfin, draw the spline shown in Figure T3-13. Then, extrude the spline 5.0 units. Name the object Tailfin. In the Top viewport, rotate the tailfin as needed and center it left-to-right on the frame for the tailfin. Then, move the tailfin so it just touches the cylinder portion of the frame. Refer to Figure T3-12.

Materials for the Windmill

The windmill has six different materials applied to it. Three of these materials are from the default 3ds max material library. Two materials are standard materials you create. The sixth material is an advanced material you need to define.

Material Library Materials

Start by getting and applying the materials from the 3ds max material library. Select an unused material sample slot in the **Material Editor**. Get the material Metal_Black_Plain from the material library. Apply this material to:

- Axle
- Hub, Vanes
- Plate, Middle
- Plate, Top
- Pump Shaft
- Tail Frame Bracket

Figure T3-12. The Tail Frame Bracket object is made up of three objects. Notice the correct positioning of the tailfin and bracket.

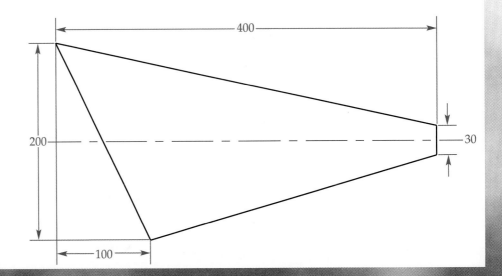

Figure T3-13. The spline used to form the tailfin.

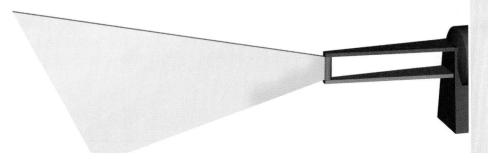

Select another unused material sample slot. Get the material Metal_Steel from the material library. Apply this material to:

- Gearbox Unit
- Gearbox Plate
- Pump Base
- Tower

Finally, get the material Concrete_Cement from the material library. Assign this material to the pad.

Apply UVW map modifiers as necessary. Some objects may not require this modifier, but you may want to change the default mapping coordinates.

Creating the Standard Materials

A yellow material is used for the Pump Linkage. Refer to Figure T3-1. This material needs to be defined. Select an unused material sample slot in the **Material Editor**. Set the material type to standard and the shading to Blinn. Define a bright yellow (R255, G255, B0) diffuse color. Lock the diffuse and ambient colors. Then, change the specular color to pure white (R255, G255, B255). Set the specular level to 50 and the glossiness to 25. Name this material Linkage Yellow and apply it to the Pump Linkage object.

Now, you need to define a copper metal material for the Pump Spigot and each Vane Plate. Select an unused material sample slot. Set the material type to standard and the shading to Metal. Define an orange-brown diffuse color (R230, G160, B50). Lock the diffuse and ambient colors. Set the specular level to 100 and the glossiness to 50. Name this material Copper and apply it to the Pump Spigot and all Vane Plate objects.

Creating the Advanced Material

The material used for the vanes and the tailfin is a mapped material. First, select an unused material sample slot in the **Material Editor**. Set the material type to standard and the shading to Blinn. Name the material Red Windmill Wood.

Define a medium red (R200, G50, B50) for the diffuse color. Define a dark red (R75, G15, B15) for the ambient color. Define the specular color as an almost white, red color (R255, G230, B230).

Next, assign a diffuse color map. Pick the wood map type. Name the map Windmill Wood. Define the two colors for the map using the same settings for the ambient and diffuse colors. Adjust the other settings for the map as necessary. However, the default settings should be fairly close to those needed.

Return to the Red Windmill Wood level of the material tree. Create an instance of the wood map for the bump map. Set the diffuse color map percentage to about 25. Set the bump map percentage to about 15.

Finally, apply the Red Windmill Wood material to the tailfin. Also apply the material to all of the vanes. You do not need to apply a UVW map modifier for the material to render correctly. However, if you want to change the mapping coordinates of the tailfin or vanes, apply UVW map modifiers as needed.

Help Cel

The default number of frames (100) is used for this tutorial. However, if you want to increase the animation length, do so now before adding animation keys. Remember, a computer plays animations at 30 frames per second. Therefore, 90 frames is equal to 3 seconds of playback.

Animating the Windmill

The animation for this scene is fairly simple. The vanes, vane plates, hub, and axle rotate about the center of the axle. A dummy object is created to transfer the rotation of the axle into vertical motion for the pump shaft. At the same time this action is taking place, the entire top of the windmill rotates, pauses, and rotates back to the original position.

To create the animation, you need to create a hierarchy of linked objects. However, before creating the hierarchy, it is good practice to align all pivots to the world coordinates. You can do this for each object individually. You can also select all objects and align all pivot points at the same time. Refer to Chapter 12 if you need to review aligning pivot points.

Help Cel

Before actually linking objects, it is a good idea to save or "hold" the scene. Sometimes undoing links can shift objects, resulting in a lot of "fixing" time.

Creating the Hierarchy

Now that all pivot points are aligned to the world coordinates, you can begin creating the hierarchy. Look at the windmill in Figure T3-1. Sketch a hierarchy on paper. The hierarchy should be created in two general "steps." The first step should be similar to the following sequence.

- Vane to Vane Plate
- Vane Plate to Hub, Vanes
- Hub, Vanes to Axle
- Axle to Gearbox Unit
- Gearbox Unit to Gearbox Plate

There are, of course, six vanes and six vane plates. You will also need to link the Tailfin to the Tail Frame Bracket, and the Tail Frame Bracket to the Gearbox Unit. Make sure you link objects on frame 0. You will also need to set inheritance as needed. When finished linking and setting inheritance, continue with the second hierarchical step. The second step should be similar to the following sequence.

- Pump Linkage to Pump Shaft
- Pump Shaft to vertical motion of the axle

A dummy needs to be created to transfer the rotation of the axle into vertical motion for the Pump Shaft. The Pump Shaft, therefore, is linked to the dummy. Note: Since the connection between the Pump Shaft and the Axle is enclosed inside the gearbox and cannot be seen, the actual connection is not modeled.

Draw a dummy object in any viewport. It can be any size, but an object about 15 units square results in a convenient size. Next, in all viewports, center the dummy on the offset portion of the axle. Finally, link the dummy to the axle.

Set the inheritance for the dummy. The inheritance for the other objects is not as critical as that for the dummy and the Pump Shaft. The dummy should inherit movement on the X, Y, and Z axes. It should also inherit rotation on the Z axis. All other inheritance should be off.

Next, link the Pump Shaft to the dummy on frame 0. Make sure the shaft is positioned vertically just below the axle offset before linking. You will also need to move the shaft's pivot point to the center of the dummy object. Then, link the shaft to the dummy and set the inheritance. Since the shaft only moves up and down, it should inherit the movement of the dummy object on the Z axis only. Also, remember the Pump Linkage is linked to the shaft. This cannot rotate. Therefore, the shaft should not inherit any rotation.

Setting the Animation

There are really just two motions for the scene. The vanes of the windmill rotate. In addition to that, the entire top of the windmill turns. The pump shaft moves up and down. However, this is tied to the motion of the dummy object, which, in turn, is tied to the rotation of the axle.

First, move to frame 100. Then, animate the rotation of the axle 720° about its longitudinal axis. With this setting, the vanes, vane holders, hub, and axle will rotate two complete rotations over the length of the animation.

Now, the entire top of the windmill needs to be animated. Move to frame 50. Next, animate the rotation of the Gearbox Plate object 30° clockwise in the Top viewport. Move to frame 100. Animate the rotation of the Gearbox Plate object 30° counterclockwise back to its original position.

The basic animation for the scene is now complete. Make and view a preview animation of the Perspective viewport. Notice that the top of the windmill rotates 30° and immediately rotates back. A pause needs to be added before the top rotates back to its original position. Also, make sure all other motion is correct. Observe the vertical position of the Pump Shaft and Pump Linkage. If any adjustments need to be made, move to frame 0. Then make the adjustments. Unlink and relink objects as necessary.

Help Cel

If you look closely at the rotation of the vanes and think about the curvature on the vanes, the positive 720° rotation may be "backward." In this case, change the rotation value to –720°.

Adjusting Keys

To add the pause to the rotation of the windmill top, the keys need to be adjusted. The animation key added at frame 50 has the correct rotation values. Move this key to frame 30. Now, to add the pause, copy the key at frame 30 to frame 60. The windmill top will now fully rotate by frame 30, stay there until frame 60, and rotate back to its original position by frame 100.

Make and view a preview animation. Notice the "swooping" motion or "bounce" of the windmill top. As you learned in this section, the bounce is due to the default transition into and out of keys. 3ds max attempts to create a smooth motion into and out of every key. Since the windmill is a piece of machinery, its movement should be more mechanical.

The rotation keys have TCB controllers. To change the rotation to a more mechanical motion, change the **Continuity:** value to 10 on all rotation keys for the Gearbox Plate object. By using a value of 10 instead of 0, the rotation will be mechanical, but it will also "ease into" the keys. Think of an oscillating fan. The head of the fan slows down as it approaches the end of its rotation.

Make and view another preview animation. Further refine the keys as needed.

Drawing the Barn

The barn may not look simple to draw, but it really is. The details on the barn are added as a material. The barn doors are added as geometry and placed on the end face of the barn.

Start creating the barn by drawing the spline shown in Figure T3-14 in the Front viewport. Name the spline Barn. Next, extrude the spline 2500 units using the default settings. The basic barn object is now complete and ready for materials.

Figure T3-14. The spline used to form the barn.

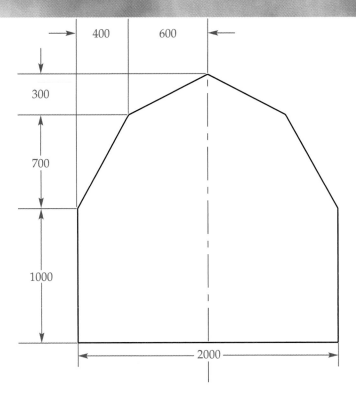

Next, draw one barn door and then clone it to create the other door. Draw the splines shown in Figure T3-15. Attach the inner spline to the outer spline. Then, extrude the spline 15 units and name the object Door Frame01. Now, draw a box 852 units by 552 units and 5 units in height. Name the box Door Panel01 and center it in the frame. The "back" of the panel and the "back" of the frame should be on the same plane. This will allow both the frame and the panel to sit flat on the barn wall. Copy the panel and frame to create a second door. Finally, move all four objects so they are flush with the barn wall. Refer to Figure T3-1.

With the barn and barn doors drawn, they need to be placed in their final position. Select the barn, both door frames, and both door panels. Then, in the Top viewport, rotate the objects 20° clockwise. You can use your own rotation. However, be sure to write down how much you rotate the objects in case you need it for future reference.

Defining the Barn Material

The barn material is a combination of several material types and maps. Start by opening the **Material Editor** and selecting an unused material sample slot. Next, get the material Wood_Cedfence from the default 3ds max material library. Rename the material Barn Red. Change the material type to composite and keep the material as a sub-material.

In the **Composite Basic Parameters** rollout, pick the **Mat. 1:** button labeled **None**. Define a standard material named Red Barn Paint. The diffuse color should be a medium red, the ambient color a deep red, and the specular color a light red. The defaults can be used for all other settings. Return to the Barn Red level of the material tree and change the percentage of Red Barn Paint material to 60 with additive color.

Next, select an unused material sample slot and get the material Concrete_Asphalt from the default 3ds max material library. Change the material type to blend and keep the material as a sub-material. Name the blend material Shingles. In the **Blend Basic Parameters** rollout, Concrete_Asphalt should be listed as one of the materials. Pick the other material button to navigate to that material level. Name the material Shingle Tiles. Define a diffuse color map as bricks. Set the brick color to a dark grey (R51, G51, B51) and the mortar color to a light grey

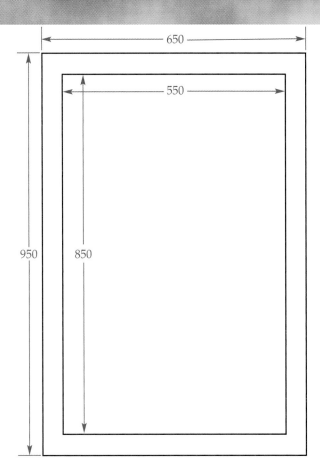

Figure T3-15. The two splines used to form the frame of one barn door.

(R184, G184, B184). Also, set the pattern as running bond. Navigate to the Shingle Tiles level of the material tree and set the diffuse color as 100% the brick map. Finally, navigate to the Shingles level of the material tree and enter 25.0 in the **Mix Amount:** spinner.

To finish the barn material, you must create a multi/sub-object material composed of the Barn Red and Shingles materials. Select an unused material sample slot. Change the material type to multi/sub-object. Discard the existing material. Name the material Barn Material and set the number of sub-materials to two. Then, drag the Barn Red material sample and drop it onto the first material button in the **Multi/Sub-Object Basic Parameters** rollout. When prompted, place the copy as an instance. In the **Name** column, enter Sides. Finally, drag and drop an instance of the Shingles material onto the second material button in the **Multi/Sub-Object Basic Parameters** rollout. In the **Name** column, enter Roof. The material sample should appear similar to the one shown in Figure T3-16.

The barn material is now complete. In the next section, you will apply the material to the barn.

Help Cel

By placing copies of the materials as instances when defining a multi/sub-object material, it is easier to edit the original material.

Applying Materials to the Barn

The first step in putting the barn material on the barn is to actually apply the material to the object. You can do this with any method you like. Next, apply a mesh select modifier. At the face sub-object level, select all faces on both ends of the barn. Apply a planar UVW map

Figure T3-16. The Barn Material should look similar to the material shown here.

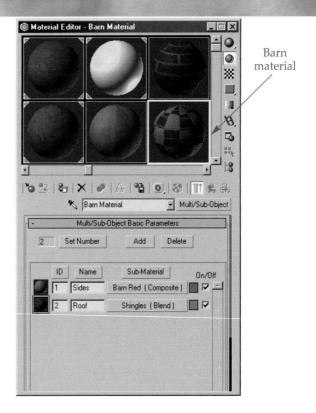

Barn material

modifier to the selection. Then, apply a material modifier to the selection. If you followed the earlier directions, the Barn Red material is ID 1, which should be used for the ends of the barn.

Next, apply another mesh select modifier. At the face sub-object level, select all faces on both sides of the barn. Apply a planar UVW map modifier to the selection. Then, apply a material modifier to the selection. Set the material ID for the Barn Red material.

Apply a final mesh select modifier. At the face sub-object level, select all faces on the four roof surfaces. Apply a box UVW map modifier to the selection. Then, apply a material modifier to the selection. The material ID for the Shingles material should be 2, which should be used for the roof.

Make any adjustments necessary to the UVW map modifiers. Adjust the gizmos as needed. As you navigate the modifier stack for the barn, you will get a warning message. Since you are only changing mapping coordinates, you can disregard this message. However, do *not* change any geometry.

Finally, the doors need materials. Apply the Barn Red material to the door panels. Then, get the material Wood_Driftwood from the default 3ds max material library and apply it to the door frames. You will also need to apply a UVW map modifier to each of the door objects and adjust mapping coordinates.

Help Cel

If you want to be very precise with the shingle placement, a mesh select and UVW map modifier should be applied independently to each flat surface of the roof.

Drawing the Ground and Sky

To draw the ground, create a quad patch in the Top viewport. The patch is 10,000 units square. You can also use a plane object. Name the patch Ground. Position the object as necessary so the barn and windmill sit directly on top of the ground. See Figure T3-17. Apply the material Ground_Grass from the default 3ds max material library to the object. Also, apply a UVW map modifier to the object and increase the tiling. For the rendering in Figure T3-1, the **U Tile:** value is 8.0 and the **V Tile:** value is 10.0, but you can use your own values.

The sky is an environmental background. First, open the **Material Editor** and select any unused material sample slot. Name the material Sky Material. Define a diffuse color map as a gradient type. In the **Coordinates** rollout for the map, pick the **Environ** radio button and set the **Mapping:** option to screen. Then, define the colors of the gradient as shown in Figure T3-18. Also, change the "color 2" position as needed. Finally, name the map Sky Map in the drop-down list below the material samples.

To finish specifying the sky, open the **Environment** dialog box. Then, specify the background map as Sky Map by picking the **Environment Map:** button to open the **Material/Map Browser**. Get the map from the **Material Editor** and place it as an instance. The map Sky Map is now displayed as the background in renderings and by ActiveShade.

Adding Lights and a Camera

Before adding a camera, adjust the Perspective viewport to get a view close to the one you want displayed for the final rendering. Then, draw a target camera in any viewport. Use the **Match Camera to View** function to match the camera to the Perspective viewport. Finally, make any fine-tuning necessary to get the view you want.

There are only two lights in this scene. A free directional light provides the overall illumination. A target spotlight is used to simulate sunlight streaming through a break in cloud cover. If you look at Figure T3-1, you can see this effect.

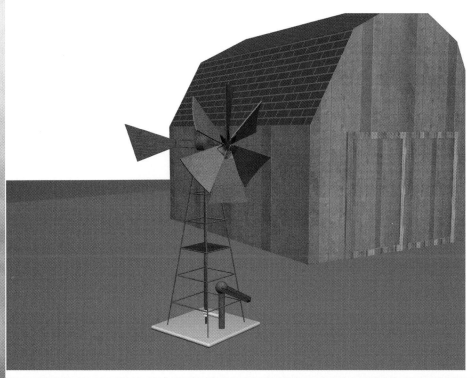

Figure T3-17. All objects are correctly placed on the ground.

Figure T3-18. The settings for the background map.

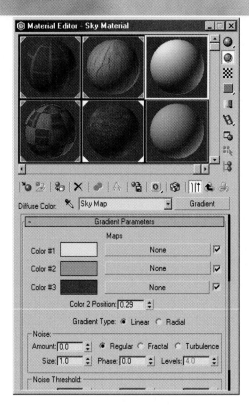

First, draw a free directional light in the Top viewport. Adjust the hotspot so the entire ground object falls within the hotspot. Set the **Multiplier:** spinner to a value of about 1.0 or slightly less. Also, turn off shadow casting for this light. Next, move the light so it is above all objects. Finally, rotate the light in the Front and Left viewports so the side and end of the barn are illuminated.

Now, draw a target spotlight. Place the target somewhere close to the base of the windmill. Place the spotlight above the scene and to the left. Turn on shadow casting for the spotlight. Set the intensity of the light as needed, probably between .75 and 1.0. Adjust the hotspot so the windmill is completely inside the hotspot. Adjust the falloff to a slightly larger size by about five units. You may also want to change the light's color to a very light, almost white, blue.

Add a volumetric light atmospheric effect to the spotlight. Make any adjustments to the default settings as necessary. You can probably use the default settings for everything except density. The density value must be very low, probably around 0.125 or just slightly higher.

Help Cel

If you are making further refinements to the scene after adding the volumetric lighting, you may want to deactivate the effect when performing test renderings. This can reduce rendering time.

Other Details

If you like and have the time, you can add other details to the scene. For example, the rendering shown in Figure T3-1 has a water trough with water placed next to the pump. Also, a split rail fence is added at the back of the barn. You may also want to add some animals to the scene or crop fields in the distance. The rendering in Figure T3-1 also has a dirt path leading from the barn doors. This is simply an irregular, closed spline extruded 1 unit. You can add a sign to your barn if you like.

In the next section of the text, you will learn about particle systems. After you learn how to simulate fluid using a particle system, you may want to come back to this scene and add water flowing from the pump.

Other Materials

If you added a dirt road, as shown in Figure T3-1, you can assign the material Ground_Sand from the default material library. The material Wood_Grey_Plank might be used for a split rail fence. The material Wood_Cedfence can be used for the water tank shown in Figure T3-1. Use your imagination to fill in the detail for the scene.

Rendering the Final Scene

Before rendering the final animation, make a preview animation. Check the motion in the preview to make sure the hierarchy and motion are set correctly. Then, render three or four still images, such as frames 15, 50, and 75. Use these renderings to check materials, lighting, and shadows. Alternately, you can use ActiveShade on three sample frames.

When completely satisfied with the scene, render a final animation to a file named tut03.avi in the folder of your choice. Render every frame of the active time segment. To save time and hard drive space, use the 320×240 resolution setting. If you have time and space, you can use the 640×480 resolution setting, but this will require perhaps an hour or more to render, and, depending on compression, the file may be over 10MB in size.

When the rendering is complete, view the animation. If necessary, make any adjustments and render the scene again.

Discussion Questions

1) The pump spigot is created by extruding the spline shown in Figure T3-5. How else can the spigot be created?
2) When drawing the first vane, why must the spline be lofted, instead of using an extrude modifier?
3) When the twist modifier is applied to the vane plate, why is the gizmo's center point moved?
4) When creating the hierarchy, why are the pivot points aligned to the world coordinates before linking any objects?
5) Why are UVW map modifiers applied separately to the ends and sides of the barn?
6) When making final adjustments to linked objects, why might you need to unlink and relink the objects? Are there any other ways to achieve the same result?
7) Volumetric lighting is applied to the spotlight to simulate sunlight streaming through a break in the clouds. How else might you give the impression of sunlight coming through a break in the clouds?

Section Four

OBJECTS IN MOTION

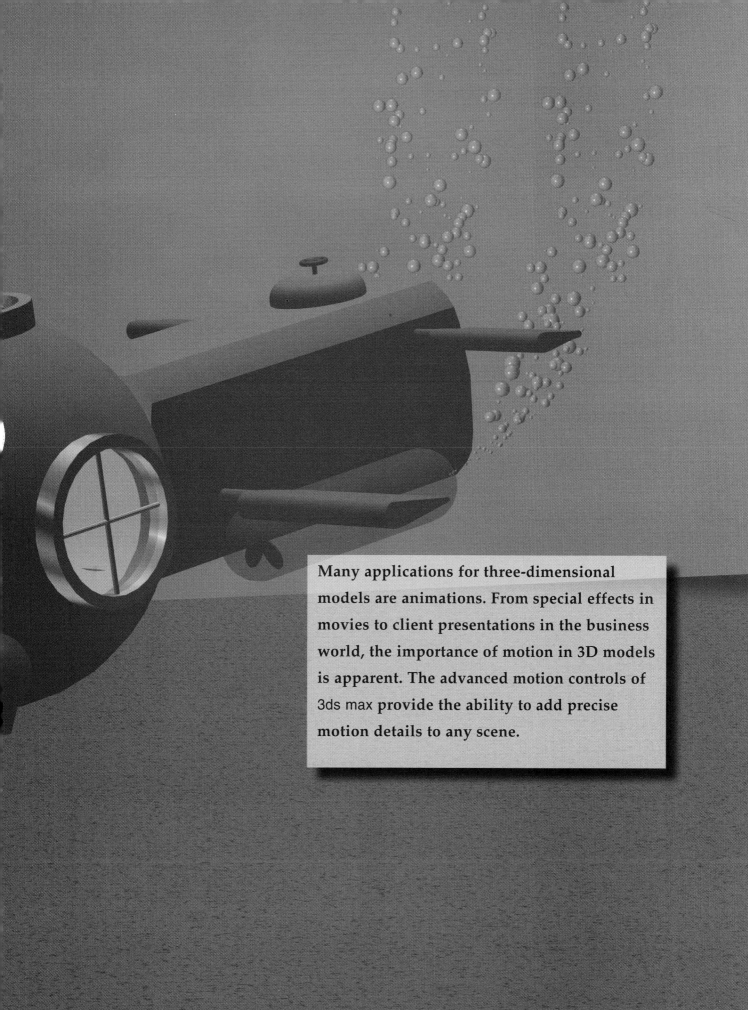

Many applications for three-dimensional models are animations. From special effects in movies to client presentations in the business world, the importance of motion in 3D models is apparent. The advanced motion controls of 3ds max provide the ability to add precise motion details to any scene.

Chapter 20

Creating Systems and Wiring Parameters

Objectives

After completing this chapter, you will be able to:

- Define a system as used in 3ds max.
- Explain the bones system.
- Give an example of where a bones system is used.
- Explain the ring array system.
- Create a ring array.
- Substitute objects for the default ring array boxes.
- Explain the sunlight system.
- Create a sunlight system.
- Explain parameter wiring.
- Wire parameters.

What Is a System?

A *system* in 3ds max is a process of automating objects, links, and controllers. The animation process of a system can often be replicated manually. However, using a system greatly simplifies the process and reduces production time. 3ds max comes with three built-in systems. These are the bones, ring array, and sunlight systems. In addition, third-party software developers have created hundreds of other systems available as plug-ins.

Create

Systems

To create a system, pick **Create** in the **Command Panel**. Then pick the **Systems** button. See Figure 20-1. In the drop-down list, select the type of system. Unless plug-ins are loaded, the only option is **Standard**. Then, in the **Object Type** rollout, pick the button for the system you want to create.

Bones

The *bones system* allows you to create a hierarchical network of joints and "bones." This network can be animated using inverse kinematics (IK). *Bones* are wireframe objects that can be transformed, but not modified. Bones are not rendered with the scene by default. However, you can set bones to be renderable. Inverse kinematics and bones are discussed in Chapter 21.

A big advantage of using bones with IK is ease of animation. A complex object can have a bone system created for it. The object can then be hidden and the bones animated. The object is then displayed for the final rendering.

The network of bones is used to control the motion of other objects. A very common application of this is to animate humans, animals, or SciFi creatures. See Figure 20-2. However, bones can also be used to control the animation of mechanical objects, such as a spring-loaded door closer or an oil well pump.

Figure 20-1. The bones, ring array, and sunlight systems come with 3ds max.

Figure 20-2. A—A bones system is used to animate this model of a cartoon rabbit. B—The bones used in the rabbit model. A combination of bones and box primitives used as bones is applied to the model. (Discreet, a division of Autodesk)

A

B

Ring Array

A *ring array system* is a circular arrangement of boxes with a dummy object at the center. You can set the number of objects (boxes) in the ring array. The objects can be placed on one plane or along a sinusoidal wave. See Figure 20-3. The parameters of the ring array can be animated and the ring array can be transformed.

Drawing and Animating a Ring Array

Create

Systems

Ring Array

Ring Array

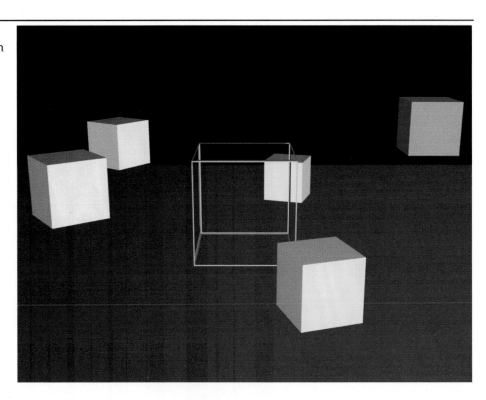

Motion

To draw a ring array, pick **Systems** in the **Create** tab of the **Command Panel**. Then, pick the **Ring Array** button in the **Object Type** rollout. The **Parameters** rollout is displayed. See Figure 20-4. Then, pick in the viewport to set the center of the array. Drag the cursor to set the radius of the array. The exact radius can be set later. Notice one of the boxes is a different color and selected after the array is drawn. This box is the first in the array and is the "control center" for the parameters of the array.

With the **Create** tab still active and the array selected, you can set the parameters of the array in the **Parameters** rollout. Otherwise, select any box in the array and pick **Motion** in the **Command Panel**. The **Parameters** rollout also appears in this panel. See Figure 20-5.

Set the exact radius of the array in the **Radius:** spinner. The value in the **Amplitude:** spinner determines the height of the sinusoidal wave. It is measured in current drawing units from the dummy object's center. The value in the **Cycles:** spinner sets the number of peaks in the sinusoidal wave around the circumference of the array. The **Phase:** spinner is used to rotate the sinusoidal wave around the array. Whole numbers entered in this spinner have no visible effect, but change the position of the first object. The number of boxes in the array is set using the **Number:** spinner.

Figure 20-3. A ring array is a system with boxes placed about a dummy object. The dummy is not rendered.

Figure 20-4. The ring array is defined in the **Parameters** rollout.

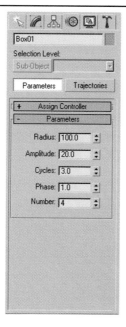

Figure 20-5. After the ring array is created, the **Motion** tab in the **Command Panel** is used to adjust the parameters of the array.

You can animate the radius, amplitude, cycles, and phase of the ring array. The number of objects in the array cannot be animated. Transforms can be added to the dummy. Modifiers can be added to the objects. Any modifier applied to any object is applied to all objects. Modifiers applied to the dummy are *not* applied to the objects and are, therefore, essentially useless.

Materials can be assigned to the objects in an array. Each object can have a different material. Animated materials can also be assigned.

Using Other Objects in a Ring Array

So now you can automatically create a ring of boxes. This probably does not seem very useful, and you may be right. However, you can replace the objects (boxes) in a ring array with other objects. See Figure 20-6. You can use copies or instances. All objects (boxes) can be replaced with the same object. You can also replace each box with a different object. Replacing the objects in a ring array is done using **Track View**. **Track View** is covered in Chapter 16 if you need a review.

Copy Object

Paste Object

Before replacing the objects in a ring array, the replacements and the array must be drawn. Then, open **Track View**. Move through the hierarchy tree until the container for the replacement object is displayed. See Figure 20-7. Select the container and pick the **Copy Object** button on the **Track View** toolbar. In order to replace the objects in a ring array with a modified object, you must select the modified object container. Next, move through the hierarchy tree until the containers for all box objects in the ring array are displayed. Select each container and pick the **Paste Object** button.

Once the **Paste Object** button is picked, the **Paste** dialog box appears. See Figure 20-8. In the **Paste as:** area, select whether you want to paste a copy or an instance. Often, an instance is pasted so modifications to the original object are transferred to the objects in the array.

If you check the **Replace all instances** check box in the **Paste Target:** area, all of the array objects are replaced with the new object. If this check box is unchecked, you can copy and paste different objects to each array object.

Often, the instanced geometry is not properly aligned with the ring array. To correct this problem, pick **Hierarchy** in the **Command Panel**. Then pick the **Pivot** button and the **Affect Object Only** button. Finally, transform each instance in the ring array as needed.

Figure 20-6.
Geometry, such as these frogs, can be substituted for the default boxes in a ring array.

Figure 20-7. Track View is used to substitute geometry for the default boxes in a ring array.

Replacement object

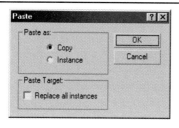

Figure 20-8. The **Paste** dialog box appears when pasting geometry in **Track View**.

Help Cel

To pass a rotate or scale transform on to the instanced object in the ring array, you must transform the original object with the xform modifier. Only modifiers are passed on to instanced objects.

Exercise 20-1

1) Draw a cylinder in the Top viewport. Use your own dimensions, but make it about 30 units in radius and 150 units in height. Increase the height segments to about 15.
2) Name the object Replacement Object.
3) Apply a bend modifier. Animate the bend from 0° on frame 0 to 180° on frame 50 and back to 0° on frame 100.
4) Draw a ring array in the Top viewport. Make the radius about 200. Set the amplitude and cycles to 0. Set the number in the array to five.
5) Animate the rotation of the dummy 720° on its Z axis on frame 100.
6) Animate the amplitude of the ring array from 0 on frame 0 to 100 on frame 50, and back to 0 on frame 100.
7) Using **Track View**, replace all of the ring array box objects with the Replacement Object cylinder. Be sure to create instances.
8) Apply a different material to each of the objects in the array.
9) Draw a small sphere in the middle of the array. This is used as a reference during animation playback.
10) Adjust the Perspective viewport as necessary to see the array during playback.
11) Render an animation of the Perspective viewport. Set the resolution to 320 x 240. Save the animation as ex20-01.avi in the folder of your choice.
12) When the animation is rendered, view the file.
13) Save the scene as ex20-01.max in the folder of your choice.

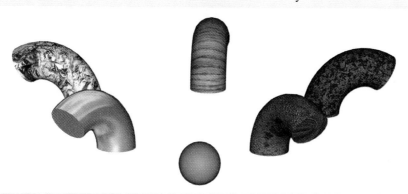

Exercise

Sunlight

The *sunlight system* is used to simulate geographically accurate illumination from the sun. You can select a preset location on any continent or you can manually enter settings. A 3ds max free direct light provides the illumination. You can have more than one sunlight system in a scene.

The position of the "sun" can be animated. See Figure 20-9. This can be useful for doing a shadow study of a proposed building, for example.

Creating a Sunlight System

To draw a sunlight system, pick **Systems** in the **Create** tab of the **Command Panel**. Then, pick the **Sunlight** button in the **Object Type** rollout. The **Control Parameters** rollout is displayed.

You can also pick **Lights** in the **Create** pull-down menu. Then, pick **Sunlight System** in the cascading menu. This opens the **Create** tab in the **Command Panel**, "picks" the **Systems** button, and selects the **Sunlight** button in the **Object Type** rollout.

Create

Systems

Sunlight

Sunlight

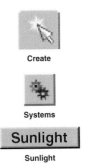

Figure 20-9. An animated sunlight system can be used to simulate the passing of a day, from sunrise to sunset. Notice, however, how the background is not affected by the sunlight.

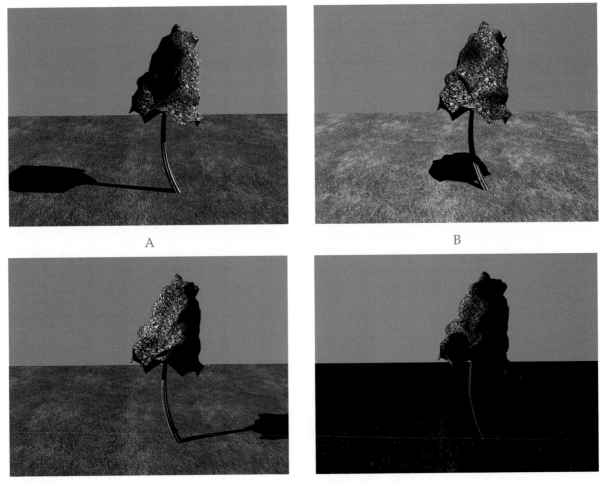

A

B

C

D

Pick in the viewport to set the center of the compass rose. This should be near the center of your scene. Then, drag to set the radius of the compass rose. Finally, drag and pick to set the distance of the light from the compass rose. The light can be any distance since the rays are parallel. The compass rose and a directional light are placed in the viewports. The default name of the light is Sun01.

The *compass rose* is a helper object used to define north in the scene. It looks similar to the "north" indicator found on many maps. The direct light always points to the center of the compass rose. The compass rose does not render.

The default "sun" is created based on the current date, time, and time zone settings on your computer. The light is by default pure white. These and other parameters can be changed after the system is created.

Setting Sunlight Parameters

When the sunlight system is created, parameters can be changed while the **Create** tab is still active and the system is selected. Later, the parameters can be changed by selecting the light and picking **Motion** in the **Command Panel**. The **Control Parameters** rollout is displayed. See Figure 20-10. The basic light parameters can be changed in the **Modify** tab of the **Command Panel**.

Motion

The **Azimuth** and **Altitude** labels in the **Control Parameters** rollout display the current settings for the sun. *Azimuth* is a measure of degrees on a compass, where north is $0°$. *Altitude* is height measured in degrees from the horizon. These labels change based on the rest of the settings in the rollout.

The **Time** area of the **Control Parameters** rollout is used to set the time of day. The time zone is also set in this area and can be corrected for daylight savings time. In the **Hours**, **Mins.**, and **Secs.** spinners, enter the time of day. This follows the 24-hour clock, where noon is 12 and midnight is 0. In the **Month**, **Day**, and **Year** spinners, enter the date.

Figure 20-10. After a sunlight system is created, the **Motion** tab in the **Command Panel** is used to adjust parameters.

Checking the **Daylight Savings Time** check box automatically adjusts the altitude and azimuth when necessary.

The **Time Zone** spinner is used to specify the time zone of your scene. This value can range from 12 to –12. It is based on Greenwich mean time. This is a system of time measurement where Greenwich, England, is +0. Time zones are plus or minus values from this location, based on the sun's movement. For example, the sun rises in Chicago six hours after it does in Greenwich. Therefore, the time zone in Chicago is –6.

The **Location** area is used to set the geographic location of the scene. You can manually enter values in the **Latitude:** and **Longitude:** spinners. If you do not have the exact measurements, you can select from several presets. Pick the **Get Location**... button. The **Geographic Location** dialog box is displayed. See Figure 20-11. Select a preset location from the **City:** list at the left. You can also pick on the map image tile. Other tiles are displayed by selecting a continent or region from the **Map:** drop-down list. If you check the **Nearest Big City** check box and pick on the map image tile, the closest large city is highlighted in the **City:** list. Select a location and pick the **OK** button. The name of the location is displayed in the **Location** area. The values in the **Latitude:** and **Longitude:** spinners reflect the selected location.

The **Site** area of the **Control Parameters** rollout is used to set the direction of north. Enter a degree value in the **North Direction:** spinner. This is measured clockwise from the world origin. The value in the **Orbital Scale:** spinner is the distance from the direct light to the compass rose. It is measured in current drawing units. This value really has little effect. Just make sure the light is in front of the scene and not behind it.

Animating Sunlight

You can animate all of the sunlight properties except the time zone. Most likely, you will only animate the time and date. Animating these values animates the altitude and azimuth. The longitude and latitude are not often animated. An example of when you might animate these values is a scene where the camera follows a sailboat or plane across a long distance.

Modify

You can also animate the intensity and color of the sunlight. To do this, select the direct light. Then, pick **Modify** in the **Command Panel**. Finally, animate the parameters just as you would for a normal direct light. Refer to Chapter 10 for a discussion on how to change light parameters.

Figure 20-11. A sunlight system allows you to choose an actual geographic location for your scene. The sunlight is based on the location you choose.

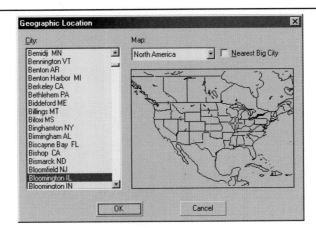

Help Cel

If you animate the month setting through 12 months, the light actually moves through 24 hours for each of 365 days. In other words, the light may spin wildly in your animation, especially for a low number of frames.

Exercise 20-2

1) Draw a park bench similar to the one shown below. Use your own dimensions. Apply materials and mapping as needed.
2) Create a camera. Change the Perspective viewport to display the camera. Adjust the viewport as needed to get a good view of the bench.
3) Create a sunlight system. Center the compass rose on the bench. Orient the north direction so the bench is facing south.
4) Set the location as the nearest big city to where you live. Set the date as today's date.
5) Change the color of the sunlight to a very light blue.
6) Set the total number of frames in the animation to 240.
7) On frame 0, set the time of day to midnight.
8) On frame 240, animate the time of day to one second before midnight.
9) Make and play a preview animation of the camera viewport.
10) Adjust the intensity of the sunlight as necessary.
11) Draw a large quad patch for the ground. Assign a material and mapping as needed.
12) Assign a bitmap of clouds for the environment background.
13) Render the animation to a file named ex20-02.avi in the folder of your choice. Use a 320 x 240 resolution and render the active time segment.
14) View the rendered animation. Notice that the background is not affected by the sunlight. How can this be corrected?
15) Save the scene as ex20-02.max in the folder of your choice.

Introduction to Parameter Wiring and Manipulators

Parameter wiring allows you to link any parameter that can be animated on one object to another object. This is a simple way of placing constraints on an object without having to assign and set up a controller. A wired parameter can be one-way or two-way. If set as two-way, a change in the parameter for either object is passed to the other object. Parameter wiring is also referred to as *wire parameters* in the 3ds max documentation.

Parameter wiring is designed to streamline animation. There are also three helper objects that can be used in conjunction with wired parameters. These helpers are called *manipulators.* They provide a "control interface," serving a purpose somewhat like that of linking an object to a dummy for animation purposes.

Help Cel

Parameters should be wired after any hierarchies are defined. Altering a hierarchy that contains wired parameters may produce unexpected and unwanted results.

Parameter Wiring Dialog Box

The **Parameter Wiring** dialog box is used to wire parameters between two objects. See Figure 20-12. To open this dialog box, first pick **Wire Parameters** in the **Animation** pull-down menu. Then, pick **Parameter Wire Dialog** from the cascading menu. This opens a "blank" dialog box.

On the upper left and upper right of the dialog box are hierarchy trees similar to the one found in **Track View**. Use the trees to locate the two object parameters that will be wired. Select a parameter from the left and one from the right.

Notice in between the two trees are three buttons. The top button is used to set a two-way relationship. The middle button sets the parameter

Figure 20-12. The **Parameter Wiring** dialog box is used to connect, or "wire," selected parameters of two objects.

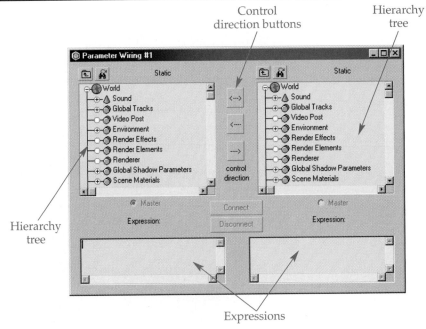

in the right-hand tree to control the parameter in the left-hand tree. The bottom button sets the parameter in the left-hand tree to control the parameter in the right-hand tree.

Once the two parameters are selected and the direction of control is set, you must actually wire the parameters. To do so, pick the **Connect** button in the middle of the dialog box. If the parameters are already wired, this button is labeled **Update** and is used to update any changes made. The **Disconnect** button is used to remove the wire from two wired parameters.

You can also begin the parameter wiring process from the quad menu. First, select an object and right-click on it to display the quad menu. Then, select **Wire Parameters** from the lower-right quadrant. Alternately, you can select **Wire Parameters** from the **Wire Parameters** cascading menu in the **Animation** pull-down menu. A shortcut menu appears on the object. From the shortcut menu, select the parameter you want to wire. A rubber band appears attached to the object. Drag and pick the object to which you are wiring the parameter. The **Parameter Wiring** dialog box is opened with the two parameters selected. Then, complete the wiring as described above.

At the bottom of the **Parameter Wiring** dialog box are two text boxes. Displayed in these boxes are the text equivalent expressions for the parameter wiring set in the dialog box.

Exercise 20-3

Exercise

1) Draw a sphere and a teapot. Use the same radius for both objects.
2) Draw a pyramid with a base approximately the same size as the sphere. Make the height approximately the radius of the sphere.
3) Select the sphere. Right-click to display the quad menu. Select **Wire Parameters** from the lower-right quadrant.
4) The quad menu is replaced with a shortcut menu on the sphere. Select **Object (Sphere)** in the shortcut menu, and then select **Radius** from the cascading menu.
5) A rubber band line appears attached to the pivot of the sphere and the cursor. Drag to the teapot and pick. A shortcut menu appears on the teapot. Select **Object (Teapot)** in the shortcut menu, and then select **Radius** from the cascading menu.
6) The **Parameter Wiring** dialog box is opened. Verify that **Radius** is selected on the left for the sphere and on the right for the teapot. Then, pick the two-way control direction button. Finally, pick **Connect** and then close the dialog box.
7) Using Steps 3 through 6, wire the radius of the sphere to the height of the pyramid. However, make the relationship one-way with the sphere controlling the pyramid.
8) Using the **Modify** tab in the **Command Panel**, adjust the height of the pyramid. The spinner is unavailable, correct? Why?
9) Adjust the radius of the teapot. What happens? Why?
10) Adjust the radius of the sphere. What happens? Why?
11) Save the scene as ex20-03.max in the folder of your choice.

Create

Helpers

Slider

Slider

Manipulator Helper Objects

As previously discussed, manipulators are helper objects used in parameter wiring. Adding manipulators to a scene can streamline the animation process. When parameters are wired to the manipulators, the manipulators become "control knobs" for animation. There are three different types of manipulators available in 3ds max. These are slider, cone angle, and plane angle.

To draw a manipulator, select **Create** in the **Command Panel**. Then, pick the **Helpers** button. Pick **Manipulators** from the drop-down list. Finally, select the appropriate button in the **Object Type** rollout.

Slider

The *slider manipulator* is a straight line that appears in the current viewport. See Figure 20-13. A slider has a value parameter that can be wired to a parameter on an object. Then, you can manipulate the slider to change the parameter on the wired object.

To draw a slider, pick the **Slider** button in the **Object Type** rollout. Then, pick anywhere in any viewport. The slider always appears in the current viewport, so the viewport in which it is drawn does not matter. Also, a slider can be moved without affecting its value parameter, so it can be drawn anywhere in the viewport.

In the **Name and Color** rollout, you can enter a name for the slider. This is the name of the manipulator object. At the top of the **Parameters** rollout, you can enter a name for what the slider controls. Refer to Figure 20-13. For example, you might enter Sphere Radius if the slider is

Figure 20-13. A slider manipulator appears only in the active viewport. The label entered in the **Name:** text box appears above the slider in the viewport.

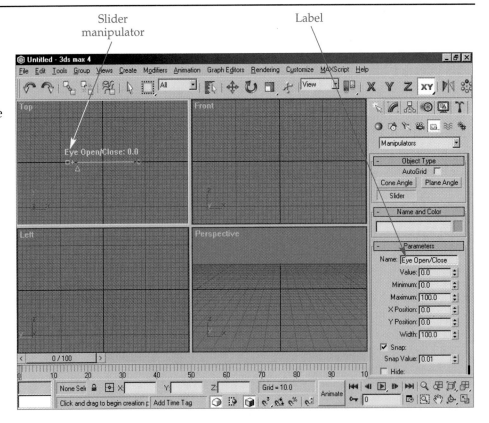

wired to the radius of a sphere. This name also appears above the slider in the viewport.

The **Value:** spinner indicates the current "position" of the slider. This is the parameter that is typically wired to other object parameters. The default value is 0 and, by default, can range from 0 to 100. The **Minimum:** and **Maximum:** spinners set the lowest and highest possible values for the slider.

The **X Position:** and **Y Position:** spinners indicate where the slider is located in the viewport. The position can be changed with these spinners, or it can be changed by moving the slider in the viewport. The **Width:** spinner sets the length of the slider in current drawing units. Changing the value in this spinner does *not* change the minimum, maximum, or current parameter values.

Cone Angle

The *cone angle manipulator* is designed to have its angle value wired to the parameter of another object. For example, as you manipulate the angle of the cone, the field-of-view of a camera can be changed. This manipulator is also good for animating the hotspot or falloff of a spotlight.

The cone angle manipulator, as you might guess from the name, appears as a cone in the viewports. See Figure 20-14. The base (circle) of the manipulator is plan to the viewport in which the manipulator is drawn. The cone comes "out" of the viewport. Unlike a slider, the cone angle manipulator maintains this orientation and does not change based on the current viewport.

To draw a cone angle manipulator, pick the **Cone Angle** button in the **Object Type** rollout. Then, pick in the viewport where you want the cone base to be plan. A cone angle manipulator can be moved without changing its angle, so you can draw it anywhere in the viewport. Drag the cursor to set the height of the cone and release.

Cone Angle

In the **Name and Color** rollout, you can enter a name for the manipulator. This is the name of the manipulator object. Unlike a slider, there is no additional text label in the **Parameters** rollout. Refer to Figure 20-14.

The value in the **Angle:** spinner in the **Parameters** rollout is the parameter to which other objects are typically wired. As you manipulate the cone angle manipulator, the **Angle:** value changes. The value in the **Distance:** spinner is the height of the cone.

By checking the **Use Square** check box, the cone is changed to have a square base instead of a circular base. This may be useful if the manipulator is wired to a camera or a rectangular spotlight. The value in the **Aspect:** spinner determines the aspect ratio. This value is similar to the aspect ratio for a rectangular spotlight.

Plane Angle

The *plane angle manipulator* is designed to have its angle value wired to the parameter of another object. It is intended for animating rotation angles in a plane. For example, you may wire the angle value of a plane angle manipulator to a door. When manipulating the plane angle manipulator, its name is displayed in the viewport with the current angle. See Figure 20-15.

Figure 20-14. A cone angle manipulator appears in the shape of a cone in all viewports.

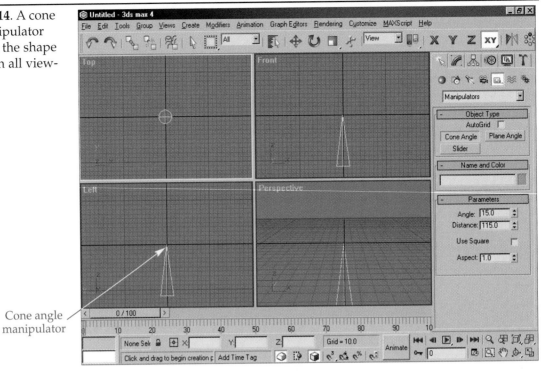

Cone angle manipulator

Figure 20-15. When a plane angle manipulator is being manipulated, its name and value are displayed above the cursor.

Plane angle manipulator

Name and value are displayed when manipulating

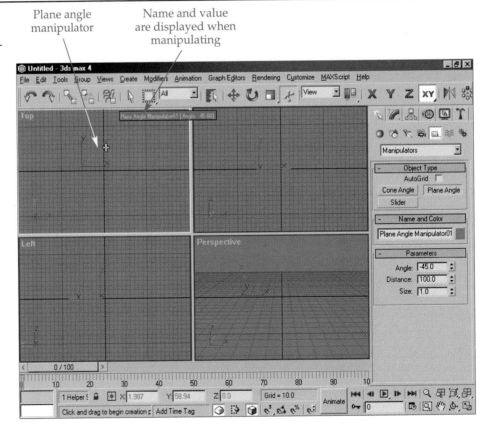

To draw a plane angle manipulator, pick the **Plane Angle** button in the **Object Type** rollout. Then, pick and hold in the viewport representing the plane in which you want to control a rotation angle. The point you pick is the pivot point about which the angle is measured. Finally, drag to set the distance of the "handle" from the pivot point.

Plane Angle

In the **Name and Color** rollout, you can enter a name for the manipulator. This is the name of the manipulator object. Unlike a slider, there is no additional text label in the **Parameters** rollout. Refer to Figure 20-15.

In the **Parameters** rollout, there is a **Size:** spinner. This is the relative size of the "handle." The **Distance:** spinner value is the distance of the handle from the pivot point. The default value is the distance set by dragging when the manipulator is created. The value in the **Angle:** spinner is the parameter to which other objects are typically wired. As you manipulate the plane angle manipulator, the **Angle:** value changes.

Manipulating Manipulators

Once parameters are wired to one another, whether object-to-object or object-to-manipulator, you can change the control parameters using the **Modify** tab of the **Command Panel**. However, you can also use the **Select and Manipulate** button on the **Main** toolbar. This button is used to manipulate an object or manipulator helper.

Select and Manipulate

When you pick the **Select and Manipulate** button, it is depressed until you pick it again. You can also enter and exit "manipulate mode" by selecting **Manipulate** in the quad menu. When a check mark appears next to the quad menu entry, you are in "manipulate mode." Once in manipulate mode, select the object or manipulator to manipulate. Hold and drag to change the wired parameter. If animation mode is turned on, an appropriate key is placed. When finished manipulating objects and manipulators, exit manipulate mode and continue modeling.

Help Cel

You can "manipulate" the UVW map modifier without wiring a manipulator to the modifier.

Exercise

Exercise 20-4

1) In this exercise, you will create two camera "eyeballs" for a robot. You will then wire parameters to a manipulator to control the "focusing" of the eyeballs.

2) Start by drawing two concentric spheres in the Front viewport. Set one radius to 25 and the other to 26. Name the smaller sphere Eye Left and the larger sphere Lid Left. In the Top viewport, rotate each sphere 180° about its pivot point.

3) In the Front viewport, make a copy of each sphere about 60 units to the right of the first two. Name the copies Eye Right and Lid Right.

4) Draw and extrude an ellipse to use as a backing plate as shown below.

5) Select or define materials of your choice and assign them to the objects.

6) In any viewport, draw a slider manipulator.

7) In the **Name:** text box for the slider, enter Lens Focus as the label. Also, change the **Minimum:** value to .15 and the **Maximum:** value to .33, and enter .15 in the **Value:** spinner.

8) In the active viewport, select the slider, right-click on it, and select **Wire Parameters** in the quad menu.

9) In the shortcut menu that appears, select **Object (Slider)** to display a cascading menu. Then, pick **Value** in the cascading menu. Drag the "rubber band" to the Lid Left sphere and pick.

10) In the shortcut menu that appears, select **Object (Sphere)** to display a cascading menu. Then, pick **Hemisphere** in the cascading menu.

11) In the **Parameter Wiring** dialog box, verify that "value" is selected for the slider and "hemisphere" is selected for the sphere. Then, pick the control button so the slider controls the sphere. Finally, pick the **Connect** button and then close the dialog box.

12) Repeat Steps 8 through 11 using the same slider and the Lid Right sphere.

13) Pick the **Select and Manipulate** button on the **Main** toolbar. Then, pick the triangle on the slider and move it left and right in the viewport. Notice how the outer spheres change to simulate the focusing of a camera or opening of an eye's iris.

14) Define and render a short animation of your own design. Save the animation to a file named ex20-04.avi in the folder of your choice.

15) Save the scene as ex20-04.max in the folder of your choice.

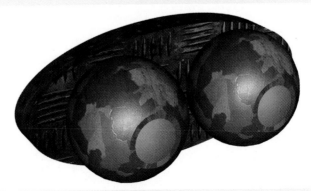

Chapter Snapshot

Chapter Test

1) What is a system in 3ds max?
2) What is a bones system used for?
3) Explain a ring array system.
4) List the basic settings for a ring array.
5) When a modifier is applied to the dummy object in a ring array, which array object(s) inherit the modifier?
6) Which parameter of a ring array cannot be animated?
7) How can different modifiers be applied to each object in a ring array?
8) Which function of 3ds max is used to substitute geometry for the boxes in a ring array?
9) Explain a sunlight system.
10) What type of 3ds max light is created in a sunlight system?
11) Define compass rose.
12) The default sun in a sunlight system is created based on what?
13) Define altitude and azimuth.
14) Which parameters of a sunlight system are most often animated?
15) Which parameter of a sunlight system cannot be animated?
16) _____ allows you to link any parameter that can be animated on one object to another object.
17) Manipulators are classified as what type of 3ds max objects?
18) What is the name of the dialog box used to connect parameters together? Which two menus can be used to open this dialog box?
19) List the three manipulators that come with 3ds max.
20) The control direction of wired parameters can be _____ or _____.

Modeling Problems

Unless otherwise directed, draw the objects shown using your own dimensions. Define and apply materials as needed. Add lights and a camera as needed. Pay attention to shadow location and color. When finished, save each scene as p20-xx.max in the folder of your choice.

Yard Swing 1

Open problem p12-01.max from Chapter 12. Save the scene as p20-01.max in the folder of your choice. Create a sunlight system for the scene. Specify the nearest big city to your home town as the location. Animate the light through a 24-hour day. Also, animate the swing moving back and forth. Render the animation to a file named p20-01.avi in the folder of your choice.

2 Concert Lighting
Open problem p12-08.max from Chapter 12. Save the scene as p20-02.max in the folder of your choice. Create a slider manipulator for each of the three spotlights. The minimum value for the slider should be 15 and the maximum value should be 5 units greater than the falloff for the spotlights. Label the sliders Red Hotspot, Green Hotspot, and Blue Hotspot. Wire the hotspot of each spotlight to the appropriate slider. Animate the sphere moving around the stage. (The spotlight targets should be linked to the sphere.) Also, using the sliders, animate changes in the hotspots for each light. Then, render the scene to a file named p20-02.avi in the folder of your choice. Save the scene.

3 Ferris Wheel
Open problem p14-06.max from Chapter 14. Save the scene as p20-03.max in the folder of your choice. Create a sunlight system for the scene. Specify the nearest big city to your home town as the location. Animate the light through 12 months. Render the animation to a file named p20-03.avi in the folder of your choice.

4 Carousel
Draw the carousel shown below. Use a ring array and instanced geometry to complete the carousel. Add materials, lights, and a camera as needed. Render the final scene to a file named p20-04.jpg in the folder of your choice.

Pea Shooter **5**

Draw a tube and a sphere, as shown below. The radius of the sphere should be equal to the inner radius of the tube. Define and apply a transparent material to the straw. Add lights and a camera as needed. Wire the sphere's radius to control the inner radius of the tube. Create a slider manipulator to control the sphere's radius. The maximum value should be the original radius of the sphere. Finally, animate the pea shooting through the straw. Also, using the slider, animate the radius of the sphere from small to maximum. Render the animation to a file named p20-05.avi in the folder of your choice. Save the file.

Sofa and Sunlight **6**

Open problem p10-09.max from Chapter 10. Save the scene as p20-06.max in the folder of your choice. Delete the light created to simulate sunlight. Add a sunlight system to take its place. Animate the sunlight through a 24-hour day. Render the animation to a file named p20-06.avi in the folder of your choice.

Robot Quadruped **7**

Open problem p12-09.max from Chapter 12. Save the scene as p20-07.max in the folder of your choice. Add a quad patch or plane as the ground. Create a sunlight system centered on the quadruped. Create a plane angle manipulator and wire its value to the solar date of the sunlight system. Add materials, other lights, and a camera as needed. Using the manipulator, animate the sun through a few hours of the day. Render the animation to a file named p20-07.avi in the folder of your choice. Save the scene.

8 Dancing Bears
Use a ring array and instanced geometry to create the dancing bears shown below. Add materials, lights, and a camera as needed. Render the final scene to a file named p20-08.jpg in the folder of your choice.

9 Jack-O'-Lantern
Open problem p15-02.max from Chapter 15. Save the scene as p20-09.max in the folder of your choice. Define a volumetric light effect for the omni light inside the jack-o'-lantern. Create a slider manipulator with a minimum value of 0.5 and a maximum value of 3. Wire the slider to the multiplier of the omni light. Using the slider, animate the omni light so it flickers. Render the animation to a file named p20-09.avi in the folder of your choice. Save the scene.

Amusement Park Ride **10**

Use a ring array and instanced geometry to create the amusement park ride shown below. Add materials, lights, and a camera as needed. Render the final scene to a file named p20-10.jpg in the folder of your choice.

Chapter 21

Introduction to Inverse Kinematics

Objectives

After completing this chapter, you will be able to:

- Define inverse kinematics.
- Identify inverse kinematics methods.
- Explain applied inverse kinematics.
- Explain interactive inverse kinematics.
- Explain the inverse kinematics solver.
- Draw bones.
- Set IK joint parameters.
- Bind an object to a follow object.
- Create an end effector for a bones system.
- Animate using the three inverse kinematics methods.

What Is Inverse Kinematics?

In Chapter 12, you learned how to create a hierarchy and link objects using forward kinematics. *Forward kinematics* is a process where the movement of a parent object is passed down a linked hierarchy to its child object. The movement can then be passed further down the hierarchy to that object's children. This is a one-way relationship. If the child is transformed, the parent is not affected. Since the movement is passed forward down the hierarchy, this is called "forward kinematics." Kinematics is the science of motion or movement.

Inverse kinematics (IK) is the opposite of forward kinematics. If the child object at the end of the linked hierarchy is transformed, the movement of the child is passed up the hierarchy to each ancestor. IK is useful when animating characters or linkages in machinery. There are three ways to use IK on a hierarchy. These methods are applied IK, interactive IK, and IK solvers. With applied IK, a "solution" must be calculated. Interactive IK allows you to manipulate objects in real time. You can also switch between IK and forward kinematics. IK solvers apply a controller, called an IK solver, to a bone structure, such as a bones system. IK solvers utilize both IK and forward kinematics in real time. This chapter provides an introduction to the IK systems available in 3ds max.

Inverse kinematics has changed significantly in 3ds max r4. In previous versions of 3D Studio, IK used a mathematical algorithm that was dependent on the history of the IK chain. This "version" of IK is available in 3ds max r4 as the history-dependent IK solver. In addition to this solver, there are two new solvers. The history-independent solver is probably the best choice in most situations, since the IK solution is not based on the history of the IK chain. The limb solver can be used to apply a "sub" IK solution to two bones in the IK chain.

It is important to realize this chapter is merely an introduction to IK. The software Character Studio, a companion to 3ds max, is used to perform many of the IK operations discussed in this chapter much more quickly. In addition, IK in 3ds max can get very complicated very fast. Character Studio is designed to make working with IK much easier. Character Studio is a completely separate software program and is not covered in this text.

Help Cel

Nonuniform scaling should not be applied to objects used for IK. If you need to apply nonuniform scaling, first apply an xform modifier. Then, apply the nonuniform scaling to the modifier.

IK Terminology

There are several key terms associated with inverse kinematics. Understanding these terms is important when working with IK. The following list contains definitions for some of the more commonly used IK terms.

- *Binding.* Binding is the process of "locking" or "pinning" an object to any other object that is not its descendant. Often, objects are bound to dummy objects. Binding is very similar to linking. An object can also be bound to the world.
- *Bone.* A bone object is part of a system to which IK is applied. In addition to a bones system object, any object can be used as a bone.
- *Bound object.* An object to which binding has been applied is called a bound object.
- *End effector.* The object moved or animated to create the IK solution in history-dependent IK is called the end effector. For example, if you have modeled a leg, the foot might be the end effector. Note: An end effector is created in a history-independent solver, but the goal is animated instead of the end effector.
- *Follow objects.* An object to which another object is bound is called a follow object.
- *Goal.* The goal is used in history-independent IK to manipulate the IK chain. It is similar to an end effector.
- *IK solution.* The IK solution is the set of parameters that result from the transformation of the object from the previous frame to the current frame. In other words, it is the values required to get the object to where it is on the current frame.
- *Initial state.* The beginning, or initial, position of a bone (frame 0) is called its initial state.

- *Joint.* An object's joint is the point about which transforms are applied with respect to its parent object. Therefore, an object's joint is its pivot point. The location of the parent's pivot point is also part of the IK solution.
- *Joint parameters.* The behavior of a joint is referred to as the joint parameters. You can constrain movement for a joint, set the axes of movement, and set the type of joint.
- *Kinematic chain.* The kinematic chain is the selected object and all objects above and below it in the linked hierarchy up to, and including, the terminator object.
- *Root bone.* The root bone is the top-most bone in an IK hierarchy.
- *Solver.* A solver applies the IK solution calculated based on joint parameters and animated bones to the IK chain.
- *Terminator.* The terminator is the object that determines the end of the kinematic chain. This object can be the root of the entire hierarchy or an object you specify.

Applied IK

Applied IK uses a hierarchy of linked objects to produce very accurate motion. When using applied IK, "follow objects" are created and animated. The end effector for the hierarchy is linked to the follow object. Once all motion is complete, you must instruct 3ds max to calculate an IK solution for each object in the hierarchy for *every frame* in a specified range.

The motion of applied IK is very accurate because 3ds max is not required to make many interpolations between keyframes. Accurate motion is the big advantage of applied IK. The disadvantage of applied IK is that keys are created for every object in the hierarchy on *every* frame. This makes altering the motion later much more than a bit challenging.

Help Cel

The history-independent IK solver is typically the best choice in most situations. Applied IK is most likely used only when very precise motion is needed.

Interactive IK

Interactive IK allows you to dynamically animate the objects. IK solutions are only calculated for the keyframes you specify. As a result, the motion on tweens is interpolated. This method produces a slightly less accurate motion. However, altering the motion later is very easy. Animating with interactive IK is very similar to animating with forward kinematics.

IK Solver

The *IK solver* applies an IK solution based on the animated IK controller applied to a bone structure. The bone structure can be a bones system or "regular" objects used as a bone structure. The bones structure to which an IK solver is applied is animated interactively, as with interactive IK. A controller is applied to each bone in the system. The motion is passed up the hierarchy to the root bone. Keys are only set for an object called the IK "goal." In addition, a "sub solution" can be applied to only two bones in the structure.

Help Cel

Do not confuse a "bone structure" with a bones system. A bone structure can contain bones and "regular" objects set up to act as bones. A bones system is an automated function used to create bone objects.

Creating Bones

The bones system is introduced in Chapter 20. To create a network of bones, open the **Create** tab in the **Command Panel**. Pick the **Systems** button. Then, pick the **Bones** button in the **Object Type** rollout. The **Name and Color**, **IK Chain Assignment**, and **Bone Parameters** rollouts are displayed. See Figure 21-1. The **Name and Color** rollout is used to change the name of a bone and its display color.

IK Chain Assignment

The **IK Chain Assignment** rollout is used to select the "version" of IK to apply automatically. In the **IK Solver:** drop-down list, you can pick **History Dependent**, **IKHISolver**, or **IKLimb**. The **History Dependent** option is the IK method used in previous versions of 3D Studio. The **IKHISolver** option is the history-independent IK solver. The **IKLimb** option is a "sub solution" applied to only two bones in a larger IK chain.

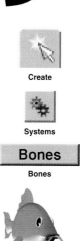

Create

Systems

Bones

Bones

Figure 21-1. The rollouts displayed when drawing bones.

Below the drop-down list are two check boxes. When the **Assign To Children** check box is checked, the IK solver displayed in the drop-down list is applied to all children of the first bone drawn in the network. This check box is unchecked by default. This means a standard position, rotation, scale (PRS) controller is applied to all bones in the network. In other words, by default, no IK solver is applied to a bone network when it is created.

When the **Assign To Children** check box is checked, the **Assign To Root** check box is enabled and, by default, checked. Checking this check box applies the IK solver displayed in the drop-down list to the first bone drawn in the network. When unchecked, the solver is not applied to the first bone. Instead, the solver "starts" with the second bone and a standard PRS controller is applied to the first bone.

Help Cel

In most situations, it is probably better to not automatically assign an IK solver. The IK solver is generally added later to allow for various adjustments and setups.

Bone Parameters

The **Bone Parameters** rollout is used to set how the bones appear in the viewports. See Figure 21-2. This rollout is available in the **Create** tab and **Modify** tab of the **Command Panel**.

The **Width:** and **Height:** spinners in the **Bone Object** area set the "thickness" of the currently selected bone. The "length" of the bone is set by the points you pick when creating the bone. The **Taper:** spinner sets the percentage of taper along the length of the bone.

Figure 21-2. On the left is the default "shape" of a bone. Next, side fins are added, then a back fin, and finally a front fin.

In addition to changing the "thickness" of each bone, you can add fins to the sides of the bone. See Figure 21-2. This can help you visualize the skin that the bones are controlling. For example, if you have modeled a leg and are using bones to control the animation of the leg, you may want to add fins to each bone. The fins can be set to extend to the skin. In this way, the skin does not need to be displayed when the bones are animated.

The **Bone Fins** area is used to add fins and set their size. You can choose to add fins on each side, on the front, and on the back. Check the **Side Fins**, **Front Fin**, or **Back Fin** check box to turn on the corresponding fin. The **Size:**, **Start Taper:**, and **End Taper:** spinners below each check box control how the fin appears. Adding fins does not alter the function of the bone, just its appearance.

The **Generate Mapping Coords.** check box at the bottom of the **Bone Parameters** rollout is used to automatically calculate mapping coordinates and apply them to the selected bone. The **Refine** button is available in the **Modify** tab. It allows you to split the selected bone in two. Pick the button, then pick on the bone at the location where you want the new joint. Right-click to end the command.

Making Bones Renderable

Bones can be set up so they appear in renderings. To do this, first select the bone. Then, display the quad menu and select **Properties**... from the lower-right quadrant. You can also select **Object Properties**... from the **Edit** pull-down menu. The **Object Properties** dialog box is displayed. See Figure 21-3.

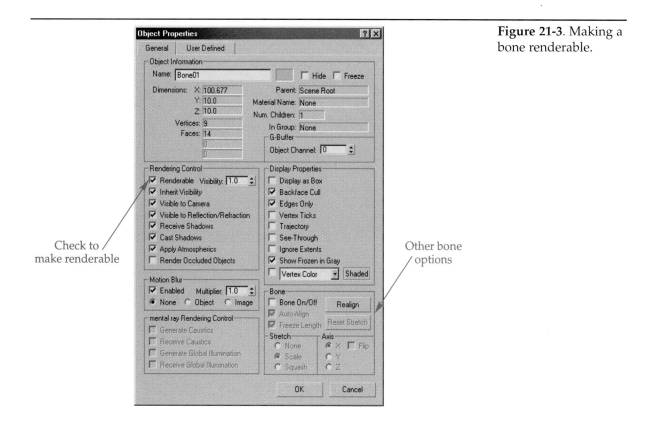

Figure 21-3. Making a bone renderable.

Check to make renderable

Other bone options

In the **Rendering Control** area, check the **Renderable** check box. The bone is rendered with the scene in the next rendering. When the check box is checked, other options in the **Rendering Control** area are made available. You can set the visibility for the bone, set the bone to receive and cast shadows, and set it to receive atmospheric effects, among other things.

Drawing Bones

You must draw the bone hierarchy using the cursor. First, make the necessary settings in the **Bone Parameters** rollout. Then, pick in the viewport to place the base of the hierarchy. See Figure 21-4. Move the cursor to define the length and orientation of the first bone. Pick to place the end of the first bone and the beginning of the second bone. Continue placing bones until the hierarchy is complete. Right-click to end the command.

You can connect a new bone hierarchy to an existing one. The new hierarchy can be connected to the end of the first hierarchy, or in the middle to create a branched network. Activate the command just as you would to create a new hierarchy. Then, move the cursor over the joint to which you want to connect. The cursor changes to a large crosshairs. This indicates you can connect to the joint. Pick to connect. Then, draw the branched hierarchy as you would a normal bone hierarchy. Right-click to end the command.

Figure 21-4. Drawing bones.

Bone network

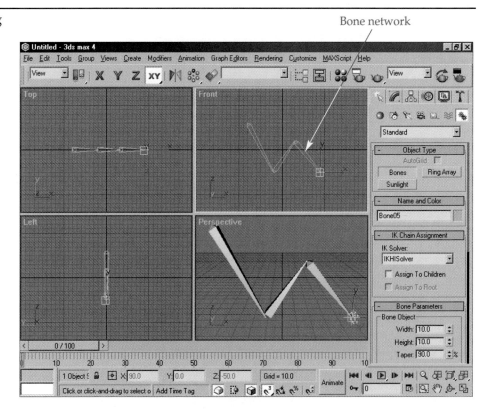

Using Any Hierarchy as a Bone Network

Any hierarchy can be set up to use as bones. First, select all objects in the linked hierarchy. Then, open the **Object Properties** dialog box by picking **P**roperties... from the lower-right quadrant of the quad menu or by selecting **Object P**roperties... in the **E**dit pull-down menu. The **Bone** area of the **General** tab is used. You can also use the **Bone Options** dialog box. See Figure 21-5. This dialog box is opened by selecting **Bone Options** in the **A**nimation pull-down menu. The two dialog boxes share many of the same options.

Check the **Bone On/Off** check box to set up the linked hierarchy as a bone network. Once this check box is checked, an IK solver can be applied. Be sure to set the appropriate IK parameters before applying the solver.

Initial Bone Position

The initial position of a bone or object in an IK hierarchy is its position before an IK solution is calculated. The initial position of a bone is very important because the IK solution is based on movement and parameters set for the bone from its initial position.

Before an IK solver is applied to the bone network, setting the initial position is easy. Simply transform the bones or objects as you would normally using standard transform tools. As long as an IK solver is not applied, you are transforming the bone's initial position. After an IK solver is applied, you can delete the solver, adjust the initial position, and reapply the solver. As you can see, it is much better to properly set the initial position before applying an IK solver.

Creating an Object Hierarchy for IK

The same rules that apply to forward kinematics apply to IK. These rules are covered in Chapter 12. In general, a parent should move less than a child. Also, the hierarchy from parent to child should be logical.

When setting up a hierarchy for IK, there are two additional considerations. First, the links and pivot points must be located to best reproduce natural or "real-world" movement. Second, the root of the hierarchy should be near the center of gravity for all objects in the hierarchy. For example, if you are animating a dog, the center of gravity is near its shoulders. See Figure 21-6. If you animate the dog with the head as the root, you may accidentally animate the dog into a seizure.

When determining which object to use as the root, look at how often other objects should follow a given object when it is moved. If no objects, or very few objects, should follow the given object, the object is

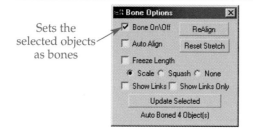

Sets the selected objects as bones

Figure 21-5. Setting objects to act as bones.

Figure 21-6. The center of gravity of the dog is near its shoulders. As such, this point is used as the root for the bone network.

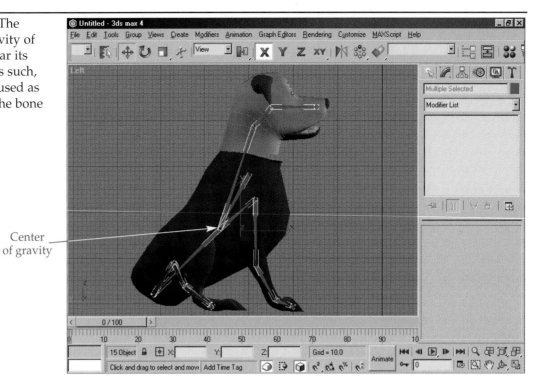

Center of gravity

probably not the best choice for the root. On the other hand, if nearly all other objects should follow the given object, it may make a good root object. In addition, a good root object should not be animated often.

Once you have determined the best root object and the most logical hierarchy, you can link the objects. The procedure is the same as that used to create a hierarchy for forward kinematics. After the objects are linked, you must set the joint parameters.

Hierarchy

Help Cel

It is best to align object pivot points to world coordinates whenever possible. If you do not do this, you may have problems later when animating the hierarchy using IK.

Exercise 21-1

1) Draw the three objects shown below. Use your own dimensions. These objects form one knee, one hip joint, and one ankle joint for a biped (two-leg) robot. Feel free to make "design" changes, but be sure to make a knee, ankle, and hip joint. Note: The assembled model below is shown with the upper leg rotated for illustration purposes only. For this exercise, construct the model so the leg is "straight."

2) Move the pivot point for the upper leg to the center of the hip joint.

3) Move the pivot point for the lower leg to the center of the knee joint.

4) Move the pivot point for the foot to the center of the ankle joint. Finally, align all pivot points to the world.

5) Link the foot to the lower leg. Inherit movement and rotation on all axes. Lock the scale and movement on all axes.

6) Link the lower leg to the upper leg. Inherit movement and rotation on all axes. Lock the scale and movement on all axes. Lock the rotation on the Y and Z axes, assuming the local X axis runs from side to side through the knee joint.

7) Move the leg and foot to verify correct linking and motion.

8) Assign the material Metal_Chrome to the upper leg.

9) Assign the material Metal_Dark_Gold to the lower leg.

10) Assign the material Metal_Brushed to the foot.

11) Use the UVW map modifier to assign mapping coordinates as necessary.

12) Save the scene as ex21-01.max in the folder of your choice. This file is used in later exercises in this chapter.

Freezing Objects

Often, a model can get "cluttered" with objects. This is especially true of complex models with many overlapping objects. You can hide objects, as described in Chapter 5. However, you may want to be able to see the objects, just not select them. This is accomplished by *freezing* the objects. Freezing objects is especially useful when working with bones. When frozen, linked objects still transform with their parents/children. Reference and instanced objects also behave as if they are not frozen.

Display

Freeze Selected

To freeze a selected object, pick **Display** in the **Command Panel**. Then, expand the **Freeze** rollout. See Figure 21-7. Finally, pick the **Freeze Selected** button in the rollout. The selected object is frozen. You can also freeze the selected object without using the **Display** tab by pressing the [6] key or using the quad menu. Frozen objects are displayed in dark grey by default and cannot be selected. See Figure 21-8.

The **Freeze** rollout provides other options for freezing and unfreezing objects. You can freeze all unselected objects, select objects to freeze by their name, or pick objects to freeze in the viewports. You can unfreeze objects by specifying their name or by picking on them in the viewport, or you can unfreeze all objects.

Instead of the default grey, you can set individual objects to display in their normal color when frozen. To do this, select the object and open the **Object Properties** dialog box. Then, in the **Display Properties** area of the **General** tab, uncheck the **Show Frozen in Gray** check box. When this check box is checked, the object is displayed in grey whenever it is frozen.

Help Cel

The hiding and freezing options can also be accessed in the **Display Floater**. This is a modeless dialog box that is opened by selecting **Display Floater**... from the **Tools** pull-down menu.

Figure 21-7. Options for freezing and unfreezing objects are located in the **Freeze** rollout.

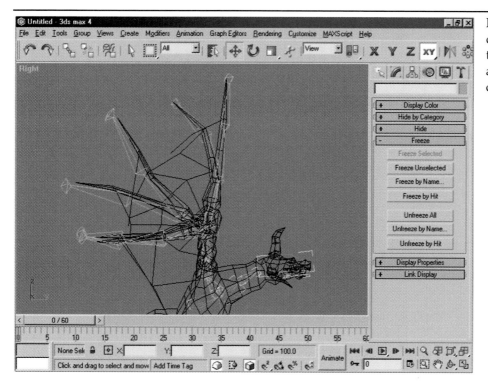

Figure 21-8. This dragon is frozen, but the bones in its wings are not. (Discreet, a division of Autodesk)

Exercise 21-2

1) Open the file ex21-01.max from Exercise 21-1.
2) Select the lower leg.
3) Right-click in the viewport to display the quad menu. Then, pick **Freeze Selection** in the upper-right quadrant.
4) Pick the **Select and Move** button. Attempt to move the lower leg. What happened? Press the [H] key and attempt to select the lower leg by its name. What happened?
5) Pick the **Select and Rotate** button. Select and rotate the upper leg. What happened?
6) Attempt to rotate the lower leg. What happened?
7) Unfreeze the lower leg and select it.
8) In the **Display** tab of the **Command Panel**, pick the **Hide Selected** button in the **Hide** rollout.
9) Attempt to move the lower leg. You cannot move it, can you? Why not?
10) Reset 3ds max without saving.

Setting IK Joint Parameters

Joint parameters for IK are similar to lock and inherit properties for linked objects. They define the type of joint and how it moves. Joint parameters can also be used to limit movement. There are six possible axes for each joint—the X, Y, and Z axes on each of two joint types. See Figure 21-9. Joint parameters control the motion of the joint on these axes. IK joint parameters override any settings made for lock and inherit properties.

Help Cel

When transforming a bone network, you must make sure an IK solver has not been applied to the network. Otherwise, an IK solution is calculated as you transform the bones.

Joint Axes

The axes of motion for a child object are based on the local axes of the parent object. If the child object is rotated about the Z axis, the rotation is applied about the Z axis of the parent object, not the object's own Z axis. For this reason, always orient pivot points to world coordinates whenever possible before creating and animating a hierarchy.

Joint Types

There are two basic types of IK joints. These are sliding and rotation. Using one or the other produces a distinct motion. Using both types on the same joint creates complex motion.

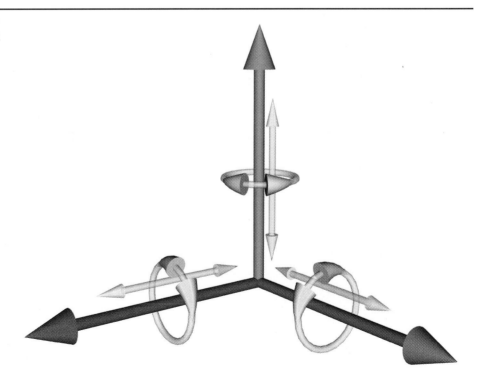

Figure 21-9. There are three possible rotation axes and three possible sliding axes for a joint.

A *rotation joint* allows an object to rotate about one or more axes of its pivot point. The parameters for a rotation joint determine the axes about which the object can rotate. The parameters can also be used to limit rotation on one or more of these axes.

A *sliding joint* allows an object to move along one or more axes of its pivot point. The parameters for a sliding joint determine which axes the object can slide along. The parameters can also be used to limit movement on one or more of these axes.

There are other types of joints, including path, surface, and a combination of sliding and rotation joints. These joint types are not covered in this text.

Setting Joint Parameters

With IK, it is extremely important to correctly set all joint parameters prior to animating the objects. If you fail to do so, you will quickly have a mess that cannot be fixed. To set the joint parameters, select the object and then pick **Hierarchy** in the **Command Panel** and pick the **IK** button. Then, expand either the **Sliding Joints** or **Rotational Joints** rollout, depending on which settings you are making.

Hierarchy

IK

Both rollouts contain similar settings for the X, Y, and Z axes. See Figure 21-10. The rollouts displayed for an object with the history-independent IK solver applied are slightly different from those for an object with the history-dependent IK solver. The joint parameter settings available for an object with the history-independent IK solver are available after the solver is applied. Otherwise, the joint parameter settings for an object with the history-dependent IK solver are displayed in the **Hierarchy** tab. Applying different IK solvers is discussed later in this chapter.

Figure 21-10. A—Joint parameters for a joint using a history-independent IK solver. B—Joint parameters for a joint using a history-dependent IK solver.

A

B

At the top of each "axis" area are three check boxes. Checking the **Active** check box turns on movement or rotation on the axis. Checking the **Limited** check box applies the limits set in the **From:** and **To:** spinners. These are the only settings available if a history-independent IK solver is applied. However, the history-independent IK solvers also have a **Preferred Angle:** spinner. This sets the preferred angle, which is the "default" angle at the joint between objects in the hierarchy.

When the **Limited** check box is checked, you can pick directly on the **From:** and **To:** labels to show the limits in the viewports. The object is moved to the limit as long as you hold the mouse button. When you release the mouse button, the object returns to its original position.

Checking the **Ease** check box forces the object to slow down as it approaches the limits. The "spring" settings for a joint add an element of dynamics to the joint. Every joint has a "natural" position. This is the position to which the object tries to return. When the **Spring Back** check box is unchecked, there is no attempted return. When checked, the object attempts to return to its natural position, based on the other "spring" settings.

The value in the **Spring Back** spinner determines the "natural" position. For sliding joints, this value is in current drawing units relative to the object's pivot point. For rotational joints, this value is in degrees. If you use the spinner arrows to set the value, the object dynamically changes in the viewport to show the natural position. However, as soon as you release the mouse button, the object returns to its original position.

The **Spring Tension:** spinner determines how strong of a pull the object's natural position has. In other words, the higher this value, the more the object is drawn back to its natural position. Increasing the value in the **Damping:** spinner applies the tension over the entire range of joint movement. This can be used to simulate an organic joint, such as a knee, or a worn mechanical joint, such as a rusty hinge.

Help Cel

You can press the [Page Up] and [Page Down] keys on the keyboard to select the object above or below the selected object in a hierarchy. This works with bones as well.

Exercise 21-3

1) Open the file ex21-01.max created in Exercise 21-1. Save the scene as ex21-03.max in the folder of your choice.
2) Create hips, as shown below.
3) Unlink all objects. Then, align all pivot points to the world.
4) Link the foot to the lower leg, the lower leg to the upper leg, and the upper leg to the hips.
5) Set IK joint parameters, as described next. The axes indicated and the to/from settings are based on the figure shown below. However, the correct axes are determined by how you drew the object. *The correct axes and settings for your model may be different from the ones indicated!*
6) The movement on all sliding joint axes should be turned off for all objects.
7) The foot should have one rotational axis active. Limit the axis rotation with a **From:** (back) value of about 25 and a **To:** (forward) value of 0. Pick on the labels to preview the limits.
8) The lower leg should also have one rotational axis active. Limit the axis rotation with a **From:** (forward) value of 0 and a **To:** (back) value of about 75. Pick on the labels to preview the limits.
9) The upper leg should have one rotational axis active. Limit the axis rotation with a **From:** (back) value of about 50 and a **To:** (forward) value of about –50. Pick on the labels to preview the limits.
10) Finally, the hips should have the movement on all rotation and sliding axes turned off.
11) Save the scene. This model is used for other exercises in this chapter.

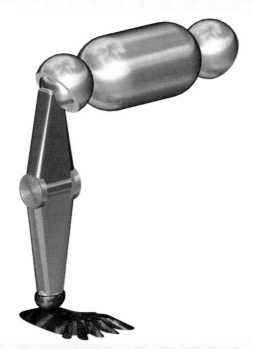

Binding

Binding is the process of "locking" or "pinning" an object to any other object that is not its descendant. Binding objects to follow objects is primarily used for applied IK. However, there can be other applications for bound objects. As you gain practice and experience in using the types of IK solvers, you will be able to identify other applications for bound objects. However, this chapter focuses on binding for applied IK.

Binding Objects

Hierarchy

IK

IK

To bind an object to a follow object, first select the original object. Next, pick **Hierarchy** in the **Command Panel**. Then, pick the **IK** button and expand the **Object Parameters** rollout. See Figure 21-11. In the **Bind To Follow Object:** area, pick the **Bind** button so it is on (depressed).

Pick on the original object. Then, drag to the follow object. The cursor changes to a push pin when over a valid follow object. Finally, release the mouse button when over the follow object. In the **Bind To Follow Object:** area, the name of the follow object is displayed. Picking the **Unbind** button removes the binding.

Setting Binding Parameters

You can set binding to the orientation or position of the follow object, or both. The **Orientation:** and **Position:** areas in the **Object Parameters** rollout have the same settings. Checking the **Bind Position** or **Bind Orientation** check box turns on binding for position or orientation. When the **R** button is on (depressed), the relationship between the object and the follow object is relative. When the button is off (the default setting), the relationship is absolute based on the world.

The **Axis:** check boxes are used to turn the binding effect on each axis on and off. For example, if both **X** check boxes are unchecked and the follow object moves along the X axis only, the bound object is unaffected.

Figure 21-11. The **Object Parameters** rollout is used to bind an object to a follow object.

The value in the **Weight:** spinner determines the influence of the follow object on the hierarchy. This spinner allows you to set the relative influence of multiple follow objects in the IK solution. The higher the value, the higher the priority in calculating the IK solution.

Help Cel

If you only have one follow object in the IK chain, increasing the weight value has no effect.

Exercise 21-4

1) Open the file ex21-03.max saved in Exercise 21-3. Save the scene as ex21-04.max in the folder of your choice.
2) Draw a dummy object. Make the dummy the size you want, but do not make it too large or too small.
3) Move the dummy object so its pivot point aligns with the pivot point of the foot. Align the pivot point to the world.
4) Bind the foot to the dummy object. Bind the position on the X, Y, and Z axes. The binding should be based on the world. Enter 1.0 in the **Weight:** spinner.
5) Save the scene. This model is used in Exercise 21-5.

Animating with Applied IK

To animate with applied IK, a little preparation is required. First, draw all objects. Link the objects to create the hierarchy. Set all IK joint parameters as necessary. Finally, animate the follow object as necessary with the **Toggle Animation Mode** button on. Now, you are ready to use applied IK on the hierarchy.

Select the bound object or the follow object and pick **Hierarchy** in the **Command Panel**. Then, pick the **IK** button and expand the **Inverse Kinematics** rollout. See Figure 21-12. At the bottom of the rollout are the **Start:** and **End:** spinners. These determine the range of frames over which the IK solution is calculated.

In the middle of the rollout are three check boxes. Checking the **Apply Only To Keys** check box calculates IK solutions only on keyframes for the follow object. This can reduce the complexity of the calculation, but at the same time, it eliminates the advantage of this IK method. When the **Update Viewports** check box is checked, the progress of the IK calculation is reflected in the viewports. When unchecked, the result is displayed after the calculation is complete. When the **Clear Keys** check box is checked, any existing keys for objects are removed when the IK solution is calculated.

When all options are set as needed, pick the **Apply IK** button at the top of the rollout. 3ds max calculates the IK solution for all objects in the hierarchy. The **Time** slider moves along the current time segment as the calculation is being performed. If the selected object requires keys, the new keys appear above the **Time** slider as the calculation is performed.

Toggle Animation Mode

Hierarchy

IK

IK

Apply IK

Apply IK

Help Cel

Applied IK results in movement that very precisely matches the follow object. For this reason, applied IK may be best used for animating mechanical movement, such as machinery.

Figure 21-12. The **Inverse Kinematics** rollout is used to animate with applied IK and interactive IK.

Exercise

Exercise 21-5

1) Open the file ex21-04.max saved in Exercise 21-4. Save the scene as ex21-05.max in the folder of your choice.
2) Move to frame 25 and turn on animation mode.
3) In the Left viewport, animate the dummy object to a position in front of and above the foot.
4) Move to frame 50. Animate the dummy object straight back (to the left in the viewport) behind the leg.
5) Move to frame 75. Animate the dummy object straight down in the viewport below the foot.
6) Move to frame 100. Animate the dummy object back to its original location.
7) Exit animation mode.
8) With the dummy selected, apply the IK solution.
9) Select the foot. Notice the keys below the **Time** slider. Select the other objects and notice the keys created for them.
10) Render a final animation to a file named ex21-05.avi in the folder of your choice.
11) Save the scene.

Exercise 21-8

1) Open ex21-07.max saved in Exercise 21-7. Save the scene as ex21-08.max in the folder of your choice.
2) Using the **Left** viewport (the side view of the leg), animate the end effector that was automatically created when the IK solver was applied in Exercise 21-7. Animate the end effector so the leg moves as shown below. Approximate the position of the end effector on each keyframe. The exact movement of your model may vary slightly, depending on how it was drawn.
3) Make and view a preview animation.
4) If necessary, make any changes to the keys for the end effector. In **Track View**, the keys appear in the **End Effector Position** track under **Transform** for the dummy object.
5) Render a final animation to a file named ex21-08.avi in the folder of your choice.
6) View the animation.
7) Save the scene.

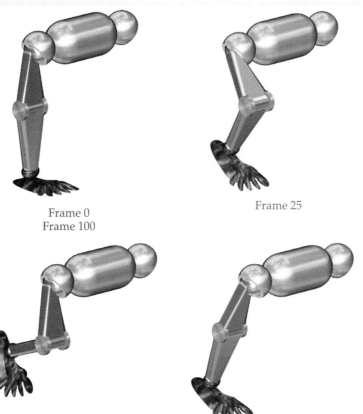

Frame 0
Frame 100

Frame 25

Frame 50

Frame 75

Animating with the History-Independent IK Solver

Using the history-independent IK solver is very similar to using the history-dependent IK solver in many aspects. However, the IK solution is not based on the history of the IK chain. In this way, the time required to calculate the IK solution is not related to the number of frames over which the solution is applied. You can also apply overlapping IK chains when using the history-independent IK solver. In addition, the resulting IK chain is typically more stable than one with a history-dependent IK solver applied.

History-Independent IK Solver Basics

The IK solution for the history-independent IK solver is calculated in a flat plane called the *solver plane.* The plane is used as a basis for the calculation. However, the movement of the bone chain is not limited to this plane. The plane is formed by the joint of the first bone and the joint of the second bone, and comes as close as possible to passing through all other joints in the bone chain. In world coordinates, this orientation of the plane is at a 0 swivel angle. The *swivel angle* is the rotation of the solver plane about an axis formed from the first joint to the last joint. This axis is called the *end effector axis.* See Figure 21-15. The value of the swivel angle can be changed and animated.

The end effector axis and swivel angle are actually calculated based on "parent space" of either the first joint or the IK goal. *Parent space* is the local coordinate system of a parent object. Parent space settings are

Figure 21-15. A history-independent IK solver is calculated in a solver plane, which can be rotated by adjusting the swivel angle.

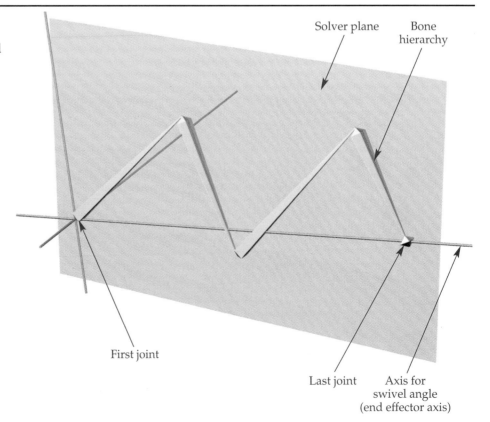

Solver plane

Bone hierarchy

First joint

Last joint

Axis for swivel angle (end effector axis)

important when the first joint or the goal is *not* rooted in world space. This may occur when overlapping hierarchies exist, but it may also occur in a single hierarchy.

The *goal* is somewhat like a dummy object, but tied to a specific IK chain to which a history-independent IK solver has been applied. To animate the IK chain, the goal is animated. The IK solver then attempts to match the end effector of the IK chain to the transformation of the goal.

Applying the History-Independent IK Solver

To apply a history-independent IK solver, first draw a bone hierarchy or set up an existing linked hierarchy as a bone network. Select the first bone in the hierarchy. Then, select **HI Solver** from the **IK Solvers** cascading menu in the **Animation** pull-down menu. A dashed white line appears connected to the first bone and the cursor. Pick on the last bone in the hierarchy. The solver is applied. A goal is shown in white and appears at the last bone. See Figure 21-16. The **Motion** tab in the **Command Panel** is also automatically displayed. The currently selected object is IK Chain*xx*, which is the goal for the history-independent IK solver. You can now finalize the settings.

IK Solver Rollout

The **IK Solver** rollout is located in the **Motion** tab when the goal is selected. The drop-down list in the rollout allows you to choose between the history-independent IK solver and the limb IK solver. If any third-party history-independent IK solver plug-ins are loaded, they will appear in the drop-down list as well.

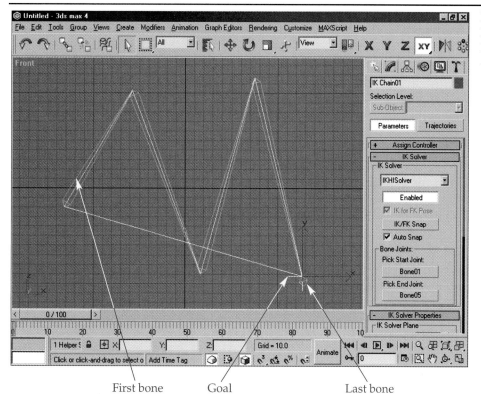

First bone   Goal   Last bone

Figure 21-16. A history-independent IK solver is applied to this bone network.

Below the drop-down list is the **Enabled** button. This button allows you to switch between animating the chain with IK and animating the chain with forward kinematics. When the button is on (depressed), an IK solution is applied to the transformation of the hierarchy. When the button is off, forward kinematics is used to calculate the transformation of the hierarchy.

When the **Enabled** button is off, the **IK for FK Pose** check box is made available. When the check box is checked (default), the hierarchy can be transformed using forward kinematics. However, if the goal is transformed, the solution automatically switches to IK.

The **IK/FK Snap** button is used to "align" controller values to prevent a jump or jerk when switching between IK and forward kinematics. When the **Auto Snap** check box is checked (default), this is automatically done when switching between IK and FK. Otherwise, pick the **IK/FK Snap** button *before* switching to prevent a jump or jerk in the bone network.

The **Bone Joints:** area displays the current first and last bone in the IK chain. The names of the bones appear on the buttons in this area. To pick a new first or last bone, select either the **Pick Start Joint:** button or **Pick End Joint:** button and select the new starting or ending bone.

IK Solver Properties Rollout

The **IK Solver Properties** rollout is displayed in the **Motion** tab of the **Command Panel** when the goal is selected. This rollout provides additional controls for the IK solver. The **IK Solver Plane** area of the rollout contains settings for the swivel angle and the parent space, as discussed earlier. You can also select a target object to control the swivel angle. Select the **Pick Target:** button and choose an object to use as the target. The target object's name is displayed on the button. When the **Use** check box is checked, the target object is used.

Also found in the **IK Solver Properties** rollout are the **Position:** and **Rotation:** spinners for setting thresholds and the **Iterations:** spinner for limiting the solution calculation. These spinner values perform the same functions as their counterparts for a history-dependent IK solver.

IK Display Options Rollout

The **IK Display Options** rollout is available in the **Motion** tab of the **Command Panel** when the goal is selected. This rollout is used to control the display of the end effector, goal, and solver. You can also enable the swivel angle manipulator in this rollout.

To turn on the display of the end effector, check the **Enabled** check box in the **End Effector Display** area. The value in the **Size:** spinner determines the size of the end effector, in current drawing units. The size of the end effector has no effect on the IK solution.

To turn on the display of the goal, check the **Enabled** button in the **Goal Display** area of the rollout. The value in the **Size:** spinner determines the size of the goal, in current drawing units. The size of the goal has no effect on the IK solution.

To turn on the display of the IK solver, check the **Enabled** button in the **IK Solver Display** area. The IK solver is displayed as a white line between the first bone in the chain and the last bone in the chain, when the goal is selected. When the goal is not selected, the IK solver is not displayed by default. Checking this check box displays the IK solver as a blue line when the goal is not selected.

To turn on the swivel angle manipulator, check the **Enabled** button in the **Swivel Angle Manipulator** area of the rollout. When this check box is unchecked, the **Select and Manipulate** button on the **Main** toolbar cannot be used to adjust the swivel angle. The **Size:** and **Length:** spinners in this area are used to control the size and length of the manipulator.

Help Cel

Displaying the IK solver can be helpful when overlapping IK solvers are applied.

IK Joint Parameters

The joint parameters for joints to which the history-independent IK solver is applied have "stripped-down" settings. See Figure 21-17. These settings are located in the **Hierarchy** tab. Each joint can potentially rotate about X, Y, and Z axes, and slide along X, Y, and Z axes. The transformation can be turned on or off for each of these axes. In addition, you can limit the transformation using the **From:** and **To:** spinners for each axis. However, there is no "ease" setting for any joint axis when using the history-independent IK solver. In addition, there are no "spring" settings.

For rotational axes, there is a **Preferred Angle:** spinner. The value in this spinner sets the initial rotation for the joint. The "sign" of the value (positive or negative) also indicates in which direction the joint will prefer to rotate in the IK solution.

Animating with the History-Independent IK Solver

When all IK properties are correctly set, animating the history-independent IK solver is quite easy. First, identify keyframes for the IK chain and the movement required. Then, move to the first keyframe and enter animation mode. Finally, transform the goal to achieve the first movement. The IK chain moves interactively as you transform the goal, based on the display settings. When all keys are set, exit animation mode and preview the animation.

Figure 21-17. Setting joint parameters for a joint using a history-independent IK solver.

You can also animate changes to the swivel angle. This can be done by animating the **Swivel Angle:** spinner value in the **IK Solver Plane** area of the **IK Solver Properties** rollout. In addition, you can manipulate the angle in the viewport. The manipulator must be enabled in the **Swivel Angle Manipulator** area of the **IK Display Options** rollout. Then, use the **Select and Manipulate** button on the **Main** toolbar to change the swivel angle. The value in the **Swivel Angle:** spinner is updated to reflect the change.

Select and Manipulate

Exercise

Exercise 21-9

1) Open ex21-03.max from Exercise 21-3. Save the scene as ex21-09.max in the folder of your choice.
2) Rotate the upper leg 45°, as shown below. Rotate the lower leg 45° in the opposite direction.
3) Draw a bone hierarchy, starting with the hip joint. Refer to the figure below (the bones are shown out of place for illustration). Do not automatically assign an IK solver to the children. You should have a bone from the hip joint to the knee joint, from the knee joint to the ankle joint, and from the ankle joint to the ball of the foot. When you right-click to end bone creation, a fourth bone (single diamond) is created at the ball of the foot. There will be four total bones when you are done.
4) Select the first bone. Apply a history-independent IK solver and pick the bone drawn from the ankle to the ball of the foot (Bone03).
5) Set the IK joint parameters as needed. Refer to the values given in Exercise 21-3. However, these values may need to be modified as appropriate for this IK chain.
6) When all IK parameters are set, link the upper leg to Bone01 and the lower leg to Bone02. Make sure the foot is linked to the lower leg.
7) In the Left viewport, pick the goal. Transform the goal in the viewport and observe the motion.
8) Make any adjustments necessary to the IK parameters.
9) Save the scene.

Using the Limb Solver

The IK limb solver is specifically designed for character animation. The solver works on two bones in a hierarchy. In order to work properly, the hierarchy must have three bones. To apply the limb solver, select the first bone in a three-bone network. Then, select **IK Limb Solver** in the **IK Solvers** cascading menu in the **Animation** pull-down menu. A dashed white line appears from the root bone to the cursor. Pick on the *third* bone in the chain. This sets the solver correctly on the chain. Now, you can animate the goal, which is on the second bone in the chain.

Help Cel

Be sure to correctly set joint parameters and the initial position of each bone before applying a limb solver.

Skin and Bones

The skin modifier is specifically designed for use with a bones system and another object. By applying the modifier to an object, you can "bind" the object to each bone in the bones system. When the bones are animated, the object is deformed to reflect the movement of the bones. See Figure 21-18. A brief tutorial using the skin modifier is presented in Chapter 8.

The modifier allows you to adjust the sphere of influence, or envelope, around each bone. If the envelope is not large enough, the modifier will not be able to deform the parent object. To adjust the envelope, select a bone in the list in the **Parameters** rollout for the modifier. Then, pick the **Edit Envelopes** button. In the viewport, select the inner or outer gizmo. In the **Parameters** rollout, adjust the properties of the envelope for the end of the bone selected.

Figure 21-18.
A—The skin modifier is applied to the cylinder so the bone network can deform the cylinder.
B—You can adjust the envelope for each bone assigned to the skin modifier. The gizmo is displayed on the selected bone.

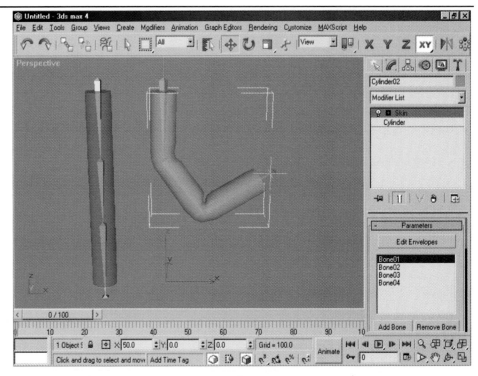

A

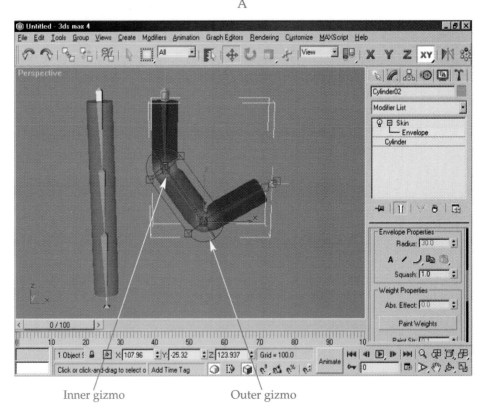

Inner gizmo   Outer gizmo

B

Exercise 21-10

1) Draw the simple loft object shown below on the left.
2) Draw a bone hierarchy of 10 or 11 bones inside the loft object. Set IK joint parameters as necessary. Then, apply a history-dependent or history-independent solver.
3) Apply a skin modifier to the loft object. Add all bones to the modifier. Adjust the envelope settings for the bones as necessary.
4) Animate the bones to achieve a shape similar to the one shown below on the right. This should be on frame 50. On frame 100, animate the bones back to their original position, or close to it.
5) Render a preview animation of the Perspective viewport.
6) When satisfied with the motion, render a final animation to a file named ex21-10.avi in the folder of your choice.
7) Save the scene as ex21-10.max in the folder of your choice.

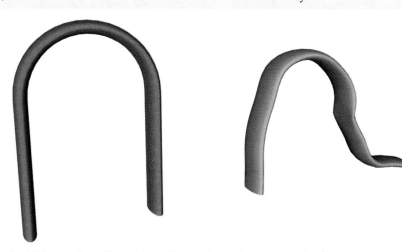

Exercise

Chapter Snapshot

Chapter Test

1) Define inverse kinematics.
2) List the three methods of utilizing inverse kinematics.
3) Define IK solution.
4) What is an end effector?
5) Which IK method calculates an IK solution for every frame?
6) The _____ and _____ IK methods allow you to dynamically animate objects.
7) Which IK method is designed for use with bones systems?
8) Define goal.
9) Which IK method is primarily designed to use follow objects?
10) What is an initial state?
11) What does freezing an object allow?
12) There are _____ possible joint axes for each joint when setting joint parameters for IK.
13) What are the basic types of IK joints?
14) What is the function of the **Spring Back** spinner value?
15) What is the preferred angle?
16) Where is the **Interactive IK** button located?
17) Which rollout is used to manually create an end effector?
18) How do you transform a bone without an IK solution being calculated?
19) What is a threshold in relation to IK?
20) The _____ modifier is used to deform an object based on the transformation of a bones system.

Modeling Problems

Unless otherwise directed, draw the objects shown using your own dimensions. Define and apply materials as needed. Add lights and a camera as needed. Pay attention to shadow location and color. Apply IK solvers as needed. When finished, save each scene as p21-xx.max in the folder of your choice.

Sliding Drawer **1**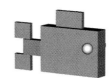

Once you have created the objects, adjust pivots and link objects as needed. Adjust and limit the IK joint parameters as needed. Animate the drawer sliding open, pausing, and sliding shut. Render the animation to a file named p21-01.avi in the folder of your choice.

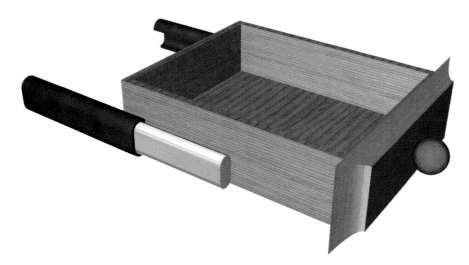

Cartoon Bee **2**

Open problem p07-03.max from Chapter 7. Save the scene as p21-02.max in the folder of your choice. Adjust pivot points as needed. Create a logical hierarchy and link objects. Define IK joint parameters as needed for the legs. Create a bone network for the wings. Use the skin modifier to link each wing to its bone network. Animate the legs and wings using your own design. Render the animation to a file named p21-02.avi in the folder of your choice.

3 Robot Biped
Open problem p12-10.max from Chapter 12. Save the scene as p21-03.max in the folder of your choice. Double-check the linking created for the robot. Create a bone network from the existing objects. Adjust IK joint parameters as needed. Animate the arms lifting and the torso turning. Render the animation to a file named p21-03.avi in the folder of your choice.

4 Snork 2000 Security System
Open problem p07-05.max from Chapter 7. Save the scene as p21-04.max in the folder of your choice. Draw a bone network for the Snork. A hierarchy was not created in Chapter 7, so you will not be able to set up the existing objects as bones. After drawing the bones, adjust the IK joint parameters as needed. Create end effectors as needed. Animate the Snork with simple movement, such as lifting a leg or turning its head. Render the animation to a file named p21-04.avi in the folder of your choice.

5 Folding Chair
When the chair is folded closed, the back of the seat should slide up toward the backrest. When the model is complete, animate the chair closed and then open again. Render the animation to a file named p21-07.avi in the folder of your choice.

Robot Quadruped **6**

Open problem p12-09.max from Chapter 12. Save the scene as p21-06.max in the folder of your choice. Draw a new bone network for the quadruped (do not create it from the existing hierarchy). Adjust the IK joint parameters as needed. Limit the joints as appropriate. Create end effectors as needed. Animate the quadruped with a simple motion, such as lifting a leg or bending its neck. Render the animation to a file named p21-06.avi in the folder of your choice.

Recoiling Cannon **7**

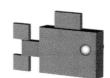

Draw the cannon as shown below. Then, animate the cannon rotating up and firing. The forward barrel section should recoil (slide) into the rear barrel section. Render the animation to a file named p21-05.avi in the folder of your choice.

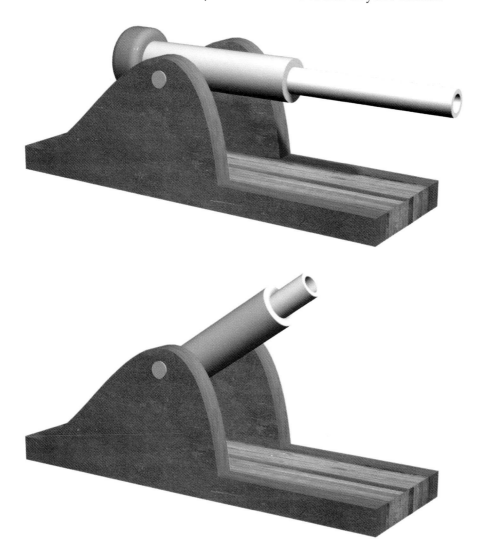

8 Desk Lamp

The head of the lamp should slide along the upper arm. The arms should rotate about the center of their "joints." When the model is complete, animate several different movements for the lamp. Be sure the light moves with the lamp head. Render the animation to a file named p21-08.avi in the folder of your choice.

9 Portable Dishwasher and Shelves

After drawing the dishwasher, define the IK joint parameters as needed so the shelves slide out as the door is opened. Then, animate the door opening, staying open for a period of time, and closing. Render the animation to a file named p21-09.avi in the folder of your choice.

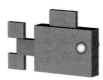

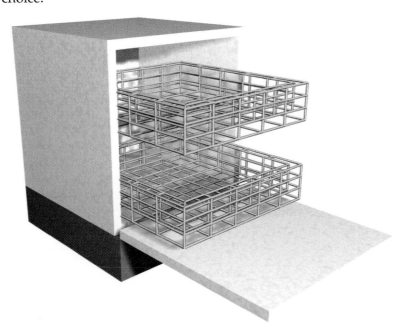

Robot Arm **10**

Open problem p12-03.max from Chapter 12. Save the scene as p21-10.max in the folder of your choice. Create a bone network from the existing hierarchy. Adjust the IK parameters as needed. Limit joint movement as needed. Create an end effector in an appropriate location. Animate the bone network so the arm performs a simple movement. Render the animation to a file named p21-10.avi in the folder of your choice.

Shaft Linkage **11**

Draw the objects shown. Add a bones system and define IK joint parameters as necessary. Animate the rotation of the purple axle through one complete rotation. The yellow shaft should move up and down only. Render the animation to a file named p21-11.avi in the folder of your choice.

Chapter 22

Introduction to Particle Systems

Objectives

After completing this chapter, you will be able to:

- Explain what a particle system does.
- Define emitter.
- List the particle systems that come with 3ds max.
- Create various particle systems.
- Modify a particle system.
- Define distribution object.
- Apply motion blur to a particle system.
- Define space warp.
- Create and utilize a deflector space warp.
- Create and utilize a gravity space warp.

What Is a Particle System?

A particle system is a special type of object that generates other objects based on parameters. Particle systems are used to create snow, rain, dust, explosion debris, and so on. Particle systems can also be used to create a flock of seagulls, a school of fish, or a herd of buffalo. See Figure 22-1.

A particle system uses a helper object called an *emitter*. See Figure 22-2. The emitter is where the particles are generated. It is also the "control center" for the particle system's parameters. For particle systems that do not generate particles, such as a PArray, the emitter's only purpose is to serve as the control center for the parameters.

Help Cel

Do not confuse a "particle system" with a "system." Systems are discussed in Chapter 20.

Figure 22-1. This alien invasion is generated using instanced geometry and a super spray particle system. The nebula behind the spacecraft is a fire atmospheric effect.

Emitter

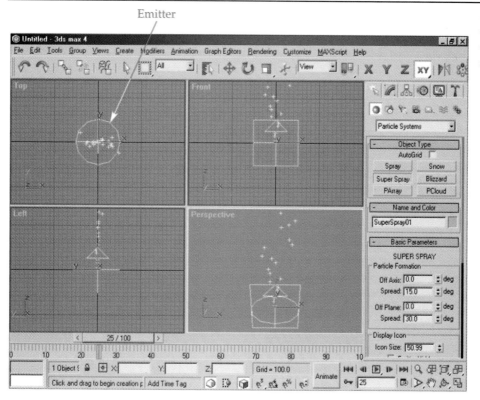

Figure 22-2. An emitter is the "control center" for a particle system.

Types of Particle Systems

There are six types of particle systems that come with 3ds max. These are spray, super spray, snow, blizzard, PArray, and PCloud. The blizzard and super spray types are similar. Snow and spray are also similar types. The PArray and PCloud types can generate "particles" of other geometry you create.

Spray

The spray particle system is a simple system that emits particles in a spray pattern. It can be used to simulate rain, dust storms, water dripping, or a cooling mist on a machine tool. It can also be used to simulate steam rising from a manhole cover or space dust in a SciFi scene. See Figure 22-3. This is an early particle system that has been carried through various releases of 3D Studio.

Super Spray

The super spray particle system is an advanced version of the spray system. It provides more control over the particles. The additional control allows you to create fountains, star fields, volcano eruptions, and many other effects. See Figure 22-4. You can also use super spray to create bubbles or even water flowing from a pipe.

Snow

The snow particle system is similar to the spray system. However, there are also "tumbling" parameters to control how the particles move. This system is designed to create snow, but it can also be used to simulate a windy rainstorm or sparks from a cauldron of molten metal. See Figure 22-5. Like spray, snow is an early particle system.

Figure 22-3. The space debris around this spacecraft is generated with a spray particle system. The nebula behind the spacecraft is a fire atmospheric effect.

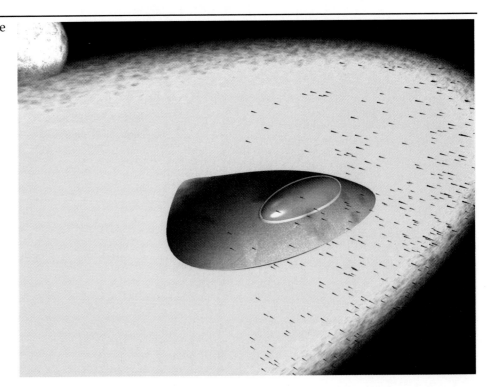

Figure 22-4. The lava spewing from this island volcano is generated using a super spray particle system.

Figure 22-5. The sparks above the cauldron of molten metal are generated using a snow particle system.

Blizzard

The blizzard particle system is an advanced version of the snow system. It provides additional control over the particles. The blizzard particle system is used in applications similar to those for the snow particle system when additional control is needed.

PArray

The PArray, or particle array, particle system allows you to use geometry as the emitter. The selected geometry can generate particles in a pattern. The PArray system can also be used to create an explosion from the selected geometry. See Figure 22-6.

PCloud

The PCloud, or particle cloud, particle system is used to create particles confined to a specified volume. This particle system is especially useful for creating scenes such as a school of fish or a pack of animals. See Figure 22-7. The "container" can be one of the presets or any renderable 3D object.

Help Cel

There are many particle system plug-ins available. Only the particle systems that come with 3ds max are discussed in this text. Refer to documentation provided by the plug-in developer for details on using after-market particle systems.

Create

Geometry

Creating Particle Systems

To create a particle system, first pick **Create** in the **Command Panel**. Then, pick the **Geometry** button and select **Particle Systems** from the drop-down list. Then, in the **Object Type** rollout, pick the button for the particle system you want to create.

You can also pick **Particles** in the **Create** pull-down menu. Then, select the desired particle system in the cascading menu. This opens the **Create** tab in the **Command Panel** and "selects" the button corresponding to the particle system in the **Object Type** rollout.

Figure 22-6. A PArray particle system is used to blow up the bomb shown on the left. The pieces of the bomb are shown on the right.

Figure 22-7. This army of mechanical space bugs is generated using a PCloud particle system.

In general, when creating a particle system, you first draw an emitter. Then, you need to set the number, size, and shape of the particles. Finally, you need to define motion parameters for the particles. The specifics of each type of particle system are covered in the next sections.

Spray

Once you pick the **Spray** button in the **Object Type** rollout, you must draw an emitter. Pick in the viewport and drag to create the rectangular emitter. See Figure 22-8. The straight line in the middle of the emitter indicates the direction the particles will travel. This direction is "into" the viewport where the emitter is drawn.

Next, you need to set parameters for the spray. At the top of the **Parameters** rollout is the **Particles:** area. The settings in this area determine how the particles are generated. The value in the **Viewport Count:** spinner is the maximum number of particles displayed in a viewport at any given time. The value in the **Render Count:** spinner is the maximum number of particles displayed in a rendered frame.

The value in the **Drop Size:** spinner sets the size of each particle in current drawing units. The value in the **Speed:** spinner sets the velocity of each particle as it leaves the emitter. The particle will remain at this velocity unless affected by a space warp. Space warps are introduced later in this chapter and covered in detail in Chapter 23. The **Variation:** spinner is used to vary the speed and direction of particles as they leave the emitter. The lower the value, the slower and more dense the spray.

The three radio buttons at the bottom of the **Particles:** area determine how the particles are displayed in the viewport. This setting does not affect the rendered particles.

The **Render:** area of the **Parameters** rollout is used to set the shape of the rendered particles. Picking the **Tetrahedron** radio button renders each

Spray

Spray

Figure 22-8. An emitter for a spray particle system is a rectangle. The line extending down from the center of the rectangle indicates the direction of particle travel.

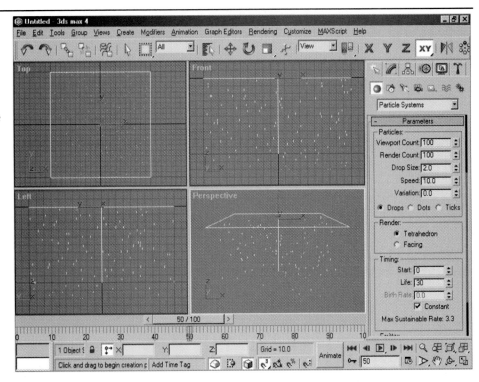

particle as a tetrahedron. The length of the tetrahedron is specified in the **Drop Size:** spinner in the **Particles:** area. Picking the **Facing** radio button renders each particle as a square face. The size of the square is specified in the **Drop Size:** spinner. The face always points toward the viewer in a camera viewport or the Perspective viewport. Using this option in other viewports will produce unwanted results. This option is designed specifically for use with mapped materials.

The **Timing:** area is used to set the life span of a particle. The value in the **Start:** spinner is the frame where the emitter begins generating particles. The value in the **Life:** spinner is the number of frames a particle will be alive. After that, the particle dies and is removed. The value in the **Birth Rate:** spinner is the number of new particles born on each frame. If the **Constant** check box is checked, the birth rate is automatically set to the maximum sustainable rate. The maximum sustainable rate is indicated at the bottom of the **Timing:** area. This is the maximum number of particles that can be born in each frame without interrupting particle generation.

The **Emitter:** area is used to set the size of the emitter. The size of the emitter determines the area over which particles are generated. Checking the **Hide** check box hides the emitter in the viewports. An emitter is not rendered, so this check box affects viewport display only.

Help Cel

When the maximum "count" value is reached, no more particles are generated until some of the existing particles die. To ensure this does not occur, either use the **Constant** check box or set the birth rate lower than the maximum sustainable rate.

Exercise 22-1

1) Draw a spray emitter in the Top viewport. Use your own dimensions and set the particle size as necessary.
2) Make the Perspective viewport active. Adjust the viewport as necessary to get a good view of the emitter. Leave enough space below the emitter to see the particles.
3) Pick the **Play Animation** button to preview the motion of the particles.
4) Assign a material of your choice to the emitter, such as a bright red or blue standard material.
5) Change the environment background to pure white (255).
6) Render the animation to a file named ex22-01a.avi in the folder of your choice. Set the resolution to 320 x 240.
7) When the rendering is complete, view the animation.
8) In the **Render:** area of the **Parameters** rollout for the spray, pick the **Facing** radio button.
9) Render the animation to a file named ex22-01b.avi in the folder of your choice. Use the same resolution as before.
10) Compare the two animations. Save the scene as ex22-01.max in the folder of your choice.

Super Spray

The super spray particle system is similar to the spray system, but it provides more control over particle generation. Once you pick the **Super Spray** button in the **Object Type** rollout, you must draw an emitter. Pick in the viewport and drag to create the emitter. See Figure 22-9. The emitter looks like a circle and rectangle intersecting at 90° with a triangle pointing in one direction. The triangle points in the direction of travel for the particles. The particles are emitted from the center of the circle. The particles generally come straight out of the viewport where the emitter is drawn.

Next, you need to set parameters for the super spray. There are several rollouts where parameters can be set. These include the **Basic Parameters, Particle Generation, Particle Type, Rotation and Collision, Object Motion Inheritance, Bubble Motion, Particle Spawn,** and **Load/Save Presets** rollouts.

Help Cel

Many of the particle systems that come with 3ds max have the same rollouts, options, and settings.

Basic Parameters

The settings in the **Basic Parameters** rollout determine how the particles are generated. The settings in the **Particle Formation** area define the basic shape of the spray. The **Off Axis:** spinner and off axis **Spread:** spinner determine the vertical shape of the spray. The **Off Plane:** spinner and off plane **Spread:** spinner determine the horizontal shape of the spray. See Figure 22-10. If the **Off Axis:** value is 0°, the **Off Plane:** setting has no effect.

Figure 22-9. The particles for a super spray are generated from the center of the emitter.

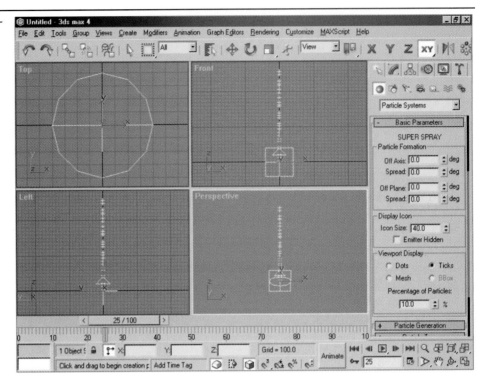

Figure 22-10. The blue triangle represents the "off axis" setting. The red triangle represents the "off plane" setting. Together, these two settings can define a cone in which particles move.

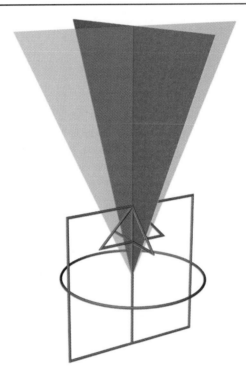

The **Icon Size:** spinner in the **Display Icon** area determines the size of the emitter. Since the super spray particle system generates particles from a single point, the size is for display only. Checking the **Emitter Hidden** check box hides the emitter in the viewports.

The **Viewport Display** area is used to set how the particles appear in the viewports. When instanced geometry is specified (in the **Particle Type** rollout), picking the **Mesh** radio button displays the geometry. Also, the **BBox** radio button is enabled. Picking this radio button displays the instanced geometry in the viewports as bounding boxes. The **Percentage of Particles:** spinner is used to display only a small percentage of the total number of particles. Generally, set this to about 10% or 20% so your system does not bog down.

Exercise 22-2

1) Draw a super spray emitter in the Top viewport.
2) Make the Perspective viewport active. Adjust the viewport as necessary to get a good view of the emitter. Leave enough space above the emitter to see the particles.
3) Pick the **Play Animation** button to preview the motion of the particles.
4) Change the off axis spread to 15. Change the off plane spread to 30.
5) Pick the **Play Animation** button to preview the motion again in the Perspective viewport.
6) Render a final animation to a file named ex22-02.avi in the folder of your choice.
7) When the rendering is complete, view the animation.
8) Save the scene as ex22-02.max in the folder of your choice.

Exercise

Particle Generation

The **Particle Quantity** area of the **Particle Generation** rollout determines how many particles are generated on each frame. When the **Use Rate** radio button is on, the spinner below it is enabled. The value in the spinner is the number of particles generated on each frame. When the **Use Total** radio button is on, the spinner below it is enabled. The value in this spinner is the total number of particles the emitter will generate over its life span.

The **Particle Motion** area is used to set the velocity of each particle. The value in the **Speed:** spinner is the velocity of each particle as it leaves the emitter. This value is the number of current drawing units the particle moves per frame. The value in the **Variation:** spinner is a percentage by which the velocity of each new particle will vary from the value in the **Speed:** spinner.

The **Particle Timing** area is used to control the life span of the particles. The values in the **Emit Start:** and **Emit Stop:** spinners set the first and last frames for particle generation. The value in the **Display Until:** spinner is the frame where all particles are removed from the scene. The value in the **Life:** spinner is the number of frames a particle is alive. The value in the **Variation:** spinner is the number of frames a particle's life can randomly vary from the **Life:** setting.

The **Subframe Sampling:** check boxes at the bottom of the **Particle Timing** area allow you to increase the particle sampling rate. If the rate is too low, particles may be emitted in groups as opposed to a continuous stream.

The **Particle Size** area is used to set the size of each particle. The value in the **Size:** spinner is the size of the particle. What this value represents depends on the type of particle. The **Variation:** spinner is used to vary the size of particles. The value in the **Grow For:** spinner is the number of frames it will take for the particle to be fully grown from small to the **Size:** value. The value in the **Fade For:** spinner is the number of frames before the particle's death it will take the object to shrink to $1/10^{th}$ the **Size:** value. If these values are set to 0, the particles are always the same size.

The **Uniqueness** area is used to assign a seed to the emitter. This allows different particles to be generated by different emitters with all other settings the same. Pick the **New** button to randomly generate a seed. You can also manually enter a value in the spinner.

Exercise

Exercise 22-3

1) Open ex22-02.max from Exercise 22-2. Save the scene as ex22-03.max in the folder of your choice.
2) In the **Particle Generation** rollout, change the emitter stop time to frame 100.
3) Change the particle speed to 5.
4) Change the particle size to about 5 or slightly less. Also, set the particle size variation to 50.
5) Render the animation to a file named ex22-03a.avi in the folder of your choice.
6) When the rendering is complete, view the animation.
7) Change the particle speed to 20.
8) Render the animation to a file named ex22-03b.avi in the folder of your choice.
9) Compare the particle motion in the two animations.
10) Save the scene.

Particle Type

The **Particle Type** rollout allows you to choose the type of geometry used for the particle. In the **Particle Types** area of the rollout, you can select the **Standard Particles**, **MetaParticles**, or **Instanced Geometry** radio button. The corresponding area on the rollout is enabled.

Standard Particles

In the **Standard Particles** area, you can choose from eight different types of particle shapes. Picking the **Triangle** radio button renders each particle as a triangle. Picking the **Cube** radio button renders each particle as a cube. Picking the **Special** radio button renders each particle as three intersection planes, or squares. This type is intended to be used with a face-mapped material. Picking the **Facing** radio button renders each particle as a square facing the viewer. Picking the **Constant** radio button renders each particle as a circle. The size of the circle remains constant regardless of the distance from the camera. Picking the **Tetra** radio button renders each particle as a tetrahedron. Picking the **SixPoint** radio button renders each particle as a flat, six-pointed star. Picking the **Sphere** radio button renders each particle as a sphere.

Exercise 22-4

1) Open ex22-03.max from Exercise 22-3. Save the scene as ex22-04.max in the folder of your choice.
2) In the **Particle Type** rollout, change the particle type to the standard particle sphere.
3) Render a final animation to a file named ex22-04a.avi in the folder of your choice.
4) Change the particle type to the standard particle six-pointed star.
5) Render a final animation to a file named ex22-04b.avi in the folder of your choice.
6) Compare the two animations.
7) Save the scene.

MetaParticle Parameters

The **MetaParticle Parameters** area of the **Particle Type** rollout allows you to set the parameters for particles known as metaparticles, or meta-balls. *Metaballs* are special spherical geometry with organic properties. Metaballs can join with each other to form other particles. They can also have a skin to create one large mass or "blob." Metaparticles are used to create streams of liquid, flowing lava, mudslides, and other similar "flowing" objects.

The value in the **Tension:** spinner determines the surface tension of each metaball. The higher the tension, the harder it is for two particles to join. The value in the **Variation:** spinner sets a percentage of allowed variation for tension.

The **Evaluation Coarseness:** spinners determine the precision of the equation used to calculate metaball interaction. The **Render:** spinner determines coarseness for rendering. The **Viewport:** spinner determines coarseness for viewport display. The higher the coarseness value, the less precise the calculation. However, if the coarseness is too low, the calculation can take forever. These spinners are disabled if the **Automatic Coarseness** check box is checked, which is the default setting.

The **One Connected Blob** check box is used to calculate and display only the metaballs that touch and connect. Particles separate from the "mass" are not displayed. This option should be used on a particle system where the metaballs are positioned tightly together, such as for a flowing liquid. Checking the check box enables the calculation "shortcut" and can reduce rendering time.

Help Cel

The **One Connected Blob** option may produce animations where the mass of particles "disappears" on certain frames of the animation. If this happens, increase particle size, reduce particle speed, reduce tension, or simply turn this option off.

Exercise

Exercise 22-5

1) Open ex22-04.max from Exercise 22-4. Save the scene as ex22-05.max in the folder of your choice.
2) In the **Particle Type** rollout for the super spray emitter, change the particle type to metaparticles. Also, enter 2.0 in the **Tension:** spinner.
3) In the **Particle Generation** rollout, set the speed at 2.0 and the size to about 5 or a little less.
4) Render a final animation to a file named ex22-05a.avi in the folder of your choice.
5) When the rendering is complete, view the animation.
6) Enter 0.5 in the **Tension:** spinner.
7) Change the particle speed to 3.5 or a little lower.
8) Render a final animation to a file named ex22-05b.avi in the folder of your choice.
9) Compare the two animations.
10) Save the scene.

Instancing Parameters

The **Instancing Parameters:** area of the **Particle Type** rollout allows you to use instanced geometry in a particle system, when the particle type is set to **Instanced Geometry**. At the top of the **Instancing Parameters:** area is the **Object:** label. This indicates the name of the object instanced by the particle system. Each particle in the system is an instance (copy) of the geometry. If no object has been selected, this label is displayed as **<None>**.

To choose an object to use as instanced geometry, select the **Pick Object** button. Then, select the object in the viewport. You can use the [H] key to select the object by its name. Picking a group includes all objects in the group as particles. If the selected object has children, you can include the children as particles by checking the **Use Subtree Also** check box. Right-click or pick the button again to exit the "select" mode.

Pick Object

Pick Object

The **Animation Offset Keying** radio buttons allow you to set how animation of the instanced geometry is applied to the particles. See Figure 22-11. Picking the **None** radio button animates each particle at its birth as the first frame of the animated instanced geometry. This results in identically animated particles. Picking the **Birth** radio button animates each particle at its birth as the equivalent animation frame of the instanced geometry. Picking the **Random** radio button enables the **Frame Offset:** spinner below it. Entering a value other than 0 in this spinner in effect randomizes the **Birth** option. Entering a value of 0 is the same as applying the **None** option.

Material Mapping and Source

The **Mat'l Mapping and Source** area of the **Particle Type** rollout is used to control the source of material for the particles and how a mapped material is applied. At the bottom of this area are the **Icon** and **Instanced Geometry** radio buttons. When the **Icon** radio button is on, the material

Figure 22-11. When instanced geometry is animated, you can set how the timing of the animation is carried over to the particles. In this example, the emitter begins generating particles on frame 40.

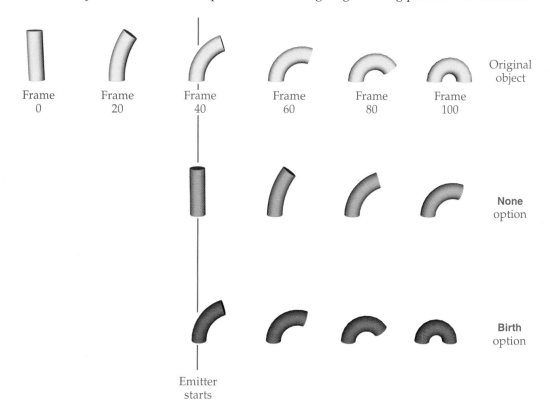

assigned to the emitter is used for the particles. When the **Instanced Geometry** radio button is on, the material assigned to the instanced geometry is used for the particles. This button is greyed out unless the particle type is set to instanced geometry. Picking the **Get Material From:** button loads the material from the specified source to the particles. Once you load the material from instanced geometry, the material for the particles is always from the instanced geometry. The **Icon** radio button is greyed out, making it impossible to later load the material from the emitter.

The radio buttons and spinners at the top of the **Mat'l Mapping and Source** area are used to control the mapping of a mapped material applied to the particles. If the mapped material is not animated, these settings have no effect. Picking the **Time** radio button enables the spinner below it. The value in this spinner is the number of frames it takes for one mapping cycle of the material to be completed. Picking the **Distance** radio button enables the spinner below it. The value in this spinner is the distance of a particle from the emitter when one mapping cycle is complete. This value is in current drawing units. Both of these options are disabled when the **Instanced Geometry** option is used.

Help Cel

Tetrahedron particles have their own material mapping.

Exercise

Exercise 22-6

1) Open ex22-05.max from Exercise 22-5. Save the scene as ex22-06.max in the folder of your choice.
2) Draw a hedra using the **Star1** shape option. Make the radius about 1 or 1.5, but not much larger.
3) In the **Particle Type** rollout for the super spray emitter, change the particle type to instanced geometry. Then, pick the hedra as the geometry.
4) Assign a red standard material to the super spray emitter. Assign a blue standard material to the hedra.
5) Change the particle speed to 7 or a little higher. Change the particle size to 2.5 or a little lower.
6) Render a final animation to a file named ex22-06a.avi in the folder of your choice.
7) When the rendering is complete, view the animation.
8) In the **Mat'l Mapping and Source** area of the **Particle Type** rollout, pick the **Instanced Geometry** radio button. Then, pick the **Get Material From:** button.
9) Render a final animation to a file named ex22-06b.avi in the folder of your choice.
10) Compare the two animations. Then, save the scene.

Rotation and Collision

The **Rotation and Collision** rollout is used to control how particles interact with each other. You can also add motion blur to the particles in this rollout. Motion blur is used to help simulate a high velocity for the particles. Particle motion blur is covered in detail later in this chapter.

The settings in the **Spin Speed Controls** area of the **Rotation and Collision** rollout determine how a particle rotates. The value in the **Spin Time:** spinner is the number of frames it takes the particle to complete one rotation. The value in the **Variation:** spinner below the **Spin Time:** spinner is the percentage of variation allowed in the spin time. The **Phase:** spinner sets the initial rotation of the particle at birth. The **Variation:** spinner below the **Phase:** spinner sets the variation in phase.

The **Spin Axis Controls** area sets the axis of rotation for the particles. Picking the **Random** radio button randomizes the axis of rotation for each particle.

Picking the **Direction of Travel/Mblur** radio button specifies the axis of rotation as the vector along which the particles travel. The **Stretch:** spinner is also enabled. This spinner allows you to set a percentage of stretch for each particle. Generally, use low stretch values. These two settings also allow you to simulate motion blur, as discussed later in the chapter.

Picking the **User Defined** radio button enables the spinners below it. The values in the **X Axis:**, **Y Axis:**, and **Z Axis:** spinners define a point from the particle's origin. The axis of rotation is about a vector drawn from the particle's origin to the specified point. See Figure 22-12. The **Variation:** spinner sets the allowed variation from this vector, measured in degrees.

The **Interparticle Collisions** area of the **Rotation and Collision** rollout is used to fine-tune how the particles interact, or collide, with each other.

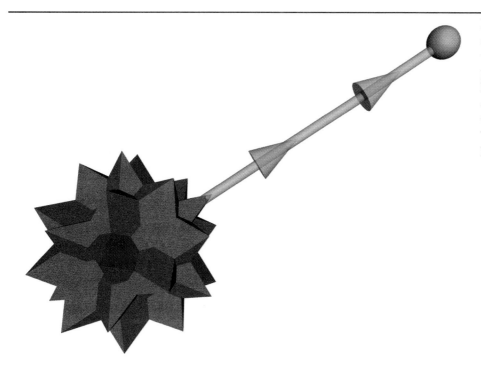

Figure 22-12. You can specify an axis of rotation for particles. The point you pick, shown here in orange, defines a vector from the particle's center. The vector is shown here in blue.

To turn this option on, check the **Enable** check box. The value in the **Calc Intervals Per Frame:** spinner is the number of times the collision calculation is applied for *each frame* of the animation. The value in the **Bounce:** spinner determines how quickly a particle returns to its velocity setting after a collision. In effect, this determines if the particles are soft or hard. The **Variation:** spinner sets the allowed variation in bounce.

Help Cel

Enabling the **Interparticle Collisions** options dramatically intensifies the calculations required to render a scene. These options should only be enabled when you need to provide additional control.

Object Motion Inheritance

The **Object Motion Inheritance** rollout is used to set how the motion of the emitter affects the particles. The particles generated by a stationary emitter travel along their own path of travel. However, as the emitter moves, the particles move along their own path of travel *and* the emitter's path of travel. See Figure 22-13. You can fine-tune this motion or turn it off completely.

The value in the **Influence:** spinner is the percentage of total particles that will be affected by the motion of the emitter. When this value is 0, none of the particles are affected by the movement of the emitter. When the value is 100, all of the particles follow the emitter as it moves.

The value in the **Multiplier:** spinner determines the strength of the effect. When set to 1, there is a 1:1 ratio between emitter movement and the influence on the particles. When set to 3, the effect of the emitter movement is three times stronger on the particles. Negative values can also be entered in this spinner. The **Variation:** spinner sets the allowed variation in the multiplier value.

Figure 22-13. You can set how the motion of the emitter affects the motion of the particles. The yellow arrows show the direction of travel. The blue particles are set so that 100% of the particles are affected by emitter travel. The red particles are set so that 50% of the particles are affected by emitter travel. Notice how half of the red particles move with the emitter and half do not.

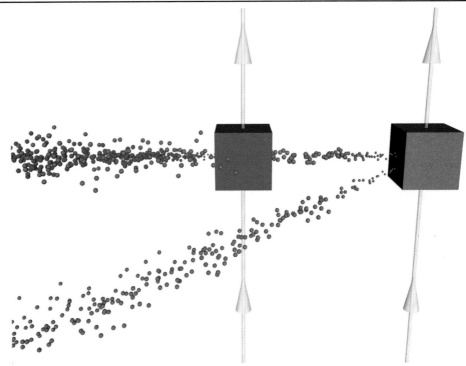

Exercise

Exercise 22-7

1) Open ex22-06.max from Exercise 22-6. Save the scene as ex22-07.max in the folder of your choice.
2) Change the particle type to the standard particle sphere.
3) Set the particle size to 3 or a little lower. Also, change the particle speed to about 5 or a little higher.
4) On frame 0, move the emitter to the far left side of the Perspective viewport. Then, on frame 100, turn the **Toggle Animation Mode** button on and move the emitter to the far right side of the Perspective viewport. Turn the **Toggle Animation Mode** button off.
5) Render a final animation to a file named ex22-07a.avi in the folder of your choice.
6) When the rendering is finished, view the animation.
7) In the **Rotation and Collision** rollout for the emitter, pick the **Direction of Travel/Mblur** radio button. Enter a value of about 50 in the **Stretch:** spinner.
8) In the **Object Motion Inheritance** rollout, enter a value of 5 in the **Influence:** spinner. Also, enter 0.5 in the **Multiplier:** spinner.
9) Render a final animation to a file named ex22-07b.avi in the folder of your choice.
10) When the rendering is complete, compare the two animations. Then, save the scene.

Bubble Motion

The **Bubble Motion** rollout allows you to define a waveform motion path for particles. This allows the particles to stagger or wobble as they travel away from the emitter. However, they still travel along the vector of the travel path. This is different from the "off axis" and "off plane" options because those settings alter the vector. The options in this rollout are designed to make the generated particles look like bubbles. See Figure 22-14.

The value in the **Amplitude:** spinner sets the height of each wave. Since the waveform is sinusoidal, the height applies to both sides of the vector. The **Period:** spinner sets the number of frames it takes a particle to travel from the beginning of the wave to the end. The **Phase:** spinner determines the initial position of a particle along the wave. All three of these spinners have a **Variation:** spinner to set the allowed variation in the value.

Help Cel

The **Period:** spinner value defaults to 100,000. This may be too high for many applications. At 30 frames per second, this is nearly an hour of animation to complete one cycle.

Figure 22-14. The settings in the **Bubble Motion** rollout allow you to simulate bubbles. The bubbles from the left-hand propulsion tube (foreground) have bubble settings applied. The bubbles from the right-hand propulsion tube (background) do not have bubble settings applied. Therefore, they travel in a straight line.

Exercise

Exercise 22-8

1) Open ex22-07.max from Exercise 22-7. Save the scene as ex22-08.max in the folder of your choice.
2) Delete the movement keys for the emitter. Then, move the emitter to the middle of the Perspective viewport.
3) In the **Rotation and Collision** rollout for the emitter, enter a value of 0 in the **Stretch:** spinner.
4) In the **Object Motion Inheritance** rollout, enter a value of 100 in the **Influence:** spinner. Also, enter a value of 1 in the **Multiplier:** spinner.
5) In the **Bubble Motion** rollout, enter a value of 20 in the **Amplitude:** spinner. Also, enter a value of 20 in the **Period:** spinner.
6) Render a final animation to a file named ex22-08a.avi in the folder of your choice.
7) When the rendering is complete, view the animation.
8) In the **Basic Parameters** rollout for the emitter, change the off axis spread value to 0. Also, change the off plane spread value to 0.
9) Render a final animation to a file named ex22-08b.avi in the folder of your choice.
10) Compare the two animations. Then, save the scene.

Particle Spawn

The **Particle Spawn** rollout is used to control how a particle reacts when it dies or collides with a particle deflector. See Figure 22-15. A particle deflector is a special type of 3ds max object called a space warp. Space warps are introduced later in this chapter and covered in detail in Chapter 23. Using the **Particle Spawn** rollout, you can set particles to generate, or *spawn,* new particles when they die or collide. You can also set the particle system so no particles are spawned.

When the **None** radio button is on, particles do not spawn. The settings of the particle deflector object control how the particles bounce on collision. The particles die after their life span is reached.

When the **Die After Collision** radio button is on, particles die after colliding into their particle deflector. The value in the **Persist:** spinner is the number of frames that the particle remains alive after the collision. The **Variation:** spinner sets the allowed percentage of variation in the persist value.

When the **Spawn on Collision** radio button is on, the particle spawns after colliding with its particle deflector. When the **Spawn on Death** radio button is on, the particle spawns at the end of its life span, based on the settings in this rollout. When the **Spawn Trails** radio button is on, particles are spawned from each existing particle on every frame of the particle's life. These three particle spawn options generate particles based on the remaining settings in the rollout.

The **Spawns:** spinner determines how many times particles are generated. This is, in effect, a time limiter. If "particle 1" is set to spawn three times, the third set of spawns will not spawn themselves. This is not to be mistaken for a multiplier.

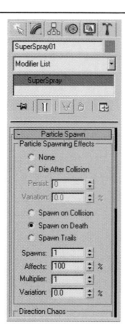

Figure 22-15. The **Particle Spawn** rollout is used to control how a particle reacts when it dies or collides with a particle deflector.

The **Multiplier:** spinner determines how many particles are spawned from each existing particle. For example, if the **Spawns:** spinner is set to 3 and the **Multiplier:** spinner is set to 2, the first spawn produces 2 particles. However, the second spawn produces 4 particles, and the third spawn produces 8 particles. The **Variation:** spinner sets the allowable percentage of variation for the multiplier value.

The **Affects:** spinner sets the percentage of particles in the system that will spawn. For example, if this value is 50, only 50% of the particles produce spawn on death or collision. This spinner can be used to reduce the total number of particles while still maintaining the spawn effect.

Chaos

The **Direction Chaos** area is used to vary the direction of each spawned particle. Enter a percentage of variance in the **Chaos:** spinner. A value of 0 means that spawned particles follow the path of the original particle. A value of 100 produces random direction paths for the spawned particles.

The **Speed Chaos** area is used to vary the speed of each spawned particle. The value in the **Factor:** spinner is a maximum percentage of the original particle's speed by which each particle can vary. A value of 0 means the spawned particle speed can vary by 0%, or not at all. When the **Slow** radio button is on, the change in speed slows down the spawned particles. When the **Fast** radio button is on, the change in speed increases the velocity of spawned particles. When the **Both** radio button is on, the change in speed slows some particles while speeding up others.

When the **Inherit Parent Velocity** check box in the **Speed Chaos** area is checked, the speed of the spawned particles is the sum of the parent's velocity and the "factor" velocity. When the **Use Fixed Value** check box is checked, the percentage of original velocity set in the **Factor:** spinner is applied to all spawned particles. When unchecked, the **Factor:** spinner sets an allowable range from which the speed of individual spawned particles is randomly selected.

The **Scale Chaos** area is used to vary the size of each spawned particle. The value in the **Factor:** spinner sets a percentage by which spawned particles can vary in size from the original. When the **Down** radio button is on, the spawned particles are scaled down in size. When the **Up** radio button is on, the spawned particles are scaled up in size. When the **Both** radio button is on, some particles are scaled up in size while others are scaled down. When the **Use Fixed Value** check box is checked, the value in the **Factor:** spinner defines a set value instead of a range of values. This is similar to the **Use Fixed Value** option for speed chaos.

Exercise

Exercise 22-9

1) Reset 3ds max.
2) Draw a super spray emitter in the Top viewport.
3) Adjust the Perspective viewport to get a good view of the emitter. Be sure to leave enough room above the emitter for the particles.
4) Set the particle type as the standard particle sphere with an off axis spread of 10. Set the speed to 3, the particle life to 25, and the particle size to 1.5. Set the emitter to stop on frame 100.
5) Render a final animation to a file named ex22-09a.avi in the folder of your choice.
6) When the rendering is complete, view the animation.
7) In the **Particle Spawn** rollout for the emitter, pick the **Spawn on Death** radio button. Then, enter a value of 10 in the **Spawns:** spinner and 2 in the **Multiplier:** spinner.
8) Render a final animation to a file named ex22-09b.avi in the folder of your choice.
9) Compare the two animations.
10) Save the scene as ex22-09.max in the folder of your choice.

Queues

The **Lifespan Value Queue** area in the **Particle Spawn** rollout allows you to define unique life spans for each generation of spawned particles. These life spans are independent of the life span setting for the particle system. To create a queue, or sequence, enter a value in the **Lifespan:** spinner and pick the **Add** button. That value appears at the top of the list. See Figure 22-16. The value sets the number of frames for the corresponding life span. Continue adding life span settings for as many generations as you want. If there are more generations than settings in the queue, the last (bottom) setting is used for all remaining generations.

To change an existing value in the life span queue, first enter the new value in the **Lifespan:** spinner. Then, highlight the value in the queue and pick the **Replace** button. If you want to delete an existing value from the queue, simply highlight the value in the list and pick the **Delete** button.

The **Object Mutation Queue** area allows you to specify different instanced geometry for each spawn generation. This option is only

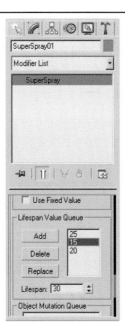

Figure 22-16. The **Lifespan Value Queue** area allows you to define unique life spans for each generation of spawned particles.

Figure 22-17. The **Object Mutation Queue** area allows you to specify different instanced geometry for each spawn generation.

available when the particle type for the particle system is set to instanced geometry. To add geometry to the queue, the geometry must first exist in the scene. Then, select the **Pick** button and pick the first object in a viewport. The object's name appears at the top of the list. See Figure 22-17. Continue instancing geometry for each generation of particle spawning.

Now, when a particle spawns for the first time, the original instanced geometry is replaced by the geometry at the top of the queue. At the second spawn, the particle uses the instanced geometry listed second in the queue, and so on. See Figure 22-18. If there are more generations than geometry in the queue, the last (bottom) instance is used for the remaining spawns.

To delete instanced geometry from the queue, highlight the name in the list and pick the **Delete** button. To replace existing geometry in the queue with different geometry, first highlight the name of the existing geometry. Then, pick the **Replace** button. Finally, pick the new geometry in a viewport.

Help Cel

Use particle spawning very carefully. If you do not watch what you are doing, you can quickly create a scene with literally millions of particles. You will also quickly find out the hard way why this is bad.

Figure 22-18. The particles of the super spray particle system emitted from the teapot spout start as red cubes, mutate on first collision to orange spheres, and finally mutate on second collision to yellow tori.

Exercise 22-10

1) Reset 3ds max.
2) In the Top viewport, draw a 5-unit cube, a 4-unit-radius sphere, and an 8-unit-radius teapot.
3) Define a blue standard material and assign it to the teapot. Define a red standard material and assign it to the box. Define a white standard material and assign it to the sphere.
4) In the Top viewport, draw a super spray emitter. Make the icon about 25 units in size.
5) In the **Basic Parameters** rollout for the super spray emitter, enter 15 for the off axis spread value and 30 for the off plane spread value.
6) In the **Particle Generation** rollout, set the particle speed to 5 and change the emitter stop time to frame 100. Set the particle life to 10. Also, make sure the particle size is set to 1.
7) In the **Particle Type** rollout, set the particle type as instanced geometry. Pick the box as the instanced geometry.
8) In the **Particle Spawn** rollout, set the particles to spawn on death and set the number of spawns to 4.
9) In the **Object Mutation Queue** area of the **Particle Spawn** rollout, select the **Pick** button and select the box in any viewport. Select the **Pick** button again and select the sphere. Finally, select the **Pick** button again and select the teapot. The list should read from top to bottom: box, sphere, teapot. Also, set the particle system to get the material from the instanced geometry.
10) Move to frame 50 in the animation. Adjust the Perspective viewport so all particles are visible in the viewport. Render a still frame. Readjust the viewport if necessary.
11) Render a final animation to a file named ex22-10.avi in the folder of your choice. This may take several minutes, depending on the speed of your computer. Be sure to use a low resolution (320 x 240) to save time.
12) When the rendering is complete, view the animation.
13) Save the scene as ex22-10.max in the folder of your choice.

Load/Save Presets

The **Load/Save Presets** rollout allows you to load, name, and save particle system settings. See Figure 22-19. This can be a valuable time-saver when creating similar particle systems. For example, if you are modeling an assembly line with robotic spot welders, you may create a particle system for the welding sparks. Once you have set all of the parameters for the first system, you can save those parameters. Then, as you create the other particle systems for the remaining welding robots, you can load the saved parameters instead of recreating them.

3ds max comes with seven presets for the super spray particle system. These are the bubbles, fireworks, hose, shockwave, trail, welding sparks, and default presets. To load an existing preset, highlight its name in the **Saved Presets:** area of the **Load/Save Presets** rollout. Then, pick the **Load** button.

Figure 22-19. The **Load/Save Presets** rollout allows you to load, name, and save particle system settings.

To save the existing parameters as a new preset, first name the parameters in the **Preset Name:** text box. The name should be something logical, like Fish Bubbles or Plasma Rifle. Then, pick the **Save** button. The parameters are saved and the name now appears in the **Saved Presets:** area.

Snow

Snow

The snow particle system is used to simulate snow and other forms of particles. It is similar to the spray particle system. Once you pick the **Snow** button in the **Object Type** rollout, you must draw an emitter. Pick in the viewport and drag to create the rectangular emitter. This emitter appears the same as the one for a spray particle system. See Figure 22-20. The straight line in the middle of the emitter indicates the direction the particles will travel. This direction is "into" the viewport where the emitter is drawn.

Next, you need to set parameters for the particles. At the top of the **Parameters** rollout is the **Particles:** area. The value in the **Viewport Count:** spinner is the maximum number of particles displayed in a viewport at any given time. The value in the **Render Count:** spinner is the maximum number of particles displayed in a rendered frame. This is the same as with a spray particle system.

The value in the **Flake Size:** spinner sets the size of each particle in current drawing units. This is similar to the **Drop Size:** spinner for a spray particle system. The value in the **Speed:** spinner sets the velocity of each particle as it leaves the emitter. The particle will remain at this velocity unless affected by a space warp. The **Variation:** spinner is used to vary the speed and direction of particles as they leave the emitter. The smaller the value, the slower and more dense the particles.

Tumble is particle rotation about a randomly selected axis. The amount of tumble is set in the **Tumble:** spinner. The value can range from 0 to 1. With a value of 0, the particles will not tumble. The **Tumble Rate:** spinner sets how fast the particles tumble.

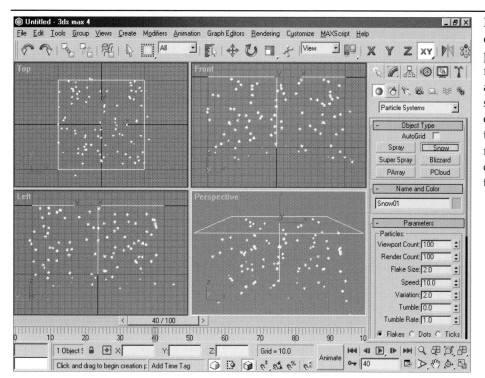

Figure 22-20. An emitter for a snow particle system is a rectangle, just as with a spray particle system. The line extending down from the center of the rectangle indicates the direction of particle travel.

The three radio buttons at the bottom of the **Particles:** area determine how the particles are displayed in the viewport. This setting does not affect the rendered particles.

The **Render:** area of the **Parameters** rollout is used to set the shape of the rendered particles. Picking the **Six Point** radio button renders each particle as a flat, six-sided star. You can assign a material to both sides of the particle. Picking the **Triangle** radio button renders each particle as a flat triangle. A material can be assigned to one side of the triangle. Picking the **Facing** radio button renders each particle as a square face. The size of the square is specified in the **Flake Size:** spinner. The face always points toward the viewer in a camera viewport or the Perspective viewport. This option is designed specifically for use with mapped materials. Snowflakes can be quickly created using this option and an opacity map.

The **Timing:** area is used to set the life span of a particle. The value in the **Start:** spinner is the frame where the emitter begins generating particles. The value in the **Life:** spinner is the number of frames a particle will be alive. After that, the particle dies and is removed. The value in the **Birth Rate:** spinner is the number of new particles born on each frame. If the **Constant** check box is checked, the birth rate is automatically set to the maximum sustainable rate. The maximum sustainable rate is indicated at the bottom of the **Timing:** area. This is the maximum number of particles that can be born in each frame without interrupting particle generation. These options are the same as those for a spray particle system.

The **Emitter:** area is used to set the size of the emitter. The size of the emitter determines the area over which the particles are generated. Checking the **Hide** check box hides the emitter in the viewports. An emitter is not rendered, so this check box affects viewport display only. This is the same option as the **Hide** option for a spray particle system.

Exercise

Exercise 22-11

1) Reset 3ds max. Draw a snow emitter in the Top viewport. Use your own dimensions.
2) Make the Perspective viewport active. Adjust the viewport as necessary to get a good view of the emitter. Leave enough space below the emitter to see the particles.
3) Pick the **Play Animation** button to preview the motion of the particles.
4) In the **Parameters** rollout for the snow emitter, enter a value of 500 in the **Render Count:** spinner. Also, change the flake size to about 3 and enter a value of 15 in the **Speed:** spinner.
5) Render a final animation to a file named ex22-11.avi in the folder of your choice.
6) When the rendering is complete, view the animation.
7) Save the scene as ex22-11.max in the folder of your choice.

Blizzard

Blizzard

Blizzard

The blizzard particle system is similar to the snow system and is used when additional control over the particles is needed. Once you pick the **Blizzard** button in the **Object Type** rollout, you must draw an emitter. Pick in the viewport and drag to create the emitter. See Figure 22-21. The emitter looks like a rectangle with a straight line pointing in one direction. This is the same as the spray and snow particle system emitters. The line points away from the rectangle in the direction of travel for the particles. The particles generally go straight into the viewport where the emitter is drawn.

Next, you need to set parameters for the blizzard. There are several rollouts where parameters can be set. The **Basic Parameters** and **Particle Generation** rollouts are covered here. The options and settings in the **Particle Type**, **Rotation and Collision**, **Object Motion Inheritance**, **Particle Spawn**, and **Load/Save Presets** rollouts are exactly the same as those for a super spray system. There are, however, four different presets available. These are blizzard, rain, mist, and snowfall.

Basic Parameters

The **Basic Parameters** rollout for a blizzard is very similar to the **Basic Parameters** rollout for a super spray. See Figure 22-22. The main difference is the lack of **Particle Formation** settings.

In the **Display Icon** area of the **Basic Parameters** rollout, you can specify the width and length of the emitter. The height of the particle system is determined by particle settings. Unlike a super spray, the size of the emitter for a blizzard *does* affect the particle system. The particles are generated over the entire surface of the emitter. Therefore, a small emitter creates tightly packed particles.

You can hide the emitter in viewports by checking the **Emitter Hidden** check box in the **Display Icon** area. However, the emitter is not rendered even when visible.

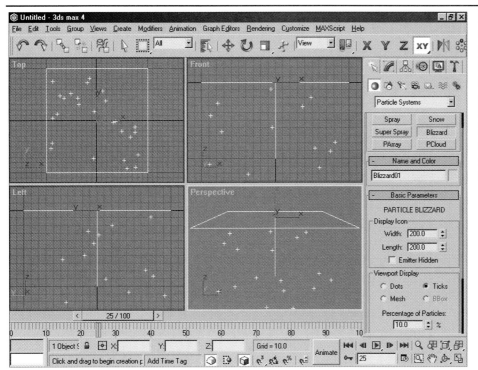

Figure 22-21. An emitter for a blizzard particle system is a rectangle, just as with the spray and snow particle systems. The line extending down from the center of the rectangle indicates the direction of particle travel.

Figure 22-22. The **Basic Parameters** rollout for a blizzard is very similar to the **Basic Parameters** rollout for a super spray.

The **Viewport Display** area is used to set how the particles appear in the viewports. The options found in this area are the same as those for a super spray. As with a super spray, you should generally set the particle system to display only 10% to 20% of the total number of particles. This helps prevent overloading your computer.

Particle Generation

The **Particle Quantity** area of the **Particle Generation** rollout for a blizzard determines how many particles are generated on each frame. The options in this area are the same as those for a super spray.

The **Particle Motion** area is used to define how each particle moves. See Figure 22-23. The **Speed:** spinner sets the velocity of the particle at its birth. This value is the number of current drawing units the particle moves per frame. The **Variation:** spinner sets a percentage by which the speed can vary. The value in the **Tumble:** spinner sets the random rotation for each particle. This value can range from 0 to 1. The speed of rotation is set in the **Tumble Rate:** spinner.

The **Particle Generation** rollout also has the **Particle Timing**, **Particle Size**, and **Uniqueness** areas. The options and settings in these areas are the same as those for a super spray.

Figure 22-23. The **Particle Motion** area of a blizzard's **Particle Generation** rollout is used to define how each particle moves.

Exercise 22-12

1) Draw a blizzard emitter in the Top viewport. Use your own dimensions.
2) Make the Perspective viewport active. Adjust the viewport as necessary to get a good view of the emitter. Leave enough space below the emitter to see the particles.
3) Pick the **Play Animation** button to preview the motion of the particles.
4) In the **Particle Generation** rollout, change the emitter stop time to frame 100. Also, change the particle size to about 3 and the speed to about 5.
5) In the **Particle Type** rollout, set the particle type to the six point standard particle.
6) Render a final animation to a file named ex22-12.avi in the folder of your choice.
7) When the rendering is complete, view the animation.
8) Save the scene as ex22-12.max in the folder of your choice.

PArray

The PArray (particle array) particle system is used to generate particles from selected geometry. The geometry you use acts as an emitter and is called the *distribution object*. A PArray can also be used to create the effect of an explosion from the selected geometry. To create a PArray, you must draw the particle system and the distribution object. First, draw the distribution object. Then, pick the **PArray** button in the **Object Type** rollout, or select **Particles** in the **Create** pull-down menu and then **PArray** from the cascading menu. Finally, pick in the viewport and drag to create the emitter. See Figure 22-24. The emitter looks like a wireframe cube with three wireframe pyramids inside.

Next, you need to set parameters for the PArray. There are several rollouts where parameters can be set. There are the **Basic Parameters, Particle Generation, Particle Type, Rotation and Collision, Object Motion Inheritance, Bubble Motion, Particle Spawn,** and **Load/Save Presets** rollouts. These rollouts share many of the same options and settings with the similar rollouts for a super spray. The following sections cover the differences. The presets for a PArray include bubbles, comet, fill, geyser, shell trail, shimmer trail, blast, disintegrate, pottery, stable, and the default preset.

PArray

PArray

NEW

Basic Parameters

The **Basic Parameters** rollout for a PArray is used to assign the distribution object and define how the particles are formed from the object. Select the **Pick Object** button in the **Object-Based Emitter** area. Then, select the distribution object in a viewport. The distribution object can be any object with renderable faces. Once selected, the distribution object's name appears at the bottom of the **Object-Based Emitter** area. See Figure 22-25.

Figure 22-24. A PArray emitter appears as a cube with three pyramids inside it.

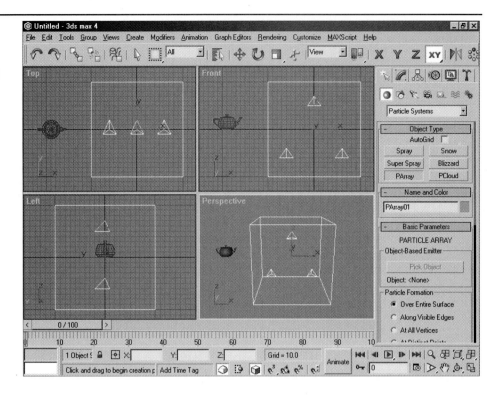

Figure 22-25. The **Basic Parameters** rollout for a PArray is used to assign the distribution object and define how the particles are formed from the object.

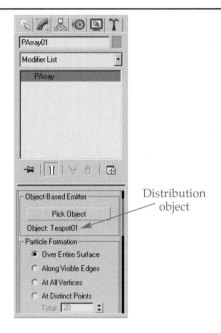

Distribution object

The **Particle Formation** area of the **Basic Parameters** rollout is used to set how particles are formed on the surface of the distribution object. When the **Over Entire Surface** radio button is on, particles are randomly generated over the entire distribution object. When the **Along Visible Edges** radio button is on, particles are randomly generated only along the distribution object's visible edges. When the **At All Vertices** radio button is on, particles are randomly generated only from the distribution object's vertices. When the **At Face Centers** radio button is on, particles are randomly generated only from the center of faces on the distribution object.

When the **At Distinct Points** radio button is on, the **Total:** spinner is enabled. The value in this spinner is the total number of points where particles are generated. These points are randomly placed on the surface of the distribution object.

The **Use Selected SubObjects** check box at the bottom of the **Particle Formation** area is used to limit particle generation to a sub-object selection set. The sub-object selection is passed up the modifier stack. For example, suppose you select one-half of the faces on a sphere. Then, you assign the sphere as a distribution object. Even if the **Over Entire Surface** radio button is on, particles are only generated on the selected half when the **Use Selected SubObjects** check box is checked. See Figure 22-26.

The **Basic Parameters** rollout also contains the **Display Icon** and **Viewport Display** areas. The options and settings in these areas are the same as those available with a super spray.

Particle Generation

The **Particle Generation** rollout for a PArray is identical to that of a super spray with one exception. In the **Particle Motion** area, a PArray has the **Divergence:** spinner. The value in this spinner is an angle measured in degrees. The direction of travel for a particle can vary within this range. In effect, this setting creates a "spread" of particles. The angle is applied to both sides of the emitter's normal. For example, if the **Divergence:** spinner is set to 45, the spread of particles can fall anywhere in a 90° cone projected out from the emitter. See Figure 22-27.

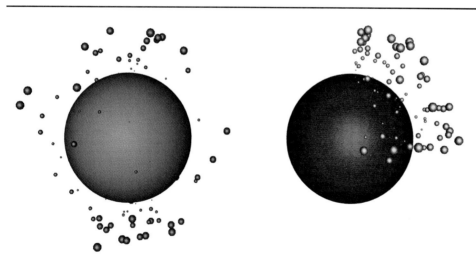

Figure 22-26. When the **Use Selected SubObjects** check box is checked, particles are generated from sub-object selection sets only, as shown on the red sphere.

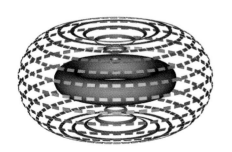

Figure 22-27. The divergence setting defines a range in which a particle can travel. On the left, a divergence value of 0 produces object fragments that travel straight out. On the right, a divergence setting of 45 produces particle travel in a more "jumbled" pattern.

Particle Type

The particles generated by a PArray can be of the same three types available with a super spray. These types are standard, metaparticles, and instanced geometry. In addition, the particles generated by a PArray can be of a fourth type—object fragments. This option generates particles from fragments of the distribution object. It can be used to make existing geometry explode.

When the **Object Fragments** radio button is selected in the **Particle Types** area of the **Particle Type** rollout, the options in the **Object Fragment Controls** area are enabled. See Figure 22-28. The **Thickness:** spinner is used to extrude the exploded fragments. By default, this value is 0 and creates single-sided fragments with no thickness.

When the **All Faces** radio button is on, each face of the distribution object becomes a fragment. For complex objects, this option may create too many particles. This option also produces a fairly regular explosion. This may or may not be what you need.

When the **Number of Chunks** radio button is on, the distribution object is fragmented into randomly sized chunks. See Figure 22-29. Also, the **Minimum:** spinner below the radio button is enabled. The value in this spinner is the lowest number of fragments generated. There may be more than this value, depending on how the fragments are calculated.

Picking the **Smoothing Angle** radio button fragments the distribution object based on the angle between normals. When this radio button is on, the **Angle:** spinner below it is enabled. The value in the **Angle:** spinner sets the smoothing angle. If two adjacent face normals form an angle *greater* than this setting, the two faces are fragmented. Therefore, a high angle setting generally produces fewer fragments. If the value is too high, no fragments are produced. There will be only one particle generated, which is identical to the distribution object.

Figure 22-28. The **Object Fragment Controls** area is used to define how an object explodes into pieces.

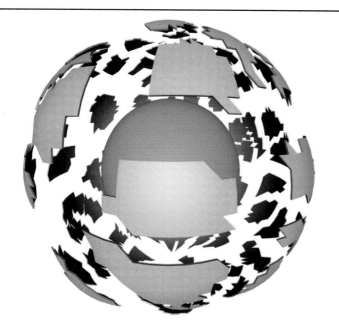

Figure 22-29. When the **Number of Chunks** radio button is on, the distribution object is fragmented into randomly sized chunks.

Help Cel

When using a PArray to make an object explode, you will need to turn the visibility of the original object off on the same frame where the emitter starts. Otherwise, the original object remains visible after the explosion.

Exercise 22-13

1) Reset 3ds max.
2) Draw a tetra-shaped hedra in the Top viewport.
3) Apply a mesh select modifier to the hedra. Select the top half of the hedra faces.
4) Draw a PArray emitter in the Top viewport. Make it about the same size as the hedra.
5) Adjust the Perspective viewport so both the hedra and emitter are visible.
6) In the **Basic Parameters** rollout for the emitter, pick the hedra as the object-based emitter.
7) In the **Particle Generation** rollout for the emitter, set the speed to 5, the particle size to 5, and the emitter stop time to 100.
8) In the **Particle Type** rollout for the emitter, set the particle type to the sphere standard particle.
9) Render a final animation to a file named ex22-13a.avi in the folder of your choice.
10) When the rendering is complete, view the animation.
11) In the **Basic Parameters** rollout for the emitter, check the **Use Selected SubObjects** check box.
12) Render a final animation to a file named ex22-13b.avi in the folder of your choice.
13) Compare the two animations.
14) Save the scene as ex22-13.max in the folder of your choice.

PCloud

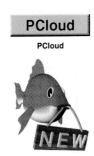

PCloud

The PCloud, or particle cloud, particle system is used to create particles confined to a specified volume. To draw a PCloud particle system, pick the **PCloud** button in the **Object Type** rollout, or select **Particles** in the **Create** pull-down menu and then **PArray** from the cascading menu. Next, pick in a viewport and draw an emitter. See Figure 22-30. The emitter looks like a wireframe box with the letter C inside. You can generate particles from the emitter or assign any 3D geometry as a distribution object.

Next, you need to set parameters for the PCloud. There are several rollouts where parameters can be set. There are the **Basic Parameters**, **Particle Generation**, **Particle Type**, **Rotation and Collision**, **Object Motion Inheritance**, **Bubble Motion**, **Particle Spawn**, and **Load/Save Presets** rollouts. These rollouts share many of the same options and settings with similar rollouts for a super spray. The following sections cover the differences. The presets for a PCloud include cloud/smoke and the default preset.

Basic Parameters

If you are using geometry as a distribution object, select the **Pick Object** button in the **Object-Based Emitter** area of the **Basic Parameters** rollout. Then, select the distribution object in a viewport. The name of the currently selected distribution object is displayed at the bottom of the **Object-Based Emitter** area. See Figure 22-31. The particle system emitter also displays the word FILL instead of the letter C.

The **Particle Formation** area of the **Basic Parameters** rollout is used to define the basic shape of the particle cloud. You can select a preset shape of a box, sphere, or cylinder. If you have selected a distribution object,

Figure 22-30. The emitter for a PCloud particle system looks like a wireframe box with the letter C inside.

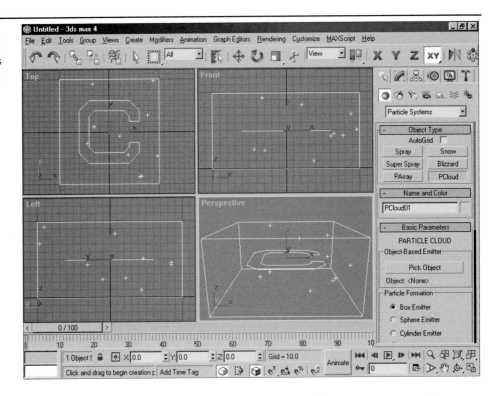

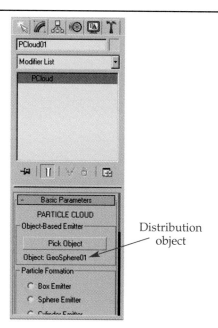

Figure 22-31. The **Basic Parameters** rollout for a PCloud is used to assign the distribution object and define how the particles are formed from the object.

Distribution object

the **Object-based Emitter** radio button is automatically on. However, you can switch to one of the other shapes.

The **Display Icon** area allows you to change the size of the emitter icon. This affects the size of the particle cloud. If a distribution object is assigned and selected, changing the size of the emitter icon does not affect the size of the cloud. The **Viewport Display** area contains the same settings and options available with a super spray.

Particle Generation

The **Particle Generation** rollout contains some of the same options available with a super spray. There are also additional options. The **Particle Size** and **Uniqueness** areas of the rollout are the same as those for a super spray. The **Particle Timing** area is very similar to that of a super spray. However, there are no subframe sampling options.

The **Particle Motion** area of the **Particle Generation** rollout contains the **Speed:** and **Variation:** spinners. These function in a similar manner to those for a super spray. The **Particle Motion** area also contains settings to fine-tune the path of travel for particles. When the **Random Direction** radio button is on, particles travel in random directions from the emitter. When the **Direction Vector** radio button is on, particles travel along a user-defined vector. The vector is defined by a line running through the local axis origin and the values in the **X:**, **Y:**, and **Z:** spinners.

When the **Reference Object** radio button is on in the **Particle Motion** area, particles travel along a vector defined by the local Z axis of a selected object. The name of the currently specified object is displayed below the radio button. To choose a reference object, select the **Pick Object** button. Then, pick an object in a viewport.

The **Variation:** spinner allows you to set a percentage by which the particles can vary their travel. This spinner is enabled when the **Direction Vector** or **Reference Object** radio button is on.

Help Cel

By default, a PCloud generates all of its particles on one frame. The particles have a speed of 0. Increasing the speed results in the particles leaving the volume. PCloud is designed to create a static volume of unmoving particles. Animated, instanced geometry can be used to provide motion to the PCloud. In addition, the cloud itself can have animated transforms.

Exercise

Exercise 22-14

1) Reset 3ds max.
2) Draw a teapot in the Top viewport with a radius of 5.
3) Draw a 200-unit cube PCloud emitter in the Top viewport.
4) Change the emitter to a sphere shape.
5) Adjust the Perspective viewport so the entire emitter is shown. Move the teapot so it is not displayed in the viewport.
6) In the **Particle Type** rollout for the emitter, set the particle type to instanced geometry. Pick the teapot as the geometry.
7) Render a final animation to a file named ex22-14.avi in the folder of your choice.
8) When the rendering is complete, view the animation.
9) Save the scene as ex22-14.max in the folder of your choice.

Adding Motion Blur to Particles

The particle mblur, or motion blur, map is used to add motion blur to particles. Motion blur is simulated by varying the opacity of the leading and trailing edges of a particle, and the particle's length, based on the particle's speed. As such, the map is typically applied as an opacity map. However, by applying a particle mblur map to other material components, different effects can be achieved. The material must be assigned to the particle system as a single material, not a multi/sub-object material.

The particle systems that support the use of particle mblur mapping are PArray, PCloud, spray, and super spray. In addition, the particle mblur map is *not* supported for the constant, facing, metaparticle, and PArray fragment particle types.

Defining a Motion Blur Map

To define a motion blur map for particles, first assign the particle mblur map to a material component. As stated earlier, the map is usually applied as an opacity map. Next, define the particle mblur map at the map level of the material tree. See Figure 22-32.

The map is the color in the **Color #1:** color swatch at the particle's slowest speed. The default color is white. White in an opacity map is 100% opaque. At the particle's fastest speed, the map is the color displayed in the **Color #2:** color swatch. The default color is black. Black in an opacity map is 100% transparent.

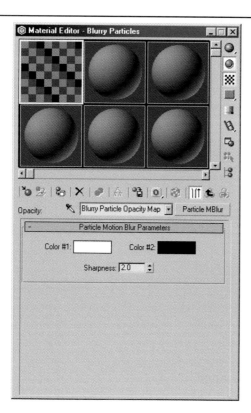

Figure 22-32. The particle mblur map level of a material definition.

The **Sharpness:** spinner is used to adjust the transition between color 1 and color 2, based on speed. When this spinner is set to 0, color 2 is the predominant color, regardless of particle speed. When the particle mblur map is assigned as an opacity map and color 2 is black, this means the particle is blurry even when at a standstill. As the value in the **Sharpness:** spinner is increased, color 1 becomes the predominant color. The default value is 2.0 and works well in most applications.

When the map is defined, complete any other definitions for the material. Then, assign the material to the particle system. Remember, the material cannot be assigned as a multi/sub-object material.

Help Cel

If you assign a particle mblur map to a material's diffuse color with red and yellow as color 1 and color 2, you can simulate particles heating up as they enter the atmosphere or being fired from a SciFi plasma rifle.

Setting Motion Blur for a Particle System

Simply defining a particle mblur map in the material for a particle system will not result in particle motion blur. You must also make a couple of settings to the particle system itself. First, in the **Rotation and Collision** rollout for the particle system, the **Direction of Travel/MBlur** radio button in the **Spin Axis Controls** area must be on.

In addition, the value in the **Stretch:** spinner must be greater than 0. This value is a percentage of the particle's length by which the particle is stretched, based on the speed set for the particle. For example, if this spinner is set to 5 and the particle speed is set to 10, the particle is stretched by 50% (5 x 10) along the direction of travel.

Gravity, Deflectors, and Other Space Warps

As you worked through this chapter, you may have noticed that particles do not fall to the "ground." You may have also noticed particles pass through other objects. In order to correct these problems, special objects called *space warps* need to be used. Space warps affect the appearance of other objects. There are space warps that help simulate gravity and wind, deflect particles and objects, and force particles to follow a path. Space warps are introduced here and covered in detail in Chapter 23.

Deflector Example

To introduce space warps, work through the following brief example using a super spray and a deflector. Use your own dimensions. First, draw a chamfer cylinder in the Left viewport. Then, draw a flat, thin box perpendicular to the cylinder. Finally, draw a super spray pointing out of the cylinder and at the box. See Figure 22-33. Change the emitter stop frame to 50. Also, change the particle type to sphere. Set the particle system to spawn on collision with a 15% direction chaos.

Now, pick **Create** in the **Command Panel**. Then, pick the **Space Warps** button. Select **Deflectors** in the drop-down list and pick the **Deflector** button. In the Left viewport, pick and drag to draw a deflector about the same size as the box. Finally, center the deflector on the box. Also, place it on the surface facing the particle system.

Make the Perspective viewport active. Adjust the view as necessary. Then, pick the **Play Animation** button. Observe the motion of the particles.

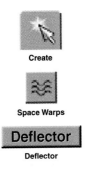

Create

Space Warps

Deflector

Deflector

Figure 22-33. Draw and position the objects shown here for the deflector space warp example given in the text.

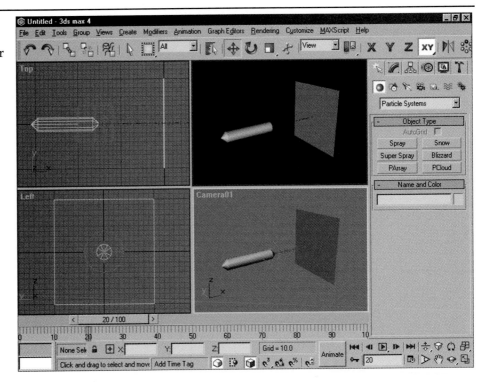

They pass right through the deflector, right? In order for a space warp to affect an object, the object must be bound to the space warp.

Activate the Top viewport. Select the particle system. Then, pick the **Bind to Space Warp** button on the **Main** toolbar. Move the cursor over the particle system. The cursor changes. Pick and drag to the space warp. The cursor changes when over a valid space warp. Then, release. Now, make and play a preview of the Perspective viewport. The particles now ricochet off the deflector. Render a final animation of the scene. See Figure 22-34. Save it in the folder of your choice.

Play Animation

Bind to Space Warp

Gravity Example

The following example uses a gravity space warp to simulate the effect of gravity on a super spray system. First, draw a fountain similar to the one shown in Figure 22-35. Place a super spray in the middle of the fountain head. Change the emitter stop time to 100. Set the spread for both off axis and off plane to 15. Also, set the particle system to spawn on collision with a 5% direction chaos.

Adjust the Perspective viewport as necessary. Pick the **Play Animation** button. Notice the particles just spray straight up.

Next, pick **Create** in the **Command Panel**. Then, pick the **Space Warps** button. Select **Forces** in the drop-down list and pick the **Gravity** button. In the Top viewport, pick and drag to draw a gravity space warp about the same size as the fountain. Finally, center the space warp on the fountain. Also, move it vertically below the fountain. Bind the particle system to the space warp.

Make and play a preview animation of the Perspective viewport. Do you notice any problems? Do the particles drop through the fountain? Can you come up with a solution for this? When your solution has been applied, make a final rendering of the animation. See Figure 22-36. Save the animation in the folder of your choice.

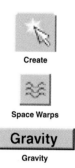

Create

Space Warps

Gravity

Gravity

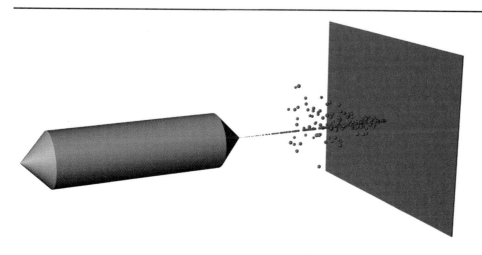

Figure 22-34. The particles appear to deflect from the box. In reality, the particles are deflected from the deflector on the surface of the box.

Figure 22-35. The fountain used in the gravity space warp example. At first, the space warp draws the particles through the fountain.

Figure 22-36. After a deflector is added to the surface of the water, the particles bounce on the water surface rather than pass through the fountain.

Exercise 22-15

1) Reset 3ds max.
2) Draw the fire hose shown below. Use your own dimensions, but make the hose diameter about 5 units.
3) Draw the brick wall shown below. Use your own dimensions.
4) Assign the material Bricks_Bricks_1 to the wall. Apply mapping coordinates as necessary.
5) Assign the material Fabric_Tan_Carpet to the hose. Assign the material Metal_Dark_Gold to the nozzle. Apply mapping coordinates as necessary.
6) Draw a super spray emitter. Center the emitter at the outlet of the nozzle. Assign a light blue standard material to the emitter.
7) In the **Basic Parameters** rollout for the emitter, change the off axis spread to 5 and the off plane spread to 10.
8) In the **Particle Generation** rollout for the emitter, change the particle quantity rate to 20. Change the particle speed to 8. Change the emitter stop time to frame 100. Change the particle life to 50. Change the particle size to 5. Also, enter 0 in the **Grow For:** and **Fade For:** spinners.
9) In the **Particle Type** rollout for the emitter, change the particle type to metaparticles. Also, enter 0.1 in the **Tension:** spinner.
10) Draw a deflector space warp the same size as the brick wall. Place it directly on the wall. In the **Parameters** rollout for the deflector, enter 0.125 in the **Bounce:** spinner.
11) Bind the super spray to the deflector.
12) Render a final animation to a file named ex22-15.avi in the folder of your choice. This may take a few minutes. Use a low resolution (320 x 240) to save time.
13) When the rendering is complete, view the animation.
14) Save the scene as ex22-15.max in the folder of your choice.

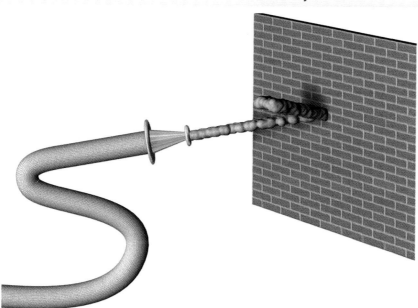

Chapter Snapshot

Chapter Test

1) Define particle system.
2) Define emitter.
3) List the six types of particle systems that come with 3ds max.
4) Which two particle systems appeared in early versions of 3D Studio and are carried through to the current release of 3ds max?
5) _____ is an advanced version of _____. Both particle systems can be used to simulate rain, dust storms, star fields, and sparks.
6) _____ is an advanced version of _____. These particle systems have a "tumbling" component to particle movement.
7) _____ allows you to use geometry as the emitter to generate particles in a pattern.
8) _____ allows you to use geometry as the emitter to confine particles to a specific volume.
9) List the basic steps to drawing a particle system.
10) What does the value in the "off axis" **Spread:** spinner determine?
11) What does the value in the "off plane" **Spread:** spinner determine?
12) What is the difference between the **Use Rate** setting and the **Use Total** setting for particle generation?
13) How can you control when an emitter begins and ends particle generation?
14) What determines how long a particle is displayed?
15) What is a metaparticle?
16) Explain the purpose of the **Object Mutation Queue** area.
17) Define particle spawn.

18) How is using bubble motion different from using the "off axis" and "off plane" settings?
19) Define space warp.
20) What does a gravity space warp do?

Modeling Problems

Unless otherwise directed, draw the objects shown using your own dimensions. To save rendering time when the particle type is meta-particle, use the **One Connected Blob** option. If the particle size is not large enough, the particle stream may "disappear" on certain frames of the animation. Use the gravity and deflector space warps described in this chapter as needed. Define and apply materials as needed. Add lights and a camera as needed. Pay attention to shadow location and color. When finished, save each scene as p22-xx.max in the folder of your choice.

Outdoor Drinking Fountain **1**

When the objects are created, set up the particle system to produce a continuous stream of water over the entire animation. Then, render the animation to a file named p22-01.avi in the folder of your choice.

2 Blacksmith's Forge
When the objects are created, add a combustion effect and a particle system. The particle system should produce sparks from the forge. Render the animation to a file named p22-02.avi in the folder of your choice.

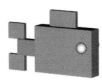

3 Aquarium Air Pump
When the scene is completed, render the animation to a file named p22-03.avi in the folder of your choice.

Grinding Wheel **4**

When the scene is complete, animate the rotation of the grinding wheel, axle, nut, and retaining plate. Render the animation to a file named p22-04.avi in the folder of your choice.

Snowman **5**

Open problem p13-04.max from Chapter 13. Save the scene as p22-05.max in the folder of your choice. Using a PCloud particle system, create a snowstorm inside the sphere, as shown below. Render the scene to a file named p22-05.jpg in the folder of your choice.

6 Spawning Bounce
Create and set up a particle system to reproduce the particle spawning shown here. Render the final animation to a file named p22-06.avi in the folder of your choice.

7 Campfire
After the objects are drawn, create and set up a particle system for sparks in the fire. Animate the combustion effect. Render the animation to a file named p22-07.avi in the folder of your choice.

Ceiling-Mounted Fire Sprinkler System **8**

When the objects are created, set up a particle system to produce the spray. Animate the rotation of the sprinkler head through several rotations. The spray should follow the rotation. Set up the particle system to properly inherit the motion. Render the final animation to a file named p22-08.avi in the folder of your choice.

Lava Flow **9**

Set up a particle system for the lava flow. The lava should not be visible on the first frame of the animation. On the final frame of the animation, the lava should stretch across the view. Render the animation to a file named p22-09.avi in the folder of your choice.

Chapter 23

Introduction to Space Warps

Objectives

After completing this chapter, you will be able to:

- List the general categories of space warps.
- Identify the space warps in each general category.
- Explain modifier-based space warps.
- Create various space warps.
- Bind space warps to geometry and particle systems.

Space Warp Basics

Space warps are objects that affect the motion or appearance of other objects, but are not themselves rendered. Space warps are used to create a variety of special effects in animations. For example, gravity and wind space warps can be used to simulate blowing and drifting snow. A path follow space warp or vortex space warp might be used to create a genie leaving a bottle.

There are different categories of space warps in 3ds max. Selected space warps in the forces, deflectors, and geometric/deformable categories are discussed in detail in this chapter.

Supported Object Types

A given space warp can only be used with certain types of objects. When you create or select a space warp, a **Supports Objects of Type** rollout is made available. Expanding this rollout reveals a list of all types of objects the space warp can affect. See Figure 23-1.

Binding Objects to Space Warps

Before a space warp can affect an object, that object must be "bound" to the space warp. *Binding* to a space warp is very similar to linking objects. First, select the objects in the scene you wish to be affected by the space warp. Next, pick the **Bind to Space Warp** button on the **Main** toolbar. When this button is active, you can also select objects. In any viewport, position the cursor over one of the selected objects. A helper

Bind to Space Warp

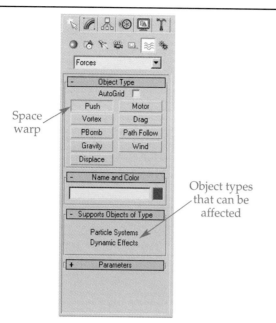

Space warp

Object types that can be affected

Figure 23-1. The **Supports Objects of Type** rollout lists the types of objects that can be bound to a given space warp.

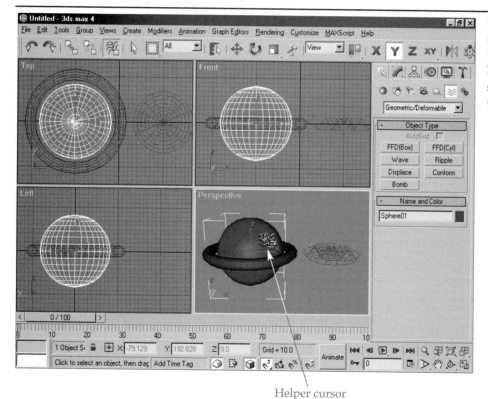

Helper cursor

Figure 23-2. The selected sphere is in the first stage of being bound to a ripple space warp. Notice the helper cursor.

cursor appears. See Figure 23-2. Pick on the object and drag the cursor to the space warp object. If the cursor passes over an invalid object, a prohibitive helper cursor appears. See Figure 23-3. When the cursor is positioned over a valid space warp object, the helper cursor changes to indicate it is a valid space warp. See Figure 23-4. Release the mouse button to bind the selected objects to the space warp.

Figure 23-3. The **Bind to Space Warp** helper cursor changes as it passes over an invalid object.

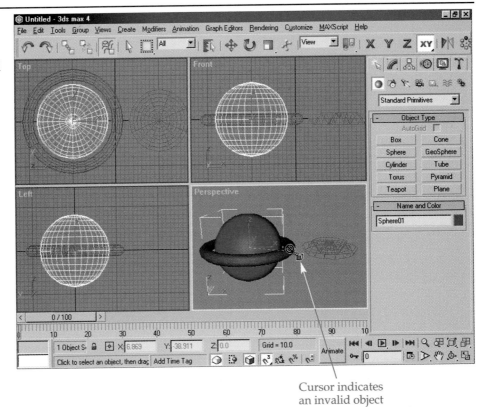

Cursor indicates an invalid object

Figure 23-4. The **Bind to Space Warp** helper cursor changes again as it passes over the ripple space warp object. Releasing the mouse button at this point binds the sphere to the ripple space warp.

Cursor indicates a valid space warp

Multiplying the Effects of Space Warps

The effects of many space warps can be multiplied in various ways. An object can be bound to a space warp multiple times. In many instances, this will increase the effect of the space warp. Often a space warp object can be scaled to either increase or decrease its effect on objects, even if the original effect is not dependent on the size of the space warp object. Objects bound to wave and ripple space warps have a **Flexibility:** spinner used to increase or decrease the space warp's effect on that object. A **Flexibility:** setting of 1 produces a normal effect. Decreasing the spinner setting decreases the space warps effect, while increasing the spinner setting increases the space warp's effect on that object. The flexibility setting is discussed later in this chapter.

Forces

As the name implies, space warps in the forces category simulate the effect of natural forces on the objects bound to them. The space warps in this category can be used to create a variety of real-world phenomena. This category includes the push, vortex, PBomb, gravity, displace, motor, drag, path follow, and wind space warps. The push, vortex, gravity, path follow, and wind space warps are discussed in the following sections.

Push

The *push space warp* is very similar to the gravity and wind space warps discussed later in this chapter. It applies a unidirectional force to particle systems bound to it. You can use the push space warp to create such effects as a sudden gust of wind. You can bind particle systems and dynamics effects to a push space warp.

To add a push space warp to a scene, pick the **Create** tab in the **Command Panel**. Pick the **Space Warps** button, and select **Forces** from the drop-down list. Pick the **Push** button on the **Object Type** rollout. In the appropriate viewport, pick and drag to create the push space warp icon. The size of the icon does not matter. The force created by the push icon is initially directed along the positive Z axis of the viewport in which it is drawn. The icon can be moved or rotated to change the direction of the force.

The **Parameters** rollout contains controls to adjust the effect of the push space warp. See Figure 23-5. The **Timing** area contains two spinners that let you determine the beginning frame and ending frame for the push effect. The **On Time:** spinner sets the beginning frame of the effect. The **Off Time:** spinner sets the ending frame for the effect.

The **Strength Control** area of the **Parameters** rollout contains controls that set the strength of the force created by the push space warp. The force of the space warp is set using the **Basic Force:** spinner, with either the **Newtons** or **Pounds** radio button active to determine the units. The value is exactly measured in these units when a dynamic system is bound to the space warp, but the setting is only subjective when a particle system is bound.

When the **Feedback On** check box is unchecked, the force remains constant throughout the active frames of the space warp. When the **Feedback On** check box is checked, the force varies as the speed of the

Create

Space Warps

Push

Push

Figure 23-5. The **Parameters** rollout for a push space warp.

bound particles approach the target speed. If the particles exceed the target speed, when the **Reversible** check box is checked, the force is reversed. If the **Reversible** check box is unchecked, the force is removed until the affected particles drop below the target speed. The target speed is set using the **Target Speed:** spinner. The **Gain:** spinner setting determines how responsive the feedback settings are to the particles' approach of the target speed.

The controls in the **Periodic Variation** area of this rollout allow you to create sinusoidal variations in the strength of the force generated by the space warp. If these controls are not enabled, the force applied by the space warp is either constant, or varied by the feedback controls. This results in a uniform deflection of particles. When periodic variation is enabled, the force applied changes, creating a serpentine effect in the deflection of a linear stream of particles. See Figure 23-6.

Check the **Enable** check box to activate periodic variation. Set the rate of variation using the **Period 1:** and **Period 2:** spinners. The rate of variation is the number of frames it takes to complete one cycle of variation in strength of the space warp. The **Amplitude 1:** and **Amplitude 2:** spinners set the amount of variation, or height of the sine wave, for each period. The **Phase 1:** and **Phase 2:** spinners setting determine at what stage, in the sinusoidal cycles, the period 1 and period 2 variations begin.

Checking the **Enable** check box in the **Particle Effect Range** area of the rollout limits the effect of the push space warp. A white sphere, which marks the limits of the space warp's effect, is displayed in the viewports. The force of the space warp diminishes as the particles move away from the center of the sphere. At the very edges of the sphere, the force is negligible. The size of the sphere, and the range of the space warp, is adjusted by changing the **Range:** spinner setting.

The **Icon Size:** spinner in the **Display Icon** area of the rollout sets the size of the push space warp icon. Changing this setting does not alter the effect of the push space warp. The size of the icon is for display only.

Particle stream   Particle emitter   Space warp

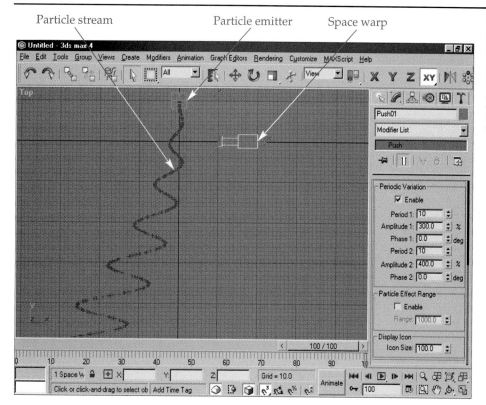

Figure 23-6. A linear stream of particles being affected by a push space warp. Notice the serpentine path of the particles caused by the **Periodic Variation** settings.

Vortex

The *vortex space warp* is used to create interesting funnel effects. A vortex space warp can be used to simulate a whirlpool, tornado, or any number of phenomena. The vortex space warp pulls bound particles along an axis, while simultaneously rotating the particles about that axis and tapering the particle stream. You can bind particle systems to a vortex space warp.

To add a vortex space warp to a scene, pick the **Create** tab from the **Command Panel**. Pick the **Space Warps** button, and select **Forces** from the drop-down list. Pick the **Vortex** button from the **Object Type** rollout.

Pick in the appropriate viewport to place the center of the vortex icon. See Figure 23-7. The axis of the space warp, and the motion of affected particles, is initially along the negative Z axis of the viewport in which the space warp is drawn. After it is created, the space warp can be transformed as necessary. Drag the mouse to size the icon, and when the object is the desired size, release the mouse button. The size of the vortex object has no bearing on the effect produced by the space warp.

The **Parameters** rollout contains controls to adjust the effect of the vortex space warp. The **Timing:** area of the **Parameters** rollout contains two spinners, which set the span of frames during which the space warp is active. The **Time On:** spinner sets the frame on which the space warp activates. The **Time Off:** spinner sets the frame on which the space warp deactivates.

Controls in the **Vortex Shape** area of the **Parameters** rollout are used to define the shape of the affected particle streams. The **Taper Length:** spinner sets the relative length of the tapering effect. By default, this value is 100. Increasing the value spreads the tapering effect over a greater distance. Decreasing the value condenses the tapering effect. The **Taper Curve:**

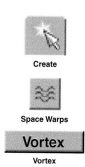

Create

Space Warps

Vortex

Vortex

Figure 23-7. The **Parameters** rollout for a vortex space warp.

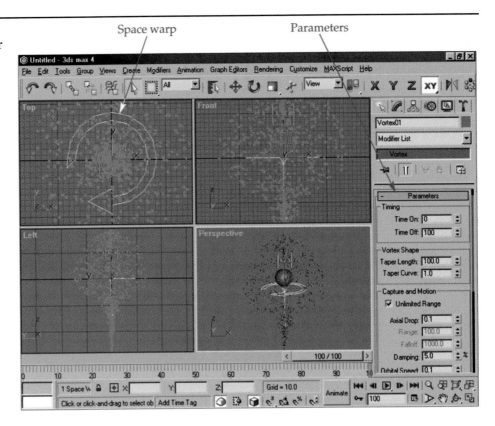

spinner determines the general shape of the taper. A value of 1.0 through 4.0 can be entered in this spinner. A value of 1 creates the most gradual taper, giving the affected particle stream a conical shape. A value of 4 creates a flared taper, giving the affected particle stream a flared funnel shape.

The **Capture and Motion** area of the **Parameters** rollout contains controls that determine which particles are affected, and the motion of the affected particles. The **Unlimited Range** check box appears at the top of this area. Checking this check box causes the space warp to exert its full strength throughout space. When this check box is unchecked, the strength of the space warp's effect is determined by the **Range:** and **Falloff:** spinners, and it's distance from the affected particle stream.

The **Axial Drop:** spinner setting determines how quickly the affected particles are "sucked down" the space warp's axis. The **Damping:** spinner sets the percentage of particle motion along the space warp's axis that is diminished each frame. The **Range:** spinner sets the maximum distance from the space warp center at which the full strength of the damping is applied to particles. The **Falloff:** spinner sets the maximum distance at which the damping affects the particles.

The **Orbital Speed:** spinner setting determines the speed at which the affected particles revolve around the space warp axis. Increasing the orbital speed of the particles, while the Radial Pull: spinner setting remains constant, increases the size of the orbit around the space warp axis. The **Damping:** spinner sets the percentage of orbital motion of the particles that is diminished each frame. The **Range:** and **Falloff:** spinners set the limits for the orbital motion damping.

The **Radial Pull:** spinner sets the relative distance at which the affected particles revolve around the space warp axis. This spinner's setting, in conjunction with the **Orbital Speed:** spinner setting, determines the orbital circumference of the affected particles. The **Damping:** spinner sets the percentage of radial pull effect that is diminished for each particle on each frame. The **Range:** spinner sets the maximum distance from the space warp center at which the full strength of the damping is applied to particles. The **Falloff:** spinner sets the maximum distance at which the damping affects the particles. Damping gradually decreases from the **Range:** setting to 0 at the **Falloff:** setting.

At the bottom of the **Capture and Motion** area are two radio buttons that determine the direction of spin for the affected particles. When the **CW** radio button is active, captured particles spin clockwise around the space warp's axis. When the **CCW** radio button is active, the captured particles spin counterclockwise around the space warp axis. The direction is determined by looking down the space warp's Z axis, from positive to negative. You cannot animate a change in direction.

The **Icon Size:** spinner, located in the **Display** area of the rollout, sets the size of the vortex space warp object. Changing this setting does not alter the effect of the gravity space warp. The size of the object is for display purposes only.

Exercise 23-1

Exercise

1) Create a PCloud particle emitter in the Top viewport. Select the **Box Emitter** radio button. Set the **Rad/Len:** spinner to 200, the **Width:** spinner to 300, and the **Height:** spinner to 40. Display the particles as ticks in the viewport.

2) In the **Particle Generation** rollout, set the **Rate:** spinner to 75. You may choose to use a lower value in this setting if you experience sluggish system performance. In the **Particle Timing** area, set the **Emit Stop:** spinner to 100. Set the **Particle Size:** spinner to 3. Center the PCloud on the origin, and move it up 50 units on the world Z axis.

3) In the Top viewport, create a vortex space warp centered at the origin. Move the space warp 70 units along the world Z axis so it originates at the center of the PCloud. Set the **Axial Drop:** spinner to 0. Accept all other default settings and bind the particle system to the space warp.

4) Adjust the Perspective viewport so the PCloud is near the top and its "side" spans the width of the viewport. Make a preview animation.

5) Set the **Orbital Speed:** and **Radial Pull:** spinners to 0. Pick the **Animate** button and move to frame 30. Set the **Radial Pull:** spinner to .5. Move to frame 100 and animate the **Axial Drop:** spinner to .15, and the **Orbital Speed:** spinner to .5.

6) Make a preview animation.

7) Render a final animation to a file named ex23-01.avi in the directory of your choice. Render all frames. You will need to use a light-colored particle on a dark background, or dark-colored particle on a light background.

8) When the rendering is complete, view the animation.

9) Save the scene as ex23-01.max in the folder of your choice.

Figure 23-8. A super spray particle system bound to a gravity space warp using the planar setting.

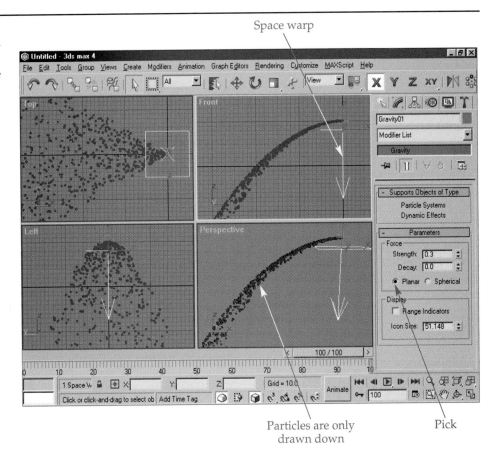

Space warp

Particles are only drawn down

Pick

Gravity

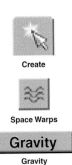

Create

Space Warps

Gravity

Gravity

As its name implies, the *gravity space warp* pulls the particles of bound particle systems in a certain direction. Particles affected by the gravity space warp are accelerated in the direction of gravity. When gravity is planar, it pulls the bound particles in a direction perpendicular to its plane. See Figure 23-8. When gravity is spherical, it pulls the bound particles toward the center of the sphere. See Figure 23-9. In an animation of a comet orbiting the sun, you would use a spherical gravity space warp centered on the sun. To create falling confetti during a ticker tape parade, you would use a planar gravity space warp placed on the road surface. You can bind particle systems and dynamics effects to a gravity space warp.

To add a gravity space warp to a scene, pick the **Create** tab in the **Command Panel**. Pick the **Space Warps** button, and select **Forces** from the drop-down list. Then, pick the **Gravity** button in the **Object Type** rollout.

Pick in the appropriate viewport to place the center of the gravity object. Drag the mouse to set the size of the space warp object. When the object is the desired size, release the mouse button. The size of the gravity icon has no bearing on the effect produced by the space warp. Initially, the force of the gravity space warp is applied along the negative Z axis of the viewport in which it is drawn. The space warp object can be transformed as needed to adjust the effect.

The **Parameters** rollout contains controls that allow you to adjust the gravity space warp effect. See Figure 23-10. The **Strength:** spinner in the

Space warp

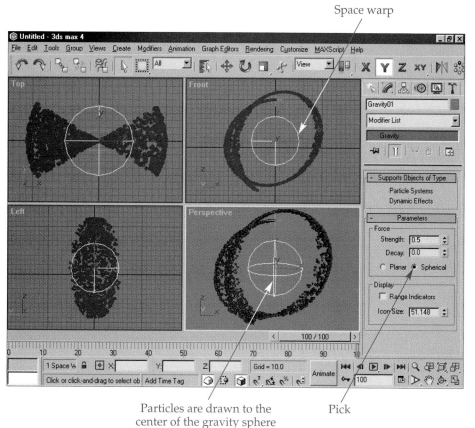

Figure 23-9. A super spray particle system bound to a gravity space warp using the spherical setting.

Particles are drawn to the center of the gravity sphere

Pick

Figure 23-10. The **Parameters** rollout for a gravity space warp.

Force area of the rollout determines the amount of influence the gravity space warp exerts over bound particle systems. Increasing the value of this spinner increases the force of gravity. Setting this value to zero creates no gravity. Setting this spinner to a negative value creates negative gravity, in which bound particles are repelled from the gravity icon.

If the **Decay:** spinner is set to a value greater than 0, the strength of the gravity space warp is inversely proportional to the distance between space warp and the particles bound to it. Increasing this value decreases the influence of the space warp at a set distance. If this value is set to 0, then the influence of the space warp is constant throughout space.

When the **Planar** radio button is active, the gravity space warp is planar. Particles are drawn in a direction perpendicular to the gravity plane. When the **Spherical** radio button is selected, the gravity space warp is spherical. Particles are drawn toward the center of the gravity sphere.

The **Icon Size:** spinner sets the size of the gravity space warp object. Changing this setting does not change the effect of the gravity space warp. Checking the **Range Indicators** check box places icons in the viewports to indicate the effect of the gravity space warp when the **Decay:** spinner value is greater than 0. At these settings, the range indicator icons represent the locations in space where the effect of gravity is half of its maximum force. Plane icons are used with planar gravity, and sphere icons are used with spherical gravity space warps.

Drag

Create

Space Warps

Drag

Drag

The *drag space warp* slows the motion of bound particles that pass through it. This effect can be used to simulate drag, created by wind resistance or fluid viscosity, or the dampening effects of opposing magnetic fields. You can bind particle systems to a drag space warp.

To add a drag space warp to a scene, pick the **Create** tab in the **Command Panel**. Then, pick the **Space Warps** button and select **Forces** from the drop-down list. Finally, pick the **Drag** button in the **Object Type** rollout. Pick in any viewport to place the center of the drag space warp. Drag the cursor to the desired extent of the space warp and release the mouse button. By default, the linear dampening option is selected, and the space warp icon appears as a box within a box. See Figure 23-11.

The **Parameters** rollout contains controls that allow you to adjust the drag space warp effect. The two spinners found in the **Timing** area of the **Parameters** rollout allow you to set the span of frames over which the space warp is active. The **Time On:** spinner setting determines the frame on which the space warp becomes active. The **Time Off:** spinner setting determines the last frame for which the space warp is active.

The controls in the **Damping** area of the **Parameters** rollout control the effect of the space warp on the particle systems bound to it. Checking the **Unlimited Range** check box at the top of this area causes the full strength of space warp to be exerted on all bound particles, regardless of their distance from the space warp.

When the **Linear Damping** radio button is active, the effect of the space warp is applied at linear vector levels. The motion of affected particles is broken down into X, Y, and Z axis vectors through the space warp, and the dampening effect is applied individually to each vector. These vectors are based on the space warp's local coordinate system and are transformed as the space warp object is transformed. The **X Axis:**, **Y Axis:**, and **Z Axis:** spinners set the percentage of particle motion that is affected along that vector. For example, if the **X Axis:** spinner is set to 10 percent and the **Unlimited Range** check box is unchecked, the bound particles lose 10 percent of their velocity along the space warp's X axis per frame. The full strength of the space warp is exerted on bound particles whose distance from the space warp

Figure 23-11. The **Parameters** rollout for a drag space warp.

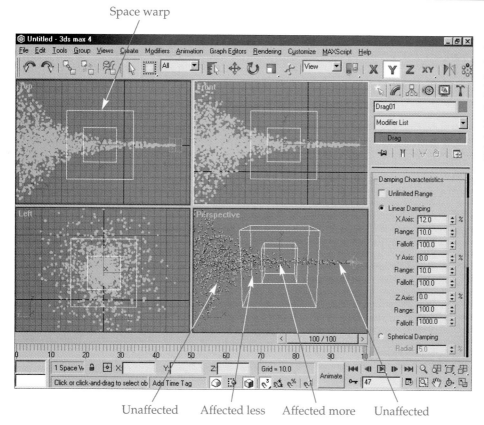

Space warp

Unaffected   Affected less   Affected more   Unaffected

Figure 23-12. A drag space warp with linear damping active affecting a super spray particle system. Notice that the linear damping slows the forward motion of the particles, causing a funneling effect.

object is less than the **Range:** spinner setting. At the distances greater than or equal to the distance specified by the **Falloff:** setting, the space warp exerts no force on particles bound to it. The effect of the space warp gradually diminishes in the distances between the **Range:** setting and the **Falloff:** setting. See Figure 23-12.

Figure 23-13. A drag space warp with spherical damping active affecting a super spray particle system. Notice that the radial damping slows the particles' motion toward the center of the sphere, causing them to flow around it.

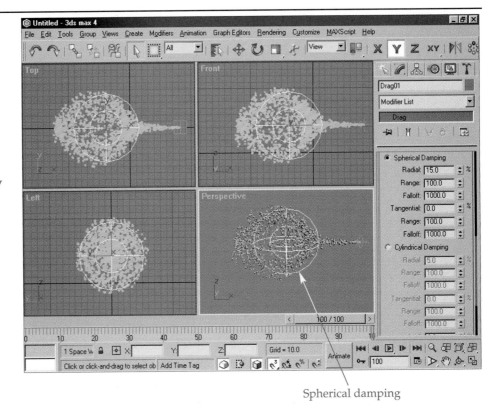

Spherical damping

When the **Spherical Damping** radio button is active, the bound particles' motion is broken into radial and tangential vectors. See Figure 23-13. The **Radial:** spinner sets the percent of motion of the particles toward, or away from, the space warp's center that is affected by the space warp. This has the effect of bending the particles' trajectories around the space warp. The **Tangential:** spinner sets the percentage of the motion, tangential to the space warp, that is affected by the space warp. This has the effect of pulling the particles' trajectories toward the center of the space warp. The **Range:** spinners, located under the **Radial:** and **Tangential:** spinners, set the range of the full effect of the drag force for the corresponding vectors. Beyond this limit, the strength of the space warp's effect diminishes. The **Falloff:** spinners, located beneath each **Range:** spinners set the maximum range of the space warp's effect.

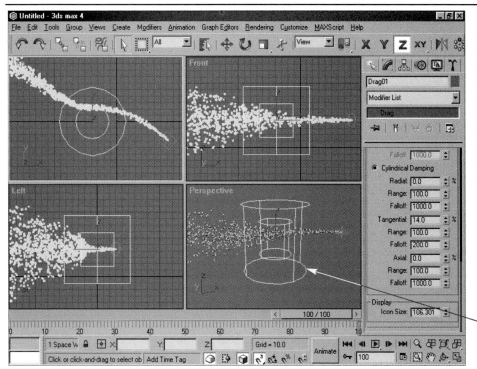

Figure 23-14. A drag space warp with cylindrical damping active affecting a super spray particle system. Notice that the tangential damping slows the particles' motion tangential to the object, drawing them toward the object's vertical axis.

Cylindrical damping

When the **Cylindrical Damping** radio button is active, the motion of the bound particles is broken into radial, tangential, and axial vectors. See Figure 23-14. The **Radial:** spinner sets the percentage of motion of the particles, perpendicular to the wall of the cylinder, that is affected by the space warp. The **Tangential:** spinner sets the percentage of motion of the particles, tangential to the wall of the cylinder, that is affected by the space warp. The **Axial:** spinner sets the percentage of motion of the particles, parallel to the wall of the cylinder, that is affected by the space warp. The **Range:** spinners, located under the **Radial:**, **Tangential:**, and **Axial:** spinners, set the range of the full effect of the drag force for the corresponding vectors. Beyond this limit, the strength of the space warp's effect diminishes. The **Falloff:** spinners, located beneath each **Range:** spinners set the maximum range of the space warp's effect.

The **Display** area contains the **Icon Size:** spinner, which is used to set the size of the space warp icon. Changing the size of the space warp icon does not alter the effect of the space warp.

Exercise

Exercise 23-2

1) In the Left viewport, create a super spray particle emitter. Position it at world coordinates X:75, Y:0, Z:0. Set the **Off Axis Spread:** spinner to 8 and the **Off Plane Spread:** spinner to 180. In the **Particle Generation** rollout, set the **Rate:** spinner to 30.
2) In the Top viewport, create a drag space warp. Set the **Icon Size:** spinner to 75. Position the space warp at world coordinates X:–50, Y:0, Z:0 and bind the particle emitter to the space warp. Play the animation.
3) Uncheck the **Unlimited Range** check box and set the linear damping X axis **Range:** spinner to 30 and the **Falloff:** spinner to 50. Play the animation in the Perspective viewport, then in the Left viewport.
4) Increase the **Y-Axis:** spinner to 20 and play the animation in the Left viewport. Notice the difference. Increase the **Z-Axis:** spinner to 20. Play the animation and notice the difference.
5) Select the particle emitter and then select **SuperSpray** in the modifier stack. In the **Particle Generation** rollout, set the **Speed:** spinner to 15.
6) Select the space warp. Select the **Spherical Damping** radio button in the **Parameters** rollout. Set the **Radial:** spinner to 30, the **Range:** spinner to 60, and the **Falloff:** spinner to 100. Play the animation.
7) Set the **Radial:** spinner to 0 and set the **Tangential:** spinner to 30.
8) Select the particle system and set the **Off Axis Spread:** spinner to 60. Play the animation.
9) Set the space warp to **Cylindrical Damping** and play the animation. Set the **Axial:** spinner to 75 and play the animation. Set the **Axial:** spinner back to 0 and increase the **Radial:** spinner setting to 30. Activate the Top viewport and play the animation.
10) Set the **Radial:** spinner to 10, the **Tangential:** and **Axial:** spinners to 30. Play the animation. Think about the forces at work causing the particles to stick in the center of the cylindrical icon.
11) Save the scene as ex23-02.max in the folder of your choice.

Path Follow

The *path follow space warp* allows you to select a spline or NURBS curve to use as a motion path for particles. NURBS curves are discussed in Section Five of this book. Additional controls associated with the path follow space warp are used to spin the particles about the path as they advance. The particles can also be made to converge or diverge as they progress along the path, creating a funneling effect. The path follow space warp supports particle systems.

You can create a new spline shape or NURBS curve to use as the particle path. You can also use an existing spline or curve. If the object you select as the path is constructed from multiple splines or curves, only the spline or curve with the lowest vertex count is used for the path.

To add a path follow space warp to a scene, pick the **Create** tab in the **Command Panel**. Then, pick the **Space Warps** button and select **Forces** from the drop-down list. Finally, pick the **Path Follow** button in the **Object Type** rollout. Pick, drag, and release in any viewport to create the path follow object. The size and orientation of this icon have no bearing on the path follow space warp effect.

The **Basic Parameters** rollout contains the controls used to fine tune the path follow space warp. See Figure 23-15. The name of the space warp (particle path follow) appears as a text label at the top of the rollout.

The **Current Path** section contains the controls to select the path and limit the range of the space warp. The name of the object used as the path is displayed in the **Object:** label. To select an object to use as a path, select the **Pick Shape Object** button. Then, pick the shape in a viewport.

Checking the **Unlimited Range** check box allows the path follow space warp to control particle systems regardless of their distance from the path object. When this box is unchecked, the space warp affects only the particle's that are within range. The **Range:** spinner is used to set the range. The value in this spinner specifies the maximum distance a particle can be from the starting point, or vertex, of the path object and still fall under the space warp's control. Particles outside this range are unaffected by the space warp.

The **Motion Timing:** area of the **Basic Parameters** rollout contains controls for specifying how long the space warp is active and how fast affected particles travel. The **Start Frame:** spinner sets the frame on which the path follow space warp first becomes active. The **Last Frame:** spinner sets the frame on which the path follow space warp is deacti-

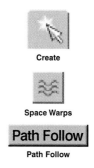

Create

Space Warps

Path Follow

Path Follow

Pick Shape Object

Pick Shape Object

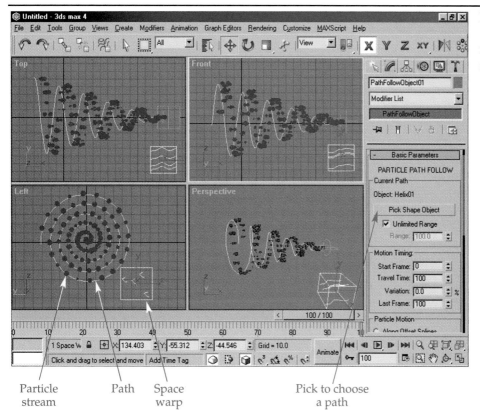

Figure 23-15. The **Basic Parameters** rollout for a path follow space warp.

Particle stream

Path

Space warp

Pick to choose a path

vated. The **Travel Time:** spinner setting determines how many frames each particle takes to move from the starting point of the path to the endpoint. You can vary the particle travel times using the **Variation:** spinner. When this spinner value is low, the particles move at a very uniform rate. As this spinner setting is increased, the particle velocities appear more random.

The **Particle Motion** area of the **Basic Parameters** rollout contains controls affecting particle motion as particles move along the path. When the **Along Offset Splines** radio button is active, the path followed by the particles is affected by the distance between the starting point of the path object and the particle system emitter. As this distance increases, the path followed by the particles becomes an exaggeration of the path object. See Figure 23-16. When the **Along Parallel Splines** check box is checked, the dimensions and curvature of the path the particles follow exactly matches those of the path object, regardless of the position of the particle emitter. Checking the **Constant Speed** check box causes affected particles to maintain a constant speed, regardless of the shape of the path.

The **Stream Taper:** spinner sets the amount the stream of affected particles is tapered during its trip along the path. The **Variation:** spinner setting determines how far individual particles can deviate from the taper value. Particles create the taper by converging, diverging, or both. See Figure 23-17. Pick the appropriate radio button to set the stream tapering method.

The **Stream Swirl:** spinner setting determines how many revolutions, or "orbits," the particles make around the path as they travel. A setting of 0 for this spinner causes particles to progress along the path without orbiting it. A setting greater than 0 causes the particles to orbit the path as they advance along it, creating a corkscrew motion. The **Variation:** spinner sets the maximum percentage an individual particle can deviate from the stream swirl setting. Particles can be made to orbit the path

Figure 23-16. Three identical particle systems affected by the path follow space warp, with the **Follow Offset Splines** option active. The emitter for the orange particles is at the origin of the path object. The emitter for the yellow particles is a short distance away from the origin, and the emitter for the red particles is twice that distance from the origin. Notice the differences in trajectory, and effect of the **Swirl Stream:** setting.

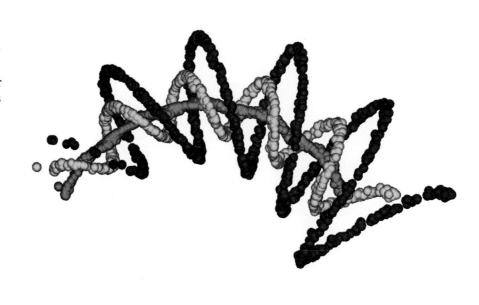

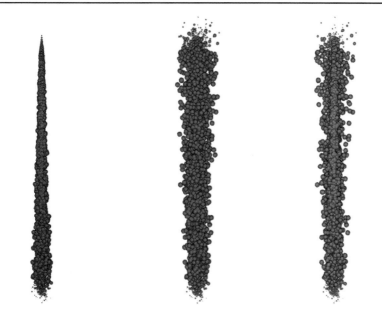

Figure 23-17. The red particle stream is tapered using the **Converge** option. The green particle stream is tapered using the **Diverge** option. The blue particle stream is tapered using the **Both** option.

clockwise, counterclockwise, or bidirectionally by activating the appropriate radio button. Checking the **Bidirectional** radio button splits the particle stream, with some particles rotating clockwise and others rotating counterclockwise.

Changing the **Seed:** spinner setting, in the **Uniqueness** area, can subtly change the effect of the space warp on the bound particles. In addition, each path follow space warp in a scene should have a different seed value or they will tend to produce similar effects.

The **Icon Size:** spinner sets the display size of the path follow space warp object. Changing the size, position, or orientation of the path follow object does not change the space warp's effect.

Help Cel

The stream swirl effect is much more pronounced when the **Along Offset Splines** radio button is active and the particle emitter is some distance from the path.

Exercise

Exercise 23-3

1) In the Top viewport, create a 50-unit-radius teapot. Now, create a second teapot to the right of the first. Make its radius 25 units. Also, create only the body and handle of the teapot. Rename the second teapot Mug and rotate it 180 degrees about the Z axis.

2) In the Top viewport, create a super spray. Move the emitter to the opening in the teapot spout. Set the **Off Axis Spread:** to 30 degrees. Set the **Off Plane Spread:** to 180 degrees. Select to display the particles as mesh, and set to display 50 percent of the particles. Set the **Emit Stop:** to 30, and **Life:** to 80. Set the **Particle Size:** to 3. Choose to emit standard particles, and activate the **Sphere** radio button.

3) Create a looped spline running from the opening in the teapot spout to the opening in the top of the mug, as shown below. Rename the spline Path.

4) Create a path follow space warp in any viewport.

5) Bind the particle system to the path follow space warp.

6) Select the path follow object. Pick the **Modify** tab in the **Command Panel**. Select the **Pick Shape** button in the **Basic Parameters** rollout and then pick the path. Uncheck the **Unlimited Range** check box and set the **Range:** spinner to 20. Set the **Travel Time:** spinner to 70. Set the **Stream Taper:** spinner to 99 percent. Activate the **Diverge** radio button.

7) Render the animation to a file named ex23-03.avi in the folder of your choice. When the rendering is complete, view the animation.

8) Save the scene as ex23-03.max in the folder of your choice. Reset 3ds max.

Wind

The *wind space warp* is very similar to the gravity space warp. Both space warps accelerate the particles of bound particle systems in a particular direction. The wind space warp offers the additional effect of turbulence, which is unavailable in the gravity space warp settings. You can bind particle systems and dynamics effects to a wind warp.

To add a wind space warp to a scene, pick the **Create** tab on the **Command Panel**. Pick the **Space Warp** button, and select **Forces** from the drop-down list. Pick the **Wind** button in the **Object Type** rollout. Pick and drag in the appropriate viewport to create the wind space warp icon. Wind direction is initially in the positive Z direction of the local coordinate system of the viewport in which it is drawn. The space warp can be transformed to change the direction of the effect. The size of the wind space warp object does not alter the effect of the space warp.

The **Parameters** rollout contains controls for customizing the effect of the wind space warp. See Figure 23-18. The controls in the **Force** area are identical in name and function to their counterparts in the **Force** area of the gravity space warp's **Parameters** rollout.

The controls in the **Wind** area of the **Parameters** rollout are what make the wind space warp different from the gravity space warp. The **Turbulence:** spinner value determines the amount of random variation in the motion of particles as the wind space warp propels them. This feature is important in creating realistic effects, because naturally occurring wind is not perfectly uniform. The **Frequency:** spinner determines how the turbulence varies over time. The **Scale:** spinner sets the scale of the turbulence.

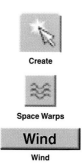

Create

Space Warps

Wind

Wind

Space warp

Figure 23-18. The **Parameters** rollout for a wind space warp.

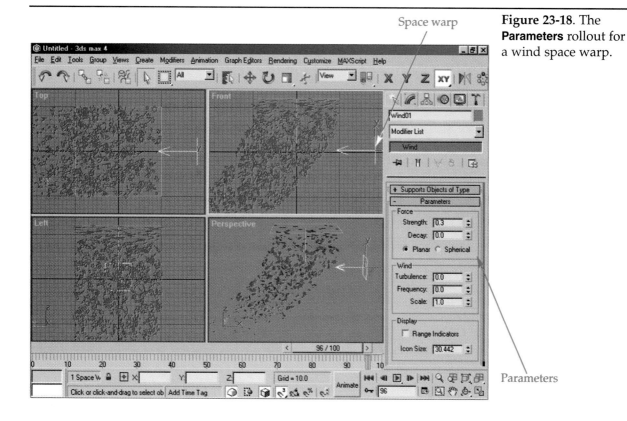

Parameters

The **Icon Size:** spinner in the **Display** area is used to change the size of the wind space warp object. Changing this setting does not alter the wind effect. The function of the **Range Indicators** check box is the same as that for the gravity space warp.

Exercise 23-4

1) In the Top viewport, create a super spray particle system. Set the **Off Axis Spread:** to 30 degrees. Set the **Off Plane Spread:** to 180 degrees. In the **Particle Generation** rollout, activate the **Use Rate** radio button and set the spinner to 30. Set the **Emit Stop:** spinner to 100. Set the **Life:** spinner to 60.
2) Draw a wind space warp in the Left viewport. Pick and drag to create the wind icon. Set the **Strength:** spinner to .2.
3) Bind the particle system to the wind space warp. Play the animation.
4) In the Top viewport, draw a gravity space warp. Set the **Strength:** spinner to .4.
5) Bind the particle system to the gravity space warp. Play the animation.
6) Reset 3ds max. Do not save the file.

Deflectors

Space warps in the deflector category have the ability to reflect or refract particles that strike the space warp. This category includes the POmniflect, SOmniflect, UOmniflect, SDeflector, Deflector, PDynaflect, SDynaflect, UDynaflect, and UDeflector space warps.

Deflector

The *deflector space warp* repels particles generated by a particle system. It can halt the motion of particles that collide with it, or it can reflect those particles with more or less energy than they had prior to the collision. You can use the deflector space warp to accumulate snow on a rooftop, or to bounce rubber balls dropped from the sky. The deflector space warp is introduced in Chapter 22. Refer to that chapter for an example scene containing a deflector.

Create

Space Warps

Deflector

Deflector

To add a deflector to a scene, pick the **Create** tab in the **Command Panel**. Pick the **Space Warps** button, and select **Deflectors** from the drop-down list. Pick the **Deflector** button in the **Object Type** rollout. Pick and drag in the appropriate viewport to create the deflector space warp. The deflector space warp object appears as a rectangle in the viewports. Next, bind the particle systems you wish to affect to the deflector space warp.

The **Parameters** rollout contains a few spinners used to modify the deflector space warp. See Figure 23-19. At the bottom of the rollout, the **Width:** and **Length:** spinners determine the size of the deflector space warp. Unlike some other space warps, the size and location of the object affects the functions. The space warp affects only the particles striking the space warp object.

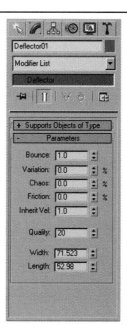

Figure 23-19. The **Parameters** rollout for the deflector space warp.

The **Bounce:** spinner in the **Parameters** rollout adjusts the energy level of the particle after it collides with the deflector space warp. When this spinner is set to 0, the particles do not bounce off the deflector, but rather accumulate on or slide along the deflector. As the value of this spinner is increased, the particles bounce off the deflector with increasing velocity. When this spinner is set to a value of 1, the particles bounce off the deflector at the same speed with which they hit it. When this value is greater than 1, the particles bounce off the deflector at a higher velocity than they had when they hit it. The **Variation:** spinner setting determines the amount that a particle's bounce can vary from the value specified in the **Bounce:** spinner. The **Chaos:** spinner setting determines the degree of randomness in the bounce trajectories of the particles. At 0%, the particles reflect at the ideal angles; the angle of incidence equals the angle of reflection. At 100%, the particles' reflection angles may vary up to 90 degrees from the perfect reflection angle.

The **Friction:** spinner setting determines the percentage decrease, in the particle's speed as the particle moves across the deflector's surface. In effect, this simulates the friction coefficient of the deflector. The **Inherit Velocity:** spinner setting determines the degree to which the motion of the deflector is passed on to affected particles. When the spinner is set to 0, the particles do not inherit the motion of the deflector. When the spinner is set to a value greater than 0, the setting in effect changes the mass ratio between the deflector and the affected particles. At a setting of 1, the particles are of the same relative mass as the deflector, and are propelled forward at the collision velocity. At a setting of 100, the particles are of much smaller relative mass, and are propelled ahead of the deflector at a great velocity. See Figure 23-20. The **Quality:** spinner setting determines the quality of equations used to determine the effect of collisions between stationary particles and the deflector. A low setting in this spinner speeds up computation time, but may allow some particles to pass through the deflector unaffected.

Figure 23-20.
Deflector space warps colliding with three identical particle streams. Each deflector space warp has a different **Inherit Vel:** setting. Notice the difference in the reflected particles.

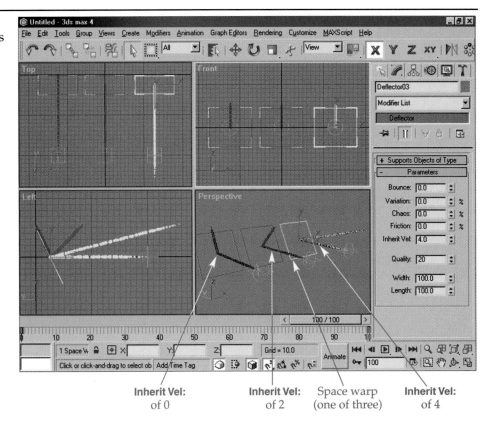

Inherit Vel: of 0   Inherit Vel: of 2   Space warp (one of three)   Inherit Vel: of 4

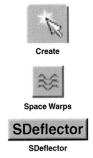

Help Cel

Use a low **Chaos:** spinner value to simulate particles reflecting from a perfectly smooth, even surface. Use higher **Chaos:** spinner values to simulate particles reflecting off a rough or uneven surface.

SDeflector

The *SDeflector space warp* is similar to the deflector space warp. However, the standard deflector space warp is planar and the SDeflector is spherical. The controls for the two space warps are identical. You can bind particle systems and dynamics effects to SDeflector space warps.

To add an SDeflector to a scene, pick the **Create** tab in the **Command Panel**. Pick the **Space Warps** button, and select **Deflectors** from the drop-down list. Pick the **SDeflector** button in the **Object Type** rollout. Then, pick and drag in the appropriate viewport to create the SDeflector space warp. The SDeflector space warp object appears as a sphere in the viewports. Next, bind the particle systems you wish to affect to the SDeflector space warp.

Create

Space Warps

SDeflector

SDeflector

UDeflector

The *UDeflector space warp* is very similar to both the deflector and the SDeflector space warp. Its **Parameters** rollout contains many of the controls of those deflector space warps. However, instead of the space warp object deflecting particles, you can specify *any* object in the scene as the deflector. You can bind particle systems and dynamics effects to UDeflector space warps.

To add a UDeflector to a scene, pick the **Create** tab in the **Command Panel**. Pick the **Space Warps** button, and select **Deflectors** from the drop-down list. Pick the **UDeflector** button in the **Object Type** rollout. Pick and drag in the appropriate viewport to create the deflector space warp. The space warp object appears in the viewports. Next, bind the particle systems you wish to affect to the UDeflector space warp.

At the top of the UDeflector space warp's **Parameters** rollout is the **Object-Based Deflector** area. Selecting the **Pick Object** button in this area allows you to choose an object in the scene to be the deflector. The name of the selected object appears in the **Item:** label above the button. Until an object is selected, the space warp has no effect on bound particle systems.

At the bottom of the **Parameters** rollout is the **Display Icon** area. Changing the **Icon Size:** spinner setting resizes the space warp object. Changing the size or position of the UDeflector space warp object does not alter the effect of the space warp. The effect of the space warp is based on the selected object deflector.

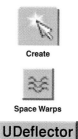

Omniflectors

Omniflectors are very similar to the deflector space warp. However, omniflectors offer an expanded variety of capabilities. The ability to spawn and the ability to refract particles are among the extended effects available with the omniflector space warps. Also, omniflectors can be set up to allow a percentage of the particles to pass through the space warp unaffected.

There are three types of omniflector space warps. A POmniFlect space warp is a planar omniflector. A SOmniFlect space warp is a spherical omniflector. A UOmniFlect space warp allows you to select an object to use as the omniflector. The controls for the three types are nearly identical. You can bind particle systems to all three types of omniflectors.

To draw an omniflector, select **Create** in the **Command Panel**. Then, pick the **Space Warps** button and select **Deflectors** in the drop-down list. Pick the appropriate button in the **Object Type** rollout. Finally, pick in a viewport and drag to set the size of the space warp object. The size of POmniFlect and SOmniFlect space warp objects is a factor in the effect on bound particle systems. The size of the UOmniFlect space warp object does not matter, as the effect is based on the size of the selected omniflector object.

The **Parameters** rollout contains controls for adjusting the effects of the various omniflector space warps. See Figure 23-21. The controls in the **Timing** section of this rollout are common to all three types of omniflectors. The spinners in this area determine span of frames over which the omniflector is active. The **Time On:** spinner sets the frame on which the omniflector activates. The **Time Off:** spinner sets the frame on which the omniflector deactivates.

When a UOmniFlect space warp is drawn or selected, the **Parameters** rollout contains the **Object-Based OmniFlector** area. The UOmniFlect space warp uses an object in the scene as the deflector, instead of the space warp object itself. To choose an object to act as the deflector, select the **Pick Object** button. Then, select the object in any viewport. Once selected, the object name appears in the **Item:** label above the button.

Figure 23-21. The
Parameters rollout for
the POmniFlector
space warp.

Reflection Area

The controls of the **Reflection** area of the **Parameters** rollout for any
of the three omniflectors determine how bound particles are reflected by
the omniflector. The **Reflects:** spinner sets the percentage of bound particles reflected by the omniflect when they collide. When this setting is
less than 100, some of the bound particles pass through the omniflector.

The **Bounce:** spinner setting determines the speed of reflected particles.
When this value is 0, the particles collect at the surface of the omniflector.
When this value is 1, the particles bounce off the omniflector at the same
speed with which they hit it. When the value of this spinner is greater than
1, particles bounce off the omniflector at a greater speed than they had
when they hit it. The **Variation:** spinner setting determines how much an
individual particle's rebound speed can deviate from the bounce setting.

The **Chaos:** spinner setting determines the amount of randomness in
the trajectories of the reflected particles. When this value is set to 0, the
particles are reflected perfectly; the angle of reflection equals the angle of
incident. Increasing the value of the **Chaos:** spinner allows the particles
to deviate a certain percentage from the perfect trajectory.

Refraction Area

The controls in the **Refraction** area of the **Parameters** rollout for any
of the three omniflectors determine how the omniflector affects the particles that pass through it. The **Refracts:** spinner sets the percentage of
particles that are refracted as they pass through the omniflector.
Refraction is a bending or altering of the particle's travel vector as it
passes through the space warp. In other words, a refracted particle is not
traveling along the same vector when it leaves the omniflector as it was
when it entered. In 3ds max, a particle's direction *or speed* can be affected
by the refraction settings of the omniflector. Only particles that are not
reflected can be refracted.

The **Pass Vel:** spinner sets the speed for particles refracted by the omniflector. A setting of 1 causes refracted particles to continue moving at the

speed they were traveling when they entered the space warp. A setting of .5 for this spinner causes refracted particles to move at one half of their original speed. A setting of 2 causes refracted particles to move at twice their original speed. The **Variation:** spinner setting determines by what percentage an individual particle's speed can deviate from the pass velocity.

The **Distortion:** spinner affects the angle of refraction. Values between −100 and 100 can be entered with this spinner. The effect of this spinner setting is based on the direction in which the particles pass through the omniflector. When particles enter the omniflector in the direction of the arrow on the omniflector object, one effect is produced. When particles enter from the opposite direction, the opposite effect is produced. For a POmniFlect, a setting of 100 causes particles traveling in the direction of the arrow to be refracted perpendicular to the plane. The resulting particle movement is perpendicular to the surface of the omniflector. A setting of −100 causes the particles to be refracted parallel to the plane. The movement of the refracted particles is parallel to and on the surface of the omniflector. A setting of 50 refracts the particles at a 45 degree angle. For a SOmniFlect, a setting of −100 causes particles traveling in the direction of the arrow to be refracted tangentially to their point of collision. A setting of 100 causes the particles to be refracted perpendicular to their point of collision. The **Variation:** spinner sets the percentage that an individual particle's trajectory can vary from the expected trajectory.

The **Diffusion:** spinner setting is the angle at which all refracted particles are scattered. For example, if this spinner were set to 30 degrees, then all particles refracted by the omniflector space warp would have their refraction trajectories altered by 30 degrees in random directions, creating a hollow cone effect. See Figure 23-22. The **Variation:** spinner setting determines the percentage by which an individual particle's trajectory can vary from diffusion trajectory. Increasing this value causes particles to stray to the inside and outside of the diffusion cone.

Figure 23-22. The hollow cone effect created with the **Diffusion:** setting on an omniflector.

Common Area

The **Inherit Vel:** spinner in the **Common** area of the **Parameters** rollout for any of the three omniflector types determines how a moving omniflector passes on its speed to affected particles. When this value is set to 1, a collision between a moving omniflector and a stationary particle propels the particle ahead of the omniflector at the omniflector's rate of speed. If this value is set to 2, then the particle is propelled ahead of the omniflector at twice the omniflector's velocity.

The speed set in the **Inherit Vel:** spinner is added to the speed created by the particle's bounce setting. However, the bounce velocity is in the direction of reflection, and the inherited velocity is in the direction of the omniflector's movement.

The **Friction:** spinner setting determines the percentage of decrease in the particle's speed as the particle moves across the omniflector's surface. A setting of 0 means the particle does not loose any speed due to the surface friction on the omniflector.

Spawn Effects Only Area

The **Spawn Effects Only** area of the **Parameters** rollout for any of the three types of omniflectors contains controls for enabling and adjusting spawning for particles that pass through the space warp. These settings only affect particle systems set to spawn on collision, and to those particles that are not reflected or refracted by the space warp.

The **Spawns:** spinner setting determines the percentage of eligible particles that are affected by the spawn effect. The effect of the **Pass Vel:** spinner setting is very similar to the effect of the **Pass Vel:** spinner setting in the **Refraction** area of the rollout. This setting determines the speed of the particles that are affected by the spawn controls. The **Variation:** spinner setting determines the maximum percentage that an individual particle's speed can deviate from the speed set by the **Pass Vel:** spinner setting.

Collision Quality Area

The **Collision Quality** area contains the **Quality:** spinner. The value of this spinner determines the accuracy of the equations used to calculate collisions between stationary particles and moving omniflectors. A low setting in this spinner reduces computation time, but may allow some particles to pass through the omniflector unaffected. This area is only available with a POmniFlect space warp.

Display Icon Area

The **Display Icon** area, at the bottom of the rollout, contains controls for changing the size of the space warp object. In the case of SOmniFlect and POmniFlect space warps, the object size determines the range of the space warp. In the case of UOmniFlect space warps, the size of the selected omniflector object, not the space warp object size, determines the extents of the space warp. The size of an SOmniFlect object is set with the **Radius:** spinner. The size of a POmniFlect object is set with **Width:** and **Height:** spinners. The UOmniFlect object size is set with the **Icon Size:** spinner.

Exercise 23-5

1) Open ex23-03.max from Exercise 23-3.
2) In the Top viewport, create a cylinder that is nearly as wide as the mug at its widest point and about half as tall. Position the cylinder so it is completely inside the mug.
3) Pick the **Space Warp** button, and select **Deflectors** from the drop-down list. Pick the **UOmniFlect** button from the **Object Type** rollout. In any viewport, pick and drag to create the omniflector.
4) Select the **Pick Object** button in the **Parameters** rollout. Pick the cylinder. In the **Reflection** area of the **Parameters** rollout, set the **Reflects:** spinner to 100. Set the **Bounce:** spinner to 0.
5) Bind the particle system to the UOmniFlect space warp. Play the animation.
6) Reset 3ds max. Do not save the file.

Dynaflectors

Dynaflectors are very similar to deflector and omniflector space warps. While dynaflector space warps can be used as standard deflector space warps, they are intended for dynamics effects. However, their dynamics attributes make them more mathematically intensive than a standard deflector or omniflector. For this reason, use dynaflectors only for dynamics simulations.

Geometric/Deformable

The space warps in the geometric/deformable category are used to deform mesh and NURBS objects. This category includes FFD (box), FFD (cyl), wave, ripple, displace, conform, and bomb space warps. Bomb, wave, ripple, and conform space warps are covered in the next sections.

Wave

The *wave space warp* creates a linear wave in space to distort objects bound to it. See Figure 23-23. The effect of the wave space warp is identical to the effect of the wave modifier. It can be used for such obvious purposes as creating a waving flag or a rolling sea. It can also be used to quickly create a corrugated tin roof. You can bind any deformable object to a wave space warp.

To add a wave space warp to a scene, pick **Create** in the **Command Panel**. Pick the **Space Warps** button and select **Geometric/Deformable** from the drop-down list. Then, pick the **Wave** button in the **Object Type** rollout. In any viewport, pick to set the center of the wave space warp. Then, drag the cursor to set the size of the space warp. Now, move the mouse up or down and pick to set the amplitude, or height, of the waves. The height of the waves is initially along the local Z axis of the viewport in which the space warp is created. See Figure 23-24. You can transform the space warp to adjust the wave effect.

Create

Space Warps

Wave

Wave

Figure 23-23. A wave space warp affecting various objects.

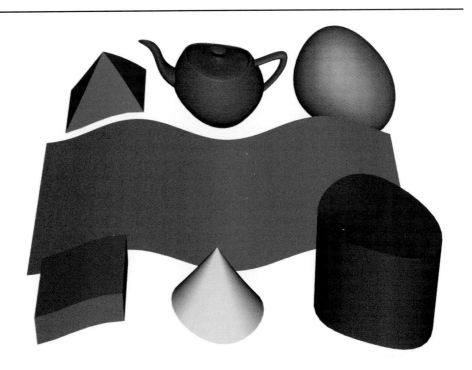

Figure 23-24. Setting the amplitude of the wave space warp.

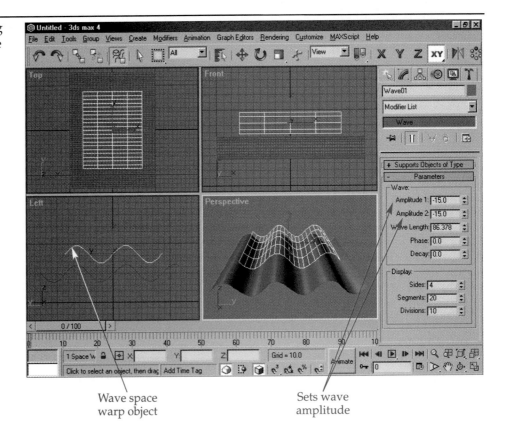

Wave space warp object

Sets wave amplitude

Exercise

Exercise 23-5

1) Open ex23-03.max from Exercise 23-3.
2) In the Top viewport, create a cylinder that is nearly as wide as the mug at its widest point and about half as tall. Position the cylinder so it is completely inside the mug.
3) Pick the **Space Warp** button, and select **Deflectors** from the drop-down list. Pick the **UOmniFlect** button from the **Object Type** rollout. In any viewport, pick and drag to create the omniflector.
4) Select the **Pick Object** button in the **Parameters** rollout. Pick the cylinder. In the **Reflection** area of the **Parameters** rollout, set the **Reflects:** spinner to 100. Set the **Bounce:** spinner to 0.
5) Bind the particle system to the UOmniFlect space warp. Play the animation.
6) Reset 3ds max. Do not save the file.

Dynaflectors

Dynaflectors are very similar to deflector and omniflector space warps. While dynaflector space warps can be used as standard deflector space warps, they are intended for dynamics effects. However, their dynamics attributes make them more mathematically intensive than a standard deflector or omniflector. For this reason, use dynaflectors only for dynamics simulations.

Geometric/Deformable

The space warps in the geometric/deformable category are used to deform mesh and NURBS objects. This category includes FFD (box), FFD (cyl), wave, ripple, displace, conform, and bomb space warps. Bomb, wave, ripple, and conform space warps are covered in the next sections.

Wave

The *wave space warp* creates a linear wave in space to distort objects bound to it. See Figure 23-23. The effect of the wave space warp is identical to the effect of the wave modifier. It can be used for such obvious purposes as creating a waving flag or a rolling sea. It can also be used to quickly create a corrugated tin roof. You can bind any deformable object to a wave space warp.

To add a wave space warp to a scene, pick **Create** in the **Command Panel**. Pick the **Space Warps** button and select **Geometric/Deformable** from the drop-down list. Then, pick the **Wave** button in the **Object Type** rollout. In any viewport, pick to set the center of the wave space warp. Then, drag the cursor to set the size of the space warp. Now, move the mouse up or down and pick to set the amplitude, or height, of the waves. The height of the waves is initially along the local Z axis of the viewport in which the space warp is created. See Figure 23-24. You can transform the space warp to adjust the wave effect.

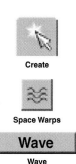

Create

Space Warps

Wave

Wave

Figure 23-23. A wave space warp affecting various objects.

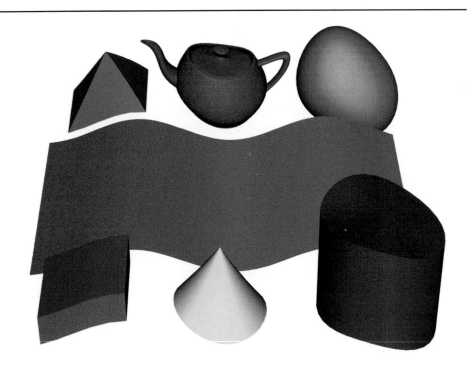

Figure 23-24. Setting the amplitude of the wave space warp.

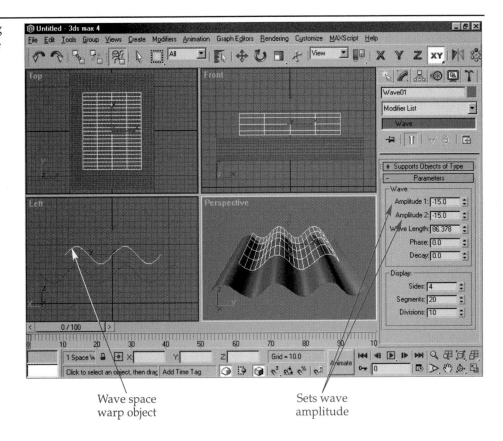

Wave space warp object

Sets wave amplitude

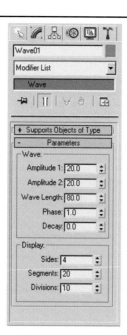

Figure 23-25. The **Parameters** rollout for a wave space warp.

The **Parameters** rollout contains controls that allow you to fine-tune the effect of the wave space warp. See Figure 23-25. Finally, bind the objects in the scene to be affected by the wave space warp.

Wave Area

The **Wave:** area of the **Parameters** rollout contains the controls determining the effect of the space warp. The value in the **Amplitude 1:** spinner is the amplitude at the left-right center of each wave. The value in the **Amplitude 2:** spinner sets the amplitude for the left and right edges of each wave. When these values are identical, the wave has a uniform height across its crests and troughs. When the value in the **Amplitude 2:** spinner is very different from the value in the **Amplitude 1:** spinner, an effect similar to a stingray swimming under water is produced.

The **Wave Length:** spinner sets the distance, in current drawing units, between crests of the waves. This value also affects the overall size of the space warp. However, the strength of the space warp is not affected.

The **Phase:** spinner determines the stage of the sine wave at the origin. When this value is set to 0, the wave is beginning its cycle at the center of the space warp. This means the center lies between a crest and a trough. When this value is set to .25, the center lies at the bottom of a trough. When the value of this spinner is set to .75, the center lies at the top of a crest. The value in the **Phase:** spinner refers to complete cycles. This spinner can be animated to produce motion in the space warp.

Increasing the value of the **Decay:** spinner from 0 causes the amplitude of the waves to decrease as the wave travels from the center of the space warp. The decay is inversely proportional to the distance from the center of the wave space warp. When this spinner is set to 0, the waves have the same amplitude throughout space.

Display Area

The controls in the **Display:** area of the **Parameters** rollout alter the appearance of the wave space warp icon. Increasing the value of the

Sides: spinner increases the number of segments across the width of the wave. Increasing the value of the **Segments:** spinner increases the number of segments across the length of the wave. The **Divisions:** spinner sets the number of divisions used to define a complete cycle. Increasing the value of the **Divisions:** spinner while keeping the **Segments:** spinner value constant refines the curvature of the wave space warp icon while making it shorter. Changes to the settings in the **Display:** area do not change the wave effect.

Bound Object Settings

In addition to the controls in the **Parameters** rollout for the space warp, each object bound to the space warp is affected by an adjustable **Flexibility:** setting. The flexibility setting determines how much the object is deformed by the wave space warp. It is essentially a multiplier.

To change the flexibility setting of a bound object, first select the object, *not* the space warp. Then, pick the **Modify** tab in the **Command Panel**. Select the **Wave Binding** level in the modifier stack. The **Parameters** rollout is displayed and the **Flexibility:** spinner can now be changed to adjust the effect of the space warp on the selected object.

Exercise

Exercise 23-6

1) In the Top viewport, create a quad patch. Make the X dimension 200 and the Y dimension 400 units. Set the **Length Segs:** and **Width Segs:** spinners to 1.
2) In the Top viewport, create a sphere with a radius of 25 units and 16 segments. Position it near the center and slightly above (local Z axis) the quad patch.
3) In the Top viewport, create wave space warp. Set the **Wave Length:** spinner to 200. Set the **Amplitude 1:** and **Amplitude 2:** spinners to approximately 15.
4) In the Top viewport, rotate the wave 90 degrees. Bind the quad patch and the sphere to the wave space warp. Notice the quad patch is only slightly affected by the wave space warp.
5) Select the quad patch and pick the **Modify** tab in the **Command Panel**. Select **Quad Patch** in the modifier stack. Increase the **Length Segs:** and **Width Segs:** spinners for the quad patch to 5. Select the **Wave Binding** level in the modifier stack. Notice the shape of the quad patch now closely matches the wave.
6) Select the wave space warp. Move to frame 100 and activate the **Toggle Animation Mode** button. Increase the **Phase:** spinner setting to 2.
7) Render the animation to a file named ex23-06.avi in the folder of your choice. View the animation when the rendering is complete.
8) Save the scene as ex23-06.max in the folder of your choice. Reset 3ds max.

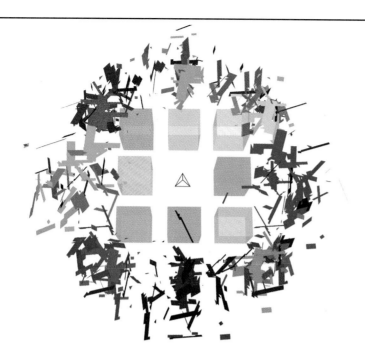

Figure 23-26. The effects of the bomb space warp. The trajectory of each box's fragments is dependent on the box's position relative to the bomb space warp at the time of detonation.

Bomb

The *bomb space warp* explodes bound objects into fragments. The fragments are formed from the faces of the bound objects. The fragments are blown outward in a direction normal to the blast sphere of the space warp. Therefore, if the bomb space warp icon is placed behind an object, all faces of the object are blown forward. See Figure 23-26. However, if the bomb space warp icon is placed inside an object, the faces of the object are blown outward in every direction. You can bind any geometric object to a bomb space warp.

To place a bomb space warp in a scene, pick **Create** in the **Command Panel**. Pick the **Space Warps** button and select **Geometric/Deformable** from the drop-down list. Then, pick the **Bomb** button from the **Object Type** rollout. Pick in any viewport to place the bomb space warp. The space warp object appears as a small wireframe pyramid. The default name for the space warp object is MeshBomb*xx*. Finally, bind the objects in the scene to be affected by the bomb space warp.

The **Bomb Parameters** rollout contains the controls used to adjust the bomb's effect. See Figure 23-27. This rollout contains the **Explosion:**, **Fragment Size:**, and **General:** areas. The options in these areas are discussed in the following sections.

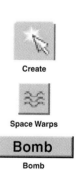

Create

Space Warps

Bomb

Bomb

Help Cel

When an object is bound to a bomb space warp, the bomb space warp is referred to as a "mesh bomb."

Explosion

The settings in the **Explosion:** area of the **Bomb Parameters** rollout determine the effect of the bomb's explosion. The value in the **Strength:** spinner determines the velocity of the fragments. Increasing the strength setting allows fragments to travel further outward before they succumb entirely to the space warp's gravity setting.

Figure 23-27. The
Bomb Parameters
rollout.

The value in the **Spin:** spinner sets the rate of rotation, in revolutions per second, for the fragments. This setting defines the initial state of the fragments, but the fragment spin rate is also affected by the **Chaos:** and **Falloff:** settings.

When the **Falloff On** check box is checked, the falloff feature is activated. A yellow falloff gizmo is displayed in the viewports. The falloff gizmo marks the extents of the bomb space warp's effects. Fragments lying outside the gizmo are affected only by the space warp's gravity setting.

The value in the **Falloff:** spinner determines the blast radius of the bomb. Faces of the affected object lying outside the falloff area are not propelled outward. They are, however, affected by gravity. As a fragment's position nears the edge of the falloff sphere, the effect of the bomb diminishes for that fragment.

Fragment Size

The two spinners in the **Fragment Size:** area of the **Bomb Parameters** rollout determine the size of the fragments created by the bomb space warp. The **Min:** spinner sets the minimum number of faces a fragment can have. The **Max:** spinner sets the maximum number of faces a fragment can have. Each fragment consists of a random number of faces between these two values. If the values are the same, the explosion effect appears very uniform. If both are set to 1, each face becomes a fragment. Increasing the difference between these values creates a more random effect.

General

The **General:** area of the **Bomb Parameters** rollout contains a variety of controls used to fine-tune the effects of the space warp. The **Gravity:** spinner is used to set the strength with which gravity affects the fragments. Increasing the value of the **Gravity:** spinner increases the fragments' rate of acceleration along the world Z axis. A positive value in this spinner accelerates the fragments in the negative Z direction. A negative value in this spinner accelerates the fragments in the positive Z direction. The gravity generated by this space warp is always along the world Z axis, regardless of the orientation of the space warp or bound objects.

The **Chaos:** spinner is used to add a degree of randomness to the explosion effect. A setting of zero in this spinner creates a uniform explosion. A setting of 1 adds a realistic amount of randomness to the fragments' outward acceleration, direction, and rate of spin. Increasing the setting increases the degree of randomness of the effect.

The **Detonation:** spinner setting determines the frame on which the explosion begins. The **Seed:** spinner adjusts the random numbers generated for the explosion. Changes to the seed setting have less effect the more uniform the explosion is. In a more chaotic explosion, the seed setting can have a significant effect. If you have multiple bomb space warps in a scene, each should have a different seed to produce different exploding effects.

Help Cel

On the frame set with the **Detonation:** spinner, the smoothing groups for objects bound to the bomb space warp are removed. If the bound object is created from too few segments, this transition is very obvious. Increase the number of segments in the bound object to smooth the transition.

Exercise 23-7

1) In the Top viewport, create a 200-unit cube. Leave all the segment spinner values at 1.
2) Pick **Create** in the **Command Panel**. Pick the **Space Warps** button and select **Geometric/Deformable** from the drop down list. Pick the **Bomb** button from the **Object Type** rollout. Pick in any viewport to create the bomb icon. Move the bomb icon to the center of the cube. Zoom extents in all viewports.
3) Bind the cube to the bomb space warp.
4) Define a simple material, and check the **2-Sided** check box to make it two sided. Apply this material to the box.
5) Select the Perspective viewport and pick the **Play Animation** button.
6) Select the bomb space warp, and then open the **Modify** tab in the **Command Panel**. Increase the **Spin:** spinner setting to 1. Play the animation in the Perspective viewport.
7) Select the box, and then pick **Modify** in the **Command Panel**. Select the **Box** level in modifier stack. Increase the number of segments for length, width, and height to 10.
8) Select the bomb, and set the **Spin:** spinner to 0. Play the animation in the Perspective viewport. Increase the **Chaos:** spinner value to 1. Play the animation again.
9) Move the bomb space warp icon down near the bottom of the box. Check the **Falloff On** check box. Increase the **Falloff:** spinner value to 200. Set the **Spin:** spinner to 1. Play the animation in the Perspective viewport.
10) Render the animation to a file named ex23-01.avi in the folder of your choice. Save the scene as ex23-01.max in the folder of your choice.

Figure 23-28. A ripple space warp affecting a thin cylinder and an array of boxes.

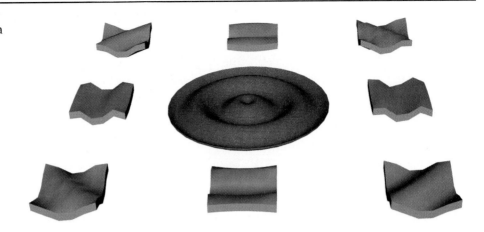

Ripple

The ripple space warp is very similar to the wave space warp. However, the ripple space warp generates circular, concentric deformation waves. See Figure 23-28. This is similar to the waves created by throwing a rock in a pond. The wave space warp, on the other hand, generates waves similar to the waves on a large lake or ocean. You can bind any deformable object to a ripple space warp.

To add a ripple space warp to a scene, pick the **Create** tab in the **Command Panel**. Pick the **Space Warps** button and select **Geometric/Deformable** from the drop-down list. Pick the **Ripple** button from the **Object Type** rollout. In any viewport, pick to set the center of the ripple space warp. Then, drag the cursor to determine the diameter of the object. Since the space warp is applied throughout space, the object size is for display only. When the object is the size you would like, release the mouse button. Now, move the cursor up and down to set the amplitude of the waves. When the amplitude is the height you want, pick the mouse button. The height of the waves is initially along the Z axis of the viewport in which the space warp is created. You can transform the space warp to adjust the effect. Finally, bind any objects to the ripple space warp.

The **Parameters** rollout contains the controls used to edit the ripple effect. See Figure 23-29. The controls in the **Ripple:** area are identical in name and function to their counterparts in the **Wave:** portion of the **Parameters** rollout for a wave space warp.

The controls in the **Display:** area of the rollout alter the appearance of the ripple space warp object. Increasing the value of the **Circles:** spinner increases the number of concentric circles used to display the object. Increasing the value of the **Segments:** spinner increases the number of pie-shaped segments formed from the concentric circles. The **Divisions:** spinner sets the number of divisions used to define a complete cycle. Changing these values does not alter the effect of the space warp.

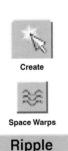

Create

Space Warps

Ripple

Ripple

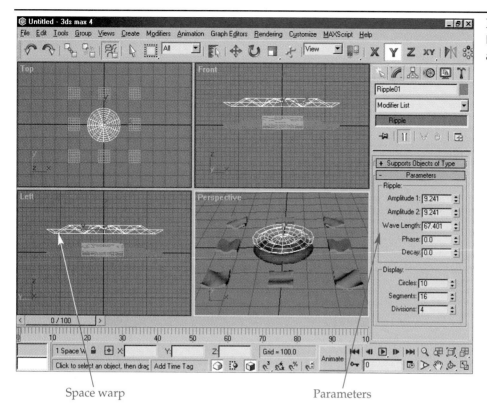

Figure 23-29. The **Parameters** rollout for a ripple space warp.

Space warp   Parameters

As with the wave space warp, bound objects have an adjustable **Flexibility:** setting. This is a multiplier used to determine how much the space warp affects the object. To change the flexibility setting of an object, select the object. Pick the **Modify** tab of the **Command Panel**. Then, select the **Ripple Binding** level in the modifier stack. The **Flexibility:** spinner in the **Parameters** rollout can then be used to adjust the effect of the space warp on the selected object.

Help Cel

Like waves in the real world, the effects of wave and ripple space warps are additive. This means wave space warps in phase with one another combine in strength. Wave space warps of equal amplitude and frequency that are one-half cycle out of phase with one another cancel out each other.

Exercise

Exercise 23-8

1) In the Top viewport, create a tube. Set the **Radius 1:** spinner to 100 units. Set the **Radius 2:** spinner to 95 units. Set the height to 40 units. Increase the number of sides to 32. Name the tube Pan.
2) Create a cylinder in the center of the tube. Make the cylinder radius 97.5 units. Give the cylinder a height of 25 units. Set the **Cap Segments:** spinner to 9. Set the **Sides:** spinner to 32. In the Front viewport, move the cylinder 3 units on the positive Y axis. Name the cylinder Water.
3) In the Top viewport, create a ripple space warp centered on the tube and cylinder. Make the object roughly the same diameter as the cylinder. Set the **Amplitude 1:** and **Amplitude 2:** spinners to approximately 5 units.
4) Bind the cylinder to the ripple space warp.
5) On frame 100, animate the **Phase:** spinner setting to a value of 3. Pick the **Play Animation** button to preview the animation.
6) Exit animation mode and move to frame 0. Select the cylinder. Set the **Flexibility:** spinner to 0.
7) Move to frame 50 and turn animation mode on. Animate the **Flexibility:** spinner to a value of 1 or a little higher. Move to frame 100. Animate the **Flexibility:** spinner to a value of .25 or a little lower.
8) Render the animation to a file named ex23-08.avi in the directory of your choice.
9) When the rendering is complete, view the animation.
10) Save the scene as ex23-08.max in the directory of your choice. Reset 3ds max.

Conform

Suppose you have modeled waves using a quad patch. You have also drawn an extruded spline, representing seaweed floating on the surface of the water. The seaweed's shape must match, or conform, to the waves. You can accomplish this using the conform space warp. The *conform space warp* reshapes objects bound to it so they match the shape of a target object. The waves are the target, or "wrap to," object. The extruded spline is bound to a conform space warp. The "seaweed" can then be animated moving across the waves, and its surface always conforms to the waves.

The conform space warp works by moving vertices of the bound object until they are displaced a preset amount, or contact the surface of the target object. See Figure 23-30. You can bind any deformable object to a conform space warp.

To add a conform space warp to a scene, pick the **Create** tab in the **Command Panel**. Pick the **Space Warp** button and select **Geometric/ Deformable** from the drop-down list. Then, pick the **Conform** button in the **Object Type** rollout.

Now, pick and drag in any viewport to create a conform space warp. The conform space warp object is a rectangle with an arrow at its center, similar to some particle systems. The arrow indicates the direction in which selected vertices of the bound objects will be moved. The arrow initially points down the negative Z axis of the viewport in which the space warp is created.

Create

Space Warps

Conform

With the space warp created, bind the objects you wish to be affected by the conform space warp. Finally, set the parameters for the space warp.

To adjust the conform space warp, select the conform space warp object. Pick the **Modify** tab in the **Command Panel** and expand the **Conform Parameters** rollout. This rollout contains the controls needed to adjust the conform space warp. See Figure 23-31.

Wrap To Object Area

The **Wrap To Object:** area of the **Conform Parameters** rollout contains a single button. Picking this button allows you to select the object to which the bound objects will conform. This is called the target, or "wrap to," object. To choose a target object, select the **Pick Object** button in the **Wrap To Object:** area. Then, pick the target object in any viewport. The name of the target object is displayed under the button.

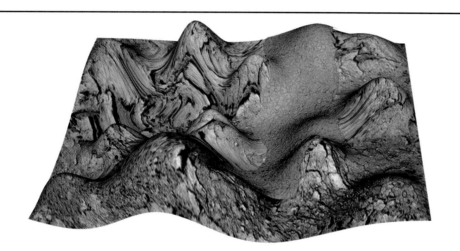

Figure 23-30. The conform space warp used to create lava flowing over rugged terrain.

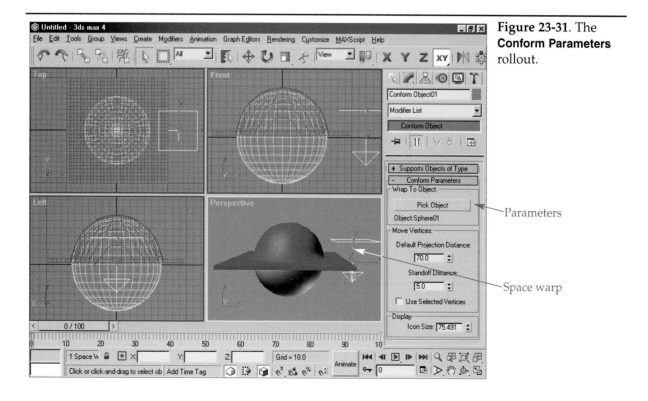

Figure 23-31. The **Conform Parameters** rollout.

Move Vertices Area

The **Move Vertices:** area of the **Conform Parameters** rollout determines how the space warp deforms the objects that are bound to it. The **Default Projection Distance:** spinner determines how far the vertices of bound objects can be displaced. The value of the **Standoff Distance:** spinner is the gap between the bound objects and the object to which they conform.

Checking the **Use Selected Vertices** check box applies the space warp only to those vertices that are selected on a bound object. This, in effect, allows you to bind a sub-object selection to the space warp. When this check box is unchecked, every vertex in a bound object is displaced until it reaches the **Default Projection Distance**, or encounters the surface of the target object. If the **Use Selected Vertices** option is on and there are no selected vertices, the effect of the space warp is *not* applied.

Display Area

The **Icon Size:** spinner in the **Display** area of the **Conform Parameters** rollout sets the size of the conform space warp object in the viewports. Changing this setting does not alter the conform space warp effect.

Help Cel

The effectiveness of the conform space warp is, in part, determined by the segmentation of the bound object and the wrap object. In order for conform to be effective, the bound object must be sufficiently segmented to match the contours of the wrap object.

Exercise

Exercise 23-9

1) In the Top viewport, create a quad patch. Make the quad patch approximately 250 units long by 350 units wide. Set the **Length Segs:** and **Width Segs:** spinners to 6.
2) In the Top viewport, create two boxes. Make each of the boxes approximately 30 units long, 50 units wide, and 1 unit high. Set the segments to 6 on all sides. Position the boxes at opposite ends of the quad patch and approximately 5 units above it.
3) In the Top viewport, draw a conform space warp. Select the **Pick Object** button and pick the quad patch. Increase the **Standoff Distance:** spinner setting to 10 units.
4) Select the boxes and bind them to the conform space warp.
5) Select the quad patch and apply a noise modifier to it. Check the **Fractal** check box and increase the **Roughness:** spinner setting to 1 or a little higher. In the **Strength:** area of the rollout, increase the **Z:** spinner setting to 10 or a little higher.
6) On frame 100, animate each of the boxes moving to the opposite corner of the quad patch. Preview the animation.
7) Render the animation to a file named ex23-09.avi in the folder of your choice. When complete, view the animation.
8) Save the scene as ex23-09.max in the folder of your choice. Reset 3ds max.

Modifier-Based

The *modifier-based space warps* create identical effects to their modifier counterparts. However, they are a great time-saver when you want to modify numerous objects using the same parameters. Unlike the modifier gizmos, which must be transformed at the sub-object level, the modifier-based space warp icons can be transformed directly. Also, additional objects can be easily added to the set of affected objects by binding them to the space warp.

Chapter Snapshot

Chapter Test

Answer the following questions on a separate sheet of paper.
1) When creating a push space warp, what is the effect of checking the **Feedback On** check box?
2) How are the **Orbital Speed:** and **Radial Pull:** settings of a vortex space interrelated?
3) What type of objects can be used as the path for the path follow space warp?
4) How does the effect of activating the **Along Offset Splines** radio button differ from the effect of activating the **Along Parallel Splines** radio button in the **Basic Parameters** rollout for a path follow space warp.
5) What are the three options available for tapering the stream of particles affected by the path follow space warp?
6) In the **Basic Parameters** rollout for a path follow space warp, what does the **Stream Swirl:** spinner setting determine?
7) What is the difference between reflection and refraction of particles?
8) For deflector and omniflector space warps, what effect would a **Bounce:** spinner setting of 1.5 have on reflected particles?
9) When creating an omniflector space warp, how do the effects of the **Bounce:** spinner and **Inherited Vel:** spinner differ?

10) In the **Parameters** rollout for a wave space warp, what does the **Amplitude 1:** spinner setting determine? What does the **Amplitude 2:** spinner setting determine?

11) In the **Parameters** rollout for a wave space warp, what does the **Phase:** spinner determine?

12) How can you animate wave motion using the wave space warp?

13) If three identical objects are bound to a wave space warp, how can you increase the effect of the space warp on one object, decrease the effect of the space warp on one object, and leave the third object unchanged?

14) What does the **Strength:** spinner in the **Bomb Parameters** rollout control?

15) How do you increase the randomness of an explosion created with the bomb space warp?

16) What is the primary difference between the ripple space warp and the wave space warp?

17) In the **Parameters** rollout for the ripple space warp, what function does the **Decay:** spinner serve?

18) Which spinner would you adjust to increase the distance between the crests of a ripple space warp's waves?

19) In the **Conform Parameters** rollout, what function does the **Standoff Distance:** spinner serve?

20) Describe two ways a modifier-based space warp differs from its modifier counterpart.

Modeling Problems

Draw the following models using your own dimensions. Use the 3ds max objects presented in this and earlier chapters. Create and apply materials as needed, similar to those shown. Add lights and cameras as needed to create the shadows and views shown. When finished, save each scene as p23-xx.max in the folder of your choice.

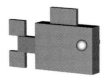

1 Exploding Firecracker

Bobber in a Pond **2**

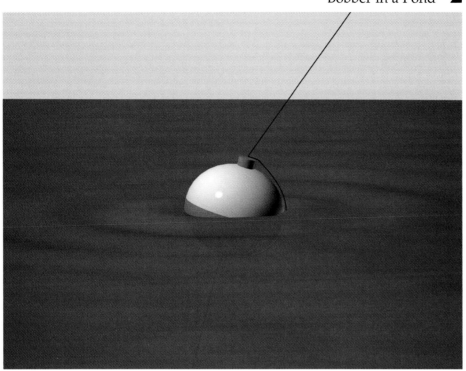

Magic Carpet **3**
A suitable diffuse color map for the carpet can be found in the
3ds max \Maps\Fabric folder. Examine the rendering closely. You may
need to use more than one map.

4 Soap Bubbles

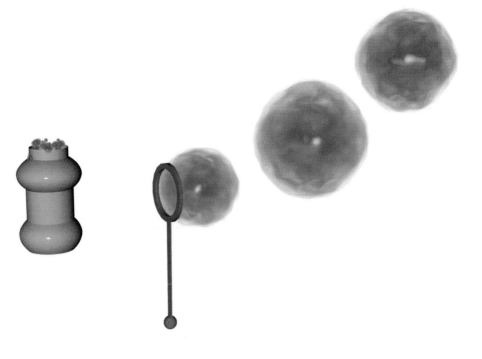

5 Filling a Water Bowl

Washboard **6**

Umbrella in the Rain **7**

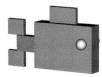

8 Comet

The purple nebula is on the environmental background. This map can be found in the **3ds max** \Maps\Space folder.

9 Ball Breaking a Window

Marbles in a Funnel **10**

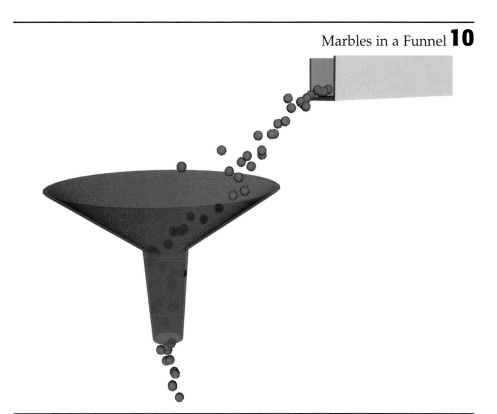

Genie in a Bottle **11**

Section Four Tutorial

Overview

For the Section Four tutorial, you will create an animation of a 19th century steam loco-motive. This model requires you to create advanced compound and loft objects. In addition, you must create particle systems, and a bone network. To put the finishing touches on the scene, you must create and apply environmental effects and advanced materials.

A final rendering of the model is shown in Figure T4-1. Start by looking at the model and determining basic components of the locomotive. For example, you can draw the boiler first, the body and cab next, then the wheels, and finish the scene by adding the remaining components.

Help Cel

Save and save often. It is up to you to determine how often to save. However, a general rule of thumb is every 10 to 15 minutes. Also, you will probably want to perform test renderings during the modeling process. Use the **Quick Render (Draft)**, **Quick Render (Production)**, and **ActiveShade** settings to your advantage.

Drawing the Locomotive

As just mentioned, the locomotive can be divided into several basic components. Logically, you might start by drawing the boiler or cab, and then add the rest of the parts. However, for this tutorial, the wheels and linkages are drawn first. The reason for this is that the positioning and orientation of the bones used for the linkages are critical. Once the wheels and linkages are in place, the rest of the locomotive can be assembled around them.

Figure T4-1. The completed Section Four tutorial model with details added.

Wheels and Linkage Assembly

First, you will draw one of the large wheels. Then, you will copy the wheel to create the other three. Next, the linkage is created. For the animation described in this tutorial, only the left side of the locomotive is visible. Therefore, only the wheels on the left side are created.

First Wheel

Start by drawing a donut in the Front viewport with an outer radius of 100 and an inner radius of 80. Place the center of the donut at the world origin (0,0). Extrude the donut 20 units. This forms the outer "ring" of one wheel. In the Top viewport, center the wheel on the world origin.

Next, draw a tube in the Front viewport with an outer radius of 110 units and an inner radius of 90 units. Make the height 5 units. Center the tube on the extruded donut. Also, in the Top viewport, move the tube so the "back edges" of the two objects are flush. The total thickness of the wheel should be 20 units. Union the two objects and name the new object Wheel, Left 01.

In the Left viewport, draw a cylinder with a radius of 7 units and a height of 170 units. Center the cylinder on the wheel left-to-right and top-to bottom. In the Front viewport, center the cylinder left-to-right. Name the cylinder Spoke, Left 01. See Figure T4-2. In the Front viewport, rotate three copies of the spoke at 45° so there are four total cylinders. It will appear as if there are eight spokes.

Draw a cylinder in the Front viewport with a radius of 30 units and a height of 20 units. This is the hub for the wheel. Center the hub in the wheel. The hub should be centered front-to-back as well. Name the object Hub, Left 01.

Looking at Figure T4-1, there is a linkage connecting the wheels and the steam engine. Each wheel has a "linkage hub" where the motion from the linkage is transferred to the wheel. In the Front viewport, draw a chamfer cylinder with a radius of 10 units and a height of 50 units. Center the chamfer cylinder at (60,0) in the Front viewport. Create a fillet of 2 units and set the fillet segments to 5 or a little higher. In the Top viewport, align the object so its

Figure T4-2. The outer portion of the first wheel with one spoke added.

"maximum Y" is the world origin. Move the object's pivot point to the center of the wheel. Then, rotate the object 22.5° about the world origin in the Front viewport. Name the object Link Hub, Left 01.

Now, you need to create a plate between two spokes on which the link hub will sit. In the Front viewport, draw a triangle as shown in Figure T4-3. The edges of the triangle should be "inside" the spokes and the rim. Extrude the spline 10 units and name the object Link Plate, Left 01. In the Top viewport, center the plate front-to-back on the spoke.

Finally, a counterweight needs to be created. In the 3ds max model, the counterweight is for appearance only. However, on a real locomotive, the counterweight offsets the weight of the linkage plate to keep the wheel in balance. In the Front viewport, draw a donut with an outer radius of 80 units and an inner radius of 50 units. Center the donut on the wheel and convert the donut to an editable spline. In sub-object mode, delete three of the "quadrants" of the donut. Refer to the final shape shown in Figure T4-3. Next, draw two lines connecting the inner and outer arcs. Extrude the spline 15 units. In the Top viewport, center the counter-weight front-to-back on the spokes. Finally, rotate the extruded object 22.5° about the center of the wheel in the Front viewport to place it opposite the linkage hub. Name the object Counterweight, Left 01.

The counterweight, linkage plate, and linkage hub should remain separate from the wheel. However, you can attach the spokes to the wheel. Select the wheel. Then, union each of the spokes to the wheel. You can also union the hub to the wheel. Next, make sure the pivot point for the wheel is located in the center of the hub. Also, make sure the pivot is aligned to the world.

Make a copy of the linkage hub in the same location as the original. Name this Linkage Pivot Temp 01. You will need this later to set a pivot point. Now, the linkage plate and linkage hub can be unioned together. Name the new object Linkage Pivot, Left 01. Then, move the pivot point of the new object to the center of the wheel. Also, align the pivot to the world.

Move the pivot of the counterweight to the center of the wheel. Align its pivot to the world. Link the counterweight to the wheel. Inherit rotation and movement on all axes. Link the Linkage Pivot, Left 01 object to the wheel. Inherit rotation and movement on all axes.

Figure T4-3. The first wheel completed with spokes, linkage pivot, counterweight, and hub.

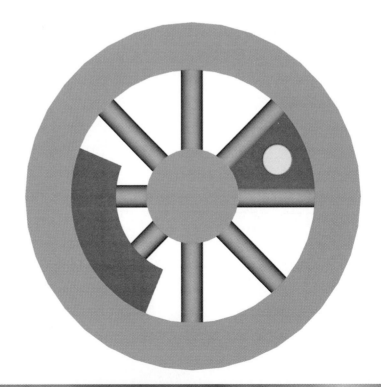

Three More Wheels

Now, you need to create three copies. Select all parts of the wheel and the temporary linkage pivot in the Front viewport. Rotate all objects 22.5° about the center of the wheel to align the linkage hub with the X axis.

Before creating copies of the wheel assembly, add animation keys for the wheel. In this way, copies of the wheel also have keys. First, change the total number of frames in the animation to 300 so the final animation is 10 seconds. Then, move to frame 300 and animate the rotation of the wheel in the Front viewport. The rotation value should be 3600° so the wheel rotates once every 10 frames.

Next, clone copies of all objects. In the Front viewport, move the copies 250 units on the X axis. Clone copies of the second wheel. Move the copies 250 units on the X axis. Repeat this procedure once more to create the fourth wheel assembly. If you pick the **Play Animation** button, you can see the wheels move in perfect unison.

Linkages

There are five linkages for the wheels. Refer to Figure T4-1. Each one is the same. Start by drawing the spline shown in Figure T4-4. Then, extrude the spline 10 units. Name the object Linkage, Left 01. Center the linkage on the linkage pivots of the first and second wheels. It should be flush to the front surface on the wheel. Next, make two copies. Locate the copies between the second and third, and third and fourth wheels. The first and third linkage should be flush to the front surface of the wheels. The second linkage should be offset as shown in Figure T4-5.

Adjust the pivot points for the linkages as necessary. The pivot point for the first linkage should be in the center of the linkage pivot of the first wheel. See Figure T4-6. The pivot point for the second linkage should be in the center of the linkage pivot of the second wheel. Finally, the pivot point for the third linkage should be in the center of the linkage pivot of the third wheel. Use the "temporary linkage" objects to your advantage.

Now, make another copy of the first linkage. Move its pivot point to the center of the linkage pivot of the second wheel. In the Front viewport, rotate the copy 30°, as shown in

Figure T4-4. The dimensions of the spline used to create the linkages.

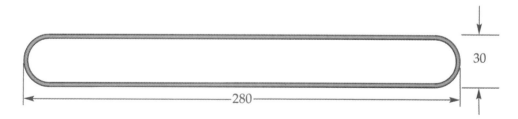

30

—280—

Figure T4-5. The alignment of the first three linkages, as seen in the Top viewport.

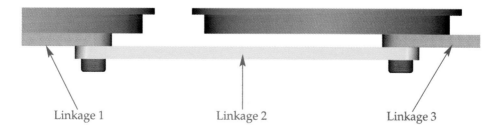

Linkage 1   Linkage 2   Linkage 3

Figure T4-6. The pivot point of the first linkage should be located in the center of the cylinder portion of the linkage plate. Use the temporary pivot object to align the pivot.

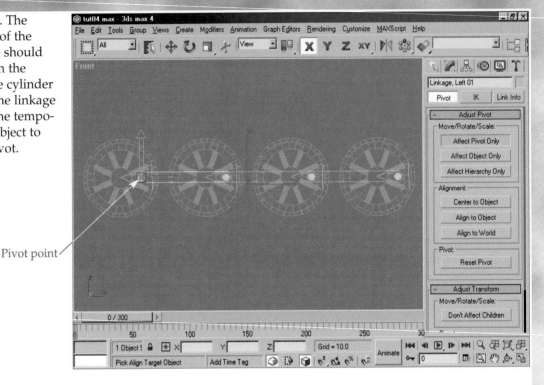

Pivot point

Figure T4-7. The completed wheel and linkage assembly.

Figure T4-7. In the Top viewport, move the linkage down so it is flush with the second linkage. The end of the linkage pivot for the second wheel should stick out slightly from the fourth linkage. Refer to Figure T4-1. Now, make a final copy of the first linkage. Move it straight up in the Front viewport so it is in line with the end of the angled linkage, as shown in Figure T4-1. Then, move it to the left so the centers of the round portions of the fourth and fifth linkages match. The fifth linkage should also be flush with the "back" of the fourth linkage.

Align the pivot points of all objects to the world. Then, link Linkage, Left 01 to Linkage Pivot, Left 01. Link Linkage, Left 02 to Linkage Pivot, Left 02. Link Linkage, Left 03 to Linkage Pivot, Left 03. You do not need to link Linkage, Left 04 or Linkage, Left 05 to any objects at this point. All "linkage" objects should inherit movement on the X and Z axes only. They should not inherit *any* rotation.

Steam Piston Tube

The top horizontal linkage (Linkage, Left 05) slides in and out of a steam piston tube at the front of the locomotive. Refer to Figure T4-1. This is created from a chamfer box and an oil tank.

In the Left viewport, draw an oil tank with a radius of 30 units and a height of 150 units. Make the cap height 5 units. Center the oil tank on the Linkage, Left 05 object. Name the object Piston Tube, Left. In the Top viewport, move the oil tank to the left (negative X) 150 units.

Next, draw a chamfer box in the Top viewport. Make it 50 units in length, 120 units in width, and 70 units in height. It should have a fillet of 5 units with about 5 fillet segments. In the Top viewport, center the chamfer box on the oil tank. Then, in the Front viewport, align the chamfer box so its "bottom" is in the center of the oil tank. Select the Piston Tube, Left object and union the chamfer box to it.

Bones

You may think of bones as something used for people and animals. However, as you will see, they can be used for mechanical linkages as well. In the Front viewport, draw a bone network as follows. Do not assign an IK solution at this point. Be sure to precisely locate the bones. Refer to Figure T4-8.

- Draw the first bone from the center of Piston Tube, Left to the midpoint of Linkage, Left 05.
- Draw the second bone from the midpoint of Linkage, Left 05 to the center of the joint between Linkage, Left 05 and Linkage, Left 04.
- Draw the third bone from the center of the joint between Linkage, Left 05 and Linkage, Left 04 to the center of Linkage Pivot, Left 02.

The bones will be offset from the linkage network when viewed in the Top viewport. Select all of the bones and move them straight down in the Top viewport so they are centered on Linkage, Left 05. Be sure to move them straight down in the viewport (negative local Y). Now, set Linkage, Left 04 and Linkage, Left 05 to inherit movement and rotation on all axes. This may seem a bit illogical, but be patient. Also, set the IK joint parameters for the bones as follows.

Bone01 should have all rotational and sliding axes inactive. Bone02 should have all rotational axes inactive. In addition, Bone02 should have a sliding joint active on the X axis only. Bone03 should have all sliding axes inactive. In addition, Bone03 should have a rotating joint active on the Z axis only. Bone04 should have all rotational and sliding axes inactive.

Now, you need to assign an IK solver. Pick Bone01 and apply a history-dependent IK solver. Pick Bone04 as the last bone in the chain. Then, link the end effector on Bone04 to Linkage Pivot, Left 02.

Bones

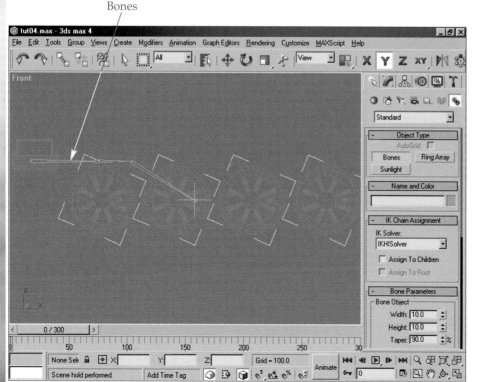

Figure T4-8. The bone network for the wheels and linkages.

Figure T4-9. The top and angled linkages should follow the motion of the linkages connecting the wheels.

Now, to complete the linkage assembly, the Linkage, Left 04 and Linkage, Left 05 objects need to be linked to the bone network. Select Linkage, Left 04 and link it to Bone03. Select Linkage, Left 05 and link it to Bone02. Now, pick the **Play Animation** button with the Perspective viewport active. The wheels should rotate in unison, the three linkages connecting the wheels should follow the wheels, and the top linkage should move in and out of the piston tube as the angled linkage follows it and the wheels. See Figure T4-9.

You can hide the "temp linkage" objects now. You do not need them any longer.

Help Cel

Remember, when linking the end effector for the animation, you do not use the **Select and Link** button.

Guide Wheels and Main Body

Looking at Figure T4-1, there are two guide wheels on the front of the locomotive. These wheels have a smaller diameter than the other four wheels. Even though there are really four small guide wheels on the locomotive, we will only model the two on the left side that will be visible in the animation.

Start by drawing a tube in the Front viewport. Make the outer radius 50 units and the inner radius 40 units. Make the tube 20 units in height. Next, draw a cone centered on the tube. Make the first radius 50 units, the second radius 0 units, and the height 20 units. The back edge of the tube and the cone should be flush. Union the tube and cone. Name the object Guide Wheel, Left 01.

Move the guide wheel down in the Front viewport so its bottom is level with the bottom of the other wheels, not counting the "lip." Then, center the guide wheel left-to-right in the Front viewport with the piston tube. Also move the guide wheel so its back is flush with the backs of the larger wheels. Animate rotation of the wheel in the Front viewport. On frame 300, the guide wheel should rotate 7200°, since it is ½ the diameter of the larger wheels. Now, make a copy of the guide wheel. Move the copy to the left (negative X) 150 units in the Front viewport. See Figure T4-10.

Figure T4-10. Two smaller guide wheels are added to the front of the larger wheels.

Now, you need to create the main body to which the wheels, boiler, and cab connect. In the Top viewport, draw a box with a length of 300 units, width of 1300 units, and height of 140 units. The box should start at X=–400 and end at X=900. The bottom of the box should be in line with the centers of the large wheels. Align the box so it is flush with the "back" of the wheels. Also draw a box with a length of 300 units, width of 200 units, and height of 50 units. In the Front viewport, align the second box so its left edge is flush with the left edge of the first box. Also, move the second box down so its top is flush with the bottom of the first box. Union the two boxes. Name the object Body. See Figure T4-11.

Help Cel

If you want to create an animation where the right side of the locomotive is visible, you will need to draw another set of wheels and bones for the right side.

Boiler and Smokestack

The boiler is simply an oil tank. In the Left viewport, draw an oil tank with a radius of 170 units and an overall height of 1200 units. Set the cap height to 45 units. Center the oil tank left-to-right with the Body in the Left viewport. In the Front viewport, move the oil tank so its left edge extends past the left edge of the body by 100 units. Also, vertically align the oil tank so its center is level with the top of the Piston Tube. Name the oil tank Boiler.

The smokestack is a simple loft object with scale deformation. First, in the Top viewport, draw a donut with an outer radius of 100 units and an inner radius of 80 units. The X coordinate of the center should be –300. This locates the smokestack near the front of the Boiler. Also, draw a straight line 300 units in length. Select the donut and create a loft object by "getting" the straight line as the path. Name the object Smokestack.

Next, apply scale deformation to the smokestack. First, add control points at 25, 80, and 90 percent along the path. Then, scale the points as follows. Refer to Figure T4-12.
- Point 0 to 45
- Point 25 to 45
- Point 80 to 100
- Point 90 to 100
- Point 100 to 50

In the Left viewport, center the smokestack left-to-right with the Boiler. Then, move the smokestack vertically until its bottom is just inside the top of the Boiler.

Help Cel

Looking at the Left viewport, the Boiler overlaps the Body and the Piston Tube.

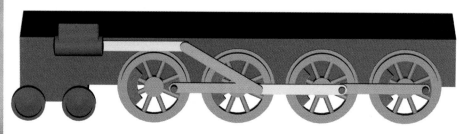

Figure T4-11. The body is created from two boxes.

Figure T4-12. The smokestack is a loft object with a scale deformation applied.

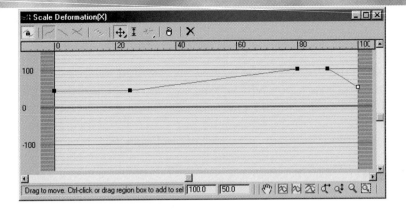

Figure T4-13. The dimensions for the spline used to create the cab.

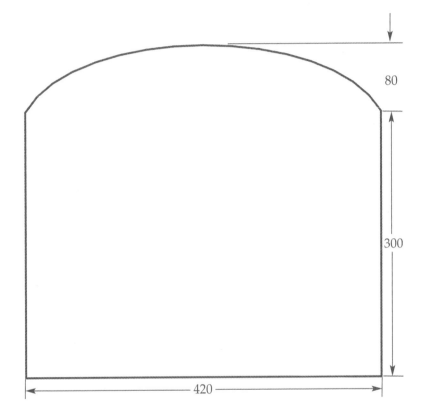

Cab

To draw the cab, first create the spline shown in Figure T4-13 in the Left viewport. Center the shape left-to-right on the Boiler. Also, align the bottom of the shape with the top of the body. Loft the shape along a 600-unit straight line. Finally, in the Top viewport, move the cab so the back overlaps the back of the body by 100 units. Refer to Figure T4-1. Name the object Cab. Make a copy named Cab Drill.

In the Front viewport, draw a box 400 units in length, 200 units in width, and 700 units in height. This box is used to cut the "notch" in the back of the cab. Align the box so that 100 units overlaps the back of the cab. In other words, the box will cut a 100-unit notch. The upper edge of the box should be just below the curved portion of the roof. In the Top viewport, center the box top-to-bottom on the cab. Finally, select the cab and subtract the box. If the drill object is displayed, you will not be able to see the notch.

In the Left viewport, select Cab Drill. Apply a nonuniform scale to 90% on the X and Y axes. In the Top viewport, move the drill object so 20 units protrude from the back of the Cab. The drill object should be centered on the Cab in the Left viewport. Select the Cab and subtract the Cab Drill object.

Now, you need to make some windows in the cab. In the Front viewport, draw a box 80 units in length, 150 units in width, and 700 units in height. Name the object Window Drill 01. Make a copy named Window Drill 02. Locate the boxes on the side of the cab as shown in Figure T4-14. In the Top viewport, center the boxes across the cab. Then, subtract the boxes from the Cab.

In the Left viewport, draw a box 60 units in length, 100 units in width, and 80 units in height. In the Top viewport, center the box across the front "wall" of the cab. Name the box Window Drill 03. Make a copy named Window Drill 04. In the Left viewport, locate the drill objects as shown in Figure T4-14. Then, subtract the boxes from the cab.

Cow Catcher and Light

The cow catcher is the pointed "nose cone" on the front of the locomotive. Start by drawing an ellipse in the Top viewport centered on the front of the Body. The length of the ellipse is 300 units (the width of the Body). The width of the ellipse is 800 units. Convert the ellipse to an editable spline. Then, delete the right-hand vertex, which is the one overlapping the body. Convert the top and bottom vertices to Bézier corners. Also, convert the left-hand vertex to a Bézier corner and "point" the shape slightly. Finally, make the right-hand segment a straight line. See Figure T4-15.

Next, loft the shape along a 200-unit straight line. Name the object Cow Catcher. Apply a scale deformation to the loft object. Scale Point 100 to 30%. Also, change the path steps to 0 and increase the shape steps to 10.

Apply a lattice modifier to the Cow Catcher. Turn off joints in the modifier. Change the radius of the struts to 10, enter 1 for the segments, and change the number of sides to 4. Do not apply smoothing to the struts. Finally, in the Front viewport, move the Cow Catcher 90 units down.

The light is basically a box with an oil tank lens. In the Left viewport, draw a box with a length of 150 units, width of 100 units, and height of 75 units. Center the box left-to-right on the Boiler. Also, move the box so its bottom rests on top of the Boiler. In the Front viewport, move the box so it is flush with the point where the Boiler end cap begins. See Figure T4-16. Name the object Light.

Figure T4-14. Place the "drill" boxes in locations similar to those of the yellow boxes shown here. These are used to create the windows.

Figure T4-15. The spline used to create the cow catcher.

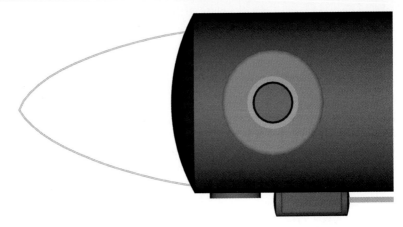

Partial Top View

Figure T4-16. The light correctly positioned on top of the Boiler.

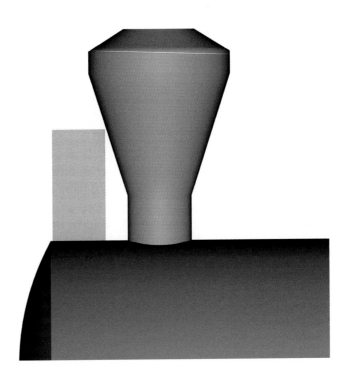

Partial Side View

In the Left viewport, draw an oil tank with a radius of 40 units and a height of 30 units. The end cap should have a height of 14.85, which is the minimum allowed. Name the oil tank Lens. Center the Lens on the upper third portion of the Light. In the Front viewport, move the Lens so its center is on the edge of the Light.

Smoke and Sparks

Two different particle systems are used to create smoke and sparks from the smokestack. First, create a super spray in the Top viewport centered on the smokestack. In the Front viewport, move the super spray up so the particles are emitted from the very top of the smokestack. Name the super spray Sparks. Make a copy named Smoke.

Next, select the Sparks super spray. Load the preset configuration named Welding Sparks. Then, change the particle quantity to a rate of 1. Change the particle speed to 10. Change the "emitter stop" and "display until" times to 300. Change the "emitter start" time to −100. Change the particle life to 10 and the particle size to 5. Change the particle type to the standard sphere. Finally, change the **Off Axis:** setting to 0.

Select the Smoke super spray. Change the particle speed to 5, the emitter start time to −100, the emitter stop time to 300, the "display until" time to 300, and the particle life to 75. Change the particle size to 175. Set the particle type to metaparticle with a tension of 0.1. Change the off axis spread to 90 and the off plane spread to 180. Check the **Automatic Coarseness** and **One Connected Blob** check boxes to turn those options on.

Finally, draw a gravity space warp in the Left viewport. Place it at the back of the Cab and perpendicular to the Boiler. Set the strength of the gravity to .25. Bind the Smoke particle system to the gravity. The Sparks particle system is not bound to any space warps.

Help Cel

Be certain you turn on the **One Connected Blob** option. The disadvantage of this option is the smoke may "disappear" on certain frames of the animation. However, if you do not use this option, rendering the animation may take literally hours or days.

Materials

Refer to Figure T4-17 and create the materials needed to complete the locomotive. A bright red material with red self-illumination is used for the sparks. A semitransparent white material is used for the smoke. The cab has a multi/sub-object material. The linkages have a composite material applied based on Metal_Black_Plain, Metal_Chrome, and the bright red material used for other parts on the locomotive. A bright yellow material is used for the light lens. Define and apply other materials as needed.

Figure T4-17. Refer to the materials shown here when defining and applying materials for the locomotive.

Details

You may want to draw two rails and some railroad ties to add detail to the model. You may also want to add ground and some sort of background, such as Meadow1.jpg located in the 3ds max \Maps\Backgrounds folder.

Create a spotlight to provide illumination from the Light and Lens. Add volumetric light to the spotlight as appropriate. Add additional lights to provide overall illumination to the scene. See Figure T4-18.

You may want to create some trees and bushes to provide more detail. Keep these simple. They are not the primary focus of the scene.

Rendering the Animation

The animation for the scene is already created. The primary motion is the wheels and linkages. These were animated at the beginning of this tutorial. To provide the illusion of motion, the locomotive stands still while all objects around it move. In order to do this, animate any railroad ties, bushes, trees, or background image you added as detail.

When all the necessary animation has been added, render a final animation to a file named tut04.avi in the folder of your choice. There are 300 frames in the animation, so this may take a while. Also, render the animation at a resolution of 320 x 240 to reduce time and save hard drive space. At higher resolutions, even 640 x 480, 300 frames of animation can quickly (or not so quickly) reach several megabytes in size, depending on the codec.

Help Cel

If you want to change the number of frames in the animation, you can use the re-scale time option in the **Time Configuration** dialog box.

Figure T4-18. Several details are added to create a realistic scene.

Questions for Discussion

1) Why is animation added to the first wheel before copies are made? How else can you achieve the same results *without* animating each individual wheel?
2) When creating the Cow Catcher object, why is the ellipse lofted instead of extruded?
3) Why is the **One Connected Blob** option used for the Smoke super spray? If the smoke disappears on some frames of the animation, how can this be corrected?
4) In this animation, the illusion of motion is conveyed by moving the scenery as opposed to the locomotive. What are some reasons why you may want to convey motion this way?

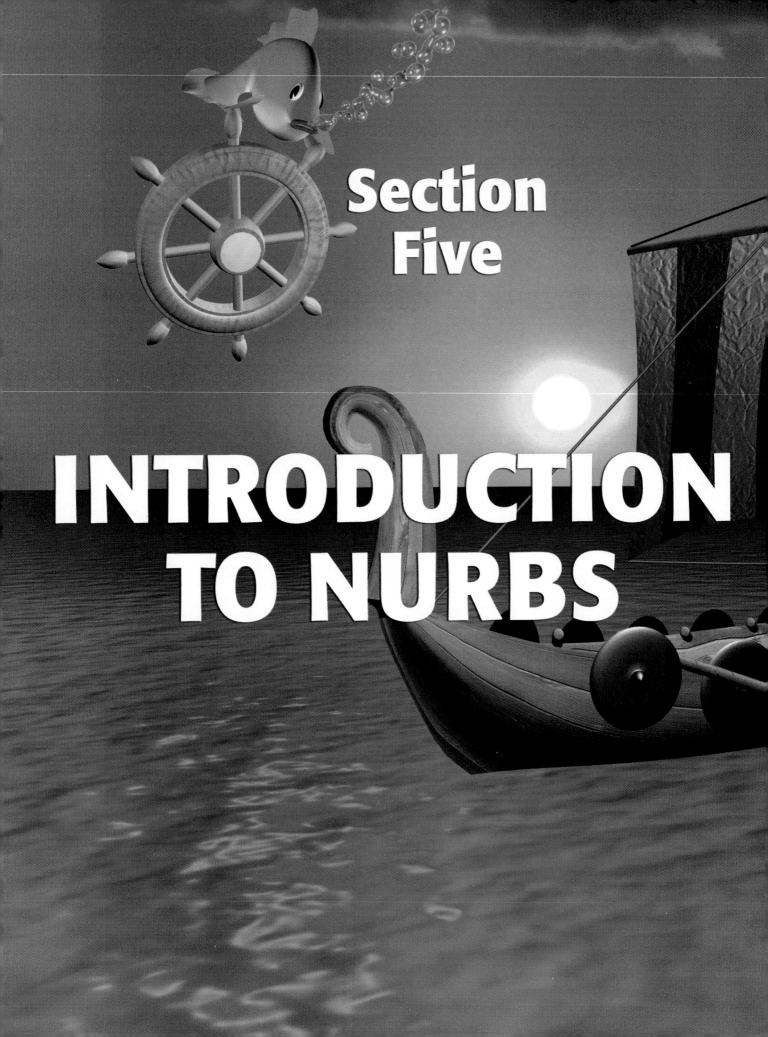

Section
Five

INTRODUCTION TO NURBS

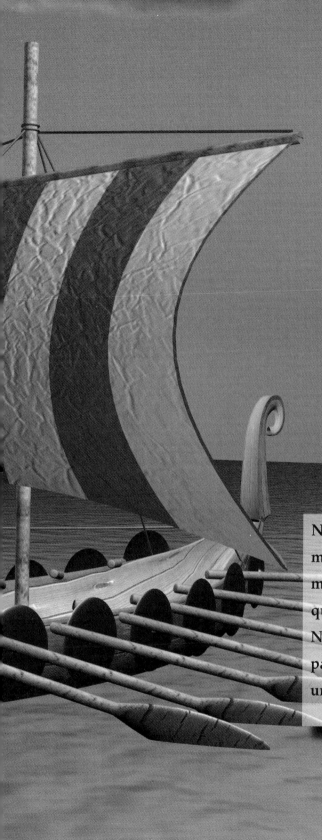

Nonuniform Rational Basis Splines, or NURBS, modeling is ideally suited for creating organic models. There are modeling tools that allow quick and easy creation of complex surfaces. NURBS models are easy to edit. Many NURBS parameters can be animated, allowing for unique and interesting animation effects.

Chapter 24

Introduction to NURBS

Objectives

- Define NURBS.
- Explain the purpose of a control vertex.
- Explain the purpose of a control lattice.
- Create independent NURBS curves.
- Create independent NURBS surfaces.
- Convert splines into NURBS curves.
- Convert standard primitives into NURBS surfaces.

What Are NURBS?

NURBS is an acronym for Nonuniform Rational Basis Spline. This chapter introduces the use of NURBS as a modeling tool within 3ds max. The name NURBS refers to the mathematical calculations used to create 3D objects. However, it is not necessary to understand the mathematics of NURBS objects to use them effectively.

Why Model with NURBS?

NURBS modeling is ideally suited for creating organic models. NURBS modeling tools make it easy to create complex surfaces, and NURBS models can offer a higher degree of smoothness than traditional mesh objects. NURBS models can also be edited easily and extensively. Many of the NURBS editing parameters can be animated, allowing for some interesting animation effects.

NURBS Components

A *NURBS model* is a collection of NURBS sub-objects that function together as a single object. Do not confuse a *NURBS model* with the scene, which is sometimes referred to as a model or 3D model. A scene, or "3D model," can contain many NURBS models. A NURBS model can contain four types of sub-objects. These are surfaces, curves, points, and control vertices.

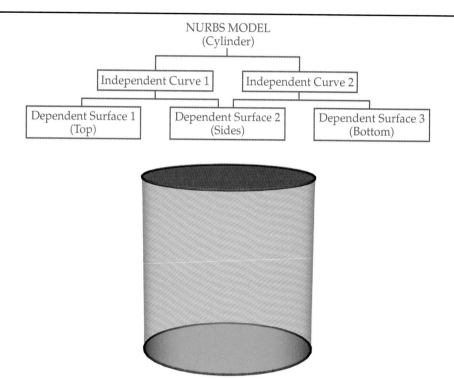

Figure 24-1. The red circles are NURBS curves, the green sides and ends are NURBS surfaces. Together, these objects constitute a NURBS model.

NURBS Hierarchy

In the hierarchy of sub-objects, *surfaces* are at the top. *Curves* follow next in the sub-object hierarchy. *Point* and *control vertex (CV)* sub-objects are at the bottom of the sub-object hierarchy. Points and CVs can exist only at the sub-object level. Curves and surfaces can exist at the top level of a NURBS model. This means that all NURBS models must contain surface or curve sub-objects, or both. For example, the following process illustrates how NURBS sub-objects are used to create a cylinder. The actual commands are discussed later.

First, begin by creating a single, circular NURBS curve. Refer to Figure 24-1. The curve is then cloned and displaced vertically to form the top and bottom edges of the cylinder. The NURBS curves are shown in red in Figure 24-1. The second curve sub-object is then attached to the first, giving you a single NURBS object, or model, consisting of two curve sub-objects. A surface sub-object is then created from the curve sub-objects, forming the visible sides of the cylinder. This surface is shown in green in Figure 24-1. Two cap surfaces are then created from the two curves, creating the visible ends of the cylinder. These surfaces are shown in dark green in Figure 24-1. The final NURBS model consists of three surface sub-objects and two curve sub-objects.

Dependent and Independent NURBS Sub-Objects

NURBS curve and surface sub-objects can be either dependent or independent. In other words, they may be child or parent objects, depending on how they are created. In some ways, you can think of this as a linked hierarchy similar to an IK hierarchy. However, these "linked" relationships can only exist between sub-objects of the same NURBS model. If the sub-objects are made independent and detached from the NURBS model, the parent-child relationship is lost.

Dependent sub-objects are the children of other sub-objects, and are affected by changes made to the parent sub-objects. Likewise, transformations applied to the dependent child sub-objects are transferred to the parent sub-objects. *Independent sub-objects* are sub-objects that are "created from scratch". This means that their geometry is in no way determined by the geometry of other sub-objects in the model.

In the previous example of the cylinder, the two curves (circles) are independent, since they are not created from another sub-object. The first surface, the outside of the cylinder, is created from the curves, and therefore a child of the curves and dependent. Any change made to either of the curves is reflected in the surface. The caps are also dependent surfaces. Each one is created from a curve, and therefore a child of the curve from which it was created.

In the viewports, dependent sub-objects are displayed in green. Occasionally, a surface sub-object cannot be properly calculated, in which case it is displayed as a group of orange lines. See Figure 24-2.

NURBS Curves

NURBS curves create the framework for NURBS models. They are used to create complex surfaces and to trim surfaces. Two basic types of NURBS curves can be created. These are CV curves and point curves. You may find point curves easier to manipulate, but using point curves to create surfaces requires more system resources.

CV Curves

CV curves are NURBS curves with control vertices (CVs). *Control vertices* are the points that lie outside the curve and define the curve's shape. The control vertices of a NURBS curve are connected by a

Figure 24-2. Two identical U loft surfaces. The surface displayed in orange has been trimmed with an open surface curve, creating an error state.

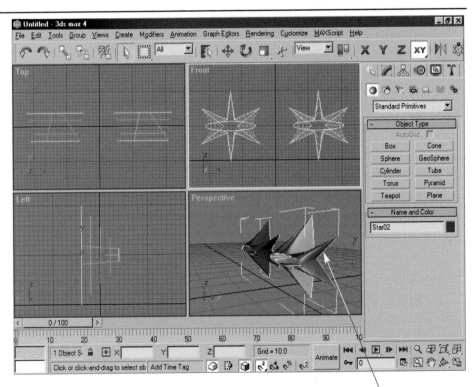

Surface edited incorrectly

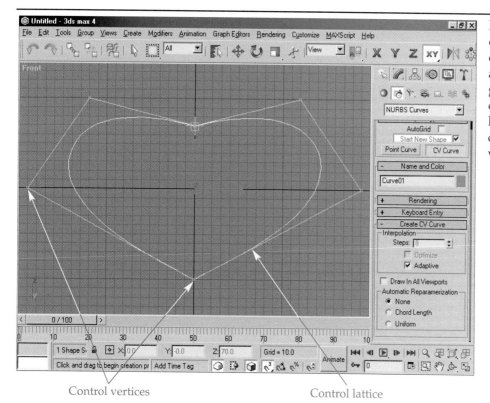

Control vertices   Control lattice

Figure 24-3. The control lattice of a CV curve is displayed as a yellow line. The green boxes connected by the lattice represent the curve's control vertices.

"control lattice," which encloses the curve. See Figure 24-3. When the CVs are moved, the control lattice is changed, in turn changing the curve's shape.

In addition, control vertices are weighted. Their assigned weight dictates how much influence they exert on the shape of the curve. As the weight of a CV is increased, the curve is drawn closer to the CV. As the weight of a CV is decreased, the CV's influence on the shape of the curve is decreased, and the curve falls away from the CV. See Figure 24-4. It is important to remember that a particular CV's influence is determined by its weight *relative* to the weight of the other CVs in the sub-object.

When control vertices are stacked directly on top of one another, they are called **coincidental CVs.** The use of coincidental CVs provides additional control over the shape of a CV curve. Two coincidental CVs increase the influence of a single point, creating a tighter curvature by pulling the curve closer to the point in space that they occupy. Three coincidental CVs cause the curve to pass directly through the point in space that they occupy. An angle or corner is created in the curve through the coincidental CVs. See Figure 24-5.

Help Cel

It is important to note that coincidental CVs can be moved individually at the sub-object level. To avoid accidentally moving coincidental CVs, it may be necessary to "fuse" them. This process is explained in Chapter 26.

Figure 24-4. Although these curves have identical control lattices and an equal number of CVs, the shapes of the two curves are different. The weight values of the corner CVs of the curve on the right have been increased.

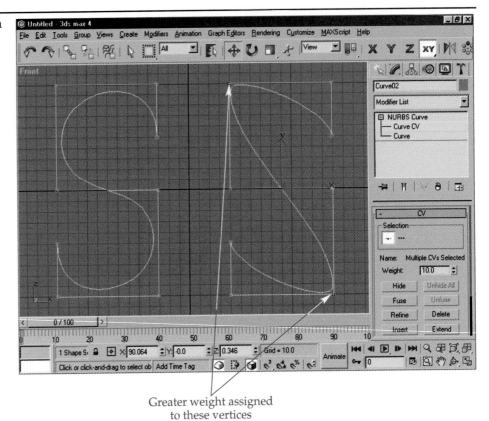

Greater weight assigned
to these vertices

Figure 24-5. The curve on the top has a single center CV. The curve in the middle has two coincidental CVs in the center. The curve on the bottom has three coincidental CVs in the center.

Single CV

Two
coincidental
CVs

Three
coincidental
CVs

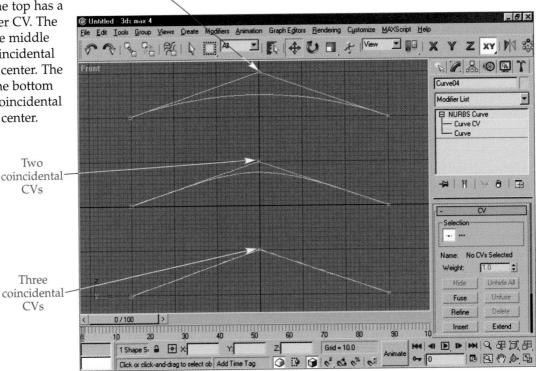

Point Curves

At the mathematical level, point curves and CV curves are the same. However, many users find it difficult to draw with CV curves. You may find it easier to draw with point curves. When creating a point curve, you simply pick points through which the curve will pass. For this reason, it is easier to "see" where points should be placed, in order to create the shape you want. However, using point curves to create surface sub-objects reduces system performance.

NURBS Surfaces

It is useful to think of NURBS surfaces as the "skin" of the NURBS model. In most instances, surface sub-objects represent the part of a NURBS model visible in the final rendering. There are two types of NURBS surfaces, CV surfaces and point surfaces.

CV Surfaces

CV surfaces are controlled by a network of control vertices, which may lie outside the surface. The network of CVs functions much like the network of control points of an FFD modifier. As with a CV curve, the control vertices of a CV surface are weighted. Their weight determines the amount of influence they exert on the geometry of the surface. The control vertices of CV surfaces can be stacked, or made coincidental, just as with CV curves. Also, as with CV curves, coincidental CVs in the control lattice may be fused to avoid accidental relocation.

Help Cel

Regardless of the creation method, all NURBS surfaces are converted into CV surfaces when made independent.

Point Surfaces

The geometry of a point surface is determined by a number of points that lie directly on the surface. When the points are moved, the geometry of the surface changes so the surface continues to pass directly through those points. This type of surface is useful in creating basic geometry, but it is not as easy to edit as a CV surface.

Forcing Two-Sided Rendering

NURBS surfaces are single-sided. Often, the normals of the NURBS model face away from the viewer. If a single sided material is applied, the surfaces may not be visible. Therefore, it may be necessary to apply a double sided material type or a material with the **2-Sided** option active. Refer to Chapter 13 *Creating Basic Materials* and Chapter 17 *Creating Advanced Materials*.

As an alternative, you can force two-sided rendering in the shaded viewport and in the final rendering. This option requires more system resources because it affects all objects in the scene. Therefore, it may be best to apply two-sided materials.

To force two-sided rendering in a shaded viewport, right-click on the viewport label. Pick **Configure**... at the bottom of the shortcut menu. Finally, check the **Force 2-Sided** check box in the **Rendering Options** area of the **Rendering Method** tab in the **Viewport Configuration** dialog box. Pick **OK** to close the dialog box.

To force a two-sided rendering, open the **Render Scene** dialog box. Pick either the **Production**, **Draft**, or **ActiveShade** radio button. Then, check the **Force 2-Sided** check box in the **Options:** area and pick the **Close** button. The next rendering created with that setting (production or draft) is rendered as if all materials are two sided. Also, **ActiveShade** forces two-sided rendering.

NURBS Snaps

You will find NURBS snaps quite handy when creating the framework for NURBS surfaces. The NURBS snaps function in the same manner as standard snaps. They make it easy to position the cursor at a specific location on an existing NURBS sub-object. For example, if you need to create a NURBS curve that runs from the endpoint of one curve to the normal of another, NURBS snaps make the job easy and precise. Some editing functions require a level of precision that cannot be accomplished using freehand techniques. In these instances, NURBS snaps are essential.

To use NURBS snaps, right-click on one of the snap buttons in the status bar, other than the **Spinner Snap Toggle** button. You can also pick **Grid and Snap Settings**... from the **Customize** pull-down menu. This opens the **Grid and Snap Settings** dialog box. Pick the **Snaps** tab and select **NURBS** from the drop-down list.

Ten check boxes are displayed for the various types of NURBS snaps. To activate a snap, simply check its check box. As soon as a check box in this dialog box is checked, the snap is activated or deactivated. This dialog box is a modeless dialog box and can remain open as you draw. Depending on which object snaps are active during a command when an object snap button is on, a cyan (light blue) helper cursor appears indicating what is being snapped to. The helper cursor icon is the same as the corresponding snap icon in the **Grid and Snap Settings** dialog box. See Figure 24-6.

Figure 24-6. The NURBS snap settings in the **Grid and Snap Settings** dialog box.

Creating NURBS Curves

There are two basic methods for creating top-level NURBS curves. They can be created from scratch, or they can be converted from existing spline shapes.

Creating CV Curves

Create

Shapes

CV Curve
CV Curve

To create a CV curve, pick **Create** in the **Command Panel**. Then, pick the **Shapes** button. Select **NURBS Curves** in the drop-down list and pick the **CV Curve** button in the **Object Type** rollout.

Notice the **Start New Shape** check box is checked by default. This check box serves the same function as it does when a spline is created. Unchecking this check box will add new curves to the current model.

A CV curve can be created using the cursor, or by using the **Keyboard Entry** rollout. See Figure 24-7. Because it can be difficult to envision the effects of CV locations on the shape of the curve when entering exact coordinates, the keyboard entry option has limited usefulness. However, it does offer the ability to adjust the weight of CVs during creation.

The procedure for creating a CV curve using the **Keyboard Entry** rollout is similar to that for creating a spline. The coordinates for each CV location are entered in the **X:**, **Y:**, and **Z:** spinners. The weight of each CV can be adjusted by changing the value in the **Weight:** spinner. Increasing the weight of a CV increases its influence on the curve's shape. Decreasing its weight decreases its influence. The **Add Point** button is then picked to create a CV at the specified coordinates. Picking the **Finish** button ends the command. Picking the **Close** button closes the curve.

When using the **Keyboard Entry** rollout, coincidental CVs are added by picking the **Add Point** button multiple times for the same coordinates. Picking the **Add Point** button twice for the same coordinates creates two coincidental CVs, increasing the curvature. Picking the **Add Point** button three times for the same coordinates creates three coincidental CVs,

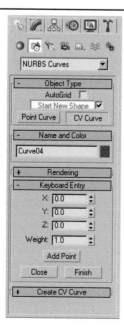

Figure 24-7. The **Keyboard Entry** rollout for a CV curve.

resulting in an angle or corner through those coordinates. Notice that as coordinates are typed in and the CVs are added, the curve appears as a solid white line.

To create a CV curve using the cursor, simply pick the first point in a viewport where the CV should be placed. A single pick (left mouse click) creates a single CV. Picking twice on the same location creates two coincidental CVs. Picking three times on the same location creates three coincidental CVs. Pressing the [Backspace] key removes the previously placed CV. Pressing [Esc] or right-clicking ends the command.

Help Cel

You may find it necessary to pause between picks, without moving the mouse, in order to create coincidental CVs.

Rendering Rollout

The **Rendering Rollout** contains controls that determine how curves are displayed in the viewports and rendered. See Figure 24-8. At the top of the rollout are the **Viewport** and **Renderer** radio buttons. When the **Renderer** radio button is active, changes made to the settings are applied to the renderer. When the **Viewport** radio button is active, changes made to settings are applied to the viewport displays. Enabling the **Viewport** radio button is discussed at the end of this section.

The value set in the **Thickness:** spinner determines the diameter of the curve. The **Sides:** spinner sets the number of sides in the curve's cross section. The **Angle:** spinner setting determines the orientation of the curve cross section. Changing this value rotates the cross section around its center point.

Checking the **Renderable** check box causes the curves to be visible in renderings. When unchecked, the curves are visible in the viewports, but not in renderings. Checking the **Generate Mapping Coordinates** check box creates mapping coordinates for the curve. Checking the **Display Render**

Figure 24-8. The **Rendering** rollout for a CV curve.

Mesh check box displays the curve as a mesh object in the viewports and makes the **Use Viewport Settings** check box available.

The **Use Viewport Settings** check box is unavailable unless the **Display Render Mesh** check box is checked. Checking **Use Viewport Settings** displays the curve "mesh" in the viewport using the current settings in the **Rendering** rollout for the **Viewport** radio button. When this check box is unchecked, the curve is displayed in the viewports using the renderer settings, and the **Viewport** radio button is disabled.

Create CV Curve Rollout

The settings in the **Interpolation** area in the **Create CV Curve** rollout determine how the curve is generated and displayed. Checking the **Adaptive** check box creates the curve with more segments in highly curved areas, and fewer segments in relatively straight areas. Unchecking the **Adaptive** check box enables the **Steps:** spinner and the **Optimize** check box. The **Steps:** spinner value determines the number of line segments used to create the curve. Checking the **Optimize** check box creates the curve using the number of segments set with the **Steps:** spinner. However, if two segments are collinear, then only a single segment is used.

Checking the **Draw In All Viewports** check box allows you to place CVs in any viewport, active or not, using the cursor. This is very useful in creating curves with CVs in three dimensions.

The **Automatic Reparameterization** area in the **Create CV Curve** rollout contains radio buttons that allow you to enable or disable automatic reparameterization. *Reparameterization* is the recalculation of a curve or surface. This recalculation is necessary when CVs are added, either by refinement or insertion.

The **Chord Length** and **Uniform** automatic reparameterization settings automatically reparameterize the curve when necessary. Chord length reparameterization is usually the best choice. This is set by activating the **Chord Length** radio button. However, with chord length reparameterization, there is the potential for the movement of a single CV to alter the entire curve. When the **Uniform** radio button is activated, uniform reparameterization is enabled and the influence of a single CV ends at its neighboring CVs. Activating the **None** radio button turns off automatic reparameterization for the selected curve.

Help Cel

Because of the hierarchical structure of NURBS models, every NURBS object created using the **Create** tab is a sub-object of a NURBS model, even if it is the only object in a scene. For this reason, the **Parameters** rollout for the object is not immediately available when the **Modify** tab is selected. The object must be selected at the sub-object level before its parameters can be changed. The editing of NURBS sub-objects is covered in detail in the next chapter.

Exercise

Exercise 24-1

1) Pick **Create** in the **Command Panel**. Next, pick the **Shapes** button and select **NURBS Curves** from the drop-down list. Finally, pick **CV Curve** in the **Object Type** rollout.
2) Activate and maximize the Top viewport.
3) Using a single pick, pick a point anywhere in the viewport. This point becomes the starting point of the CV curve. Pick again, anywhere, using a single pick to create a second point. Now move the cursor to a third location. Notice how the curve reacts as you move the cursor.
4) Select a third point and pick twice to create two coincidental CVs. As you move the cursor to select a fourth point, notice the curve passes closer to the third CV than to the second CV.
5) Select a fourth point and pick three times to create three coincidental CVs. Move the cursor back to the first CV. Notice the curve passes directly through the fourth set of CVs, forming a corner.
6) Single-pick on the first CV. When prompted, choose to close the curve. Notice how the curve is reformed.
7) Repeat Steps 3 through 6, but do not close the curve when picking on the first CV to specify the last CV. Notice the CVs remain in the locations where they were created. Right-click to end the command.
8) Expand the **Keyboard Entry** rollout.
9) Type in coordinates of your choice for the first CV of a third curve and pick the **Add Point** button. Notice nothing appears in the viewport.
10) Type in the coordinates of your choice for a second CV and pick the **Add Point** button. Notice that a straight line has formed connecting the first and second CVs. Type in coordinates of your choice for a third CV, increase the value of the **Weight:** spinner to 5, and pick the **Add Point** button. Type in coordinates of your choice for a fourth CV and pick the **Add Point** button twice. Type in coordinates of your choice for a fifth set of CVs and pick the **Add Point** button three times. Type in the coordinates of the first CV, pick the **Add Point** button, and then pick the **Finish** button.
11) Repeat Steps 9 and 10 but in the final step, pick the **Close** button instead of the **Finish** button. Notice how the curve is reshaped.
12) Reset 3ds max. Do not save the file.

Creating Point Curves

To create a point curve, pick **Create** in the **Command Panel**. Then, pick the **Shapes** button and select **NURBS Curves** in the drop-down list. Finally, pick the **Point Curve** button in the **Object Type** rollout. You can create the point curve using the cursor or the **Keyboard Entry** rollout. The options and procedures involved are the same as those for creating a CV curve.

Create

Shapes

Point Curve

Point Curve

Placing *two points* at the same coordinate location creates a corner in the curve. This can be done by picking twice at the desired coordinates for the corner, or by picking the **Add Point** button twice while the same coordinates are entered. Right-clicking or pressing the [Esc] key ends the command.

The controls in the **Create Point Curve** rollout and their functions are nearly identical to those in the **Create CV Curve** rollout. The exception to this is the automatic reparameterization function, which is not available for point curves.

Exercise 24-2

1) Pick **Create** in the **Command Panel**. Then, pick the **Shapes** button and select **NURBS Curves** from the drop-down list. Pick **Point Curve** in the **Object Type** rollout.
2) Activate and maximize the Top viewport.
3) Using a single pick, pick a point anywhere in the viewport to specify the first point of the point curve. Pick again anywhere using a single pick to create a second point. Now move the cursor to a third location. Notice how the curve reacts as you move the cursor.
4) Select a third point and pick twice to create two coincidental points. As you move the cursor to select a fourth point, notice the line remains straight, creating a corner.
5) Select a location for the fourth set of points and pick twice. Press the [Backspace] key. Notice only one of the coincidental points has been removed. Move the cursor back to the first point and single-pick. When prompted, choose to close the curve. Notice the final point is removed.
6) Repeat Steps 3 through 5, but do not close the curve. Notice the final point is made coincidental to the first. Right-click to end the command.
7) Reset 3ds max. Do not save the file.

Exercise

Converting Splines

In addition to creating NURBS models from CV curves and point curves, you can also convert a spline shape into a NURBS model. To do this, select a shape in any viewport and pick **Modify** in the **Command Panel**. Then, right-click on the spline name in the modifier stack. Select **NURBS** in the **Convert To:** area of the shortcut menu. You can also convert to a NURBS model using the quad menu. With the spline selected, right-click in the active viewport to display the quad menu. Then, select **Convert To:** in the lower-right quadrant. Finally, select **Convert to NURBS** from the cascading menu.

There are several factors to consider when converting splines to NURBS curves. First, only splines constructed from smooth or Bézier vertices will convert into a *single* NURBS CV curve. Splines that contain corner vertices or Bézier corner vertices in any location other than the endpoints will convert into *multiple* CV curve sub-objects. For this reason, it may be necessary to convert the individual vertices of a shape before changing it into a NURBS curve. However, be aware that this may alter the shape of the original spline. If the vertices are converted into Bézier vertices, the resulting shape of the spline can be adjusted using the Bézier handles. Moving the handles directly on top of the vertex creates a square corner.

Shapes constructed using Bézier corner or corner vertices include NGons, text, rectangles, and helixes. In order to create a single CV curve from one of these shapes, the shape must be collapsed to an editable spline, or it must have an edit spline modifier applied. Then, at the sub-object level, each vertex must be converted into either a smooth or Bézier vertex. It may then be necessary to reshape the spline. When this is done, the spline can be converted into a single CV curve.

Help Cel

All vertices of a spline can be converted to the same type at one time. First, convert the shape to an editable spline, or apply an edit spline modifier. Next, enter vertex sub-object mode, select all vertices in the shape, and right-click on a single vertex to display the quad menu. Select the type of vertex to convert to in the upper-left quadrant. This converts all selected vertices.

Exercise 24-3

1) In any viewport, create a spline using only Bézier and smooth vertices.
2) Select the spline and then pick the **Modify** tab in the **Command Panel**.
3) Right-click on the spline name in the modifier stack and select **NURBS** from the **Convert To:** area in the shortcut menu.
4) Expand the sub-object tree, and select the **Curve** level. Make sure the **Single Curve** button in the **Selection** area of the **Curve Common** rollout is on (depressed).
5) Select the curve. Notice the NURBS model is composed of a single curve, as indicated by the entire curve being selected with one pick.
6) Reset 3ds max without saving.
7) Create a spline using smooth and corner vertices.
8) Convert the spline to a NURBS curve.
9) Expand the sub-object tree, and select the **Curve** level. Make sure the **Single Curve** button in the **Selection** area of the **Curve Common** rollout is on (depressed).
10) Select the curve. Notice the NURBS model is composed of multiple curve sub-objects, each terminating at a former corner vertex.
11) Reset 3ds max. Do not save the file.

Creating NURBS Surfaces

Like top-level NURBS curves, top-level NURBS surfaces can be created from scratch or converted from existing geometry. The procedures involved in creating CV surfaces, point surfaces, and NURBS surfaces from existing geometry are discussed in the following sections.

Creating CV Surfaces

To create a CV surface, pick **Create** in the **Command Panel**. Then, select the **Geometry** button. Select **NURBS Surfaces** from the drop-down list, and then pick the **CV Surf** button in the **Object Type** rollout.

Create

Geometry

CV Surf

To create a CV surface using the cursor, expand the **Create Parameters** rollout. Pick the first corner of the CV surface in a viewport. Hold down the left mouse button and drag the cursor to locate the opposite corner. Then, release the mouse button. All CV surfaces created this way are rectangular, but they can be easily edited for shape later.

When a CV surface is created, a grid of white lines, yellow lines, and green rectangles is displayed between the coordinates that you specified. The white lines are the iso lines and edges of the surface. *Iso lines* represent the curvature of the surface. The yellow lines represent the control lattice for the surface. The green boxes represent the control vertices.

The control lattice indicates the extents of the influence of the CVs. A surface with many CVs has a dense control lattice, and each CV affects only a very localized area. A surface with fewer CVs has a less dense control lattice, and each vertex affects a larger area of the surface. See Figure 24-9.

Figure 24-9. The surface on the left contains 16 CVs. The surface on the right contains 49 CVs. Identical move transforms were applied to the corresponding CVs on each surface. Notice the more localized effect on the surface on the right.

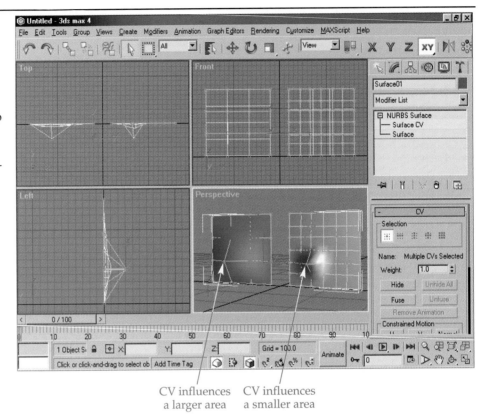

CV influences   CV influences
a larger area   a smaller area

In the **Create Parameters** rollout, dimensions for the surface can be specified in the **Length:** and **Width:** spinners. Also, the number of CVs for the surface can be changed in the **Length CVs:** and **Width CVs:** spinners. By default, this is set to 4 × 4, or 16 CVs, which allows the individual CVs very generalized influence over the shape of the surface. Adding more CVs will localize the influence of individual CVs, but it does so at the expense of system performance. Additional CVs can be added later.

Activating the **Generate Mapping Coordinates** check box in the **Create Parameters** rollout automatically generates mapping coordinates for the newly created surface. Activating the **Flip Normals** check box reverses the "up" and the "down" sides of the surface. The **Automatic Reparam.** (reparameterization) area of this rollout contains controls for setting up automatic reparameterization for the surface. Chord length reparameterization is usually the best choice. This is set by activating the **Chord Length** radio button. When the **Uniform** radio button is activated, uniform reparameterization is enabled. Activating the **None** radio button turns off automatic reparameterization for the selected surface. Reparameterization is discussed earlier in this chapter.

To create a CV surface using the keyboard, expand the **Keyboard Entry** rollout. The coordinates for the center of the surface are entered in the **X:**, **Y:**, and **Z:** spinners. Note that the surface is created on the local XY plane of the active viewport. The length and width values of the surface are entered in the **Length:** and **Width:** spinners. The number of columns and rows of CVs can be adjusted by entering new values in the **Length CVs:** and **Width CVs:** spinners. When all values are set, pick the **Create** button to create the new surface.

Exercise 24-4

1) Pick the **Create** tab in the **Command Panel**. Then, pick the **Geometry** button and select **NURBS Surfaces** from the drop-down list. Pick **CV Surf** in the **Object Type** rollout.
2) Draw a CV surface of any size in any viewport and leave it selected.
3) In the **Create Parameters** rollout, change the values in the **Length CVs:** and **Width CVs:** spinners to 6. Observe the change in the object.
4) Delete the object and activate a different viewport.
5) Create another CV surface using the **Keyboard Entry** rollout. Type in coordinates for the center of the NURBS surface, and enter values for the length and width. Pick the **Create** button. Select another viewport and pick the **Create** button again. Notice the surface is oriented to the viewport in which it is drawn.
6) Reset 3ds max. Do not save the file.

Creating Point Surfaces

The procedure for creating a NURBS point surface is the same as that for a CV surface. However, instead of a grid of control vertices, a grid of points is created. These points lie on the surface, and their positions in space directly determine the shape of the surface.

To create a point surface, pick **Create** in the **Command Panel**. Then, pick the **Geometry** button and select **NURBS Surfaces** from the drop-down list. Finally, pick the **Point Surf** button in the **Object Type** rollout.

Create

Geometry

Point Surf

To create the point surface using the cursor, expand the **Create Parameters** rollout. Pick the first corner of the point surface in a viewport. Hold down the left mouse button and drag the cursor to locate the opposite corner. Then, release the button. All point surfaces created this way are rectangular, but they can be easily edited for shape later.

The **Length Points:** and **Width Points:** spinners are used to adjust the number of points on the surface. The default is set to 4 × 4, or 16 points. Adding points to the surface gives you greater control over its shape, but decreases system performance. The other options in the **Create Parameters** rollout are the same as the corresponding options in the **Create Parameters** rollout when creating a CV surface.

When a point surface is created, a series of white lines and green boxes is displayed. The white lines are the iso lines of the surface. The green boxes represent the points. Notice the iso lines pass directly through the points. See Figure 24-10. Also notice the green boxes are "rotated" from those appearing with a CV surface. This gives a visual indication of which type of surface the model is.

To create a point surface using the keyboard, expand the **Keyboard Entry** rollout. Enter the coordinates for the center of the surface in the **X:**, **Y:**, and **Z:** spinners. Also, enter the length and width of the surface using the **Length:** and **Width:** spinners. If you wish to increase or decrease the number of points on the surface, adjust the **Length Points:** and **Width Points:** spinners. When all values are set, pick the **Create** button to create the new surface.

Figure 24-10. A point surface. Notice the white iso lines pass directly through the green diamond-shaped points.

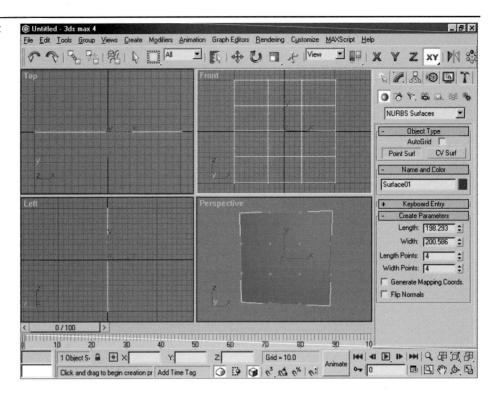

Exercise

Exercise 24-5

1) Pick **Create** in the **Command Panel**. Then, pick the **Geometry** button and select **NURBS Surfaces** from the drop-down list. Finally, pick **Point Surf** in the **Object Type** rollout.
2) Draw a point surface of any size and keep the surface selected.
3) In the **Create Parameters** rollout, change both of the values in the **Length Points:** and **Width Points:** spinners to 6. Observe the change in the object.
4) Delete the object and activate a different viewport.
5) Create another point surface using the **Keyboard Entry** rollout. Type in coordinates for the center of the NURBS surface, and enter values for the length and width. Pick the **Create** button. Select another viewport and pick the **Create** button again. Notice the surface is oriented to the viewport in which it is drawn.
6) Reset 3ds max. Do not save the file.

Converting Primitives and Other Geometry

Standard primitives, loft objects, and patch objects in 3ds max can be easily converted into NURBS surfaces. First, select the object you wish to convert, and then pick **Modify** in the **Command Panel**. Right-click on the highlighted object in the modifier stack, and select **NURBS** in the **Convert To:** area of the shortcut menu. Or, you can select the object, right-click in the viewport to display the quad menu, select **Convert To:** in the lower-right quadrant, and select **Convert to NURBS**.

When converting a primitive, you will notice NURBS surface iso lines replace the mesh lines of the primitive. The primitive is converted into a model which may contain multiple surface and curve sub-objects. Green iso lines in the model represent dependent surface sub-objects. Dependent and independent surface sub-objects are discussed in Chapter 25. You will also notice that the NURBS surface sub-objects are not affected by certain creation parameters of the original primitive, such as smoothing or segment parameters. The NURBS surface generated from a four-segmented sphere is as smooth as the NURBS surface generated from a 32-segmented sphere. See Figure 24-11.

Other types of geometry, such as extended primitives, may also be indirectly converted into NURBS models. In these cases, you must first convert the object into an editable patch. The editable patch can then be converted into a NURBS object.

Help Cel

An editable mesh cannot be directly converted into a NURBS model.

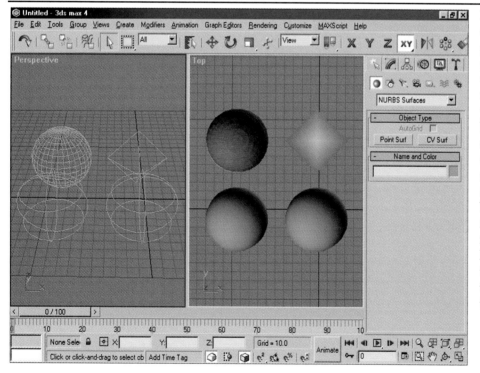

Figure 24-11. The red object in the background is a sphere primitive constructed with 32 segments, and no smoothing. The yellow object in the background is a sphere primitive constructed with four segments, and smoothing active. The blue objects in the foreground are the resulting converted NURBS objects. The two dissimilar primitives produce identical NURBS objects.

Exercise

Exercise 24-6

1) Draw a standard primitive sphere (not a geosphere) of any size in any viewport.
2) Reduce the number of segments for the sphere to 4. Uncheck the **Smooth** check box.
3) Right-click on the sphere and select **Convert To:** in the lower-right quadrant of the quad menu. Then, select **Convert to NURBS** in the cascading menu. Notice the change in the viewports.
4) Reset 3ds max. Do not save the file.

Chapter Snapshot

Chapter Test

Answer the following questions on a separate sheet of paper.

1) NURBS is an abbreviation for what?
2) How do you make a NURBS curve visible in a final rendering?
3) What is the order of objects in the NURBS sub-object hierarchy, from top to bottom?
4) What are the two basic types of NURBS curves?
5) What are coincidental CVs, and how do they affect a curve?
6) What is a control lattice?
7) How is a control lattice displayed in the viewports when a NURBS curve is drawn?
8) What effect will two coincidental points have on a point curve?
9) How do you set NURBS snaps?
10) What happens when you convert a rectangle into a NURBS object?
11) How do you convert a standard primitive into a NURBS surface?
12) How is an invalid NURBS surface displayed in the viewports?
13) How are dependent surface sub-objects displayed?
14) What happens to a point curve sub-object which is made independent?
15) How are a primitive's smoothing groups affected when the primitive is converted into a NURBS surface?

16) How are a primitive's segment parameters affected when it is converted into a NURBS curve?
17) What types of geometry can be directly converted into NURBS objects?
18) How can an extended primitive be converted into a NURBS model?
19) What are the advantages of increasing the number of CVs for a surface?
20) What is the disadvantage of increasing the number of CVs for a surface?

Modeling Problems

Draw the following models using standard and NURBS modeling techniques and your own dimensions. Convert all objects to NURBS models. Use the 3ds max objects presented in this and earlier chapters. Create and apply materials as needed, similar to those shown. Add lights and cameras as needed to create the shadows and views shown. When finished, save each model as p24-xx.max in the folder of your choice.

Memorial **1**

3-Ring Binder **2**

3 Jack-in-the-Box

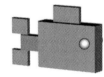

4 Snowman

Silo **5**

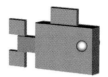

Telescope **6**

7 Whisk

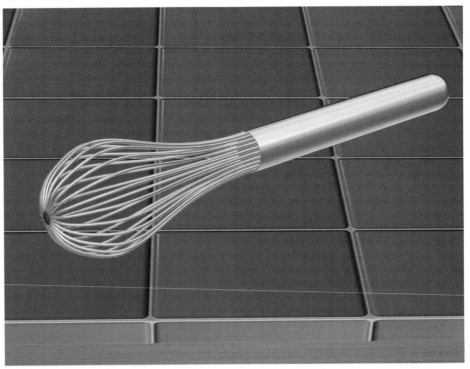

8 Banjo

Satellite Re-Entering the Atmosphere **9**

Chattering Teeth **10**

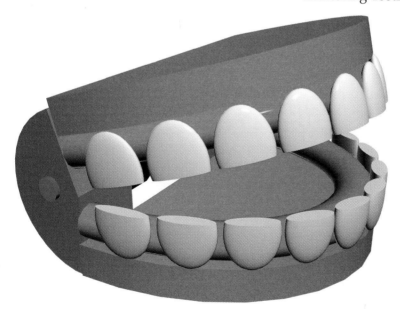

Chapter 25
NURBS Modeling

Objectives

After completing this chapter, you will be able to:

- Identify NURBS modeling components in the **Modify** tab.
- Add modifiers to NURBS models.
- Set parameters for curve approximation.
- Set parameters for surface approximation.
- Add point sub-objects to a NURBS model.
- Add curve sub-objects to a NURBS model.
- Add surface sub-objects to a NURBS model.

In Chapter 24, you learned how to create basic NURBS curves and surfaces. One of the advantages of NURBS modeling over other modeling techniques is the ease with which basic NURBS objects can be edited. In this chapter, you will learn how to manipulate basic objects to create complete NURBS models. In doing so, you learn how to modify existing objects as well as create new sub-objects.

Help Cel

The parameters rollout for a NURBS sub-object disappears once the sub-object is deselected. For the exercises in this chapter, make sure you have made all the adjustments that you wish to make to the sub-object before deselecting it. In the next chapter, you will learn how to select and adjust the parameters of sub-objects.

Modify Tab Layout

When a NURBS model is modified, the modifier that is used is added to its modifier stack. When the stack is collapsed, the effects of the modifiers are applied to the NURBS model. The resulting collapsed object is a NURBS model.

As is the case with other editable objects, modifying tools for NURBS objects are found in the **Modify** tab. The **General,** and **Curve Approximation, Create Points, Create Curves,** and **Create Surfaces** roll-outs are common to the **Modify** tab layout whether a NURBS curve or a

NURBS surface is selected. The basic **Modify** tab layout for NURBS objects is discussed in the following sections. Many of the options should be familiar from previous sections of this book. Creating sub-objects using the various rollouts is discussed in the second part of this chapter.

Applying Modifiers

To apply a modifier to a NURBS object, select the object. Then, pick the **Modify** tab in the **Command Panel**. The **Modifiers List** drop-down list contains all modifiers available for that object. When you select a modifier, it is applied to the modifier stack. You can also apply a modifier using the **Modifiers** pull-down menu.

Modifiers applied at the top level of the sub-object hierarchy affect all sub-objects in the NURBS model. Applying modifiers to only selected sub-objects of a model is covered in Chapter 26.

Modifier Stack

The modifier stack appears under the **Modifiers List** drop-down list. It serves the same function for NURBS objects as it does for other object types. The NURBS model type appears at the bottom of the modifier stack. This will be either NURBS Curve or NURBS Surface depending on the sub-objects that compose the model. All modifiers placed in the stack are added above the NURBS model type in the order in which they are applied. A plus sign next to an item in the modifier stack hierarchy indicates an expandable hierarchy tree.

General Rollout

The **General** rollout is available for all NURBS models. See Figure 25-1. Some of the controls in this rollout determine the way in which a NURBS model is displayed. Other controls are used to import or attach additional objects as sub-objects of the selected model.

Figure 25-1. The **General** rollout is displayed in the **Modify** tab when a NURBS object is selected.

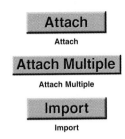

Attach

Attach Multiple

Import

Import Multiple

At the top of the **General** rollout are the **Attach, Attach Multiple, Import**, and **Import Multiple** buttons. Since most NURBS modeling is done at the sub-object level, the functions performed by these buttons are essential. Picking the **Attach** button allows you to add selected objects to a NURBS model. When added, the objects are converted to NURBS, they become sub-objects of the NURBS model, and their history is lost. Picking the **Attach Multiple** button allows you to select and add more than one object to a NURBS model at the same time.

When NURBS curves are added, they become curve sub-objects of the original NURBS model. When splines or shapes are added, they are converted into NURBS curves and are added as curve sub-objects of the original NURBS model. When standard primitives or patch objects are added, they are converted into NURBS surfaces and become surface sub-objects of the original NURBS model. The histories of the objects are lost when they are attached.

The **Import** and **Import Multiple** buttons allow you to add similar object types, but the objects retain their history. When an object is added to a NURBS model using one of the **Import** buttons, it becomes an import sub-object of the NURBS model. Imported sub-objects are displayed in green in the viewports.

Below the **Attach** and **Attach Multiple** buttons in the **General** rollout is the **Reorient** check box. Checking this check box orients the attached or imported object so its local coordinate system aligns to the local coordinate system of the NURBS model.

Help Cel

In 3D Studio MAX release 2.5 and earlier, surface objects can only be attached to NURBS models that already contain at least one surface sub-object. When working with a NURBS model containing only curve sub-objects, this can be overcome by first converting the model into a surface object by selecting **NURBS** under **Convert to:** in the **Edit Stack** shortcut menu. Additional surfaces can then be attached to the model.

Display Area

The settings in the **Display** area of the **General** rollout control how elements of NURBS objects are displayed in the viewports. Each element in the selected NURBS model is listed along with a check box. Checking the check box allows the corresponding element type to be visible in the viewports.

Checking the **Lattices** check box displays control lattices as yellow lines. You may have noticed when working with NURBS in Chapter 24 that the lattice was only displayed when the NURBS object was created. This is because the **Lattices** check box is off by default.

Checking the **Curves** check box allows the model's curve sub-objects to be visible. Checking the **Surfaces** check box allows the model's surface sub-objects to be visible. Checking the **Dependents** check box displays dependent sub-objects in green.

Checking the **Surface Trims** check box displays the effects of surface trims. Surface trims are discussed in detail later in this chapter.

Figure 25-2. The **NURBS** toolbox.

Checking the **Transform Degrade** check box allows NURBS models to degrade their display in shaded viewports during transformations. By allowing "transform degradation," system performance can be improved.

NURBS Creation Toolbox

To the right of the **Display** area in the **General** rollout is the **NURBS Creation Toolbox** button. Picking this button activates the floating NURBS toolbox. See Figure 25-2. The toolbox contains buttons that correspond to the functions found in the **Create Points**, **Create Curves**, and **Create Surfaces** rollouts. The buttons on the toolbox and the buttons in the rollouts perform identical operations. By default, the **NURBS Creation Toolbox** button is on, which is why the **NURBS** toolbox is automatically displayed when the **Modify** tab is opened with a NURBS selected.

NURBS Creation Toolbox

Help Cel

When the **NURBS** toolbox is used to create a NURBS sub-object, that sub-object's rollout becomes the only rollout available in the **Modify** tab. Once the button in the **NURBS Creation Toolbox** is disabled, all appropriate rollouts once again become available in the **Modify** tab.

Surface Display Area

The **Surface Display** area in the **General** rollout contains two radio buttons to control the display of NURBS surfaces in the viewports. For either option to be seen, the **Surfaces** check box in the **Display** area of the rollout must be checked.

Activating the **Tessellated Mesh** radio button displays the NURBS model in either iso lines or as a mesh in the viewports, depending on the viewport's setting. The precise settings for the model's appearance are made in the **Display Line Parameters** rollout.

Activating the **Shaded Lattice** radio button displays only the control lattice of a NURBS surface. In shaded viewports, the control lattice is displayed as a shaded lattice. It is important to remember that a control lattice's shape can vary greatly from the shape of the surface that it defines. See Figure 25-3.

Relational Stack

When the **Relational Stack** check box in the **General** rollout is unchecked, dependent surface sub-objects are converted into independent

Figure 25-3. These NURBS objects are identical. However, the teapot on the right (in yellow) is displayed as a shaded lattice.

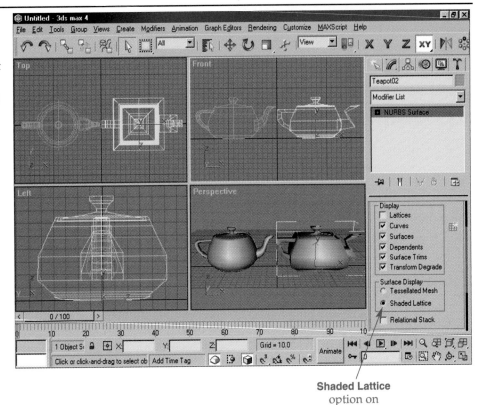

Shaded Lattice
option on

surface sub-objects before a modifier is applied to the model. This speeds up system performance, but it may result in inaccuracies in the display. When the **Relational Stack** check box is checked, dependent sub-objects retain their relationships with their parent sub-objects as modifiers are applied to the model.

To speed up system performance, apply modifiers to a NURBS model while the **Relational Stack** check box is unchecked. Once you have applied all the desired modifiers, you can restore relational modeling to ensure accuracy in the rendered file. To do this, select the base object in the modifier stack and check the **Relational Stack** check box in the **General** rollout. When you return to the top of the modifier stack, relational modeling will be restored.

Display Line Parameters Rollout

Additional display options for the appearance of NURBS models can be set in the **Display Line Parameters** rollout. The **U Lines:** and **V Lines:** spinner values set the number of iso lines used to display the NURBS model's wireframe. A higher setting increases the number of iso lines used to create the wireframe display. A large number of iso lines may be desirable when precision is important, but increased detail slows system performance. These settings have no effect on the final rendering.

The **U Lines:** and **V Lines:** spinner settings control the display of the NURBS model only when the **Iso Only** or **Iso And Mesh** check box is checked. Checking the **Iso Only** check box displays only the iso lines of the selected NURBS model in all viewports, regardless of the viewport display settings. Checking the **Iso And Mesh** check box displays the

NURBS model as iso lines in the viewports set for wireframe display. In shaded viewports, the NURBS model is displayed as a shaded surface. Checking the **Mesh Only** check box displays the NURBS model as a mesh in viewports configured for wireframe display. In shaded viewports, the NURBS model is displayed as a shaded surface.

Surface Approximation Rollout

The settings in the **Surface Approximation** rollout allow you to determine the way in which NURBS surfaces are displayed and rendered. The settings are applied to all shaded viewports or rendering displays by selecting the **Viewports** or **Renderer** radio button at the top of the rollout. See Figure 25-4.

Picking the **Base Surface** button applies the settings in the **Tessellation Method** area of the rollout to entire surfaces in the model. Picking the **Surface Edge** button allows you to set the tessellation settings for surface edges created by trim curves. Trim curves are discussed later. Picking the **Displaced Surface** button allows you to set the tessellation settings for surfaces that have a displacement map or a disp approx modifier applied to them.

Activating the **Lock** button causes 3ds max to change the tessellation settings for trimmed surface edges automatically as the **Base Surface** settings are modified. If the **Lock** button is deactivated, the tessellation settings for surfaces and trimmed edges are independent of each other, and must be set separately.

Tessellation Presets Area

The three buttons in the **Tessellation Presets** area of the **Surface Approximation** rollout allow you to apply prerecorded surface approximation settings to the model. Picking the **Low** button configures the surface approximation settings to produce a low-quality approximation. Picking the **Medium** button configures the surface approximation settings to produce a medium-quality approximation. Picking the **High** button configures the surface approximation settings to produce a high-quality approximation.

Figure 25-4. The **Surface Approximation** rollout.

Tessellation Method Area

The settings in the **Tessellation Method** area of the **Surface Approximation** rollout determine the way mesh surface approximations are calculated for NURBS objects. The settings entered with these controls only affect the viewports when the **Iso And Mesh** option or the **Mesh Only** option is activated in the **Display Line Parameters** rollout. In addition, changes made to these settings are only visible in wireframe viewports when the **Mesh Only** option is selected. These settings tessellate the model's mesh in different ways. The advantages and disadvantages of each are briefly described in the next sections.

Regular

Picking the **Regular** radio button approximates the NURBS surface with a standard, fixed tessellation based on U and V step values you enter. This method offers the quickest performance, but the least degree of accuracy. The accuracy of the mesh can be increased by increasing the values of the **U Steps:** and **V Steps:** spinners. Using the **Regular** setting may lead to unpredictable results when dealing with curved surfaces, however. As discussed in Chapter 17, UVW is another way of labeling the local XYZ axes on a given object.

Parametric

Picking the **Parametric** radio button approximates the NURBS surface with a uniform tessellation based on U and V step values you enter. This option provides a higher degree of accuracy than the **Regular** option. The accuracy of the mesh can be increased by increasing the values of the **U Steps:** and **V Steps:** spinners.

Spatial

Picking the **Spatial** radio button approximates the NURBS surface with a uniform tessellation consisting of triangular faces. The **Edge:** spinner, located under the **Spatial and Curvature** radio button, is enabled when the **Spatial** radio button is picked. This spinner allows you to set a maximum length for the faces that make up the mesh. Decreasing this value increases the accuracy of the surface approximation, but decreases system performance.

Curvature

Picking the **Curvature** radio button approximates the NURBS surface with a variable tessellation based on the surface's shape. When the surface's curvature increases, the mesh is made up of smaller faces. When the surface is flatter, the mesh is made up of larger faces. If the surface is modified, the tessellation changes to match.

The **Distance:** and **Angle:** spinners is enabled when the **Curvature** radio button is picked. The **Distance:** spinner value sets the maximum distance that the approximated mesh can stray from the actual NURBS surface. The value entered is a percentage of the diagonal length of the surface's bounding box. For this reason, meshes calculated with the curvature method can be scaled without affecting the tessellation. As this value is made smaller, accuracy increases, but at the cost of system performance. If this value is set to 0, the setting is ignored. In this case, 3ds max uses only the **Angle:** setting to calculate the accuracy of the approximated mesh. The **Angle:** spinner is used to set the greatest angle that can exist between adjoining faces in the mesh. As this angle is decreased, more faces may be created to compensate. Values ranging from 0° to 180° can be entered. If the **Angle:** setting is 0, 3ds max ignores the setting and uses the **Distance:** setting to approximate the surface.

Spatial and Curvature

Picking the **Spatial and Curvature** radio button approximates the NURBS surface with a tessellation calculated by a combination of the curvature and surface methods. For this reason, the **Edge:**, **Distance:**, and **Angle:** spinners are all active. The **Edge:** spinner value sets the maximum length of the individual faces. When this value is 0, only the **Distance:** and **Angle:** spinner settings determine the tessellation. The **Distance:** spinner value sets the maximum distance that the approximated mesh can stray from the actual NURBS surface. When this value is 0, the tessellation is determined by only the **Angle:** and **Edge:** spinner settings. The **Angle:** spinner value sets the maximum angle between adjoining faces. When this value is 0, only the **Edge:** and **Distance:** spinner settings determine tessellation.

View-Dependent

When setting surface approximation values for the renderer, the **View-Dependent** check box becomes available. Checking this check box causes 3ds max to consider the distance from an object to the camera when calculating its tessellation. This results in less accuracy but greater rendering speed for distant objects. This option only affects the rendering of perspective and camera views. It does not affect renderings of orthographic views.

Merge

The **Merge:** spinner setting determines how 3ds max matches tessellation between adjoining, or nearly adjoining, sub-object surface edges. Increasing this value increases the area considered in calculating matching tessellations for adjoining edges. This value is based on 0.1 percent of the diagonal length of the object's bounding box. Increasing this value increases rendering time, and offers quickly diminishing returns in terms of increased accuracy. In most cases, it will not be necessary to adjust the default setting. If a rendered model shows gaps between adjoining edges, you can increase the **Merge:** value until the gaps are eliminated. Be aware that this will slow system performance.

Advanced Parameters

Picking the **Advanced Parameters** button displays the **Advanced Surface Approx.** dialog box. This dialog box is used to set subdivision parameters for the **Spatial**, **Curvature**, and **Spatial and Curvature** surface approximation methods.

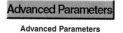

Advanced Parameters

Clear Surface Level

When the **Clear Surface Level** button in the **Surface Approximation** rollout is picked, all surface approximation settings applied to specific surface sub-objects are removed. Also, the **Lock to Top Level** check box is checked in the **Surface Approximation** rollout for all surface sub-objects. This causes all surface sub-objects to use the surface approximation settings applied at the top level.

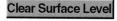

Clear Surface Level

Exercise

Exercise 25-1

1) Create a sphere in any viewport. Right-click on the sphere, select **Convert To:** from the quad menu, and then select **Convert to NURBS**.
2) The **Modify** tab should be automatically displayed. If not, display it. Then, expand the **Surface Approximation** rollout. Next, pick the **Viewports** radio button. This applies changes to only the viewport display and not the renderer.
3) Expand the **Display Line Parameters** rollout and select the **Iso Only** radio button. Notice the change in the shaded viewport. Now, select the **Iso And Mesh** radio button, and increase the **U Lines:** spinner value to 3. Increase the **V Lines:** spinner value to 5. Notice the change in the viewports.
4) Pick the **Mesh Only** radio button. In the **Tessellation Method** area of the **Surface Approximation** rollout, pick the **Regular** radio button. Notice the change in the viewports. Increase the **U Step:** and **V Step:** spinner values to 4 and notice the change.
5) Now select the **Parametric** radio button. Decrease the values in the **U Steps:** and **V Steps:** spinners to 3. Notice the change in the viewports. Decrease the spinner values to 1, and notice the difference.
6) Pick the **Spatial** radio button. Increase the value of the **Edge:** spinner to 50. Notice the change in the viewports.
7) Pick the **Curvature** radio button. Increase the value of the **Distance:** spinner to 50 and then decrease the spinner value to 1. Notice the change in the viewports. Set the spinner back to the default 20. Decrease the value of the **Angle:** spinner to 10. Notice the change in the viewports.
8) Reset 3ds max. Do not save the file.

Curve Approximation Rollout

The **Curve Approximation** rollout allows you to determine the way in which NURBS curves are displayed and rendered. When the **Adaptive** check box is checked, 3ds max determines the proper number of line segments needed to create a smooth curve. When the **Adaptive** check box is unchecked, the **Optimize** check box can be checked. A new value can then be entered using the **Steps:** spinner. More steps produce a smoother curve. However, the increased precision of the curve requires more processing time and may slow system performance.

Help Cel

The **Curve Approximation** rollout is similar to the **Interpolation** rollout for a spline.

Creating Point Sub-Objects

It may be necessary to create point sub-objects during the NURBS modeling process. Point sub-objects can be dependent or independent. They can lie on surfaces, on curves, or in space. Points are used to create fit curves, or to trim curves. The following sections briefly discuss the various types of point sub-objects that can be added to a NURBS model. Point sub-objects are added using the **Create Points** rollout in the **Modify** tab, or the corresponding button in the **NURBS Creation Toolbox**.

In viewports, 3ds max represents independent point sub-objects with white triangles. Dependent point sub-objects are displayed as green asterisks in the viewports.

Point

To add an independent point sub-object to a NURBS model, first select the model. Next, select the **Modify** tab in the **Command Panel**. Expand the **Create Points** rollout and pick the **Point** button. See Figure 25-5. You can also pick the **Create Point** button in the **NURBS** toolbox. Move the cursor to the desired coordinates in any viewport and pick. The new point appears as a white triangle in the viewports. Continue adding points or right-click to end the command. Use snaps to your advantage.

Create Point

Offset Point

Offset points are dependent point sub-objects. They are points that lie a specified distance from a parent point. To create an offset point sub-object, pick **Modify** in the **Command Panel**. Expand the **Create Points** rollout and pick the **Offset Point** button from the **Dependent Points** area. You can also pick the **Create Offset Point** button in the **NURBS** toolbox. See Figure 25-6. Select the parent point in any viewport. As the cursor passes over a potential parent, that point turns blue and the cursor turns into a cross. Pick the parent point. Right-click to end the command.

Create Offset Point

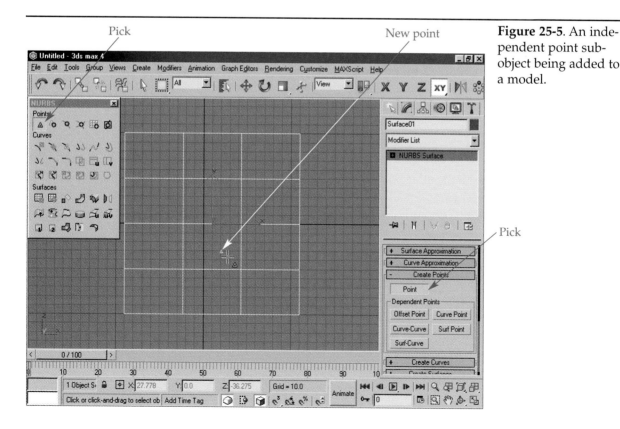

Figure 25-5. An independent point sub-object being added to a model.

Figure 25-6. An offset point sub-object being added to a model.

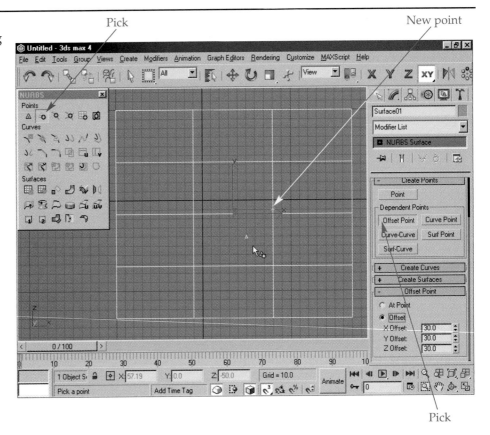

When the parent point has been picked, the **Offset Point** rollout becomes available. If the button is selected in the toolbox, this rollout is displayed immediately. Selecting the **At Point** radio button in the **Offset Point** rollout places the offset point at precisely the same coordinates as its parent. Selecting the **Offset** radio button applies the values in the **X Offset:**, **Y Offset:**, and **Z Offset:** spinners. The values entered in these spinners determine where the offset point is placed relative to its parent. Notice that as the values are changed, the distance between the offset point and its parent is represented as a dotted red line.

Curve Point

Curve points are dependent point sub-objects that either lie directly on a curve, or are offset from it. To create a curve point, pick **Modify** in the **Command Panel** with the curve selected. Expand the **Create Points** rollout and pick the **Curve Point** button in the **Dependent Points** area. You can also pick the **Create Curve Point** button in the **NURBS** toolbox. Move the cursor to the curve that is to act as a parent for the point. See Figure 25-7. Notice as the cursor passes over a NURBS curve, that curve turns blue. Also notice a blue box forms on the curve. The center of this box represents the cursor's U location on the curve. Position the box where you wish to create the point and pick. The **Curve Point** rollout is displayed. If the button is selected in the toolbox, the rollout is displayed immediately, as shown in Figure 25-7.

A curve point can lie either directly on the curve or at a position in space relative to its U location along the curve. If the point is to lie directly on the curve, pick the **On Curve** radio button. You can then set its precise

Create Curve Point

Pick   New point   **Figure 25-7.** A curve point being offset.

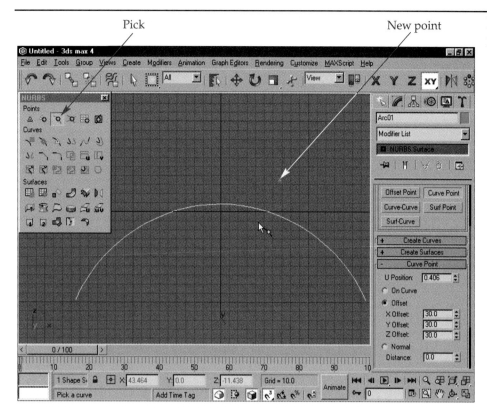

location on the curve by adjusting the **U Position:** spinner. The **U Position:** spinner value determines the point's position along the curve's U axis, where 0.0 is the starting point and 1.0 is the endpoint of the curve.

If the point is to lie away from the curve, one of three methods for placing the point must be chosen. Picking the **Offset** radio button in the **Curve Point** rollout places the point at a location in space relative to the curve's location. Picking the **Normal** radio button places the point at a specific distance along the curve's normal at the point's U position. Picking the **Tangent** radio button places the point at a specific distance along the curve's tangent at the point's U location.

If the point is to be offset from the curve, pick the **Offset** radio button. This applies the values in the **X Offset:**, **Y Offset:**, and **Z Offset:** spinners. The values entered in these spinners determine the point's location in space. Notice that a dotted red line is drawn between the point's U position and its relative position in space. The point's U location can be adjusted using the **U Position:** spinner.

Pick the **Normal** radio button if you wish to offset a point along the curve's normal at the point's U location. When this option is selected, the value in the **Distance:** spinner is applied. The value entered in this spinner determines how far along the curve's normal the point is placed. A dotted red line represents the distance between the point on the normal and the point's U location. Changing the value of the **U Position:** spinner changes the point's U position on the curve.

Pick the **Tangent** radio button if you wish to offset a point at a position tangent to the point's U location. The **U Tangent:** spinner is used to move the point away from the curve, along its tangent at the point's U location.

Checking the **Trim Curve** check box in the **Trimming** area of the **Curve Point** rollout trims the curve at the location of the point. Checking the **Flip Trim** check box switches the portion of the curve that is kept with the portion that is trimmed. After a NURBS curve is trimmed, it is still possible to adjust the point's U location and offset values.

Curve-Curve Intersection Point

A *curve-curve point* is a dependent point sub-object that lies at the intersection of two NURBS curve sub-objects. To create a curve-curve point, select a NURBS model that has two intersecting curve sub-objects. Next, open the **Modify** tab. Expand the **Create Points** rollout and pick the **Curve-Curve** button in the **Dependent Points** area. You can also pick the **Create Curve-Curve Point** button in the **NURBS** toolbox.

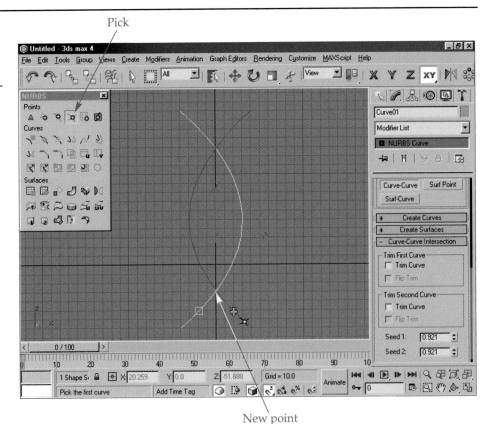

Create Curve-Curve Point

As the cursor passes over NURBS curve sub-objects, those curves turn blue. A blue box appears on the curve, and follows the cursor's movement along the curve. Pick the first of two intersecting curves. The U location of the point you pick becomes the location of the first seed. 3ds max uses seeds to determine the nearest point of intersection between the two curves in case they intersect more than once. Move the cursor to the second curve and pick a point for the second seed. 3ds max locates a point where the two curves intersect nearest to the two seeds. The point appears as a green asterisk, and the seed locations are marked by yellow boxes. See Figure 25-8.

When both parents for the curve-curve point have been chosen, the **Curve-Curve Intersection** rollout is displayed. This rollout is displayed immediately if the button is selected from the toolbox. The **Trim First Curve**

Figure 25-8. A curve-curve intersection point (displayed as a green asterisk) being placed at the intersection determined by the seeds (displayed as blue and yellow boxes).

area of this rollout contains the **Trim Curve** and **Flip Trim** check boxes. Checking the **Trim Curve** check box trims the first parent curve at the point of intersection. Checking the **Flip Trim** check box switches the portion of the curve that is kept with the portion that is discarded. The **Trim Second Curve** area of the **Curve-Curve Intersection** rollout contains identical controls for trimming the second parent curve.

The **Seed 1:** and **Seed 2:** spinners in the **Curve-Curve Intersection** rollout are used to relocate the seeds. If the parent curves intersect at multiple locations, adjusting the values of these spinners allows you to place the curve-curve point at the desired intersection. For CV curves, these spinner values can range from 0 to 1, where 0 is the beginning of the curve and 1 is the end of the curve. For point curves, these spinner values can range from 0 to the length of the curve. As with CV curves, the starting point of the curve is located at a U position of 0.

If you choose two nonintersecting curves as the parents for a curve-curve point, 3ds max places an orange asterisk at the location of the first seed. This indicates the program is unable to locate an intersection between the parent curves. However, if the parent curves are later edited so they intersect, the curve-curve point will jump to the intersection and turn green.

Exercise 25-2

Exercise

1) In any viewport, create two separate CV curves that intersect in two locations, similar to those shown in Figure 25-8. With the second curve selected, open the **Modify** tab in the **Command Panel**. Pick the **Attach** button in the **General** rollout, and pick the first curve to attach it to the second.

2) Expand the **Create Points** rollout and pick the **Point** button.

3) Pick anywhere in the viewport to create an independent point sub-object.

4) Pick the **Offset Point** button in the **Create Points** rollout. Pick the point you created in Step 3.

5) In the **Offset Point** rollout, enter a value of 30 in each of the **X Offset:**, **Y Offset:**, and **Z Offset:** spinners. Notice the new position of the offset point in the viewport.

6) Pick the **Curve Point** button in the **Create Points** rollout. Pick anywhere on either curve to create a curve point.

7) In the **Curve Point** rollout, pick the **Offset** radio button. Set the **X Offset:**, **Y Offset:**, and **Z Offset:** spinner values to 30. Notice the new position of the curve point.

8) Pick the **Normal** radio button and set the **Distance:** spinner value to 30. Notice the new location of the curve point.

9) Pick the **Tangent** radio button and set the **U Tangent:** spinner value to 100. Notice the location of the point. Now, set the **U Tangent:** spinner value to –100. Notice the change. Check the **Trim Curve** check box, and notice where the curve is trimmed. Now check the **Flip Trim** check box.

(continued)

Exercise

Exercise 25-2 *(Continued)*

10) Uncheck both trim check boxes and pick the **Curve-Curve** button in the **Create Points** rollout.

11) Pick a point on one of the curves near an intersection. Next, pick a point on the second curve near the same intersection.

12) In the **Curve-Curve Intersection** rollout, set the **Seed 1:** and **Seed 2:** spinner values to 0. Now, gradually increase the value of the **Seed 1:** spinner until the intersection point jumps to the other curve intersection. If the point does not jump to the other intersection, gradually increase the **Seed 2:** spinner value until it does.

13) Experiment with the **Trim Curve** and **Flip Trim** check boxes as you adjust the seeds.

14) Reset 3ds max. Do not save the file.

Surf Point

Create Surf Point

Surface points are dependent point sub-objects that have surfaces as their parents. Surface points can either lie directly on a surface or at a location in space relative to a fixed location on the surface.

To create a surface point sub-object, select a NURBS model containing at least one surface sub-object. Open the **Modify** tab and expand the **Create Points** rollout. In the **Dependent Points** area of the rollout, pick the **Surf Point** button. You can also pick the **Create Surf Point** button in the **NURBS** toolbox

Position the cursor over the surface sub-object. A pair of intersecting blue lines form on the surface. These intersecting blue lines represent the U and V locations for the point. Pick at the desired location to create the surface point. If the surface is not planar, you will need to be careful that you place the point on the appropriate "side" of the surface.

Once the point is created, you can change its location using the spinners in the **Surface Point** rollout. Changing the **U Position:** and **V Position:** spinners repositions the point on the surface. If the **On Surface** radio button is active, the point's location is determined by its U and V values alone (no W).

If the **Offset** radio button is active, the point's location in space is determined by a combination of the **X Offset:**, **Y Offset:**, and **Z Offset:** spinner values, and the **U Position:** and **V Position:** spinners. The U and V positions determine the point's base position on the surface. The **X Offset:**, **Y Offset:**, and **Z Offset:** spinners determine the direction and distance that the point is offset from its U and V position on the surface. A dotted red line is drawn between the point and its UV position on the surface. See Figure 25-9.

If the **Normal** radio button is activated, the point's location in space is determined by a combination of its UV position on the surface and a distance perpendicular to the surface at that location. Increasing the value of the **Distance:** spinner moves the point away, perpendicular to the surface. Entering negative values moves the point away from the surface in a direction opposite to the normal. A dotted red line is drawn between the point and its UV position on the surface.

If the **Tangent** radio button is activated, the point's location in space is determined by its UV position on the surface and a distance tangent to

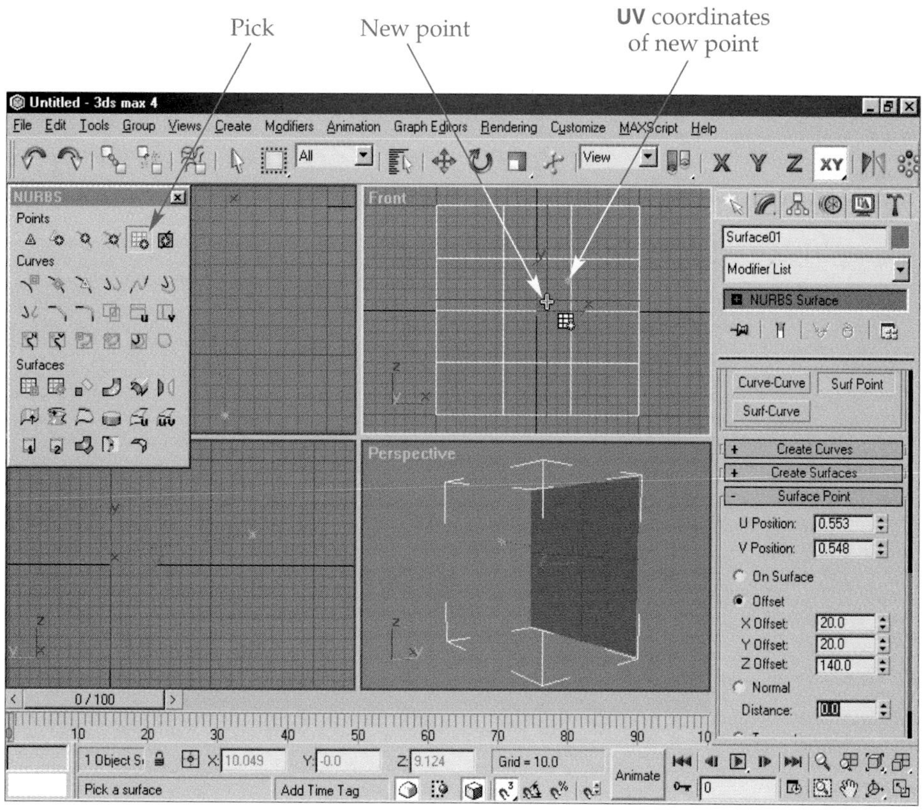

Pick　　New point　　**UV** coordinates
of new point

Figure 25-9. A surface point being offset.

[Screenshot of 3ds max 4 interface showing NURBS surface point being offset, with Surface Point rollout displaying U Position: 0.553, V Position: 0.548, Offset selected with X Offset: 20.0, Y Offset: 20.0, Z Offset: 140.0]

the surface at that location. The point can be placed anywhere in the plane defined by the U and V tangents. The **U Tangent:** spinner value determines the point's position along the axis defined by the U tangent. The **V Tangent:** spinner value determines the point's position along the axis defined by the V tangent.

Surf-Curve Intersection Point

A *surface-curve intersection point* is a dependent point sub-object that lies at the intersection of a parent curve sub-object and a parent surface sub-object. To create a surface-curve intersection point, select a NURBS model with intersecting curve and surface sub-objects. Open the **Modify** tab and expand the **Create Points** rollout. Finally, pick the **Surf-Curve** button. You can also pick the **Create Surface-Curve Point** button in the **NURBS** toolbox.

Move the cursor over the curve. The curve is highlighted in blue, and a blue box trails the cursor. Position the cursor over the desired location for the seed and pick. 3ds max will place the point at the intersection nearest to this seed. Now, move the cursor to the surface sub-object. The surface is highlighted in blue as the cursor passes over it. Pick anywhere on the surface to create a surface-curve intersection point at the intersection nearest to the seed on the curve. See Figure 25-10.

The **Surface-Curve Intersection Point** rollout is displayed when the **Surf-Curve** button or **Create Surface-Curve Point** button is selected. The **Trim Curve** area in this rollout is used to control trimming of the curve. The **Seed:** spinner at the bottom of the rollout is used to reposition the seed along the curve. If there are multiple intersections between the surface and the curve, 3ds max creates the point at the intersection nearest to the seed.

Create Surface-Curve Point

Figure 25-10. A surface-curve intersection point being placed at the intersection determined by the seed.

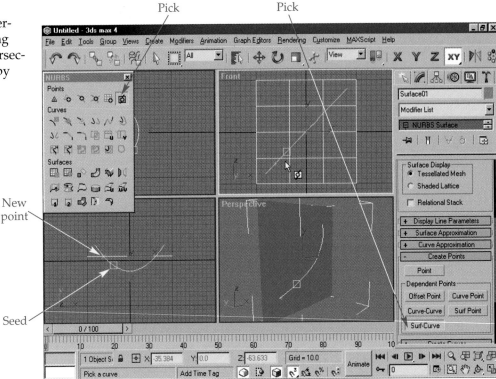

Exercise

Exercise 25-3

1) Create a sphere in any viewport. Right-click on the sphere and select **Convert To:** and then **Convert to NURBS** from the quad menu.
2) In the **Modify** tab of the **Command Panel**, expand the **Create Points** rollout and pick the **Surf Point** button.
3) Move the cursor over the surface of the sphere. The intersection of the blue iso lines shows the cursor's relative position on the surface. Pick to place a point anywhere on the surface.
4) In the **Surface Point** rollout, adjust the **U Position:** and **V Position:** spinners to relocate the point on the surface. Now, select the **Offset** radio button and set each of the three **Offset:** spinners to 30. Notice the new position of the point.
5) Select the **Normal** radio button and set the **Distance:** spinner to 50. Notice the new location of the point. Adjust the **U Position:** and **V Position:** spinners. What happens to the point's location?
6) Select the **Tangent** radio button. Set both **Tangent:** spinners to 50. Notice the point's new location. Now, set both **Tangent:** spinners to –50. Notice the change in the point's location.
7) Open the **Create** tab and draw a CV curve. Position it so it passes through the sphere. Next, attach the curve to the sphere.
8) Pick the **Surf-Curve** button from the **Create Points** rollout. Pick the curve at a location near an intersection with the surface. Next, pick the surface. Notice the position of the point. Now, gradually increase or decrease the value in the **Seed:** spinner in the **Surface-Curve Intersection Point** rollout. Continue to adjust the spinner value until the surface-curve intersection point jumps to the other curve intersection.
9) Reset 3ds max. Do not save the file.

Creating Independent Curve Sub-Objects

Independent CV curve and point curve sub-objects can be added to an existing NURBS model. An independent curve added using the **Modify** tab automatically becomes a sub-object of the NURBS model that is selected when it is created. The same result is accomplished when a NURBS curve is created using the **Create** tab, and then attached to an existing NURBS model.

Independent CV Curves

To draw an independent CV curve sub-object, select a NURBS model and open the **Modify** tab. Then, pick the **CV Curve** button in the **Create Curves** rollout. The **CV Curve** rollout is displayed. See Figure 25-11. You can also pick the **Create CV Curve** button in the **NURBS** toolbox.

Checking the **Draw In All Viewports** check box in the **CV Curve** rollout allows you to place CVs in any viewport, whether it is active or not. To place a single CV, position the cursor over the appropriate coordinates and click once. To create two coincidental CVs, position the cursor over the appropriate coordinates and click twice. To create three coincidental CVs, position the cursor over the appropriate coordinates and click three times. Two coincidental CVs increase the amount of curvature in the curve. Three coincidental CVs create a sharp angle or corner in the curve. Right-click to end the command.

The **Automatic Reparam.** (reparameterization) area in the **CV Curve** rollout contains radio buttons that allow you to enable or disable

Create CV Curve

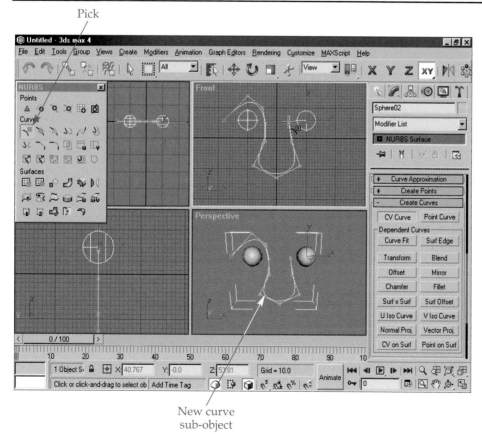

Pick

New curve
sub-object

Figure 25-11. Creating an independent CV curve.

automatic reparameterization. Chord length reparameterization is usually the best choice. This is set by picking the **Chord Length** radio button. However, with chord length reparameterization, there is the potential for the movement of a single CV to alter the entire curve. When the **Uniform** radio button is activated, uniform reparameterization is enabled and the influence of a single CV ends at its neighboring CVs. Activating the **None** radio button turns off automatic reparameterization for the selected curve.

Independent Point Curves

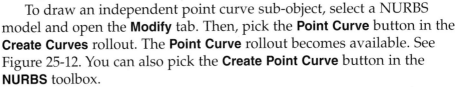

Create Point Curve

To draw an independent point curve sub-object, select a NURBS model and open the **Modify** tab. Then, pick the **Point Curve** button in the **Create Curves** rollout. The **Point Curve** rollout becomes available. See Figure 25-12. You can also pick the **Create Point Curve** button in the **NURBS** toolbox.

Checking the **Draw In All Viewports** check box allows you to place points in any viewport, whether it is active or not. To place a single point, position the cursor over the appropriate coordinates and click once. To create coincidental points, position the cursor over the appropriate coordinates and click twice. Coincidental points create a sharp angle or corner in the curve. Right-click to end the command.

Figure 25-12. Creating an independent point curve.

Pick

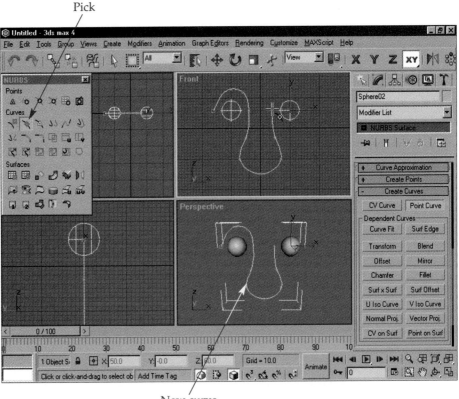

New curve
sub-object

Creating Dependent Curve Sub-Objects

Various types of dependent curve sub-objects can be added to NURBS models using the **Create Curves** rollout in the **Modify** tab. The following sections discuss the types of dependent curves that use point, curve, and surface sub-objects as their parents.

Help Cel

Dependent curves contain no point or CV sub-objects. Their shapes are dependent on their parent sub-objects rather than their own point or CV sub-objects.

Fit Curve

A *fit curve* is a dependent point curve sub-object between existing point sub-objects in the NURBS model. Any combination of existing point sub-objects can be used to create fit curves. They can be drawn between independent points, offset points and curve points, intersection points and surface points, and so on. The only restriction is that all points used in a fit curve must be sub-objects of the same NURBS model.

To create a fit curve, select the NURBS model and open the **Modify** tab in the **Command Panel**. Expand the **Create Curves** rollout and pick the **Curve Fit** button in the **Dependent Curves** area. You can also pick the **Create Fit Curve** button in the **NURBS** toolbox. Pick the points through which you wish the new curve to pass. Right-click to end the command. See Figure 25-13.

Create Fit Curve

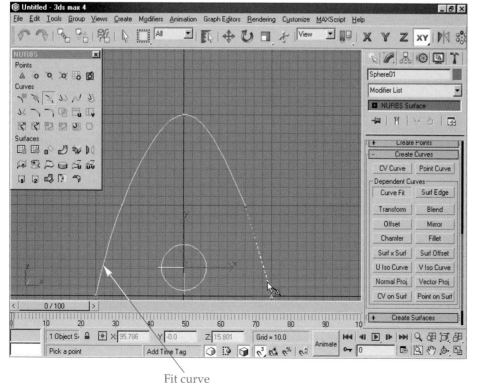

Figure 25-13. A fit curve being created between independent points.

Fit curve

Help Cel

A fit curve is unique among dependent curve sub-objects. You will notice that, unlike other dependent curve sub-objects, the fit curve is displayed in white rather than green. For all practical purposes, a fit curve behaves as an independent point curve. However, it is classified as dependent because it is created between existing points. If a fit curve is deleted, the points used to create it remain.

Transform Curve

A *transform curve* is a duplicate of its parent curve. Transform curves can be transformed or modified at the sub-object level without affecting the parent curve. However, if the parent curve is transformed or modified, that change is reflected in the transform curve.

To create a transform curve, select a NURBS model containing a curve and open the **Modify** tab in the **Command Panel**. Expand the **Create Curves** rollout and pick the **Transform** button in the **Dependent Curves** area. You can also pick the **Create Transform Curve** button in the **NURBS** toolbox.

Create Transform Curve

As the cursor passes over a NURBS curve sub-object, that curve turns blue and the cursor becomes a white cross. Pick the curve. Holding down the mouse button, drag the transform curve to the location you wish to place it. See Figure 25-14. Release the mouse button to place the curve. The transform curve is a duplicate of the parent curve, but the point sub-objects of the parent curve are not duplicated.

Figure 25-14. Creating a transform curve.

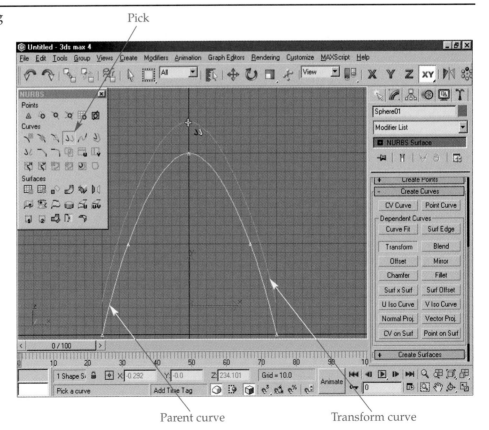

Pick

Parent curve

Transform curve

Offset Curve

An *offset curve* is a dependent curve sub-object that is perpendicular to the normals of its parent curve at all points, regardless of its distance from the parent. For this reason, the curvature of the offset curve is adjusted according to its distance from the parent curve.

To create an offset curve, select a NURBS model containing a curve and open the **Modify** tab in the **Command Panel**. Expand the **Create Curves** rollout and pick the **Offset** button in the **Dependent Curves** area. The **Offset Curve** rollout is displayed. You can also pick the **Create Offset Curve** button in the **NURBS** toolbox.

Create Offset Curve

When the cursor is over a NURBS curve, the curve turns blue and the cursor becomes a white cross. Pick the curve. Hold down the mouse button and drag the offset curve the desired distance from the parent. You can only move the offset curve in a direction normal to the parent curve. Notice that the curvature of the offset curve increases the farther it is dragged from its parent. See Figure 25-15. The **Offset:** spinner in the **Offset Curve** rollout can also be used to set the offset distance. The point sub-objects of the parent curve are not duplicated in the offset curve.

Figure 25-15. Creating offset curves. Notice the change in curvature as the distance between the parent curve and offset curve increases.

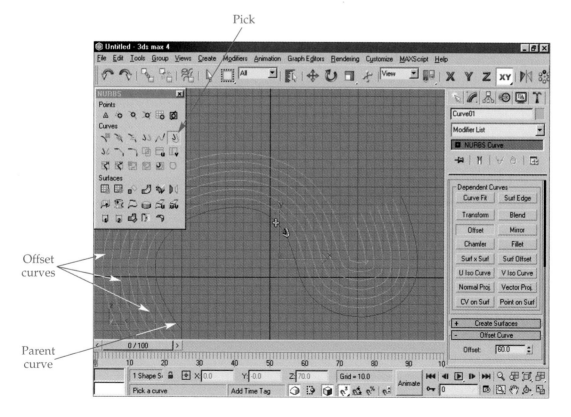

Exercise

Exercise 25-4

1) In any viewport, create two point curves. Either uncheck the **Start New Shape** check box when creating the second curve or attach it to the first curve.
2) Open the **Modify** tab in the **Command Panel** and expand the **Create Curves** rollout. Pick the **Curve Fit** button.
3) Pick the starting point of the first curve. Pick any point on the second curve, and then any point on the first curve. Right-click to end the command.
4) Pick the **Transform** button. Pick the fit curve you just created. While holding down the mouse button, drag the transform curve away from its parent. Release the mouse button to locate the new curve.
5) Pick the **Offset** button in the **Create Curves** rollout. Pick the curve that has the most curvature. While holding down the mouse button, drag the offset curve away from its parent. Notice the change in the curvature of the offset curve. Now, move the offset curve away from its parent in the opposite direction. Notice the change in the curvature of the offset curve. Release the mouse button to end the command.

Chamfer Curve

A *chamfer curve* is a straight line between two intersecting parent curve sub-objects. Chamfer curves can be used to trim one or both of the parent curves. You can also choose to leave the parent curves untrimmed.

To create a chamfer curve, select a NURBS model containing intersecting curve sub-objects. Open the **Modify** tab in the **Command Panel** and expand the **Create Curves** rollout. Pick the **Chamfer** button from the **Dependent Curves** area. The **Chamfer Curve** rollout is displayed. You can also pick the **Create Chamfer Curve** button in the **NURBS** toolbox.

Create Chamfer Curve

Position the cursor over the first curve. The curve turns blue and a blue box follows the cursor along the curve. Position the blue box over the location where you wish to place the first seed. The seeds are used to determine which intersection is chamfered. Now position the cursor over the second intersecting curve. A dotted white line extends between the first seed and the cursor. See Figure 25-16. Pick any point along the curve to place the second seed and create the chamfer curve.

If 3ds max is unable to calculate a valid chamfer for the curves, an orange line is drawn between the two seeds. You will need to adjust the chamfer curve's parameters in order to create a valid chamfer.

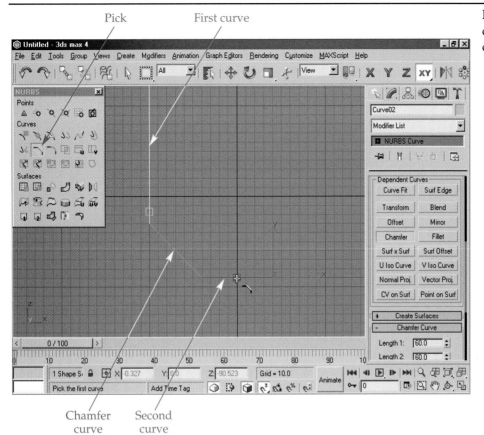

Figure 25-16. A chamfer curve being created.

The **Chamfer Curve** rollout allows you to modify the chamfer curve's parameters. The **Length 1:** spinner value sets the location of the chamfer curve's starting point. The **Length 2:** spinner value sets the endpoint for the chamfer curve. These values represent the starting point and endpoint distances from the intersection.

Checking the **Trim Curve** check box in the **Trim First Curve** area trims the first parent curve at the starting point of the chamfer curve. Checking the **Flip Trim** check box switches the portion of the curve that is kept with the portion that is discarded. Checking the **Trim Curve** check box in the **Trim Second Curve** area trims the second parent curve at the endpoint of the chamfer curve. Checking the **Flip Trim** check box switches the portion of the curve that is kept with the portion that is discarded.

Changes to the **Seed 1:** and **Seed 2:** spinners reposition the seeds, allowing you to change the intersection that is being chamfered, or change which side of an intersection is being chamfered. Four different chamfer curves can be created for a single intersection, so placement of the seeds is critical. See Figure 25-17.

Figure 25-17. A chamfer curve can be created in four locations on a pair of crossing curves. The seeds determine the placement of the chamfer curve.

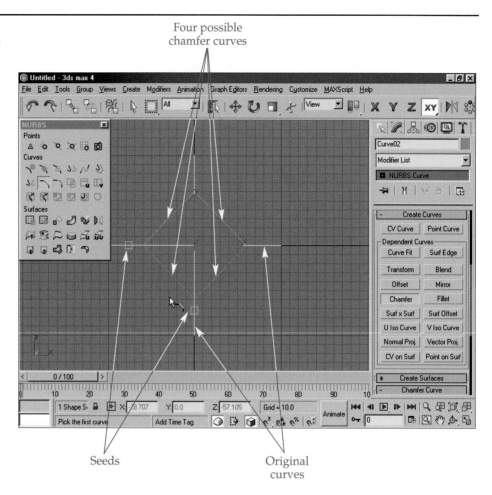

Four possible chamfer curves

Seeds

Original curves

Exercise

Exercise 25-5

1) In any viewport, create two CV curves that intersect in two locations. Then, open the **Modify** tab in the **Command Panel**. Pick the **Attach** button and attach the first curve to the second.

2) Expand the **Create Curves** rollout and pick the **Chamfer** button.

3) Pick a point on the first curve near one intersection. Next, pick a point on the second curve near the same intersection. Increase the values of the **Length 1:** and **Length 2:** spinners. Notice what happens to the chamfer curve.

4) Experiment with changing the values of the **Seed 1:** and **Seed 2:** spinners. Notice how the chamfer curve jumps from one side of the intersection to the other, and from intersection to intersection.

5) Check the **Trim Curve** check boxes. Note the results. Now check the **Flip Trim** check boxes and note the results.

6) Reset 3ds max. Do not save the file.

Blend Curve

A *blend curve* is a dependent curve sub-object that connects the endpoints of two parent curve sub-objects. The curvature of the blend curve is extrapolated from the parent curves. Blend curves can be created between any two curve sub-objects of the same model, regardless of their type.

To create a blend curve, select a NURBS model that contains two or more curve sub-objects. Open the **Modify** tab in the **Command Panel** and expand the **Create Curves** rollout. Pick the **Blend** button in the **Dependent Curves** area. The **Blend Curve** rollout is displayed. You can also pick the **Create Blend Curve** button in the **NURBS** toolbox.

Position the cursor over the first curve to use in the blend. The curve turns blue and the cursor changes to a white cross. A blue box appears at the endpoint nearest to the cursor. Pick the endpoint where you wish to start the blend. Move the cursor to the second curve to be used in the blend. A dotted white line is drawn between the first endpoint and the cursor. The second curve turns blue and a blue box appears at the endpoint nearest to the cursor. Pick the appropriate second endpoint to create the blend curve.

You can modify the blend curve with the spinners in the **Blend Curve** rollout. Increasing the values of the tension spinners pulls the blend curve closer to the tangent of each parent curve, creating a smoother transition. Decreasing the values allows the blend curve to fall farther from the tangent of each parent, creating a less smooth transition. The **Tension 1:** spinner value affects the transition between the first parent curve and the blend curve. The **Tension 2:** spinner value affects the transition between the second parent curve and the blend curve. See Figure 25-18.

Create Blend Curve

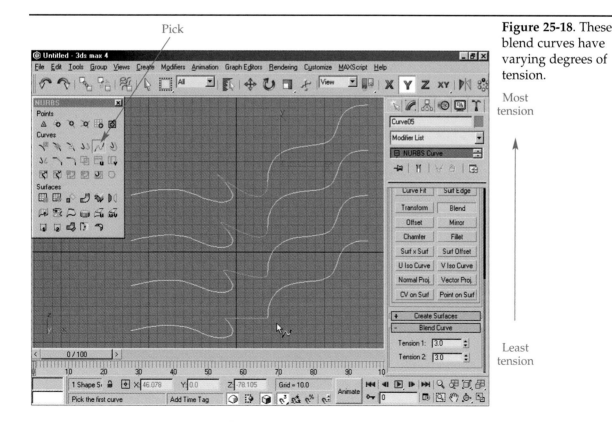

Figure 25-18. These blend curves have varying degrees of tension.

Most tension

Least tension

Exercise

Exercise 25-6

1) In any viewport, create one L-shaped point curve and one L-shaped CV curve. Draw the curves so that the endpoints are roughly in line with each other, as seen in the figure below. Then, open the **Modify** tab in the **Command Panel**. Attach the first curve to the second.
2) Expand the **Create Curves** rollout and pick the **Blend** button.
3) Pick an endpoint on the first curve. Next, pick the endpoint on the second curve that is the closest to the point you just selected.
4) Increase the value of the **Tension 1:** spinner in the **Blend Curve** rollout. Notice the change in the blend curve. Next, increase the value of the **Tension 2:** spinner. Notice the change in the blend curve.
5) Create a second blend curve using the remaining two endpoints. Experiment with changing the values of the tension spinners.
6) Reset 3ds max. Do not save the file.

Mirror Curve

As its name implies, a *mirror curve* is a mirror image of its parent curve. To create a mirror curve sub-object, first select a NURBS model with at least one curve sub-object. Next, open the **Modify** tab in the **Command Panel**. Expand the **Create Curves** rollout and pick the **Mirror** button in the **Dependent Curves** area. The **Mirror Curve** rollout becomes available. You can also pick the **Create Mirror Curve** button in the **NURBS** toolbox. The **Mirror Curve** rollout is displayed.

Create Mirror Curve

The **Mirror Axis:** area in the **Mirror Curve** rollout contains six radio buttons that allow you to set the initial mirror axis. These correspond to the world axes. Pick the radio button that corresponds to the axis about which you wish to mirror the parent curve. Next, place the cursor over the curve you wish to mirror. Notice the curve turns blue and the cursor becomes a white cross. Pick the curve and a yellow gizmo appears. The

Pick   Mirror curve   Original curve   **Figure 25-19.** A mirror curve being created.

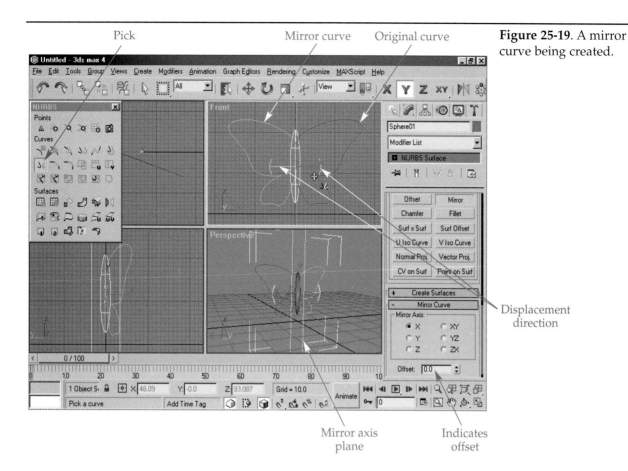

Displacement direction

Mirror axis plane   Indicates offset

rectangular portion of the gizmo represents the mirror plane, while the arrows on the gizmo represent the direction of displacement. See Figure 25-19. Drag the curve up or down while holding the mouse button to set the offset distance. Once you have the mirror curve placed where you want it, release the mouse button.

Increasing or decreasing the value in the **Offset:** spinner in the **Mirror Curve** rollout repositions the mirror curve along the displacement axis. The offset is also dynamically displayed in this spinner as you drag to create the mirror curve.

The mirror axis can be changed by selecting the appropriate radio button in the **Mirror Axis:** area in the **Mirror Curve** rollout. The mirror axis can also be transformed at the sub-object level, allowing you to mirror the parent curve about an axis other than one of the six presets. Transforming the mirror axis at the sub-object level is discussed in the next chapter.

Fillet Curve

Where a chamfer curve is a straight line, a *fillet curve* is a rounded corner between two parent curves. To create a fillet curve, first select a NURBS model that contains at least two curve sub-objects. Next, open the **Modify** tab in the **Command Panel**. Expand the **Create Curves** rollout and pick the **Fillet** button in the **Dependent Curves** area. The **Fillet Curve** rollout is displayed. You can also pick the **Create Fillet Curve** button in the **NURBS** toolbox.

Create Fillet Curve

Move the cursor over the first curve to be used in the fillet. Notice the curve turns blue and the cursor becomes a white cross. A blue box trails the cursor along the path of the curve. Move the cursor to the desired location for the first seed and pick. Next, move the cursor to the second curve to be used in the fillet. A dotted white line connects the first seed to the cursor. Place the cursor at the desired coordinates for the second seed and pick.

After you pick the second seed, the blue seed boxes on each of the parent curves turn yellow. The dependent fillet curve sub-object is created between the two parent curves. Its location is dependent on the relative positions of the two curves and the fillet radius. See Figure 25-20. If 3ds max is unable to create a valid fillet, the curve is represented in the viewports as a straight orange line. To make the fillet valid, you may either reposition the parent curves or adjust the fillet radius, depending on your needs.

The **Radius:** spinner in the **Fillet Curve** rollout is used to adjust the radius of the fillet. By default, this value is set to 10. It may be necessary to adjust this value before 3ds max can calculate a proper fillet. Checking the **Trim Curve** check boxes trims the parent curves at their intersection with the fillet curve. Checking the **Flip Trim** check boxes switches the portions of the curves that are kept with the portions that are discarded. The **Seed 1:** and **Seed 2:** spinners are used to adjust the U location of each seed along the parent curves. 3ds max uses the seed locations to determine which parent curve endpoints are used in creating the fillet curve.

Figure 25-20. A fillet curve can be created in four different locations between a pair of crossing curves. The location of the fillet curve is determined by the locations of the seeds. The fillet radius determines the locations of the fillet curve's endpoints on the parent curves.

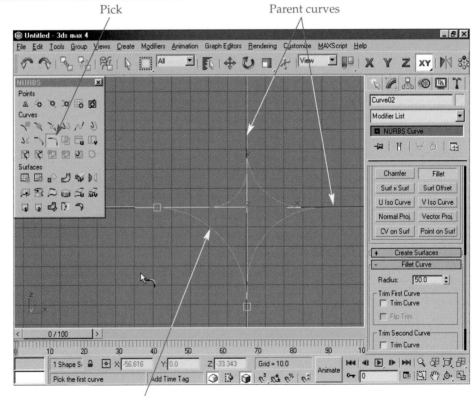

Pick

Parent curves

Fillet curve

Exercise 25-7

1) In the Front viewport, create a CV curve that begins horizontally and then curves down vertically, as shown in the figure below. Next, open the **Modify** tab in the **Command Panel**.
2) Expand the **Create Curves** rollout and pick the **Mirror** button. In the **Mirror Curve** rollout, pick the **XY** radio button in the **Mirror Axis:** area.
3) Pick the curve and drag the copy a short distance from the parent. Release the mouse button to create the mirror curve. Note the value in the **Offset:** spinner.
4) Zoom extents all.
5) Pick the **Fillet** button in the **Create Curves** rollout. Pick the parent curve at one endpoint. Pick the mirror curve at the endpoint nearest the endpoint you just selected.
6) Enter the same value as the offset in the **Radius:** spinner in the **Fillet Curve** rollout. If the fillet curve is invalid, and the curve is displayed as a straight orange line, increase the value in the **Radius:** spinner until a fillet curve is created.
7) Reset 3ds max. Do not save the file.

Surface Edge Curve

A *surface edge curve* is a dependent curve sub-object created from the edges of a surface. The edges can be either outside edges or inside edges, such as trim edges.

Create Surface Edge Curve

To create a surface edge curve, select a NURBS model that contains a surface. Open the **Modify** tab in the **Command Panel** and expand the **Create Curves** rollout. Pick the **Surf Edge** button in the **Dependent Curves** area. The **Surface Edge Curve** rollout is displayed. You can also pick the **Create Surface Edge Curve** button in the **NURBS** toolbox. Position the cursor over an edge. When the edge is highlighted, pick it. See Figure 25-21. This creates the edge curve.

Changing the values of the **Seed 1:** and **Seed 2:** spinners in the **Surface Edge Curve** rollout moves the seed around the surface. 3ds max uses the edge closest to the two seeds to create the surface edge curve.

Surface-Surface Intersection Curve

A *surface-surface intersection curve* is a dependent curve sub-object created at the intersection of two surface sub-objects. To create a surface-surface intersection curve, select a NURBS model containing intersecting surface sub-objects. Open the **Modify** tab in the **Command Panel** and expand the **Create Curves** rollout. Pick the **Surf x Surf** button in the **Dependent Curves** area. You can also pick the **Create Surface-Surface Intersection Curve** button in the **NURBS** toolbox. This displays the **Surf-Surf Intersection Curve** rollout.

Create Surface-Surface
Intersection Curve

Figure 25-21. Creating a surface edge curve.

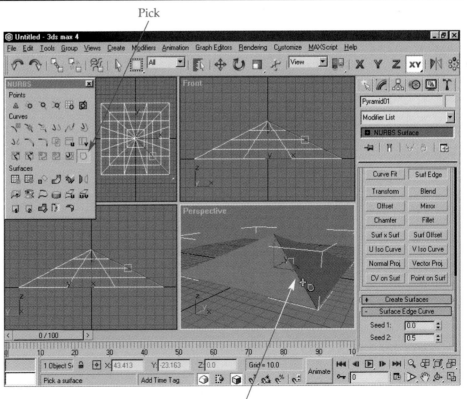

Surface edge
curve

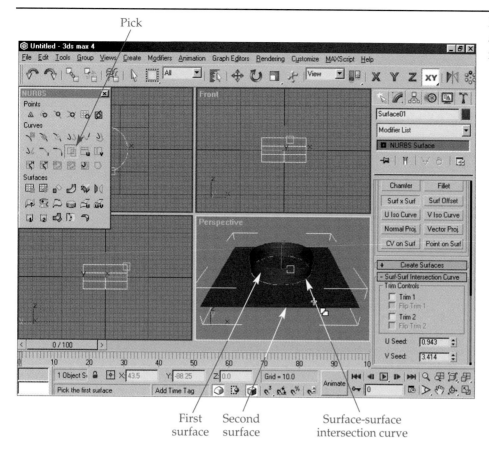

Pick

Figure 25-22. Creating a surface-surface intersection curve.

First surface   Second surface   Surface-surface intersection curve

In any viewport, move the cursor over the first intersecting surface. The surface turns blue as the cursor passes over it. Pick the first surface. Next, position the cursor over the second intersecting surface. It also turns blue. Pick the second surface to create the surface-surface intersection curve. See Figure 25-22.

If the surfaces intersect one another in multiple places, the intersection nearest to the seed is used to create the new curve. The seed, represented in the viewports as a yellow box, can be relocated using the **U Seed:** and **V Seed:** spinners in the **Surf-Surf Intersection Curve** rollout. By changing the location of the seed, you can select a different intersection to be used in forming the curve.

The **Trim Controls** area of the **Surf-Surf Intersection Curve** rollout contains controls for trimming. Checking the **Trim 1** check box trims the first selected surface. Checking the **Trim 2** check box trims the second selected surface. Checking the **Flip Trim** check boxes reverses the portion of the surface that is trimmed away with the portion that remains.

U Iso Curve

U iso curves are dependent curve sub-objects that lie directly on a NURBS surface, run parallel to the surface's U axis, and follow the contours of the surface. It may help to think of U iso curves as lines of longitude and V iso curves as lines of latitude, or vice versa.

To create a U iso curve, select a NURBS model that contains at least one surface sub-object. Open the **Modify** tab in the **Command Panel** and expand the **Create Curves** rollout. Pick the **U Iso Curve** button in the

Create U Iso Curve

Figure 25-23. Creating a U iso curve. The blue line is displayed where the curve will be created.

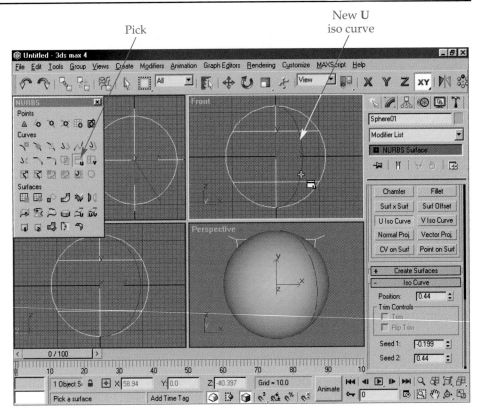

Pick

New **U** iso curve

Dependent Curves area. This displays the **Iso Curve** rollout. You can also pick the **Create U Iso Curve** button in the **NURBS** toolbox.

Move the cursor over the surface on which the iso curve is to be placed. This causes a blue line, which runs parallel to the iso lines of the surface, to appear. See Figure 25-23. As you move the cursor, the blue line follows. Pick at the desired location on the surface to create the U iso curve.

The position of the U iso curve can be modified by adjusting the value of the **Position:** spinner in the **Iso Curve** rollout. Checking the **Trim** check box in the **Trim Controls** area trims the surface at the U iso curve's location. Checking the **Flip Trim** check box switches the portion of the surface that is displayed with the portion that is discarded.

V Iso Curve

Like U iso curves, *V iso curves* are dependent curve sub-objects lying on a NURBS surface. They run parallel to the iso lines of the surface and follow the surface's contour.

To create a V iso curve, select a NURBS model that contains at least one surface sub-object. Open the **Modify** tab in the **Command Panel** and expand the **Create Curves** rollout. Pick the **V Iso Curve** button in the **Dependent Curves** area. This displays the **Iso Curve** rollout. You can also pick the **Create V Iso Curve** button in the **NURBS** toolbox.

Move the cursor over the surface on which the iso curve is to be placed. This causes a blue line, which runs parallel to the iso lines of the surface, to appear. As you move the cursor, the blue line follows. See Figure 25-24. Pick at the desired location on the surface to create the V iso curve.

Create V Iso Curve

Pick

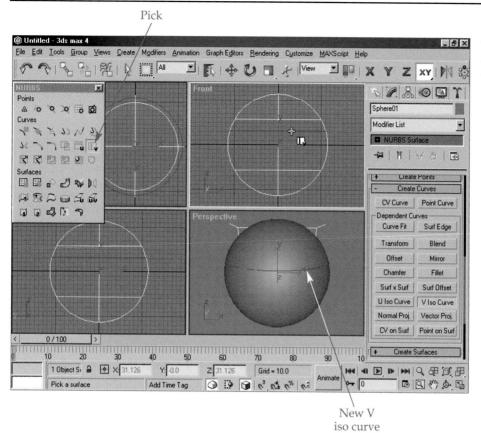

Figure 25-24. Creating a V iso curve. The blue line is displayed where the curve will be created.

New V
iso curve

Adjusting the value of the **Position:** spinner in the **Iso Curve** rollout repositions the V iso curve. Checking the **Trim** check box in the **Trim Controls** area trims the surface at the iso curve's location. Checking the **Flip Trim** check box switches the portion of the surface that is displayed with the portion that is discarded.

Exercise 25-8

1) In any viewport, create two overlapping spheres. Convert one sphere to a NURBS object. With the converted sphere selected, open the **Modify** tab in the **Command Panel** and pick the **Attach** button. Attach the second sphere to the first to make them both sub-objects of the same NURBS model.
2) Expand the **Create Curves** rollout and pick the **Surf x Surf** button. Pick the first surface, and then pick the second surface. Observe the surface-surface intersection curve.
3) Pick the **U Iso Curve** button in the **Create Curves** rollout and draw two U iso curves on one of the spheres. Then pick the **V Iso Curve** button and create two V iso curves on the other sphere. Notice the difference between the U and V iso curves.
4) Reset 3ds max. Do not save the file.

Exercise

Normal Projected Curve

A *normal projected curve* is a dependent curve sub-object that lies directly on a surface. To create the dependent curve, a parent curve sub-object is projected onto a parent surface sub-object in the direction of the surface's normal. Because the curve is projected normal to the parent surface rather than along a set vector, curvature in the parent surface creates distortion in the projected curve. The normal projected curve is created at the intersection of the projection and the parent surface.

Create Normal Projected Curve

To create a normal projected curve, select a NURBS model that contains at least one curve and one surface. Open the **Modify** tab in the **Command Panel** and expand the **Create Curves** rollout. Pick the **Normal Proj.** button in the **Dependent Curves** area. The **Normal Projected Curve** rollout is displayed. You can also pick the **Create Normal Projected Curve** button in the **NURBS** toolbox.

Move the cursor over the curve to be projected. The curve turns blue. Pick the curve. A dashed white line appears from the curve to the cursor. Move the cursor to the surface. The surface turns blue. Pick the parent surface to create the normal projected curve.

If you check the **Trim** check box in the **Trim Controls** area of the **Normal Projected Curve** rollout, 3ds max attempts to trim the surface with the projected curve. An error state results if the projected curve does not stretch across the extents of the surface, or is not closed. Checking the **Flip Trim** check box switches the portion of the surface that is retained with the portion that is not. See Figure 25-25.

On surfaces where multiple projections are possible, 3ds max picks the projection nearest to the seed. You can relocate the seed by adjusting

Figure 25-25. Three identical spheres trimmed by normal projected curves. The sphere on the left uses normal trimming. The sphere in the middle has trimming "flipped." The sphere on the right is trimmed by an open projected curve, resulting in an error state.

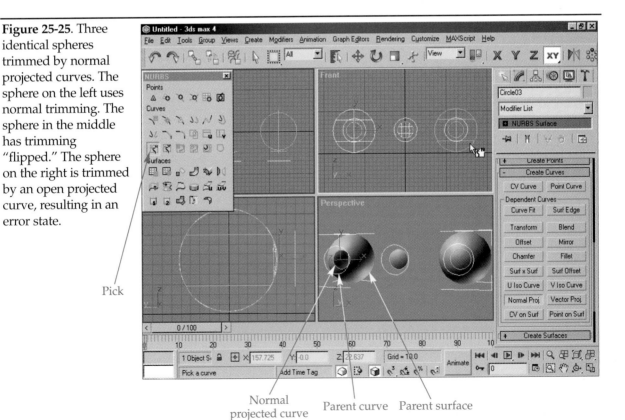

Pick

Normal projected curve   Parent curve   Parent surface

the values of the **U Seed:** and **V Seed:** spinners in the **Normal Projected Curve** rollout.

Vector Projected Curve

A *vector projected curve* is very similar to a normal projected curve. It is a dependent curve sub-object that lies directly on a surface. A parent curve is projected onto a parent surface. The vector projected curve is created at the intersection of the projection and the surface. The projection vector of a vector projected curve can be transformed, while a normal projected curve is always projected on a vector normal to the surface. Because the curve is projected along a set vector, localized curvature in the parent surface does not result in dramatic distortion of the projected curve. However, as the direction of the vector gizmo is rotated to a direction less perpendicular to the surface, the distortion of the projected curve increases.

To create a vector projected curve, select a NURBS model containing at least one surface and one curve. Open the **Modify** tab in the **Command Panel** and expand the **Create Curves** rollout. Pick the **Vector Proj.** button in the **Dependent Curves** area. The **Vector Projected Curve** rollout is displayed. You can also pick the **Create Vector Projected Curve** button in the **NURBS** toolbox.

Create Vector Projected Curve

Move the cursor over the curve to be projected. The curve turns blue. Pick the curve. A dashed white line appears from the curve to the cursor. Move the cursor to the surface. The surface turns blue. Pick the parent surface to create the vector projected curve.

A yellow box appears on the surface. This yellow box indicates the location of the seed. On surfaces where multiple projections are possible, 3ds max picks the projection nearest to the seed. You can relocate the seed by adjusting the values of the **U Seed:** and **V Seed:** spinners in the **Vector Projected Curve** rollout.

A yellow line also appears in all viewports. This yellow line is a gizmo representing the projection vector. See Figure 25-26. The initial vector always lies along the Z axis of the viewport's local coordinate system. For this reason it is important that you create the vector projected curve in the viewport that faces the direction you wish to project the curve. If the projected curve is not positioned exactly the way you want, do not worry. In the next chapter you will learn how to rotate the vector gizmo.

If you check the **Trim** check box in the **Trim Controls** area of the **Vector Projected Curve** rollout, 3ds max attempts to trim the surface with the projected curve. An error state results if the projected curve does not stretch across the extents of the surface, or is not closed. Checking the **Flip Trim** check box switches the portion of the surface that is retained with the portion that is not.

Help Cel

An analogy can be drawn between the parent surface of a projected curve and a funhouse mirror. If a person stands in front of a funhouse mirror, the reflection appears drastically distorted. This is analogous to a normal projected curve. However, if the same mirror is painted flat white, and a flashlight is used to project the person's shadow onto the mirror, the shadow appears much less distorted. This is analogous to a vector projected curve.

Figure 25-26. A vector projected curve being created. The projection vector gizmo can be transformed at the sub-object level.

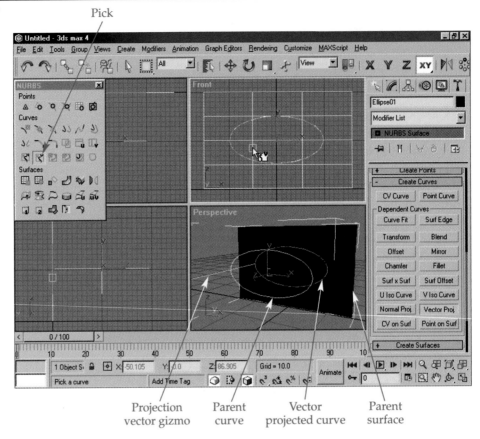

Projection vector gizmo   Parent curve   Vector projected curve   Parent surface

Exercise

Exercise 25-9

1) In any viewport, create a CV surface. In the same viewport, create a circle spline shape above the CV surface.

2) Convert the circle into a NURBS object. Open the **Modify** tab in the **Command Panel** and attach the CV surface to the curve. Hold the model at this point.

3) Expand the **Create Curves** rollout and pick the **Normal Proj.** button. Pick the curve, and then pick the surface.

4) In the **Normal Projected Curve** rollout, check the **Trim** check box to create a circular hole in the CV surface. Check the **Flip Trim** check box, if necessary.

5) Fetch the model. Pick the **Vector Proj.** button in the **Create Curves** rollout. Pick the circle, and then pick the CV surface. In the **Vector Projected Curve** rollout, check the **Trim** check box to create a circular hole in the CV surface. Check the **Flip Trim** check box, if necessary.

6) Reset 3ds max. Do not save the file.

Surface Point Curve

A *surface point curve* is a dependent curve sub-object that lies directly on a surface. When you draw a surface point curve, 3ds max automatically places the points of the curve directly on the surface, regardless of the viewport used.

To create a surface point curve, select a NURBS model that contains at least one surface. Open the **Modify** tab in the **Command Panel** and expand the **Create Curves** rollout. Pick the **Point on Surf** button in the **Dependent Curves** area. The **Point Curve On Surface** rollout is displayed. You can also pick the **Create Point Curve On Surface** button in the **NURBS** toolbox. At this point, there are two methods for continuing to create the point curve.

Create Point Curve On Surface

One method is to pick points on the surface in any viewport. The cursor's position is projected along the viewport's local Z axis, and a point is placed where the projection and surface intersect. See Figure 25-27. If the projection and the surface do not intersect, no point is placed. Click once to create a single point or click twice to create coincidental points. Right-click to end the command. Unfortunately, with this method, points cannot be placed in areas of the surface that are hidden from view. In other words, you cannot place points on the "back side" of a surface.

You can also draw a surface point curve two dimensionally. To do this, first check the **2D View** check box in the **Point Curve On Surface** rollout, and then pick the surface on which to draw the curve. This opens the **Edit Curve on Surface** dialog box, which is a modeless dialog box. See Figure 25-28.

Pick

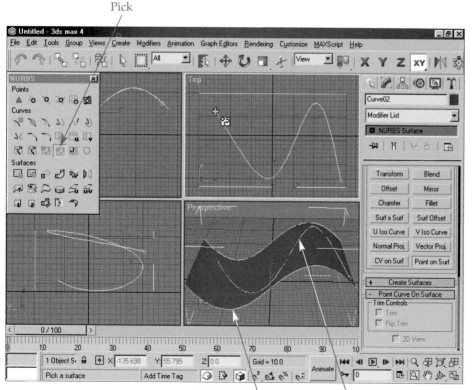

Parent surface   Point curve

Figure 25-27. Creating a surface point curve by drawing directly on the surface.

In the viewports, a blue box appears on the surface at the coordinates you picked. However, no point is added at that location. There is also a blue box at the corresponding coordinates in the 2D viewport of the **Edit Curve on Surface** dialog box. See Figure 25-28. This helps you visualize the relationship between 2D point coordinates in the dialog box and their relative position on the 3D surface. The entire 3D surface is represented as the square area in the 2D viewport. Place points by picking at the appropriate coordinates in the 2D viewport. Click twice to create coincidental points. As you add points, the viewports are updated so you can see the results. Right-click to end the command and close the dialog box. With this process, you can draw the curve on areas of the surface that are hidden in the viewports.

If you check the **Trim** check box in the **Trim Controls** area of the **Point Curve On Surface** rollout, 3ds max attempts to trim the surface with the newly created curve. An error state results if the projected curve does not stretch across the extents of the surface, or if it is not closed. Checking the **Flip Trim** check box switches the portion of the surface that is retained with the portion that is not.

Help Cel

When drawing a point curve on surface in the viewports, pressing the [Backspace] key removes the point last placed. However, the viewport is not updated until the mouse is moved. Keep this in mind to avoid accidentally removing points.

Figure 25-28. Creating a surface point curve using the **Edit Curve on Surface** dialog box. Notice the blue seed on the surface corresponds with the seed in the dialog box.

Drawing the curve in **2D**   Extent of the surface

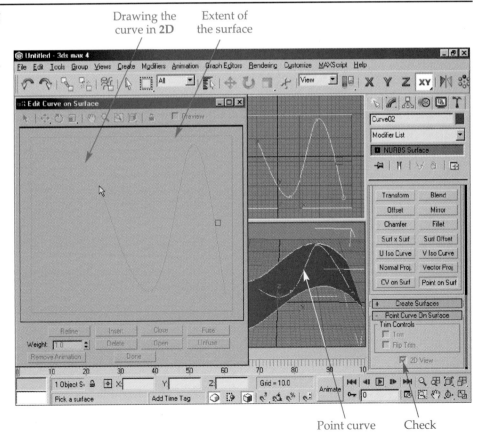

Point curve   Check

Surface CV Curve

A *surface CV curve* is very similar to a surface point curve. Both are dependent curve sub-objects that lie directly on a parent surface. However, with a surface CV curve you do not place points through which the curve passes, as you do when creating a point curve. Instead, you place CVs, the influences of which combine to determine the curve's shape.

To create a surface CV curve, select a NURBS model containing at least one surface sub-object. Open the **Modify** tab in the **Command Panel** and expand the **Create Curves** rollout. Pick the **CV on Surf** button in the **Dependent Curves** area. The **CV Curve On Surface** rollout is displayed. You can also pick the **Create CV Curve on Surface** button in the **NURBS** toolbox. As with a surface point curve, you can draw the surface CV curve directly in the viewports, or in the **Edit Curve on Surface** dialog box by checking the **2D View** check box in the **CV Curve On Surface** rollout.

Create CV Curve On Surface

Once you have drawn the surface CV curve, you can use it to trim the parent surface by checking the **Trim** check box in the **Trim Controls** area of the **CV Curve On Surface** rollout. Checking the **Flip Trim** check box switches the portion of the surface that is trimmed away with the portion that remains. The **Automatic Reparameterization** area contains controls for setting automatic reparameterization. These are the same as for a CV curve.

Surface Offset Curve

A *surface offset curve* is a dependent curve sub-object that is offset from a parent surface curve. The parent surface curve sub-object can be a normal or vector projected curve, a U or V iso curve, or a surface point or surface CV curve.

To create a surface offset curve, select a NURBS model that contains at least one surface curve sub-object. Next, open the **Modify** tab in the **Command Panel** and expand the **Create Curves** rollout. Pick the **Surf Offset** button in the **Dependent Curves** area. The **Surface Offset Curve** rollout is displayed. You can also pick the **Create Surface Offset Curve** button in the **NURBS** toolbox.

Create Surface Offset Curve

Move the cursor over the surface curve that is to be duplicated and offset. When highlighted, the curve turns blue. Pick the curve. In the **Surface Offset Curve** rollout, use the **Offset:** spinner to set the distance that the new curve is offset from the surface curve. Increasing the value of this spinner moves the curve away from the surface in the direction of the surface's normal. Entering a negative value in this spinner moves the curve away from the surface in a direction opposite to the surface's normal. See Figure 25-29.

Figure 25-29. Creating a surface offset curve.

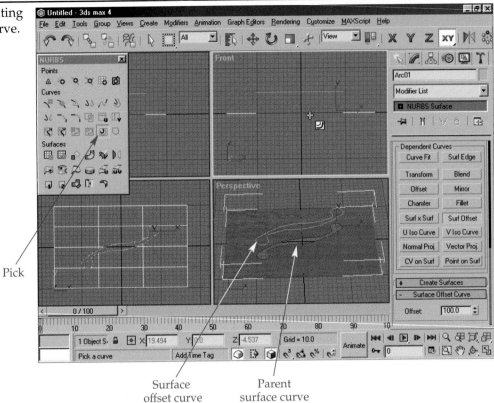

Pick

Surface
offset curve

Parent
surface curve

Exercise

Exercise 25-10

1) In the Left viewport, create a sphere. Convert the sphere to a NURBS model. With the sphere selected, open the **Modify** tab in the **Command Panel.**

2) Expand the **Create Curves** rollout and pick the **Point on Surf** button. In the **Point Curve on Surface** rollout, check the **2D View** check box.

3) In the Front viewport, pick a point on the surface. This opens the **Edit Curve on Surface** dialog box. Notice the blue box in the **Edit Curve on Surface** dialog box. This box corresponds to the blue box on the surface. Move the **Edit Curve on Surface** dialog box so you can see the Front viewport.

4) Pick points in the **Edit Curve on Surface** dialog box to create the smile of a smiley face. You can monitor your progress in the Front viewport. Close the curve by picking the last point on top of the first point.

5) When you have drawn the mouth, check the **Trim** check box and the **Flip Trim** check box in the **Point Curve on Surface** rollout as needed.

6) Now, pick the **CV on Surf** button. Uncheck the **2D View** check box in the **CV Curve On Surface** rollout if it is checked. In the Front viewport, draw a closed curve for the right eye. When you have finished the eye, check the **Trim** check box in the **CV Curve On Surface** rollout. Flip the trim if needed. Now draw a closed surface CV curve for the left eye. Once again, check the **Trim** check box and flip the trim if needed.

7) Save the scene as **ex25-10.max** in the folder of your choice. Reset 3ds max.

Creating NURBS Surface Sub-Objects

Many types of surface sub-objects can be added to NURBS models. Dependent surfaces are created from existing sub-objects, and are related to them. This means the surface sub-object is affected by changes made to its parent curves or surfaces. Independent surfaces are not related to other sub-objects in the NURBS model.

Creating Independent Surface Sub-Objects

When you are editing a NURBS model, you can add independent surface sub-objects to the model. The procedure is similar to that used to draw NURBS surfaces using the **Create** tab in the **Command Panel**. However, the NURBS surfaces drawn using the **Create Surfaces** rollout in the **Modify** tab are added as sub-objects to an existing NURBS model. The surfaces drawn using the **Create** tab are the top level of a new NURBS model.

To create independent NURBS surface sub-objects, select a NURBS model. Next, open the **Modify** tab in **Command Panel**. Expand the **Create Surfaces** rollout and pick the **CV Surf** or **Point Surf** button. The **CV Surface** or **Point Surface** rollout is displayed. You can also pick the **Create CV Surface** or **Create Point Surface** button in the **NURBS** toolbox. Pick the coordinates for one corner in any viewport. Then, while holding down the mouse button, drag the cursor to the coordinates for the opposite corner. Finally, release the mouse button. See Figure 25-30.

Create CV Surface

Create Point Surface

Pick

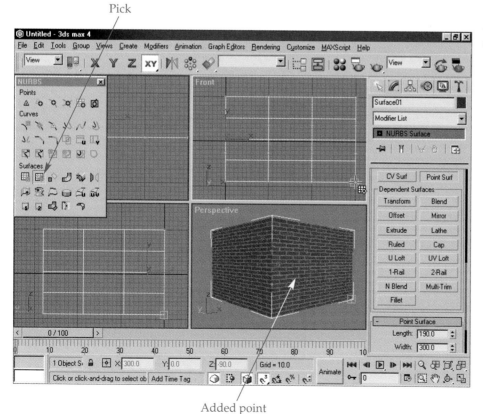

Figure 25-30. Creating an independent point surface.

Added point surface sub-object

NURBS surface sub-objects are changed using the spinners in the **Point Surface** or **CV Surface** rollout. The procedures are identical to those for creating top-level NURBS surfaces. Creating top-level NURBS surfaces is covered in Chapter 24.

Creating Dependent Surface Sub-Objects

Dependent surface sub-objects are created from existing curve and surface sub-objects. The sub-objects used to create dependent surface sub-objects are known as parent sub-objects. Changes made to parent sub-objects are passed onto the dependent child sub-objects. In addition, changes made to the dependent surfaces may also affect the surfaces' parent sub-objects. The following sections discuss the types of dependent surfaces that use curve and surface sub-objects as their parents.

Help Cel

Like dependent curves, dependent surfaces contain no point or CV sub-objects. Their shapes depend on their parent sub-objects rather than their own point or CV sub-objects.

Transform Surface

A *transform surface* is a duplicate of its parent. Transform surfaces can be transformed at the sub-object level without affecting their parent sub-objects. However, if the parent surface is changed, that change is reflected in the transform surface.

To create a transform surface, select a NURBS model that contains at least one surface. Open the **Modify** tab in the **Command Panel** and expand the **Create Surfaces** rollout. Pick the **Transform** button in the **Dependent Surfaces** area. The **Transform Surface** rollout is displayed. You can also pick the **Create Transform Surface** button in the **NURBS** toolbox.

Create Transform Surface

Move the cursor over the surface to be duplicated. When the surface is highlighted, it turns blue. Pick the surface. While holding down the mouse button, drag the cursor to the desired location for the transform surface. Then, release the mouse button. See Figure 25-31. Checking the **Flip Normals** check box in the **Transform Surface** rollout changes which "side" of the surface is facing outward.

Changes made to the parent surface at the sub-object level are passed on to the transform surface. However, changes made to the transform surface are not passed back to the parent surface.

Offset Surface

An *offset surface* is a dependent surface sub-object that is positioned normal to its parent surface. The contour of the offset surface is adjusted according to its distance from the parent surface. As the offset surface is moved away from its parent, its curvature is exaggerated. As it is moved closer to the parent, its curvature becomes more like that of the parent.

To create an offset surface, select a NURBS model that contains at least one surface. Open the **Modify** tab in the **Command Panel** and expand the **Create Surfaces** rollout. Pick the **Offset** button in the

Create Offset Surface

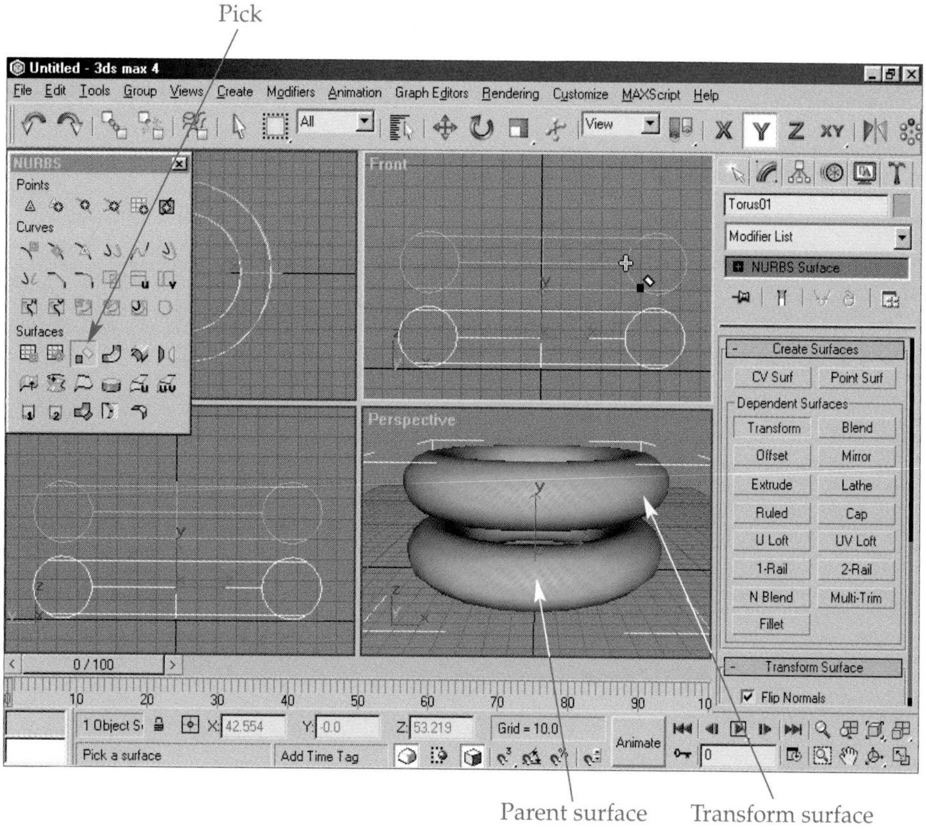

Pick

Figure 25-31. Creating a transform surface.

Parent surface   Transform surface

Dependent Surfaces area. The **Offset Surface** rollout is displayed. You can also pick the **Create Offset Surface** button in the **NURBS** toolbox.

Position the cursor over the surface to be offset. When the surface is highlighted, pick and hold the mouse button. Drag the cursor the desired distance away from parent surface and release the mouse button. Use the **Offset:** spinner in the **Offset Surface** rollout to adjust the offset surface's location. See Figure 25-32. You can flip the normals of the offset surface by checking the **Flip Normals** check box.

Checking the **Cap** check box creates new curves at the edges of the offset surface and its parent. Ruled surfaces are then created between these curves. These ruled surface sub-objects are dependent on, but separate from, the offset surface and its parent.

Extruded Surface

An *extruded surface* is a dependent surface sub-object created by extruding a NURBS curve sub-object. Using the **Extrude** button in the **Create Surfaces** rollout is similar to applying an extrude modifier to a curve. However, when you use the **Extrude** button in the **Create Surfaces** rollout, the vector of the extrusion can be rotated.

To create an extruded NURBS surface, select a NURBS model containing at least one surface and one curve. Open the **Modify** tab in the **Command Panel** and expand the **Create Surfaces** rollout. Pick the **Extrude** button in the **Dependent Surfaces** area. The **Extrude Surface** rollout is displayed. You can also pick the **Create Extrude Surface** button in the **NURBS** toolbox.

Create Extrude Surface

Position the cursor over the curve to be extruded. When the curve is highlighted, it turns blue. Pick the curve. A yellow gizmo appears in the viewports as a line. This gizmo represents the axis of extrusion. Drag the cursor the desired length of the extrusion while holding down the mouse button. Finally, release the mouse button. See Figure 25-33.

Figure 25-32. Creating an offset surface. Notice the difference in curvature between the parent surface and the offset surface.

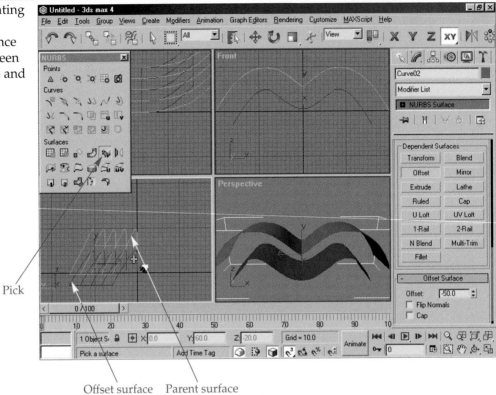

Pick

Offset surface   Parent surface

Figure 25-33. Creating an extruded surface. The extrude gizmo, displayed in yellow, can be transformed at the surface sub-object level.

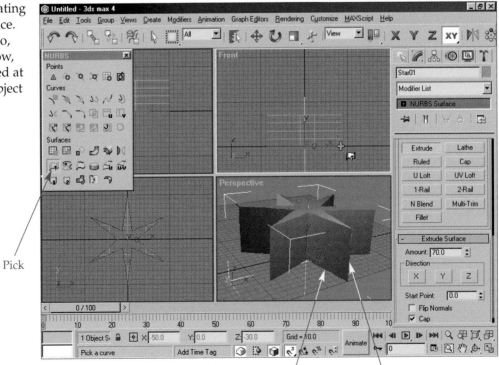

Pick

Parent curve   Extruded surface

At this point, the extruded surface may not be the length that you want, or it may be extruded along the wrong axis. These settings can be adjusted using the controls in the **Extrude Surface** rollout. Picking the **X**, **Y**, or **Z** button in the **Direction** area sets the axis of extrusion. The **Amount:** spinner value sets the length of the extruded surface. You can flip the normals of the extruded surface by checking the **Flip Normals** check box.

The **Start Point:** spinner is used to reposition the starting point of the parent curve. This option is only available if the parent is a closed curve. If the parent curve is closed, checking the **Cap** button creates cap surfaces at the ends of the extruded surface. These caps are separate surface sub-objects.

Ruled Surface

A *ruled surface* is a dependent surface sub-object created between two curve sub-objects. The parent curves form the edges of the surface. If the curves are different in shape, the contour of the surface gradually changes to match the contour of the curves at either edge.

To create a ruled surface, select a NURBS model that contains at least two curves. Open the **Modify** tab in the **Command Panel** and expand the **Create Surfaces** rollout. Pick the **Ruled** button in the **Dependent Surfaces** area. The **Ruled Surf** rollout is displayed. You can also pick the **Create Ruled Surface** button in the **NURBS** toolbox.

Create Ruled Surface

Position the cursor over the first curve to be used in creating the ruled surface. When highlighted, it turns blue. Pick the curve, and then position the cursor over the second curve. When it is highlighted, pick the second curve.

The calculation of the ruled surface is based on the location of the first point on each parent curve. That is, the iso lines of the ruled surface run from the starting point of the first curve to the starting point of the second, and so on. If the curves run in opposite directions, the resulting surface is twisted. See Figure 25-34. Checking the **Flip Beginning** check box in the **Ruled Surf** rollout reverses the direction of the first curve. Checking the **Flip End** check box reverses the direction of the second curve. You can flip the normals of the ruled surface by checking the **Flip Normals** check box.

Sometimes, flipping the curves will not fix a twist. This is because the starting points do not align. The **Start Point 1:** and **Start Point 2:** spinners in the **Ruled Surf** rollout allow you to reassign the starting points of the edges of the ruled surface. Doing so can fix unwanted twists and deformities created in the surface. This option is only available if the edges of the ruled surface are closed.

Cap Surface

A *cap surface* is a dependent surface sub-object created within the boundaries of a closed curve or the edge of a closed surface, such as an extruded closed curve. To create a cap surface, select a NURBS model that contains at least one closed curve or an open-ended closed surface. Open the **Modify** tab in the **Command Panel** and expand the **Create Surfaces** rollout. Pick the **Cap** button in the **Dependent Surfaces** area.

Create Cap Surface

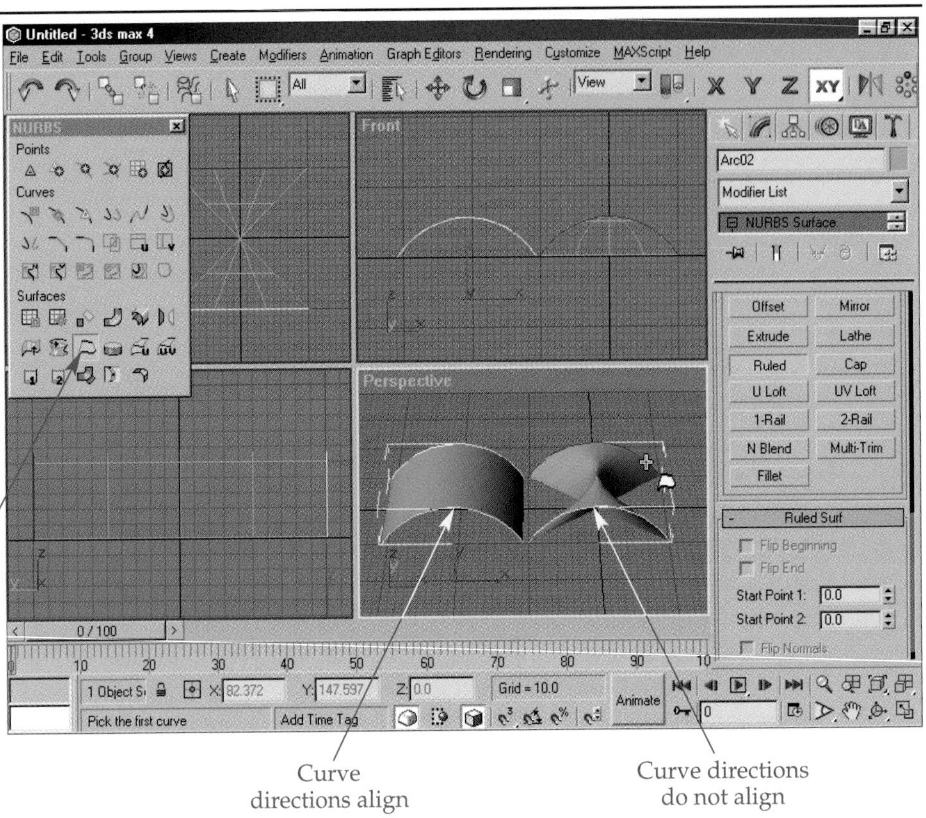

Figure 25-34. Two ruled surfaces created from similar curves. The parent curves of the surface on the left both run in the same direction. The parent curves of the surface on the right run in opposite directions, resulting in a twist in the surface.

Pick

Curve directions align

Curve directions do not align

The **Cap Surface** rollout is displayed. You can also pick the **Create Cap Surface** button in the **NURBS** toolbox.

Position the cursor over the closed curve or the closed surface. If you position the cursor over a closed curve, the curve turns blue. Pick the curve to end the command.

If you position the cursor over an open-ended closed surface, the surface turns gold (dark yellow), and the edge nearest to the cursor is highlighted in blue. Move the cursor to select the edge of the surface you wish to cap, and pick the surface. See Figure 25-35.

You can flip the normals of the cap surface by checking the **Flip Normals** check box in the **Cap Surface** rollout. The **Start Point:** spinner can be used to reassign the starting point of the cap's parent sub-object.

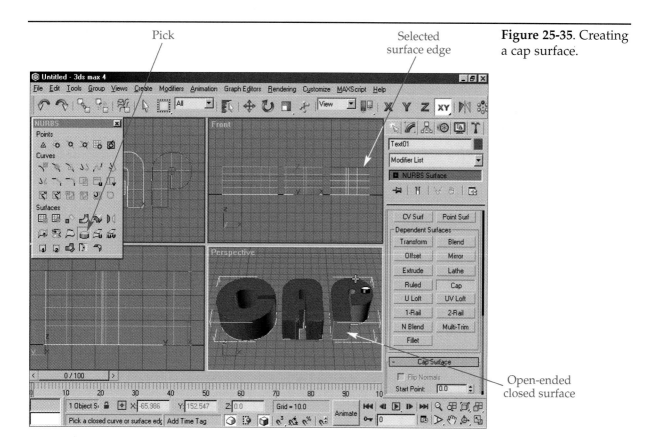

Pick

Selected
surface edge

Figure 25-35. Creating
a cap surface.

Open-ended
closed surface

Exercise 25-11

1) In the Top viewport, create a rectangle of any size. Convert the spline to a NURBS model. Next, open the **Modify** tab in the **Command Panel**.

2) Expand the **Create Surfaces** rollout and pick the **Extrude** button. In the Top viewport, pick a side of the rectangle. Pick the **Z** button in the **Direction** area of the **Extrude Surface** rollout. Increase the value of the **Amount:** spinner to an appropriate height. Repeat this step for all four sides.

3) Pick the **Ruled** button in the **Create Surfaces** rollout. Pick one curve of the original rectangle. Now, pick the curve opposite to it. If the resulting surface has a twist in it, check the **Flip Beginning** or **Flip End** check box.

4) In the Top viewport, create a circle. Next, select the NURBS model and open the **Modify** tab in the **Command Panel**. Attach the circle to the NURBS model.

5) In the **Create Surfaces** rollout, pick the **Extrude** button. Pick the circle. Pick the **Z** button and, in the **Amount:** spinner, enter the same height value used for the sides.

6) Pick the **Cap** button in the **Create Surfaces** rollout. Pick the top edge of the extruded circle. Now pick the bottom edge of the extruded circle.

7) Save the scene as ex25-11.max in the folder of your choice. Reset 3ds max.

Exercise

Create Mirror Surface

Mirror Surface

A *mirror surface* is a mirror image of its parent surface. To create a mirror surface sub-object, select a NURBS model containing at least one surface. Open the **Modify** tab in the **Command Panel** and expand the **Create Surfaces** rollout. Pick the **Mirror** button in the **Dependent Surfaces** area. The **Mirror Surface** rollout is displayed. You can also pick the **Create Mirror Surface** button in the **NURBS** toolbox.

The **Mirror Axis:** area of the **Mirror Surface** rollout contains six radio buttons that allow you to set the initial mirror axis. These are world axes. Pick the radio button that corresponds to the axis you wish to use to mirror the parent surface. Next, place the cursor over the surface you wish to mirror. Pick the surface when it is highlighted, and hold down the mouse button. A yellow gizmo appears. See Figure 25-36. The rectangular portion of the gizmo represents the mirror plane, while the arrows represent the axis of displacement. Drag the surface to set the offset distance. Once you have the mirror surface placed where you want it, release the mouse button.

Increasing or decreasing the value of the **Offset:** spinner in the **Mirror Surface** rollout adjusts the offset distance. A new mirror axis can be assigned by selecting the appropriate radio button in the **Mirror Axis:** area. The mirror axis can be transformed at the sub-object level, allowing you to mirror the parent surface about an axis other than that of one of the six presets. You will learn how to transform the mirror axis in the next chapter. You can flip the normals of the mirror surface by checking the **Flip Normals** check box.

Figure 25-36. Creating a mirror surface.

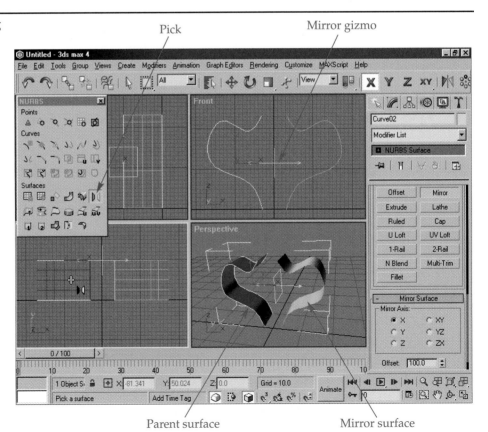

Lathe Surface

A *lathe surface* is a dependent surface sub-object created by rotating a parent curve. Creating a NURBS lathe surface is similar to creating a mesh object using the lathe modifier.

To create a lathe surface, select a NURBS model that contains at least one curve. Open the **Modify** tab in the **Command Panel** and expand the **Create Surfaces** rollout. Pick the **Lathe** button in the **Dependent Surfaces** area. The **Lathe Surface** rollout is displayed. You can also pick the **Create Lathe Surface** button in the **NURBS** toolbox.

Create Lathe Surface

Position the cursor over the curve you wish to lathe. When the curve is highlighted (blue), pick the curve to create the lathe surface. By default, the lathe surface is rotated 360° around the world Y axis.

The axis of rotation and the amount of rotation can be adjusted using the spinners in the **Lathe Surface** rollout. The **Degrees:** spinner value sets the amount of rotation of the lathe surface. A value of 360° causes the curve to spin completely around the axis, creating a closed surface. A value less than 360° causes the curve to rotate only partially around the axis, creating an open surface. See Figure 25-37.

The **X**, **Y**, and **Z** buttons in the **Direction** area of the **Lathe Surface** rollout determine the axis of rotation. A yellow gizmo represents the axis of rotation in the viewports. This gizmo can be rotated when the surface is edited at the sub-object level. This allows you to create a lathe surface whose axis does not align with the world coordinate axes. See Figure 25-38.

The three buttons in the **Align** area are used to position the axis in relation to the parent curve. Picking the **Min** button, which is active by default, places the axis at the minimum X coordinate of the curve. In other words, if you have selected the Y axis as the lathe axis, picking the **Min** button places the lathe axis to the "inside" of the curve. Picking the **Center** button places the axis through the midpoint between the curve's minimum and maximum X coordinates. In other words, if you have chosen the Y axis as the lathe axis, picking the **Center** button runs the lathe axis through the center of the curve. Picking the **Max** button

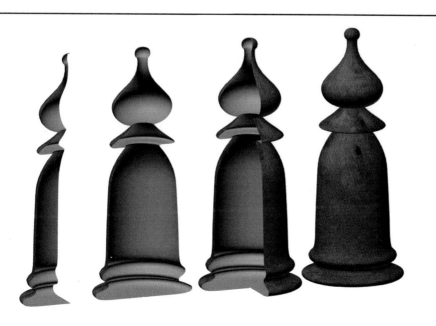

Figure 25-37. These four lathe surfaces result from rotating an identical curve in 90° increments.

Figure 25-38. Creating a lathe surface. The lathe axis gizmo can be edited at the surface sub-object level.

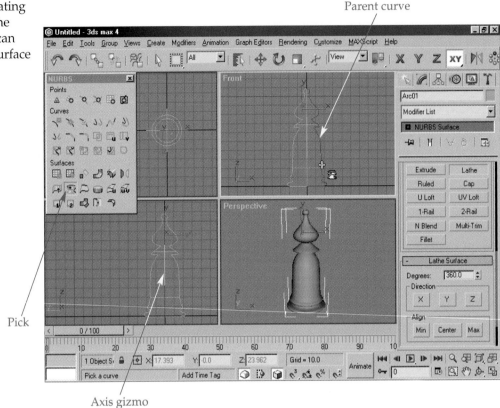

Parent curve

Pick

Axis gizmo

positions the lathe axis at the maximum X coordinate of the curve. Thus, if you pick the Y axis as the lathe axis, picking the **Max** button places the lathe axis to the "outside" of the curve.

For CV curves, the alignment of the lathe axis gizmo is dependent on the curve's CVs rather than the curve itself. The lathe axis aligns with the CVs at the extremes. For this reason, the lathe axis gizmo may not appear where you expect it.

You can flip the normals of the lathe surface by checking the **Flip Normals** check box in the **Lathe Surface** rollout. The **Start Point:** spinner allows you to reassign the starting point of the curve. This option is only available for closed curves. Checking the **Cap** check box automatically caps any open ends on a lathe surface. This feature is only available if the lathe surface is created with 360° rotation.

Help Cel

You may find it useful to review the lathe modifier information in Chapter 5.

Exercise 25-12

1) In the Front viewport, create two CV curves to form the outside edges of a sugar bowl and lid, as shown in the figure below.
2) Open the **Modify** tab in the **Command Panel**. With one of the curves selected, pick the **Attach** button to attach it to the other curve.
3) Expand the **Create Surfaces** rollout and pick the **Lathe** button. Pick the curve that is to form the bowl. In the **Lathe Surface** rollout, make sure the lathe axis is the Y axis, and the lathe is set to rotate 360 degrees. Now pick the curve that is to form the lid. Make sure the lathe axis is the Y axis, and the lathe is set to rotate 360 degrees.
4) Save the file as ex25-12.max in the folder of your choice. Reset 3ds max.

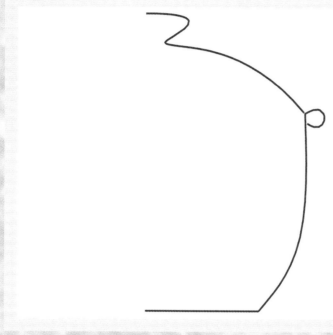

U Loft Surface

A *U loft* is a dependent surface sub-object contoured to match a series of curve "cross sections." For best results, the cross sections should have the same number of points or CVs. In addition, unless it is your intention to have the surface twist, all curves used as cross sections should have the same direction.

A U loft is similar to a standard loft object, but it does not have a path. A U loft surface is also similar to a ruled surface, but it can be created between more than two curves. When three or more nonaligned shapes are used to create a U loft, the resulting surface is smoothly curved, whereas the corresponding ruled surfaces are angular. See Figure 25-39.

To create a U loft surface, select a NURBS model that contains at least two curves. Open the **Modify** tab in the **Command Panel** and expand the **Create Surfaces** rollout. Pick the **U Loft** button in the **Dependent Surfaces** area. This displays the **U Loft Surface** rollout. You can also pick the **Create U Loft Surface** button in the **NURBS** toolbox.

Create U Loft Surface

Position the cursor over the curve that forms the first cross section of the U loft surface. When the curve is highlighted, pick it. This adds the name of the curve to the **U Curves:** window in the **U Loft Surface** rollout. Each curve's name appears here as it is added to the loft.

Now, position the cursor over the curve that forms the second cross section of the U loft. When it is highlighted, pick it. The green iso lines of the U loft surface are now displayed in the viewports. A dashed white line appears connected to the cursor. You can continue to add curves to the U loft by picking them in order. The U loft surface grows with each curve you pick. See Figure 25-40. Pressing the [Backspace] key removes the last curve added. Right-click to end the command.

Figure 25-39. The elbow on the left is created with ruled surfaces. The elbow on the right is created with a U loft surface. Both objects are formed from identical curves.

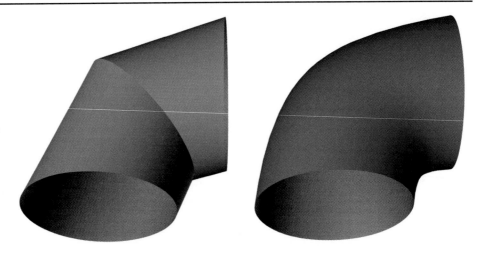

Figure 25-40. Creating a U loft surface. The fins shown here are not part of the U loft surface.

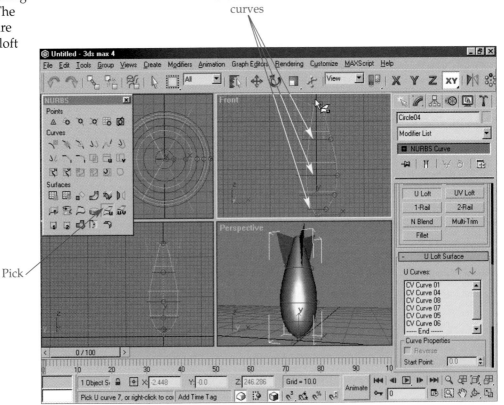

Once the U loft command is exited, the arrows in the upper-right corner of the **U Loft Surface** rollout can be used to change the order of the curves. To reposition a curve, highlight the curve's name in the **U Curves:** window. The curves appear in this window in the order they are added. Once a curve name is selected, pick the appropriate arrow to move the curve up or down the list. The loft changes to reflect the new order.

Additional changes can be made to the U loft in the **Curve Properties** area of the **U Loft Surface** rollout. These controls affect only the curve highlighted in the **U Curves:** window. Checking the **Reverse** check box reverses the direction of the selected curve. Use this check box to remove twists from the loft.

The **Start Point:** spinner in the **Curve Properties** area allows you to switch starting points in closed curves. If the selected curve is not closed, this option is unavailable. The **Tension:** spinner can be used to adjust the tension of the loft where it intersects the selected curve.

The **Use COS Tangents** check box in the **Curve Properties** area is available if the selected curve is a surface curve. Checking this check box causes the loft to match the surface tangents, creating a smooth transition between the surface and the loft. Checking the **Flip Tangents** check box reverses the direction of the tangents. If the selected curve is not a surface curve, this check box is unavailable.

Checking the **Auto Align Curve Starts** check box aligns the starting points of closed curves used in the loft. Unaligned starting points in the loft's parent curves can cause twists in the surface. Checking the **Close Loft** check box creates a new surface segment between the first curve and the last curve of the loft.

Picking the **Remove** button removes the selected curve from the loft. Removing the curve causes the loft to ignore the selected curve, and span from the curve before it to the curve after it.

The **Insert**, **Refine**, and **Replace** buttons are disabled when creating a U loft. When modifying a U loft surface, the **Insert** button can be used to add a curve to the U loft. The curve added is placed before the currently highlighted curve in the **U Curves:** window. Picking the **Refine** button allows you to refine a U loft surface by selecting a curve on the surface and adding it to the **U Curves:** window. Picking the **Replace** button allows you to replace an existing curve in the **U Curves:** window with a new one.

Checking the **Display While Creating** check box allows you to see the loft as it is being created. This may slow system performance when an intricate surface is being created. You can flip the normals of the U loft surface by checking the **Flip Normals** check box.

Curves and splines can be automatically attached to U lofts and UV lofts using the automatic curve attachment feature. This feature is unavailable in some older versions of 3D Studio. You can simply pick a top-level curve or spline, and it will be automatically converted to a NURBS object, attached to the selected model, and added to the loft. Keep in mind, if the spline has Bézier corner or corner vertices, multiple curve sub-objects are created from it as a result. When you automatically attach a spline with corner or Bézier corner vertices, only one of the resulting curve sub-objects is added to the loft.

UV Loft Surface

A *UV loft* is a dependent surface sub-object. UV loft surfaces are very similar to U loft surfaces. However, the surface of a UV loft is defined by curves along both its U and V dimensions.

To create a UV loft surface, select a NURBS model that contains the curve sub-objects you wish to use to define the surface. Open the **Modify** tab in the **Command Panel** and expand the **Create Surfaces** rollout. Pick the **UV Loft** button in the **Dependent Surfaces** area. The **UV Loft Surface** rollout is displayed. You can also pick the **Create UV Loft Surface** button in the **NURBS** toolbox.

The prompt line indicates to select the first U curve. Position the cursor over the first U curve. When the curve is highlighted, pick it. The curve's name is added to the **U Curves:** window in the **UV Loft Surface** rollout. As each U curve is added, its name appears in this window. Repeat this process for all of the U curves. When you have added the last U curve, right-click to finish adding U curves.

The prompt line indicates to select the first V curve. Now, position the cursor over the first V curve. When it is highlighted, pick the curve. The curve's name appears in the **V Curves:** window in the **UV Loft Surface** rollout. Repeat this process until all V curves have been added. When a valid surface can be calculated, it is created. Right-click to end the command. See Figure 25-41.

As with a U loft, the curves making up a UV loft surface can be rearranged. To rearrange the order of the U or V curves, simply highlight a curve in the **U Curves:** or **V Curves:** window and pick the appropriate arrow to the right. A curve can be removed from the list by highlighting it and picking the **Remove** button. The functions of the **Insert**, **Refine**,

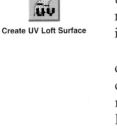

Create UV Loft Surface

Figure 25-41. Creating a UV loft surface.

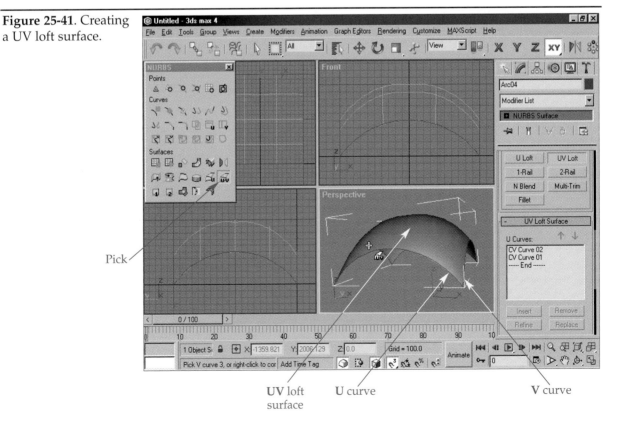

Pick

UV loft surface

U curve

V curve

and **Replace** buttons are the same as those of the corresponding buttons for a U loft surface, and are only available when the UV loft surface is edited at the sub-object level.

Checking the **Display While Creating** check box allows you to see the loft as it is being created. This may slow system performance when an intricate surface is being created. You can flip the normals of the UV loft surface by checking the **Flip Normals** check box.

Exercise 25-13

1) In the Front viewport, create an ellipse. Convert it to a NURBS model. Using the **Uniform Scale**, **Move**, and **Rotate** tools, create nine copies of the curve and arrange them in the Left viewport as shown in A below.

2) Open the **Modify** tab in the **Command Panel**. Attach all curves together. Expand the **Create Surfaces** rollout and pick the **U Loft** button. Pick the first curve, and then the second curve. Continue adding curves until all have been added. Right-click to end the command.

3) Save the scene as ex25-13a.max in the folder of your choice. Reset 3ds max.

4) Create a CV curve in the Front viewport and copy it three times in the Top viewport. Arrange the curves as shown in B below. Use the **Align** tool or NURBS snaps to precisely locate the curves.

5) Open the **Modify** tab in the **Command Panel**. Attach all four curves together.

6) Expand the **Create Surfaces** rollout and pick the **UV Loft** button. Pick the first U cross section curve. Pick the second U cross section curve opposite the first, and then right-click. Next, pick the V cross section curves. Right-click to finish. The UV loft surface should appear similar to the one shown below. Flip normals if needed.

7) Save the scene as ex25-13b.max in the folder of your choice. Reset 3ds max.

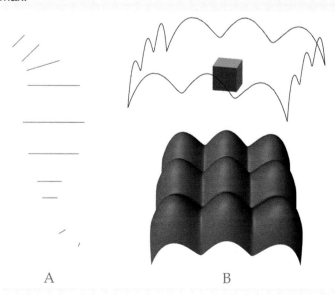

A   B

One-Rail Sweep Surface

A *one-rail sweep surface* is a dependent surface sub-object defined by curves forming cross sections and one curve forming an edge or "path." The curve acts as the edge of the sweep surface is called the *rail*. The other curves are used to form the cross sections of the sweep surface. As with curves used in U and UV lofts, the curves used to form the cross sections of the sweep should all have the same direction. In addition, the cross section curves should intersect the rail. The first cross section curve should intersect the starting point of the rail, and the final cross section curve should intersect the rail at the endpoint. Use snaps and the **Align** tool in order to precisely locate the curves.

To create a one-rail sweep surface, select a NURBS model with the rail and cross section curves positioned as you need them. Open the **Modify** tab in the **Command Panel** and expand the **Create Surfaces** rollout. Pick the **1-Rail** button in the **Dependent Surfaces** area. The **1-Rail Sweep Surface** rollout is displayed. You can also pick the **Create 1-Rail Sweep** button in the **NURBS** toolbox.

Create 1-Rail Sweep

Position the cursor over the curve that is to be used as the rail. When the curve is highlighted, pick it. The curve's name appears in the **Rail Curve:** window in the **1-Rail Sweep Surface** rollout. Now, position the cursor over the first cross section curve. When it is highlighted, pick it. If there are multiple cross sections, add the cross sections sequentially. As cross section curves are added, their names are displayed in order in the **Section Curves:** window in the **1-Rail Sweep Surface** rollout. The green iso lines of the sweep surface expand as you add more curves. Right-click to end the command. See Figure 25-42.

Figure 25-42. Creating a one-rail sweep surface.

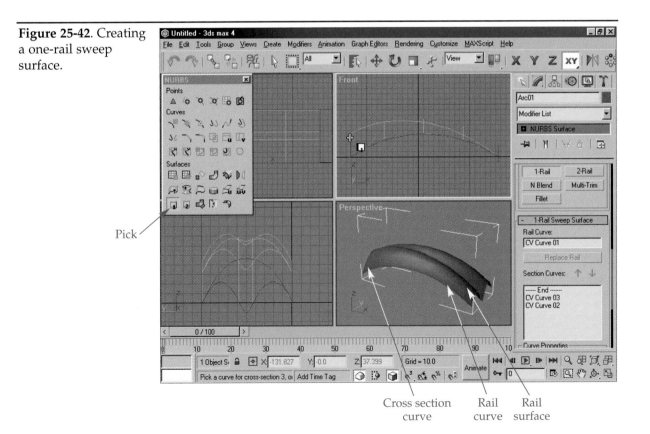

Pick

Cross section curve

Rail curve

Rail surface

You can change the order of the cross section curves by highlighting a curve name in the **Section Curves:** window and picking an arrow. To remove a curve from the sweep, highlight the curve and pick the **Remove** button. The functions of the **Insert**, **Refine**, and **Replace** buttons are the same as those of the corresponding buttons for U and UV loft surfaces.

Checking the **Reverse** check box in the **Curve Properties** area reverses the direction of the highlighted curve. This removes twists in the sweep between curves with opposite directions. The **Start Point:** spinner can be used to reassign a closed curve's starting point, allowing you to remove buckles and twists, which may form in sweeps between curves with misaligned starting points.

When the **Sweep Parallel** check box is checked, the sweep surface's normal is parallel to the rail's normal. When this check box is unchecked, the surface's normal may not match the rail's normal. The effect is most noticeable when forming sweeps between parallel curves. In this case, when the **Sweep Parallel** check box is checked, the U iso lines of the surface run parallel to the cross section curves. When the **Sweep Parallel** check box is unchecked, the U iso lines of the surface are slightly rotated to match the contour of the rail. See Figure 25-43.

When the **Snap Cross-Sections** check box is active, 3ds max automatically interprets the cross sections as if they intersect the rail. The first curve picked is placed at the rail's starting point. The last curve picked is placed at the rail's endpoint. The curves picked between are placed at the points of intersection closest to their endpoints.

Checking the **Road-Like** check box causes the sweep surface to bank through curves in the rail. You can later edit the surface at the sub-object

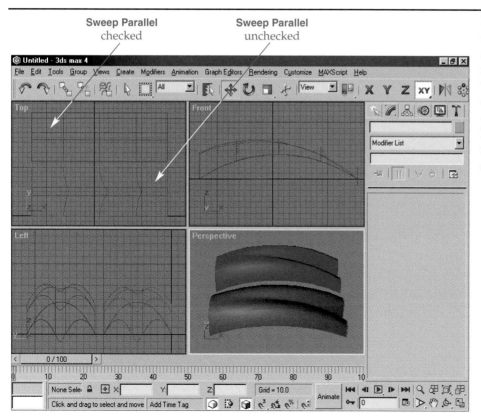

Sweep Parallel checked   Sweep Parallel unchecked

Figure 25-43. Two one-rail sweep surfaces created from identical curves with the **Sweep Parallel** check box checked and unchecked. Notice the difference in the resulting surfaces.

level and change the banking angle by rotating the corresponding vector gizmo. Since banking a surface alters its normal, activating the **Road-Like** check box automatically deactivates the **Sweep Parallel** check box.

Checking the **Display While Creating** check box allows you to see the sweep as it is being created. This may slow system performance when an intricate surface is being created. You can flip the normals of the sweep surface by checking the **Flip Normals** check box.

As is the case with U and UV loft surfaces, curves and splines can be automatically attached to one-rail and two-rail sweep surfaces. You can simply pick a top-level curve or spline, and it is automatically converted to a NURBS object, attached to the selected model, and added to the sweep. Keep in mind, if the spline has Bézier corner or corner vertices, multiple curve sub-objects are created from it as a result. Only one of the resulting curve sub-objects is added to the sweep.

Two-Rail Sweep Surface

A *two-rail sweep surface* is a dependent surface sub-object defined by curves forming cross sections. A two-rail sweep surface is very similar to a one-rail sweep surface. However, *two* rail curves are used to define the edges of a two-rail sweep surface. Additional curves define the surface's cross sections between the rails. As with a one-rail sweep surface, the cross section curves should all have the same direction, and they should intersect the rails. In addition, the endpoints of the initial cross section should meet the rail curves' starting points. Use snaps and the **Align** tool to precisely locate curves.

To create a two-rail sweep surface, select a NURBS model with the rail and cross section curves positioned as you need them. Open the **Modify** tab in the **Command Panel** and expand the **Create Surfaces** rollout. Pick the **2-Rail** button in the **Dependent Surfaces** area. The **2-Rail Sweep Surface** rollout is displayed. You can also pick the **Create 2-Rail Sweep** button in the **NURBS** toolbox.

Create 2-Rail Sweep

Position the cursor over the curve that is to be used as the first rail. When the curve is highlighted, pick it. Next, position the cursor over the second rail. When it is highlighted, pick it. The names of the rails are added to the **Rail Curves:** window in the **2-Rail Sweep Surface** rollout. Now, pick the cross section curves in order, just as you would in creating a one-rail sweep. As cross section curves are added, their names are displayed in order in the **Section Curves:** window in the **2-Rail Sweep Surface** rollout. When all of the cross section curves have been added, right-click to end the command. See Figure 25-44.

You can change the order of the cross section curves by highlighting a curve name in the **Section Curves:** window and picking the up or down arrow. To remove a curve from the sweep, highlight the curve and pick the **Remove** button. The functions of the **Insert**, **Refine**, and **Replace** buttons are the same as those of the corresponding buttons for one-rail sweep surfaces.

Checking the **Reverse** check box in the **Curve Properties** area reverses the direction of the highlighted curve. This removes twists in the sweep between curves with opposite directions. The **Start Point:** spinner can be used to reassign a closed curve's starting point, allowing you to remove

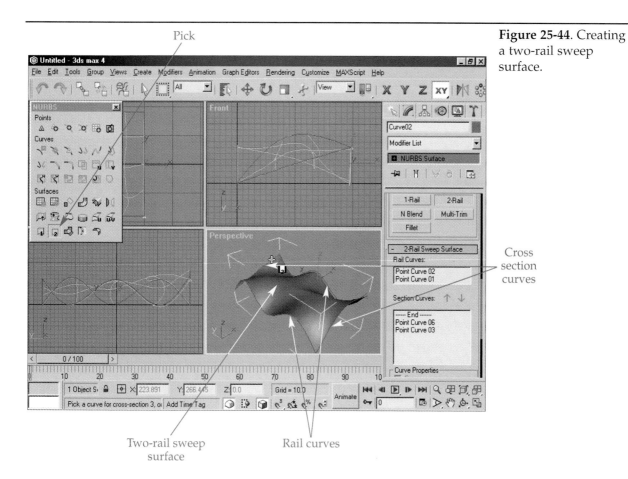

Figure 25-44. Creating a two-rail sweep surface.

buckles and twists, which may form in sweeps between curves with misaligned starting points.

Checking the **Sweep Parallel** check box causes the surface normals to be parallel to the rail normals. Checking the **Sweep Scale** check box allows the sweep to scale cross sections uniformly in all directions. When this check box is off, the cross sections of the sweep will only be scaled across the rails. When the **Snap Cross-Sections** check box is checked, 3ds max automatically interprets the cross sections as if they intersect the rail.

Checking the **Display While Creating** check box allows you to see the sweep as it is being created. This may slow system performance when an intricate surface is being created. You can flip the normals of the sweep surface by checking the **Flip Normals** check box.

Exercise

Exercise 25-14

1) Create a series of CV curves and arrange them as shown below. Be creative in drawing the cross section curves, but make sure that they intersect the rail as shown. You will need to use snaps or the **Align** tool to achieve this.
2) Open the **Modify** tab in the **Command Panel**. Attach all curves together. Expand the **Create Surfaces** rollout and pick the **1-Rail** button.
3) Pick the curve for the rail. Next, pick the first cross section curve, and then pick one of the other cross-section curves. Right-click to end the command.
4) Pick the **Undo** button in the **Main** toolbar.
5) Expand the **Create Curves** rollout and pick the **CV Curve** button. Create a curve that will be used as the second rail in a two-rail sweep. Use snaps to ensure the endpoints of the cross section curves intersect the rail curve.
6) Pick the **2-Rail** button in the **Create Surfaces** rollout. Pick the curve to be used as the first rail, and then pick the curve to be used as the second rail. Now, pick the cross section curves in order. Right-click to end the command. The resulting sweep surface should appear similar to the one shown below.
7) Save the scene as ex25-14.max in the folder of your choice. Reset 3ds max.

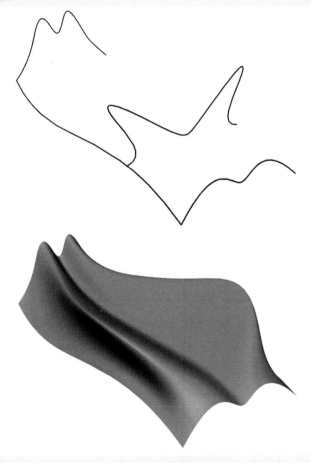

Blend Surface

A *blend surface* is a dependent surface sub-object formed between the edges of parent curves or surfaces. 3ds max analyzes the curvature of the parent sub-objects and contours the blend surface to form a smoothly curved transition between the two.

To create a blend surface, select a NURBS model that contains two or more curve and/or surface sub-objects. Open the **Modify** tab in the **Command Panel** and expand the **Create Surfaces** rollout. Pick the **Blend** button in the **Dependent Surfaces** area. The **Blend Surface** rollout is displayed. You can also pick the **Create Blend Surface** button in the **NURBS** toolbox.

Position the cursor over the first edge to be blended. If this is the edge of a surface, then the surface turns yellow, and the edge nearest to the cursor is highlighted. If you position the cursor over a curve, the curve turns blue. Pick the first edge and then position the cursor over the second edge to be blended. Then, pick the second edge. The blend surface is created. See Figure 25-45.

You can modify the blend surface using the spinners in the **Blend Surface** rollout. Increasing the values of the **Tension:** spinners causes the blend surface to more closely match the curvature of the parent edges, creating a smoother transition. Decreasing the values makes the blend surface less tangential to the parent, creating a less smooth transition. The **Tension 1:** spinner value affects the transition between the first parent edge and the blend surface. The **Tension 2:** spinner value affects the transition between the second parent edge and the blend surface.

Create Blend Surface

Pick

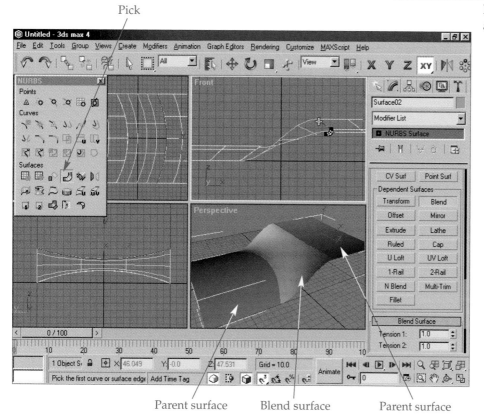

Parent surface · Blend surface · Parent surface

Figure 25-45. Creating a blend surface.

Checking the **Flip End 1** check box reverses the direction of the first surface's normals. This in effect reverses the direction of the edge used to form the blend surface. Checking the **Flip End 2** check box reverses the direction of the second surface's normals. If there are unwanted twists in the blend surface, caused by parent surfaces with opposing normals, checking one of these check boxes will solve the problem.

Checking the **Flip Tangent 1** or **Flip Tangent 2** check box reverses the angle at which the blend surface approaches the parent edge. The **Flip Tangent 1** check box controls the intersection of the first parent edge and the blend surface. The **Flip Tangent 2** check box controls the intersection of the second parent edge and the blend surface. You can flip the normals of the blend surface by checking the **Flip Normals** check box.

The **Start Point 1:** and **Start Point 2:** spinners allow you to reassign the starting points of the edges of the blend. This helps to fix unwanted twists and deformities created in the blend by unaligned starting points. These options are only available if the edges of the blend are closed.

Help Cel

The **Flip Tangent** and **Tension:** settings affect only blend surfaces created between edges of surfaces, or surface curves. They do not affect blend surfaces created from curves.

Multisided Blend Surface

A *multisided blend surface*, or *N blend surface*, is a dependent surface sub-object that caps the area enclosed by facing edges of adjoining curves or surfaces. The parent edges of a multisided blend surface must completely enclose a space without overlapping. See Figure 25-46.

Create a Multisided Blend Surface

To create a multisided blend surface, select a NURBS model in which three or four surface or curve edges form a closed loop. Open the **Modify** tab in the **Command Panel** and expand the **Create Surfaces** rollout. Pick the **N Blend** button in the **Dependent Surfaces** area. The **Multisided Blend Surface** rollout is displayed. You may also pick the **Create a Multisided Blend Surface** button in the **NURBS** toolbox.

Position the cursor over the first edge to be blended. When that edge is highlighted, pick it. Do the same for the adjacent edge. Continue picking the edges until you have completed the loop. Right-click to end the command. You can flip the normals of the multisided blend surface by checking the **Flip Normals** check box in the **Multisided Blend Surface** rollout.

Multi-Trim Surface

A *multi-trim surface* is simply a surface sub-object trimmed with multiple surface curve, iso curve, or projected curve sub-objects. When you trim a surface with a single curve, that curve must be closed, or it must stretch across the extent of the surface. However, with multi-trimming, you can use multiple curves to perform the same function. The group of curves used to create a multi-trim surface must, together, form a closed loop or stretch across the extent of the surface. See Figure 25-47. You can use surface curves, projected curves, or iso curves to create a multi-trim.

Multisided
blend surface

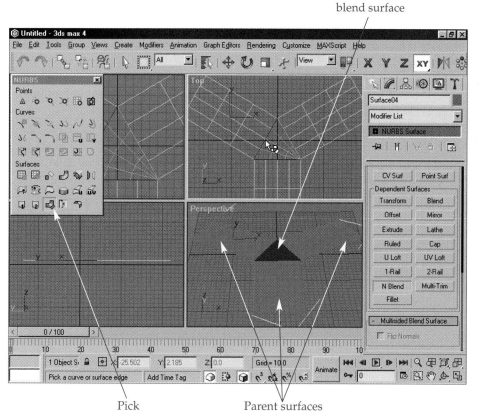

Pick   Parent surfaces

Figure 25-46. Creating a multisided blend surface. Notice the parent edges form an enclosure, which is then filled by the blend surface.

Valid   Invalid

Figure 25-47. The combinations of curves on the left side of the figure represent valid curve configurations for creating a multi-trim surface. Notice each curve is a different color. The combinations of curves on the right side of the figure are invalid configurations for creating multi-trim surfaces. A multi-trim surface is shown in the center of the figure.

To create a multi-trim surface, select a NURBS object that contains at least one surface sub-object and a group of curve sub-objects. The group of curves must form a complete circuit on the surface, or stretch across the extent of the surface. Next, open the **Modify** tab in the **Command Panel** and expand the **Create Surfaces** rollout. Pick the **Multi-Trim** button in the **Dependent Surfaces** area. The **Multicurve Trimmed Surface** rollout is displayed. You can also pick the **Create a Multicurve Trimmed Surface** button in the **NURBS** toolbox.

Create a Multicurve Trimmed Surface

First, pick the surface to be trimmed. Then, pick the first curve that is to be used in the trim. The surface turns blue when highlighted and orange when picked. Its name appears in the **Trim Curves:** window in the **Multicurve Trimmed Surface** rollout. A dashed white line is connected to the surface and the cursor. Next, add the curves of the loop in sequence. Their names appear in the **Trim Curves:** window as they are added. When the last curve is added, right-click to end the command. See Figure 25-48.

A curve can be removed from the trim by highlighting its name in the **Trim Curves:** window in the **Multicurve Trimmed Surface** rollout and picking the **Remove** button. Checking the **Flip Trim** check box switches the portion of the surface that is kept with the portion that is trimmed. You can flip the normals of the multi-trim surface by checking the **Flip Normals** check box.

Fillet Surface

A *fillet surface* is a curved surface connecting two parent surfaces. You can use the fillet surface edges to trim the parent surfaces, creating a smooth transition between the two.

To create a fillet surface, select a NURBS model that contains at least two surface sub-objects. Open the **Modify** tab in the **Command Panel** and

Figure 25-48. Creating a multicurve trim surface.

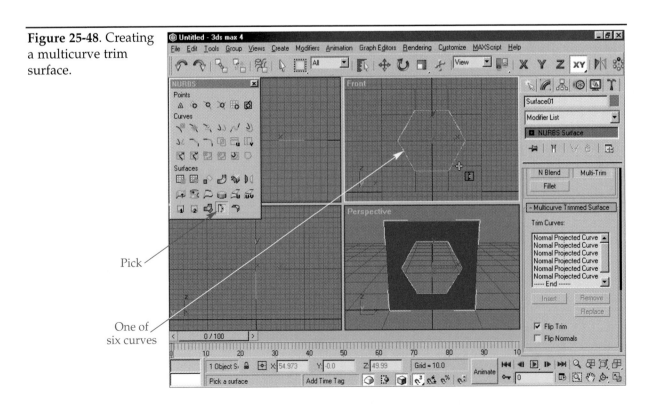

expand the **Create Surfaces** rollout. Pick the **Fillet** button in the **Dependent Surfaces** area. The **Fillet Surface** rollout is displayed. You can also pick the **Create Fillet Surface** button in the **NURBS** toolbox.

Create Fillet Surface

Pick on the first surface near the point where you want the fillet to intersect. Next, pick on the second surface near the point where you want the fillet to intersect. A yellow "seed" box is created on each parent surface, and the fillet surface is created between the two surfaces. If multiple fillets are possible, as when two surfaces form a T-intersection, the fillet is created at the location nearest to the seeds. See Figure 25-49. However, the size of the fillet surface is determined by the fillet radius.

You can adjust the radius of the fillet surface by changing the values of the **Start Radius:** and **End Radius:** spinners in the **Fillet Surface** rollout. Picking the **Lock** button sets the end radius at the same value as the start radius. This creates a uniform fillet.

The **Radius Interpolation** area contains two radio buttons that allow you to determine how the fillet radius is calculated. For these settings to affect the fillet, the start radius and the end radius must have different values. In addition, at least one of the parent surfaces must be curved. When the **Linear** radio button is active, the change in the radius distance is distributed evenly across the entire length of the fillet surface. When the **Cubic** radio button is active, the change in the fillet radius is calculated as a function of the parent surfaces' curvature, and is distributed unevenly across the length of the fillet surface. The effects of each method are most noticeable when the viewing plane is parallel to one of the parents. See Figure 25-50.

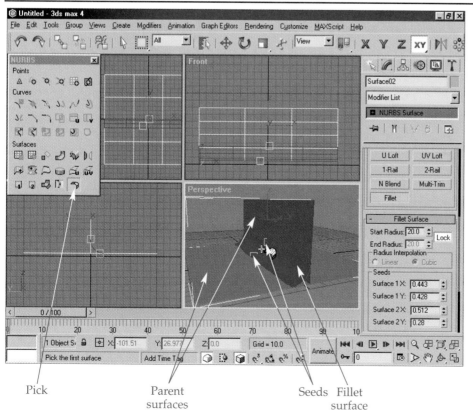

Figure 25-49. Creating a fillet surface. The locations of the seeds determine which side of the intersection is used to create the fillet surface.

Pick   Parent   Seeds Fillet
            surfaces   surface

Figure 25-50. These two fillet curves have identical radius values and the intersecting surfaces are identical.

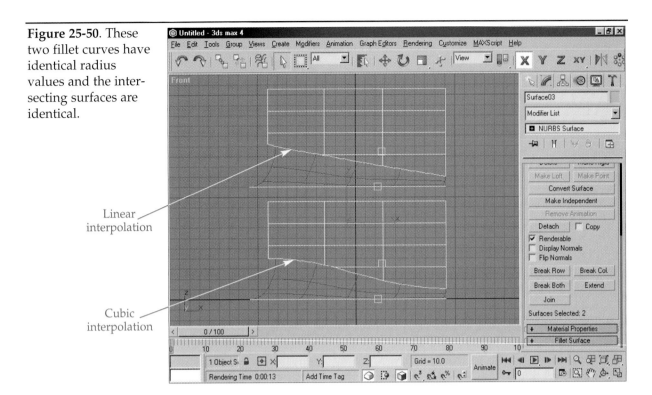

The **Seeds** area of the **Fillet Surface** rollout contains four spinners used to relocate the position of the seeds. 3ds max uses the seeds to determine the location of the fillet surface.

You can use the check boxes in the **Trim First Surface** and **Trim Second Surface** areas to trim the parent surfaces with the edges of the fillet surface. You can flip the normals of the fillet surface by checking the **Flip Normals** check box.

Chapter Snapshot

Chapter Test

Answer the following questions on a separate sheet of paper.
1) Explain the difference between dependent and independent sub-objects.
2) How are independent point sub-objects displayed in the viewports?
3) What is the difference between attaching an object and importing an object to a NURBS model?
4) If gaps are visible between adjoining NURBS surfaces in a rendered scene, how do you correct the problem?
5) What happens to dependent surface sub-objects when a modifier is applied to a NURBS model while the **Relational Stack** check box is unchecked?

6) How are dependent point sub-objects displayed in the viewports?
7) What is a fit curve?
8) What is the primary difference between a normal projected curve and a vector projected curve?
9) How do you correct a twist in a ruled surface?
10) What types of sub-objects can serve as the parents for a cap surface?
11) What is the function of the **Road-Like** check box in the **1-Rail Sweep Surface** rollout?
12) What is represented by the yellow line that is displayed in the viewports during the creation of a lathe surface?
13) What do the **Length 1:** and **Length 2:** spinner values represent when creating a chamfer curve?
14) How does the **Offset:** spinner setting affect the curvature of an offset curve or offset surface?
15) What is the difference between a CV surface created from the **Create** tab in the **Command Panel** and a CV surface created from the **Create Surfaces** rollout in the **Modify** tab?
16) How do you access the **Edit Curve on Surface** dialog box in order to create a surface point curve?
17) What is the function of seeds when creating a chamfer curve?
18) How do you remove a cross section curve from a U loft without deleting the loft surface?
19) How do you change the order of the V cross section curves in a UV loft without deleting the loft surface?
20) Briefly explain the relationship between a transform curve and its parent curve.

Modeling Problems

Draw the following models using NURBS modeling techniques and your own dimensions. Use the 3ds max objects presented in this and earlier chapters. Create and apply materials as needed, similar to those shown. Add lights and cameras as needed to create the shadows and views shown. When finished, save each model as p25-xx.max in the folder of your choice.

1 Barbed Wire

2 Clothespin

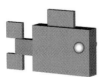

Antique Telephone **3**

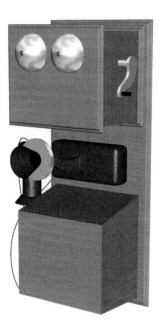

Oil Lamp **4**

5 Jug

6 Anvil

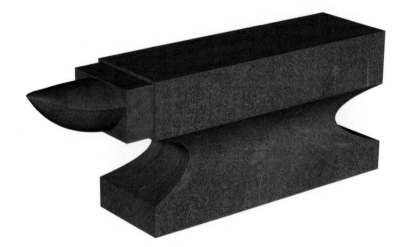

Milk Jug **7**

Drop Light **8**

9 Martin Birdhouse

10 Aluminum Cans

Coat Rack **11**

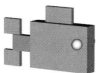

Chapter
26
Editing and Animating NURBS Models

Objectives

After completing this chapter, you will be able to:

- Identify the five sub-object selection levels.
- Use the nsurf sel modifier to modify sub-objects.
- Identify which sub-object transforms can be animated.
- Edit all types of NURBS sub-objects.
- Identify controls for applying materials to NURBS sub-objects.
- Edit a texture surface.

Editing NURBS Sub-Objects

In Chapter 24 and Chapter 25, you learned how to create various types of NURBS sub-objects. This chapter discusses how to edit, apply materials to, and animate NURBS sub-objects. As you have seen, there are many different types of NURBS sub-objects. Since each type has different characteristics and parameters, this chapter focuses primarily on the editing controls that are not available when a specific sub-object is created.

When you select a NURBS sub-object for editing, the rollouts related to the sub-object are displayed in the **Modify** tab. The parameters set when the sub-object was created can be edited. If there are additional parameters that can be changed, such as those of a mirror or lathe axis, those adjustments can also be made at the sub-object level. Many of the modifications and transformations of sub-objects can be animated, giving life to your model.

Selection Levels

The current sub-object selection level determines which NURBS sub-objects can be selected and edited. Sub-object editing can be performed at the top, surface, surface CV, curve, curve CV, and point levels. When a level is selected, you can select, transform, and edit any sub-object in the model that is on that level.

To enter sub-object mode, pick the plus sign next to the NURBS model in the sub-object tree in the modifier stack. This expands the tree and displays the sub-objects in the model. To select a level, simply highlight the sub-object name. You can also enter sub-object mode using the quad menu in a viewport. Open the quad menu and select **Sub-Objects** in the upper-left quadrant. Finally, select the appropriate level in the cascading menu.

Top Level

When editing NURBS objects, the term *top level* refers to a NURBS model. At this level, new sub-objects are created and added to the existing NURBS model. Modifiers and transforms applied at this level affect the entire NURBS model.

Surface

The *surface level* allows you to edit surface sub-objects. If the selected surface sub-objects are the children of curve sub-objects, you may be able to edit the parent curves from this level as well.

Surface CV

You can edit the control vertices of a surface at the *surface CV level*. Fine detail can be added to a NURBS model at this level. For example, if you want to model an apple from a spherical surface, much of your modeling will be done at this level. Manipulating surface CVs changes the shape of a surface, and all sub-objects related to that surface. Additional surface CVs can be added at this level as well.

Curve

The *curve level* is used for editing all types of curve sub-objects. Editing the parent curve of a dependent sub-object changes that sub-object as well as the curve. So, if you edit the parent curves of a ruled surface, you are changing the curves, the ruled surface, and any other related sub-objects.

Curve CV

At the *curve CV level,* you can add CVs, or manipulate all of the existing CVs of a CV curve, changing the curve's shape. As you manipulate a CV and change the curve's shape, you also alter all sub-objects related to the CV curve.

Point

The *point level* allows you to manipulate all point sub-objects. These can be independent points, surface points, or curve points. Transforming a point may alter related sub-objects.

Cloning NURBS Sub-Objects

When a NURBS curve or surface sub-object is cloned, you must specify how the new object is created in the **Sub-Object Clone Options** dialog box. See Figure 26-1. This dialog box is only available when

Figure 26-1. The **Sub-Object Clone Options** dialog box is used to clone NURBS curve and surface sub-objects.

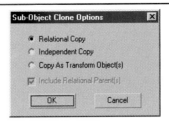

cloning a sub-object using the [Shift] key and a transform tool. Independent or dependent NURBS objects can be cloned at the sub-object level. You *cannot* clone a NURBS sub-object using the **Edit** pull-down menu.

The **Sub-Object Clone Options** dialog box contains three radio buttons that allow you to determine what type of copy is created. Picking the **Relational Copy** radio button creates a copy of the dependent object and any related parent sub-objects. This radio button is unavailable if an independent sub-object is cloned. The **Independent Copy** and **Copy As Transform Object(s)** radio buttons are available when a dependent or independent sub-object is selected for cloning. Picking the **Independent Copy** radio button creates the clone as an independent CV curve or CV surface. Picking the **Copy As Transform Object(s)** radio button creates the clone as a transform curve or transform surface dependent on the original object.

Applying Modifiers to Sub-Objects

The *nsurf sel modifier* (NURBS surface select modifier) is used to apply multiple modifiers to NURBS sub-objects without collapsing the modifier stack. Using this modifier is the only way to animate the effects of modifiers on multiple sub-objects within a NURBS model. When a modifier is applied to a sub-object without using the nsurf sel modifier, the modifier stack must be collapsed before another modifier can be applied to a sub-object selection. Applying the NURBS surface select modifier to the model allows you to select and modify additional sub-objects.

The nsurf sel modifier is used to select and modify surface, point, CV, or curve sub-objects in a model. In order to select curve, point, and curve CV sub-objects, the **Relational Stack** check box must be checked in the **General** rollout of the **Modify** tab. When the **Relational Stack** check box is not checked, the application of a modifier to a surface sub-object removes all curve sub-objects from the model.

Modifiers cannot be applied to dependent curve sub-objects. However, the curve can be made independent, and then a modifier can be applied. Modifiers can only be applied to dependent surface sub-objects when the **Relational Stack** checkbox is unchecked in the **General** rollout. When the **Relational Stack** check box is unchecked, dependent surfaces are treated as independent surfaces.

If a modifier is applied to a surface and the modifier stack is collapsed with the **Relational Stack** check box unchecked, all surfaces in the model are converted to dependent surfaces. However, the resulting dependent sub-objects have no parent sub-objects.

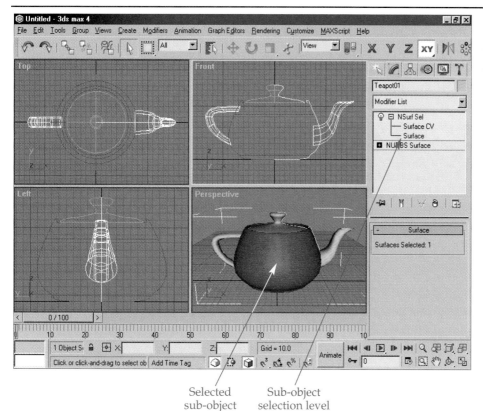

Figure 26-2. Selecting a sub-object level in the NURBS surface select modifier's hierarchy tree.

Selected sub-object

Sub-object selection level

To modify a NURBS sub-object using the nsurf sel modifier, select the NURBS model and apply the modifier. The modifier is located in the **Selection Modifiers** area of the **Modifier List** drop-down list as **NSurf Sel**. You can also apply the modifier by selecting **NURBS Surface Select** in **Selection Modifiers** or **NURBS Editing** cascading menus in the **Modifiers** pull-down menu.

Next, expand the sub-object tree in the modifier stack by picking the plus sign to the left of the modifier's name. Select a sub-object level from the expanded hierarchy tree. In a viewport, select the sub-object(s) you wish to modify. See Figure 26-2. Apply the modifiers of your choice. If you wish to modify additional sub-objects, apply additional NURBS surface select modifiers and repeat the process.

Help Cel

When the **Relational Stack** checkbox is checked, changing the shape of a parent sub-object will indirectly affect the shape of its child sub-objects as well.

Exercise

Exercise 26-1

1) Open file ex25-12.max created in Chapter 25. Select the model and open the **Modify** tab in the **Command Panel**. For this exercise, make sure the **Relational Stack** check box is unchecked in the **General** rollout.

2) Hold the project at this point. You will fetch the file to complete the second part of this exercise.

3) Select the surface sub-object level.

4) Select the bowl portion of the sugar bowl and apply a taper modifier. Set the taper **Amount:** spinner to 0.

5) Move to frame 100 and activate the **Toggle Animation Mode** button.

6) Set the taper **Amount:** spinner to 1, the primary axis to Z, and the effect axis to XY.

7) Collapse the modifier stack and select the surface sub-object. Select the lid of the sugar bowl.

8) Move to frame 0. Apply a taper modifier to the lid of the sugar bowl and set the taper amount to 0. Then, move to frame 100 and set the taper amount to –1.1. Leave the other settings at their defaults. Pick the **Play Animation** button and observe the results. When you collapsed the modifier stack, you removed the animation controllers for the base of the sugar bowl.

9) Now fetch the project. Move to frame 0, if not already on that frame.

10) Select the sugar bowl and apply the **NURBS Surface Select** modifier. Expand the modifier's hierarchy and select the surface sub-object level. Select the bowl portion of the sugar bowl.

11) Apply a taper modifier to the bowl and set the taper amount to 0.

12) Move to frame 100. While in animation mode, set the taper amount to 1.

13) Apply another **NURBS Surface Select** modifier. Expand the modifier's hierarchy and select the surface sub-object level.

14) Move to frame 0. Select the lid and apply a taper modifier. Set the taper amount to 0. Then, move to frame 100 and set the taper amount to –1.1. Leave the other settings at their defaults. Play the animation and observe the results.

15) Save the scene as ex26-01.max in the folder of your choice. Reset 3ds max.

Common Sub-Object Editing Rollouts

As discussed earlier, the rollouts available in the **Modify** tab when creating NURBS sub-objects are redisplayed when editing sub-objects, allowing you to change parameters as necessary. Many of these rollouts are common for all sub-objects at a particular sub-object selection level. The following sections discuss the common settings within the **Modify** tab rollouts, depending on which type of sub-object mode is selected for editing.

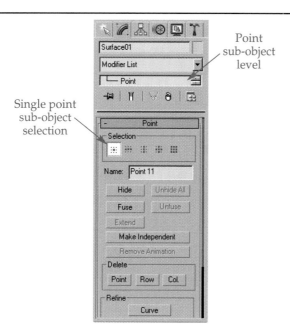

Point sub-object level

Single point sub-object selection

Figure 26-3. The **Point** rollout.

Point Rollout

Selecting the point sub-object selection level makes the **Point** rollout available. See Figure 26-3. The controls in this rollout determine the way in which point sub-objects are selected and transformed. Additional rollouts may also be made available, depending on the specific type of point sub-object selected.

Selection

The five toggle buttons in the **Selection** area of the **Point** rollout control the way point sub-objects are selected. When the **Single Point** button is active, points are selected individually. Picking a single point selects only that point. You can add additional points to the selection set by holding down [Ctrl] while picking the points. If you pick an already selected point while holding down [Ctrl], the point will be removed from the selection set. When the **Row of Points** button is active, picking a single point selects all the points in the selected point's row. A curve consists of a single row of points. Therefore, picking a curve point when the **Row of Points** button is active selects all points in the curve. When the **Column of Points** button is active, picking a single point selects all the points in the selected point's column. When the **Row and Column of Points** button is active, picking a single point selects all the points in the selected point's row and column. When the **All Points** button is active, picking a single point selects all the points in the sub-object that contains the selected point. See Figure 26-4. When the selected NURBS model contains only curves and points, the **Single Point** and **All Points** buttons are the only ones available.

At the bottom of the **Point** rollout is a label displaying the number of points currently selected. This can be useful in determining if any fused or coincidental points are selected.

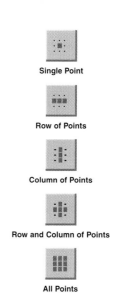

Single Point

Row of Points

Column of Points

Row and Column of Points

All Points

Figure 26-4. The effects of the different selection buttons.

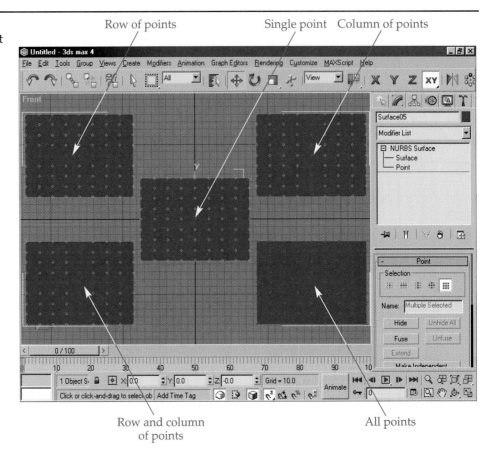

Row of points · Single point · Column of points

Row and column of points · All points

Name

The **Name:** window in the **Point** rollout displays the name of the selected point. If the point has not been specifically named, it is assigned a number. You can enter a custom name for the point in this text box. Default point names may not be meaningful.

In the case of the points in a point surface, the numbers are assigned in ascending order from bottom to top in each column. In a 4 × 4 point surface, the first point in the first column is numbered as 01. The second point in the first column is numbered as 02. The first point in the second column is numbered as 05, and so forth. In the case of a point curve, which is composed of a single row of points, the numbers are assigned in ascending order from the starting point to the endpoint.

Hide

Picking the **Hide** button in the **Point** rollout hides the selected point. Once a point has been hidden, it cannot be selected. Picking the **Unhide All** button redisplays all hidden points. Once points have been unhidden, they can be selected.

Fuse

Picking the **Fuse** button in the **Point** rollout fuses two points together. Although they remain separate sub-objects, the fused points act as a single point. This is useful in connecting curve or surface sub-objects together. The fuse function is also useful in preventing the accidental movement of coincidental points. Fused points are displayed in purple when unselected.

To fuse points together, you must be at the point sub-object level. Pick the **Fuse** button and then pick the first point you wish to fuse, turning it blue. Carefully pick the second point you wish to fuse. If the points are not coincidental, the first point is moved to the second point. The points are made coincidental and affect the curves, or surfaces, as such.

The **Unfuse** button becomes available when a set of fused points is selected. Picking the **Unfuse** button unfuses the points, but this action does not relocate the points if they were moved during the fusing process.

Exercise 26-2

Exercise

1) Create a point surface and a point curve in any viewport. Open the **Modify** tab in the **Command Panel**, and attach the point curve to the point surface.
2) Expand the sub-object hierarchy tree and select the point sub-object level.
3) Activate the **Single Point** selection button and select individual points on the surface, observing their numbers in the **Name:** window. Before picking a point, try to predict its name. Now, activate the other selection buttons one at a time, and experiment with using them to select points.
4) Pick the **Fuse** button, and then pick the starting point on the point curve. Next, pick one corner of the point surface. The starting point on the curve is moved to the corner of the surface.
5) While the **Fuse** button is still active, pick the endpoint on the curve, and then pick another corner of the surface. Notice the result. Pick the **Fuse** button again to deactivate it.
6) Activate the **All Points** selection button. Select a point on the curve. Lock the selection set using the space bar. Using the **Select and Move** button, drag the curve around the viewport. Notice the effect on the surface. Why is the surface affected in this way?
7) Reset 3ds max. Do not save the file.

Extend

Picking the **Extend** button in the **Point** rollout allows you to add additional points to the end of an open point curve, thereby extending the curve. The extension of a point curve cannot be animated.

To extend a point curve, you must be at the point sub-object level. Pick the **Extend** button and position the cursor over the curve you wish to extend. The curve is highlighted blue and a blue box forms at the endpoint nearest to the cursor. Pick the endpoint and drag the cursor to the desired location. See Figure 26-5. Release the mouse button to add the point and extend the point curve.

Figure 26-5.
Extending a point
curve.

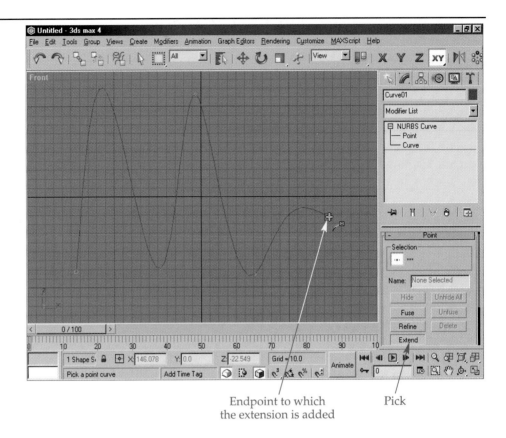

Endpoint to which
the extension is added

Pick

If you extend the curve from its starting point, the new point
becomes the starting point for the curve. Points cannot be added to a
closed point curve using the **Extend** function.

To add coincidental points, drag the cursor to the desired location for
coincidental points. Release the mouse button to add the first point. Pick
the newly added endpoint, drag the cursor outward, and then drag it
back to the endpoint. When the cursor is positioned over the endpoint,
release the mouse button to create the coincidental point.

Exercise

Exercise 26-3

1) Create an open point curve in any viewport. Select the curve and
   open the **Modify** tab in the **Command Panel**.
2) Expand the sub-object hierarchy tree and select the point sub-
   object level.
3) Pick the **Extend** button. Pick and drag an endpoint of the curve to
   create a new point. Now, pick and drag the opposite endpoint of
   the curve.
4) Reset 3ds max. Do not save the file.

Make Independent and Remove Animation

Picking the **Make Independent** button in the **Point** rollout converts a dependent point into an independent point. Making a dependent point independent removes its animation controllers.

Picking the **Remove Animation** button in the **Point** rollout removes animation controllers for the selected points. However, this does not affect dependency.

Delete

Picking the **Delete** button in the **Point** rollout deletes the selected points from a point curve or surface. If the NURBS model contains a point surface, three buttons appear in the **Delete** area of the **Point** rollout. Picking the **Point** button deletes only the selected point. This is the only button available unless the selected point is on a point surface. Picking the **Row** button deletes all the points in the selected point's row. Picking the **Col.** button deletes all points in the selected point's column. Deleting points cannot be animated.

Refine

There are many instances when it is necessary to add points to sub-objects. This is called *refining.* For example, it may be necessary to add points to create fine detail in a model. You may also add points to isolate specific areas of a sub-object. Remember, however, that as you increase point density in your model, you also increase computation time. The refinement of a curve or surface cannot be animated.

If the NURBS model contains only curves and points, the **Refine** button is displayed in the **Point** rollout. Picking this button allows you to add a point on the curve.

If the NURBS model contains a point surface, four buttons are available in the **Refine** area of the **Point** rollout. Picking one of these buttons allows you to add points to a point curve or surface.

Picking the **Curve** button in the **Refine** area allows you to add a single point to a point curve sub-object. To refine a point curve, pick the **Curve** button and then pick anywhere on the curve to create the new point. Right-click or pick the button again to cancel the command.

Picking the **Surf Row** button in the **Refine** area allows you to add a row of points to a surface. To add a row of points, simply pick the **Surf Row** button, and then pick anywhere on the surface to create the points. The new row of points intersects the picked point. Right-click or pick the button again to cancel the command.

Picking the **Surf Col.** button in the **Refine** area allows you to add a column of points to a surface. To create a new column of points, pick the **Surf Col.** button. Next, pick anywhere on the surface to create the new column of points. The new column of points intersects the picked point. Right-click or pick the button again to cancel the command.

Figure 26-6. An extra row and column of points being added to the surface at a location intersecting the cursor.

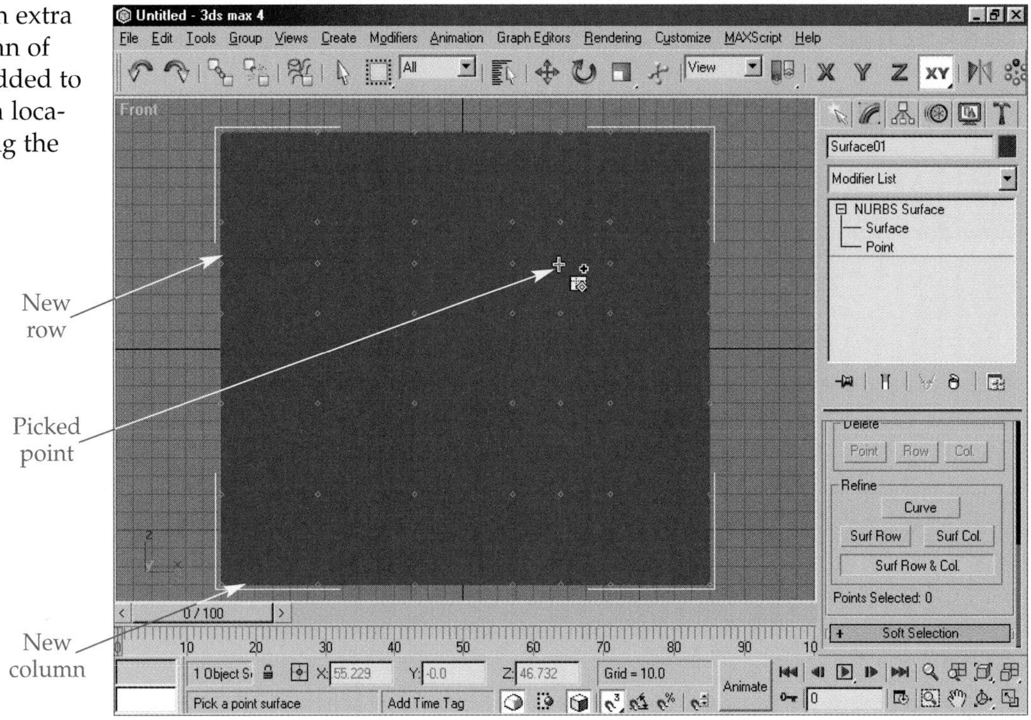

New row

Picked point

New column

Picking the **Surf Row & Col.** button in the **Refine** area allows you to add both a row and a column of points to a surface. To create a new row and column of points, pick the **Surf Row & Col.** button. Then, pick any location on the surface. A new row of points and a new column of points are formed, intersecting at the picked point. See Figure 26-6. Right-click or pick the button again to cancel the command.

Exercise 26-4

1) Create a point surface of any size in the Top viewport. Use the default values for the length and width points. Select the surface, and then open the **Modify** tab in the **Command Panel**.
2) Expand the sub-object hierarchy tree and select the point sub-object level.
3) Select the four corner points of the surface, and lock the selection set.
4) Move to frame 100 and activate the **Toggle Animation Mode** button.
5) Uniformly scale the points in the selection set to about 150%. Play the animation and observe the motion.
6) Move to frame 0. Pick the **Surf Row** button in the **Refine** area of the **Point** rollout. Add a new row of points just inside the top and bottom horizontal edges.
7) Pick the **Surf Col.** button. Add a new column of points just inside each of the vertical edges of the surface. Refer to the figure shown.
8) Play the animation and observe the motion.
9) Reset 3ds max. Do not save the file.

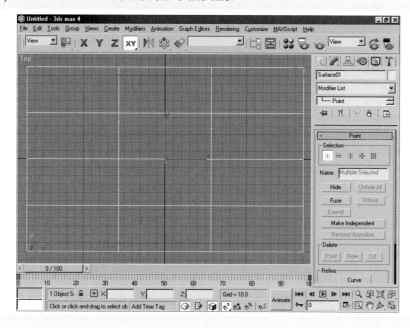

Soft Selection Rollout

The **Soft Selection** rollout is available at the point sub-object level. It contains controls that determine the way in which the transformation of a point or CV affects its neighbors. In 3D Studio MAX Release 2.5 and earlier, these controls are called **Affect Region** controls.

When the **Soft Selection:** check box in the **Soft Selection** rollout is unchecked, a point's influence does not extend beyond its neighboring points. Therefore, when a surface has more points, each point affects a smaller area. If a surface has few points, then each point affects a large surface area. See Figure 26-7.

Figure 26-7. The surface on the right contains twice as many points as the surface on the left. When an identical transform is applied to a corresponding point on each surface, the effect is more localized in the surface with the higher point density.

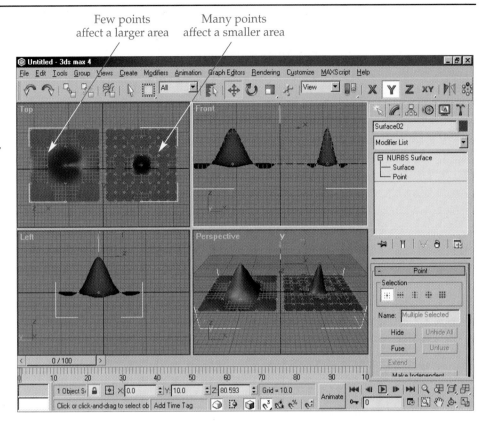

When the **Soft Selection:** check box in the **Soft Selection** rollout is checked, a point's influence is adjustable. You can adjust not only the extent of a point's influence, but also the way surrounding points are affected by the transformation of the selected point. The area of influence of a selected point is indicated by the color of the surrounding points. The amount of red in a point's color corresponds to the amount of influence the selected point exerts over it. Points that are mostly red are greatly influenced by a transformation in the selected point. Points that are mostly green are only slightly affected. See Figure 26-8.

Checking the **Affect Neighbors** check box allows a point's influence to affect points in neighboring sub-objects. Checking the **Same Type Only** check box restricts a selected point's influence to only points of the same type.

Beneath the check boxes is a graphic representation of a point's influence. If you select a single point on a planar surface and move it normal to the surface, a side view cross section of the result will loosely resemble this graph. See Figure 26-9.

The **Falloff:** spinner value sets the diameter of a point's sphere of influence. The **Pinch:** spinner value determines the curvature of the resulting geometry. A setting of zero produces a smooth curvature, while the maximum setting of 10 produces a very sharp point. A negative setting causes neighboring points to rise above the selected point, resulting in dimpled geometry. The **Bubble:** spinner value determines the "fullness" of the curve. A setting of 1 produces a smooth bulge. Greater values cause the resulting geometry to curve back on its self, forming a dimple or crater. Negative values cause a depression to form at the edge of the affected region.

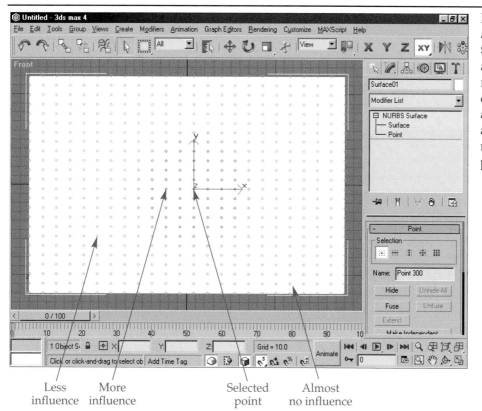

Figure 26-8. Selecting a point while the **Soft Selection** setting is active. The amount of red in a point's color corresponds to the amount that it will be affected by a transformation of the selected point.

Less influence   More influence   Selected point   Almost no influence

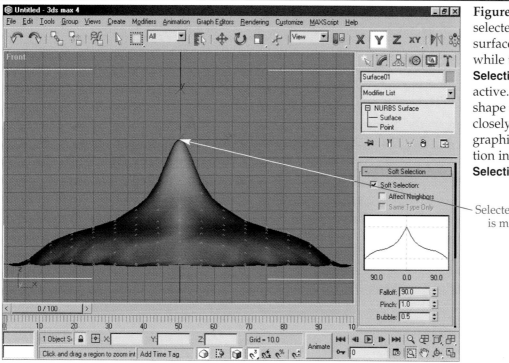

Figure 26-9. A selected point on a surface being moved while the **Soft Selection** setting is active. The resulting shape of the surface closely resembles the graphic representation in the **Soft Selection** rollout.

Selected point is moved

Help Cel

Transformations made with soft selection are not dynamically updated when the settings are changed. This means that changing the settings for **Falloff:**, **Pinch:**, and **Bubble:** will only affect transformations made after the settings are changed. The changes are not applied to previous transformations.

Exercise

Exercise 26-5

1) Create a point surface in the Top viewport. Make the length approximately 150 units. Make the width approximately 250 units. Set the number of points to 12 for both the width and length.
2) Select the surface and open the **Modify** tab in the **Command Panel**. Expand the sub-object hierarchy tree and select the point sub-object level.
3) Select Point 23 on the surface. This is one in from the top, left corner. Lock the selection. Pick the **Select and Move** tool. In the Front viewport, move the point 30 units in the local Y direction.
4) Expand the **Soft Selection** rollout and check the **Soft Selection:** check box. Increase the **Falloff:** spinner value to 60.
5) Unlock the selection, select Point 18 on the surface, and lock the selection. In the Front viewport, move the point 30 units in the local Y direction.
6) In the **Soft Selection** rollout, increase the **Pinch:** spinner value to 1. Unlock the selection, select Point 70, and lock the selection. In the Front viewport, move the point 30 units in the local Y direction.
7) In the **Soft Selection** rollout, increase the **Bubble:** spinner value to 2. Unlock the selection, select Point 63, and lock the selection. In the Front viewport, move the point 30 units in the local Y direction.
8) In the **Soft Selection** rollout, set the **Pinch:** spinner value to –2. Unlock the selection, select Point 118, and lock the selection. In the Front viewport, move the point 30 units in the local Y direction.
9) In the **Soft Selection** rollout, set the **Bubble:** spinner value to –2, and decrease the **Falloff:** spinner value to 40. Unlock the selection, select Point 111, and lock the selection. In the Front viewport, move the point 30 units in the local Y direction.
10) Save the scene as ex26-05.max in the folder of your choice. Reset 3ds max.

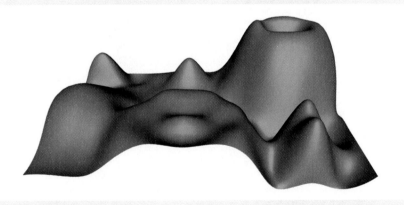

Point Type-Specific Rollouts

In addition to the **Point** rollout common to the point sub-object level, the selection of many types of points activates additional rollouts in the **Modify** tab. These rollouts are essentially the same as the rollouts used to create the points. However, additional controls may be activated at the sub-object level. The options not yet covered are discussed in detail in the following sections. If a control is not specifically mentioned, it is covered in detail in Chapter 25.

Curve Point

Selecting a curve point at the sub-object level activates the **Curve Point** rollout. See Figure 26-10. The spinners in this rollout can be adjusted to relocate the point on the curve, or to make and adjust the point's offset. Check boxes at the bottom of this rollout allow you to trim the parent curve. The **Replace Base Curve** button allows you to select a new parent curve for the point.

The U position and offset position settings can be animated. When a change is made to these settings while in animation mode, a key is created for the spinner. The point's position changes gradually from the previous key to the new key, as controlled by the key settings.

The trim settings and parent curve selection cannot be animated. If you trim the parent curve or select a new parent curve while in animation mode, the change is transferred to frame 0 and no animation key is set.

Offset Point

When an offset point is selected at the sub-object level, the **Offset Point** rollout is displayed. See Figure 26-11. The point can be placed directly on its parent by activating the **At Point** radio button. Its offset can be adjusted using the spinners in this rollout. Picking the **Replace Base Point** button allows you to select a new parent point.

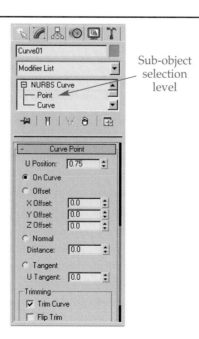

Sub-object selection level

Figure 26-10. The **Curve Point** rollout.

Adjustments made to the point's offset can be animated. However, you cannot animate the selection of a new base point. In addition, you cannot animate the effects of the **At Point** radio button.

Surface Point

When a surface point is selected at the sub-object level, the **Surface Point** rollout is displayed. See Figure 26-12. The surface point can be repositioned on the surface, or its offset adjusted using the spinners in this rollout. In addition, a new parent surface can be chosen by picking the **Replace Base Surface** button.

The changes in the point's position can be animated. However, a change in the type of offset cannot be animated. The selection of a new parent curve also cannot be animated.

Figure 26-11. The **Offset Point** rollout.

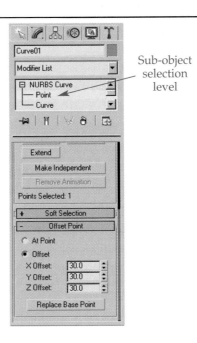

Figure 26-12. The **Surface Point** rollout.

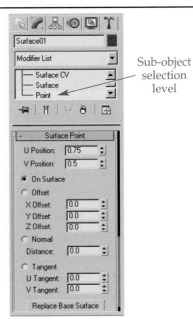

Exercise 26-6

1) In the Top viewport, create a CV surface roughly 150 units by 150 units. Open the **Modify** tab in the **Command Panel** and expand the **Create Curves** rollout. Pick the **Point Curve** button. In the Front viewport, create an S-shaped curve that passes through the surface.
2) Expand the **Create Points** rollout and pick the **Curve Point** button. Create a curve point at the starting point of the point curve. In the **Curve Point** rollout, check the **Trim Curve** and **Flip Trim** check boxes. The curve should disappear, leaving only the point.
3) Pick the **Surf Point** button and create a surface point anywhere on the CV surface.
4) Pick the **Offset Point** button, and select the surface point as the parent point. In the **Offset Point** rollout, set the **X Offset:**, **Y Offset:**, and **Z Offset:** spinners to 20.
5) In the **Create Curves** rollout, pick the **Curve Fit** button. Pick the surface point as the fit curve's starting point. Pick the offset point next. Finally, pick the curve point. Right-click to complete the curve.
6) Move to frame 100 and activate the **Toggle Animation Mode** button.
7) Expand the sub-object hierarchy tree and select the point sub-object level.
8) Pick the surface point and move it to a different location on the surface. Pick the offset point and increase its **Z Offset:** spinner value to 60. Finally, pick the curve point and increase its **U Position:** spinner value until the point roughly touches the surface.
9) Pick the **Play Animation** button and observe the results.
10) Save the scene as ex26-06.max in the folder of your choice. Reset 3ds max.

Surface-Curve Intersection Point

When a surface-curve intersection point is selected at the sub-object level, the **Surface-Curve Intersection Point** rollout is displayed. The controls in this rollout allow you to trim the curve, move the seed to select a different intersection, and select different parent sub-objects. No changes made to the settings in this rollout can be animated.

Curve-Curve Intersection

When a curve-curve point is selected at the sub-object level, the **Curve-Curve Intersection** rollout becomes available. The controls in this rollout can be used to trim either of the parent curves, to reposition the seeds to select a new intersection, and to replace either of the parent curves. None of these changes can be animated.

CV Rollout

When the sub-object selection level is set to surface CV or curve CV, the **CV** rollout is displayed. See Figure 26-13. The settings in this rollout control CV selection and transformation. The controls function primarily in the same manner whether the sub-object selection level is set to curve CV or to surface CV. However, more controls are available when the sub-object selection level is set to surface CV.

Figure 26-13.
The **CV** rollout for a surface CV.

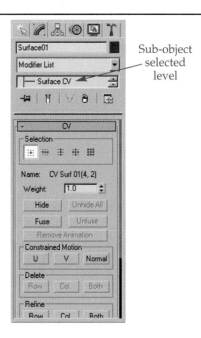

Sub-object selected level

Selection

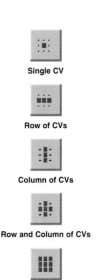

Single CV

Row of CVs

Column of CVs

Row and Column of CVs

All CVs

The toggle buttons in the **Selection** area of the **CV** rollout control the way in which CV sub-objects are selected. Five buttons are available when the surface CV sub-object selection level is selected. When the **Single CV** button is active, CVs are selected individually. Picking a CV selects only that CV. Pressing [Ctrl] while selecting a point adds the CV to the selection set. To remove a single CV from the selection set, hold [Ctrl] while selecting the point. When the **Row of CVs** button is active, picking a CV selects all the CVs in the same row as the selected CV. When the **Column of CVs** button is active, picking a CV selects all the CVs in the same column as the selected CV. When the **Row and Column of CVs** button is active, picking a CV selects all the CVs in the same row and all the CVs in the same column as the selected CV. When the **All CVs** button is active, picking a CV selects all the CVs in the sub-object. Only the **All CVs** and **Single CV** buttons are available when the curve CV sub-object selection level is selected.

At the bottom of the **CV** rollout, the number of CVs currently selected is displayed. This is extremely useful in determining whether any fused or coincidental CVs are selected.

Name

The **Name:** listing in the **CV** rollout displays the name of the selected CV. If no CVs are selected, No CVs Selected is displayed. If multiple CVs are selected, Multiple CVs Selected is displayed. If a single CV is selected at the curve CV sub-object selection level, the curve name is displayed followed by the CV's number. If a single CV is selected at the surface CV sub-object selection level, the surface's name is displayed followed by the CV's row and column in parentheses. You *cannot* use this listing to customize a CV's name.

Weight

The **Weight:** spinner setting in the **CV** rollout determines the amount of influence the selected CVs exert on the shape of the curve or surface. This setting is available at both the surface CV and curve CV sub-object selection levels. Increasing the value of the spinner pulls the curve or surface closer to the CV. Decreasing the value of the spinner causes the curve or surface to fall away from the CV. The change in a CV's weight can be animated.

Hide

The **Hide** button in the **CV** rollout is available at both the surface CV and curve CV sub-object selection levels. Picking this button hides selected CVs. Once a CV is hidden, it cannot be selected. However, its influence remains. Picking the **Unhide All** button displays all hidden CVs, allowing them to be selected. The hide and unhide functions have no effect on animation.

Fuse

Picking the **Fuse** button in the **CV** rollout allows you to fuse two CVs together. Although they remain separate sub-objects, the fused CVs are selected as a single CV. The CVs are made coincidental and affect the curves, or surfaces, as such. This is useful in connecting curve or surface sub-objects together. The fuse function is also useful in preventing the accidental movement of coincidental CVs. Fused CVs are displayed in purple when not selected.

To fuse CVs together, you must be in the curve CV or surface CV sub-object editing mode. Pick the **Fuse** button in the **CV** rollout and pick the first CV you wish to fuse, turning it blue. See Figure 26-14. A dashed

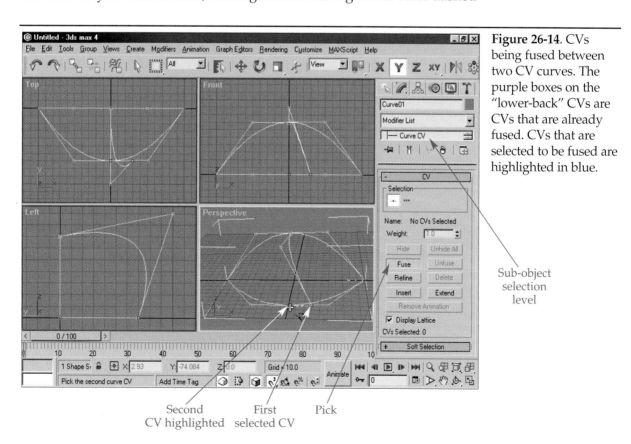

Figure 26-14. CVs being fused between two CV curves. The purple boxes on the "lower-back" CVs are CVs that are already fused. CVs that are selected to be fused are highlighted in blue.

Sub-object selection level

Second CV highlighted   First selected CV   Pick

white line is attached to the first CV and the cursor. Carefully pick the second CV you wish to fuse. You can use the [H] key to select by name. If the CVs are not coincidental, the first CV is moved to the second CV.

The **Unfuse** button is available when a set of fused CVs is selected. Picking the **Unfuse** button unfuses the CVs. However, this action does not relocate them even if they were moved during the fusing process. When the CVs are unfused, all previously fused CVs inherit the weight of the last CV fused.

When CVs are fused, the change is applied to all frames of the animation. The fused CVs inherit the animation controllers of the last CV fused. When the CVs are unfused, all animation controllers for those CVs are lost.

Remove Animation

The **Remove Animation** button in the **CV** rollout is available at both the curve CV and surface CV sub-object selection levels. Picking this button removes all animation controllers from the selected CVs. The button is greyed out unless the selected CV has an animation controller applied to it.

Exercise

Exercise 26-7

1) In any viewport, create a CV curve containing five CVs.
2) Open the **Modify** tab in the **Command Panel**. Expand the sub-object hierarchy tree and select the curve CV sub-object level.
3) Move to frame 100 and activate the **Toggle Animation Mode** button.
4) Select and move each CV individually. Play the animation. When you have finished, return the time slider to frame 100
5) Turn on animation mode, if not already on. Fuse any two of the center CVs. Play the animation. What happens? When the animation has finished, return the time slider to frame 100.
6) Turn on animation mode, if not already on. Select the third center CV and increase its weight to 10. Play the animation. What happens? When you have finished, return the time slider to frame 100.
7) Turn on animation mode, if not already on. Select the fused CVs, and unfuse them. Select the two endpoints of the curve and pick the **Remove Animation** button. Play the animation. What happens?
8) Reset 3ds max. Do not save the file.

Refine

When the sub-object selection level is set to curve CV, a single button in the **CV** rollout is available to refine a curve. Picking the **Refine** button allows you to place CVs between existing CVs on the curve's control lattice. This does not change the curve's shape, but it uses more CVs to define it. Adding CVs allows for finer tuning of the curve's shape later.

To refine a curve, simply pick the **Refine** button. Position the cursor over the control lattice where you wish to refine the curve. All CVs of the curve are highlighted and rearranged to make room for the new CV. A blue box appears on the control lattice at the location where the new CV will be placed. You can move this box by repositioning the cursor. When the blue box is in the proper position, simply pick to create the new CV.

When the sub-object selection level is set to surface CV, three buttons in the **Refine** area of the **CV** rollout are available to refine a network of surface CVs. When the **Row** button is picked, the surface's CVs are displaced by rows to make room for the new CVs. Picking on the surface creates a new row of CVs between the two existing rows closest to the cursor. When the **Col.** button is picked, the surface's CVs are displaced by columns. Picking on the surface creates a new column of CVs between the two existing columns closest to the cursor. When the **Both** button is picked, the surface's CVs are displaced by both rows and columns. Picking on the surface creates a new row and a new column of CVs between the existing rows and columns nearest to the cursor's location. See Figure 26-15.

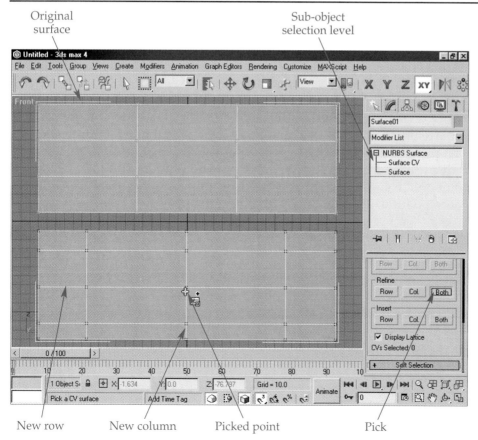

Original surface

Sub-object selection level

Figure 26-15. Refining a CV surface. Existing CVs are moved to accommodate the new CVs being created.

New row   New column   Picked point   Pick

When a network of curve or surface CVs is refined, all CVs in that sub-object lose their animation controllers. In other words, any animation of that sub-object done at the CV level is lost. The sub-object appears in its altered state in all frames of the animation.

Delete

When the sub-object selection level is set to curve CV, a single button in the **CV** rollout is available to delete a selected CV. Picking the **Delete** button permanently removes the selected CV from the curve.

When the sub-object selection level is set to surface CV, three buttons in the **Delete** area of the **CV** rollout can be used to remove selected CVs. When the **Row** button is picked, all rows containing selected CVs are deleted. When the **Col.** button is picked, all columns containing selected CVs are deleted. Picking the **Both** button deletes all rows and all columns containing selected CVs. CVs cannot be deleted if the action will result in fewer than four rows *or* four columns of CVs in the surface. The deletion of CVs cannot be animated.

Help Cel

Deleting CVs probably will affect the shape of a surface or curve.

Insert

When the sub-object selection level is set to curve CV, a single **Insert** button is available in the **CV** rollout. The insert function is very similar to the refine function. However, when the **Insert** button is used, existing CVs are not relocated. For this reason, inserting CVs may affect the curve's shape. To insert a curve CV, simply pick the **Insert** button, and then pick the location on the control lattice where you wish to place the new CV.

When the sub-object selection level is set to surface CV, three buttons in the **Insert** area of the **CV** rollout can be used to insert CVs. To insert a row of CVs, pick the **Row** button, and then pick a location on the surface to place the row. To insert a column of CVs, pick the **Col.** button, and then pick a location on the surface to create the new column. To insert both a row and column of CVs, pick the **Both** button, and then pick a point on the surface where the new row and new column of CVs will intersect. Inserting new CVs cannot be animated.

Display Lattice

If the **Display Lattice** check box is checked in the **CV** rollout, the control lattice for the selected object is displayed in all viewports at the curve CV and surface CV sub-object selection levels. This setting has no effect on animation.

Extend

The **Extend** button is available in the **CV** rollout only when the sub-object selection level is set to curve CV. It is used to add CVs to the end of a CV curve, thus extending the curve. To extend a CV curve, pick the **Extend** button and position the cursor over one endpoint of the CV curve. Pick the endpoint and drag to the desired location for the new endpoint. Release the mouse button to create a pair of new CVs between the former endpoint CV and the new endpoint CV. The extension of a curve cannot be animated.

Constrained Motion

The buttons in the **Constrained Motion** area are available in the **CV** rollout when the sub-object selection level is set to surface CV. These buttons allow you to limit the movement of surface CVs to a particular dimension. Picking the **U** button, or pressing [Alt][U], restricts the movement of the selected CVs to the surface's U dimension. Picking the **V** button, or pressing [Alt][V], restricts the movement of the selected CVs to the surface's V dimension. Picking the **Normal** button, or pressing [Alt][N], restricts the movement of the selected CVs to the normal of the surface at each point's location.

To use this feature, select a CV or a group of CVs. Pick the appropriate constraint button or key combination. Drag the CVs to the desired position and release the mouse button. This deactivates the constraint.

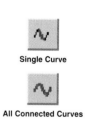

Curve Common Rollout

When the sub-object selection level is set to **Curve** in the **Modify** tab, the **Curve Common** rollout is displayed. See Figure 26-16. This rollout contains controls to help you select and manipulate curve sub-objects. The rollout controls discussed in the following sections are available for all curve types.

Selection

The two buttons in the **Selection** area of the **Curve Common** rollout determine how curves are selected. When the **Single Curve** button is active, picking a curve selects only that curve. When the **All Connected Curves** button is active, picking a curve selects all connected curves.

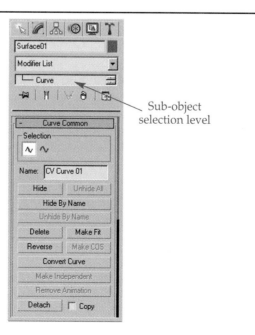

Sub-object selection level

Figure 26-16. The **Curve Common** rollout.

Connected curves include curves that share fused points, dependent curves that link the selected curve to another curve, and curves that are linked to the selected curve by dependent curves.

The number of curves currently selected is displayed at the bottom of the **Curve Common** rollout. This is useful when working with a model containing many curve sub-objects.

Name

The **Name:** window in the **Curve Common** rollout displays the name of the currently selected curve. By default, the name is the type of curve followed by an assigned number. You can change the name of the currently selected curve by typing a new name in this window.

Hide

Picking the **Hide** button in the **Curve Common** rollout hides the selected curve. Once a curve is hidden, it cannot be selected. You can also hide a curve by name. To do this, pick the **Hide By Name** button and select the name of the curve in the **Select Sub-Objects** dialog box. Picking the **Unhide All** button reveals all hidden curves. Once curves are redisplayed, they can be selected. The **Unhide By Name** button allows you to select and reveal a hidden curve by name. To do this, pick the **Unhide By Name** button and select the curve's name from the **Select Sub-Objects** dialog box. The hide and unhide controls have no effect on animation.

Delete

Picking the **Delete** button deletes the selected curve sub-object. Deleting a curve cannot be animated.

Make Fit

The **Make Fit** button in the **Curve Common** rollout is used to convert a CV curve into a point curve. It is also used to change the number of points contained within a selected point curve.

To convert a CV curve, first select the CV curve. Next, pick the **Make Fit** button to open the **Make Point Curve** dialog box. See Figure 26-17. The **Number of Points:** spinner in this dialog box sets the number of points the converted curve will contain. The display of the curve in the viewports is automatically updated to reflect the change in the number of points. Pick the **OK** button to complete the conversion.

To change the number of points in a point curve, first select the curve. Next, pick the **Make Fit** button. This opens the **Make Point Curve** dialog box. Use the **Number of Points:** spinner to add or subtract points from the curve. If you are adding points, the result is similar to refining the curve. Existing points are displaced to make room for the new points without changing the shape of the curve. If points are being removed,

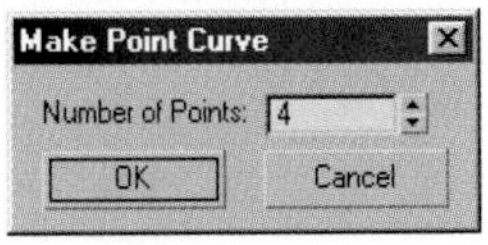

Figure 26-17. The **Make Point Curve** dialog box.

the shape of the curve is changed. Once the points have been removed, and the shape of the curve has changed, increasing the number of points in the curve will not restore the original shape. Changes made using the **Make Fit** button cannot be animated.

Reverse

Picking the **Reverse** button in the **Curve Common** rollout reverses the direction of the curve. Curve direction is extremely important in creating many surface sub-objects. If two parent curves of a surface sub-object have opposite directions, the resulting surface will be twisted.

The direction of a curve always progresses from the starting point to the endpoint. At the curve sub-object level, a small circle at one end of the curve denotes its starting point. In a closed curve, a small plus sign appears on the curve to one side of the small starting point circle. A closed curve's direction runs from the starting point circle in the direction of the plus sign.

If the selected curve is open, picking the **Reverse** button switches the endpoint and the starting point, and reorders the points or CVs between. If the selected curve is closed, picking the **Reverse** button causes the plus sign to jump to the other side of the starting point circle, and all points or CVs in the closed curve are reordered. See Figure 26-18. You cannot animate the reversing of a curve's direction.

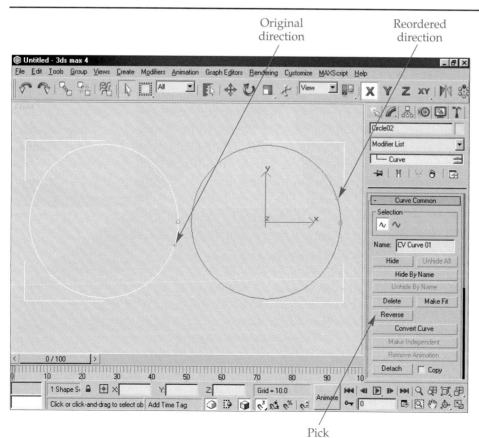

Original direction — Reordered direction

Pick

Figure 26-18. The direction of the curve on the right is reversed from the original on the left. Notice the relocation of the green plus sign.

Help Cel

A new starting point can be assigned in a closed curve by using the **Make First** button. This is discussed in detail later in this chapter.

Exercise

Exercise 26-8

1) In the Top viewport, create a straight point curve, starting near the upper-left edge of the viewport and ending near the upper right edge of the viewport.
2) In the same viewport, create a straight CV curve. Begin this curve near the lower-*right* corner of the viewport, and end it near the lower-*left* corner of the viewport.
3) Open the **Modify** tab in the **Command Panel** and attach the first curve to the second.
4) Expand the sub-object hierarchy tree and select the curve sub-object level. Select the CV curve, and pick the **Make Fit** button. Set the **Number of Points:** spinner to 2 and pick the **OK** button.
5) Select the top (NURBS curve) level in the sub-object hierarchy tree. Create a ruled surface between the two curves. Notice that the resulting surface is shaped like a bow tie.
6) Return to the curve sub-object selection level, and select one of the curves. Pick the **Reverse** button in the **Curve Common** rollout. Notice the change in the surface.
7) Reset 3ds max. Do not save the file.

Make Curve on Surface (COS)

The **Make COS** button in the **Curve Common** rollout is used to convert iso curves, projected curves, surface edge curves, and surface-surface intersection curves into surface curves. It can also be used to add or subtract points or CVs from existing surface curves. Picking the **Make COS** button opens the **Convert Curve On Surface** dialog box. See Figure 26-19. The **Convert Curve On Surface** dialog box contains the **CV Curve On Surface** radio button and the **Point Curve On Surface** radio button.

When the **CV Curve On Surface** radio button is active, the selected curve is converted into a surface CV curve. The **Number of CVs:** spinner allows you to set the number of CVs the converted curve contains. The default value in this spinner generally retains the curve's shape, but it may use an excessive number of CVs to do so. Entering a value greater than the default

Figure 26-19. The **Convert Curve On Surface** dialog box.

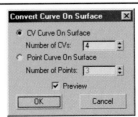

value has the same effect as refining the curve. Entering a value lower than the default value may change the shape of the curve. Checking the **Preview** check box allows you to preview the results before converting the curve. If the results are acceptable, pick the **OK** button to complete the conversion.

When the **Point Curve On Surface** radio button is active, the selected curve is converted into a surface point curve. The **Number of Points:** spinner is used to set the number of points the converted curve contains. The default value in this spinner generally retains the curve's shape once it has been converted, but it may use an excessive number of points to do so. Entering a value greater than the default value produces the same effect as refining the curve. Entering a value lower than the default value may change the shape of the curve. Checking the **Preview** check box at the bottom of the dialog box allows you to see the results before you convert the curve. Pick the **OK** button to complete the conversion.

Help Cel

If you press [Enter] when the **Convert Curve On Surface** dialog box is first opened, the dialog box is closed and the default settings applied.

Convert Curve

Picking the **Convert Curve** button in the **Curve Common** rollout allows you to convert point curves to CV curves, and vice versa. There are also controls that allow you to adjust certain parameters for the selected curve. Picking the button opens the **Convert Curve** dialog box. See Figure 26-20.

The **Convert Curve** dialog box contains the **CV Curve** tab and the **Point Curve** tab. Picking one of the tabs converts the selected curve into that type of curve. If the selected curve is already that type, then adjusting the controls of the tab simply changes the parameters of the curve.

In the **CV Curve** tab, activating the **Number** radio button allows you to use the spinner to set the number of CVs contained within the curve. Activating the **Tolerance** radio button causes 3ds max to calculate the number of CVs in the curve. The value entered in the **Tolerance** spinner determines how accurately the converted curve's shape matches its initial shape. Decreasing the value of this spinner increases accuracy. Increasing the value of this spinner decreases accuracy. A less accurate conversion requires fewer CVs.

The **Reparameterization** area of this dialog box contains radio buttons that allow you to choose between two types of reparameterization. Chord length reparameterization is usually the best choice. This is selected by activating the **Chord Length** radio button. However, with chord length reparameterization, the movement of a single CV may alter

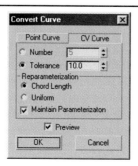

Figure 26-20. The **Convert Curve** dialog box.

the entire curve. When reparameterization is set using the **Uniform** option, the influence of a single CV ends at its neighboring CVs. Checking the **Maintain Reparameterization** check box automatically reparameterizes the curve as it is edited.

In the **Point Curve** tab, activating the **Number** radio button allows you to use the spinner to set the number of points contained within the curve. Activating the **Tolerance** radio button causes 3ds max to calculate the number of points contained within the converted curve. The **Tolerance** spinner setting determines how closely the converted curve's shape matches the initial curve shape. As this value is increased, the curve's accuracy is reduced, and fewer points are used. As this value is decreased, the curve's accuracy increases, and more points are used. The settings in the **Reparameterization** area are unavailable in the **Point Curve** tab.

In both the **Point Curve** tab and the **CV Curve** tab, checking the **Preview** check box allows you to preview the effects of the conversion. In either tab, picking the **OK** button completes the curve conversion. Using the **Convert Curve** dialog box to modify or convert a curve removes all animation controllers for that curve.

Make Independent

The **Make Independent** button in the **Curve Common** rollout is available only if a dependent curve or a point curve is selected. Picking the **Make Independent** button converts the selected curve into an independent CV curve. Making a curve independent removes all animation controllers for that curve.

Remove Animation

Picking the **Remove Animation** button in the **Curve Common** rollout removes all animation controllers for the selected curves. However, any individual points or CVs within the curve that are animated at the point or CV sub-object level remain unaffected. Picking the **Remove Animation** button also will not remove any animation of the curve created at the top, or model, level.

Detach

Picking the **Detach** button in the **Curve Common** rollout removes the selected curve from the current NURBS model, and places it at the top level of a new NURBS model. If the **Copy** check box is checked, the selected curve is not removed from the current NURBS model. Instead, a copy of the selected curve is placed at the top level of a new NURBS model.

When the **Detach** button is picked, the **Detach** dialog box appears. The **Detach as:** text box in this dialog box allows you to name the detached curve by typing a new name in the field. When the **Relational** check box is unchecked and the selected curve is dependent, the curve is made independent when it is detached. When the **Relational** check box is checked and the selected curve is dependent, both the selected curve and its parents are detached, and the selected curve retains its dependency. Picking the **OK** button completes the detachment.

Detached curves retain their animation controllers. However, any children of the detached curve are made independent, or converted into a different type of dependent curve, and lose their animation controllers.

Make First

The **Make First** button in the **Curve Common** rollout is used to relocate the starting point of a closed curve. After picking the **Make First** button, you can pick anywhere on a closed curve to define a new starting point. A new CV or point is added to the curve, and becomes the new starting point for the curve. The relocation of a closed curve's starting point cannot be animated.

Break

The **Break** button in the **Curve Common** rollout is used to break a single curve sub-object into two curve sub-objects, or to change a closed curve into an open curve. To break a curve, pick the **Break** button, and then pick anywhere on the curve to create the break. Two coincidental points are placed at the break. One point is the starting point of the new curve, and the second point is the endpoint of the old curve. The breaking of a curve cannot be animated.

Help Cel

If a closed curve is broken, the starting point of the closed curve is automatically relocated to the break point. Breaking a closed curve creates a single, open curve sub-object.

Join

The **Join** button in the **Curve Common** rollout is used to join two curve sub-objects together into a single curve sub-object. To join two curves, pick the **Join** button and pick the endpoint of one curve that is to be joined. Drag it to the endpoint of the second curve, and release the mouse button. This opens the **Join Curves** dialog box. See Figure 26-21. This dialog box allows you to choose the way the new, joined curve is created.

The **Join Curves** dialog box contains two tabs: the **ZIP** tab and the **Join** tab. In some previous releases of 3D Studio, only the **Join** method is available. The **ZIP** tab contains controls for joining curves using the zip method. The zip method combines the CV lattices of the two curves. Although it can change the shapes of the initial curves, it often provides a better result than the **Join** method.

If the gap distance between the endpoints being joined is greater than the **Tolerance:** spinner setting, a new segment is created between the two endpoints. Both the initial curves and the new segment are joined into the final curve. If the gap distance between the two endpoints is less than the **Tolerance:** spinner setting, the two endpoints are made coincidental and become a single point or CV.

Figure 26-21. The **Join Curves** dialog box.

When the **Join** tab is active, a different algorithm is used to extrapolate the joined curve. Often, this involves the creation of a blend curve between the two initial curves. The two curves and the blend curve are then combined into a single curve sub-object. If the endpoints of the two initial curves are not coincidental, then the value of the **Tolerance:** spinner determines how the gap between the two curves is bridged. If the gap between the curves is greater than the **Tolerance:** spinner setting, then a blend curve is created between the two curves. The two original curves and the blend curve are joined into a single curve sub-object. If the gap between the two original curves is less than the **Tolerance:** spinner setting, then the endpoints of the original curves are made coincidental and become a single point in the joined curve.

The **Tension 1:** and **Tension 2:** spinner values set the tangency of the blend curve. As the values of these spinners decrease, the transition between the blend curve and the initial curves becomes smoother. As the values of these spinners are increased, the transition between the blend curve and the initial curves becomes sharper. These spinners are disabled in the **ZIP** tab.

Whether the **Join** tab or the **ZIP** tab is active, checking the **Preview** check box allows you to see the results before joining the curves. Picking the **OK** button completes the joining. If both initial curves were point curves, then a point curve is created. In all other cases, a CV curve is created.

The joining of two curves cannot be animated. The curves, and all CVs or points in the curves, lose their animation controllers when the curves are joined.

Material ID

The **Material ID:** spinner in the **Curve Common** rollout allows you to assign a material ID to the selected curve. When you apply a multi/sub-object material to a NURBS model, the material IDs of the sub-objects determine which materials are applied to them. Of course, the material is only visible on renderable curves. Refer to Chapter 17 *Creating Advanced Materials* for a discussion on multi/sub-object materials.

Select By ID

Picking the **Select By ID** button in the **Curve Common** rollout opens the **Select By Material ID** dialog box. This dialog box allows you to add all curves with a specific material ID to the current selection set. You can also replace the current selection set with the curves of a particular material ID. Use the **ID:** spinner in the **Select By Material ID** dialog box to select the material ID. All curves with that ID are added to the selection set. If the **Clear Selection** check box is checked, then the material ID selection replaces the previous selection. If the **Clear Selection** check box is unchecked, the new selection is added to the current selection. Pick the **OK** button to complete the selection process.

Help Cel

Curve sub-objects are not renderable in NURBS models containing surfaces. If the curves are detached from the model, they can be made renderable. In addition, all curves sub-objects within a model have the same thickness when rendered.

Exercise 26-9

1) Create a CV surface in the Front viewport. Open the **Modify** tab in the **Command Panel**.
2) Create two arc-shaped CV curves, one at each end of the surface. Position the arcs in front of the surface. You may want to draw an arc shape, position it, convert it into a NURBS curve, mirror it, and then attach both curves to the surface.
3) Create two normal projected curves on the CV surface, using the CV curve arcs as parent curves. Refer to the figure shown.
4) Expand the sub-object hierarchy tree and select the curve sub-object level.
5) Select one of the projected curves and pick the **Make COS** button in the **Curve Common** rollout. Choose **CV Curve On Surface** and use the default number of CVs.
6) Move to frame 100 and activate the **Toggle Animation Mode** button.
7) Select the curve CV level sub-object selection level. Select several of the CVs on each of the original curves, and move them. Notice the difference in behavior between the projected curve and the surface point curve. Play the animation. When the animation has finished, return to frame 100.
8) Select the curve sub-object level from the sub-object hierarchy tree. Select one of the original CV curves, and then pick the **Convert Curve** button. Pick the **Point Curve** tab in the **Convert Curve** dialog box, and use the default number of points. Play the animation again. Notice the change in the animation. Return to frame 100.
9) At the curve sub-object level, pick the **Join** button, and join the two original curves together at their starting points using the zip method. Select the curve CV sub-object level from the sub-object hierarchy tree. Notice that the projected curve has been converted into a surface CV curve. Play the animation again. There is no animation because all of the curves have been converted from their original forms, removing the animation controllers.
10) Reset **3ds max**. Do not save the file.

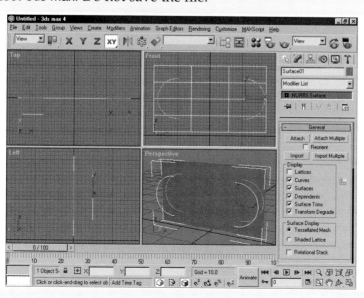

Curve Type-Specific Rollouts

In addition to the **Curve Common** rollout, selecting specific types of curves makes additional rollouts available in the **Modify** tab. The editing rollouts for these curve types and the controls available are basically the same as those used to create them. However, certain rollout controls may only be available in sub-object editing mode.

Point Curve

Selecting an independent point curve at the curve sub-object selection level makes the **Point Curve** rollout available. Independent point curves can be transformed using the transformation tools on the **Main** toolbar. Transformations made to the curve can be animated. However, the closing of a point curve cannot be animated.

CV Curve

Selecting an independent CV curve at the curve sub-object selection level makes the **CV Curve** rollout available. See Figure 26-22. An independent CV curve can be transformed using the transform tools on the **Main** toolbar. These transformations can be animated. However, none of the changes made in the **CV Curve** rollout can be animated.

Degree

The **Degree** spinner in the **CV Curve** rollout allows you to change the mathematical equation that defines the curve. For most applications, a degree of three is sufficient. Equations of higher degrees are more likely to be unstable.

Close

The **Close** button in the **CV Curve** rollout is used to close a CV curve. When this button is picked, a new curve segment is created between the starting point and endpoint, closing the selected curve. If the starting point and endpoint CVs are coincidental, no segment is drawn.

Figure 26-22. The **CV Curve** rollout.

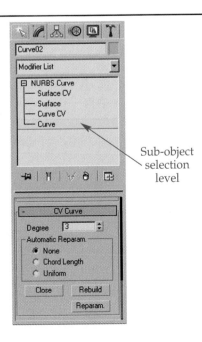

Sub-object selection level

Rebuild

Picking the **Rebuild** button in the **CV Curve** rollout opens the **Rebuild CV Curve** dialog box. Rebuilding a curve simply means reconstructing the curve with a specific number of points. There are two methods for rebuilding a CV curve: by number of CVs or by accuracy of the rebuild.

Activating the **Number** radio button in the **Rebuild CV Curve** dialog box allows you to use the spinner to set the number of CVs contained in the rebuilt curve. Activating the **Tolerance** radio button causes 3ds max to calculate the number of CVs contained in the rebuilt curve. The **Tolerance** spinner setting determines how closely the rebuilt curve's shape matches the initial curve shape. As this value is increased, the rebuilt curve's accuracy is reduced, and fewer CVs are used. As this value is decreased, the rebuilt curve's accuracy is increased, and more CVs are used. Checking the **Preview** check box allows you to preview the results before reconstructing the curve.

Reparameterization

Picking the **Reparameterization** button at the bottom of the **CV Curve** rollout opens the **Reparameterize** dialog box. See Figure 26-23. If the **Maintain Parameterization** check box is checked, or if automatic reparameterization is on, then the reparameterization for the selected curve is automatic. Otherwise, a one-time reparameterization is applied by picking the **OK** button.

Point Curve On Surface

Selecting a surface point curve at the curve sub-object selection level makes the **Point Curve On Surface** rollout available. The entire curve sub-object can be transformed using the transform tools on the **Main** toolbar. However, the transforms applied to the surface point curve are passed on to the parent surface. So, if you scale a surface point curve, you also scale the surface that it is on. Such transformations can be animated. However, trimming changes to the "trim controls" cannot be animated.

Help Cel

The points of a surface point curve can be transformed at the point sub-object selection level.

Replace Surface

Picking the **Replace Surface** button in the **Point Curve On Surface** rollout allows you to replace the parent surface of the surface point curve. After picking the **Replace Surface** button, pick the new surface. The curve then lies at the same UV coordinates on the new surface. This can cause the curve to be scaled or distorted if the two surface dimensions do not

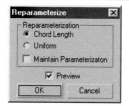

Figure 26-23. The **Reparameterize** dialog box.

match. If the UV axes of the two surfaces are not aligned, a surface point curve that appeared to be on the "front" of the old surface may appear to be on the "back" of the new surface. See Figure 26-24. The replacement of a surface point curve's parent surface cannot be animated.

Edit Curve on Surface

Picking the **Edit** button in the **Point Curve On Surface** rollout opens the **Edit Curve on Surface** dialog box. See Figure 26-25. This dialog box is used to edit surface curves in a two-dimensional environment based on the U and V axes of the surface. A toolbar appears at the top of the dialog box. The buttons in this toolbar are used to select and transform the curve's points, and to change the view.

Select

Picking the **Select** button activates the selection tool. When this button is active, picking a curve point selects it. Holding down the [Ctrl] key while picking additional points adds them to the selection set. Dragging a window with the selection tool selects all points within the window. Picking a selected point while holding down the [Ctrl] key removes the point from the selection set. Activating the **Lock Selection** button locks the selection set.

Figure 26-24. The sphere on the right, identical in size and shape to the sphere on the left, has been rotated 90° about the Z axis, and 180° about the Y axis. When it is selected as the new parent surface for the surface point curve, the trimmed area appears on the back-side of the sphere.

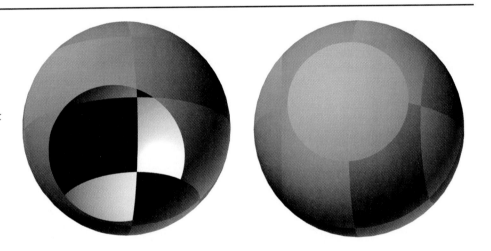

Figure 26-25. Using the **Edit Curve on Surface** dialog box to edit a surface point curve.

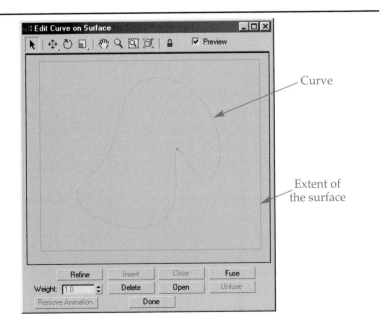

The **Move** flyout is used to choose an appropriate move tool. The **Move** button in the flyout allows selected points to be moved along the surface's U and V axes. The **Move Horizontal** button in the flyout limits the movement of selected points to the U axis. The **Move Vertical** button in the flyout limits the movement of selected points to the V axis.

Picking the **Rotate** button activates the rotate tool. The rotate tool rotates selected points around the surface's W axis.

The **Scale** flyout is used to choose an appropriate scale tool. The **Scale** button in the flyout scales selected points uniformly. The **Scale Horizontal** button in the flyout scales selected points nonuniformly across the surface's U axis. The **Scale Vertical** button in the flyout scales selected points nonuniformly across the surface's V axis.

The **Pan, Zoom, Zoom Window,** and **Zoom Extents** tools allow you to change the portion of the curve and surface that is visible in the dialog box. You can also pan in the 2D viewport by holding down the center mouse button and dragging. This method of panning is only available if you have a three-button mouse.

The dark grey frame centered in the dialog box viewport represents the U and V extents of the surface. In the dialog box, the U axis runs from left to right, and the V axis runs up and down. The 2D representation of the curve is only accurate if the curve's parent surface is perfectly flat and square. Variations in the world space dimensions of the surface, or in the surface's shape, cause the actual surface curve to vary from its 2D representation. For this reason, it is helpful to check the **Preview** check box and observe the changes you are making in one of the 3ds max viewports. See Figure 26-26. You may need to move the dialog box to see the viewports.

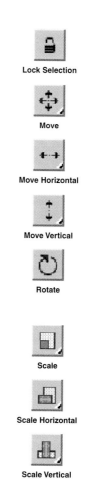

Lock Selection

Move

Move Horizontal

Move Vertical

Rotate

Scale

Scale Horizontal

Scale Vertical

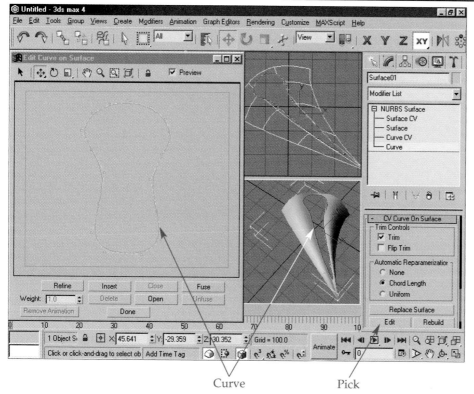

Figure 26-26. The shape of a surface point curve can appear differently in the **Edit Curve on Surface** dialog box than it does on the surface.

Curve   Pick

Beneath the dialog box viewport is a series of buttons. These buttons are used to edit the points of the curve. Picking the **Refine** button allows you to add points to the curve without changing its shape. Picking the **Delete** button deletes the selected points from the curve. Picking the **Close** button closes the curve. Picking the **Open** button unfuses the starting point and the endpoint of a closed curve, creating an open curve. Picking the **Fuse** button fuses two points together. If the two points are not coincidental, the first point selected is made coincidental with the second point before the points are fused. Picking the **Unfuse** button unfuses a set of fused points. Picking the **Remove Animation** button removes the animation controllers for the selected points. Picking the **Done** button closes the **Edit Curve on Surface** dialog box. You can also pick the Windows close button (X) to close the dialog box. The **Insert** button and the **Weight:** spinner are disabled when editing a surface point curve.

The transformations you apply to the curve's points using the **Move**, **Rotate**, and **Scale** tools can be animated. The changes you make to the curve using the **Refine**, **Delete**, **Fuse**, **Unfuse**, **Open**, and **Close** buttons cannot be animated.

Help Cel

In some instances, you may find it easier to edit a surface point curve at the point sub-object level than to edit it using the **Edit Curve on Surface** dialog box.

CV Curve On Surface

Selecting a surface CV curve at the curve sub-object selection level makes the **CV Curve On Surface** rollout available. See Figure 26-27. Surface CV curves can be transformed using the tools on the **Main** toolbar. The parent surface inherits the transformations applied to the curve. Such transformations can be animated. However, changes to trimming and reparameterization cannot be animated.

Figure 26-27. The **CV Curve On Surface** rollout.

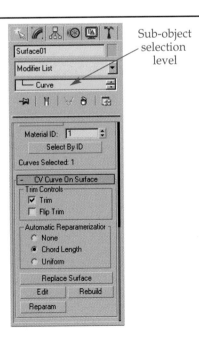

Sub-object selection level

Help Cel

Replace Surface

Picking the **Replace Surface** button allows you to replace the parent surface of the surface curve. After picking the **Replace Surface** button, pick the new surface. The curve then lies at the same UV coordinates on the new surface. This can cause the curve to be scaled or distorted if the two surface dimensions do not match. If the UV axes of the two surfaces are not aligned, a surface curve that appeared to be on the "front" of the old surface can appear to be on the "back" of the new surface. The replacement of a surface curve's parent surface cannot be animated.

Edit Curve on Surface

Picking the **Edit** button activates the **Edit Curve on Surface** dialog box. This dialog box is used to edit surface curves in a two-dimensional environment. It shares some common functions with the dialog box used to edit surface point curves. In addition, several functions specific to surface CV curves are made available when editing a surface CV curve.

When a surface CV curve is selected, the **Insert** button is made available in the **Edit Curve on Surface** dialog box. Picking the **Insert** button allows you to place additional CVs in the surface curve's control lattice. Unlike refining a curve, adding CVs using the **Insert** button can change the shape of the curve. The **Weight:** spinner is also only available for surface CV curves. Adjusting the value of this spinner increases or decreases the influence of the selected CVs.

The transformation of the surface curve's CVs can be animated. The adjustment of the weight of a CV can also be animated.

Exercise

Exercise 26-10

1) Create a sphere in the Top viewport and convert it to a NURBS object. Now create a second sphere that fits just inside the first. Assign a bright yellow material to the first sphere. Assign a black material to the second sphere.

2) Create two ovals and a crescent-shaped CV curve and position the objects in the Front viewport, as shown in the figure below. You may want to draw these objects as splines, convert them into NURBS curves, and attach them to the outer sphere NURBS surface.

3) Create vector projected curves using the CV curves as the parents and the outer sphere as the surface. Check the **Trim** and **Flip Trim** check boxes as needed so the area inside each of the projected curves is trimmed. Refer to the figure below.

4) Expand the sub-object hierarchy tree and select the curve sub-object level. Pick one of the projected curves, and then pick the **Make COS** button in the **Curve Common** rollout. Select **CV Curve On Surface**. Make sure the **Preview** check box is checked. Adjust the **Number of CVs:** spinner to the lowest value that retains the shape of the curve, and pick **OK**. Repeat this process for each of the projected curves.

5) Move to frame 20 and activate the **Toggle Animation Mode** button. Select all three of the vector projected surface curves, and pick the **Edit** button in the **CV Curve On Surface** rollout. Use the transform tools in the **Edit Curve on Surface** dialog box to create a new expression with the surface curves. Refer to the figure shown. Be careful; if you alter the curves too much, you may create an invalid surface.

6) Move to frame 40 and create another new expression.

7) Create and play the animation.

8) Save the scene as ex26-10.max in the folder of your choice. Reset 3ds max.

Transform Curve

Selecting a transform curve at the curve sub-object selection level makes the **Transform Curve** rollout available. The entire curve sub-object can be transformed using the transform tools on the **Main** toolbar. Transformations, such as scaling, rotating, and moving the transform curve, can be animated.

The **Replace Base Curve** button in the **Transform Curve** rollout can be used to replace the parent curve of the transform curve. You cannot animate the replacement of a transform curve's parent.

Blend Curve

Selecting a blend curve at the curve sub-object selection level makes the **Blend Curve** rollout available. See Figure 26-28. Blend curves can be transformed using the tools on the **Main** toolbar. The parent curves inherit the transformations applied to the curve. Such transformations can be animated, as can changes to the tension spinners.

The **Replace First Curve** and **Replace Second Curve** buttons allow you to choose new parents for the blend curve. To replace a parent, pick the **Replace First Curve** or **Replace Second Curve** button. Then, pick an endpoint on a new curve. One endpoint of the blend curve moves to the endpoint that you select. The replacement of parent curves cannot be animated.

Offset Curve

Selecting an offset curve at the **Curve** sub-object selection level makes the **Offset Curve** rollout available. Offset curves can be transformed using the tools on the **Main** toolbar. The parent curve inherits the transformations applied to the curve. Such transformations can be animated, as can changes to the **Offset:** spinner.

The **Replace Base Curve** button allows you to replace the curve's parent. Replacing a parent curve cannot be animated.

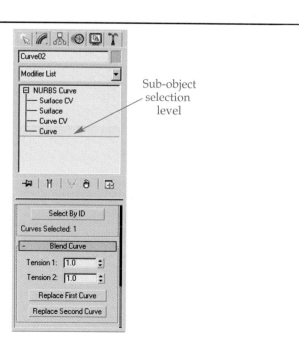

Figure 26-28. The **Blend Curve** rollout.

Mirror Curve

Selecting a mirror curve at the curve sub-object selection level makes the **Mirror Curve** rollout available. See Figure 26-29. Mirror curves can be transformed using the tools on the **Main** toolbar. Transformations can be applied to both the curve and its mirror gizmo on the sub-object level. Transformations applied to the curve are inherited by the parent curve. Transformations applied to the gizmo are not. The gizmo can be moved and rotated, but not scaled. Transformations to both the gizmo and the curve can be animated, as can the offset distance.

The radio buttons in the **Mirror Axis:** area in the **Mirror Curve** rollout can be used to assign a new mirror axis to the curve. Any transforms applied to the gizmo are still applied after the mirror axis is changed. Changing a mirror axis, using the radio buttons, cannot be animated.

The **Replace Base Curve** button allows you to replace the curve's parent. Replacing a parent curve cannot be animated.

Figure 26-29. Editing a mirror curve. The mirror axis gizmo can be transformed at the sub-object level.

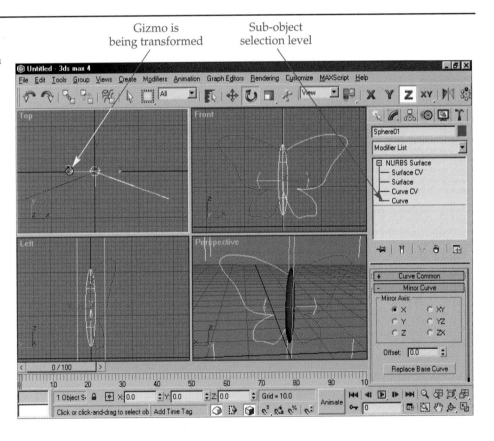

Gizmo is being transformed

Sub-object selection level

Exercise 26-11

1) Create a CV curve in any viewport. Open the **Modify** tab in the **Command Panel**.
2) Create a mirror curve of the CV curve.
3) Expand the sub-object hierarchy tree and select the curve sub-object level.
4) Move to frame 100 and activate the **Toggle Animation Mode** button.
5) Pick the mirror curve. Rotate the mirror gizmo 30° around each of two different axes. Now, activate the **Z** radio button in the **Mirror Axis:** area of the **Mirror Curve** rollout. Notice the mirror axis does not match the world Z axis. Change the **Offset:** spinner value.
6) Play the animation and observe the results.
7) Reset 3ds max. Do not save the file.

Surf-Surf Intersection Curve

Selecting a surface-surface intersection curve at the curve sub-object selection level makes the **Surf-Surf Intersection Curve** rollout available. All transformations applied to the curve are inherited by the curve's parent surfaces. These transformations can be animated.

The **Replace First Surface** and **Replace Second Surface** buttons are used to replace the parent surfaces of the intersection curve. The replacement of a parent surface cannot be animated. The relocation of seeds or changes in trimming cannot be animated.

Surface Offset Curve

Selecting a surface offset curve at the **Curve** sub-object selection level makes the **Surface Offset Curve** rollout available. All transformations applied to the curve are inherited by the curve's parent surface curve. These transformations can be animated, as can changes to the offset distance.

The **Replace Curve** button allows you to replace the surface offset curve's parent curve. The replacement of a parent curve cannot be animated.

Chamfer Curve

Selecting a chamfer curve at the curve sub-object selection level makes the **Chamfer Curve** rollout available. See Figure 26-30. All transformations applied to the curve are inherited by the curve's parent curves. These transformations can be animated.

You can also animate changes in the chamfer's length. However, changes in the parent curves' trimming cannot be animated. The relocation of seeds cannot be animated. The replacement of a parent curve cannot be animated.

Fillet Curve

Selecting a fillet curve at the curve sub-object selection level makes the **Fillet Curve** rollout available. See Figure 26-31. All transformations applied to the curve are inherited by the curve's parent curves. These transformations can be animated.

Changing a fillet curve's radius can be animated. Changes in the parent curves' trimming cannot be animated. Changing a seed's location cannot be animated.

The **Replace First Curve** and **Replace Second Curve** buttons are used to replace the fillet curve's parents. The replacement of a parent curve cannot be animated.

Figure 26-30. The **Chamfer Curve** rollout.

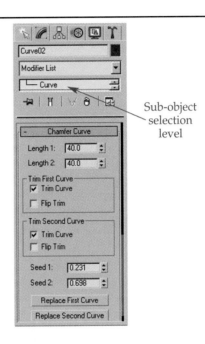

Sub-object selection level

Figure 26-31. The **Fillet Curve** rollout.

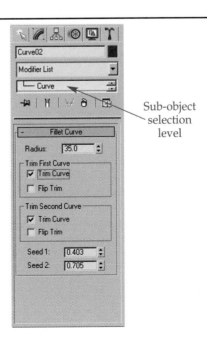

Sub-object selection level

Iso Curve

Selecting a U or V iso curve at the curve sub-object selection level makes the **Iso Curve** rollout available. All transformations applied to the curve are inherited by the curve's parent surface. These transformations can be animated. You can also animate the repositioning of a U or V iso curve.

The **Replace Base Surface** button is used to replace the parent surface. Changes in the parent curves' trimming and the replacement of a parent surface cannot be animated.

Projected Curve

When a projected curve is selected at the curve sub-object selection level, the **Vector Projected Curve** or **Normal Projected Curve** rollout becomes available. The controls in these rollouts are identical.

When a projected curve is transformed at the sub-object level, the transformations are passed on to the parent curve and parent surface. When a vector projected curve is selected, the projection gizmo becomes visible in the viewports. The projection gizmo can be rotated, moving the projected curve on the surface. See Figure 26-32. These transformations can be animated.

A change in the parent surface's trimming cannot be animated. Changing of the seed location also cannot be animated.

The **Replace Curve** and **Replace Surface** buttons are used to replace the parent curve and parent surface of the projected curve. The replacement of a parent sub-object cannot be animated.

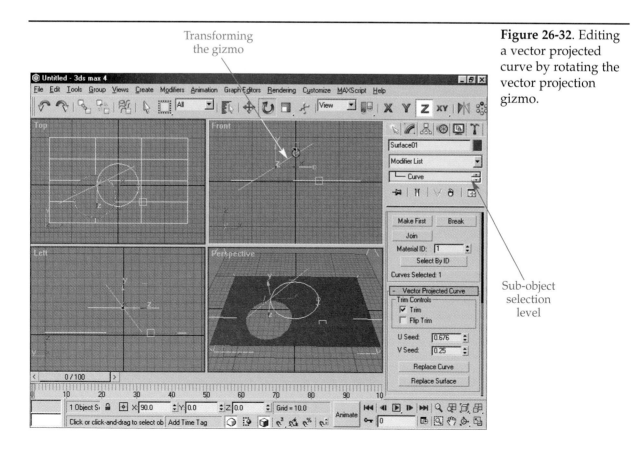

Figure 26-32. Editing a vector projected curve by rotating the vector projection gizmo.

Exercise

Exercise 26-12

1) In the Front viewport, create a point surface. Next, create a circle spline near the center of the point surface. Make the diameter of the circle approximately one-fourth the height of the surface. Position the circle in front of the point surface at a distance equal to its diameter.
2) Convert the circle to a NURBS object. Open the **Modify** tab in the **Command Panel** and attach the circle to the point surface.
3) Create a vector projected curve using the circle as the parent curve. Project it onto the point surface. Check the **Trim** check box in the **Vector Projected Curve** rollout. Flip the trim if needed. Refer to the illustration.
4) Move to frame 25 and activate the **Toggle Animation Mode** button.
5) Expand the sub-object hierarchy tree and select the curve sub-object level. Select the vector projected curve, and rotate the projection gizmo so the projected curve is in the upper left-hand corner of the point surface. You will have to use the Top and Left viewports to accomplish this.
6) Move to frame 50. Rotate the projection gizmo so the projected curve is in the lower right-hand corner.
7) Move to frame 100. In the Top viewport, rotate the parent curve (the circle) 360° about the Z axis. Play the animation. Why does the surface disappear for a time, leaving only the area within the projected curve?
8) Save the scene as ex26-12.max in the folder of your choice. Reset 3ds max.

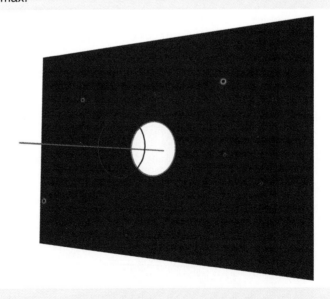

Surface Common Rollout

When the sub-object selection level is set to surface in the **Modify** tab, the **Surface Common** rollout is displayed. This rollout contains general controls for selecting and editing surface sub-objects. See Figure 26-33. The available controls are discussed in the following sections.

Selection

The two toggle buttons in the **Selection** area of the **Surface Common** rollout determine how surfaces are selected. When the **Single Surface** button is active, picking a surface selects only that surface. When the **All Connected Surfaces** button is active, picking a surface selects all connected surfaces.

For two surfaces to be classified as connected surfaces, all the CVs or points along the common edge of one surface must be fused with their counterparts on the other surface. Connected dependent surfaces, such as blend surfaces, are also considered connected surfaces.

At the bottom of the **Surface Common** rollout the number of surface sub-objects currently selected is displayed. This is useful when working with a model containing many surface sub-objects.

Single Surface

All Connected Surfaces

Name

The **Name:** window in the **Surface Common** rollout displays the name of the currently selected surface. The default name is the surface type followed by an assigned number. You can enter a new name in this window to change the name of the selected surface.

Hide

Picking the **Hide** button hides the selected surface. A surface hidden at the sub-object level is still rendered, but it cannot be selected. Hidden surfaces are still affected by changes made to related sub-objects, or the NURBS model as a whole.

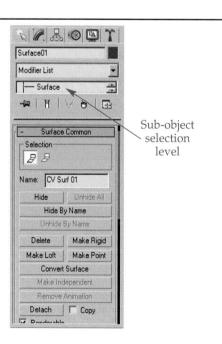

Sub-object selection level

Figure 26-33. The **Surface Common** rollout.

Picking the **Hide By Name** button opens the **Select Sub-Objects** dialog box. This dialog box allows you to hide a surface by selecting its name. Picking the **Unhide All** button in the rollout reveals all hidden surfaces. Picking the **Unhide By Name** button allows you to reveal only the surface you select by name in the **Select Sub-Objects** dialog box. The hide and unhide controls have no effect on animation.

Delete

Picking the **Delete** button deletes the selected surface sub-object. The deletion of a surface cannot be animated.

Make Rigid

The **Make Rigid** button is used to make a surface rigid. When a surface has been made rigid, its points or CVs can no longer be edited. Making a surface rigid also removes all animation controllers for the surface's points or CVs. Using the **Make Point**, **Make Independent**, or any of the **Break** functions on the surface removes its rigidity.

Help Cel

Making a surface rigid speeds up system performance.

Exercise

Exercise 26-13

1) Create an S-shaped CV curve in the Front viewport with an overall shape roughly 100 units square. In the Top viewport, make a copy of the curve and move it 60 units along the Y axis.
2) Open the **Modify** tab in the **Command Panel** and attach the first curve to the second. Use the two curves to create a U loft surface.
3) Move to frame 100 and activate the **Toggle Animation Mode** button.
4) Expand the sub-object hierarchy tree and select the curve CV sub-object level. Select and move various CVs on each curve. Play the animation. When you have finished playing the animation, return to frame 100.
5) Select the surface sub-object level, and select the U loft. With animation mode off, pick the **Make Rigid** button in the **Surface Common** rollout. Play the animation. What happens? Why?
6) Reset 3ds max. Do not save the file.

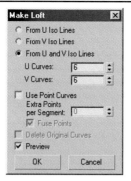

Figure 26-34. The **Make Loft** dialog box.

Make Loft

Picking the **Make Loft** button in the **Surface Common** rollout activates the **Make Loft** dialog box. See Figure 26-34. The **Make Loft** dialog box is used to convert the selected surface, regardless of its type, into a U or UV loft surface.

If the **From U Iso Lines** radio button is active, the new loft surface is constructed from the existing surface's U iso lines. New curves are created, based on the surface's contours, and spaced evenly across the surface's U axis.

If the **From V Iso Lines** radio button is active, the new loft surface is constructed from the existing surface's V iso lines. New curves are created, based on the surface's contours, and spaced evenly across the surface's V axis.

If the **From U and V Iso Lines** radio button is active, the new loft surface is constructed from the existing surface's U and V iso lines. New curves are created, based on the surface's contours, and spaced evenly across both axes, creating a UV loft surface.

The **U Curves:** and **V Curves:** spinner values set the number of curves used to create the new loft surface. Increasing these values increases the accuracy of the loft surface, but decreases system performance. Decreasing these spinner values decreases the accuracy of the loft surface, but increases system performance.

Checking the **Use Point Curves** check box causes the new loft surface to be constructed with point curves, rather than CV curves. Increasing the value of the **Extra Points per Segment:** spinner adds evenly spaced points between each U and V curve intersection. Checking the **Fuse Points** check box fuses the points at the intersections of the curves. This ensures the curves continue to intersect as they are edited.

If the selected surface is a loft surface, checking the **Delete Original Curves** check box deletes the curves originally used to create the loft surface. If this check box is unchecked, the original loft curves remain in place.

Checking the **Preview** check box allows you to preview changes made to the surface. None of the changes made to a surface in the **Make Loft** dialog box can be animated.

Exercise

Exercise 26-14

1) Create a sphere of any size in the Top viewport. Convert the sphere into a NURBS object.
2) Open the **Modify** tab in the **Command Panel**. Expand the sub-object hierarchy tree and select the surface CV sub-object level. Select the top and bottom "rings" of CVs as shown in the figure below. Scale the selection down to 60%.
3) Change to the surface sub-object selection level. Select the surface. Pick the **Make Loft** button in the **Surface Common** rollout. With the **Preview** check box checked in the **Make Loft** dialog box, activate each of the three radio buttons in order. Notice the differences in the viewports.
4) Pick the **Cancel** button and reset 3ds max. Do not save the file.

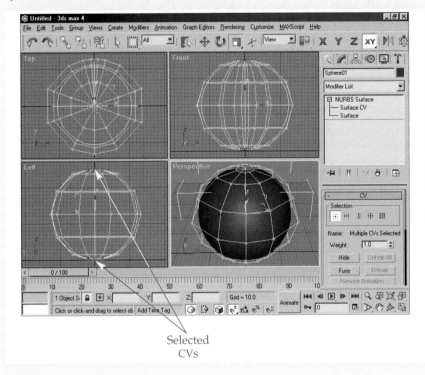

Selected
CVs

Make Point

Picking the **Make Point** button in the **Surface Common** rollout opens the **Make Point** dialog box. See Figure 26-35. This dialog box is used to convert the selected surface into a point surface.

The **Number in U:** spinner value sets the number of columns in the point surface. The **Number in V:** spinner value sets the number of rows in the point surface. Increasing these values increases the accuracy of the point surface, but decreases system performance. Checking the **Preview** check box allows you to preview the changes made to the surface. Changes made in the **Make Point** dialog box cannot be animated.

Figure 26-35. The **Make Point Surface** dialog box.

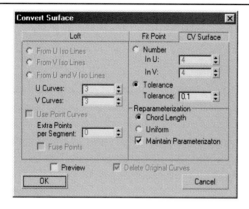

Figure 26-36. The **Convert Surface** dialog box.

Convert Surface

Picking the **Convert Surface** button in the **Surface Common** rollout opens the **Convert Surface** dialog box. See Figure 26-36. This dialog box provides a simple method for converting the selected surface into a different type of surface.

The **Loft** button provides controls that are identical to their counterparts in the **Make Loft** dialog box. These controls allow you to convert the selected surface into a loft surface with the specified settings.

The controls activated by the **Fit Point** button and the **CV Surface** button are very similar. The **Fit Point** controls allow you to convert the selected surface into a point surface. The creation method is selected by picking the **Number** or **Tolerance** radio button. When the **Number** radio button is active, enter the desired number of rows for the point surface in the **In U:** spinner. The **In V:** spinner is used to set the number of columns in the point surface. If the **Tolerance** radio button is active, the point surface is created with the minimum number of points needed to achieve the desired level of accuracy. The accuracy of the point surface is adjusted with the **Tolerance:** spinner.

The **CV Surface** button provides controls to convert the selected surface into a CV surface. The **Number** and **Tolerance** radio buttons are used to select a creation method for the CV surface. If the **Number** radio button is active, the CV surface is created with a specified number of rows and columns of CVs. The **In U:** spinner value sets the number of rows. The **In V:** spinner value sets the number of columns. If the **Tolerance** radio button is active, then the CV surface is created with the minimum number of CVs required to attain the desired level of accuracy. Increasing the value of the **Tolerance:** spinner decreases the level of accuracy, and the number of CVs used. Decreasing the value of the **Tolerance:** spinner increases accuracy, but also reduces system performance. The **Reparameterization** area contains controls for the reparameterization of the surface.

The conversion of a surface into a different type cannot be animated. Converting a surface removes all animation controllers from the surface's CVs or points.

Make Independent

Picking the **Make Independent** button in the **Surface Common** rollout converts a dependent surface sub-object into an independent surface sub-object. Making a surface independent removes the animation controllers for that surface and for all its dependent sub-objects.

Remove Animation

Picking the **Remove Animation** button in the **Surface Common** rollout removes the animation controllers for the selected surface. However, any points or CVs within the surface that are animated at the point or CV sub-object level remain unaffected. Picking the **Remove Animation** button also will not remove any animation of the surface created at the top, or model, level.

Detach

Picking the **Detach** button in the **Surface Common** rollout removes the selected surface from the current NURBS model, and places it at the top level of a new NURBS model. If the **Copy** check box is checked, the selected surface is not removed from the current NURBS model. Instead, a copy of the selected surface is placed at the top level of a new NURBS model.

When the **Detach** button is picked, the **Detach** dialog box appears. The **Detach as:** text box allows you to rename the surface. When the **Relational** check box is unchecked, and the selected surface is dependent, the surface is made independent when it is detached. When the **Relational** check box is checked, and the selected surface is dependent, both the selected surface and its parents are detached, and the selected surface retains its dependency. Picking the **OK** button completes the detachment.

Detached surfaces retain their animation controllers. However, children of the detached surface are made independent and lose their animation controllers when their parents are detached.

Renderable

If the **Renderable** check box in the **Surface Common** rollout is checked, the selected surface will be rendered. If the check box is not checked, the selected surface will not render. This option cannot be animated.

Display Normals

Checking the **Display Normals** check box in the **Surface Common** rollout displays normal icons at the UV origins of the selected surfaces. The icons are colored in a gradient of dark blue to white. See Figure 26-37. It may be necessary to zoom in to see the icons. The normal icons are not rendered, and have no effect on animation.

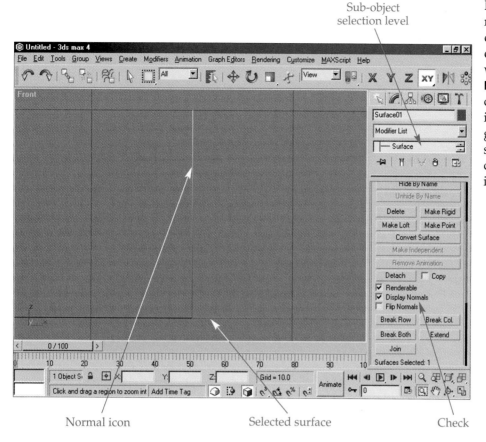

Sub-object selection level

Figure 26-37. A normal icon is displayed at the origin of a surface when the **Display Normals** check box is checked. The normal icon shown here is greatly magnified to show detail. Icons are displayed as 10 units in height.

Normal icon   Selected surface   Check

Break

Picking the **Break Row**, **Break Col.**, or **Break Both** button, in the **Surface Common** rollout, divides the selected surface into two or four separate surfaces. See Figure 26-38. When a surface is broken, all children of that surface are made independent. Breaking a surface removes all animation controllers for that surface.

Picking the **Break Row** button slices the selected surface along the U axis at the cursor's location, forming two independent surfaces. Picking the **Break Col.** button slices the selected surface along the V axis at the cursor's location, creating two independent surfaces. Picking the **Break Both** button slices through the surface along both the U and V axes, forming four independent surfaces.

Extend

Picking the **Extend** button in the **Surface Common** rollout allows you to increase the selected surface's dimension along the U or V axis. The **Extend** function displaces the selected edge without distorting it and extends the center of the surface to change the surface's dimension. This is unlike nonuniform scaling, in which all areas of the surface are affected equally along the scale axis.

To extend a surface, pick an independent surface at the sub-object level. Next, pick the **Extend** button, and position the cursor over the surface you wish to extend. The surface is highlighted in yellow. The

Figure 26-38. A sphere broken into quadrants by using the **Break Both** button. The "pieces" are moved for illustration.

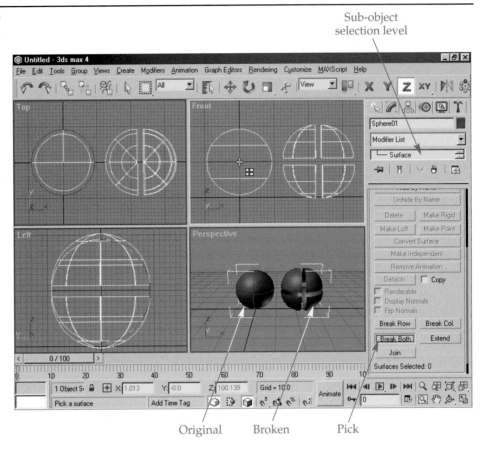

Sub-object selection level

Original   Broken   Pick

edge that will be extended is highlighted in blue. The highlighted edge determines which dimension will be scaled.

When the desired combination is highlighted, pick and drag the cursor up or down in the viewport. See Figure 26-39. Dragging the cursor up moves the surface edge outward from its starting place. Dragging down moves the selected edge toward its starting place. If you continue dragging the cursor down past its starting position, the opposite edge is extended outward. Extending a surface removes all animation controllers for the surface.

Join

The **Join** button in the **Surface Common** rollout is used to join two surface sub-objects in the same NURBS model together. This results in a single, independent surface sub-object. The joining of two surface sub-objects removes the animation controllers for the surfaces.

To join two surfaces, pick the **Join** button. Then, position the cursor over the first surface at the edge you wish to join. The selected surface is highlighted in yellow, and the selected edge is highlighted in blue. Pick the highlighted edge. Next, pick the edge on the second surface you wish to join. The **Join Surfaces** dialog box is opened.

The controls in the **Join Surfaces** dialog box are very similar to the controls in the **Join Curves** dialog box. The controls in the **ZIP** button are used to join the surfaces using the zip algorithm. The **Tolerance:** spinner sets the minimum distance the surfaces can be apart before a row of CVs or points is removed in the joining process. If the distance between the

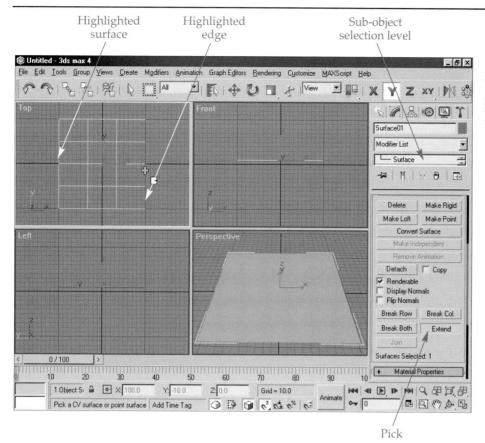

Figure 26-39.
Extending a surface. The selected surface is highlighted in yellow. The edge that is used in the extension is highlighted in blue.

surfaces is less than the distance in the **Tolerance:** spinner, then one row of CVs or points is removed to avoid the accidental creation of coincidental points or CVs.

When the **Join** button is selected, the surfaces are joined with the "join" algorithm. The value entered in the **Tolerance:** spinner sets the minimum distance between the surfaces before a blend surface is created between them. The distance between the surfaces exceeds the **Tolerance:** spinner setting, then a blend curve is created between the surfaces, and all three surfaces are joined.

The **Tension 1:** spinner setting determines the way the blend curve approaches the first parent curve. Increasing this value causes the blend to be more tangential to the edge of the first parent curve. The **Tension 2:** spinner setting determines the way the blend curve approaches the second parent curve. Increasing the value causes the blend to be more tangential to the second parent curve. If the two parent surfaces are closer together than the **Tolerance:** spinner setting, the tension spinners have no effect.

Exercise

Exercise 26-15

1) Create a CV surface of any size in the Top viewport. Use the default number of CVs to create the surface.
2) Open the **Modify** tab in the **Command Panel**. Expand the hierarchy tree and select the surface CV sub-object level.
3) Move to frame 100 and activate the **Toggle Animation Mode** button.
4) Select the two inside rows of CVs on the surface and uniformly scale the selection to 200%. Play the animation. Return to frame 100.
5) Activate the **Toggle Animation Mode** button. Select the surface sub-object level from the sub-object hierarchy tree. Pick the **Break Both** button in the **Surface Common** rollout, and break the surface in the center. Play the animation.
6) With the **Toggle Animation Mode** button inactive, select the surface sub-object level from the sub-object hierarchy tree. Select the surface sub-objects one at a time, and move them 10 units (positive and/or negative) in the X and Y direction, away from the origin.
7) Pick the **Join** button in the **Surface Common** rollout and rejoin the pieces.
8) Save the scene as ex26-15.max in the folder of your choice. Reset 3ds max.

Surface Type-Specific Rollouts

In addition to the **Surface Common** rollout, selecting certain types of surfaces at the sub-object level displays additional rollouts in the **Modify** tab. The controls in these rollouts are nearly identical to the controls used to create the surface. However, when a surface is edited, certain options may be available that were not available when the surface was created. Some of the parameters set with these controls can be animated, others cannot.

CV Surface

When a CV surface is selected at the surface sub-object selection level, the transforms applied to it, such as moving, scaling, or rotating transforms, can be animated. Selecting a CV surface at the surface sub-object level makes the **CV Surface** rollout available. See Figure 26-40. The controls in this rollout are discussed in the following sections.

U and V Degree

The **U Degree** and **V Degree** spinners in the **CV Surface** rollout are used to set the degree of the equation used to define the surface. Increasing the values of the spinners increases the level of continuity between surface segments. However, equations above a degree of three tend to be unstable, and require more calculation time. For most purposes, a setting of three in both of these spinners is recommended. Changes to these settings cannot be animated.

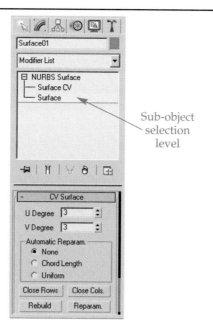

Sub-object selection level

Figure 26-40. The **CV Surface** rollout.

Automatic Reparameterization

The **Automatic Reparameterization** area in the **CV Surface** rollout contains radio buttons that allow you to automatically reparameterize the surface every time it is edited. Activating the **None** radio button disables automatic reparameterization. Activating the **Chord Length** radio button applies the chord length method of reparameterization to the surface each time it is changed. Activating the **Uniform** radio button applies the uniform method of reparameterization to the surface each time it is changed. Reparameterization has no effect on animation.

Close Rows and Columns

Picking the **Close Rows** button in the **CV Surface** rollout while a CV surface is selected at the sub-object level closes the surface by joining the ends of the rows. If the **Close Cols.** button is picked, the surface is closed by joining its columns. The closing of a surface cannot be animated.

Rebuild

Picking the **Rebuild** button in the **CV Surface** rollout opens the **Rebuild CV Surface** dialog box. See Figure 26-41. This dialog box is used to reconstruct a CV surface. The controls in this dialog box allow you to create a new surface with more or fewer CVs.

When the **Tolerance** radio button in the **CV Surface** rollout is active, the surface is rebuilt with the minimum number of CVs necessary to

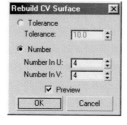

Figure 26-41. The **Rebuild CV Surface** dialog box.

achieve a desired level of accuracy. The value of the **Tolerance:** spinner determines the level of accuracy. A higher value for this spinner creates fewer CVs, and less accuracy, in the rebuilt surface. A lower value for this spinner rebuilds the surface with more CVs, and greater accuracy. Increasing the accuracy increases computation time.

When the **Number** radio button is active, the surface is rebuilt using a specified number of CVs. The **Number In U:** spinner value sets the number of CV rows in the rebuilt surface. The **Number In V:** spinner value sets the number of CV columns in the rebuilt surface.

If the surface is rebuilt, all animation controllers are removed from the surface's CVs. Checking the **Preview** check box allows you to preview the changes made to the surface.

Reparameterize

Picking the **Reparam.** button in the **CV Surface** rollout opens the **Reparameterize** dialog box. This dialog box allows you to reparameterize the surface. When the **Chord Length** radio button is active, the surface is reparameterized using the chord length method. When the **Uniform** radio button is active, the surface is reparameterized using the uniform method. Checking the **Maintain Parameterization** check box automatically reparameterizes the surface when it is edited. Checking the **Preview** check box allows you to preview the changes made to the surface. Reparameterization has no effect on animation.

Exercise

Exercise 26-16

1) Create a CV surface of any size in the Top viewport. Create the surface with eight length CVs, and eight width CVs.
2) Open the **Modify** tab in the **Command Panel**. Expand the sub-object hierarchy tree and select the surface CV sub-object level.
3) Move to frame 100 and activate the **Toggle Animation Mode** button. Select five or six CVs and move them "up" to create a hilly landscape from the planar CV surface. Play the animation. Return to frame 100.
4) Select the surface sub-object level from sub-object hierarchy tree. Select the surface.
5) In the **CV Surface** rollout, pick the **Rebuild** button. Make sure the **Preview** check box is checked in the **Rebuild CV Surface** dialog box. Pick the **Tolerance** radio button, and set the **Tolerance:** spinner value to 50. Notice the change in the viewports. Now, set the **Tolerance:** spinner value to 90. Notice any difference in the viewports.
6) Pick the **Number** radio button and decrease the number of U and V CVs to 6. Notice the change in the viewports. Pick **Cancel**.
7) Reset 3ds max. Do not save the file.

Point Surface

Selecting a point surface at the surface sub-object selection level makes the **Point Surface** rollout available. Transforms applied to the surface, such as moving, scaling, or rotating transforms, can be animated.

The **Point Surface** rollout contains a **Close Rows** button and a **Close Cols.** button. These buttons allow you to close the surface by rows or columns, similar to a CV surface. The closing of a point surface cannot be animated.

Transform Surface

Selecting a transform surface at the surface sub-object selection level makes the **Transform Surface** rollout available. Transforms applied to the transform surface can be animated.

The **Replace Base Surface** button in the **Transform Surface** rollout allows you to select a new parent surface for the transform surface. The replacement of a parent surface cannot be animated.

Blend Surface

Selecting a blend surface at the surface sub-object selection level makes the **Blend Surface** rollout available. See Figure 26-42. Transforms applied to the blend surface are inherited by the parent surfaces. These transforms can be animated.

Changes made to the tension spinners can be animated. However, you cannot animate the flipping of a normal. You also cannot animate the flipping of a tangent.

The **Replace First Edge** and **Replace Second Edge** buttons are used to select a new edge from which to form the blend. The replacement of a parent edge cannot be animated.

Offset Surface

Selecting an offset surface at the **Surface** sub-object selection level makes the **Offset Surface** rollout available. Transforms applied to the

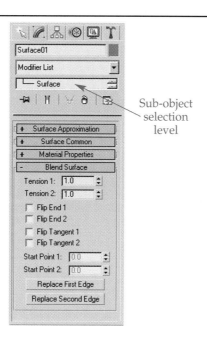

Sub-object selection level

Figure 26-42. The **Blend Surface** rollout.

offset surface are inherited by the parent surface. These transforms can be animated, as can changes made to the **Offset:** spinner.

Picking the **Replace Base Surface** button allows you to choose a new parent surface for the offset surface. The selection of a new parent surface cannot be animated.

Mirror Surface

Selecting a mirror surface at the surface sub-object selection level makes the **Mirror Surface** rollout available. See Figure 26-43. Transforms applied to the mirror surface are inherited by the parent surface. You can also rotate and move the mirror axis gizmo at the surface sub-object level. These changes can be animated.

Changes made to the mirror surface's offset distance can be animated. However, you cannot animate the selection of a new mirror axis.

Picking the **Replace Base Surface** button allows you to choose a new parent surface for the mirror surface. The selection of a new parent surface cannot be animated.

Extruded Surface

Selecting an extruded surface at the surface sub-object selection level makes the **Extrude Surface** rollout available. When the extruded surface is transformed, the transforms applied are inherited by the parent curve. When an extruded surface is selected, you can also rotate the extrusion gizmo. See Figure 26-44. These transformations can be animated.

Changes made to the **Amount:** spinner can be animated. Changes made to the other parameters in this rollout cannot be animated.

Figure 26-43. Editing a mirror surface. The mirror axis gizmo can be transformed at the sub-object level.

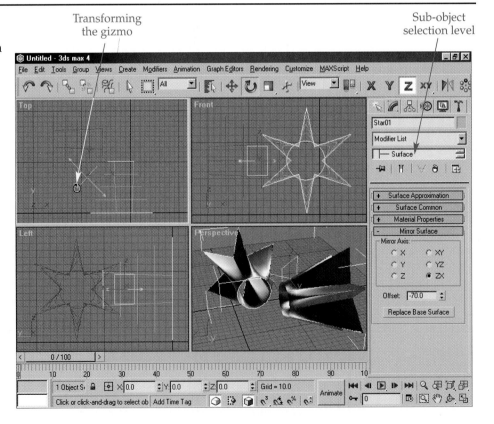

Transforming
the gizmo

Sub-object
selection level

Figure 26-44. Editing an extruded surface. The extrusion gizmo can be transformed at the sub-object level.

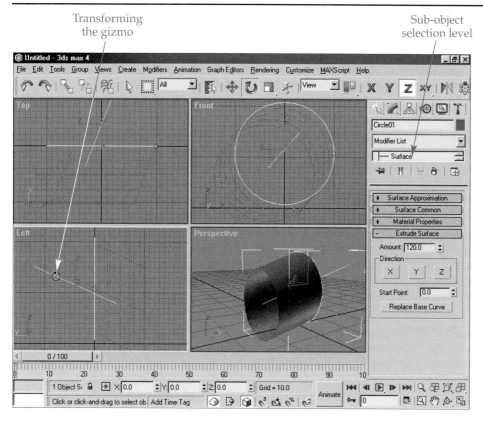

Exercise 26-17

1) In the Top viewport, create a circle spline with a diameter of 50 units. Convert the circle into a NURBS object and open the **Modify** tab in the **Command Panel.**

2) Expand the **Create Surfaces** rollout, and pick the **Extrude** button. Extrude the circle 200 units along the Z axis.

3) Expand the sub-object hierarchy tree and select the surface sub-object level.

4) Move to frame 100 and activate the **Toggle Animation Mode** button.

5) Select the extruded surface. In the Front viewport, rotate the extrusion gizmo 45° about the local Z axis and 30° about the local X axis.

6) Play the animation.

7) Return to frame 100. Activate the **Toggle Animation Mode** button and select NURBS surface selection level. In the **Create Surfaces** rollout, pick the **Mirror** button. Pick the extruded surface. Set the mirror axis to X, and the **Offset:** spinner value to 0. Play the animation.

8) Return to frame 100. Select the surface sub-object level from the sub-object hierarchy tree. Activate the **Toggle Animation Mode** button.

9) Select the mirror surface in the Front viewport, and rotate the mirror axis gizmo 45° about the local Y axis. Play the animation.

10) Save the scene as ex26-17.max in the folder of your choice. Reset 3ds max.

Exercise

Figure 26-45. Editing a lathe surface. The red and green surfaces have identical parent curves, and both are rotated 360° about the Y axis. However, the lathe axis gizmo of the red surface is rotated slightly, creating a different shape in the surface.

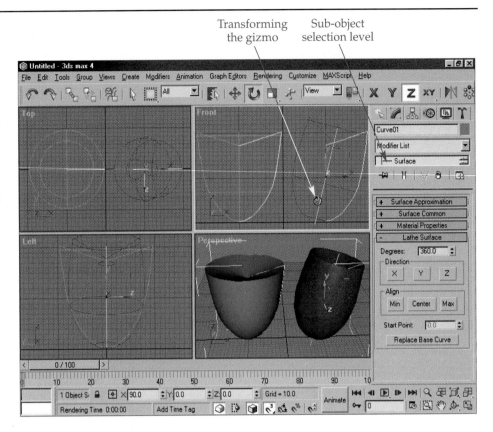

Lathe Surface

Selecting a lathe surface at the surface sub-object selection level makes the **Lathe Surface** rollout available. When the lathe surface is transformed, the transforms applied to it are inherited by its parent curve. The lathe axis gizmo can also be rotated and moved at the sub-object level. See Figure 26-45. These changes can be animated.

Picking the **Replace Base Curve** button allows you to select a new parent curve. This cannot be animated. Changes made to the **Degrees:** spinner value can be animated. The effects of all other controls in the **Lathe Surface** rollout cannot be animated.

Exercise 26-18

1) Create an arc of any size in the Front viewport. Use the illustration below as a guide. Convert the arc into a NURBS object and open the **Modify** tab in the **Command Panel.**

2) Expand the **Create Surfaces** rollout, and pick the **Lathe** button. Use an appropriate axis as the lathe axis. Select an appropriate alignment option. Set the **Degrees:** spinner to .1 degree.

3) Expand the sub-object hierarchy tree and select the surface sub-object level. Pick the lathe surface. Position the lathe axis gizmo as shown in the illustration.

4) Move to frame 100 and activate the **Toggle Animation Mode** button. Set the **Degrees:** spinner in the **Lathe Surface** rollout to 360. Play the animation.

5) Return to frame 100. Activate the **Toggle Animation Mode** button. Pick the lathe surface. In the Top viewport, rotate the lathe gizmo 45° about the local Z axis. In the Left viewport, rotate the lathe gizmo 45° about the local Z axis. Play the animation.

6) Save the scene as ex26-18.max in the folder of your choice. Reset 3ds max.

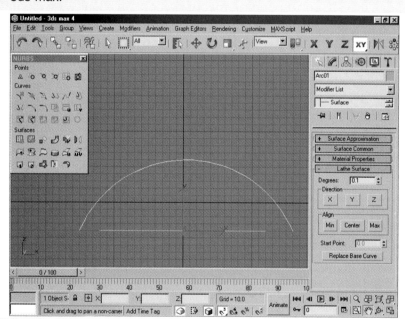

Ruled Surf

Selecting a ruled surface at the surface sub-object selection level makes the **Ruled Surf** rollout available. See Figure 26-46. When a ruled surface is transformed, the transforms applied to it are inherited by its parent curves. These transforms can be animated.

The **Replace First Curve** and **Replace Second Curve** buttons are used to replace the parent curves. None of the changes made in this rollout can be animated.

Cap Surface

Selecting a cap surface at the surface sub-object selection level makes the **Cap Surface** rollout available. Transforms applied to a cap surface are passed on to its parent curve or edge. These transforms can be animated.

The **Cap Surface** rollout contains only a **Replace Curve** button, and a **Start Point:** spinner. Changes made with these controls cannot be animated.

U and UV Loft Surface

When a U loft or UV loft surface is selected at the surface sub-object selection level, its corresponding rollout becomes available. See Figure 26-47. When a U or UV loft surface is transformed, all transforms applied to it are inherited by the parent curves. The transforms can be animated.

The **U Loft Surface** and **UV Loft Surface** rollouts are almost identical to the rollouts that are available when the loft surface is created, with the exception of the **Edit Curves** toggle button at the bottom.

When the **Edit Curves** button is active, the points or CVs of the loft's parent curves are visible. You can edit the parent curves as if you are at the **Point** or **Curve CV** sub-object selection level. You can edit a different parent curve by highlighting its name in the **U Curves:** or **V Curves:** window in the rollout. In addition, all rollouts related to the parent

Figure 26-46. The **Ruled Surf** rollout.

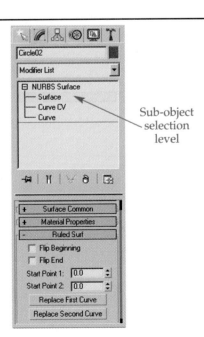

Sub-object selection level

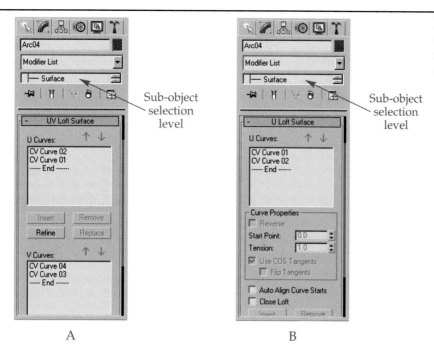

curves are also made available. Deactivate the **Edit Curves** button to complete the edit.

Transforms applied to the parent curves' points or CVs can be animated. The effects of all other changes made in the rollout cannot be animated.

Sweep Surface

When a one-rail or two-rail sweep surface is selected at the surface sub-object selection level, its corresponding rollout becomes available. See Figure 26-48. When a sweep surface is transformed, all transforms applied to it are inherited by its parent curves. These transforms can be animated.

The controls in the **1-Rail Sweep Surface** and **2-Rail Sweep Surface** rollouts are nearly identical. For a two-rail sweep surface, the **Rail Curves:** window displays the names of the curves chosen to be the rails. Highlighting the curve's name selects it. Picking the **Replace Rail 1** or **Replace Rail 2** button allows you to replace the highlighted rail curve with another curve. You cannot animate the replacement of a rail curve.

The **Section Curves:** window displays the names of all curves selected as sections, in the order they were chosen. Highlighting a curve name selects it. Picking one of the arrow buttons at the top of this window changes the selected curve's position in the list. Changes in the order of section curves cannot be animated.

The **Curve Properties:** area has controls for altering a highlighted section curve. The **Reverse Curve** check box, when checked, reverses the direction of the selected curve. The **Start Point:** spinner is used to relocate a closed curve's starting point. None of the changes made to these controls can be animated.

Picking the **Insert** button allows you to pick a new curve to be inserted, as a section, into the sweep surface. The new curve is added

Figure 26-48. A—The **1-Rail Sweep Surface** rollout. B—The **2-Rail Sweep Surface** rollout.

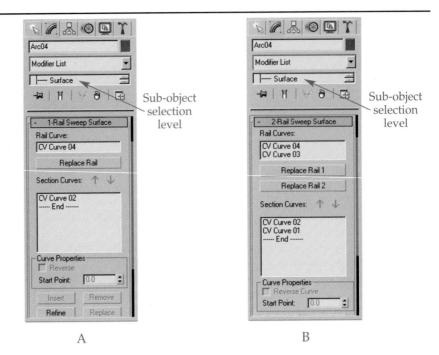

A

B

before the curve currently highlighted in the **Section Curves:** window. The insertion of a new curve into a sweep surface cannot be animated.

Picking the **Remove** button removes the currently selected curve from the sweep surface. Picking the **Replace** button allows you to replace an existing curve in the **Section Curves:** window with a new one. You cannot animate the removal or replacement of a curve.

Picking the **Refine** button allows you add a iso line cross section to your sweep surface. To do this, pick the **Refine** button. Position the cursor over an iso line. Pick the line when it is highlighted. The new section is inserted into the appropriate place in the **Section Curves:** window. You cannot animate the refinement of a sweep surface.

When the **Road-Like** check box is checked for a one-rail sweep surface, you can also edit the road-like gizmo. Rotating this gizmo changes the banking of the sweep surface. See Figure 26-49. You can animate changes to the road-like gizmo.

Picking the **Edit Curves** toggle button allows you to edit the parent curves' CVs or points without changing the sub-object selection level. Changes made to the parent curves' points and CVs can be animated.

Applying Materials to a NURBS Model

The typical NURBS model is an assembly of different sub-objects. Therefore, you will most likely apply a multi/sub-object material to the model. This allows the model to remain a single object, but appear as though the components are separate. Refer to Chapter 17 *Creating Advanced Materials* for detailed information about multi/sub-object materials. The rollouts and editing controls used in applying materials to NURBS sub-objects are discussed in the following sections.

When a surface sub-object is selected, the **Material Properties** rollout becomes available in the **Modify** tab. See Figure 26-50. The controls in this rollout determine how a material is applied to the selected surface.

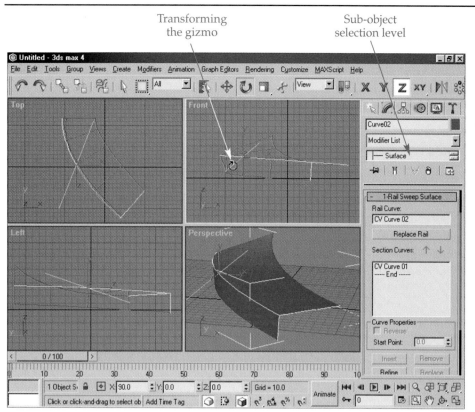

Transforming
the gizmo

Sub-object
selection level

Figure 26-49.
Transforming the
road-like gizmo while
editing a one-rail
sweep surface. The
rotation of the gizmo
causes the surface to
bank.

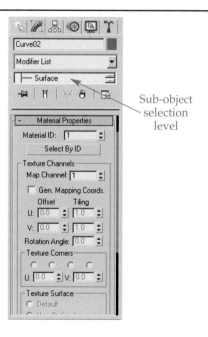

Sub-object
selection
level

Figure 26-50. The
Material Properties
rollout.

Help Cel

Materials can also be applied to renderable NURBS curves, and the
Material IDs adjusted in the **Curve Common** rollout.

Material ID

The **Material ID:** spinner in the **Material Properties** rollout allows you to assign a material ID to the selected surface. When a multi/sub-object material is applied to the model, a sub-object's material ID determines which "sub-material" is applied to it.

Picking the **Select By ID** button opens the **Select By Material ID** dialog box. This dialog box allows you to select a sub-object by the material ID assigned to it.

Texture Channels

The controls in the **Texture Channels** area of the **Material Properties** rollout determine the way in which maps are applied to a surface. The **Map Channels:** spinner is used to select a map channel. A single surface sub-object may contain up to 99 map channels. Checking the **Generate Mapping Coordinates** check box automatically generates mapping coordinates for the selected sub-object.

The **U:** and **V: Offset** spinners are used to relocate the origin of mapping coordinates. The default mapping coordinates origin is the sub-object's UV origin. Changing these values moves the mapping origin away from the sub-object's origin along the selected axis. You can animate changes made to these settings.

The **U:** and **V: Tiling** spinners determine the number of times a map is repeated across the U and V extents of the surface. You can animate adjustments made to tiling.

The **Rotation Angle:** spinner setting determines how the map is oriented on the sub-object. Increasing or decreasing the value of this spinner rotates the map around the mapping origin. You can animate the rotation of a map.

Texture Corners

The controls in the **Texture Corners** area of the **Material Properties** rollout allow you to change the UV mapping coordinates at the corners of NURBS surface sub-objects. This helps you match textures between adjacent surfaces.

The four radio buttons at the top of the **Texture Corners** area correspond to the four corners of the selected surface sub-object. As a radio button is selected, the corresponding corner is highlighted with a blue box. See Figure 26-51. The **U:** and **V:** spinners are used to move the mapping coordinates for the selected texture corner.

Texture Surface

Texture surfaces are the surfaces on top of surface sub-objects, onto which maps are placed. Texture surfaces are presented as a grid of transformable control points, which allow you to make localized changes in UVW mapping of a surface. Areas of the texture surface may be stretched, shrunk, or rotated, changing the appearance of the map while maintaining the sub-object's shape. As an analogy, think of an image printed on thin plastic film, with the film then tightly wrapped around an object. You can heat and stretch the film in certain areas, and cool and shrink the film in other areas. The printed image is altered when you

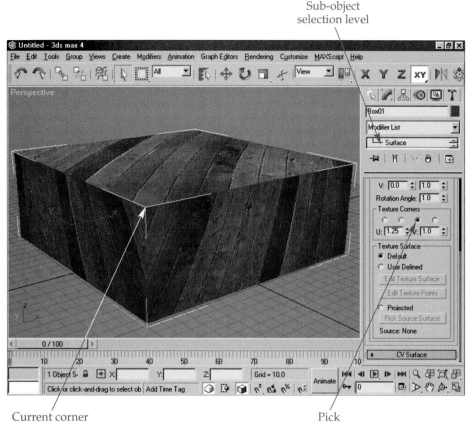

Sub-object
selection level

Current corner

Pick

Figure 26-51. The mapping coordinates for the texture surface corners of these three surfaces are repositioned, changing the way the mapped material appears on the surface.

make these changes, but the plastic film still perfectly conforms to the object that it is wrapped around.

When the **Default** radio button is active in the **Texture Surface** area of the **Material Properties** rollout, 3ds max automatically generates a texture surface. This texture surface is adjusted automatically as the surface sub-object is edited. When the **User Defined** radio button is active, 3ds max generates a texture surface that can be edited.

Edit Texture Surface

The **Edit Texture Surface** button in the **Texture Surface** area is enabled when the **User Defined** radio button is activated. Picking this button activates the **Edit Texture Surface** dialog box. See Figure 26-52. This dialog box should look very familiar. It is very similar in layout and function to the **Edit Curve on Surface** dialog box. The transform, select, and zoom tools in the toolbar perform functions that are identical to those of their curve-editing counterparts. Like the **Edit Curve on Surface** dialog box, the **Edit Texture Surface** dialog box contains a 2D viewport, which provides a 2D representation of the 3D texture surface.

The texture surface is displayed as a network of green points, interconnected by a dotted yellow control lattice. These texture points behave in the same manner as regular surface points. Transformations applied to selected points can be animated. Picking the **Remove Animation** button removes animation controllers from the selected texture points.

Additional rows of points are added by picking the **Insert Row** button, and then picking a location in the 2D view. A new row of texture

Figure 26-52. The **Edit Texture Surface** dialog box.

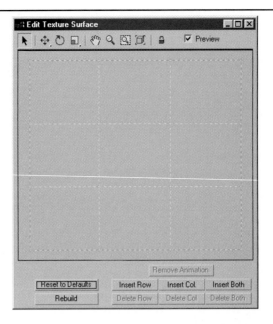

points appears at the cursor's U location. Additional columns are similarly added by picking the **Insert Col.** button. A new column of texture points is then added at the cursor's V location. Picking the **Insert Both** button adds a row of texture points at the cursor's U location, and a column of texture points at the cursor's V location. Picking the **Delete Row** button removes the highlighted row of texture points. Picking the **Delete Col** button removes the highlighted column of texture points. Picking the **Delete Both** button removes the highlighted row and column of texture points. The addition and deletion of texture points cannot be animated. Picking the **Reset to Defaults** button restores the default texture surface.

Picking the **Rebuild** button opens the **Rebuild Texture Surface** dialog box. The **Number in U:** and **Number in V:** spinners are used to specify the number of texture points contained in the new texture surface. Pick **OK** to rebuild the texture surface. Rebuilding a texture surface removes all animation for the texture surface.

Sub-object
selection level

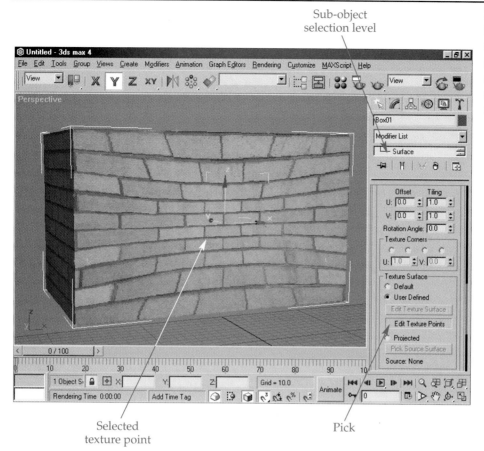

Selected
texture point

Pick

Edit Texture Points

When the **User Defined** radio button is active in the **Texture Surface** area, picking the **Edit Texture Points** button makes the points of the texture surface visible in the 3ds max viewports. See Figure 26-53. These points can then be selected and transformed in the 3ds max viewports.

Projected

Picking the **Projected** radio button in the **Texture Surface** area allows you to project the texture surface of another surface sub-object onto the selected surface.

To project a texture surface, pick the **Pick Source Surface** button. Highlight and pick the new surface that has the texture surface you wish to project. The texture surface of the second surface sub-object is then projected onto the original surface sub-object.

Chapter Snapshot

Chapter Test

Answer the following questions on a separate sheet of paper.
1) What are the five sub-object selection levels for a NURBS model?
2) What modifier is used to apply multiple modifiers to a surface sub-object?
3) Explain the difference between the **Refine** and **Insert** functions in relation to NURBS curves.
4) What function does the **Affect Neighbors** check box perform in the **Soft Selection** rollout?
5) What happens to two non-coincidental, animated CVs when they are fused?
6) What happens to an animated dependent curve sub-object that is made independent?
7) What happens to the parent curves when a blend curve is scaled?
8) How do you convert a projected curve into a surface point curve?
9) What are the two methods of editing a surface curve?
10) How do you convert a point curve into a CV curve?
11) How do you convert a CV curve into a point curve?
12) What happens when you drag the cursor downward in a viewport while extending a surface?
13) What are connected surfaces?
14) What happens when an animated CV surface, trimmed by a normal projected curve, is broken by row?
15) What happens when two non-adjacent surfaces are joined?
16) What is the function of the **Make Rigid** button?
17) How do you change the material ID of a surface sub-object?
18) How do you access the **Edit Texture Surface** dialog box? What is the other method for editing a texture surface?
19) How do you convert a two-rail sweep surface into a UV loft?
20) Although any given surface can be defined by U curves alone, it is often advantageous to use UV lofts when creating complex surfaces. Explain why this is so.

Modeling Problems

Draw the following scenes using NURBS modeling techniques and your own dimensions. Use the 3ds max objects presented in this and earlier chapters. Create and apply materials as needed, similar to those shown. Add lights and cameras as needed to create the shadows and views shown. When finished, save each model as p26-xx.max in the folder of your choice.

Toothbrush **1**

2 Cartoon Jet

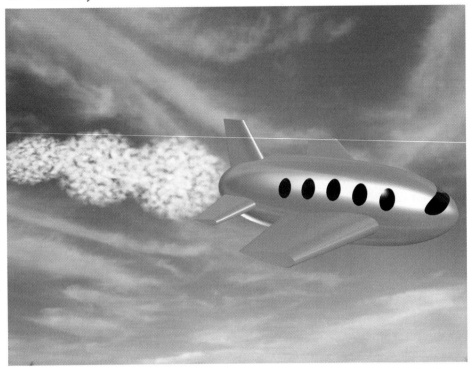

3 Apple

Hammer **4**

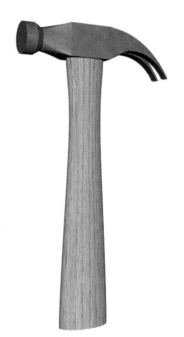

Teddy Bear **5**
A displacement map is used to give the rough fur look.

6 Covered Wagon

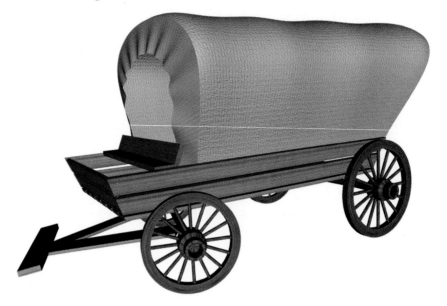

7 Lava Lamp

Toy Putty **8**

A suitable diffuse color map for the image of the woman can be found in the 3ds max \maps\characters folder.

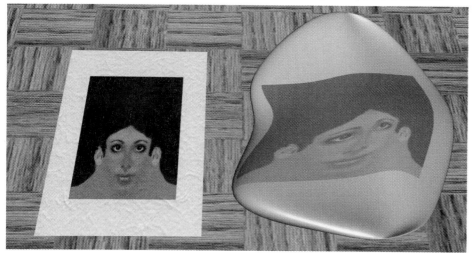

Novelty Glasses **9**

Ballpoint Pen and Refill **10**

Section Five Tutorial

Overview

In this tutorial, you will model and animate a Viking longship sailing at dusk. See Figure T5-1. In the first step of this tutorial, you will create the hull of the Viking ship. In the second step, you will add the ship's sail and oars. Next, you will create the "world" surrounding the ship, including the ocean and the background. In the fourth step, you will apply materials, and also add lights and a camera. In the final step, you will create an animation of the longship making its journey.

Creating the Hull

The hull of the ship is created by drawing a cross section, and then scaling and repositioning the initial cross section to create additional cross sections. These cross sections define the size and shape of the hull. The surface is defined by the cross sections in the same way the skin of a ship or the skin of a wing is defined by the ribs underneath.

As you work through the tutorial, refer to the views shown in Figure T5-2, Figure T5-3, and Figure T5-4 to duplicate the precise curvature and taper of the hull. If you have access to a scanner, you may choose to scan these sketches and load them as viewport background images in your drawing. The images can then be traced as necessary using the appropriate viewport. Displaying a viewport background using a bitmap is discussed in Chapter 11 of this text.

Creating a Cross Section

To create the first cross section, draw the rib shown in Figure T5-4 in the Front viewport using the dimensions provided. This rib is the widest and tallest rib in the hull of the ship. It will be copied, scaled down, rotated, and repositioned to create the other ribs of the hull.

Figure T5-1. The completed Section Five Tutorial.

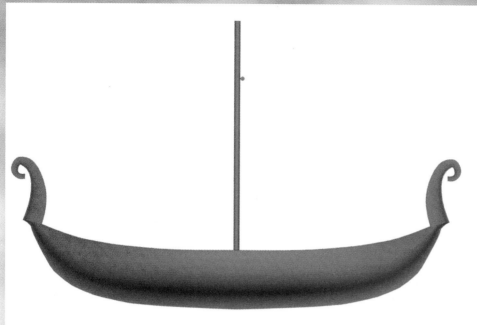

Figure T5-2. A sketch of the left view of the Viking ship.

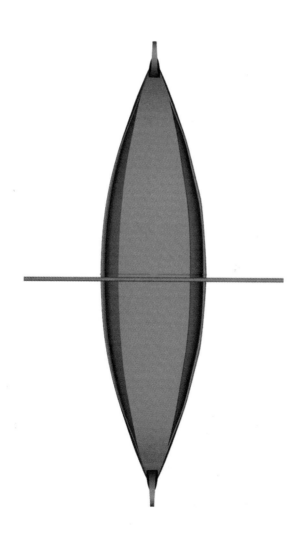

Figure T5-3. A sketch of the top view of the Viking ship.

Figure T5-4. A sketch of the center rib (partial front view) of the Viking ship.

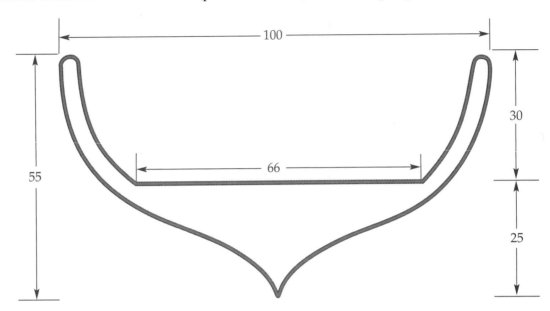

You can create the cross section in a variety of ways. The recommended method is to draw it as a CV curve. This may take some time to edit the CVs, but it is the best method. You can also create it as a point curve. After the cross section is created, name it Rib01.

Help Cel

When creating the first cross section as a CV curve, set automatic reparameterization to **Chord Length**. This prevents distortions from forming when transforming the cross sections.

Scaling and Positioning Cross Sections

Now that one cross section has been drawn, you can copy it to create the remaining cross sections. In the Top viewport, create four copies of the cross section and place them as shown in Figure T5-5. The first copy is moved –70 units from the original along the local Y axis. The second copy is moved –120 units from the original along the local Y axis. The third copy is moved –160 units from the original along the local Y axis. The last copy is moved –190 units from the original along the local Y axis.

Once the ribs are positioned, they must be rotated and scaled to match the contours of the hull. See Figure T5-6. Use the Top viewport to uniformly scale and rotate the ribs. Use the Front viewport to move and nonuniformly scale the ribs. All of the following instructions refer to the local coordinate systems of those viewports. Be sure to use the correct viewport for these operations!

The first copied rib (Rib02) should be rotated –6° about the local X axis, and then nonuniformly scaled along the X axis to 90%. The second copied rib (Rib03) should be uniformly scaled to 95%, rotated –12° about the local X axis, moved 6 units up the local Y axis, and nonuniformly scaled to 74% along the local X axis. The third copied rib (Rib04) should be uniformly scaled to 80%, rotated –41° about the local X axis, moved 20 units along the local Y axis, and nonuniformly scaled to 56% along the local X axis. The last copied rib (Rib05) should be uniformly scaled to 28%, rotated –80° about the local X axis, and nonuniformly scaled to 56% along the local X axis. Move the last rib 51 units up on the local Y axis and 5 units up on the local Z axis.

You now have all the ribs from the middle of the ship to one end. You still need to make the ribs for the area between the middle of the ship and the other end. This is done by selecting the ribs and mirroring them about the middle of the ship. First, attach all of the rib copies to the first rib so they are all part of the same model. Then, move the pivot point for the model to the world origin (0,0,0), if it is not already there. Select the model and mirror a copy about the Y axis in the Top viewport using the **Mirror** command. Set the mirror's **Offset:**

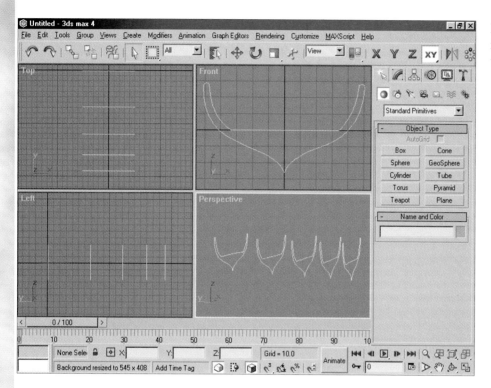

Figure T5-5. The initial positions of the copied ribs.

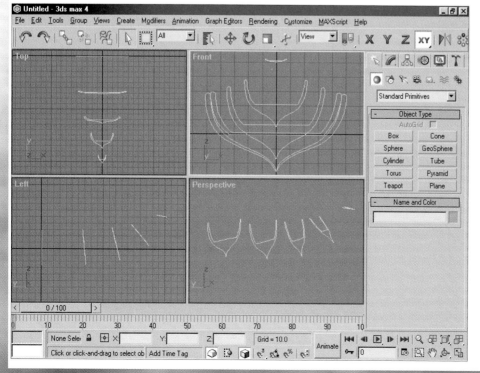

Figure T5-6. The ribs after being scaled and repositioned.

spinner value to 0. When the ribs are mirrored, enter sub-object mode and delete the copy of the center rib. Next, return to the top level and attach the second set of ribs to the first. You should now have all the ribs necessary to create the hull of the Viking ship. See Figure T5-7.

Creating the Hull Skin

Now you need to create the skin of the ship. You will do this by creating a U loft surface from the ribs.

Activate the Left viewport and perform a zoom extents. Select the hull's cross sections, and open the **Modify** tab in the **Command Panel**. Expand the **Create Surfaces** rollout and pick the **U Loft** button. Pick the cross sections in order, from left to right. When you have picked the last cross section, right-click to end the command. The skin of the Viking ship is now visible in the viewports. See Figure T5-8. Name the U loft surface Hull.

Now you will create a path along which the oars and shields will be arranged. The path is created as a V iso curve of the hull. The iso curve is then detached.

First, select the hull. Open the **Modify** tab in the **Command Panel**, and expand the **Create Curves** rollout. Pick the **V Iso Curve** button, and then pick a point near the edge of the hull. See Figure T5-9. Now, at the curve sub-object level, select the V iso curve and detach it as Path. Make sure the **Relational** check box is unchecked before detaching the curve.

Creating the Figureheads

The decorative, carved scrolls at the bow and stern of the ship are called figureheads. These are created by copying and modifying the last rib of the hull and using it as a cross section for a one-rail sweep. To do this, select the hull. At the curve sub-object level, pick the far right cross section in the Left viewport, and detach a copy of the rib, making sure the **Relational** check box is unchecked. Name the curve Fig01.

Reposition the pivot point as indicated in Figure T5-10, and pick the **Align to World** button. In the Left viewport, rotate the curve 10° about the local Z axis using the pivot point as the center of rotation. Edit the CVs of the cross section to create the shape shown in Figure T5-11.

Figure T5-7. All of the ribs required for the hull.

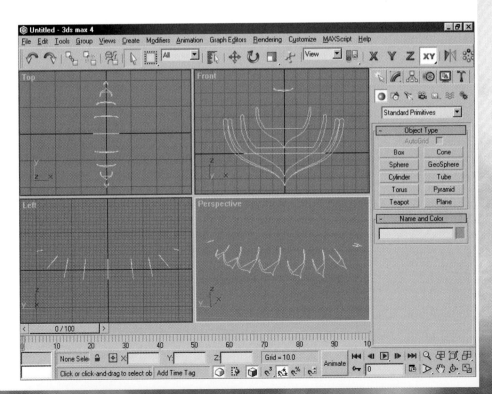

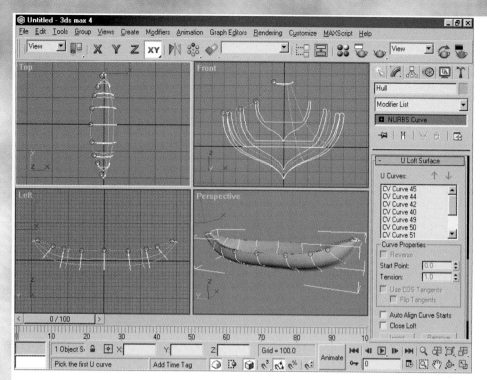

Figure T5-8. The hull is created as a U loft surface.

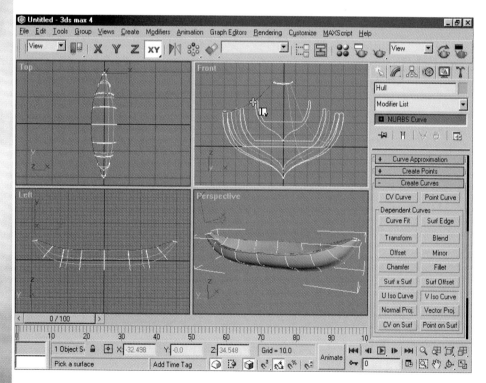

Figure T5-9. Creating a V iso curve at the edge of the hull.

In the Left viewport, move the curve 5 units along the local X axis and 2.5 units along the local Y axis. This gives the curve the orientation and position shown in the figure. Finally, rotate the curve an additional 15° about the local Z axis.

In the Left viewport, create a CV curve to serve as the rail for the figurehead. See Figure T5-12. Make the curve approximately 55 units in height and 22.5 units wide at the extents. Clone, scale, and rotate the Fig01 curve to create the additional cross sections. You

Figure T5-10.
Repositioning the
pivot point of the
detached curve.

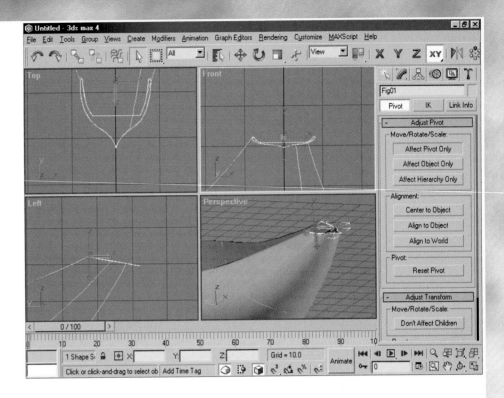

Figure T5-11.
Creating the first
cross section for the
one-rail sweep
surface. This
becomes the base of
the figurehead.

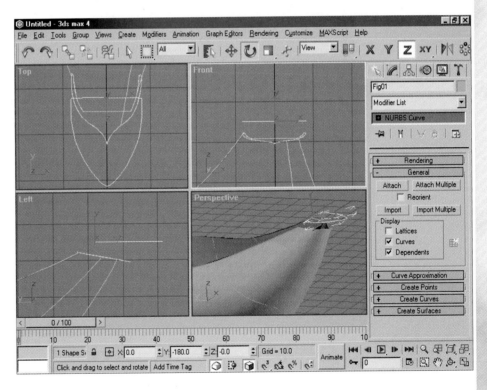

will need to create five total cross sections. Referring to Figure T5-12, position the cross sections so they are approximately perpendicular to the rail.

Create a one-rail sweep. When the surface is created, uncheck the **Sweep Parallel** check box. If there are additional deformities in the surface, you can edit the curves at the sub-object level to correct the problems. Name the sweep surface Fighead01.

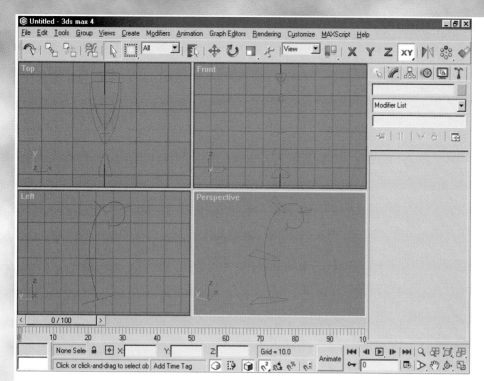

Figure T5-12. The curve and all of the segments used to create the figurehead. Notice the cross sections are rotated according to their position on the rail.

Maximize the Left viewport, and perform a zoom extents. Position the sweep surface's pivot point at the world origin, and align it to the world. Create a mirror copy of the figurehead using an **Offset:** spinner value of 0. Mirror the copy about the X axis. Attach both sweep surface figureheads to the hull.

Next, create a blend surface between the right-most cross section of the hull and the first cross section of the corresponding figurehead. See Figure T5-13. Do the same between the left-most cross-section of the hull and the first cross section of the other sweep surface.

Adding the Shields, Oars, Mast, and Sail

Now you must complete the Viking ship by adding details. A good deal of the animation is also added when these components are created. For example, the sail billows in the wind, and the oars cycle through their stroke.

Creating the Shield

The shields are simple lathe surfaces. Rather than draw and position each shield individually, you will create a single shield. That shield and a single oar are used to create an array of identical objects, using the edge of the hull as a path. The array is then mirrored to create the shields and oars along the other side of the hull.

The first step is to create the outline for the shield. Create this as a CV curve in the Front viewport. Draw the curve just to the outside of the widest rib, and position it so the top of the rib roughly lines up with the midpoint of the curve. The approximate dimensions of the curve are 16 units by 4 units. See Figure T5-14. Create a lathe surface using the curve rotated 360° about the local X axis. Edit the gizmo as needed at the surface sub-object level to create the proper shield shape, as shown in Figure T5-15.

Assign a material ID of 3 to the shield surface. When the shields are attached to the Viking ship, the material ID determines the sub-material assigned to the shields. Name the lathe surface Shield01.

Figure T5-13. The gap between the hull and the figurehead is filled with a blend curve.

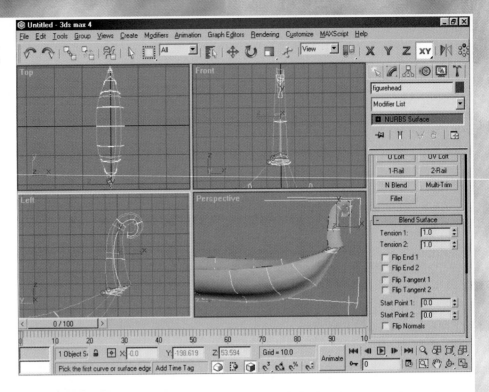

Figure T5-14. The outline of the shield. Notice its position relative to the hull.

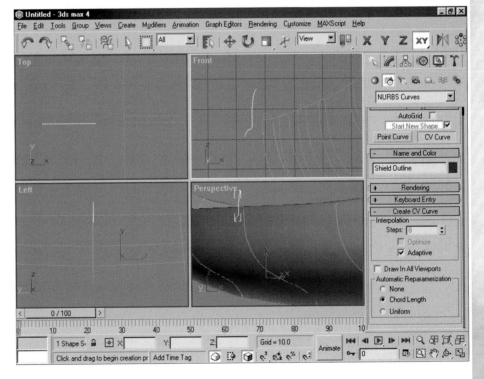

Creating the Oar

Like the shield, the oar is constructed from a lathe surface. The first step is to create the outline for the oar. In the Top viewport, create a CV curve outline that resembles the curve in Figure T5-16. The overall dimensions for the oar should be 10 units by 150 units. When the curve is satisfactory, create a lathe surface using the curve rotated 360° about the local X axis. Edit the gizmo as needed at the surface sub-object level to create the proper oar shape.

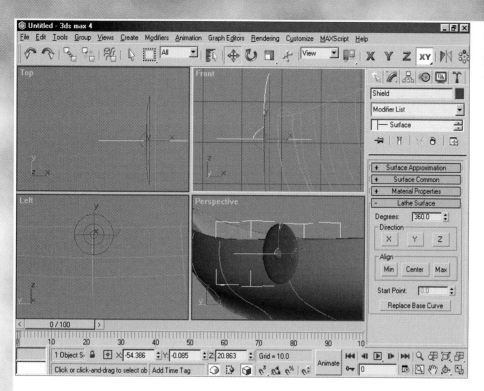

Figure T5-15. The completed shield. Notice the location of the lathe axis gizmo.

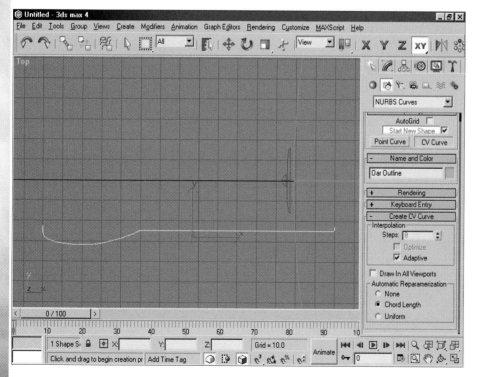

Figure T5-16. Creating the outline for the oar.

Next, pick the **Convert Surface** button in the **Surface Common** rollout. Make sure **CV Surface** is active in the **Convert Surface** dialog box. Leave the default settings and pick **OK**. At the surface CV sub-object level, select the rings of CVs that form the blade of the oar in the Top viewport. Nonuniformly scale the selected vertices to approximately 25% on the local Y axis. The width of the blade should be approximately the same as the width of the handle. See Figure T5-17. Name the surface **Oar01**.

Adjusting the Oar's Pivot

Next, you need to adjust the pivot point of the oar. Doing so helps create the illusion that the oar is fastened to the edge of the hull. First, select the oar, and then move it to the position shown in Figure T5-18. Next adjust the pivot so it is directly above the rim of the hull, and centered in the handle of the oar. Also, make sure the pivot is aligned to the world. See Figure T5-18.

Figure T5-17. Scaling down the rings of CVs to complete the oar.

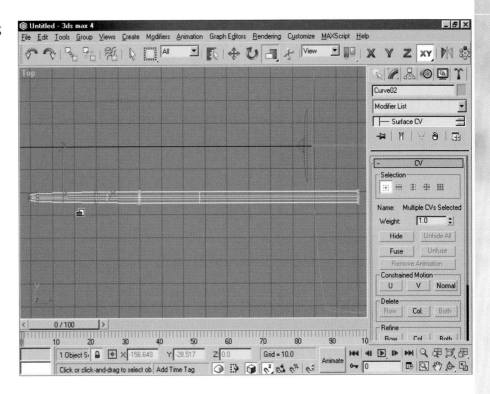

Figure T5-18. Adjusting the pivot point of the oar.

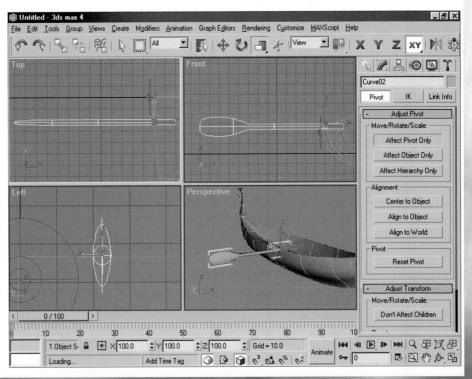

Animating the Oar

It is easiest to add the animation keys for the oars at this point. A complete cycle of the oars takes 100 frames, the total length of the animation. It is recommended that you use the **Transform Type-in** dialog box to apply the transforms at each key. Use the Left viewport to set all keys.

The first key is placed at frame 15. This key is created in the Left viewport by rotating the oar 30° about the local Y axis. The next key, at frame 30, is created by rotating the oar –30° about the local Z axis. The key at frame 40 is created by rotating the oar –5° about the local Y axis. The key at frame 70 is created by rotating the oar –55° about the local Y axis. The key at frame 85 is created by rotating the oar –30° about the local Z axis. The key at frame 100 is created by rotating the oar 36° about the local Y axis, 3.5° about the local X axis, and 48.5° about the local Z axis (in that order). Check the animation to see if the oar slices through the shield at any point. Reposition the oar if it passes through the shield.

Creating the Remaining Shields and Oars

To add the remaining shields and oars, first select the oar and the shield and group them. In the Top viewport, rotate the oar and shield group –90° about the Z axis. Pick the **Spacing Tool** button from the **Array** flyout. Select **Divide Evenly, No Objects at Ends** from the drop-down list in the **Parameters** area of the dialog box. Set the **Count:** spinner to 7. Select the **Pick Path** button, and select the iso curve named Path. Pick the **Edges** radio button and check the **Follow** check box in the **Context** area of the dialog box, and pick the **Apply** button. Close the dialog box.

Delete the original oar and shield. Position the array, as a group, along the rim of the hull. If all of the shields do not meet the side of the hull, you can adjust the oar and shield groups individually to achieve the desired configuration. Next, ungroup the shields and oars. Select the oar farthest to the left in the Left viewport and delete it. This end of the ship is the bow, or front.

Select all the shields and oars, and then mirror them to create the shields and oars for the other side of the hull. Use the world X axis as the mirror axis, and displace them approximately 150 units. See Figure T5-19.

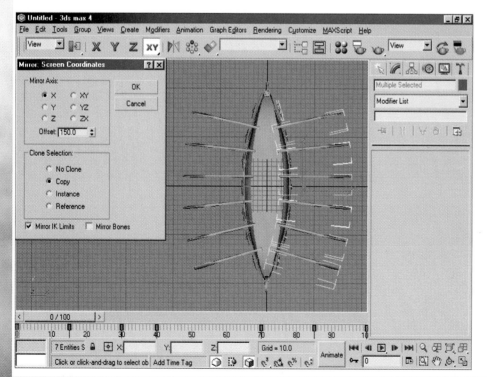

Figure T5-19.
Mirroring the oars and shields.

You may need to change the viewport display to **Smooth and Highlights** in order to accurately see the side of the hull. Finally, attach all of the shields to the hull model. Do not attach the oars!

Help Cel

After using the spacing tool, the oars rotate in the opposite direction from their original animation. This is correct.

Creating the Mast

The mast and the boom are simply cylinder primitives converted to NURBS objects and attached to the ship model. The mast has a radius of 3 units, and it is 250 units in height. It can be constructed of a single height segment. The mast is placed in the center of the ship, with its base at the world origin.

The boom should have a radius of 2 units, and a height of 250 units. It should be centered on the mast, about 50 units from the top. It should not pass through the mast. Instead, it should be just to the left of the mast, when viewed in the **Left** viewport. Like the mast, the boom can be constructed with a single height segment. Both the mast and the boom should be converted to NURBS objects. Rename the surfaces Mast and Boom. Assign both surfaces a material ID of 2, and then attach them to the ship. See Figure T5-20.

Help Cel

Do not forget to change the material IDs of the cap surfaces when you change the material IDs of the converted cylinders. Remember that each cylinder is converted into three surface sub-objects, and each of those surface sub-objects has a material ID.

Figure T5-20. The boom and mast are attached to the ship.

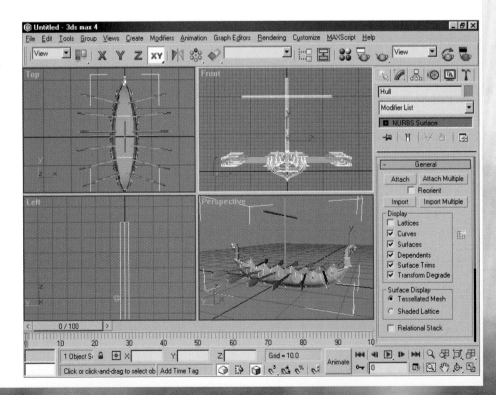

Creating the Sail

The sail is a CV surface, in which certain CVs are moved to create the billowing effect. To create the sail, first create an independent CV surface in the Front viewport. The surface should be 140 units high by 250 units wide. Use the default setting of 4×4 CVs. The top of the sail is fixed to the boom, so position the top edge of the sail inside the cylinder of the boom.

Make sure the **Relational Stack** check box is checked for the NURBS model. At the surface CV selection level, select all CVs but those in the top row and the two corner CVs on the bottom row. See Figure T5-21. In the Left viewport, move the CVs –30 units along the local X axis. This creates the billow effect. Next, deselect the four center CVs, and uniformly scale the remaining six CVs to 65%. In the Front viewport, move the selected CVs 10 units along the local Y axis. This recenters the curvature of the sail. Assign the sail a material ID of 4. Attach the sail to the ship.

Next, apply an nsurf sel modifier to the ship. Expand the nsurf sel hierarchy tree and select the surface CV sub-object level. Select all of the CVs in the sail surface except those in the top row and the two corner CVs in the bottom row. See Figure T5-22. Apply a noise modifier to the selected CVs. Activate the **Fractal** check box, and set the **Roughness:** spinner value to 1. Set the **Strength:** spinner value for the **X:** direction to 2, and the **Strength:** spinner value for the **Z:** direction to 10. Check the **Animate Noise** check box, and set the **Frequency:** spinner to .12.

Linking the Parts

The oars are not part of the longship model, because attaching them to the ship model would remove their animation controllers. However, they must follow the movement of the ship. Select all of the oars, and then link them to the ship model. This causes them to move and turn with the ship model.

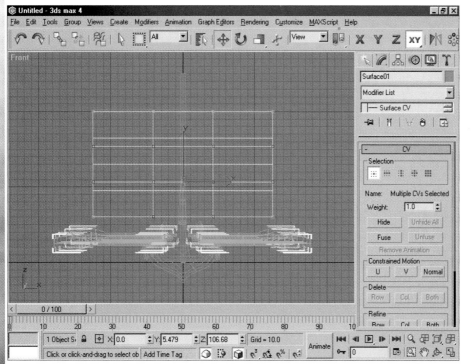

Figure T5-21. The selection set of CVs used to create the billowing effect in the sail.

Figure T5-22.
Applying a noise modifier to this selection set of CVs will keep the wind in your sail.

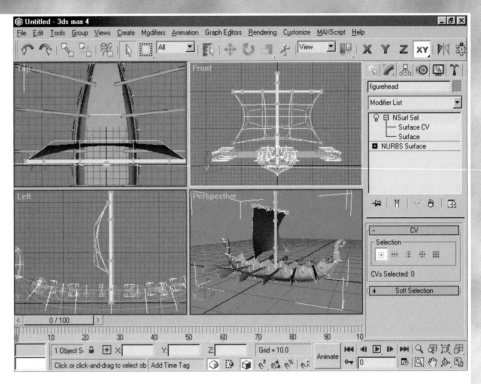

Creating the Ocean

The next step is to create the ocean. In the Top viewport, create a 5000 unit by 5000 unit quad patch, and name it Ocean. Give the quad patch 10 length segments and 10 width segments. Generate mapping coordinates for the quad patch. Move the center of the quad patch 2000 units from the origin along the world X axis and –1500 units from the origin along the Y axis.

Also, in the Top viewport, just outside of the quad patch, create a wave space warp. Set the **Amplitude 1:** spinner to 5, and the **Amplitude 2:** spinner to 5. Set the **Wave Length:** spinner to 125. See Figure T5-23. Bind the Ocean to the wave space warp. Next, move to frame 100 and activate animation mode. Set the **Phase:** spinner to 2. This creates gentle rising and falling action in the ocean.

Creating and Applying Materials

Now, create and assign materials to the various objects in the scene. Since the ship model consists of various sub-objects that all have different appearances, you will assign a multi/sub-object material to it. The materials for the oars and the ocean and the map for the background are also created.

Loading Default Materials

The first step is to determine the default materials to be used, and to load those materials in the **Material Editor**. The default material Wood_Cedfence is used for the hull and figurehead sub-objects. The default material Wood_Oakgrtrt is used for the mast and boom sub-objects. The default material Metal_Black_Plain is used for the shield sub-objects. The default material Wood_Driftwood is used for the oars. Load these materials into empty sample slots in the **Material Editor**. Assign the material Wood_Driftwood to the oars.

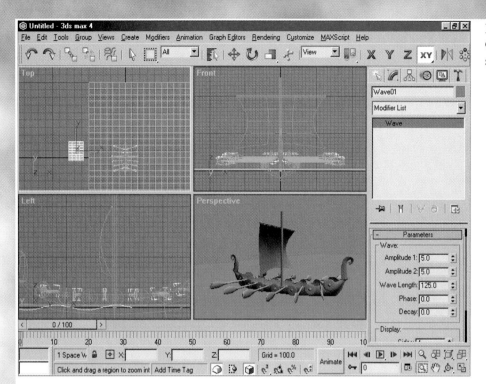

Figure T5-23. Creating the wave space warp.

Creating the Blend Material for the Sail

Now you need to create the custom materials used for the sail. Detailed instructions follow for creating the red and off-white canvas materials shown in Figure T5-1. However, you are encouraged to experiment with materials of your own design.

To create the sail material, begin by selecting an unused sample slot in the **Material Editor**. You are going to create a new standard material. Set the ambient color to R126 G92 B33. Next, set the diffuse color to R234 G231 B227. Set the specular color to white (R255 G255 B255). Set the **Specular Level:** spinner 5 and the **Glossiness:** spinner to 12. Name the material Canvas White and check the **2-Sided** check box. Use the bitmap file Crumple4.jpg located in the \Maps\organics\ folder as a bump map. Set the U and V tiling to 2. Name the map Sail Bumps. Set the **Amount:** spinner in the **Maps** rollout to 90.

Copy the material to a different sample slot, and name it Canvas Red. Change the color settings as follows. First, set the ambient color to R110 G62 B62. Next, set the diffuse color to R161 G89 B89. Leave the specular color as white.

Pick another unused sample slot and create a new blend material. Choose to discard the existing material. Name the material Sail. Assign an instance of Canvas Red as **Material 1**, and an instance of Canvas White as **Material 2**. Apply a checker map as a mask. Set the **U Offset:** spinner to .35, and the **U Tiling:** spinner to 3.5. Set the **V Offset:** spinner to .5, and the **V Tiling:** spinner to 0. See Figure T5-24. Name the map Sail Mask.

Creating the Multi/Sub-Object Material for the Ship

All of the materials used for the ship are now loaded in the **Material Editor**. However, they must be combined to create a multi/sub-object material so they can be assigned to the appropriate sub-objects.

Select an empty sample slot and create a new multi/sub-object material. Choose to discard the old material. Name the material Ship. Set the number of materials to four. Place an instance of Wood_Cedfence in the first material slot. Place an instance of Wood_Oakgrtrt in the second material slot. Place an instance of Metal_Black_Plain in the third material slot. Place an instance of Sail in the fourth material slot.

Double-check the material IDs of the surfaces in the ship model. The hull, figureheads, and the blend surfaces between them should all have a material ID of 1. The mast and boom should both have a material ID of 2. The shields should all have a material ID of 3. The sail should have a material ID of 4. When you have ensured that all of the material IDs are correctly set, assign the material Ship to the longship model. See Figure T5-25.

Figure T5-24.
Creating the blend material Sail.

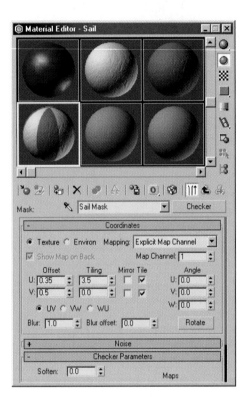

Figure T5-25.
Applying the material Ship to the scene.

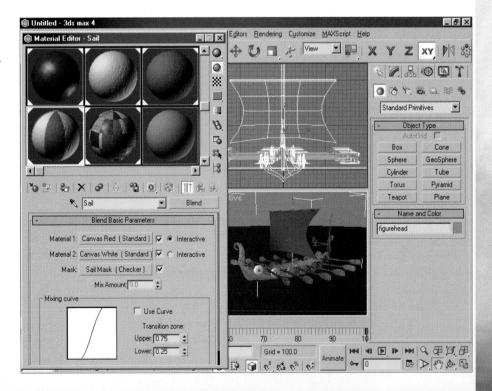

Creating the Material for the Ocean

Now you will create the material for the ocean. Pick an empty sample slot in the **Material Editor** and create a new standard material. The material for the water is slightly transparent, allowing the portion of the hull and oars below the waterline to show through. The water is also reflective, allowing the sunset to shimmer on its surface.

Begin by setting the shading type to Blinn. Now, set the ambient color to R24 G16 B78. Set the diffuse color to R61 G57 B97. Set the specular color to R228 G232 B255. Set the **Opacity:** spinner to 95. Set the **Specular Level:** spinner to 45, and the **Glossiness:** spinner to 60. Name the material Water.

In the **Maps** rollout, set the bump map **Amount** spinner to 30, and assign a noise map with fractal noise. Name the map Water Noise. Next, move to frame 100 and activate animation mode. In the **Noise Parameters** rollout for the Water Noise map, increase the value of the **Phase:** spinner to 3. In the **Maps** rollout for the material, set the reflection map **Amount:** spinner to 30 and assign a reflect/refract map. Name the map Water Reflect. See Figure T5-26. Accept the default settings. Assign the material to the quad patch named Ocean.

Loading the Environment Map

The next step is to load the background for the scene. Although the map can be loaded directly through the **Environment** dialog box, you will have more control over its appearance if you first load it as a map for a material. Then, the material map can be loaded as a background map.

To set up the background, open the **Material Editor**. Pick any unused sample slot. Expand the **Maps** rollout and add a bitmap as a diffuse color map. Load the image Skysun2.jpg located in the \Maps\Skies\ folder as the diffuse color map. See Figure T5-27. Name the map Background Sun. In the **Coordinates** rollout, activate the **Environ** radio button and set the **V:** offset spinner to .40. This positions the sun slightly above the quad patch ocean when the map is used as a background image in the scene. Also, set the mapping to **Screen**.

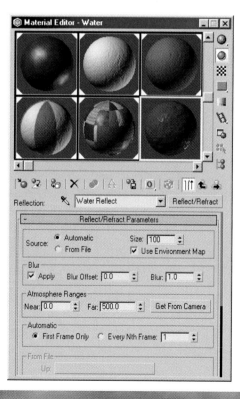

Figure T5-26. Creating the material for the ocean.

Figure T5-27. Setting up the background image as a material map.

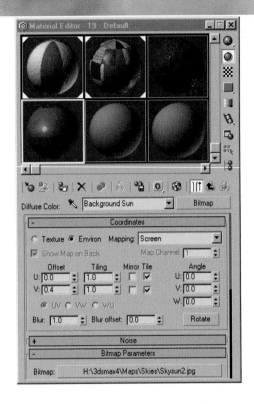

Finishing the Scene

In the final step of this tutorial, you will add the touches that give the scene realism. You will load the sunset background, add lights and a camera, and finish animating the ship.

Adding the Background

First, load the background. Open the **Environment** dialog box and pick the **Environment Map:** button. Next, get the Background Sun map from the **Material Editor**. In the **Material/Map Browser**, activate the **Mtl Editor** radio button. Locate and select the Skysun2.jpg map. Choose to make it an instance of the material map.

Adding the Lights

Three lights illuminate the scene. The first is a fill light at a high altitude in the front of the scene. The second light is a backlight, colored orange like the sunset. This is the light that casts the shadows and creates highlights on the water. It is also the light that creates the warm highlights on the ship. The third light is a directional light, which simulates the parallel rays of the setting sun.

First, create the fill light as an omni light. Position it at world coordinates X=-420, Y=120, Z=700. Set the color for the light at 255 white. Leave all other settings at their defaults. Name the light Fill.

Next, create the backlight as another omni light. Position the light at world coordinates X=420, Y=120, and Z=180. These coordinates position the backlight lower in the sky than the fill light, creating warm highlights at the edges of the ship. Name the light Backlight. Set the color for the backlight to R235 G120 B18. Check the **Cast Shadows** check box. Accept the defaults for all other settings.

Finally, create a direct light to simulate the parallel rays of the sun. Begin by creating a free direct light in the Top viewport. Position the light at world coordinates X=4500, Y=-3000, and Z=175. Name the light Sun. Make the light the same color as the backlight. Check the **Cast Shadows** check box.

In the **Directional Parameters** rollout, set the **Target Distance:** spinner to 6000. Set the **Hot Spot:** spinner to 600, and the **Falloff:** spinner to 800. Aim the light as necessary so the ship and an area slightly larger are in the hotspot of the directional light. The light should be almost, but not quite, parallel to the ocean and aimed at the ship.

Adding the Camera

For this animation, use a free camera. The camera's position and its target remain static. Create the camera in the Left viewport and position it at world coordinates X=–350, Y=500, and Z=93. In the Top viewport, rotate the camera –2° about the local Y axis, and –47° about the local Z axis. Use the 28mm stock lens. Finally, change the Perspective viewport to a camera viewport.

Completing the Animation

The final step in completing the scene is to finish adding the animation. The rowing motion of the oars was added when they were created. The movement of the sail and the rising and falling of the ocean have also been added. However, for all the movement in the scene, the ship is going nowhere. You need to add some forward motion.

To do this, select the ship in the Top viewport. Move to frame 100 and activate animation mode. Move the ship 150 units along the local Y axis. Check the camera viewport to make sure the ship is still within the safe frame.

Rendering the Final Scene

Before rendering the final animation, make a preview animation. Check the motion in the preview to make sure it is correct. You may also want to render five still images, such as frames 1, 25, 50, 75, and 100.

When completely satisfied with the scene, render a final animation to a file named tut05.avi in the folder of your choice. To save time and hard drive space, use the 320 × 240 resolution. If you have time and space, you can use the 640 × 480 resolution.

When the rendering is complete, view the animation. If necessary, make any adjustments and render the scene again.

Questions for Discussion

1) In this tutorial, the hull of the ship is created with a U loft. What other methods might be used to create the hull? What would be some advantages and disadvantages of each?
2) Why is it important to make sure that the **Relational** check box is unchecked when detaching the V iso curve?
3) What changes could be made to make the seas rougher?
4) How could rigging be added to the Viking ship? How could the rigging be animated to add realism?
5) What other methods may have been used to add the lighting effect of the setting sun?

Index